July 3–5, 2012
Haifa, Israel

Association for
Computing Machinery

Advancing Computing as a Science & Profession

ITiCSE'12

Proceedings of the ACM Conference on

Innovation and Technology in Computer Science Education

Sponsored by:

ACM SIGCSE

Supported by:

Technion-Israel Institute of Technology, The Open University of Israel, Machshava - Israel National Center for Computer Science Teachers, Computer Science Teachers Association, and Microsoft

Association for
Computing Machinery

Advancing Computing as a Science & Profession

The Association for Computing Machinery
2 Penn Plaza, Suite 701
New York, New York 10121-0701

ISBN: 978-1-4503-1246-2 (Digital)

ISBN: 978-1-4503-1736-8 (Print)

Additional copies may be ordered prepaid from:

ACM Order Department
PO Box 30777
New York, NY 10087-0777, USA

Phone: 1-800-342-6626 (USA and Canada)
+1-212-626-0500 (Global)
Fax: +1-212-944-1318
E-mail: acmhelp@acm.org
Hours of Operation: 8:30 am – 4:30 pm ET

Printed in the USA

Foreword

Welcome to Haifa, Israel

We are proud to host the 17th ACM Innovation and Technology in Computer Science Education (ITiCSE) conference at the Technion – Israel Institute of Technology in Haifa. We hope you will find this venue a great choice for the conference.

The theme of ITiCSE 2012 is Computing Sciences Education: Legacy, Innovation and Future Trends. Accordingly, the conference offers a variety of opportunities to learn from and interact with colleagues, researchers and professionals from all over the world.

The program consists of invited keynotes, working groups, exhibits, and technical sessions featuring papers, panels, posters, tips, techniques, and student posters.

The three keynotes of ITiCSE 2012 are in conjunction with the Alan Turing Centenary events. The three speakers are: Prof. Michael Rabin, 1976 Turing Award winner, of the Hebrew University in Jerusalem and Harvard University; Prof. Lenore Blum of Carnegie Mellon University; and Prof. David Harel of the Weizmann Institute of Science.

We accepted 61 excellent papers for presentation from among the 134 papers submitted—an acceptance rate of 45%. Each paper was reviewed by at least four reviewers. Additionally, 4 working groups, 3 panels, 24 posters and 13 tips, techniques, or courseware presentations were accepted.

Here are some details about the conference schedule:
Working groups begin on Sunday, July 1st, and will work in earnest throughout the conference, with a presentation of their preliminary results on Wednesday.
The ITiCSE 2012 reception will take place on Monday evening.
Tuesday morning will be devoted to conference excursions.
The conference itself will begin on Tuesday afternoon with a keynote, followed by a poster session, two parallel paper presentation sessions, and one panel.
Wednesday and Thursday will each begin with a keynote, followed by three parallel paper presentation sessions, panels, tips, techniques, or courseware presentations.
The conference banquet will take place on Wednesday evening in Acre, where we will enjoy excellent food, lively music, and the breathtaking scenery of Haifa Bay and the walls of the old city of Acre.

Israel is a tiny country, and yet it is a place of amazing variety, rich history, varied geography, an ancient background and a modern present, with globally unique contrasts. Haifa, the largest city in northern Israel, is a city of tolerance where people of all religions live together. We hope that ITiCSE 2012 will provide a fitting platform for attendees to become acquainted with the Israel experience.

We would like to thank our reviewers and conference committee members. It was a pleasure working with such motivated and experienced scientists.

Tami Lapidot and Judith Gal-Ezer
ITiCSE 2012 Conference Co-Chairs

Michael Caspersen and Orit Hazzan
ITiCSE 2012 Program Co-Chairs

Table of Contents

Session 4: Systems

Session 5: CS1/2 I

Session 6: Testing

Session 7: Assessment I

Session 8: CS1/2 II

Session 9: Technologies in CSE

Session 10: Assessment II

Session 11: Classroom Management

Session 12: K-12 II

Session 13: Short Presentations I

Session 14: Pedagogical Tools

Session 15: Computers and Society

Session 16: Short Presentations II

Session 17: Interface-Related Tools

Session 18: Curriculum Issues

Panels

Tips, Techniques and Courseware I

Tips, Techniques and Courseware II

Posters

ITiCSE 2012 Conference Organization

Conference Co-Chairs: Tami Lapidot *(Technion, Israel)*
Judith Gal-Ezer *(The Open University, Israel)*

Program Co-Chairs: Michael E. Caspersen *(Aarhus University, Denmark)*
Orit Hazzan *(Technion, Israel)*

Panels: Ronit Ben-Bassat Levy *(Weizmann Institute of Science, Israel)*
Bruce Klein *(Grand Valley University, USA)*

Working Groups Coordinators: Elizabeth S. Adams *(James Madison University, USA)*
Noa Ragonis *(Beit Berl College, Israel)*

Tips, Techniques and Courseware: Arnold N. Pears *(Uppsala University, Sweden)*
Tamar Vilner *(The Open University, Israel)*

Posters: Michal Armoni *(Weizmann Institute of Science, Israel)*
John Impagliazzo *(Emeritus, Hofstra University, USA)*

Treasurer/Registrar: Cary Laxer *(Rose-Hulman Institute of Technology, USA)*

Proceedings & Publicity: Michael Goldweber *(Xavier University, USA)*
Don Goelman *(Villanova University, USA)*

Evaluations: Mats Daniels *(Uppsala University, Sweden)*
Ela Zur *(The Open University, Israel)*

System Administrators: John Dooley *(Knox College, USA)*
Henry M. Walker *(Grinnell College, USA)*

High School Projects: Bruria Haberman *(Weizmann Institute of Science, Israel)*
Cecile Yehezkel *(Weizmann Institute of Science, Israel)*

Local Committee: Dan Aharoni *(Kinneret College on the Sea of Galilee, Israel)*
Niv Kfir *(Technion, Israel)*
Tamar Paz (*Oranim College, Israel)*
Bella Furman *(Technion, Israel)*

ITiCSE 2012 Working Groups

Working Group 1: Academic Integrity Policies: Addressing Best Practices in Education and Industry

Leader: Charles P. Riedesel (*University of Nebraska - Lincoln*)

Participants: Alison Clear (*Christchurch Polytechnic Institute of Technology*)
Gerry Cross (*Mount Royal University*)
Jitender Deogun (*University of Nebraska - Lincoln*)
Janet Hughes (*University of Dundee*)
Simon (*University of Newcastle - Ourimbah*)
Henry Walker (*Grinnell College*)

Working Group 2: First Year Programming Projects for Computing for the Social Good

Leader: Michael Goldweber (*Xavier University*)

Participants: John Barr (*Ithaca College)*
Tony Clear (*Auckland University of Technology*)
Renzo Davoli (*University of Bologna)*
Samuel Mann (*Otago Polytechnic*)
Elizabeth Patitsas (*University of Toronto*)
Scott Pornoff (*Downtown Magnets High School, Los Angeles*)

Working Group 3: Teaching Modeling in Computing Curricula

Co-Leaders: Carl Alphonce (*University at Buffalo)*
Jürgen Börstler (*Bleginge Institute of Technology*)
Ludwik Kuzniarz (*Bleginge Institute of Technology*)

Participants: William B. Sanders (*University of Hartford*)
Michal Smialek (Warsaw University of Technology)

Working Group 4: Educating for Mobile Computing: Addressing the New Challenges

Leader: Barry Burd (*Drew University*)

Participants: João Paulo Barros (*Polytechnic Institute of Beja*)
Mark Chang (*Olin College of Engineering*)
Chris Johnson (*University of Wisconsin – Eau Claire*)
Stanislav Kurkovsky (*Central Connecticut State University*)
Arnold Rosenbloom (*University of Toronto – Mississauga*)
Taly Sharon (*University of Liverpool*)
Nikolai Tillman (*Microsoft*)

ITiCSE 2012 Sponsors & Supporters

Sponsor:

SIGCSE

Supporters:

Technion Israel Institute of Technology

The Open University of Israel

מחשבה
מרכז המורים הארצי למדעי המחשב

csta Computer Science Teachers Association

Microsoft®

ITiCSE 2012 Reviewers

Elizabeth S. Adams, *James Madison University*
Rajeev Agrawal, *North Carolina A & T State University*
Hend Al-Khalifa, *King Saud University*
Hana Alnuaim, *King Abdulaziz University*
Barbara Anthony, *Southwestern University*
Michal Armoni, *Weizmann Institute of Science*
Doug Baldwin, *SUNY Geneseo*
Valerie Barr, *Union College*
Michael Bauer, *University of Hawaii - Leeward Community College*
Tim Bell, *University of Canterbury*
Mordechai Ben-Ari, *Weizmann Institute of Science*
Mikael Berndtsson, *University of Skovde*
Anne Beug, *California Polytechnic State University*
Steven Bogaerts, *Wittenberg University*
Dennis Brylow, *Marquette University*
Kevin Burger, *Arizona State University*
Andre Paul Calitz, *Nelson Mandela Metropolitan University*
Vivian Campbell, *ECU*
Daniel Canas, *Wake Forest University*
Steven Case, *University of the Virgin Islands*
Maiga Chang, *Athabasca University*
Wei Kian Chen, *Champlain College*
Jayan Kurian Chirayath, *Royal Melbourne Institute of Technology*
David Chiu, *Washington State University, Vancouver*
Tony Clear, *Auckland University of Technology*
Joe Clifton, *University of Wisconsin, Platteville*
Randy Connolly, *Mount Royal University*
Andrew Dalton, *Western Carolina University*
Adrienne Decker, *Rochester Institute of Technology*
Katherine Deibel, *University of Washington-Seattle*
Rafael del Vado, *Universidad Complutense de Madrid*
Barbara Demo, *University Torino*
Peter DePasquale, *The College of New Jersey*
Molisa Derk, *Dickinson State University*
William Doane, *Bennington College*
Zachary Dodds, *Harvey Mudd College*
John Dooley, *Knox College*
Peter Drexel, *Plymouth State University*
J. Philip East, *University of Northern Iowa*
Joseph Ekstrom, *Brigham Young University*
Stephanie Elzer, *Millersville University*
Alec Engebretson, *Doane College*
Henry Etlinger, *Rochester Institute of Technology*
Alan Fekete, *University of Sydney*
Ernest Ferguson, *Northwest Missouri State University*
Samantha Foley, *Oak Ridge National Laboratory*
Sumit Garg, *Argonne National Laboratory*
Alessio Gaspar, *University of South Florida Polytechnic*
Rick Gee, *Okanagan College*
Paul Gestwicki, *Ball State University*
Don Goelman, *Villanova University*
Michael Goldweber, *Xavier University*
Jean Goulet, *Universite de Sherbrooke*
John Hamer, *University of Glasgow*
Sarah Heckman, *North Carolina State University*
David Hemmendinger, *Union College*
Tyson Henry, *California State University, Chico*
Matthew Hertz, *Canisius College*
Joe Hollingsworth, *Indiana University*
William Hooper, *Belmont University*
Brian Howard, *DePauw University*
James Howatt, *Luther College*
Jorge Eduardo Ibarra-Esquer, *Universidad Autonoma de Baja California*
Petri Ihantola, *Aalto University*
Mike Jipping, *Hope College*
Mark Johnson, *Central College*
Daniel Joyce, *Villanova University*
Viggo Kann, *KTH*
Elizabeth Katz, *Millersville University*
David Kauchak, *Middlebury College*
Petros Kefalas, *International Faculty of the University of Sheffield*
Mark Kerstetter, *Western Michigan University*
Nancy Kinnersley, *University of Kansas*
Benjamin Kuperman, *Oberlin College*
David Largent, *Ball State University*
Mary Last, *Self-Employed*
Alina Lazar, *Youngstown State University*

Byong Lee, *Bennett College*
Cynthia Lee, *UCSD*
Gilliean Lee, *Lander University*
Chi Un Lei, *University of Hong Kong*
Joan Lucas, *State University of New York, College at Brockport*
Bonnie MacKellar, *St John's University*
Lester McCann, *The University of Arizona*
O. William McClung, *Nebraska Wesleyan University*
Pedro Medeiros, *Universidade Nova de Lisboa*
Antonio Jose Mendes, *University of Coimbra*
Joe Miro, *Universitat de les Illes Balears*
Srikanth Mudigonda, *Saint Louis University*
Michael Murphy, *Concordia University Texas*
William Myers, *Belmont Abbey College*
Robert Noonan, *College of William and Mary*
Keith O'Hara, *Bard College*
David Parker, *Salisbury University*
James Paterson, *Glasgow Caledonian University*
Elizabeth Patitsas, *University of Toronto*
Arnold Pears, *Uppsala University*
Andrew Petersen, *University of Toronto Mississauga*
Vreda Pieterse, *University of Pretoria*
Nelishia Pillay, *University of KwaZulu-Natal*
Wayne Pollock, *Hillsborough Community College*
Jon Preston, *Southern Polytechnic State Unviersity*
John-Paul Pretti, *University of Waterloo*
Sarah Monisha Pulimood, *The College of New Jersey*
Muthu Ramachandran, *Leeds Metropolitan University*
Samuel Rebelsky, *Grinnell College*
Christian Roberson, *Plymouth State University*
Stefan Robila, *Montclair State University*
Guido Roessling, *Technische Universitaet Darmstadt*
Krishnendu Roy, *Valdosta State University*
Martin Ruckert, *Munich University of Applied Sciences*
Anthony Ruocco, *Roger Williams University*
Mehran Sahami, *Stanford University*
Ian Sanders, *University of South Africa*
André Santos, *Lisbon University Institute*
Otto Seppälä, *Aalto University*
Amber Settle, *DePaul University*
Behrooz Seyed-Abbassi, *University of North Florida*
Mark Sherriff, *University of Virginia*
Yasuto Shirai, *Shizuoka University*
Raja Sooriamurthi, *Carnegie Mellon University*
Jaime Spacco, *Knox College*
Kazunari Sugiyama, *National University of Singapore*
Valerie Summet, *Emory University*
James Teresco, *Siena College*
William Thacker, *Winthrop University*
Megan Thomas, *California State University Stanislaus*
Rebecca Thomas, *Bard College*
Neena Thota, *Uppsala University*
William Turner, *Wabash College*
Ian Utting, *University of Kent at Canterbury*
Jan Vahrenhold, *Technische Universität Dortmund*
Tammy VanDeGrift, *University of Portland*
Jorge Vasconcelos, *Johns Hopkins University*
Troy Vasiga, *University of Waterloo*
Kam Vat, *University of Macau*
Gabriela Vilanova, *National Patagonia Austral University*
Sally Wahba, *Clemson University*
Henry Walker, *Grinnell College*
Xinli Wang, *Michigan Technological University*
Thomas Way, *Villanova University*
Howard Whitston, *University of South Alabama*
Gary Ka Wai Wong, *The Community College at Lingnan University*
Arthur Yanushka, *Christian Brothers University*
Fani Zlatarova, *Elizabethtown College*

Keynote Talk

Never Too Early to Begin: Computer Science for High-School Students

Michael Rabin
Hebrew University and Harvard University
rabin@seas.harvard.edu

Abstract

Computer science and technology innovated over the past sixty years, have revolutionized science, the economy and societal interactions. Inherently CS constitutes a new science combining mathematics, logic, information theory and electronics, on par with physics, chemistry and the life sciences. It is appropriate to educate students in the fundamentals of this science. The curriculum should emphasize the scientific content rather than provide mere training in some programming language.

Categories and Subject Descriptors: K.3.2 [**Computers and Education**]: Computer and Information Science Education – *Computer Science Education*

Keywords: High School Education

Bio

Rabin is Professor of Computer Science at Harvard SEAS. He received his Ph.D. in Mathematics at Princeton University. His contributions include innovation of non-deterministic computations, probabilistic automata, the first paper on complexity of computations, non-deterministic automata on infinite trees applicable to decision problems in logic and program verification, randomized algorithms including randomized test for primality, PKE system provably as safe as factorization, oblivious transfer, asynchronous parallel computing, a practical provably unbreakable encryption system recently implemented as a Masters Thesis Project by a student jointly supervised by Rabin and Ron Rivest Currently Rabin is working on a practically efficient zero-knowledge proof system with application to privacy and financial processes such as secure auctions, matching, and regulation compliance.

Rabin's awards include the ACM Turing Award, the Dan David Prize in Computation and Communication, the Israel Prize in Computer Science, the Harvey Prize in Science and Technology, the ACM Paris Kanellakis Prize for Theory and Practice, and the Rothschild Prize in Mathematics. His academy memberships include the US National Academy of Science, the American Philosophical Society, the French Academy of Sciences, the Royal Society and the Israel Academy of Sciences. He holds six honorary degrees. He was Albert Einstein Professor at the Hebrew University where he was also Rector (academic head). He was Visiting Professor at Berkeley, Columbia, Yale, Paris University, University College London, MIT, Cal Tech, ETH, NYU Courant Institute. He was Saville Fellow at Merton College Oxford and Steward Fellow at Gonville and Caius College Cambridge. During Spring 2009 he was Visiting Researcher at Google lab New York.

ITiCSE'12, July 3--5, 2012, Haifa, Israel.
ACM 978-1-4503-1246-2/12/07.

Keynote Talk

Alan Turing and the Other Theory of Computation

Lenore Blum
Carnegie Mellon University
lblum@cs.cmu.edu

Abstract

The two major traditions of the Theory of Computation, each asking claim to similar motivations and aspirations, have for the most part run a parallel non-intersecting course. On one hand, we have the tradition arising from logic and computer science addressing problems with more recent origins, using tools of combinatorics and discrete mathematics. On the other hand, we have numerical analysis and scientific computation emanating from the classical tradition of equation solving and the continuous mathematics of calculus. Both traditions are motivated by a desire to understand the essence of computation, of algorithm; both aspire to discover useful, even profound, consequences. While the logic and computer science communities are keenly aware of Alan Turing's seminal role in the former (discrete) tradition of the theory of computation, most remain unaware of Alan Turing's role in the latter (continuous) tradition, this notwithstanding the many references to Turing in the modern numerical analysis/computational mathematics literature. In this talk I recognize Turing's work in the foundations of numerical computation. I also indicate its role in complexity theory today, and how it provides a unifying concept for the two major traditions in the Theory of Computation.

Categories and Subject Descriptors: K.3.2 [**Computers and Education**]: Computer and Information Science Education – *Computer Science Education*

Keywords: Numerical Computation, Complexity Theory

Bio

Blum received her Ph.D. in mathematics from M.I.T. in 1968. She then went to UC Berkeley as a Postdoctoral Fellow and Lecturer in Mathematics. In 1973 she joined Mills College where she founded the Dept. of Mathematics and Computer Science. In 1979 she was awarded the first Letts-Villard Chair at Mills. In the fall of 1999, Blum joined Carnegie Mellon, where she is Distinguished Career Professor of Computer Science, as well as co-Director on the NSF-ITR ALADDIN Center for ALgorithm ADaptation Dissemination and INtegration. Blum's research, from her early work in model theory and differential fields to her more recent work in developing a theory of computation and complexity over the real numbers has focused on merging seemingly unrelated areas. Blum is well known for her work in increasing participation of girls and women in STEM fields. She was instrumental in founding the Assoc. for Women in Mathematics (serving as its President from 1975 to 1978), the Math/Science Network and its Expanding Your Horizons conferences for high school girls, and served as co-PI for the Mills Summer Mathematics Institute for undergraduate women. At CMU she has been faculty advisor to the Women@SCS and a member of the President's Diversity Advisory Council. Furthermore, Blum has served on the Council and as Vice President of the AMS (1990-1992). After representing the AMS at the Pan African Congress of Mathematicians in 1991, she became committed to building links between the American and African mathematics communities.

ITiCSE'12, July 3--5, 2012, Haifa, Israel.
ACM 978-1-4503-1246-2/12/07.

Keynote Talk

Standing on the Shoulders of a Giant: One Person's Experience of Turing's Impact

David Harel
The Weizmann Institute of Science, Israel
david.harel@weizmann.ac.il

Abstract

The talk will briefly describe three of Turing's major achievements, in three different fields: computability, biological modeling and artificial intelligence. Interspersed with this, I will explain how each of them directly motivated and inspired me to carry out a variety of research projects over a period of 30 years, the results of which can all be viewed humbly as extensions and generalizations of Turing's pioneering and ingenious insights.

Categories and Subject Descriptors: K.3.2 [**Computers and Education**]: Computer and Information Science Education – *Computer Science Education*

Keywords: Turing, Computability, Biological Modeling, AI

Bio

David Harel has been at the Weizmann Institute of Science in Israel since 1980. He was Department Head from 1989 to 1995, and was Dean of the Faculty of Mathematics and Computer Science between 1998 and 2004. He was also co-founder of I-Logix, Inc. He received his PhD from MIT in 1978, and has spent time at IBM Yorktown Heights, and sabbaticals at Carnegie-Mellon, Cornell, and the University of Edinburgh. In the past he worked mainly in theoretical computer science (logic, computability, automata, database theory), and he now works mainly on software and systems engineering and on modeling biological systems. He is the inventor of Statecharts and co-inventor of Live Sequence Charts (LSCs), and co-designed Statemate, Rhapsody, the Play-Engine and PlayGo. Among his books are "Algorithmics: The Spirit of Computing" and "Computers Ltd.: What They Really Can't Do", and his awards include the ACM Karlstrom Outstanding Educator Award (1992), the Israel Prize (2004), the ACM Software System Award (2007), the Emet Prize (2010), and four honorary degrees. He is a Fellow of the ACM, the IEEE and the AAAS, and a member of the Academia Europaea and Israel Academy of Sciences.

ITiCSE'12, July 3--5, 2012, Haifa, Israel.
ACM 978-1-4503-1246-2/12/07.

Activities, Affordances and Attitude — How Student-generated Questions Assist Learning

Andrew Luxton-Reilly, Paul Denny, Beryl Plimmer, Robert Sheehan
The University of Auckland
Auckland, New Zealand
andrew|paul|beryl|robert-s@cs.auckland.ac.nz

ABSTRACT

Recent research has focused on tools that support the creation, review and sharing of student-generated content for peer learning. However, we know little about the student perspective of such activities. In this paper, we identify what students believe is most helpful for their learning by analysing open-ended comments from students engaged in creating, answering and reviewing exam-style questions generated by their peers. Students report learning about content and appropriate standards of work, both individually and through interaction with peer generated resources.

Categories and Subject Descriptors

K.3.2 [**Computers and Education**]: Computer and Information Science Education—*computer science education*

General Terms

Design, Human Factors

Keywords

StudySieve, question-generation, peer-review, free-response, student-generated, contributing student pedagogy, constructive evaluation

1. INTRODUCTION

Technology has enabled new pedagogies that place students in the centre of learning by involving them in the *process* of education [4]. Although studies involving these pedagogies have reported quantitative evidence of positive feedback from students, few of the studies have employed qualitative measures. We argue that greater insights may be gleaned from an analysis of open-ended comments from students.

In these "contributing student" pedagogies, students take on roles traditionally occupied by teachers, generating resources for peer learning. There are many benefits claimed by advocates of these pedagogies, perhaps most important, moving students towards the goal of being independent learners. Students are encouraged to focus on determining the quality of their own work and that of others, and selecting, filtering and creating course related material that meets appropriate standards [8].

One approach, categorised by Hamer et al. [9] as *activity creation*, requires students to generate exam-style questions, with sample solutions, and submit them to an online repository. Other students may answer the questions, and having answered, may evaluate the quality of the questions and answers contributed by their peers. This pedagogy has been previously termed *constructive evaluation* [16].

The activity of generating questions for peer learning has been supported by a number of purpose-built tools [5, 11, 13, 17, 22, 23, 24]. Studies involving some of these tools show improved learning outcomes [13, 15]. However, we know little about the student perspective of these tools. In this study, we present qualitative findings from a questionnaire administered to students engaged in constructive evaluation.

2. RELATED WORK

Numerous tools that support the generation and sharing of questions created by students have been reported in the literature. The evaluations of student attitudes towards these tools have been predominantly conducted using quantitative feedback from students obtained using Likert-scale questions.

Quantitative analysis of student attitudes show that students believe creating questions is beneficial for learning in studies of QPPA [24], ExamNet [22], Concerto [11], PeerWise [5], QuARKS [23], CodeWrite [6] and StudySieve [17]. Answering questions in drill-and-practice form was also reported as beneficial for learning in studies of QPPA, CodeWrite, PeerWise and StudySieve.

Quantitive results from student surveys also show that viewing the questions authored by peers was reported as beneficial for learning in studies of ExamNet [22], QuARKS [23] and StudySieve [17]. Students using CodeWrite reported that seeing solutions of other students helped them learn [6], as did students using StudySieve. The evaluation phase (i.e. peer assessment) was reported as useful in QPPA [24], PeerWise [5], QuARKS [23] and StudySieve. Summary statistics and online ranking lists (features also present in PeerWise) were noted as being beneficial for learning by students using QPPA.

Only studies with QPPA [24] and Concerto [11] have reported qualitative findings. Although open-ended comments

ITiCSE'12, July 3–5, 2012, Haifa, Israel.

were collected from students about how QPPA helped them to learn, the analysis of the data was not reported in detail. Comments from students using Concerto were also collected, but few of the students who answered the survey had used Concerto to write questions (of the 77 students enrolled in the course, 66 completed the survey, but only 20 had used the system to author questions). A few exemplar student comments were presented, but no systematic analysis of the qualitative data was performed.

3. METHODOLOGY

StudySieve [17] is a web-based system designed to support student-generated free-response questions. Students in three large undergraduate courses were required to use StudySieve to author questions, answer questions created by their peers and evaluate both questions and answers. After the deadline for completing the tasks, a questionnaire consisting of both Likert-scale and open-response questions was administered to students.

Qualitative data were collected from students in response to the questions "What was most helpful for your learning?" and "What improvements would you like to see?". Comments about improvements tended to be system-specific and have been used to inform the modification of the interface and workflow of StudySieve. However, the focus of this paper is to analyse student responses to the question "What was most helpful for your learning?". In this section, we report on the context in which the activities took place, the questionnaire response rates and the analysis procedures.

3.1 Context of use

StudySieve was used as part of the teaching and assessment activities used in three large undergraduate courses (COMPSCI 111, COMPSCI 101 and COMPSCI 105) taught at The University of Auckland during 2010 and summer 2011. All students were provided with written information that explained the philosophy underlying student-generated content and a simple guide that outlined different kinds of questions. In all courses, students were required to submit questions and answers for a small portion of their final grade. When students answer a question, StudySieve requires them to evaluate that question, their own answer to the question and a minimum of one other answer, although students may choose to evaluate more than one other answer if they choose. The courses involved in this study, and the requirements for the activities involving student-generated content are described below.

COMPSCI 111 — Mastering Cyberspace: An Introduction to Practical Computing (hereafter referred to as CS0) is a service course that provides non-majors with an introduction to computing concepts and their practical application. Students enrolled in CS0 during the second semester 2010 and the summer semester 2011 were surveyed. In both semesters, students were required to author 2 questions and answer 10 questions for a small percentage of their final grade (1% in 2010 and 2% in 2011).

COMPSCI 101 — Principles of Programming (hereafter referred to as CS1) is a standard introduction to programming using Java. Students enrolled in the second semester 2010 were surveyed. Each student was required to author 1 question and answer 5 questions to receive 1% of their final grade.

COMPSCI 105 — Principles of Computer Science (hereafter referred to as CS2) is a standard introduction to data structures and algorithms using Java. This course is normally taken by students who have completed CS1. Students enrolled in the second semester 2010 were surveyed. Each student was required to author 1 question and answer 5 questions for 1% of their final grade.

3.2 Questionnaire response rates

Across the first-year cohort surveyed, 853 students participated in the activities and 54.6% of those students returned the questionnaire. Of the 466 questionnaires returned, 218 included responses to the open-ended question "What was most helpful to your learning?".

Table 1 summarizes the courses, the number of students that used StudySieve in each course, and the percentage of students that completed the questionnaire. The low response rate to the questionnaire in the CS1 course was a consequence of distributing the questionnaire during lectures (which have a relatively low attendance rate), rather than during tutorials/labs as in the other courses.

Course	Users	Survey	Response rate
CS0	491	333	67.8%
CS1	173	27	15.6%
CS2	189	106	56.1%
Overall	853	466	54.6%
Complete		218	25.5%

Table 1: Questionnaire response rates

3.3 Analysis procedure

The qualitative feedback provided by students was data-entered prior to being coded. Initially, the data was *open-coded* [20] by the first author. The procedure of open-coding focuses on individual words and phrases in detail, generating a multitude of codes which are grounded in the data. During the open-coding process, the comments provided by students were broken into units of meaning, each containing one distinct idea [18]. In most cases, individual sentences acted as a unit of meaning, but compound sentences were frequently divided into component parts.

Through an iterative process of refinement, the first author grouped the initial codes into topics, constantly comparing [20] the topics with the original data to ensure that the topics adequately captured the meaning inherent in the data. These topics were subsequently grouped into categories, which were in turn grouped into themes.

To determine the reliability of the coding scheme, a second researcher coded the data according to the list of topics, and the inter-rater reliability was calculated using Cohen's kappa. An almost perfect [14] level of agreement was found (κ=.83).

4. RESULTS

Three main themes were identified during the analysis of student responses to the question "What was most helpful to your learning?". No negative feedback was provided in response to this question. The three themes distinguished between *activities* described by students, the *affordances* provided by StudySieve, and the *attitudes* of students. The activity theme includes categories that distinguish between individual learning and peer learning, and between content knowledge and knowledge about a course (i.e. the standards and expectations of performance).The following subsections describe the major themes and categories that emerged through the analysis of the qualitative data.

4.1 Activities

Student feedback about the activities that were most helpful for their learning are organised into the categories of: individual content; peer content; individual standards; and peer standards. Figure 1 summarizes the different categories of student activity and lists the topics that belong to each category. The activity categories are described in more detail in this section, along with comments that exemplify the different topics.

4.1.1 Activities – Individual content

Individual learning about content occurs when a student interacts with resources that are not peer generated, or when they create material in response to requests from teachers. Most of the learning activities in traditionally delivered courses would fit into this category. For example, students may read a textbook or complete an individual programming assignment set by their teacher.

In this study, activities involving writing questions, reviewing study material, or reflecting on the content they have learned in class are all classified as individual learning of content. In all of these cases, the learning occurs through interaction with traditional course material rather than peer generated content, although it is possible that peer interaction acts as a catalyst for learning.

The most frequent activity mentioned by students was **writing questions**. The following comments are typical:

> *Having to develop a question.*
>
> *Writing a question of my own.*

In addition, some students gave an explanation of *why* writing questions helped them to learn. Students described how the act of creating a question caused them to return to the instructional material delivered during the course and **review content** (described by students as revising content) before they were able to generate a question. For example:

> *The fact that we had to create our own questions and provide the answers. Need to do some revision first in order to complete them*
>
> *When developing new questions I had to revise the course book*

Similarly, when students described why *answering questions* helped them to learn, they explained that they used resource material to try and find a solution to questions they couldn't answer. In other words, they **reviewed content** in order to answer a question. Although some students used the term "research", all the questions in the repository involved material that had been presented during lectures or laboratories. The use of "research" in this context is therefore interpreted as trying to understand course content that was previously missed, either by reviewing the instructional material, or by finding alternate explanations. For example:

> *This means we have to try to solve it ourselves to understand the topic or to find more info in the Internet.*
>
> *. . . because research needed*
>
> *. . . you would have to find out the answer*

Writing questions, and the sample solutions to those questions, caused some students to **reflect on the content** they had learned during the course. Students felt that the *process* of creating a question (and associated solution) required them to really focus on the course content and engage in analysis of the material. For example:

> *Having to think more deeply about the info in order to create questions (interact with the study material)*
>
> *The construction of questions I thought was useful. And by this I mean the process of thinking of a question and logically finding a good response to own question was useful*

4.1.2 Activities – Peer content

Peer learning of content occurs when a student learns from material produced by their peers. The quantity and variety of content produced by students can act as a valuable learning resource. In this study, reading the questions authored by peers, reading the answers authored by peers, and answering the questions authored by peers are all activities classified as learning about content from peer-generated resources.

Students reported that **viewing questions** contributed by their peers was beneficial, although it is unclear *how* simply seeing the questions helped them. The following examples are typical of student comments categorized as **viewing questions**

> *That I could look at other people's questions*
>
> *Seeing other student's questions*

Students also reported that **answering questions** improved their understanding of the course material.

> *Answering questions from other students helped me with difficult topics*
>
> *Access to the database of questions allowing me to answer the questions as it allowed me to understand the coursework better*

Using the questions generated by their peers for drill and practice helped students to prepare for tests and exams. For example:

> *The large database of questions allows for a lot of practice which I find is essential to doing well in tests/exams*

The large number of questions available in the repository was appreciated, and both the variety of topics covered and the different styles of questions were described as being beneficial.

> *Having a lot of questions to answer covering all topics*

	Content	Standards
Individual	• Write question • Review content • Reflect on content	• Evaluate self • Check content • Establish expectations
Peer	• View questions • Answer questions • View answers	• Evaluate others • Receive feedback • Compare self with others

Figure 1: Categorization of activities that help students learn.

> *Many new questions on the StudySieve these new questions I never see before*
>
> *I feel it was really helpful being able to answer other peers questions because they would often be quite different to questions asked by the examiners/lecturers etc.*

Students also felt that **viewing the answers** contributed by other students was helpful, particularly when the answers varied. For example:

> *Seeing other student's answers as most questions can be solved multiple ways so it is interesting to see the different approaches to solve the problem*

Exposure to solutions of varying levels of correctness was identified as being valuable by some students. The better solutions provided an opportunity to learn by modelling a high quality answer, while poor solutions highlighted mistakes that students could avoid. The following comments illustrate how students used both high and low quality answers to learn.

> *I can see some other programming codes that give me more ideas on how to implement mine*
>
> *Having a reference answer/template helps me understand what to put in my own answers to get the best possible mark*
>
> *By seeing the common mistakes made by other students allowed me to make sure I avoid that pitfall*
>
> *If some other students answer is wrong then I can learn what errors student occurred in particular question. This thing help me a lot and I never made that mistake in future*

4.1.3 Activities – Individual standards

Individual learning about appropriate standards of work occurs when a student engages in self-assessment to determine their own knowledge or judges the quality of their own work. These evaluations are typically based on criteria specified by an external authority such as a teacher or a textbook. In this study, activities in which students evaluate their own knowledge, check the correctness of their own work, or make judgements about the nature of course content (such as difficulty or relative importance) are classified as individual learning about standards.

There are many different kinds of judgements that students make when using StudySieve. Students reported that they focused internally through **self-evaluation**, either by evaluating their own work, or by assessing their understanding. For example:

> *Evaluating my own question*
>
> *Writing and answering questions helped test my knowledge*

Students also described how they **checked content** by verifying the accuracy or correctness of material in external, authoritative sources.

> *Checking the coursebook to be sure I had it right*
>
> *Anything I was unsure of I went back to notes and the manuals to check my answers. I also did this to clarify answers posted by other students.*

The entire process encouraged them to think about the **expectations** of the course, reflecting on the topics that would be examined and the relative difficulty of those topics.

> *Actually having to do it made you think about things what would be the most difficult*
>
> *... think about what kind of questions might be asked in a text/exam*
>
> *... give a good idea of what to focus on.*

4.1.4 Activities – Peer standards

Learning about standards from peer-generated resources occurs when students focus on judging the quality of those resources. In this study, both the giving and receiving of feedback is categorised as learning about standards through interaction with peers. Situations in which students compare their own work against the work produced by their peers also fall into this category.

Students reported that **evaluating others** by rating the quality of peer content (both questions and answers) helped them to learn, as did **receiving feedback** from their peers.

> *Evaluating other student's questions*
>
> *... rating other student's answers*
>
> *Seeing how other students rated my answer*

More commonly, students described how they used the peer content to **compare themselves with their peers**. The answers contributed by peers acted as sample solutions against which students could benchmark their own solutions, identify errors and note possible improvements. For example:

> *After answering you can compare your question with others and find out that there were more correct solutions or more effective ones*
>
> *It was good being able to check answers against other people because you could see where you had gone wrong.*

4.2 Affordances

Although the majority of comments from students were related to their activities, the functions provided by StudySieve were also mentioned. Since these features were described in response to the question "What was most helpful for your learning?", we assume that students found these features to be critically important to the usability of the system.

The most common function identified was the ability to organize the questions in different ways using filtering and sorting. The filtering and sorting features make it much easier to find relevant questions, which is particularly important when there is a large number of questions present in the repository.

> *Being able to choose questions by topic*
>
> *View all the questions before answering, browse by rank*
>
> *The difficulty of each question shown is helpful.*
>
> *The ability to choose which questions does mean you can only do easy questions, but it also means that you can pick questions relevant to what you are studying and matching your difficult without being forced to answer a multitude of bad or easy questions*

4.3 Attitude

The final category captures comments that describe the emotional state of a student. Some students describe how the activities or features experienced when they interact with StudySieve improved engagement, confidence or enjoyment.

Students noted that the ranking and overall statistics were motivating and enjoyable.

> *I found the personal ranking and stats motivating, made me want to do more.*
>
> *Seeing my statistics compared to the rest of the students is motivating to answer more questions*
>
> *I think the ratings and comments systems along with the large amount of statistics and "achievements" were fun*

The anonymity and student-centric focus of the activities were described favourably. The activities were considered to be low-risk by students, which made it easy to practice and interact with other students.

> *Mainly the viewing of questions from other students. This helped to familiarize me with CS topics in a more communicatively approachable manner*
>
> *It was like exam questions but the pressure was not there so it is a small confidence booster*
>
> *The anonymity of questions and answering made it "safe" to have a go.*

A few students also noted that they had fun being involved in the question-generation and answering process and that it was interesting.

> *The system was relatively fun to use.*
>
> *I think the system itself was very interesting and useful for learning.*

5. DISCUSSION

We have focused on identifying the major themes and categories of activity evident in students' comments, rather than quantifying the comments falling into each category. These themes and categories may inform future studies of student-generated questions for peer learning. Students report that they learn from both individual activities and from interacting with resources generated by their peers. In addition, students report that they learn not only context specific knowledge (course content), but also metacognitive knowledge such as the standards and expectations of a given course.

The comments from students provide evidence that they are engaged in both *comprehension fostering* and *comprehension monitoring activities* [19].

Comprehension fostering activities such as **writing questions** resulted in students **reviewing content** and **reflecting on course content** which are strategies that promote deeper learning. Students also report learning vicariously [2] from the behaviour of their peers by modelling the examples of good solutions and avoiding the errors present in poor solutions.

Students engaged in **answering questions** for drill and practice, **evaluating** their own questions and answers, or **comparing themselves with others** are monitoring their own understanding, and having identified their strengths and weaknesses, may be able to use their study time more efficiently. Such comprehension monitoring activities are described by Boud [3] as being essential for successful life-long learning.

Although there have been no previous qualitative studies of student-generated exam-style questions, there are reports on the student perspective of peer review activities that show similar findings to this study. Williams [21] found that students valued being able to compare different solutions, being able to compare standards of work, and exchanging information and ideas, all of which are also mentioned by students in this study. Similarly, Hanrahan and Isaacs [10] found that students enjoyed the opportunity to compare their own work with others, that it was useful to see examples of good and bad work, that it gave students a good idea of the expected standards and it helped to develop critical thinking skills.

The large size of the repository and the variety of questions and answers is reported as valuable. Sharing such a large resource within a learning community is only possible when a tool is provided to assist with the administrative burden imposed by activities that involve peer assessment [1]. The focus on student-generated content and the anonymity provided by the online tool both helped to create an environment in which students felt confident to contribute.

Howe, McWilliam and Cross [12] suggest that peer interaction does not result in immediate gains in learning, but rather acts as a catalyst for future learning. Students who engage in peer discussion or generate a solution that disagrees with peers are *primed* to learn when they encounter that topic in future. Draper [7] suggests that interacting with peers is more effective than interacting with teachers in this regard because the opinion of teachers are accepted without thinking, while peer opinions are treated with an element of suspicion and encourage students to verify material for themselves. In this study, students do indeed report checking content with authoritative sources and engaging in research to resolve conflicts in understanding.

6. CONCLUSIONS & FUTURE WORK

The results from this study are consistent with findings from studies involving self- and peer-assessment. Students learn from a wide variety of activities, both individually and through interaction with peer-generated resources. The qualitative analysis of student feedback confirms that they are engaged in activities that promote deeper learning while developing important metacognitive skills. In future, we hope to use the categories identified in this study to quantify the proportion of students engaged in these various kinds of learning to improve our understanding of how student-generated questions can be used most effectively in the classroom.

7. REFERENCES

[1] R. Ballantyne, K. Hughes, and A. Mylonas. Developing procedures for implementing peer assessment in large classes using an action research process. *Assessment and Evaluation in Higher Education*, 27(5):427–441, 2002.

[2] A. Bandura. *Social foundations of thought and action: A social cognitive theory.* Prentice-Hall, 1986.

[3] D. Boud. Sustainable assessment: rethinking assessment for the learning society. *Studies in Continuing Education*, 22(2):151–167, 2000.

[4] B. Collis and J. Moonen. *An on-going journey: Technology as a learning workbench.* University of Twente, Enschede, The Netherlands., 2005.

[5] P. Denny, A. Luxton-Reilly, and J. Hamer. The PeerWise system of student contributed assessment questions. In Simon and M. Hamilton, editors, *Tenth Australasian Computing Education Conference (ACE 2008)*, volume 78 of *CRPIT*, pages 69–74, Wollongong, NSW, Australia, 2008. ACS.

[6] P. Denny, A. Luxton-Reilly, E. Tempero, and J. Hendrickx. Codewrite: supporting student-driven practice of java. In *Proceedings of the 42nd ACM technical symposium on Computer science education*, SIGCSE '11, pages 471–476, New York, NY, USA, 2011. ACM.

[7] S. W. Draper. Catalytic assessment: understanding how MCQs and EVS can foster deep learning. *British Journal of Educational Technology*, 40(2):285–293, March 2009.

[8] J. Hamer, Q. Cutts, J. Jackova, A. Luxton-Reilly, R. McCartney, H. Purchase, C. Riedesel, M. Saeli, K. Sanders, and J. Sheard. Contributing student pedagogy. *SIGCSE Bull.*, 40(4):194–212, 2008.

[9] J. Hamer, H. C. Purchase, A. Luxton-Reilly, and J. Sheard. Tools for "contributing student learning". In *Proceedings of the 2010 ITiCSE working group reports on Working group reports*, ITiCSE-WGR '10, pages 1–14, New York, NY, USA, 2010. ACM.

[10] S. J. Hanrahan and G. Isaacs. Assessing stlf- and peer-assessment: the students' views. *Higher Education Research & Development*, 20:53–69, 2001.

[11] Y. Hirai and A. Hazeyama. A learning support system based on question-posing and its evaluation. *Creating, Connecting and Collaborating through Computing, International Conference on*, 0:178–184, 2007.

[12] C. Howe, D. McWilliam, and G. Cross. Chance favours only the prepared mind: Incubation and the delayed effects of peer collaboration. *British Journal of Psychology*, 96(1):67–93(27), February 2005.

[13] Y.-F. Lan and P. C. Lin. Evaluation and improvement of student's question posing ability in a web-based learning environment. *Australasian Journal of Educational Technology*, 27(4):581–599, 2011.

[14] J. R. Landis and G. G. Koch. The measurement of observer agreement for categorical data. *Biometrics*, 33(1):pp. 159–174, 1977.

[15] A. Luxton-Reilly, D. Bertinshaw, P. Denny, B. Plimmer, and R. Sheehan. The impact of question generation activities on performance. In *SIGCSE '12: Proceedings of the 43rd ACM technical symposium on Computer Science Education*, Raleigh, NC, USA, February 29 – March 3rd 2012. ACM.

[16] A. Luxton-Reilly and P. Denny. Constructive evaluation: a pedagogy of student-contributed assessment. *Computer Science Education*, 20:145–167, 2010.

[17] A. Luxton-Reilly, P. Denny, B. Plimmer, and D. Bertinshaw. Supporting student-generated free-response questions. In *Proceedings of the 16th annual joint conference on Innovation and technology in computer science education*, ITiCSE '11, pages 153–157, New York, NY, USA, 2011. ACM.

[18] M. B. Miles and A. M. Huberman. *Qualitative Data Analysis.* SAGE Publications Inc., 1994.

[19] A. S. Palincsar and A. L. Brown. Reciprocal teaching of comprehension-fostering and comprehension-monitoring activities. *Cognition and Instruction*, 1(2):117–175, 1984.

[20] A. L. Strauss. *Qualitative Analysis for Social Scientists.* Cambridge University Press, 1987.

[21] E. Williams. Student attitudes towards approaches to learning and assessment. *Assessment & Evaluation in Higher Education*, 17(1):45–58, 1992.

[22] E. V. Wilson. Examnet asynchronous learning network: augmenting face-to-face courses with student-developed exam questions. *Computers & Education*, 42(1):87 – 107, 2004.

[23] F.-Y. Yu. Scaffolding student-generated questions: Design and development of a customizable online learning system. *Computers in Human Behaviour*, 25:1129–1138, 2009.

[24] F.-Y. Yu, Y. H. Liu, and T.-W. Chan. The efficacy of a web-based domain independent question-posing and peer assessment learning system. *Computers in Education, International Conference on*, 0:641, 2002.

Maximizing Learning and Guiding Behavior in Free Play User Generated Content Environments

Acey Boyce, Antoine Campbell, Shaun Pickford, Dustin Culler, and Tiffany Barnes

Department of Computer Science
University of North Carolina at Charlotte
9201 University City Blvd., Charlotte, NC, USA
1-704-687-8577

Tiffany.Barnes@uncc.edu

ABSTRACT

Providing users the ability to create their own unique content in educational software and games can be highly effective at motivating the users to use and reuse the system. It is especially popular with students who self identify as creative or wanting to do their own thing rather than a prescribed activity. Due to the popularity of user generated content modes, some users may ignore other modes the software has to offer and only create new original content. Therefore it is important to maximize the learning potential and effectively guide user behavior in a constructivist free play environment. However, in doing so it is vital that we do not hamper the creative freedom of the user, the very reason users enjoy content creation. Here we present effective strategies for meeting these goals, provide an example implementation, and present results of a study using the example.

Categories and Subject Descriptors

K.3.2 [**Computers and education**]: Computer and information science education. – computer science education.

General Terms

Design, Human Factors

Keywords

Game development, education, motivation, evaluation.

1. INTRODUCTION

Educational software, including games, is rapidly increasing in complexity and number of features. One area that shows great promise for motivating students is user generated content. User generated content is additional original content that is created by the user rather than the developer to be used by other users in the software. Examples of user generated content could include art assets, sounds, music, questions, puzzles, or games. There are numerous examples in both industry and academia for the power of user generated content. The largest commercial success is Little Big Planet and its sequel Little Big Planet 2. Little Big Planet is a platforming game for the Playstation 3 that allows its players to make their own levels within the game. The sequel takes this a step farther and allows players to make entire games. In total the community has generated over six million levels and games in Little Big Planet 2. The result of this is an active creative community and nearly infinite replayability [7]. In academia the WeScheme programming environment is being used to support Bootstrap, an educational program for middle and high school students. With WeScheme users can create full games in their browsers then publish the games and share them through WeScheme or social media sites such as Facebook, Reddit, and Twitter [9]. Another successful example of user-generated content is the Scratch programming environment. Scratch has a very active online community where users can upload their Scratch creations. It has developed into "a vibrant online community, with people sharing, discussing, and remixing one another's projects" [8]. In the 27 months following Scratch's launch more than 500,000 projects were published on the Scratch website [8].

The addition of user generated content has many advantages. By allowing users to create additional content you can greatly increase the replayability of the software. This increased motivation to play and replay the game is a key feature of the most successful educational software [5]. This content creation can also decrease the amount of content the developers must generate. In some cases the content generated by users can surpass that of the original developers [3].

Creating user-generated content can appeal to users who self-identify as creative, who may not like the rigid goal based systems of typical educational software. Giving these users an environment where they are free to create and express themselves helps make your software appeal to a wider range of users. This can also create a content generation loop where the creative users are creating content for other, more goal-oriented users. In turn the goal-oriented users demand even better new content. This loop motivates both competitive and creative players to continue to return to the game [3].

Motivating users to use the content generation features is only half of the equation, when the goal is to promote learning. It is not uncommon for some users to use only the content creation feature rather than using all the features of the software as it was designed. Even if the rest of the software shows great learning gains, if the isolated content creation environment is not an effective learning environment then users who primarily use this feature will not get the vital learning from the educational software. Therefore we must ensure that the content creation environment is effective for learning. This is a difficult challenge because of the inherent free play nature of content creation environments. In a free play environment without interference a majority of users will default to the simplest solution to a problem [1,2]. This simplest solution may avoid exposure to and learning

ITiCSE'12, July 3–5, 2012, Haifa, Israel.

of targeted learning objectives. Thus the challenge is how to guide behavior in order to maximize learning in a free play environment without impacting creative freedom. Here we present our solution to this problem for BeadLoom Game and the results of a study using the new user generated content environment.

2. BEADLOOM GAME

BeadLoom Game (BLG) [community.game2learn.com] is an educational puzzle game designed to teach basic mathematical principles including geometry and Cartesian coordinates as well as more advanced concepts like iteration and optimization. In BLG players are given a goal image on a 21x21 Cartesian grid. They are tasked with recreating it in the fewest moves possible, where a move consists of drawing beads using one of the six functions available. The Point function plots a single point at a time. Line, Rectangle, and Triangle Functions plot multiple points at a time creating a line, rectangle, or triangle of beads. Linear Iteration and Triangle Iteration functions use an iterative pattern to plot complex patterns. Although all the goal images could be created using the simple point function, in order to get better scores players must use and learn the material associated with the more complex functions. In other words, using the more complex functions is the desired behavior and using the simple functions is a less desirable behavior but is permitted especially with new or novice players. The game encourages a transition to the desired behavior through performance medals and high score tables which rank the players. This system was found to be more effective at teaching the learning objectives than similar software with no game elements [1,2].

The original implementation of a content creation environment was very simple. Players had a blank 21x21 Cartesian coordinates grid and could fill it using as many moves as they wanted. Once they were done, they could publish their design so that other players can play it. Published designs also appear in the custom puzzle showcase where players view and rate each others' designs. The showcase is ordered by ratings, with the highest rated puzzles appearing first.

Studies on this version of the user generated content environment found it to be extremely effective at motivating students to play both in the classroom and at home. The custom puzzle showcase also pushed players to create very complex and interesting designs in a constant effort to reach the top of the showcase [3]. However, later analysis of the logs revealed that a majority of players were creating these complex designs using the simple functions with almost no use of the iterative functions, because there was no motivation to do otherwise. Although the content that was being created was of high quality and could be used to teach in the main game environment, the act of creating it in the content creation environment had only minimal educational value. This meant that players who primarily played this way were not learning as much as they could.

We developed a new content creation environment to fix the problems in the old version. Like the previous version, this one has the player using the six functions to create an image on a 21x21 Cartesian grid. However, this version imposes a limitation on the number of functions that can be used. Each function is assigned a cost: point function 5 points, line function 4 points, rectangle function 3 points, triangle function 2 points, and the iterative functions 1 point. The total number of points used is tracked and when the player submits their design they are placed into one of four showcases based on points used. There is a general showcase and one for puzzles using under 25, 50, and 75 points. Thus in order to reach the top of the most prestigious 25-point showcase players will need to master the cheaper but more complex functions to optimize their designs.

3. EFFECTIVE STRATEGIES

In this section we present the strategies we used to implement a free play content creation environment that is effective for learning. Our goal was to guide behavior without limiting the user's creative freedom. These strategies are:

1) Integrate learning objectives into content creation

First and most importantly we want the user to learn while they create. The very act of creating the new content should give exposure and practice with the desired material. If we separate the content creation from the learning, for example by having content creation as a reward, separate from the main learning activity, then it loses some of its appeal for more creative students since they will still have to perform the less enjoyable task.

In BeadLoom Game, the user creates bead patterns on a grid. This could have been accomplished with a point and click interface, but that interaction would avoid learning of Cartesian coordinates, one of the key learning objectives of the software. The user must enter (x,y) coordinates for each use of the Point tool, and for 2-3 vertices when using the Line, Rectangle and Triangle functions. This helps users overcome common errors such as confusing x and y, or forgetting which directions are positive and negative. The line, rectangle, and triangle function all integrate basic geometry while the iterative functions introduce simple iterative logic. While every student learns to plot points, since there is no way to avoid it, most avoid using the iteration tools. The new point system was constructed to strongly encourage their use.

2) Provide multiple levels of success

We had to keep in mind that users will not start out as masters of the material or the software. Thus there must be options for how to complete each task according to different levels of ability. Therefore, BLG provides simple options that only require basic understanding of the material as well as better, but more challenging, options, which require deeper understanding. Users will start with the basic strategies and gradually master and use the more complex ones. Rather than forcing the user to use the more complex strategies, we provide different levels of success. These levels motivate users to improve and learn harder material without discouraging them.

BLG does this in two ways. First, novice users can be successful simply by mastering the Point function. It is possible to create any design with the point function. Although this function teaches less than the other options it provides a simple way to become familiar with the environment and start the creation process. We could have provided just the iterative functions, which utilize both Cartesian coordinates and iteration, but this would be a very large learning curve and could easily discourage novice users.

The second way BLG provides multiple levels of success is the tiered showcase. Although users will strive for the 25-point showcase, if they reach that point limit and are not completely finished they can submit what they have, then roll into the 50-point showcase. This represents different levels of success. It also does not overly punish or discourage newer users because even if they do not achieve the target goal they can still submit their unique creation to a showcase. An earlier prototype did not have these rolling point limits. Instead, when the user ran out of points they could not add more to the design. This proved to be discouraging because it meant they would have to restart their design in order to complete it. We added the rolling limits to provide more options while maintaining several levels of success.

3) Implement limitations

By providing options with differing skill intensities we have given the user the ability to create content in a simple way with minimal learning, but also a complex way with more learning. Unfortunately, in a completely free play environment a majority of users will default to the simple method and never fully explore the other options. Therefore, it is necessary to implement certain limitations on the free play nature of the environment. These limitations should be designed in a way, which rewards the more desirable behavior and punishes or provides less reward for less desirable behavior. These limitations should not negate the user's ability to perform the less desirable behavior because this behavior is important for new and less experienced users. Instead, it should make it clear that other options are available and that exploring these options will have a better overall outcome. It should also limit how much of the less desirable behavior is permitted from the more experienced users.

The original content creation environment in BLG lacked this important strategy. Although all the functions were available, we did not limit the user so they defaulted to using points and rectangles. There was simply little reason to use the harder functions. By assigning each function a different point value and limiting how many points could be used for each showcase, we made it clear that the harder functions were the more desirable option without removing the important simple functions. Additionally, this limits how many point functions can be used at the higher levels of performance. As shown in Figure 1, for the 25-point showcase users can use at most 5 single point functions (a crude smiley face at best) or up to 25 iterations, which allows for highly complex and interesting designs.

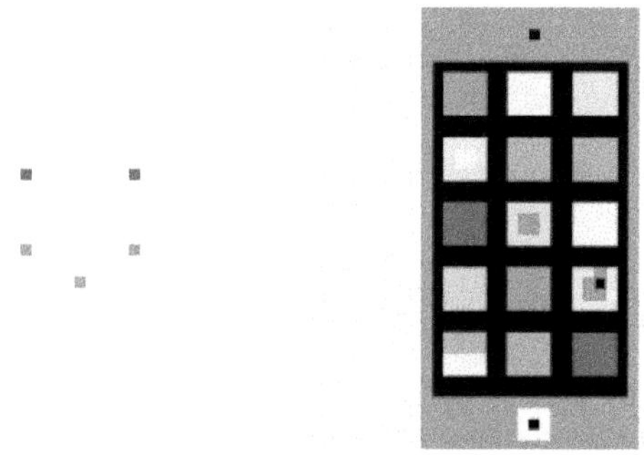

Figure 1: Two 25-point custom puzzles

4) Ensure the limitations do not limit creativity

This strategy reminds us that the primary audience for the content creation environment is users with a strong desire to express their individual creativity. It is therefore extremely important that the limitations used in the prior strategy do not limit user creativity. Ideally, all of the content that could possibly be created without the limitation should be creatable with the limitation. It is acceptable, and even preferable, to require the user to work harder in order to achieve the same goal. Users are most frustrated when they get an idea, but later find it to be unobtainable simply because of the new limitations. It should be clear to the user that their idea can be made; it may simply require a more complete mastery of the learning objective in order to achieve it.

Since there is a general showcase without any point limit any puzzle can be made in the BLG however, it is actually possible to create a vast majority of puzzles in under 25-points. This is because it is possible to create almost any design using only iteration. Points, straight lines, rectangles, and most triangles can all be defined iteratively. Thus a user can save points through the use of iteration. For example, creating three rectangles will cost 9 points but only 3 points using iteration and the savings are even more for lines and points. In fact, over 90% of the current custom designs could potentially be made in 25 points or less.

5) Allow for peer review

Finally part of the motivation for the creative students is the ability to show their work off for others. They want their work to be seen and liked by other users. We can use this desire to our advantage. Since all the preexisting content is accessible, users can see what is popular and attempt to out do it. This results in ever more complex and creative works being added to the system. In a system without reviews, users may instead be driven to recreate rather than improve. We saw this in our original version of the BLG, where students could not publish their designs. When they saw another person make something they liked, users would attempt to recreate it on their own computer to save. Publishing prevents that, and encourages more creativity, since, instead of copying a design, users riff off of the designs they see. The showcases work like those for Scratch – showing users what they can create and sparking new ideas [8]. Through the use of peer review we create a strong internal motivator and are able to generate an ever-flowing stream of content. Users can also look to the peer review system for inspiration on what to create next.

The different levels of custom puzzle showcases provide an additional incentive for these socially-sensitive creative users. Not only does it meet the peer review strategy, it encourages users to find more and more optimal ways of creating a design so that it can be in the lesser point showcases. By "saving" points, users often have a few left over for additional details at the end. Users often create similarly-themed designs but work to shave points so they could add in further details and out-do other designs.

4. PROTOTYPE EXPERIMENTAL METHOD

We have run a series of experiments to evaluate the success of the custom puzzle creation (CPC) with the new limitations developed following our strategies. The first utilized a mixed-fidelity prototype involving the old, fully free play content creation environment augmented with paper worksheets. Using this system players create a BLG custom puzzle on the computer, but use a paper worksheet to record the puzzle name, their target point limit, the point value for each function, the number of times each function was used, and the final point usage. This prototype featured the hard point limits we would later remove.

Although this method of testing was simple, it did provide a few benefits. By testing the system prior to development we could validate the idea with minimal development time as well as incorporate user feedback into the final design. This style of game design is supported both by our own previous work with BLG [1] as well as Fullerton [4]. By integrating the pencil and paper version with the functioning custom puzzle mode we could avoid the traditional problems with pure paper prototypes like abstractness and response lag [6].

We used this system at four one-week summer camps in 2011. All of these camps were for middle school students with one camp focused on the use of educational tools and the three focused on video game design. In total, we had 57 participants. On the first day, the students were introduced to the BLG and walked through a short tutorial showing them how to use each of the different functions. They were then given an hour and a half to play the original free play custom puzzle mode. On days two, three, and four we had daily custom puzzle contests. These contests were used to approximate the showcase reward system.

During each contest, students took one hour to create a design while tracking the actions used on their worksheets. At the end of the hour, camp counselors gave small rewards for the best designs. Campers who had not won a prize by the end of the week received a participation prize then. The first contest used a 100-point hard limit. A hard limit means that puzzles were not allowed to use more than 100 points. The second contest had a 50-point hard limit. To encourage players who thought this was too few points, an announcement was made informing everyone that all shapes but irregular lines and irregular triangles could be created using iteration. The final contest had a 25-point hard limit.

Players were also given an hour on each day during which they were allowed to play the original free play custom puzzle mode. Students also had access to the game after camp by visiting the website. Logs were saved of each submitted puzzle including CPC, free play custom puzzle, and for puzzles made outside camp hours. On the final day, the campers were given a short survey asking their opinions on various aspects of the CPC mode. These questions included "which point limit was your favorite?" and "do you feel the point limit motivated you to use the advanced functions like iteration more than the free play mode?"

Figure 2: 100-point (left) and 50-point (right) custom puzzles

5. PROTOTYPE RESULTS

In order to evaluate how the prototype CPC mode altered player behavior, we collected logs during both the CPC play time as well as the free play times, during and after the camps. In total, we had 279 puzzles created during the camps and an additional 34 made afterwards. Figures 1 (right) and 2 show some of the designs. We grouped these puzzles by creation mode and by camp session. Figure 3 shows how the average number of iterations per puzzle varied with these groups.

The players averaged .725 iterations per puzzle during the free play time on the first day of camp. During the following days' free play times they averaged 1.3, .957, and .56 iterations per puzzle, and after the camp was over students continued to make new content which averaged .79 iterations each. Puzzles made during the CPC 100 point contest averaged 5.85 iterations per puzzle. The 50 point and 25 point contest puzzles had an average of 7.80 and 9.80 respectively. Our results exclude two puzzles from the 25-point challenge, one from the 50-point challenge, and one from the 100-point challenge which were begun during the contest but completed during the free play session.

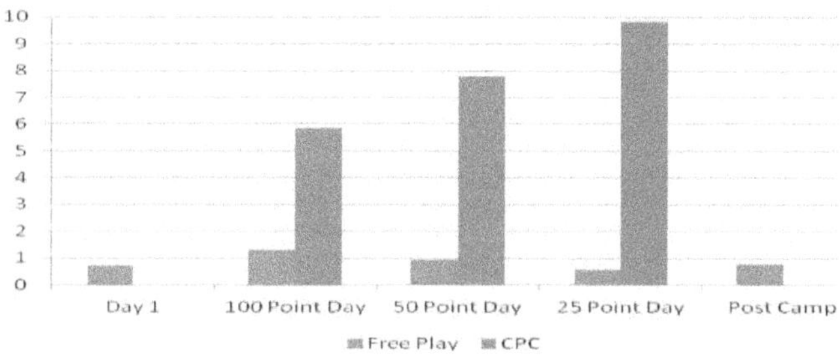

Figure 3: Average iterations per puzzle

When asked about their favorite point limits, 24 students preferred 100 points, 17 students preferred 50 points, and 16 students preferred 25 points. The overwhelming majority (46/57) felt that the point limit motivated them to use the iterative functions.

Although this was only a prototype we learned a great deal about the new point limits for the custom puzzle creation (CPC) mode. First was that this mode and our strategies were effective at altering player behavior. In the free play creation environment each day the created content only had on average about 1 iteration per puzzle while in the CPC mode this rose sharply. It is important to note that this number rose each day despite decreasing limits on total allowed points. It could have happened that users made less and less complex designs, by being de-motivated to explore complicated ideas or by being impeded because of a strict point limit. Instead, the use of iteration went up while design complexity seemed to stay steady. This could be caused by the increasing mastery of the subject area. We also found, based on the survey results and observations of the participants, that we were not providing the users with enough options. Users ranged widely on favorite point limit and many wanted to continue their work past the point limit. Based on these findings we created a new version of BLG which incorporated the new CPC mode as well as soft point limits and multiple showcases.

6. FINAL EXPERIMENTAL METHOD

Although we were happy to find that our strategies could be used to alter player behavior we also wanted to ensure that this custom puzzle creation environment and others like it could truly produce learning outcomes. We also wanted to ensure that such an environment could be utilized in a shorter classroom environment as opposed to the longer summer camp environment. To do this we had three middle school computer and business education classes (one sixth, one seventh, and one eighth grade) take a 12 question pretest. This test evaluated their understanding of Cartesian coordinates, iteration, and optimization. Figure 4 shows an example iteration question, while the coordinate questions asked students to plot points, and the optimization questions asked students to identify minimal shapes needed to create patterns.

After the pretest students were led through a thirty-minute demonstration of the various functions. During the next class (two days later) the students were given 40 minutes to use the new CPC mode. They were told they could aim for any showcase they wanted but were encouraged to go for 25 or 50. Afterwards the students were given an isomorphic posttest. In total 44 students from all three classes were present for both days of the activity.

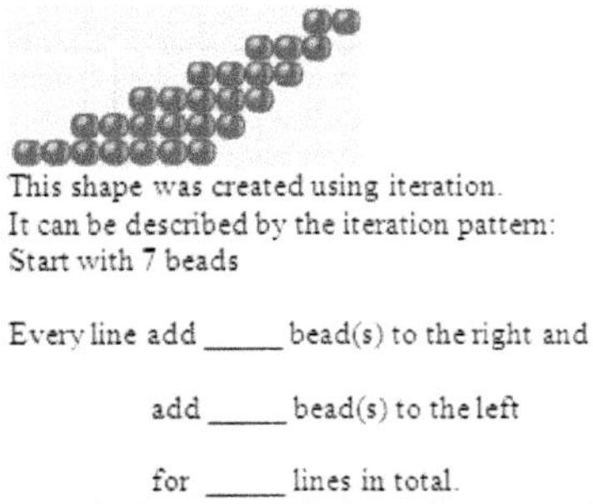

Figure 4: An example iteration question

7. FINAL RESULTS

In total, 42 puzzles were submitted during the 40 minute activity while many more were left unfinished. For the published puzzles the average number of iterations per puzzle was 5.38. This is very close to the value we saw on the first day of the mixed fidelity prototype study. This shows that even given a short amount of time and the freedom to set their own point limit, our strategies were effective at guiding user behavior. We also believe that given continued exposure in or out of class that the use of iteration would rise similar to the trend in the prototype study.

A 2-tailed matched paired t-test was performed on the pre and posttest data. Students performed significantly better, $t(43) = 3.86$, $p<.001$, $d=.82$ on the post test ($M=5.69$, $SD=1.72$) than on the pre test ($M=4.18$, $SD=1.96$). Cohen's d indicates that students improved from pretest to post test by .82 of a standard deviation. Thus we see that the CPC mode developed following our strategies is able to produce significant learning gains in a classroom environment.

8. DISCUSSION

Free play custom content creation environments are highly motivating and can greatly increase the replayability of any software. Through the use of our guidelines it is also possible to have these environments result in learning gains. BLG illustrates how these guidelines can be used to enhance an educational game. We feel all educational games should incorporate some form of user content generation to enhance its replayability and learning gains. These principles can also be applied to more traditional educational software systems. The puzzles in BLG can be viewed as questions and the solution is the act of creating it. Thus these principles can be applied to any question and solution environment as long as the motivation to use it is present. One way to create this motivation would be to sign questions with the creator's name that way those that make questions know that others will be able to see that they created interesting and challenging questions. This is further enhanced by letting other users rate the quality of the created questions.

These guidelines can also be used to enhance existing free play content creation environments. For example, the very successful Scratch programming environment already follows a majority of these suggestions. The learning objectives are directly tied with the creation process and there are multiple ways to accomplish the same goal. for example novice users may shy away from loops until they are more familiar with the environment but can still create great programs. Scratch is also well known for its peer review and online community. However, Scratch provides no internal motivation to explore more complex or efficient methods of coding. If limitations were implemented then users would need to think about efficient ways in which to code their creations. This could be accomplished with a kind a showcase that orders on blocks used or challenges to make cool programs in under a certain number of blocks. As long as these additions had optional rewards that players could eventually move towards it would not limit their creativity. In fact the addition of the limits could lead to a new form of creativity as users find more and more interesting ways to accomplish the same objectives. This could more easily allow Scratch to transition from teaching the basics of computer science to encouraging more complex computer science practices.

9. CONCLUSION

We have found custom content environments that promote user-generated content to be highly effective at motivating users to use and reuse software. Due to the popularity of such modes it is important that they be capable of guiding user behavior and producing significant learning gains on their own. Therefore we have produced five effective strategies for maximizing the learning gains and guiding users towards desired behavior:

1) Integrate learning objectives into the content creation

2) Provide multiple levels of success

3) Implement limitations

4) Ensure the limitations do not limit creativity

5) Allow for peer review

Similar strategies have been shown to be effective in other computing learning environments such as Scratch. In our experience, however, without guided help, some kids never get the internal motivation to explore beyond basic instructions, and aren't sure what they can make in the environment. Instituting some goal-directed modes may reach some students that open-ended environments do not, spark curiosity and creativity, and eventually lead students to be the creators we want them to become.

By following these strategies we created a user generated content environment for the educational puzzle game BeadLoom Game. Through our study of the prototype we were able to show that this mode can guide behavior, and have a large impact on desired behavior over time. Follow up studies with the completed software in a classroom environment revealed similar impacts on desired behavior as well as significant learning gains in the understanding of Cartesian coordinates and the advanced subjects of iteration and optimization. We believe that by following these strategies it is possible to improve other educational software systems through the addition of motivating and educational content creation environments.

10. ACKNOWLEDGMENTS

We thank Ron Eglash for making the Virtual Bead Loom, the original inspiration for BLG, Kera Bell-Watkins' 2009 software engineering class for making a Java version of VBL, and Carmen Lucas for allowing us to test BLG in her classroom. This work was partially supported by National Science Foundation grants CNS-0634342, CNS 0739216, CNS 0540523, IIS-0757521 and the UNCC Diversity in IT Institute.

11. REFERENCES

[1]Boyce, A, and T. Barnes. BeadLoom Game: Using Game Elements to Increase Motivation and Learning. *ACM FDG 2010.* Monterey, CA, USA, June 19-21, 2010.

[2]Boyce, A, A. Campbell, S.Pickford, D. Culler, T. Barnes. Experimental Evaluation of BeadLoom Game: How Adding

Game Elements to an Educational Tool Improves Motivation and Learning. *ACM ITiCSE 2011*,

[3]Boyce, A., A. Campbell, S. Pickford, D. Culler, T. Barnes. BeadLoom Game: Adiing Competitive, User Generated, and Social Features to Increase Motivation. *ACM FDG 2011*

[4]Fullerton, T., Swain, C., ,Hoffman, S. *Game Design Workshop: Desigining,Prototyping and PlayTesting Games.* CMP Books, Feb 2004.

[5]Garris, Ahlers, & Driskell. Games, motivation, and learning: a research and practice model. Simulation and Gaming, Vol. 33, No. 4, 2002, 441-467.

[6]Lim, Y., A. Pangam, S. Periyasami,A.Sheweta. Comparative Analysis of High- and Low-fidelity Prototypes for More Calid Usability Evaluations of Mobile Devices. *NordiCHI 2006.*

[7] LittleBigPlanet.com/en/community Accessed Jan. 12, 2012.

[8]Resnick, M., J. Maloney, A. Monroy-Hernandez, N. Rusk, E. Eastmond, K. Brennan, A. Millner, E. Rosenbaum, J. Silver, B. Silverman, Y. Kafai. 2009. Scratch: Programming for all. *Comm. ACM 52,* 11, 60-67.

[9]Yoo, D, E. Schanzer, S. Krishnamurthi. WeScheme: The Browser Is Your PROGRAMMING ENVIRONMENT. *ACM ITiCSE 2011*

Lectures Abandoned: Active Learning by Active Seminars

Henrik Bærbak Christensen
Computer Science – Aarhus University
8200 Aarhus N – Denmark
hbc@cs.au.dk

Aino Corry
Computer Science – Aarhus University
8200 Aarhus N – Denmark
aino@cs.au.dk

ABSTRACT

Traditional lecture-based courses are widely criticized for being less effective in teaching. The question is of course what should replace the lectures and various *active learning* techniques have been suggested and studied. In this paper, we report on our experiences of redesigning a software engineering course in *software architecture* to employ a range of active learning techniques. The course was constrained by the study administration's traditional assignment of a three hour lecturing slot and as such we had to make techniques that fitted this imposed constraint. Our contribution is *active seminars* as a replacement of traditional lectures, an activity template for the contents of active seminars, an account on how *storytelling* supported the seminars, as well as reports on our and the students' experiences.

Categories and Subject Descriptors

D.2.11 [**Software**]: Software Architectures; K.3 [**Computing Milieux**]: Computers and Education; K.3.2 [**Computing Milieux**]: Curriculum

General Terms

Design

Keywords

Curriculum design, Education, Software architecture.

1. INTRODUCTION

Much university level teaching is still centered on lectures [15] even though research has established that lecturing is a mediocre learning source [12, 14, 6]. Lectures even fail in conveying hard facts—only 30% of unknown key concepts are mastered by students after a traditional lecture course [10]. Then why do we continue to lecture? One answer is probably that we miss alternatives. Given our university administrations that assign lecturing slots for our courses we have some hours we need to fill by something. For many teachers that have a curriculum to cover the obvious choice is to encode the curriculum's topics into decks of slides that are then presented in the lecture hall. Slide decks have the added benefit for teachers that they present a comfort zone in an otherwise strenuous situation: "what should I say next?" is answered just by flipping the next slide.

Our contribution is to propose replacing lecturing with *active seminars* which basically replaces the students' passiveness of lecturing by active learning tasks. We present the mindset as well as a set of ideas, techniques and structuring mechanisms that can be used to make the seminars fun and rewarding for both students and teachers. Specifically, we present experience from a master level course on software architecture. While the presented active learning techniques necessarily are geared towards the concrete course's curriculum we postulate they can be used as inspiration in other course settings especially in courses that are oriented towards teaching application-oriented software engineering techniques.

Furthermore we present data from course evaluations and exam grading that outline preliminary results of applying active seminars.

The paper is organized as follows. In section 2 we outline our motivation and ideas for restructuring our course while section 3 describes the active seminar concept. Section 4 provides examples of the contents and learning activities in our active seminars for the software architecture course. In section 5 we discuss the benefits and liabilities of the approach and broaden the techniques, as well as present our data from exam grading and evaluations. Finally, we conclude in section 6.

2. RETHINKING A COURSE

The course is a 7-week (half semester) Master's course for 4th year CS and engineering students. It is a 5 ECTS (European Credit Transfer and Accumulation System) course which correlates to an expected workload of 140 hours. Typically around 50 students enroll. The primary learning objectives are the operational aspects of software architecture: to enable them to understand and document architectural requirements, to produce a software architecture that obeys these requirements, and to evaluate it. Secondary learning objectives are academic aspects looking at current research in the field. The primary literature is a classic book within software architecture from Software Engineering Institute (SEI) by Bass et al. [4]. It covers the basic concepts

ITiCSE'12, July 3–5, 2012, Haifa, Israel.

and techniques, like documentation using viewpoints, quality attributes, architectural style and patterns, architectural tactics, as well as evaluation and process techniques.

The course had up until our revision been taught four times with a three hour lecturing slot (Monday 2–5 PM) that has used the traditional lecturing scheme: PowerPoint slides were presented by the lecturer basically covering the contents of the book's chapters or research papers and spiced up with some anecdotes or experiences from the lecturers' research projects.

In addition to the Monday lecturing the course has three mandatory deliveries by groups of 2–3 students on key techniques. Furthermore it has a 20 minute oral exam with 20 minutes preparation. In the preparation, the student is given a concrete but unknown case to prepare.

When we were assigned as teachers on the course, we set out to revise the lecturing time slot of the course fundamentally with three objectives in mind:

- As argued in the previous section there is much research that demonstrates that traditional lectures aid little in learning. Thus we wanted to avoid using the three hour slot for traditional lecturing.
- As we both were part of a departmental initiative on improving teaching, we wanted to experiment with active learning techniques [13] in general, including specific techniques like clickers [11] and strip-sequences [5].
- One of the teachers had previously developed a course using a *story-telling* approach [8] that had resulted in a book on software design [9]. We wanted to test if the story-telling approach would work in a more abstract course as well.

This lead us to make statements that were to become the premises of the course redesign.

Change our terminology. The word "lecture" has a lot of connotations. As we wanted a radical shift away from standard lecturing we decided to rename our three hour Monday afternoon slot and call it "active seminar" instead. The very renaming sends a clear signal to student to expect something else.

Abandon lecturing slides. A well prepared set of slides present many advantages for the lecturer: preparing them is a great learning vehicle for the lecturer himself and they serve as a path to steer you safely through the strenuous situation of lecturing. However, as they often are transcriptions of the contents of the reading material they send a signal to the student that reading is not necessary as the lecturer will go over it anyway. And—students who do prepare are bored as little new material is presented. We replaced slide presentations by active learning activities rooted in the learning topics.

Storytelling approach. In storytelling you structure your choice of topics as an unfolding story rooted in actual requirements. This teaching style supports several findings in cognitive learning theory [7]. We identified a story of a complex architecture that supported all learning activities in the course.

3. ACTIVE SEMINARS

In this section, we present the story we used to ground the techniques as well as the template we developed for how to execute the active seminars.

3.1 Choosing a Story

As the course covers techniques designed for "heavy lifting" it was important to pick a story with a "heavy" case: many of the SEI techniques for documenting, designing, and evaluating architectures are powerful but effort-intensive and forcing students to apply them to toy projects that are easily handled without them is demotivating at best and stupid at worst. Thus, with regards for the story the most important criteria was to pick a case with a sufficiently complex architecture to study and a second criteria was to pick something appealing to a relatively young audience.

The choice fell on the "World of Warcraft" (WoW) universe by Blizzard Entertainment[1]. WoW is a massive multiplayer online role playing game (MMORPG) and we will give a brief introduction here for readers unfamiliar with this type of game.

In WoW a player controls his/her avatar in a virtual landscape as shown in Figure 1. Using the mouse you move your avatar around exploring the world, interacting with other players, solving quests, and often joining battles in which you team up with other players in "hack-and-slash" action. To access the online universe, you must have a subscription and as of November 2011 there are 10.3 millions paying subscribers.

Figure 1: Avatar "Relota" in the streets of Stormwind

From a software architecture standpoint WoW represents extreme architectural requirements. Players need precise and responsive control over their avatar in a world that needs to be rendered in high resolution at high frame rates to provide a meaningful experience. And interaction with the potential 10 million other avatars in the same world puts extreme requirements in keeping state synchronized across servers and a large set of clients.

Thus, WoW served our pedagogical purpose. It is extremely complex, warranting demanding techniques, and certainly well beyond what students can master, and finally it appeals to many as an entertainment product or at least as a challenging system from a software engineering perspective.

3.2 Overall Structure of a Seminar

Active seminars replace *presenting a topic* by *actively working with a topic.* As such the three hour slot settled into a form containing two or more instances of a *learning session*:

[1] www.blizzard.com

1. Short recap of prerequisites. Typically 5 minutes. We present very briefly the key concepts/techniques that this session will build upon.

2. Case/exercise introduction. Typically 5–15 minutes. A short introduction by the teachers to the case or exercise and an outline of the intended learning outcome. This was presented using power-point slides, and usually the final slide was a "quick reference" that contained for instance a writing template, the UML notation for a particular viewpoint, the Quality Attribute Workshop process points, etc. This final slide then served as reference point for the students' work.

3. Case work. Typically 30–60 minutes. Students group up in two–three person groups and work on the case. Meanwhile the teacher(s) roam around and ensure that every group is visited. If a group has no questions the teachers pose open-ended question like "what are you working at now?", "what is the most difficult aspect of you have been doing so far?" etc. This phase is eminent as teacher to gather common misunderstandings, spot aspects that are particularly difficult to master, as well as bright ideas that has surfaced.

4. Plenum discussions. Typically 20 minutes. In this concluding session we again focus all students' attention. We go over the collected misunderstandings, bright ideas, etc. as well as sketch and discuss all or part of a solution to the posed problems. Again we strive for open discussions so questions from the audience is not just answered but directed back for other students to comment and discuss.

5. Break. We do not obey the standard lecturing time table (at our university it is 45 minute lecture and 15 minute break), but put the breaks between the learning sessions within the three hour slot.

The room we had available was a classic lecturing theater which is inconvenient for group work and thus more or less dictates a maximal group size of three as they can work while sitting in a row. Still, with this size it seemed to work out all right.

4. EXAMPLES

Below we present some examples of how learning sessions in the active seminars have been unfolded.

4.1 The Introduction Seminar

Many courses start with an introductory lecture that tries to convince students that this particular course is interesting and relevant. The previous instances of the course had upheld this tradition. And as is often the case, the only effect had been to put the audience severely to sleep.

This year we made a radical shift away from this approach. After the mandatory two minute welcome we started our WoW story with the following exercise:

You are now all employed in our company as software architects. You have 30 minutes in groups of 2–3 persons to design an architecture for WoW to support:

- *Fluent user experience of controlling his/her avatar in the virtual world—1600x1200 full color rendering at minimum 30 frames per second.*
- *10 million avatars on-line at the same time, all being able to see all other avatars in the same region of the virtual world.*

Two groups will be picked to present their solution at the blackboard. GO GO GO! In contrast to previous years' sleepy audience this created a flurry of activity! The air was thick with discussions in the groups while we as teachers roamed around to discuss issues, hear their thoughts, and detail requirements!

It was indeed very difficult to call the audience's attention again for the two groups' presentations. The first group drew a lot of boxes and lines and used words like "server" and "databases"; while the next group drew quite a few unconnected circles using words like "peers" and "data packets". Both presentations generated a lot of discussions and comments from the audience which again was difficult to stop as people got absorbed by the exercise. However, our learning goal was not a sketch of a World of Warcraft architecture. It was the following statement from the course's book:

> *Hence, most of the box-and-line drawings that are passed off as architectures are in fact not architectures at all. They are simply box-and-line drawings. [3, p. 22].*

In that moment, the audience was dead silent as the message came across: *The groups had absolutely no language to express software architecture.* Even though they might have come up with some good architectural designs they had just drawn boxes and lines without any semantics: "does this box represent a class, a server, a computer, a process, a jar file, or?" Nobody really knew.

As teachers we had traded a one hour (boring) slide show on how important it is to have well defined semantic in your diagrams for one hour of fun with a clear morale at the end. Furthermore, it provided a basic understanding of the WoW domain to be built upon in all the following weeks of seminars.

4.2 QAW Seminar

In a later seminar, the learning objectives were a way of expressing architectural requirements, *quality attribute scenarios* [4, Chap. 4], and a lightweight workshop to find these in collaboration with the architecture's stakeholders, *quality attribute workshop* [1].

We organized the seminar accordingly in two sessions. In the first session we used *strip sequences* [5]. Strip sequences are scissors cut pieces of paper on which a permutation of information is printed: one piece of information on each strip of paper and the exercise's goal is for students to put the pieces back into the right ordering. This type of learning aid fits the quality attribute scenarios (QAS) well as this technique defines a standard writing template to express quality requirements consisting of six entries (source, stimuli, artifact, environment, response, and response measure.) The template is well suited for detailing otherwise vague requirements. For instance, a performance requirement on a web server like "the web server shall handle 1000 page requests per second" is detailed in the QAS in Figure 2.

Note that the right column can be read as a natural requirement top to bottom while the entry headers on the left column act both to keep the requirements in a well-formed template as well as act as a checklist.

Entry	Quality: Performance
Source	A Firefox user
Stimuli	requests a web page
Artifact	from web server
Environment	under normal load.
Response	The page's data is returned
Response Measure	with maximal latency of 1 ms

Figure 2: A performance QAS

We designed six QAS for the WoW case for four different quality attributes (performance, maintainability, availability, security) which resulted in 36 pieces of paper each with a single statement. The entry header (like e.g. "Response Measure") was of course removed so the line printed on a single piece of paper would be e.g. "Maximal latency of 1 ms".

The task was thus threefold:

- Identify the entry header. That is, does this statement match a "source" or "environment" entry etc.?
- Identify the QAS. That is, match the statements under the entry headers in a manner that makes feasible requirements for WoW.
- Identify the quality attributes that the QAS covers.

The tasks above are not a sequence but an interactive process leading to a set of well-formed and meaningful QAS.

This exercise is easier than asking the students to generate QAS from scratch and thus represents both as less steep learning curve as well as exemplify the *example completion effect*[7] that has been shown to increase the *germane cognitive load* that contributes positively to learning.

The second session revolved around the quality attribute workshop (QAW). QAW is a four phased workshop in which stakeholders (a) brainstorm to produce a set of QAS (b) prioritize these by voting and (c) refine the 5–7 top priority QAS. While QAWs are meant to be used in small groups of around 5-15 persons we managed to engage all 50 students.

During the brainstorm, one teacher acted as the facilitator that listens to the audience's suggested vague QAS and clarifies any uncertainties while the other teacher acted as the note keeper, writing them down on the whiteboard. This process continued until a set of 25-30 QAS were on the whiteboard. The prioritization phase had to be tailored as we wanted to use electronic clickers [11]. Each student had a clicker with numbers 0–9 which they could press. Software on the teacher's laptop then accumulates the count of students that has pressed each of the ten digits. In QAW each stakeholder has a number of votes that can be freely distributed among all scenarios. We handled this discrepancy by having a short break in which we selected the ten most interesting proposed QAS (from a learning perspective, ensuring they covered different quality attributes as well as had sufficient complexity), and then allowed the students one vote each. In the final phase the students again worked in groups of 2–3 taking the top three priority QAS on the whiteboard and refined them into the full QAS writing template. The session was ended by a couple of groups presenting their final results.

These two sessions present a learning curve: in the first session they get acquainted with the QAS writing template by trying to assemble them from scrambled bits developed by the teachers while in the last session they get to work on their very own QAS that they themselves have suggested as well as voted on.

4.3 Other Examples

One active seminar had architectural design techniques as learning topic: tactics and architectural patterns. Again a stepwise approach was adapted. The first session on tactics consisted of 10 minutes overview followed by a 20 minutes clicker-based Q/A session. In this session we presented a QAS to fulfill and the students voted on architectural tactics to satisfy the quality requirement using clickers. As an example we posed the following availability QAS: *An internal crash happens in a world of warcraft realm server in normal operation, the crash is detected, recorded in a log, and the server returns to normal operation within one hour.* A set of failure detection techniques (heartbeat, ping-echo, etc.) was enumerated and each student would vote on the detection technique best suited to support the QAS. After a period of work, voting was made, and finally we discussed the various proposals.

After this gentle introduction we had a 30 minute work session in which all students were given five full QAS and asked to select and argue for a selection of tactics to support each. A discussion concluded this session.

Another active seminar was devoted *architectural prototyping* [2]—a technique for exploring and evaluating the architectural design space by building executable prototypes that focus solely on architectural properties. One interesting aspect we wanted to try was if it was possible for students to actually get to the point where they program in order to experiment with architectural issues. We took a relatively large software system from another course designed with a single threaded Model-View-Controller (MVC) architecture. We next augmented it with a tracing tool that allowed call sequences to be recorded. The exercise's goal was to investigate how the system could be refactored to become a distributed system having the model component of the MVC on a server side while view and controller components on the client side. Unfortunately this exercise was never realized due to the active seminar being cancelled due to sickness.

5. DISCUSSION

Are active seminars better than lectures is of course the important question to try to answer? This leads to an analysis of what "better" means. A primary concern may be to increase exam pass rates and/or grades as this must be assumed to correlate to student's learning. A secondary concern is the teacher's perspective—is teaching more fun and rewarding?

Concerning the students Table 1 shows grade data from the last five exams[2]. Examiners have varied over the years but one of the authors has acted as censor in exams from 2006–2009 and both authors acted alternating as examiner or censor in 2011. The table shows pass rates as well as mean grades (counting all grades in column 3 and counting just passed grades in column 4). Note that other aspects of the course have been stable over these five exams: mandatory exercises as well as the exams have been the same and

[2]Grades are in the Danish 7-step scale that has grades: 12(best), 10, 7(good), 4, 02 (pass), 00(fail).

Year	Count (students)	Pass ratio	Mean grade (all)	Mean grade (pass)	Performance (p)
2011	47	76.6	7.0	9.1	**698**
2009	25	76	6.3	8.3	632
2008	46	65.2	5.6	8.5	557
2007	25	88	6.4	7.3	644
2006	27	81.5	6.7	8.3	674
Mean	-	77.5	6.4	8.3	641

Table 1: Exam grades. Grade 7 roughly equals C in U.S. grades.

	Active seminars contribute to my learning				
	No	Less degree	Somewhat	High degree	Very high degree
Count	0	1	2	7	4
%	0	6.7	13.3	46.7	26.7

Table 2: Perceived outcome of the active seminars.

thus it is only the lecturing aspect that has been special in the 2011 edition of the course. The measure "Performance" (p) is calculated as "Pass ratio" times "Mean grade (pass)" and thus increases faster as more students pass and/or get better grades. Looking over the table, $p = 698$ is the highest of all years in our active seminar structured 2011 course. Likewise the mean grade (both counting all and only passed grades) is the highest. Unfortunately the standard deviation σ of p is 48.1 and thus p for *all* years is within the 95% confidence interval. Thus we cannot make any statistically sound conclusions.

Another source is the anonymous course evaluations that are collected via web forms just before the exams. Using a five point Likert scale the students answered the question "Did the active seminars contribute to your learning of the course techniques?" Table 2 shows the perceived outcome. That is 79% of the students felt that active seminars either to a high or very high degree contributed to their learning. However, the evaluation is not mandatory and only 14 out of the around 50 students filled the form. Still it is an encouraging result.

While students' outcome is the ultimate goal we must not forget ourselves as teachers: *what is in it for us?* We found that replacing traditional lectures with active seminars has several benefits but also has its requirements. A primary benefit is you see the *real* problems that students struggle with as you look over their shoulders and discuss with them during the seminars. In traditional lecturing it is generally only strong students that dare pose questions and teaching assistants unconsciously act as filters so you have little feeling for the problems felt by the students. In active seminars you stand a better chance of discovering them and actively do something about it.

The secondary benefit is that *it is simply more fun.* After years of teaching, the task of "going over the slides once more" can become pretty boring! Active seminars replace the monologue with engaging dialogue that cast new light on the topics taught.

A third benefit is that it becomes *obvious for students that they need to prepare for the seminars.* The seminars assume they have read about the techniques because they are going to apply them actively during the seminars.

We also noted some requirements on our teaching. First of all *you have to know you stuff very well.* Students ask questions and good students sometimes ask really tricky questions so you need to have expert level skills to handle these. Also you do not have the safety-net for timing and completeness that a well prepared set of slides represents. We therefore will not recommend active seminars if it is the first time you run a course in a subject that you are not well acquainted with.

We also noted that our old, abandoned, lecturing slides held quite a few "deep insights" on the topics that do not get communicated during seminars. Often they represent long term experience with a topic that of course will not surface during the students' first exposure during the seminar; or the case or exercises chosen for the seminar will not exhibit that particular property. While we on one hand feel the "loss" of missed insights we also acknowledge that these insights are probably lost anyway as novice students scrambling to understand their first exposure to a technique simply lack the foundation to anchor their learning anyway.

A final but import point of discussion is scale and topic choice. Regarding scale we acknowledge that discussion and exercise focus of active seminars scale poorly. In some sessions one teacher handled a maximum of 50 students during the three hour slot and this is probably close to the maximal number of students you can adequately handle. If many more students enroll too many students may get stuck for too long time before you get around to them.

Regarding choice of topics our software architecture course generally has topics characterized by "easy to learn, difficult to master": a quality attribute scenario is simply a six entry writing template but the real challenge is mastering how to correctly encode a real case's requirements into the template. This class of topics are suitable for active seminars because students can prepare without getting stuck, and we are around in the "getting stuck" phase. Also the techniques are generally of the pen-paper-brains class that does not require computers. It is not obvious that active seminars will do just as well for heavy math or computer programming topics. On the other hand, traditional lectures are known not to do well either.

As a final note, we found that storytelling worked well in this course just as it has been shown to work well in a more programming oriented course [8]. The high complexity of WoW served the learning domain well, allowed all aspects of the learning topics to be demonstrated, and seminars profited from the domain quickly being known to the students and thus valuable time was not wasted on introducing new domains. A potential problem in that some students "do not like this game/games in general" was not raised, at least not to our attention.

6. CONCLUSION

We have presented a case study in active learning in which we have replaced traditional lecturing with *active seminars.* Active seminars are characterized by *student learning through activities rather than teachers going over slides.*

Active seminars are structured around exercises and discussions on the core topics instead of presenting core topics. Generally the three hour time slot was divided into two or three learning sessions, each focusing on a case and associated exercises that required students to apply and master techniques from the learning topic.

We have presented statistics for exam grades of the course and compared it to earlier, lecturing-based, instances of the course. Though no statistical evidence can be found the numbers are still encouraging. The same encouragement can be found in students' evaluation of the learning outcome of the seminars. As teachers, we found the active seminars more fun and rewarding that traditional lecturing primarily because we get a much deeper insight into the real problems that students struggle with. However, active seminars also put high demands on your expertise in the subject area. In conclusion, we will continue with active seminars in this course in the following years, and hope other teachers in the community will try some or all of our ideas.

7. REFERENCES

[1] M. Barbacci, R. Ellison, A. Lattanze, J. Stafford, C. Weinstock, and W. Wood. Quality Attribute Workshops (QAW). Technical Report CMU/SEI-2003-TR-016, Software Engineering Institute, 2003.

[2] J. E. Bardram, H. B. Christensen, and K. M. Hansen. Architectural Prototyping: An Approach for Grounding Architectural Design. In *Proceedings of Fourth Working IEEE/IFIP Conference on Software Architecture (WICSA4)*, pages 15–24, Oslo, Norway, June 2004.

[3] L. Bass, P. Clements, and R. Kazman. *Software Architecture in Practice, 1st Ed.* Addison-Wesley, 1998.

[4] L. Bass, P. Clements, and R. Kazman. *Software Architecture in Practice, 2nd Ed.* Addison-Wesley, 2003.

[5] R. Bhatt. *Modern Methods of Teaching Biology.* A P H Publishing Corporation, New Delhi, 2008.

[6] D. A. Bligh. *What's the use of lectures?* John Wiley & Sons, 2000.

[7] M. E. Caspersen and J. Bennedsen. Instructional design of a programming course: a learning theoretic approach. In *Proceedings of the third international workshop on Computing education research*, ICER '07, pages 111–122, New York, NY, USA, 2007. ACM.

[8] H. B. Christensen. A story-telling approach for a software engineering course design. *SIGCSE Bull.*, 41:60–64, July 2009.

[9] H. B. Christensen. *Flexible, Reliable Software—Using Patterns and Agile Development.* CRC Press, 2010.

[10] R. Hake. Interactive-engagement versus traditional methods: A six-thousand-student survey of mechanics test data for introductory physics courses. *The American Journal of Physics*, 66(64), 1998.

[11] A. A. Levesque. Using Clickers to Facilitate Development of Problem-Solving Skills. *CBE–Life Sciences Education*, 10:406–417, 2011.

[12] E. Mazur. Farewell, Lecture? *Science*, 323(50–51), Jan. 2009.

[13] D. A. McConnell, D. A. McConnell, and D. A. McConnell. Assessment and Active Learning Strategies for Introductory Geology Courses. *Journal of Geoscience Education*, 51(2):205–216, 2003.

[14] C. Wieman. Why Not Try a Scientific Approach to Science Education? *Change*, September/October 2007.

[15] C. Wieman, K. Perkins, and S. Gilbert. Transforming Science Education at Large Research Universities: A Case Study in Progress. *Change*, March/April 2010.

Infusing Computational Thinking into the Middle- and High-School Curriculum

Amber Settle
DePaul University
243 S. Wabash Avenue
Chicago, IL 60604
(312) 362-5324
asettle@cdm.depaul.edu

Baker Franke, Ruth Hansen, Frances Spaltro, Cynthia Jurisson, Colin Rennert-May, Brian Wildeman
The University of Chicago Laboratory Schools
1362 E. 59th Street
Chicago, IL 60637
(773) 702-9450
{bfranke, rhansen, fspaltr, cjurisson, crenner, bwildem} @ucls.uchicago.edu

ABSTRACT
In recent years there have been significant efforts to revamp undergraduate and K-12 curricula to emphasize computational thinking, a term popularized by Jeannette Wing in 2006. We describe work introducing and enhancing computational thinking activities and assessments in the middle- and high-school curriculum at the University of Chicago Lab Schools. In total six courses were altered as a part of the Computational Thinking across the Curriculum Project: middle-school and high-school computer science, and high-school Latin, graphic arts, English, and history. We detail the modifications to the curriculum and discuss the successes and challenges of the project.

Categories and Subject Descriptors
K.3.2 [**Computers and Education**]: Computer and Information Science Education – *curriculum.*

General Terms
Management, Design, Standardization.

Keywords
Computational thinking, K-12, high school, middle school, history, English, Latin, computer science, graphic arts.

1. INTRODUCTION
In her seminal article, Jeannette Wing argues that computational thinking is an emerging basic skill that should become an integral part of education. "To reading, writing, and arithmetic, we should add computational thinking to every child's analytical ability" [16]. In a subsequent article, Wing formally defined computational thinking as "the thought processes involved in formulating problems and their solutions so that the solutions are represented in a form that can be effectively carried out by an information-processing agent" [17]. Spurred by the creation of the NSF CPATH (CISE Pathways to Revitalized Undergraduate Computing Education) Program, researchers have considered how to revamp undergraduate courses and entire curricula to place a greater emphasis on computational thinking concepts. A number of CPATH projects have focused on finding ways to enhance computational thinking in undergraduate courses outside the standard computing curriculum [5, 6, 8, 10, 14, 15]. These projects have the potential to expand the number of college graduates who have exposure to computational thinking, an important goal in a world in which computational competency is increasingly important for people in all professions.

However, a small minority of people worldwide attends and graduates from colleges and universities. The potential of any approach to integrating computational thinking into the curriculum will be limited by a focus on undergraduate education. A much greater impact can be obtained by modifying the K-12 curriculum to include a stronger emphasis on computational thinking. This is especially true if the goal is to reach a larger number of students for the anticipated information technology workforce shortage. This idea has been embraced in the United States and has resulted in a great deal of activity in the computer science education community. It has been justifiability recognized that the K-12 arena is a complex and politicized environment, where multiple competing priorities exist [1]. Having outsiders inject computational thinking into an already overburdened curriculum is not a formula for success, and it has been suggested that inviting teachers into the process is a promising technique [19]. Further, a practical approach that demonstrates how computational thinking can be achieved in the curriculum is crucial [1].

Additional complexities in the United States are that computer science is not a core topic covered in high school, and there are too few K-12 computing teachers to implement a national-scale computing requirement [3]. Focusing on high school is a good start but may not be the ultimate goal since motivational concerns need to be addressed as early as middle school [11], particularly for girls and underrepresented minorities. Reaching students who do not consider themselves candidates for Science, Technology, Engineering, and Mathematics (STEM) disciplines is also important if the broadest audience possible is to be engaged [19].

In 2008 we began a project at DePaul University to modify existing general education courses to teach computational thinking concepts in context, funded under the CPATH program described previously. Our project is described in more detail in the next section. A natural extension of our project was to move into the K-12 arena, and in 2010 we began work with teachers at the University of Chicago Laboratory Schools. During the next two years we worked both with teachers trained in computer science and with teachers in the language and visual arts and humanities to develop computational thinking activities and assessments for their courses. The courses are at the middle- and high-school levels for students ages 10 through 18, and the materials were developed by the teachers responsible for the courses in consultation with the principal investigators of the DePaul University project. Using a process of iterative design, refinement, and reflection that is recommended in the literature [1], we found ways to integrate computational thinking into six courses: middle-school and high-school computer science, and high-school Latin, graphic arts, English, and history.

2. BACKGROUND

In the Computational Thinking across the Curriculum project we focused on modifying existing general education courses to teach computational thinking concepts in context. Our approach was to begin with courses closest to computing and work our way out to faculty in non-computing disciplines, creating a framework that all instructors teaching undergraduates could use to deepen their treatment of computational thinking in their courses and discipline. Because computational thinking involves a broad set of approaches and skills and because we were interested in finding commonalities across disciplines, we adopted a set of categories from Peter Denning's "Great Principles of Computing" project [4] for classification. According to Denning, the Great Principles of Computing are: computation, communication, coordination, recollection, automation, evaluation, and design. We used these categories throughout the project to identify types of computational thinking.

During the 2008 – 2009 academic year ten faculty from the College of Computing and Digital Media were recruited. They worked to modify courses from cryptography to screenwriting highlighting or including for the first time computational thinking class activities and assignments. The widest variety of courses possible were chosen so that the materials produced could provide inspiration for the second year of the project. During 2009 – 2010, eight additional faculty members from the College of Liberal Arts and Sciences joined the project. They developed materials for courses in the sciences and humanities. Over the life of the project faculty from eight different departments or schools modified 19 courses across five different areas in the Liberal Studies Program. In a previous publication we discussed the first two years of the project [10], and all of the materials created for the project are available online [9].

In an extension of the project funded through a Research Experience for Teachers (RET) supplement from the NSF three teachers from the University of Chicago Laboratory Schools extended the project into the K-12 curriculum in the academic year 2010-2011. The University of Chicago Laboratory Schools, denoted the Lab Schools in the remainder of this paper, was founded in 1896. The mission statement of the Lab Schools includes among its goals, "to provide an experience-centered, rigorous and well-rounded education for a diverse community" [13]. The school enrolls nearly 1800 students in nursery school through 12th grade, 44% of whom identify as students of color, and there are over 200 faculty employed at the school. The Lab Schools teachers planned to modify three courses, a high-school and a middle-school computer science class and a high-school Latin class, to include computational thinking activities and exercises. Their work then inspired further modifications during the 2011-2012 academic year by three additional teachers. Like the part of the project conducted at DePaul, the second year at the Lab Schools involved reaching out to teachers in areas other than computer science. The goal was to experiment with computational thinking in various courses and disciplines, and the strong support for professional development at the Lab Schools provided a unique environment for this work.

3. CURRICULAR MODIFICATIONS

In total six courses were altered for this project: middle-school and high-school computer science, and high-school Latin, graphic arts, English, and history. The changes in the computer science and Latin classes were made in 2010-2011 academic year as part of the RET supplemental grant. In the 2011-2012 academic year the project was expanded to include high school graphic arts, English, and history classes.

Our work on integrating computational thinking into the curriculum at the Lab Schools involved several distinct approaches. As an extension of the project at DePaul, we investigated the ways that computational thinking could be used to teach discipline-specific topics outside of computing, specifically history, graphic arts, English, and Latin. We were also interested in how computational thinking could be used in an interdisciplinary setting earlier in the curriculum, which was the focus of the work done in the middle-school computer science course. We also considered the effectiveness of several pedagogical approaches to computational thinking in a high-school computer science course.

3.1 Computational Thinking in High School

Four high-school courses were modified to include computational thinking approaches to teaching discipline-specific topics.

3.1.1 English

Students in high-school English classes often make generalizations about authors and their work. Sophomores who have read a single play by Shakespeare have no issues making major claims about his entire oeuvre. Erroneous generalizations can be corrected directly by the teacher or can be handled by asking students to support them, which they typically cannot. But while this approach may encourage students to think seriously about offering support and evidence for their arguments, it may also discourage them from thinking broadly about the texts they read. To test intuitions that deal with large number of texts, for example the 37 plays written by Shakespeare, one needs an efficient way to deal with a large amount of information. The widespread availability of digital texts and free online tools for analyzing them makes it relatively easy to generate data about texts. Even for intuitions that focus on only one text, these tools can still be efficient and illuminating.

The implementation of the project began in the Winter 2012 as a part of the ten-week term spent studying *Romeo and Juliet*. In addition to having read *Macbeth* in the ninth grade, students read several sonnets by Shakespeare. The central focus of the unit is a close reading of the text based on an examination of word choice, imagery, and syntax. The work for the project involves three to four class days of work as well as some related homework. The unit is divided into three parts: introducing the approach, using the approach on *Macbeth* and *Romeo and Juliet*, and finally generating and testing intuitions independently. The teacher models the process of testing intuitions using text analysis as follows:

1. Form or identify intuitions
2. Hypothesize results – what results would suggest/confirm your claims?
3. Apply the tool(s), for example TAPor (http://portal.tapor.ca) and TagCrowd (http://tagcrowd.com)
4. Analyze results and assess the intuition
5. Form conclusions

This process involves computational thinking in every step. To form an intuition students must abstract ideas from the text to design an intuition and then construct results that would confirm their claims. Abstraction is a part of the design category in the Great Principles of Computing [4]. Finally, the connection between the intuition and the hypothesis must be evaluated. Using the tool(s) involves computation, albeit indirectly. Analyzing the results is a form of evaluation, and drawing conclusions involves both evaluation and abstraction.

When modeling intuitions, there are two types of thoughts that can be considered. The first are intuitions that could be answered through a traditional reading of the text but for which textual analysis might provide support, such as "Macbeth is the most violent character in the play". The second are claims that must be supported by evidence drawn from a number of texts, such as "Shakespeare's plays are violent." For both types of intuitions, the instructor goes through the five steps given above, so that students could see that while the tools produce results quickly, it is necessary to spend time reviewing the results to see if they produce useful evidence for the claims.

After the introduction of the textual analysis process, students work in small groups to use a tool to answer a question that relates to the class's work on *Romeo and Juliet* or the sonnets. Each group is assigned to use one of the tools demonstrated, including programs that allow users to examine collocation and word frequency. Students follow the process, write a report describing their findings, present that report to the class, and offer an assessment of the tool's capabilities and drawbacks. Finally, later in the term, students are asked to form intuitions independently and to explain how they would apply one of the text analysis tools to test that hypothesis.

3.1.2 History

Effective note taking is essential for every student, but it is usually assumed and rarely verified. In a subject like history where understanding and classifying information during a lecture is important this is particularly problematic. Efficacious note taking is not a passive activity, since a good set of notes should be an accurate record not just of what the teacher said, but also of the broader discussion including student comments and questions, and is a multi-stage process. The goals of the activities introduced into the year-long required American history course taken by the 11th and 12th grade students are to use computational thinking to help students:

- Improve their note-taking ability
- Improve their active-listening skills
- Recognize the difference between homework and studying
- Improve their recall skills

The activities ask students to use hashtags to improve their understanding of the process of note taking. The activities involve abstraction (to identify appropriate hashtags), evaluation (to consider if an effective set of hashtags has been chosen and applied correctly), and recollection (because the purpose of the hashtags is to allow classification and recall of information). The activities are sequenced as follows:

Step 1: Give a formal presentation on the definition and value of efficacious note taking. Preface the presentation with a discussion of note taking and affirm student observations whenever possible.

Step 2: Introduce the idea of hashtagging. This activity will help students to understand that hashtags are useful for note taking because it allows someone to choose the term or phrase that will best help them retain and retrieve the information they have recorded. It is important to convey that effective hastags are based on a thoughtful abstraction of the material and will not be proper nouns or words from the lecture. Assign as homework a short reading on hashtagging, to be discussed during lecture the next day.

Step 3: Present a short, formal lecture of approximately twenty minutes in length, during which students need to take class notes. The instructor should identify in advance up to ten key ideas that students might plausibly tag. At the end of the lecture students will be asked to quietly read over their lecture notes, adding or correcting information as necessary and supplying a maximum of ten tags for key ideas in their notes. Finally students will, in small groups, compare, contrast, and debate their hash tag choices and then present a summary of their work to the group for consideration.

Step 4: Present a longer, formal history lecture of about thirty minutes in duration for which students need to take notes. As with the last step, the teacher will have identified up to ten likely ideas that the students might plausibly tag. This time students will correct and augment their notes as homework, again identifying a maximum of ten hashtags in the margins of their notes. The ten tags will also be recorded on a separate piece of paper to be submitted to the teacher. In the following class their work will be reviewed in small groups and then with the larger class.

This process, and variations of it, will be repeated with regularity throughout the year. It will be applied not only to lectures but also to large group discussions and other classroom activities. Later a similar process will be used to improve students' critical reading skills.

3.1.3 Latin

This part of the project was designed to implement three particular exercises for learning Latin that require and encourage computational thinking: grammar notation, sentence diagramming, and metaphrasing. Notation involves identifying the grammatical parts of sentences as well as their relationship to the rest of the sentence, maintaining the integrity of the Latin syntax or sentence structure. Notating primarily uses abstraction. Diagramming requires a spatial realignment of sentence parts according to a precise visual diagram of English syntax. When one diagrams a Latin sentence, one moves the sentence out of its natural order and into English word order, a process that involves evaluation in addition to abstraction. Finally, metaphrasing involves analyzing each component of the Latin sentence in its given word order, establishing its various possible uses and meanings, and trying to predict into which of three general Latin clause patterns it falls. This process also involves evaluation. Notating, diagramming, and metaphrasing were used in the course prior to the project, but typically on an ad-hoc basis in response to the needs of a particular class or student, or as a short-term activity designed to illuminate a difficult grammatical or syntactical concept. The project inspired the systematic use of the methods, with the intent that the students would learn the associated computational thinking skills.

The implementation of the new activities was in a class of twenty-two students with a broad range of ability and achievement. The teacher intended to introduce the activities as a part of a layered curriculum, or differentiated instruction, so that each student could find success with at least one of the practices. For the study data was gathered from weekly reading comprehension exercises and self-assessments or surveys administered every four weeks. The project began in the winter with notation exercises. The stronger students quickly moved onto diagramming and metaphrasing. But the other students had extreme difficulty with the notation as soon as the English sentences became more complex, providing some evidence that abstraction is crucial and challenging to teach in more than just computer science classes [7]. Those students then moved to notating Latin sentences, but it seemed best to keep those students working in Latin so the diagramming was skipped for the whole class. By the spring the whole class was either notating Latin sentences or metaphrasing them. Throughout the project data collection proved difficult. No usable data could be obtained from the monthly survey, as only seven students consistently completed them. On the reading comprehension quizzes, only two students seemed to perform more solidly and seemed to be making mistakes in reading rather than from simply guessing. For the rest, comprehension did not seem to increase or decrease notably.

There were unanticipated difficulties in the project, mainly the late start and the reduced amount of time devoted to it in the class. The teacher also hadn't anticipated how much notating or diagramming Latin sentences would confuse some students. In the end, only a handful of the students seemed to have acquired the particular skill set (notation, diagramming, metaphrasing) for reading Latin, and these were either the high achieving students, or in two cases, the students who struggle with language study. Moving forward, this work has helped to more clearly define the parameters for continued and regular computational thinking activities in the Latin classroom which the teacher is hopeful will produce more consistent results. Diagramming sentences will be avoided in the future since it forces English word order on Latin sentences and undermines the goals of the activities and class. In the 2011-2012 academic year notation or metaphrasing will be made a regular part of exercises, activities, and quizzes, with the hope that it becomes automatic when the students read Latin prose or poetry.

3.1.4 Graphic Arts

The fine arts course modified for the project is Digital Design for Communication, a year-long class in graphic design that is taken by students in grades 9 through 12. The activities added to the course have the students design a prototype for an object to be printed using a 3D printer off site, as well as design packaging for the item. The duration of the computational thinking activities is approximately one month, with the following objectives:

- To explore the nature of a designer and client relationship
- To learn about the concept of a prototype
- To experience what it is like to be a part of a design team where individuals are responsible for different aspects of product design and development, but where no single individual controls all phases of a project
- To learn how to use a simple 3D modeling software system such as Sketchup
- To learn about package design

The primary computational thinking focus of the activities is abstraction, with the various stages of the project designed to help students understand how to do graphic reduction and how and why to leave out details in that process. A second computational thinking concept that will be revealed is communication and how difficult it can be to specify information well enough to avoid ambiguity. The included activities are done in stages:

Stage 1: Introduce students to the concept of a prototype. Ask them to sketch out ideas for a small object that they would like to make. Each student should produce at least five different ideas, but these should be simple sketches rather than rendered images. Next a group critique of the sketches is conducted. The students are asked to pick one of their prototype sketches that they would like to develop further. This choice must be fixed at this stage.

Stage 2: Introduce Google's Sketchup software. First students will be given some in-class sessions where they play with the software but are not yet allowed to use it to design one of their prototypes.

Stage 3: Ask students to trade their hand-drawn sketches with each other and use the software to design each other's prototype. There should be no communication between the person who made the sketch and the person who reproduces it with the software. Once the prototypes are designed they will be sent off site to be printed on a 3D printer.

Stage 4: Introduce students to the concept of package design, including logo design, pamphlet design, and hands-on experimentation with paper folding to create packages. During this stage the difficulties of communication will be discussed in the abstract by playing fax machine, a telephone-like game that involves passing drawings around the group rather than whispering messages.

Stage 5: Bring students together to compare the results of the sketches to the printed 3D objects. The student who drew the original sketch and the student who designed it will come together to compare notes. These pairs of students will then describe and explain their prototype to another pair of students, with the second pair responsible for designing the packaging for that prototype. Communication between prototype teams and packaging teams is not only allowed but also considered very important.

A last step is to critique the final projects. The focus here is on emphasizing how the students felt about the trading back and forth that was designed into the activities.

3.2 Interdisciplinary Computational Thinking

The project modified in the middle-school curriculum is a creative-writing assignment with an implementation in Logo to create an interactive, text-based adventure game. Like other similar projects [11, 18], the goal is to allow middle school students to learn some programming in a more creative context. The modified curriculum is part of a fifth-grade class required of all students. The first part of the class relevant for the project focuses on graphics and design and the second on programming in Logo using MicroWorlds. For the latter, students work through a series of assignments, beginning with learning to control the turtle's movements one command at a time and then writing new procedures for the turtle. It culminates in two major assignments: a Pac-Man style maze game and a choose-your-own-adventure story with interactive text.

For the project the choose-your-own-adventure story assignment was modified. The middle-school teacher collaborated with all of the fifth-grade homeroom teachers during the 2010-2011 academic year to write an interdisciplinary curriculum unit based on the project. The curriculum required students to write their stories in the language arts class with the homeroom teacher and then bring the stories to the computer science classroom, where they learned how to use Logo to turn their stories into an interactive, text-based game. The collaboration between the homeroom teachers and the computer science teacher was novel and inspired by the project.

The goal for the students is to apply computational thinking to the task of writing a story. Because the choose-your-own-adventure story is necessarily segmented, students need to think about writing in a new and different way. The story is non-linear, and keeping track of the various threads of the story requires them to abstract portions of the plot. The students were encouraged in particular to use graphs to visualize and organize their plot lines. Graphs assist students in seeing that they have sufficient material for an interesting story and also how various pieces of the story can be reused in different plot lines. For example, a story involving three choices at each branch and allowing two plot progressions but containing no duplicated elements will result in $1 + 3 + 9 + 27 = 40$ story segments. Allowing reuse of story lines can dramatically reduce the writing while not hindering the story.

When the change to the class was implemented during the 2010-2011 academic year, some challenges were identified. Some students struggled conceptually with creating a coherent, non-linear story. The project is also not very portable, since many students do not have the MicroWorlds software at home. A goal for the future is to find a way to publish or present their finished work outside of that environment. It was also difficult to identify ways to formally assess the project's goals and outcomes. However, there is a wealth of anecdotal evidence that the project was successful. Student engagement was improved. The students produced longer, and more complicated stories than students had in the past. There were more student questions about complex ways of traversing the story paths, and more students completed their stories as planned than in previous years. The students also seemed to enjoy the projects more, and many students chose to revisit the project during free-choice class time. Another success of the project was the collaboration between the teachers. Other fifth grade teachers have contacted the participating co-author, asking about possible collaborations on interdisciplinary projects.

3.3 Different Pedagogical Approaches

The portion of the study designed by the high school computer science teacher considered the efficacy of two different instructional approaches to teaching computer programming. The modified course provides instruction in Python to 9th grade students in a required computer science course. For most of the students in the class it was their first programming experience. The students were taught some basics of programming in Python during two weekly 45-minute class sessions for approximately two months. Prior to the programming unit students had done some CS Unplugged activities [2], learned about the history of computing, and created some web pages with HTML and CSS. The goal in teaching the basics of Python was to make students familiar with how computational solutions to problems are implemented in a real language.

Students in four sections of the course were split into two groups, roughly even in number and gender. The two groups produced the same programs and output but were instructed differently. The first group used a worked examples approach [12]. This group received a lecture on a topic, where the instructor programmed examples in front of them, a process known as live programming. The teacher would pose a problem orally and ask the group through discussion and brainstorming to suggest a solution. The teacher would demonstrate how to program that solution in Python and illuminate any nuances of the language that arose when solving the problem. At the end of the lecture, the teacher handed out a packet containing lightly annotated copies of each of the examples that the class had generated during the discussion. In the packet were a series of problems that the students were asked to solve. The required solutions ranged from near verbatim copying of the examples seen during the lecture to problems that required more abstract thinking and application of the programming concepts to new situations. In this group the students were instructed, verbally and on the assignment sheet, to study the worked examples in the packet provided and use them as a guide to solve the problems.

The second group used a modified examples approach. Instead of a lecture and demonstration, these students receive a work packet that guided them through the problem making a series of modifications to some starting code that ultimately led them through the same series of problems and solutions that the lecture-and-worked-examples group received. This group was able to work at their own pace, following the packet and getting a much more hands-on approach to developing the solutions to the example problems.

The programming skills of the students were measured using a commercial online tutoring system, and the data is still being analyzed. Anecdotally there was not much difference between the two groups in terms of student performance, ability, confidence or stress. It is likely that the largest contributing factor to student performance is the small and infrequent amount of contact time with the students. Because giving homework was not possible, there was a lot of momentum lost between each instructional period and the students' opportunities for practice were not contiguous enough to make a difference.

Interestingly, the number of students in a given section seemed to be a larger determining factor in which instructional method worked over another. In larger sections the self-paced modified examples packet seemed to work better. Students were encouraged to help each other and in the larger sections they seemed more willing to do so. The teacher was also able give attention to those students who asked for it or were clearly in need of it. In smaller sections the modified examples were not received well, as the students seemed reluctant to work together. In the smaller groups the lecture and worked example approach seemed better because the interactive demonstration felt more like a conversation or brainstorming session in which each student was able to make a contribution.

4. DISCUSSION

The work done at the Lab Schools has demonstrated how computational thinking can be integrated into middle- and high-school courses. Examples of computational thinking in non-computer-science disciplines are particularly important for progress in this area [1]. The project has also identified a number of challenges in implementing computational thinking activities into the 5-12 curriculum, including student participation, differences in student ability, and the difficulty in assessing the effectiveness of the new activities. Recognition that failed attempts are nevertheless beneficial to the effort is something that has both been identified by the project participants and in the wider literature [1].

One of the clear successes of this project has been the way in which it has impacted the participating teachers. This project has impacted the participants' teaching in courses beyond the one selected for modification. Like many professional development opportunities, it has provided a new lens through which to view existing courses, and the changes from the project are expected to filter through the curriculum. Fostering such professional development activities has been recognized as a crucial step in bringing computational thinking to the K-12 curriculum [1, 19].

Another benefit to come from the project has been the student response. Across a variety of classes, the instructors observed that student engagement and enthusiasm were improved during the project. The activities were also seen by teachers as a way to address heterogeneous student populations, which is a possible explanation for increased student engagement. Investigating the motivational and pedagogical impact of computational thinking activities and assignments in disciplines outside of computing is a fruitful area for future work.

5. ACKNOWLEDGMENTS

Funding for this project was provided by the National Science Foundation under Grant Number 0829671. We are grateful to Ljubomir Perkovi½ for his instrumental role in the project. We thank Randy Connolly for feedback on earlier drafts of the article.

6. REFERENCES

[1] Barr, V. and Stephenson, C. 2011. Bringing Computational Thinking to K-12: What is Involved and What is the Role of the Computer Science Education Community? In *ACM Inroads*, 2:1, pp. 48 – 54.

[2] Bell, T., Witten, I., and Fellows, M. Computer Science Unplugged, www.csunplugged.org, accessed December 2011.

[3] Cooper, S., Pérez, L.C., and Rainey, D. 2010. K-12 Computational Learning. In *Communications of the ACM*, 53:11, pp. 27 – 29.

[4] Denning, P. 2003. Great Principles of Computing. Communications of the ACM, 46:11, pp. 15-20.

[5] Dierbach, C. et al. 2011. A Model for Piloting Pathways for Computational Thinking in a General Education Curriculum. In *Proceedings of the 42nd SIGCSE Technical Symposium on Computer Science Education*, Dallas, Texas.

[6] Fox, E. et al. 2008. LIKES (Living in the KnowlEdge Society). In *Proceedings of the 39th SIGCSE Technical Symposium on Computer Science Education*, Portland, Oregon.

[7] Kramer, J. 2007. Is Abstraction the Key to Computing? *Communications of the ACM*, 50:4, pp. 37-42.

[8] Martin, F. et al. 2009. Joining Computing and the Arts at a Mid-Size University. *Journal of Computing Sciences in Colleges*, 24:6.

[9] Perkovi½ L. and Settle, A. 2010. Computational Thinking across the Curriculum: A Conceptual Framework. *College of Computing and Digital Media Technical Report 10-001*, DePaul University.

[10] Perkovi½ L., Settle, A., Hwang, S., and Jones, J. 2010. A Framework for Computational Thinking across the Curriculum. In *ITiCSE 2010: The 15th Annual Conference on Innovation and Technology in Computer Science Education*, Ankara, Turkey.

[11] Repenning, A., Webb, D., and Ioannidou, A. 2010. Scalable Game Design and the Development of a Checklist for Getting Computational Thinking into Public Schools. In *Proceedings of the 41st SIGCSE Technical Symposium on Computer Science Education*, Milwaukee, Wisconsin.

[12] Trafton, J.G. and Reiser, B.J. 1993. The contributions of studying examples and solving problems to skill acquisition. Proceedings of the 15th Conference of the Cognitive Science Society, pp. 1017-1022.

[13] The University of Chicago Lab Schools, http://www.ucls.uchicago.edu/, accessed December 2011.

[14] Wallace, S.A., Bryant, R., Orr, G. 2009. The Northwest Distributed Computer Science Department. In *Journal of Computing Sciences in Colleges*, 25:1.

[15] Way, T. et al. 2010. A Distributed Expertise Model for Teaching Computing Across Disciplines and Institutions. In *Proceedings of the International Conference on Frontiers in Education: Computer Science and Computer Engineering*, Las Vegas, Nevada.

[16] Wing, J. 2006. Computational Thinking. In *Communications of the ACM*, 49:3, pp. 33-35.

[17] Wing, J. 2011. Research Notebook: Computational Thinking – What and Why? http://link.cs.cmu.edu/article.php?a=600, accessed December 2011.

[18] Werner, L., Denner, J., Bliesner, M., and Rex, P. 2009. Can Middle-Schoolers use Storytelling Alice to Make Games? Results of a Pilot Study. In the *Proceedings of ICFDG: International Conference on Foundations of Digital Games*, Orlando, Florida.

[19] Wolz, U. et al. 2011. Computational Thinking and Expository Writing in the Middle School. In *ACM Transactions on Computing Education*, 11:2.

Pseudo Abstract Composition: The Case of Language Concatenation

Ronnie Alankry
CS Group, Science Education Department
Tel-Aviv University, Israel
ronnieal@post.tau.ac.il

David Ginat
CS Group, Science Education Department
Tel-Aviv University, Israel
ginat@post.tau.ac.il

ABSTRACT
Composition is a fundamental problem solving heuristic. In computer science, it primarily appears in program design with concrete objects such as language constructs. It also appears in more abstract forms in higher-level courses. One such form is that of language concatenation in the Computational Models course. This concatenation involves the composition of two specifications of infinite sets (source languages) into a third one, and requires both abstraction and non-deterministic conception. In this paper, we illuminate behaviors of advanced high school students, with such composition. Students who encountered difficulties offered pseudo solutions, which enclosed only "surface" features and observations. We orderly display their solutions, discuss them, and offer suggestions for educators to cope with this phenomenon.

Categories and Subject Descriptors
K.3.2 **[Computers and Education]:** Computer and Information Science Education – Computer science education.

General Terms
Design, Theory.

Keywords
Computational models, composition, concatenation, abstraction, non-determinism.

1. INTRODUCTION
Consider the following basic composition task in the fundamental course of Computational Models: "Given the two regular languages L1={words that do not contain *aba*} and L2={words that end with the letter *a*}, formulate the specification of the concatenation language L^c=L1·L2, that is – the language in which each word may be viewed as a word composed of a first part that belongs to L1 and a second part that belongs to L2".

An answer provided by some students encloses a simple composition of the two languages: "L^c is the language of words that do not contain *aba* and end with the letter *a*". Simple. But is it correct? Not quite. A word in L^c may contain *aba*. In fact, it may contain many *aba*'s. The correct answer is: L^c={words that end with the letter *a*}. This is due to the observation that if a word *w* in L^c contains *aba*'s, then we may consider the first *aba* appearance in *w* as starting the part of *w* that belongs to L2. We may also take another view of dividing *w*, such as: the *ab* of the first *aba* ends the part of *w* that belongs to L1, and the *a* that follows starts the part in *w* that belongs to L2.

The key point here is to notice that if there exists some *pasting* point in a word *w*, which splits *w* into a left part that belongs to L1 and a right part that belongs to L2, then *w* belongs to L^c (=L1·L2). Comprehension of the latter notion, and suitable formulation of L^c requires abstraction and a non-deterministic conception.

Why abstraction? First, the required composition involves languages, which are usually infinite sets of elements (words). The composition is in the form of concatenation, which is less familiar than the more common set operations of union and intersection. Second, the objective is to combine two specifications into a third one. In seeking the solution, one needs to take into account various cases of splitting a word into two parts (one belonging to L1 and the other belonging to L2), and identify a pasting point for each word. Different sub-sets of words may be characterized by different pasting points. Third, the characteristics of the pasting point(s) may be kept implicit, and not explicitly appear in the resulting specification.

Why non-determinism? The requirement here is that for each word "there will exist" a pasting point of a part that belongs to L1 and a part that belongs to L2. One may identify many relevant pasting points, even for a particular word (or a sub-set of words), but may only need to capitalize on the characteristic that there is at least one such point.

The composition, abstraction, and non-determinism needed in tasks like the one above encapsulate essential skills in computational thinking that we would like our students to acquire and demonstrate (e.g., [13]). Do students demonstrate these skills? Not necessarily. In this paper we unfold student behavior that yields only "pseudo" outcomes, of limited computational thinking.

Difficulties with composition were studied in the development of computer programs with programming constructs (e.g. [12]) and with design/algorithmic patterns (e.g., [7]). Difficulties with abstraction and non-determinism were studied with respect to student ways to reduce abstraction [6], and students' (inelegant) ways to "bypass" abstract and non-deterministic notions (e.g., [1-3]). The latter was particularly noticed in Computational Models tasks that involved <u>de</u>composition.

No study was conducted on the composition of sets, such as regular languages (as in the example above). In this paper we shed light on such composition, in the form of language concatenation. Our study extends the perspective of student difficulties with composition, abstraction, and non-determinism. In particular, we illuminate a new angle of student behaviors – the angle of *pseudo solutions*. We elaborate on this term in the discussion section. Unlike the tasks mentioned in [1-3], in which students could find ways to reduce or avoid abstraction, the tasks in this study could

ITiCSE'12, July 3-5, 2012, Haifa, Israel

not be solved in such ways. One had to express suitable abstraction and non-determinism. As a result, in places of difficulty, students yielded solutions that reflected only limited, "surface" characteristics.

In the next section, we present a short background on previous studies of composition, abstraction, and non-determinism; and further motivate our study. In the section that follows we present our study of composition in the form of language concatenation. We then discuss our findings, and offer some suggestions for tutors, of coping with the non-trivial comprehension of abstraction and non-determinism, with respect to language concatenation.

2. BACKGROUND AND RATIONALE

Program design involves decomposition of a problem into sub-problems, and the composition of the solutions to these sub-problems. The sub-problems are often familiar, and their solutions are regarded as algorithmic patterns, or design patterns, from which the end result is composed [4]. Previous studies named a variety of basic, generic patterns, or templates such as counting, and linear search (e.g., [7,9]).

The composition of patterns, which yields the solution to a given problem, may be obtained from one or more kinds of compositions. Soloway [11] identified four particular composition types: *Abutement* – patterns appear one after the other ("pasting"); *Nesting* – a pattern is a subset of another pattern; *Merging* – patterns are interleaved; *Tailoring* – patterns need to be altered in order to fit the needs of the problem at hand.

Spohrer et al. [12] revealed several kinds of mistakes that occur during composition (and particularly during Merging), and named them *Missing* (pieces), *Malformed* (pieces), *Misplaced* (pieces), and *Spurious* (misused/unnecessary pieces). Muller, Haberman, and Ginat illuminated difficulties with Nesting and Merging, and partly explained these difficulties with respect to cognitive (over)load of the problem solver [7].

An additional, rather different CS domain, which involves composition and decomposition, is that of Computational Models. In this domain, composition is required in operations such as union, intersection, and concatenation of automata and languages. Decomposition often appears in proofs of language properties, in which one capitalizes on closure properties that are applied on decomposed parts.

Armoni and Gal-Ezer illuminated student difficulties of various kinds with Computational Models tasks. Students refrained from capitalizing on abstract closure properties, and non-deterministic notions, in solving tasks that could be elegantly solved by combing these notions with decomposition [1-3]. Instead, students (both in college and in high-school) followed a concrete approach, and constructed complex, deterministic automata "from scratch". Armoni and Gal-Ezer's findings add to Hazzan's findings of students' reduction of abstraction in both mathematics and computer science [5,6].

In the domain of program design, the composition facets that were examined involved the objects of programming templates and patterns. The objects composed were concrete, specific, and very few. In the domain of Computational Models some of the composed objects are concrete (the automata), and some are more abstract (the languages). The previous studies (mentioned above) in this domain examined student tendencies to compose concrete objects rather than decompose the more abstract ones while capitalizing on abstract properties.

Student behaviors in the composition of abstract entities, such as languages, were not studied so far. Yet, CS students are required to compose abstract entities, in the Computational Models course, and in additional theoretical courses. They also need the skill of abstract composition in their analysis of complex systems and algorithm behaviors. A study of their behavior in this respect may shed light on possible difficulties that they may demonstrate, and of which educators should be aware.

In what follows we display such study, on composition of the form of language concatenation, which is one of the essential set operations employed in the course of Computational Models. In language concatenation one needs to compose two set specifications that may overlap, and combine them into one, in a way that will preserve the features of each of the sets with respect to its role (as a prefix or a postfix of the whole). The challenge may be posed in gradual levels of difficulty, as will be shown in the next section.

3. A STUDY OF CONCATENATION

3.1 The Research Question

In our experience with students who study Computational Models, we noticed that some indeed demonstrate difficulties with language concatenation. Following the above rationale we posed the following research question:

> *What behaviors do students demonstrate in solving language concatenation tasks, and how is it reflected in terms of the notions of composition, abstraction, and non-determinism?*

3.2 Population

Computational Models is a fundamental course in college CS curriculum. In Israel, it also is an advanced course, or unit, studied in the late year of high-school.

In Israeli high schools, every student must study at least one area in depth, in addition to her studies of Mathematics, English, History, Literature etc. The highest level of studies is the 5-units level, where each unit involves 90 class hours. Computer science is one of the areas that may be studied in depth.

The high-school CS curriculum is modular, and composed of three basic units and two advanced ones. The three basic units primarily involve Fundamentals of Computer Science, and focuses on programming and the particular notions of correctness, efficiency, and modularity. The 4-th unit involves Data Structures (in which "Trees" is the most advanced topic), and the 5-th unit offers a few alternatives, of which one is the 90 class hours of Computational Models.

The Computational Models unit includes the topics of: finite state automata (deterministic/non-deterministic), regular languages, pushdown automata (deterministic/non-deterministic), and Turing machines. (Context free languages are only briefly mentioned.) In the final exam students may be required to compose finite-state and pushdown automata, explain whether a language is regular or irregular, apply closure operations, such as union, intersection, concatenation and complement, and construct a simple Turing machine. In tasks that involve regular languages, the languages are usually specific (i.e., specified with specific features).

Our study involved 46 12th graders from three different high schools. We posed them a questionnaire on language concatenation, after they have learnt the topics of finite-state automata and regular languages. They all practiced various kinds of compositions, including language concatenation, as well as the utilization of closure properties. All these students studied mathematics at the higher levels of 4 or 5 units.

3.3 Tools

The research tools consisted of a questionnaire and interviews. Students were asked to answer the following eight questions, which were ordered according to their level of difficulty. Most questions directly ask for language concatenation, while others involve related questions, from which we could infer one's insight. We display the desired answers together with the questions.

Question 1: L1={*ε, aab, bb, ac*}, L2={*a ,cc, d*}. Specify L1·L2.
[**Answer**:{*a, cc, d, aaba, aabcc, aabd, bba, bbcc, bbd, aca, accc, acd* }]

Question 2: L1={words that begin with the letter *a*}, L2={words that end with the letter *b*}. Specify L1·L2.
[**Answer**:{words that begin with the letter *a* and end with the letter *b*}]

Question 3: L1={words that begin with the letter *b*}, L2={words that begin with the letter *a*}. Specify L1·L2.
[**Answer**:{words that begin with the letter b and contain the letter *a*}]

Question 4: L1={words of an even length}, L2={words that begin with the letter *a*}. Specify L1·L2.
[**Answer**:{words that contain the letter *a* at least once in an odd position}]

Question 5: L1={words that begin with the letter *a*}, L2={words of an even length }.

a. What is the shortest word in L1·L2?
b. Do *abbb* and *abaab* belong to the language L1·L2?

[**Answer**: *a* is the shortest word; both words belong to L1·L2]

Question 6: L1={words that do not contain the sequence *aba*}, L2={words that end with the letter *a*}. Specify L1·L2.
[**Answer**:{words that end with the letter *a*}]

Question 7: L1={a^nb^m| $n>m$, $m>=0$}, L2={words that begin with the letter *b*}. Is L1·L2 a regular language? Explain.
[**Answer**: Yes. The concatenation language is {words that begin with a sequence of one or more *a*'s, followed by a *b*}]

Question 8: L1={$\#_aw = \#_bw$, $\#_aw>0$, $\#_bw >0$}, L2={$\#_aw \neq \#_bw$}. Is L1·L2=L2? Explain.
[**Answer**: No. (The combined characteristic that the number of appearances of the letter *a* is different than that of the letter *b*, is insufficient for the specification of L1·L2.)]

We explain below the objectives in selecting the above questions. (In what follows we call L1 and L2 the source languages, and L1·L2 the target, or concatenation language.)

Question 1 – the source languages are finite, the number of words is limited, and all the words are given. The objective here is to make sure that students understand the meaning of concatenation as a Cartesian product between the words of the source languages.

Questions 2-3 – each of the source languages is specified by a simple (one letter) prefix or postfix; thus the specification of the concatenation language is trivial. In Question 2 one may keep explicit the features of both of the source languages in specifying the concatenation language. In Question 3 one may keep one of the features and slightly modify the other.

In both cases, the pasting point between a part that belongs to L1 and a part that belongs to L2 is straightforward – in Question 2 the features of the two languages do not overlap, and the pasting point may be anywhere after the first letter and before the last letter in the target (concatenation language) word; and in Question 3 the overlap of the features is trivial and the pasting point is just before the letter featuring the prefix of L2.

Questions 4-7 – one source language is defined with a simple (one letter) prefix or postfix, and the other source language is specified with a feature that applies to the whole word. In Question 4 the result (the specification of the concatenation language) is an insightful combination of the two languages' features; in Questions 5 and 6 the result is the cancellation of the whole-word features (easier to see in Question 5); in Question 7 one of the source languages in irregular, but the concatenation yields a regular language.

At first glance, one may get the impression that the feature that applies to the whole word in one source language yields complex overlapping with the feature that applies to the prefix or the postfix in the other language. However, this impression is misleading. In all four cases one may "dissolve" the overlapping by recognizing suitable pasting points.

In Question 4, the pasting point is in any *a* that appears in an odd position. This is also explicitly indicated in the specification of the concatenation language. In Question 5, the pasting point may be at the very end of the word, leaving the word ε, of length 0, as the part that belongs to L2. The pasting point for Question 6 was described in the Introduction section. In Question 7, the pasting point may be right after a^n. Notice that the part that belong to L2 may include any number of b's (possibly larger than a^n), thus the concatenation language is regular even though the source language L1 is irregular.

Question 8 – the features of both of the source languages apply to the whole word. This strengthens the phenomenon of overlapping features. One needs to be very careful upon attempting to combine both features. In this case, it is impossible to delete the feature of L1 in the specification of the concatenation language.

3.4 Procedure

Students were given 60 minutes to answer the questionnaire. Following an initial analysis of their answer sheets, several students were interviewed about their answers. We selected for the interviews eight students who offered typical (sometimes erroneous) solutions. In the interviews they were asked to describe their train of thought, and elaborate on points where they felt uncertain about their solutions. Following the interviews, we carefully analyzed all the student answers and interview responses. We display our findings in the next section.

3.5 Results

Figure 1 below shows the statistics of the correct student answers to the eight questions.

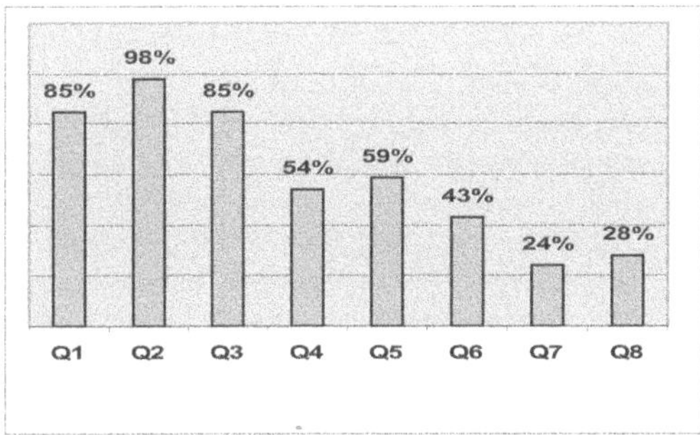

Figure 1.

As can be seen above, about 90% of the answers to Questions 1-3 were correct, while only 42% of the answers to Questions 4-8 were correct. In careful examination of the student answers, including their explanations, we noticed five different categories of answers:

1. Irrelevant answers.
2. No composition of the source languages' features.
3. Expansion of a source language feature.
4. Cancellation of a source language feature.
5. Suitable feature composition.

All in all, 58% of the answers to all the eight questions were inappropriate or incorrect (and 42% – correct). In what follows, we describe the five categories, while displaying the part of each of the categories 1-4 in the total amount of incorrect answers.

3.5.1 Irrelevant Answers

A total of 3% of the inappropriate answers were no-answer, and 7% were answers of another question (e.g., switching L1 and L2).

3.5.2 No Composition of the Languages' Features

A total of 30% of the incorrect answers involved no composition of the source languages L1 and L2. A typical answer structure was: "The concatenation language is a language in which each word can be divided into two parts – a first part that belongs to L1 and a second part that belong to L2". Such answers appeared particularly in response to Questions 4, 5, 6, and 7.

For example, an answer to Question 6, in which L1={words not containing the sequence *aba*} and L2={ words that end with the letter *a*}, was the following:

> "The concatenation language is words that can be divided into two words, when the first word does not contain the sequence *aba* and the second word ends with the letter *a*".

Question 7 asked whether the concatenation of L1 and L2 yields a regular language, where L1=$\{a^nb^m|\ n>m,\ m>=0\}$ and L2={words that begin with the letter *b*}. Many answered that the concatenation language is not a regular language, since:

> "The concatenation language involves words that can be divided into two part, one of the form $\{a^nb^m|\ n>m,\ m>=0\}$, and the other – words that begin with a *b*. And, since the first part is irregular, and cannot be implemented with a deterministic finite state automaton, then the concatenation language is irregular."

One of the students who provided such answer was Rotem, whom we interviewed about her solution. A part of the interview is displayed in Figure 2 below.

***Interviewr**: L1=$\{a^nb^m|n>m,m>=0\}$ and L2=$\{b\Sigma^*\}$. What is L1·L2?*
***Rotem**: $\{a^nb^mb\Sigma^*|\ n>m\}$, and it is irregular, because you need to compare the amount of a's to the amount of b's.*
***Interviewer**: does the word aaabbbbbbbb belong to L1·L2?*
***Rotem**: Yes.*
***Interviewer**: But the number of a's is smaller than that of the b's.*
***Rotem**: True, but I can divide the word into two parts so that the first belongs to L1 and the second belongs to L2, like this: (aaabb) and (bbbbbb).*
***Interviewer**: Can you think of a word that begins with an a and doesn't belong to this "outcome" language?*
***Rotem**: um... aabbb is ok, so is abb... wait! The word a isn't ok.*
***Interviewer**: Nice.... Can you think of a word that begins with some a's followed by a b that isn't in L1·L2?*
***Rotem**: ... No.*
***Interviewer**: What do you think this means?*
***Rotem**: Well ... maybe the concatenation is actually words that begin with a's followed by a b ... but it still does not make sense to me, where did the condition (of L1) that there are less b's than a's disappear?*
***Interviewer**: Let's look at your answer to Question 5. You had to specify L1·L2 and you did so correctly, saying that the concatenation language is {words that begin with an a}. Where did the condition "words of an even length" disappear?*
***Rotem**: Because ... I can divide a word in more than one place ... wait, now I realize ... I can divide the "outcome" word here in more than one place ... so I don't need to check the ratio between the number of a's and the number of b's ...*
***Rotem**: I did not think that such a significant condition (the irregularity of L1) can be cancelled out like that ...*

Figure 2.

Roten did solve Question 5 properly, and combined the features of the two source languages. In Question 5, she recognized a suitable pasting point of the two parts (the one that belongs to L1 and the one that belongs to L2), and offered a combined, elegant solution. However, in Question 7, which is harder, she did not recognize a pasting point, and offered the typical, "no-composition" solution displayed above. During the interview she gradually realized the suitable composition, and were rather surprised that it also yielded a regular language (from an irregular source language).

3.5.3 Expansion of a Source Language Feature

A Total of 32% of the incorrect answers involved an improper expansion of one of the source languages' features to the whole word. That is, rather than being characteristic of only one of the two parts of a word in the concatenation language, their feature characterized the whole word. This phenomenon particularly appeared in the answers to Questions 4, 5, and 6.

For example, an answer to Question 5, in which L1={words that begin with the letter *a*} and L2={words of an even length}, was the following:

> "Words of an even length that begin with the letter *a*."

In this answer the feature {an even length} that should only characterize the second part of a word in the concatenation language is *imposed* on the whole word.

A similar answer was provide to Question 4, in which L1 and L2 switch "roles": L1={words of an even length} and L2={words that begin with the letter *a*}. Some answers were the following:

"Words of an even length that include an *a*."

Here too, the feature {an even length} is imposed on the whole word. Since the parity was imposed on the whole word, the location on the *a* became unimportant, and it just had to be "somewhere". If the problem solver would have applied the parity property only on the first part of the word (that belongs to L1), she would require that the *a* that starts the second part of the word will be in an odd position (and not just anywhere). In this case, the explicit indication of this position is actually an explicit indication of the pasting point (between the two parts) in the specification of the concatenation language.

In an answer to Question 6, in which L1={words not containing the sequence *aba*} and L2={words that end with the letter *a*}, students imposed again, improperly, the feature that characterizes L1 on the whole word:

"Words that do not contain *aba* and end with an *a*."

As seen already in the Introduction section, this answer is incorrect, as *aba* may appear many times in a word of the concatenation language. Unlike the answer to Question 4, here the correct answer – {words that end with an *a*} – does not include an explicit specification of the pasting point.

3.5.4 Cancellation of a Source Language Feature

A Total of 28% of the incorrect answers involved an improper cancellation of one of the source language features. Such answers appeared particularly in responses to Questions 4 and 8.

In the previous sub-section we described erroneous answers that imposed the parity property in Questions 4 and 5 on the whole word, rather than on a part of it. Some students took the opposite course. Instead of imposing the parity property on the whole word, they just cancelled it out. Their answer to Question 4, in which L1={words of an even length}, L2={words that begin with the letter *a*} was:

"Words that contain an *a*."

As we may see, the parity property was completely omitted. Some properly handled the parity property here, but improperly cancelled out a source language feature in Question 8.

Question 8 asks whether L1·L2=L2, when L1={$\#_a w = \#_b w$, $\#_a w>0$, $\#_b w >0$} and L2={$\#_a w \neq \#_b w$}. The student Elad answered "Yes" (though the correct answer is "No"). In a following interview he explained his answer as displayed below:

> ***Elad:*** *The claim is correct, because in words that belong to L1, the number of appearances of a is equal to that of b, and if we concatenate L2, in which the number of appearances of a is different than that of b, then there's no need for L1's feature anymore. It is as if it does not exist because it is just adding length to the words.*

Elad identified correctly that the total number of appearances of *a* should be different than that of *b*. So it may seem that L1's feature is not relevant anymore. This, however, is not true. In the beginning of a word in the concatenation language the number of a's must equal the number of b's. There may be words, like *aaba*, in which the total numbers of *a*'s and *b*'s are different, but there is no prefix in which the amounts of *a*'s and *b*'s are equal. The cancellation of a feature must be suggested only after one carefully examined all the possible cases of pasting words of L1 with words of L2.

3.5.5 Suitable Feature Composition

In each of the previous sub-sections (3.5.1 – 3.5.4), we examined the percentage of each category among the set of erroneous answers. In examining the whole (correct and incorrect) set of answers given to Questions 4-8, we may extract from Figure 1 that 42% of these answers (to Q4, Q5, Q6, Q7, and Q8) were correct. These answers reflect suitable abstract composition, which involves proper consideration of all the possible cases of pasting words of L1 with words of L2.

4. DISCUSSION

In answering the research question we may notice that the results of the previous section illuminate several patterns of student behaviors. About 40% of the answers to Questions 4-8 involved correct composition that encapsulated suitable abstraction and non-deterministic conception. Yet, more than 50% of the answers revealed no composition, or erroneous composition. (We should note that we did not ask the students about their confidence in their solutions, though quite a few seemed comfortable with their answers, without carefully checking them.)

Unlike some tasks in previous studies (e.g., [1-3]), which could be solved by "bypassing" abstraction and non-determinism, the tasks posed in this study could only be solved with suitable demonstration of abstraction and non-deterministic conception. Those who could not properly employ such conception turned to an ally of "kind of", or pseudo solutions.

Pseudo solutions were of two kinds. One kind of such solutions appeared in the student answers displayed in sub-section 3.5.2. These involved arguments in the form "The concatenation language is a language in which each word can be divided into two parts – a first part that belongs to L1 and a second part that belong to L2". Such arguments *only enclose the definition* and meaning of language concatenation, but do not reflect any composition of the specifications of L1 and L2.

The other kind of pseudo solutions is apparent in the student answers in sub-sections 3.5.3 and 3.5.4. In these answers students did attempt composition of the source languages' specifications. However, their "picture" of the desired composition was vague. In particular, they did not demonstrate insightful analysis of the given specifications, and offered *oversimplified solutions*, some which involved unsuitable expansion of source language features, and others which involved cancellation of source language features. In both cases, they did not express recognition of pasting points of words of the concatenation language, which divide the words into a first part that belongs to L1 and a second part that belongs to L2.

The pseudo solutions described above reflect difficulties with composition, abstraction, and non-determinism. Composition is a fundamental heuristic in problem solving [8,10]. It is apparent in a variety of occasions in mathematics, engineering, science in general, and computer science in particular. In programming it involves a few composition types, among them Merging and Concatenation. Merging is considered the harder type, and Concatenation – the easier one. Concatenation is considered easy as one just needs to paste the beginning of one concrete object to the end of another concrete object. Yet, when the concatenated objects are not concrete, the composition becomes subtler.

Question 1 of our set of questions involved only several concrete objects (words) in each language, and the vast majority of the student compositions were correct. In Questions 2 and 3, many still performed well, as there was no overlap in the features that characterized the composed languages. But, in the questions that followed (4-8), the picture changed.

Questions 4-8 involved overlapping features of the composed languages. In solving them, students had to demonstrate both abstraction and non-deterministic conception in carefully seeking the existence of pasting points that divide the words of the concatenation language into two parts. Many students avoided or oversimplified the view of the concatenation language words, and particularly did not examine all the possible divisions of these words. It seems that the notion of only seeking an existence of a suitable division point, among many possible alternatives, was not properly conceived and applied.

We should note that the studied population was that of high-school students. Yet, these were senior students, studying at the most advanced level. Previous studies of both high-school and college students revealed related difficulties in approaching tasks in the Computational Models course.

How may one address the difficulties revealed in this study? Hazzan presented three different ways by which students attempt to reduce abstraction: the way of turning to the more familiar, the way of turning to a procedure, and the way of decreasing complexity by "narrowing", or simplifying the object(s) to handle [5,6]. In our case, we the teachers, may capitalize on these observations and apply them in our teaching.

We may try to cope with the abstraction and non-determinism challenge of language concatenation by combining all the three ways indicated above. In particular, we may gradually familiarize students with a procedure of seeking pasting points in words of the concatenation language. This can be done by gradually posing to students subtler tasks, and examining with them the different cases that may be relevant for dividing words into two parts. Some of the tasks may require different considerations for different subsets of words. Moreover, some resulting specifications may explicitly encapsulate references to the pasting points, while other will not. The set of questions posed to the students in this study may serve as an initial example for the above.

In addition, in order to reduce complexity, source languages may be initially be presented with finite, rather small number of words. Students will not be expected to offer the Cartesian product of the words in these languages, but rather apply the same procedure we indicate above. Since the number of words, and therefore cases to consider is small, the task of conducting the procedure becomes simpler and more concrete. After teaching concatenation in this form, we may "fade out" and expand the practice to languages that are infinite sets.

5. CONCLUSION

The phenomenon of "pseudo" solving the task at hand may be apparent in occasions other than language concatenation. CS educators should be aware of this phenomenon, and seek ways to cope with it, such as the suggestions we offered above. It may also be relevant to examine whether our suggestions for educators can help students with abstraction and non-determinism. In addition, further studies may examine both this phenomenon and ways to cope with it in domains other than Computational Models.

6. ACKNOWLEDGMENTS

We would like to thank Ela Zur and Tami Lapidot for their helpful feedback and remarks.

REFERENCES

1. Armoni, M. and Gal-Ezer, J. (2006). Introducing non-determinism, *Journal of Computers in Mathematics and Science Teaching*, 25(4), 325-359.
2. Armoni M. and Gal-Ezer, (2006). Reduction – an abstract thinking pattern: the case of the computational models course, *SIGCSE'06*, 389-394.
3. Armoni, M. and Gal-Ezer, J. (2007). Non-determinism: an abstract concept in computer science studies, *Computer Science Education*, 17(4), 243-262.
4. Astrachan, O., Berry, G., Cox, L., and Mitchener, G. (1998). Design patterns: an essential component of CS Curricula. *SIGCSE'98*, 153-160.
5. Hazzan, O. (1999). Reducing abstraction level when learning abstract algebra concepts, *Educational Studies in Mathemartics*, 40, 71-90.
6. Hazzan, O. (2003). How students attempt to reduce abstraction in the learning of mathematics and in the learning of computer science, *Computer Science Education* 13(2), 95-122.
7. Muller, O., Ginat, D., and Haberman, B. (2007). Pattern-oriented instruction and its influence on problem decomposition and solution construction, *ITiCSE'07*, 151-155.
8. Polya, G. (1954). *How to Solve It.* Princeton University Press.
9. Schank, P. K., Linn, C. M., and Clancy, J. M. (1993). Supporting Pascal programming with an on-line template library and case studies, *International Journal of Man-Machine Studies*, 38(6), 1031-1048.
10. Schoenfeld, A. E. (1992). Learning to think mathematically: problem solving, metacognition, and sense making in mathematics, in Grouws D. A. (ed.), *Handbook of Research on Mathematics Teaching and Learning,* 334-370.
11. Soloway, E. (1986). Learning to program=learning to construct mechanisms and explanations. *Communications of the ACM*, 29(9), 1031-1048.
12. Sphorer, J., Soloway, E., and Pope, E. (1985). A goal/plan analysis of buggy Pascal programs. *Human-Computer Interaction*, 1(2), 163-207.
13. Wing, J. (2006). Computational thinking. *Communications of the ACM*, 49(3), 33-35.

Teaching Graph Algorithms To Children Of All Ages

J. Paul Gibson
Département LOR (SAMOVAR UMR 5157)
Telecom Sud Paris, France
paul.gibson@it-sudparis.eu

ABSTRACT

We report on our experiences in teaching graph theory and algorithms to school children, aged 5 to 17. Our objectives were to demonstrate that children can discover quite complex mathematical concepts, and are able to work with abstractions and use computation reasoning from quite an early age. We provide details of our incremental approach, which can be used with students of a wide range of abilities. Also, we comment on the importance of problem based learning where the algorithms are presented as possible solutions to games or puzzles. Finally, we conclude with a number of important observations with regard to the introduction of computer science into schools.

Categories and Subject Descriptors

K.3.2 [**Computer and Information Science Education**]: Computer science education; G.2 [**Discrete Mathematics**]: Graph Theory—*Graph algorithms*

General Terms

Human Factors, Experimentation

Keywords

Computational thinking, K-12 education, Problem based learning, Modelling, Abstractions

1. INTRODUCTION

There has been much recent debate concerning the teaching of computer science in schools. Within the computer science community (acdemia and industry) there is general agreement that computer science <u>is not</u> about how to use a computer through the applications that it can execute, but it <u>is</u> about knowing how these applications work. For example, in the UK the *NextGen 2011 report on CS education* criticises "a school curriculum that focuses in ICT on office skills rather than the more rigorous computer science and programming skills which high-tech industries [...] need". Similar stories and reports have appeared in the media around the world, with politicians and policy-makers finally listening to the message. (For example, Michael Bloomberg, the mayor of New York, has publically endorsed a course on learning to program that he is taking, and which is targetted at school children.) We welcome these recent events, even if we strongly believe that computer science in schools needs to be broader than just learning to program[9]; it needs to be about computational thinking[23], algorithmic thinking[8] and algorithmic learning[12]. Programming in schools is important, but teaching about abstraction may be even more so[18].

This paper supports the move towards this new type of computer science education. However, we note that in making such an educational change, one should not forget about the teachers who are expected to teach this "new" material. It is critical that teachers understand computer science if they are to teach it well. Such an observation has already been made by Ball[1] with respect to mathematics education, where she notes (page 36):

> "Making the judgments about which student suggestions to pursue, developing the tasks that encourage certain kinds of exploration, and conducting fruitful class discussions — all these tasks depend heavily on the teacher's subject matter knowledge"

In the same report (page 37), a teacher acknowledges the importance of learning while teaching:

> "When I decided to be a teacher, I knew there were a lot of things I had to learn about teaching, but I felt I knew everything there was to teach my students. [...] I found I was as much a learner of subject matter as I was a learner of the art of teaching. My education in the future will not be limited to 'how to teach', but also what it is I'm teaching."

We propose that the best way to prepare teachers of computer science is for them to actually teach it. Thus, experimental computer science sessions should be introduced into the classroom in order to teach the teachers, as well as to introduce computer science to the students, and to help develop or improve the computer science curriculum. This would address many of the issues raised by Guzdial[13] when he states:

> "We need more education research that is informed by understanding CS — how it's taught,

> what the current practices are, and what's important to keep as we change practice."

Our research was motivated by the Bruner's famous educational challenge from 1960[4](page 33):

> "We begin with the hypothesis that any subject can be taught effectively in some intellectually honest form to any child at any stage of development. It is a bold hypothesis and an essential one in thinking about the nature of a curriculum"

We wished to validate this hypothesis within the domain of computer science, and chose the subject of graph algorithms as our test case. This subject is foundational to all computer science and it provides an excellent example of the importance of mathematics[15] and the mathematical nature of algorithms and programming[20].

The structure of the remainder of the paper is as follows. In section 2 we provide a brief review of recent related work. Section 3 provides details concerning some of the sessions that we have run in schools. During the sessions, a number of important observations were made: section 4 reports on these. In section 5 we conclude the paper and make suggestions for future work.

2. RELATED WORK

Previous work that has most unfluenced our research falls under the following themes —

1. Teaching computer science without using a computer: The CS Unplugged programme as first introduced by Bell[2] inspired and motivated our teaching in the classroom, where the computer is no longer a distraction to learning about computing.

2. Preparing school teachers to teach computer science: Hazzan et al.[14] propose a model for high school computer science education, where our paper makes a contribution to 3 of the 4 key elements that they identify: teacher preparation, pedagogic research and curriculum development.

3. Teaching computer science to young children: Work with very young children has been reported by Gibson, where children of all ages (starting from 5) have been introduced to formal methods through reasoning about algorithms and proofs[11]. Many different programming languages have been developed specifically for teaching children. Feurzig et al., as early as 1969, proposed using programming to teach about mathematics[7] and demonstrate how the programming language LOGO can be used by young children. More recently researchers have reported success in schools with languages oriented towards children (and beginners) such as Alice[17]. Further, evidence suggests that young children are also able to program using standard (real world) languages such as Java[10]. Teaching young children about computers and computer architecture has been the subject of research by Bianco and Tinzanni[3], where they use interactive stories to introduce the main concepts. This approach could be complementary to our use of stories when describing the problems to be solved.

4. Teaching (graph) algorithms: Researchers have also suggested teaching algorithms during mathematics classes in schools. A typical example is from daRosa[6], where sorting and searching algorithms are used to teach about algorithm analysis. There has been much research into innovative ways of teaching graph algorithms, with most results focussing on animation and simulation[5]. However, such tools are aimed at University level students rather than for use in schools.

5. Teaching using puzzles and games: Levitin and Papalaskari propose using games and puzzles in the teaching of algorithms[19] and this approach has been successsful in other computing disciplines[21], including topics such as operating systems[16]. More formal resoning about algorithms has also been linked to puzzles and games[12].

It is beyond the scope of this paper to review all relevant publications in the teaching of computing at schools. We choose to conclude this section by referencing a paper, by Pollard and Duvall[22], that considers the knowledge transfer in the other direction: namely from schools to university. It is worthy of note that they comment on the how teaching CS at University could be improved and informed by experiences with teaching at kindergarten.

3. THE INCREMENTAL PBL APPROACH

Our teaching approach is founded on a sequence of sessions where we (aided by the teachers) work through each session at a speed that is dictated by the age and ability of the class. No session in the sequence should be skipped, but all sessions are open-ended so that more advanced students can advance at their own pace. Due to lack of space, we report only on 4 sessions that we run (each of these sessions can take between 30 minutes and 4 hours, depending on the students). Each session is divided into classes whose duration is also dictated by the level of the students. The youngest students may have 30 minute classes whilst older students may manage 90 minute classes. Our approach is to be as flexible as possible, and to follow the advice of the teacher (who is always present). All schools involved were non-fee paying and could be considered typical, with pupils' abilities following an unexceptional normal distribution.

At this experimental stage, we have no fixed learning objectives: the goal is to observe the students and to assess the impact of the classes on their general school behaviour and performance. We believe that improving their computational thinking — with emphasis on abstraction — will have a positive impact on all other classes that they study. We return to this claim in section 4.

3.1 The first session: graph concepts

This session was one of the first that we tried when we first started visiting schools more than ten years ago. It has been run twelve times in five different schools (in Ireland and France) and with five different age groups — the youngest group aged 5-6, the oldest group aged 14-15. The class sizes varied from 12 to 32 children. In the first few years in which we ran the sessions, we focused on the oldest pupils at primary school (aged 10-11). Then we extended the session with more difficult puzzles in order to use it with the oldest group of children (from secondary school) who were participating in a summer science camp. Finally, in the last year, we have adapted the session for very young children and have used it in two different classes.

Working with the youngest school children, one cannot assume that they are able to read or write. Consequently, with our first lessons we are obliged to use less abstract forms of 'language' for describing graphs. Rather than inventing such languages, we try to adapt the skills of the children to the creation of their own syntax and semantics.

Experience has shown that the youngest children are particularly motivated by drawing. Thus, we introduce a drawing game, whereby we restrict them to using only circles and lines. The game is to construct drawings — using paper and pencils — that have to follow rules that are specified using spoken natural language. For example, we start by asking them to draw "two circles connected by a single line". Typically, we see a variety of drawings, such as seen in figure 1. (Note that we have coloured the drawings to clarify the illustration, but that — at this stage in the session — the children do not yet use different colours in their drawings.)

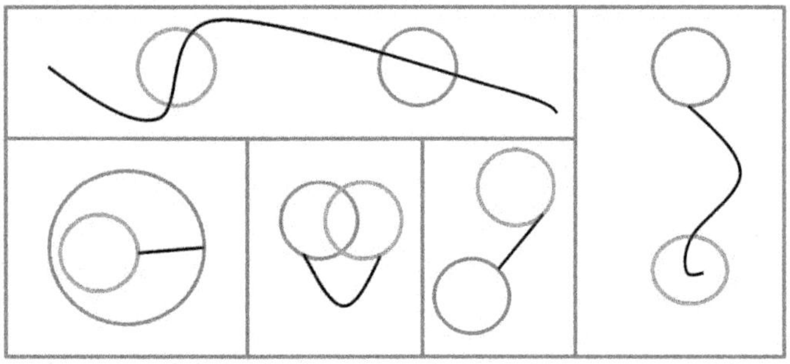

Figure 1: Two circles connected by a single line

The children than get to vote on which drawings follow the rule, and comment on whether the rule was easy to understand. At this stage, they are unsure about which drawings are right and which are wrong — so we tell them that all (within reason) are right but some are better than others. They will get to judge on which are best as they are asked to carry out more drawings.

After a few more examples we introduce colours for the circles. A typical puzzle will be for them to draw "a red circle connected to a blue circle and a green circle connected to a red circle". The two most interesting variations of drawings proposed for this problem are shown in figure 2)

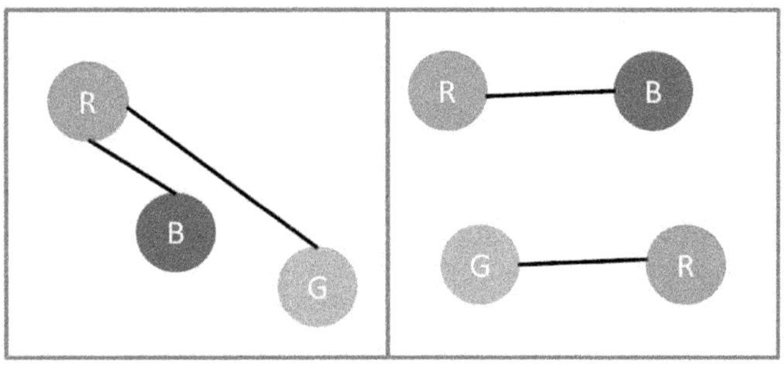

Figure 2: Red-Blue and Green-Red

At this stage, the students openly discuss about how to decide whether 2 drawings are the same, posing questions such as:

Does it matter if the lines are straight or curved?
Can the circles touch?
Can one circle be inside another?
Where can the lines start/stop?
Does it matter if the circles are different sizes?
Can the lines cross?
Do the circles have to be aligned vertically or horizontally?
Does the distance between the circles matter?

It is important to let the students decide on the answers to these questions, and very important that they understand that they can change their answers as the session progresses.

The two graphs in figure 2 usually lead to clear disagreement in the class, with 3 different opinions coming to the fore:

- The 2 drawings (we start to call them graphs in the next session) are correct and so they can be considered to be the same (or equal or equally good)
- The 2 drawings are correct but they are different
- Only 1 of the drawings is correct.

The final case usually involves heated argument concerning the meaning of the word 'and', as the students who agree that only one drawing is correct cannot agree which one.

We next introduce a description game, where the teacher no longer describes what is to be drawn (using only circles and lines) but the children have to do a drawing and to describe it to a partner, who has to reproduce the drawing without seeing their partner's original creation. The teams (in pairs) are awarded points when the rest of the class agrees that the two drawings are the same. Now, due to the competitive nature of the game, students identify the need to agree on rules for 'sameness'. Interestingly, when they re-assess the drawings in figure 2 the students almost always state that they are not the same because the number of circles is different. Asked who is to blame for their initial confusion, they usually state that the description from the teacher should have been better.

The next step is to introduce the concept of a property of a drawing that can be checked even if it is not mentioned in the description. We start with the idea of connectivity. Students have no problem in identifying connectivity in the left side of figure 2, and absence of connectivity in the right side. More advance students will even start to define connectivity in terms of paths.

For younger students, who cannot read or write, we now use the drawings as building plans for constructing models of coloured balls connected by string. These children are quite comfortable following such plans (from games such as LEGO) and so find no difficulty in making the constructions. The advantage with this approach is that the constructions are flexible and even when they change shape the students consider them not to have changed. This is the beginning of them starting to reason about semantics in terms of equivalence classes, and they return to the rules concerning sameness in the description game.

For students who are able to read and write, we introduce another challenge: to write down a textual description of the drawings using as few letters as possible. In the beginning they just write the natural language description, but the game environment motivates them to find a more concise, unambiguous syntax. Typically, the students will describe the drawings in figure 2 in the following sequence of improvements: "Red to Blue and Green to Red", "Red-Blue,Green-Red","RBGR". At this stage, we ask about the equivalence of two textual descriptions. For example, is "RBGR" the same as "GRRB" or "RRBG"? Further we ask about the meaning of strings such as "RBGRR" where there is redundant information in the textual description. In later sessions we return to this type of issue when we look at using graphs to describe languages or strings in a password game.

Finally, with the oldest students, we ask them to reason about paths. We ask if there is a path from red to blue and a path from red to green then is there a path from blue to green. This leads to interesting questions concerning whether paths are uni-directional or bi-directional, and whether different circles can have the same colour. To further the discussion, we ask if it would make any difference if the circles were locations (towns, for example) instead of colours. The question of which drawing is correct is then addressed when we talk to them about merging 2 drawings (in order to merge paths). In the merge game, we divide the textual description into two parts and give a single part to each member of a pair. We then ask them to merge their individual drawings into one. Most pairs perform a merge as seen in the right of figure 2. However, when asked "if there is a path from town1 to town2 and a path from town2 to town3 then must there be a path from town1 to town3?", students often spend some time rethinking the merging puzzle. They start to see that merging as in the drawing on the left of figure 2 may be more useful when thinking about paths.

To complete this first session we ask the oldest students to reason about the drawings by considering only the textual representation. For example, we introduce the concept of a circuit (where lines are uni-directional) and ask them to read the textual description of a drawing (following their own syntax) and decide whether there is a circuit or not. With the visual representation the students spot circuits immediately but find it very difficult to explain how they do it. With the textual representation there is a real struggle to check for a circuit (initially) but when they explain how they do it (or try to do it) we see the start of an algorithmic reasoning, and abstract modelling.

3.2 A simple session: algorithmic concepts

Not all of the schools participated in this follow-up session: the 2 largest classes did not continue (but feedback from the teachers led us to believe that the size of the class had no influence on their decision to stop).

It has been run eight times in three different schools (in Ireland and France) and with four different age groups — the youngest group aged 5-6, the oldest group aged 14-15. The class sizes varied from 12 to 28 children. The subgraph problem was our first attempt to observe algorithmic reasoning.

To start, we explain the concept and terminology of graphs and subgraphs through the operation of erasing lines and circles in drawings (or removing balls and strings in the physical constructions). We then provide 2 drawings and ask whether one can be made simply through erasing or removing elements of the other.

It is interesting to note that nearly all students count the circles (balls) because they intuitively know that the subgraph cannot have more balls than its supergraph. However, very few count the number of lines (pieces of string).

In figure 3, we show a typical subgraph problem that students of all ages are able to reason about: are any 2 of the 3 graphs related by the subclassing relation?

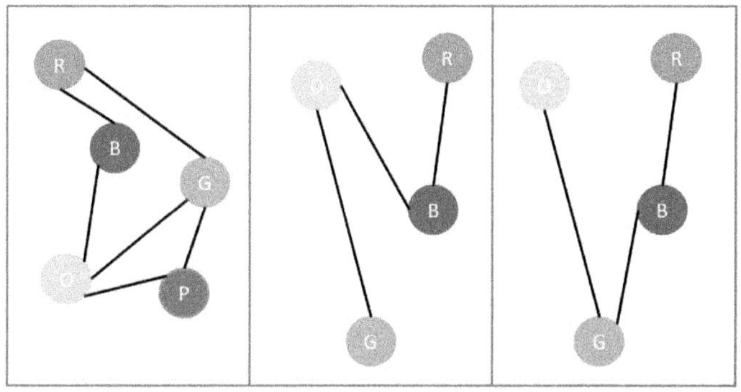

Figure 3: Typical Subgraph Problem

We then give them the same problem, but with all the balls being the same colour. This is quite challenging for the younger children, but the older children enjoy the puzzle for graphs of large numbers of circles (balls). What is interesting — for us — is to see how the older students rise to the challenge of checking for a subgraph when they have only the textual representations to play with and manipulate.

3.3 An intermediate session: shortest paths

This session has been run five times in two different schools (in Ireland and France) and with two different age groups — the youngest group aged 8, the oldest group aged 14-15. The class sizes varied from 20 to 28 children. We note that students younger than 8 were not asked to participat: speaking to the teachers we realized that the younger children did not have enough understanding of length (or size) to be able to reason about shortest paths.

To begin, we introduce the notion of different types of line. First we start with colours (and coloured string). Then we cut the coloured string into fixed constant integer lengths (in cms). The younger students can then measure paths in a relative fashion by joining up strings and comparing their lengths. The older children quickly tire with measuring strings and ask if they can just write the numbers beside the coloured lines. As a final step, they forget about colouring the lines and just write the numbers. At this point we introduce the puzzle of finding shortest paths in graphs.

We start with a very small example, and build it up in a number of steps, as illustrated in figure 4.

With the more advanced students, we allow them to collectively construct their own graphs — on the black/white board at the front of the class — to see who can find the shortest path between a start and end colour, in a limited amount of time. The students often wish to make things as complicated as possible so they add lines with enormous values (usually integers with 10+ digits), they also "sneakily" add lines with zero values, and in some instances negative values. A typical student constructed shortest path problem will look like the graph in figure 5.

After playing with a number of such puzzles, the students are invited to make comments, ask questions, propose answers to questions and to try out new instances of the problem to demonstrate the issues at hand. Interestingly, different classes often address the same issues:

Does it matter if you flip the start and end points?

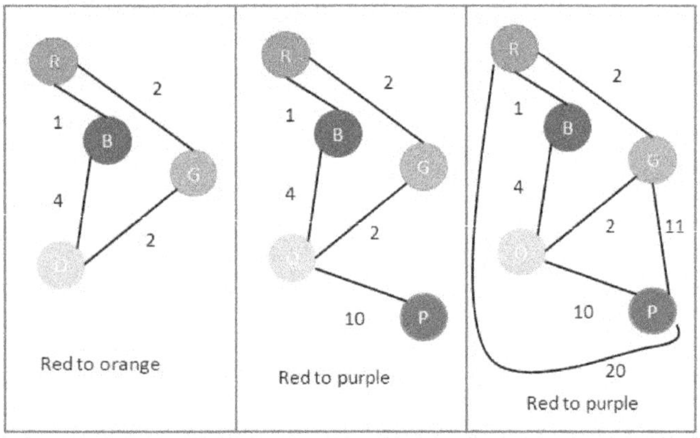

Figure 4: Shortest Path Problems — Increasing in difficulty

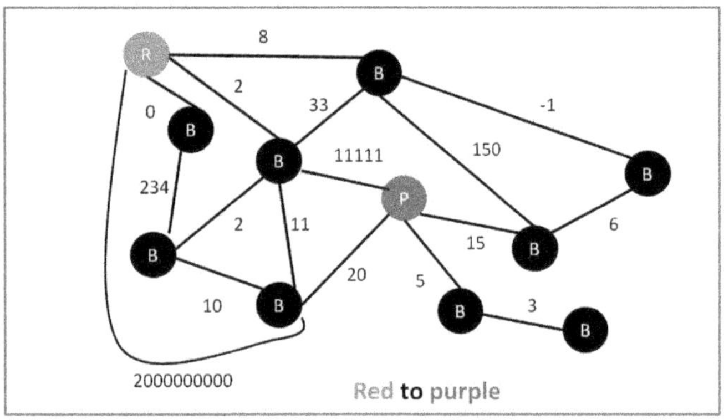

Figure 5: A typical student-generated shortest path problem

> *Can you ignore parts of the graph (as in links with values 5 and 3 in figure 5)?*
> *What happens if a negative value is in a loop?*
> *Is it always best to take the path with the least value from your current position in the graph?*
> *Is it always best to avoid the path with the biggest value from your current position in the graph?*
> *Is the shortest path (in terms of the sum of the values) always the shortest in terms of the number of connections?*
> *Is it more difficult to find the longest or the shortest path?*

The role of the teacher is not to answer such questions but to encourage the students to think about them amongst themselves. It is surprising how many times they find the right answer through collective discussion and creation of counter-examples.

3.4 Formal reasoning

Once the students have developed a thirst for reasoning about problems like the shortest path, we attempt to get them to reason using what they know about integer mathematics, together with their intuitive understanding of properties of graphs.

A good step for this is to introduce a problem, often as a story that involves a puzzle. For example, with the shortest path, we can phrase the problem in terms of a magician who wishes to get to a certain town and the links are distances to travel between towns. In some cases, towns are not directly connected because of physical or magical barriers.

We state that the magician already knows the shortest path between any two towns, through the large number of trips that he has made in the last few years. However, he has now been given a magic transporter wand which he can use once only for every trip in order to travel along an existing road without incurring any cost (distance or time). The question is, how does he know where he should use the wand when making the trip.

Most children, without hesitation, choose to use the wand on the connection with the highest value (on the known shortest path). We ask them to explain why. It is usually only through trying to "prove" that they are right, that they see that they are wrong. At this point the next most common suggestion is to just use the wand on the connection with the largest value (anywhere in the graph). Again, it does not take them long to see that this reasoning is also wrong. After multiple similar attempts, we explain to them that this is not a simple problem and that finding the solution is a good example of computer science in action. At this point we introduce the notion of an algorithm and proving that an algorithm is correct.

4. IMPORTANT OBSERVATIONS

Our experience shows that these sessions work only if there is an enthusiastic teacher involved. It is not critical that the teacher has each session explained to them beforehand — they can participate and interact with the children, learning with them rather than teaching them. However, it is also sometimes useful that the teacher is prepared for a particular session in advance — in order to better observe the childen learning instead of being wrapped up in the learning process themselves. When possible, it is best to have 2 teachers involved — an observer and a participant. These teachers can swap roles in order to get a better understanding of the learning process and the computer science.

Children who lacked confidence in fundamental skills such as literacy and numeracy often gained confidence from playing with the graphs and the graph problems. They were delighted to see that sometimes there was not just a right answer and a wrong answer — and that every answer (even their own) had good points, as well as bad. As a result, many of these classes have had an indirect positive impact on students' peformance throughout their schooling; and even though some of the teachers involved were sceptical at first, their feedback became more positive as the sessions progressed.

It is possible to base a whole semester of work around these graph sessions (for students ranging from 5 to 17 years old). The key is for each session to naturally progress into the next, and at the same time for the teacher be ready to add ever more difficut challenges to any particular session.

For the older students, we saw that they quite naturally started to work on algorithmic solutions to some problems by looking at the textual descriptions (using their own abstract syntax). The better students even asked about choosing the best syntax to help solve the problems. Thus, they discovered the link between data structures and algorithms.

5. CONCLUSIONS AND FUTURE WORK

This research is purely observational and we have not collected hard data in order to test any hypotheses that we may have about this teaching approach. An empirical study across many different classes could lead to interesting results. However, this paper is more about convincing teachers and CS educators to try out this type of educational process in schools near to them.

A long term research goal is a curriculum for teaching computer science to children as soon as they go to school — that is primary school, not secondary school. Children aged from 5-11 have so much potential for learning about algorithms and computation that it would be a shame to wait until they are teenagers before we teach them the foundations. We believe that our work shows that you can start teaching computer science before students even know how to read and write.

We have risen to the challenge of Bruner — as stated in the introduction to this paper — and we have shown, through our teaching of graph algorithms, that this small, but important, part of computer science can be taught effectively to most children of school age. The challenge is to extend this to cover as much of our discipline as possible.

6. REFERENCES

[1] D. Ball, U. S. O. of Educational Research, and Improvement. *Research on teaching mathematics: Making subject matter knowledge part of the equation.* National Center for Research on Teacher Education, Michigan State University, 1988.

[2] T. Bell. A low-cost high-impact computer science show for family audiences. *23rd Australasian Computer Science Conference*, 00:10–16, 2000.

[3] G. M. Bianco and S. Tinazzi. One step further the ACM K-12 final report: a proposal for level 1: computer organization for K-8. In *ITICSE '06: Proceedings of the 11th annual SIGCSE conference on Innovation and technology in computer science education*, pages 207–211, New York, NY, USA, 2006. ACM.

[4] J. Bruner. *The process of education.* Harvard University Press, 1960.

[5] M. D. Byrne, R. Catrambone, and J. T. Stasko. Evaluating animations as student aids in learning computer algorithms. *Comput. Educ.*, 33:253–278, December 1999.

[6] S. da Rosa. Designing algorithms in high school mathematics. In C. N. Dean and R. T. Boute, editors, *TFM*, volume 3294 of *Lecture Notes in Computer Science*, pages 17–31. Springer, 2004.

[7] W. Feurzeig, S. Papert, M. Bloom, R. Grant, and C. Solomon. Programming-languages as a conceptual framework for teaching mathematics. *SIGCUE Outlook*, 4:13–17, April 1970.

[8] G. Futschek. Algorithmic thinking: The key for understanding computer science. In R. Mittermeir, editor, *ISSEP*, volume 4226 of *Lecture Notes in Computer Science*, pages 159–168. Springer, 2006.

[9] J. Gal-Ezer, C. Beeri, D. Harel, and A. Yehudai. A high school program in computer science. *IEEE Computer*, 28(10):73–80, 1995.

[10] J. P. Gibson. A noughts and crosses Java applet to teach programming to primary school children. In J. F. Power and J. Waldron, editors, *Proceedings of the 2nd International Symposium on Principles and Practice of Programming in Java (PPPJ 2003)*, volume 42 of *ACM International Conference Proceeding Series*, pages 85–88, Kilkenny City, Ireland, 2003. ACM.

[11] J. P. Gibson. Formal methods — never too young to start. In Z. Istenes, editor, *Formal Methods in Computer Science Education (FORMED 2008)*, pages 151–160, Budapest, Hungary, Mar. 2008.

[12] J. P. Gibson and J. O'Kelly. Software engineering as a model of understanding for learning and problem solving. In *ICER '05: Proceedings of the 2005 international workshop on Computing education research*, pages 87–97, New York, NY, USA, 2005. ACM.

[13] M. Guzdial. Learning how to prepare computer science high school teachers. *Computer*, 44:95–97, 2011.

[14] O. Hazzan, J. Gal-Ezer, and L. Blum. A model for high school computer science education: the four key elements that make it! In *Proceedings of the 39th SIGCSE technical symposium on Computer science education*, SIGCSE '08, pages 281–285, New York, NY, USA, 2008. ACM.

[15] O. Hazzan and I. Hadar. Reducing abstraction when learning graph theory. *Journal of Computers in Mathematics and Science Teaching*, 24(3):255, 2005.

[16] J. M. D. Hill, C. K. Ray, J. R. S. Blair, and C. A. Carver, Jr. Puzzles and games: addressing different learning styles in teaching operating systems concepts. *SIGCSE Bull.*, 35:182–186, January 2003.

[17] C. Kelleher, R. Pausch, and S. Kiesler. Storytelling alice motivates middle school girls to learn computer programming. In *Proceedings of the SIGCHI conference on Human factors in computing systems*, CHI '07, pages 1455–1464, New York, NY, USA, 2007. ACM.

[18] J. Kramer. Is abstraction the key to computing? *Commun. ACM*, 50(4):36–42, 2007.

[19] A. Levitin and M.-A. Papalaskari. Using puzzles in teaching algorithms. *SIGCSE Bull.*, 34:292–296, February 2002.

[20] P. Martin-Löf. Constructive mathematics and computer programming. *Logic, Methodology and Philosophy of Science VI*, pages 153–175, 1982.

[21] B. Parhami. Puzzling problems in computer engineering. *Computer*, 42(3):26–29, 2009.

[22] S. Pollard and R. C. Duvall. Everything I needed to know about teaching I learned in kindergarten: bringing elementary education techniques to undergraduate computer science classes. *SIGCSE Bull.*, 38:224–228, March 2006.

[23] J. Wing. Computational thinking and thinking about computing. *Philosophical Transactions of the Royal Society A: Mathematical, Physical and Engineering Sciences*, 366(1881):3717–3725, 2008.

Forming Project Groups while Learning about Matching and Network Flows in Algorithms

Dinesh Mehta
Colorado School of Mines
dmehta@mines.edu

Tina Kouri
Colorado School of Mines
tkouri@mines.edu

Irene Polycarpou
Colorado School of Mines
ipolycar@mines.edu

ABSTRACT

The matching problem in bipartite graphs is the basis for many applications that have become especially prominent with the advent of online markets that connect two entities (e.g., job-seekers and employers). Its algorithmic basis is the max-flow problem in networks, a topic that is often covered in introductory algorithms texts and courses.

Separately, the Computer Science education literature is abundant with examples which indicate that the quality of the experience in the implementation of programming tasks is enhanced when done in groups.

In this paper, we describe the application of a network-flow-based matching algorithm in bipartite graphs to form project groups in the algorithms course at the Colorado School of Mines (CSM). This activity simultaneously provides students with an immersive experience in a bipartite matching application. We present a small exploratory study on the effectiveness of the activity.

Categories and Subject Descriptors

K.3.2 [**Computers and Education**]: Computer and Information Science Education—*Computer science education, curriculum*

General Terms

Algorithms

Keywords

algorithms, matching, group learning, group formation, bipartite graphs

1. INTRODUCTION

Network Flows and Matching

Network flows and the related problem of matching and assignment in graphs lie at the intersection of the Computer Science Algorithms and Operations Research/Mathematical Programming/Optimization disciplines. Although this topic area is not explicitly mentioned under the list of Algorithms topics in the joint ACM and IEEE Computer Society "Computer Science Curriculum 2008: An Interim Revision of CS 2001" report [3], there are several popular Algorithms texts that include sections or chapters on network flows such as [5, Chapter 26] and [13, Chapter 7].

Matching and assignment problems have numerous applications. Perhaps one of the higher-impact applications is the National Resident Matching Program (NRMP), which matches residency applicants' preferences with program directors' preferences. The algorithmic basis for this is the "stable marriage" problem [9]. The underlying algorithms are beyond the scope of an introductory undergraduate-level algorithms class. However, its cousin, the simpler problem of bipartite matching is well within the scope of a first undergraduate course in algorithms.

The advent of the internet and its role as a marketplace with interactions between buyers and sellers has revived the importance of matching problems. Easley and Kleinberg have recently authored an excellent book that describes this emerging interdisciplinary "science of networks" [8] In particular, they discuss the concept of Matching Markets [8, Chapter 10], where "interaction among buyers and sellers" can be modeled by "implicit network encodings."

Collaborative Learning

The use of cooperative and collaborative learning instructional methods date back to the first century [10]. Within Computer Science, collaborative learning has been seen as a technique that ameliorates some of the difficulties and frustrations associated with learning programming. The National Center for Women and Information Technology (NCWIT) has identified collaborative learning as a key practice for retaining undergraduate CS students [1]. In fact, Joseph et al. show that the more a student participates in out-of-class collaborative activity, the higher the student's academic achievement [11]. In addition to programming courses, team projects are also used in software engineering, HCI, database, and multimedia courses [2]. We are not aware of literature that describes the use of team projects in an algorithms course. In the context of the algorithms course at our University, collaborative learning allows instructors to assign larger and more comprehensive projects, which enables students to develop a broader perspective on practical problems. In addition, it provides students with valuable experience working in groups. Most employment opportunities

ITiCSE'12, July 3–5, 2012, Haifa, Israel.

after graduating with an undergraduate degree in Computer Science have a significant team-work component [17].

Group Formation

In our earlier offerings of the course (in the early 2000s), groups were formed by allowing students to self-organize. Our (anecdotal) experience was that students would self-organize into groups of friends. The workload was not distributed evenly and the group would rely on one member to do much of the work, but they would report that the effort had in fact been evenly distributed among the members. Our goal was to create groups that did not merely consist of friends, but instead operated more professionally and responsibly. This point of view is supported by studies such as [6]. On the other hand, we did not want to impose groups on the students because this might result in students who did not know or get along with each other being placed in the same group. Since the group-work primarily occurred outside of class, we would not be aware of any problems and therefore not be able to intervene in a timely fashion. This is also supported by other studies that show that the level of interaction in a group is greater if there is some existing friendliness among group members [15]. The ideas described next are a result of wanting an approach that served as a middle-ground between the two extremes of allowing students complete control versus giving the instructor complete control. We are not aware of strategies that seek to do this in the group formation literature.

Automated group-formation has been studied in the Computer Supported Collaborative Learning (CSCL) community. In this context, a variety of factors such as gender, personality, and level of experience with the content have been proposed as being useful in synthesizing optimal groups. There are also similar studies in the context of pair programming [12]. The literature describes several techniques that seek to obtain optimal groups including fuzzy C-Means ([4]), particle swarm optimization ([14]), genetic algorithms ([18]), etc. All of these first require the instructor to collect the required information. This adds a layer of overhead that may not be practical in some situations.

Our Approach

In this paper, we describe an innovative activity that simultaneously meets both needs, namely (a) Exposes students to a simple matching application through an immersive experience. (b) Forms project groups through a process that distributes control between the instructor and the students. We are also presenting a small exploratory study on students' experience with group activity and their ability to work with matching problems. The study was conducted in Spring 2011 and Fall 2011 semesters. The results of the study suggest that students benefited from the group activity and that the immersive experience involving matching markets consolidated their ability to apply network flows to matching problems.

2. GROUP FORMING ALGORITHM

2.1 Our Algorithms Course

"Algorithms" is a required course in our eight-semester undergraduate curriculum. Students are expected, but not required, to take it in semester six. Prerequisites for it are our "Data Structures" (CS2) and Discrete Mathematics courses. Graduate students who have not previously taken this course are also required to take it for graduate credit. Topics covered in the course include asymptotic analysis, data structures, sorting, unweighted and weighted graphs, dynamic programming, and NP-completeness. (Some of the material in asymptotic analysis, data structures and sorting is a review of concepts learned earlier in CS2, but a significant portion is devoted to advanced topics in these areas.) We have adopted a mixed model for teaching the course consisting of (i) traditional homework assignments and exams and (ii) four significant projects (contributing to 40% of the total grade), each of which includes a conceptual and an implementation component. While the specific content of the projects varies from one semester to the next, the theme remains the same. In general, Project 1 is to implement and evaluate exhaustive and heuristic algorithms for an NP-hard optimization problem, Project 2 is related to dynamic programming, Project 3 is based on using LEDA to solve a graph maze problem and Project 4 to develop a heuristic for an NP-hard optimization problem.

2.2 Group Projects

Projects 1 and 3 are individual projects, while Projects 2 and 4 are group projects, with three students per group. Our rationale for using groups of three rather than pairs is as follows: Groups are formed in Week 4 or 5 of a 15-week semester in time for Project 2. Project 4 is typically assigned in Week 11 or 12. By this point, students have received their evaluations for mid-semester examinations and quizzes. This causes a small number to drop the course, which in turn reduces group sizes. If we had started with pairs, some students would be left without partners, making the final project overwhelming. At this stage, we want to avoid merging or changing groups in other ways because members of newly formed groups will have to undergo the overhead of familiarizing themselves with each other.

To ensure that students are motivated to contribute substantially to their group projects, the grading rubric consists of two components to evaluate group projects. The first is a score assigned by the instructor that is based on the quality of the work. The second is based on effort pecentages based on each member's contribution. The group is expected to arrive at a consensus on this quantity and provide it to the instructor. If the group does not arrive at a consensus, the instrutor allocates effort percentages based on an interview with the students. We also caution the students that we may modify the effort percentages if we do not think they represent an accurate distribution of effort based on our observations and the end-of-semester interview. This approach is similar to the "bonus money" idea in [16]. An alternative approach to assigning grades in a programming project is to assign an individual student credit if his/her module works [7]. This is not feasible in algorithms because a significant portion of the activity is conceptual.

2.3 Network Flows

Network flows are discussed toward the end of the material on graph algorithms in approximately Week 12 or 13 of a 15-week semester. It follows algorithms for graph traversal, minimum spanning tree, and shortest paths. The presentation focuses on defining the problem and describing Ford-Fulkerson and the Edmonds-Karp algorithms, including the min-cut max-flow theorem. This is followed by an introduction to Bipartite Matching using an example and by a description of its solution through the reduction to Network Flows. (Note that groups were formed in Weeks 4 or 5, approximately 8 weeks earlier, so students have typically forgotten about the group-formation algorithm at this stage.) This is then followed by the pre-test worksheet, a discussion of the group example, and the post-test worksheet, all in one class. Any homework assignments on network flows focus on students' understanding of the mechanics of the algorithms rather than on modeling problems by networks. The final exam takes place approximately three weeks after the pre/post-test worksheets are administered.

2.4 Our Group Formation Algorithm

Student groups in the algorithms course are selected using our group formation algorithm, based on network flows, which is discussed below. For simplicity, we assume that the number of students n in the class is an exact multiple of three. [1]

Algorithm

1. The instructor selects $n/3$ students and designates them to be "hiring managers." Note that instead of selecting the hiring managers randomly, we can use alternative strategies such as ranking students based on their GPAs and their performance in the Discrete Mathematics prerequisite and then picking the middle third to be hiring managers.
2. Each hiring manager must select and request *four* students from the remaining $2n/3$ students (the candidate pool) to be potential group members.
3. When a student from the candidate pool receives such a request, s/he is required to accept the request unless s/he has already received and accepted *two* requests.
4. Each hiring manager turns in a list of four names to the instructor.
5. The instructor takes all of the lists and runs a "mystery algorithm" such that each hiring manager is assigned two students chosen from the list of four students that s/he provided and such that no two hiring managers are assigned the same student.
6. This results in $n/3$ groups of three students each.

Note: before we start forming the groups, we explain the "rules" a few days in advance so that students have time to reflect on the process. We then announce the list of hiring managers and ask them to submit their four names within a week. Some turn in partial lists because they don't know which students are still available. We then facilitate the process by listing candidates who haven't yet received two requests. Figure 1 illustrates this with an example. We first show that the algorithm is internally consistent.

THEOREM 1. *On completion of Step 4, exactly four candidates are linked to each hiring manager and each candidate is linked to exactly two hiring managers.*

[1] If n is not a multiple of three, groups can be fixed "by hand." Since $n \mod 3$ is at most 2, this results in at most two groups with 4 members.

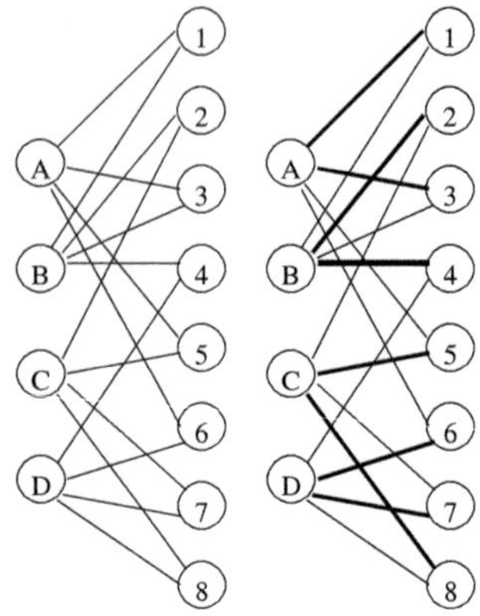

Figure 1: The figure on the left shows the situation after Step 4 of the algorithm. The vertices on the left (A,B,C,D) denote hiring managers, while those on the right denote candidates (vertices 1 ... 8). Each hiring manager vertex has edges to its four candidates. Similarly, each candidate has edges from the two hiring managers that sent it a request. The figure on the right depicts the situation after Step 5. Thick edges denote the matching: each hiring manager has exactly two thick edges to its candidates and each candidate has exactly one thick edge from a hiring manager. In this example, the four groups that result are (A,1,3), (B,2,4), (C,5,8), and (D,6,7).

PROOF. Each hiring manager selects four candidates for a total of $\frac{n}{3} \times 4 = \frac{4n}{3}$ candidates. There are $\frac{2n}{3}$ distinct candidates. The average number of candidates per hiring manager is $\frac{4n}{3} / \frac{2n}{3} = 2$. Since no candidate may accept more than two requests, all candidates must accept *exactly* two requests. □

Note that there is no guarantee that the four candidates selected by a hiring manager are distinct.

EXAMPLE 1. *Consider a class with $n = 9$ students with hiring managers A, B, and C and candidates D through I. Suppose A and B both approach D, E, F, and G. Each of these four candidates has now been spoken for twice. Candidates H and I have not received any requests, while hiring manager C has not issued any requests. To satisfy the algorithm's criteria, C will have to issue two requests to both H and I.*

It is possible to guarantee that each hiring manager is assigned four distinct candidates; however, this would require additional rounds between the instructor and the students and is not practical in our classroom setting. In practice, the situation described in Example 1 occurs very rarely and does not impact the instructor's ability to execute Step 5 of the group formation process. We can turn this into a learning experience by telling them there is a flaw and asking them to find it.

The following theorems explore how successful the approach is at separating friends.

THEOREM 2. *Suppose two students A and B are friends such that the entire student population is conspiring to place them in the same group. The probability that they end up* *in the same group assuming (i) n is large (ii) each hiring manager issues requests to distinct candidates and (iii) all instructor selections are made randomly is $\frac{4}{9}$.*

PROOF. *Case 1: A and B are both selected to be hiring managers.* In this case, A and B are guaranteed to be in different groups. This case occurs with probability $\frac{1}{3} \times \frac{n/3-1}{n-1}$. Since n is large, we ignore the "minus 1" in both the numerator and denominator of the second term to get $\frac{1}{3} \times \frac{1}{3} = \frac{1}{9}$. *Case 2: A is a hiring manager, but B is not.* This case occurs with probability $\frac{1}{3} \times \frac{2}{3} = \frac{2}{9}$. Since A and B are determined to be in the same group, we assume that A picks B as one of four potential group members. Assuming the instructor randomly picks two out of the four candidates for A's group, A and B end up on the same group with probability $\frac{1}{2}$. *Case 3: B is a hiring manager, but A is not.* This case is symmetric to Case 2 and yields the same analysis. *Case 4: Neither A nor B are selected to be hiring managers.* This case occurs with probability $\frac{2}{3} \times \frac{2}{3} = \frac{4}{9}$. Let's assume that two hiring managers C and D select both A and B among their four candidates as this maximizes the probability that A and B will be in the same group. The probability that C gets A (or B) is $\frac{1}{2}$. Similarly, the probability that D gets A (or B) is also $\frac{1}{2}$. The probability that A and B end up in the same group is $\frac{1}{2} \times \frac{1}{2} + \frac{1}{2} \times \frac{1}{2} = \frac{1}{2}$. Combining the four cases, we get an overall probability that A and B are in the same group of $\frac{1}{9} \times 0 + \frac{2}{9} \times \frac{1}{2} + \frac{2}{9} \times \frac{1}{2} + \frac{4}{9} \times \frac{1}{2} = \frac{4}{9}$. □

THEOREM 3. *Suppose three students A, B and C are friends such that the entire student population is conspiring to place them in the same group. The probability that they end up in the same group assuming (i) n is large (ii) each hiring manager issues requests to distinct candidates and (iii) all instructor selections are made randomly is $\frac{1}{9}$.*

PROOF. Similar to the proof for Theorem 2. □

If we allow hiring managers to select the same candidate multiple times as in Example 1, the probabilities for Theorems 2 and 3 become $\frac{8}{9}$ and $\frac{4}{9}$ respectively.

Once again, these represent the results under the unlikely assumption that all of the n students (not just A, B and C) are conspiring to achieve a desired outcome. Note also that it is not our intention to make it impossible to allow friends to work together. We just want to make it less likely than when students are allowed to self-organize.

2.5 Algorithm for Step 5

In what follows, we describe how Step 5 of the group-forming process presented in Section 2.4 can be solved by reducing the problem to the maximum flow problem in networks:

1. Add source vertex s and sink vertex t.
2. Add edges from s to the hiring manager vertices and from the candidate vertices to t.
3. Direct the edges from left to right.
4. Edges from s to the hiring managers are given capacities of 2. All other edges have capacity 1.
5. Run the max-flow algorithm from s to t.

Figure 2 shows the graph of Figure 1 augmented to form a network.

THEOREM 4. *The algorithm for Step 5 finds a valid assignment ($n/3$ groups of 3 members each).*

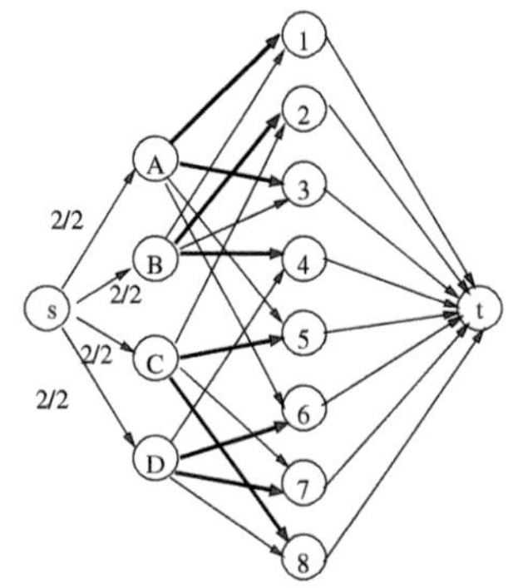

Figure 2: Bipartite graph of Figure 1 augmented to form a network. Only edges from s to hiring managers have been labeled to simplify the figure. (An edge label of the form a/b denotes that the edge's capacity is b and the flow on it is a.) All of the remaining edges have capacity 1. The thick edges from hiring managers to candidates would have label 1/1, while the thin edges have label 0/1. Edges from candidates to t all have label 1/1.

PROOF. Consider any cut (S, T) with $s \in S$ and $t \in T$ in the flow network constructed in Step 5. Let n_a be the number of hiring manager vertices and n_b the number of candidate vertices in S. Then, the total capacity of outedges from source s to vertices in T is $2(n/3 - n_a)$. The total capacity of outedges from the n_b candidate pool vertices to t is n_b. Finally, the maximum total capacity of outedges from hiring manager vertices to vertices in T is $\max(4n_a - 2n_b, 0)$. There are 4 edges that leave each of the n_a hiring manager vertices. Of these, the total number that can be absorbed within S is $2n_b$ leaving the difference which represents the total capacity into T. Adding these three quantities gives the total capacity of the cut.

Case 1: if $4n_a \leq 2n_b$, we get $2n/3 - 2n_a + n_b + 0 \geq 2n/3$.
Case 2: if $4n_a > 2n_b$, we get $2n/3 - 2n_a + n_b + 4n_a - 2n_b = 2n/3 + 2n_a - n_b > 2n/3$.

The capacity of any cut is therefore $\geq 2n/3$. Therefore, the maximum flow in the network is guaranteed to be $\geq 2n/3$. Exactly two out-edges from each of the $n/3$ hiring manager vertices must have flow 1. Exactly one of the in-edges to each of the $2n/3$ candidate vertices must have flow 1, guaranteeing a valid assignment. □

3. RESULTS

We conducted an exploratory study during Spring 2011 and Fall 2011. Participants were 55 undergraduate students taking an introductory algorithms class (25 in Spring 2011 and 30 in Fall 2011). The goals were to ascertain (1) the effectiveness of the group-formation algorithm in forming good groups and (2) whether the immersive experience in matching markets aided students' understanding of network flow applications. The study was designed as follows: (1) Students self-reported background data including name, age, gender, ethnicity, GPA, and their declared major. Students were permitted to not participate in the study and not report any or all of the requested data. Unique IDs were associated with student names. (2) A pre-test and post-test worksheet were administered to assess changes in students' knowledge and confidence of bipartite matching and network flow. The pre-test worksheet was administered after bipartite matching was discussed in class. The post-test worksheet was administered after discussing the group-formation algorithm for Step 5. (This was the only activity between the pre-test and post-test.) The instructor assigned scores to the worksheets for comparison purposes. (3) A group experience questionnaire was given to the students to obtain student information such as attitude about group-work. The instructor was only given access to this information after the co-investigators replaced student names with unique IDs. In addition to quantitative ratings, students were asked to provide comments.

The problem used in the pre- and post-test worksheets was adapted from Problem 16 in the Network Flow chapter in [13]. It asks how to show ads on a website to users belonging to certain demographics. Its solution involves setting up a non-trivial flow network.

Table 1: Response to: On a scale of 1 (not effective) to 5 (very effective), how effective do you think your group was?

Scale	1	2	3	4	5
# Students	0	1	8	20	23

Table 2: Response to: On a scale of 1 (not satisfied) to 5 (very satisfied), how satisfied were you with your group?

Scale	1	2	3	4	5
# Students	1	1	4	15	31

Table 3: Response to: For each statement in the table below, check the column that applies to you for your assigned group (52 students).

Question	Very Much	Somewhat	Not at all
Working in a group promoted creativity	29 (55.77%)	21 (40.38%)	2 (3.85%)
Working with the group motivated me	35 (67.31%)	16 (30.77%)	1 (1.92%)
I felt comfortable contributing within my group	48 (92.31%)	4 (7.69%)	0
The group was conflict-free	40 (76.92%)	10 (19.23%)	2 (3.85%)
I had fun working with the group	41 (78.85%)	10 (19.23%)	1 (1.92%)
I learned a great deal from the people in my group	34 (65.38%)	16 (30.77%)	3 (5.77%)
My group work and interaction made me feel confident	32 (61.54%)	18 (34.62%)	2 (3.85%)

Tables 1, 2 and 3 report the results of the group experience questionnaire. (52 students responded to the questionnaires.) Almost all students rated the effectiveness of their group at 3 or above (51 students) as well as their satisfaction with their group (50 students). One student felt that his/her group was not effective, thus was not satisfied with his group, and one other student reported that s/he was not satisfied with his group. According to their comments, these two students felt that the programming load within the group was unbalanced. Table 3 indicates group work was viewed favorably by the students. Most students responded positively to all questions related to their experience working in groups. Based on their comments, the "not at all" responses can be attributed to communication problems with team members and work load balance. Some positive comments from the students include: "Not as bad as all other groups have been in my life. I liked the team selection system."; "We worked well together, didn't have any problems getting the work. I would definitely work with them again."; "Group projects work well because we all have different backgrounds so we all have different ideas."; "I worked with people that I'm accustomed to working with, so we already had a good system in place and worked well together."; "I enjoyed the group work and thought it was effective for learning."; Some additional comments include "No conflicts but a lot of arguing at times," "there were few conflicts and those were resolved quickly," "I felt slightly intimidated at some times," "It was just hard finding times to meet."

Tables 4, 5 and 6 report on the effectiveness of the group formation example (only 50 students responded to this questionnaire). Table 4 shows a moderate increase of confidence from a mean of 3.17 on the pre-test to 3.93 on the post-test. 30 students rated their confidence at 3 or more in the pre-test. This quantity increased to 36 in the post-test. In

Table 4: Response to: On a scale of 1 (low confidence) to 5 (high confidence), rate your confidence in modeling a bipartite matching problem. (Only 41 students responded to this question on both the pre- and post-tests.)

Scale	1	2	3	4	5
# Students (pre-test)	3	8	12	15	3
# Students (post-test)	2	3	4	19	13

Table 5: Response to: On a scale of 1 (not helpful) to 5 (very helpful), rate how helpful the group formation example was for your understanding of bipartite matching/network flow? (50 students)

Scale	1	2	3	4	5
# Students	3	4	8	26	9

Table 6: Pre-test and post-test Worksheet and Final Exam grades (Fall 2011 data only, 27 students)

Grade	0	1	2	3	4	5	Mean	Median
# Students (pre-test)	1	1	5	8	5	7	3.33	3.00
# Students (post-test)	0	0	0	6	7	14	4.30	5.00
Final Exam Problem	5	0	1	1	2	18	3.81	5.00

Table 5, 43 students rated the group example at 3 or above, while seven rated it at 2 or below. Four of the seven were still unclear how to solve the problem while three students figured it out on the pre-test so the group example was redundant. Table 6 reports students' grades in the pre-test and post-test worksheets along with the grade of a complex network flow modeling question in the final exam. (Note that this was a different question than the one employed in the pre-test and post-test and arguably of comparable, if not greater, difficulty.) We only include data from Fall 2011 because the final exam question was not administered in Spring 2011. The results show a significant improvement in both the mean (from 3.33 to 4.30, approximately 1 grade level) and median (from 3.00 to 5.00) from the pre-test to the post-test. The median stayed at 5.00 for the final with an impressive two-thirds of the class getting a perfect score (in comparison to the pre-test, where one-fourth of the class received a perfect score and the post-test where about half the class received a perfect score). However, the mean dropped to 3.81 primarily because of five students who received 0s. (These students did not model the question as a network flow even though the problem statement explicitly suggested this approach, suggesting they did not read the question carefully.) Note that the pre-test and post-test were conducted on the same day separated only by our discussion of the group formation algorithm, whereas the final exam question was administered approximately three weeks later.

4. CONCLUSIONS

We have presented a group-formation algorithm that distributes control between the instructor and the students and at the same time can be used to help students understand bipartite matching. We have also presented an exploratory study. The results from our study and the overall feedback from participating students are encouraging. They suggest that groups formed using the proposed algorithm were successful, i.e., most students reported that they were very satisfied with their group, they felt that the group work was effective for their learning, and they had a positive experience working with their groups. Moreover, the presentation of the group formation algorithm to the students helped them feel more confident about bipartite matching and student performance improved significantly from pre-test to post-test.

5. ACKNOWLEDGMENTS

T. Kouri and D. Mehta were funded in part by the National Science Foundation under Grant Nos. BPC-DP-0739233 and CNS-0931748. Any opinions, findings, and conclusions or recommendations expressed in this material are those of the authors and do not necessarily reflect those of the NSF. I. Polycarpou was supported by a NCWIT Academic Alliance Seed Fund grant, sponsored by Microsoft Research.

6. REFERENCES

[1] L. Barker and J. M. Cohoon. Key Practices for Retaining Undergraduates in Computing. http://www.ncwit.org, Sept. 2009.

[2] J. Brown and G. Dobbie. Supporting and evaluating team dynamics in group projects. In *The proceedings of the 30th SIGCSE technical symposium on Computer science education*, SIGCSE '99, pages 281–285, 1999.

[3] L. Cassel, A. Clements, G. Davies, M. Guzdial, R. McCauley, A. McGettrick, B. Sloan, L. Snyder, P. Tymann, and B. Weide. Computer Science Curriculum 2008: An Interim Revision of CS 2001. http://www.acm.org/education/curricula.html, 2008.

[4] C. Christodoulopoulos and K. Papanikolaou. A group formation tool in an e-learning context. In *Proc. 19th IEEE International Conference on Tools with Artificial Intelligence*, Oct. 2007.

[5] T. Cormen, C. Leiserson, R. Rivest, and C. Stein. *Introduction to Algorithms.* MIT Press, Cambridge, Massachussetts, third edition, 2009.

[6] K. Deibel. Team formation methods for increasing interaction during in-class group work. In *Proceedings of the 10th annual SIGCSE conference on Innovation and technology in computer science education*, ITiCSE '05, pages 291–295, 2005.

[7] A. Diwan, W. M. Waite, and M. H. Jackson. An infrastructure for teaching skills for group decision making and problem solving in programming projects. In *Proceedings of the 33rd SIGCSE technical symposium on Computer science education*, SIGCSE '02, pages 276–280, 2002.

[8] D. Easley and J. Kleinberg. *Networks, Crowds, and Markets: Reasoning About a Highly Connected World.* Cambridge University Press, 2010.

[9] D. Gusfield and R. Irving. *The Stable Marriage Problem.* The MIT Press, 1989.

[10] D. Johnson, R. Johnson, and K. Smith. *Active Learning: Cooperation in the college classroom.* Interaction Book Company, 1991.

[11] A. Joseph and M. Payne. Group dynamics and collaborative group performance. In *Proceedings of the 34th SIGCSE technical symposium on Computer science education*, SIGCSE '03, pages 368–371, 2003.

[12] N. Katira, L. Williams, E. Wiebe, C. Miller, S. Balik, and E. Gehringer. On understanding compatibility of student pair programmers. In *Proceedings of the 35th SIGCSE technical symposium on Computer science education*, SIGCSE '04, pages 7–11, 2004.

[13] J. Kleinberg and E. Tardos. *Algorithm Design.* Pearson, 2006.

[14] Y.-T. Lin, Y.-M. Huang, and S.-C. Cheng. An automatic group composition system for composing collaborative learning groups using enhanced particle swarm optimization. *Computers & Education*, 55:1483–1493, 2010.

[15] H. Simon. *Models of Man.* John Wiley, 1957.

[16] D. Smarkusky, R. Dempsey, J. Ludka, and F. de Quillettes. Enhancing team knowledge: instruction vs. experience. In *Proceedings of the 36th SIGCSE technical symposium on Computer science education*, SIGCSE '05, pages 460–464, 2005.

[17] W. M. Waite, M. H. Jackson, A. Diwan, and P. M. Leonardi. Student culture vs group work in computer science. In *Proceedings of the 35th SIGCSE technical symposium on Computer science education*, SIGCSE '04, pages 12–16, 2004.

[18] D.-Y. Wang, S. Lin, and C.-T. Sun. Diana: A computer-supported heterogeneous grouping system for teachers to conduct successful small learning groups. *Computers in Human Behavior*, 23:1997–2010, 2007.

Refinement of an Experimental Approach to Computer-Based, Active Learning of Greedy Algorithms

J. Ángel Velázquez-Iturbide
Departamento de Lenguajes y Sistemas Informáticos I
Escuela Técnica Superior de Ingeniería Informática
Universidad Rey Juan Carlos
C/ Tulipán s/n, 28933 Móstoles, Madrid, Spain
angel.velazquez@urjc.es

ABSTRACT

Some years ago we presented a novel approach to the active learning of greedy algorithms. The approach was two-fold: an experimental method and the interactive assistant GreedEx that supports it. In this paper we present a refinement of the different elements of our approach, based on our experience of 5 years using and evaluating it in a course on algorithms. Firstly, usability evaluations were conducted to check the adequacy of GreedEx to its intended aims, so they guided the evolution of GreedEx. Secondly, the analysis of students' reports allowed us to identify unexpected misconceptions, which convinced us of the necessity of several didactic interventions. Our findings suggest that we succeeded both in obtaining an attractive and effective tool and in removing severe students' misconceptions. We consider that the paper is interesting to CS education researchers because of its specific contributions to the teaching of algorithms, and also as an example of a multifaceted, medium-term CS education research.

Categories and Subject Descriptors

K.3.1 [**Computers and Education**]: Computer Uses in Education; K.3.2 [**Computers and Education**]: Computer and Information Science Education – *computer science education.*

General Terms

Algorithms, Experimentation, Human Factors.

Keywords

Computer Science Education, Greedy Algorithms, Active Learning, Visualization, Usability, Misconceptions.

1. INTRODUCTION

Algorithms are a core element of computer science (CS) curricula [1]. Unfortunately, algorithms have received less attention than CS1 with respect to innovative methods for active learning. An outstanding exception is David Ginat's emphasis on the creative design of algorithms [6].

ITiCSE'12, July 3–5, 2012, Haifa, Israel.

Some years ago we presented a novel approach to the active learning of greedy algorithms [13] which was aimed at achieving one key learning goal: "Discover an optimal selection function for a problem". Depending on the problem difficulty, this goal can be placed at the application or synthesis level in Bloom's taxonomy [3]. Our approach was two-fold [13]: an experimental method and the interactive assistant GreedEx that supports it.

Proposing a new didactic method does not guarantee success, so it must be evaluated. In this paper we present a refinement of the different elements of our approach, based on our experience of 5 years using it in a course on algorithms and on the different evaluations conducted. We consider that they are valuable contributions to the teaching of algorithms. Furthermore, we consider that it also is an example of a multifaceted, medium-term CS education research, and provides an example of action research [4].

The main contributions of our work follow. Firstly, usability evaluations guided the evolution of GreedEx. As a consequence, we succeeded in obtaining a balance between comprehensiveness and attractiveness of the tool. Secondly, the analysis of students' reports allowed us to identify unexpected misconceptions. These findings convinced us of the necessity of several didactic interventions, which made severe misconceptions disappear.

The paper is structured as follows. In section 2, we outline the basic elements of our approach, namely the experimental method and the interactive assistant GreedEx. Section 3 presents the usability evaluations conducted over GreedEx, as well as its evolution. Section 4 presents the results of analyzing students' reports of assignments performed using GreedEx, as well as the didactic modifications introduced to address students' misconceptions. Finally, the two last sections contain a short personal recapitulation and our conclusions.

2. BACKGROUND

Typically, a first phase in solving optimization problems consists in designing a multistage process to incrementally construct an optimal solution from candidates. This process takes distinct forms in the different algorithm design techniques. In particular, greedy algorithms [5][9] only take at each step one candidate into consideration. The candidate is chosen by a selection function which therefore is the key design element. Well-known examples of greedy algorithms are Kruskal's and Prim's algorithms for the minimum-cost spanning tree problem, and Dijkstra's algorithm for the single-source shortest paths problem.

Our original approach consisted of an experimental method to discover optimal selection functions and an interactive assistant that supported it [13]. We outline both elements in this section.

2.1 Experimental Method

The core of our active-learning proposal consists in asking the student to find out the selection functions that may characterize optimal greedy algorithms for a given optimization problem.

A selection function is defined on the set of available candidates, returning at each step the most promising candidate according to some measure. If we want to make explicit the design process, we may first identify a list of possible selection functions and then experiment with them for optimality. In general, the set of possible selection functions is not very large, as they are restricted to the values of some parameters or to values derived from them, sorted in increasing or decreasing order.

For instance, consider the activity selection problem [5]. Given a set of n activities, each one with a start time s_i and a finish time f_i, we seek selecting a maximum-size subset of non-overlapping activities. For instance, given the set of activities in Table 1, the subset composed of activities {2,0,5} is a valid solution, while subset {2,0,1,4,3} is a maximum-size solution.

Table 1. An instance of the activity selection problem

i	0	1	2	3	4	5	6	7	8	9
s_i	6	13	2	23	14	13	14	0	20	23
f_i	9	14	4	29	23	24	28	29	25	29

We may think of the following selection functions:

1. Increasing order of start time (denoted S↑).
2. Decreasing order of start time (S↓).
3. Increasing order of finish time (F↑).
4. Decreasing order of finish time (F↓).
5. Increasing order of duration (D↑).
6. Decreasing order of duration (D↓).

Given a set of possible selection functions, experimentation allows filtering non-optimal ones: we just need to find a counter-example to a selection function to discard it. After this discarding process, the remaining selection functions are plausible candidates, but they must still be proved for optimality.

If we solve the example given above with the former six selection functions, we obtain the results of Table 2.

Table 2. Results of applying different selection functions to the activity selection problem

Selection function	Selected activities	#activities
S↑	{7}	1
S↓	{3,4,1,0,2}	5
F↑	{2,0,1,4,9}	5
F↓	{3,4,1,0,2}	5
D↑	{1,2,0,9,4}	5
D↓	{7}	1

As a consequence of this execution, the two selections functions that yielded fewer activities (i.e. S↑ and D↓) can be discarded. If we now use new input data, the four remaining selection functions can be reduced to three (see Table 3, 2nd run). Further experimentation with additional input data also produces optimal values for three selection functions (see Table 3, 3rd and 4th runs).

Consequently, we conclude that there is empirical evidence about the plausibility of S↓, F↑ and D↑ as optimal selection functions.

We could go on experimenting with new input data, or stop and try to formally prove the optimality of the three selection functions. Notice, however, that the function D↑ is not optimal.

Table 3. Results of applying different selection functions over several input data to the activity selection problem

Selection function	1st run	2nd run	3rd run	4th run
S↑	1	–	–	–
S↓	5	3	3	3
F↑	5	3	3	3
F↓	5	1	–	–
D↑	5	3	3	3
D↓	1	–	–	–

More detailed recommendations about how to use the experimental method as an introduction to greedy algorithms and to other algorithm design techniques can be found elsewhere [12].

2.2 The Interactive Assistant GreedEx

The experimental method described above is supported by an interactive assistant, called GreedEx. Given the big differences among different greedy algorithms, GreedEx only supports a fixed (but extensible) set of problems, some of them not optimally solvable with greedy algorithms, in order to leave experimentation open. Currently, GreedEx supports 6 optimization problems:

1. The activity selection problem [5].
2. Knapsack problems: the fractional and the 0/1 knapsack problems [5][9], as well as three variations with different maximization measures: the number of objects introduced into the knapsack, the weight of these objects, and the number of objects provided two knapsacks are available.

We had several design goals for GreedEx:

1. It must aid in achieving the following levels of Bloom's taxonomy for every greedy algorithm:
   - Comprehension level. The student must understand the problem and the greedy algorithm that solves it.
   - Analysis level. The student must be able to analyze the effect of applying a greedy algorithm to the same input data with different selection functions.
   - Evaluation level. The student must be able to evaluate the outcome of different selection functions and select the optimal ones.
2. It must support related, mundane educational tasks.
3. It must be easy to learn and use.
4. It must be visually appealing in order to promote motivation.

Fig. 1 shows the user interface of GreedEx in a session with the activity selection problem.

Three areas can be clearly distinguished, apart from the window title, the main menu and the icon bar. The top area is the visualization panel, which graphically displays data. The lower left area is the theory panel, which consists of two tabs: the problem tab contains the problem statement (visible in the figure), and the algorithm tab contains a greedy algorithm in Java pseudocode. Finally, the lower right area is the table panel, with four tabs containing the input data table, the results table, the history table (visible in the figure), and the summary table.

When the user launches the application, only the theory panel hosts visible contents. Its two tabs can be read to understand the problem. Afterwards, the user may generate input data from three sources: from the keyboard, randomly or from a file. Some limits are imposed on data size to keep it manageable for learning and for visualization. Input data are displayed in the visualization panel and the user may choose any selection function from those available in the application. In order to make the experiment a bit more complex and interesting, two additional selection functions are available for any problem (see Fig. 1, table panel): increasing/decreasing order of index.

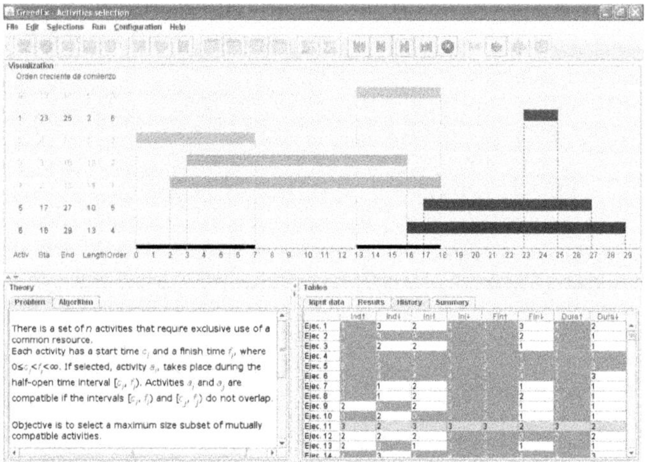

Fig. 1. User interface of the GreedEx system

Every time the user selects a selection function, she may execute it flexibly with four execution/animation controls: step forward, full forward, step backward, and rewind. As animation controls are clicked, the visualization is accordingly updated. After a selection function has been completely executed, its results are stored in the results table and in the history table. The summary table shows the percentage of optimal results obtained by each selection function along past executions.

Additional facilities are provided for faster experimentation: executing all the selection functions over the current input data, executing a subset of the selection functions, and executing all the selection functions over a very large number of randomly generated input data.

Finally, GreedEx includes a number of educational facilities. GreedEx is internationalized to support multiple languages (currently, English and Spanish), and allows exporting visualizations, animations and tables into graphical formats.

GreedEx is available at the following URL: http://www.lite.etsii.urjc.es/greedex/.

3. USABILITY EVALUATIONS OF GREEDEX

We conducted usability evaluations [8] to check the adequacy of the interactive assistant GreedEx for its intended aims. In particular, we measured ease of use, user's satisfaction and task effectiveness. In this section we review evaluations based on questionnaires and on other methods, and the evolution of GreedEx to overcome the difficulties encountered.

3.1 Lab Sessions with GreedEx

Our approach has been used for five academic years in a course on algorithms. The course schedule included one laboratory session for an assignment on greedy algorithms. We made use of this session to conduct 5 usability evaluations based on questionnaires. They were held in January 2008, May 2008, January 2009, November 2009, and November 2010, respectively.

The procedure was similar for all the evaluations. Students downloaded all the materials at the beginning of the session: the assignment statement, GreedEx, and a report template. Besides, they were given an opinion questionnaire in a sheet of paper. The assignment statement contained the problem statement and a short description of GreedEx. They had to perform three tasks:

1. Use GreedEx to determine the optimal selection functions for a problem. In the first evaluation the knapsack problem was used, but in successive evaluations the selection activity problem was preferred because of the higher difficulty of showing the non-optimality of the D↑ selection function (see Section 2.1).
2. Fill and deliver electronically a short report, following a template with a simple outline.
3. Fill and deliver the opinion questionnaire (optional).

The assignment could be solved either individually or in pairs, but the questionnaire had to be filled individually. The questionnaire consisted of three parts: multiple-choice questions on general issues, multiple-choice questions on specific elements, and open questions on general issues. Answers to multiple-choice questions were in a Linkert scale ranged from 1 (very bad) to 5 (very good).

Despite this common structure, some changes were introduced in the fourth and fifth evaluations (a consequence of interventions in the course to reduce misconceptions, see Section 4.2):

- 4th evaluation. A second lab session was introduced, where the optimal selection functions were identified, and students had to analyze their past report and identify the errors committed.
- 5th evaluation. An introductory lab session was introduced, where students experimented with a simpler problem (i.e. the knapsack problem) using GreedEx.

The number of questionnaires gathered in these evaluations was 40, 11, 28, 27 and 36, respectively.

3.2 Usability Evaluations Based on Questionnaires

Let us review the results of the three parts of the questionnaire. Table 4 shows the results for multiple-choice questions on general issues. The table contains five columns, labeled "A.n", each one containing the average value of students' answers collected in the n-th evaluation. The last column contains the global average.

Notice that very high results were obtained, especially for ease of use (row 1). Students also gave very high ratings to effectiveness (rows 2 and 3) and satisfaction (row 4). Only one mark under 4 was obtained (due to the limited set of facilities that GreedEx had in that evaluation for non-trivial problems, such as the activity selection problem).

The second part of the questionnaire measured the perceived quality of the main elements of GreedEx.

Table 5 shows that their values also are very high for the most relevant elements of the user interface. (Some cells do not have a value because either that element did not exist at the time of the evaluation or the questionnaire did not include it.) Most elements with lower values either are less critical for experimentation (e.g. interactive help) or are the most static elements (e.g. theory tabs).

Table 4. Evolution of answers on general issues

Question	A.1	A.2	A.3	A.4	A.5	Avg.
Easy to use	4.54	4.64	4.42	4.38	4.29	4.45
Useful for analyzing the effect of every selection function	4.20	4.50	4.36	4.19	4.43	4.34
Useful for identifying optimal selection functions	4.55	3.60	4.04	4.04	4.57	4.16
Overall, you liked it	4.25	4.27	4.32	4.19	4.12	4.23

Table 5. Evolution of answers on user interface elements

Element	A.1	A.2	A.3	A.4	A.5	Avg.
Tab for results table	4.28	4.18	4.36	4.31	4.00	4.23
Execution/animation			4.33	4.19	4.00	4.17
Introduction/generation of input data	4.30	4.45	4.04	3.96	4.07	4.16
Main menu	4.00	4.45	4.11	4.08	4.04	4.14
Tab for historic table			4.39	3.88	4.14	4.14
Tab for input data	4.03	4.18	4.07	4.15	4.11	4.11
Visualization panel	4.17	4.18	4.46	4.00	3.89	4.14
Choice of selection functions			4.07	4.00	4.00	4.02
Tab for algorithm (code)	3.80	4.09	4.11	3.85	3.93	3.96
Icons	3.80	4.64	3.96	3.77	3.61	3.96
Tab for problem (explanation)	3.60	3.91	3.82	3.58	3.89	3.76
Interactive help			3.81	3.40		3.61
Exporting/storing facilities	3.48	4.00	3.93	3.76	2.82	3.60

Finally, the questionnaire included open questions:

1. Positive elements. This is the open question with the most answers. The most frequent comment was that GreedEx is simple, pleasant, or easy to use. Other appreciated elements of GreedEx were its visualizations and its usefulness to understand and compare results.
2. Elements that students would include. The answers to these questions were the main source of information about how to enhance GreedEx. They varied greatly along the five evaluations, according to GreedEx evolution. Relevant suggestions were: better support for tables, enhancements of the visualization format, and better support for exportation.
3. Elements which are negative, more difficult to use, or that students would suppress. The answers to these questions also varied considerably and often suggested enhancements. Other complaints were: the static nature of the theory panel, and the narrow domain of the tool.

3.3 Other Kinds of Usability Evaluations

We have conducted two additional classes of usability evaluations. Firstly, we conducted an observational study. Its primary goal was triangulation [4] with the results obtained with other methods. Given that most observations were consistent with the results of other evaluation methods and the lack of space, we do not include them here.

We also conducted expert evaluations [8], mainly in the first stages of GreedEx or when substantial changes were introduced. They were conducted by the author, as an "expert" on the teaching of algorithms. The number of these evaluations can be counted in hundreds. Their purpose varied for each session, but they always had at least one of the following goals:

1. Testing. The goal was to check that the new assistant release satisfied the specifications and that it did not contain bugs.
2. Heuristic evaluation. The goal was to check that the assistant user interface was conformed to good principles (e.g. homogeneity or standardization).
3. Cognitive walkthrough. The goal was to check that the tool supported the experimental process well.

Typically, the expert had a list of changes to be checked or he simply performed some tasks, representative of typical scenarios. The result of each expert evaluation was a list of items marked (either as done, partially done, or pending), as well as a list of new changes to be introduced.

3.4 Evolution of GreedEx

The evaluations of GreedEx, mainly those based on questionnaires, allowed gathering much information about its drawbacks. New functions were incorporated along these years:

1. Tables. Initially, GreedEx only provided two tables [13], namely the input data table and the results table. It was later considered convenient to include two additional tables: the history table, and the summary table.
2. Execution. Initially, GreedEx only allowed choosing and executing selection functions individually [13]. Afterwards, a number of execution functions were included for higher speed: executing all the selection functions with current input data, executing a subset of the selection functions with current input data, and executing all the selection functions over a very high number of input data randomly generated.
3. Export. A number of functions to export visualizations, animations, and tables were included.
4. Internationalization. GreedEx can be customized to any natural language. Currently, it supports English and Spanish.

Two additional elements that received much attention in expert evaluations were: the menu structure and the icon bar. They were key means for keeping the user interface simple while the number of functions supported by GreedEx increased. The scores on ease of use obtained from students (see Table 4) remain constant, thus we succeeded in keeping interaction simple.

Finally, many minor details were changed and enhanced, such as:

1. Graphical format of visualizations.
2. More flexible generation of random input data.
3. Deletion operations in tables.
4. Customization options.

4. ANALYSIS OF STUDENTS' REPORTS

The success of a didactic method rarely relies only on technology, but technology itself must be integrated into the educational practice. Consequently, we analyzed the reports delivered by students in the three last evaluations identified in Section 3.1. In this section, we review the procedure and findings of these analyses, and the interventions performed to address the misconceptions identified.

4.1 Analysis of Students' Reports

We analyzed the students' reports elaborated in the three last usability evaluations conducted, i.e. January 2009, November 2009, and November 2010. The reports were analyzed according to the principles of grounded theory [7]. Initially, we thought that the number of relevant misconceptions would be limited to two:

1. Proposal of suboptimal selection functions. In particular, D↑ (see Section 2.1) is a good, but sub-optimal selection function.
2. Inconsistency in the deductive reasoning. We expected some students to be inconsistent, so that they would either propose sub-optimal selection functions (even after finding a counterexample) or discard optimal selection functions (even without finding a counterexample).

We analyzed the reports exhaustively three times, several months apart. In each loop, each report was analyzed and re-analyzed as many times as necessary. We built a table where we summarized many aspects of each report, the most relevant being: the selection functions proposed as optimal, quality of their (informal) justification, quality of the evidence provided, and quality of global reasoning. In addition, we also recorded: the number of executions performed, number of examples included, size of examples, and number of selection functions executed per input data.

Even in the first analysis loop, it was evident that some reports had more severe misconceptions than those listed above. Finally, we identified two additional misconceptions:

3. Additional optimization criterion. Some students proposed an additional criterion, e.g. maximizing time usage of the resource or minimizing waiting time of activities. The rationale was that students considered "optimal" as a synonym of "unique".
4. Proposal of different selection functions for different input data. Here, the misconception is even stronger, as these students do not consider "optimal" as a synonym of "always" but of "particular".

During the different analyses, these four coding schemes were invariant, but their role changed. Initially, we considered each of these misconceptions as a different category in a hierarchy (being 1 the least severe misconception and 4 the most severe) and we tried to classify each report into one of them. However, it became apparent that it was better to simply list, for each report, the misconceptions it exhibited. Finally, we obtained the categories shown in Table 6. Notice that category A does not hold any misconception.

The seven categories are very different with respect to viability of their underlying mental models. Notice that the least severe misconception is number 1. Therefore, categories A and B were viable, given that they solve the problem (almost) correctly and consistently. Next, categories C and D only exhibited one additional misconception. Finally, categories E-G exhibit two or three additional misconceptions.

Table 6. Relation between categories and misconceptions

Category	Misconceptions
A	–
B	1
C	1-2
D	1-3
E	1-2-3
F	1-3-4
G	1-2-3-4

As we explain in the following subsection, we addressed these misconceptions, and they evolved as shown in Table 7.

Table 7. Evolution of category percentages

	1st eval.	2nd eval.	3rd eval.
A	22.22%	28.57%	47.83%
B	5.56%	23.81%	39.13%
C	16.67%	23.81%	13.04%
D	11.11%	19.05%	0%
E	16.67%	4.76%	0%
F	22.22%	0%	0%
G	5.56%	0%	0%

Notice that misconceptions 3 and 4 disappear in the third evaluation. If we group categories according to their degree of severity, we obtain the evolution shown in Table 8. In summary, we may conclude that we were successful in removing severe misconceptions, which are now limited to a small percentage of students who do not fully understand the experimental method.

Table 8. Evolution of percentages of category groups

	1st eval.	2nd eval.	3rd eval.
A-B	27.78%	52.38%	86.96%
C-D	27.78%	52.86%	13.04%
E-F-G	44.45%	4.76%	0%

4.2 Didactic Interventions

The results of the analysis of the first batch of students' reports were unexpected and shocking for us. Consequently, we introduced (and later reinforced) several changes in our didactic practice. The most important interventions follow. (Notice that experimentation with selection functions makes more sense at the beginning of the chapter on greedy algorithms.)

The most obvious interventions were in lectures. We scheduled more time at the beginning of the chapter on greedy algorithms. In this extra time, we explicitly identified possible selection functions for all the problems, formulated the experimental method, used GreedEx, identified counterexamples, and related these experiments to others known by students (mainly, scientific experimentation and software testing). We have claimed elsewhere [12] that giving emphasis to the searching of counterexamples rather than to proofs of optimality, in the initial phases of greedy algorithms, has didactic benefits.

A related, second intervention was the elaboration of lecture notes. In an effort to remove misconceptions, they explicitly addressed optimization problems, experimentation, and GreedEx.

A third intervention was an increase in the number of lab sessions (see Section 3.1). We introduced a last lab session where students were given the optimal selection functions, and they had to analyze their past report and to identify the errors committed. In addition, we introduced an introduction session where students could experiment with a simpler problem (typically, the knapsack problem). In this way, they got hands-on experience with experimentation and became familiar with GreedEx.

We also introduced changes in the reports that students had to fill for the assignment. A more structured template was given, that made experimental evidence clearer. Notice also that the new functions of GreedEx to export figures and tables (see Section 3.4) facilitates students to focus on the assignment goals.

Finally, we have spread the experimental method along our course on algorithms to introduce backtracking and dynamic programming. We use GreedEx to show that some problems cannot be solved optimally with greedy algorithms, so they must be solved using other design techniques. Using variations of known problems (i.e. the 0/1 knapsack problem instead of the knapsack problem) allows accommodating this approach without extra time.

5. RECAPITULATION

We started our research effort trying to follow clear principles. In particular, we adopted Bloom's taxonomy [3] as a framework to specify the learning goals of both our experimental method and GreedEx. However, we expanded our interests as our research advanced, so we have been influenced by a number of methods, experiences and authors. Given the lack of space, we regret only citing some of the relevant works.

Usability evaluations are nowadays common practice, but they are not very common in educational software (see a review on visualization tools in [11]). We also are influenced by previous works on students' misconceptions on programming concepts. In particular, Sanders et al.'s work [10] identified mental models of recursion and intervened to eliminate unviable ones. The joint use of software tools and written materials has been advocated by some authors as a key element in successful experiences [2].

6. CONCLUSIONS

We have presented an innovative approach, its evaluation, and its refinement for the active learning of greedy algorithms. To our knowledge, the approach is unique within the CS education research community focused on algorithms. Initially, we proposed an experimental method and constructed a tool to support it. The tool was specified with explicit pedagogical aims. The tool was later evaluated with respect to usability and it was enhanced to fully support the experimental method. We also analyzed students' products in order to detect misunderstandings. Consequently, we intervened in a number of activities to eliminate such misconceptions. Both the results of the usability evaluations and of the last reports' analysis suggest that we succeeded.

Our approach has some limitations, the main one being the narrowness of its domain. We have tried to alleviate it by using the approach in the introduction to other algorithm design techniques (i.e. dynamic programming and backtracking). This required extending GreedEx with some problems which cannot be optimally solved with greedy algorithms.

We plan to further develop our efforts. Firstly, GreedEx has been modified to support collaborative discussion. Secondly, we plan to observe and analyze student activity with GreedEx in detail in order to know more about the students' problem solving process. Finally, an open issue is whether we could design and construct a similar, interactive tool, usable in a broader domain.

7. ACKNOWLEDGMENTS

This work was supported by research grant TIN2011-29542-C02-01 of the Spanish Ministry of Science and Innovation.

8. REFERENCES

[1] ACM, Interim Review Task Force (2008). *Computer Science Curriculum 2008*. ACM & IEEE Computer Society. Retrieved January 10, 2012, from http://www.acm.org// education/curricula/ComputerScience2008.pdf.

[2] Bazik, J., Tamassia, R., Reiss, S.P., and van Dam, A. 1998. Software visualization in teaching at Brown University. In *Software Visualization*, J. Stasko, J. Domingue, M.H. Brown and B.A. Blaine, Eds. MIT Press, Cambridge, MA. 383-398.

[3] Bloom, B., Furst, E., Hill, W., and Krathwohl, D. R. 1956. *Taxonomy of Educational Objectives: Handbook I, The Cognitive Domain*. Addison-Wesley, Reading, MA.

[4] Cohen, L., Manion, L., and Morrison, K. 2011. *Research Methods in Education*, 7th ed. Routledge, London.

[5] Cormen, T. H., Leiserson, C. E., Rivest. R. L., and Stein, C. 2009. *Introduction to Algorithms*, 3rd ed. MIT Press.

[6] Ginat, D. 2008. Learning from wrong and creative algorithm design. In *Proceedings of the 39th SIGCSE Technical Symposium on Computer Science Education*. SIGCSE'08. ACM Press, 26-30.

[7] Glaser, B., and Strauss, A. 1967. *The Discovery of Grounded Theory: Strategies for Qualitative Research*. Aldine, Chicago, IL.

[8] Rubin, J., and Chisnell, D. 2008. *Handbook of Usability Testing: How to Plan, Design, and Conduct Effective Tests*. John Wiley, New York, NY.

[9] Sahni, S. 2004. *Data Structures, Algorithms, and Applications in Java*, 2nd ed. Silicon Press, Summit, NJ.

[10] Sanders, I., Galpin, V., and Götschi, T. 2003. Mental models of recursion revisited. In *Proceedings of the 8th Annual Conference on Innovation and Technology in Computer Science Education*. ITiCSE'06. ACM Press, 138-142.

[11] Urquiza-Fuentes, J., and Velázquez-Iturbide, J. Á. 2009. A survey of successful evaluations of program visualization and algorithm animation systems. *ACM Transactions on Computing Education*, 9, 2, article 9.

[12] Velázquez-Iturbide, J. Á. 2011. The design and coding of greedy algorithms revisited. In *Proceedings of the 16th Annual Conference on Innovation and Technology in Computer Science Education*. ITiCSE'11. ACM Press, 8-12.

[13] Velázquez-Iturbide, J. Á., and Pérez-Carrasco, A. 2009. Active learning of greedy algorithms by means of interactive experimentation. In *Proceedings of the 14th Annual Conference on Innovation and Technology in Computer Science Education*. ITiCSE'09. ACM Press, 119-123.

Digging for Algorithmic Nuggets in the Land of Polyominoes

Anany Levitin
Department of Computing Sciences
Villanova University
Villanova, PA 19085, USA
anany.levitin@villanova.edu

ABSTRACT

This paper seeks to demonstrate that tiling with polyominoes, almost entirely neglected by textbooks on algorithms, can provide valuable examples of applications of algorithm design techniques, some of which are not easy to illustrate by examples from other domains.

Categories and Subject Descriptors

F.2.2 [**Analysis of Algorithms and Problem Complexity**]: Nonnumerical Algorithms and Problems

General Terms

Algorithms

Keywords

Algorithm design techniques, polyominoes

1. INTRODUCTION

When teaching courses on algorithms, it is very helpful to provide examples beyond traditional CS problems such as sorting, searching, graphs, and so on. First, such examples demonstrate generality of algorithm design techniques as problem solving tools. Second, they help crystallize the techniques in question by divesting them from low-level computing minutia. One domain that can provide such examples is tiling with polyominoes.

Polyominoes are shapes made by connecting certain numbers of equal–sized squares, each joined together with at least one other square along an edge [6, 10]. There is one monomino and one domino, two trominoes (or triominoes), and five tetrominoes (see Figure 1); we are not going to consider polyominoes made of more than four squares here.

The first puzzle involving polyominoes was published in the first decade of the last century by the great English inventor of puzzles Henry E. Dudeney [4]; many such problems under the name of "dissection problems" appeared in the 1930s and 1940s in the British puzzle journal *The Fairy Chess Review*. The name "polyominoes" was introduced in 1953 by a prominent U.S. mathematician Solomon W. Golomb who is justly considered the father of this field. Since then, a voluminous literature on the subject has appeared, both as a subarea of combinatorial geometry and a genre of recreational mathematics. The popularization of polyominoes by Martin Gardner in his *Scientific American* columns [5] played an important role in the latter.

ITiCSE'12, July 3–5, 2012, Haifa, Israel.

This paper seeks to demonstrate that this area, almost completely neglected by textbooks on algorithms, contains valuable pedagogical examples, some of which are difficult to find elsewhere. Section 2 introduces polyominoes and the tiling problem and then provides examples from this area that are valuable for teaching algorithmics. Section 3 discusses these examples and points out several other interesting problems involving polyominoes.

2. TILING WITH POLYOMINOES

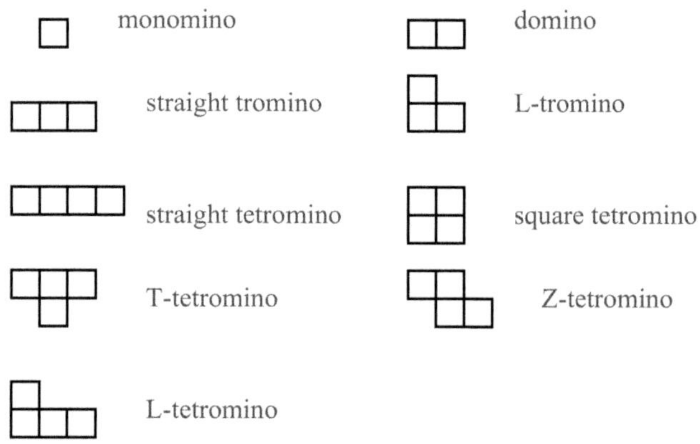

Figure 1. Polyominoes with 1, 2, 3, and 4 squares

Most problems involving polyominoes deal with tiling. To tile a given region (such as a chessboard or, more generally, an $n \times n$ square or a rectangle) with prescribed types of polyominoes is to cover the region with copies of the polyominoes exactly and without overlaps. Note that copies of a polyomino may be rotated, flipped over, or slid around to tile the region given.

2.1 Tiling with Dominoes

To begin, consider the following questions: Which of the regions listed below can be tiled with dominoes?

a. an $n \times n$ square

b. an $n \times n$ square with a 1×1 square cut off from one of its corners

c. an $n \times n$ square with two 1×1 squares cut off from two corners on the same side

d. an $n \times n$ square with two 1×1 squares cut off from two diagonally opposite corners

e. an $n \times n$ chessboard with two arbitrary 1×1 squares of opposite colors removed

The first three of these questions are, of course, very easy but even they can serve a useful pedagogical purpose. First, they send a very important message that not all algorithmic problems have a solution; with an exception for an occasional reference to the Halting Problem, this fundamental fact is neglected in current algorithm textbooks. Second, they draw attention to importance of parity as a principal invariant that may signal impossibility of a solution.

Question d is a generalization of a well-known puzzle about covering with dominoes an 8×8 chessboard without two diagonally opposite squares. It requires a coloring argument (i.e., taking into account colors of the squares) to establish that the problem does not have a solution for even n's. (Of course, it has no solution for odd n's either because of the parity argument.)

Finally, when n is even, an $n \times n$ chessboard without two arbitrary 1×1 squares of opposite colors can always be tiled with dominoes, but the proof requires an ingenious device called the Gomory barriers (see Figure 2). These barriers partition the board into two "corridors" with the endpoints at the removed squares if the latter are not next to each other and just one "corridor" if the removed squares are next to each other. Dominoes of a tiling can always be laid in a unique way along these "corridors" [6, p. 111]. Note that from the algorithm design technique perspective, the Gomory barriers can be interpreted as *input enhancement* [8, p. 253].

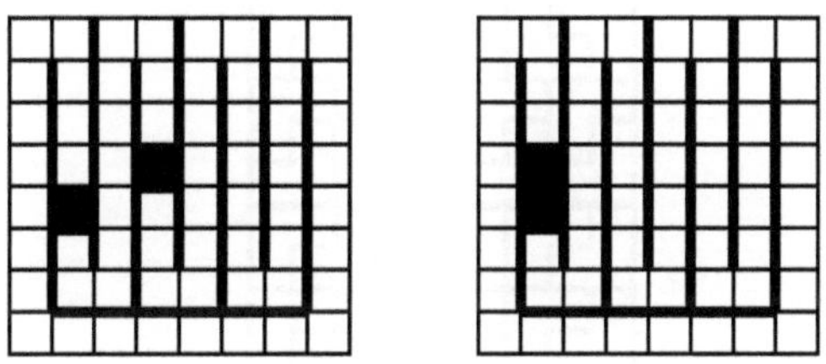

Figure 2. Two cases of the Gomory barriers: with nonadjacent and adjacent squares removed

The question about a domino tiling of a $w \times h$ rectangle has an obvious answer: it exists if and only if at least one of the rectangle's sides is even. A much more interesting problem is to tile a region bounded by a polygonal line made up of alternating vertical and horizontal segments (see Figure 3 for an example). Since this problem, obviously, does not always have a solution, one can ask instead about the largest number of dominoes that can be placed within such a region. The problem can be solved by representing the region by a graph in which vertices represent 1 × 1 squares of the region and edges connect every pair of vertically or horizontally adjacent squares. Such a graph will always be bipartite since it will have no odd-length cycles. Hence the problem in question can be solved by a standard maximum cardinality matching algorithm for bipartite graphs (e.g., [8, Sec. 10.3]).

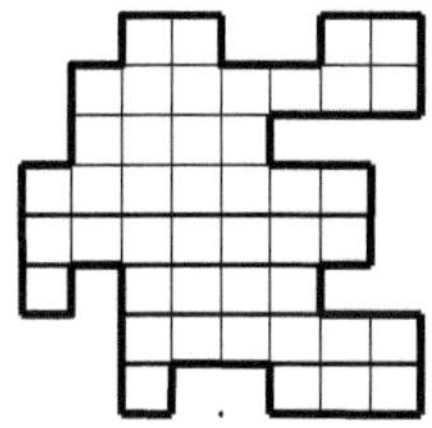

Figure 3. Region with a polygonal boundary

There is also a puzzle about the number of ways one can tile an $n \times 2$ rectangle without regard for possible symmetries (see [6, 7]). Since such a tiling must start either with one vertically placed domino or with two horizontally placed ones, we immediately obtain the Fibonacci recurrence for the number of tilings $C(n)$:

$$C(n) = C(n\text{-}1) + C(n\text{-}2) \text{ for } n > 2, \; C(1) = 1, C(2) = 2.$$

Its solution is $C(n) = F(n+1)$, where $F(n)$ is the nth Fibonacci number with the standard initial conditions $F(0) = 0$, $F(1) = 1$.

2.2 Tiling with Straight Trominoes

Obviously, any region that can be tiled with trominoes must have the number of squares divisible by 3. The well-known problem here is the question about tiling an 8×8 chessboard with one square missing (or covered with a monomino). By recoloring the board into three colors, one can show (e.g., [6, pp. 4–5]) that the problem has a solution if and only if the missing square is located in one of the four symmetric positions shown in Figure 4a. Figure 4b shows such a tiling, which can be easily obtained by tiling the board with rectangular "blocks" of two trominoes until a room for just a single tromino is left.

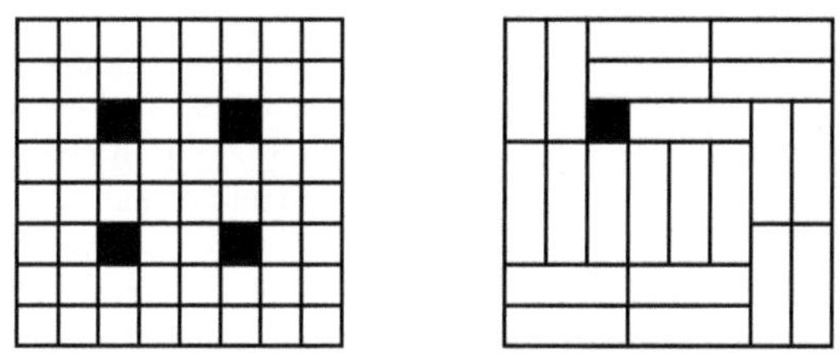

(a) (b)

Figure 4. (a) The four symmetric positions for a removed square making tiling with straight trominoes possible. (b) One such tiling.

Consider now the general question about tiling an $n \times n$ square, where $n \geq 3$, with straight trominoes. If n is divisible by 3, the problem has two obvious solutions made up with all the tromino tiles placed either horizontally or vertically. If n is not divisible by 3, then $n^2 \bmod 3 = 1$, and one monomino is necessary and, in fact, also sufficient for tiling. Indeed, if $n \bmod 3 = 1$ and $n \geq 3$, i.e., $n = 4 + 3k$ where $k \geq 0$, we can divide the square into three subregions (note the divide-and-conquer idea in action!): the 4×4 square in, say, the upper left corner, the $4 \times 3k$ rectangle, and $3k \times (4+3k)$ rectangle (see Figure 5). The 4×4 square requires a monomino placed in one of its corners to make it possible to tile the rest of it; tiling the other two rectangles (if $k > 0$) is trivial since both of them have a side equal to $3k$.

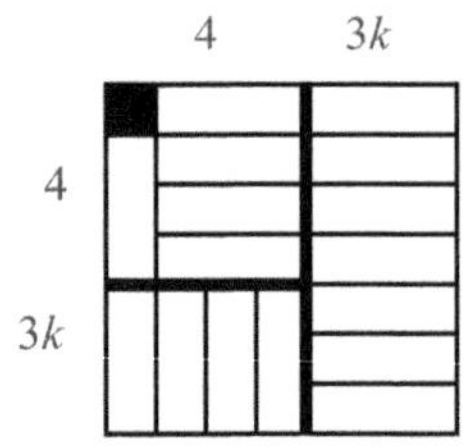

Figure 5. Tiling a (4+3k) × (4+3k) square with straight trominoes and one monomino (shown for k = 1)

Similarly, if n mod 3 = 2 and $n \geq 3$, i.e., $n = 5 + 3k$ where $k \geq 0$, we can tile the board as shown in Figure 6.

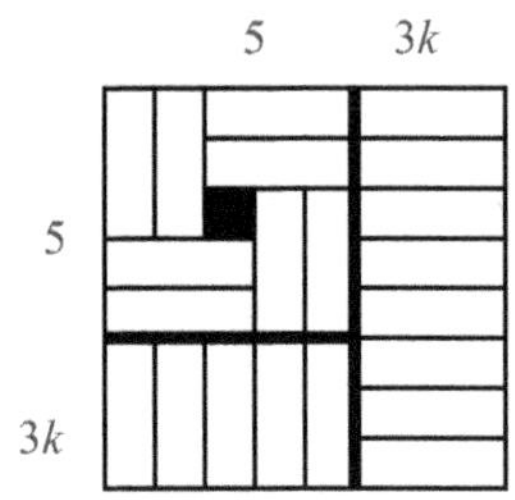

Figure 6. Tiling a (5+3k) × (5+3k) square with straight trominoes and one monomino (shown for k = 1)

Note that the preceding algorithm can also be considered as based on the decrease-by-3 technique: there is a simple way to tile an $n \times n$ square once an (n-3) × (n-3) square has already been tiled.

2.3 Tiling with L-trominoes

Tiling with L-trominoes a $2^n \times 2^n$ board with one removed square seems to be the only tiling problem that has appeared in algorithm textbooks with some regularity (e.g., [8, p. 175]). It does provide an excellent demonstration of the divide-and-conquer strategy: by placing a properly oriented copy of the L-tromino at the center of the board, the problem's instance of size n is reduced to four instances of size n-1 (Figure 7).

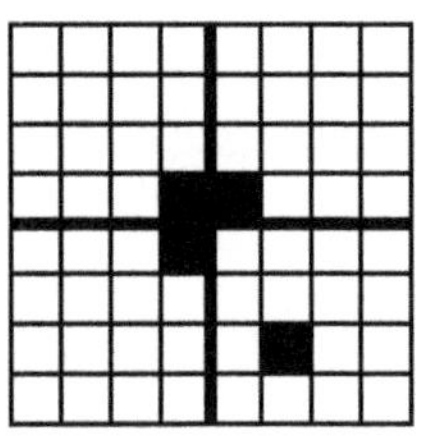

Figure 7. Tiling with L-trominoes a $2^n \times 2^n$ board with one removed square by divide-and-conquer

The problem of tiling a square board of an arbitrary size is significantly more difficult although it does have a solution with a single exception: Any $n \times n$ square with n divisible by 3 except for n = 3 can be tiled with L-trominoes; if n is not divisible by 3, the square can be tiled with L-trominoes and one monomino, which can always be placed at the square's corner [10, p. 31]. Each size $1 \leq n \leq 9$ has to be considered separately. The cases of n = 1 and n =2 are trivial; n = 4 and n = 8 are special cases of powers of 2 discussed at the beginning of this subsection; the case of n = 6 is very simple because the 6 × 6 square can be covered by six 2 × 3 rectangular "blocks" made up of a pair of L-trominoes. A tiling for n = 5 can be found by trial-and-error or backtracking. The 7 × 7 square can be partitioned into a 5 × 5 square, 3 × 2 and 2 × 3 rectangles, and an L-shaped region obtained by increasing each side of the L-tromino by the factor of 2; each of them can be easily tiled with L-trominoes (Figure 8).

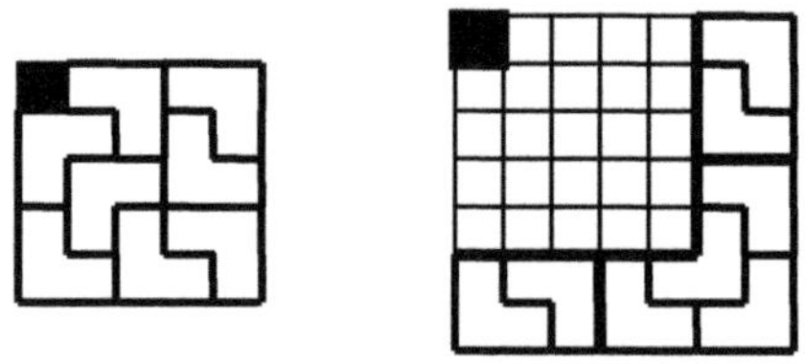

Figure 8. Tiling 5 × 5 and 7 × 7 squares with L-trominoes and one monomino

The most difficult case here is that of a 9 × 9 square. It takes advantage of the remarkable tiling of a 9 × 5 rectangle, which can be found by backtracking, and the straightforward tiling of a 9 × 4 rectangle obtained by dividing it into six 3 × 2 blocks (Figure 9).

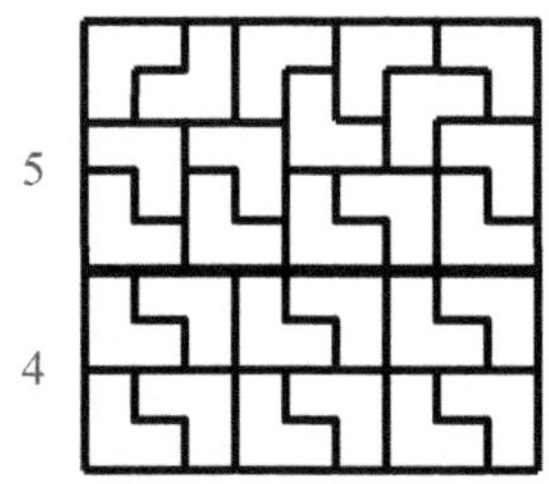

Figure 9. Tiling of a 9 × 9 square with L-trominoes

An algorithm for tiling squares larger than 9 × 9 can be based on the decrease-by-6 technique: a tiling of an $n \times n$ square can be obtained by tiling an (n-6) × (n-6) square recursively, and tiling a 6 × 6 square, an (n-6) × 6 rectangle, and a 6 × (n-6) rectangle. Figure 10 illustrates the solutions for even and odd n's by depicting the cases of n =10 and n = 11, respectively.

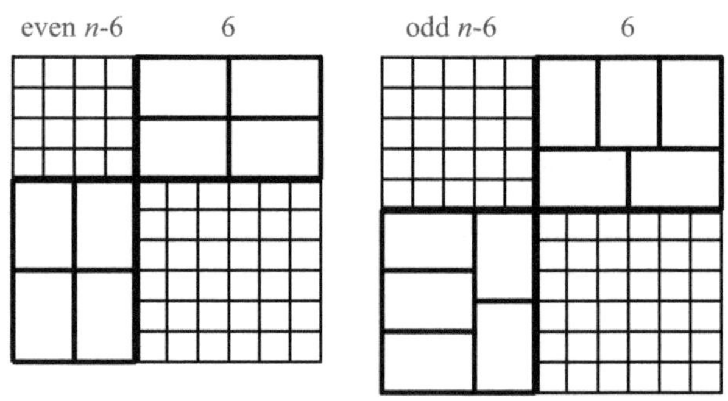

Figure 10. Tiling an $n \times n$ square with L-trominoes by using a tiling of an (n-6) × (n-6) square

Instead of tiling a square, one can also pose a closely related problem of tiling an L-shaped region obtained by cutting out a quadrant off a $2r \times 2r$ square. Such a region can be alternatively obtained by stretching each side of the L-tromino by the factor of r. (An example of such a region for $r = 2$ can be seen inside the 7×7 square in Figure 8.) Any such region can be tiled by r^2 copies of the L-tromino. Using the term introduced by Golomb, the L-tromino is a *reptile of order* r^2 for any positive integer $r > 1$.

2.4 Tiling with Tetrominoes

Following the divide-and-conquer partition of the chessboard into four 4×4 squares, it is easy to see that the board can be tiled with 16 copies of either straight tetromino, or square tetromino, or T-tetromino, or L-tetromino by tiling each of the 4×4 squares as shown in Figure 11.

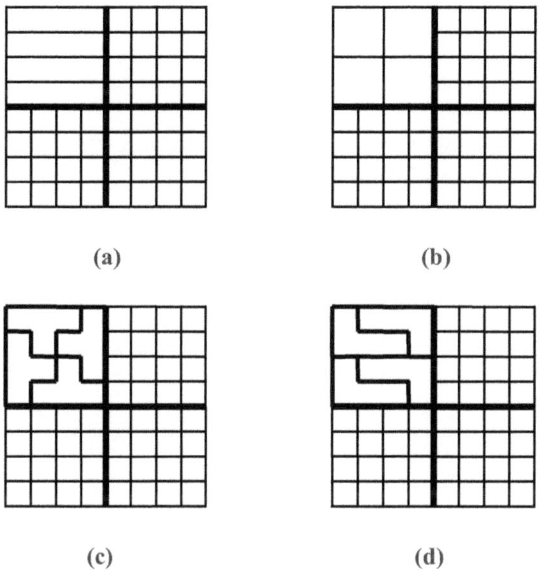

Figure 11. Tiling the chessboard with (a) straight tetrominoes; (b) square tetrominoes; (c) T-tetrominoes; (d) L-tetrominoes

On the other hand, by starting at a corner and trying to cover the squares along one side of the board, it is easy to see that it is impossible to tile the chessboard with Z-tetrominoes.

Consider now the problem of tiling with straight tetrominoes an arbitrary $n \times n$ square. The problem has a solution if and only if n is divisible by 4 [10, p. 41], with an obvious tiling of each 4×4 region illustrated in Figure 11a. If n is odd and not equal to 3, an $n \times n$ square can always be tiled with straight tetrominoes and one monomino. A tiling algorithm can be based on the decrease-by-4 technique: to tile an $n \times n$ square, partition it into the $(n\text{-}4) \times (n\text{-}4)$ square (say, in its upper left corner), the $(n\text{-}4) \times 4$ rectangle in the lower left corner, and the remaining $4 \times (n\text{-}4)$ rectangle. The $(n\text{-}4) \times (n\text{-}4)$ square can be tiled recursively, while the tiling of the other two rectangles is obvious because they have a side equal to 4. If $n = 1 + 4k$, $k \geq 0$, the recursive calls stop with the trivial tiling of the 1×1 square with one monomino (see Figure 12a for the case of $n = 5$ as an example); and if $n = 7 + 4k$, $k \geq 0$, the recursive calls can stop with tilling the 7×7 square as shown in the upper left corner of Figure 12b.

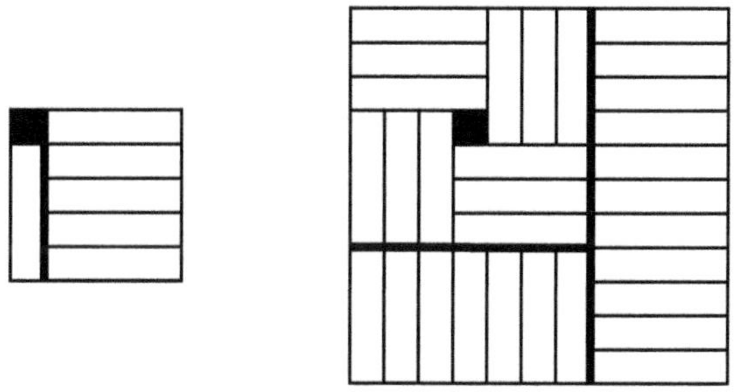

(a) (b)

Figure 12. Tiling (a) a 5×5 square and (b) an 11×11 square with straight tetrominoes and one monomino

Consider now the problem of tiling an arbitrary $n \times n$ square with L-tetrominoes. It follows from a more general theorem (see [10, p. 48]) that the problem has a solution if and only if n is divisible by 4. A tiling similar to the one shown in Figure 11d provides a solution. If n is odd, an $n \times n$ square can always be tiled with L-tetrominoes and one monomino. A tiling algorithm can be based on the decrease-by-4 technique: a tiling of an $n \times n$ square can be obtained by tiling recursively the $(n\text{-}4) \times (n\text{-}4)$ square at its center and by tiling the remaining two-square-wide border surrounding it as shown in Figure 13. The recursive calls stop by obvious tilings of the smallest squares in the two series $n = 1 + 4k$, $k \geq 0$, and $n = 3 + 4k$, $k \geq 0$, which are shown in Figures 13a and 13b, respectively. (The 4×2 and 2×4 rectangles in Figure 13 can be obviously tiled by two L-tetrominoes, which are not shown for the sake of clarity.)

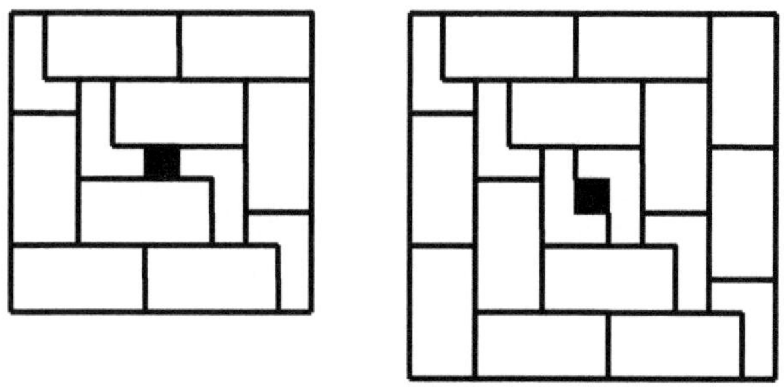

(a) (b)

Figure 13. Tiling (a) a 9×9 square and (b) an 11×11 square with L-tetrominoes and one monomino

3. DISCUSSION

The preceding section of the paper provides several examples of polyomino tilings that exemplify some major algorithm design techniques: divide-and-conquer, decrease-and-conquer, input enhancement, and backtracking. Divide-and-conquer examples are valuable because outside traditional computer science topics there seems to be surprisingly few pedagogically sound examples illustrating it. The tiling problem provides a natural source of such examples. It should be noted, however, that in many of them one needs to partition a region in question into smaller regions that are not necessarily of the same shape as the original one. This is a point worth drawing students' attention to.

Decrease-and-conquer (called by some the inductive or incremental approach) is based on finding a solution to an instance of size n by exploiting a solution to a smaller instance. Most often, this smaller instance has the size n-1. Section 2 contains examples where the constant size reduction differs from 1, namely, 3, 4, and 6.

Input enhancement is also a technique that is not very easy to illustrate by an example. The Gomory barriers provide such an opportunity. Backtracking, on the other hand, has a multitude of examples. Still, its application to tiling can serve as a no-routine programming exercise.

Speaking of programming exercises, it should be noted that tiling problems in general provide attractive assignments because of the visual nature of their output. Such assignments can also be enhanced by asking students to color tiles with a minimum number of colors so that no two polyominoes sharing a border are colored the same color. While the Four-Color Theorem guarantees that four colors always suffice, this might not be the smallest number necessary. For example, Chu and Johnsonbaugh [3] gave an algorithm for tiling a $2^n \times 2^n$ board without a square with L-trominoes colored in at most three colors.

Finally, tiling problems provide a wide variety of natural problems that do not have solutions. We believe that the lack of such problems in algorithm textbook is unfortunate and should be rectified. Although some books on discrete mathematics (e.g., [12]) do provide such examples when discussing existence proofs, it is important, in our view, not to miss this topic in algorithm courses.

Many other tiling examples useful for teaching algorithmics can be found in the two monographs on polyominoes [6, 10] and the recently published collection of algorithmic puzzles [9]. In the former, the problems are grouped by the polyomino types; in the latter, the puzzles are grouped by difficulty levels and indexed by algorithm design and analysis techniques.

Of course, there are many other polyomino problems that can be of interest to teachers of algorithms. We would like to mention three of them. The first is the so-called Pentomino Game [6, pp. 8–9]. Two players play with a set of twelve pentominoes (polyominoes made up of five squares) by alternating their moves. On each move, a player places one of the remaining pentominoes on a chessboard (with no two pieces allowed to overlap). The first player who cannot make a move loses the game. The game will last at least five and at most twelve moves and cannot end in a tie. It turns out that the first player can always win [11].

The second — and much more serious from a scientific point of view — is the problem of enumerating polyominoes of different orders. For a brief survey of the problem and algorithms for solving it, see the Wikipedia article on the subject at http://en.wikipedia.org/wiki/Polyomino.

Finally, we would be remiss not to mention Tetris, one of the all-time favorite computer games, which asks a player to manipulate a randomly generated sequence of falling tetrominoes. The game is simple enough to be assigned as a project in an advanced programming class. On the other hand, it has motivated some serious research, including the possibility of the game continuing forever [2] and NP-completeness of several problems related to the offline version of the game [1].

4. REFERENCES

[1] Breukelaar, R. et al. Tetris is hard, even to approximate. International *Journal of Computational Geometry and Applications*, *14* (1), 41–68.

[2] Brzustowski, J. 1992. *Can You Win in Tetris?* Thesis. University of British Columbia.

[3] Chu, I.-P., and Johnsonbaugh, R. Tiling and recursion. SIGCSE '87, 261–263.

[4] Dudeney, H. E. *The Canterbury Puzzles*. Dover Publishing, 2002.

[5] Gardner, M. *Martin Gardner's Mathematical Games* (CD-ROM). Mathematical Association of America, 2005.

[6] Golomb, S. W. *Polyominoes: Puzzles, Patterns, Problems, and Packings*. 2nd edition. Princeton University Press, 1994.

[7] Knott, R. Easier Fibonacci Puzzles page, 2007. http://www.mcs.surrey.ac.uk/Personal/R.Knott/Fibonacci/fibpuzzles.html (retrieved January 3, 2012)

[8] Levitin, A. *Introduction to the Design and Analysis of Algorithms*, 3rd edition. Pearson, 2012.

[9] Levitin, A., and Levitin M. *Algorithmic Puzzles*. Oxford University Press, 2011.

[10] Martin, G. E. *Polyominoes: A Guide to Puzzles and Problems in Tiling*. The Mathematical Association of America, 1996.

[11] Orman, H. K. Pentominoes: a first player win. In Nowakowski, R. J., ed. *Games of No Chance*. MSRI, 1994. 339–344.

[12] Rosen, K. H. *Discrete Mathematics and Its Applications*, 7th edition. McGraw-Hill, 2011.

The Empirically Refined Competence Structure Model for Embedded Micro- and Nanosystems

Andre Schäfer,
Rainer Brück
Institute of Microsystems Technology
University of Siegen
Germany
andre.schaefer@uni-siegen.de

Steffen Büchner,
Steffen Jaschke,
Sigrid Schubert
Didactis of Informatics and E-Learning
University of Siegen
Germany
steffen.buechner@uni-siegen.de

Dietmar Fey,
Bruno Kleinert,
Harald Schmidt
Chair of Computer Science 3
University of Erlangen-Nürnberg
Germany
dietmar.fey@informatik.uni-erlangen.de

ABSTRACT

Teaching the development of embedded micro- and nanosystems needs a well structured foundation. In this paper, we show how we refined our normative competence structure model (NCSM) to an empirical competence structure model (ECSM) by incorporating the results of a survey of German experts in the field of embedded systems. In addition, we introduce a course concept for a new internship which takes the results of the ECSM into account.

Categories and Subject Descriptors

K.3.2 [**Computer and Information Science Education**]: Computer science education

General Terms

Human Factors, Theory, Experimentation.

Keywords

Competence development, Systems engineering education, Embedded systems

1. INTRODUCTION

Embedded systems are present in more and more application areas and their pervasiveness will increase with their power. Today, the number of processors built for embedded systems already exceeds the number of processors built for classical PCs and this trend is expected to continue [10].

Grimheden and Törngren [7] have already shown that the need for suitable education of embedded systems is even more important than ever before. Nevertheless, embedded systems are under-represented in teaching. That is, among other reasons, because of the lack of comprehensive equipment needed to teach embedded systems in an appropriate way [10]. Up to now, embedded systems education is often limited to the programming of microcontrollers. This is neglecting the link to the physical environment of the system. The physical aspects of hardware design and operation in many curricula and practical hardware courses as a part of computer science education are often assigned to electrical engineering. Compared to electrical engineering, computer science education is primarily limited to theoretical and algorithmic aspects [4]. This position is no longer appropriate in teaching embedded systems, because knowledge of the physical level or the hardware is necessary [13], [14]. The Japanese "Software Engineering Centre" (SEC)[1] has defined the "Embedded Technology Skill Standard" (ETSS) [11]. According to this, even the pure software developer of embedded systems must have knowledge of the hardware. Hardware related courses with actuators and sensors are needed because they are widely used in the context of embedded systems [10].

The domains of embedded systems need a structured basis in the form of a competence model for the education of computer scientists and engineers who develop future embedded systems. In the project *Competence development with embedded micro- and nanosystems* (KOMINA), we developed a NCSM in a first step [12]. This paper describes the empirical procedure to an ECSM.

The paper is organised as follows: In the next section we introduce our research approach and mainly sketch the way to the NCSM. In section three we explain in detail how we attained the ECSM from the NCSM. Section four shows how the ECSM serves us as basis for the design of courses. The last sections contain conclusion and further work.

2. PREVIOUS WORK

Within the KOMINA project, we particularly research on engineering in the context of embedded micro- and nanosystems (EMNS). Our aim is to make a contribution to the system oriented didactics of computer engineering which includes skill-building experiments for practical courses. In addition, the development of an ECSM is necessary to progress from a subjective and content oriented design of courses

[1] http://www.ipa.go.jp/english/sec/index.html

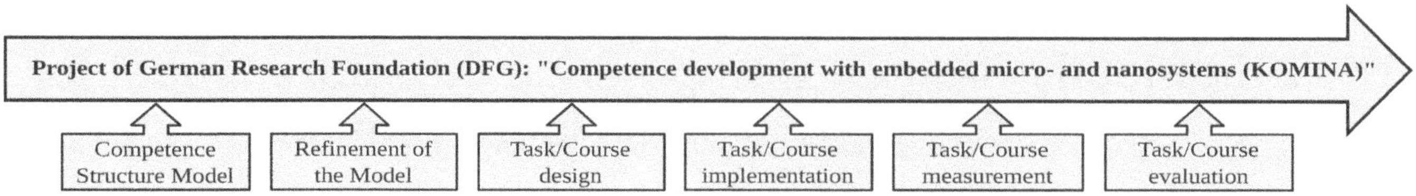

Figure 1: Research approach

and tests to traceable and outcome oriented courses [3, 8]. This means that aligned tasks and associated assessments have to deal with the same topics and related competencies. The recommended procedure is described in [6]. Up to day, neither a competence model for EMNS nor for computer engineering has been developed.

Figure 1 depicts the research methodology of our proceeding. According to [9], we developed the competence structure model in a normative way by analysing the module descriptions of excellent rated universities in the field of computer engineering and embedded systems. In addition, we analysed the curricula recommendations of the Association for Computing Machinery (ACM) as well as the Institute of Electrical and Electronics Engineers (IEEE)[1] and the German Informatics Society (GI) [5]. As a result, we clustered the competencies in four dimensions (C1-C4). While we chose a strictly thematic division for breaking down C1 (competencies as preconditions) and C2 (development competencies) to subdimensions, we recommend dividing C3 (competencies for multi-level development) into solution approaches and their interconnections. The competence dimension C4 (non-cognitive competencies) includes the attitudes, social-communicative competencies, motivational and volitional skills with their strong interconnections to the cognitive dimensions [12].

Afterwards, two surveys have been sent to 171 German experts to rate the importance of our normative derived competencies. The group of experts consisted of professors from German universities and universities of applied sciences in the field of EMNS exclusively. The refinement of the NCSM towards an ECSM is based on the results of the two surveys. The amount of 58 feedbacks confirms the necessity of our research work.

3. FROM AN NCSM TO A ECSM

In our surveys, we asked the experts to rate all aspects of our NCSM. The rating has been separated into the four categories *very important*, *rather important*, *rather unimportant* and *very unimportant*. All questions (aspects of competencies) are taken from the module descriptions of the subjects, *embedded systems* and *computer engineering*, from the GI curriculum for computer engineering [5] or from the ACM/IEEE Computer Science Curriculum [1]. Figure 2 shows the results of the survey.

Due to the fact that the whole competence model with all competence descriptions would oversized to be presented in a single graphic, Figure 2 only contains the numbers of the competence dimensions and subdimensions and not the competence descriptions. The names of all competence dimensions and subdimensions is shown in Figure 3. The descriptions of the best voted competences are shown in Table 2.

We assigned a categorization scheme in order to classify the rated competence descriptions. In the first step, the whole competence range is divided into two sets. One set contains the *important (I)* ratings, which includes all *very important (VI)* and *rather important (RI)* ones, the other one the *unimportant (U)* ones, thus all *very unimportant (VU)* and *rather unimportant (RU)* ones accordingly Figure 3. However, a division into only two sets is too ague, as almost all of the aspects would be in the *important* set (45 of 47) (see Figure 2).

In a second step, the *important* set is further classified into three subsets (A-C) to gain a better distinguishability. The *unimportant* set is also divided accordingly (D-F) to have a symmetric scale. In total, six classes can now be distinguished, where class A is rated the most and class F the least important one. The class definitions can be described as follows:

A: The majority of all experts rated this aspect as *very important.* (VI $>$ 50%)

B: The majority of all experts rated this aspect as *important.* The number of *very important* ratings is greater than the number *unimportant* ratings. Class A should not be a subset of Class B. (I $>$ 50%, VI $>$ U, A $\not\subseteq$ B)

C: The majority of all experts rated this aspect as *important.* The number of *unimportant* votes is greater or equal to the number of *very important* ratings. (I $>$ 50%, VI $\leq$ U)

D: 50% or more of all experts rated this aspect as *unimportant.* The number of *important* ratings is larger than the number *very unimportant* ratings. (U $\geq$ 50%, I $>$ VU)

E: 50% or more of all experts rated this aspect as *unimportant.* The number of *very unimportant* ratings is larger or equal than the number of *important* ratings. Class F should not be a subset of class E. (U $\geq$ 50%, I $\leq$ VU, F $\not\subseteq$ E)

F: The majority of all experts rated this aspect as *very unimportant.* (VU $>$ 50%)

Afterwards, the different aspects have been classified as shown in Figure 3. The *Analysis & Classification* column has two types of entries. The one written in black coloured font describes in which class the majority of the descriptions of a dimension has been placed. The white coloured font is used on those cases, where a specific description does not fit

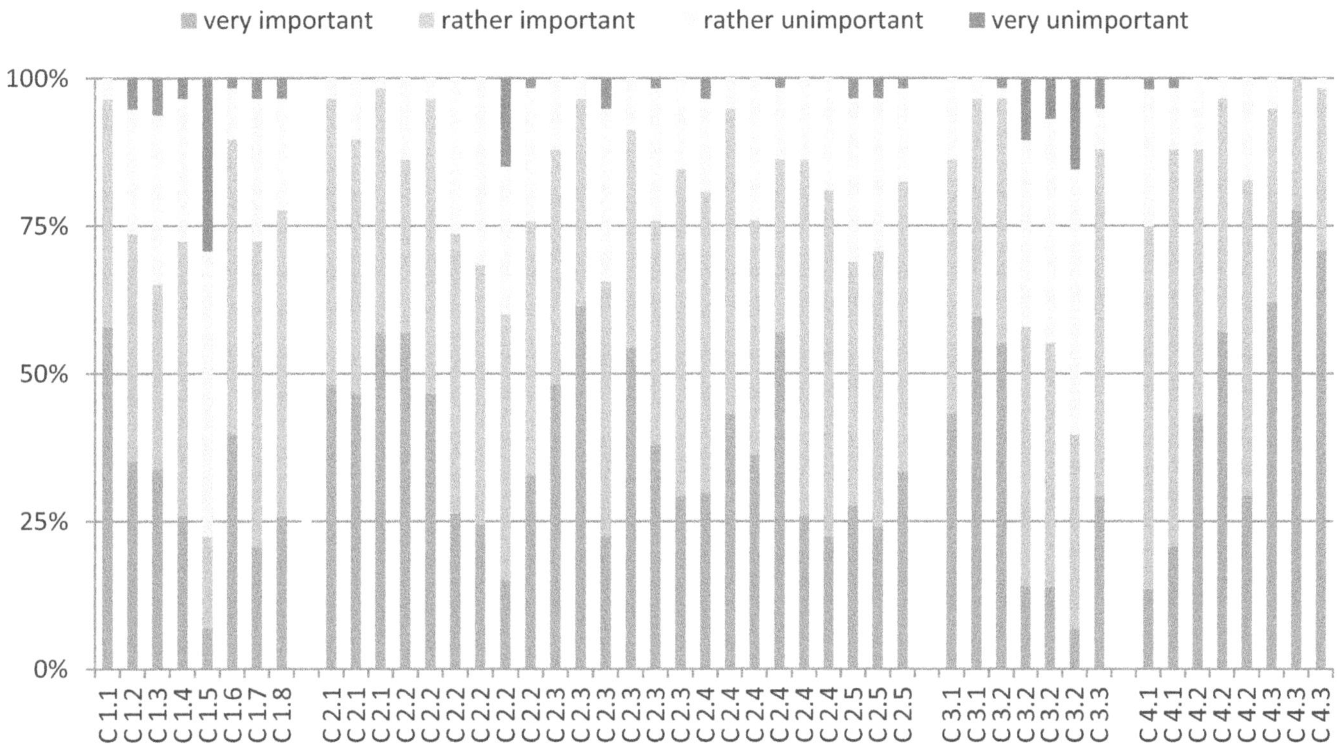

Figure 2: First results

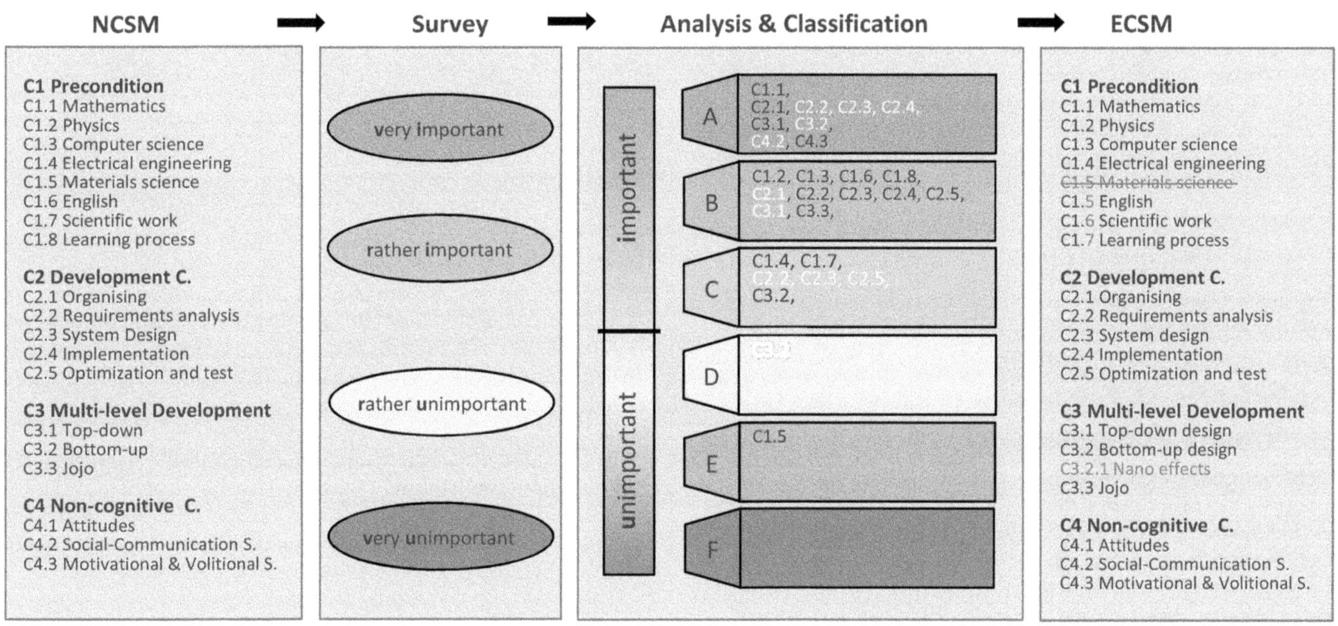

Figure 3: From a NCSM to an ECSM

into the same class as its siblings from the same subdimension. For example, in average the descriptions of dimension C2.1 are placed in class A. However, according to our classification scheme, some descriptions from C2.1 have to be put in class B. The classification of competencies in the various categories must not be seen absolutely, because in some cases, the distinction between two categories is very small.

In almost all cases, all aspects of a subdimension were rated similarly well. An exception for the summary of subdimensions is C3.2 *bottom-up design*. This one was initially described by four aspects (see Table 1). After applying our categorisation rules, we noticed that aspect one was clearly better voted than the other three. The average sub-dimension C3.2 (black) is in class C, but some aspects are also in class A and class D. Because of that C3.2 is the only subdimension which includes aspects which are not in directly adjacent classes.

Table 1: Aspects of sub dimmension 3.2

Classification of C3.2	VI	RI	RU	VU	Cl.
C3.2 Bottom-Up-Design	22,5	39,8	29,0	8,7	C
C3.2	55,2	41,4	1,7	1,7	A
They have the ability to understand the relationship between hardware concepts and the impact on the software, to create and apply efficient programs as well as building a computer of basic components					
C3.2	14,0	43,9	31,6	10,5	C
They have the ability to understand the problems in dependability of nanoelectronic devices					
C3.2	13,8	41,3	39,0	6,9	C
They can understand and apply self-organising principles, e.g., self-adaptivity by reconfiguration to make nanoelectronic systems more reliable					
C3.2	6,9	32,8	44,8	15,5	D
They understand the physical first principles of new basic nano assembly parts for the IT, like nano tubes, nano crossbars or quantum cellular automata					

The reason for this is likely to be the thematic orientation towards nano effects within almost all aspects. The first aspect, however, describes the more general subdimension. Because of that we decided to add a further subdimension C3.2.1 to our ECSM which includes nano related design topics.

As already mentioned before (see Figures 2 and 3) almost all sub dimensions were rated by most experts as *important*. Only the subdimension C1.5 *material science* was estimated to be *unimportant* by 75% of all experts. Due to the low experts rating in case of C1.5, we decided to exclude the subdimension from the ECSM.

Apart from these two peculiarities the results of the survey shows that the experts consider the NSCM as important. The resulting ECSM is shown on the right side of Figure 3 with the changes highlighted in dark-red font.

Twelve competence descriptions are included in class A, when the described categorization algorithm is applied (see Table 2). The highest important rated descriptions are the non-cognitive ones from competence dimension C4. In contrast, the majority of A-rated competence descriptions are in competence dimension C2, which for example, contains approaches to development organisation as well as describing design circuits in description languages.

4. COURSE DESIGN

In this section, we first describe which competences should be supported in our new internship, and then introduce the subject of the practical course as well as the connections to the competence classes.

4.1 Competence selection

The results gained from our experts survey can be used to support competence oriented teaching in the field of embedded systems engineering. Thus, our new practical course design takes these results into account and supports the most important rated competencies. At this time, all classes from *class B* downwards are not considered for the internship.

The strict separation of all competencies is not possible in each case. This is due to the definition of competence dimensions. Each dimension clusters subdimensions and competencies which logically belong to each other. According to this, for the categorization, it is not important if some dimensions overlap, take example, the A-rated competence C2.2:

> *They know the special constraints of the design of embedded systems*

However, developing competencies in the field of requirements and constraints for designs of embedded systems influence multi-level-development competencies as well (e.g., *C3.3 - Yoyo design*, rated as class B).

The second category (*class B*) is obviously not as important as *class A*, but still includes the rather important ones. We will combine competencies from category A and B to support learners by getting a deeper understanding of the whole topic whenever synergies are possible.

4.2 Course concept

As one can see in Table 2, the highest rated competence dimension is C4. In addition, the most important rated competencies are contained in this dimension, too. Some of them exceeds 98 %, when adding very and rather important to one scale. Therefore almost no expert considered the non-cognitive competencies as unimportant.

In contrast, to other competence dimensions, motivational skills cannot be taught, but they can be supported. Doing so, one requirement for our new course is a task which on one side is a topic in today's technical industry and on the other side has strong relations to students' everyday life.

To encourage the students' motivation, our first tasks includes the programming of a smartphone application for the Android operating system[2]. On the one hand, this life-world related topic of embedded systems' development motivates students, e.g. due to the direct results on the screen or the

[2]http://www.android.com/

Table 2: All class A aspects of the ECSM

Class A competencies	VI	RI	RU	VU
C1.1	57,9	38,6	3,5	0
Mathematics				
C2.1	56,9	41,4	1,7	0
They learn goal-orientated and structured proceeding for design				
C2.2	56,9	29,3	13,8	0
They know the special constraints of the design of embedded systems				
C2.3	61,4	35,1	3,5	0
They gain elementary knowledge and basic comprehension about the most important technologies and about the most important concepts that are needed for design and analysis of computer-assisted systems				
C2.3	54,4	36,8	8,7	0
They understand the assembly and the function of all important basic circuits and computer units				
C2.4	56,9	29,3	12,7	1,7
They can design circuits using a description language				
C3.1	59,7	36,9	3,5	0
They learn the acquaintance of the programming language C and its interplay with the hardware. At the same time basic functionalities and the interplay of basic components of an operating systems, with the focal point on efficient resource management, are procured				
C3.2	55,2	41,4	1,7	1,7
They have the ability to understand the relationship between hardware concepts and the impact on the software, to create and apply efficient programs as well as building a computer of basic components				
C4.2	56,9	39,7	3,4	0
They can communicate competently in a professional field with engineers and eletrical engineering technicians as users of computer science				
C4.3	62,1	32,8	5,2	0
They have the openness for new ideas/requirements				
C4.3	77,6	22,4	3,5	0
They show willingness to learn				
C4.3	70,7	27,6	1,7	0
They show willingness for commitments				

possible solutions in their private life. On the other hand, programming smartphones affects many embedded systems topics like reading sensors, driving actuators and considering limited resources.

It can be assumed that a majority of the computer science students own an Android-based or comparable smartphone. Nevertheless, to ensure a smooth entry to the laboratory experiments, we will provide additional smartphones as well as tutorials and sample code. Furthermore we will provide a sensor-/actuator simulation to permit training at home without direct access to a smarthphone. The smartphone part of our new course will not be very extensive because the implementation of simple programs with the Java language is one of the previously achieved competencies (*C1.3 Computer Science*).

The second component of our new course design has to be relevant in case of EMNS requirements and implementation. Whereas the Android programming part focuses towards software skills with some embedded specific issues, this one aims to convey technical aspects. The access to sensors/actuators is highly abstracted in smartphones and not representative for e.g., reactive EMNS, which interact with sensors and actuators on a much lower and hardware-related level. Other course designers reported that students do understand the functional principle of those units, but in most cases, they are not able to implement a given task (e.g., [2, p. 168]). Often a trial-and-error strategy is applied by the students. In practice, this strategy is not appropriate due to costs, hardware functionalities as well as complexity also. This can be seen in Table 2 where the experts rated "*... goal-oriented and structured proceeding for design*" as one of the most important competencies. Nevertheless, some particularities of typical sensors/actuators should be covered.

The main project in our new course design is a miniature home automation, which consists of three parts. First, an embedded system with attached components like brightness or temperature sensors and the corresponding actuators like LEDs and heating elements. First experiments are currently executed with an microcontroller based and an FPGA based evaluation kit. The second part is an Android smartphone with a simple user interface for setting nominal values like room temperature or reading sensor data like current power consumption. The third component is related to the communication of the embedded system and the smartphone as they will communicate over bluetooth.

The students do not need to implement all functionality in the three areas by themselfes. For example, a large part of the bluetooth functionality will be available in the form of callable functions, which can be directly used by the students. The same is true for the Android part that is initially supposed to support the motivation and identification with at least one part of the project, as well as the ease of the introduction.

Nevertheless, the project is still too huge for one student alone. To encourage communication among the students and to promote team work, we plan to design the internship with small groups, each focussing on a specific couple of sensors and actuators. At the end of the internship, every set of sensors and actuators can be tested with every embedded system to check the quality of the implementation. The students have to communicate with different groups to provide an appropriate interchangeability.

In addition, to the competence development, the presented

concepts must be proofed in regards of costs and applicability, too. This implies the costs of equipment and staff as well as the necessary support per student or group.

5. CONCLUSION

The competence structure model, which we had originally derived in a normative way, was almost fully confirmed by our expert surveys. There were no significant differences between the two professorial expert groups (universities and universities of applied sciences). Most competence dimensions and subdimensions were rated predominantly important. Nevertheless, slight adjustments were made to the NCSM. *Material science (C1.5)* was excluded due to the unimportant ratings. In addition, the subdimension *Bottom-Up-Design* was further subdivided into the rather general competencies and the exclusive nano related competencies.

The conceptual design of the new practical course is based on the competence structure model and the classification (A-F). Hence, the most important rated competencies were addressed first and in particular. The less important the competencies were rated, the later they will be considered within course and task design. Nevertheless, no strict separation of competencies is often possible so that the less important rated competencies are included casually.

Since the non-cognitive competencies were rated as the most important ones, we will take motivational and social-communicative aspects particularly into account.

6. FURTHER WORK

The initial conceptual design of the new practical course will be stated more precisely in the next research step. Therefore, every educational unit in the laboratory will be checked for its relation to the competencies of the ECSM. At the moment, we focus on all competencies assigned to *class A* which represent the most important competencies for future developers of EMNS. Subsequently, we will integrate as many tasks as possible considering *class B*. Tasks supporting the development of *class C* competencies are not disclosed because of their often strong connections to the other ones. However, they will not be particularly addressed in the course concept nor in the course evaluation.

In a further research step, the designed course and its tasks will be evaluated via direct observation. Each experiment will also be analyzed by video recordings that document possible learning difficulties. With the method of thinking aloud, a review of suspected barriers will be made. Furthermore, new tasks, transferred from the system-oriented didactics will be checked for the efficiency of their competence development.

7. ACKNOWLEDGMENT

The KOMINA project is promoted by the German Research Foundation (DFG).

8. REFERENCES

[1] ACM/IEEECS, editor. *Computer Science Curriculum 2008: An Interim Revision of CS 2001*. 2008.

[2] K. Berns. *Eingebettete Systeme*. Studium. Vieweg + Teubner, Wiesbaden, 1 edition, 2010.

[3] C. Brabrand. Constructive alignment for teaching model-based design for concurrency. In K. Jensen, W. M. P. Aalst, and J. Billington, editors, *Lecture Notes in Computer Science*, pages 1–18. Springer Berlin Heidelberg, Berlin, Heidelberg, 2008.

[4] CE2004, editor. *Curriculum Guidelines for Undergraduate Degree Programs in Computer Engineering: A Report in the Computing Curricula Series*. 2004.

[5] GI, editor. *Curriculum Technische Informatik in Bachelor- und Masterstudiengängen Informatik: Empfehlung der Gesellschaft für Informatik e. V.* Gesellschaft für Informatik e. V., Bonn, 2011.

[6] GRF, editor. *Competence Models for Assessing Individual Learning Outcomes and Evaluating Educational Processes: Priority Research Program*. Berlin, 2007-2013.

[7] M. Grimheden and M. Törngren. What is embedded systems and how should it be taught?—results from a didactic analysis. *ACM Transactions on Embedded Computing Systems*, 4(3):633–651, 2005.

[8] S. Jaschke, S. Schubert, A. Schäfer, R. Brück, B. Kleinert, H. Schmidt, and D. Fey. Competence research: Teaching embedded micro/nano systems. In J. Jackson, P. Marwedel, and K. Ricks, editors, *Workshop on Embedded Systems Education*, Taipei, Taiwan, 2010. ACM.

[9] J. Magenheim, W. Nelles, T. Rhode, N. Schaper, S. Schubert, and P. Stechert. Competencies for informatics systems and modeling: Results of qualitative content analysis of expert interviews. In *IEEE EDUCON 2010 Conference*, pages 513–521. IEEE, 2010.

[10] P. Marwedel. *Embedded System Design: Embedded Systems Foundations of Cyber-Physical Systems*. Embedded Systems. Springer Science+Business Media B.V, Dordrecht, 2011.

[11] H. Mitsui, K. Hidetoshi, S. Endo, and H. Koizumi. A student experiment method for learning the basics of embedded software development including hw/sw co-design. In *22nd International Conference on Advanced Information Networking and Applications - Workshops, 2008*, pages 31–37. IEEE, 2008.

[12] A. Schäfer, R. Brück, S. Jaschke, S. Schubert, D. Fey, B. Kleinert, and H. Schmidt. A normative competence structure model for embedded micro- and nanosystems development. In *Proceedings of the 16th annual joint conference on Innovation and technology in computer science education - ITiCSE '11*, page 375. ACM Press, 2011.

[13] J. Sztipanovits, G. Biswas, K. Frampton, A. Gokhale, L. Howard, G. Karsai, T. J. Koo, X. Koutsoukos, and D. C. Schmidt. Introducing embedded software and systems education and advanced learning technology in an engineering curriculum. *ACM Transactions on Embedded Computing Systems*, 4(3):549–568, 2005.

[14] W. Wolf and J. Madsen. Embedded systems education for the future. *Proceedings of the IEEE*, 88(1):23–30, 2000.

Supporting Operating Systems Projects using the μMPS2 Hardware Simulator

Michael Goldweber
Xavier University
mikeyg@cs.xu.edu

Renzo Davoli
Università di Bologna
renzo@cs.unibo.it

Tomislav Jonjic
Università di Bologna
tjonjic@gmail.com

ABSTRACT

We live in a multicore world. In spite of this observation, none of the available system emulators designed for undergraduate education and for use in operating systems courses support multiprocessors. This paper presents μMPS2, a pedagogically undergraduate-appropriate multiprocessor system emulator/architecture. Using μMPS2 educators now have the ability to structure realistic operating system projects to maximize student exposure to the ubiquitous parallelism and concurrency present in current computing devices.

Categories and Subject Descriptors

K.3.2 [**Computer and Information Science Education**]: [Computer Science Education]

General Terms

Design, Experimentation

Keywords

Operating Systems, Multiprocessors, Emulation

1. INTRODUCTION

The study of operating systems is a standard component of virtually all undergraduate computer science programs. Given the concurrency that operating systems both implement and exhibit, and the complexity they both hide and possess, the study of operating systems, which usually happens towards the end of an undergraduate curriculum, often provides a capstone-like experience[9]. Adopting the taxonomy proposed by Pfaff, et. al.[14], the projects that support the operating systems course can be characterized by two orthogonal axes: concrete vs abstract, and internal vs external. Projects with an external perspective take the role of the programmer using an OS's API, while those projects which consider the role of the operating system designer/writer are ones with an internal perspective. Furthermore, projects implementing the abstract perspective may include partial implementations and/or simulation exercises. Concrete projects focus on the design and implementation of realistic artifacts.

We advocate for the concrete/internal perspective. Clearly, studying, designing and finally implementing key OS structures allow students to attain a deeper understanding than those who simply study them abstractly. Similarly, projects whose components interconnect (e.g. term-long multi-phase implementation projects) are superior to those that do not. It is the interconnectedness of an operating system's complex concurrent components that make OS's such interesting artifacts to study. While one could design a concrete/internal operating system project for real bare hardware, such approaches are most often supported by a machine, or system emulator with which students experiment with.

Goldweber, et. al. in [7], and Anderson and Nguyen in [2] both provide enumerations of the available undergraduate-education focused hardware/system emulators available for use. Newer systems/projects that have been developed since these two surveys appeared include Pintos[14], BabyOS[10], Xv6[4], in addition to a couple of unnamed ones[8, 13]. Each system has its own particular focus. For example BabyOS[10] endeavors to reflect the properties of embedded systems. Pintos[14] runs on real (or emulated) x86 hardware and comes bundled with a bootable kernel that students first read and then build upon. μMPS[7] provides a simplified MIPS-like system emulator upon which students write a complete operating system (e.g. Kaya) from scratch. One common attribute among all these systems is that the system being emulated or built upon is a uniprocessor system.

Today's machine architectures are all shared memory multicore processors, while all of the undergraduate-education focused hardware/system emulators are based on uniprocessor architectures. Given the importance of educating students to maximize their leveraging of the concurrency and parallelism offered by multiprocessor and/or multicore systems[1, 3, 5, 15] and the capstone nature of the operating systems course and its employment of hardware/system emulators, there is a disconnect between practice and desired outcomes. μMPS2 is a new undergraduate-education focused hardware/system emulator that supports up to sixteen processors all sharing the same memory and a robust set of peripherals.

The remainder of this paper is organized as follows. Section 2 contains a thorough description of the μMPS2 system emulator. Section 3 discusses some of the μMPS2-based

ITiCSE'12, July 3–5, 2012, Haifa, Israel.

projects one might employ. Finally, our conclusions are presented in Section 4.

2. THE μMPS2 EMULATOR

2.1 The μMPS Emulator

The μMPS system emulator[7] was created expressly to support undergraduate education. It was a direct outcome of the MPS system emulator[11]. The MPS system emulator was designed to faithfully emulate the architecture of the MIPS R3000. Not surprisingly, it turned out that MPS, due to the complexity of MIPS' virtual memory management was, as determined via class testing, unsuitable for undergraduates. In the MIPS architecture, virtual memory is always on, all address translation is performed through a small fixed size TLB, and hence even the OS maintained page tables for itself and user processes are kept in virtual memory. Furthermore, the physical address space for the kernel and its data structures are permanently disjoint from its virtual address space. While these RISC-design features allow for an extremely fast CPU they complicate undergraduate students' understanding; in particular with the circularity of an OS always running with VM on and whose page tables are kept in virtual memory.

A design goal of μMPS was to implement a virtual memory management subsystem that more closely matched the conceptual description found in the current introductory OS texts of the day[12, 16, 17]. More specifically:

- A VM bit was introduced into the **STATUS** control register allowing for address translation to be turned on and off.
- Formal segment table and page table formats were introduced.
- If the TLB does not contain the appropriate entry, μMPS, via the appropriate segment and page tables locates the missing entry and inserts it into the TLB. That is, TLB-Refill events are handled by the system. This functionality is performed by the supplied system ROM code and not by the system emulator. Since the ROM code can be changed, this affords the opportunity for advanced projects in addition to modeling the practice of altering/updating system behavior via ROM updates versus actual hardware changes.
- All of the segment and page tables, both for the kernel and for user processes are stored in permanent physical locations. This eliminates the circularity of having the OS data structures for supporting virtual memory being kept in (and hence managed by the) virtual memory.
- The cross compiler that accompanies μMPS compiles the student OS to reside in a different segment than the one the user programs are compiled to reside in.
- The number of segments was reduced to three with one of these segments (*ksegOS*) reserved for kernel use only.
- The size of the TLB was made user configurable.
- Two new TLB-Mgmt. exceptions were introduced:
  - Bad-PTE: For when a incorrectly formed page table is discovered.
  - PTE-MISS: For when a (well-formed) page table is searched unsuccessfully for a given entry.
- The virtual address space of *ksegOS* overlaps in a one-to-one fashion the physical address space of the installed RAM. This allows for the construction of a page table for *ksegOS* such that a virtual address within this segment maps to a physical address that is identical to the virtual address one started with. Note; this overlap may be partial or full depending on the amount of installed RAM.

Additionally, μMPS also simplified exception and interrupt handling. In the MPS architecture, when an interrupt or exception is raised, the hardware stores off the **PC**, performs two stack pushes within the **STATUS** register and loads the **PC** with a computed exception vector address. In μMPS instead of the minimal context switch a MIPS machine would perform, the complete processor state is atomically stored and a new one loaded. As with TLB-Refill events, the μMPS emulator performs as a MIPS machine would, while the complete processor state store/load-operation is completed via the supplied ROM code.

Outside of these simplifications of the virtual memory management subsystem and interrupt/exception handling, μMPS is virtually identical to the MPS emulator upon which it is based. This includes:

- Support for up to eight memory-mapped DMA disk and eight memory-mapped DMA tape devices.
- Support for up to eight memory-mapped printers and eight read/write capable terminal devices.
- Support for up to eight memory-mapped ethernet network devices.
- A sophisticated development, user interface, testing, and debugging environment.

While the MIPS architecture was designed to achieve super fast operation, μMPS was designed to maximize undergraduate student understanding – something we call the μMPS philosophy. By providing a realistic-like architecture that more closely matches the conceptual architectures described in popular operating system textbooks, one maximizes the potential that undergraduates in a single term can successfully write a complete (though sparse) operating system. The Kaya operating system[6, 7] is one such operating system design that runs on the μMPS system. Kaya, which undergraduates at universities all over the world have been successfully implementing since its publication in 2004, supports up to eight, potentially cooperating, concurrently running processes executing with virtual memory.

2.2 The μMPS2 Emulator

μMPS2 extends the μMPS philosophy to a multiprocessor environment. Furthermore μMPS2 is fully backward compatible with μMPS: Any operating system that runs on μMPS will run unaltered on μMPS2 when running in single processor mode (the default).

At boot time, on a μMPS2 machine, only a single processor, processor 0, is started/running. To boot additional processors, processor 0 must explicitly start up another processor. Except for processor 0, which is automatically started at boot time, a processor begins execution only when explicitly commanded to by another processor.

As with TLB-Refill events, and exception/interrupt handling in μMPS, there is a "raw" action performed by the μMPS2 emulator for processor startup, in addition to a simplifying ROM service that closely resembles the conceptual understanding that undergraduates have regarding processor startup.

For example, in μMPS2 there are three relevant machine registers for processor startup: **ResetCPU**, **BootPC**, and **BootSP**. One loads **BootPC** and **BootSP** with initial values for the processor's **PC** and **SP** registers. The processor begins execution when the processor's ID is written into the **ResetCPU** register. Other control registers have their startup default values. Furthermore, this "raw" processor startup procedure does not update the ROM tables which also needs to be done for correct ROM code execution. Hence, μMPS2 also contains the ROM service **InitCPU** which not only accomplishes the above, but also allows one to specify a complete processor start state in addition to performing all the necessary updates to the ROM tables.[1]

μMPS2 extends μMPS in the following ways.

- Support for up to sixteen processors, all sharing the same peripheral devices and primary memory.
- In addition to the system-wide Interval Timer and Time of Day Clock, each processor has its own local timer. Processor local timers behave similarly to the system-wide Interval Timer; each local timer is automatically decremented by one every clock cycle. Each timer will generate an interrupt when it makes the 0x0000.0000 $\Rightarrow$ 0xFFFF.FFFF transition. Furthermore, unlike the system-wide Interval Timer, processor local timers can be disabled/enabled via a Timer Enable bit in the **STATUS** register.
- Processor i can both **HALT** and **RESET** (i.e. restart) processor j.
- Processors now support an *IDLE* (or *WAIT*) state. A processor in a *WAIT* state is not executing instructions, but unlike a **HALT**ed CPU, maintains its state. Processors exit this state by either receiving an interrupt or by receiving a **RESET** command. While processor i can **HALT** processor j, a processor wishing to be idled must itself execute a **WAIT** instruction.
- On a device by device basis, interrupts can be routed to a processor based on either a static or a dynamic interrupt routing mechanism. All interrupts are always routed to at most a single processor.
  - Static Interrupt Routing: All interrupts from a specified device are always routed to an operating system designated processor.
  - Dynamic Interrupt Routing: All interrupts from a specified device are routed to the processor out of an operating system designated set of processors currently executing the lowest priority task. Each processor has a **Task Priority Register** which needs to be set periodically by the operating system - say at process dispatch time.
- Support for inter-processor interrupts (IPIs). An IPI represents an inter-processor signaling mechanism used by a processor to request the attention of another processor. IPI's are commonly used by operating systems for issuing rescheduling requests, maintaining TLB consistency, and any other task which requires one processor to request the attention of another.
  - Each IPI can carry an arbitrary 8-bit data field (message). This feature is provided solely for software convenience and has no side effects on the IPI delivery subsystem.
  - Processor i can signal multiple processors simultaneously, sending each processor the same message.
  - Multiple IPIâĂŹs may be pending at the same time for a given processor.
  - Only one pending IPI may be acknowledged at a time.
  - There is no built-in delivery status notification mechanism.
  - There is a limit of one pending IPI per originating processor. For example, if processor i IPI signaled processor j, processor i cannot IPI signal processor j again until after processor j has acknowledged the first IPI from processor i. IPI signal requests that violate this limit are ignored.
  - μMPS2 maintains IPI delivery order. IPI messages are always retrieved in the order they were received by the processor interface.
- Support for an atomic **COMPARE-and-SWAP** instruction.

One can observe that not only does μMPS2 implement a complete and full functioning multiprocessor environment, but it does so preserving the μMPS philosophy. This is particularly evident with the

- **InitCPU** command described above.
- **WAIT** (for event) command. RISC processors typically do not support wait-states. Instead, OS programmers must load a busy-wait processor state –an interrupt enabled, CPU wasting infinite loop that accomplishes nothing while waiting for an event to occur.
- **COMPARE-and-SWAP** command. RISC machines in general, including the MIPS architecture, achieve a lock-free atomic read-modify-write operation via the **Load-Link** and **Store-Condition** pair of instructions. While **COMPARE-and-SWAP** is functionally equivalent to the **LL/SC** pair, it is far simpler for students to both understand and correctly use.

[1] Since the ROM code atomically stores the complete processor state when an exception/interrupt is raised, each processor needs to have a disjoint exception/interrupt vector registered with the ROM code. The **InitCPU** command is parameterized to allow the caller to specify the processor ID to be started, its initial processor state, and the address of its exception/interrupt vector.

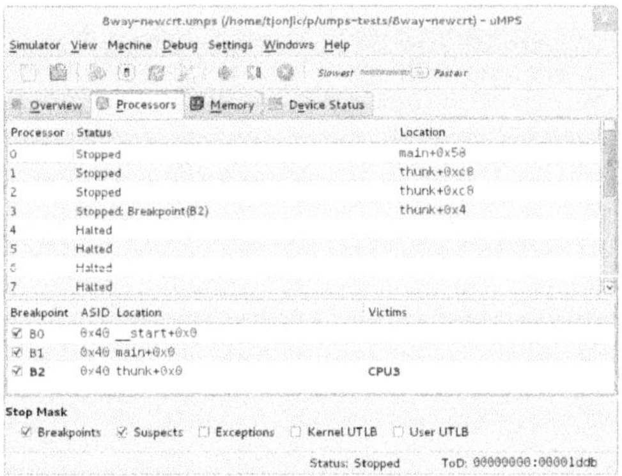

Figure 1: Primary Processor View Window Tab

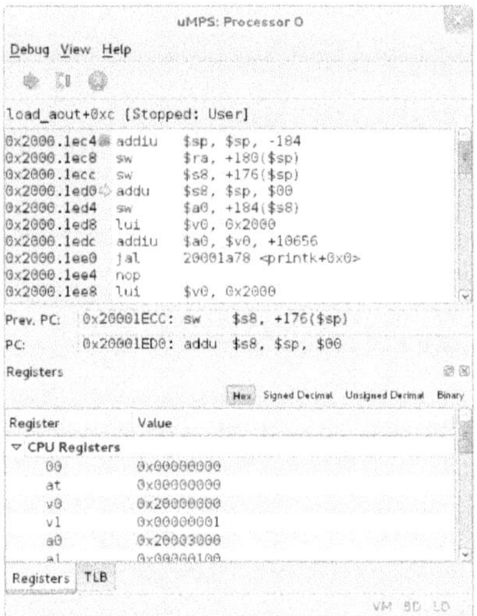

Figure 2: Individual Processor Window

2.3 User Interface

An important under-the-hood improvement between μMPS and μMPS2 was the user interface. Technical details notwithstanding, without a sufficient user interface, the system will not be used. While it is impossible to satisfactorily quantify the quality of the user interface, after two semesters of class testing μMPS2 and its user interface at two different institutions, not a single complaint has been registered. In particular, the user interface is set up to support a wide range of debugging styles/approaches.

The GUI from μMPS was based on the Tcl/Tk libraries. The GUI for μMPS2 is based on quicktime. Not only does this provide a better "look and feel," but provides superior performance along with a greater degree of portability. Figures 1–4 present some screen shots of the user interface.

As is typical of machine debuggers, breakpoints can be set in a variety of ways: Function entry (step in & step over), whenever an arbitrary memory location is read/written, TLB events, etc. Particular consideration was given to the design and functionality of the debugger. Up until the operating system course, students are often successful debugging via side effects – sprinkle the code full of print statements. This approach is clearly unsuitable for debugging a scheduler or a pager; hence the need for a top quality debugging facility. An oft-heard comment from students after a μMPS/μMPS2-based course was that it was in this course that they finally learned how to debug.

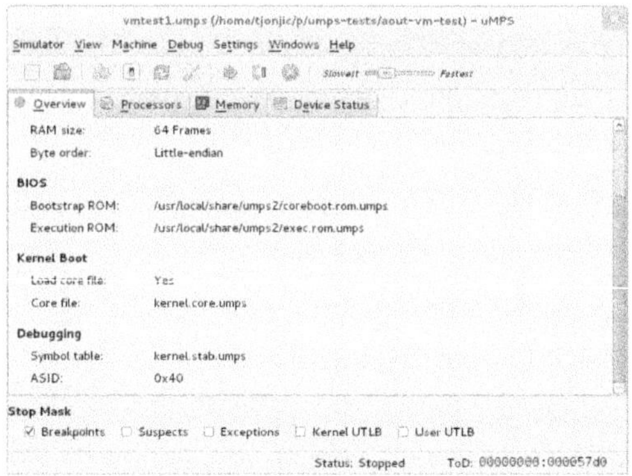

Figure 3: Primary GUI Window Tab

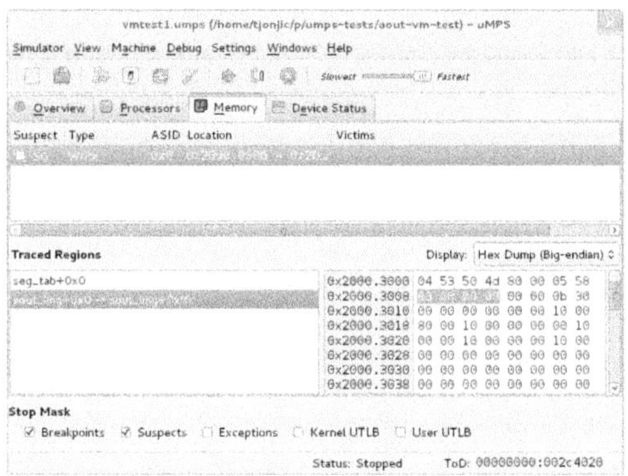

Figure 4: Memory View Window Tab

3. μMPS2 PROJECTS

μMPS2 is 100% backward compatible with μMPS. This implies that ALL projects designed for μMPS (e.g. Kaya) will work unchanged on μMPS2. This permits a smooth upgrade path for the existing μMPS user base.

There are different kinds of projects for kernels exploiting the multi-core architecture of μMPS2. The following list presents some options in increasing order of complexity.

- Probably the easiest operating system project to exploit μMPS2's multiprocessor support would be a non-symmetric operating system. With this approach, all interrupt handling is performed by a single processor. (Exception handling is always performed by each individual processor.) A project of this nature, though resulting in a rather inefficient operating system, still requires the student to manage several of the basic synchronization problems associated with multiprocessor systems. (e.g. spinlocks)

- It is also possible to create a project for an SMP kernel. Such projects would be more difficult since an SMP kernel requires more complex interactions among the processors. Unlike a non-symmetric operating system, an SMP operating system would require the use of inter-processor interrupts (IPIs).

- One simple implementation strategy for an SMP kernel is based on the "big kernel lock" approach: every time any processor begins to run kernel code, it enters a spinlock controlled mutex. This *single-threads* the kernel, guaranteeing that at most one processor is executing kernel code at any point in time.
- A more sophisticated SMP student project option would be to only protect (small) portions of the kernel with specific spinlocks. This not only increases the level of parallelism of the system, but also the complexity of the project, especially in its debugging phase.

Test programs designed for the Kernel and VM/IO layers of Kaya (named "Phase 2" and "Phase 3") can also run on multicore kernels. Furthermore, one might design, or more appropriately ask students to design, additional specific test programs whose purpose is not to validate kernel correctness, but to measure kernel effectiveness.

Students, after a successful implementation, can test the scalability of their kernels: Run the same workload of processes using differing numbers of processors. The workload mix can also be varied: I/O bound jobs only, CPU intensive jobs only, and mixed type job loads. Hopefully, such testing will expose students to the subtleties of multiprocessor efficiencies and how which kind of workload is more affected by each design choice.

While μMPS2 is designed primarily for undergraduate use, μMPS2, more than μMPS is capable of supporting advanced operating system projects. This can be either a second semester operating system course/project, master's level courses, or even a master's level thesis dissertation.

μMPS, μMPS2, and Kaya are all products of the Virtual Square Lab. While μMPS supports a plethora of operating system projects, only one is from the Virtual Square Lab – the Kaya project. This is possible because the emulator is designed to be a courseware tool independent of any project designed to run on it. μMPS2 was designed with the same goal in mind – it is an independent courseware tool. We anticipate, that as with μMPS there will eventually be a plethora of projects designed to run on μMPS2. One such project is Kaya$_n$, which is currently under development at the Virtual Square Lab.

4. CONCLUSIONS

The reality is, we now live in a multicore world. It appears that even mobile devices are soon to support multicore CPUs. Currently, none of the available undergraduate-education focused hardware/system emulators support multiprocessors. This paper presents μMPS2, a multiprocessor extension to the μMPS system emulator.

Like μMPS, μMPS2 is designed, not to achieve super fast throughput, nor for a 100% authentic emulation of an existing real hardware system, but to achieve the greatest degree of undergraduate student mastery. We call this the μMPS philosophy – to design the system emulator to more closely represent the uncluttered/abstract hardware presented in undergraduate texts rather than high speed achieving real systems. Towards that end, μMPS2 supports many pedagogically justified *simplifications*. Some of these include the **WAIT**, **COMPARE-and-SWAP**, and **InitCPU** commands, both static and dynamic interrupt routing and a simplified inter-processor interrupt model.

It is imperative that computing curricula keep pace with the hardware advances of the real world. μMPS2, the first multiprocessor supporting system emulator designed specifically for undergraduates is an important step in achieving this goal.

5. REFERENCES

[1] J. C. Adams, D. J. Ernst, T. Murphy, and A. Ortiz. Multicore education: pieces of the parallel puzzle. In *Proceedings of the 41st ACM technical symposium on Computer science education*, SIGCSE '10, pages 194–195, New York, NY, USA, 2010. ACM.

[2] C. L. Anderson and M. Nguyen. A survey of contemporary instructional operating systems for use in undergraduate courses. *J. Comput. Small Coll.*, 21:183–190, October 2005.

[3] R. Brown, E. Shoop, J. Adams, C. Clifton, M. Gardner, M. Haupt, and P. Hinsbeeck. Strategies for preparing computer science students for the multicore world. In *Proceedings of the 2010 ITiCSE working group reports*, ITiCSE-WGR '10, pages 97–115, New York, NY, USA, 2010. ACM.

[4] R. Cox, F. Kaashoek, and R. Morris. Xv6, a simple unix-like teaching operating system. http://pdos.csail.mit.edu/6.828/2011/xv6.html.

[5] D. J. Ernst and D. E. Stevenson. Concurrent CS: preparing students for a multicore world. In *Proceedings of the 13th annual conference on Innovation and technology in computer science education*, ITiCSE '08, pages 230–234, New York, NY, USA, 2008. ACM.

[6] M. Goldweber and R. Davoli. *Student Guide to the Kaya Operating System Guide*. LuLu Publishing, 2011.

[7] M. Goldweber, R. Davoli, and M. Morsiani. The kaya OS project and the μmps hardware emulator. In *Proceedings of the 10th Annual Conference on Innovation and Technology in Computer Science Education ITiCSE '05*, 2005.

[8] J. C. Guzmán and P. O. Bobbie. Hands-on operating systems made easy. *J. Comput. Small Coll.*, 22:145–151, April 2007.

[9] Joint IEEE Computer Society/ACM Task Force on Computing Curricula. Computing curricula 2001: Computer science - final report, 2001.

[10] H. Liu, X. Chen, and Y. Gong. Babyos: a fresh start. In *Proceedings of the 38th SIGCSE technical symposium on Computer science education*, SIGCSE '07, pages 566–570, New York, NY, USA, 2007. ACM.

[11] M. Morsiani and R. Davoli. Learning operating systems structure and implementation through the MPS computer system simulator. In *Proceedings of the 30th SIGCSE Technical Symposium on Computer Science Education*, 1999.

[12] G. Nutt. *Operating Systems: A Modern Perspective*. Addison Wesley, 3rd edition, 2004.

[13] T. Peterson and S. Crosby. Teaching os design through implementation of a simulated operating system. *J. Comput. Sci. Coll.*, 23:119–126, October 2007.

[14] B. Pfaff, A. Romano, and G. Back. The pintos instructional operating system kernel. In *Proceedings*

of the 40th SIGCSE Technical Symposium on Computer Science Education, 2009.

[15] S. Rivoire. A breadth-first course in multicore and manycore programming. In *Proceedings of the 41st ACM technical symposium on Computer science education*, SIGCSE '10, pages 214–218, New York, NY, USA, 2010. ACM.

[16] A. Silberschatz, P. Galvin, and G. Gagne. *Operating System Concepts*. Wiley, 6th edition, 2001.

[17] A. Tanenbaum. *Modern Operating Systems*. Prentice Hall, 2nd edition, 2001.

Integrating Data-Intensive Cloud Computing with Multicores and Clusters in an HPC Course

Atanas Radenski
Chapman University
Orange, CA 92869, USA
1-714-744-7657
radenski@chapman.edu

ABSTRACT
This paper presents the design and implementation of a new High-Performance Computing (HPC) course. This course amalgamates the emerging trend of *data-intensive cloud computing* with the dominant innovation of *multicore computing* and the important legacy of *cluster computing*. While others have reported the development of novel HPC courses, we are the first, to our knowledge, to report an upper-level HPC course that introduces the increasingly popular data-intensive cloud computing paradigm - integrally with the better-established shared memory and message-passing models. This course is entirely based on free digital reading resources and open source software. The course's design rationale and implementation - including the use of open source software tools and reading resources - may be beneficial for educators who need to design HPC courses or modules, and especially for those who wish to cover data-intensive cloud computing.

Categories and Subject Descriptors
K.3.2 **[Computers & Education]**: Computer and Information Science Education - *computer science education, curriculum*

General Terms
Human Factors, Performance.

Keywords
Cloud computing, MapReduce, OpenMP, MPI, AWS

1. RATIONALE
This section is intended to serve as a systematic justification for our choices of specific HPC course topics rather than as a mere introduction to such topics. The section evolves around the theme on legacy, innovation and future trends in computing, and the integration of technologies. This theme has guided us in the choice of specific contents in our HPC course.

1.1 Trends, Innovation, and Legacy in HPC
We are witnessing an acceleration of computer architectures' evolution towards significant hardware parallelism. The utilization of multicore processors has transformed off-the-shelf servers and desktops into symmetric multi-processors. Leading companies such as Google, Amazon, and Microsoft base much of their data processing on large multicore clusters; such companies also use their data centers to offer cloud computing services to external clients.

1.1.1 Current Trend: Data-Intensive Processing
Traditionally, HPC applications have been *compute-intensive*, involving relatively small amounts of data but demanding significant processor resources. In recent years, however, the HPC domain is being transformed with the proliferation of *data-intensive* applications, both business and scientific. Data-intensive applications involve large volumes of data, measured in terabytes and petabytes, with much of the processing time devoted to I/O and relatively simple data manipulation. Space exploration, meteorology, and the sciences in general are already known for very large data sets. Beyond the sciences, business data processing is challenged by an explosive growth of machine-generated, extra-large data sets in recent years [25]. Internet search indexing is a common example of a large text-data problem, and Google's MapReduce is a typical example of software platform specially designed to process large text-data. Apache's Hadoop is a free implementation of MapReduce capable of processing petabytes of data on extra-large clusters [4].

1.1.2 Current Trend: Cloud Computing
Traditionally, organizations have relied on dedicated computing infrastructures, such as organizations' own servers and networks. Recently, *cloud computing* has provided organizations with computer infrastructure, computing platforms, and software applications as services that are typically remote, on-demand, and on a pay-per-use basis. While cloud computing has become a buzzword in recent years, it is not a completely new concept: cloud computing can be viewed as a descendant of grid computing - enhanced with instant provisioning and utility computing [13].

Amazon Web Services (AWS) is the first – and currently the largest – publicly available cloud computing platform that provides virtual computing resources on a metered, pay-per-use basis [3]. Examples of available AWS pay-per-use services include Elastic MapReduce, and also multicore and GPGPU instances on AWS's Elastic Compute Cloud (EC2).

1.1.3 Dominant Innovation: Multicore Processors
While *multicore processors* have already become the de facto standard on desktops and servers, they are growing increasingly common on smaller devices such as laptops and smartphones. As of the writing of this paper, mainstream commercial processors are built with up to 8 physical cores that can potentially be expanded to 16 virtual processors by means of hyper-threading – as in Intel's Nehalem-EX Xeon processor, for example.

Meanwhile, Intel has already built a research prototype of its Polaris processor which incorporates 80 cores on a single chip. Popular software platforms that are used to develop shared memory parallel applications for multicore systems include lower-level thread libraries and higher-level threading abstractions such as OpenMP [10] and TBB [26].

Highly *specialized co-processors*, most notably general purpose graphics processing units (GPGPU) are also gaining popularity in upper-end installations. Modern GPGPUs "have ten or more cores, each optimized for SIMD data processing done via hundreds or thousands of simplified threads per core" [29]. Popular software platforms that are used to develop vector-parallel applications for GPGPU systems include Nvidia's CUDA [18] and the open-standard OpenCL [17].

1.1.4 Innovation in Legacy: Multicore Clusters
Heterogeneous clusters of tightly-coupled commodity grade computers have long been used as cost-effective HPC platforms. In recent years, the proliferation of relatively inexpensive multicore nodes has permitted the design of super-productive *multicore clusters*. Multicore clusters are used both in industry and in scientific computing. Google, for example, supports its Web-search applications with extra-large clusters of tens of thousands of commodity multicore PCs [6]. From a scientific computing perspective, the Top 500 list presents the five hundred most powerful computer systems, all ranked against the LINPACK Benchmark [30]. At present, cluster architectures dominate the Top 500 list: in November 2011, 82% of the Top 500 systems were clusters. The Japanese K computer, for example, currently number one on the Top 500 list, is a cluster of 88,128 8-core SPARC64 processors. While Intel processors are used by 77% of the Top 500 systems, some are boosted by GPGPU co-processors, such as the Chinese Intel-based Dawning (ranked fourth in November 2011). Hence, multi-core clusters are an important topic to be incorporated in an HPC course.

A variety of open source and proprietary software platforms are used to develop cluster applications. On scientific computing clusters in particular, MPI [19] implementations are used to develop message passing distributed applications. On multicore nodes, MPI can be combined with OpenMP and on nodes with GPGPU processors MPI can be combined with CUDA/OpenCL to build multi-level, hybrid parallel applications.

1.2 Curriculum Development in HPC
While parallel computing has been around for a long time, the recent proliferation of multi-cores has motivated educators to intensify and accelerate the expansion of parallel computing in the core CS/CE curriculum. While most curriculum developments have been focused on compute-intensive processing, this paper reveals curricular experience with the less understood data-intensive processing.

1.2.1 ACM / IEEE Curricula Recommendations
In 2008, an Interim Review Task Force commissioned by ACM and the IEEE Computer Society produced Computer Science Curriculum 2008 (CS2008), an Interim Revision of CS2001 [1]. CS2008 places a greater emphasis than CS2001 on the principles, techniques and technologies of concurrency. CS2008 now recommends a standalone course (outside of the 14 knowledge areas of CS2008) entirely dedicated to Parallel Computation, a course that should repackage relevant material from eight advanced courses from the older CS2001 [1].

In 2010, a working group from the IEEE Technical Committee on Parallel Processing (TCPP), NSF, ACM and other communities began work on a parallel and distributed computing proposal for computer science and computer engineering undergraduates. The current goal of this active working group is to propose a detailed set of topics to be included in the undergraduate CS curriculum, preferably by "changing the approach of teaching traditional topics to encompass the opportunities for thinking in parallel" [23]. A preliminary proposal was published in December 2010 [21], including a detailed set of recommendations – based on Bloom's classification – of parallel and distributed computing topics to include in the undergraduate curriculum.

1.2.2 Adapting Existing Curricula versus Dedicated Course Design
A number of educators prefer to adapt existing curricula by including parallelism modules in traditional courses [21, 8]. Garrity et al. [14] advocate the need for and the benefits from teaching MapReduce to beginning CS students; these authors promote a simplified user interface for the Apache Hadoop implementation of MapReduce. This interface is "designed so that novice programmers in an introductory CS courses can perform authentic data-intensive scalable computations using the programming language they are learning in their course." Brown et al. [8] review and advocate incremental approaches to parallel computing education though enhancements of established curricula with concurrency and parallelism. Rague [24] makes the case for a concepts-first approach, emphasizing conceptual design rather than implementation issues – an approach that seems suitable at the early introductory level. Ernst [12] proposes "extending the performance coverage of a traditional computer organization course to include an exploration of the quantitative characterization of a program's performance on a variety of architectural platforms, including modern GPU hardware".

Alternatively, some educators choose to develop new standalone courses dedicated to important aspects of parallel computing, rather than extend existing courses with parallelism [28, 22]. Cunha and Lourenço [9] advocate an "integrated approach" to concurrency, parallelism, and distributed computing in a breadth-first undergraduate course. Sadowski et al. [28] promote a breadth-first approach to teaching parallel and concurrent programming in a course that is oriented towards shared memory multi-threading. Ortiz [22] puts the emphasis on program correctness and promotes Erlang as a teaching environment for correct concurrent programming – an approach that is implemented by the author in a new course on concurrency-oriented programming. Apart from Erlang, the long list of languages that have been used to teach concurrency and parallelism includes Java, C#, Ada, Cilk, Occam, Concurrent ML, Concurrent Haskel, and others.

1.3 Our Approach: Integration of Established and Emerging Parallel Models
To address the growing importance of parallel computation, we developed a new upper-level course on High-Performance Computing (details of its implementation follow in section 2). With this course, we aimed to integrate both emerging and established knowledge and techniques in the areas of data-intensive cloud computing, multicore, and cluster computing.

Because multicore processors are becoming the norm in the realm of desktops and servers, so are multicore nodes in the realm of computer clusters. This is why we chose to systematically cover (i) multicore computing and (ii) computing in multicore clusters in our HPC course. The fast growing areas of (iii) data-intensive computing and (iv) cloud computing have yet to become common practice and to form well established bodies of knowledge which is why we chose to cover only *the intersection of the two areas*, namely *data-intensive cloud computing*. This approach permits the introduction of the fascinating novel areas of data-intensive computing and cloud computing with exciting opportunities for projects and self-study (as discussed later in section 2) while providing full coverage of multicore and clusters.

Parallel computation through *software parallelism* becomes essential to gaining sustained performance on current parallel systems and is therefore a necessary part of the computer scientist's and engineer's core knowledge. Thus, our HPC course evolves around several parallel programming models: (i) *shared memory* for multicore systems; (ii) *message passing* and also *hybrid* (i.e., message passing plus shared-memory) for multicore clusters; and (iii) *MapReduce* model for *data-intensive cloud computing*. While parallel programming models are central to our HPC course, the course also aims to provide ample background in parallel architectures, efficiency, algorithms, and applications.

2. IMPLEMENTATION

We have implemented this HPC at Chapman University (est. 1861), Orange, California. The university's mission is to provide personalized education of distinction, with programs and classes that are rigorous but small in size. The HPC course was first offered in the fall of 2010 as an elective in computer science and several other computing-related programs.

2.1 Parallelism Prerequisites

While our HPC course is intended to be self-contained as much as possible, it still relies on traditional courses for preliminary coverage of some aspects of concurrency and parallelism. In particular, the HPC course relies on the preliminary study of threads; these are covered in our Java-based CS2 course. Python and Java events are studied in our CS1 and CS2 courses correspondingly. Parallel processes are covered in our Operating Systems (OS) course, and selected types of parallelism – such as instruction-level parallelism for example - are studied in a Computer Architecture course. While CS1 and CS2 are required courses for all majors who may possibly enroll in the HPC course, OS and Computer Architecture courses are required only for Computer Science majors. This is why in our HPC course, OS and architecture knowledge is not strictly expected. Instead, the HPC course itself offers sufficient coverage of parallel architecture and OS concepts and techniques.

2.2 Course Content

In our upper-level undergraduate HPC course, students understand parallel computing architectures and learn parallel programming techniques through the study of the shared memory, message passing, and MapReduce parallel programming models. The course of study starts with the better understood and well-published shared-memory and message-passing models, and concludes with the emerging yet less documented domain of data intensive cloud computing.

This HPC course approaches parallel computation from the perspective of students who are comfortable with software design and development but are familiar with only a few basic parallel computing concepts, such as threads and processes. Accordingly, the course includes the following modules: (i) Parallel computing overview; (ii) Computing in Unix and C; (iii) Shared memory computing with OpenMP; (iv) Performance; (v) Message passing computing with MPI; (vi) Cloud computing with MapReduce; (vii) Course project.

Parallel computing overview. Students learn primary concepts and terminology, as related to parallelism in programs (data and task parallelism); parallelism in hardware; parallel architectures; performance measures. Students explore the Top 500 list of parallel computers.

Computing in Unix and C. In an intensive, tutorial-based approach, students review and practice Unix (including parallel processes) and C programming. We chose Unix because it is the de facto standard OS for HPC. We chose ANSI C as an implementation language for parallel programs because C is fast and available on virtually any platform, and because C can be used to implement parallelism with both OpenMP and MPI.

Shared memory computing with OpenMP. Students learn and practice shared memory computing using C and OpenMP. We chose OpenMP because (i) it is standardized and comes ready-to-use with contemporary C compilers, including compilers that are freely available; (ii) it is easier to use than various thread libraries because it supports a higher level parallel programming model; (iii) it can work on a wide number of shared memory platforms as opposed to other interesting yet less available higher-level frameworks, such as UPC [11].

Performance. Students are introduced to principal performance concepts (such as speedup, efficiency, and scalability) and to Unix performance measurement tools. Students learn how to measure and evaluate performance of shared memory OpenMP programs.

Message-passing computing with MPI. Students learn and practice message passing computing (including performance) using C and MPI. Students also get acquainted with hybrid parallel computing with MPI and OpenMP. We chose MPI because (i) it is implemented for a broad variety of architectures, including implementations that are freely available; (ii) MPI is well documented; (iii) MPI has grown much more popular than alternative platforms such as PVM [15].

Cloud computing with MapReduce. Students learn and practice data-intensive computing with MapReduce (i) on our university Rocks cluster and (ii) on Amazon's Elastic MapReduce (EMR) cloud, a member of AWS [5]. In the process, students get conceptually and practically acquainted with some of Amazon's primary clouds, such as (i) Elastic Compute Cloud (EC2) and (ii) Simple Storage Service (S3). We chose the MapReduce parallel programming model because (i) although its first implementation is property of Google, free open source implementations are now available for various platforms; (ii) it is easy and stimulating to learn; (iii) commercial-grade MapReduce clusters are instantly available on the AWS's EMR cloud. We chose to use AWS as it is the world largest and fast-developing cloud computing platform.

2.3 Computing Platforms

For experiments, labs, and projects with OpenMP and MPI, students use a five-node Rocks 5.2 cluster with GNU/Linux. Each cluster node contains two Intel Xeon quad-core processors, for a total of 40 cores. This cluster is hosted in the School of Computational Sciences at Chapman University. For experiments, labs, and projects with MapReduce, students initially use a single-node Hadoop server, also hosted in the School of Computational Sciences. Tested and debugged MapReduce applications are then uploaded and executed on Amazon's Elastic MapReduce.

Amazon supports teaching and research through grants that involve a simple application process. We have been awarded a teaching grant that has provided sufficient semester-long student access to the Amazon clouds.

2.4 Digital Learning Resources and Software

The HPC course is based on free digital reading resources and on open source software.

For reading resources, we prefer free open-access online resources. The course is heavily based on a selection of open-access online courses on parallel computing, OpenMP, and MPI, developed by the National Center for Supercomputing Applications (NCSA) at the University of Illinois at Urbana-Champaign [20]. Additionally, the course employs selected parts from (i) Apache's online guides and tutorials on Hadoop MapReduce [4], (ii) Amazon's online guides and tutorials on Elastic MapReduce [5], and (iii) popular online Unix and C tutorials.

There is a good selection of high quality books on parallel computing in general, and on OpenMP, MPI, MapReduce, and Unix/C in particular. We realize that some open-access resources can be of somewhat lower quality than commercially published books. If we had chosen to support our selected course contents (section 2.2) with commercial books instead of open-access resources, then the list of required textbooks would have been prohibitively long and expensive. Hence, we chose open-access online resources because they are both free and highly accessible. To supplement open-access resources, we placed a representative collection of parallel computing paper books on reserve in the university library for our HPC students. An advantage of open-access online resources to printed ones is the opportunity to promptly introduce corrections and improvements. In particular, we communicated with developers of the NCSA open-access courses who responded by improving parts of their courses.

For parallel programming, we prefer open-source platforms and tools to commercial ones. We chose well-established open-source platforms and tools that are well-documented and that have good community support. Open source tools that are used in this HPC course include the Rocks cluster, the GNU C compiler with OpenMP, the MPICH MPI implementation, Apache Hadoop MapReduce, and others. While Amazon clouds are available on a pay-per-use basis, Amazon is willing to grant free use for educational purposes.

We recognize the quality and the benefits of commercial platforms, most notably from Intel and Microsoft (Intel's OpenMP-enabled C compiler is known to be of better quality than the GNU C compiler, for example); at the same time, we have not acquired any commercial software for this HPC course, mainly because of the availability of high quality open source software that is free to use and is reasonably easy to install and maintain.

2.5 Online Study Pack

We developed a special online study pack that uniformly integrates all resources and activities for our HPC course. The HPC study pack is based on the Moodle open-source course management system. The home page of the HPC study pack is organized in Moodle's weekly format. The appearance of a single week on the HPC home page is depicted in Fig. 1.

The *E-Text* page contains links to one or more principal reading resources. The E-text customizes open-access resources through a detailed list of required sections, plus an indication of sections that are optional. The *Annex* offers recommendations for supplemental reading resources, tutorials, and also custom *how-to* instructions developed by the instructor.

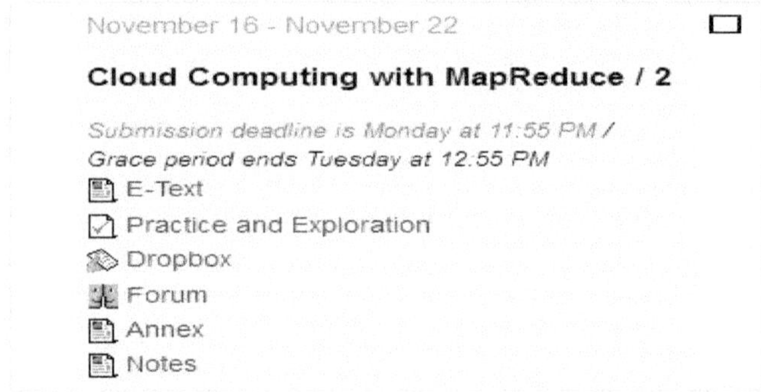

Figure 1. Week 2 for Cloud Computing with MapReduce in the HPC study pack home page

The *Practice and Exploration* section is a detailed list of all *homework* activities that are to be performed in sequence during the current week. Activities include reading of various parts of the *E-Text* and the *Annex*; running sample parallel programs; developing and running parallel programs; measuring parallel performance; working on projects; submitting completed code and execution snapshots in the *Dropbox*; sharing experiences in the *Forum*.

Our HPC study pack is a portal that creates order and uniformity for a set of diverse open-access resources and activities. It is free for students and available 24/7.

2.6 Active Learning

Part of the open-access resources that are adopted in the HPC study pack are detailed *tutorials* that guide students in parallel computing experiments for active learning. For example, such tutorials direct students to run sample parallel programs and to measure performance.

A substantial active learning component of the HPC course is its set of three individually chosen *mini-projects* on OpenMP, on MPI, and on Cloud Computing with MapReduce. In addition, the last two weeks of the HPC course are dedicated to an individual *course project* that is unique for each student. During these two weeks, scheduled class meetings are used for group project discussions and also for technical assistance from the instructor and peers. All projects incorporate experimental components, such as development of parallel programs from scratch, or adaptation and extension of existing parallel programs. Course projects stimulate active learning because students are given the opportunity to choose their topics and projects' experimental components.

3. EVALUATION

This HPC course was offered in the fall of 2010 as an elective for Computer Science, Computer Information Systems, Mathematics, Mathematics and Engineering majors. These are vibrant yet small personalized education programs and many courses – including the HPC course – are scheduled to be offered in alternate years. While it may take years to accumulate more substantial evaluation data for our HPC course, we believe in the importance of a timely dissemination – as provided by this paper - of novel experiences in this rapidly changing area. (In the fall of 2011, Chapman University launched a new MS program in computational science; a PhD program in the same area will begin in the fall of 2012. A graduate-level sister course in HPC - a core course for the Computational Science graduate studies – is included in the core graduate curriculum.)

3.1 Lessons Learned

Cloud computing with MapReduce is attractive for students. During the three weeks of study of MapReduce, we witnessed a growing enthusiasm about the framework and about its use on the Amazon cloud. Our impression that MapReduce won students' interest was confirmed by the fact that MapReduce was the top choice for term projects, as seen in Table 1; this table presents the percentage of final course projects that dealt with (i) shared-memory computing with OpemMP, (ii) message-passing computing with MPI, and (iii) cloud computing with MapReduce. Note that some projects covered more than one of the above areas and are counted in each covered area in Table 1. The significant interest in MapReduce can possibly be attributed (i) to MapReduce being a higher-level platform than OpenMP and MPI, (ii) to MapReduce being a modern emerging framework, and (iii) to the intriguing exposure - through MapReduce - to the emerging novel domain of data-intensive cloud computing.

Table 1. Percentage of term projects by platform

OpenMP	MPI	MapReduce
33%	11%	56%

Message-passing computing with MPI is least attractive for students. Four weeks were allocated to this technically challenging topic: the largest time slot among all topics. While students succeeded in learning MPI, it could not win and retain their attention. That students succeeded in obtaining sufficient technical knowledge on MPI was confirmed by good MPI scores for Practice and Exploration homework and for the Final Exam as seen in Fig. 2; this figure hints that students' knowledge of MPI was roughly the same as their knowledge of OpenMP and MapReduce. Our impression that MPI failed to ignite students' interest is confirmed by the fact that students avoided choosing MPI for their term projects (Table 1). Insufficient interest towards MPI can possibly be attributed (i) to the fact that MPI is a lower-level platform than OpenMP and MapReduce, and (ii) also to the fact that typical MPI applications require particularly rigorous background in mathematics and sciences. (Note that we did not find explanation for the significant discrepancy in *Unix and C* scores, as seen in Fig. 2, between (i) Practice and Exploration and (ii) Final Exam.)

Cloud computing is beneficial for this HPC course. In the absence of a dedicated MapReduce cluster in our university, Amazon's Elastic MapReduce cloud turned out to be indispensible in the study of data-intensive computing. Students - being aware that cloud computing is a popular emerging trend - became interested, motivated, and involved in its study and utilization.

Local MapReduce development should precede running on the cloud. In our opinion, and in accordance with our experience MapReduce applications are faster to develop and easier to debug on a standalone Hadoop server rather than on the Amazon Elastic MapReduce cloud. On the other end, Amazon's Elastic MapReduce is a suitable multi-node platform for final testing and high-performance execution with real data.

Final course projects were the culmination of this course. Project topics were individually chosen by students; every individual project had to include a significant experimental component. At the end of the course, students wrote project papers and gave oral project presentations. Examples of successful projects include (i) large prime number calculations in OpenMP, MPI, and MapReduce, and a comparison of the three platforms; (ii) text document analysis and Markov Model generation with MapReduce; (iii) using MapReduce to count frequencies of first names in the USA in the period 1913-2000.

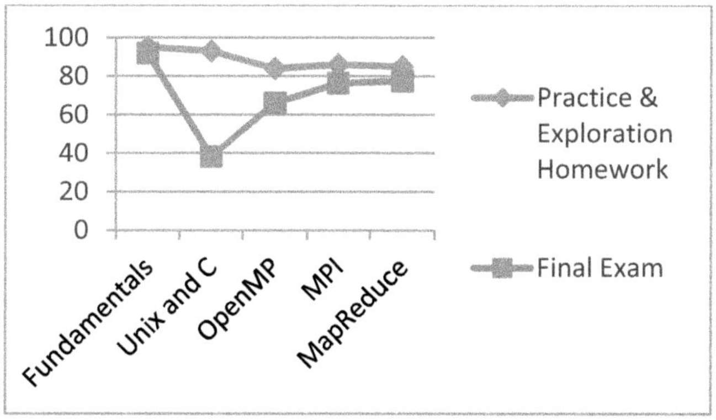

Figure 2. Average homework and exam scores by topic

This HPC course can be challenging yet beneficial for reasonably motivated students. From the nine students who enrolled in this challenging course in the fall of 2010, six completed it successfully. The course grade distribution was: A(2), B+(2), B-(1), C-(1), F(2), W(1). The high failure rate was caused by the lack of adequate commitment from the failing students, rather than by complexity of the course material itself. Anonymous student evaluations of teaching – as administered by the university – resulted in an overall rating of 4.15 on a 1-5 scale. We consider this to be a high rating, especially given the high failure rate in the course. In anonymous comments, student expressed satisfaction with various course aspects, such as projects, practice and exploration activities, online tutorials, and the study pack. One student wished for more defined project goals and ideas.

3.2 Evaluation of Alternative Contents

General Purpose Graphics Processing Units (GPGPUs). For possible inclusion in this course, we evaluated two popular platforms that are available for parallel GPGPU programming: OpenCL and CUDA. The newer OpenCL is an open standard that is implemented by a number of vendors. OpenCL is designed around a relatively low-level programming model that falls short of high-level abstractions. As a low-level platform, OpenCL is complex. OpenCL is "a low-level programming language, and given that these devices can have very different types of compute capabilities, careful tuning is often required to get close to peak performance" [2, Sect. 4]. CUDA's programming model is low-level, too - much like OpenCL's programming model.

A dedicated on-campus server with an appropriate GPGPU co-processor is currently unavailable for this HPC course. An alternative solution would be to use Amazon's GPGPU cloud instances. We believe that using a cloud instance for entry-level GPGPU computing would impose a learning curve that is too steep for students. Instead of GPGPUs, we decided to embed in our HPC course emerging higher-level big-data approaches, such as MapReduce and cloud computing. In the current HPC course edition, the GPGPU theme is an option that students may choose for their course projects. In the absence of an on-campus server with an appropriate GPGPU processor, such projects require use of students' own hardware (when available), or the use of GPGPU-equipped instances on AWS.

Parallel Languages. While parallel languages have been in the focus of active research for years, they have yet to become dominant in the realm of practical parallel programming. Some parallel languages, such as Cilk [7] or UPC [11], can be relatively easily understood in terms of OpenMP and MPI techniques [2,

Sect. 4]. Others, such as Concurrent ML [27] and Concurrent Haskel [16], offer very high level parallel programming abstractions and can be useful in building concise prototypes and/or specifications of parallel applications and libraries. While we appreciate the unquestionable benefits from parallel languages, we have left all parallel languages – and parallelizing compilers for that matter - out of our HPC course, to provide for a more rigorous technical study of well-established or emerging practical platforms, such as OpenMP, MPI, and MapReduce.

4. CONCLUSION

In this paper we report the design and implementation of a new HPC course which amalgamates the emerging data-intensive cloud computing paradigm with the dominant trend towards multi-core computing and the legacy of cluster computing. Our work builds on the experience of others who have previously reported the design parallel computing courses [1, 8, 9, 12, 14, 21, 22, 23, 24, 28], but this paper is the first to report experience with an upper-level HPC course that integrates the evolving MapReduce parallel model with the better-established shared memory and message-passing models. The course's design choices – such as specific contents, software tools, and reading resources – may be beneficial for the computer science education community in the design of HPC courses and parallel computing modules, including data-intensive cloud computing modules.

5. ACKNOWLEDGMENTS

This work was supported by an *AWS in Education* research grant award from Amazon.

6. REFERENCES

[1] ACM, 2008. Computer Science Curriculum 2008: An Interim Revision of CS 2001, Interim Review Task Force. ACM, IEEE Computer Society.

[2] ACM, 2010. ACM's Parallel Computing Techpack. http://techpack.acm.org/parallel/.

[3] Amazon Web Services. http://aws.amazon.com/.

[4] Apache Software Foundation. Apache Hadoop™ MapReduce. http://hadoop.apache.org/mapreduce/.

[5] AWS. Amazon Elastic MapReduce Developer Guide. http://docs.amazonwebservices.com/ElasticMapReduce/latest/DeveloperGuide/.

[6] Barroso L. et al., 2003. Web search for a planet: The Google cluster architecture. IEEE Micro, 23(2), 22–28.

[7] Blumofe R. et al, 1995. Cilk: an efficient multithreaded runtime system. PPOPP '95, New York, 207-216.

[8] Brown R. et al., 2010. Strategies for preparing computer science Students for the multicore world. ITiCSE-WGR'10, Ankara, Turkey, 97-115.

[9] Cunha J., Lourenço, J., 1998. An integrated course on parallel and distributed processing. SIGCSE '98, Atlanta, Georgia, 217-221.

[10] Dagum L., Menon R., 1998. OpenMP: an industry standard API for shared-memory programming. IEEE Computational Science & Engineering, 5(1), 46-55.

[11] El-Ghazawi T. et al, 2003. UPC: Distributed Shared Memory Programming. Wiley.

[12] Ernst D., 2011. Preparing students for future architectures with an exploration of multi- and many-core performance. ITiCSE'11, Darmstadt, Germany, 57-62.

[13] Foster I. et al., 2008 Cloud computing and grid computing 360-degree compared. GCE '08, the Grid Computing Environments Workshop, Austin, Texas, 1-10

[14] Garrity P. et al., 2011. WebMapReduce: An accessible and adaptable tool for teaching Map-Reduce Computing. SIGCSE'11, Dallas, Texas, 183-188.

[15] Geist A. et al., 1994. PVM: Parallel Virtual Machine. MIT Press.

[16] Jones S. P. et al., 1996. Concurrent Haskell. 23rd ACM SIGPLAN-SIGACT symposium on Principles of Programming Languages, St. Petersburg Beach, Florida, 295-308.

[17] Khronos Group. OpenCL - The open standard for parallel programming of heterogeneous systems. http://www.khronos.org/opencl/.

[18] Lindholm E. et al., 2008. NVIDIA Tesla: A unified graphics and computing architecture, IEEE Micro 28(2), 39–55.

[19] MPI Forum. Message Passing Interface Forum. http://www.mpi-forum.org/.

[20] NCSA-UIUC. Cyberinfrastructure Tutor. http://citutor.org/.

[21] NSF/IEEE-TCPP, 2010. Curriculum Initiative on Parallel and Distributed Computing – Core Topics for Undergraduates. http://www.cs.gsu.edu/~tcpp/curriculum/index.php.

[22] Ortiz A., 2011. Teaching concurrency-oriented programming with Erlang. SIGCSE'11, Dallas, Texas, 195-200.

[23] Prasad, S. et al., 2011. NSF/IEEE-TCPP Curriculum Initiative on Parallel and Distributed Computing – Core Topics for Undergraduates. SIGCSE'11, Dallas, Texas, 617-618.

[24] Rague, B., 2011. Measuring CS1 perceptions of parallelism. 41st ASEE/IEEE Frontiers in Education Conference. http://fie-conference.org/fie2011/papers/1686.pdf.

[25] Ranganathan P., 2011. From microprocessors to nanostores: Rethinking data-centric systems. IEEE Computer, 44(1), 39–48.

[26] Reinders J., 2007. Intel Threading Building Blocks, O'Reilly Media.

[27] Reppy, J., 1999. Concurrent programming in ML. Cambridge University Press.

[28] Sadowski C. et al., 2011. Practical parallel and concurrent programming. SIGCSE'11, Dallas, Texas, 189-194.

[29] Sodan, A. et al., 2010. Parallelism via Multithreaded and Multicore CPUs. Computer, 43(3), 24–32.

[30] TOP500.Org. Top 500 Supercomputer Sites. http://top500.org.

All Syntax Errors Are Not Equal

Paul Denny, Andrew Luxton-Reilly, Ewan Tempero
Department of Computer Science
The University of Auckland
Auckland, New Zealand
{paul,andrew,ewan}@cs.auckland.ac.nz

ABSTRACT

Identifying and correcting syntax errors is a challenge all novice programmers confront. As educators, the more we understand about the nature of these errors and how students respond to them, the more effective our teaching can be. It is well known that just a few types of errors are far more frequently encountered by students learning to program than most. In this paper, we examine how long students spend resolving the most common syntax errors, and discover that certain types of errors are not solved any more quickly by the higher ability students. Moreover, we note that these errors consume a large amount of student time, suggesting that targeted teaching interventions may yield a significant payoff in terms of increasing student productivity.

Categories and Subject Descriptors

K.3.2 [**Computers and Education**]: Computer and Information Science Education—*computer science education*

General Terms

Design, Human Factors

Keywords

Syntax errors, Java, CodeWrite, drill and practice, assessment

1. INTRODUCTION

Syntax errors are frequently encountered by the novice programmer. As educators, the more we understand about the nature of these errors and how students respond to them, the more effective our teaching can be [12]. In particular, if there are certain errors that students spend much of their time struggling with, targeted support may be effective.

Previous research examining students working on typical Java programming assignments, involving multiple class and method definitions, has shown that a few types of syntax errors occur much more frequently than most [4, 6]. While the time elapsed between successive compilations is generally short [5], it is not known if students spend more time solving *certain kinds* of syntax errors than others.

In this paper, we examine the syntax errors encountered by students writing short fragments of Java code when implementing single methods. Despite differing from previous work in the length of the code being written, we confirm earlier results that a small number of errors are highly represented. We also show that students spend a large proportion of their time fixing problems associated with these most common errors, and that the highest performing students take as long to correct certain errors as any other students.

2. RELATED WORK

Understanding syntax has long been a source of difficulty for programming students [11]. Many novices find it frustrating to struggle with syntax errors [7], and given that programming is a subject in which the cumulative effects of previous learning are critical to progression [10], this has the potential to hinder long-term success.

A varied body of research concerning how novices encounter and respond to syntax errors exists. A number of tools have been developed and evaluated to help students fix syntax errors in their programs. SyntaxTrain [9] parses a student's source code and, if it detects a syntax error, displays a syntax diagram illustrating the required syntax. Another example in this category is the Expresso tool [3], which operates as a pre-compiler, producing detailed messages from a set of pre-defined common syntax errors.

Other research has explored, in controlled conditions, how students approach syntax error correction. Kummerfeld et al. [7] deliberately inserted errors into a set of 10 programs and then observed how a small number of students, of varying programming experience, went about correcting them. Participants were provided with a web-based guide cataloguing a number of common errors that they could use as a reference. Among their conclusions they report that more experienced programmers adopt clear strategies for detecting and fixing errors, and that for all students syntax error correction can be very time consuming.

More closely aligned with the work we present here, several studies examine and categorize the error messages actually generated by students when programming. Reports of this nature tend to use technology to automatically capture students' compilations. Jackson et al. [4] utilize their web-enabled Gauntlet IDE, which logs all student errors while a session is active, sending the full collection of errors to a

ITiCSE'12, July 3–5, 2012, Haifa, Israel.

remote server once the student exits the IDE. They tabulate the most common errors, and report that based on teaching experience, faculty successfully predicted 5 of the 10 most common errors.

Jadud [5] used a modified version of the popular BlueJ IDE that collected relevant information every time a student compiled their program on campus. The collected data included a snapshot of the complete program and the result of each compilation. The most common errors were reported, as well as the average time taken between successive compilation events. The two most common errors, "Missing ;" and "Cannot resolve identifier/symbol", match the result of Jackson et al. although their order is reversed. There is also some agreement amongst the less frequent errors, however a comparison is complicated by the fact that the two studies define different error categories.

Previous work has not attempted to measure the time that students spend solving *particular kinds* of syntax errors. Our expectations were that more capable students would identify and solve syntax errors more quickly than their weaker counterparts. In addition to our intuitive feelings about this, it is supported by previous research in which the differences between the kinds of tasks achievable by students in different performance quartiles has been examined. In the domain of code comprehension, Lister et al. [8] applied the SOLO taxonomy to describe how novice programmers manifest their understanding of code. Their data show that the more capable students are far more likely to successfully integrate parts of a problem into a coherent structure. They propose that this difference may account for the particular difficulty students in the lower quartiles of a class experience when writing code.

3. METHODOLOGY

In this paper, we analyse the syntax error messages encountered by students when writing short fragments of Java code. The data were collected using CodeWrite [1], a web-based drill and practice tool with which students tackle exercises requiring the completion of a single method body. As a consequence, submissions are typically short, and students focus on just the syntax and logic for the one method being implemented without concern for larger program design issues. Figure 1 illustrates the length of all submissions in our data set containing at least one syntax error. The average over all such submissions is 6.5 lines of code.

When a student chooses an exercise to answer, they are shown the method signature (the return type, method name, and names and types of the parameters), a textual description of the purpose of the method, and the expected output for one example input. Students type and edit their code directly in the browser, and submit when they are ready to receive feedback. Their submitted code is compiled on the server, and if syntactically correct, is executed against a set of test cases. If the code contains syntax errors, the corresponding error messages are displayed.

We report here on data collected from the Semester 1 (March-June) offering of the COMPSCI 101 (CS1 in Java) course taught at the University of Auckland in 2011. Of the 478 students enrolled, 430 sat the final exam (a 10% withdrawal rate is typical). Each student was given approximately three weeks to correctly answer 30 exercises on CodeWrite for which they could earn a total of 2% credit towards their final grade in the course. This period of participation spanned parts of Weeks 6 and 7 (of the 12 week teaching semester) and included a two-week mid-semester break. At the point of the course that the CodeWrite activity was introduced, students had already completed their first programming assignment and attended 10 hours of supervised lab sessions. Importantly, while the second half of the course covers object-oriented design, for the period in which the data was collected for this study Java was only used for teaching basic programming concepts such as primitive and array variables, control structures, basic functions from the Java API, and methods and parameter passing.

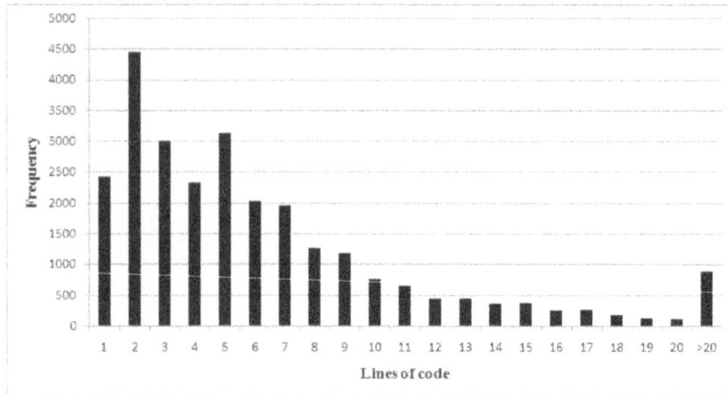

Figure 1: Length of all submissions containing at least one syntax error

In the following sections, we use the term *submission* to represent a single fragment of code submitted to one exercise by one student, and the term *exercise attempt* to represent the full set of submissions made by a single student to a particular exercise. Each submission can be classified into one of the three types listed in Table 1.

Table 1: Submission types

Type	Explanation
"P"	the submission compiles and passes all of the exercise test cases
"F"	the submission compiles but does not pass all of the exercise test cases
"X"	the submission does not compile

Following each submission, a student receives immediate feedback, which in the case of an "X" submission would include the error messages from the compiler. Note, there may be several error messages generated for each submission of type "X". The failing test cases are displayed for a submission of type "F". A timestamp records when each submission is received by the CodeWrite server.

As an example, Figure 2 shows an exercise attempt consisting of four submissions made by one student when solving an exercise to calculate the volume of a cube given the side length. Upon making their first submission, the student receives a "Cannot resolve identifier" type error for not declaring the variable `volumeOfACube`. For their next submission, they replace the expression calculating the volume with a call to `Math.pow()`. In this case, they receive the same error message as before, as the compiler still cannot resolve the identifier `volumeOfACube`. They then declare `volumeOfACube` to be of type `int`, which exposes the "type mismatch" error introduced by the use of `Math.pow()`. The student suc-

```
Submission type: X (9 Mar 2011, 11:36:59 PM)
Error: volumeOfACube cannot be resolved

public int volumeOfACube(int side) {
        volumeOfACube=side*side*side;
        return volumeOfACube;
}
--------------------
Submission type: X (9 Mar 2011, 11:37:36 PM)
Error: volumeOfACube cannot be resolved

public int volumeOfACube(int side) {
        volumeOfACube=Math.pow(side,3);
        return volumeOfACube;
}
--------------------
Submission type: X (9 Mar 2011, 11:39:59 PM)
Error: Type mismatch: cannot convert from double to int

public int volumeOfACube(int side) {
        int volumeOfACube;
        volumeOfACube=Math.pow(side,3);
        return volumeOfACube;
}
--------------------
Submission type: P (9 Mar 2011, 11:40:29 PM)

public int volumeOfACube(int side) {
        int volumeOfACube;
        volumeOfACube=side * side * side;
        return volumeOfACube;
}
```

Figure 2: Example of an exercise attempt for one student

cessfully corrects this mistake by reverting to the expression they used previously.

A student who completed the requirements for the activity as described previously would therefore have made at least 30 exercise attempts, where each one includes at least one submission of type "P". Figure 3 illustrates the data we have collected from this course for a single student that is relevant to the analysis presented in this paper.

3.1 Research questions

We know that students of all levels of ability frequently write code that does not compile, and that weaker students are often unable to solve their syntax problems [2]. Our interest in this paper is to investigate the kinds of syntax errors that students are most commonly making, and measure the time they spend solving these errors. This also provides us with an opportunity to replicate the results of earlier studies in this area, but in a context where students are writing short fragments of code. We outline our three research questions in this section.

> RQ1: Which syntax errors do students most commonly encounter, and how does this compare with previous work?

Our examination of the common types of syntax errors is based upon the error messages generated by the compiler rather than on inspection of the code. To tabulate the error frequencies we analysed all submissions of type "X" and, for each, processed every error message generated by the compiler. Error messages were aggregated and duplicates

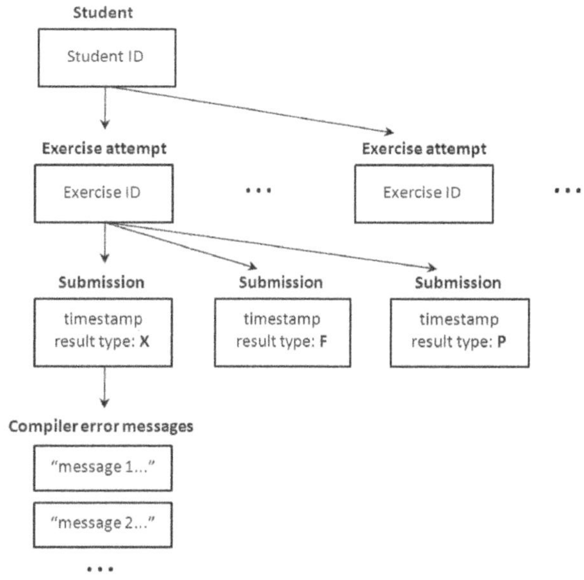

Figure 3: Data collected for each student

removed, so that for any given submission, a particular *type* of syntax error was either present or not. For example, if two variable identifiers, `i` and `j`, were used in one submission without first being declared, then error messages "`i` cannot be resolved" and "`j` cannot be resolved" would both be generated by the compiler. Likewise, if the variable identifier `i` appeared in multiple places in a submission without first being declared, the compiler would generate the error message "`i` cannot be resolved" for each occurrence. In either case, we classified the multiple error messages under the single, more general, type "Cannot resolve identifier".

When defining syntax error categories, we attempted to align them with previously published results where possible, however there has not been agreement on this in the past. For example, in [5] the category "bracket expected" is reported, whereas four separate categories "`{` expected", "`(` expected", "`}` expected" and "`)` expected" are reported in [4].

> RQ2: How long do the different kinds of syntax errors take students to solve, and does this vary by level of ability?

It is difficult to measure precisely, through a purely automated analysis, how long it takes a given student to successfully fix a given error that occurs during an exercise attempt. Our analysis relies on the assumption that if a submission contains a particular type of error, then the compiler will generate a corresponding error message. This is often, but not always, the case. For example, certain types of errors in a submission may prevent the compiler from discovering and listing all errors.

Given this assumption, the first "X" submission of an exercise attempt that generates a particular type of error represents the point at which the error was introduced into the code. Of all subsequent submissions, the first one that does not generate the same type of error represents the point at which the error was corrected. A timestamp records when every submission is made. Therefore, the *time difference* between the submission that first generates the error, and

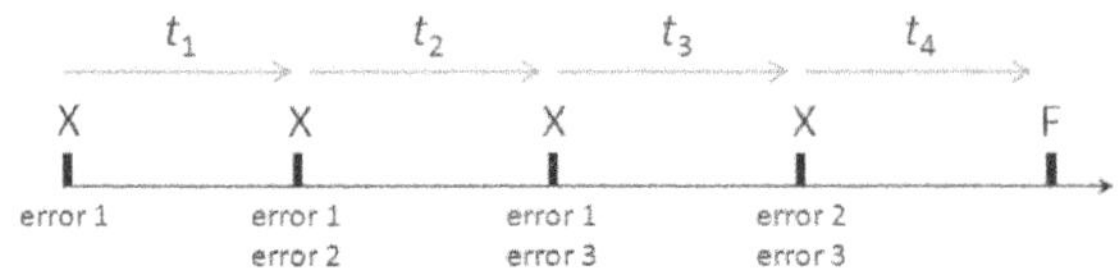

Figure 4: An example exercise attempt consisting of five submissions

the next submission in which the error is not generated is an approximate measure of how long the student spent solving that error. Of course, for any given submission there may be multiple errors generated (about 30% of "X" submissions generated more than a single error message), and a student may focus on fixing just one of these errors for every submission they make. Nevertheless, the period of time described above is a measure of the length of time that a particular error existed in the student's code prior to being corrected.

For example, the diagram in Figure 4 illustrates the timeline of an exercise attempt consisting of five submissions (X, X, X, X, F). The first submission of type "X" generates a single kind of error, whereas the next three submissions each generate two kinds of errors. The arrows, t_i, shown in the diagram represent the time differences between consecutive pairs of submissions. In this particular example, the time taken to correct "error 1" is $t_1 + t_2 + t_3$, and the time taken to correct "error 3" is $t_3 + t_4$. There are two separate occurrences of "error 2", the first of which took t_2 and the second of which took t_4 to correct. In this case, the average time taken to correct "error 2" is therefore $(t_2 + t_4)/2$.

To investigate this research question, for every kind of syntax error, we calculate the average time taken by each student across all of their submissions to correct that error. We only consider students who encountered the error at least once when calculating this average.

As student participation is unsupervised, we must be aware of the fact that an individual time measurement may be inflated if a student is interrupted or leaves a task and then returns to it at a later time. A simple heuristic for handling such cases is to ignore time periods greater than a particular threshold. A suitable threshold value would be one that captures a high percentage of the data yet represents a reasonable maximum period of time for a student to be working on preparing a submission.

To determine possible threshold values, we examined the elapsed times between all consecutive pairs of submissions for all exercises. A histogram of this data is shown in Figure 5. The majority of elapsed times are short, nearly half (45%) being less than 30 seconds, and the frequency of the periods reduces rapidly with their length. Roughly 8% of the periods are longer than 380 seconds.

We repeated our analysis 8 times using threshold values between 120 and 540 seconds inclusive (at 60 second intervals). For simplicity in presenting the data in this paper, unless otherwise specified, a threshold value of 300 seconds has been used.

We were interested in how the time spent solving errors varied by student ability. Students were split into quartiles based on their performance in the course overall. The final course mark was based on assignment, laboratory, midterm test and final exam marks. Our analysis only considers students who participated with CodeWrite, and because students in the lower quartiles were less likely to participate, there are fewer students in these quartiles. Table 2 summarizes the number of students who sat the exam, the number who participated with the CodeWrite activity, the total number of exercises attempted, the total number of submissions, and the number of submissions of type "X" for students in each quartile (Q1 is the top quartile).

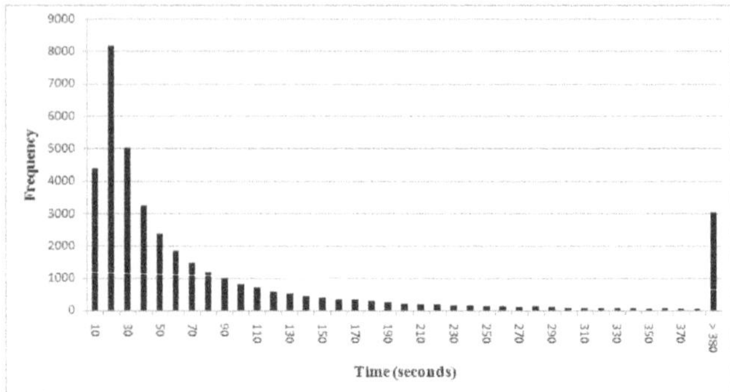

Figure 5: Elapsed times between consecutive submission pairs

Table 2: Student participation data by quartile

	All	Q1	Q2	Q3	Q4
Sat exam	430	108	107	107	108
Participated	385	106	105	97	77
Exercises	15481	4923	4281	3814	2463
Submissions	53888	18022	15917	12282	7667
... of type "X"	26387	7853	8138	6305	4091

RQ3: How much student time, in total, was spent on the most common syntax errors?

Focusing our teaching efforts on the types of syntax problems for which students are spending a disproportionate amount of time may help to assist learning and increase student productivity. To explore this idea, we determined the total amount of time that all students spent on each error, and the average amount of time spent per student on each error.

4. RESULTS

4.1 RQ1: Most common errors

Of the 53888 submissions made by all students, 26387 contained at least one syntax error (i.e. were "X" submissions). The most common type of error, "Cannot resolve identifier", appeared in 6344 of these submissions. Table 3 lists the ten most common error messages, the total number of submissions in which they each occurred, and the percentage of all "X" submissions that this represents.

These results agree moderately with previous work. Our three most common error messages appear 2nd, 7th and 1st in Jadud's table [5] and 1st, 7th and 2nd in Jackson's table [4], respectively. We note that "Type mismatch" errors occured much more frequently in our study than in previous work. One possible explanation for this is the nature of the exercises students work on. As every exercise involves implementing a method body, students must always ensure

Table 3: Most common syntax errors (all students)

Error type	Total	%
Cannot resolve identifier	6344	24.0%
Type mismatch	4847	18.4%
Missing ;	3436	13.0%
Token should be deleted	2712	10.3%
Method not returning correct type	1743	6.6%
Missing }	1450	5.5%
Missing)	1213	4.6%
Missing {	512	1.9%
Using .length as a field	433	1.6%
Insert "AssignmentOperator"	339	1.3%

that the type of the return expression matches the return type of the method. We noticed many errors as a result of this kind of mismatch.

We also note that the Sun/Oracle JDK compiler was used in both of the previous studies. CodeWrite uses the batch compiler that is part of the Java Development Tools (JDT) Core component of the Eclipse development environment. The error messages produced by this compiler, which evolved from IBM's VisualAge environment, differ from those produced by the Sun/Oracle JDK. For example, consider the following expression with unmatched parentheses:

```
double result = Math.round(value * 100)) / 100.0;
```

The Sun/Oracle JDK produces the following error message:

```
';' expected
```

whereas the JDT batch compiler (used by CodeWrite) would generate:

```
Syntax error on token ")", delete this token
```

A full comparison of error messages is beyond the scope of this paper, however, as in this example, we often found the messages produced by the JDT batch compiler more informative than those produced by the Sun/Oracle JDK.

Despite these differences, although in our study students were practicing with short fragments of code, they still frequently encountered the same kinds of errors as in previous research where students were developing complete programs.

4.2 RQ2: Time to solve errors by quartile

We measured the time a student took to solve a particular type of syntax error as the time that elapsed while the corresponding error message was generated for consecutive submissions of type "X". Figure 6 shows the time students in different quartiles spent, on average, solving errors of the three most common varieties.

Both "Cannot resolve identifier" and "Type mismatch" errors took longer for students to solve than "Missing ;" errors. As expected, more capable students tended to spend less time solving "Missing ;" errors than weaker students (students in the top quartile, Q1, solved these errors more than twice as quickly as students in the bottom quartile). Interestingly, this did not appear to be the case for the other two errors. To investigate the significance of any differences between quartiles we ran a Kruskal-Wallis test for independent samples (this non-parametric method was selected because the samples did not have similar variances and ANOVA is

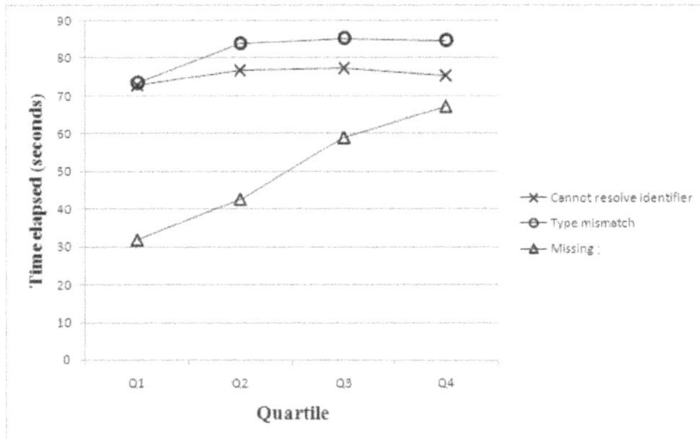

Figure 6: Average time spent correcting submissions (with a single error message) by quartile

not robust to violations of this assumption when the sample sizes are unequal).

The differences between quartiles for the "Missing ;" error were highly significant ($p \ll 0.001$), whereas the time spent solving "Cannot resolve identifier" errors did not vary by quartile ($p = 0.534$). These were very robust results, and held across all threshold values we investigated.

For "Type mismatch" errors, students in the top quartile solved them marginally more quickly than other students however these differences were not significant ($p = 0.073$). This held when the analysis was performed using threshold values less than 300 seconds, however for threshold values greater than 300 seconds the differences were significant at the 0.05 level ($0.027 < p < 0.050$).

In summary, although more capable students spend far less time solving certain kinds of errors than other students, somewhat surprisingly this is not the case for all kinds of errors.

4.3 RQ3: Cumulative time solving errors

Throughout the practice activity for which we have collected data, not all students encountered every kind of syntax error. The total amount of time a student spent tackling a particular type of error was dependent both on how frequently the error occurred and how long it took to solve.

Table 4 summarises, for each of the most common kinds of errors, the number of students that encountered the error at least once, the cumulative total time all students spent solving errors of that kind (in hours) and the average amount of time per student spent solving errors of that kind (in minutes). Of the 385 students who participated, 356 encounterd at least one "Cannot resolve identifier" error. This error stands out, along with the next most common type of error, "Type mismatch", as consuming a particularly large amount of student time – twice that of any other error.

5. DISCUSSION

Our interest was in understanding where beginners spend most of their time due to failed compilation when implementing short methods. From earlier work in this area, we expected to see a few kinds of errors making up the majority, and we confirmed previous results in this respect. We speculated that as these errors were so common, the amount of *time* spent on them may have been proportionally less, how-

Table 4: Number of students, total time by all and average time per student spent on each error

Error type	n	Total (hrs)	Avg. (mins)
Cannot resolve identifier	356	70.7	11.9
Type mismatch	341	57.1	10.0
Missing ;	347	26.8	4.6
Token should be deleted	316	26.7	5.1
Method not returning correct type	268	22.6	5.1
Missing }	234	14.3	3.7
Missing)	251	11.5	2.8
Missing {	110	4.7	2.6
Using .length as a field	118	4.9	2.5
Insert "AssignmentOperator"	90	3.6	2.4

ever the two most common errors also dominated students' time. Finally, we predicted more capable students would solve all types of errors in less time than the weaker students in class. Although this was sometimes the case, quite unexpectedly we found that all students spent a similar amount of time solving the most common errors no matter what quartile they were in.

That all students struggle equally with these errors, and spend so much time with them, suggests there is some fundamental issue that needs to be addressed. It also suggests that providing specific support for these errors may be particularly useful.

Given the surprising nature of our result, we must consider other possible explanations (or, threats to validity) for it. One possible factor is that when a student makes a submission of type "X" that contains multiple errors, we do not know their strategy for correcting those errors. Some students may attempt to fix all errors before making their next submission, while others may attempt to fix what they perceive is the simplest error first. To investigate this, we repeated our analysis considering only submissions of type "X" for which a single error message was generated. In other words, we ignored the 30% of "X" submissions containing more than one kind of error that may contribute to this threat. This analysis did not affect our conclusions.

It should also be noted that students are free to choose which exercises they answer. It is possible that students with lower capability tend to choose easier exercises than those with higher capability. Although this may be true, there is no obvious reason why the "Cannot resolve identifier" and "Type mismatch" errors are any harder (or easier) to solve due to the difficulty of the exercise. However this might be true of other errors – for example it may be harder to determine where the missing "}" should go in more complex code than in simple code.

6. CONCLUSIONS AND FUTURE WORK

In this paper, we investigated the types of errors most frequently encountered by students practicing writing short fragments of Java code using the CodeWrite practice tool. We discovered, confirming previous work in different contexts, that students encounter a small number of errors much more frequently than others.

Our expectations were that the most capable students in class would be able to resolve errors more quickly than less able students, and this result was confirmed for one of the top three most frequent errors, the classically well-known "Missing ;". However, quite unexpectedly, we found that for the two most common errors, the time taken to correct the corresponding mistakes did not vary by quartile. This result indicates that specific teaching support around the causes of these errors may be particularly effective.

In future work, we will develop interventions to provide teaching support for these common mistakes, and measure their success against the baseline data collected in this study.

The data reported here was collected over a fairly short period of time that included a mid-semester break and coincided with just one week of class time. Additional future directions will examine the way in which student responses to particular types of errors change over time as their learning progresses and their experience grows.

7. REFERENCES

[1] P. Denny, A. Luxton-Reilly, E. Tempero, and J. Hendrickx. CodeWrite: Supporting student-driven practice of Java. In *Proceedings of SIGCSE '11*, pages 471–476, 2011.

[2] P. Denny, A. Luxton-Reilly, E. Tempero, and J. Hendrickx. Understanding the syntax barrier for novices. In *Proceedings of ITiCSE '11*, pages 208–212, 2011.

[3] M. Hristova, A. Misra, M. Rutter, and R. Mercuri. Identifying and correcting Java programming errors for introductory computer science students. *SIGCSE Bull.*, 35:153–156, January 2003.

[4] J. Jackson, M. Cobb, and C. Carver. Identifying top Java errors for novice programmers. In *Proceedings of ASEE/IEEE Frontiers in Education Conference*, FIE '05, pages T4C24–T4C27, 2005.

[5] M. C. Jadud. A first look at novice compilation behaviour using BlueJ. *Computer Science Education*, 15:1–25, 2005.

[6] M. C. Jadud. Methods and tools for exploring novice compilation behaviour. In *Proceedings of ICER '06*, pages 73–84, 2006.

[7] S. K. Kummerfeld and J. Kay. The neglected battle fields of syntax errors. In *Proceedings of ACE '03*, pages 105–111, 2003.

[8] R. Lister, B. Simon, E. Thompson, J. L. Whalley, and C. Prasad. Not seeing the forest for the trees: novice programmers and the solo taxonomy. *SIGCSE Bull.*, 38:118–122, June 2006.

[9] A. L. A. Moth, J. Villadsen, and M. Ben-Ari. SyntaxTrain: relieving the pain of learning syntax. In *Proceedings of ITiCSE '11*, pages 387–387, 2011.

[10] A. Robins. Learning edge momentum: A new account of outcomes in CS1. *Computer Science Education*, 20:37–71, 2010.

[11] D. Sleeman, R. T. Putnam, J. A. Baxter, and L. Kuspa. *An introductory Pascal class: A case study of students' errors*, pages 207–235. Lawrence Erlbaum Associates, Hillsdale, NJ, USA, 1988.

[12] J. C. Spohrer and E. Soloway. Novice mistakes: are the folk wisdoms correct? *Commun. ACM*, 29:624–632, July 1986.

Code Comprehension Problems as Learning Events

Leigh Ann Sudol
Computer Science Department
Carnegie Mellon University
Pittsburgh, PA
lsudol@andrew.cmu.edu

Mark Stehlik
Computer Science Department
Carnegie Mellon University
Pittsburgh, PA
mjs@cs.cmu.edu

Sharon Carver
Psychology Department
Carnegie Mellon University
Pittsburgh, PA
sc0e@andrew.cmu.edu

ABSTRACT

Code comprehension problems have been shown to be effective assessment items in computer science education. In this paper we present qualitative and quantitative results of a study evaluating the effectiveness of code comprehension questions with feedback as learning events. Students taking an introductory programming course that satisfies a university requirement interacted with an online tutoring system using code comprehension problems about simple array algorithms as a part of a homework assignment. Students answered the problems in their own words first, before selecting a multiple choice option from the system.

Both the open-ended and multiple-choice responses were collected and analyzed. Results indicate that code comprehension questions with appropriate feedback can be learning events. The use of open-ended and multiple choice responses to the same question is also shown to be useful in refining distracter items for future assessment. Recommendations from this study can be applied not only to tutoring systems, but also to the type of interactions used in worked examples in class lecture and textbook production.

Categories and Subject Descriptors

I.2.6 [**Computing Methodologies**]: Learning;Concept Learning; K.3.2 [**Computers & Education**]: Computer and Information Sciences Education;Computer Science Education

General Terms

Human Factors

Keywords

Code Comprehension, Worked Examples, Tutoring System, Feedback

1. INTRODUCTION

Code comprehension problems are often used for assessment in computer science education, especially at the introductory level [1]. These problems require the student to read a segment of code, and then answer a question about the code. There are many types of code comprehension problems, as described in 1.1, and each type has different assessment implications. Code comprehension questions are an often-employed method of assessment because performance on code comprehension questions often correlates with code production or code writing [2]. Code comprehension questions also allow for more detailed analysis of student ability than code production [3] because descriptions of code in natural language can expose mental models and misconceptions held by the student.

Although code comprehension problems are a popular assessment item, little work has been done to evaluate their viability as a learning task when accompanied by appropriate feedback. Textbooks and teachers often use worked examples during instruction [4], and many of the papers published about peer instruction [5] include code comprehension questions in the instruction.

The work presented in this paper explores code comprehension questions that are learning tasks as a part of an online computer-supported tutoring assignment. Both open ended responses and multiple choice selections are analyzed, and results indicate appropriate code comprehension questions with feedback can produce both increasingly accurate multiple choice answers and more sophisticated open ended responses over time.

1.1 Code Comprehension Problems

Code comprehension problems are presented in many different ways. The type of question asked about the code varies depending on the goals of the assessment [6]. Students may be asked to trace the code with a specified set of input values to determine output, reason about the code abstractly (without specified inputs) to make a generic statement about the output, produce invariants about the code's performance, or describe the code in their own words often classifying the algorithm in the process. Just as the questions can vary, the type of responses expected and the grading of those responses will vary as well [7]. Two of the most common types of responses are multiple choice and open ended.

Both multiple choice and open ended responses have benefits and weaknesses. Multiple choice responses are easy to grade, especially by automated systems, while open ended responses are more difficult to score automatically. Multiple choice however constrains the possibilities offered the student and makes it more possible to guess the correct answer, while an open ended response will give more detail about a student's true mental model. Open ended responses also provide the opportunity to classify the student's level of reasoning when answering the problem against one of several appropriate taxonomies [8].

There is a difference between the ability to trace code and reason about code. Tracing can be seen as a precursor skill to reasoning about code [9]. However, tracing ability alone is not sufficient for skill at writing code, as students must also be able to explain the code and the abstractions contained within to develop code production skills [10].

The tutoring environment used for this study contained two types of code comprehension questions, tracing and algorithmic abstraction questions. In the tracing questions, students are presented with a code snippet and input values for any parameters or variables required. The students are then asked to calculate the resulting value contained in a variable after the code has executed. Algorithmic abstraction questions focus on primarily on two key student abilities. One type of algorithmic abstraction question asks the student to make a general observation about the behavior of the code (What does this code do? It finds the sum of all the numbers in the list). The second type of algorithmic abstraction question asks about the role of a particular variable within the algorithm. The three questions analyzed in Section 3 ask about the role of variables related to the accessing of individual elements within the arrays used in the questions.

1.2 Questions as Learning Events

There is a rich history in intelligent tutoring systems (ITS) of using questioning with feedback as learning events for students [11, 12]. Within computer science education, many of the tutors have focused on the code writing ability of students [13, 14, 15, 16]. Many experts believe that in addition to code production, code comprehension is an important skill for novices to learn [17, 18]. In addition to using comprehension skills to troubleshoot and debug their own code, comprehension skills are also important for parsing and integrating concepts demonstrated in worked examples. In addition, code comprehension problems themselves can be viewed as worked examples, and the questions asked about the code can draw a student's attention away from surface features of the problem, to the deeper algorithmic abstractions in the example. There is evidence for the need to explicitly draw students' attention to the algorithms, as students seem not to make the connection from simple tracing problems and translate the observed algorithm to code production [10].

The tutor discussed in this work uses code comprehension questions and is part of a larger study published in [19]. The goal of the larger study was to evaluate the impact on student learning of questions regarding algorithmic abstractions compared to tracing questions on the same code. We focus here specifically on open-ended student responses to a series of similar algorithmic abstraction questions in the tutor.[1] We describe the change that occurs through the sequence of questions, highlighting the improved performance and explanations students provide as they encounter learning events involving questions with feedback.

[1]Student responses to the tracing questions were mostly the singular value the function returned and therefore we deemed them uninteresting for this analysis.

2. METHODOLOGY

This paper includes data collected as a part of a larger study [19] focused on instructing students in algorithmic abstractions. Participants engaged with an online tutoring system comprised of 30 multiple choice questions as a part of a larger homework assignment in an introductory computer science course. As a part of the data collection, students were asked to submit open ended responses to the questions prior to selecting from the provided responses. This section describes the participants, the assignment, and the type of data collected and analyzed for this paper.

2.1 Participants

In the Fall of 2010, students (N=435) enrolled in an introductory computer science course at a major university were assigned a problem set from an online tutoring system as a part of a homework. The course is a first course in Java programming, including topics such as control structures, variables, lists, and simple array algorithms. The course was comprised of a section of students majoring in Computer Science (N=44) as well as sections from two other instructors with non-major students completing a university-wide requirement. Students were given the ability to opt-out of the study; however, they were still required to complete the homework assignment for course credit. Because the study involved random assignment to experimental condition, different questions were provided to students in the same course. In order to mitigate any learning differences across groups, all students were given access to the other tutoring sequences of the study for "extra practice" after completing the required homework.

2.2 The Task

The tutoring system designed for this study presented students with a code snippet and a question about the code on each screen. Students were required to first answer the question by typing an open ended response in a textbox, and then selecting a multiple choice style response from a drop down list. The system automatically provided feedback based upon the answer chosen in the drop down list, and incorrect answers needed to be corrected, by selecting a different response, before the student could continue. The student did not have to re-enter an open ended response in order to progress to the next question. The open ended responses were saved by the system for later analysis by researchers.

The code snippets used for the questions were implementations of 10 array algorithms, and within the tutoring environment there were three questions presented for each code snippet. The first six code snippets were selected to be common algorithms including an implementation of a sum, incrementing all elements in an array, a count of values less than a given, and a max search. The last four code snippets were designed to be more complex and included a sort, and a check for duplicates within the array. Students were randomly assigned to one of four experimental conditions in the tutor, and all students saw multiple choice questions about the same 10 code segments in the same order.

The experimental conditions varied in two ways, which

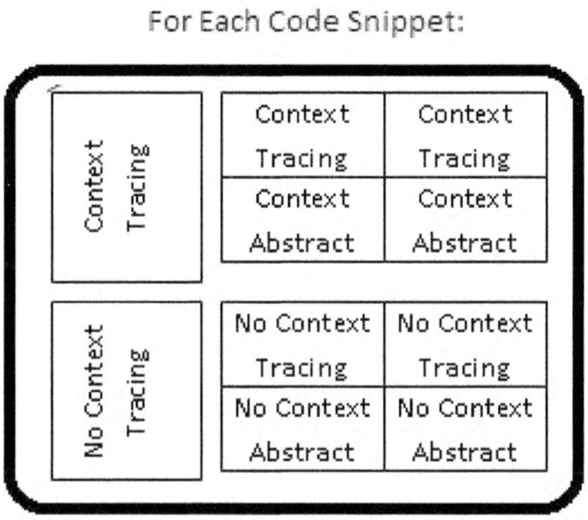

Figure 1: Question Sequence for Each Code Snippet

are illustrated in Figure 1. Two groups of students saw code with no contextual explanation (i.e., the code simply had a list of numbers and performed some operation), while two groups of students saw the code with an additional sentence offering context for the code snippet (i.e., the list contains the total number of votes cast for each candidate in an election). Two groups of students saw only code tracing questions (i.e., given some values already stored in the list, what is the result of the code), and two groups of students saw one tracing question and two questions asking about algorithmic abstractions (i.e., what is the role of the variable x in the following code) for each code snippet. These variables were crossed yielding four conditions for students, Abstract Questions No Context (AQNC), Abstract Questions with Context (AQC), Tracing Questions No Context (TQNC), and Tracing Questions with Context (TQC). Results of performance across condition are available in [19].

In this paper we analyze the responses students had to questions regarding algorithmic abstraction within the tutoring sequence. Although the students in the experimental conditions with only tracing questions (TQNC, TQC) saw the same code snippets, the open ended responses were the numeric answer produced by the code trace, and not useful for qualitative coding or analysis. We will be focusing on the students in the Abstract Question conditions (AQNC, AQC)(N=113).

2.3 Data Analysis

The student responses were classified based on alignment with any of the possible choices from the multiple choice question, and also on the correctness of the statement made. A response was judged to be correct if it matched the correct option for the multiple choice options provided, or if it made a factual statement relevant to the question asked that did not match one of the incorrect multiple choice options. Table 1 describes the codes employed to classify responses.

Although students contributed an open ended response to every question, in this paper we present the analysis of three particular questions due to their similarity, and the complexity of student responses and analysis. By limiting

Code	Description
NR	Non-Responsive Answers categorized as non responsive were single letters, "no answer" or other nonsense words.
MA-C	Matches Answer Correct The student's response matched an answer provided in the multiple choice selections and was correct.
MA-I	Matches Answer Incorrect: The student's response matched an answer provided in the multiple choice selections but was incorrect
NM-C	No Match Correct: The student's response did not match an answer provided in the multiple choice selections, however was an accurate statement.
NM-I	No Match Incorrect: The student's response did not match an answer provided in the multiple choice selection and was incorrect.

Table 1: Classification Codes for Student Responses

our question choice, we reduce variance in student responses and in correctness rate due to additional knowledge needed to answer the other questions. The questions we present were asked in regards to code snippets 3 (Sum), 4 (Count) and 5 (Increment). The questions asked about code snippets 3 and 4 ask about the role of a temporary variable used to store the current array element within the for loop in the algorithm. Question 5 asks about the role of the indexing variable (i) which is initialized, and updated as a part of the for loop. By evaluating the performance on question 4 we can determine if the experience of answering question 3 with feedback changed students behavior on the next question. Although question 5 is slightly different, it can be seen as a near-transfer question as the indexing variable is used to access each value in the list, as opposed to storing the value.

2.4 Feedback

Feedback was provided to the students upon selecting from the multiple choice options. The feedback was generated automatically by the system using a platform designed with the Cognitive Tutor Authoring Tools (CTAT) [20]. If the answer was correct, it would turn green and the student would be allowed to proceed to the next question. If the answer was incorrect, it would turn red, a message would appear at the bottom of the screen, and students would need to select the correct answer before continuing in the tutor.

The feedback was constructed to point out any flaws in reasoning that resulted in an incorrect choice. For example, when asked about the purpose of a variable that temporarily represents each element in the list (x = myList[i];) students had the option of choosing "It holds all the values in myList". The correct answer was "It temporarily represents each value in myList" and the feedback presented for the incorrect answer is "Can one variable hold all the values in the list at the same time? What might be a better description for what x does?". See Table 2 for question 3 including choices and feedback.

3. RESULTS

Student responses were analyzed in three ways using a mixed methods approach. First, the responses were qualitatively coded to determine if they matched any of the multiple

Description	Text

Code	public void code(int []myList){
	int x=0;
	for(int i=0; i<myList.length; i++){
	x = x + myList[i];
	}
	return x;
	}

Question	What purpose does the variable x serve in the algorithm implemented above?
Choice	It stores the value 0 (Feedback: That is the starting value of x, does x get changed at any point in the algorithm?)
Choice	It stores the last value in the list (Feedback: The variable x does get changed by the last value in the list, but is that the only value that changes x?)
Choice	To store the sum of all the values in the list (Feedback: This is the final result of the code, is it the purpose of x throughout the execution?)
Choice	It maintains the sum of all the values in the list encountered so far (Feedback: Correct)

Table 2: A Full Problem, The feedback would be displayed after the choice was selected.

choice answers. Then the responses were coded to determine if they were an accurate statement about the code snippet and answering the question asked. Quantitative methods were used to look at the difference in performance across questions and conditions, and to compare the open-ended responses with the multiple choice selection across questions. For this analysis we focus on the three questions described in Section 2.3.

3.1 Results from Qualitative Coding

The results of the coding for the three questions are shown in table 4. Although students received no feedback after typing their open ended response, there was a higher success rate on the first attempt at answering the multiple choice question than the open ended response questions. On question 3, 67% of students wrote a correct open ended response (55% matching the correct option), however 74% of students chose the correct response from the options available. Question 4 was much more consistent with 80% of students providing a correct open ended response (63% matching the correct multiple choice option) and 75% of students choosing the correct option on their first attempt. Question 5 was harder for students with only 34% of students providing a correct open ended response (20% matching the correct multiple choice option) and 37% of students selecting the correct multiple choice option on their first attempt.

As a group, the students who answered question 3 incorrectly showed improvement on question 4. Forty (40) students answered question 3 in an incorrect manner (NM-I, MA-I, NR) in their open ended response, however only 12 of those students answered question 4 incorrectly and of those 7 were non-responsive answers. The pattern is even more interesting because there were two additional questions asked between what we have designated question 3 and question 4 in this paper (one on code base 3 regarding an overall de-

Example	Code	Student Response	Explanation
A	NM-I	Represents the number of minutes in one song in the list	The variable represents each element at some point in the algorithm, not just one song.
B	MA-I	It gets added to the variable that represents the sum of the list	While this is a correct statement, it was judged to be a direct translation of the code and not the role of the variable in the algorithm.
C	NM-C	It is the current value to be added	This is a correct statement, however the matching answer references the sum of all values so far.

Table 3: Example Student Responses to Problem 3

scription of the algorithm, and one on code base 4 asking the student to trace the code with given input values).

Table 3.1 contains sample student responses. The No Match Incorrect (NM-I) responses often did not express the algorithms as a process, but instead a singular action. Notice the language in response B. The student indicated that the variable only represented the minutes in one song in the list. These responses echo difficulties students have during code production, where they have trouble understanding or writing algorithmic components with constantly changing state. Similar to the NM-I responses, the Match Incorrect (MA-I) responses did not express either the changing or temporary nature of the variable in the algorithm.

The number of students who incorrectly answered the open-ended question and then correctly answered the multiple choice question could indicate that the constraint of choices acted as feedback to the students about the correct answer, or that some students made appropriate guesses. In Section 4.1 we offer additional distractors appropriate from student responses.

3.2 Statistical Models

Student responses varied across question and experimental condition (No Context or Context). Table 4 shows the number of responses in each category by question. Figure 3.2 shows the number of students whose open ended answer matched a researcher created multiple choice response, whose open ended answer was coded to be accurate, and who answered the multiple choice question correctly on their first attempt. An ANOVA indicates that there is a significant effect of question ($p<.001$) on students' ability to answer correctly, but no significance was attributed to contextual condition ($p=.48$). A linear regression model did indicate significance in matching a multiple choice answer ($p<.05$) in the contextual condition. The regression results indicated that for students in the contextual condition they were less likely to construct an open ended response matching a predetermined distractor. The regression result is an indication

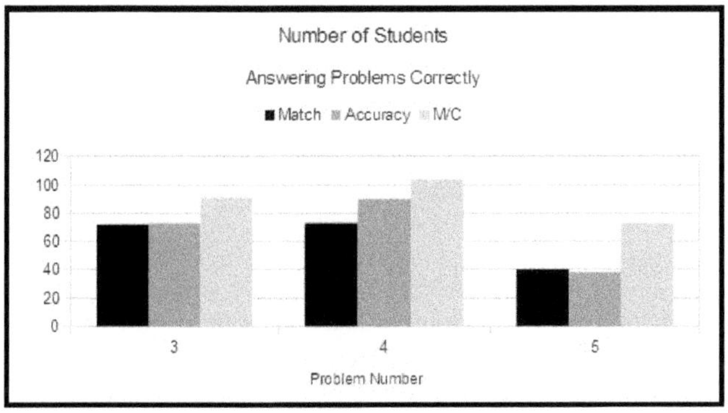

Figure 2: Student Performance by Question

that context may have some impact on student's thought process, and should be studied in more detail.

Student performance increased from question 3 to question 4, indicating some learning had taken place. Student performance decreased for question 5, however it is seen as a near-transfer question, so some performance decrease is expected.

Question	MA-C	MA-I	NM-C	NM-I	NR
No Context 3	37	6	3	7	4
Context 3	23	6	11	13	0
No Context 4	40	2	5	4	6
Context 4	31	0	14	8	3
No Context 5	15	10	1	27	7
Context 5	8	9	15	20	4

Table 4: Student Performance by Question

Question 3 Student performance on the first attempt of the multiple choice response of question 3 was only significantly affected by whether their response matched an answer available in the multiple choice selections ($p<.05$). The condition that the student was in, and the accuracy of the statement made by the student was not significant with respect to answering the multiple choice selection.

Question 4 Student performance on the first attempt multiple choice response of question 4 was significantly impacted by their correct choice response in question 3 ($p<.001$) and whether their open ended response for question 4 was categorized as accurate ($p<.001$). Eighty-six (86) percent of students who answered the multiple choice option incorrectly for question 3, answered the multiple choice option correctly for question 4. While it may be argued that the students just remembered the last option (even with the questions between) and re-chose it, there is evidence that it was more than simple recognition. Of the students who answered question 3 incorrectly, and then question 4 correctly, 74% of them also wrote a correct open-ended response as well.

Question 5 Student performance on the first attempt multiple choice response of question 5 was significantly impacted by their correct choice response in question 3 ($p<.01$), their accuracy in the open ended part of question 4 ($p<.05$) and their accuracy in the open ended part of question 5 ($p<.01$).

4. CONCLUSIONS

The significant performance improvement from the first to second question indicates that code comprehension questions can be used as learning activities when accompanied by feedback. Just as a teacher would use a worked example in class, and use the class to answer questions regarding the example, code comprehension activities can be used as a part of problem sets to highlight features of code. Future work is planned to evaluate the impact of code comprehension learning activities on code production with introductory students.

4.1 Using Open-Ended and Multiple Choice

Together, the first and third authors of this paper have over 30 years of teaching experience in both high school and college settings. Although the incorrect responses were designed to be effective distracters, analysis of the open ended responses provided data indicating that students had alternative models of the code. As online and automated assessment becomes increasingly popular, the use of multiple choice items for their ease of grading will be common. We hope that this work highlights the additional data collection that can be done using open ended responses, not to be used in scoring the students, but instead to offer assessment designers a way to evaluate the distracters used in multiple choice style questions.

Within the three questions analyzed in this paper, the most common incorrect answers that did not match a response shared language referring to "an element" or "the value". This would indicate the need for a distractor focused on a singular state held by variables that are updated as the loop continues through the algorithm. If these questions are reused in a future study we will include a response in the multiple choice answers addressing this misconception.

4.2 Recommendations for the Use of Worked Examples

Computer programming requires reasoning on multiple levels of abstraction during problem solving. In order to comprehend code, novices must understand (parse) individual commands, and attempt to construct a larger understanding of the algorithm as a whole[21, 18]. Novices often can understand the individual parts, but struggle with formulating a coherent complex representation of all of the parts of the algorithm[3].

The responses discussed in this paper highlight a particular misconception that students struggle with, the "in motion" properties of algorithms. Unlike the solving of algebraic expressions in mathematics classes, the addition of looping constructs means that a single variable, in the same line of the worked example, can represent multiple values. Algorithmic animations do a good job of emphasizing the change, especially if they include simultaneous code highlighting.

For instructors and textbook authors who present worked examples in code, emphasis on the change that occurs to variables over time within the algorithm is recommended. The authors plan to explore this misconception and appropriate instructional methods in future studies.

5. ACKNOWLEDGMENTS

The authors would like to thank Matt Jadud for helping to facilitate access to his students and computers at Allegheny

College. This work was supported through the Program for Interdisciplinary Education Research (PIER) at Carnegie Mellon University, funded through Grant R305B040063 to Carnegie Mellon University, from the Institute of Education Sciences, US Department of Education. The opinions expressed are those of the authors and do not represent the views of the Institute or the US Department of Education.

6. REFERENCES

[1] Carsten Schulte, Teresa Busjahn, Tony Clear, James Paterson, and Ahmad Taherkhani, "An introduction to program comprehension for computer science educators", in *ITiCSE '10: Proceedings of the fifteenth annual conference on Innovation and technology in computer science education*, New York, NY, USA, 2010, pp. 108–112, ACM.

[2] Mike Lopez, Jacqueline Whalley, Phil Robbins, and Raymond Lister, "Relationships between reading, tracing and writing skills in introductory programming", in *ICER '08: Proceeding of the Fourth international Workshop on Computing Education Research*, New York, NY, USA, 2008, pp. 101–112, ACM.

[3] Raymond Lister, "The neglected middle novice programmer: Reading and writing without abstracting", *In Proceedings of the 20th Annual Conference of the National Advisory Committee on Computing Qualifications*, 2007.

[4] John Sweller and Graham Cooper, "The use of worked examples as a substitute for problem solving in learning algebra", *Cognition and Instruction*, vol. 2, pp. 59–89, 1985.

[5] Beth Simon, Michael Kohanfars, Jeff Lee, Karen Tamayo, and Quintin Cutts, "Experience report: peer instruction in introductory computing", in *Proceedings of the 41st ACM technical symposium on Computer science education*, New York, NY, USA, 2010, SIGCSE '10, pp. 341–345, ACM.

[6] Raymond Lister, Tony Clear, Simon, Dennis J. Bouvier, Paul Carter, Anna Eckerdal, Jana Jacková, Mike Lopez, Robert McCartney, Phil Robbins, Otto Seppälä, and Errol Thompson, "Naturally occurring data as research instrument: analyzing examination responses to study the novice programmer", *SIGCSE Bull.*, vol. 41, pp. 156–173, January 2010.

[7] Raymond Lister, Elizabeth S. Adams, Sue Fitzgerald, William Fone, John Hamer, Morten Lindholm, Robert McCartney, Jan Erik Moström, Kate Sanders, Otto Seppälä, Beth Simon, and Lynda Thomas, "A multi-national study of reading and tracing skills in novice programmers", *SIGCSE Bull.*, vol. 36, pp. 119–150, June 2004.

[8] Laurie Murphy, Renee McCauley, and Sue Fitzgerald, "'explain in plain english' questions: Implications for teaching", *Proceedings of the fourty-third ACM Special Interest Group on Computer Science Education*, 2012.

[9] A. Philpott, P. Robbins, and J. Whalley, "Assessing the steps on the way to relational thinking", *Proceedings of the 20th annual conference of the National Advisory Committee on Computing Qualifications*, p. 286, 2007.

[10] T. Clear, J. Whalley, P. Robbins, A. Philpott, A. Eckerdal, M. Laakso, and R. Lister, "Report on the final bracelet workshop", *Journal of Applied Computing and Information Technology*, vol. 15 (1), 2011.

[11] National Research Council, *How People Learn: Brain, Mind, Experience and School*, National Academy Press, 2000.

[12] Steve Ritter, John Anderson, and Ken Koedinger, "Cognitive tutor: Applied research in mathematics education", *Psychonomic Bulletin & Review*, vol. 14(2), pp. 249–255, 2007.

[13] J. Anderson and B. Reiser, "The lisp tutor: it approaches the effectiveness of a human tutor", *Lecture*, vol. 174, 1985.

[14] C. Areias and A. Mendes, "A tool to help students to develop programming skills", *Proceedings of the 2007 International Conference on Computer Systems and Technologies*, 2007.

[15] Nick Parlante, "Codingbat: Practice java and python problems".

[16] Elliot Soloway, Beverly Woolf, Eric Rubin, and Paul Barth, "Meno-ii: an intelligent tutoring system for novice programmers", *Proceedings of IJCAI'81, Proceedings of the 7th international joint conference on artificial intelligence*, 1981.

[17] Anne Venables, Grace Tan, and Raymond Lister, "A closer look at tracing, explaining and code writing skills in the novice programmer", in *ICER '09: Proceedings of the fifth international workshop on Computing education research workshop*, New York, NY, USA, 2009, pp. 117–128, ACM.

[18] Jacqueline L. Whalley, Raymond Lister, Errol Thompson, Tony Clear, Phil Robbins, P. K. Ajith Kumar, and Christine Prasad, "An australasian study of reading and comprehension skills in novice programmers, using the bloom and solo taxonomies", in *Proceedings of the 8th Austalian conference on Computing education - Volume 52*, Darlinghurst, Australia, Australia, 2006, ACE '06, pp. 243–252, Australian Computer Society, Inc.

[19] Leigh Ann Sudol-DeLyser and Jonathan Steinhart, "Factors impacting novice code comprehension in a tutor for introductory computer science", *In Proceedings of the 2nd Annual Conference in Educational Data Mining.*

[20] Vincent Aleven, Bruce McLaren, Johnathan Sewall, and Ken Koedinger, "A new paradigm for intelligent tutoring systems: Example-tracing tutors", *International Journal of Artificial Intelligence in Education*, vol. 19(2), pp. 105–154, 2009.

[21] Carsten Schulte, "Block model: an educational model of program comprehension as a tool for a scholarly approach to teaching", *Proceedings of the Fourth Annual Workshop on Computer Science Education*, 2008.

An Open-Ended Environment for Teaching Java in Context

André L. Santos[*†]
andre.santos@iscte.pt

[*]Faculty of Sciences, University of Lisbon
LASIGE, Bloco C6, Piso 3, Campo Grande
1749-016 Lisboa, Portugal

[†]Instituto Universitário de Lisboa (ISCTE-IUL)
Av. das Forças Armadas, Edifício II
1649-026 Lisboa, Portugal

ABSTRACT

Teaching programming in context, i.e. having students learning how to program by manipulating artifacts of a familiar domain (e.g. images, card games), has demonstrated convincing results in terms of raising student retention and interest in CS. This paper presents a pedagogical environment for teaching Java in context that is extensible with respect to the domains it supports. Instructors model domains and develop visualization widgets for rendering their objects. In turn, students use the environment to visualize and manipulate objects of the domain when solving exercises. The advantage and originality of the proposed environment is that it embodies an open-ended platform for creating diverse contexts at a low cost, standing as an enabler for widening the spectrum of abstractions for programming in context.

Categories and Subject Descriptors

K.3.2 [**Computers and Education**]: Computer and Information Science Education; D.1.5 [**Programming Techniques**]: Object-oriented Programming

General Terms

Design, Human Factors

Keywords

Object-oriented programming, contextualized programming, Java

1. INTRODUCTION

When teaching computer science in *context* [2], programming is introduced using domains that are familiar and relevant to students, such as image manipulation or card games. This teaching strategy has proven successful (e.g. [9]), especially in non-CS majors (e.g. [4]), demonstrating a significant impact on retention and student satisfaction.

This paper presents an extensible environment[1] for teaching and learning Java in context. When using the environment, instructors may adopt existing or create new *domain contexts* for programming exercises. Such domain contexts may be, for instance, board games, card games, image manipulation, charts, maps, etc, and basically anything that can be modeled and visualized. In order to supply the environment with a domain context, one has to provide a set of classes that models that domain and view widgets that are capable of rendering objects of those classes.

When developing and testing programs, students manipulate and visualize objects of the domains provided by the extensions available in the environment. In a first step, a student may explore a domain in order to learn what can be done with its objects. This is achieved by interactively creating and manipulating objects through the environment's GUI. Upon understanding the domain, students instantiate its classes in their programs when solving exercises. The role of the environment is to enable experimentation of the developed code, through a GUI that adapts itself to the user classes.

The advantage of the proposed environment is that it embodies an open-ended means to support various domains for programming in context. The environment extensibility allows domain contexts to be added at a low cost, in the order of a few tens of lines of code. Standing as an affordable means to develop new contexts, the environment has the potential for widening the spectrum of solutions for contextualized programming.

The proposed environment has been used during one delivery of the introduction to programming course at our department. We have carefully analyzed its impact with respect to two different student populations (CS majors and non-CS majors). Results reveal higher success rates in both populations, however, with more expressive impact on non-CS majors. Moreover, we found that non-CS majors tend to like and feel more comfortable with the environment than CS majors.

This paper proceeds as follows. Section 2 presents an overview on the proposed environment. Section 3 explains how the environment can be used by students. Section 4 details how extensions for supporting new domains can be developed. Section 5 presents the results of using the proposed environment in our introduction to programming course. Section 6 situates our approach regarding related work, and Section 7 concludes the paper.

2. OVERVIEW

The proposed environment is an Eclipse-based tool supporting Java that capitalizes on our previous work on AGUIA/J [8]. The essence of the environment's role is to graphically render objects of a certain domain context, while enabling users to manipulate them. The domain contexts supported by the environment are provided by means of plugins. In this way, the environment is not targeting any particular domain, but it rather consists of an open-ended platform for supporting different domains, which may be combined.

[1]available at *http://www.aguiaj.org.pt*

ITiCSE'12, July 3–5, 2012, Haifa, Israel.

For the purpose of illustrating our approach, consider a basic domain context of board games. Many board games involve a rectangular board, composed of several positions that are referenced by a coordinate (line and column). Positions may have different colors and may hold an image (icon) that represents a game entity (e.g. a chess piece). Figure 1 presents a conceptual model for board games according to what is described, and a picture representing an instance of that model.

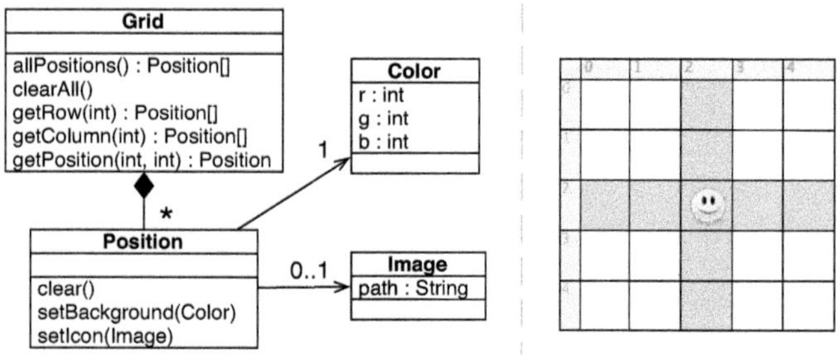

Figure 1: Board games context: a UML class diagram (left) describing the domain model and a picture (right) representing an example instance of the model.

We refer to the objects that instantiate the domain classes as being a *model* of a particular board in a certain state, whereas we refer to the several possible visual representations of that model as its *views*, as in the the well-known *model-view-controller* architectural pattern. For instance, the graphical representation of the board shown in Figure 1 is one out of many possible representations, from which the actual *domain model* is independent. When developing a domain context for our environment, one has to model it in terms of Java classes.

The environment customization relies on a plugin-based architecture, which we illustrate in Figure 2. A plugin is essentially composed of a *domain model* and *view* widgets. The domain model is given as a set of classes, whereas the views are widget implementations for rendering objects of those classes. The environment acts as a *controller* that coordinates the domain objects and the views that render them. There are two clearly distinct environment stakeholders. On the one hand we have *instructors*, which prepare the environment to be used in accordance with the proposed course exercises. On the other hand we have *students*, which use the environment as a learning tool and solve exercises using it.

The role of an instructor is to customize the environment for a given programming course (or a course involving programming). The customization can be achieved by means of: (a) using existing plugins that address domain contexts, (b) developing a plugin for supporting a new domain context, or (c) adapting/extending an existing plugin. Naturally, the proposed course exercises have to take into account the domain contexts available in the customized environment.

In turn, students solve exercises involving the creation and manipulation of objects of the domain contexts offered by the environment. In a first contact with a new domain, a student may create its objects solely through the environment's GUI, in order to easily see what the objects are representing and understand their behavior in terms of the available operations. Upon a domain being understood, students may start to manipulate the domain objects in their Java programs. Furthermore, if inheritance is a topic of the course contents, the exercises may involve specialization of domain classes.

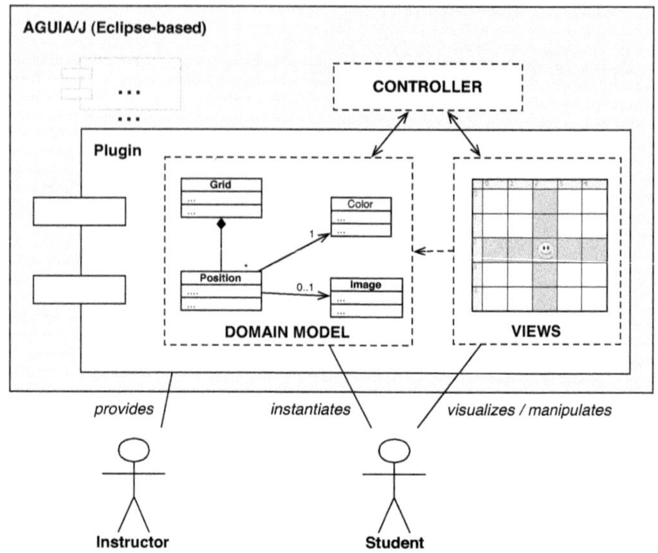

Figure 2: Environment overview: instructor and student roles.

3. ENVIRONMENT USAGE

This section explains how students use the environment, detailing the user experience when solving programming exercises.

3.1 Domain exploration

As explained, a domain is modeled in a set of classes. These classes conceptually define the set of possible objects of the domain. When faced with an unfamiliar domain, a student may explore it through experimentation in order to understand its objects. Domain objects are created and manipulated in the environment, enabling the user to see the changes in the objects' state while interacting with them. This is illustrated in Figure 3 using the board games domain introduced previously. The boxes represent the objects and the buttons represent commands (i.e. operations) that can be instructed to the object (by pressing them). While interacting with the objects, the user visualizes their state in a view widget on the upper part. Following the annotations in the figure, in step one the Grid object was created by pressing the button new. Upon creation, all the positions of the grid were white. In step two, the method getPosition(..) was invoked on the grid, causing the corresponding position object to be brought into the environment. Finally, in step three, the method setBackground(..) is invoked on the position fetched in step two, changing its color to gray. The color changes in both widgets (grid and position), since we have the position object visualized in two different views.

During interaction, the environment displays a documentation view that shows the relevant Javadoc snippets when the mouse hovers class/object members. For instance, when the mouse is over an object's button, the documentation view displays the Javadoc description of that operation (as illustrated in the figure).

3.2 Domain instantiation

After gaining contact with a given domain context, students will have grasped what can be done with the domain objects. This will in principle make it easier to instantiate the domain classes in Java programs, given that the objects should feel less abstract after being materialized in the environment.

In order to use a domain context, its classes have to be imported as if using a library. The output of the exercises relies on the envi-

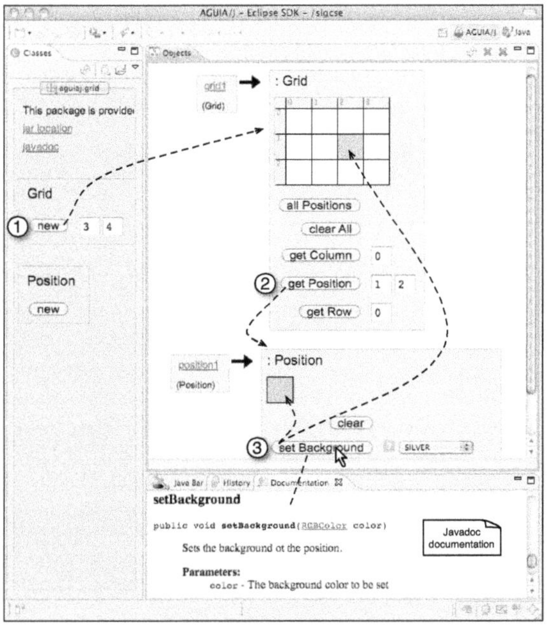

Figure 3: Domain exploration: platform screenshot illustrating the experimentation of the board games domain.

```
1  import aguiaj.board.Grid;
2  import aguiaj.board.Position;
3  import aguiaj.colors.Color;
4
5  public class CheckersGame {
6     private static final int SIDE = 8;
7     private static final Color BLACK = new Color(0, 0, 0);
8
9     private Grid board;
10    ...
11    public CheckersGame() {
12       board = createBoard();
13    }
14
15    public static Grid createBoard() {
16       Grid board = new Grid(SIDE, SIDE);
17       for(int i = 0; i < SIDE; i++) {
18          for(int j = (i+1) % 2; j < SIDE; j+=2) {
19             Position p = board.getPosition(i, j);
20             p.setBackground(BLACK);
21          }
22       }
23       return board;
24    }
25
26    public Grid getBoard() { return board; }
27    public void setupGame() { ... }
28    ...
29 }
```

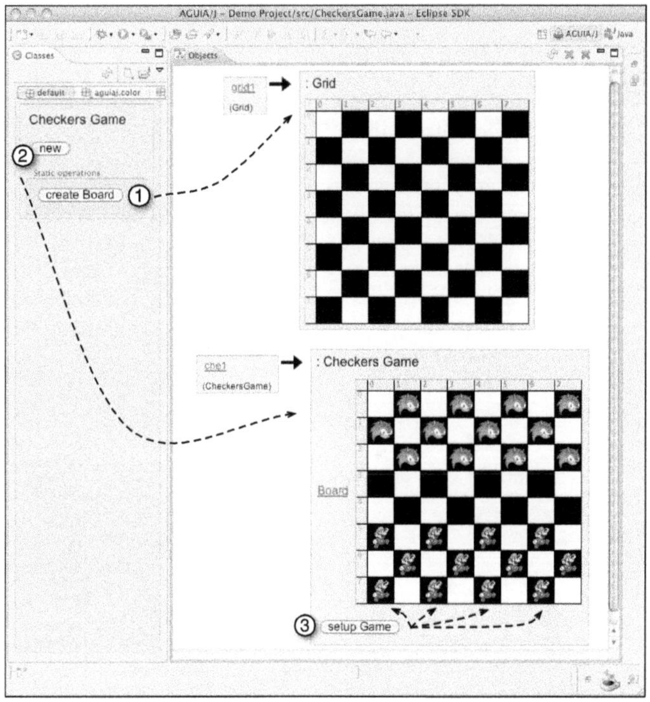

Figure 4: Domain instantiation: using the board games domain to develop a checkers game.

ronment, which is where users see the objects that their code outputs. The environment adapts its GUI to the structural elements of the user classes.

As an example, Figure 4 presents a part of an exercise for creating a checkers game using the board games' domain classes, omitting attributes and methods related with the game state. The class CheckersGame is the main class of the game, holding a reference to a Grid object, which displays the board view. In this example we can see two forms of experiencing the visualization of domain objects in the environment. The first form is direct object instantiation, illustrated with the static method given on lines 15-24. Given that the method is public, a button for invoking it is displayed in the GUI. When pressing it (step one), the method is invoked and the resulting Grid object is placed in the environment. The second form is when domain objects are part of objects of a user class, as illustrated with CheckersGame. Such a class has a constructor, which determines the existence of the new button. When pressed (step two), the created object of type CheckersGame is brought into the environment. Due to the existence of the accessor method getBoard(), the object displays the current game board using the available widget to render Grid objects. In step three, the method setupGame() is invoked by pressing the button, setting up the initial state of the game.

4. PROVIDING DOMAIN CONTEXTS

Providing a domain context for the environment can be achieved by means of developing a plugin. Given that the plugin-based architecture of the environment is built on Eclipse, the extension points are based on its standard mechanisms. Although we have assumed that plugins would be developed by instructors or anyone with a reasonable programming background, we consider that the necessary programming skills for doing so are not demanding.

A plugin has to provide a *model* for the domain and *view* widgets for rendering objects of that domain. The model is composed of a set of classes, which are completely independent from environment classes or any other classes (such as Swing/AWT). Therefore, the development of the model does not involve subclassing environment classes nor implementation of interfaces. The domain should be modeled abstractly and independently of how its objects might be visualized (recall Figure 1). The domain classes are intended to be a "pure" and conceptually clean model of the domain that one wants to support in the environment. Given that domain classes are going to be used and inspected by students, their code should be clean and without any awkward workarounds that could be considered pedagogically incorrect. Finally, the code should include Javadoc comments, so that students can have access to documentation when exploring the domain (recall Section 3.1). The effort of creating the domain model is orthogonal to our approach, given that it directly relates to the complexity of the domain itself.

In addition to the domain model, a plugin should provide view widgets that are responsible for rendering the domain objects. The widget classes have to implement an interface of the environment's framework. The classes of the view widgets depend on the model classes (while the opposite should not happen). Given that Eclipse is built on SWT, the view widgets have to be implemented using it. As a reference in terms of effort, the implementation of the grid viewer that was used throughout the examples in the previous section had approximately 150 LOC. This domain also included a view widget for the position in isolation (as in Figure 3), which had approximately 60 LOC.

4.1 Card games domain context

In order to give another example of a domain context, here we present a domain context for *card games* that we developed for the introduction to programming course at our institution. Besides having course exercises making use of this domain, students also had to develop a small project using it, as part of their evaluation.

Card games are known almost everywhere in the world and are very popular in some countries. Possible programming exercises span across the domain of known card games. Algorithmic topics involving sorting, shuffling, randomness, and array manipulation, naturally fit within this context. Figure 5 illustrates the playing cards domain by presenting a screenshot taken from a student project (object visualized in the environment) and the related domain model. As we can see in the domain model, the concepts of *rank* and *suit* were represented as object enumerations. Besides the concept of card object, the domain also considered data structures for cards, namely, for representing *hands* and *stacks* of cards.

The implementation of the card views totalized approximately 60 LOC, comprising two widgets (for cards and suits). The card stack widget had approximately 50 LOC, while the card hand widget had approximately 70 LOC.

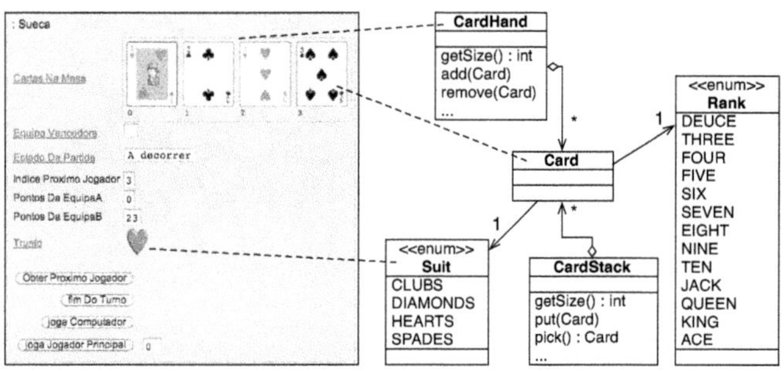

Figure 5: Playing cards context: Screenshot of a student project and domain model.

5. EVALUATION

At our institution, we have redesigned the introduction to programming course taking into account the proposed environment, while shifting to a conservative contextualized programming teaching strategy. By conservative we mean that the course still remains partially traditional. In our case, the first half of the course is taught using traditional exercises that mostly involve numeric calculations and algebra, whereas in the second half the different domain contexts come into play.

5.1 Context

The introduction to programming course is offered to several degrees, which are all related to Information Technology. In this section we report the results of the last delivery of the course for two of those degrees, namely Computer Science and Engineering (CSE, CS major) and Informatics and Management (IM, non-CS major).

The course lasts for 12 weeks, each week having a lecture of 1.5 hour and a lab class of 3 hours. Table 1 presents the course topics, grouped in three stages of 4 weeks.

Stage	Weeks	Topics
1	4	Variables, loops, selection statements, functions
2	4	Arrays, references, objects, procedures
3	4	Object classes, encapsulation, enum types

Table 1: Introduction to programming course topics.

Each group of students — CSE and IM — has a common lecture given for all the students of that degree and 4 lab class groups running in parallel. The lectures were all given by a single teacher (the main author of this paper), whereas 4 different teachers (including the lecturer) gave one lab class to CSE and one lab class to IM.

Every year, up to 65 new students from each degree enroll in the course. In addition to the students enrolling for the first time there is a significant number of students reenrolling (about 25%).

In order to obtain approval in the course, a student has to perform the final exam. Attending the final exam requires the student to obtain prior approval in the lab classes (minimum of 45% score), by means of tests and a small project. Throughout the 12 weeks there were three evaluation items for qualifying for the final exam: (a) Test-1 at week 4, (b) Test-2 at week 8, and (c) individual project to hand in at week 12.

The environment was used throughout the 12 weeks. In the lectures the environment served the purpose of aiding the explanation and illustration of concepts. In the lab classes the environment was used by the students to develop exercises. The environment played a minor role in the first stage of the course, given that students only developed static functions using primitive types. The main advantage was to avoid having to deal with the main() method and I/O.

Besides the lab class exercises, students also used the environment to develop and test their project. The project goal was to model a popular card game using object classes. The game was simulated in an object representing the game state (e.g. see Figure 5). Students tested their card games in the environment and concentrated solely on game logic without worrying about user interface issues, given that the environment works as GUI for their objects. In addition to the card games domain, the course also included exercises using the domains of image manipulation (binary, grayscale, and color) and board games (illustrated in Section 2) in the course exercises.

5.2 Methodology

We decided to investigate and present the results of the degrees CSE and IM in parallel because they had approximately equal population sizes and were taught exactly by the same teachers in equal proportions. Moreover, given that IM is a non-CS major, we could evaluate the impact of the approach on two substantially different student populations.

We have measured the impact of using the environment in terms of approval rates (objective) and student satisfaction (subjective). The evaluation is not only evaluating the impact of the environment itself in isolation, but rather the impact of using the tool in our context together with the course restructuring towards a contextualized programming teaching strategy.

We compared the approval rates among first-time enrollment (i.e. the set of students enrolling for the first time in the course) between the restructured course delivery and the previous delivery (before adopting the environment). We decided to focus only on first-time enrollment in order to evaluate the impact of the environment independently of student experience gained in previous enrollments, which naturally influences student performance.

The student satisfaction measurement was achieved by means of a survey handed in to students that have qualified for the exam. We decided to survey only these students in order to guarantee that the respondents had experienced the whole process. One of the survey questions had the purpose of characterizing the population in terms of prior programming experience. The other three questions were related with the way the course was conducted and the involvement of the tool environment in the process. Additionally, in order to complement the comparison of approval rates, the survey included a question only for reenrolling students that asked how difficult they felt the course delivery was when compared to the previous year. The survey was optional and we had 100 respondents, 47 out of 49 in CSE (96%), and 53 out of 55 in IM (95%).

5.3 Results

The two student populations — CSE and IM — are significantly different. Two of the main distinctive characteristics are with respect to prior programming experience and student background. In CSE there are clearly more students with previous programming experience. In IM there are several students with a high school background on Economics and Business Administration. Moreover, the IM degree is more competitive, in the sense that degree enrollment applications normally register a minimum mark that is 5-10% higher than in CSE.

5.3.1 Success rates

Taking into account first-time enrollment only, Table 2 presents how the approval rates evolve as the semester progresses towards the final exam (qualify). The values correspond to the number of students that succeeded in obtaining positive mark (>=50%) on the different evaluation items. We can see that within first-time enrollment roughly two thirds of the students make it to the final exam. We speculate that the remarkable higher success of IM students in the written tests is due to the higher competitiveness.

Table 3 presents the approval rates of first-time enrollment in two course deliveries: *Fall 2010* (previous year) and *Fall 2011* (present year, restructured taking into account the proposed environment). The rates are not definitive, they were originated after the first exam was due (students have a second opportunity). We can observe increased approval rates in both degrees, being the improvement more expressive in IM. We have performed a two proportion Z-test to compare the approval rates of the different course deliveries, revealing a statistically significant ($\alpha = 0.05$) improvement in the Fall 2011 course delivery within IM ($p = 0.0436$). With respect to CSE, the rate improvement did not prove to be statistically significant ($p = 0.2676$).

We have asked students reenrolling how they perceive the difficulty of the current course delivery when compared to the previous year. The question in the survey was *"When compared to the previous course delivery, how do you classify the effort required to obtain approval in this course delivery?"*. Within the possible answers: *much easier (-2)*, *easier (-1)*, *equivalent (0)*, *harder (1)*, and *much harder (2)*, we obtained average values of 0.56 for CSE and 0.81 for IM. This poll strengthens the result of improved approval rates, given that a course restructuring that would require less student effort would likely raise approval rates *per se*.

5.3.2 Survey

The survey contained a question that asked students to characterize their programming experience before starting the course (see Table 4). We can see that in CSE there is a significant proportion of students that states that it has considerable prior programming experience, whereas in IM more than 50% of the students stated that they did not have any programming experience at all.

Another question of the survey had the purpose of measuring to what extent students felt that the tool environment helped them (see Table 4). We have segmented students according their answer regarding programming experience ("none" or "little" vs. "fair" or "considerable") and degree. We can see that students that have no significant programming experience tend to answer clearly positively (stating that the environment helped them "somewhat" or "much"), being the tendency stronger in the case of IM (non-CS major). When analyzing students that have stated to have "fair" or "considerable" programming experience we can observe less positive answers. However, in the case of IM there is still 72% of students with programming experience that state that the environment has helped them "somewhat" or "much". It is clearly noticeable that CS majors (CSE) tend to be less positive in their perception of the usefulness of the environment when compared to non-CS majors. It is also worth mentioning that being IM students more positive towards the tool environment they have also been more successful in obtaining approval in the course. Although more CSE students had prior programming experience, their success rate was clearly inferior. Based on comments that we (teachers) heard in the lab classes, we feel that some CSE students tend to not fully enjoy the tool environment due to the frustration of their programming activity not resulting in a "real" program with full control of interaction. This was especially evident in students with prior programming experience.

The survey contained two other questions, which due to space constraints are only reported briefly here. Given that the answers to these two questions did not differ significantly between CSE and IM, we present the results here as a whole. One of such questions was: *"To what extent do you consider the process of developing*

Degree	Enrolled	Test-1	Test-2	Project	Qualify
CSE	62	44 (71%)	39 (63%)	34 (55%)	40 (65%)
IM	59	53 (90%)	45 (76%)	36 (61%)	42 (71%)

Table 2: Evaluation and success rates of first-time enrollment throughout the semester.

Course delivery	CSE	IM
Fall 2010	30.3% (22/66)	33.9% (21/62)
Fall 2011	35.5% (22/62)	49.2% (29/59)

Table 3: Comparison of approval rates of first-time enrollment.

How do you characterize your prior programming experience?

Degree	None	Little	Fair	Considerable
CSE	36%	23%	24%	17%
IM	56%	17%	23%	4%

To what extent do you consider that the tool environment has contributed positively to overcome your difficulties in programming with objects?

Degree	Nothing	Little	Somewhat	Much
CSE	7%	25%	43%	25%
CSE (with experience)	32%	42%	21%	5%
IM	0%	8%	33%	59%
IM (with experience)	7%	21%	43%	29%

Table 4: Survey questions and results.

the project fun (i.e. not tedious, stimulating)?". A great majority of students answered positively, namely 46% answered "very" and 43% answered "fair" (other options: "little" and "nothing"). We concluded that choosing a popular theme (card game) for the project and having the tool environment for developing it was a good option. The other question was: *"Supposing that you have a friend enrolled in a non-CS major degree that has interest in programming, would you recommend him/her this course?"*. A great majority of students answered positively, namely 26% answered "definitely" and 60% answered "yes" (other options: "maybe" and "no"). The goal of this question was to measure to what extent students consider the course to be interesting for non-CS majors.

6. RELATED WORK

The Media Computation [3] approach for introductory programming courses advocates the construction of media through programming, where images, sounds, and videos, are manipulated in students' programs. Our environment, when supplied with a domain context for image manipulation (which may be custom-designed by an institution), is adequate as courseware for a Media Computation course. Moreover, the image manipulation context may coexist with other domain contexts in the environment.

The Inverted Curriculum teaching strategy [7] involves addressing introduction to programming using an "outside-in" approach, where right from the start software construction relies on existing reusable components. These are embodied in a large software framework that the students start to use as consumers, and progressively move on to be producers, exploring, modifying, and augmenting its implementation. The introductory programming course that applies Inverted Curriculum as described by its proponents [7] uses a single, large software framework (named Traffic). Our environment relates to the Inverted Curriculum approach in the sense that students are also provided with a set of classes to work with. Although we have envisioned the domain contexts for our environment as being small, simple, and focused, there is no restriction with respect to their size and complexity. However, using large classes in the domain models would certainly affect environment usability due to the resulting large object widgets.

BlueJ [6] is a pedagogical IDE for Java where users can experiment the creation of objects and method invocations. Despite some usability differences, our environment has a similar interaction style. However, our environment was designed for programming in context upfront. Although BlueJ was not primarily targeted for programming in context, one may use it for that purpose. For instance, the "shapes" example project that ships with BlueJ can be considered to a certain extent a form of contextualized programming, where we have a canvas containing geometrical figures that can be added, moved, etc. However, in this example there is no separation between model and view, since its classes depend on the AWT graphical library (they represent both the concept of geometrical figures and its visualization). Given that one of the central goals of BlueJ is to relieve beginners of having to deal with pedagogically-uninteresting language-specific issues (e.g. main() method), we argue that early exposure to graphical libraries somewhat conflicts with this goal. We are in favor of providing students with conceptually clean models, given that it avoids exposing advanced topics (for a first programming course), while it promotes conceptual modeling (the essence of object-orientation).

Greenfoot [5] is a pedagogical environment for Java (based on BlueJ), suitable for developing programs that consist of 2D simulations in a *scenario* where several *actors* live in a *world*. Greenfoot is extensible with respect to its scenarios, having necessarily every class of visual objects as a subclass of Greenfoot's framework classes (World and Actor). Greenfoot can be thought of as being a means to program in the context of 2D simulations with scenario variability, and naturally, the set of possible domains is constrained to 2D simulations. For instance, it is possible to represent a card game in terms of a world with actors, but nevertheless, it leads to an unnatural modeling of the game.

In a similar vein as Greenfoot, Alice [1] consists of a programming environment, also supporting Java (as of version 3.0), that addresses the domain of creating 3D animations in the style of storytelling. Both Greenfoot and Alice enable students to create animations, a stimulating form of program visualization that we did not consider upfront in our approach. Although these systems may be used in CS1, they were designed to target younger age groups when compared to our approach. We believe that for teaching more advanced concepts, such as algorithms, data structures, and design patterns, the tool support has to move into a more "real" solution.

7. CONCLUSION

In this paper we have proposed an open-ended environment for programming in context whose design considered context variability upfront. An essential aspect of the novelty of our work is the fact that our environment is a means to program in context that is not tied to any particular context. At our institution, we have adopted the environment in the introduction to programming course along with a course restructuring towards a contextualized programming teaching strategy. Results revealed good levels of student satisfaction, as well as a significant improvement in approval rates with respect to non-CS majors.

8. REFERENCES

[1] S. Cooper. The design of alice. *ACM Transactions on Computing Education*, 10:15:1–15:16, November 2010.

[2] S. Cooper and S. Cunningham. Teaching computer science in context. *ACM Inroads*, 1:5–8, March 2010.

[3] M. Guzdial. A media computation course for non-majors. In *Proceedings of the 8th annual conference on Innovation and technology in computer science education*, ITiCSE '03. Thessaloniki, Greece, June 2003.

[4] M. Guzdial and A. Forte. Design process for a non-majors computing course. In *Proceedings of the 36th SIGCSE technical symposium on Computer science education*, SIGCSE '05, St. Louis, Missouri, USA, February 2005.

[5] M. Kölling. The greenfoot programming environment. *ACM Transactions on Computing Education*, 10:14:1–14:21, November 2010.

[6] M. Kölling, B. Quig, A. Patterson, and J. Rosenberg. The BlueJ system and its pedagogy. *Journal of Computer Science Education, Special issue on Learning and Teaching Object Technology*, 13(4):249–268, December 2003.

[7] M. Pedroni and B. Meyer. The inverted curriculum in practice. In *Proceedings of the 37th SIGCSE technical symposium on Computer science education*, SIGCSE '06, Houston, Texas, USA, March 2006.

[8] A. L. Santos. AGUIA/J: a tool for interactive experimentation of objects. In *Proceedings of the 16th annual conference on Innovation and technology in computer science education*, ITiCSE '11. Darmstadt, Germany, June 2011.

[9] B. Simon, P. Kinnunen, L. Porter, and D. Zazkis. Experience report: CS1 for majors with media computation. In *Proceedings of the 15th annual conference on Innovation and technology in computer science education*, ITiCSE '10, Bilkent, Ankara, Turkey, June 2010.

On Teaching Arrays with Test-Driven Learning in WebIDE

Michael Hilton, David S. Janzen
California Polytechnic State University
San Luis Obispo, California USA
{hilton,djanzen}@calpoly.edu

ABSTRACT

Test-driven development (TDD) has been shown to reduce defects and to lead to better code, but can it help beginning students learn basic programming topics, specifically arrays? We performed a controlled experiment where we taught arrays to two CS0 classes, one using WebIDE, an intelligent tutoring system that enforced the use of Test-Driven Learning (TDL) methods, and one using more traditional static methods and a development environment that instructed, but did not enforce the use of TDD. Students who used the TDL approach with WebIDE performed significantly better in assessments and had significantly higher opinions of their experiences than students who used traditional methods and tools.

Categories and Subject Descriptors

K.3.2 [**Computers and Education**]: Computer and Information Science Education—*Computer Science Education*

General Terms

Experimentation

Keywords

CS0, CS1, computer science education, intelligent tutor

1. INTRODUCTION

Test-driven development (TDD)[1] is a software engineering best practice that involves writing fine-grained automated unit tests prior to corresponding code, then refactoring in short, rapid increments. Numerous studies have examined the efficacy of test-driven development (TDD)[13, 3] with encouraging, but sometimes mixed results. For instance, TDD studies generally report improved software quality, but sometimes at the expense of lower productivity [2]. In addition, while many of these studies report very promising results with advanced students, incorporating TDD with beginning students has been more challenging. Desai et al. [4] report that introductory students who were taught TDD wrote higher quality code as measured through code-coverage. However, there was not significant change in the quality of source-code, the time spent on projects, attitudes towards testing or overall comprehension of material. It was their conclusion that simply incorporating TDD into current course materials with existing tools was not ideal, and that what was needed was some re-ordering and re-emphasizing of the material. We consider whether teaching an introductory programming topic, namely arrays, in a test-driven manner with the support of WebIDE, a novel web-based intelligent tutoring system that can enforce the test-driven approach, has any effect on student learning. Section 2 discusses related work, establishing context and motivation for this work. Section 3 describes the lab we created for teaching beginning programming students about arrays. Section 4 reports results from a controlled experiment to evaluate the new instructional materials, and Section 5 suggests some conclusions and future work.

2. RELATED WORK

2.1 Test-Driven Learning

Test-Driven Learning (TDL) [6] was proposed as an approach to teach computing students new topics using automated tests as examples. The basic idea is that TDD can be taught for free by simply incorporating a TDD approach to the material being taught. When an instructor introduces a topic such as recursion, as they present examples they can include automated tests as the first step of writing a source code implementation.

2.2 WebIDE

Although demonstrating TDD to students can be motivating, actually getting them to write code in a test-first manner can be challenging. WebIDE [5] is a novel intelligent tutoring system framework for delivering interactive web-based labs designed specifically for applying TDL in the first few weeks of introductory programming courses. WebIDE helps students during these difficult early weeks by offering a one-button interface in a ubiquitous and familiar web context that requires no additional installation.

Significant work on intelligent tutors exists [14], but WebIDE appears to be the first open and scalable system designed to incorporate TDL. WebIDE's architecture separates lab specification, lab rendering, and automated evaluation. Labs are specified in an xml file located at any URL. Labs embed references to evaluators that process and respond to student submissions. WebIDE includes internal evaluators such as regular expression matching. An unlimited number of external evaluators can be located on any Internet-accessible server. External evaluators can range from generic evaluators that compile and/or execute complete programs or test suites, to custom evaluators that parse very specific expressions (e.g. the sum of two integers).

Dvornik et al. [5] conducted a pilot study in 2010 using WebIDE to teach students using TDL. Although WebIDE was still under development they did see significant improvement in students developing a beginning Android application over the non-WebIDE students. However, the WebIDE students did not perform better on programming tasks overall. During the experiment students experienced significant evaluator timeouts on some labs that prevented them from completing all labs. This was a significant threat to validity. The timeout issue and other reliability issues were resolved prior to conducting the study reported in this paper.

2.3 Beginning Programmer Experiments

While most of the research into TDL and TDD has been with advanced students, there has been some research into TDL and TDD for beginning students.

2.3.1 Effects on Student Learning

Janzen and Saiedian [6] conducted a short experiment in two sections of a CS1 course that used C++. The experiment was conducted in three fifty-minute lectures and one fifty-minute lab that covered the introduction of classes and arrays. While both sections had been introduced previously to the assert() macro, during this experiment the first section was instructed using TDL and the second section was presented examples in a traditional manner using standard output with the instructor explaining the expected results. At the end of the experiment, all students were given the same short quiz. The quiz covered concepts and syntax from the experiment topics. The section that had been instructed using TDL scored a higher average on the test than the non-TDL section by a margin of 7.84 to 7.14. The sample size was relatively small with only 27 participants, so broad conclusions cannot be made.

2.3.2 Beginning Programmer Resistance

Many TDD studies address student appreciation of TDD and willingness to adopt TDD with mixed results. Janzen and Saiedian [7] performed an examination of acceptance of TDD by students at various levels. They found that after learning about TDD in the study, over 60% of mature developers would choose test-first over test-last, while only 10% of beginning developers would choose test-first methods. However, among several confounding factors they note that the mature developers used Java and JUnit while the beginners used C++ and assert statements.

2.3.3 Few choosing TDD

Garcia et al. [8] report that teaching beginning students in a test-driven manner resulted in only 10% of students choosing to use automated tests. However, there were several differences in their approach that may account for why so few students chose to use TDD. The students were taught in a classical procedural language and therefore they were taught a specially designed testing framework called tpUnit. The creators of the study chose not to use JUnit because they felt it would be too complex for beginning students. By using WebIDE we were able to abstract out the more complex features, and thereby teach beginning students Java and testing with JUnit at the same time. Garci et al. did find that the students who choose to write the tests scored higher than the students who did not, but due to low participation rates they couldn't draw definitive conclusions.

2.3.4 TDD least popular of XP practices

A study performed by Keefe [9] introduced students to four XP practices: Pair Programming, Test Driven Development, Simple Design, and Refactoring. Of the four practices TDD was least preferred by the students in the study. There were several reasons why students did not like TDD. They found that students did not have a sufficient understanding of testing to be able to write tests effectively. Many of the students found JUnit to be too complicated for them. They also found that many of the students had difficulty understanding why testing was important, and felt as if it was a waste of their time. While the authors recommended that testing needs to be introduced to programming students, they believed that their study was inconclusive on whether beginning students are capable of test first development.

2.3.5 Age and attitudes towards TDD

An investigation into students' perceptions of Extreme Programming (XP) practices conducted by Melnik [10] found a positive correlation between a students' age and a positive attitude towards TDD. They considered that this might be explained by a higher level of discipline of more mature students. They believe that this is because TDD is not about testing but about design. They feel that the older students are better at design, which in turn leads to them having a better opinion of TDD than beginning students.

2.3.6 Proper incentives needed

To help students appreciate TDD, Spacco and Pugh [11] developed a system called Marmoset for student project programming and submission. They would distribute projects to students including documentation, skeleton code, and several test cases in order to give the students a starting place. They found that as students had not yet learned the value of TDD, they needed to incentivize the students to write tests. In order to do that, they based a part of the students' grades on the amount of automated testing code coverage delivered. They also tried to design the system to encourage students to write tests. They found that as a result of their efforts, the students did indeed write and submit test cases as part of their final submission. However, upon further exploration, they found that a significant number of students did substantial work on their test cases after they had passed all the submission tests. It is their conclusion that without the proper incentive to write test cases early, many students do not adopt a test-first mentality, but rather stick to the test-late mentality of writing their implementation and then testing it at the very end.

3. TDL ARRAY LESSON

We created a new lab to teach introductory students about the topic of arrays in Java using the TDL approach and WebIDE. Each step is described below.

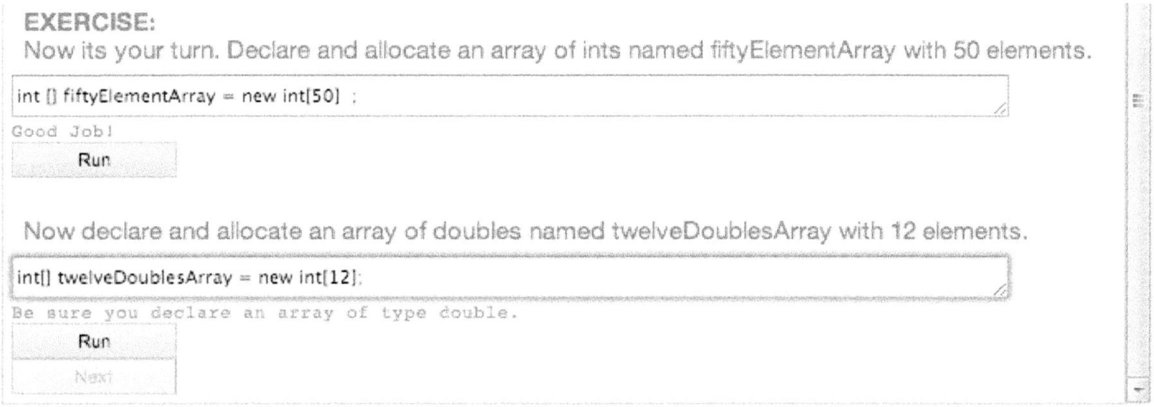

Figure 1: WebIDE lab step 1 exercise with sample error feedback

3.1 Step 1: Introduction to Arrays

The first step of the WebIDE lesson is titled "Introduction to Arrays". The purpose of this step is to introduce the students to the basics of Java arrays including the concepts of indexes and declaration, along with basic syntax. The lab targets beginning students so we assume the students do not have any knowledge about arrays before coming into this class. After seeing examples of array declarations, students are asked to declare two simple arrays before being allowed to move to the next step. Figure 1 shows a sample input where the student entered the first declaration correctly, but forgot to change the data types in the second declaration. These very simple first steps are to help the student build confidence and to not be overwhelmed too early. This will attempt to break down some of the initial resistance to TDL other studies have found to be common in beginning students [9, 8].

3.2 Step 2: Populating Arrays

The second step is "Populating Arrays". We emphasize how indices start at 0, a common source of confusion when dealing with arrays. We also introduce the first test in an exercise for the students. We assume that they have already been exposed to tests as part of their coursework in this class, so we do not need to go into detail about what the tests are or how they will work. Others [7, 10] have reported that beginning students feel test-last is more intuitive to them than test-first, so we start with one test-last example to help them feel comfortable before we move on to test-first. The exercise in this step is a simple task, to populate an array with the first five prime numbers. We give them the first five prime numbers to minimize external barriers to success with the topic at hand. Since we have assumed familiarity with the concept of variables, we do a simple assignment much like they have done with integers in the past.

3.3 Step 3: Retrieving Values from Arrays

The next step is "Retrieving Values from Arrays" and is shown in Figure 2. Here we want to introduce students to the concept of retrieving a value from an array and using that value. The exercise that the students will need to do this time is to sum all the values that they put into the array in the previous step. Before they write this code, they will set up a test to ensure that they have the correct sum. We have gradually been introducing testing, but at this point they are now doing test-first development. In order to avoid the confusion that has bothered other students in the past [9] we attempt to make the tests as straight forward as possible and directly related to the outcome of the code.

3.4 Step 4: Out of Bounds

Step 4 is designed to help students learn more about array indices. It also is designed to introduce them to the concept of Java exceptions. This step uses a WebIDE external Java Evaluator so that students could see an actual Java exception being thrown based on the code. We assume that the students at some point would write some code in which the array index is out of the bounds of the array, resulting in an exception being thrown. This step also provides an additional opportunity to work with array indices which must be mastered before they move on to more advanced exercises. This step starts with erroneous code that throws an exception. After running the code and seeing the exception, the student must fix the defect and see the code run successfully.

3.5 Step 5: Looping with Arrays

Now that we have been over the basics of arrays, we will start to cover concepts that are a little more complicated. This step will teach students how to work with arrays in loops. Since the students have already covered loops in this course, we do not need to introduce them as a new concept. Our focus is on teaching students to understand how they can use a loop to work with an array. We are also using this as an opportunity to continue to develop their understanding of test-first development. Since TDD has been shown to help programmers design better code [6], we will guide the students to write tests that will help them with their code design, as the exercises get to be more complicated. In this step, we give them the first test, then we use the internal WebIDE Regular Expression evaluator to ensure that they write the correct test for each test case, which in this instance corresponds to each index of the array that they will be populating. Once the students have written the correct test cases, they will get feedback as they write their code. If their design is incorrect, the test cases will show them.

3.6 Step 6: Functions with Arrays

This step focuses on teaching students how to use arrays with functions. As with the previous step, since they have

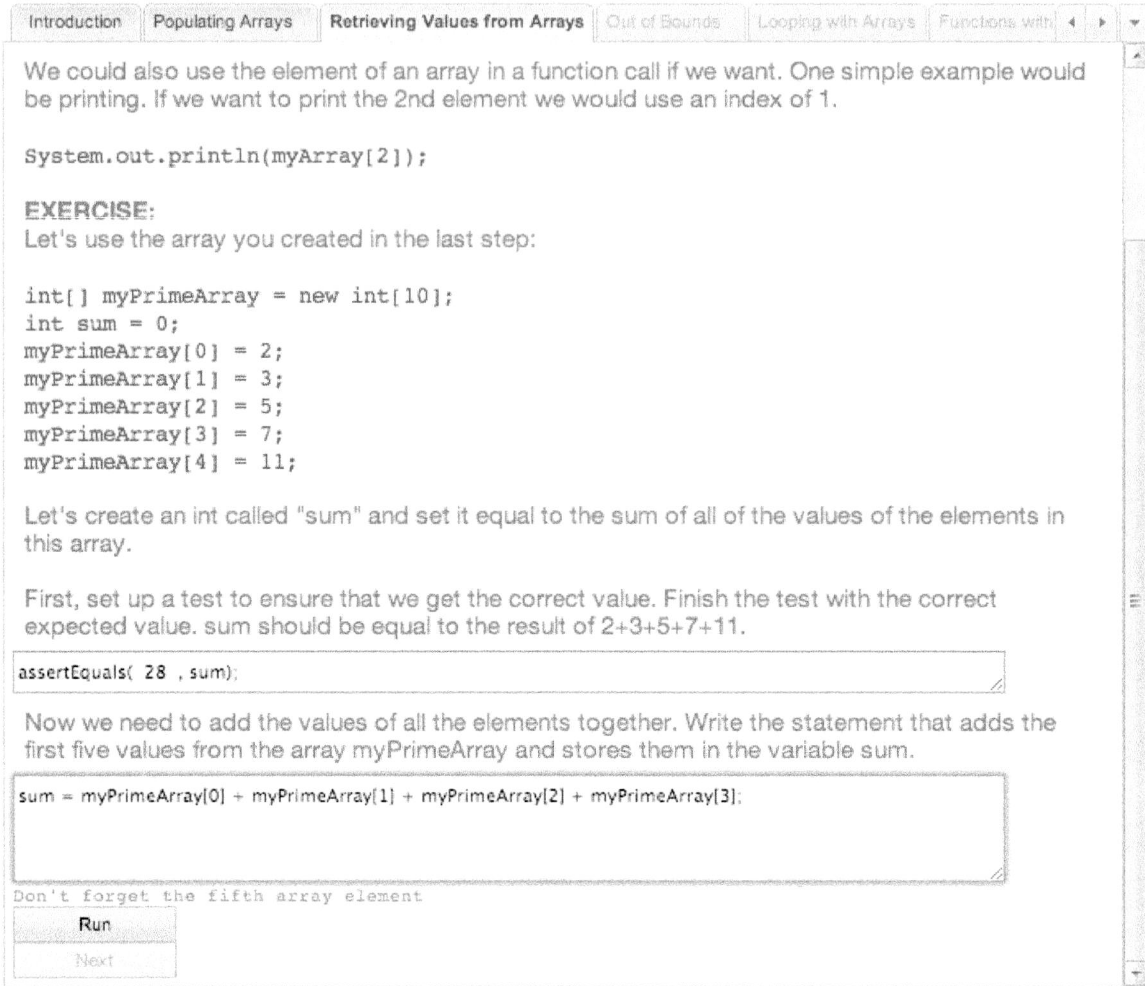

Figure 2: WebIDE lab step 3 with sample error feedback

covered functions previously in the course we will not have to introduce functions from scratch, but will focus on what the students will need to know to work with functions and arrays. The two main concepts that we want to teach the students are how to pass arrays into functions as parameters and how to return arrays from functions. We provide the students with some example code that is very similar to the code that we wish them to write. Then we set them up with some partial test cases so that they will be able to develop the test cases before they write the code. The code required to complete this exercise involves writing a function that takes an array as a parameter and then returns an int that is the count of the number of positive integers in the array. This exercise was designed with the goal of not only forcing the student to understand the information that was just given to them about arrays and functions, but also to reinforce the last step, where they learned how to use loops to deal with arrays. By building on the previously taught concepts we hope to reinforce the students' understanding.

3.7 Step 7: Array of Objects

We will continue to build on previous information with this step. Up until this point we have only used arrays of primitive types. In this step we will introduce arrays of objects. As before, we are assuming that they are familiar with objects and so we are only concerned with this lesson covering the information that the students will need to be able to use an array of objects. We give them an example of an array of PlayingCards. For the exercise we will ask them to write a piece of code that will declare an array of type President and fill it with some information about four presidents. However, before they write this code we will give them an example test and a partial test, and ask them to finish the partial test. Once they have written this code, we will use this array for the next step. Since we can use WebIDE to force them to finish this step correctly before they move on, we know that they will have answered this step correctly when we arrive at the next step.

3.8 Step 8: Operations On Array Elements

As the eighth and last step, we will tie in all the concepts that we have taught in the previous steps of this lesson. We will have the students iterate through the array that they created in the previous step which contains four presidents and the years that they started their presidency and the year that they ended their presidency. We will start the students off with part of a test, which they will need to complete. This test will be straight forward as it will test the sum of all the years in office of all the presidents in the array. This test was chosen because in order to complete it, the student will have to figure out on paper how they will come up with a number of years based on the information that they have been given. This computation is the type of design work that we would like them to do before they begin to write code. It also benefits the student because once they have that number, it will provide them with a test so that they know that their code is working properly once they have written it. In order to complete this assignment, the student will have to use concepts that we have previously taught in the lesson such as array indices, looping, functions, arrays of objects and array values. By continuing to use the same concepts repeatedly, we hope to reinforce the learning.

4. RESULTS

In order to evaluate the effects of the TDL arrays lab, we conducted a controlled experiment with 72 students in two sections of an introductory computing course (CS0) for students who had selected a computing major. Students were given a pre-study programming quiz at the beginning of the course to determine their programming skills entering the course. Results on this quiz indicated no statistically significant difference in previous programming experience between the WebIDE and control groups, although the WebIDE group did score slightly lower. Students completed the new array lab in the eighth week of the ten week course during a 90 minute closed lab period. This particular course introduced students to computing in the context of mobile applications. Prior to the lab on arrays, students completed labs using Scratch, App Inventor, and Java including Java basics (data, operators, expressions), methods, selection, looping, and classes. Each section contained 36 students and was taught by the same instructor with identical content. The independent variable was the use of WebIDE. Students in the control section were presented the same content in static html lab pages, and they used the Eclipse integrated development environment and were provided boiler-plate code for completing the exercises (e.g. Java and JUnit classes). Students in the control group had been using Eclipse for three weeks prior to this lab, whereas students in the WebIDE section had been introduced to Eclipse, but were completing their labs in WebIDE. Students in both sections were required to demonstrate proficiency in Eclipse by creating an Android app in a six-week group project.

4.1 Overall Quiz Scores

At the end of the lab period, students were given a six question on-line quiz on array concepts and syntax in Java worth a total of 22 points. The control group had 36 students take the quiz and the experimental group had 35 students take the quiz. One week later, students were also given a comprehensive lab quiz that included a question on Java arrays and loops. Students were encouraged to redo and study the lab outside of class in preparation for the comprehensive lab quiz. Table 1 reports student performance on the computer programming assessments, demonstrating the weaker performance on the pre-experiment assessment, and better performance after the introduction of WebIDE. Statistical significance was determined with $p < .05$ using a one-tailed univariate analysis of covariance test controlling for each student's score on the pre-study programming quiz.

4.2 Individual Question Scores

Since TDD has been shown to help improve software design [6], we would expect that TDL would be more beneficial for the more complicated problems, and there to be less of a difference on the less complicated quiz questions. That is exactly what we see in Table 2. Questions two and three were the simplest questions, requiring the least recall and corresponding to steps one and two. Questions two and four were both multiple choice, requiring more recognition over recall, but question four covered the more difficult topic of arrays of objects, corresponding to step seven. Questions five and six were the most open-ended and challenging, requiring students to write entire tests and methods based only on a problem description. Consequently, the control group even performed slightly better than the experiment group on question two, which was a very simple question. On the most complicated question (number six) we see the largest difference of 19%.

4.3 Student Opinions

Students were asked their opinions on the course, the labs, and their perspectives on the course topics (Java and Android) in a post-experiment on-line survey. Table 3 reports these results based on a five point Likert scale with one being "Strongly Agree" and five being "Strongly Disagree." The WebIDE students were more positive about the array lab than the control group.

4.4 Threats to Validity

As with any academic study there are unavoidable threats to validity such as the course time of day and external social or academic factors. One main threat to validity is that we are unable to determine if the better test scores were due exclusively to students using WebIDE, and that if they had used WebIDE with a different learning style they would have shown similar improvement over the control group.

5. CONCLUSIONS AND FUTURE WORK

This experiment has shown that students who were taught arrays in a TDL manner with a system that enforced the TDL approach performed better on assessments of the array topics than students who were taught the same material in a more traditional manner. Further, the students who used WebIDE were more positive about the course and the labs, than students who used a traditional development environment.

Future work includes extending the same concepts that were used to teach beginning students arrays in a test-driven manner, to other CS0/CS1 topics, such as functions and loops. Also, since WebIDE is not intrinsically built on TDL, an experiment could be devised that compares teaching the same material using WebIDE and TDL, and also using WebIDE but with a different teaching paradigm.

6. ACKNOWLEDGMENTS

We would like to thank Clark Turner for his work reviewing early versions of this paper, John Clements, Thomas Dvornik, and Karl Bell for their work developing WebIDE, and Olga Dekhtyar for reviewing all statistical analyses.

Assessment	Total Possible	WebIDE Mean	Control Mean	Significant?
Pre-Study Programming Quiz	25	2.72	3.50	No
Lab 8 Quiz: Java Arrays	22	13.75	11.44	Yes
Comp. Lab Quiz: Java Arrays/Loops	12	10.17	8.75	Yes

Table 1: Student Performance on Programming Assessments

Question	WebIDE Mean	Control Mean	Difference	Total Possible	Percent Difference
1 (declare array)	1.80	1.58	.22	2	10.83
2 (last element m/c)	1.83	1.94	-.12	2	-5.80
3 (first element)	1.29	1.19	0.091	2	4.56
4 (array of objects m/c)	1.6	1.39	.211	2	10.55
5 (test for getSmallest method))	3.49	2.72	0.76	6	12.72
6 (method getSmallest)	4.14	2.61	1.53	8	19.15

Table 2: Quiz Scores by Question

Question	WebIDE Mean	Control Mean	Significant?
I liked this course	1.59	2.03	Yes
I am comfortable with Java	2.38	2.47	No
Labs helped learn Java	2.21	2.64	Yes
Liked Lab 8	2.34	2.81	Yes

Table 3: Student Opinions

This material is based upon work supported by the National Science Foundation under Grant No. 0942488. Any opinions, findings, and conclusions or recommendations expressed in this material are those of the author(s) and do not necessarily reflect the views of the National Science Foundation.

7. REFERENCES

[1] K. Beck "Test Driven Development: By Example," *Addison Wesley,* November 2002.

[2] S. Kollanus, "Test-driven development - still a promising approach?" *7th Int. Conf. on the Quality of Information and Communications Technology (QUATIC),* Porto, Portugal, Oct. 2010, pp. 403 - 408.

[3] C. Desai, D. Janzen, and K. Savage "A survey of evidence for test-driven development in academia," *SIGCSE Bulletin,* vol. 40, no. 2, 2008, pp. 97 - 101

[4] C. Desai, D. Janzen, and J. Clements, "Implications of integrating test-driven development into CS1/CS2 curricula," in *Proceedings of the 40th ACM technical symposium on Computer science education.* New York, NY, USA: ACM, 2009, pp. 148–152

[5] T. Dvornik, D. Janzen, J. Clements, O. Dekhtyar, "Supporting introductory test-driven labs with WebIDE" *24th IEEE-CS Conference on Software Engineering Education and Training (CSEE and T), 2011* 22–24 May 2011, pp. 51–60.

[6] D. Janzen and H. Saiedian, "Test-Driven Learning: Intrinsic Integration of Testing into the CS/SE Curriculum." *In Proc. 37th Technical Symposium on Computer Science Education (SIGCSE),* pages 254–258. ACM, 2006.

[7] D. Janzen and H. Saiedian, "Test-Driven Learning in Early Programming Courses." *In Proc. 39th Technical Symposium on Computer Science Education (SIGCSE).* ACM, 2008.

[8] E. Barriocanal, M. Urban, I. Cuevas, and P. Perez, "An Experience in Integrating Automated Unit Testing Practices in an Introductory Programming Course." *ACM SIGCSE Bulletin,* 34(4):125–128, December 2002.

[9] K. Keefe, J. Sheard, and M. Dick, "Adopting XP Practices for Teaching Object Oriented Programming." *In Proc. 8th Australian Conf. Computing Education,* volume 52, pages 91–100, 2006.

[10] G. Melnik and F. Maurer, "A Cross-Program Investigation of Students' Perceptions of Agile Methods." *In Proc. 27th Intl. Conf. on Software Eng. (ICSE),* pages 481–488. ACM Press, 2005.

[11] J. Spacco and W. Pugh, "Helping Students Appreciate Test-Driven Development (TDD)." *In Companion to 21st. ACM SIGPLAN Conf. Object-Oriented Prog. Systems, Languages, and Applications (OOPSLA),* pages 907–913, 2006.

[12] D. Janzen and H. Saiedian, "A Leveled Examination of Test-Driven Development Acceptance." *In Proc. 29th Intl. Conf. on Software Engineering (ICSE),* pages 719–722. IEEE Press, 2007.

[13] R. Jeffries and G. Melnik, "Guest Editors' Introduction: TDD–The Art of Fearless Programming." *IEEE Software,* volume 24, pages 24–30. IEEE Computer Society, 2007.

[14] R. Raga and J. Raga, "A Survey on Intelligent Tutoring Systems (Its) and it's Authoring in the Context of Features Promoting the Human-Teacher Factor." *Journal of Business, Education and Law,* volume 14, no 1, Jose Rizal University, 2010.

JUG: A JUnit Generation, Time Complexity Analysis and Reporting Tool to Streamline Grading

Christopher Brown, Robert Pastel and John Earnest
Michigan Technological University
Houghton, MI
cdbrown, rpastel, jwearnes @mtu.edu

Bill Siever
Northwest Missouri State University
Maryville, MO
bsiever@nwmissouri.edu

ABSTRACT

The JUnit Generation (JUG) system provides fast, semi-automated feedback to students. It uses a Java-like script to generate unit tests and time complexity tests, then runs those tests to generate reports. The goals for JUG are improved feedback for students, and decreased preparation and grading time for instructors and grading assistants.

Categories and Subject Descriptors

D.2.5 [**Software Engineering**]: Testing And Debugging - *Testing tools*;
F.3.1 [**Logics and Meanings of Programs**]: Specifying and Verifying and Reasoning about Programs;
K.3.2 [**Computers and Education**]: Computer Uses in Education - *Computer-managed instruction*

General Terms

Documentation, Measurement

Keywords

Automated Testing, Evaluation, Generative Programming

1. INTRODUCTION

One decision that introductory programming instructors must make is balancing the number of programming exercises with the amount of time available for preparation and grading. Additional practice of new skills and ideas helps developing programmers, but can increase the amount of work an instructor must do. Although automated systems can decrease the time spent grading an individual student, the time spent setting up the automated system and managing unusual cases still makes fewer assignments a more appealing option.

There are fundamental differences between a classroom grading system and professional software testing. In a professional environment, tests are meant to identify and prevent problems with the software. Often those tests are designed with edge cases and provided data structures in mind. In a classroom environment, the instructor must assign weight to different aspects of the program, and in certain courses (such as a Data Structures course), students are expected to write those objects that industry takes for granted. In addition, an industry project may be developing the same code for months, without much need to write new tests. An instructor must prepare tests for each assignment, where a single assignment is only used once during a week. Finally, reports given to a grader or student must include more detailed reference to how the test was executed, since the student would not have direct access to the test.

The two major goals for the JUnit Generation (JUG) system are: 1) providing strong supplemental feedback to improve student learning, and 2) ease of use for the assignment developer and grader. The JUG system combines automated tests, evaluation and reporting to fulfill those goals.

Our first goal, course improvement through fast, useful feedback, is attained by providing concise but clear test descriptions and results, and by including important supplemental information into the automated process, such as time complexity analysis. We measure the success of this method by examining the types of assignments and grading techniques used as our automated grading system evolved. In addition, we have interviewed the instructors and graders, and surveyed students to gain more insight into the success and future work of the system.

To create an easy system for instructors developing assignments and graders, we create an environment where a single, simple test requires only a single, simple line of code. The system is flexible enough to incorporate multi-line tests, and can assign point weight to different test groups. A report generator can also produce a graded or partially graded report for the grader.

2. BACKGROUND

Automated testing is not new, in fact, one of the first publications using tests in the classroom is from 1960[13], with a goal of saving the then precious machine operation time. As additional resources have been developed, and resources available to instructors improve, automated instruction has increased potential. Although many automated grading systems already exist[14], the fact that they are still being developed indicates the strong need for adaptive systems.

ITiCSE'12, July 3–5, 2012, Haifa, Israel.

2.1 Previous work on Automated Grading

Recently, Ihantola et al. reviewed a number of automated grading programs with associated publications between 2005 and 2010. Their assessment indicated that programs should include stronger sandbox/security systems, more public distribution methods, and combine automatic feedback with manual feedback[14]. We have attempted to follow these guidelines through our goals by using JUnit, publishing JUG (see Section 4.4), and creating reports ready for the grader to examine.

Venables and Haywood stress the importance of feedback when developing their web-based grading tool, *submit*. They used a comparative output providing the difference between the expected and provided results[21]. We also adopt this technique, although JUnit provides some utility for more succinct comparisons (see Section 4.1). Finally, Kay et al. provide a set of important ideas regarding the philosophy behind grading[15]. We address many of these ideas in Section 3.

2.2 Test Driven Development

The **Test-Driven Development** (TDD) methodology is based on the mantra: "write a test; make it run; and make it right"[10]. In other words, tests are a fundamental step in agile programming. TDD practices can demonstrate improvement in both productivity and quality of the final product[5]. Erdogmus et al. demonstrate that the test-first approach, when used with incremental development, promotes the creation of more tests, thereby providing stronger code [9]. By focusing the JUG unit tests in a TDD style, especially in Data Structures, students experience first-hand the benefits of making tests for their own projects. In addition, since JUG is publicly available, students and other developers can use it to easily create and maintain tests.

2.3 JUnit

JUnit [4] was developed as a tool for test driven development, and has been expanded to serve in different ways [16, 18, 19]. JUnit developers use the terms *test cases* and *test suites* to represent the organization of tests. Often, these tests are organized by what aspects of a class they test. This is similar to a point distribution organization in any graded assignment, so JUG exploits this similarity. JUnit also has the benefit of running the tests as separate threads, avoiding complications from errors propagating into the testing environment.

2.4 Generative Programming

Generative programming techniques provide the means to combine domain specific abstract concepts and template structures to create code in a general purpose language, such as C++ or Java. Czarnecki and Eisenecker standardized generative practices in 2000, focusing on constructive techniques to use abstract terms to describe a system, without manually creating each part [7]. Since then, a number of domains have begun using generative programming, including embedded systems, scientific applications and user interface generation[2, 3, 8, 11, 12, 20]. While our automated testing evolved, we noticed a few recurring patterns in the test styles and overhead, making templating techniques the natural choice for generating tests. This evolved into JUG as a domain-specific language for automated testing.

3. PHILOSOPHY OF JUG

Kay et al. provide a set of issues that an automated grading system should address, followed by a breakdown of the aspects of an automated grading system[15]. Although we diverge on some of the thoughts behind their proposed ideas, it serves as a good baseline for discussing the decisions behind JUG.

3.1 General Issues with Automated Grading

The general issues Kay emphasizes are security from tampering, scalability to large class sizes, flexibility to varying assignments, and robustness toward bugs. Many of these issues have been solved through JUnit, since the unit tests are run in separate processes, can handle many different types of code, and are usually robust in dealing with errors. However, to resist tampering, JUG uses Java's Security Manager class to avoid improper student calls, such as `System.exit`, which would end the entire testing process.

Our system scales by separating the test generation from report generation. The tests for all students are the same; therefore, generating the JUnit tests once is sufficient for the entire class. When compiling and running the tests, however, each student is graded independently. We use `BASH` scripts to direct the processes, avoiding processor scalability issues by operating on one student at a time. This process is completely automated and does not requiring human intervention that can slow the process down for large classes. Afterward, the human grader can examine and finish grading the stored reports. To add to the robustness, timeouts can be set so that a student with an infinite loop can still receive a readable report, and the system can grade the other students.

3.2 The Automated Process

3.2.1 Submission

The first suggestion from Kay et al. is that a submission system should allow for multiple source files and ancillary files[15]. With object-oriented design integrated into early programming courses, this is a necessity. Fortunately, our department has a submission procedure established. However, with the ability to export projects through Eclipse, create branches using version software, and additional means for students to provide code to the instructor, this aspect is left to `BASH` scripts. The JUG framework includes appropriate `BASH` scripts to manage code for compilation and testing (see Section 4.4).

3.2.2 On-Submit Feedback

In addition to submission, Kay et al. suggest that feedback be provided immediately after each submission, such as compilation information and results of tests against published cases[15]. Instead, we consciously do not permit students to see this type of feedback before the due date. This prevents students from solving the problems by trial and error or using the grading program as a debugging tool, as experienced by Malmi et al.[17]. The experience of compiling, testing and debugging is part of the programming process, and once a student begins using the grading system as a debugging tool, they lose the experience of testing their own code.

3.2.3 *Two-Phase Feedback*

To provide students with the benefits of near-immediate knowledge of the results, we use JUG in a two-phase submission process. At the due date, reports are generated by JUG, but not evaluated by a human grader. Those ungraded reports are emailed to students, giving them the ability to see compilation errors and failed tests. A few days later, they may choose to resubmit a fixed program for a small penalty. JUG creates reports for the resubmits, then the human grader evaluates the programs. This means that the human grader only looks at each student's grade once, but students get the benefit of immediate feedback and the opportunity for improvement.

3.2.4 *Test Components*

The obvious role of test components is to determine whether the student's code works as required. However, the more subtle aspect of this role is the pedagogical feedback provided. To assist in improving student understanding, we want students to be able to recreate the test case and know exactly what is expected. For this, JUG uses annotated comments, and includes more descriptive feedback.

3.2.5 *Scoring*

Kay et al. suggest that grades or point assignments not be calculated, but left for a human grader. Their reasoning includes adjudication of common mistakes, such as spelling and whitespace in the results. Although these common errors are important to adjust for, we have found that presenting students with a low score due to minor errors emphasizes the importance of attention to detail required for programming. In addition, with the regrade policy described above, a quick fix of these minor errors creates a minimal penalty. On the other hand, including a grade calculation can reduce the grader's time spent adding and calculating grades, which can cut grading time significantly.

3.2.6 *Plagiarism*

Kay emphasizes the importance of automated plagiarism detection, and we agree with that assessment. Our department uses the freely available plagiarism detection system, Moss[1], to evaluate student code. Through some simple organizational scripts, Moss has allowed us to compare students in the same course with each other and those from previous semesters.

4. THE JUG SYSTEM

JUnit Generator, or JUG, consists of two parts: a test generator, and a report description. By mixing of natural language and Java code, JUG's input syntax can provide sets of simple JUnit tests, while maintaining an overview of all tests.

4.1 JUnit Generation - The JUG File

The JUG system uses templates to generate JUnit tests. Our objective for the generator was to have one line of JUG for each test. Although this meets our secondary goal of simplifying the grading process, tests must also be able to provide adequate feedback to students so that they can recreate the tests and improve their programs.

For each simple test, we use the form [`code keyword code;`] to represent a JUnit test statement. Some of the common

```
fixture Matrix {
    /* @name Addition and Subtraction T = {{7,8,9},{4,5,6},{1,2,3}} */
    test AddSub{
        /* @name after addition, T is still T */
        {
            Matrix.identity(3).add(T);
            T equals new Matrix(new double[][]
              {{7.0, 8.0, 9.0},
               {4.0, 5.0, 6.0},
               {1.0, 2.0, 3.0}});
        }
        /* @name new Matrix(5,3) + T (IllegalArgumentException) */
        new Matrix(5,3).add(T) throws IllegalArgumentException;
    }
}
```

A line or bracketed group of instructions becomes a single test. The test output includes the name, the result, and the point value. Points are divided evenly, and added automatically.

```
Addition and Subtraction T = {{7,8,9},{4,5,6},{1,2,3}}
        2.00 / 3.00
  identity(3) + T => {{8,8,9},{4,6,6},{1,2,4}}
     Test Successful                                          -0.00
  after addition, T is still T
     Test Successful                                          -0.00
  new Matrix(5,3) + T (IllegalArgumentException)
     Expected: an instance of java.lang.IllegalArgumentException   -1.00
       got: <java.lang.ArrayIndexOutOfBoundsException: 3>
```

Figure 1: Test Generator File and Report Samples

keywords include `equals`, `arrayequals`, `isinstanceof` and `throws`. These terms use templates to expand to a single JUnit test statement within a test method. Since this type of statement indicates both the call and the result, it can be easily reproduced, and clearly represents the test being called. This test statement is used in the report to describe the test to the student.

Sometimes more complex tests are necessary, however. Therefore, JUG allows a block to be created representing a single test, where the last line of the block is the test statement. Any valid Java code can be placed within the block, allowing any kind of set up to be made prior to the test. In this case, the test statement may not be adequate, so a simple javadoc-style annotation can be added as a descriptor for the test, allowing the test developer to describe the test. See Figure 1.

4.2 JUG/JUnit Reports - The JUR File

The reports are defined using JavaScript Object Notation (JSON), which uses simple formatting rules to divide data into generic lists and maps[6]. We chose this notation over other standards, such as XML and HTML, because the notation is straightforward and intentionally human-readable. In addition, by using a standard convention, code highlighting is already available.

The report format is based on various section types. The most complex section type is the test section, allowing the instructor to set the number of points for the section, or for individual test suites. Test suites are referenced by name to the JUG file. Additional sections provide annotation tables, plots and source code (see Figure 2, Figure 3 and Section 4.3).

Generating the report uses an abstract report generation class, with abstract methods for "printing" the various components of a report (i.e. tests, headers, plots, etc). Through these methods, a subclass generates an XHTML document which can be posted online, emailed to students, printed, or converted to a pdf. Currently, we convert the files to pdfs, however, the system is flexible enough that one could generate reports in many formats.

```
{   "header" : "Program 8 main() Run",
    "points" : 40,
    "type" : "tests",
    "timeout" : 20,
    "fixture" : "Program8",
    "tests" : [ "Prog8Main", "Tickets"]
},
{   "type" : "header",
    "text" : "Vehicle Heirarchy Decisions",
    "points" : 10
},
{   "type" : "header",
    "text" : "Style & Commenting",
    "points" : -40
},
{   "type" : "code",
    "class" : "Vehicle"
}   "header" : "Vehicle.java"
```

Figure 2: JUnit Report File (JUR)

4.3 Tables and Data Plots

Another objective for improving supplemental feedback is providing students with real analytic data concerning their programs. Therefore, the JUG system supports programmatic plot generation and annotation tables. See Figure 4.

Instructors can generate tables based on custom annotations. A reference to the class, method and annotation type allows instructors to acquire meta-data from the students, and print that information to the report. In our use of JUG with Data Structures (see Section 5.1), we used these annotations to require students to include time and space complexity information concerning their data structures.

For a data plot, the instructor includes code for two Java methods which will generate and return data arrays for the plot axes. They can include calls to known student methods, and time those methods or reference results. In our use, we included time complexity plots by running methods with various inputs and data structure sizes.

4.4 Using the JUG System

The JUG system uses a series of scripts to aid in use of the test generator and report generator. First, the instructor must create a solution, a test file (JUG) and a report file (JUR). Next, the instructor modifies a configuration file for the BASH scripts. Finally, a grader can run scripts to gather student submissions, generate JUnit tests, create the reports, and email the reports to students. If any students need to be tested again, scripts include options to restrict a run to individual students. The JUG system, the scripts, and the Java source code are freely available at http://www.csl.mtu.edu/~cdbrown/JUG/.

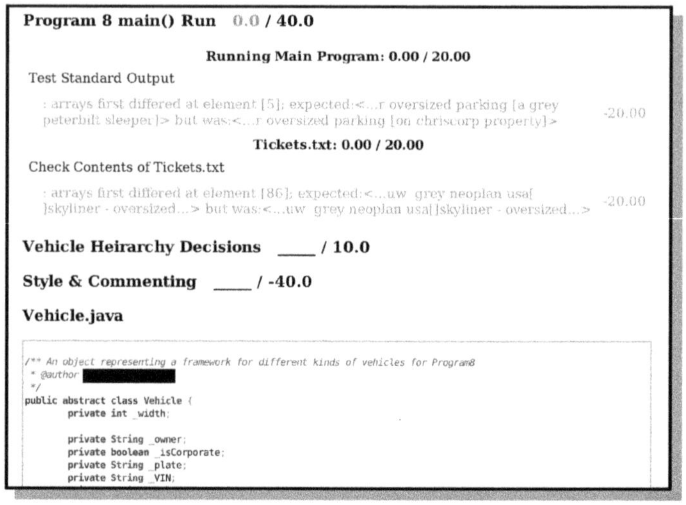

Program 8 main() Run 0.0 / 40.0

Running Main Program: 0.00 / 20.00

Test Standard Output

: arrays first differed at element [5]; expected:<...r oversized parking [a grey peterbilt sleeper]> but was:<...r oversized parking [on chriscorp property]> -20.00

Tickets.txt: 0.00 / 20.00

Check Contents of Tickets.txt

: arrays first differed at element [86]; expected:<...uw grey neoplan usa[ ]skyliner - oversized...> but was:<...uw grey neoplan usa[]skyliner - oversized...> -20.00

Vehicle Heirarchy Decisions ____ / 10.0

Style & Commenting ____ / -40.0

Vehicle.java

```
/** An object representing a framework for different kinds of vehicles for Program8
 * @author [redacted]
 */
public abstract class Vehicle {
        private int _width;

        private String _owner;
        private boolean _isCorporate;
        private String _plate;
        private String _VIN;
```

Figure 3: JUnit Report Output

5. APPLICATION

We have used versions of the JUG system over the past three years. The system has been evolving as we get feedback and new ideas for the system. It was first developed for a Data Structures course, and recently used for an accelerated introductory programming course.

5.1 Case Study: Data Structures

Our first case study was a data structures course. Before automating the system, the course included five assignments. Four of the assignments required creating a data structure and an application of that data structure. The fifth assignment compared the time complexities of various sorting algorithms, requiring students to graph and report their results. Observations of student programs indicated that they would use incomplete data structures, meeting the minimum requirements for the application. In addition, the assignment provided little distinction between the data structure and the application, and often students had difficulty getting various components to work together correctly.

We introduced unit testing for the data structures component of the assignment, and generated reports for students. This divided each assignment into two separate parts, the data structure and the application, eventually becoming two distinct assignments. It also allowed us to include elements of time complexity analysis into the data structure assignments. The difficulty in automation was writing the unit tests and the report generator for each assignment. Often, the largest time costs were specifying the form of the report in code, and formatting the unit tests appropriately for unusual types of tests. In addition, our original version had points assigned per test, creating problems when tests were added or removed—many times the total points for an assignment was an unusual value. Automating these aspects

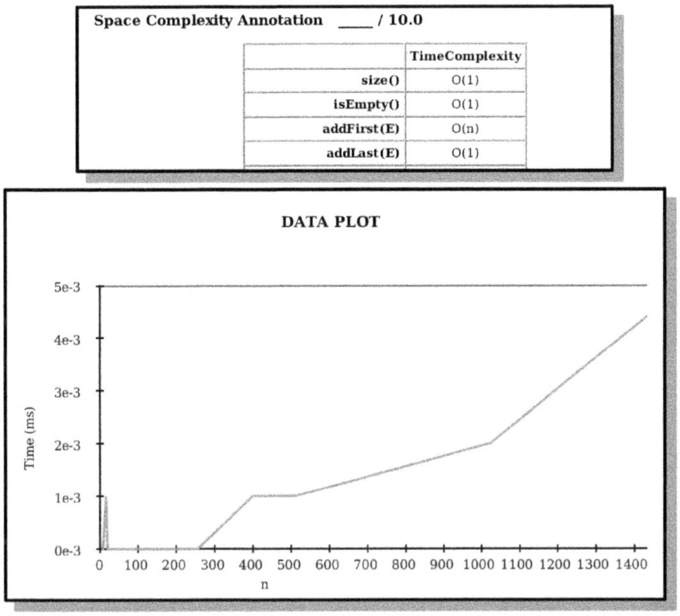

Figure 4: A Time Complexity Table and Graph

led to the template based test generator, and a simplified report system that automatically divided test points.

Students responded well to the JUG reports, using them to discuss their expectations and grades. We conducted a survey of the students to determine the perceived impact, and attempted to infer the real impact. Two questions from the survey directly inquired about the JUG reports: 1) "Did the auto-graded tests match your expectations of the requirements?"; 2) "Did the preliminary reports from the auto-grader clarify how your code should behave?" The results of the survey are shown in Figure 5.

We believe that these results indicate that students found that the reports helped them better understand the data structures and their applications after seeing specific tests run. For instance, a student may not understand why specific types of exceptions are thrown. Seeing a test cases throwing those exceptions can improve that understanding through the experience.

5.2 Case Study: Introductory Programming

The second case study incorporated the JUG system into an accelerated introductory programming course. The accelerated course covered material from two introductory courses in one semester. The course was presented in an algorithm-first approach, incorporating object-oriented design practices in the fourth week (of fifteen). Due to its accelerated nature, the course included 15 assignments, meaning that the turnaround time for a program was often less than a week. Because of this, we decided that resubmissions would only be allowed in special cases, but often there was no penalty associated with resubmission.

The results provided strong evidence that JUG improved the efficiency of the grading process. The assignments were all new, but tests were simple to generate and most reports could be copied from one assignment to the next with minimal changes. One major problem was testing extremely long outputs. One report printed two pages of "expected" output, followed by another two pages of slightly incorrect output. To alleviate this, JUG allows output to be split by line into an array. An example of a result like this is displayed in Figure 3—students were simply told that the array index represented the line number of the first error.

6. RESULTS

When observing students as they argue for better grades, certain patterns emerge. In programming assignments, students will often make claims that the program "works" to an extent better than their grade reflects. Of course, this is a very subjective statement and often difficult to argue against. However, when the grade is presented as a series of rewards and penalties, students instead tend to argue against those penalties they believe are incorrect or inconsistent. This provides a moment where the instructor either a) finds an error in their requirements, tests or grading policy, or b) provides an instructional moment with the inquiring student. Both are positive situations which result in a satisfactory conclusion for both instructor and student.

One of the unexpected benefits we found using this system was the adaptability and reusability that the system provided. After writing only a few sets of tests, we found we could copy and paste sets of tests within an assignment, and quickly modify them to a new case. We could also take series of tests from one assignment to another and make minor modifications. Often, between one semester and another, we would make minor changes to the assignments and our solution. We could then use JUG to run the old test on the new solution, generating a report of which tests needed adjustment. The JUG and JUR files are now regular components of our assignments with the description and solution, and are easy to port from one semester to another.

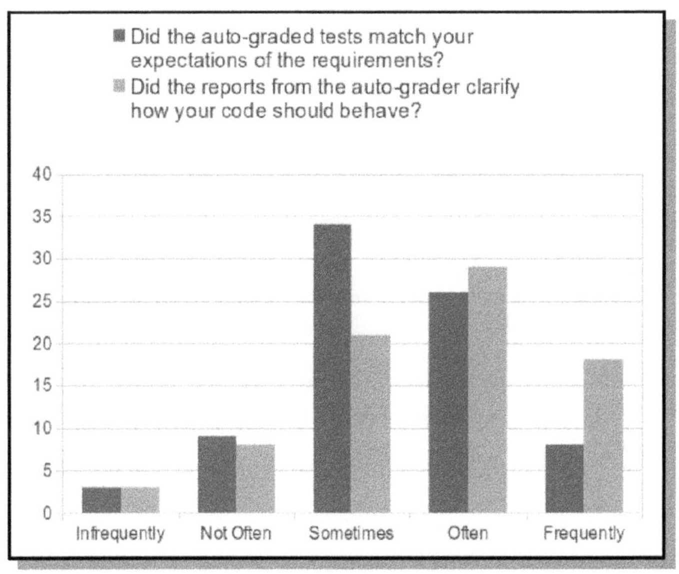

Figure 5: Student Survey Results

7. CONCLUSIONS

The goals of the JUG system were improving student understanding and easing the grading process. Based on the evidence presented, we believe this was the case, and that the results of streamlining grading exceeded our expectations. Based on the case studies, students found that JUG helped their understanding of various aspects of programming, and we, as instructors, found the system easy to incorporate into our classroom, improving the efficiency of our work.

8. FUTURE WORK

As JUG evolves, there is opportunity to examine the ability of the system to adapt to changing needs. Specifically, students are commonly developing web and mobile device applications. Automated evaluation of GUIs often requires event simulation and display evaluation. These elements may be a future objective for another domain-specific testing language, and generative techniques could provide much needed simplification for test developers.

Acknowledgments

We would like to thank the Computer Science Department at Michigan Technological University, and the Faculty, Teaching Assistants and Graders for participating in this study and providing feedback on their experiences. We would also like to thank the students of both courses for allowing us to study and publish their feedback.

9. REFERENCES

[1] A. M. Aiken. Moss: a system for detecting software plagiarism. `http://theory.stanford.edu/~aiken/moss/`, 1994.

[2] R. Arora, P. Bangalore, and M. Mernik. Developing scientific applications using generative programming. In *Proceedings of the 2009 ICSE Workshop on Software Engineering for Computational Science and Engineering*, SECSE '09, pages 51–58, Washington, DC, USA, 2009. IEEE Computer Society.

[3] G. Attardi, A. Cisternino, and A. Kennedy. Codebricks: code fragments as building blocks. In *Proceedings of the 2003 ACM SIGPLAN workshop on Partial evaluation and semantics-based program manipulation*, PEPM '03, pages 66–74, New York, NY, USA, 2003. ACM.

[4] K. Beck. Junit: Resources for test driven development. `http://www.junit.org/`, 1994.

[5] B. Beizer. *Software system testing and quality assurance*. Van Nostrand Reinhold Co., New York, NY, USA, 1984.

[6] D. Crockford. Javascript object notation (json). `http://www.json.org/`, 2006.

[7] K. Czarnecki and U. W. Eisenecker. *Generative programming: methods, tools, and applications*. ACM Press/Addison-Wesley Publishing Co., New York, NY, USA, 2000.

[8] A. M. R. da Cruz and J. a. P. Faria. A metamodel-based approach for automatic user interface generation. In *Proceedings of the 13th international conference on Model driven engineering languages and systems: Part I*, MODELS'10, pages 256–270, Berlin, Heidelberg, 2010. Springer-Verlag.

[9] H. Erdogmus, M. Morisio, and M. Torchiano. On the effectiveness of the test-first approach to programming. *Software Engineering, IEEE Transactions on*, 31(3):226 – 237, march 2005.

[10] S. Fraser, K. Beck, B. Caputo, T. Mackinnon, J. Newkirk, and C. Poole. Test driven development (tdd). In *Proceedings of the 4th international conference on Extreme programming and agile processes in software engineering*, XP'03, pages 459–462, Berlin, Heidelberg, 2003. Springer-Verlag.

[11] P. Grigorenko, A. Saabas, and E. Tyugu. Visual tool for generative programming. In *Proceedings of the 10th European software engineering conference held jointly with 13th ACM SIGSOFT international symposium on Foundations of software engineering*, ESEC/FSE-13, pages 249–252, New York, NY, USA, 2005. ACM.

[12] F. Heidenreich, J. Johannes, M. Seifert, C. Wende, and B. Marcel. Generating safe template languages. *SIGPLAN Not.*, 45:99–108, October 2009.

[13] J. Hollingsworth. Automatic graders for programming classes. *Commun. ACM*, 3:528–529, October 1960.

[14] P. Ihantola, T. Ahoniemi, V. Karavirta, and O. Seppälä. Review of recent systems for automatic assessment of programming assignments. In *Proceedings of the 10th Koli Calling International Conference on Computing Education Research*, Koli Calling '10, pages 86–93, New York, NY, USA, 2010. ACM.

[15] D. G. Kay, T. Scott, P. Isaacson, and K. A. Reek. Automated grading assistance for student programs. In *Proceedings of the twenty-fifth SIGCSE symposium on Computer science education*, SIGCSE '94, pages 381–382, New York, NY, USA, 1994. ACM.

[16] J. Link and P. Frolich. *Unit Testing in Java: How Tests Drive the Code*. Morgan Kaufmann Publishers Inc., San Francisco, CA, USA, 2003.

[17] L. Malmi, V. Karavirta, A. Korhonen, and J. Nikander. Experiences on automatically assessed algorithm simulation exercises with different resubmission policies. *J. Educ. Resour. Comput.*, 5, September 2005.

[18] V. Massol and T. Husted. *JUnit in Action*. Manning Publications Co., Greenwich, CT, USA, 2003.

[19] J. B. Rainsberger and S. Stirling. *JUnit Recipes: Practical Methods for Programmer Testing*. Manning Publications Co., Greenwich, CT, USA, 2004.

[20] M. Schlee and J. Vanderdonckt. Generative programming of graphical user interfaces. In *Proceedings of the working conference on Advanced visual interfaces*, AVI '04, pages 403–406, New York, NY, USA, 2004. ACM.

[21] A. Venables and L. Haywood. Programming students need instant feedback! In *Proceedings of the fifth Australasian conference on Computing education - Volume 20*, ACE '03, pages 267–272, Darlinghurst, Australia, Australia, 2003. Australian Computer Society, Inc.

Exploring Influences on Student Adherence to Test-Driven Development

Kevin Buffardi
Virginia Tech
114 McBryde Hall (0106)
Blacksburg, Virginia
+1 540-231-5723
kbuffardi@vt.edu

Stephen H. Edwards
Virginia Tech
114 McBryde Hall (0106)
Blacksburg, Virginia
+1 540-231-5723
edwards@cs.vt.edu

ABSTRACT

Test-Driven Development (TDD) is a software development process with a test-first approach that shows promise for improving code quality. Our research addresses concerns raised in both academia and industry about a lack of motivation or acceptance in adopting TDD. In a CS2 class, we used an automated testing tool and post-class surveys to observe patterns of behavior in testing as well as changes in attitudes. We found significant positive outcomes for students following TDD. We also identified obstacles deterring students from adhering to TDD and discuss reasons and possible remedies.

Categories and Subject Descriptors

K.3.2 [**Computers and Education**]: Computer and Information Science Education; D.1.5 [**Programming Techniques**]: Object oriented Programming; D.2.5 [**Software Engineering**]: Testing and Debugging.

General Terms

Measurement, Human Factors, Verification.

Keywords

Test-Driven Development (TDD), Automated Testing, Adherence, Affect, Procrastination, Software Engineering, Agile, Extreme Programming, JUnit, Web-CAT.

1. INTRODUCTION

Test-Driven Development (TDD) is a strategy emphasizing testing source code in the software development process. In particular, TDD advocates a test-first approach where writing test cases precedes writing the corresponding portion of the implementation. Unit testing is also central to TDD, since programmers focus tests on the smallest level of testable code—often a function or method. Agile methods such as Extreme Programming (XP) popularized TDD in industry [2].

Meanwhile in academia, educators have integrated TDD into computer science curricula and observed beneficial results [5][8]. However, several studies recognize a challenge of promoting student acceptance of TDD. Barriocanal identified a need to motivate students to write tests when they are new to TDD [1]. Other academic studies also acknowledged a reluctance to adopt TDD, particularly by younger and less experienced programmers [12][15][18].

At our university, we teach TDD with Java in our introductory programming courses. TDD is introduced early using the JUnit framework [13] and is reinforced throughout the course. Programming project grades include assessment on design as well as on the comprehensiveness of student-written tests. However, project grades only evaluate individual, completed submissions. They cannot definitively reveal whether or not students followed a test-first approach when writing their solutions.

Grading test code in programming projects may offer insight to students' abilities to produce adequate tests. However, by incorporating TDD into the computer science curriculum, we intend to not only expose students to testing, but to also prepare them in software development methods applied in industry. Therefore, we are interested in both the software they produce and the processes to which they adhere.

In our CS2 course, Software Design and Data Structures, students submit their code to Web-CAT [19], an on-line automated grading tool that provides students feedback including static analysis, test coverage, and solution correctness evaluated by undisclosed instructor-written reference tests. Students may submit their programming projects as many times as they wish without penalty and only their final submission is considered for grading.

By allowing students to submit their work-in-progress, we also gain access to snapshots of students' progress as they develop their software. These series of snapshots provide some insight into students' behaviors and the development methods they follow. Consequently, this study addresses student adherence to TDD and investigates reasons for their adherence or lack thereof.

2. RELATED WORK

Many leading industrial software development organizations have adopted Test-Driven Development (and Agile development in general) [11]. Empirical research on TDD in industry suggests that TDD improves the quality of both code and testing [3][4]. Several academic studies have identified benefits of TDD as well.

Studies in academia have shown similar results to those in industry: while TDD may increase workload, quality of testing and code improves [6]. One study in particular found when pairing TDD with an automated testing tool, students produced programs with 45% fewer defects per line of code compared to students in a class not using TDD [8]. Moreover, Edwards argues that students' analytical skills improve by encouraging the practice of "reflection in action" rather than using trial-and-error strategies.

Educators have also developed tools to assist TDD in the computer science curriculum. Both Web-CAT [15] and Marmoset [17] are automated testing tools that provide feedback based on instructor-written tests in addition to students' own tests. In contrast, ComTest uses a simple macro language for writing shorter and easier unit tests than JUnit [14]. However, Lappalainen, et al., also acknowledge ComTest's limitation—like other test-driven learning tools, while unit testing may be required in assignments, ComTest does not strictly enforce a test-first approach.

Janzen and Saiedian found that students' experience with TDD and their maturity as developers influenced their willingness to adopt TDD. Spacco and Pugh also suggest that students require adequate incentives to accept a "test-first mentality" or otherwise they will resort to writing the code first and waiting to test until the end. Given the concern for motivating students to adopt TDD, understanding their attitudes and influences toward adherence to TDD principles is imperative.

3. METHOD

3.1 Research Design

In order to understand student behavior and affect—including their attitudes and emotional valence—with regards to adhering to TDD, we collected data from a semester of CS2 assignments via Web-CAT. We collected both project submissions and attitudinal surveys. Participation was voluntary and no compensation was offered. Consent was acquired for Web-CAT assignment data analysis and for survey analysis separately.

The survey consisted of 5-point interval scale items. First, students were asked to "Rate each item individually on the 5-point scale from 1 (Very Unimportant) to 5 (Very Important) on *how important the skill is in Computer Science*" for: time management, problem solving, attention to detail, writing solution code, and writing test code. They then repeated ratings for the same skills according to "*how strong you are in the skill*" from "Very Poor" to "Very Good."

Next, students rated "*the impact of the following behaviors have on developing programs*" from "Very Harmful" to "Very Helpful," for the following behaviors: beginning work *as soon as it is assigned*, beginning work *near its deadline*, developing thorough test code, developing code and corresponding tests in *small units* at a time, developing code and corresponding tests in *large portions* at a time, developing tests *before* writing solution code, and developing tests *after* writing solution code. Correspondingly, they also rated these behaviors according to "*how often you practice the behavior*" from "Very Rarely" to "Very Often."

Students then rated their agreement with the following statements from "Strongly Disagree" to "Strongly Agree," "*based on your experience with Test-Driven Development (TDD)* by incrementally developing tests and then solution code one unit at a time:" *I consistently followed TDD in my programming projects during this course*; *TDD helped me write better test code*; *TDD helped me write better solution code*; *TDD helped me better design my programs*; and *In the future, I will choose to follow TDD when developing programs outside of this course*.

On the same scale, the students then rated the following items "based on *your experience with Web-CAT automated results* (NOT TA/instructor feedback):" *Web-CAT helped me improve writing test code*; *Web-CAT helped me improve writing solution code*; *Web-CAT helped me improve designing my programs*; *Web-CAT helped me follow Test-Driven Development*; *Web-CAT helped improve my time management*; and *Web-CAT helped improve my attention to detail*.

To explore relationships between psychological affect and TDD and instructional technology interaction, the survey included the Brief Fear of Negative Evaluation Scale (BFNES) [16] and the Westside Test Anxiety Scale (WTAS) [7]. Both are brief (5-point scale, 8- and 10-item, respectively), validated questionnaires. The adaptation of WTAS specifically addressed working on programming projects with the following items:

- *The closer I am to a programming project deadline, the harder it is for me to concentrate on it*
- *When I prepare for programming projects, I worry I will not understand the necessary material*
- *While working on programming projects, I think that I am doing awful or that I may fail*
- *I lose focus on programming projects, and I cannot understand material that I knew before the project*
- *I finally understand solutions to programming projects after the deadline passes*
- *I worry so much before a programming project deadline that I am too worn out to do my best on the project*
- *I feel out of sorts or not really myself when I work on programming projects*
- *I find that my mind sometimes wanders when I am working on important programming projects*
- *After the project deadline, I worry about whether I did well enough*
- *I struggle with developing programming projects, or avoid them as long as I can. I feel that what I do will not be good enough.*

Statistical analysis concentrated on evaluating the following hypotheses:

(1) Students will rate importance of skills and their corresponding strengths with a positive correlation

(2) Students will rate helpfulness of and their adherence to behaviors with a positive correlation

(3) Students more likely to adhere to TDD principles will rate TDD's helpfulness more positively

(4) Students with higher programming anxiety (according to WTAS) will adhere less to starting work early and to principles of TDD

(5) Students with higher programming anxiety will rate Web-CAT as more helpful

(6) Students with higher evaluation anxiety (according to BFNES) will rate Web-CAT as less helpful.

All participants were students in CS2 in the Fall 2011 semester. 87 students consented (66% of 131 enrolled) to release their project data on Web-CAT for analysis and 61 students (47%) voluntarily completed the survey. Of the survey respondents, 84% were computer science majors and others either belonged to a different department or had no declared major. Before the course began, 48% of respondents had previously used Web-CAT, 61% had previously written test code, and 52% had previously followed TDD.

4. RESULTS

Ratings on skill strength and importance to computer science were generally positive for each skill. The mean and standard deviation for each item is shown in Figure 1, below. Analysis of paired ratings using Pearson's product-moment correlation coefficient did not reveal any significant relationships except for a small, positive correlation between the importance of writing test code and personal strength at it (r^2=0.26, p=0.02).

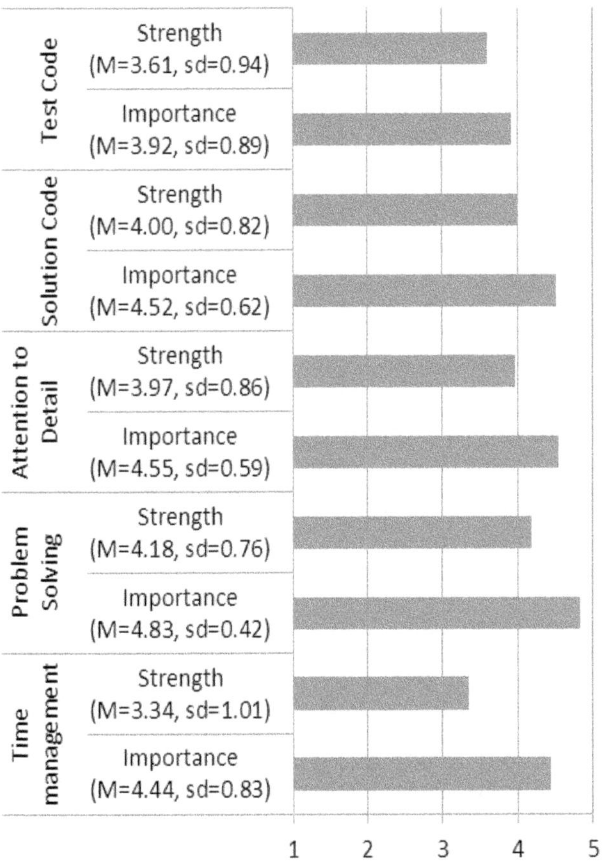

Figure 1. Personal strength and importance of skills in computer science with mean and standard deviation

Hypothesis (1) cannot be supported given the lack of either correlation or statistical significance for time management (r^2=0.08, p=0.54), problem solving (r^2=0.00, p=1.00), attention to detail (r^2=0.07, p=0.60), and writing source code (r^2=0.03, p=0.80).

On the other hand, positive correlations between ratings of helpfulness and adherence support Hypothesis (2). Figure 2 shows a summary of the ratings.

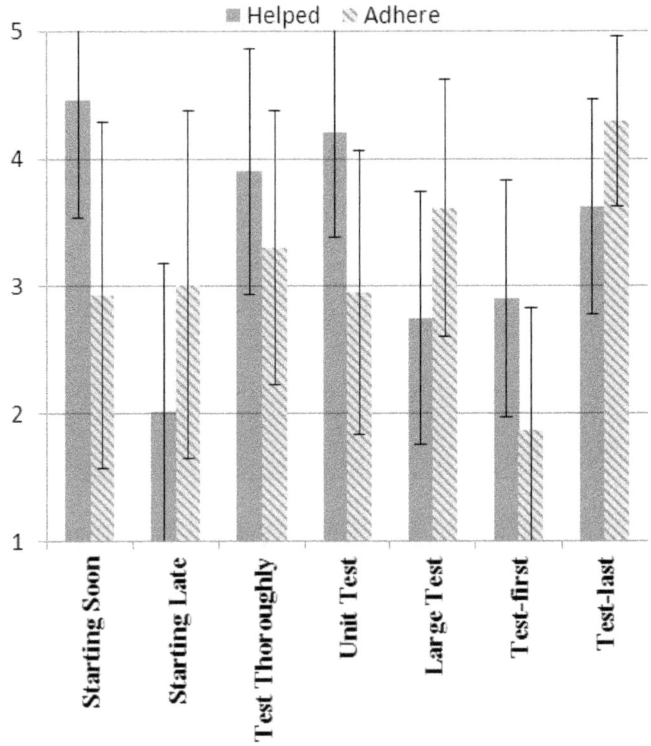

Help (M, sd)	4.46, 0.92	2.02, 1.16	3.90, 0.96	2.02, 1.16	2.02, 1.16	2.02, 1.16	2.02, 1.16
Adhere (M, sd)	2.93, 1.35	3.01, 1.36	3.30, 1.08	3.30, 1.08	3.30, 1.08	3.30, 1.08	3.30, 1.08
r^2, p	**0.42, <0.01**	**0.33, =0.01**	**0.55, <0.01**	**0.57, <0.01**	**0.39, <0.01**	**0.49, <0.01**	0.23, =0.07

Figure 2. Behavior adherence and helpfulness ratings graph (above) with correlation data (below)

All items demonstrate positive correlations that are statistically significant except for *test-last*, which has a correlation approaching significance.

Likewise, Hypothesis (3) was supported with significant correlations between self-reported adherence to TDD and perceived helpfulness of TDD. Often adhering to TDD has a strong, positive correlation with agreement to: "TDD helped me write better test code" (r^2=0.67, p<0.01), "TDD helped me write better solution code" (r^2=0.65, p<0.01), "TDD helped me better design my programs" (r^2=0.60, p<0.01), and "In the future, I will choose to follow TDD when developing programs outside of this course" (r^2=0.57, p<0.01). Figure 2 illustrates the ratings and correlations.

For both the Brief Fear of Negative Evaluation Scale (BFNES) and Westside Test Anxiety Scale (WTAS), ratings were averaged to score each participant where higher scores represent higher anxiety. On a 5-point scale, WTAS found moderately-low project anxiety (M=2.16, sd=0.81) and BFNES found slightly higher evaluation anxiety (M=2.7, sd=1.08). Cronbach's coefficient confirmed that BFNES (a=0.96) and WTAS (a=0.88) were reliable and the Shapiro-Wilk test found the results were not normally distributed for either BFNES (W<0.01) or WTAS (W=0.02).

Hypothesis (4) suggested that project anxiety (WTAS) would correlate with avoiding TDD, in starting work late, and in not testing thoroughly. However, no conclusion can be made because no correlations were found between project anxiety and: "Beginning work as soon as it is assigned" (r^2=-0.08, p=0.54), "Developing thorough test code" (r^2=0.08, p=0.54), "Developing code and corresponding tests in small units at a time" (r^2=-0.02, p=0.87), nor "Developing tests before writing solution code" (r^2=0.03, p=0.82).

Moderate positive correlations between project anxiety and some ratings of Web-CAT's helpfulness suggest some support for Hypothesis (5) with significance for: "Web-CAT helped me improve writing solution code" (r^2=0.26, p<0.05), "Web-CAT helped me improve designing my programs" (r^2=0.36, p<0.01), and "Web-CAT helped me follow Test-Driven Development" (r^2=0.45, p<0.01). However, correlations with some other items were not significant: "Web-CAT helped me improve writing test code" (r^2=0.17, p=0.19), "Web-CAT helped improve my time management" (r^2=0.15, p=0.27), and "Web-CAT helped improve my attention to detail" (r^2=0.21, p=0.11).

In addition, programming project submissions to Web-CAT allowed for analysis of patterns in student software development. It should be noted, however, that submissions to Web-CAT did not equally represent the code in all stages of development. On average, the first submission by a student already represented nearly 65% of the number of the statements in that student's final submission. Therefore, the snapshots of work-in-progress are sometimes limited in what they reveal about early work habits.

However, when comparing the relationship between the time of first submission and eventual final test coverage of statements, there was a significant difference between those who achieved 100% coverage and those who did not. The median time of first submission for students who achieved 100% coverage was 3.18 days before the deadline, while students who did not achieve 100% coverage had a median time of first submission 1.22 days before the deadline. According to the Mann-Whitney U test, the time remaining before the project deadline had a significant effect on final test coverage achieved (Z=-4.37, p<0.01).

We also compared the test coverage of each snapshot in the series of submissions for each student's project. We investigated relationships between the following metrics:

- Average test coverage — Percent of statements covered by tests at time of each submission to Web-CAT, averaged for each student on each project
- Total coverage rate — Percent of submissions that achieved 100% statement coverage at time of submission to Web-CAT, measured for each student on each project
- Final coverage — Percent of statements covered by tests on student's final submission for a project
- Final correctness — Correctness of solution code on student's final submission for a project, as determined by instructor-written tests
- Final Test NCLOC — Amount of student-written test code, in terms of the number of non-comment, non-blank lines of code
- Final Solution NCLOC — Amount of student-written solution code, in terms of the number of non-comment, non-blank lines of code

The relationships between these metrics are summarized in Table 1, below. We found that the average test coverage (M=82%, sd=19.08) had a strong, positive correlation with both the project's final correctness and final coverage. It also had moderately positive correlations with final test and solution non-comment lines of code (NCLOC). Similarly, the total coverage rate positively correlated with final coverage and final correctness. A combination of high average test coverage and consistent total coverage rate would suggest incremental, thorough testing on behalf of the student.

Table 1. Correlations between test coverage and the quality and quantity of the final product submission

	Mean, sd	Avg Test Coverage (r^2, p)	Total Coverage Rate (r^2, p)
Final Coverage	97.49%, 0.09	*0.72, <0.0001*	*0.28, <0.0001*
Final Correctness	88.06%, 20.60	*0.55, <0.0001*	*0.39, <0.0001*
Final Test NCLOC	235.43, 108.01	*0.38, =0.0001*	-0.06, 0.3097
Final Solution NCLOC	355.37, 120.61	*0.21, <0.0001*	*-0.24, <0.0001*

5. DISCUSSION

While Hypothesis (1)'s prediction—that students' perceived importance of skills would be positively correlated to their self-assessments—was not supported, the results may be interpreted with a positive outlook. Students' ability to separate their own ability from what they consider important skills in computer science may allow them to recognize their strengths and identify important skills they may lack.

Additionally, the strong relationship between what students characterize as helpful practices and their adherence illustrates reciprocity between affect and behavior in learning. A positive attitude toward good programming practices will encourage a student to act accordingly, which should reinforce that attitude with positive outcomes. The supportive result for Hypothesis (3) strengthens this reciprocal model of learning, where we observe students who have adhered to Test-Driven Development (TDD) characterize the method as helpful.

Students who adhered to TDD also benefited with significantly better test coverage and solution correctness. The observations of high average coverage per submission and percentage of submissions with 100% coverage associate with incrementally testing and developing a solution in tandem. While one cannot irrefutably conclude that these students were following the test-first principle of TDD, the pattern strongly suggests behavior consistent with unit testing. The adherents' improved outcomes also corroborate with other studies' findings that TDD improves quality of code and testing.

Interestingly, in post-hoc analysis we found that adherence to TDD principles of test-first and unit testing also correlated with adherence to the good practice of starting work early. Survey data showed modest, positive correlations between starting work early with both test-first ($r^2=0.28$, $p<0.05$) and unit testing ($r^2=0.33$, $p<0.01$).

Despite these encouraging results, our conclusions must also acknowledge two concerning findings. Foremost, both survey results and Web-CAT data showed trends in procrastinating before starting work. Procrastination should be discouraged and the data show negative effects on test coverage. This finding is consistent with other studies that found that students who earn A and B grades start work significantly earlier than those who earn lower grades [10]. There is opportunity for research in dissuading this counterproductive behavior, perhaps through pedagogical or instructional technology interventions.

Secondly, survey results showed discouragingly low ratings for both helpfulness and adherence to test-first development (Figure 2). In fact, the Wilcoxon signed-rank test found that the mean score for helpfulness (M=3.62, SD=0.84) and adherence (M=4.29, SD=0.67) to test-last is significantly greater ($p<0.01$ and $p<0.01$, respectively) than the helpfulness (M=2.90, SD=0.93) and adherence (M=1.87, SD=0.96) to test-first. Snapshots of project submissions to Web-CAT may indicate whether students tested early or not, but they cannot concretely determine whether a unit test was written before or after its corresponding solution code. Consequently, we can only rely on the survey data to evaluate student adherence to test-first.

It is not entirely surprising that the test-first aspect of TDD garners more resistance than unit testing. For students with experience programming but not with TDD, the behavior of designing tests first is a considerable departure from immediately developing the solution. As mentioned previously, studies in both academia and industry found programmers who were younger and less experienced were less accepting of TDD. Our study suggests that student attitudes towards test-first development may be the primary hindrance for new novices accepting and adhering to TDD. Accordingly, therein lies an opportunity for computer science educators to explore ways to persuade students to use test-first development. We plan to investigate this opportunity in future research.

Finally, our research investigated possible relationships between psychological anxiety and the adherence to TDD and attitudes toward Web-CAT. Both Brief Fear of Negative Evaluation Scale (BFNES) and Westside Test Anxiety Scale (WTAS) were internally consistent. There was no observable relationship between project anxiety and adherence to TDD principles.

According to the Yerkes-Dodson law [20], stress has a positive effect on performance until surpassing threshold where stress becomes too great and produces a negative effect on performance. Likewise, stress may motivate students to follow recommended methods unless the stress is so great that it encourages bad habits. Further investigation into individual differences in response to project anxiety is necessary to conclude how stress may influence software development behaviors. Meanwhile, the positive correlation found between project anxiety and Web-CAT helpfulness was modest, but indicates opportunity for easing disruptive affect with instructional technology.

On the contrary, we hypothesized (6) that instructional technology that includes feedback on test failures and other negative results would have an adverse effect on those with fear of evaluation (BFNES). However, the results of evaluation anxiety relating to impression on Web-CAT's helpfulness were inconclusive. It is important though to design feedback with sensitivity to possible negative student affect.

6. CONCLUSION

Our research investigated adherence to Test-Driven Development (TDD) with particular attention to the role of student affect, or attitudes and emotions. As we observed, attitudes toward TDD influenced both negative and positive outcomes in students new to the method. Understanding the reciprocal nature of affect in learning appears to be especially important when teaching methods. Methods like TDD are taught but not necessarily assessed directly. Consequently, it is vital to evaluate whether students are adhering to the methods as well as understand their attitudes that will likely inform their behavior.

This study found significant results that emphasize beneficial outcomes of following TDD. However, it also identified challenges to persuade both desired affect and behavior. We hope this research will mark grounds for progress in designing instructional technology and computer science curriculum to improve TDD education.

7. REFERENCES

[1] Barriocanal, E.G., Urban, M.S, et al., "An experience in integrating automated unit testing practices in an introductory programming course," SIGCSE Bull., vol. 34., no. 4., pp. 125-128, 2002.

[2] Beck, K "Embracing change with extreme programming." Computer, vol. 32, no. 10, pp. 70-77, 1999.

[3] Bhat, T. and Nagappan, N. "Evaluating the efficacy of test-driven development: industrial case studies," Proceedings of the 2006 ACM/IEEE international symposium on Empirical software engineering, ACM, Rio de Janeiro, Brazil, pp. 356-363, 2006.

[4] Canfora, G., Cimitile, A. et al., "Evaluating advantages of test driven development: a controlled experiment with professionals," Proceedings of the 2006 ACM/IEEE international symposium on Empirical software engineering, Rio de Janeiro, Brazil, pp. 364-371, 2006.

[5] Desai, C., Janzen, D.S., and Clements, J. "Implications of integrating test-driven development into CS1/CS2 curricula," SIGCSE Bull., vol. 41., issue 1, pp. 148-152, 2009.

[6] Desai, C., Janzen, D.S., and Savage, K. "A survey of evidence for test-driven development in academia," SIGCSE Bull., vol. 40, issue 2, pp. 97-101, 2008.

[7] Driscoll, R. (2007). "Westside Test Anxiety Scale Validation." Education Resources Information Center: 6.

[8] Edwards, S.H. "Improving student performance by evaluating how well students test their own programs." *J. Educational Resources in Computing*, 3(3): 1-24, September 2003.

[9] Edwards, S.H. "Using software testing to move students from trial-and-error to reflection-in-action," SIGCSE Bull., vol. 36, issue 1, pp. 26-30, 2004.

[10] Edwards, S.H., J. Snyder, et al (2009). "Comparing effective and ineffective behaviors of student programmers." Proceedings of the fifth international workshop on Computing education research workshop. Berkely, CA, USA, ACM: 3-14.

[11] Fraser, S., Astels, D. et al., "Discipline and practices of TDD: (test driven development)," Companion of the 18th annual ACM SIGPLAN conference, ACM, Anaheim, California, pp. 268-270, 2003.

[12] Janzen, D.S. and Saiedian, H. "A leveled examination of test-driven development acceptance," Proceedings of the 29th international conference on Software Engineering, IEEE Computer Society, pp. 719-722, 2007.

[13] JUnit.org Resources for Test Driven Development. Web page last accessed Sept. 23, 2011: <http://www.junit.org/>

[14] Lappalainen, V. , Itkonen, J. ,et al., "ComTest: a tool to impart TDD and unit testing to introductory level programming," Proceedings of the fifteenth annual conference on Innovation and technology in computer science education, ACM, Bilkent, Ankara, Turkey, pp. 63-67, 2010.

[15] Melnik, G. and Maurer, F. "A cross-program investigation of students' perceptions of agile methods," Proceedings of the 27th international conference on Software engineering, ACM, St. Louis, Missouri, pp. 481-488, 2005.

[16] Rodebaugh, T. L., C. M. Woods, et al. (2004). "More Information From Fewer Questions: The Factor Structure and Item Properties of the Original and Brief Fear of Negative Evaluation Scale." Psychological Assessment 16(2): 169-181.

[17] Spacco, J., Hovemeyer, D. et al., "Experiences with marmoset: designing and using an advanced submission and testing system for programming courses," SIGCSE Bull., vol. 38, issue 3, pp. 13-17, 2006.

[18] Spacco, J. and Pugh, W. "Helping students appreciate test-driven development (TDD)," Companion to the 21st ACM SIGPLAN symposium, ACM, Portland, Oregon, pp. 907-913, 2006.

[19] Web-CAT. Web page last accessed Sept. 23, 2011: <http://web-cat.cs.vt.edu>

[20] Yerkes, R.M. and J.D. Dodson. "The relation of strength of stimulus to rapidity of habit-formation." *Journal of Comparative Neurology and Psychology* 18(5): 459-482, 1908.

Statistical Evidence of the Correlation between Mental Ability to Compute and Student Performance in Undergraduate Courses

Osvaldo Luiz de Oliveira
Faculty of Campo Limpo Paulista
Rua Guatemala, 167, Jardim América
Campo Limpo Paulista, SP, Brazil
55 11 4812-9407
osvaldo@faccamp.br

ABSTRACT

In recent years, many studies have suggested the hypothesis that mental ability to compute is essential for many activities and is as fundamental as reading, writing and arithmetic. This work provides mathematical arguments to verification of this hypothesis. Assuming a precise statement of what is to compute, based on the model of computation "Turing Machine", we found experimentally the existence of a correlation, statistically significant, between mental ability to compute and student performance in four different university courses.

Categories and Subject Descriptors

K.3.2 [**Computers and Education**]: Computer and Information Science Education - *Computer Science Education.*

General Terms

Human Factors, Experimentation.

Keywords

Computational Thinking, Computing Education, Model of Computation, Empirical Research.

1. INTRODUCTION

This article addresses computation by people rather than by computers. In recent years, several studies have suggested that mental ability to compute is crucial for the realization of many human activities [2, 3, 4, 5, 6, 9, 11].

When a physician examines a patient, he computes a set of symptoms to determine a diagnosis. An architect computes the needs and possibilities of occupying a space to develop an architectural design. A lawyer computes facts, evidence, circumstances and norms to establish defense or prosecution arguments to convince juries and judges. In these and many other cases, an intuitive notion of computation is present, even if the physician, architect and lawyer are not aware of it.

From this perspective, computation is important for everyone and this generates a lot of confusion regarding its meaning. The term "computation" means different things to different people, depending on the type of system with which they are dealing. Alfred Aho discusses this problem by suggesting use of the term "computation" in conjunction with a model of computation with clear and well-defined semantics. "Since computation refers to a process that is defined in terms of some underlying model of computation, we would achieve clearer communication if we made clear … the underlying (model)" [1, p. 2].

Motivated by the hypothesis that mental ability to compute is fundamental, we investigated the correlation between this ability and the performance of students on four different undergraduate courses provided by the Faculty of Campo Limpo Paulista, Brazil.

In Section 2 we develop a computation model for use in studies to verify the mental ability to compute. This model was used in an experiment in which we tested the computation ability of students from different courses. The test score for each student was compared to his course performance, as described in Section 3. Sections 4 and 5 present the results and our conclusions.

2. A MODEL OF COMPUTATION FOR PEOPLE TO THINK

In this section we present, in an intuitive way, the computation model we developed. A formal definition this model is omitted. We chose the set P of plane geometric figures as the universe on which computations are performed. This set was chosen because it is familiar to every undergraduate student. Psychology departments have successfully used geometric figures in psychological tests for many years [8]. A **computation** is a function f: P $\rightarrow$ P carried out by a machine M. For example, Figure 1-a shows a computation by machine M that involves a 90° clockwise rotation of the figure given as input.

ITiCSE'12, July 3–5, 2012, Haifa, Israel.
Copyright 2012 ACM 978-1-4503-1246-2/12/07...$10.00.

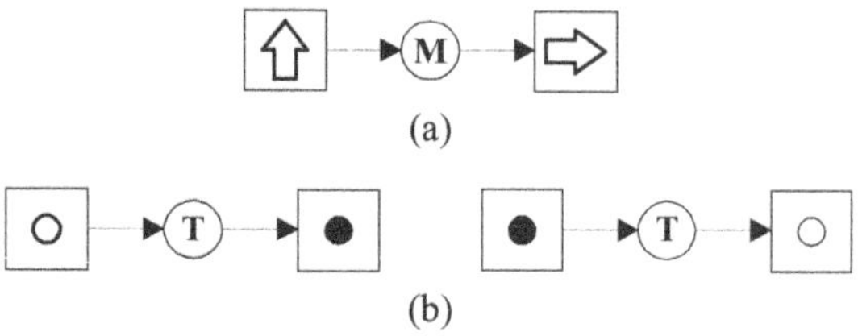

Figure 1. (a) Computation by machine M; (b) Two computations by machine T.

We identified four types of human reasoning about computation by a machine:

- Knowing one or more input values (function domain) and output (function image) of a machine M, **abstract** what it does (i.e., find the function). For example, using information about the two computations by machine T in Figure 1-b, we can abstract that T reverses the fill color (black or white) of the plane figure presented as input.
- Knowing one or more inputs (function domain) for a machine M and a description of its computation mechanism (description of the function), **calculate** the output (function image) of M.
- Knowing one or more input and output pairs (domain and image of function) of a machine M, abstract and **write** the computation mechanism (function).
- Knowing the mechanism of computation of a machine (function), **analyze** how efficient it is in terms of resources needed to compute, for example, how fast it reaches a result.

We developed a **computation mechanism** used by machines, taking the "Turing Machine" computation model as a reference [10]. A Turing Machine computes on sets of binary numbers and its programs are defined by mathematical relations. These concepts are very specific and people from different backgrounds find them difficult to use. Thus, we developed the computation mechanism described below.

A machine operates on a tape divided into small units called cells and has a read–write head that can read and write content in a cell. The read–write head of a machine can move to the left and right of the tape. The symbols used in the computing mechanism for the machine are shown in Figure 2.

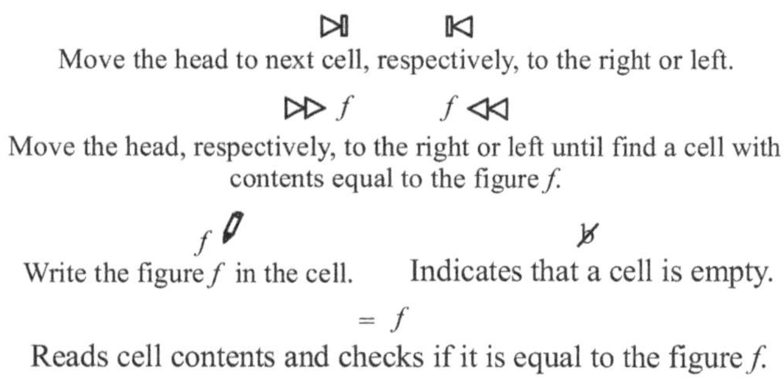

Figure 2. Symbols used to describe the computation mechanism for a machine.

As an example, Figure 3-a presents the computation mechanism used by a machine M. Figures 3-b to 3-f show the sequence of computation of machine M on a tape initially filled with three white circles and the read–write head positioned at the leftmost cell. The final tape configuration is the output of machine M.

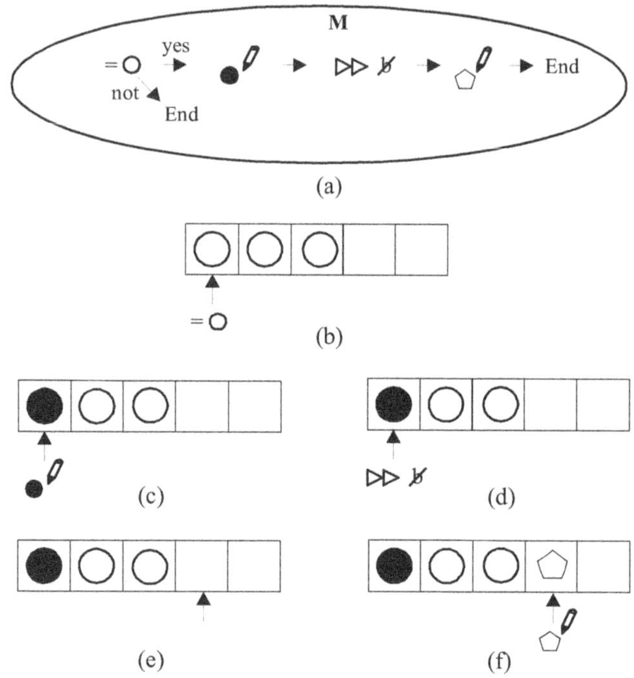

Figure 3. (a) Computation mechanism used by machine M. (b) M reads the cell content and compares it with a white circle. If what is read is a white circle, the machine prepares to execute the instruction to write a black circle. Otherwise, the computation is terminated. (c) M writes a black circle in the cell. (d) M moves the head to the right until (e) it finds a blank cell. (f) M writes a pentagon, after which the computation is terminated.

3. MATERIALS AND METHODS

3.1 A Test of Mental Ability to Compute

Using the computation model described in Section 2, we designed a test to measure a person's ability to compute (Appendix I). The test was validated in two successive pilot tests with subsequent refinement twice applied to groups of 12 and 10 students who did not participate in the final experiment. In the refinements, some very easy or very difficult questions were replaced. The computation mechanism that was initially proposed evolved, giving rise to the model presented in Section 2.

After the refinements, the test comprised seven objective questions, each containing five alternatives. The test was divided into two parts:

- Part 1 (questions 1–4) evaluates a person's ability to abstract what one or more machines compute, knowing the input and output of some of its computations.
- Part 2 (questions 5–7) focuses on the computation mechanism. Question 5 measures a person's ability to calculate the output of a machine, knowing the mechanism of computation and an input. Question 6 evaluates a person's ability to write down the computation mechanism of a machine, knowing input and output pairs. Question 7

assesses a person's ability to recognize the more efficient of two distinct mechanisms developed to perform the same computation.

The questions in Parts 1 and 2 of the test were preceded by explanatory text. Appendix I lists the test questions.

3.2 Subjects

A total of 79 students in their penultimate year of courses in computer science (sixth semester), law (eighth semester), education (sixth semester) and pharmacy (sixth semester) at a university in Brazil participated in the survey (Table 1). Students were randomly selected to give a sample of approximately 70% of students enrolled on a particular course/semester.

Table 1. A profile of the survey participants.

Course / semester	Gender, *n* (%)		Age, years		
	Female	Male	Range	Mean	Median
Computer science / 6	2 (13%)	14 (87%)	20–34	23	21
Law / 8	11 (55%)	9 (45%)	21–60	37	32
Education / 6	21 (100%)	0 (0%)	20–49	28	28
Pharmacy / 6	14 (64%)	8 (36%)	20–57	30	29

3.3 Experimental Setup

The students individually answered the test questions in their classrooms at the beginning of an academic day. The maximum duration for responses to the test was set to 20 minutes. The evaluators did not interact with the students during the test.

A score from 0 to 7, corresponding to the number of questions answered correctly, was assigned to each student.

Student performance in a course (course score) was measured as the average score obtained in common disciplines taken by the students in the same period and taught by the same teacher. This average was calculated as follows. Student transcripts were provided by the academic registry of the university. We identified the following numbers of disciplines in common among the participants: computer Science, 26 (83%); law, 40 (75%); education, 33 (79%); and pharmacy, 33 (81%). The course score obtained by a student was calculated taking into account only the common disciplines among participants on a course.

For each course, we created tables listing the test score and course score for each student. Appendix II provides an example of these tables developed for the computer science students.

4. RESULTS AND DISCUSSION

Pearson's correlation coefficient, typically denoted by r, is a measure of the linear correlation between two variables [7] and is a real value between 0 (no systematic concordance) and 1 (perfect agreement). Student's t-test is usually applied to check the statistical significance of r. We consider a value of r coefficient statistically significant when p-value ≤ 0.01 in Student t–test. Values of Pearson's r for correlation between the test scores and course scores are presented in Table 2.

Table 2. Pearson's r correlation coefficients between the test scores and course scores.

Course/semester	Number of pairs	Pearson's r	t	p-value
Computer Science / 6	16	0.69 (strong)	3.57	0.003
Law / 8	20	0.59 (moderate)	3.11	0.006
Education / 6	21	0.51 (moderate)	2.57	0.010
Pharmacy / 6	22	0.50 (moderate)	2.59	0.010

The results show that for computer science, law, education and pharmacy students, there was a statistically significant ($p \leq 0.01$) correlation between the test scores and the course scores.

The results are restricted to small groups of students from a single institution. Although limited, they suggest a strong correlation between the ability to compute, as measured by the proposed model, and student performance in a computer science course, as expected. The results also present less obvious things. They present statistical evidence of a moderate correlation between computation ability and student performance for groups from three careers that are not computational (law, education and pharmacy).

Correlations are not cause and effect relations. Our results may indicate that the ability to compute is a fundamental element of the disciplines for the courses surveyed. However, they also may indicate that the ability to compute and skills in performing activities in courses surveyed rely on fundamental factors common to these areas.

Whatever the case, the results are important because they indicate a way to investigate and establish mathematical argumentation to verify the hypothesis that mental ability to compute is fundamental. If the objective is to verify this hypothesis, then the generality of our results needs to be investigated in a larger population comprising a large number of students from different universities and courses.

5. CONCLUSION

The main aim of this study was mathematical verification of the hypothesis that mental ability to compute is fundamental. The results provide three contributions for verification of the hypothesis.

The first contribution is a computation model to assess the human capacity to compute. Instead of some vague notion of computation, the model proposed clearly defines what we understand by computation. The model is based on the classical Turing Machine model of computation, which has well-defined semantics, and uses plane geometric figures as the computation universe, which makes it suitable for students of different courses.

The second contribution is statistical evidence of correlation between mental ability to compute, as measured by the test proposed, and the student performance in four different undergraduate courses.

The third contribution is motivation for new research questions. Is the evidence we found present in larger populations comprising students from different courses and universities? What explains the correlation observed? Is computation a fundamental skill underlying different careers and (or) there are basic factors common to computation and other areas?

6. ACKNOWLEDGMENTS

We would like to thank all subjects who volunteered for the experiment for their invaluable contribution to this work.

7. REFERENCES

[1] Aho, A. V. 2011. Computation and Computational Thinking. *Ubiquity* 2011, January (Jan. 2011), article no. 1. DOI=10.1145/1922681.1922682.

[2] Basawapatna, A., Koh, K. H., Repenning, A., Webb, D. C. and Marshall, K. S. 2011. Recognizing Computational Thinking Patterns. In *Proceedings of the 42nd ACM Technical Symposium on Computer Science Education* (Dallas, Texas, USA, March 09 - 12, 2011). SIGCSE'11. ACM, New York, NY, 245-250. DOI= 10.1145/1953163.1953241.

[3] Guzdial, M. 2009. Teaching Computing to Everyone. *Communications of the ACM* 52, 5 (May 2009), 31-33. DOI=10.1145/1506409.1506420.

[4] Hu, C. 2011. Computational Thinking: what it might mean and what we might do about it. In *Proceedings of the 16th Annual Joint Conference on Innovation and Technology in Computer Science Education* (Darmstadt, Germany, June 27 - 29, 2011). ITiCSE'11. ACM, New York, NY, 223-227. DOI=10.1145/1999747.1999811.

[5] Kafura, D. and Tatar, D. 2011. Initial Experience with a Computational Thinking Course for Computer Science Students. In *Proceedings of the 42nd ACM Technical Symposium on Computer Science Education* (Dallas, Texas, USA, March 09 - 12, 2011). SIGCSE'11. ACM, New York, NY, 251-256. DOI= 10.1145/1953163.1953242.

[6] Lu, J. J. and Fletcher, G. H. L. 2009. Thinking about Computational Thinking. In *Proceedings of the 40th ACM Technical Symposium on Computer Science Education* (Chattannoga, Tennesse, USA, March 03 - 07, 2009). SIGCSE'09. ACM, New York, NY, 260-264. DOI=10.1145/1508865.1508959.

[7] Miles, J. and Shevlin, M. 2004. *Applying Regression and Correlation: A Guide for Students and Researchers*. Sage Publications, London, UK.

[8] Plotnik, R. and Kouyoumdjian, H. 2010. *Introduction to Psychology*. Wadsworth, Belmont, CA, USA.

[9] Qualls, J. A., Grant, M. M. and Sherrell, L. B. 2011. CS1 Students' Understanding of Computational Thinking Concepts. *Journal of Computing Sciences in Colleges* 26, 5 (May. 2011), 62-71.

[10] Turing, A. M. 1936. On Computable Numbers, with an Application to the Entscheidungsproblem. In *Proceedings of the London Mathematical Society* (London, UK, 1936), Ser. 2, vol. 42, 230-265. [Also available on-line at january 02, 2012: http://www.cs.ox.ac.uk/activities/ieg/e-library/sources/tp2-ie.pdf].

[11] Wing, J. 2006. Computational Thinking. *Communications of the ACM* 49, 3 (Mar. 2006), 33-35. DOI=10.1145/1118178.1118215.

Appendix I - A Test of Mental Ability to Compute

1)

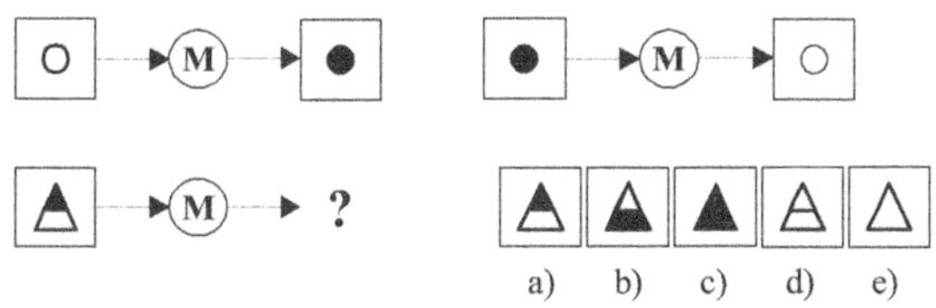

2)

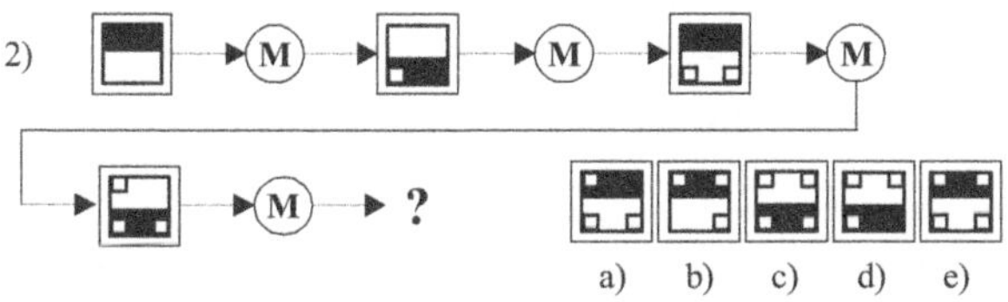

3)

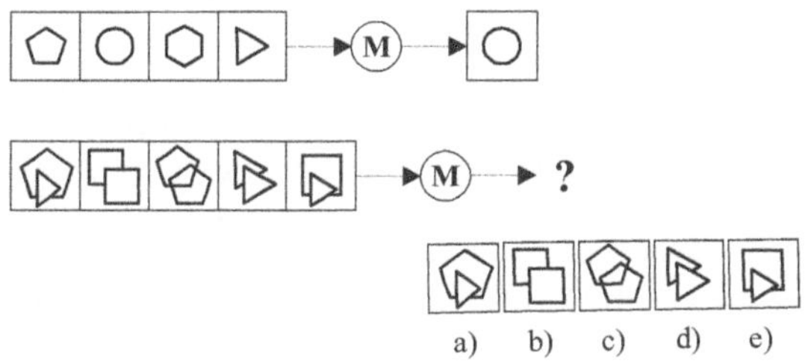

4)

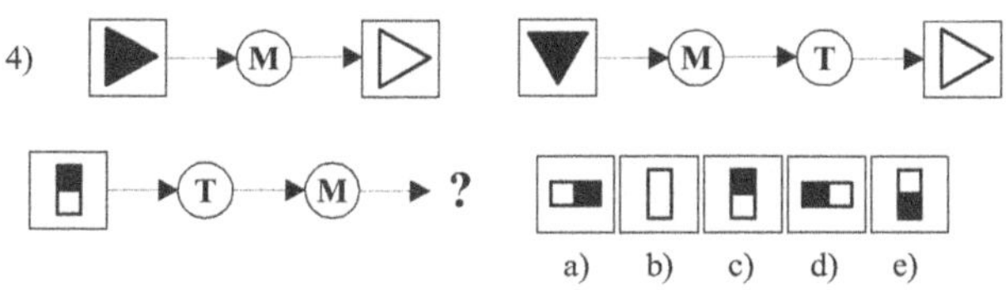

5)

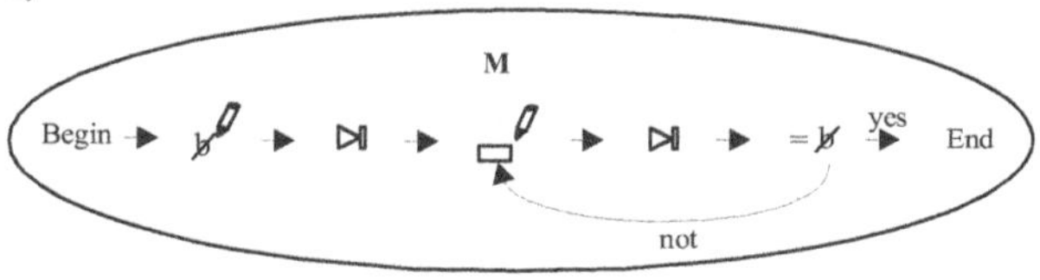

Before the M computation.

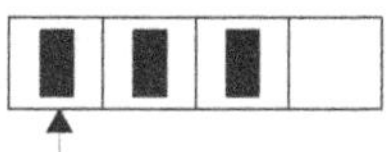

After the M computation.

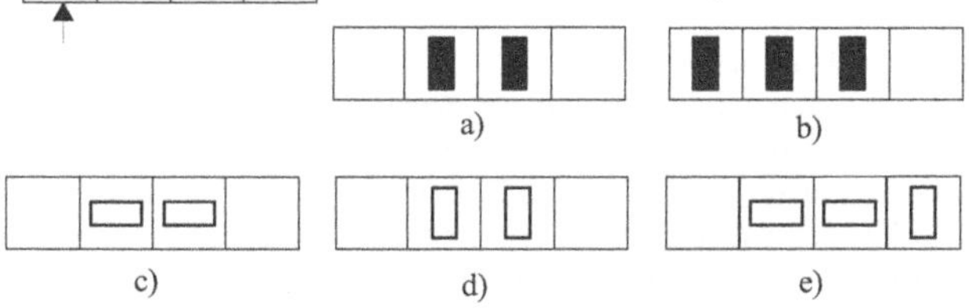

6)

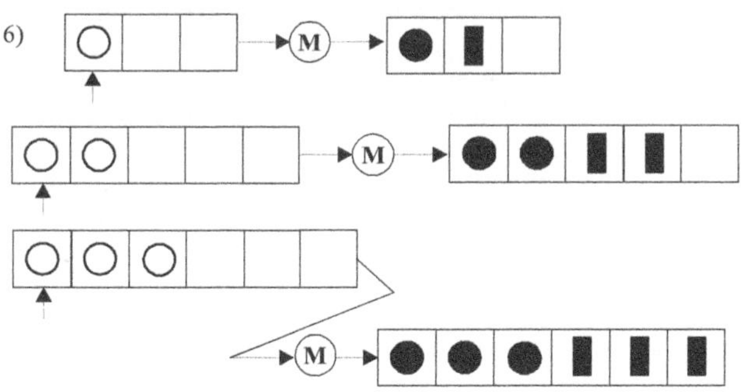

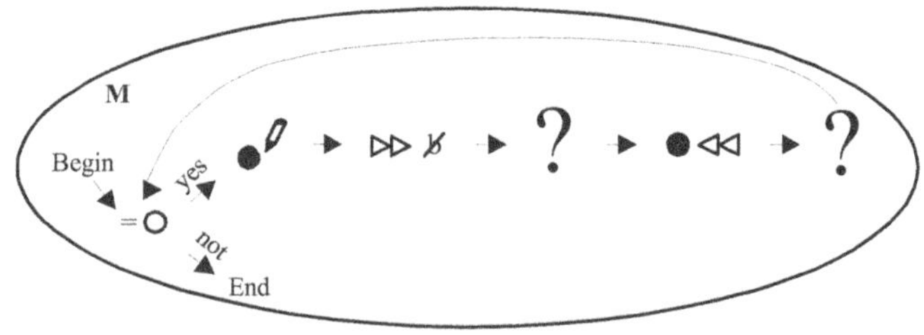

You should complete the two questions (?), with:

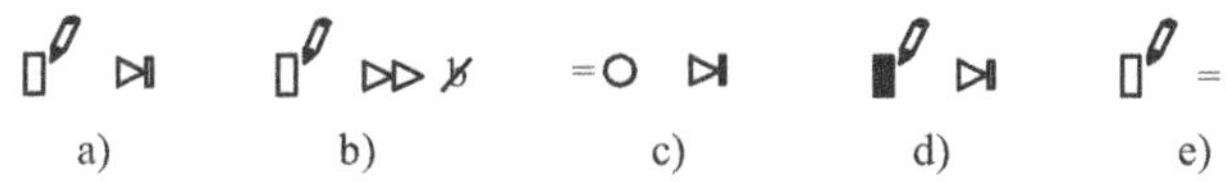

7)

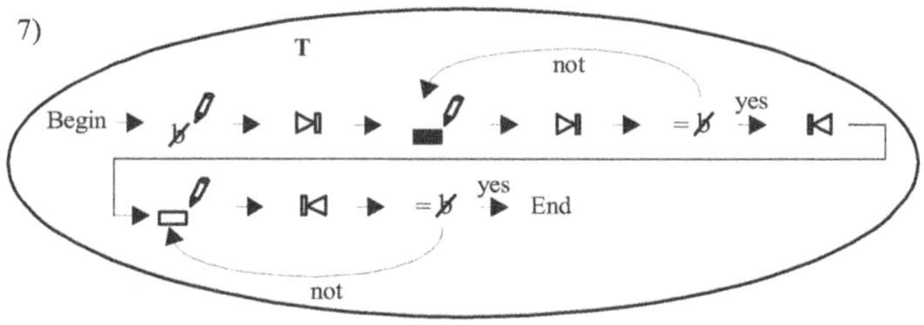

Before the M computation.

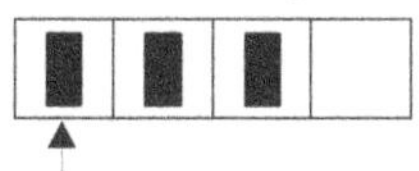

Considering the computations, on the tape above, of the M (question 5) and T machines (described above), it can be stated that:

a) The results of computations of M and T are different.

b) The results of the computations of M and T are equal, and they do the same amount of movement of the read-write head.

c) The results of computations of M and T are equal, and T does less movements of the read-write head than M.

d) The results of computations of M and T are equal, and M does less movimentes of read-write head than T.

e) None of the previous alternatives is correct.

Appendix II - Test Score and Course Score by Computer Science Students.

Student	Test (0 .. 7)	Course (0 .. 10)
A	4	8.23
B	1	6.32
C	3	6.99
D	6	8.84
E	4	8.71
F	3	7.33
G	6	7.58
H	6	9.50

Student	Test (0 .. 7)	Course (0 .. 10)
I	6	9.52
J	6	7.59
K	2	5.56
L	3	8.02
M	6	8.68
N	4	9.16
O	4	6.49
P	5	8.21

Grade Inflation, What Students Value, and the Necessity of Suffering

Taly Sharon
University of Liverpool
Computer Science Department
(Online Degree Programmes)
Ashton Building, Ashton Street
Liverpool, UK, L69 2BX
Taly.Sharon@liverpool.ac.uk

Paul Kingsley
University of Liverpool
Computer Science Department
(Online Degree Programmes)
Ashton Building, Ashton Street
Liverpool, UK, L69 2BX
Paul.Kingsley@liverpool.ac.uk

ABSTRACT
This paper questions whether there is a conflict between the academic and business interests of a university in combating grade inflation. A survey of online Master's degree students in Computing at a British university was carried out. It examined variations in the perceived value of a degree or the university's perceived reputation as a result of a number of possible changes aimed at reducing the sacrifices involved in gaining a degree; making it less likely that students would fail modules or their degree; and reducing the degree dropout rate to almost zero. The conclusion is that students saw such changes as reducing the value of their degree. The research suggests that in certain circumstances, academic and business interests can be aligned in opposing grade inflation.

Categories and Subject Descriptors
K.3.2 [**Computers and Education**]: Computer and Information Science Education – *computer science education, curriculum.* K.3.1 [**Computers and Education**]: Computer Uses in Education – *distance learning.*

General Terms
Measurement, Performance, Economics, Experimentation, Human Factors, Theory.

Keywords
Grade inflation, perceived value, online education, higher education, sacrifice, failure rates, dropout rates.

1. BROADENING THE PERSPECTIVE
The theme for this year's conference challenges educationalists to think about future trends in computing sciences research. Part of that future, and only part of it, lies in "broadening the perspective", the title of one of the paper sessions at ITiCSE 2011. As well as being able to describe how to teach computing topics well, at least some of the profession should be able to research the great educational controversies of the day, such as plagiarism and grade inflation. It would be profitable if some computer scientists were known for their contribution to education beyond the boundaries of computer science. In this we have been inspired by our own computer science colleagues Paul Leng, who became the University of Liverpool's first Professor of E-Learning, and Kathleen Kelm, who, as Director of Faculty Development, is responsible for the training of all online teachers, regardless of subject.

ITiCSE'12, July 3–5, 2012, Haifa, Israel.

2. THE BUSINESS OF GRADE INFLATION
Many university teachers may often feel that the pressure in favour of grade inflation and a lowering of standards is relentless. They may be tempted to identify such pressure as being exerted by the business interests of their university, driven in turn by student demands to make courses easier.

It is understandable in such situations to regard teaching staff as defending academic standards on largely ethical grounds in opposition to business interests which would be served by easier degree courses. This would be unfortunate. By broadening the perspective and looking at some of the economic forces that influence demand for Computing degrees, it can be seen that well established and validated marketing theory does not suggest that there will always be this conflict between academic and business interests.

Kotler and Armstrong, in their classic work, *Principles of Marketing*, state that "consumers usually perceive higher-priced products as having higher quality" [5]. This implies that the cost of goods can be too low as well as too high. Teas and Agarwal write about extrinsic product cues, such as price and brand name, affecting in a positive way perceptions of quality [12]. Marketing theory is flexible enough to realize that there are costs which are not related to financial price involved in the acquisition of goods and services. These total costs are often referred to as the give or sacrifice. The latter term is particularly pertinent to university students taking a degree. The stress involved in balancing competing demands on time can be considerable. The suffering involved in acquiring a degree is particularly acute among part-time mature students who have so many more commitments than their younger full-time counterparts. These are the kind of students that are taught on a completely online Master's degree programme in Computing run by Laureate Online Interactive Education on behalf of the University of Liverpool. The university is believed to be the biggest provider of online Master's degrees in Europe. The students have an average age of around 36, and are drawn from all parts of the world.

The current authors' research focused on the question of whether it is possible that, in certain circumstances, degrees that involve greater sacrifice are perceived as having more value. If this is so, then there might well be an alignment of academic and business interests. The teacher who protects academic standards could be maintaining the value and economic desirability of the product.

A decision was taken to gather students' views through the medium of an anonymous online survey. What the survey sought to measure was perceived value. Students were not asked to apply a range of objective criteria in making their judgments. In general they were simply asked whether certain things increased or decreased the value or quality of their degree in their eyes.

3. THEORY

Alves conducted a wide ranging review of the literature on perceived value in higher education [1]. Sancjez-Fernandez and Iniesta-Bonillo performed a similar service in looking at perceived value in general. [10]. Some of the literature treats perceived value as the net value of a product after all the pluses and minuses have been added up. In the definition of Zeithaml, perceived value is "...the consumer's overall assessment of the utility of a product based on perceptions of what is received and what is given" [14]. The weakness of this is that it hides much of the detail. In particular, it does not tell us whether a high level of sacrifice is perceived as a plus or a minus. Too often the sacrifice is seen as unambiguously negative, ignoring the obvious example of luxury goods where a high price is often seen as a positive feature.

In this study the approach was to isolate a number of variables to see if something interesting, and possibly unexpected, could be identified. A cluster of three issues was identified which might be seen as associated with grade inflation and a lowering of academic standards.

1. The level of sacrifice involved in obtaining a student's degree. We asked respondents to ignore the cost of fees and concentrate on other sacrifices they had made. The question of tuition fee cost as a sign of quality was tested separately.
2. The proportion of students who failed their degree or individual modules (a module is an intensive class lasting 8 weeks). The survey asked about the case where the number of failures was very low. It was reasoned that where grades were uniformly inflated, the number of failures would fall, and that questions like this would be the easiest way of testing attitudes towards grade inflation.
3. The numbers of students who dropped out of their degree. Ormond Simpson, in a book based on his experiences at the Open University in the UK, expressed the opinion that "an institution that awarded its own qualifications and had zero dropout might have difficulty in persuading both its students and the general public that its qualifications were worth having." [11]. Part of the current authors' research was aimed at establishing how far this was true.

The responses to some of the questions would probably depend on the current situation. The reaction of students could be different if they were enrolled on a degree course where grades were already inflated. It should therefore be made clear that the degree programmes described in this paper apply very strict grading criteria. Only around 15% of students could expect to receive A or A* grades. This can be contrasted with the case at Princeton University, which reported as a success the fact that the proportion of A+, A, and A- grades on undergraduate courses had fallen from 47.9% in 2002-2003, to 39.7% in 2008-2009 [9]. International students are generally advised that a grade C at Liverpool is equivalent to grade B in the United States.

What might be called the baseline position was that grade inflation was not a problem, and students would therefore be expected to work hard for good grades. It could not be considered easy to pass the Computing degrees in question. This is consistent with what colleagues in marketing would call the positioning of the degrees.

Two authors who pioneered the programmes, Kalman and Leng, wrote about "the widespread public suspicion that this educational [online] paradigm will be associated with low standards and quality." They concluded that, in overcoming this perception, "quality cannot be bought cheaply" [4]. Computing colleagues, Grasso and Leng, stated that "We believe firmly that the successful programmes of the future will be those that focus on pedagogy, and give precedence to academic standards and quality assurance, rather than those that emphasize technological aspects or focus on low-cost delivery." [3]. This meets the concerns expressed by Thirunarayanan a decade ago that online education might lead to people receiving degrees who did not really deserve them [13].

4. SURVEY OF COMPUTING STUDENTS

An online survey was carried out in 13 small Research Methods modules of the University of Liverpool's online Computing Master's degrees programme. This is the module students take towards the end of their degree immediately before attempting their dissertation, and after completing 8 other modules (a module is an 8 week class). Some 101 students completed the survey anonymously with a response rate of 62%.

Many respondents did not have English as their first language, and so they were asked to indicate whether any question in the survey was so difficult for them to understand that their reply might not reflect their true opinion. Where a student indicated that a question fell into that category, the response to that question was discounted. After applying this procedure there were at least 98 responses to each question.

Students were asked for their age and gender, and the survey service that was used, SurveyGizmo, identified their location from their IP address. Students were asked about the actual sacrifices they had made compared with the sacrifices they expected to make; how important it was to them that their degree was being awarded by the University of Liverpool; their level of satisfaction with their degree course; and the survey asked about their views on the relationship between tuition fees and course quality.

The core of the survey addressed questions of perceived value in situations where changes were made that would generally make the course easier. These were grouped as follows:

1. Questions that asked about the effect on the perceived value of the degree if, shortly after the student's graduation, changes were made that resulted in modules being much easier to pass, students being unlikely to drop out of their degree because it was too difficult, or

students finding that gaining a degree involved far fewer sacrifices.

2. Questions about the effect on the perceived value of the degree if it involved very little non-monetary sacrifice, students hardly ever failed, or the dropout rate was close to zero.
3. Questions about the effect on the University of Liverpool's reputation if students rarely failed modules or rarely dropped out because the work was too hard.

For the most part semantic differential questions were used, with possible options ranging from 7 (Increased Value/Higher Reputation) to 1 (Decreased Value/Lower Reputation). This has been treated as interval data for which the mean score can legitimately be calculated. The choice by participants of the mid-point value 4 was assumed to indicate a degree of neutrality or indifference towards the issue in question; scores of 5 to 7 were interpreted as being broadly positive, and scores of 1 to 3 negative. The results consistent with the authors' expectations would involve a mixture of high and low scores.

5. RESULTS

5.1 Sacrifice and Tuition Fees

Some 72% of students indicated that their degree had involved greater sacrifices than they had expected. Only 5% thought it involved less sacrifices. The mean score was 5.24. At the same time, 86% of the sample were satisfied with their degree (mean = 5.6) and 89% would recommend their degree to others (mean = 5.9). It can therefore be seen that there is no incompatibility between high student satisfaction and a higher than expected degree of sacrifice.

The assumption had been that high tuition fees would not be a strong indicator of course quality, and that other aspects of the give or sacrifice involved in obtaining a degree would be more important. This was confirmed by the survey. When asked whether courses with high tuition fees were typically of better quality than those with lower tuition fees, respondents produced a mean score of 3.87 (median = 4). The number of positive, neutral and negative responses were almost precisely equal.

5.2 Changes to Degrees After Graduation

Possibly the most significant results from the survey were produced by the questions which asked about future changes that would make degrees easier in certain specified respects after the student had graduated. The general conclusion was that students would see such changes as devaluing their degree. This would be likely to generate significant negative word-of-mouth (as well as negative social network and email traffic) about their degree programme.

If, in future, it would be much easier to pass each module on the degree, 74% of respondents felt that that this would decrease the value of their degree and only 8% believed that its value would increase (mean = 2.6, median = 2). Similarly 68% saw a future degree that would involve far fewer sacrifices on the part of students as involving a lowering of value. Just 12% of the sample thought this would increase the degree's value (mean = 3.0, median = 3).

Throughout the survey, respondents were less concerned about low dropout rates as a negative indictor, but 59% of the sample believed that a future in which students would be unlikely to drop out of their degree because it was too difficult would signal a qualification that had less value. 18% took the contrary view (mean = 3.2, median = 3). The mean scores for these three questions are highlighted in Figure 1. The percentage of respondents who thought these changes would be positive or negative is represented in Figure 2.

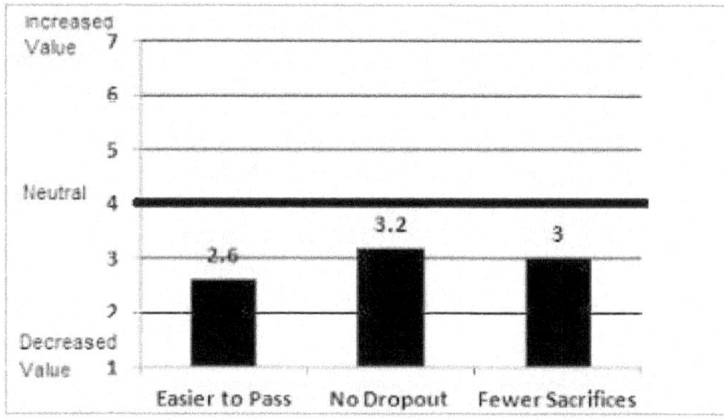

Figure 1. Mean Values for the Assessment of Future Changes

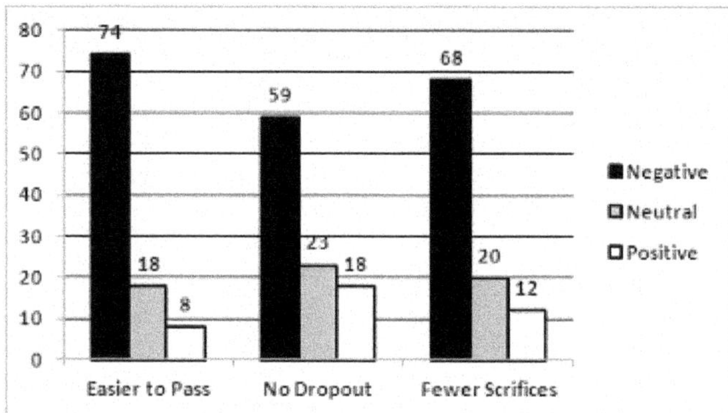

Figure 2. Percentages of those who saw changes as having a positive or negative effect on the value of the degree

5.3 Less Sacrifice, Low Failure/Dropout Rates

The next set of questions involved subtle differences in wording. Instead of being asked about failing modules, students were quizzed about their view if people hardly ever failed their degree. 62% of respondents felt this would decrease the value of the qualification. This represented a slight softening of attitudes, because degree failure was clearly a harsher penalty than module failure, and hence a higher price to pay for degree quality. However, the polarity of student opinion was clear, with only 13% feeling the degree would increase in value (mean = 3.0, median = 3).

When asked how they would rate their degree if it involved very little sacrifice on their part, 58% said their qualification would decrease in value, with 15% taking the contrary view (mean = 3.2, median = 3). A dropout rate close to zero was seen as a negative thing by 46% of respondents, while 20% saw it as positive (mean = 3.6, median = 4). In this case, the reason for dropping out was not mentioned in the question. A summary of the relevant percentages is set out in Figure 3.

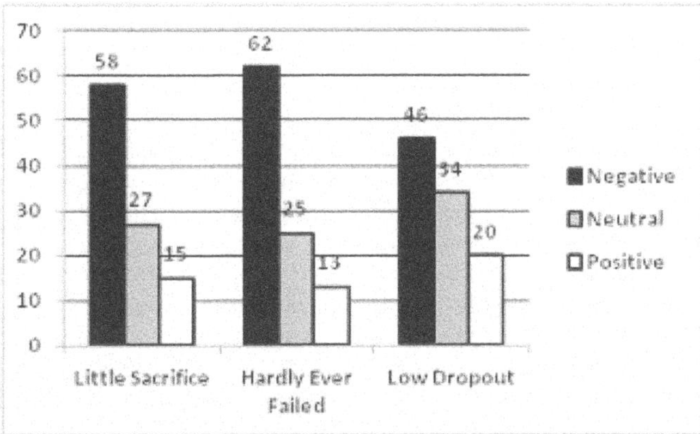

Figure 3. Percentages of those who saw features as having a positive or negative effect on the value of the degree

5.4 The University's Reputation

The University of Liverpool brand proved to have been an important factor in attracting students to their degree programme. Many online degrees are offered by institutions whose names are not immediately recognizable. Liverpool is one of the older British civic or redbrick universities formed around the turn of the 20th century. It is a member of the Russell Group, a collection of research-intensive universities in the UK.

In the survey, 87% of students indicated that the fact that the University of Liverpool was offering their degree was important or very important. Only 5% thought this factor was unimportant (mean = 6.1, median = 7). Students were therefore asked about the effect of certain scenarios on the Liverpool brand. The result of students rarely failing modules on their degree course would, in the opinion of 51% of respondents, lower the reputation of the university (mean = 3.4, median = 3).

A very significant 30% of the sample opted for the mid-point value on the scale, indicating some degree of indifference. If that assumption of indifference is correct then the natural conclusion is that the university does not need to worry about the reaction of a certain proportion of its students to modules getting easier. The reaction is likely to be neither positive nor negative. The focus will therefore switch to the proportions of students who react positively (19% in this case) and negatively (51%). On balance, therefore, it was concluded that modules that are rarely failed would damage the reputation of the university.

The sample was also asked about the effect on the University of Liverpool's reputation if students rarely dropped out because the work was too hard. Here the results were inconclusive. The split meant that 37% thought this change would lower the reputation of the university, 30% thought it would give Liverpool a higher reputation, and 33 % were indifferent (mean = 3.9, median = 4).

Although the question did specify a particular reason why students might drop out of degree courses, informal feedback suggested some participants might have taken account of other reasons, such as illness or a change in personal circumstances. The retention of students under these difficult circumstances would be seen as a positive sign. It was also likely that the reputation of the university was considered so robust that changes were less likely to damage its image.

It was concluded that the use of dropout rates as a signal of perceived value was problematical and any future research would require more incisive questioning to separate out the various factors involved.

5.5 Demographics

Just 12% of the survey sample was female. This was broadly in line with the gender composition of the degree programme. Although female students were a little more satisfied with their course than their male counterparts, there were no other statistically significant differences ($p < 0.05$) in the answers provided by men and women. This was the first of a number of indications that the results we had obtained had a general validity. They pointed to stable and pervasive attitudes.

In analyzing the sample according to the part of the world in which students were resident, the only significant differences were between the 15% of students who came from Africa and the rest. African students were more likely to value the Liverpool brand in choosing their degree ($p = 0.02$). They were less likely to believe that Liverpool's reputation would be harmed by a degree in which students rarely failed modules ($p = 0.01$), or rarely dropped out ($p = 0.04$). They were more satisfied with their degree and more likely to recommend it to someone else (in both cases $p = 0.01$). Otherwise the differences were minor and conclusions had a general applicability.

Although age was not generally a determinant of outcomes, there was a small cluster of differences when comparing students who were over 40 (30% of the sample) with the rest. The damage to the university's reputation from modules that were rarely failed ($p = 0.01$) or degrees where students rarely dropped out ($p = 0.003$) was judged to be much less than it was in the eyes of younger students. Similarly the over 40s were less concerned by future changes that would make it much easier to pass each module or would make it unlikely that students would drop out of degrees because they were too difficult (in both cases $p = 0.03$). They did, however, still believe that these changes would be detrimental.

6. DISCUSSION

The results of the survey show that, at least in certain circumstances, students do perceive high pass rates, low dropout rates, and degrees that involve very little sacrifice on their part as reducing the value of their qualification. This perception is particularly strong in the case where post-graduation changes are proposed that would make the degree easier to obtain. Students who have made great sacrifices to gain a Master's degree would be particularly unhappy at seeing their degree devalued.

The survey sample consisted of students who were survivors. Those who had dropped out (typically in the first or second module of the degree) could have a different view. However, the authors' informed conjecture is that the support services offered to online students by Laureate and Liverpool are gradually eliminating avoidable dropouts. Those who leave are increasingly likely to be those who see how hard the online programme is and realize that they cannot fit it into their schedule.

If this is true, then at least some of these early dropouts are possibly a necessary evil in proving that this example of online education is not an easy option. It would seem a far better business option to appeal to those who are similar to the people in the sample who had demonstrated that they were retainable. Their desire is for degrees which, through the sacrifices involved, indicate their high value.

The authors' research highlighted a cluster of interesting variables. It is possible that other variables will have an effect on students' attitudes towards degrees which are challenging. Further research in comparing the influence of different variables would be welcomed.

The high proportion of students who felt that their degree had involved greater sacrifices than they expected does suggest that, at the time of their enrolling for the degree, the marketing and other university literature did not prepare them satisfactorily for what was to come. This may have changed in more recent times.

This does point to the dangers of being unduly positive in promotional material. It can inflate avoidable dropout rates. Firstly, because those who have believed the myths about online education being an easy option do not have those myths sufficiently dispelled by what they read about their degree. This encourages applications from people who are not suited to the workload or the pedagogical/andragogical model employed. Such people might not apply if promotional material consistently pointed out how difficult study was likely to be.

Secondly, being more realistic in public statements would reduce the number of avoidable dropouts amongst students who felt that they were failures because they found online education extremely challenging. A university might say: "This degree course is going to be very difficult, but ultimately rewarding. You will experience many problems in balancing all your commitments, but we have the support services that can help you."

Such an approach would tend to engender different expectations, so that the student might think, "I have problems, but this is normal. It does not mean that I am inadequate." It is also likely that there are strong potential students who have believed the stories about online education being an easy, low quality option (which in some cases might be true). It is possible that more honest marketing, telling them that they will have to suffer to gain a degree, would actually have a positive appeal. It could open up new markets by astute product positioning.

The data suggests that retainable students taking the Master's degrees in Computing discussed in this paper see factors that add to the difficulty in obtaining their qualification as increasing its perceived value. This will inevitably influence their word-of-mouth recommendations (and that includes recommendations made by electronic means of communication). In this case, there is strong evidence that academic and business interests are aligned. Pressures for grade inflation and a degree obtained with fewer sacrifices are likely to undermine the value of the product and make it less attractive in the eyes of retainable students.

A business manager who was asked "How difficult is it to resist the temptations of grade inflation ?" could reasonably reply, "It is quite easy. Grade inflation would damage our business by making the product less attractive."

7. CONCLUSION

Under what circumstances is this consideration likely to apply ? What is the scope of these conclusions ? Marketing theory suggests that when an organization is selling a high value, high price product, the high price can be a positive attraction. This is because it makes the product exclusive. The owner possesses something that others do not have.

In education it is the total sacrifice involved in obtaining a degree, rather than the level of fees, that provides this exclusivity. Conversations between the authors and online students after graduation ceremonies suggest that it is precisely because students have suffered to gain their degree that they regard it as having a high value. Under no circumstances would they accept that studying online was an easy option.

Are all degrees likely to engender this feeling in their students ? Almost certainly not. A Master's degree, particularly one from a reputable university (one with a strong brand) is still something that sets an employee apart from others. It does, in many circumstances, still provide a career advantage. It is exclusive because large numbers of people do not have a Master's degree. In such circumstances the business pressures to combat grade inflation are likely to be strong. Although the amount of fees charged is not in itself crucial in indicating the quality or value of the degree, it is likely that students who perceive their degree as having a high value are more willing to pay high fees.

On the other hand, where the possession of certain kinds of degrees becomes commonplace (a Bachelor's degree in certain countries, for instance) then the product takes on more of the features of mass produced consumer goods. Here there are more pressures to drive the price down. In education terms, the emphasis switches to the importance of the grade that is obtained, because the mere possession of a degree has a reduced value. The pressure here is often to reduce the amount of sacrifice involved in getting a good grade. Pressman would identify this as demand-pull inflation, where too many students are chasing too few jobs [8].

It is clearly much easier to prevent grade inflation that has not historically taken place than it is to reduce grades that have become inflated. Once the proportion of A grades has risen over 40%, it is difficult to get the genie back in the bottle. However, the business case for doing so is suggested by the results of this research. There is a market for high value degrees, the acquisition of which involves a significant amount of suffering on the part of the student. Indeed it is possible to argue for the necessity of suffering. The student who has suffered is likely to believe that he or she has obtained a prize of great value.

Where degree programmes require a high level of student participation, such as in the numerous assessed asynchronous online discussions favoured by Liverpool, a campaign against grade inflation might also be a good way of getting students to work harder and participate to the desired extent. Babcock, in surveying a large number of students at the University of California, San Diego, concluded that "Holding fixed instructor and course, classes in which students expect higher grades are found to be classes in which students study significantly less. Results indicate that average study time would be about 50% lower in a class in which the average expected grade was an 'A' than in the same course taught by the same instructor in which students expected a 'C'." [2].

Although the University of Liverpool Computing degrees are delivered in conjunction with an American private sector organization, Laureate Online Interactive Education, the authors have noted no pressures for grade inflation from their paymasters in their day to day teaching. There is therefore little cost-push pressure for grade inflation where teachers are encouraged to give higher grades by their institution [8]. Why ? Because it would be bad for business.

The pressure is likely to be in the opposite direction, particularly in the case of Americans and other instructors who might be operating in on-campus courses characterized by rampant grade inflation. When they become online instructors at Liverpool, they have to adjust quickly to their new environment.

Oleinik pessimistically concluded that "grade inflation results from the substitution of criteria specific to the search for truth by criteria of quality control generated outside of academia" [7]. He did not foresee that certain systems of quality control would be aimed at preventing grade inflation on the understanding that courses with inflated grades are of reduced quality.

On the demand side of the equation, Liverpool students may wish that the assignment they are currently completing were not so time consuming. In the passing moment they may wish for an easier life. However, in the longer term, they value the suffering they have had to undergo. This may not be universally true, but it would be surprising if there were not general lessons to be learned here.

A search for papers on grade inflation in ACM and IEEE publications yields a very modest return. It suggests that this profession has been very good at writing about Computing but, with some honourable exceptions, has not adopted the broader perspective that would help it to contribute fully to the great Education debates of our time [6][13]. The current authors hope that this paper will make some small contribution in making good that omission.

8. REFERENCES

[1] Alves, H. 2010. *The Measurement of Perceived Value in Higher Education: a Unidimensional Approach.* Universidade da Beira Interior, Portugal. http://www.dge.ubi.pt/investigacao/TDiscussao/2010/TD04_2010.pdf

[2] Babcock, P. 2009. Real Costs of Nominal Grade Inflation ? New evidence from Student Course Evaluations. *Economic Inquiry* 48 (4), October, pp.983-996.

[3] Grasso, F. and Leng, P.H. 2005. Quality Assurance Issues for Online Universities. In *Encyclopedia of Information Science and Technology*, Idea Group, Hershey, USA, pp.2382-2386.

[4] Kalman, Y.M. & Leng, P.H. 2007. A Distributed model for managing academic staff in an international online academic programme. *Interactive Learning Environments* 15(1), pp.47-60.

[5] Kotler, P. and Armstrong, G. 2010. *Principles of Marketing, Thirteenth Edition.* Prentice Hall, Upper Saddle River, New Jersey.

[6] Modelski, J.W. 2008. Facing Grade Inflation in Engineering Education. *IEEE Microwave Magazine*, May 2008.

[7] Oleinik, A. 2009. Does education corrupt ? Theories of grade inflation. *Educational Research Review* 4 , 156–164.

[8] Pressman, S. 2007. The Economics of Grade Inflation. *Challenge* 50 (5) (September/October 2007), 93-102.

[9] Quinones, E. 2009. *Princeton achieves marked progress in curbing grade inflation.* Princeton University. http://www.princeton.edu/main/news/archive/S25/35/65G93

[10] Sancjez-Fernandez, R. and Iniesta-Bonillo, M.A. 2007. The concept of perceived value: a systematic review of the research. *Marketing Theory* 7, 4, 427-451.

[11] Simpson, O. 2003. *Student Retention in Online, Open and Distance Learning.* Kogan Page, London.

[12] Teas, R.K. and Agarwal, S. 2000. The Effects of Extrinsic Product Cues on Consumers' Perceptions of Quality, Sacrifice and Value. *Journal of the Academy of Marketing Science.* 28, 2, 278-290.

[13] Thirunarayanan, M.O. 2001. Technology and Degree Inflation. *Ubiquity* May 2001.

[14] Zeithaml, V.A. 1988. Consumer Perceptions of Price, Quality and Value: A Means-End Model and Synthesis of Evidence. *Journal of Marketing* 52, 3, 2-22.

Instructor-Centric Source Code Plagiarism Detection and Plagiarism Corpus

Jonathan Y. H. Poon
National University of Singapore
Computing 1,
13 Computing Drive
Singapore 117417
poonyanh@comp.nus.edu.sg

Kazunari Sugiyama
National University of Singapore
Computing 1,
13 Computing Drive
Singapore 117417
sugiyama@comp.nus.edu.sg

Yee Fan Tan *
KAI Square
33 Ubi Avenue 3,
#07-58 Vertex Tower A
Singapore 408868
yeefan@kaisquare.com

Min-Yen Kan
National University of Singapore
Computing 1,
13 Computing Drive
Singapore 117417
kanmy@comp.nus.edu.sg

ABSTRACT

Existing source code plagiarism systems focus on the problem of identifying plagiarism between pairs of submissions. The task of detection, while essential, is only a small part of managing plagiarism in an instructional setting. Holistic plagiarism detection and management requires coordination and sharing of assignment similarity – elevating plagiarism detection from pairwise similarity to cluster-based similarity; from a single assignment to a sequence of assignments in the same course, and even among instructors of different courses.

To address these shortcomings, we have developed Student Submissions Integrity Diagnosis (SSID), an open-source system that provides holistic plagiarism detection in an instructor-centric way. SSID's visuals show overviews of plagiarism clusters throughout all assignments in a course as well as highlighting most-similar submissions on any specific student. SSID supports plagiarism detection workflows; *e.g.*, allowing student assistants to flag suspicious assignments for later review and confirmation by an instructor with proper authority. Evidence is automatically entered into SSID's logs and shared among instructors.

We have additionally collected a source code plagiarism corpus, which we employ to identify and correct shortcomings of previous plagiarism detection engines and to optimize parameter tuning for SSID deployment. Since its deployment, SSID's workflow enhancements have made plagiarism detection in our faculty less tedious and more successful.

Categories and Subject Descriptors

K.3.2 [**Computer Science and Information Science Education**]: Computer science education; I.2.7 [**Natural Language Processing**]: Text analysis; H.5.2 [**User Interfaces**]: User-centered design

*This work was done while he was a doctoral student at the National University of Singapore.

General Terms

Algorithms, Experimentation, Languages, Performance

Keywords

Plagiarism assessment, Plagiarism detection, Programming, Similarity, User interface, Corpus studies

1. INTRODUCTION

Plagiarism is a serious issue in undergraduate courses involving programming assignments [20]. In 2004, 181 students at School of Computing at the National University of Singapore admitted to committing source code plagiarism [16]. In 2005, the Centre for Academic Integrity (CAI) reported that almost 40% of 50,000 students at more than 60 universities admitted in plagiarism [12].

Plagiarism detection and subsequent disciplinary actions are of paramount importance in education. If students involved in plagiarism are not identified and proper action is not taken, it unfair to their peers whom produced and submitted original works. Furthermore, the students involved learn less than their hardworking counterparts, tarnish the reputation of their own institutions, and reduce the value of their own degrees.

Detecting plagiarism, however, is a time-consuming and tedious process when performed manually. Inspecting n assignment submissions for plagiarism could require instructors to access all $n \times (n-1)/2$ pairs of submissions. Furthermore, the process becomes more difficult when students actively attempt to obfuscate the traces of plagiarism by modifying the plagiarized copies. Thus, according to [15], research on automated source code plagiarism detection was started in the mid-1970s [17, 4, 9, 2, 6].

The basic task in (source code) plagiarism detection, to decide whether one input is plagiarized from another input, has been studied extensively. However, a holistic plagiarism management system requires expanding the basic task to a larger scope: allowing instructors to zoom in on the suspicious code segments (rather than at the assignment level), support detection on a set of inputs (rather than single files; as code submissions often contain several files), support the input of the instructor's skeleton code (when the instructor provides some template code for students to start from). Furthermore, an instructor-centric system needs to provide visualization to see these suspected cases at a cluster level, across assignments and help fellow instructors pin down plagiarism across courses. All of these issues are addressed in our implemented Student Submissions Integrity Diagnosis (SSID), an open-source system that provides holistic plagiarism detection reported here.

```java
import java.util.*;

public class A{
    public static void main(String[] args){
        for(int i=0; i<100; i++){
            System.out.println("Here");
        }
    }
}
```

(a) Original submission

```java
import java.util.*;

public class A{
    public static void main(String[] args){
        for(int i=0+0+0; i<100; i++){
            System.out.println("Here");
        }
    }
}
```

(b) Plagiarised copy

Figure 1: Original and plagiarized code pair that goes undetected by MOSS, where the bolded text indicates modification. MOSS reports a similarity value of 97% when the original is submitted against itself (*i.e.*, (a) and (a) as the input pair), but 0% similarity when the (a) original submission and (b) plagiarized copy are input.

A key contribution of our work is our source code plagiarism corpus. To gain insight on how source code plagiarism happens, we asked volunteers to plagiarize sample input code. The subsequent analysis of the plagiarized examples allows us to classify attacks into two classes and identifies attack modes that current plagiarism systems do not handle. This corpus is also publicly available, which we hope will spur development in future plagiarism benchmarking and studies.

2. RELATED WORK

Plagiarism detection systems typically perform pairwise comparison of submissions to detect plagiarism and do so in two ways, using: (1) attribute-counting metrics, or (2) structure metrics.

In attribute-counting metric systems, code similarity is based on counts of particular entities. In Ottenstein's system [17], Halstead's software science metrics [10] are used with the number of unique operators and operands. To improve upon this, subsequent attribute-counting systems have added metrics for counting the number of loops [4], control statements [9], keywords [2], as well as measuring the average length of the procedure or function [6].

Structure metrics compute similarities based on code structure. An essential property in structure matching is that many spurious matches can involve small code fragments, thus the *Minimum Match Length* (MML) parameter is important to set correctly. As it has been shown that structure metrics produces better plagiarism detection results [21], many of the widely used plagiarism detection systems, such as MOSS (Measure Of Software Similarity) [1], the YAP (Yet Another Plague) family [22, 24], sim [8], and JPlag [18] are based on structure metrics. From our understanding, MOSS and JPlag are the current benchmark systems for code plagiarism detection [3]. However, even these systems can be easily confused; plagiarists can insert non-functional code to ensure that no plagiarised code segments are larger than the MML. An example of this problem is shown in Figure 1, in which a plagiarized copy goes undetected by MOSS.

The aforementioned systems deal with plagiarism at the pairwise level. In recent work, Freire [7] and Meyer [14] also developed a plagiarism detection system for programming assignments that allows pairwise comparison. However, as stated earlier, a real-world plagiarism detection system needs to perform n-way plagiarism detection. Two systems that are not publicly available – PDetect [15], an attribute-counting metric system, and PDE4Java [11], a structure metric system – provide the capability to detect plagiarism clusters.

In summary, currently available systems focus on the core problem of detecting plagiarism in a pairwise or clusterwise manner. But crucially, the current state-of-the-art misses in-depth knowledge about how plagiarism is actually carried out (from the plagiarists' view), as well as the knowledge of how the core problem affects an instructor's workflow (from the instructor's view).

3. PLAGIARISM DETECTION METHOD

In implementing SSID, we take the structure metric method but make changes to improve detection accuracy and efficiency. For clarity, we review the entire working of our core algorithm, which is largely in common with other structure metric systems, but highlights salient differences between SSID and other structure metric systems. SSID follows a three step pipeline to judge the plagiarism status of a set of submissions:

Tokenization is the first step. We note that tokenization is programming language specific, as the tokenizer needs to know the syntax and keywords associated with the inputs. Correct identification of keywords and syntax has been shown to be an important factor in any programming language specific support tool [19]. SSID is implemented for Java and C input. We use Java in our examples.

Our tokenizer currently ignores differences in whitespaces and comments, as format alteration is commonly employed in plagiarism [13]. We define four token types: constants, keywords, symbols, and variables. Our Java tokenization scheme merges both numbers and characters into a single *constant* category, as Java allows easy conversion of character comparisons to numeric ones and vice versa. We also remove string constants, as suggested by Wise *et al.* [24]. We also assign an integer hash value to each unique string instead of storing each keyword and symbol as a string, to facilitate fast string comparison. Also, as structure metrics can generate spurious matches, we differentiate between tokens used at the end or beginning of statements. As a result of the tokenization phase, the token N-grams that represent each submission are indexed into a hash table.

Pairwise, asymmetric similarity is computed per input submission pair. We adopt the *Greedy-String-Tiling* algorithm [23], but modify the *Minimum Match Length* (MML) termination criterion. We deem two statements identical if and only if their contiguous tokens are identical. We also make a small efficiency improvement by using hash value comparison, as suggested by Prechelt *et al.* [18] in their JPlag system. This step creates a hash table representation for each submission. Then, retrieving the indices of a N-gram is done in $O(1)$ time instead of $O(n)$ time, reducing the practical average submission comparison complexity to $O(c^2)$ from $O(c^3)$, where c is the number of tokens in a submission.

A crucial extension in SSID is the support of skeleton code. Instructors often provide students with skeleton code as a framework to start structuring their programming assignments. Such code, if not properly considered by the plagiarism system, will indicate plagiarism when in fact the suspicious code was initially provided by the instructor. We thus extend the basic algorithm to exclude skeleton code from comparison. SSID does this by adding a *mark* property to differentiate between the ordinary *match marks* that are determined by the *Greedy-String-Tiling* algorithm [23], and the *skeleton marks* that match both submissions and the instructor provided skeleton code. We consider a match as valid (to be flagged as part of plagiarism) if and only if the number of *match-marked* statements within a marked region satisfies the MML.

To further improve the efficiency of the algorithm, we leverage our tokenization scheme, which distinguishes tokens that form the beginning of statements. Instead of considering all N-grams, SSID only considers the ones where the first token is marked as the beginning of a statement. This significantly reduces the practical runtime by about 4 times and reduces spurious matching.

The algorithm finds the matched regions in the input submissions A and B in decreasing sizes of contiguous identical statements, until no more matches satisfying MML can be found. To provide the user with a clear notion of the similarity of two submissions, we define a similarity measure to reflect the percentage of tokens that are covered by matches. For example, if the code for submission A is entirely embedded within another submission B, the similarity from A to B is 100%, but is smaller in the opposing direction. This results in the asymmetric similarity measure $sim(A \rightarrow B) = \frac{\text{\# of match marked tokens in } A}{\text{\# of tokens in } A}$. We then define the symmetric similarity score $sim(A, B)$ as the maximum of the two asymmetric values $sim(A \rightarrow B)$ and $sim(B \rightarrow A)$.

Determining plagiarism clusters is the final step. SSID groups submissions that are all highly similar to each other. The clustering employed uses a similarity threshold to assign each submission into at most one group (plagiarism cluster) or as a singleton (original submission), in a deterministic, reproducible manner. These clustering requirements are fulfilled by *DBScan* [5].

Finally, we note that **the real-time performance** of SSID is also critical. Instructors need immediate feedback for incorporating plagiarism detection into their already busy workflows. On an ordinary modern generation 2.8 GHz Linux laptop, SSID evaluates datasets consisting of 80+ introductory programming assignment submissions, amounting to over 3600 submission pairs, in less than 4 seconds on average, tested over three runs. This is an adequately short delay for most instructors.

4. PLAGIARISM CORPUS

Prechelt *et al.* [18] noted that the success of plagiarists is proportional to their effort in attempting plagiarism. However, we hypothesize that plagiarists might find certain types of plagiarism easier to perform than others.

To better understand how plagiarism works in practice, we asked student volunteers to actively plagiarize submissions from two individual in-lab introductory level programming assignments. As the assignments are carefully monitored, we have a large set of true negative examples. The attempted modifications then constitute positive known examples of plagiarism, while the original submissions for the assignments constitute negative examples. To begin with, we picked four of the known original submissions from each assignment as samples for participants to perform plagiarism. The four samples were picked as they constituted different means to solve the problem and our asymmetric similarity metric indicated that these were substantially different.

28 student volunteers participated in our corpus collection work. They generated a plagiarized version of their given source code sample, under time pressure to simulate the limited time and effort that plagiarists commonly have in practice. In total, $28 \times 2 = 56$ positive and about 180 negative examples are given in our corpus. The corpus is also distributed along with the SSID system at the SSID website[1]. Using our symmetric similarity metric $sim(A, B)$, when the size of the N-grams used is set to 2, and MML is set to 2 statements, our system successfully differentiates between the plagiarized positives and original negatives with 100% accuracy. The parameter settings were set by using the standard method of cross validation, where different subsets of the corpus are rotated for determining optimal parameter settings and accuracy testing. Figure 2 shows the similarity distribution for the first assignment.

4.1 Attack Types

We analyzed the different types of plagiarism attempts (termed *attacks*) that participants attempted. For example, a detection failure (termed *confusion*) can occur when lines of code are inserted into the copied code segment, splitting the original code segment in two. As SSID is structure metric based, insertions can prevent SSID from identifying the copied code segments. In our description of each attack, we include a ratio in parenthesis that indicates the attack's effectiveness, as measured by the number of times the attack confused SSID (left number), over the total number of times the attack was observed (right number).

[1] http://wing.comp.nus.edu.sg/downloads/SSID/PlagiarismCorpus.html

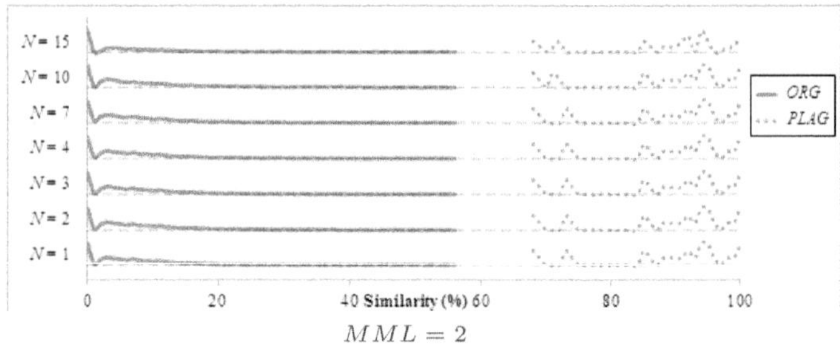

Figure 2: Similarity distributions for the first assignment in the corpus for various sized N-gram lengths where MML is set to 2. Note the perfect separation between original non-plagiarized submissions (*ORG*) and plagiarized ones (*PLAG*).

Note while individual attacks may confuse SSID, a single plagiarized assignment consists of many attacks, and perfect separation of positive and negative cases does not require perfect per-attack detection; indeed, it is a collective decision over all attacks present in a plagiarism attempt. We classify the observed attacks into three broad categories, as follows:

1. *Immutable attacks* do not modify the token sequences and are not effective against SSID. We first list them and then collectively discuss salient points about individual attacks. This was the largest category of observed attacks, amounting to 122 observed attacks, out of 246 in total or about 40%.

1) Insertion, modification or deletion of comments (0/35)
2) Indention, spacing or line breaks modifications (0/38)
3) Identifier renaming (0/41)
4) Constant modification (0/2)
5) Insertion, modification, or deletion of modifiers (0/6)
6) No change (0/0)

Structure metric systems are all immune to Attacks 1, 2, 3 and 4 as the conversion of the program into token types canonicalizes any renaming. For Attack 5, the Java tokenizer in SSID specifically ignores changes in access modifiers (*e.g.*, `public`, `protected`).

2. *Size dependent attacks* may confuse SSID, dependending on the size of the modified code segment. 64 instances were observed in our corpus. They are most effective in short programs, where the modification is proportionally large compared to the original source. But in large programs, they may be inefficient due to the amount of effort needed to perform the modifications.

7) Reordering of independent statements (6/10)
8) Reordering of methods (6/16)
9) Insertion or removal of parentheses (0/20)
10) Inlining or refactoring of code (13/18)

For Attacks 7 and 8, SSID correctly detected a portion of the attacks. When the original code segment were split into chunks smaller than $MML = 2$, SSID failed. For example, one attack reordered all of the three contiguous and independent statements within a block. Since the resultant code segment was a single state-

(a) Original submission	(b) Plagiarised copy
left = tree.getLeft(); right = tree.getRight();	right = tree.getRight(); left = tree.getLeft();

Figure 3: A reordering statement attack (Attack type 7) that is successfully detected by SSID.

(a) Original submission	(b) Plagiarised copy

if(myString.equals("right")) return 1;
if(myString.equals("left")) return 1;
return 0;
	if(myString.equals("right")) ||
	myString.equals("left")) return 1;
	return 0;

Figure 4: A refactoring attack (Attack type 10) that confused SSID.

ment in length, the code segments did not exceed the MML threshold and went undetected. Attacks were detected by SSID when the reordered statements consisted of two large blocks or were structurally identical. In Figure 3, the resulting token sequence is the same even after the statement reordering, and can be detected as a match.

Attack 9 modifies the syntactic scheme of the code, by adding or removing parentheses that are optional in Java. SSID's tokenization step automatically canonicalizes the Java syntax used in most cases, inserting missing parentheses to single-lined conditional statements and loops; in those cases the attacks failed.

Inlining and refactoring (#10) requires more effort. Six of the inlining attacks confused SSID as the inlined method length caused the original code segments to be less than MML in length, or were combined with other successful attacks like statement reordering. Seven refactoring attacks, by combining conditional statements together (as in Figure 4), succeeded.

3. *Successful Attacks* confused SSID in all instances. They were observed in our corpus 60 times.

11) Redundancy (8/8)
12) Scope modification (7/7)
13) Modification of control structures (14/14)
14) Declaration of variables (10/10)
15) Modification of method parameters (1/1)
16) Modification of import statements (2/2)
17) Introduction of bug (1/1)
18) Modification of temporary variables in expressions (10/10)
19) Modification of mathematical operations and formulae (2/2)
20) Structural redesign of code (5/5)

We comment briefly on the more common attacks. Redundancy attacks (#11) remove or insert non-functional code. Scope modifications (#12) involve moving variable declarations to larger or smaller scope, which make it similar to size-dependent attacks. Control constructs were modified (#13) by changing looping variables, initialization and termination conditions, running loops in reverse. In conditional statements, the logic is changed by swapping the `if` and `else` blocks, or refactoring `if-else` compounds into separate `if` blocks. For variable declaration (#14), plagiarists combined several variable declarations into a single compound statement, or separated a compound statement into components. Finally, plagiarists expanded or compressed expressions, using or dropping temporary variables to store the return values from expressions, accessing them later when needed.

5. USER INTERFACE WORK FLOW

In addition to comparing pairwise similarity between submissions and detecting plagiarism clusters, SSID has a Web-based log

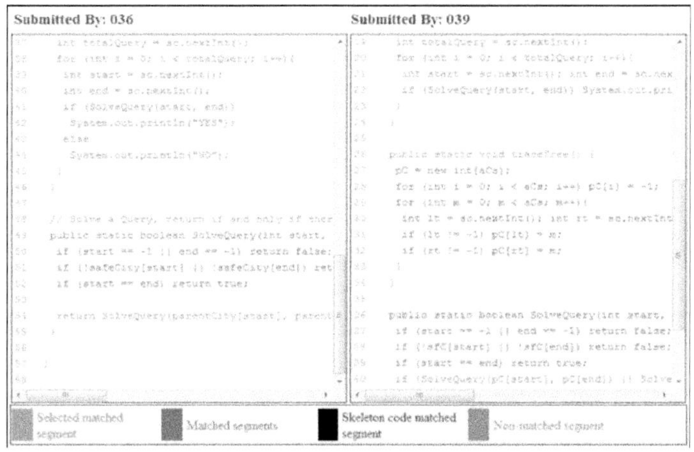

Figure 5: Snapshot of *Pairwise Comparison* interface. Codes in red and dark red denote the matched regions the instructor selected and matched regions in the displyed submissions, respectively. Code in green denotes no identical region is found in the other submission.

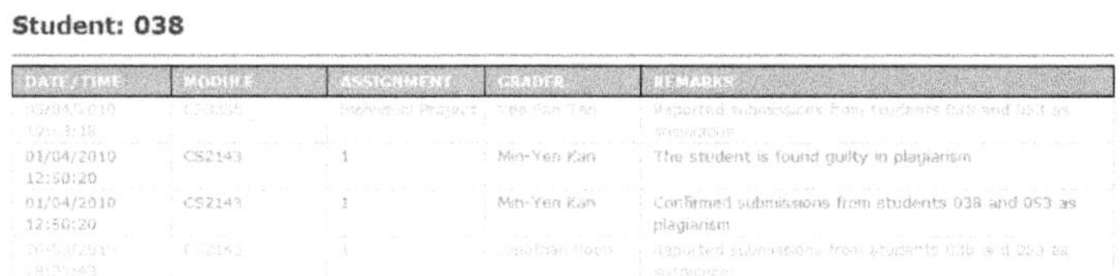

Figure 6: Snapshot of log system interface.

system that records plagiarism activities for each student, as well as visuals to illustrate plagiarism clusters and other plagiarism-related information for gathering evidence on plagiarism.

(1) Pairwise Comparison Interface. As described in Section 3, we employ the structure metric method in our SSID. An advantage of the structure metric method is that the comparison results can be easily displayed. While user interface of MOSS uses the small number of colors for matched code regions, our interface uses several colors to display the comparison between assignments. Figure 5 shows a partial snapshot of the *Pairwise Comparison* interface. The interface allows the user to have a quick overview on the code segments found identical in both submissions.

(2) Log System. One of the major differences between our SSID and other similar systems is that SSID has a log system. Every report of suspicious pairs, confirmation of plagiarism cases and results of investigation (if the student is found guilty or innocent) is recorded in the system.

In Figure 6, student '038' is under investigation by an instructor from the course CS3256 for plagiarizing the submission from student '053.' '038' has denied committing plagiarism and reasoned that both their submissions were similar because they solved the assignment together. Through the records on '038' in the log system, the instructor can see that '038' has been found guilty of plagiarizing another submission from '053' in another course CS2143. Therefore, the instructor can conclude that student '038' has probably committed plagiarism in CS3256 as well.

(3) Detecting Plagiarism Clusters. Once a group that conducts plagiarisms is defined, the group can be displayed in the *Cluster Summary* interface. For example, Figure 7 shows the (partial) *Clus-*

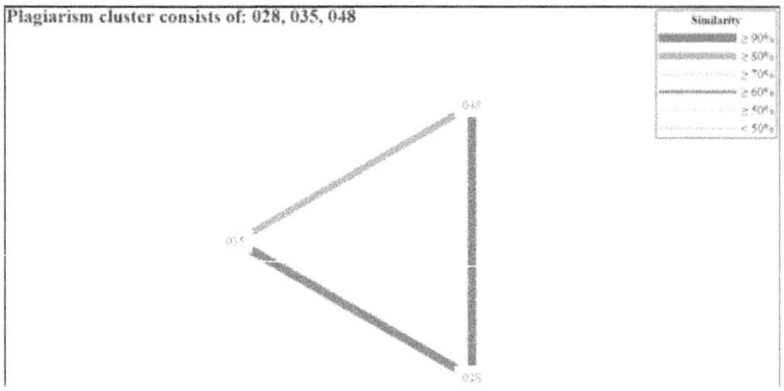

Figure 7: Snapshot of *Cluster Summary* interface (partial). Vertices and edges denote students' ids and the maximum similarity between two students' submission, respectively.

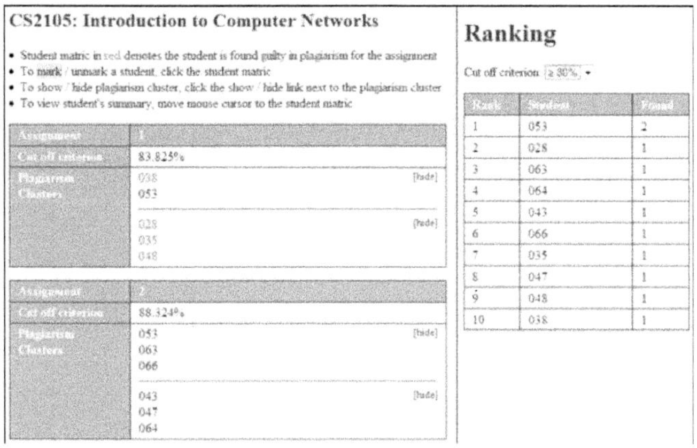

Figure 8: Snapshot of *Assignments* interface. The left frame shows the overview of each plagiarism clusters in assignments. The right frame show the statistics of the top 10 students being detected in a plagiarism cluster.

ter Summary interface which consists of students '028,' '035,' and '048.' Each vertex and each edge in the interface represent a student id and the maximum similarity value of the submission pair between two students, respectively. In addition, edges are represented with different colors and thickness. Based on the evidence given in this interface, the instructor may consider forming a learning group consisting of the students '028,' '035,' and '048' to enhance their learning experience. Since the edges connected to '028' are thicker than the one connecting '035' and '048,' it is highly possible that '035' and '048' have both copied their assignment from that of '028.'

(4) Finding Plagiarism Activities. After checking a number of assignments through SSID, an instructor wants to know the statistics on the students who often conduct plagiarism. This can be done through *Assignments* interface as shown in Figure 8. This interface provides a summary of plagiarism clusters for each assignment (left in Figure 8). Furthermore, the interface also provides a list of the top 10 students in plagiarism clusters, which helps the instructor in monitoring plagiarism activity (right in Figure 8).

(5) Similarity between Students. According to Figure 8, student '038' and '053' belong to the same group. An instructor also wants to verify whether '038' belong to another plagiarism cluster where student '053,' '063,' and '066' belong. To address this issue, our SSID provides the *Between Individual* interface (see Figure 9). After selecting the target group of students, this interface displays the similarity between their submission pairs.

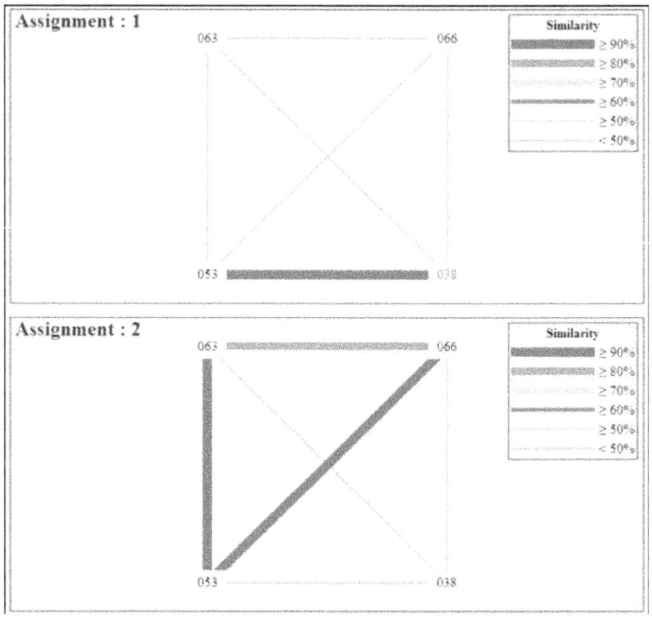

Figure 9: Example of *Between Individual* interface.

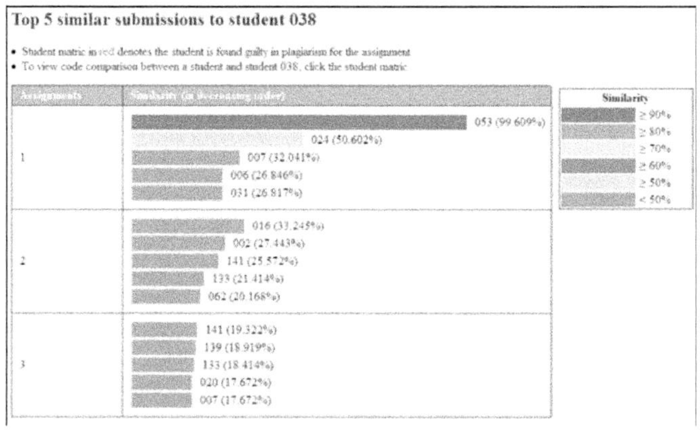

Figure 10: Snapshot of *Top Similarities* interface. This interface displays the top 5 similar submissions in each assignment for student '038.'

According to Figure 9, the similarities between the submission from '038,' and the submission from '063' and '066' are below 50% for both Assignments 1 and 2 (upper and lower in Figure 9, respectively). While '038' has similarity of 90% with '053' in Assignment 1, the similarity between the submissions from these students dropped to less than 50% in Assignment 2. This serves as a strong evidence to support the fact that '038' has probably stopped plagiarizing the work of others.

(6) Finding the Submissions Most Similar to a Student's Submission. SSID provides the *Top Similarities* interface (see Figure 10) to inform the instructor whether a suspicious student who may perform plagiarism has stopped plagiarizing other students' assignments.

Suppose that our target student is '038' as shown in Figure 10. After an instructor selects the target student and entering the number of candidates (K) to display, the K students are paired up with the target student '038' based on similarities between submissions of '038' and those of others. SSID sets the default value of K to 5. In Figure 10, an instructor has chosen to display the top 5 similar submissions in each assignment for student '038.' Since there are no similarities greater than 50% in Assignments 2 and 3, the instructor can conclude that '038' has been working on his own since his submission of Assignment 2.

6. CONCLUSION

We have presented a plagiarism detection system that assists instructors with the tedious task of detecting and reporting source code plagiarism cases. We extended the core task of detecting plagiarism between a pair of students, to a clustering framework, in order to support detection of plagiarism done by groups. To support instructors, SSID extends the visualization of assignment similarity to a group level and offers database views of code similarities across assignments and courses. Currently, our SSID only accepts Java programs as inputs. However, the system can be easily adapted by comparing other program languages if a tokenizer for the target language is introduced.

To better understand code plagiarism, we asked student volunteers to plagiarize input code samples in the Java programming language to build a corpus. On our corpus, our SSID is able to distinguish between original and plagiarized submissions with 100% accuracy. Our analysis of the resultant corpus identified two major categories of attacks: immutable attacks and size dependent attacks. However, we also identified 10 other modes of attacks that are not properly identified by current detection systems (including SSID), which serve as an agenda for future work in source code plagiarism detection.

7. REFERENCES

[1] A. Aiken. Moss: A System for Detecting Software Plagiarism. 1994. http://theory.stanford.edu/~aiken/moss/.

[2] H. L. Berghel and D. L. Sallach. Measurements of Program Similarity in Identical Task Environments. *ACM SIGPLAN Notices*, 19(8):65–76, 1984.

[3] V. Ciesielski, N. Wu, and S. Tahaghoghi. Evolving Similarity Functions for Code Plagiarism Detection. In *Proc. of the 10th Annual Conference on Genetic and Evolutionary Computation (GECCO'08)*, pages 1453–1460, 2008.

[4] J. L. Donaldson, A.-M. Lancaster, and P. H. Sposato. A Plagiarism Detection System. In *Proc. of the 12th SIGCSE Technical Symposium on Computer Science Education (SIGCSE '81)*, pages 21–25, 1981.

[5] M. Ester, H.-P. Kriegel, J. Sander, and X. Xu. A Density-Based Algorithm for Discovering Clusters in Large Spatial Databases with Noise. In *Proc. of the 2nd International Conference on Knowledge Discovery and Data Mining (KDD-96)*, pages 226–231, 1996.

[6] J. A. Faidhi and S. K. Robinson. An Empirical Approach for Detecting Program Similarity and Plagiarism within a University Programming Environment. *Computers & Education*, 11(1):11–19, 1987.

[7] M. Freire. Visualizing Program Similarity in the AC Plagiarism Detection System. In *Proc. of the Working Conference on Advanced Visual Interfaces (AVI'08)*, pages 404–407, 2008.

[8] D. Gitchell and N.Tran. Sim: A Utility for Detecting Similarity in Computer Programs. In *Proc. of the 30th SIGCSE Technical Symposium on Computer Science Education (SIGCSE '99)*, pages 266–270, 1999.

[9] S. Grier. A Tool That Detects Plagiarism in Pascal Programs. In *Proc. of the 12th SIGCSE Technical Symposium on Computer Science Education (SIGCSE '81)*, pages 15–20, 1981.

[10] M. H. Halstead. *Elements of Software Science*. Elsevier Science Ltd., 1977.

[11] A. Jadalla and A. Elnagar. PDE4Java: Plagiarism Detection Engine for Java Source Code: a Clustering Approach. *International Journal of Business Intelligence and Data Mining*, 3(2):121–135, 2008.

[12] C. L. Jocoy and D. DiBiase. Plagiarism by Adult Learners Online: A case study in detection and remediation. *The International Review of Research in Open and Distance Learning*, 7(1), 2006.

[13] C. Liu, C. Chen, J. Han, and P. S. Yu. GPLAG: Detection of Software Plagiarism by Program Dependence Graph Analysis. In *Proc. of the 12th ACM SIGKDD International Conference on Knowledge Discovery and Data Mining (KDD'06)*, pages 872–881, 2006.

[14] C. Meyer, C. Heeren, E. Shaffer, and J. Tedesco. CoMoTo – the Collaboration Modeling Toolkit. In *Proc. of the 16th Annual Conference on Innovation and Technology in Computer Science Education (ITiCSE'11)*, pages 143–147, 2011.

[15] L. Moussiades and A. Vakali. PDetect: A Clustering Approach for Detecting Plagiarism in Source Code Datasets. *The Computer Journal*, 48(6):651–661, 2005.

[16] W. T. Ooi and T. C. Tan. A Survey on Awareness and Attitudes towards Plagiarism among Computer Science Freshmen. *CDTLink*, 9(3), 2005.

[17] K. J. Ottenstein. An Algorithmic Approach to the Detection and Prevention of Plagiarism. *ACM SIGCSE Bulletin*, 8(4):30–41, 1976.

[18] L. Prechelt, G. Malphol, and M. Philippsen. Finding Plagiarisms among a Set of Programs with JPlag. *Journal of Universal Computer Science*, 8(11):1016–1038, 2002.

[19] S. Schleimer, D. S. Wilkerson, and A. Aiken. Winnowing: Local Algorithms for Document Fingerprinting. In *Proc. of the 2003 ACM SIGMOD International Conference on Management of Data (SIGMOD'03)*, pages 76–85, 2003.

[20] P. Vamplew and J. Dermoudy. An Anti-Plagiarism Editor for Software Development Courses. In *Proc. of the 7th Australasian Conference on Computing Education (ACE'05)*, pages 83–90, 2005.

[21] K. L. Verco and M. J. Wise. Software for Detecting Suspected Plagiarism: Comparing Structure and Attribute-counting Systems. In *Proc. of the 1st Australasian Conference on Computer Science Education (ACSE '96)*, pages 81–88, 1996.

[22] M. J. Wise. Detection of Similarities in Student Programs: YAP'ing may be Preferable to Plague'ing. In *Proc. of the 23rd SIGCSE Technical Symposium on Computer Science Education (SIGCSE '92)*, pages 268–271, 1992.

[23] M. J. Wise. String Similarity via Greedy String Tiling and Running Karp-Rabin Matching. 1993. ftp://ftp.cs.su.oz.au/michaelw/doc/RKR_GST.ps.

[24] M. J. Wise. YAP3: Improved Detection of Similarities in Computer Program and Other Texts. In *Proc. of the 27th SIGCSE Technical Symposium on Computer Science Education (SIGCSE '96)*, pages 130–134, 1996.

Enriching Introductory Programming Courses with Non-Intuitive Probability Experiments Component

Yana Kortsarts
Department of Computer Science
Widener University, Chester, PA
ykortsarts@mail.widener.edu

Yulia Kempner
Department of Computer Science
Holon Institute of Technology, Holon, Israel
yuliak@hit.ac.il

ABSTRACT

Probability theory is branch of mathematics that plays one of the central roles, not only in computer science, but also in science at large. We present a way to integrate non-intuitive probability experiments into introductory programming courses. We consider a set of the probability problems in which the intuitive approach leads to the wrong solution. These problems are based on interesting scenarios, attractive to students, and could be successfully "translated" into programming assignments. We present and discuss numerical simulations and verification of the correct solution through the computational approach. The proposed enrichment provides opportunity to engage students in experimental problem solving. Surprising computational results enhance students' curiosity and interest. This component promotes active involvement in the course. In addition, these problems provide an opportunity to make a connection between mathematics and computer science topics. Such non-intuitive answers may be remembered by students and may promote better understanding in the basic probability course they take later.

Categories and Subject Descriptors

K.3.2 [**Computer and Information Science Education**]: Computer science education

General Terms

Algorithms, Experimentation, Theory

Keywords

Non-intuitive probability, introductory programming

1. THE IMPORTANCE OF PROBABILITY IN COMPUTER SCIENCE

The importance of randomization in computer science cannot be overstated. There are problems that admit a faster expected running time algorithm than the best known running time of any deterministic algorithm [7], [9], [12]. There are algorithmic questions which can be solved only by using a one-sided error probabilistic algorithm but not by any deterministic algorithm [13]. Randomization is an essential tool in fast routing [4], [5], and in on-line algorithms [21], [8]. Most cryptographic protocols, including the important zero-knowledge, use randomization [20], [10]. In approximation algorithms, lower bounds had a breakthrough due to the celebrated PCP theorem [1] that gave a new characterization of NP in the language of probabilistically checkable proofs; examples are abundant. Due to the crucial importance of probability in computer science, it seems that at least some examples should be integrated into the introductory programming course - one of the first core courses in the undergraduate computer science curriculum.

ITiCSE'12, July 3–5, 2012, Haifa, Israel.

2. TEACHING PROBABILITY

2.1 Goals and objectives

The importance of adding randomization into the data structure and algorithms courses was discussed previously in [11]. The concept of probability was listed as one of the core empirical competencies for computer science in [3]. The random walks example was discussed in [2] and [19]. In addition, one of the authors of the current paper had a successful experience integrating randomized algorithms into the basic algorithms course [15, 16]. The focus of the current work is on the integration of the non-intuitive probability experiments into the introductory programming course. These examples do not require any knowledge of probability. Indeed, the value of the probability or the expectation is computed via a program that students run. All material that these problems require is covered already in the introductory programming course curriculum. The proposed enrichment helps to achieve the following goals: (1) engaging students in experimental problem solving; (2) increasing students' motivation and interest in programming; (3) increasing students' attention and curiosity during the class; (4) enhancing students' programming skills. Here we are discussing known problems drawn from the advanced algorithms and probability texts. We are emphasizing the surprising factor and non-intuitive nature of the proposed probability examples. To the best of our knowledge, these problems are not described in major introductory C/Python programming textbooks. Most of these textbooks limit probability examples to the rolling dice and coin flip problems, and in some cases, the randomized version of the rock-paper-scissors game is discussed. Proposed non-intuitive probability experiments create enjoyable programming experience, spark students' interest, and increase their engagement in the course. Students show a great interest in guessing correct answers. They become highly motivated in designing a numerical simulation for the problem to check their guesses. In addition, since students are computing results for highly non-intuitive events, the surprise increases students' attention and curiosity.

2.2 Non-intuitive testable probabilities

Since many probability statements are non-intuitive, it is difficult for students to guess a correct answer. We describe non-intuitive testable probabilities or expectations in the following way: 1. Non-intuitiveness: Intuitive problem solving leads to the wrong answer. 2. Testability: The non-intuitive probability problem could be "translated" into a programming assignment. In other words, it is possible to compute, or closely approximate, the required probability or expectation by writing a program with a low running time.

2.3 The averaging principle

While designing a numerical simulation for the probabilistic experiment, it is important to take into account that, given a single trial, the value reached can be far off the expectation. To resolve this issue we apply the averaging principle. The program simulates the experiment many times; the results for all trials are added and then averaged at the end to obtain a final answer. By simple laws of probability of sum of independent events [15], we know that the average value, produced by our program, will converge to the correct result.

3. OUR TESTABLE EXAMPLES

3.1 Is your random number generator really random?

It is known that randomized algorithms might perform poorly because the random number generator was faulty. Checking the performance of the random number generator provides a soft introduction to the subject of estimating random events. An obvious remark is that we do not know how to find even a single random bit. Still, we do know how to create pseudo-random bits [14]. To evaluate the behavior of the random number generator, we ask students to consider the simple experiment of throwing a fair coin with 'H' and 'T' 1000000 times. This is a single trial of the experiment, and we ask students to verify that, for example, the number of resulting 'H's is about 500000. For this example, it is known that standard deviation is $\sqrt{\frac{n}{4}} = 500$, n =1000000 [14].

3.2 Classical problem: "Let's Make a Deal"

How to win on the TV show "Let's Make a Deal" has been confusing players for decades. There are three curtains. Behind one of them there is an expensive car. Behind the two others there is, say, a scarecrow. The experiment is conducted as follows: (1) The player chooses a curtain; (2) As there are two curtains with a scarecrow, the host, who knows where the car is, is able, regardless of the choice of the player, to open a curtain that contains a scarecrow. If the player chooses a scarecrow curtain, the choice of the host is unique. He/she should open only the remaining scarecrow curtain; (3) Now, we have the chosen curtain, the open curtain, and the third one. At that moment, the host asks if the player wants to switch to the other (closed) curtain. The question is whether the player should switch. For almost all students, since the chosen curtain and the other closed curtain look the same, the intuitive answer is not to switch. For the numerical solution, number 1, 2, or 3 is randomly assigned for the curtain that conceals the car; we call this variable CarCurtain. In addition, number 1, 2, or 3 is randomly assigned for the curtain that is chosen by the player, PlayerCurtain. To conduct a single trial, we hold two variables: AS (after switch) and BS (before switch), both initialized to 0. Then we compare the values of CarCurtain and PlayerCurtain. In case they are equal, we increment BS by 1, since in this case the player does not need to switch. Otherwise, AS is incremented by 1. For averaging purposes, the single trial is repeated 1000000 times. The final results are surprising: with probability 2/3, one should switch, and with probability 1/3, one should not switch. This shows that the intuitive approach leads to the wrong answer. In this case, we do offer a trivial explanation that students understand immediately. We can say by symmetry, that the car is behind curtain 1. If the player chooses 1, then he should not switch. If he chooses 2, he should switch, and if he chooses 3, he should switch. This gives probability 2/3 for changing; namely, in a large number of trials, it would be worth changing to the other closed curtain about 2/3 of the time. Unfortunately, in most other examples, the derivation of the answer cannot be provided in an introductory course due to its complexity.

3.3 Another classical problem: The birthday paradox

It is natural to think that the birthdays of the students in one's class are random. The non-intuitive property is that if we have 23 students in the class, there is a probability of slightly more than 50 percent that there are two students who have the same birthday (we disregard the year of birth, and take in account only day and month). The intuition is that it cannot be that among only 23 people, there are two that were born on the same date. This is because 23 is so much smaller than 365. A way to briefly explain the error in students' thinking and why their intuition fails is to say that if there are 23 people in the class, the number of possible pairs is $253 = (23 \cdot 22)/2$. This now seems much closer to 365. For 30 students, the probability of two people being born on the same day is 0.7.

4. SOME LESSER KNOWN EXAMPLES

4.1 The "strange" behavior of the classical algorithm to find the maximum

This example discusses the classical algorithm to find the maximum that we teach in an introductory course.

Input: an array A[1..*n*] of distinct numbers. Output: M - maximum value

Algorithm:

1. M $\leftarrow$ A[1]
2. for i = 2 to *n*: if A[i] > M: M $\leftarrow$ A[i]

We ask the following question: How many times will the maximum be exchanged if the order between numbers of the array is random? The answers of the students are way off the correct value. Typical guesses are $n/2$ or $n/4$. However, the expected number of exchanges is bounded by $\ln n + O(1)$. This follows from the following analysis that is not to be taught in the course. Let X_i be the indicator variable for the event that M was replaced by A[i]. Thus the number of exchanges is $C = \sum_i X_i$. The expectation of C is $\sum_i E(X_i)$. The probability that A[i] will be the maximum of the first i elements, in a random array, is $1/i$ by symmetry, hence E(C) = $\sum_i^n \frac{1}{i} \leq \ln n + O(1)$.

The program: Since only the order of the numbers is important, we recommend the use of numbers 1, 2, . . . , *n* as the entries of an array of size *n*. To generate a random permutation of the numbers 1, 2, . . . , *n*, we recommend using the Fisher-Yates shuffle, also known as the Knuth shuffle [14] with time complexity O(*n*). First, we advise students to run the program for a relatively small *n*, *n* = 1000. As (ln 1000) is about 6.9, students are able to observe the surprising result that maximum is changed only a few times.

4.2 The strange behavior of random walks

In this section we discuss a well-known random process called random walk on the line [17]. While the random walks example was previously discussed in [2] and [19], here we introduce the simplified variation that does not require any additional resources. In our example, the random walk starts at 0, and the goal is to reach $n = 100$. At 0, the random walk must move to 1. At each step, which is not 0, the random walk moves +1 or -1 with equal probability 1/2. The process ends when the random walk reaches $n = 100$. Here, the students are asked to make predictions about the number of steps required to walk from 0 to 100. To solve this problem, one can use the Markov chains theory and a basic theorem about bridges [17] or a recursive relation (see an analysis on page 246 in [18]). It turns out that the expectation is n^2. Unfortunately, there is no way to explain to students intuitively why the correct value is n^2. It becomes clear later in a probability course. Considering the similar process of random walking on Z starting at 0, it is an elementary exercise to show that the expected position after t steps is $\sqrt{t}$. Therefore, if we want to reach *n*, we need a number of steps *t* so that $n = \sqrt{t}$. Thus, getting to *n* would take n^2 steps.

4.3 Final example

This example illustrates the known problem of faults when a collection of bits is streamed. Some 0 values change to 1 due to local interference and vice versa. The problem: A transmitter sends binary bits. For a single bit, there is a probability 0.8 that 0 is sent and probability 0.2 that 1 is sent. When a 0 is sent, a 0 will be received with probability 0.8. When a 1 is sent, the 1 will be received with probability 0.9. The question is the following: If a 1 is received, what is the probability that a 1 was sent? The correct value is 0.53. To provide an intuitive explanation of why the probability is so low, one may point out that 1 arrives not so frequently, since the probability that 1 is sent is only 0.2, and it makes a small sample. To get good, results one needs to take a large sample. This can be explained in relation to, for example, polls taken for elections.

5. ASSESSMENT AND SUMMARY

The non-intuitive probability component is successfully integrated into the introductory programming courses for a second consecutive year in both institutions. During the second iteration, multiple lab sessions were offered, and this allowed us to conduct a comparison assessment. Half of the lab sessions practiced repetition and decision structures on non-intuitive probability experiments, and the rest of the students practiced the same material on standard examples. We applied a combination of indirect and direct assessment tools. All students answered a short survey conducted before and after the programming unit was taught. Students rated the level of their engagement, interest, and curiosity during the course work, using the scale 1 through 5, where 1 indicates "very low" and 5 indicates "very high." A total of 102 students from both institutions participated in the pre- and post survey and results are presented in the table below.

Table 1: Averages for each category

Category	Pre-Survey Probability Group	Post-Survey Probability Group	Pre-Survey Non Probability Group	Post-Survey Non Probability Group
Engagement	3.7	4.1	3.8	3.7
Interest	4.3	4.5	4.1	4.2
Curiosity	3.9	4.5	4.0	3.9

One can see that the "probability" students showed increased engagement, interest, and curiosity after non-intuitive probability experiments were introduced during the laboratory sessions which supports our main claim. In addition to surveys, all students were administered the same exam to directly measure their understanding of the programming structures. The average grades for both groups of students, before and after the probability component was integrated into the course, are presented in the table below.

Table 2: Average grades

	Probability Group Before Probability Component	Probability Group After Probability Component	Non Probability Group Before	Non Probability Group After
Average Grade	78.9	80.2	78.85	78.7

It is interesting to see that while the average in the non-probability group remained about the same, the probability group performed slightly better on the exam that was introduced after the probability component. This supports our additional claim that non-intuitive probability experiments have potential to improve student learning and comprehension of the repetition and decision programming structures. In general, the assessment results support our opinion on advantages of the proposed methodology. We are planning to continue inclusion of the probability experiments in the future iterations of the course. To integrate the proposed ideas into advanced courses, some of the examples could be generalized. For example, the line in the random walk problem could be replaced by a general undirected graph and an arbitrary starting vertex. In this process we would choose the random neighbor for the next step. In this case, students would be asked to predict the number of steps required to visit all vertices. The answer is Θ(mn), where m is the number of edges in the graph [17]. On the other hand, the problem of the random walk on the directed graph is not testable, because the expected time is exponential.

6. REFERENCES

[1] S. Arora, C. Lund, R. Motwani, M. Sudan, and M. Szegedy. Proof verification and the hardness of approximation problems. Journal of ACM, 45(3): 501-555, 1998.

[2] Braught, G. Teaching Empirical Skills and Concepts in Computer Science using Random Walks, Proceedings of the of the 36th SIGCSE, pp. 41-45, 2005

[3] Braught, G., Miller, C. & Reed, D. Core Empirical Skills and Concepts for Computer Science. Proceedings of the 35th SIGCSE, pp. 245-249, 2004

[4] A Borodin and J. Hopcroft. Routing merging and sorting in the parallel model of computation. Journal of Computer and System Sciences, 30: 130-145, 1985.

[5] G. J. Brebner and L. G. Valiant. Universal schemes for parallel communication. Proceedings of the thirteenth annual ACM symposium on Theory of computing, 263-277, 1981

[6] T. Cormen, C. Leiserson, R. Rivest, and C. Stein. Introduction to Algorithms. MIT Press, third edition, 2009.

[7] D. Dor and U. Zwick. Median Selection Requires (2+epsilon)n Comparisons. SIAM Journal on Discrete Mathematics, 14(3): 312-325

[8] A. Fiat, R. M. Karp, M. Luby, L. A. McGeoch, D. D. Sleator, and N. E. Young. Competitive paging algorithms. Journal of Algorithms archive, 12(4): 685-699, 1991

[9] R. W. Floyd and R. L. Rivest. Expected time bounds for selection. Communications of the ACM, 18(3): 165-172, 1975.

[10] O. Goldreich, S. Micali, and A. Wigderson. Proofs that yield nothing but their validity or all languages in NP have zero-knowledge proof systems. Journal of the ACM, 38(3): 690-728, 1991

[11] M. T. Goodrich and R. Tamassia. Using randomization in the teaching of data structures and algorithms. Proceedings of the 30th SIGCSE, 53 - 57, 1999

[12] G. Kalai. A sub exponential randomized simplex algorithm. Proceedings of the twenty-fourth annual ACM symposium on Theory of computing, 475-482, 1992

[13] R. M. Karp, E. Upfal, and A. Wigderson. Constructing a perfect matching is in random NC. Combinatorica 6(1): 35-48, 1986

[14] D. Knuth. The Art of Computer Programming volume 2, third edition, Addison-Wesley, 1998

[15]Y. Kortsarts, J. Rufinus, Teaching a Power of Randomization Using Simple Game, Proceedings of the 37th SIGCSE, 2006

[16] Yana Kortsarts, Jeffrey Rufinus, How (and why) to introduce Monte-Carlo randomized algorithms into a basic algorithms course?, Journal of Computing Sciences in Colleges, Volume 21(2), December 2005, pp. 195 - 203

[17] R. Motwani and P. Raghavan. Randomized Algorithms. Cambridge University Press, 1995

[18] C. Papadimitriou. Computational complexity. Addison Wesley, 1994.

[19] D. Reed. The use of ill-defined problems for developing problem-solving and empirical skills in CS1. Journal of Computing Sciences in Colleges, Volume 18 Issue 1, October 2002, pp. 121 - 133

[20] R. L. Rivest, A. Shamir, and L. M. Adleman. A Method for Obtaining Digital Signatures and Public-Key Cryptosystem. Communication of the ACM, 21(2): 120-126, 1978

[21] D. Sleator and R. Tarjan. Amortize efficiency of list update and paging rules. Communication of the ACM, 28: 202 - 208, 1984

A Study on Students' Behaviours and Attitudes towards Learning to Program

Anabela Gomes
Centre for Informatics and Systems of the University of Coimbra and Engineering Institute of Coimbra
Rua Pedro Nunes
3030 Coimbra - Portugal
+351239790300
anabela@isec.pt

Álvaro Santos
Centre for Informatics and Systems of the University of Coimbra and Engineering Institute of Coimbra
Rua Pedro Nunes
3030 Coimbra - Portugal
+351239790300
ans@isec.pt

António José Mendes
Centre for Informatics and Systems of the University of Coimbra
Pólo II – Pinhal de Marrocos
3030 Coimbra – Portugal
+351239790036
toze@dei.uc.pt

ABSTRACT
Learning difficulties in introductory programming courses are well known to teachers and students. Although several types of causes for those difficulties can be pointed out, in this work we focused on student related issues, namely their study methods and attitudes towards learning to program. We found a strong correlation between students' results and their personal perceptions of competence during the course. This result raises the need for teachers to consider this issue when devising the pedagogical approaches to use in introductory programming courses.

Categories and Subject Descriptors
K.3.2 [**Computers and Education**]: Computer and Information Science Education – *computer science education*

General Terms
Experimentation, Languages.

Keywords
Programming learning, Learning difficulties, Study Methods and Attitudes.

1. INTRODUCTION
The literature includes many references to the difficulties many novice students feel in introductory programming courses throughout the world [3, 5, 17]. Winslow [26] states that learning to program is difficult and that novice programmers face a variety of difficulties. Other authors [15, 16, 19, 23] also report that the programming courses are often seen as difficult and frequently have high dropout rates. Diverse factors have been pointed out as causes of student's difficulties. Efopoulos and colleagues agree that programming is a cognitive and inherently demanding discipline, suggesting that it is the most difficult computational ability to master [8]. Several authors associate this difficulty with the abstract nature of programming [1, 2, 16]. For example, Dunican [7] states that concepts like variables, data types, dynamic memory, among others, have no correspondence in everyday life and mastering these fundamental concepts is not simple. Several authors state that programming involves a hierarchy of skills many of which have to be simultaneously active [14, 18, 24]. Dijkstra [6] also states that a particular feature of programming is that it involves intensive problem solving. To Jenkins [15] there is nothing inherently difficult in programming, but simply there are students that do not have the necessary skills, abilities and talents. It is also possible to find other studies that suggest the existence of a correlation between the student's programming abilities and their mathematical skills [4].

There are several factors that influence students' learning performance in programming, such as the students' background knowledge and attitudes, the teaching and learning methods, and the social context. Some time ago we made some studies that related freshmen difficulties to learn to program with their lack of problem solving skills and mathematical background [9, 10, 11, 21, 22]. Other studies we conducted in the past also showed that frequently the programming problems proposed by teachers are well beyond the students' cognitive development, making it difficult for them to propose even a rough solution for those problems [12, 13]. These aspects suggest that changes are necessary both in students' study methods and attitudes and also in the traditional teaching approaches.

In this paper we will focus on students' study methods and their motivation towards learning to program. We describe a study that analyses the type of study approaches and motivation of our programming students. It correlates the grades the students got in the programming courses with data about their study methods and motivation collected with the IACHE questionnaire (a Portuguese acronym of Inventory of Usual Study Attitudes and Behaviours) [25].

The IACHE instrument is a multidimensional questionnaire consisting of 44 items divided into five dimensions. Two of these dimensions refer to how students express their approach to learning, including deep (Comprehensive Approach) or superficial/memorizing learning (Memorization Approach). In the Comprehensive Approach the emphasis is on understanding. It evaluates if the student uses strategies that will ensure a deep understanding of the material studied, in other words if the student learns significantly. In the Memorization Approach the emphasis is on memorization. The questions in this topic allow to determine if the student uses strategies based on memorization and repetition of content. Another dimension includes items focusing on personal perceptions of ability and success in academic achievement (Personal Perceptions). It is related to perceptions of competence and personal achievement that the student has in himself/herself. The last two dimensions focus on students' motivation (Motivation) and organization (Organization). The Motivation approach is related to student involvement in the course. It is the intrinsic motivation that the student demonstrates in the study activities. In the Organization approach, the emphasis is obviously organization. It deals with the usual behaviour of the student, related with planning and time organization, materials and available resources. Thus the inventory includes a more behavioural aspect (actions, daily routines, time management and study materials), a more affective-motivational aspect (commitments, interests, involvement in the study and in the course) and a more cognitive aspect (personal perceptions, attitudes and approaches to learning). IACHE also includes a group of eight questions regarding students' academic expectations and satisfaction with the course and the institution. Additionally, there is another group of questions where students are asked about the causes for their possible learning difficulties. The scale format used for students to demonstrate their level of agreement with each question is a Likert-type scale with six points. Higher values correspond to a higher degree of student agreement with each statement.

2. THE STUDY

The main goal of this research was to investigate the study methods used by our students. We analysed the study behaviour of two samples of freshmen enrolled in the first programming course of a Computer Science degree. We correlated that information with the grades they obtained in the programming courses.

The study involved students enrolled in the Informatics Engineering course of the University of Coimbra (LEI-UC) and students enrolled in the Informatics Engineering course of the Superior Institute of Engineering of the Polytechnic Institute of Coimbra (LEIS-ISEC). The sample LEI-UC consisted of 166 students, 155 males and 11 females, aged between 18 and 34 years. The average age was 20.28 years, but the median was 19, an average age for students in the first year. The sample LEIS-ISEC had 175 students, 168 male and 7 female, aged between 17 and 48 years. The average age was 21.87 years and the median was 20. The higher variability of this sample is explained by the fact that LEIS-ISEC had two schedules, day (ordinary student regime) and evening classes (worker student regime). Most students who attended the latter were older than the average. Given the small number of female students we decided not to differentiate between sexes in this experiment. The students involved studied Python at LEI-UC and C at LEIS-ISEC as their first programming language, respectively, in IPRP (a Portuguese acronym for Introduction to Programming and Problem Solving) and AP (Algorithms and Programming).

3. RESULTS ANALYSIS

As IACHE had been validated for populations with characteristics similar to our samples, we did not do any study on its internal validity. Tavares *et al.* [25] present the studies leading to the current version of IACHE. However, we analysed its consistency by calculating the Cronbach's alphas, including each of the approaches (Comprehensive Approach, Memorization Approach, Personal Perceptions, Motivation and Organization). For the sample LEI-UC we obtained an $\alpha = 0.705$ and for the LEIS-ISEC sample we obtained an $\alpha = 0.785$. These results are considered satisfactory. Analysing separately each of the approaches, in the LEI-UC sample the results were reasonable or good: $\alpha = 0.777$ (for the Comprehensive Approach), $\alpha = 0.844$ (for Personal Perceptions), $\alpha = 0.773$ (for Motivation) and $\alpha = 0.847$ (for the Organization). The exception was the Memorization Approach with $\alpha = 0.616$ being weaker but still acceptable. In the LEIS-ISEC sample, the results were also considered reasonable or good: α=0.763 (for the Comprehensive Approach), $\alpha = 0.729$ (for the Memorization Approach), $\alpha = 0.773$ (for Personal Perceptions), $\alpha = 0.797$ (for Motivation) and $\alpha = 0.867$ (for Organization).

3.1 General analysis of each study approach

Tables 1 and 2 show the descriptive statistics results obtained for each of the approaches, considering all the students in each sample.

Table 1. LEI-UC Sample: Descriptive Statistic of the study approach items for all the students

	N	Min.	Max.	Med.	Stand. Dev.
Comprehension	166	23	55	38.77	6.466
Memorization	166	16	43	29.38	5.125
Personal Perceptions	166	8	45	25.73	7.883
Motivation	166	11	45	30.78	6.204
Organization	166	11	50	30.47	7.758

Table 2. LEIS-ISEC Sample: Descriptive Statistic of the study approach items for all the students

	N	Min.	Max.	Med.	Stand. Dev.
Comprehension	175	20	53	37.57	6.139
Memorization	175	13	41	29.06	5.846
Personal Perceptions	175	8	44	26.73	6.489
Motivation	175	13	47	29.85	6.430
Organization	175	10	53	28.82	8.159

The averages aren't very different from those observed in other studies in the scope of engineering education, such as the study done by Monteiro et al. [20]. However, there are large variations between the minimum and maximum values. It should be noted that the analysis of most items is straightforward, meaning that a higher classification indicates greater depth of study, more memory work, higher motivation and better organization, respectively in comprehensive, memorization, motivational and organizational approaches. In personal perceptions the analysis is done in the opposite direction, meaning that a higher value is a lower personal perception of ability. For the comprehensive and organizational approaches the maximum possible is 60 points, but for the memorization, motivational and personal perceptions approaches the maximum is 48 points.

3.2 Items analysis between independent samples

The characteristics of the studied samples allowed us to carry out tests considering different classes of students: freshmen and repeat students (those who had failed the same course in the previous year), and also students belonging to different study systems (ordinary student regime (OSR) and the student worker regime (SWR)).

We applied t-tests to determine the differences between the means. We verified that in both samples (LEI-UC and LEIS-ISEC), freshmen showed better **personal perceptions** than the repeaters (F=0.541, Sig.=0.463; t=-3.044, Sig.=0.003 in LEI-UC and F=0.084, Sig.=0.772; t=-2.921, Sig.=0.004 in LEIS-ISEC). This is probably due to the fact that repeaters had already gone through situations of failure, affecting their personal perceptions of competence to learn programming.

When we considered the regimes separately we found some variations in the samples. In the sample LEI-UC most OSR students showed better **personal perceptions** than most of the SWR students (F=1.579, Sig.=0.211; t=-2.496, Sig.=0.014 in LEI-UC). The same happened with the OSR repeaters when compared to the SWR repeaters (F=2.645, Sig.=0.108; t=-2.069, Sig.=0.042 in LEI-UC). We could not conclude whether this phenomenon was also happening among freshmen of different regimes due to lack of freshmen in the student worker regime (SWR). Maybe this result is caused by the fact that SWR students have difficulties to conciliate their studies with their jobs. Their projects are therefore hindered, affecting their self-esteem and consequently their personal perceptions of competence.

In the LEIS-ISEC sample, we also observed differences in personal perceptions between OSR freshmen and OSR repeaters (F=0.003, Sig.=0.953; t=-2.139, Sig.=0.034 in LEIS-ISEC). Repeating students' lower personal perceptions were probably due to having already failed the course in the previous year, which lowered their self-esteem and made them wonder if they would be able to learn. The fact that no differences were found in the LEIS-ISEC sample among students of the two regimes is possibly due to the fact that worker students have a particular schedule (after work), facilitating their class attendance, allowing a better performance and therefore higher personal perceptions.

We only found differences in **motivation** in the LEIS-ISEC sample when comparing OSR freshmen and SWR freshmen (F=1.315, Sig.=0.255; t=-2.05, Sig.=0.044 in LEIS-ISEC). SWR students showed more motivation, maybe because they are more mature and enroll in the course with clearer objectives. This higher motivation makes those students miss fewer classes and be more enthusiastic and participative, even after a day of work. This difference was only obtained in the freshmen sample and not in the repeater sample. This means that the SWR repeaters didn't show more motivation than the OSR repeaters. This may be related to the fact that the SWR repeaters started to lose motivation given the difficulty to balance the study with their professional and personal lives.

Also in the LEIS-ISEC sample we found differences in terms of **organization levels**. In general freshmen were more organized than repeaters (F=2.735, Sig.=0.100; t=2.241, Sig.=0.026 in LEIS-ISEC). The same conclusion was reached when considering only OSR students (F=1.160, Sig.=0.283; t=1.763, Sig.=0.080 in LEIS-ISEC) or SWR students (F=0.072, Sig.=0.791; t=3.028, Sig.=0.005 in LEIS-ISEC). The OSR freshmen also revealed to be more organized than the SWR freshmen (F=1.012, Sig.=0.317; t=-2.078, Sig.=0.041 in LEIS-ISEC). This is possibly due to the fact that OSR students have, in general, more time available than SWR students, who usually have to conciliate work and study having less time to organize themselves. This made us think that OSR repeaters should be more organized than SWR repeaters, but we couldn't find evidence to support that assumption. As we found that freshmen were more organized than repeaters, we could think that organization is correlated with learning. However, we cannot make that statement categorically. Studies conducted by other authors revealed that the level of organization of an individual is not necessarily related to their academic success [20]. On the contrary, these authors concluded that the less organized students were able to get approved in more disciplines (although with a minor difference) and had a better overall grade average.

Table 3. Personal Perceptions analysis

	Levene's Test for equality of variances		t- Test for equality of means		
	F	Sig.	t	Df	Sig. *(2-tailed)*
LEI-UC *(freshmen vs repeaters)*	0.541	0.463	-3.044	164	0.003
LEIS-ISEC *(freshmen vs repeaters)*	0.084	0.772	-2.921	173	0.004
LEI-UC *(OSR freshmen vs OSR repeaters)*	1.465	0.228	-2.659	158	0.002
LEIS-ISEC *(OSR freshmen vs OSR repeaters)*	0.003	0.953	-2.139	145	0.034
LEI-UC *(SWR freshmen vs SWR repeaters)*	*There aren't SWR freshmen in this sample*				
LEIS-ISEC *(SWR freshmen vs SWR repeaters)*	No differences.				
LEI-UC *(OSR students vs SWR students)*	1.579	0.211	-2.496	164	0.014
LEI-UC *(OSR repeaters vs SWR repeaters)*	2.645	0.108	-2.069	80	0.042
LEIS-ISEC *(OSR vs SWR, and all of these subsamples)*	No differences.				

Table 4. Motivation analysis

	Levene's Test for equality of variances		t- Test for equality of means		
	F	Sig.	t	Df	Sig. *(2-tailed)*
LEIS-ISEC *(OSR freshman vs SWR freshman)*	1.315	0.255	-2.05	83	0.044

Table 5. Organization analysis

	Levene's Test for equality of variances		t- Test for equality of means		
	F	Sig.	t	Df	Sig. *(2-tailed)*
LEIS-ISEC *(freshmen vs repeaters)*	2.735	0.100	2.241	173	0.026
LEIS-ISEC *(OSR freshmen vs OSR repeaters)*	1.160	0.283	1.763	145	0.080
LEIS-ISEC *(SWR freshmen vs SWR repeaters)*	0.072	0.791	3.028	26	0.005
LEIS-ISEC *(OSR freshmen vs SWR freshmen)*	1.012	0.317	-2.078	83	0.041

Table 6. Memorization approach analysis

	Levene's Test for equality of variances		t- Test for equality of means		
	F	Sig.	t	Df	Sig. *(2-tailed)*
LEI-UC *(repeaters vs freshman)*	0.110	0.741	-3.038	164	0.003

When looking at the **memorization approach**, differences were noted only in the LEI-UC sample, showing that freshmen used less memorization strategies than repeaters (F=0.110, Sig.=0.741; t=-3.038, Sig.=0.003 in LEI-UC). Perhaps the fact that repeating students used more surface learning strategies was one of the causes for their lack of success in programming courses, as they require a deeper study approach. We found no explanation for the fact that this difference was not detected in the LEIS-ISEC sample.

3.3 Analysis between pairing samples

To better understand some aspects we also investigated the behaviour of students throughout the school year. For that, the students were asked to answer the IACHE questionnaire again at the end of the second programming course – PPP (they had answered it for the first time during the first programming course - IPRP). The sample was reduced because many students had dropped out during the year (this is another theme that deserves more attention in further investigations).

In the LEI-UC sample we could observe that students essentially didn't change their study behaviours and attitudes. A closer look revealed that the ranks of all approaches decreased slightly, except the personal perception that was slightly higher (which is not positive). It is worth noting that the decrease in the memorization approach is regarded as positive, as students are not expected to use many memorization techniques when studying programming.

We did the same study with the LEIS-ISEC sample. However, although many students responded to the initial and final surveys, the number of students who responded to both was insufficient for a statistical treatment. However, an informal analysis showed that the results were substantially the same.

3.4 Correlation with the programming grades

It was particularly interesting to us to correlate the results obtained with IACHE with the grades the students got in the two programming courses they had in the first year. For the LEI-UC sample the courses were IPRP and PPP. The results are presented in table 3.

The results obtained were very interesting as we found correlations between the programming grades and the students' personal perceptions and motivation. The negative correlation obtained when crossing the results of the programming courses with the personal perception item has the meaning of a positive correlation, as higher values in the personal perception item represent worse personal perceptions.

These results strongly mean (at p = 0.01 two-tailed), that students who had better personal perceptions had also higher grades in the first programming courses. The same is true regarding motivational aspects, although not so strongly (p = 0.05 level two-tailed). Thus, the most motivated students are also those who got better results in the first programming courses. The results indicate that the motivation levels and personal perceptions of competence are important factors to be successful in programming learning.

Regarding the LEIS-ISEC sample it was not possible to do similar correlation tests due to the insufficient number of students that responded to the survey and took the course exam

Table 7. LEI-UC Sample: Correlation between each item and the programming results

(*at 0.05 (2-tailed), **at 0.01 (2-tailed))	IPRP	PPP
Comprehension	-	-
Memorization	-	-
Personal Perceptions	r=-0.507**	r=-0.460**
Motivation	r=0.328*	r=0.216*
Organization	-	-

3.5 Students' satisfaction analysis

As mentioned before, IACHE also has a group of eight questions concerning academic expectations. We could assess the degree of students' satisfaction with the course (subjects, materials, teachers and peers) and with the institution [general work environment, the institution itself (campus, services, information, ...), students' participation in study/work and equipment (library, equipment, computer facilities,..)]. In the LEI-UC sample, the results allowed us to affirm that students were, in general, fairly satisfied, since most of the respondents had a degree of satisfaction between 3 and 5 points. However, the only parameter that was less favorable was related to students' personal expectations with their participation in the study/work. Most of them indicated a degree of satisfaction between 3 and 4 points.

In the same sample, we also compared the students' satisfaction in the beginning and end of the year. There were some variations between the two moments, concerning the degree of satisfaction with colleagues and students' expectations with the general working environment in the institution. Even though most students continued to assign a rating between 3 and 5 to their satisfaction with the colleagues, many of them gave a lower rank in the end of the year. A similar situation was found concerning the overall working environment. The remaining parameters were essentially unchanged.

Regarding the LEIS-ISEC sample, the students' were fairly satisfied with the course and the institution, as most of the answers were between 3 and 5 or 4 and 5 points. However the parameters corresponding to the courses and their topics and students' personal expectations with their participation in the study/work were less favorable. Most of them indicated a degree of agreement between 3 and 4 points. Again it was not possible in this sample to make a longitudinal comparative analysis about the evolution of the satisfaction levels due to the insufficient number of students who answered both surveys.

3.6 Students' difficulties analysis

The third group of questions focused on the possible causes for students' learning difficulties. Students had to choose only one of the following options: "Lack of knowledge bases" (LKB), "Lack of motivation" (LM), "Intellectual difficulties" (ID), "Lack of effort or personal persistence" (LEPP), "Lack of Attention and Concentration in Class" (LACC), "Competence of Teachers" (CT), "Exam Difficulty" (ED), "Difficulties in Adapting to Higher Education" (DAHE), "Study Methods" (SM), "Bad Luck" (BL) or "Other reasons" (O).

Even though the students were told and it was written in the survey that they should only mark the most important reason for the learning difficulties they experienced, many of them marked more than one cause, making their answers not useful for our purposes.

In the first questionnaire (during the first course), applied to LEI-UC including 166 students, the most mentioned causes of difficulties were "Lack of Knowledge Bases" (LKB) (31.68%), "Lack of Effort or Personal Persistence" (LEPP) (19.25%) and "Lack of Motivation" (LM) (11.18%). Some students (3.74%) indicated other factors, such as not being in the right course, lack of time, fatigue, too much workload, the accumulation of work in certain periods, and lack of social support.

In the end of the year we wanted to compare students' answers with those the same students gave in the first semester. However, the respondents were not exactly the same, as some students that answered in the first semester did not follow or dropped out from the second semester course. So, we made a subsample including only the 74 students that answered both questionnaires. Considering only this subsample, the causes more frequently chosen in the first questionnaire were "Lack of Knowledge Bases" (LKB) (36.99%), "Lack of Effort or Personal Persistence" (LEPP) (23.29%), "Lack of Motivation" (LM) (10.96%) and "Lack of Attention and Concentration in Class" (LACC) (6.85%). In the final survey the more mentioned causes were "Lack of Effort or Personal Persistence" (LEPP) (22.97%), "Lack of Motivation" (LM), "Study Methods" (SM) and "Other reasons" (O), each mentioned by 9.46% of the sample. It is interesting to note that the "Lack of Knowledge Bases" disappeared from the top reasons mentioned, while the students seemed conscious that they should commit more to be successful, as the most mentioned reasons were student related. Curiously the percentage of students who indicated other factors more than doubled, but the factors mentioned were essentially the same as before.

We also analysed the difficulties expressed by the students in the LEIS-ISEC sample. In the first questionnaire the percentage of the 175 students who indicated several causes was very high (40.46%). The other students mentioned "Lack of Effort or Personal Persistence" (LEPP) (12.72%), "Study Methods" (SM) (9.25%) and "Lack of Motivation" (LM) (8.67%). Some students (4.62%) indicated other factors, in particular lack of time. This aspect was only mentioned by students in the worker student scheme.

In this case we also considered the subsample including the 20 students that answered both questionnaires. Considering only these students, 35% indicated several causes. The causes most frequently mentioned by the remaining students were "Competence of Teachers" (CT) (15%), "Lack of Effort or Personal Persistence" (LEPP) (10%), "Lack of Attention and Concentration in Class" (LACC) (10%), "Bad Luck" (BL) (10%) and "Other reasons" (10%). In the second survey, 70% of the students mentioned several difficulties, with "Study methods" (SM) (10%), "Lack of Effort or Personal Persistence" (LEPP) (5%), "Lack of Attention and Concentration in Class" (LACC) (5%),"Difficulty of the Exams" (DE) (5%) and "Other reasons" (O) (5%) being the most mentioned by the remaining students.

It is interesting to note that the "Competence of Teachers" and "Bad Luck" factors disappeared from the top mentioned, while the "Lack of Effort or Personal Persistence" and "Lack of Attention and Concentration in Class" continued to be mentioned. A new factor not mentioned initially appeared: “Exam Difficulty”. The students who chose the option "Other reasons" essentially mentioned the same reasons in the two surveys.

4. CONCLUSIONS

The objective of this study was to see if some connection could be made between students' behaviours and attitudes and their learning performance in introductory programming courses (measured by their final grades). The motivation for the study was the learning difficulties felt by most of our students, which often lead to dropout or poor performance in exams and other assessment activities.

The most important finding of our study was the strong correlation found between students learning performance and their personal perceptions of competence in programming. We also found some other correlations, for instance the correlation between grades and student motivation. It is important that the students feel that they are able to learn if they commit. If they lose that belief the probability of a dropout or simply a non-commitment rises, contributing to the bad results common in introductory programming courses. So, teachers should probably consider including measures to monitor and stimulate the students' perceptions of competence, making them clearly aware of the small learning improvements they show (for example, making clear that the student now is able to solve problems that she couldn't solve some time ago). To make this possible it is very important that the teacher knows very well each student programming abilities during the course. This creates the case for a course structure based on classes in groups of around 20 students where each session can be a combination of theory, lots of practice and a good level of interactivity. With this organization it is possible for the teacher to be always aware of what each student knows.

In the initial learning stages, activities are often too complex for many students, especially because they are asked to write complete programs without previously going through less demanding tasks. In this sense, we consider that the teacher should prepare alternative programming activities according to each student level. Having in consideration the Blooms' Taxonomy is a possibility. It is important that the activities proposed to each student are not too far of their current cognitive programming level, in order to improve engagement. If students feel that they are able to do a certain task their perception of competence and confidence naturally improves. Our small groups based strategy allows a more direct contact between teacher and students. It will be easier for the teacher to notice learning problems that any student might have and make direct interventions that may help to solve them. This may minimize drop out and improve success rates, as a timely teacher intervention may help students to overcome their problems. Our results open the need for further research, namely on strategies that may improve students' motivation and perceptions of competence, making them more open to the effort involved in learning to program. This type of strategy is part of a new approach we are putting in practice in our institution.

5. ACKNOWLEDGMENTS

The authors would like to thank all students that participated in the studies and to the teachers that allowed their realization.

6. REFERENCES

[1] Bennedsen, J. and Caspersen, M. E. 2006. Abstraction ability as an indicator of success for learning object-oriented programming? *SIGCSE Bulletin inroads*, 38, 2, (June 2006), 39-43.

[2] Bennedsen, J. 2008. *Teaching and Learning Introductory Programming - A Model-Based Approach*. Doctoral Thesis. University of Oslo, Norway.

[3] Bruce, C. S. and McMahon, C. A. 2002. *Contemporary Developments in Teaching and Learning Introductory Programming: Towards a Research Proposal*. Teaching and Learning Report. Faculty of Information Technology, Queensland University of Technology, Brisbane, Australia.

[4] Byrne, P. and Lyons, G. 2001. The effect of student attributes on success in programming. *SIGCSE Bulletin*, 33 3, (September 2001), 49-52.

[5] Dehnadi, S. 2006. Testing programming Aptitude. In *Proceedings of the 18th Annual Workshop of the Psychology of Programming Interest Group* (Brighton, UK, September 7-8, 2006). PPIG'06, 22-37.

[6] Dijkstra, E. W. 1989. On the Cruelty of Really Teaching Computing Science. *Communications of the ACM*, 32, 12, (December 1989), 1388-1404.

[7] Dunican, E. 2002. Making The Analogy: Alternative Delivery Techniques for First Year Programming Courses. In J. Kuljis, L. Baldwin, & R. Scoble (Ed.), PPIG 2002: *Proceedings of the 14th Annual Workshop of the Psychology of Programming Interest Group* (Brunel University, London, UK, June 18-21, 2002). PPIG'02, 89-99.

[8] Efopoulos, V., Dagdilelis, V., Evangelidis, G. & Satratzemi, M. 2005. WIPE: a programming environment for novices. *SIGCSE Bulletin*, 37, 3, (September 2005), 113-117.

[9] Gomes, A., Carmo, L., Bigotte, E. and Mendes, A. J. 2006. Mathematics and programming problem solving. In *Proceedings of 3rd E-Learning Conference - Computer Science Education* (Coimbra, Portugal, September 07-08, 2006). e-learning'06, CD-ROM.

[10] Gomes, A. and Mendes, A. J. 2007. Learning to program - difficulties and solutions. In *Proceedings of the International Conference on Engineering Education* (Coimbra, Portugal, September 03-07, 2007). ICEE'07, CD-ROM.

[11] Gomes, A. and Mendes, A. J. 2008. A study on student's characteristics and programming learning. In *Proceedings of the World Conference on Educational Multimedia, Hypermedia and Telecommunications 2008* (Vienna, Austria, June 30-July 4, 2008). EDMEDIA'08, AACE, 2895-2904.

[12] Gomes, A. & Mendes, A. J. 2009. Bloom's taxonomy based approach to learn basic programming. In *Proceedings of the World Conference on Educational Multimedia, Hypermedia and Telecommunications 2009* (Honolulu, Hawaii, USA, June 22-26, 2009). EDMEDIA'09, AACE, 2547-2554.

[13] Gomes, A. and Mendes, A. J. 2010. A study on student performance in first year CS courses. In *Proceedings of the 15th Annual Conference on Innovation and Technology in Computer Science Education* (Ankara, Turkey, June 26-30, 2010). ITiCSE'10, ACM New York, NY, 113-117.

[14] Gray, W. D., Goldberg, N. C. and Byrnes, S.A. 2007. Novices and programming: Merely a difficult subject (why?) or a means to mastering metacognitive skills? [Review of the book Studying the Novice Programmer]. *Journal of Educational Research on Computers*, 9, 1, (June 2007), 131-140.

[15] Jenkins, T. 2002. On the difficulty of learning to program. In *Proceedings of the 3rd Annual LTSN_ICS Conference* (Loughborough University, United Kingdom, August 27-29, 2002). The Higher Education Academy, 53-58.

[16] Lahtinen, E., Ala-Mutka, K. and Järvinen, H-M. 2005. A study of difficulties of novice programmers. In *Proceedings of the 10th Annual SIGCSE Conference on Innovation and Technology in Computer Science Education* (Monte de Caparica, Portugal, June 27-29, 2005). ACM New York, NY, USA, 14-18.

[17] Lister, R. 2000. On blooming first year programming, and its blooming assessment. In *Proceedings of the Australasian Conference on Computing Education* (Melbourne, Australia, December 04-06, 2000). ACM New York, NY, USA, 158-162.

[18] Lister, R., Adams, E. S., Fitzgerald, S., Fone, W., Hamer, J., Lindholm, M., McCartney, R., Moström, J. E., Sanders, K., Seppälä, O., Simon, B., Thomas, L. 2004. A multi-national study of reading and tracing skills in novice programmers. *SIGCSE Bulletin*, 36, 4, (December 2004), 119-150.

[19] Lister, R., Simon, B., Thompson, E., Whalley, J. L. and Prasad, C. 2006. Not seeing the forest for the trees: novice programmers and the SOLO taxonomy. *SIGCSE Bulletin*, 38 3, (September 2006), 118-122.

[20] Monteiro, S., Vasconcelos, R. and Almeida, L. 2005. Rendimento Académico: Influência dos métodos de estudo. *Actas do VIII Congresso Galaico Português de PsicoPedagogia* (Universidade do Minho, Braga, Portugal, September 16, 2005). ISBN: 972-8746-36-9.

[21] Pacheco, A., Gomes, A., Henriques, J., Almeida, A. M. and Mendes, A. 2008. "A study on basic mathematics knowledge for the enhancement of programming learning skills". In *Proceedings of Informatics Education Europe III* (Venice, Italy, December 04-05). IEEIII'08.

[22] Pacheco, A., Gomes, A., Henriques, J., Almeida, A. and Mendes, A. J. 2008. Mathematics and Programming: Some studies. In *Proceedings of the International Conference on Computer Systems and Technologies* (Gabrovo, Bulgaria, June 12-13, 2008). ACM New York, NY, USA, 77-82.

[23] Simon, Fincher, S., Robins, A., Baker, B., Box, I. and Cutts, Q. 2006. Predictors of success in a first programming course. In *Proceedings of the 8th Australian Conference on Computing Education* (Hobart, Australia, January 16-19, 2006). Australian Computer Society, Inc., 189-196.

[24] Sloane, K. D. and Linn, M. C. 1988. *Instructional Conditions in Pascal Programming Classes*. In R. E. Mayer (Ed.), Teaching and learning computer programming (pp. 137-152). Lawrence Erlbaum Associates.

[25] Tavares, J., Almeida, L. S., Vasconcelos, R. M. and Bessa, J. 2004. *Inventário de Atitudes e Comportamentos Habituais de Estudo - IACHE*. Universidade de Aveiro/Universidade do Minho, Centro de Investigação em Educação, Portugal.

[26] Winslow, L. E. 1996. Programming pedagogy-a psychological overview. *SIGCSE Bulletin*, 28, 3, 17-22.

Initial Results of Using an Intelligent Tutoring System with Alice

Stephen Cooper
Computer Science Department
Stanford University
Stanford, CA 94305
1.650.723.9798
coopers@stanford.edu

Yoon Jae Nam
Computer Science Department
Stanford University
Stanford, CA 94305
1.650.455.0064
namy@stanford.edu

Luo Si
Computer Science Department
Purdue University
West Lafayette, IN, 47906
1.765.496.9381
lsi@cs.purdue.edu

ABSTRACT

This paper describes the initial steps taken towards incorporating an intelligent tutoring system (ITS) into Alice. After initially describing an ITS, the paper focuses on the development of several tutorials for teaching specific introductory programming concepts that have been created using stencils. Initial results concerning usability and effectiveness of these stencil-based tutorials are provided.

Categories and Subject Descriptors

K.3.2 [**Computer and Information Science Education**]: Computer Science Education

General Terms

Algorithms, Measurement.

Keywords

Intelligent tutoring system, Alice, tutorial.

1. INTRODUCTION

Computing is becoming popular again! From the Khan Academy [27] finally offering instruction on how to program, to Jan Cuny's ambitious plans to recruit 10,000 high school teachers to provide computing capacity at the K-12 level [6], to the nearly 200,000 people who signed up for Thrun and Norvig's online Artificial Intelligence course [18], there has been an increased interest in learning computing. As Mark Guzdial noted in his keynote address at ITiCSE in July 2011, it has become increasingly difficult to use the same apprentice-based approach that has most commonly been used to teach introductory computer science (that has typically focused on teaching programming) over the past 40 or so years. It is too expensive. It doesn't scale well. And it depends quite heavily on the quality of the tutor/master.

This work proposes to use an Intelligent Tutoring System (ITS) to augment or possibly replace the role of the instructor. It is incorporated into Alice.

Intelligent Tutoring System(s) (ITS): An ITS is a computer system that provides customized instruction or feedback to students without much intervention from human teachers. An ITS can bring several benefits for delivering effective instruction: (1) An ITS can provide individualized instruction that allows all students to access the same curriculum with different entry points and learning tasks that are tailored to students' needs; (2) An ITS can enable students to achieve similar proficiency levels in a more efficient way; and (3) With appropriate design, an ITS can enable human teachers to focus on a small subset of students who need extra help besides the assistance provided by the ITS instruction, and thus delivering more effective instruction.

Alice: Alice is a programming environment designed to enable novice programmers to create 3-D virtual worlds, including animations and games [19, 20] as they learn to program. Students use a drag and drop editor to manipulate the movement and activities of these objects. Alice was designed through an iterative process of studying how novices try to describe the motions of objects in a 3-D world, and then modifying Alice so that the novices' expectations would be met [21]. Alice makes use of program visualization to allow students to immediately see how their animation programs run, enabling students to easily understand the relationship between the programming statements and constructs and the behavior of their animations. In Alice, students learn the basics of computing, but where the objects of concern are actors and scenes in a virtual world. Alice programs have a strong object-oriented flavor, allowing students to control the appearance and motion of objects, have objects respond to mouse and keyboard input, or do any sort of computation that would normally be done in an introductory programming class. Alice was chosen as the environment into which to place the ITS due to its popularity as an introductory programming language/environment.

The intent of the ITS is twofold: Initially, it is to be used to detect student progression through the tutorials. When does a student appear to have mastered a particular programming concept, and is ready to move on to the next concept? The second intent for the ITS is to detect when a student appears to be struggling while programming in Alice. Based upon where the ITS detects the student to be struggling, it will suggest one or more tutorials for the student to attempt to complete, prior to returning to the student's original program.

This paper's focus is on the tutorials that have been created to support the ITS. While a brief description of ITS's is provided, the intent is to do no more than provide a justification for our research approach. Prior to covering the overall system, it is necessary to argue that the tutorials "work" in the sense of helping students to understand a particular programming concept.

2. RELATED RESEARCH

ITS: The earliest ITSs date back at least to the 1970s. They have increased in popularity since the 1990s as more computers have been available in education applications and more intelligent methods have been utilized to improve the instructional effectiveness of ITSs. Intelligent tutoring systems have been utilized in different disciplines including mathematics, physics, chemistry and biomedical education. Some successful examples of ITSs include: ANDES for physics [8], AutoTutor for Newtonian physics, computer literacy, and scientific reasoning [11], PACT for algebra [16], SHERLOCK for electronics troubleshooting [17], and a tutor system for Chemical Engineering [4]. For example, the PCAT cognitive tutor for algebra has been studied in classrooms with 470 students for one whole year. Students in the experimental classes have been shown to outperform students in control classes (i.e., standard classes) by 50-100% on targeted practical problem solving skills and by 10-25% on standardized tests.

Some prior research work has been conducted to develop tutoring systems for computer programming education. Early systems tended to focus on identification of student errors in completed programs. These systems include Proust and Chiron [22], MENO II [26], and LispTutor [2]. Some tutoring systems use enhanced integrated development environments (IDEs). IDE tutoring systems (e.g., [23]) generally help students to identify syntactic or logic errors and students need to figure out how to fix these errors based on the information provided by the systems. The cognitive tutors go beyond the IDE approach by providing more direct feedback/suggestions. Cognitive tutors are based on the Adaptive Control of Thought-Relational (ACT-R) theory in cognitive psychology [1, 3, and 5]. In particular, cognitive tutors analyze both domain knowledge and problem-solving strategies. A cognitive model is built to represent the paths that students may use to solve problems. When a student works on the problem, the cognitive model identifies the solution path of the student and provides corresponding feedback/suggestions with respect to how the student tries to solve the task. The cognitive tutors have been applied to teach some basic programming concepts and production rules in programming [13, 5]. It has been shown by Jin in [13] that CS1 students taught with cognitive intelligent tutors outperform students in standard classrooms by more than 50% in solving targeted programming questions. However, it is generally quite time consuming to construct the cognitive models on many concepts and problems for a large population of students.

The Intelligent Learning Material Delivery Agent (ILMDA) approach uses a case-based reasoning method to suggest instructional materials through analyzing students' performance in answering questions of different topics [24, 25]. In particular, ILMDA stores different cases of instructional strategies and specific solutions. The case that best matches a current instructional situation will be retrieved and adapted in an online manner. A set of real world studies have been conducted by Soh et al. for a large CS1 course in two years to demonstrate that the intelligent ILMDA tutoring system can deliver appropriate exercise problems to students, which help them learn the materials more effectively and efficiently. WebWork is a Web-based homework delivery and grading system, which automatically compiles students' submissions and evaluates on some datasets [7, 10]. However, WebWork does not provide enough feedback/suggestions to facilitate students' learning. Its focus is more towards assessment of student learning/knowledge.

Tutorial systems: The majority of tutorial systems tend to present text based instruction as a separate window with images describing what the user should be doing. Such systems have often been shown to be hard on users [15]. Other approaches have included information within the actual context of the application itself. Such systems have included graphical overlays [9] and embedded videos [12], and have shown limited success. The system chosen here is Kelleher's stencils [14], a graphical overlay system that has been shown to be successful (in terms of speed and retention) in helping students to learn an application.

3. TUTORIALS

3.1 Stencils

Kelleher's stencils provide a means to interactively teach Alice within the Alice environment itself.

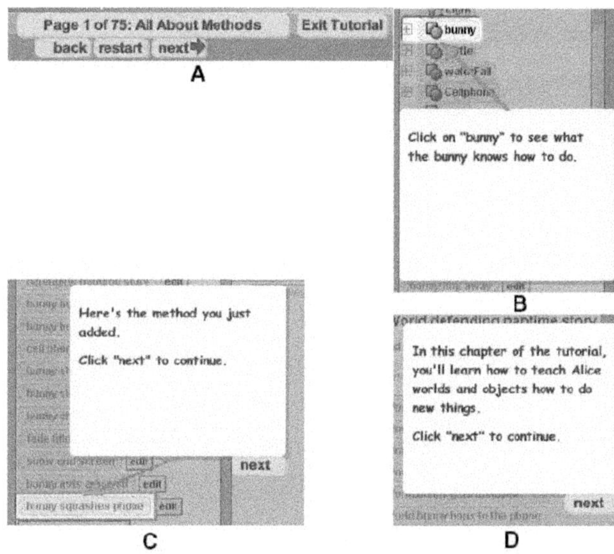

Figure 1. From [14], image A shows the navigation bar, B shows a hole with an associated note, C shows a frame with a note, and D is a standalone note.

Whereas Kelleher used stencils to teach the Alice environment, we have designed stencil tutorials to actually teach programming concepts. The appeal of Kelleher's stencils is that they provide a lovely vehicle to allow students to incrementally develop solutions to a problem. And the units of incremental development can be made arbitrarily large or small.

3.2 Teaching Alice

We developed a total of thirteen tutorials that teach basic programming concepts with which novices often have difficulties, including parameter passing, nesting of control statements, repetition (definite and indefinite loops), and list manipulation. These topics were chosen either because of their centrality in introductory programming or because they were reported as being harder to teach (as far as students' abilities to understand the concepts) as part of the annual educator survey sent out to the 3000+ member Alice educator mailing list. Along with each tutorial, a paired activity was designed to measure the extent to which the student learned the concept presented in the tutorial.

For each tutorial, we created a storyline and stated the goal of the tutorial, in order to make the tutorials engaging. This fits with our general problem solving approach we use to the teaching of Alice.

Table 1. List of tutorials and concepts taught

No.	Tutorial Name	Concepts taught
1	Snowpeople	Nesting of control statements – a general introduction to Alice programming
2	Taxi	While loops – simple conditions
3	Bunny baby	While loops – complex loop condition
4	Penguins	While loops – using a function call within the loop condition
5	Rescue	While loops – multiple loops with user-defined methods being added
6	Animals	If statement and While loops – nesting of these structures
7	Husky	If statement and While loops – a second, more complex nesting of these control structures
8	Mars Rover	For loops and parameter passing – using a simple numeric parameter
9	Jump and Spin	Parameter passing – multiple types, and more complex use of parameters
10	Moo	Lists and parameter passing
11	Gather	Parameter passing with multiple parameters
12	Midpoint	Recursion and While loops
13	Exercise	Parameter passing and lists, including some Alice idiosyncrasies

In the snowpeople tutorial, the student has to create a scene where a snowman unsuccessfully tries to grab a snowwoman's attention. In order to create this scene, the student has to nest control statements inside one another.

The goal of the taxi tutorial is to teach the concept of while loops to the student. The student has to help Alice catch up with a taxi that is already moving forward. The student has to make Alice and the taxi move while Alice has not reached the taxi's rear.

The bunny baby tutorial teaches students how to use a complex while loop condition. Three bunnies are introduced in the tutorial – a mother, a father, and a baby. Initially, the mother and the father are away from the baby. The bunny baby starts to cry, and his parents come back to the baby to soothe him. The student has to use a complex while condition to make the bunny baby cry while any of his parents is not present.

In the penguin tutorial, the student has to use a while loop to switch the positions of two penguins. The exact distance between the penguins is not given, so the student has to use a while loop and a relative distance function to switch the penguins. Initially, the two penguins are apart by a few meters; one penguin is on the other's left. The student has to use a while loop to make the penguins move while they have not switched their positions.

In the rescue tutorial, the student creates a rescue scene where a rescue ship carries people from a spaceship that is crashing into the ocean. This tutorial also makes the student create his/her own methods. The student must first use a while loop to write a method that makes the spaceship fall into the ocean while its body is still above the ocean. Then the student should create two methods, one of which makes the rescue ship approach the spaceship, and the other that makes the rescue ship approach the island. Finally, the student has to use a while loop to put things together and make the rescue ship fly back and forth between the island and the falling spaceship.

In the first part of the animals tutorial, the student has to use an if statement and a while loop to help a chicken cross the street. A bunny is sitting in the chicken's way, so the chicken has to jump over it if it gets close to the bunny. The student is provided with a method that makes the chicken hop forward a certain distance. The student must execute this method if the chicken is close to the bunny. The student must use a while loop to make the chicken move forward while it has not reached the destination at the other side of the road.

The second part of the animals tutorial introduces another way to use an if statement and a while loop to achieve the same goal. This time, the student has to make a hare cross the street by hopping over the bunny. Unlike in the first part of the tutorial, where the chicken moved forward outside the if statement, this time the student makes the hare move forward inside the if statement.

In the husky tutorial, the student creates a scene where a husky chases a chicken. A while loop is used to make the husky chase the chicken while it has not reached the chicken. However, if the husky gets too close to the chicken, the chicken runs away much faster than the husky. As a result, the husky can never catch the chicken. Also in this tutorial, the student learns how to make the camera follow the husky, so that the husky and the chicken do not go out of the student's sight.

In the mars rover activity, the student has to write a method that makes a mars rover draw a square. This method takes a numeric parameter that determines the side length of the square. In addition to learning how to create a method that takes a numeric parameter, the student learns how to use a loop in order to make the rover draw a square.

In the jump and spin tutorial, the student has to write a method that takes an object parameter in order to make several animals jump and spin at the same time.

In the moo tutorial, the student learns how to use a list of objects and a method that takes an object parameter to make five cows moo. The initial goal stated in the beginning of this tutorial is to make the five cows moo at the same time. Then, the tutorial lets the student explore what happens if he/she changes the list tile from "For All Together" to "For All In Order." After the student sees that this change makes the cows moo one by one, the tutorial goes on to show what happens if the student changes the order of items in the list.

In the gather tutorial, the student learns to create a method that takes more than one parameter. There are six animals in the tutorial – two cows, two chickens, and two bunnies. The student has to make the animals gather by species. The student must write a method that takes two object parameters and that makes the animal passed in as the second parameter to go to the animal passed in as the first parameter. Then the student should use this method to make the animals gather by species.

In the first part of the midpoint tutorial, the student learns to use a while loop in order to help a chicken find the midpoint between two cones. At the beginning of the tutorial, the chicken stands right next to one cone and is facing the other cone. The student must use a while loop to make the chicken move forward while its distance to the first cone is smaller than its distance to the second cone.

In the second part of the midpoint tutorial, the student is introduced to recursion. The student writes a recursive method called "findMid" that makes the chicken find the midpoint of the two cones by first going to the second cone and then tracing back half the distance.

In the exercise tutorial, there are four characters – three classmates and one teacher. In the first part of the exercise tutorial, the student has to make the four characters into a list, and then use that list to make the classmates turn to the teacher. In the second part of the tutorial, the student should use the same list to make the characters raise their arms. Since the student cannot directly access the parts of the item in the list, the student must use a "part named" function in order to make the characters raise their arms.

4. APPROACH

We were greatly influenced by a keynote address John Sweller gave at ICER in 2008. In a conversation with Sweller after the keynote, when asked how cognitive load theory could be applied to the teaching of introductory programming, Sweller proposed providing a great number of examples illustrating each particular programming concept. In the spirit of this suggestion, we chose to build each tutorial as a series of missteps. In other words, we intentionally have the students make all of the common mistakes we have observed as introductory computer science instructors, and observe what happens as a result. Because Alice provides such a strong visual environment, the student immediately sees what is going wrong when the animation "misbehaves". Our intent was to provide students with a collection of relationships between errors and the results of those errors. So, rather than, as Sweller suggests, providing students with a collection of working examples, we instead provide the student with an awareness of what errors lead to what incorrect results. So that later, when the student comes across a particular error, that student will recognize the error and understand what logical flaw led to its creation.

Although the tutorials themselves prevent the students from going on to the next step if the students do not follow the instructions carefully, the tutorials do have the students make mistakes so that the students can learn from them. In almost every tutorial, we introduce many errors that students often make. By having the students go through a mistake and see what happens for themselves, we made our tutorials educational and interactive. In their present form, the tutorials ask students what went wrong, but do not collect student responses, and instead provide our responses in a later tutorial frame.

We illustrate by example, the nature of the errors we introduce with while loops. We have found that while loops are a rich source of student errors, both because the Boolean condition determining whether or not the while loop is to be entered is tricky, as well as from the fact that it is often unclear exactly which instructions belong within the while loop, rather than before or after it.

Mistakes with while loops we introduce in the tutorials include:

- The opposite of the Boolean condition to determine if the while loop should be entered
- Boolean conditions that are off by one (leading to the while loop being entered one too many or one too few times.
- Using a Boolean condition of (A and B) when (A or B) is warranted, and vice versa.
- Errors with negation of Boolean conditions (such as incorrectly trying to apply DeMorgan's laws).
- Having the student place a method that should be called once, prior to entry to the while loop to instead be called within the body of the while loop.
- Having a student place a method that should be called within the body of the while loop to instead be called prior to the while loop or after the while loop.
- Errors involving nesting of control structures (multiple while loops or while loops and if statements).

After each error is made, and the student tries to run the world with the error, the tutorial asks the student to reflect on what went wrong, and how the student knew what was going wrong. As mentioned earlier, we are not presently capturing the student responses – we are simply asking the student to consider what went wrong before providing our answer.

By allowing the students to experience errors before being shown (and building) a correct solution, we try to help the students understand common mistakes.

5. DISCUSSION/RESULTS

We tested our tutorials and activities on nine undergraduates with little or no prior knowledge in computer science, students who self-reported minimal to no prior programming experience. All of the students were asked to complete the initial tutorial with no help. The initial tutorial introduced the students to programming in Alice. After completing the initial tutorial, we had the students complete differing sequences of the other tutorials. Each tutorial topic was designed to be as focused on a single programming concept as was possible. In order to determine that the student had mastered the particular programming topic, we asked the student to solve an alternate problem (we use the term activity, to differentiate it from the act of completing the tutorial). The solution to the alternate problem required an understanding of the topic that was taught in the tutorial. For the activity, we showed the student a youtube video of what a successful solution could look like, and then gave the student an initially setup world, without any code. The student was then given time to complete the activity, and we determined the extent to which the student's solution actually solved the problem posed in the activity. In addition to observing the student working on the activity, we modified Alice to capture all of the student's drags and drops, as well as the student's intended drops (when an attempt to drag and drop a syntactically invalid tile would be blocked by Alice). On average, each student spent 20 minutes on a tutorial and 11 minutes on an activity. The initial Alice tutorial took slightly longer to complete than the others.

Students were asked to describe their reactions to the tutorials. In 68% of the trials, the participant answered that the instructions in the tutorial were very clear, with the remaining students reporting that the instructions were mostly clear. In 73% of the trials, the participant answered that they learned a lot from the tutorial, with the remainder reporting that they had learned a medium amount from the tutorials. More significantly, all participants were able to correctly solve the problem posed by the activity (associated with the tutorial). Somewhat surprisingly, there were a couple of cases where we gave the student an activity that was harder than the associated tutorial (an activity that was paired with a more advanced tutorial). In each of these cases, the student was still able to complete the activity (though it took a fair bit more time).

In 60% of the trials, the participant answered that the tutorial was easy to walk through. In 30% of the trials, the participant answered that the tutorial was of medium difficulty. Based on the first students' observations, changes were made to the tutorials so that later students indicated increasing ease with the tutorials.

We tested the tutorials on both Mac and Windows. There was no significant difference between students who used Mac and those who used Windows. We tested the tutorials on students with different majors, spanning Social Science, Natural Science, Engineering, and Arts and Humanities. There was no significant difference between the performances of the students with different majors. However, some Social Science and Arts and Humanities majors performed unusually well, possibly because they seemed to have read and understood the tutorial instructions better than others.

The tutorial that took the longest time to complete was the snowpeople tutorial, which we gave to the students for their first tutorial experience. It took some time for the students to get used to the interface and the tutorial system. After the first tutorial, the students finished the tutorials in much less time and with fewer errors.

We found two somewhat significant problems with the use of Kelleher's stencils. The first was that each step of the tutorial needed to be completed exactly correctly by the student. While this makes sense in general, Alice includes a Do Together structure where the instructions within the Do Together block all occur simultaneously. Thus, the order of instructions should not matter. However, the stencils did require that the students' instructions exactly matched the "canonical solution", which seemed wrong from a pedagogic perspective. While we explained this situation within the stencil notes, this is clearly "wrong" with respect to how the stencils should work with respect to the tutorials. In the same vein, students who added extraneous parameters on method calls (such as the Style parameter), parameters that really have nothing to do with the lesson the tutorial was trying to teach, got their code flagged as being incorrect by the stencil system.

The second problem with the stencil tutorial system was that it was not possible to provide the students information about why their solution did not match the canonical solution. They were simply sent back to the last time their solution matched the canonical solution. This situation was somewhat ameliorated by the use of very small incremental steps within the tutorial system, but nevertheless, this situation was unfortunate.

Overall, we were satisfied with the performance of the stencil tutorials. Students in general felt comfortable with the tutorials themselves, and the students' abilities to correctly solve the activity problems provides evidence that the students were able to understand the concepts being presented.

During the winter 2012 quarter, we are using the tutorials we have created with a much larger group of students in an introductory programming for non-majors course (with approximately 120 students). Students are (randomly) asked to download either the standard version of Alice (which ships with four standard stencil tutorials that explain how animation works in Alice, but do not attempt to teach programming in Alice) or with a version of Alice that contains our tutorials. Pre- and post-test are being conducted (with respect to Alice programming content knowledge), and students will be asked to fill out surveys at the end of the term investigating whether they used the tutorials, and if so if they found the tutorials helpful.

6. FUTURE WORK

Work is continuing on the construction of the overall ITS. It is intended that the ITS will serve two purposes. The first is for the ITS to help the student to navigate through the tutorials as the student learns to program in Alice. Current work in this area includes designing a way to measure how close students' attempts at solutions to the activities are to a canonical solution. While the problem of determining whether two programs, in general, are equivalent is not solvable, by keeping the activities short, and using various heuristics to determine the similarities between a student's sample solution and a canonical solution. That, coupled with the time it takes for a student to complete an activity will hopefully provide enough information to the ITS to determine whether the student understands the particular topic being taught.

The second area of development for the ITS is in detecting when a student is struggling with a particular programming concept when attempting to solve a larger programming project. A student log system has been created to capture major student actions (and student intended actions) with Alice. It is in the process of being refined so as to be able to detect off-task behavior, but also to provide hint generation. It still needs to be made more robust, and then logs can be analyzed to detect when students are struggling on various concepts. In this vein, the ITS can suggest that a student take a particular tutorial when the system detects that a student is stuck in a particular area of a program.

In the interim, as the tutorials created seem to help students to learn various programming concepts in Alice, we are making the tutorials available to the 3000+ member teacher community. There has been significant interest from the community in getting additional self-guided support materials, both from those engaged in distance education as well as from those who are unable to offer their programming students sufficient in-person laboratory guidance (through open and closed laboratories, and the like).

7. ACKNOWLEDGEMENT

This work is partially supported by NSF award DUE 1021975 - Adding an Intelligent Tutoring System to Alice. Any opinions, findings, and conclusions or recommendations expressed in this material are those of the authors and do not necessarily reflect the views of the National Science Foundation.

8. REFERENCES

[1] Anderson, J. R. 1993. Rules of the Mind. Lawrence Erlbaum Associates, Publishers.

[2] Anderson, J.R. and Skwarecki, E. 1986. The automated tutoring of introductory computer programming. Communications of the ACM, 29: 842-849.

[3] Anderson, J. R., Conrad F. G. and Corbett, A. T. 1989. Skill acquisition and the lisp tutor. Cognitive Science 13(4): 467-505.

[4] Baxter, E. 1990. Comparing conventional and resource based education in chemical engineering: student perceptions of a teaching innovation, Higher Education, 19:323-340.

[5] Corbett, A. T. and Anderson, J. R. 1992. Student modeling and mastery learning in a computer-based programming tutor. Proceedings of the International Conference on Intelligent Tutoring Systems.

[6] Cuny, J. 2010. Finding 10,000 teachers. CSTA Voice, 5(6): 1-2.

[7] Gage, M. E. and Pizer, A. K. 1999. WeBWorK – Math homework on the Web. Proceedings of the Annual International Conference on Technology in Collegiate Mathematics.

[8] Gertner A. S. and VanLehn, K. 2000. ANDES: A coached problem solving environment for physics. Proceedings of the International Conference on Intelligent Tutoring Systems.

[9] Gilbert, S., Blessing, S. and Blankenship, L. 2009. The accidental tutor: overlaying an intelligent tutor on an existing user interface. In Proceedings of the 27th international conference extended abstracts on Human factors in computing systems (CHI EA '09). ACM, New York, NY, USA, 4603-4608.

[10] Gotel, O. and Scharff, C. 2007. Adapting an Open-Source Web-based assessment system for the automated assessment of programming problems. Proceedings of IASTED Web-based Education Conference.

[11] Graesser, A. C., VanLehn, K., Rosé, C. P., Jordan, P. W. and Harter, D. 2001. Intelligent tutoring systems with conversational dialogue, AI Magazine, 22(4):39-51.

[12] Grossman, T. and Fitzmaurice, G. 2010. ToolClips: an investigation of contextual video assistance for functionality understanding. In Proceedings of the 28th international conference on Human factors in computing systems (CHI '10). ACM, New York, NY, USA, 1515-1524.

[13] Jin, W. 2008. Pre-programming analysis tutors help students learn basic programming concepts. In Proceedings of the 39th SIGCSE technical symposium on Computer science education (SIGCSE '08). ACM, New York, NY, USA, 276-280.

[14] Kelleher, C. and Pausch, R. 2005. Stencils-based tutorials: design and evaluation. In Proceedings of the SIGCHI conference on Human factors in computing systems (CHI '05). ACM, New York, NY, USA, 541-550.

[15] Knabe, K. 1995. Apple guide: A case study in user-aided design of online help. In Conference companion on Human factors in computing systems (CHI '95), I. Katz, R. Mack, and L. Marks (Eds.). ACM, New York, NY, USA, 286-287.

[16] Koedinger, K. R., Anderson, J. R., Hadley, W. H., and Mark, M. A. 1997. Intelligent tutoring goes to school in the big city, Journal of Artificial Intelligence in Education. 8(1): 30-43.

[17] Lesgold, A., Lajoie, S., Bunzo, M. and Eggan. G. 1992. SHERLOCK: A coached practice environment for an electronics troubleshooting job, in J. H. Larkin and R. W. Chabay (eds.) Computer Assisted Instruction and Intelligent Tutoring Systems, 201-238.

[18] Markoff, J. 2011. Virtual and artificial, but 58,000 want course. New York Times. Available from: http://www.nytimes.com/2011/08/16/science/16stanford.html Accessed 8/31/2011.

[19] Pausch, R. and Forlines, C. 2000. Alice: Model, paint & animate — easy-to-use interactive graphics for the web. SIGGRAPH Comput. Graph., 34(2): 42-43.

[20] Pierce, J., Cobb, T., & Pausch, R. 1998. Alice. ACM SIGGRAPH 98 Conference abstracts and applications. Orlando, Florida, United States.

[21] Pierce, J. S., Christiansen, K., Cosgrove, D., Conway, M., Moskowitz, D., Stearns, B., et al. 1998. Alice: Easy to learn interactive 3d graphics, CHI 98 conference summary on Human factors in computing systems. Los Angeles, California.

[22] Sack, W., Soloway, E. and Weingrad, P. 1992. From PROUST to CHIRON: ITS Design as Iterative Engineering: Intermediate Results are Important! In Larkin, J.H. and Chabay, R.W. (Eds.), Computer-Assisted Instruction and Intelligent Tutoring Systems: Shared Goals and Complementary Approaches. Lawrence Erlbaum Associates, Hillsdale, NJ, 239-274.

[23] Shaffer, S. C. 2005. Ludwig: An online programming tutoring and assessment system, ACM SIGCSE Bulletin, 37(2):56-60.

[24] Soh, L. K., Blank, T., Miller, L. D. and Person, S. 2005. ILMDA: An intelligent learning materials delivery agent and simulation. Proceedings of International Electro-Information Technology Conference.

[25] Soh, L. K., and Blank, T. 2008. Integrating case-based reasoning and meta-learning for a self improving intelligent tutoring system. International Journal of Artificial Intelligence in Education, 18: 27-58.

[26] Soloway, E., E. Rubin, B. Woolf, W.L. Johnson and J. Bonar, 1983. MENO II: An AI-based programming tutor. J. Computer-Based Instruction, 10: 20-34.

[27] Khan Academy. http://www.khanacademy.org/ Accessed 8/31/2011.

Student Reactions to Classroom Lecture Capture

Paul E. Dickson, David I. Warshow,
Alec C. Goebel, and Colin C. Roache
Hampshire College
School of Cognitive Science
893 West St.
Amherst, MA 01002, USA
{pdickson,diw08,acg10,ccr09}@hampshire.edu

W. Richards Adrion
Department of Computer Science
Computer Science Building
University of Massachusetts
Amherst, MA 01003, USA
adrion@cs.umass.edu

ABSTRACT

This paper evaluates the benefits and drawbacks of lecture recording, which aspects of lectures and lecture capture systems are most used, and what additional features and functions would make the experience more effective. We evaluated 4 computer science courses recorded during spring 2011 using our comprehensive lecture capture system PAOL and presented with webMANIC. We discuss the results of student surveys and focus groups and compare these with prior surveys that investigated how students reacted to the availability of online lecture content and how they used these resources in large- and small-scale deployments with both home-grown and commercial lecture capture technologies. The primary motivation for this study was to analyze how lecture capture fits in the context of computer science curricula and pedagogy and about how we can enhance our systems to be more educationally effective.

Categories and Subject Descriptors

H.5.1 [**Multimedia Information Systems**]: Video; I.4.1 [**Digitization and Image Capture**]: Sampling; I.2.10 [-**Vision and Scene Understanding**]: Video analysis; K.3.0 [**Computers and Education**]: General

General Terms

Algorithms, Design

Keywords

Automatic Capture, Lecture Recording, Image Processing, Video Creation, Indexing, Evaluation

1. INTRODUCTION

Systems designed to record lectures have existed for years [2, 3, 9, 11, 21, 15, 17, 19, 28] and use has become more prevalent with increasing class sizes and growing demand for online education. Surveys have shown that various forms of online lecture recordings are extremely popular [4, 8, 20, 24, 25] among students. These systems range from audio/video podcasts to video recordings indexed by PowerPoint slides [17, 21] to comprehensive capture systems that capture whiteboard material and provide search of captured material [2, 6, 9, 28]. Developers of these systems frequently add features to make their capture systems better and we are no different [7]. Less frequently addressed are the aspects of lecture capture most useful for students and most effective for student learning, how recorded lectures fit in to a teaching and learning approach, and which features and functions contribute significantly to student learning.

We surveyed and interviewed students in 4 spring 2011 computer science courses about online lecture content, captured and presented using Presentations Automatically Organized from Lectures (PAOL) and webMANIC [5, 6, 7] (a joint project between UMass Amherst and Hampshire College). Students in each class accessed presentations online during the semester and were surveyed and/or brought into focus groups at semester's end. The information gathered was surprising and in some cases contradicted both our assumptions and results reported in the literature. We use these data to extrapolate what aspects of lecture capture are most important in computer science teaching and learning, how we might adapt PAOL/webMANIC to fit into an overall teaching and learning strategy, and which features and functions we need to (re)introduce or enhance.

2. RELATED WORK

A lot of work has gone into the creation of lecture capture software and many different approaches have been tried. In the literature, can be found research projects, campus efforts, and commercial systems that capture and deliver lecture content using a wide variety of technologies. Few studies report and address the teaching and learning outcomes.

2.1 Related Lecture Capture Systems

Automated lecture capture systems (manual systems have existed for decades) have progressed greatly from initial capture systems at Berkeley [12] and Microsoft [18] that focused on creating virtual directors. While some paths, like manual creation of presentations at UMass [19], have been replaced, others, like the automatically captured and heavily indexed presentation of eClass (originally Classroom 2000) [2], have inspired the creation of many other systems [3, 7, 9, 28].

The best example of simple video recording of lectures is Apple's Podcast Producer [1]. Podcast Producer uses video captured by a camera connected to a computer combined with screen shots from that computer to produce a video podcast of a lecture. As podcasts have simple VCR-like controls, it has minimal scroller-based search capabilities but has the advantage that the lecture presentations produced can be viewed on multiple platforms including smartphones.

Examples of systems that allow minimal indexing include Opencast's Matterhorn project [3] and Panopto [17]. Both capture material using cameras and can get some information from a lecturer's computer. Matterhorn's focus is to create software that is easily accessible and can run on any existing hardware. Panopto's focuses on instantly producing presentations for viewing. It generates index points into lecture presentations by taking snapshots at a set interval or by registering slides changes if the lecturer uses PowerPoint.

Some systems focus heavily on a particular type of content and little on video. Mediasite [21] monitors material being projected by a lecturer's computer and identifies content changes. When changes occur, the content is captured at a high resolution and a thumbnail version of the image is stored for use in an index. When the lecture presentation is viewed, the high-resolution image is displayed next to a video of the lecturer. Camtasia [23] provides software that runs on a lecturer's computer and captures everything that occurs on screen. A video of the lecturer is only included if the lecturer supplies a camera feed and indexing is only created when PowerPoint is used. Camtasia produces a fully dynamic, high-resolution screen capture.

The true descendants of eClass [2] perform total lecture capture, including video, whiteboard, and computer and have automatically generated content-based thumbnail indexes created from all content streams. TeleTeachingTool (TTT) [28] and PAOL [7] produce similar content. TTT captures information using electronic whiteboards and software installed on the lecturer's computer while PAOL uses cameras to capture whiteboard information and an analog signal converter to capture computer content. Both systems identify index points in all content streams through visual inspection and create an index point when content changes.

2.2 Studies and Evaluations

Often studies of lecture capture systems focus on technology performance with at most an effort to determine whether students and instructors "like" the systems or whether class attendance was affected. Large-scale studies have indicated that having lecture content available after class is very popular. One of the largest studies was at the University of Wisconsin Madison [25], where 82% of 7500 undergraduate and graduate students surveyed strongly preferred classes with online lecture content over those without. While this study was sponsored by Mediasite developers, other studies report similar results [4, 8, 20, 24] . Lecture capture popularity with students and (less frequently reported) with lecturers has not translated into wide-scale deployment of commercial or home-grown systems [16]. Whether this is due to the expense, difficulty of using many of the systems, constraints on teaching style and pedagogy, intellectual property issues, or instructor resistance is open for debate [10, 14]. A primary focus of the PAOL, webMANIC, and related projects [7] has been to make the systems transparent, flexible with respect to teaching style, cost effective, and educationally sound.

The results concerning attendance were mixed, with some showing little effect [2, 4, 24] and others showing an increase in absences [14] growing over the term [27].

Verramani and Bradley [25] summarize the five common categories of reasons students use captured online lectures: making up for a missed class, convenience/schedule conflicts, improving retention, improving test performance, and reviewing material in preparation for class. Category importance depends on the study. Most report that having missed class is not a primary reason for viewing lectures [8, 20] but that preparing for exams and homework is very common. The impact of lecture capture on student performance is largely inconclusive [8, 2]. Teaching style [8, 10] and the age/experience of students [13, 8] seem to be factors in the effectiveness of online lecture content.

Wieling and Hoffman [26] suggest that recording face-to-face lectures is an easy extension of a traditional course and is of practical importance, but we must consider how instructional delivery might be changed to best use these technologies. Lecture capture systems, perhaps delivered via Web2.0 cloud platforms, have significant potential [10] but need more study and adaptation before they become standard tools in teaching and learning.

3. PAOL/WEBMANIC OVERVIEW

What distinguishes PAOL/webMANIC from most other capture systems is its transparency to the instructor. One need only wear a wireless microphone (recently replaced by a ceiling microphone), no other training or positioning in the classroom is required. There are two main components to PAOL, the lecture capture and processing component and webMANIC, the web-based content interface system.

3.1 Lecture Capture Component

PAOL was designed to capture all content presented in a classroom and use it to create an easily navigable presentation. PAOL has a pair of high-resolution cameras that have fixed views of the front of the room and give complete coverage of a double-wide whiteboard (Figure 1). Images from these cameras are used to capture whiteboard content and create the lecturer video. An analog capture device captures all computer content by intercepting the signal sent to a computer projector and converting it into a sequence of images for processing. The setup runs transparently, requiring only that the lecturer wear a microphone. Lecture start and stop times with leeway for faculty running over time are scheduled on a server that captures from all devices and does all processing. The processing, presentation creation, and posting to the web occur without human intervention.

The heart of this system is the processing. The lecturer video is generated by creating a virtual pan-tilt camera that follows the lecturer by cropping smaller image frames from the larger high-resolution images (Figure 2). The high-resolution images are also processed to create clean whiteboard images with the instructor removed [6]. These images are then sequentially compared to find differences and when the differences are great enough, the image is stored and a thumbnail is created for the index. A large difference means that new content has been presented and that a new index point is necessary. The stored image is then reprocessed for clarity, with contrast being heightened and the whiteboard being made a more pure white (Figure 3).

A similar process is used for computer images. The screen is sampled, the resulting images are sequentially compared, and noisy images are removed [5]. Large differences between

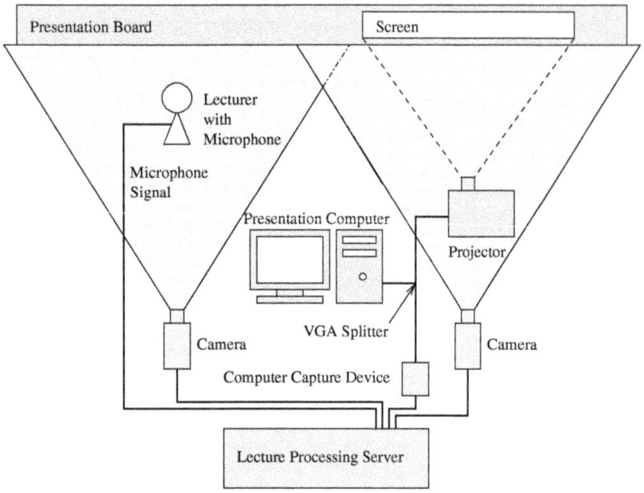

Figure 1: System configuration.

Figure 2: Original image and cropped video frame.

images cause the current computer image to be saved and a thumbnail of it created for the index (Figure 4).

The result of these processes is a video that follows the lecturer, thumbnails of content presented, and the times the content occurs, and high-resolution images of content [7].

3.2 Web-based Interface Component

webMANIC uses the basic format generally used by capture systems to present content. The presentations include the thumbnail-based index, a video of the lecturer, and a window containing an enlargement of the current captured content. When the captured content includes both whiteboard and computer information, a system that presents only one at a time does a poor job of presenting material when the lecturer refers to content in both. If the presentation system presents windows for each type of content, lack of screen real estate becomes an issue since captured content is high resolution. Our solution is web-based software with resizable and movable content windows (Figure 5).

Figure 3: Original image captured and processed saved image.

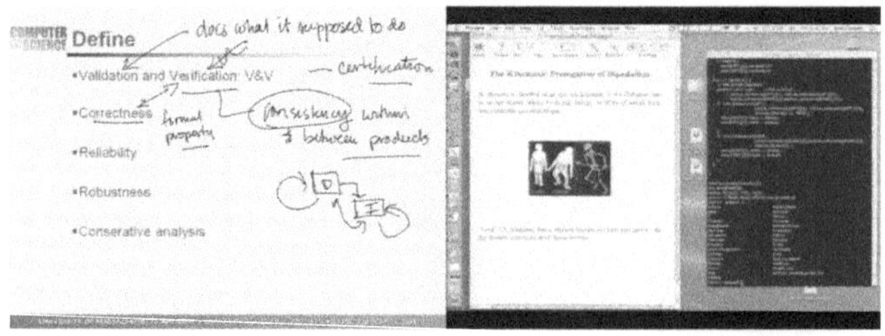

Figure 4: Sample computer captured images.

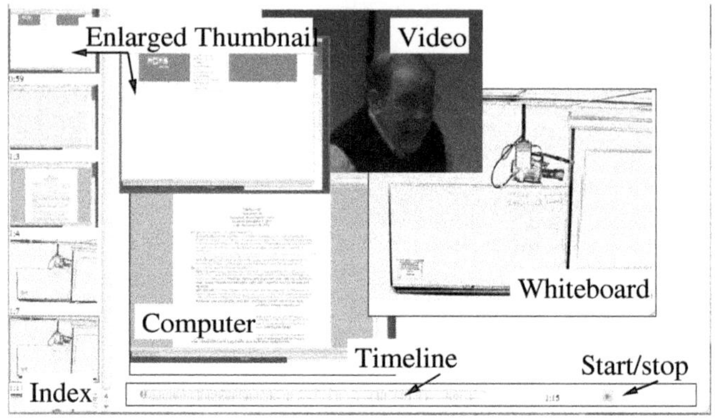

Figure 5: The webMANIC lecture presenter.

The thumbnail-based index and the timeline view of video position are fixed but all other windows are movable and resizable. enabling users to choose the content to view and the degree of detail. One major problem with thumbnail-based indexes is that thumbnails of projected content are generally so small that a viewer cannot see sufficient detail to determine whether the desired content is included. To correct this, our interface projects an enlargement of a given thumbnail in front of all content if the viewer puts the mouse over that thumbnail, (Figure 5).

4. EVALUATION

We solicited input from students in 4 computer science courses recorded at the UMass Amherst in spring 2011. The 4 courses were 220 Programming Methodology, 311 Introduction to Algorithms, and 453 Computer Networks (all undergraduate) and 677 Operating Systems (graduate).

Our goal was to examine the uptake of online lecture recordings in classes where use was not required or in some cases even encouraged. We asked faculty teaching in the PAOL-equipped classroom whether they were willing to allow us to record and deliver their lecture content. While all faculty were interested enough in our experiment to wear a wireless microphone during the lectures (the only constraint placed on the person being recorded), the level of commitment varied. We did not ask them to participate beyond allowing recording. One instructor failed to inform his students of the location of the recorded material; another scheduled extra class recordings in advance of classes he had to miss. These were available online, but a TA also showed the online content during the regularly scheduled time period. The faculty teaching two of the courses have a history of recording the audio or audio/screen capture of the lectures in their classes. None of the faculty whose classes

			Used for				
Course	Response Rate	Used > 1 or 2 Times	Homework	Exam	Missed Class	Curiosity	General Review
UGrad	28%	35%	33%	55%	50%	48%	8%
Grad	27%	67%	42%	83%	50%	17%	0%
Total	28%	42%	35%	62%	50%	40%	6%

Table 1: Survey responses by education status.

			Used for				
Course	Response Rate	Used > 1 or 2 Times	Homework	Exam	Missed Class	Curiosity	General Review
220	35%	38%	24%	57%	48%	48%	10%
311	27%	33%	33%	53%	53%	40%	7%
453	15%	25%	75%	50%	50%	75%	0%
677	27%	67%	42%	83%	50%	17%	0%

Table 2: Survey responses by course.

were recorded is associated with the lecture capture project and none of the faculty or students were trained in the use of the capture or presentation system. The captured lectures can be found at http://prussian.cs.umass.edu/S11/.

At the end of the semester, faculty members were asked to encourage students to fill out a survey about their experience using the captured lecture material. Students were also contacted via a general email invitation. A member of the PAOL/webMANIC project team attended one lecture of each course to encourage students to attend one of two focus groups held. For a voluntary survey where those surveyed were not directly involved with the courses and where students were given little incentive to participate, the response rate was very good for 3 of the 4 courses (2). Course 453, where the professor failed to mention the availability of lecture recordings nor provide a link to the lectures from the class website, was the exception. The students in the course who viewed material were either in other courses being recorded and saw that the recordings existed or were told by those students about the recordings.

We analyzed the responses into two categories: usage and features. Usage represents when and how students used the captured lectures. We asked which features students found most and least useful and which they would like to see added or enhanced in captured lecture presentations. We compare the outcomes with other studies. With the goal of increasing the use and efficacy of PAOL/webMANIC, we describe how we intend to extend functionality and make the interface more intuitive and suggest ways that instructors can incorporate lecture recordings in their classes.

4.1 Usage

Tables 1 and 2 show results by course and by level, respectively, from the sections of the surveys about frequency and mode of usage. Comparing graduate students with undergraduate (Table 1) in terms of frequency of usage shows a far greater percentage of graduate students than undergraduate students frequently accessing recorded lectures. Graduate students also used the captured material to prepare for exams and to help with homework assignments more than undergraduate students did. The higher frequency of use and the purpose for using the content by graduate students could be the result of maturity [8] or the demanding content. Significant factors clearly include strong instructor encouragement and availability of prerecorded makeup classes.

Course by course data (Table 2) show that the few students in 453 who accessed the recorded content initially did so out of curiosity but ended up using it for preparing for exams and homework. While this was only 15% of the class, the fact that they found it on their own and used it is significant. Across all of the courses, the majority of use came from students looking to review specific material for exams or to view a class that they missed; very few watched lectures for general review of material. Except for review, these results are similar to those found in other studies. The surprising lack of use for review (which we correlate with class preparation or reflecting on issues not completely understood during class) may result from how we asked the question. Most other studies showed significant use for class preparation. When instructors referenced the recorded lecture material in their teaching, usage rose.

General comments on PAOL/webMANIC showed that students liked having access to the material and felt that it improved their learning of the material. They were generally enthusiastic about the concept but had concerns with specific details in the webMANIC interface. Most indicated that they would really like to have a new and improved. version. This was not unexpected in classes where students had not been instructed on how to use the interface effectively, but it also pointed to some issues that need correction.

We have limited data regarding lecture capture's contribution to learning. Comparing grades is not the best measure, since the makeup of courses (progress through major, overall student background) may change dramatically. Of the 4 courses in this study, only 2 had previously been taught by the same professor. In the one case where enrollment was somewhat comparable (Figure 6), we can see improvement given the caveat concerning student background and preparation. Other studies [2, 20] have reported similar difficulties in correlating grades with use of lecture capture material. We are recording lectures again in spring 2012 for many of the same classes and hope to gather more conclusive results.

Overall our results were similar to those observed in earlier, smaller-scale experiments with PAOL/webMANIC. We found similar categorization to Verramani [25]. In all classes and at all levels, the online content was used to study for an exam more than or as frequently as to make up for a missed class. More aggressive and integrated use of recorded lectures within an overall teaching strategy might result in a drop in attendance. During the previous semester, we

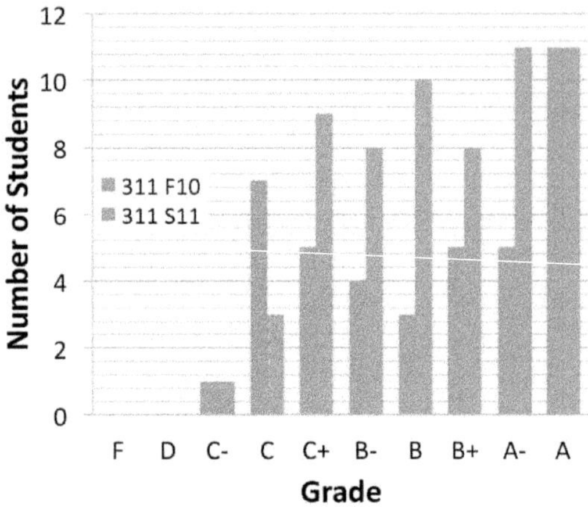

Figure 6: Final grades for 311.

recorded several lectures using a Flip camera [22] and did observe a drop in attendance toward the end of the semester.

4.2 Features

Usage data only tell half the story; the other half comes from sections of the survey covering features the students felt were missing, open-ended survey question responses, and focus groups. While many responses were directed at the webMANIC interface and not the PAOL-captured content, the information gathered can be extrapolated to lecture capture in general. Figure 7 shows that graduate students were generally more interested in more features being added than were undergraduate students. These data also suggest that while certain students would like to have certain features, a feature-rich viewing environment is not a priority for students in general. This contradicts our assumption that students would find more features more useful.

The ability to download the entire lecture and search (underlined Figure 7) were the only features that all students strongly felt would be useful. These 3 features all make it easier for students to navigate within and across lectures. Tables 1 and 2 show that students use the recorded lecture material primarily to study for exams or to work on homework assignments., and text search for a lecture and within a lecture make it easier for students to find specific information. The lectures are saved on servers but only cached for a week and initial download of uncached lectures can take some time. Thus the ability to download the entire lecture enhances navigation and improves searching within streamed material by reducing the time lag caused by jumping to a video segment not yet downloaded from the server.

Approximately half of the students felt that video was most important while the other half thought that having video linked to the corresponding whiteboard and computer images was most important. These bimodal data, when looked at in the context of usage (study, missed class), support our belief that students using the recorded material to make up a missed class are likely to watch the lectures sequentially and would prefer video, while those using content for study prefer enhanced navigation. When students were asked about the least effective feature, responses varied but were related to issues with audio syncing of the video, how video was too zoomed in on the professor, and the inability to search the text of the lecture. Thus, students priorities

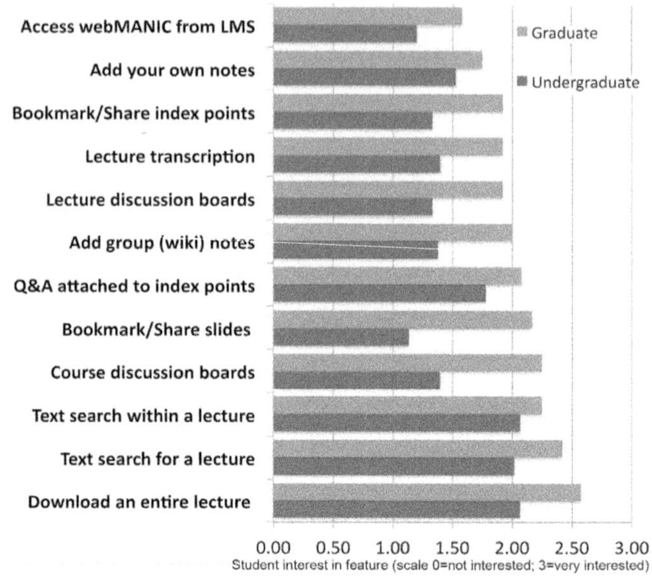

Figure 7: Desired features identified in surveys and focus groups.

are somewhat divided between wanting to review a record of the in-class experience and being able to easily search the class recordings for review and study.

Student preference for the video feature contrasts with the criticism of the quality of the video. The ability to capture and synchronize computer and whiteboard material is a strength of the PAOL capture system, but quality video was not a priority. Creating videos by animating a series of edited still images results in jerky video slightly out of sync with the audio because of inconsistent camera frame rate. These problems are currently being addressed. In some newly instrumented rooms we are directly capturing HD video rather than processing it from the same image set used for whiteboard capture. When specifically queried about their preference for the video, students responded that easy-to-read whiteboard and computer still frames makes video quality unimportant. They wanted the video to be zoomed out so that they could see lecturer gesturing.

In the focus groups, students said that the captured lectures were good for review and to make up for missed classes, but (as reported in many other studies) were not a substitute for live lectures. All students attended the recorded classes and said they only needed a recording for reviewing material. Students were very opposed to recorded lectures replacing class time. We currently have no data on live versus solely recorded classes, but student perception was that live learning was more important.

Capturing whiteboard content was one of our highest priorities but is seldom available in other systems, which limits lecture capture to slide presentations or screen capture. To ensure that nothing written or drawn on the board was missed and that the whiteboard images were easily readable, a large number of images were captured and processed. This increased the index points created from whiteboard images to over 100 index points per lecture. When asked, students responded that having a large number of index points was more a distraction than a benefit. They were less interested in missing whiteboard content than in easily navigating to material. Their answers reinforced that better search and navigation was among the students' highest priorities.

5. CONCLUSIONS

Students are interested in having recorded lectures available and believe that they help in learning. Our analysis of features supports our contention that better navigation and search coupled with cost effectiveness, ease of use, and transparency for the instructors will spur wider acceptance. We are capturing classes that are not strictly traditional lecture formats and will be increasing these in the future.

6. REFERENCES

[1] Apple. Apple-mac os x server snow leopard-podcast producer 2. http://www.apple.com/server/macosx/features/podcast-producer.html, Jan 2010.

[2] J. A. Brotherton and G. D. Abowd. Lessons learned from eclass: Assessing automated capture and access in the classroom. *ACM Trans. Comput.-Hum. Interact.*, 11(2):121–155, 2004.

[3] Opencast Community. Opencast | community | projects. http://www.opencastproject.org/, Aug 2010.

[4] S. Davis, A. Connolly, and E. Linfield. Lecture capture: Making the most of face-to-face learning. *In Engineering Education: Journal of the Higher Education Academy Engineering Subject Centre*, 4(2):4–13, 2009.

[5] P. Dickson, W. R. Adrion, and A. Hanson. Automatic capture of significant points in a computer based presentation. In *Proceedings of ISM '06*, pages 921–926, Washington, DC, 2006. IEEE Computer Society.

[6] P. E. Dickson, W. R. Adrion, and A. R. Hanson. Automatic creation of indexed presentations from classroom lectures. In *Proceedings of ITiCSE '08*, pages 12–16, New York, 2008. ACM.

[7] P. E. Dickson, W. R. Adrion, A. R. Hanson, and D. T. Arbour. First experiences with a classroom recording system. In *Proceedings of ITiCSE '09*, pages 298–302, New York, 2009. ACM.

[8] M. Gosper, D. Green, M. McNeill, R. Phillips, G. Preston, and K. Woo. The impact of web-based lecture technologies on current and future practices in learning and teaching. Technical report, Macquarie University, April 2008. http://www.cpd.mq.edu.au/teaching/wblt/research/ report.html.

[9] W. Hurst. Indexing, searching, and retrieving of recorded live presentations with the aof (authoring on the fly) search engine. In *Proceedings of SIGIR '02*, pages 447–447, New York, 2002. ACM Press.

[10] J. Kim. Capturing lectures: No brainer or sticky wicket? Research Bulletin 24, EDUCAUSE Center for Applied Research, Boulder, CO, 2009. http://www.educause.edu/ecar.

[11] Q. Liu, Y. Rui, A. Gupta, and J. J. Cadiz. Automating camera management for lecture room environments. In *Proceedings of SIGCHI '01*, pages 442–449. ACM Press, 2001.

[12] E. Machnicki and L. A. Rowe. Virtual director: Automating a webcast. In *Multimedia Computing and Networking 2002, Proc. IS&T/SPIE Symposium*, pages 208–225, 2002.

[13] R. E. Mayer. *Learning and instruction.* Prentice Hall, New Jersey, 2008.

[14] N. McKinlay. The vanishing student trick - the trouble with recording lectures. http://www.utas.edu.au/arts/flexarts/vanishing.pdf, Aug 2007.

[15] S. Mukhopadhyay and B. Smith. Passive capture and structuring of lectures. In *Proceedings of ACM MULTIMEDIA '99 (Part 1)*, pages 477–487. ACM Press, 1999.

[16] D. Nagel. Lecture capture: No longer optional? www.campustechnology.com/Articles/2008/09/Lecture-Capture-No-Longer-Optional.aspx, Sept 2008.

[17] Panopto. welcome to panopto. http://www.panopto.com/, Mar 2008.

[18] Y. Rui, L. He, A. Gupta, and Q. Liu. Building an intelligent camera management system. In *Proceedings of ACM MULTIMEDIA '01*, pages 2–11. ACM Press, 2001.

[19] A. Schapira, K. de Vries, and C. Pedregal-Martin. Manic: An open-source system to create and deliver courses over the internet. In *Proceedings of SAINT-W '01*, page 21, Washington, DC, 2001. IEEE Computer Society.

[20] A. Settle, L. Dettori, and M. J. Davidson. Does lecture capture make a difference for students in traditional classrooms. In *Proceedings of ITiCSE '11*, ITiCSE '11, pages 78–82, New York, 2011. ACM.

[21] SonicFoundry. Mediasite by sonic foundry - create online multimedia presentations, briefings and courses automatically. http://www.sonicfoundry.com/mediasite/, Jan 2010.

[22] E. Ssebanakitta, P. E. Dickson, and W. R. Adrion. Manic content delivery in a mobile application. In *Proceedings of FIE '10*, Oct 2010.

[23] TechSmith. Camtasia studio screen recorder for demos, presentations and training. http://www.techsmith.com/camtasia.asp, Dec 2007.

[24] I. N. Toppin. Video lecture capture (vlc) system: A comparison of student versus faculty perceptions. *Education and Information Technologies*, 16(4):383–393, August 2010.

[25] R. Veeramani and S. Bradley. U-w madison online-learning study: Insights regarding undergraduate preference for lecture capture. http://www.lecture capture.com/index.php?/topic/238-insights-regarding-undergraduate-preference-for-lecture-capture/, July 2008.

[26] M. B. Wieling and W. H. A. Hofman. The impact of online video lecture recordings and automated feedback on student performance. *Comput. Educ.*, 54:992–998, May 2010.

[27] J. Williams and M. Fardon. On-demand internet-transmitted lecture recordings: attempting to enhance and support the student experience. In *Proceedings of Alt-C 2005*, pages 153–161, 2005.

[28] P. Ziewer. Navigational indices and content interlinkage on the fly. In *Proceedings of ISM '06*, pages 915–920, Washington, DC, 2006. IEEE Computer Society.

Beyond PDF and ePub: Toward an Interactive Textbook

Brad Miller
Luther College
700 College Dr.
Decorah, IA 52101
bmiller@luther.edu

David Ranum
Luther College
700 College Dr.
Decorah, IA 52101
ranum@luther.edu

ABSTRACT

This paper describes a new and unique vision for electronic textbooks. It incorporates a number of active components such as video, code editing and execution, and code visualization as a way to enhance the typical static electronic book format. In addition, the textbook is created with an open source authoring system that has been developed to allow the instructor to customize the content of the active and passive parts of the text. Initial results of a semester long trial are presented as well.

Categories and Subject Descriptors

I.7.4 [**Computing Methodologies**]: Document and Text ProcessingElectronic Publishing

Keywords

CS1, Python, Sphinx, eBook

1. INTRODUCTION

Teaching introductory computer science courses, especially introductory programming courses, can be hard. Students have varying degrees of interest and varying degrees of ability. For many students this course represents their first exposure to a real computer science course taught by a real computer scientist. This means that we need to find the best way to present students with the information, tools, and techniques that will allow them to be successful learners.

As textbook authors, we desire to find ways to create a book that can be an integral part of the learning that happens in and out of the classroom. It seems that in today's world of fast-paced information and video content, reading a book may not always be the best mode for students. Perhaps students would rather watch a video rather than read the words. Perhaps they would rather try something in an interactive environment rather than see the static output printed on the page. How could we write our next book in such a way that it combines the traditional words on a page with new video and audio content while at the same time allowing a student to experiment and try examples in a safe and easy environment?

In an attempt to answer these questions and reflect on some of the underlying possibilities for assisting students as they learn computer science, we conceived of a new textbook project that was radically different from previous books. In the remainder of this paper, we will present this new model of open source electronic textbook that incorporates tools that enhance both the learning experience for students and the teaching experience for instructors. In addition, this model is supported within an extensible publishing system that allows the instructor to customize the text as desired.

ITiCSE'12, July 3–5, 2012, Haifa, Israel.

2. eBOOK DESCRIPTION

This project was driven by the following set of educational goals: 1) Encourage students to experiment with the code examples in the text. 2) Engage students using multiple learning modalities. 3) Reduce "Development Environment friction" and student frustration with homework. 4) Help students develop a mental model of flow control. We had equally important goal of creating an open source publishing system that would encourage collaboration among potential authors.

To acheive these goals we developed a set of features that could be embedded in the structure of our electronic book. These features are as follows: 1) embedded video clips, 2) active code blocks that can be edited and run right in the book, 3) a code vizualizer that allows a student to step forward and backward through example code while observing variables and program output. In the rest of this section we describe how these features are realized in our eBook.

We know that some students read their text books regularly, but we suspect that more do not. We are teaching the YouTube generation. Our own experience with providing short supplemental videos on YouTube as well as the experiences of others led us to believe that providing short videos that cover the key points in the text may appeal to students that read little or who struggle to comprehend the material based only on the written word[7, 1]. Some of our early student testers worried that we should make sure that the video covered everything in the text because if the video was there students would be more likely to watch the video than read the text. On the other hand, much of our experience indicated that keeping the videos short and limited in scope was the key to getting students to watch.

To strike a balance between coverage and usability, each

video is between five and ten minutes in length; is focused on a single topic that corresponds to the section; and is in the form of a screencast[5]. To keep the videos from visually cluttering the text we represent each video with a static thumbnail image. Each video expands to 768x590 pixels when the student clicks on the thumbnail to begin playing. It is important that the video be large enough that the student can see the code fragments being discussed, but not too big to be overwhelming. We experimented with a pop-up model, where the video would appear in a modal dialog box with the web page dimmed behind it, but early feedback indicated that was not a good idea as it prevented a student from pausing the video and referring to the text or trying an example.

We strongly believe that the best way for students to learn a programming language is to use the programming language. For years we have encouraged our students to "just try it." In theory Python makes this easy, you simply start up the command line interpreter and type in an expression. But, this is not as easy as it sounds for complete novices. Another point of frustration for novices and textbook authors alike, is to have example code that does not work. Both of these problems are solved by having runnable code embedded within the textbook. We call this runnable code **activecode**. With activecode, you have an executable Python example right in the text. To see what the code produces the student can choose to press a button to make the code run. The results are displayed right below the code itself. It is even possible for the user to write turtle graphics code in Python and see the results displayed on the web page. Figure 1 illustrates a simple turtle graphics example and the resulting output. Textual output is displayed right below the graphics, if any. Not only can the student run the example he or she can modify the example and run it again without leaving the book.

Another feature of our activecode blocks is the ability to save and reload code. The "save" button allows a student to save any modifications they make to an activecode block. These modifications can be recalled from any browser using the "load" button. In a college lab setting this is especially nice because students can use the lab computers in class and then continue their work using their own computers later on without the need for flash drives or file copying. An important detail of the activecode blocks is that the students can always get the original code that we, the authors, wrote by simply refreshing the page.

The students found the active code editors to be so useful that we eventually added scratch editors, that is windows without code, to every section of the book. Scratch editors gave the students a simple place to take notes, to try examples that we were doing in class, or to try their own programs without messing up the code in the examples provided.

Our eBook, like many textbooks, contains homework exercises at the end of each chapter. One of the things we have noticed, especially early in the CS1 course is that students get really frustrated with their homework because of simple things like getting an Integrated Development Environment (IDE) to work properly. For example, students on Windows must install Python, and then learn the difference between the editing window, and the shell. We get homeworks riddled with >>> command prompts that simply don't run. Meanwhile the frustrated students are left wondering why their programs do not run. Using an activecode window

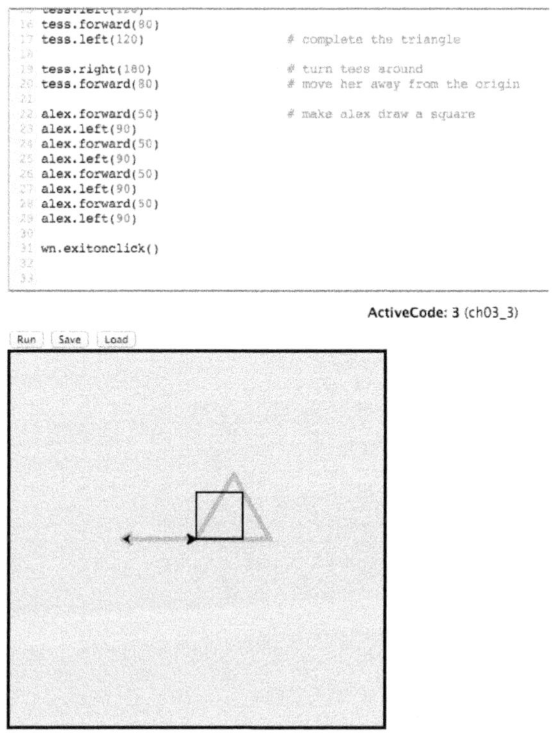

Figure 1: A Turtle Graphics Activecode

for each exercise allows the students to do their homework in an environment that is familiar, convenient, and simple.

Halfway through the semester we begin to transition the students to an IDE. This is important because it emphasizes that Python is a "real language" that exists outside the browser and can be used to solve real-world problems. Making this transition half-way through the semester works well. By Midsemester, the students are familiar enough with Python that they only have to worry about learning how to use the IDE, not the IDE and basic Python syntax at the same time. From that point forward we used the activecode windows as well as the IDE depending on the situation.

Many professors use a service like CodeLab or codingbat to give students practice exercises with feedback. It is very helpful for students to know when they have their code correct. In addition, many students have problems envisioning the kinds of corner test cases we love to use when grading. Activecode allows us to use a Python unittest framework to provide test cases and simple pass fail feedback. When we start to teach the students about functions we introduce the idea of a unittest and in their homeworks we provide them with skeleton code and a suite of test cases. Figure 2 illustrates this idea with the classic leap year problem. When the students run the code they will see whether their solution has passed or failed each of the test cases.

The final goal we had for this eBook was to help students develop a mental model of how Python works. Gone are the days when compile time was at a premium and students had to learn to trace code by hand and keep track of variable values on paper[8]. Today, beginning students often struggle with understanding the flow of the program through for loops, while loops, and conditionals. To help students visualize the flow of control, and the state of each variable

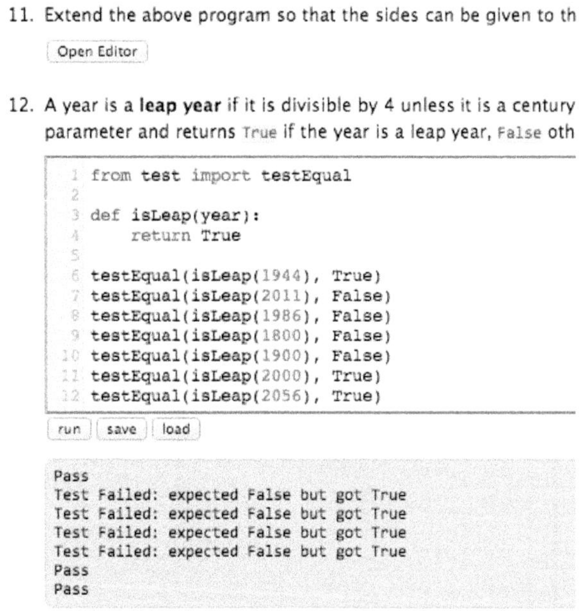

Figure 2: Using a Test Framework in Activecode

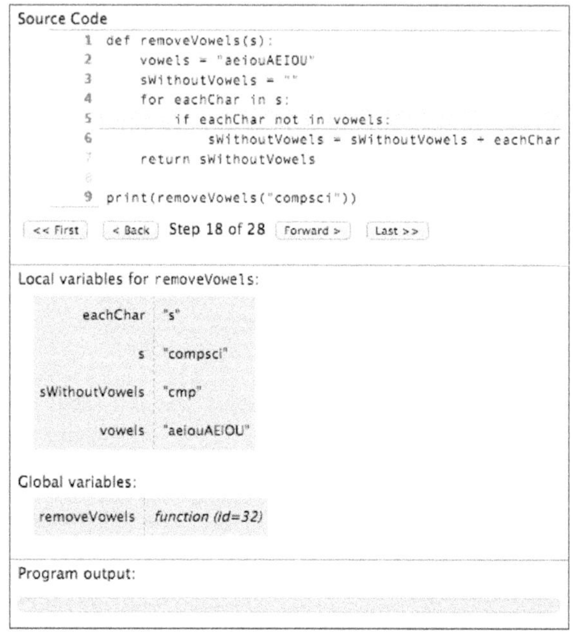

Figure 3: Visualizing Flow of Control

we introduced **codelens**. Codelens is an interactive visualization tool that highlights the currently executing line of Python, along with the state of the variables; both local and global. In some respects codelens is like a symbolic debugger. It allows you to step through a program one line at a time and observe the change in state of different variables. However, unlike most debuggers codelens also lets you go backward. This feature allows a student to quickly step forward through an algorithm, but when they get to a place where they are confused they can step backward a few steps before going through the confusing part again.

Figure 3 illustrates the interface to codelens. You can see from the yellow highlighted line that we are midway through an algorithm to remove the vowels from a string. As the students step through this example they can see the flow of control of the for loop and the if statement. Also shown is the value of the loop variable `eachChar` and the accumulated string `sWithoutVowels`.

In writing this paper we find that having been in the mode of writing for interaction, it is hard to return to a writing style that is suitable for the static printed page. We invite you to take a short break from this paper and visit our interactive book on the web at `http://thinkcspy.appspot.com`. Seeing the book in action is really the best way to understand these features.

3. IMPLEMENTATION

Having a list of features to include in an electronic book is one thing, but actually making it happen is quite another. After prototyping each of the features described above in Javascript, it is no exaggeration to say that this book would never have come about had we not first created the toolkit to allow us to easily replicate the features throughout the book. The tools that we will describe in this section address our secondary goal of creating an open source publishing toolkit.

We will continue by describing the design and implementation of the videos, activecode, and codelens features of our eBook.

Rather than invent our own new publishing system from scratch we looked at a number of existing systems before deciding that Sphinx (`sphinx.pocoo.org`) provided an ideal platform for this project. Sphinx is a document processing tool that makes it easy to generate documentation in HTML, LaTeX, and other forms. Sphinx is written in Python and makes use of the Python docutils module. All prose is written in restructuredText, which is a very minimal markup language similar to Markdown. The inclusion of figures, images, and other visual effects is achieved through the use of special directives embedded in the text. The key to our success in using Sphinx is its extension system [9]. We designed a set of new Sphinx extensions that would allow us to replicate video, activecode and codlens features easily.

The video extension is the simplest so we'll look at that in detail before discussing activecode and codelens. A directive is simply a command that you embed in the restructuredText markup that has enough information to allow sphinx to render the content in whatever output format you've chosen. In our case we were only concerned with HTML rendering since video does not work with a printed LaTeXdocument. Listing 1 shows an example of a Sphinx directive for including a video.

```
.. video:: assignvid
   :controls:
   :thumb: _static/turtleintro.png

   http://knuth.luther.edu/turtleintro.mov
   http://knuth.luther.edu/turtleintro.webm
```

Listing 1: A Video Directive for Sphinx

The first line follows the same format as all Sphinx directives: two dots followed by the name of the directive, followed by two colons. After the colons come any required parameters. In this case we give each video a unique name for logging and reference purposes. The next lines following the initial directive are optional parameters. `:controls:` is a boolean flag that indicates the video should appear with controls. The `:thumb:` parameter gives the path to an image to use as the thumbnail. After the optional parameters comes a blank line, and then the main body of the directive. In our case any lines in the body are simply URLs that point to a video file.

To implement this directive in Sphinx you must write a Python class that is a subclass of the docutils `Directive` class. At a minimum you must implement the `run` method of this class. The run method returns a node object that is inserted into the document model. In our case, this node object simply contains the raw HTML that will be inserted into the page[2]. The directive in Listing 1 produces the following HTML. The video tag is a standar HTML5 video tag, and the Javascript that follows uses jQuery to hide thumbnail and make the video visible.

```
<div id="assignvid" class="video_popup" >
<video controls   >
    <source
    src="http://knuth.luther.edu/turtleintro.mov"
    type="video/mp4"></source>
    <source
    src="http://knuth.luther.edu/turtleintro.webm"
    type="video/webm"></source>
    No supported video types
</video>
</div>
<script>
   jQuery(function($) {
      $('#assignvid_thumb').click(function(e) {
         $('#assignvid').show();
         $('#assignvid_thumb').hide();
         jQuery.get("/hsblog",{'event':'video',
         'act':'play','div_id': 'assignvid'});
         // Log the run event
      });
   });
</script>
```

Listing 2: Generated HTML for a Video

The activecode directive is also quite simple. Listing 3 shows an example of a turtle graphics program that draws a square with four different colored sides. There are no optional parameters shown in Listing 3 however the author has the option to use an `:include:` parameter to incorporate code from one or more other activecode blocks. This is extremely useful when a series of examples build on each other because it avoids the visual clutter of repeating code that has already been presented.

```
.. activecode:: ch03_forcolor

   import turtle             #set up alex
   wn = turtle.Screen()
   alex = turtle.Turtle()

   for aColor in ['yellow','red','purple','blue']:
       alex.forward(50)
       alex.left(90)

   wn.exitonclick()
```

Listing 3: An Activecode Directive for Sphinx

The activecode directive in Listing 3 generates more HTML and Javascript than we would want to include in this paper, however if you are interested, the details can be seen in the

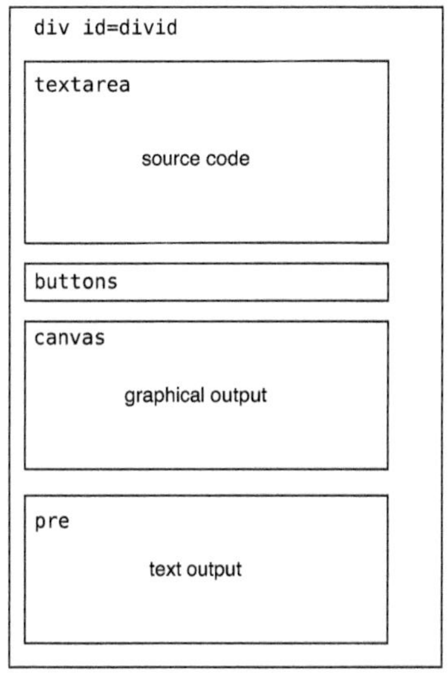

Figure 4: The HTML Structure Generated by an Activecode Directive

source of the actual web page [1]. The important thing to note is that activecode directive creates the structure shown in Figure 4

The generated activecode relies on two open source projects. The first, `Skulpt`, is a Javascript implementation of the core Python interpreter[3]. This is a very important distinction between our eBook and other tutorial web pages. Having Python in Javascript enables offline use of the eBook as well as improving the overall feel and flow of reading the book. When the run button is pressed the code from the textarea is passed to the skulpt parser and interpreter. The Python source is compiled to Javascript at runtime and run by the Javascript virtual machine right in the browser.

Although skulpt implements the core of Python none of the standard library modules are present. We've contributed the turtle graphics module as well as a math, random, image, and unittest module. Add-on modules like turtle graphics can be written in either Python or Javascript and are stored in a separate Javascript file that is loaded with the web page. The turtle graphics and image modules were written in Javscript to make use of the canvas element. The math module was also written in Javascript and simply provides a translation of the math module functions to the Javascript Math object functions. The unittest module was written in Python.

The second open source component that is critical to activecode is the Codemirror Javascript editor[6]. This is a nice, light weight editor that wraps the textarea created by the activecode directive. Codemirror does syntax highlighting and understands Python's indentation conventions. This really helps beginning students get used to the syntax and indentation patterns in Python.

The final component of our toolkit is the **codelens** code visualization tool. The directive for codelens is nearly identical to the activecode directive except for the name. A key difference between activecode and codelens is that codelens runs the Python program at the time the HTML is gen-

[1] http://thinkcspy.appspot.com/build/helloturtle.html

erated. When a codelens visualizer is created the code is traced using a regular Python interpreter and the pdb debug module. The trace function produces a list of stack frames corresponding to stepping through the code one line at a time. This list is converted to a JSON representation, stored statically with the webpage and then passed as a parameter to codelens at runtime.

As you might imagine the HTML code for codelens generates a rather complicated table structure. The code for codelens is based on the Python Tutor, another open source project[4]. You can experiment with the Python Tutor on the project website [2]. The online version relies on having a Python interpreter available for the web server. We've adapted the code to run both offline and online as a part of our eBook.

The Google App Engine (GAE) ties the entire system together and makes it possible for us to create a very rudimentary course management system. The main pages of the book are generated offline and served as static pages from GAE. To manage persistent data we developed an API that can be accessed through AJAX. The API supports saving and loading activecode blocks, listing all exercises for a student or all attempts at a specific exercise by the class. We developed a rudimentary grading interface that allows us to quickly work our way through the class and evaluate exercises by pressing the run button next to the code turned in by the student. There is a simple text entry box to enter the grade for a particular assignment, and grades are recorded and automatically saved to the Google's data store using another AJAX call.

Storing, loading, and grading all require students to have an account to use the book. GAE solves this problem easily for us because our campus uses Google Domains. This allows every student to use the same account for our book that they use for other campus activities. In general everyone can save and load their programs as long as they have a Gmail account. Of course requiring someone to log-in using their Gmail account can be off-putting at first so the book is set up such that if you are not logged in you can still run and change all of the examples and exercises, but you can't save or reload.

The fact that we were able to write this eBook in one summer is a real triumph of open source software. One critical component that we have failed to mention so far is that we were able to take the prose for this book from an existing open source textbook: *How to Think Like a Computer Scientist*[10]. Although we reorganized the chapters and added many of our own examples using things like turtle graphics and image processing it was very important to not have to rewrite core material from scratch. The ease with which we were able to convert static code examples into active parts of the book was key to our success in creating the entire work. The extensions we've written to support our eBook in Sphinx are all open source and available for download from our github repository.

4. STUDENT RESPONSE

In this section we will report some preliminary observations and make some broad commentary on usage data. In the 2011 fall semester, sixty-six students were enrolled in two sections of the first semester Introduction to Computer

[2]http://people.csail.mit.edu/pgbovine/python/tutor.html

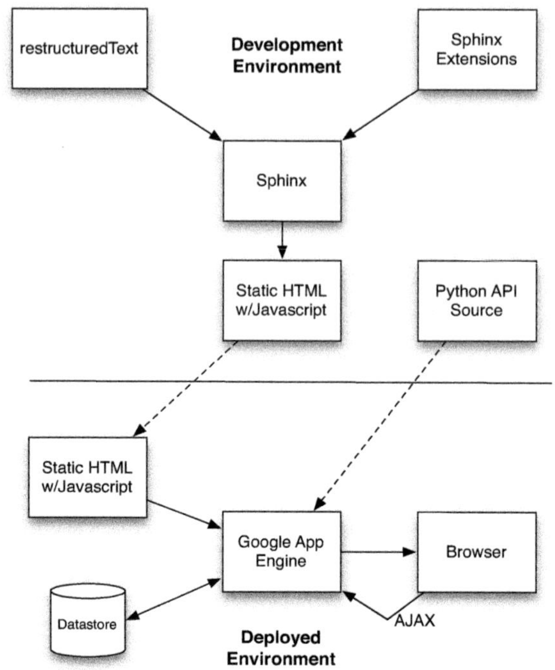

Figure 5: Block Diagram of Publishing System

Science course at Luther College. The students were all undergraduate and ranged from first-year to senior. The course was taught in a computer laboratory/classroom. All students used the eBook as described above, both as part of class lecture and as their primary textbook resource.

Throughout the semester, a large quantity of usage data was collected. This was accomplished by logging every button click made by students. In addition to usage data, students were asked to complete a comprehensive survey of their use and impressions of the textbook as a learning resource.

In all, over 240,000 events were captured for later analysis. The average student logged about 34 active book events per day throughout the semester. This includes editing and saving activecode, viewing videos, and stepping thru codelens examples. It does not count time spent simply reading static text on the page. Table 4 shows the specific usage data for each activity.

Activity	Total Events	Events per Student
activecode	224025	3394
codelens	16592	251
video	380	6

Table 1: Total Semester Activity Counts

In general, students were very pleased with the eBook format. They found it to be clearly written, easy to use, and helpful for learning the concepts that were presented in the course. When asked to rank ten items that helped in learning, from most critical to least, classroom lecture was chosen most critical. This was followed closely by (2)reading the textbook, (3)running programs from the textbook,

(4)changing programs and running the new programs in the textbook, and (5) tracing programs using codelens. This suggests that students were finding the active elements of the textbook to be very important to their learning. Related to this finding, a high degree of student satisfaction was also reported by 61 students who stated that if given the opportunity in a future computer science course, they would want to use a textbook such as this one. In particular, one with executable code examples.

When asked about their favorite aspects of the course, many students reported that the interactive, online text ranked high on their list. Reasons given included convenience, ease of testing different examples, and the ability to practice while reading the text. 88% of the students reported that the interactive nature of classtime helped them learn and 55% of the students plan to take the next computer science course in the major sequence.

5. CONCLUSIONS AND FUTURE WORK

After using the eBook in class for a semester we are very encouraged. It is clear that beginning students like the convenience of having the course organized in one place. We experienced none of the usual frustration with installing Python and learning an IDE. Perhaps the most telling and exciting feedback was the number of students who asked if there would be a similar book for them to use in the CS2 course in the Spring.

With the first version of the book in place there are many questions we want to investigate. The first of these is to investigate whether the eBook and its various features have a statistically significant impact on student learning. We've already made a start with this by collaborating with the CSLearning4U group at Georgia Tech. This group devised a set of quizzes for our students to take during the semester. Using these quizzes and the data we collected about how the students used the book we hope to be able to correlate performance and eBook features.

A second major area we want to investigate is in adding assessment features into the book. By this we mean the capability to have true/false, multiple choice, fill in the blank or short code kinds of questions right in the book. We are working on creating new Sphinx directives so that students can test their own understanding of the material. Would in-line assessment help students recognize their own problem areas more effectively? Would it help the students use the eBook more effectively? Could we use assessment to help them learn how to use codelens and activecode more effectively?

Many students commented that they would like a better way to take notes or highlight parts of the text. We are interested in whether a collaborative commenting system that allows the students to ask questions about or comment on a particularly confusing paragraph would engage students. We are planning to use this book in an experimental online course this summer and an asynchronous commenting system would be ideal to have in place for the course.

We are working with the publisher of our data structures textbook to create an electronic version of that text as well. The world of data structures opens up many new and interesting possibilities for algorithm visualization and animation in an interactive text. We envision extending codelens' capabilities to show a graphical version of a tree or graph. We know from the classroom that animating the different sort algorithms helps students learn, now these animations could be right next to the code in the book.

Finally, we are excited about the possibilities of collaborating with our colleagues around the world to improve upon our ideas here. Using open source components we envison that this could be a platform for an instructor to customize their own course organizing or adding chapters to best fit their own environment or contributing videos or exercises to a collection for others to choose from. There are other languages such as Scheme that also have Javascript implemenations, we believe it would be possible to provide activecode and codelens features for other languages. In the spirit of this book we invite you to join us in continued dialog and development at http://runestoneinteractive.org.

References

[1] Paul Carter. "An experiment with online instruction and active learning in an introductory computing course for engineers: JiTT meets CS1". In: *Proceedings of the 14th Western Canadian Conference on Computing Education*. WCCCE '09. Burnaby, British Columbia, Canada: ACM, 2009, pp. 103–108. ISBN: 978-1-60558-415-7.

[2] Dethe Elza, David Goodger, and Lea Wiemann. *Creating reStructuredText Directives*. 2009. URL: `http://docutils.sourceforge.net/docs/howto/rst-directives.html`.

[3] Scott Graham. *Skulpt*. June 2010. URL: `http://www.skulpt.org`.

[4] Philip J. Guo. *Online Python Tutor*. 2011. URL: `http://www.stanford.edu/~pgbovine/online-python-tutor.htm`.

[5] Brian Harvey. "Learning Objects and Instructional Design". In: *The International Review of Research in Open and Distance Learning* 6.2 (2005). ISSN: 1492-3831. URL: `http://www.irrodl.org/index.php/irrodl/article/view/227`.

[6] Marijn Haverbeke. *Codemirror Reference and User Manual*. 2011. URL: `http://codemirror.net/doc/manual.html`.

[7] David J. Malan. "Podcasting computer science E-1". In: *Proceedings of the 38th SIGCSE technical symposium on Computer science education*. SIGCSE '07. Covington, Kentucky, USA: ACM, 2007, pp. 389–393. ISBN: 1-59593-361-1.

[8] Thomas L. Naps et al. "Exploring the role of visualization and engagement in computer science education". In: *Working group reports from ITiCSE on Innovation and technology in computer science education*. ITiCSE-WGR '02. Aarhus, Denmark: ACM, 2002, pp. 131–152.

[9] The Sphinx Team. *Sphinx Extensions*. June 2011. URL: `http://sphinx.pocoo.org/extensions.html`.

[10] Peter Wentworth et al. *How to Think Like a Computer Scientist: Learning with Python*. 2011. URL: `http://www.openbookproject.net/thinkcs/python/english3e`.

The Future of Teaching Programming is on Mobile Devices

Nikolai Tillmann, Michal Moskal,
Jonathan de Halleux, Manuel Fahndrich,
Judith Bishop, Arjmand Samuel
Microsoft Research
One Microsoft Way
Redmond WA, USA
{nikolait,micmo,jhalleux,maf,
jbishop,arjmands}@microsoft.com

Tao Xie
Department of Computer Science
North Carolina State University
Raleigh NC, USA
xie@csc.ncsu.edu

ABSTRACT

From paper to computers, the way that we have been writing down thoughts and performing symbolic computations has been constantly evolving. Teaching methods closely follow this trend, leveraging existing technology to make teaching more effective and preparing students for their later careers with the available technology. Right now, in 2012, we are in the middle of another technology shift: instead of using PCs and laptops, mobile devices are becoming more prevalent for most everyday computing tasks. In fact, never before in human history were incredibly powerful and versatile computing devices such as smartphones available and adopted so broadly. We propose that computer programming, and thus the teaching of programming, can and should be done directly on the mobile devices themselves, without the need for a separate PC or laptop to write code. Programming on smartphones that we carry around with us at all times means instant gratification for students, as they can show their games and applications to their friends, and it means that students can do their homework or additional practicing at all times. We describe TouchDevelop, a novel mobile programming environment, and call out challenges that need to be overcome and opportunities that it creates.

Categories and Subject Descriptors

D.2.3 [**Software Engineering**]: Program editors; D.2.3 [**Software Engineering**]: Structured programming; D.2.6 [**Programming Environments/Construction Tools**]: Integrated environments; D.2.11 [**Software Architectures**]: Languages

General Terms

Human Factors, Design, Languages

ITiCSE'12, July 3–5, 2012, Haifa, Israel.

Keywords

Evolution, Mobile Devices, Touchscreen, Cloud, Type inference

1. INTRODUCTION

From scratching in sand, chiseling in stone, writing on paper, using an abacus, mechanical computers, electric computers, mainframes, minicomputers, to eventually microcomputers/PC, the way that we have been writing down thoughts and performing symbolic computations has been constantly evolving. The instruments that are available for teaching follow the prevalent technologies. Ideally, the way that a subject is taught should be closely related to how the students will apply the acquired knowledge later in their professional careers.

Right now, in 2012, we are in the middle of another technology shift: more touchscreen-based mobile devices like smartphones and tablets will be sold than PCs, laptops, and netbooks combined. In fact, in many cases, incredibly powerful and easy-to-use smartphones are going to be the first and, in less developed countries, possibly the only computing devices that virtually all people will own. Many tasks that used to require a large computer are now feasible on smaller devices. Even the tiniest smartphones are always connected to the cloud and have great email reading and internet surfing capabilities. Improvements in touchscreen technology and word prediction techniques made it possible to perform basic typing tasks with ease. Mobile devices are now often used to play games of a sophistication that would have required the most advanced PC a decade ago.

While traditional servers, PCs and embedded systems will stay around and much critical software still needs to be written for them, a significant portion of all developed programs will target mobile devices.

What has not yet happened is the shift to use the new mobile devices themselves to write applications for those devices. This shift might not seem desirable for affluent professional developers who spend the majority of their time writing code and who can afford a traditional PC development environment set up in order to be more productive with a big screen, full physical keyboard, and mouse. But note that in general non-essential input devices tend to die; witness for example the PDA stylus and tablet PC pen, and the declining popularity of slide-out keyboards for phones. If it is possible and effective to use only a mobile device with a touchscreen to program certain applications, then other more complicated approaches are likely to be eventually replaced by the single-device approach, making obsolete the PC development environment tethered to a mobile device for testing mobile applications.

Teaching of programming should follow this trend.

Students are soon more likely to personally own a smartphone than a traditional PC or laptop. Students will not only own such devices, they will carry them with them at all times. They will use them not only for communication, fun, and utility, but also to store and access their most personal digital data such as pictures, videos, and music.

This connection opens new opportunities for teaching programming. Instead of analyzing and manipulating abstract or teacher-provided data, students should write and execute programs on their own mobile devices, working with their own readily available content, making learning programming the engaging experience that it should be.

2. DISRUPTION

While some technology shifts happen gradually, they are often accompanied by fundamental changes. We believe that the way we input programs and the way we handle program state will change with the transition to mobile devices, and there will be consequences for the programming languages as well. It is important that teachers prepare students for these imminent changes, which are syntactical and conceptual in nature.

There are many precedents for the *coupling of input devices and programming languages.* Consider for example FORTRAN 77, to name one representative of the punch card era. Each punch card had 72-column lines; in FORTRAN 77, the first 5 columns were reserved for line numbers, the 6th could indicate a continuation line, and the first column could indicate a comment. All of these conventions became cumbersome once programs were not entered directly on physical punch cards anymore, but instead via a keyboard and editors with line buffers. We predict that moving away from a keyboard, a device that allows very precise entry of around 100 different characters to a touchscreen typical for mobile devices will again influence how the program syntax is structured and entered. While forward-looking predictive text input works reasonably well on virtual touchscreen keyboard, actions that require fine navigation, e.g., to make structural corrections, are awkward on a touchscreen where the size of a finger limits precision.

The capabilities of *how a computer may handle memory* also influences programming languages. Consider again FORTRAN 77. It did not allow dynamic memory allocation and had no way to represent memory references and had no safe external storage facilities, but only the unsafe COMMON blocks. Modern programming languages have greatly improved this situation, providing garbage collected object references, and routines for structured I/O. However, the modern languages were designed to handle local memory and storage, and they did not yet make the transition to cloud-connected devices where the user often perceives state as not being tied to a particular device, but instead to be rooted in the cloud, being made available as needed to fill in for the current task at hand. Besides the general hype to move storage to the cloud, mobile devices are especially affected by this trend as they have short replacement cycles, and they are easily lost or broken. Instead of burdening the programmer with the implementation of abstractions to move around and merge local and cloud data, or learning how to use add-on libraries that perform such tasks, cloud-based state and storage should be an integral aspect of a new programming language for mobile devices.

```
string ::= "Hello world!\n" | ...
number ::= 0 | 1 | 3.1415 | ...
local ::= x | y | z | foo bar | ...
action ::= frobnicate | go draw line | ...
global ::= phone | math | maps | ok button | chat roster | ...
property ::= vibrate | sin | add pushpin | disable | add | ...
exprs ::= expr | exprs , expr
parameters ::= | ( exprs )
op ::= + | − | / | * | <= | >= | > | < | = | != | and | or | ||
expr ::= local | string | number | true | false
      | − expr | not expr | expr op expr
      | action parameters | expr −> property parameters
block ::= stmt | block stmt
locals ::= local | local , locals
stmt ::= expr | locals := expr | do nothing
      | if expr then block else block
      | while expr do block | foreach local in expr do block
      | for 0 <= local < expr do block
type ::= Number | String | Song | Nothing | Phone | ...
formals ::= local : type | local : type , formals
formals-opt ::= | formals
returns-opt ::= | returns formals
action-def ::= action action ( formals-opt ) returns-opt block
```

Figure 1: Abstract syntax of TouchDevelop

3. MOBILE DEVELOPMENT ENVIRONMENT

TouchDevelop [11] is a novel programming environment, language and code editor for mobile devices that addresses some of the main consequences of the expected technology shift. TouchDevelop makes it possible to write applications directly on mobile devices, without the need for a separate PC. At its core is a typed, structured programming language that is built around the idea of using only a touchscreen as the input device to author code.

In fact, the abstract syntax, typing rules, and basic semantics of the language are fairly similar to corresponding fragments of mainstream programming languages like Java or C#. This similarity lets the user transfer expertise between the TouchDevelop language and a traditional programming environment, in both directions. The language mixes imperative, object-oriented, and functional aspects. The imperative parts are most visible: assignment statements can update local variables and state of global objects. The language has a notion of objects in order to facilitate code autocompletion by the editor — properties of objects are an easily accessible and intuitive concept. Functional features come in form of a query language.

A program consist of a set of actions; each action contains statements. Figure 1 gives an overview of the abstract syntax of statements and expressions that can appear in actions. The language provides built-in primitives that make it easy to access the rich sensor data available on a mobile device.

Instead of a traditional text editor, TouchDevelop employs a semi-structured code editor. The motivation for structured editing is not to entirely eliminate the possibility of syntax errors, but instead to ensure that every navigation task between different syntax elements can be easily achieved by tapping on a finger-sized user interface element on the screen instead of relying on a full physical or on-screen keyboard that enables editing of code at the level of individual characters from which words and in turn sentences are formed. To determine which user interface elements are shown on the limited screen space, the editor leverages inferred types and it mines previously written programs to provide highly predictive auto-completion suggestions to the user. In effect, the user only has to choose from lists of statement kinds and expression tokens instead of entering statements and expressions character by character.

In addition to the basic programming functionality (language, interpreter, editor), TouchDevelop provides a social experience, allowing users to publish and download programs, discuss them by writing comments, publish screenshots, and users can give hearts to a program or comment when they like it. A central program repository in the cloud manages all programs and analyzes them for privacy concerns and code duplication.

Figure 2 shows the different views of the code editor in TouchDevelop, including a listing of a complete program. Each screenshot captures the entire screen of a smartphone. Note that all surface areas which act as buttons are large enough to be tapped on quite precisely by a big finger. The left screenshot (a) shows a list of statements. The user can select a statement by tapping somewhere in a statement line. The middle screenshot (b) shows how the user adds additional statements by choosing from a list of possible statement kinds. It is not possible to make syntactical mistakes at the statement level. Once the statement kind is chosen, the view transitions to the expression editor to edit the expression associated with the statement. The right screenshot (c) shows the expression editor, which is implemented similar to a rich calculator. Individual built-in syntactic primitives such as numbers and operators can be accessed via nested keypads, opened by first tapping on the corresponding summary button. Other semantic procedure and function calls can be inserted by eight quick buttons, which are populated based on the type of the current scope, and historical usage information.

TouchDevelop is available as an free application on the Windows Phone Marketplace.

4. EXPERIENCE

After six months, more than 3000 games and applications have been written and published by users of TouchDevelop, using the touchscreen as the only input device. The TouchDevelop website[1] shows all games and applications.

Many games written by users leverage the accelerometer of the phone as a controller, measuring how the phone is tilted, including a fully-featured Tetris-like game, a Breakout-like game, warehouse games where boxes need to be moved to particular locations, and many more. Other applications are useful tools and utilities, including a program that queries the calendar on the phone and automatically connects to any currently scheduled online meeting, a program that queries the current state of parking meters in a city via a web service and projects the information on a map, a Siri-like application that connects the microphone, a speech recognition engine, and a search engine via web service calls, and many more.

[1] http://touchdevelop.com/

In the following, we report on our ongoing experience working with students at various levels[2].

4.1 9 Weeks with High School Students

The first indication of the feasibility of the approach was an experience with two high school students who spent 9 weeks over the course of a summer developing games and applications with an early version of TouchDevelop. The students had some previous experience with programming on PCs for PCs using Java, Python, and/or Scheme, but they had never written applications for mobile devices before. We provided them with smartphones that had TouchDevelop pre-installed, and we encouraged them to be investigative and learn by themselves how to create games and applications with the environment. The only instructional material we provided to the students was a set of sample games and applications, and a few videos that walk through the process of creating a new application, tap by tap on the touchscreen. We would help them later when they had particular questions about the language, built-in functions, the editor, or other aspects of the environment.

The students started as learners of the language and environment, and quickly became relatively experienced programmers who could write quite sophisticated games and applications by themselves. One student wrote 19 different games and applications during this time. Some of the students' games rival existing apps in software marketplaces for smartphones.

4.2 90 Minutes with 30 High School Students in a Computer Science Class

We were invited to a high school to work with 30 students in grades 11-12 in a computer science class for 90 minutes. The students had recently started the class and were already introduced to some programming concepts but they had no experience in developing mobile applications. We provided 12 phones for students to work in groups of three. After a brief introduction to TouchDevelop, the students had 45 minutes to explore the language and write their own mobile applications. All groups were able to write applications on their own, including a program that changes the color of the screen based on the direction in 3D space that the phone is facing, a peek-a-boo game that utilized the direction the phone was facing to display a covered face or an open face with the audio track to accompany it, and a role playing game where the user has to answer questions to progress. The regular computer science teacher made the following remarks: "*Even though most of the students haven't learned about some to the [techniques] before, like using a loop or a collection of objects, the concepts made sense in the context of a phone app. [It] was a fun way to learn about programming topics and obtain instant feedback on whether you did it correctly or not.*"

4.3 2 Hours with 90 Eighth Grade Students

We were invited to a middle school to work with the entire eighth grade of that school — 90 students in two sessions for 2 hours with 45 students. The students did not volunteer to be part of the sessions. We provided enough phones so that students could work together in groups of two. After a brief introduction to TouchDevelop, the students had 60

[2] http://research.microsoft.com/touchdevelop/teaching.aspx

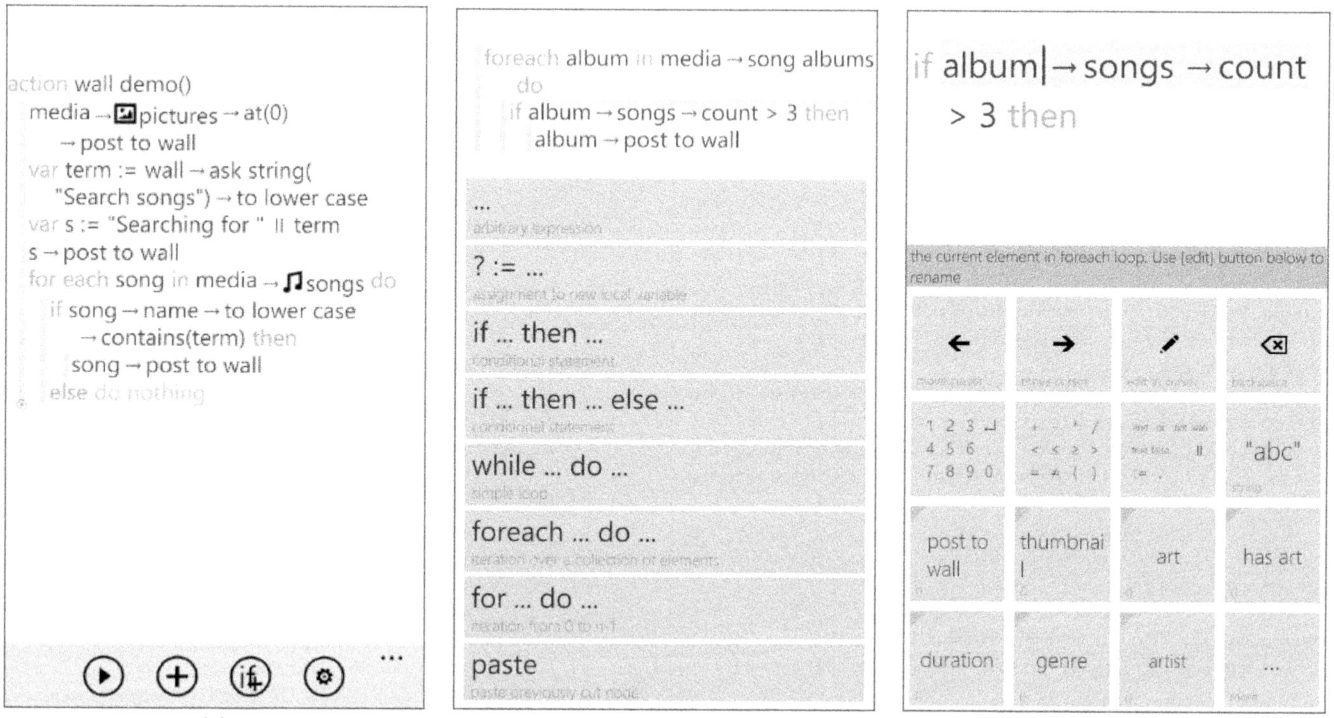

(a) (b) (c)

Figure 2: Three screenshots illustrating the TouchDevelop programming environment on mobile devices.

minutes to explore the language and write their own mobile applications.

71 students filled out questionnaires before and after the class.

Before the class,

- 12% of the students stated that they already had programming knowledge, 43% some and 43% no programming knowledge at all
- 61% of the students did not own a smartphone

After the class,

- 7% of the students stated that they thought the development of a mobile application with TouchDevelop was easy, 48% thought it was somewhat difficult, and 45% said it was difficult. However,
- 86% of the students wanted to create more applications using TouchDevelop.
- 92% of the girls wanted to continue writing applications whereas only 38% of them had an idea of what applications they could create prior to the class.

Almost all groups were able to create a unique application[3], incorporating the phone input sensors (accelerometer, camera, touchscreen, microphone) outputs (vibrator, screen, audio) and/or media libraries (songs, pictures).

[3] http://research.microsoft.com/apps/video/?id=157112

5. OPPORTUNITIES AND CHALLENGES FOR TEACHING AND LEARNING

We next discuss opportunities and challenges of teaching and learning in the context of TouchDevelop, and writing programs on mobile devices in general. The discussion is based on feedback from users and students.

5.1 Platform and Environment Support

Today's classrooms are not well equipped for the transition yet. The widespread expectation is that exercises are performed on traditional PCs and laptops. Such an expectation is reflected in the equipment made available for the students for the duration of a course. While some students may already own personal mobile devices, it is likely that with increasing adoption of various smartphone platforms we will find a heterogeneous set of incompatible phone platforms supporting vastly different programming environments that are rapidly evolving.

Mobile programming environments will have to be standardized or made available across platforms, or all students of a class must adopt a particular phone platform, or schools must make available a homogeneous set of mobile devices for teaching purposes, similar to how many schools already make available PCs or laptops.

In a classroom setting, a teacher would have to be able to project a programming session on a mobile device on a bigger screen. Some mobile devices have video-out capabilities, similar to laptops, or a teacher would need a WolfVision-like desktop visualizer[4] to capture and project the phone's screen on a larger display for students to see. Another alternative for the teacher would be to use an emulator or simulator of

[4] http://wolfvision.com/

the mobile device that runs on the teacher's laptop or PC. Finally, the programming environment itself could support a mechanism to stream its current image.

5.2 Teaching and Learning Materials

Teachers are not yet well prepared for the transition. Existing course material is tailored around programming languages that were not designed for mobile devices. Much of the existing material should be easy to adapt, as the fundamental algorithmic aspects of programming still apply. The necessary changes are foremost adaptations to language syntax and editors, with new aspects of programming with cloud state added later on.

Over time, examples and exercises could be adapted to be better suited for the nature of personal mobile devices, e.g., by letting algorithms iterate over the songs available on the actual phone instead of enumerating over fictitious payroll data.

We are in the process of creating course material for an introductory course on programming with TouchDevelop. A book[5] and slide decks[6] are already available.

5.3 Software Development Processes and Practices

There are many established development processes and practices for software development with traditional programming languages on PCs and laptops. Not all of them carry over seamlessly to an emerging mobile programming environment. Next we discuss some constraints imposed by the new programming environments and their impact on the development processes and practices.

Some processes (e.g., test-driven development) that require specific practices (e.g., testing) and supporting tools (e.g., formal unit testing frameworks and test runners) may not work well in the new programming environments at first, as the environment will not have the fully developed ecosystems that we have become accustomed to from established programming environments. This situation is likely temporary as the ecosystem is developing.

Some software development and teaching practices such as pair programming and remote assistance could be infeasible without specific platform support, e.g., live sharing of screens across phones. Even when the platform support is provided, the exact same code-editing screen without editing context may not be desirable for the observing programmer, and the platform support may need to show a different screen with more editing context for the observer.

6. DISCUSSION AND RELATED WORK

The idea of using mobile devices instead of PCs in education is not new [9]; what is new in TouchDevelop is that the mobile device is not just used as a browser-like device to access existing information and programs, but that it is used as a program creation environment itself.

Learning programming is difficult [4], as it amounts to acquiring a skill, and not just a body of knowledge. Working with mobile devices such as personal smartphones may make learning programming more interesting to students. The traditional mobile application development model centered around developing on a PC adds many complexities for teaching [3]. Nevertheless, teaching an introductory course on programming by writing code for mobile devices has been tried [8, 6, 7]; one finding was that developing mobile applications (by using a PC) was more difficult than developing desktop applications (on a PC), since the mobile programming models are typically a restricted subset of the PC model, to the extent that programming for mobile devices on PCs can be seen as a form of programming embedded systems. In contrast, TouchDevelop does not require a PC at all, offering a homogeneous development experience.

At many universities, advanced programming courses for mobile devices are becoming available. Workshops are held to make teachers familiar with mobile programming environments. An example is the Audacious Android Application Programming Workshop[7].

It has been observed that developing games for mobile devices can be a valuable tool in the CS curriculum [5], as the students can directly relate to mobile games, and because such games offer instant gratification — students can play them on the mobile devices that they carry with them at all times, and they can show them to their friends. However, it was also observed that it is difficult to develop mobile applications in the traditional development setting, and thus it is a topic that is usually delayed to advanced CS classes.

Attempts have been made to greatly simplify the programming model for mobile applications. For example, App Inventor [14] is a system that enables the visual development of Android apps by connecting blocks to define the program's behavior. This system is promising for use in introductory programming courses [13, 12]. However, even if simplifying application development, the development system is still designed around the idea of developing programs on a fully featured PC with a big screen and precise mouse. Our experience with high school students shows that a programming environment that runs directly on mobile devices has the potential to dramatically reduce the technical learning overhead; high school students whom we worked with were able to create and refine their first programs within an hour, immediately leveraging the sensors and data available on the phone, instead of having to learn concepts such as cross-compilation and application deployment first.

It has been observed that the rich sensory data available on mobile devices stimulates the use of mobile devices as learning tools [1]. However, the PC itself does not offer many of the sensors such as location and accelerometer that are often used in mobile games and applications, making it awkward to develop and test initial versions of mobile applications in a PC-based emulator; in contrast, development directly on mobile devices makes the use of such sensors easier since immediate feedback is provided.

By carrying their own mobile devices with them at all times, students will effectively carry around the entire computer programming learning and practicing environment, assuming that the programming environment runs on the device itself. The effect is an unprecedented form of mobile-device supported lifelong learning and practicing [10]. If eventually every student will own a mobile device, then this environment enables a new phase of technology-enhanced learning of programming, termed "seamless learning" [2]. This mode of learning allows students not only to learn something whenever they are curious, but also to seamlessly

[5] http://touchdevelop.com/book

[6] http://touchdevelop.com/slides

[7] http://www.harding.edu/fmccown/android/workshop.html

switch from one activity to another supported by their mobile devices.

One might argue that the smaller form factor and limited input capabilities of mobile devices make them inherently restrictive, and unsuitable for certain tasks, possibly including programming. What seems clear is that established patterns will have to change to make programming on such devices feasible. There are several programming environments already on software marketplaces for mobile devices; most are difficult to use, as they simply port existing text-editor based programming languages, but some radically adapt to the new touchscreen-based mobile paradigm, such as TouchDevelop.

Besides the small screen, the limited battery life and processors that are not as fast as those found in desktop PCs may limit the applications that run on mobile devices. However, with the omnipresent cloud, it is feasible to defer rich functionalities to remote services. Over time, more and more such services are becoming available, see for example Project Hawaii[8] which offers services for OCR, Speech to Text, and message relay. TouchDevelop makes it easy to perform such service calls, thus greatly extending the environment from the immediate sensors on the device to anything accessible via the cloud. The cloud also enables a new paradigm for data storage: the concept of distributed state will be directly incorporated into the semantics of the TouchDevelop programming language; the runtime system will take care of synchronizing and merging data between different mobile clients and the cloud, providing an abstraction at the language-level to the programmer.

The current trend to mobile devices and touchscreens may simply be a transient phenomenon, and we might soon see yet another technology emerge that will make small touchscreen considerations again obsolete. But such a development is not certain either.

7. CONCLUSION

In the foreseeable future, incredibly powerful and easy-to-use smartphones will be the first (and possibly only) computing devices that virtually all people will own, and carry with them at all times. We predict that those devices will be used as application creation environments, and propose that the teaching of programming should start from this new reality. We presented our experience with middle and high school students that indicates that programming directly on mobile devices is indeed quite accessible to students who are beginning to learn programming. By learning programming on their own personal devices, with access to personal content such as pictures, videos, songs, and sensors such as location and accelerometer, this new way of teaching programming will create a uniquely engaging and fun learning experience for students.

8. REFERENCES

[1] J. Barbosa, R. Hahn, D. N. F. Barbosa, and C. F. R. Geyer. Mobile and ubiquitous computing in an innovative undergraduate course. In *Proceedings of the 38th SIGCSE technical symposium on Computer science education*, SIGCSE '07, pages 379–383, New York, NY, USA, 2007. ACM.

[2] T.-W. Chan, J. Roschelle, S. Hsi, Kinshuk, M. Sharples, T. Brown, C. Patton, J. C. Cherniavsky, R. D. Pea, C. Norris, E. Soloway, N. Balacheff, M. Scardamalia, P. Dillenbourg, C.-K. Looi, M. Milrad, and H. U. Hoppe. One-to-one technology-enhanced learning: an opportunity for global research collaboration. *Research and Practice in Technology Enhanced Learning*, 1(1):3–29, 2006.

[3] M. H. Goadrich and M. P. Rogers. Smart smartphone development: ios versus android. In *Proceedings of the 42nd ACM technical symposium on Computer science education*, SIGCSE '11, pages 607–612, New York, NY, USA, 2011. ACM.

[4] T. Jenkins. On the difficulty of learning to program. *Language*, 4:53–58, 2002.

[5] S. Kurkovsky. Engaging students through mobile game development. In *Proceedings of the 40th ACM technical symposium on Computer science education*, SIGCSE '09, pages 44–48, New York, NY, USA, 2009. ACM.

[6] Q. Mahmoud and P. Popowicz. A mobile application development approach to teaching introductory programming. In *Frontiers in Education Conference (FIE), 2010 IEEE*, pages T4F–1 –T4F–6, oct. 2010.

[7] Q. H. Mahmoud. Best practices in teaching mobile application development. In *Proceedings of the 16th annual joint conference on Innovation and technology in computer science education*, ITiCSE '11, pages 333–333, New York, NY, USA, 2011. ACM.

[8] Q. H. Mahmoud and A. Dyer. Mobile devices in an introductory programming course. *Computer*, 41:108–107, June 2008.

[9] M. Pasamontes, J. Guzman, F. Rodriguez, M. Berenguel, and S. Dormido. Easy mobile device programming for educational purposes. In *Decision and Control, 2005 and 2005 European Control Conference. CDC-ECC '05. 44th IEEE Conference on*, pages 3420 – 3425, dec. 2005.

[10] M. Sharples. The design of personal mobile technologies for lifelong learning. *Comput. Educ.*, 34:177–193, April 2000.

[11] N. Tillmann, M. Moskal, J. de Halleux, and M. Fahndrich. Touchdevelop: programming cloud-connected mobile devices via touchscreen. In *Proceedings of the 10th SIGPLAN symposium on New ideas, new paradigms, and reflections on programming and software*, ONWARD '11, pages 49–60, New York, NY, USA, 2011. ACM.

[12] S. Uludag, M. Karakus, and S. W. Turner. Implementing it0/cs0 with scratch, app inventor for android, and lego mindstorms. In *Proceedings of the 2011 conference on Information technology education*, SIGITE '11, pages 183–190, New York, NY, USA, 2011. ACM.

[13] D. Wolber. App inventor and real-world motivation. In *Proceedings of the 42nd ACM technical symposium on Computer science education*, SIGCSE '11, pages 601–606, New York, NY, USA, 2011. ACM.

[14] D. Wolber, H. Abelson, E. Spertus, and L. Looney. *App Inventor - Create Your Own Android Apps.* O'Reilly, 2011.

[8] http://research.microsoft.com/hawaii/

Evaluation of a Collaborative Instructional Framework for Programming Learning

Luis Miguel Serrano Cámara
Universidad Rey Juan Carlos
C/ Tulipán S/N, Móstoles
28933 Madrid, Spain
0034 914887076
luismiguel.serrano.camara@urjc.es

Maximiliano Paredes Velasco
Universidad Rey Juan Carlos
C/ Tulipán S/N, Móstoles
28933 Madrid, Spain
0034 914887076
maximiliano.paredes@urjc.es

J. Ángel Velázquez-Iturbide
Universidad Rey Juan Carlos
C/ Tulipán S/N, Móstoles
28933 Madrid, Spain
0034 916647454
angel.velazquez@urjc.es

ABSTRACT
Our work lies within the collaborative approach to learning CS1. We developed an instructional framework for collaborative learning (named CIF) that is oriented by educational objectives at the analysis level of Bloom's taxonomy. Moreover, the framework is supported by a platform (named MoCAS) of collaborative tools delivered with mobile devices. In this paper an experiment is presented to evaluate the educational effectiveness of CIF and MoCAS vs. three different learning approaches. We selected a topic representative of analysis tasks, namely scope of identifiers. The experiment was conducted with four groups, respectively using a classical lecture format, a collaborative approach, the CIF framework, and CIF plus the MoCAS tool. The experiment obtains statistically significant results, showing enhanced learning with the joint use of CIF and MoCAS.

Categories and Subject Descriptors
K.3.1 [**Computers and Education**]: Computer Uses in Education; K.3.2 [**Computers and Education**]: Computer and Information Science Education – *computer science education.*

General Terms
Experimentation, Human Factors.

Keywords
CS1, Computer Supported Collaborative Learning (CSCL), Bloom's Taxonomy, Mobile Devices, Evaluation.

1. INTRODUCTION
The teaching of CS1 is an actual challenge for teachers and students and has intensively been addressed within the CS education research community [11]. There is increasing consensus in that traditional teaching models, in which the instructor is the center of the learning process while students only play a passive role (they just listen), are not the most suitable for learning in general, and for complex subjects in particular. Passive attitude produces monotony and in the sequel lack of motivation in students and, as result, about only 5% of the topics taught by the teacher are remembered by the student [8].

ITiCSE'12, July 3–5, 2012, Haifa, Israel.

There exist several active learning pedagogical approaches that improve students' motivation, for example, problem-based learning (PBL [1,3]), project-oriented learning (POL [7]), case-based learning (CBL [5]), etc. These approaches can be combined with collaborative learning if several students work together to achieve a common goal [4]. The Computer Supported Collaborative Learning (CSCL) field gives computer support to these approaches.

If we want to use these general pedagogies in any specific subject, in particular in programming, they must be adapted to the subject peculiarities. Thus, there are some CSCL tools and active learning approaches for programming learning, like the Classroom Presenter [13] and SABATO [6] approaches, and the ActiveClass [9], Group Scribbles [14] and SICAS-COL [10] tools. However, they are not guided by educational objectives so assessment is problematic. One solution consists in adopting an educational taxonomy. For example, Bloom´s taxonomy proposes a classification of educational objectives [2]. It proposes six levels of learning achievement, sorted in increasing level of difficulty: (1) knowledge, (2) comprehension, (3) application, (4) analysis, (5) synthesis, and (6) evaluation.

In a previous work, we developed an instructional framework called Collaborative Instructional Framework (CIF [12]), which is oriented by educational objectives of the analysis level of Bloom's taxonomy. Moreover, CIF is supported by the platform MoCAS (Mobile Collaborative Argument Support) of collaborative tools delivered with mobile devices such as smartphones or PDAs.

Despite the high acceptance of CIF by students, we only had anecdotal evidence of its educational efficiency. Consequently, we conducted an experiment based on the following working hypothesis: "The CIF framework improves learning efficiency". In order to obtain more an elaborated answer than yes/no, we also took into consideration the use of the MoCAS platform. Consequently, the experiment was carried out with four groups: (1) one experimental group using the CIF framework, (2) one experimental group using CIF and a PDA as an extra discussion channel, (3) one experimental group working collaboratively, and (4) a control group working with a classical lecture format. The experiment was focused on the learning of a basic programming concept, namely the scope of identifiers.

The structure of the paper is as follows. Section 2 introduces the instructional framework CIF and a software tool called MoCAS, which supports it. The experiment is described in the following two sections, the procedure in Section 3 and the results in Section 4. Finally, Section 5 contains our conclusions and future work.

2. BACKGROUND

2.1 Overview of the Instructional Framework

The collaborative instructional framework CIF provides the teacher with guidelines to create, develop, and evaluate activities under a collaborative learning paradigm. CIF is oriented to the analysis level of Bloom's taxonomy [2]. The analysis level was selected because it is especially appropriate for collaborative learning. In its original statement by Bloom et al. [2], the analysis level was divided into three sub-levels and sixteen educational objectives.

CIF is composed of sixteen Independent Domain Cards (IDCs), one for each educational objective of the analysis level. Each IDC gives a guideline to the instructor about how to achieve its corresponding analysis objective. Each IDC consists of three sections: (1) problem statement, which allows achieving the corresponding analysis objective; (2) detailed instruction on how to work collaboratively to achieve the learning goal, and (3) an assessment of learning achievements.

For the instruction in the classroom (step 2 above), CIF defines a set of elementary activities which are the building blocks of any activity. In the rest of the paper, elementary activities are called Atomic Activities (AA, see Table 1).

Table 1. Set of Atomic Activities

Code	Description
AA1	Form groups of students
AA2	Deliver the problem statements to the groups
AA3	Perform an action associated to the problem statements
AA4	Exchange problem statements among groups
AA5	Display all the answers of groups to the same problem statement
AA6	Present answers to the whole class
AA7	Debate raising disagreements
AA8	Discuss the final answers
AA9	Teacher's mediation

A collaborative class can be defined as some combination of elementary activities. The use of CIF requires the following steps: (a) the teacher chooses one of the sixteen analysis objectives provided by CIF, (b) the teacher adapts the corresponding IDC to the domain under study, obtaining as a result a Domain Card (DC), and (c) the class is organized according to the DC suggestion of elementary activities. The process can be seen in Figure 1.

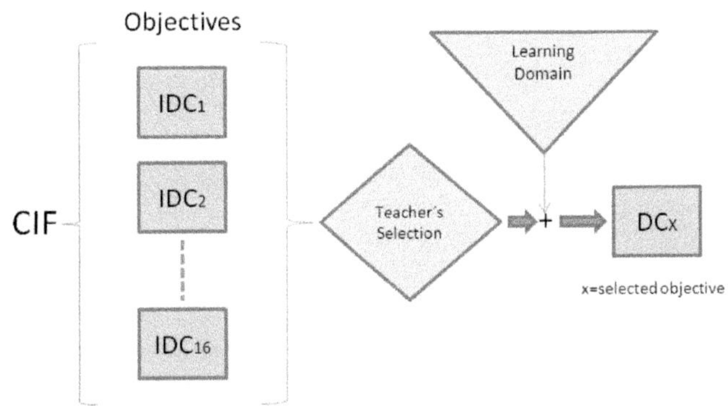

Figure 1. Usage of CIF

For the experiment reported in this paper, the teachers used the CIF framework for the domain of scope of identifiers (ID) in a structured programming language. We used the IDC corresponding to the first objective (namely "the ability to recognize unstated assumptions") belonging to the first sub-level "analysis of element" of the analysis level of Bloom's taxonomy [2].

After adapting an IDC to the domain, the resulting DC card contains the same three sections as the IDC card: (1) statement, in this case the assessment was "we propose an exercise to practice scope and visibility of identifiers in procedures, functions and the main program", (2) activity description with detailed instruction for the class, and (3) evaluation of the activity. Table 2 shows the list of activity descriptions stated to reach the objective. The sequence of Atomic Activities in column AAC must be performed, step by step, to guide the instruction of the whole activity

.

Table 2. DC - Domain Card for objective 1 under a specific domain: identifier scope in programming languages. (*) AAC= Atomic Activity Codes

Activity description	AAC(*)
Form different groups. Give each group an exercise. For example, group A and group B	AA1 AA2
Each group has to distinguish/recognize the scope of the IDs contained in a given program	AA3
The groups exchange their problem statements and repeat the second activity (previous row)	AA4 AA3
Once the problem statements have been analyzed by at least two groups, we put answers together. We check all the answers to each problem statement The answers from the different groups to each problem statement are clustered and displayed; the teacher must promote dialogue and discussion among groups The presentation of clustered answers will be made by the members of the corresponding groups	AA5 AA6
A debate about disagreements will be moderated by the teacher	AA7 AA8 AA9

2.2 MoCAS: A Tool for Collaborative Discussion in PDAs

A software tool based on the CIF framework called Mobile Collaborative Argument Support (MoCAS) was developed. In its current state of implementation, MoCAS supports several programming languages (Pascal, C and Java) and the instruction of a representative topic of analysis tasks, namely scope of identifiers (ID) in procedural programming.

MoCAS completely supports the class instruction, so it supports all the Atomic Activities of the CIF framework (see Table 1), but the different kinds of users are allowed to use different AAs. For teachers, MoCAS provides all the AAs but AA3, namely: to group students (AA1), to deliver problem statements to groups (AA2), to exchange problem statements among groups (AA4), to the result of merging the answers of groups to the same problem statement (AA5), to present answers to the whole class (AA6), to debate over disagreements (AA7), discuss the final answers (AA8) and teacher mediation (AA9).

For students, MoCAS implements: perform the action each objective indicates (AA3). Every student can view the source code given by the teacher in a PDA (Figure 2) and discuss about the ID scope contained in the code. According to the DC shown in Table 2, students must fill collaboratively a table with the scope of each ID in every section on the code -procedures, functions, and main program- (Figure 3). They can insert an ID to a section of the code, vote other insertions (confirm or dismiss) and delete IDs. MoCAS allows students to know the ownership of any contribution, to feedback from others members of the group (the acceptance or dismissal of proposals), so they build together the table that is the solution to the given exercise.

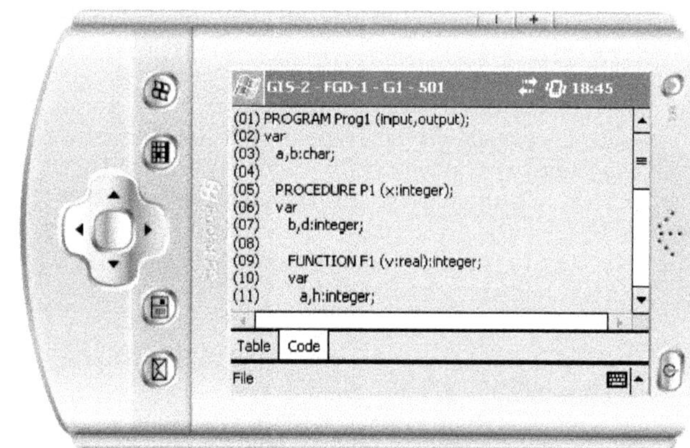

Figure 2. MoCAS´s Code Tab

MoCAS provides additional benefits such us: (1) supporting the debate and allowing to merge the contributions done not only by a group but by the whole class, (2) MoCAS provides an additional interaction channel (apart from oral exchange of information) to perform the list of activities (Table 2), and (3) MoCAS creates an automatic solution to any statement (i.e. code) and compares it with the collaborative solutions developed by the class.

MoCAS is based on a client/server architecture. A coordinator role controls all the contributions done by each member of the group. MoCAS is built under the Microsoft .Net Framework on the server site, and the .Net Compact Framework in the PDA devices. To store information, the MySQL database engine was used and to promote further functionality, communication was based on WebServices.

The hardware requirements to use the tool are: (1) a personal computer running any Windows version to install MoCAS server, (2) PDAs running Windows Mobile with MoCAS client installed, and (3) a Wireless Access point to implement the wireless net.

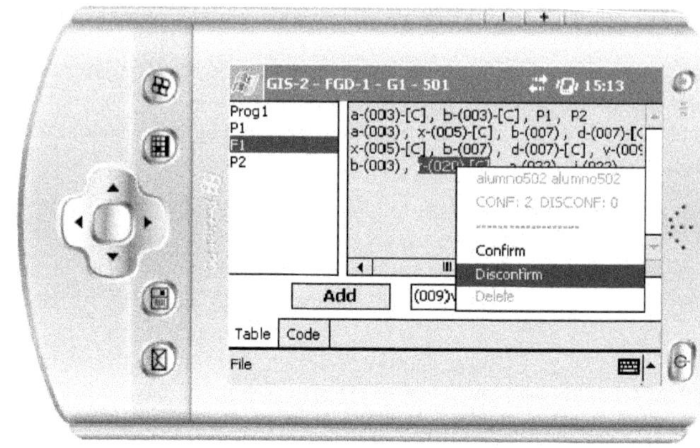

Figure 3. MoCAS´s Collaborative Table Tab

3. EXPERIMENT PROCEDURE

The aim of this experiment was to compare the learning efficiency of four kinds of teaching methodology involving collaboration or use of MoCAS: lecture, collaborative teaching, collaborative teaching using CIF, and collaborative teaching using CIF plus MoCAS.

The population contained 215 freshmen students of Computer Science, and the subject was "Introduction to Programming" (i.e. CS1), where students are introduced to procedural programming. The programming language adopted for the course currently is Pascal. Students were enrolled in two different campuses of the Rey Juan Carlos University, Móstoles and Vicálvaro, during the academic year 2010/2011. In Table 3 the sample distribution for the four different groups is shown. The groups were built up at random with the students of each campus.

Table 3. Distribution of the sample

Group Type	INDIV	C	CC	CC+MoCAS
Number of Students	57	50	42	66

We define the dependent variable, called Learning Efficiency (LE), as the level of knowledge acquired by a student on a specific concept. We define LE for each student as the difference between his/her score in the post-test and in the pre-test.

The formula is: Learning Efficiency (LE) = Post-test – Pre-test.

The pre-test and the post-test were made out of multiple-choice questions with three possible answers each one. The pre-test consisted of 12 questions, and the post-test consisted of 11 questions.

The experiment was conducted in a single session, lasting 2 consecutive hours in total (Figure 4), and consisted of four steps:

1) Pre-test. Its aim was to measure the students' dependent variable, defined as previous knowledge about the concept of ID scope in a programming language. Each test was filled individually and it lasted 20 minutes.

2) An introductory class was conducted, explaining the basic concepts of ID scope. It lasted 15 minutes with an extra period of 20 minutes to organize groups, to distribute problem statements and to explain the activity to the students.

3) Learning activity. Four groups were formed and each one performed the activity using a different approach. It took 45 minutes.

4) Pos-test. It also was filled individually in 20 minutes to measure the knowledge acquired with the learning activity.

Notice that steps 1, 2, and 4 were equal to the four groups while only step 3 differs among the experiments.

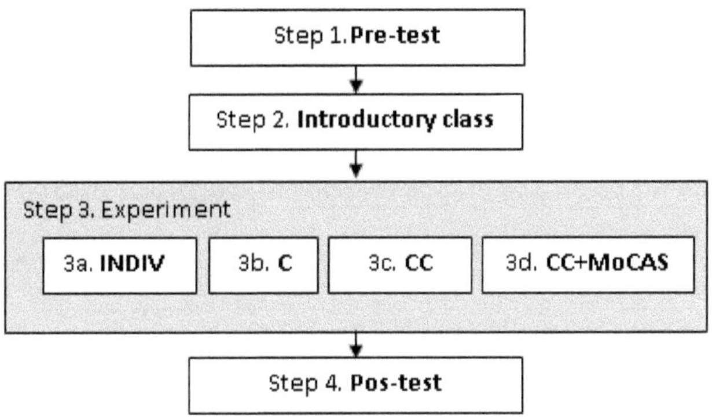

Figure 4. Parts of the experiment

The learning activity (step 3 above) was conducted as follows:

3a) Individual Control Group (INDIV). The class was based on a traditional lecture format. Students solved individually the exercises proposed by the teacher (30 minutes) and the last 15 minutes the teacher solved the exercise on the board and clarified any doubts.

3b) Collaborative Experimental Group (C). The class was conducted using a collaborative approach. The teacher formed random groups of 4 students. Each group solved different exercises (30 minutes) and the last 15 minutes the teacher solved doubts to the class.

3c) Collaborative Experimental Group based on CIF (CC). The class was conducted using a collaborative approach using the CIF methodology. The teacher guided the class according to CIF. Groups of 4 students were formed and two exercises were given to each group. Each exercise consisted in filling a table with the scope of all the identifiers found in each piece of code (30 minutes). During the last 15 minutes, a member of each group filled a table for each exercise on the board. The whole class discussed all the answers, while the teacher role was mediation.

3d) Collaborative Experimental Group based on CIF and using MoCAS (CC+MoCAS). The class was conducted under the collaborative approach using the CIF methodology and supported by the MoCAS tool. Due to the lack of PDA devices, it was conducted in five sessions in a computer laboratory with 12 students at a time. It proceeded the same way as CC, but supported by MoCAS. First, the teacher grouped the students using MoCAS (four students per group) and explained how to use MoCAS with an example (the 20 minutes used in the other approaches to organize and distribute the groups). In a second step, the teacher submitted through MoCAS an exercise to each group (the same exercise to all the groups). Each group had to fill up a table collaboratively with the ID scope on every section of the code (30 minutes). Every student had a PDA to interact with (in some cases a PDA was shared by two students). In addition, there were a board and a video projector in the class, where the source code and the tables built by the students were shown. Afterwards, the students were able to compare their solution with the solutions of other groups, creating an argumentative process. Finally, the MoCAS tool generated an automatic solution and compared it with the merged table obtained in the previous step. MoCAS showed the mistakes contained on the merged table, and these mistakes were clarified by the teacher (15 minutes).

Four teachers took part in the experiment, with more than 4 years of teaching experience on the subject. Three of them respectively participated in the INDIV, C and CC approaches, and the forth participated in the CC+MoCAS groups. The activities for the INDIV and C groups were developed by teachers without any kind of knowledge about the CIF framework in order to avoid interferences in the experiment.

The organization of the students in the CC+MoCAS approach is shown in Figure 5. Each group was placed in a row with their own PDA running the MoCAS tool. The total number of groups per session was three.

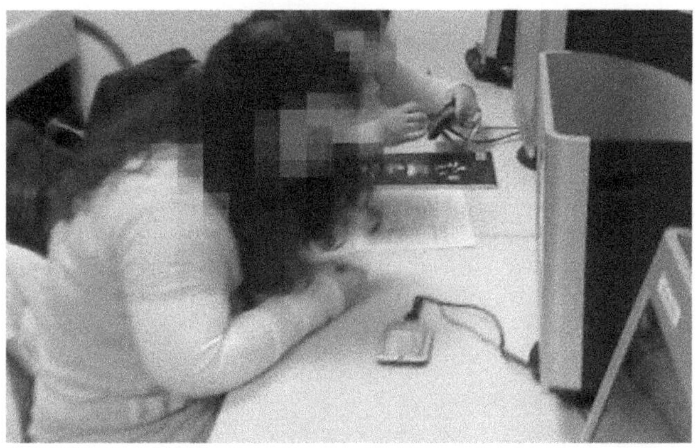

Figure 5. Students using MoCAS

4. RESULTS

In a first approach, the statistical variables that we considered were the mean and the standard deviation, both obtained from the pre- and post- tests. The resulting values are shown in Table 4 (range of values from 1 to 10).

As we can see in Table 4 (post-test mean row), the values of the arithmetic mean rise from 2.74 up to 5.63, having INDIV the lowest value (2.74), then groups C and CC follow (4.52 and 5.30), and CC+MoCAS has the highest value (5.63). Therefore, the three groups under a collaborative paradigm had better scores compared with the INDIV approach. They had about twice the score in the post-test than the INDIV group. Figure 6 shows graphically the difference in knowledge acquisition for the four approaches.

Table 4. Results of the experiments

	Learning paradigms\ Measurement	INDIV	C	CC	CC+ MoCAS
Pre-test	Mean	1.50	2.48	1.94	1.34
	Standard deviation	2.12	2.26	2.59	2.11
Pos-test	Mean	2.74	4.52	5.30	5.63
	Standard deviation	2.44	2.45	2.61	2.80
LE mean		1.24	2.04	3.36	4.29

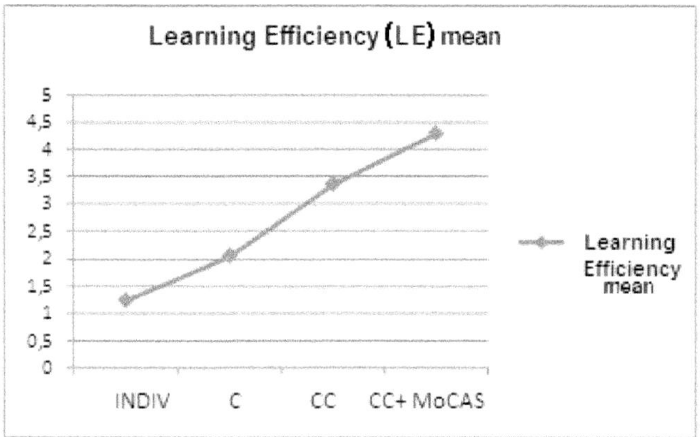

Figure 6. Variable LE mean (Learning Efficiency mean) by groups

Regarding the LE (Learning Efficiency) variable (Table 4, last row), we can see that the best scores are obtained by the two groups who used the CIF methodology (groups CC and CC+MoCAS): 3.36 and 4.29 respectively. Those values are twice the values obtained by the groups which did not follow the CIF framework (groups INDIV and C): 1.24 and 2.05 respectively.

In order to determine whether these results are statistical significant, we carried out a statistical analysis using the SPSS statistical package. To compare the mean, we computed the one-way ANOVA test. ANOVA has two prerequisites: (a) normality of the samples and (b) homogeneity of variance. In all the analysis the significant standard error was 5% (p=0.05).

To check the normality of the samples, we executed the One Simple Kolmogorov-Smirnov test. Due to the number of students of the sample (gl>40 for all the experiment types), we only used the Shapiro-Wilk result. Table 5 shows the results. As we can see in the last column (Sig column), all the Sig values are greater than the p value. Therefore, all the experiment types (INDIV, C, CC and CC+MoCAS) are normal distributed.

To test the homogeneity of variance hypothesis, Levene tests were executed, obtaining a Sig value of 0.126, greater than p. Therefore, the null hypothesis was accepted (homogeneity of variance confirmation).

Having satisfied both prerequisites, the result of the one-way ANOVA test shows Sig(ANOVA)=0.00. This accepts the alternative hypothesis (there is a difference among the experiments). However, to determinate where the differences lay, a Scheffé POS-HOC test needs to be done. Scheffé compares one experiment type with all the others, and the results are displayed in Table 6.

Table 5. Normality test

Experiment type	Shapiro-Wilk		
	Statistic	gl	Sig.
INDIV	0.961	57	0.063
C	0.963	50	0.115
CC	0.974	42	0.446
CC + MoCAS	0.985	66	0.597

Table 6. Scheffé POS-HOC test

Experiment Type	Sig. Experiment Type			
	INDIV	C	CC	CC + MoCAS
INDIV		0.633	0.015	0.000*
C	0.633		0.278	0.003*
CC	0.015	0.278		0.530
CC+MoCAS	0.000	0.003	0.530	

According to Sheffé results, only the pair (intersection between row and column) with Sig<p are statistically different. Therefore, the pairs: (INDIV,CC), (INDIV,CC+MoCAS) and (C,CC+MoCAS) are statistically different. Nevertheless, taking the Bonferroni correction used to solve the problem of multiple comparisons, the new p' is equal to 0.0083 ($p'=(p/N)$ | N=number of tests compared, in our study N=6, each approach compared with the others without repetition). This new and lower p value (p') restricts the statistical difference to pairs 2 and 3 (see Table 6, values marked with an asterisk).

Putting together the Sheffé results, the Bonferroni correction and the sample mean showed in Table 4, we can conclude the following about learning efficiency:

- Collaborative learning (C) is not statistically significant vs. traditional learning (INIDIV).
- Collaborative learning guided by CIF (CC) is close to be statistically significant vs. INDIV, but not compared to C.
- The CC+MoCAS approach compared with INDIV or C is statistically significant, thus learning efficiency is higher with CC+MoCAS.

To sum up, the key difference is caused by using together CIF and MoCAS. Taking everything into consideration, we cannot strictly assert our initial working hypothesis ("The CIF framework improves learning efficiency"), but we may claim the higher efficiency of CIF plus MoCAS. A supporting anecdote is that (Table 4) students' knowledge of the CC+MoCAS group before the experiment had the lowest score (1.34) compared to the other groups, but when the experiment finished, it was the group with best results (post-test mean 5.63)

5. CONCLUSIONS

We have introduced the instructional framework CIF, designed to guide and assist in the instruction of collaborative classes, as well as the software tool MoCAS that supports it. The main goal of this paper was to compare four different teaching approaches to determinate whether there was an improvement in learning efficiency using CIF and MoCAS. We have described the procedure and the results of an experiment conducted in the classroom about a basic programming concept (ID scope). The experiment was carried out with four groups: one experimental group (CC) used the CIF framework, a second experimental group (CC+MoCAS) used CIF and MoCAS as an extra discussion channel, a third experimental group (C) did the experiment under the collaborative paradigm, and a control group (INDIV) learned the concept in a classical lecture format.

The dependent variable was learning efficiency. The results allowed us to compare the dependent variable among the different experimental and control groups. Not only was basic analysis over the data computed, but also a deeper statistical analysis. The results prove the effectiveness of our combined proposal using CIF and MoCAS. Furthermore, the use of smartphones and PDA meant an extra motivation to CS1 students.

In the future, we plan to analyze personal interviews with students and observations in video that were gathered at the time of the sessions. This way, we expect to obtain more information about students' difficulties. We also want to check the learning effectiveness of our proposal along a longer period of instruction. Finally, we would like to implement an Android-based client to MoCAS and web-based client that could run on any browser even on mobile devices.

6. ACKNOWLEDGMENTS

This work was supported by research grant TIN2011-29542-C02-01 of the Spanish Ministry of Economy and Competitiveness.

7. REFERENCES

[1] Barrows, H.S. 1985. *How to Design a Problem-Based Curriculum for the Preclinical Years*. New York: Springer.

[2] Bloom, B.J., Englehart, M.D., Furst, M.D., Hill, E.J., and Krathwohl, D.R. 1956. *Taxonomy of Educational Objectives: The Classification of Educational Goals. Handbook 1: Cognitive Domain*. New York: David McKay Company.

[3] De la Cueva, V., De Gasperín, R., Ruiz, M., Beristain, L.M., Morales, S., Ramirez, H., and de Gasperín, A. 2000. El modelo educativito constructivista ABC2: Aprendizaje Basado en la Construcción del Conocimiento. In *Proceedings of Congreso Nacional I Retos y Expectativas de la Universidad de México* (Guadalajara, Mexico, 2000).

[4] Dillenbourg, P. 1999. Introduction: What do you mean by 'Collaborative Learning'? In Dillenbourg (Ed.), *Collaborative Learning. Cognitive and Computational Approaches*. Oxford: Elsevier Science, 1-19.

[5] Harvard Business School. 2003. How the case method works. DOI=http://www.hbs.edu/mba/experience/learn/thelearningmodel/howthecasemethodworks.

[6] Jiménez, J.A., Pavony, M.A., and Álvarez, A.F., 2008. Integration environment of PBL and CSCL for teaching algorithms and programming in engineering. *Revista de Avances en Sistemas e Informática*. 5(3), 189-194.

[7] Jones, B.F., Rasmussen, C.M., and Moffitt, M.C. 1997. *Real-Life Problem Solving: A Collaborative Approach to Interdisciplinary Learning*. Washington, DC: American Psychological Association.

[8] Kwok, R., and Ma, J. 1999. Use of a group support system for collaborative assessment. *Computers & Education*, 32, 109-125.

[9] Ratto, M., Shapiro, R.B., Truong, T. M., and Griswold, W. G. 2003. The ActiveClass project: Experiments in encouraging classroom participation. In *Proceedings of the Conference* on *Computer Support for Collaborative Learning* (Bergen, Norway, June 14-18, 2003). CSCL 2003. 477-486.

[10] Rebelo, B., Mendes, A., Marcelino, M., and Redondo, M. 2005. Sistema Colaborativo de Suporte à Aprendizagem em Grupo da Programação—SICAS-COL. In *Proceedings of the VII Simpósio Internacional de Informática Educativa* (Leiria, Portugal).

[11] Robins, A., Roundtree, J., and Roundtree, N. 2003. Learning and teaching programming: A review and discussion. *Computer Science Education*, 13(2), 137-172.

[12] Serrano-Cámara, L.M., Paredes-Velasco, M., and Velázquez-Iturbide J.A. 2010. Aprendizaje colaborativo guiado por objetivos educativos. Aplicación en el aprendizaje de la programación. In *Proceedings of the XI Simposio Nacional de Tecnologías de la Información y las Comunicaciones en la Educación* (Valencia, Spain, September 7-10, 2010). SINTICE 2010, Valencia: Gaceta Grupo Editorial, 3-10. DOI=http://eciencia.urjc.es/dspace/handle/10115/4209.

[13] Simon, B., Anderson, R., Hoyer, C., and Su, J. 2004. Preliminary Experiences with a Tablet PC Based System to Support Active Learning in Computer Science Courses. In *Proceedings of the 9th Annual SIGCSE Conference on Innovation and Technology in Computer Science Education* (Leeds, UK, June 28-30, 2004) ITiCSE 2004. ACM Press. 213-217.

[14] SRI International, Group Scribbles. 2006 DOI=http://groupscribbles.sri.com.

Capstone Project: Fair, Just and Accountable Assessment

Vivienne Farrell
Faculty of ICT
Swinburne University
Melbourne, Australia
+61 3 92145000
vfarrell@swin.edu.au

Gilbert Ravalli
Faculty of ICT
Swinburne University
Melbourne, Australia
+61 3 92145000
gravalli@swin.edu.au

Graham Farrell
Faculty of ICT
Swinburne University
Melbourne, Australia
+61 3 92145000
gfarrell@swin.edu.au

Paul Kindler
Faculty of ICT
Swinburne University
Melbourne, Australia
+61 3 92145000
pkindler@swin.edu.au

David Hall
Faculty of ICT
Swinburne University
Melbourne, Australia
+61 3 92145000
djhall@swin.edu.au

ABSTRACT

Fair, just and accountable assessment for the individual student in the capstone project requires establishing criteria beyond the final project output to meet the objectives of the capstone project experience. Current research is limited and requires solutions that are not subjective, enable formative and summative assessment with student input and are not onerous on supervisors and/or students. This paper draws on input from highly experienced academics supervising capstone projects in ICT, critically reviews recent publications pertaining to capstone project assessment and current capstone students opinions. The outcome of this input led to the development, trial and evaluation of a toolkit to assist supervisors in both formative and summative assessment of capstone projects.

Categories and Subject Descriptors

K.3 COMPUTERS AND EDUCATION

Keywords

Capstone, Project, Assessment, TCS, Peer, Group, Team, IT

1. INTRODUCTION

The capstone project experience is the culmination of a student's knowledge and skills in preparation for impending integration into the workplace. It not only offers students the opportunity to piece together their academic and technical learning but also to develop and practice a maturity towards team work, communication, client liaison, role playing, ethics, peer assessment and understanding the impact of the integration of their project on the wider community.

In offering all these benefits there are identifiable challenges of assessing the individual that have been a long-standing issue for instructors and consequently students. In order to evaluate the individual within the group it is essential to provide assessment that is not only fair and just for the individual but also accountable. Individual assessment for the capstone project or in general any team project has historically created a situation where subjective assessment is required to differentiate individual student achievements. Clear [1]identified the "3Ps" in an IT disciplined capstone projects as pertaining to Product, Process and Progression. Clear [1] recommends Product assessment (scope, expectations and outcomes) to be assessed objectively; Process (portfolio, quality management, communication etc) to be assessed objectively; Progression (professionalism, initiative, perseverance and responsibility) to be assessed subjectively, with contributions from reflective reports, evidence of improvement and "observations and opinions of supervisors.." While Clear [1] is comfortable with this subjective assessment, markers often find it difficult to justify the final grade. This is exacerbated in capstone projects where the student's individual marks can vary from a Distinction to a Fail, a situation that requires justification.

The motivation for introducing a system that identified the individual student contribution was to address the issue of "free-riders" identified by Aggarwal and O'Brien [2]. Latu [3]in their study interviewed students to identify their preferences when considering the group work grading. They found that 94% of their students wanted to identify "free-riders", defined as "an individual working in a group setting fails to contribute his or her fair share." [2]. In this study (79%) felt that individual grades were preferable to group marks.

The scope of this research has been restricted to capstone projects where students undertake a real world project within the ICT industry. We restrict the student group size from 3 to 5.
The aim of this research is to design and develop a system with supporting documentation that will enable a fair allocation of grades to individuals undertaking group work. This system is to ensure that the assessment considers the main objectives of the capstone project experience and not just the final project outcome as discussed earlier.

This paper considers the existing literature and present practices of assessment methods for capstone projects. Next it discusses the outcomes from focus groups held with experienced capstone project supervisors, representative student focus groups and surveys (pre, during and post the capstone experience). From the literature review, focus groups and surveys we next derive the criteria to optimize assessment practices. We then report on the designing and development of a manageable, verifiable Team Contribution System (TCS) as a solution to meet our derived criteria. The required documentation to support the TCS is then developed to assist capstone project assessors. Finally we discuss identified further work.

2. DEVELOPMENT PROCESS OF THE TCS

In the initial stages of this research discussions were held in the form of a focus group with academics experienced with team project supervision. The brief was to set the parameters of the study, identify issues with team project assessment, identify desired outcomes from studies and develop alternative assessment methods. Further, a preliminary literature review of capstone project assessment (CPA) research was carried out by drawing on recent studies from prominent journals and conference proceedings. Our primary focus was on identifying novel, original and grounded studies as opposed to adaptations and extensions of existing research. These studies were subsequently

analysed by the authors both independently and collectively. This approach compares to similar reviews of this nature (e.g. Tornatzky & Klein,[4]). A greater emphasis was placed on research studies that displayed a high level of rigour in terms of methodology in its establishment of practices, tools and models.
Student focus groups and surveys were undertaken to gauge student's perception of the assessment and objectives of group projects prior to commencing, during and again at the end of the capstone project experience.

The analysis of the literature as well as the cumulative experience of the authors and an extended group of experienced academics led to the establishment of a criteria for developing a Team Contribution System (TCS) for recognition of an individual student's contribution.

2.1 Academic Focus Group Discussions

We assembled a group of seven academics, experienced in supervising and coordinating software team projects. The brief was to determine the scope, direction and criteria for this study as well as discussing their needs and experiences in developing a fair and equitable marking system. The outcomes of these discussions contributed to the final study objectives as discussed in Section 2.4.

2.2 Literature Review

There are many documented methods for the grading of individual students working on team-based projects. It is often the practice of academics new to capstone project assessment, to attempt many combinations before reaching an acceptable solution [5]. Lejk and Wyvill [6] in their own practice identified six different approaches to the allocation of marks to group work that consider: individual versus group marks, student contribution to assessment distribution, weighing factors for individuals and separating individual and group assessed items. Malcolmson and Shaw[7], in the pharmaceutical educational area, espouses that " a common format for this mixed assessment [of group work] is for the product of the group work to be marked in the traditional way by the lecturer, and the contribution of the individual to the work assessed by the team members", this view is well supported [8], [9] [5] and [10].

2.2.1 Capstone Project Assessment Strategies

There are numerous factors affecting group assessment that previous research has identified, which can be divided into 2 categories, as identified by Clear [1] above, being assessment that can be validated from objective data and assessment that is subjective in nature; opinion based peer assessment, contribution to discussion and ideas, etc. Objective assessment is often used to form the basis of a group mark while subjective assessment is used to define the individual contribution to the project.

Hayes [11] suggests that a variety of assessment strategies works better when determining the portion of the subjective assessment for the individual final grade. Richards [5]and Herbert [12] consider the student evaluation in isolation is not sufficient and insists that other methods also be used to confirm them. ([13], [11], [14] [15], [12], [16], [17]). In particular Sukhodolsky [16] conducts a class room activity in the form of quizzes enabling the pin pointing of individual awareness of progress of the project. There are many who consider the continual intervention could be viewed to take away the independent nature of the capstone project. Umphress et al. [17] introduced process control, but found that the students complained about the onerous process and the number of forms, concluding that it would be advantageous to minimize the assessment, in turn reducing the burden.

2.2.2 What should be measured?

As we are interested in the student's professional development we should have an understanding of what constitutes a level of expertise in that field and how to develop it. This allows us to take students beyond minimal standards and provides them a basis and opportunity for development. In the case of capstone projects the task seems to be one of evaluating a student's current knowledge and skills to provide appropriate feedback in order to move that performance along the continuum toward expertise.

Ravalli et al suggest eleven broad categories of knowledge and skills for Information systems and classifies each as either suited for objective or subjective assessment. Objective assessment is identified with to IS development process knowledge, information systems applications knowledge, technical knowledge, problem domain knowledge, organisational knowledge and general business knowledge. Subjective assessment relates to critical thinking, interpersonal skills, communication skills, personal attitudes and aspects.

To assist with the subjective marking peer assessment and recorded meeting minutes are of particular interest to this research, deserving special attention here, as they play a major role in the TCS assessment strategy.

2.2.3 Documenting Meeting Minutes

Meeting minutes and documenting of time on tasks are methods of assessment where students can be instructed and moderated on their use as an ongoing process at each point of contact between students and supervisor. This assessment is a strong contributor to formative assessment and tracking of the individual students involvement throughout the semester, offering validation of contribution and individual grades at the completion of the unit.

2.2.4 The Role of Peer Assessment

Peer assessment (PA) requires students to formally recognize the activities and offerings of other students in their pursuit of successful delivery. Peer assessment is considered to be an important contributor to the development of essential professional skills of reflection and critical thinking. Rees (2009) states that there appears to be a link between higher quality design of assessment and the inclusion of peer assessment.
Peer assessment provides formative learning-oriented feedback to complete the learning cycle, important for models of learning. It is perceived as a means of fairness in assessment where others see it as opportunities for reflection and feedback, an important component of the learning path [19]. Latu [3] in addressing the issue recommend that peer assessment be anonymous and rigorous being utilised for the first 3 tasks of the project.
Herbert [12] questions the ability of students to be objective in peer assessment and in particular not show signs of discrimination in their assessment. However the peer assessment activity may also create a focal point for discussion at team meetings during the progression of the project for fair distribution of the workload, not just a reflection at the end of the semester.
Latu [3] observed that the majority of students believe that instructors can not evaluate individual grades alone but require peer review and self-assessment as important contributors to the process. Reily [20] states that "evaluation and criticism are high level skills in Bloom's taxonomy, students who participate in a peer review process achieve a high order educational goal."

2.2.5 Team Work Assessment Tools

Previously instructors have developed and trialed various formulae for mark distribution to address the issue of fair grade allocation.

Malcolmson and Shaw [7] used Li's [21]formula, formulated to remove a student's score of their own contribution, by calculating the "Contribution Weighting Factor" (CWF).

Software tools have been developed to assist in the self and peer assessment, such as SPARK, where the interface enables students to self and peer assess against benchmarks, encouraging academic honesty. The concern is that it was time consuming and that the projects become assessment driven. In a study undertaken by Rees, 10% considered SPARK to primarily stop free-riders, 18% thought it as a tool for reflection alone and 63% consider it useful for both. Complaints about excessive burden were received from both students and supervisors.

2.2.6 Concerns of peer assessment.

Although it is generally accepted that peer assessment has an important role to play, some voice concerns about its use. Bushell [22]and Lejk [6] both found a high correlation between student and supervisor grades, even greater when reviews were undertaken in private, conflicting with providing feedback for student improvement.

Reily [20] and Bushell [22] state that reviewers often give arbitrary scores regardless of submission quality. Reily [20] identifies the existence of rogue reviews, motivated by retaliation, collusion, competition or laziness. Richards and Reilly [5] suggests that peer assessment can be a reliable tool using aggregate student reviews, such as Hamer's algorithm that penalises the use of rogue strategies by students. It is observed that experience and training improves the accuracy of peer assessments ([20]and [22])

Norcini [23] suggests three major factors contributing to reliability: "the number of relevant performances observed, the number of peers involved, and the number of aspects of competence being evaluated." Norcini [23] suggests that the higher the stakes in an assessment the more likely it is that the assessments will be over-assessed.

In terms of preparation for PA Richards encourages teams to discuss the distribution of marks prior to submitting individual forms so as to resolve issues and minimize disputes. Given that disputes may arise the development of some mechanism for dispute resolution needs to be considered. Richards [5] provides an example of their approach.

2.3 Student Views on Group Assessment

Student Survey

Students enrolled in the capstone project were surveyed prior to commencement. Ninety-four students responded to the survey of which 16 identified as being female and 48 as male. Thirty didn't provide information regarding their gender. The majority, 75% of students had previously been involved in group projects in which a shared group mark was given without consideration of individual contribution, though only 40% of those students felt that the mark they received for those projects was fair. 85% had undertaken group projects which provided individual marks with 68% stating that the individual marks they received were fair. From this we understand that the majority of students do not believe that shared group marks are fair though individual marks received for projects are fair.

54% believed that group members should be provided with a mix of both group and individual marks for their final project mark though 30% stated that they'd prefer to receive only an individual mark. At some time during their degree, 86% of students had been "given the opportunity to contribute to the process of mark allocation through peer assessment". 75% agreed that allowing other group members to contribute to their peers final mark made the assessment fairer. These survey results gave us a clear indication that students wanted to be able to contribute to the marks of other group members.

Focus Group Findings

Focus groups were held, with undergraduate and masters students prior to them undertaking the capstone project. As is reported in the literature and as was supported in our survey, students' main issue with groupwork projects in previous units was fellow students who were seen not to be contributing equally or fairly to the group workload. This seemingly has a great impact on the enjoyment of groupwork for students.

2.4 Summary of TCS Objectives

From the literature review, academic focus group and initial feedback received from students, a list of the objectives for a fair, just and accountable assessment was compiled. The need for a marking system was identified that enabled individual assessment within group assignments that was:

1. inclusive of student participation via peer reviews and recognition of contribution statements
2. include other skills than production of project output such as team involvement, client liaison, generating ideas, etc.
3. multiple components assessed both objectively and subjectively.
4. easily accessed and analysable documentation to support the assessment process. Clearly explained to the students at the beginning of the semester to alleviate concerns and possible claims of unfair grade distribution.
5. able to be validated by more than one means
6. offer both formative and summative assessment to the student
7. offer formative feedback for the supervisor
8. not onerous on either students or supervisors

The group considered that a consistent, well informed, well supported process would enable both students and supervisors to feel confident in providing both formative and summative assessment while enabling constant improvement of project and personal development.

3. THE TEAM CONTRIBUTION SYSTEM

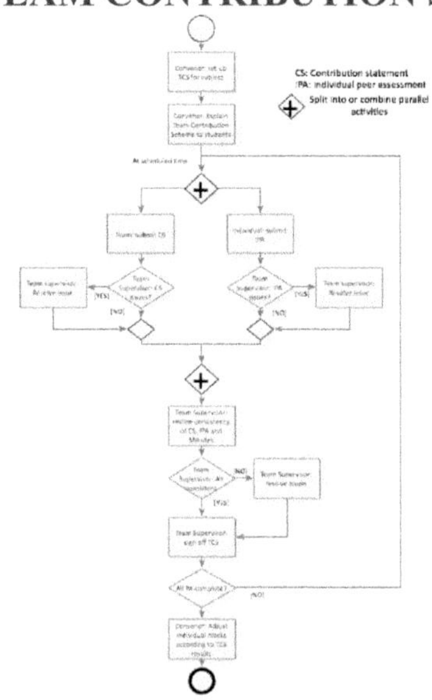

Figure 1: Team Contribution System Process

The TCS comprises of a cyclical feedback process that offers both formative and summative assessment. (see Figure 1).
In conjunction with the TCS documentation answers most of the requirements as discussed in section 2.4.
The design of the TCS was derived from the previous literature, which confirmed and expressed the experiences of the academics involved in this study adding some valuable insight into other research. The TCS is designed to answer the objectives as outlined in (Focus group discussions and lit review discussion)

3.1 The TCS Documentation

There are three types of submissions from students that make up the Team Contribution System: 'Contribution Statements' which are essentially a work log of time spent on various tasks, confidential 'Peer Assessments' of team members about themselves and their team members and finally 'Minutes' of team meetings. (Section 2.4 reqs. 1,3,4 and 5). For a project conducted over a 12 week semester there are three submissions of Contribution Statement and Peer Assessments at approximately weeks 5, 9 and at the end of the project. Contribution Statements must be signed off by all the team members and countersigned by the team's supervisor. In conjunction with the Contribution Statements, team members submit individual Peer Assessments separately and confidentially. The decision to submit the Contribution Statements and Peer Assessments approximately every four weeks was an arbitrary one based on a compromise between the tediousness of collecting, evaluating and enabling action upon the information while having information timely enough for useful formative feedback. Similarly, submission of meeting minutes is based on our experience in capstone projects. It was believed that teams needed to meet at least once each week to discuss their project and its progress, allocate work.

3.1.1 Contribution Statement (CS)

Team members are required to estimate how much time they have spent on various types of activities on their project over a particular time period (see Figure 1).

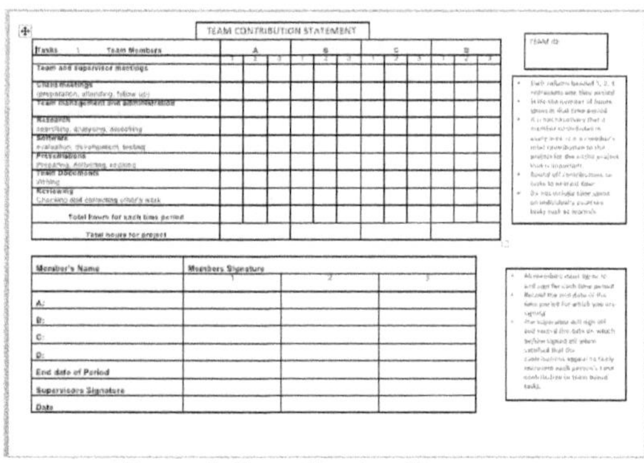

Figure 2 Contribution Statement

The CS (Figure 2) must be signed by all team members and countersigned by the team's supervisor. Students were requested to report only that time spent of activities that were team related and to exclude individual assessments such as journals or presentations that are assessed separately. The activities chosen on the contribution statement include broad categories that we believe to be relevant to requirements analysis and design projects and some technically based implementation projects relevant to our subject. The particular activities and their level of granularity is arbitrary and we have included categories of activities appropriate to what students typically do within our projects. Some obvious tasks that students report on are team meetings, interviews with clients, writing reports, developing models and presentations. Perhaps not so obvious to some students were tasks related to management, administration, review and correction of work submitted by other team members. The latter group of tasks tend to be unacknowledged or discounted in terms of the time required, which was often a source of irritation to those that performed those tasks (Section 2.4 req. 2).

When contribution statements are completed with diligence and truthfulness, they are a reasonable statement of the time spent on task. It is acknowledged that time on task does not necessarily reflect quality or quantity of contribution. However, as a first approximation, students expect that in a team project everyone is putting in a reasonable and fair effort. Where the quality or quantity of output by one or more members is not up to the standard expected, acknowledgment may appear in terms of time spent by others who take up the slack or improve the quality of products or processes. Initially, this document was seen as a tool to assist in the summative assessment of individual team members by providing a means of redistributing marks based on individual contribution as identified by Lejk and Wyvill. A number of supervisors found the contribution statement useful for formative assessment (section 2.4 req. 6 and 7). For example one poor work pattern identified was where one team member doing a substantial part of the writing of team documents while at the same time doing all the reviewing including their own work. Early detection through the use of this form enabled teams to change their work practice, allowing them to make better use of their time.

With regard to summative assessment, it should be noted that the marking of any group work components is done by academic staff. Students do not directly assess the work of other students as in some forms of peer assessment so Sadler's suggestion of potential contamination of results due to the performance of other students is not relevant to this aspect of the grading process.

3.1.2 Peer Group Assessment (PGA)

The PGA (Figure 3) requires students to evaluate their fellow team member's activities into two broad categories, the extent to which each member interacted and cooperated in group activities with other team members and the value that each member added to the progress of the project.

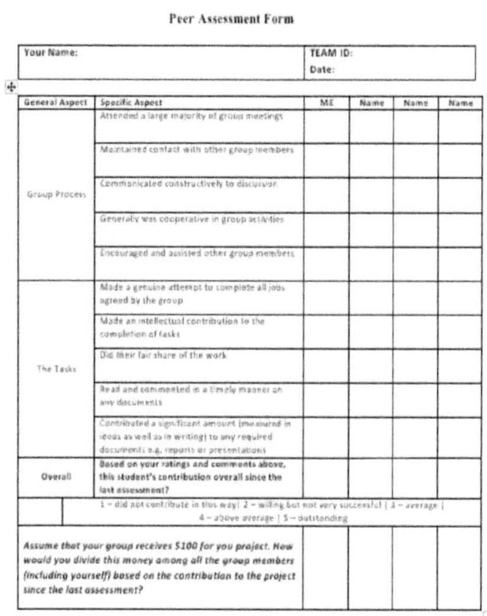

Figure 3 Peer Group Assessment

While this is subjective it represents a measure of the contribution of a person to the team as opposed to simply how much time they spent on team related tasks. Each student is finally asked to distribute an hypothetical $100 amongst the team members and decide how much to award each person. It is a common occurrence in teams that one or more team members are acknowledged as having added significantly more than others to the team overall, even though all members might contribute equally in terms of time. The PGA is submitted confidentially to the supervisor in an attempt to balance the possibility of peer coercion when filling out the CS (whether through sympathy or threat) and as recognition that this document is more personal in nature. The supervisor should review the PGAs before approving and countersigning the CS

As the first PGA and CS are completed early in the project life cycle, it provides an early warning to the supervisor of any impending issues cultivating within the project team.

3.1.3 Meeting Minutes

Teams are provided with a template (Figure 4) for meeting minutes that include areas for action items to be assigned to named individuals, a time frame for their completion and for reporting their status.

Meeting Minutes

Group name, date, and place (if it changes)

Action list from last meeting	Person	Date	Status
A description of any action that someone committed to work on or complete before the next meeting	The person or group who committed to the action	Date and time for completion or ASAP, soon, or next week.	Completed or not. Any other relevant information

Present

*Absent

Agenda items

Discussion, decisions, assignments

First agenda item.

Second agenda item.

Additional items.

Agenda items for the next meeting

Follow-up action	Person	Date
Next meeting	All	Date, time, place (if it changes)
A description of any action that someone committed to work on or complete before the next meeting	The person or group who committed to the action	Date and time for completion or ASAP, soon, or next week.

Adapted from from http://www.managementhelp.org/writing/minutes.htm

Figure 4 Meeting Minutes

Teams must formally meet at least once a week and submit their meeting minutes in a central repository accessible to all team members (but not other teams) and also to the team's supervisor. This imposes a discipline on teams to meet, discuss and distribute work and formally record what has transpired. The minutes of these team meetings and are tabled at each supervisor meeting enabling the supervisor to verify team member attendance, ensure that individual team members are meeting their committed tasks and provide a verification for the information submitted on the TCS. Meeting minutes are assessed and form part of the team marks for the project management so that there is an incentive for each team to record their minutes fully and accurately.

3.2 TCS as a Synergistic System

Independently each aspect of the TCS is not notable but we believe that their combined effect provides a reasonable window into the team's operation and the contribution made by each of the team members. While the contribution statement indicates time spent, the peer assessment is a subjective measure of soft skills to do teamwork such as communication, reliability, ideas etc. as well a subjective measure of the effectiveness of contribution rather than just time. Each aspect of the TCS can also act as a check on the other aspects so that if a team or team member provides inaccurate times in their CS then the confidential PGA can provide an opportunity for one or more team members to highlight this. The action items in meeting minutes can also be compared against the CS and PGAs to gauge what team members have been allocated and accomplished. While any one aspect of the TCS can be falsified or be filled in a biased fashion to coordinate across all three takes deliberate, systematic and cooperative effort by all team members.

The continual improvement in the student's understanding and skills in undertaking peer reviews, meeting minutes and recognition of time spent on a task were all concerns mentioned by Bushell [22], Lejk and Wyvill [6] , Norcini & Sadler [23] discussed in Section 2. With the support of team supervisors students can be guided through the problems and issues and hence arrive at more effective team interaction and improved understanding by the individual team members and the courage to be honest in their self and peer appraisal.

The TCS is designed to offer verification of the individual score by open viewing and discussions pertaining to periodical input. The TCS documentation provides triangulation in its validation in that each document validates the claims made in other documents.

With the TCS the assessor is able to validate any individual grades given that their own assumptions are underpinned by evidence from peers and the student being assessed.

3.3 Calculation of Final Mark

Like SPARK, the TCS assumes that all team based work submissions (e.g. reports, presentations, reviews etc.) are assessed by academic staff and a total mark is assigned for this work. This team mark is then redistributed amongst the team members based on a relative contribution derived from the individual peer assessments, time contribution statements and the supervisor's assessment of contribution. Meeting minutes may be examined where significant disagreement amongst team members exists regarding contribution. The precise details of the formula and approach that we have used to determine final student marks is beyond the scope of this paper and will be described in a subsequent paper. The important point to make is that final marks can be evidence based and justified even if there are some subjective aspects.

4. STUDENT RESPONSES TO TCS

Focus groups and a survey of the students enrolled in a 12 week capstone team projects in both the undergraduate and master's degrees was undertaken to gauge the student's experience with the implementation of the pilot TCS. At this stage we have some preliminary results to offer some insight into how the TCS was received and understood by the students.

The Contribution Statement was completed with varying honesty largely affected by peer pressure and friendship.

"We were pretty frank about this statement. Especially with our peer-assessment..."

"I think the contribution form is just a waste of time. Because, he's going to see what I write inside. So, I can say "he's doing the work" but then I get home and say, "he's doing less work""

In response to the concern of peer pressure other students were able to see the value in the multiple documents that either confirm or deny the claims made enabling the supervisor to be aware of an issue.

"But, because of that I suppose they will see the contribution form and the individual form and in the next meeting he'll (supervisor) say "why is there a difference between that?

Concern was raised regarding destroying team harmony and not achieving the optimal final product. It was apparent that students still considered the final product as the objective in achieving higher grades.

"I can do that..., then in the group there will be conflicts and we can't deliver a successful project... So, instead of one person getting less marks, we all get less marks."

Students commented on time contribution as a fair measurement.

I think hours are the only way you can neutrally mark.. At the end of the day, if it tallies up to be somewhat equal…

Others, conversely, felt that time was not a fair measurement of contribution. This raises the issue of effective time contribution versus time spent on task and how to rationalize these.

It's based on the number of hours. I think it's really, really poor and a terrible idea to quantify these things. My skills set is different to your skill set ….

Student stated that the most important factors regarding contribution were that the task was completed, and to an acceptable quality.

" I don't care…. I just want the task done in a perfect manner"

In summary the students were divided in their initial perception of the contribution statement, however during discussion they realised that by having the multiple forms to verify each claim they were able to alert supervisors of concerns. They also acknowledged that for some groups the contribution statement was a more reliable document whereas with others it was the peer reviews, both being substantiated by the minutes of the meetings. Students commented on the advantages of having input into the assessment and accountability to reduce freeloading.

5. CONCLUSION

Previous attempts at developing individual assessment solutions for group projects have tended to create a substantial amount of work for students and staff and be singular in the validation of the marks distribution. TCS provides a tool kit of documents that through their nature of both openness and privacy enables verification of student's honesty in their self and peer assessment as well as their contribution to the project. The TCS offers triangulation in the validation of the assigning of an individual mark through the peer reviews, meeting minutes and time contribution statements. The TCS supports personal growth as continual formative assessment enables students to reflect on their personal and group achievements such that they can recognize what is necessary for personal and group improvement. The TCS encourages supervisors to consider the overall objectives of the capstone project experience and to consider the individual as well as the group contribution while being able to account for the decisions made on the final individual grade.

6. FURTHER WORK

Although the TCS does not create a high volume of work for students, the retrieval and correlation of the various documents can be time consuming for the supervisor or assessing academic. Further work in this study will provide for an online system for entry of data by the student and assist supervisors and academics to have easy access to documents and automate document correlation for both formative and summative assessment. The system will be extended to support and automate the calculation of individual marks derived from the TCS. The new system will undergo pilot testing and refining as necessary.

7. REFERENCES

[1] Clear, T. Managing Mid-Project Progress Reviews : A Model for Formative Group Assessment in Capstone Projects. *ACM Inroads*, 12010), 14-15.

[2] Aggarwal, P. and O'Brien, C. L. 2008. Social Loafing on Group Projects: Structural Antecedents and Effect on Student Satisfaction. *Journal of Marketing Education, 30(3), pp.255-264. 30*, 2 2008), 255-264.

[3] Latu, S. and Blackshaw, R. *Group Work and Group Work Assessment for Computer Courses : A Systems Analysis and Design Case Study*. City, 2005.

[4] Tornatzky, L. G. and Klein, K. J. InnovationC har-acteristicsa nd Innovation Adoption-Implementation: A Meta-Analysis of Findings. *IEEE Transactions on Engineering Management* 29, 1 1982), 28-45.

[5] Richards, D. Designing Project-Based Courses with a Focus on Group Formation and Assessment. *ACM Transactions on Computing Education*, 9 2009).

[6] Lejk, M. and Wyvill, M. The Effect of the Inclusion of Self-assessment with Peer Assessment of Contributions to a Group Project : a Quantitative Study of Secret and Agreed Assessments. *Assessment & Evaluation in Higher Education*, 26 2001).

[7] Malcolmson, C. and Shaw, J. The Use of Self- and Peer-contribution assessments within a Final Year Pharmaceutics Assignment. *Pharmacy Education*, 52005), 169-174.

[8] Orsmond, P., Merry, S. and Callaghan, A. Communities of practice and ways to learning: charting the progress of biology undergraduates. *Studies in Higher Education*(2012/01/11, 1-17.

[9] Conway, R., Kember, D., Sivan, A. and Wu, M. Peer Assessment of an Individual ,Äôs Contribution to a Group Project. *Assessment & Evaluation in Higher Education*, 18, 1 (2012/01/11 1993), 45-56.

[10] Topping, K. Peer Assessment Between Students in Colleges and Universities. *Review of Educational Research*, 249-276.

[11] Hayes, J. H., Lethbridge, T. C. and Port, D. Evaluating Individual Contribution Toward Group Software Engineering Projects. In *Proceedings of the Proceedings of International Conference on Software Engineering,* (Portland, Oregon, 2003), [insert City of Publication],[insert 2003 of Publication].

[12] Herbert, N. *Quantitative Peer Assessment : Can students be objective ?* , City, 2007.

[13] Ge, Y., Han, P. and Xu, B. *A Comprehensive Approach for Software Group Project Assessment Based on Students' Evaluation.* IEEE, City, 2009.

[14] Wilkins, D. E. and Lawhead, P. B., , vol.32 , no. 1, 2000 . Evaluating Individuals in Team Projects. *ACM SIGCSE Bulletin archive*, 12000).

[15] Clark, N., Davies, P and Skeers, R. Self and Peer Assessment in Software Engineering Project. In *Proceedings of the Proceedings of the seventh Australasian Conference on Computing Education* (Newcastle, Australia, 2005),

[16] Sukhodolsky, J. Teaching Software Engineering to Undergraduates. *Proceedings of the International Conference on Information Systems and Engineering* (Quebec, Canada, 2003)

[17] Umphress, D., Hendrix, T. and Cross, J. " , no. 5, Sep./Oct., 2002, pp. 78-85. Software Process in the Classroom: The Capstone Project Experience. *IEEE Software*, 52002), 78-85.

[18] Ravalli, G., and Stojcevski, A. (2011). "Students Perception of Capstone Projects"*SEFI Annual Conference*. City: Lisbon.

[19] Farrell, G., and Farrell, V. (2011). "A Bifocal Information Visualisation Technique for a Multiple Choice Assessment Tool"*OzCHI*. City: Canberra, Australia

[20] Reily, K., Finnerty, P. L. and Terveen, L. *Two Peers are Better Than One: Aggregating Peer Reviews for Computing Assignments is Surprisingly Accurate*. City, 2009.

[21] Li, L., Liu, X. and Steckelberg, A. L. Assessor or Assessee: How Student Learning Improves by Giving and Receiving Peer Feedback. *British Journal of Educational Technology*, 525-536.

[22] Bushell, G. Moderation of Peer Assessment in Group Projects. *Assessment & Evaluation in Higher Education*, 91-108.

[23] Norcini, J. J. Peer Assessment of Competence. *Medical Education*, 37, 6 2003), 539-543.

Comparing the Effectiveness of Different Educational Uses of Program Animations

Jaime Urquiza-Fuentes, J. Ángel Velázquez-Iturbide
Universidad Rey Juan Carlos, LITE – Laboratory of Information Technologies in Education
C/Tulipán s/n, 28933 Móstoles (Madrid) Spain
{jaime.urquiza, angel.velazquez}@urjc.es

ABSTRACT

In this paper we study two different approaches to using program animations with educational aims: their construction by students –a constructivist and active approach– and their vision –a less active approach. In addition, we compare both approaches to a traditional teaching methodology where animations are not used. We have conducted an experiment with functional program animations using an existing IDE with visualization features called WinHIPE. We have analyzed the results in terms of Bloom's Taxonomy and the complexity of the topics covered. We have detected learning improvements in high levels of Bloom's Taxonomy, namely analysis and synthesis. Moreover, our results show that program animations are unnecessary for simple topics, support the joint use of vision and construction tasks in medium-complexity topics, and recommend vision tasks together with the typical methodology but without the use of animations in the most complex topics.

Categories and Subject Descriptors

D.2.3 [**Programming Languages**]: Coding Tools and Techniques – *pretty printers*; K.3.1 [**Computer Uses in Education**]: Computer-assisted instruction (CAI); K.3.2 [**Computer and Information Science Education**]: Computer science education

General Terms

Experimentation, Human Factors, Languages

Keywords

Program visualization, Engagement levels, Evaluation, Program animation, Funtional programming

1. INTRODUCTION

Learning to program is one of the most difficult issues in computer science curricula. Program animations, animations for the rest of the paper, are one of the existing approaches to overcome this problem. But despite its potential, it is not widely used by computer science educators. One of the main reasons, highlighted in [15], is the lack of evidence of their educational benefits.

One of the most significant results about the educational effectiveness of animations conclude that "how" students use visualization technology has a greater impact on effectiveness than "what" visualization technology shows to them [8]. Naps et al. [15] classified different educational uses of program and algorithm animations based on students' engagement. They proposed the following hypothesis: the more engagement the better the learning outcomes. In a later survey [21], it is concluded that, despite the literature supporting the educational use of animations, results are not clear regarding either the way of using them or their key features to be effective educational tools.

In this work we investigate the benefits of two different approaches: students' construction of program animations (an active, constructivist and highly engaging educational task) and students' vision of program animations (a less active approach). In addition, we compare the previous approaches with a traditional approach where program animations are not used (the *typical approach* for the rest of the paper). To this end we use a previously developed tool called WinHIPE [17] , an integrated development environment with visualization capabilities.

The rest of the paper is structured as follows. In section 2 we survey educational experiences based on viewing or constructing animations. The third section explains both approaches, i.e. vision and construction. Section 4 details the experiment and its results. Finally, we draw our conclusions in the fifth section.

2. RELATED WORK

Program animation is not a new research field. It is partially driven by a firm belief from researchers on that animations can help students in learning programming concepts. However, existing experiments do not clearly support this intuition. Hundhausen et al. [8] conclude that the more active the educational use the better the learning outcomes, but they also highlight that there are areas that need further investigation, e.g. the use of narratives and textual contents in animations [13].

Some efforts have been devoted to classify different educational uses of animations. Diehl et al. [4] described four different ways of using animations, but they were too specific, closely related to the animations' subject matter (automata theory). A broader approach was provided by the

ITiCSE'12, July 3–5, 2012, Haifa, Israel.

Engagement Taxonomy [15]. It focused on students' engagement with animations, identifying six different engagement levels: *Non-viewing*, *Viewing*, *Responding*, *Changing*, *Constructing* and *Presenting*. These levels are sorted by students' engagement with animations, being *Non-viewing* the lowest level and *Presenting* the highest one. Regarding educational effectiveness, this taxonomy proposes that the more the engagement the better the learning outcomes.

Here we briefly describe those levels involved in our study. The *Non-viewing* level represents the typical scenario without the use of animations. In the *Viewing* level the students can play animations, changing their direction, pace or abstraction level. If the animation provides multiple views, switching among them is also considered in this level. Finally, the *Constructing* level requires from students to construct explanatory animations of program/algorithm's behavior. Students need neither special construction tools nor to program and execute the program/algorithm.

In this section we survey related experiments that evaluate the educational impact of constructing and viewing animations. This educational impact can be measured in terms of knowledge acquisition, programming performance or attitude towards the subject.

2.1 Experiments with Animation Construction

We have found five studies related to animation construction. Only two of them study the pedagogical effectiveness of pure construction tasks. The other three experiments mix animation construction and presentation tasks.

Regarding pure construction tasks, Stasko [19] designed assignments where students had to construct their own animations. It was not a comparative study, but it was detected that students improved their attitude towards the subject because they dedicated more time to study the algorithms for which they had constructed animations.

Urquiza-Fuentes et al.[20] made a comparative study with vision tasks. Students who constructed animations used the WinHIPE IDE, while the others just viewed the animations produced by the instructor with the same IDE. Both groups of animations had additional textual explanations. The results showed that students who constructed animations improved their attitude towards the topic because they were longer involved with the algorithm. As a consequence, they also improved their knowledge acquisition.

The following three experiments studied animation construction and presentation tasks and used additional narrative contents. Two of them focused just on this mixture of tasks [6, 7], while the other [5] compared it with animation vision tasks.

Hundhausen [6] compared two different tools used in constructing and presenting tasks: a well-known algorithm visualization tool, and artifacts selected by the students, ranging from slides to crafts. This observational study detected improvements in the attitude of students who used their own artifacts. Based on these results, a tool to construct algorithm animations was developed and compared again with the construction artifacts selected by students [7]. In this experiment, improvements in programming performance were detected on students who worked with the new tool.

Finally, Hübscher-Younger et al. [5] made a comparative study with vision tasks. In this study, a number of volunteers developed and presented animations for a set of algorithms. They were allowed to choose the construction utilities. Then, all the students, animation developers included, had to evaluate those animations –this evaluation tasks can be considered as the vision task. The result of this study showed that the students who developed and evaluated the animations acquired more knowledge than those who just evaluated the animations.

The construction utilities play an important role in construction tasks. Thus, most studies allow students to choose the construction utilities or provide them with carefully designed interfaces for this task. In addition, the use of narratives and textual contents is present in most of the studies. We must also remark that we have only found two comparative studies. Although both studies delivered positive results, their representativeness can be questioned due to their experimental design. On the one hand, Urquiza-Fuentes et al. [20]'s study involved only fifteen subjects. On the other hand, it seems that groups from Hübscher-Younger et al. [5]'s study were biased in terms of students' motivation prior to the experiment. While the evaluation (viewing) tasks were compulsory, construction and presenting tasks were voluntary, therefore students who constructed animations were probably more motivated than those who just evaluated others' animations.

2.2 Experiments with Animation Vision

We have found five experiments for this approach. All of them detected educational improvements in terms of knowledge acquisition. Most of them compare vision tasks with, at least, the non-viewing approach.

Lawrence [12]'s study is the only one without a comparison: it just detected improvements when animations were used with textual labels.

Kann et al. [9] used animations without narratives or textual contents. They made a comparative study among different educational uses of animations. However, they only detected significant improvements between the viewing and non-viewing approaches. Crosby et al. [3] detected improvements when using multimedia materials made up of visualizations and narrative contents. Kehoe et al. [10] studied the use of animations in an environment that simulated homework. Thus, students used animations with narrative contents to complete assignments without time limit. Again, the use of animations was positive.

Finally, Kumar's problets [11] represent an auxiliary use of visualization. The main role of problets is tutoring students, providing them with automatically generated problems. His experiments showed that using visualizations within the feedback provided by the problet improves knowledge acquisition. Furthermore, students who received feedback with animations and textual contents obtained better results than those who received feedback with animations without textual contents.

In summary, narrative contents and textual explanations are used in all the experiments but one. Therefore, they seem to be features of educational tools that make animations effective, even though these features deserve more research [8].

3. EDUCATIONAL ANIMATIONS OF FUNCTIONAL PROGRAMS WITH WINHIPE

This section summarizes the features of educational animations produced with WinHIPE [17] and their construc-

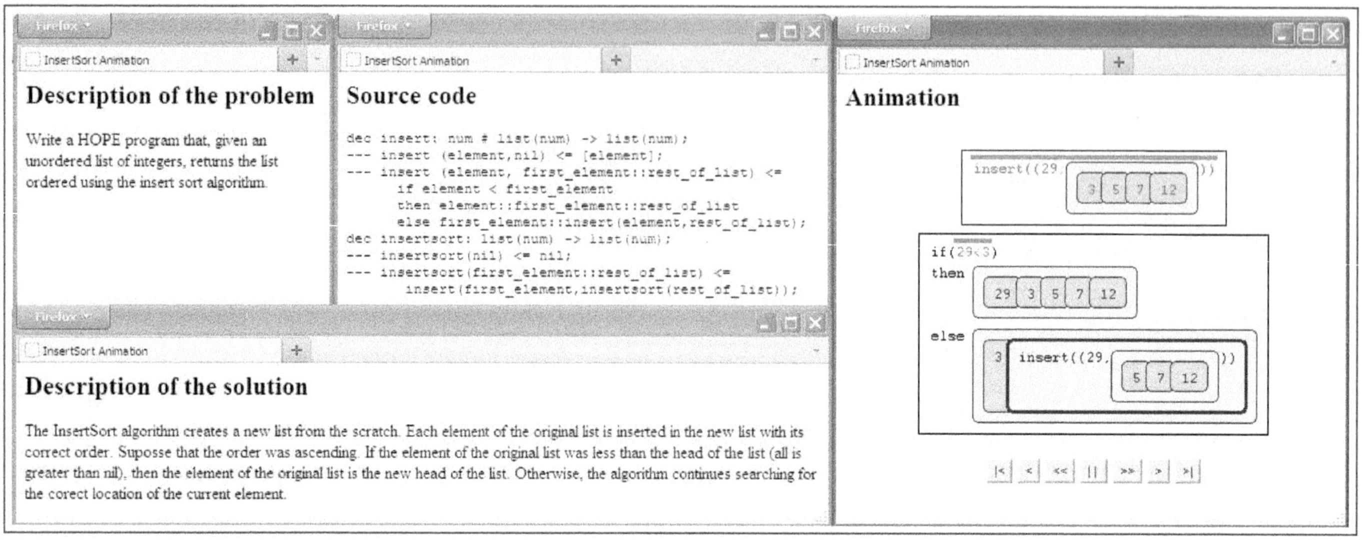

Figure 1: An educational animation of the insertion sorting algorithm

tion process; a detailed description of the later can be found elsewhere [22].

In WinHIPE, we consider animations as *documents* delivered by our programming environment. Following such a metaphor, animations are as easy to handle as any electronic document, that is, they can be easily constructed, modified, stored and retrieved with a graphical user interface.

3.1 Design and Contents of the Educational Animations

Our educational animations are web-based materials. Consequently, they can be easily shared, reused and published. In addition, they can be used either in theoretical sessions, lab sessions or at home. These animations consist of four components: a description of the problem, an explanation of an algorithm that solves the problem, the source code that implements the algorithm, and the program animation. The pace and direction of program animations can be controlled with a typical VCR interface. Besides, animations can simultaneously display one or two consecutive steps for better understanding. Fig. 1 shows an example of an educational animation about simple recursive data types (sorting a list of integers using the insertion sorting algorithm), with all its contents visible and showing two consecutive steps in the program animation.

We provide four different web formats to view our educational animations. Two of them are inspired by general principles of web pages usability [16], called *Framed1* and *Framed2*. The main usability requirements considered were: minimizing the amount of hidden information on the screen, adjusting the navigation area to a maximum of 20% of screen space, working the predictable response times (given that they depend on the number and size of animation steps), and use of linked CSS and inline frames. To sum up, the user can easily select the contents that she/he wants to view for each frame with one single mouse click. The *Framed1* format allows the user to watch one of the four contents of the educational animation. The *Framed2* format allows watching simultaneously two contents selected by the user. The third web format, called *Plain*, is an HTML page navigable by means of a local index and the scroll bar, where all the contents are available. Finally, the fourth format, called *Star*, is intended to enhance flexibility of user interaction. Here the user selects the contents that will be simultaneously visible and distributes them in the screen, Fig. 1 is an example of this web format as well. The user can change the web format to view educational animations anytime.

3.2 Producing Educational Animations with WinHIPE

Another well-known obstacle to a broader use of animations in CS education is the large amount of time that teachers have to spend to produce them [14]. This is one of the reasons why we paid special attention to achieve an effortless animation production process in WinHIPE. The other reason is that an effortless approach allows the students to produce animations focusing on educational tasks rather than on technical issues. Thus, animation construction can be used as an *active* educational task which could improve students' learning outcomes.

The construction of our educational animations is divided into two phases: generation of the program animation (the graphical representation of the execution of a program) and generation of the educational animation (the web-based materials). See Fig. 2 for a schematic view of the process.

The phase of program animation generation starts with the user typing the source code of the program and ends with a sequence of discrete visualizations of some execution steps of the program.

The execution model of the functional programming paradigm is term rewriting. In this model, running a program consists in a process of *rewriting* a starting term, the main expression, step by step, until no rewriting can be done. WinHIPE allows controlling and inspecting the execution process with typical debugging facilities. Thus the user can access to the whole trace of her/his program execution, i.e. the sequence of rewritten terms (execution steps) from the main expression to the final one.

The basis of program animations in WinHIPE are the graphical representation of these execution steps, also called

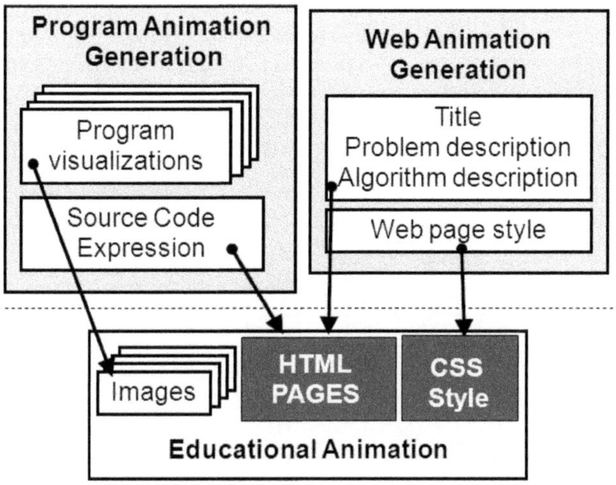

Figure 2: The construction process of educational animations

visualizations. The contents of visualizations can be pretty-printed text and/or graphical representations of data structures, i.e. binary trees and lists. These visualizations are automatically produced by WinHIPE according to a number of formatting choices made by the user with an user-friendly interface. Then, the user selects which visualizations will form part of the final program animation. Finally, the program animation is displayed in WinHIPE as a sequence of discrete of visualizations. Notice that: (1) the generation of the program animation is quite similar to the program development process (edit-compile-execute), where additional tasks are assisted by specially designed interfaces, and (2) the user is able to choose an appropriate graphical design and, more importantly, the level of detail of the animation by selecting the visualizations to show (i.e. its level of abstraction).

The educational animation is also generated through the user interface provided by WinHIPE. Then, the user must provide the information corresponding to textual contents (title, problem description, and algorithm explanation) and look contents (appearance on the web).

Notice that user interaction is limited to building the program animation, explaining the problem and its solution, and specifying the web look of the animation. Any additional processing is automatic. A final, automatic step generates the textual contents (HTML code) and the web look information (CSS code) and adds them to the program animation (images corresponding to the visualizations). Therefore we have an effortless educational animation construction process totally integrated into the development environment.

4. EVALUATION

In this evaluation we investigate the educational effect of the previously described treatments, measured in terms of knowledge acquisition. The context of this evaluation is a Programming Languages Foundations course placed in the first year of CS degrees.The evaluation took place during the second half of the course, which was focused on the functional programming paradigm.

4.1 Subjects and Experimental Design

The participants were 132 novel students enrolled in the previously mentioned course. Their participation was voluntary but incentived. Students can slightly improve their grades (0.25 out of 10) only if they pass the course exam. We discarded students who had previous knowledge of the functional paradigm.

Our study has two treatment conditions, for the viewing (TVG, n=50) and constructing tasks (TCG, n=40), respectively, and one control condition for the typical approach tasks (CG, n=42). Students were randomly assigned to the treatment/control conditions. Thus, the independent variable is the engagement level used in each group. The dependent variable is knowledge acquisition. Its measurement instrument were three knowledge tests, regarding three different topics of the course: infix operators, user defined data types and recursive data types. These topics correspond to different levels of complexity, being respectively of low, medium and high complexity. The questions of the tests are mapped into the following levels of Bloom's Taxonomy [1]: knowledge, understanding, application, analysis and synthesis.

4.2 Tasks

Each of the three groups performed different types of tasks but using the same problems/cases, all of them selected from the course book. The students in the control group (CG) worked on solving problems proposed by the teacher. They were allowed to use WinHIPE without its visualization facilities. Students had to solve problems by themselves but the teacher helped them on demand. Here, the students' attention was focused on understanding the problem and coding the solution.

The main task of the vision group (TVG) was viewing animations constructed by the teacher. For each topic they had a list of animations in a web page. They had to view them ensuring that they properly understood them. The teacher had little or no interaction with the students during the sessions of this group. Here, the students' attention was focused on understanding the description of the problem and its solution using the animation and the textual explanations.

Finally, the main task of the construction group (TCG) was constructing animations following the construction treatment described in the previous section. They had available through the web all needed materials: the description of the problem and the source code. The construction tasks consisted in studying the program, selecting an appropriate input data set, executing the program, and generating the animation using the visualization facilities provided by the IDE. Actually, the student's effort was focused on producing a representative animation –choosing suitable input data and selecting the important execution steps– and writing a correct explanation of the solution.

4.3 Protocol

At the beginning of the course, students were informed about the evaluation. The course was structured into eight topics: (1) An introduction to the functional paradigm, (2) Basic features of the functional language HOPE [18], (3) Basic concepts of recursion, (4) Prefix and infix operators, user-defined operators, priority and use, (5) User defined data types, (6) Local definitions, (7) Recursive data types, and (8) Polymorphic data types.

During the first, second and third topics, students got familiar with the IDE used in the laboratory of the subject. Also they were trained in the facilities provided by the environment related with the tasks they had to complete, either viewing or constructing animations.

The treatments were applied during the sessions corresponding to the topics 4, 5 and 7. For each topic, the protocol consisted in two parts: theoretical sessions, and a lab session. Sessions of CG followed the typical teaching methodology. TVG and TCG theoretical sessions consisted in typical lectures enhanced with the use of animations for examples and simple exercises. The lab sessions of each group consisted in the tasks previously described, vision and construction, together with a knowledge test that was completed at the end of the session.

In summary, the students participated in three evaluative sessions, completing three groups of tasks and three knowledge tests.

4.4 Results of the Evaluation

In this section we detail the measurement of the dependent variable, knowledge acquisition, and study the differences found among the three groups. Students' scores were standardized to the range [0-1]. We have used ANOVA and t-students tests for normal data sets and, Kruskal-Wallis X^2 and Mann-Whitney U for non-normal data sets.

We consider the dependent variable, knowledge acquisition, from three different points of view: global, Bloom level and topic. From the *Global* point of view we aggregate all evaluated Bloom's levels and all topics into one value per student. From the *Bloom-level* point of view, for each Bloom level we aggregate all topics into one value. Therefore, we obtained five values per student. Finally, from the *Topic* point of view, for each topic we aggregate all evaluated Bloom levels into one value. Therefore, we obtained three values per student.

Table 1 shows results from the global point of view. The ANOVA test shows significant differences among the three groups. The detailed study shows that, actually, significant differences are detected in the comparisons TCG vs. CG and TVG vs. CG. Therefore, from a global point of view, the typical approach is significantly outperformed by either vision or construction tasks in 9.26%.

Results from the Bloom-level point of view can be seen in Table 2. We have found significant differences among the three groups in the two highest evaluated levels, analysis and synthesis. A detailed study shows that significant differences, in both levels, are detected in the comparisons TCG vs. CG and TVG vs. CG. Again, vision and construction tasks outperform the typical approach, and these improvements are at the analysis, 18.6%, and synthesis, 17.7%, levels of Bloom's Taxonomy.

Finally, we have found significant differences among the three groups in the user defined data types and recursive data types topics, see Table 3. The detailed study shows that significant differences regarding the user-defined data-types topic are detected in the comparisons TCG vs. CG and TVG vs. CG. Regarding the recursive data-types topic, significant differences are detected in the comparisons TCG vs. TVG and TCG vs. CG. From this point of view, learning outcomes were improved in both topics, i.e. user-defined data types and recursive data types. In the former, vision and construction tasks improve pedagogical effectiveness in 23,2%. But in the later, either the typical approach or vision tasks outperform the construction tasks in 11.7%.

Table 1: Average grades, ANOVA, and detailed analysis from the global point of view.

GC	TVG	CG	ANOVA analysis
.6075	.6068	.5140	$F(2,120)$=3.274, p=**.041**

Groups	Stat test	Differences
TCG vs. TVG	t(78.45)=.018, p=.986	-
TCG vs. CG	t(74.36)=2.311, p=**.024**	*TCG > CG*
TVG vs. CG	t(85)=2.102, p=**.038**	*TVG > CG*

Table 2: Average grades for each group and Bloom's Taxonomy level and ANOVA, X^2 and detailed analysis of knowledge aquisition. K, U, Ap, An and S stand for their corresponding Bloom levels: Knowledge, Understanding, Application, Analysis and Synthesis.

	TCG	TVG	CG	Stat test
K	.6019	.5348	.5837	$F(2,120)$=1.084, p=.342
U	.6525	.6794	.6316	$F(2,120)$=.561, p=.572
Ap	.6623	.6988	.5972	$\chi^2(2,123)$=2.899, p=.235
An	.6675	.6009	.4487	$\chi^2(2,123)$=19.175, **p<.01**
S	.4532	.5200	.3087	$F(2,120)$=7.268, p=**.001**

Groups	Stat test for *Analysis*	Differences
TCG vs. TVG	t(78.450)=.018, p=.986	-
TCG vs. CG	U=318.0, **p<.01**	*TCG > CG*
TVG vs. CG	U=596.5, p=**.003**	*TVG > CG*

Groups	Stat test for *Synthesis*	Differences
TCG vs. TVG	t(8.784)=-.256, p=.799	-
TCG vs. CG	t(76)=2.667, p=**.009**	*TCG > CG*
TVG vs. CG	t(79.191)=3.827, **p<.01**	*TVG > CG*

Table 3: Average grades for each group and topic and ANOVA, X^2 and pairwise analysis of effectiveness. IO, UDDT and RDT stand for Infix Operators, User-Defined Data Types and Recursive Data Types respectivelly.

	TCG	TVG	CG	Stat test
IO	.5842	.5296	.4840	$F(2,123)$=1.153, p=.224
UDT	.6319	.6289	.3983	$\chi^2(2,123)$=23.26, **p<.01**
RDT	.7055	.8529	.7923	$F(2,98)$=8.019, p=**.001**

Groups	Stat test for *UDT*	Differences
TCG vs. TVG	t(79)=1.161, p=.249	-
TCG vs. CG	U=688.0, **p<.01**	*TCG > CG*
TVG vs. CG	U=415.0, **p<.01**	*TVG > CG*

Groups	Stat test for *RDT*	Differences
TCG vs. TVG	t(64)=-4.322, **p<.01**	*TVG > TCG*
TCG vs. CG	t(64)=-2.225, p=**.030**	*CG > TCG*
TVG vs. CG	t(68)=1.673, p=.099	-

5. CONCLUSIONS

In this study we have analyzed the educational impact of

two different uses of functional program animations, vision and construction tasks. Both of them were compared to a typical teaching methodology where animations are not used.

Taking into account the *Active Learning* theory [2], Hundhausen et al.'s [8] conclusions and the Engagement Theory [15], construction tasks should have overcome the other two approaches. Our results only support partially this assumption. The three approaches had similar effects on simple topics. The construction tasks produced better results than the typical approach from a global point of view, especially at the analysis and synthesis levels of Bloom's taxonomy and in medium-complexity topics. However, we have not detected any improvement with respect to viewing tasks. Furthermore, the typical and the viewing approaches outperformed the construction approach in highly complex topics.

We feel that there are other factors to take into account. In our study, viewing outperformed one of the other two approaches. In the tasks, we tried to avoid students' passive attitude by asking them to ensure their understanding of the animation contents. In addition, the animations had been produced by the instructor and enhanced with textual explanations. We think that textual explanations could be an important factor to explain these results [8, 13]. In particular, instructor's explanations (either integrated into animations or verbally expressed in class) seem to have been a significant factor for highly complex topics, such as recursive data types.

Based on our empirical results we suggest a methodological approach to the educational use of program animations. Vision and construction tasks should be integrated. Firstly, a set of animations should be facilitated for self-study. Secondly, theoretical sessions will be made of lectures with examples and specially prepared animations. Thirdly, laboratory sessions will mix the typical, viewing and constructing approaches, depending on the complexity of the concepts taught.

6. ACKNOWLEDGMENTS

This work was supported by the II Teaching Innovation Projects programme of the Rey Juan Carlos University and project TIN2008-04103/TSI of the Spanish Ministry of Science and Innovation.

7. REFERENCES

[1] B. Bloom, E. Furst, W. Hill, and D. Krathwohl. *Taxonomy of Educational Objetives: Handbook I, The Cognitive Domain.* Addison-Wesley, 1959.

[2] C. Bonwell and J. Eison. *Active Learning: Creating Excitement in the Classroom.* Jossey-Bass, 1991.

[3] M. Crosby and J. Stelovsky. From multimedia instruction to multimedia evaluation. *J. of Educational Multimedia and Hypermedia*, 4:147–162, 1995.

[4] S. Diehl and A. Kerren. Levels of exploration. *SIGCSE Bull.*, 33:60–64, February 2001.

[5] T. Hübscher-Younger and N. Narayanan. Dancing hamsters and marble statues: characterizing student visualizations of algorithms. In *SoftVis '03: Proceedings of the 2003 ACM Symposium on Software Visualization*, pages 95–104, New York, NY, USA, 2003. ACM Press.

[6] C. Hundhausen. Integrating algorithm visualization technology into an undergraduate algorithms course: Ethnographic studies of a social constructivist approach. *Comput. Educ.*, 39(3):237–260, 2002.

[7] C. Hundhausen and J. Brown. Designing, visualizing, and discussing algorithms within a CS 1 studio experience: An empirical study. *Comput. Educ.*, 50(1):301–326, 2008.

[8] C. Hundhausen, S. Douglas, and J. Stasko. A meta-study of algorithm visualization effectiveness. *J. Visual Lang. Comput.*, 13(3):259–290, 2002.

[9] C. Kann, R. Lindeman, and R. Heller. Integrating algorithm animation into a learning environment. *Comput. Educ.*, 28(4):223–228, 1997.

[10] C. Kehoe, J. Stasko, and A. Taylor. Rethinking the evaluation of algorithm animations as learning aids: An observational study. *Int. J. Hum.-Comput. St.*, 54(2):265–284, 2001.

[11] A. Kumar. Results from the evaluation of the effectiveness of an online tutor on expression evaluation. *SIGCSE Bull.*, 37(1):216–220, 2005.

[12] A. Lawrence. *Empirical studies of the value of algorithm animation in algorithm understanding.* PhD thesis, Dep. of Computer Science, Georgia Institute of Technology, 1993.

[13] R. Mayer. *Multimedia Learning.* Cambridge University Press, 2008.

[14] T. Naps, S. Cooper, B. Koldehofe, C. Leska, G. Rößling, W. Dann, A. Korhonen, L. Malmi, J. Rantakokko, R. Ross, J. Anderson, R. Fleischer, M. Kuittinen, and M. McNally. ITiCSE 2003 working group reports: Evaluating the educational impact of visualization. *SIGCSE Bull.*, 35(4):124–136, june 2003.

[15] T. Naps, G. Rößling, V. Almstrum, W. Dann, R. Fleischer, C. Hundhausen, A. Korhonen, L. Malmi, M. McNally, S. Rodger, and J. Velázquez-Iturbide. ITiCSE 2002 working group report: Exploring the role of visualization and engagement in computer science education. *SIGCSE Bull.*, 35(2):131–152, June 2002.

[16] J. Nielsen. *Designing Web Usability.* New Riders Publishing, 1999.

[17] C. Pareja-Flores, J. Urquiza-Fuentes, and J. A. Velázquez-Iturbide. WinHIPE: an IDE for functional programming based on rewriting and visualization. *SIGPLAN Not.*, 42(3):14–23, 2007.

[18] R. Paterson. The functional programming language Hope. http://www.soi.city.ac.uk/ ross/Hope/, 2009.

[19] J. Stasko. Using student-built algorithm animations as learning aids. *SIGCSE Bull.*, 29(1):25–29, 1997.

[20] J. Urquiza-Fuentes and J. Velázquez-Iturbide. An evaluation of the effortless approach to build algorithm animations with WinHIPE. *Electronic Notes in Theoretical Computer Science*, 178:3–13, July 2007.

[21] J. Urquiza-Fuentes and J. A. Velázquez-Iturbide. A survey of successful evaluations of program visualization and algorithm animation systems. *ACM Trans. Comput. Educ.*, 9:Article 9, June 2009.

[22] J. Velázquez-Iturbide, C. Pareja-Flores, and J. Urquiza-Fuentes. An approach to effortless construction of program animations. *Comput. Educ.*, 50(1):179–192, 2008.

Pros and Cons for Teaching Courses in the Classroom and Online Simultaneously

J. Mark Pullen
Department of Computer Science and C4I Center
George Mason University
mpullen@netlab.gmu.edu

ABSTRACT

In adding an online delivery option to an existing graduate program in computer science, important choices include (1) synchronous or asynchronous delivery and (2) for synchronous delivery, whether to deliver classroom and online teaching simultaneously. This paper describes the decisions made in adding an online option to an MSCS program, which now is maturing. The factors in favor of and against simultaneous delivery are discussed in detail and the conclusions reached for one particular program are described, including experience gained in the process and an open-source software system developed to support this form of delivery.

Categories and Subject Descriptors

K.3.1 **[Computing Milieux]:** Computer Uses in Education – distance learning

General Terms

Management, Performance, Human Factors

Keywords

Internet distance education, synchronous, asynchronous

1. INTRODUCTION

The impact of information technology, and in particular that of the Internet, continues to grow across nearly all domains of teaching and learning. Computer science education is in the vanguard; by the nature of their academic discipline, computer science students and faculty are well prepared to adopt new and experimental approaches including distance education (DE). Our Master of Science in Computer Science (MSCS) program has been offering courses online for over a decade, and has made a full MSCS degree available online since 2004. In the process, we have grappled with issues of effective delivery. This paper reports on our experience and conclusions.

We believe the appropriate question is "How can we best help the student to learn?" Clearly, the answer is highly dependent on the student's learning style and personal situation. We base our approach on two basic premises that have been confirmed by educational research:

1. *There is no significant difference in educational outcomes, based purely on mode of delivery*. There are differences in costs of teaching and learning and differences in student and facultyenjoyment of the educational process, but given the same goals and student motivation the outcomes are the same [16]. This premise is borne out by our own experiences over a five-year period, as shown in Figure 1, taken from [15]. It follows that educational processes should be designed to optimize other factors; generally, economic factors come to the forefront. In our own case, this has taken the form of optimizing time expenditures by the participants. We have found it most productive to minimize time spent by the student commuting to class and time required for the faculty to develop expertise and materials for online teaching.

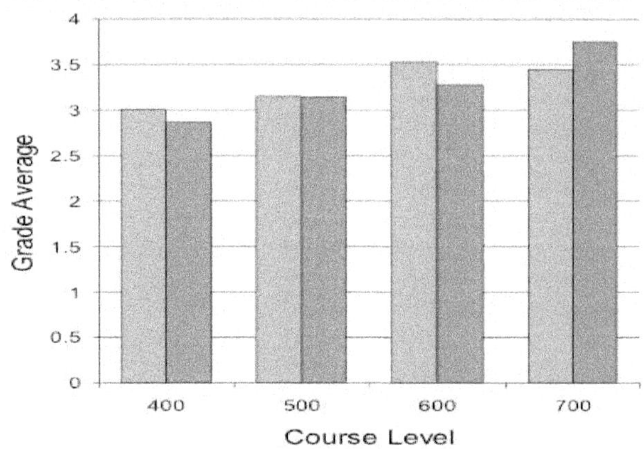

Figure 1. GMU CS grade comparisons (pink: classroom; green: online)

2. *Given technologies available today, the most effective way to present material in order to facilitate student learning is a hybrid or blended approach*, combining options for classroom learning, online synchronous delivery, and online asynchronous learning materials. This allows students to focus on the form of delivery that best suits their learning style and also allows faculty members to present material in whatever format can convey it most effectively [4,5]. Our approach to this has been to combine classroom delivery with simultaneous online delivery, in a form that maximizes the potential for student/teacher interaction and minimizes impediments presented by the technology, which we call *simulteaching*. We supplement this combination with asynchronous delivery of both recorded sessions from class and Web-based learning materials and exercises.

This paper is written to explain the choices we have made in adopting the hybrid approach and to review their validity. For this purpose, Section 2 will review the characteristics of synchronous and asynchronous online education; Sections 3 and 4 respectively will examine the pros and cons of the simulteaching approach; Section 5 will illustrate the approach as implemented in our MSCS; and Section 6 will provide an overview of the open source software we have assembled to support it, followed by conclusions. While we do not contend that the simultaneous classroom and online delivery mode is the best choice under all circumstances, we believe the discussion below shows that, as a means of expanding regional access to a quality classroom-based program, its benefits considerably outweigh its costs.

2. SYNCHRONOUS AND ASYNCHRONOUS DELIVERY TECHNOLOGIES

In this section we consider possible delivery modes for the virtual classroom for topics in engineering and technology, including CS.

2.1 Synchronous Delivery

Synchronous means "at the same time" and the synchronous mode is defined essentially by the capability for participants to interact. For many years, the capability was implemented mostly by video teleconferencing. In the past decade, expanded access to good-quality Internet, combined with good multimedia performance in inexpensive computers, has brought Internet delivery to the forefront in synchronous distance education. As a very early adopter [11], our online teaching program originally was confused with "TV teaching" (which is not necessarily interactive) and eventually came to the point of examining whether video is in fact an important medium in teaching computer science and engineering online [12]. We concluded that while video is "nice to have," the decision to provide it is an economic one because few students find video delivery of a "talking head" useful in technical teaching.

It is therefore striking that the general higher education community seems to be experimenting with video delivery today. "Classroom capture" systems [3] have emerged as a new class of teaching technology and many of them feature recording via classroom video cameras (in some cases, multiple cameras). Not all classroom capture offers synchronous delivery, and not all of it focuses on video delivery; however, its emergence as a means of distance education indicates that at least some educators find it attractive. Having concluded that video is not important in online teaching of computer science and engineering, we leave the question of its general applicability to our colleagues in the liberal arts and other academic disciplines.

However, much synchronous online teaching today is not focused on video but rather on good-quality, interactive graphics and Internet voice linked to the World Wide Web (WWW); further, it does not necessarily involve a classroom. Examples of this are Blackboard Collaborate (formerly Elluminate) [2], Adobe Connect [1], and the open-source system described in section 6 below. These systems implement an audiographic channel, with optional video, from the instructor's desktop to that of the online student, and generally support a high level of interactivity if desired by the participants. In fact, each of them has roots in online conferencing technology and can be used for teleconferencing as well as teaching, just as were the video teleconferencing systems originally used for synchronous DE.

2.2 Asynchronous Delivery

Asynchronous delivery encompasses the whole range of information conveyance that is not "at the same time" and therefore is much broader. Its original mode was the correspondence course: printed materials, delivered by postal mail or similar techniques, intended for self-study. As recording and multimedia technologies have developed, asynchronous teaching has embraced each in turn. Online and standalone "computer assisted instruction" (CAI) has a rich history of using any sufficiently inexpensive and powerful means of conveying information. The most recent, and arguably the most powerful and flexible, medium to be used for this purpose is the WWW, which can support playback of a wide range of text, audio, and video as well as interactive form that support CAI, as seen in widely-used "learning management system" (LMS) products: commercial Blackboard [2] and open source Moodle [6].

2.3 Hybrid Modes

Hybrid modes are possible in different dimensions. Hybridizing in the technology space is natural. Since we know hybrid DE delivery provides the most opportunities to support student learning styles and natural affinities of content to media, it comes as no surprise that the combining the richness of synchronous and asynchronous delivery is a productive approach. The interactive forms of desktop teaching described in the previous paragraph all feature a capability to record synchronous sessions, which results in yet another form of asynchronous delivery, as do the classroom capture systems described above. Both synchronous and asynchronous modes are accessible through a Web-browser-accessed LMS. In addition, many software packages that run on the student's computer are natural parts of today's educational environment. (An example for computer science would be the open source NetBeans Integrated Development Environment for Java [10].) Such software is generally available online; moreover, data associated with student assignments can be made available under an LMS page.

Asynchronous delivery does not necessarily mean that the student is left with complete schedule flexibility. A common experience is that many students lack the self-discipline to maintain a schedule for completion of a course; they tend to postpone required work to the end of the course and then try to complete it in a rush, resulting in a poor learning experience. The syllabus of a traditional classroom course, with its by-date assignments, helps to avoid this problem. This aspect is easily hybridized: create a syllabus with due dates where asynchronous delivery is used. We have students in our MSCS who generally do not attend class in the scheduled time slot, but instead playback the lecture recordings and complete the assignments within the scheduled week. A good way to describe this is "semi-synchronous" DE.

A different dimension of hybridization is the combination of classroom and online synchronous delivery, with students potentially able to move back and forth depending on their personal needs and preferences. This has been part of our MSCS online program from its beginning. (Administratively, we have only a single degree offering, which students access online or in the classroom at their option.) Other programs, both within our own school and across higher education in general, do the same. There are clear benefits associated with this approach, but also there are costs. The next two sections will deal with these pros and cons.

3. PROS OF SIMULTANEOUS DELIVERY

This section deals with the many benefits of simultaneous classroom and online course delivery.

3.1 Low Barriers to Participation

Most of our faculty members are motivated to provide expanded access to their courses. However, they are busy people who find it difficult to make time to master a new approach to teaching and prepare extensive new materials that accompany the approach. With synchronous online teaching, they are in essence continuing to teach as they are accustomed. While it is important to draw the online student into interaction, that is simply an extension of the need to draw the classroom student into interaction. No new materials need be prepared; whatever is used to present the existing course, so long as it is in machine-readable format, will suffice to present the course online. For office hours, simply turn on the delivery software on the office computer and use it to communicate with the student.

3.2 Good Interaction With All Students

Good quality Internet synchronous teaching software, such as the three products described in section 2.1, will support spoken and typed communication to and from all participants, including display and annotation of graphic slides. If there is a problem with interaction, it lies in the lack of interest of participants to interact. That is a pedagogical problem, which also happens in the classroom; both in the classroom and online it must be solved by the instructor, not by teaching technology.

3.3 Reduced Faculty Preparation and Support Time

Our faculty members are very busy people; most of them already work at least ten hours per day between teaching, research and service; many work even more than this. The prospect of spending extra time developing and maintaining asynchronous course materials and communicating with students by email in place of answering spoken questions is not attractive to them. Synchronous presentation reduces faculty time requirements considerably, with the result that faculty are more willing to teach DE courses. At the same time, our course-end surveys indicate that classroom students find the additional structure associated with DE (posted slides, recordings, LMS webpage, etc.) makes the learning environment more effective for them, as well as for online students.

3.4 Faculty Salary Savings from Combined Sections

Our courses have a set maximum number of students that a single instructor is expected to teach. Unless the combined enrollment of classroom and online students exceeds this number, the combined enrollment can be covered in a single presentation. The alternative would be for the instructor to make two separate presentations of the course, at twice the salary cost.

3.5 More Distance Education Courses

Most students come to us for a degree program, not just a few courses. Generally, we have enough online students enrolled in introductory graduate courses that a separate online section would fall within the allowable minimum number of students per section. For advanced graduate courses, however, in many cases there are not enough online students to justify a separate section. Offering the course simultaneously to classroom and online student addresses this problem. (In some cases, the combined numbers may be needed to justify classroom delivery also.)

3.6 Low Support Cost

Our experience is that, in order for the instructor to pay attention to both online students and classroom students, it is important to support the simultaneous teaching process by having a student assistant monitor the course to make sure all is going well, and be available to assist in case of technology problems (most often issues with sound, such as a dead microphone). However, as the program has ramped up, we discovered that one of these Information Technology Assistants can handle at least three simultaneous classes. The cost of one student assistant is a tiny fraction of the cost of even one faculty member, let alone that of three. The same assistants also maintain the course delivery software on the teaching computers and ensure that all required system functions are working before class. Further, no specialized assistance such as instructional design is required.

3.7 Enables Flexible Distance Education Delivery

The recordings of class sessions can be used in various creative ways. For example: Our university offers a very limited number of graduate courses in its summer term. We have addressed the need of students who want to continue their study in the summer by allowing individual students to work with a faculty member who taught an online course and use the recordings originally produced. The students complete all work from the syllabus under which the original course was taught, and are mentored by the instructor who made the recordings. They work on a schedule established by the mentor and must finish within the summer term. To participate, faculty members must be available ten weeks out of the summer by Internet and must have made the recordings in the prior two years. The result enables student progress, provides some extra income for faculty, and leaves all concerned with the feeling that our faculty goes out of its way to help students achieve an education.

This individualized delivery is only an example of the flexibility made possible by capturing classroom activity in recordings. Once an up-to-date set of recordings is available, it is possible to focus on other aspects of learning. The recordings can support an inverted classroom model, where students attend lectures via recordings and spend class time in group or project activities. They also can be shared across faculty teaching the same course, providing students with a variety of teaching styles to facilitate their learning.

3.8 Expansion of Local Programs

In recent years, considerable attention has been drawn to asynchronous online programs with global aspirations, such as those of the University of Phoenix [20]. Such programs undoubtedly have a place in higher education; however, so do local programs of excellence. We have chosen not to compete with global online programs. Our DE program is of regional scope, by plan; it requires that students be able to come to campus occasionally for activities such as examinations. Under this arrangement, we are able to serve more students in our metropolitan area, who otherwise would find commuting in rush-hour traffic too time consuming, or would not be able to keep up with course requirements due to work schedule and/or travel.

4. CONS OF SIMULTANEOUS DELIVERY

This section deals with the costs associated with simultaneous delivery that are not associated with independent classroom and online delivery.

4.1 Classroom Equipment Requirements

The classroom must be equipped with good quality Internet service that is not interrupted during class hours. Also we have found that some device with pen (or finger) input is essential, to support handwritten class material such as that entered on an ordinary classroom whiteboard with no online course. A tablet input device and/or a projected whiteboard such as the commercial SMART Board product [18] fill this need well at a total additional investment less than $5,000 per classroom.

4.2 Administrative Complexity

Having a different type of classroom for simultaneous online delivery requires that somebody keep track of such rooms and schedule their use. Similarly, having courses that mix online and classroom students means that such distinctions must be conveyed to students. In some cases, DE students pay an extra fee, thus both administrative systems and course delivery software (e.g. the LMS) must keep track of the two groups and provide service accordingly. While this causes extra work for administrative elements, it is financially compensated by extra tuition and also is a source of pride in that the program is serving the needs of more students and serving them better.

4.3 Faculty Technophobia

Faculty without good self-confidence in computer technology may be reluctant to take on the additional responsibility of teaching online students in addition to classroom students. This has not proved to be a particular problem in our computer science department, but in other disciplines it might become a more significant issue. We have dealt with this by providing synchronous teaching software with the simplest user interface we could imagine, and also by ensuring that help is available at all times during class as described in section 3.6 above.

4.4 Technology Problems Can Disrupt Class

If there is a problem with the computer, software, or network connection, it is possible that the instructor will be distracted in a way that detracts from educating the classroom group. Our experience is that this can be dealt with adequately by providing knowledgeable help on-call to deal with the problem, allowing the instructor to continue working with classroom students. Also any unhappiness on the part of the classroom students can be mitigated by advantages they receive from the simultaneous online delivery, for example: access to class recordings for review or makeup, or the ability to connect online when they must travel for their work.

5. EXPERIENCE WITH SIMULTANEOUS DELIVERY

Our university has some characteristics that makes a hybrid classroom/online approach particularly appealing. We are a relatively young institution, in a major urban area. Two situations, common among our students, contribute to their enthusiasm for online course delivery:

- Our urban area is well known for traffic congestion. Our graduate courses are delivered in after-work "rush hour" time, with the result that commuting to and from class can require as much of a student's time as does the class itself.
- Many of our graduate students are employed in government and industry and must travel as part of their work, but can either connect remotely or attend class "time-shifted" via recordings.

Starting with an experimental program carried out by a few "early adopters," we were able to provide enough online courses by 2004 to enable a student to complete the full MSCS degree. Since that time we have added other courses to provide the student with a variety of choices [13]. Table 1 shows the courses currently offered online. Typically we offer six to ten courses online, average classroom attendance was 16.2 students and online attendance was 9.1 students per course from 2006 to 2012. Both classroom and online enrollment has increased over time (19.1 and 15.4 respectively in Spring 2012); the fraction of students enrolled as online is 35.9% with an upward trend (44.7% in Spring 2012).

Table 1. Courses Offered in Online MSCS Program

CS 540	Language Processors
CS 555	Computer Communications and Networking
CS 571	Operating Systems
CS 580	Introduction to Artificial Intelligence
CS 583	Analysis of Algorithms
SWE 619	Object-Oriented Software Specification and Construction
SWE 620	Software Requirements Analysis and Specification
SWE 621	Software Modeling and Architectural Design
SWE 625	Software Project Management
CS 640	Advanced Compilers
CS 652	Computer Graphics
ISA 656	Network Security
CS 658	Networked Virtual Environments
CS 672	Computer System Performance Evaluation
CS 706	Concurrent Software Systems
CS 755	Advanced Computer Networks
CS 756	Performance Analysis of Computer Networks

All of this was achieved through voluntary participation; by 2009, over half of our department faculty was teaching online. The principal motivation for this was to make our courses more available to students. However, a significant enabler was the low barrier to success: a faculty member who had his or her course materials on machine-readable slides of any form could "go online" after roughly one hour of introduction to online teaching by a colleague. Undoubtedly this played a significant role in expanding course availability.

In supporting the online MSCS, it became apparent to us that every faculty member took an individual approach to online delivery, just as each of them had her or his own approach to classroom teaching. Some of them integrated various software tools into their teaching, while others developed innovative approaches to encourage interaction with online students. In the years when we were using a video camera, one professor developed the practice of turning the camera around to point at the class, based on the conviction that other students would get a better sense of inclusion from that than from seeing her "talking head." Another professor uses handwriting extensively, challenging us to improve the quality of the online whiteboard software.

6. OPEN SOURCE SOFTWARE TO SUPPORT SIMULTANEOUS DELIVERY

Starting in 2004, our C4I Center, which performs research into military information technology and systems, undertook development of an open source software system for online delivery, tailored to the simultaneous classroom and online teaching environment [14, 19]. Our MSCS program used the resulting Network EducationWare (NEW) system until 2010, when we upgraded it.

When we discovered the software integration facilities in the Modular Object-Oriented Dynamic Learning Environment (Moodle), we were motivated to rework our previous efforts into the Moodle environment. Moodle is widely recognized as a high-quality Learning Management System (LMS) supporting asynchronous DE [17], with over 66,000 currently active sites registered in 218 countries [7]. Because of its low cost and user-friendly interface, we already were using Moodle as an LMS for course delivery supported by NEW; upon discovering the developer-friendly facilities offered by Moodle [8], we factored Moodle into our development plans. The result was the Moodle Integrated Synchronous Teaching/Conferencing (MIST/C).

MIST/C thus is the result of a decade of building open-source software for simultaneous classroom and online delivery. It features the simplest user interface we have been able to devise, aimed at demanding the least possible attention from the instructor. For example: an audible chime is produced when a student's typed question is displayed, and also when the system raises a popup window that demands the instructor's attention. Also, MIST/C has a feature not available in commercial packages: a separate, full-screen copy of the whiteboard, used with the classroom projector so that classroom students are not disadvantaged by visual clutter associated with online teaching.

MIST/C is described in a nutshell by its hardware requirements (Table 2), functional capabilities (Table 3), and user interface (Figure 2). For more details, see the MIST/C website [9].

7. CONCLUSIONS

In our MSCS program, we have demonstrated that there are significant benefits to simultaneous classroom and online delivery. Operational benefits include low barriers to participation, good interaction with all students, requiring reduced faculty preparation and support time, and enabling flexible distance education delivery. Economic benefits include faculty salary savings from combined sections, enabling more distance education courses, low support cost, and enabling expansion of local programs. There are costs associated with these benefits: classroom equipment requirements (most significantly tablet input), increased administrative complexity, dealing with faculty technophobia, and impact of technology problems on classes. However, in our experience these costs are considerably more than offset by the benefits of educating more students and supporting their needs in a more effective way that can save them many hours of commuting (with no educational benefit) each semester.

Table 2. MIST/C Hardware/Software Requirements

Client Operating System: Windows XP/7; MacOS X; Linux
Browser: all major
Communication: wired/wireless Internet and dial-up
Security: LDAP authentication
Limitations: seats and classes unlimited
Remote hosting: available at moderate cost
Availability: simple download
Audio: Internet; no separate phone connection needed
Added hardware required: mouse/keyboard/mic; WebCam
Responsiveness: rapid response to user inputs

Table 3. MISTC Functional Requirements

Customizations: accessible/expandable/enhanceable
Whiteboard: able to accept graphic files in real time
Authoring formats: PowerPoint, PDF, Keynote, OpenOffice
- all participants able to annotate slides during session
Video: common computer formats (mpg, avi, mov); camera
Application sharing: able to export to students the graphic window of any application on the host computer
Recording of sessions: automatic on server; including chat
- able to render as mpeg for podcasting
Interaction: testing; polling/hand-raising; voice + chat
Student tracking: login status; participation statistics
Configurable to screen: by user
Breakout: able to partition class into separate groups

8. REFERENCES

[1] Adobe Systems Inc, Adobe Connect and Engaging Webinars, http://www.adobe.com/ConnectWebConference, as of March 2012

[2] Blackboard Inc., Blackboard Collaborate. http://www.blackboard.com/Platforms/Collaborate/Products/Blackboard-Collaborate.aspx, as of March 2012

[3] Brooks, C., C. Epp, G. Logan and J. Greer, The Who, What, When, and Why of Lecture Capture, *Proceedings of the 1st International Conference on Learning Analytics and Knowledge*, ACM, 2011

[4] Hrastinski, S. Asynchronous and Synchronous E-Learning, *EDUCAUSE Quarterly*, 31(4), 2008

[5] Latchman, H., C. Salzmann, D. Gillet and J. Kim, Learning On Demand - A Hybrid Synchronous /Asynchronous Approach, *IEEE Transactions on Education* 44(2), May 2001 208-225

[6] Moodle, Open-source Community-based Tools for Learning, http://moodle.org, as of March 2012

[7] Moodle, Site Statistics, http://moodle.org/stats, as of March 2012

[8] Moodle, Open Source Software Project Developer Documentation, http://moodle.org/development, as of March 2012

[9] George Mason University Networking and Simulation

Laboratory, Moodle Integrated Synchronous Teaching and Conferencing, http://netlab.gmu.edu/MISTC, as of March 2012

[10] NetBeans, WelcomeTo NetBeans, http://www.netbeans.org, as of March 2012

[11] Pullen, J., The Internet lecture: converging teaching and technology, *ACM Special Interest Group on Computer Science Education (SIGCSE) Bulletin* Vol 32 No 3 (Sep. 2000), 101-104

[12] Pullen, J., Applicability Of Internet video In distance education For engineering, *Proceedings IEEE Frontiers in Education 2001* (Reno, NV, October 2001), T2F-14–T2F-19, online at http://fie.engrng.pitt.edu/ fie2001/papers/1242.pdf

[13] Pullen, J., Scaling up a distance education program in computer science, *ACM Special Interest Group on Computer Science Education (SIGCSE) Bulletin 38,* 3 (Sep 2006) 33-37

[14] Pullen, J., R. Simon, and P. McAndrews, An Online Graduate Computer Science Program Delivered Via Simulteaching, *Advanced Technology for Learning* Vol 2 No 3 (Jul. 2005) 148-155, ACTA Press, Calgary, AB

[15] Pullen, J., N. Clark and P. McAndrews, MIST/C: Open Source Software For Hybrid Classroom And Online Teaching, IASTED International Conference on Technology for Education, Dallas, Texas, December 2011

[16] Russell, T., *The No Significant Difference Phenomenon: A Comparative Research Annotated Bibliography on Technology for Distance Education (5th ed.)*, IDECC, 2001

[17] Sclater, N., Large-Scale Open Source E-Learning Systems at the Open University UK, (Research Bulletin, Issue 12). Boulder, CO: EDUCAUSE Center for Applied Research, 2008, available from http://www.educause.edu/ecar

[18] SMART Board, http://smarttech.com/smartboard

[19] Snow, C., J. Pullen, and P. McAndrews (2005), An Open-Source Web-Based System for Synchronous Distance Education, *IEEE Transactions on Education 48*, 4 (Nov. 2005), 705-712

[20] University of Phoenix, Online College Degree Programs, http://www.phoenix.edu/, as of March 2012

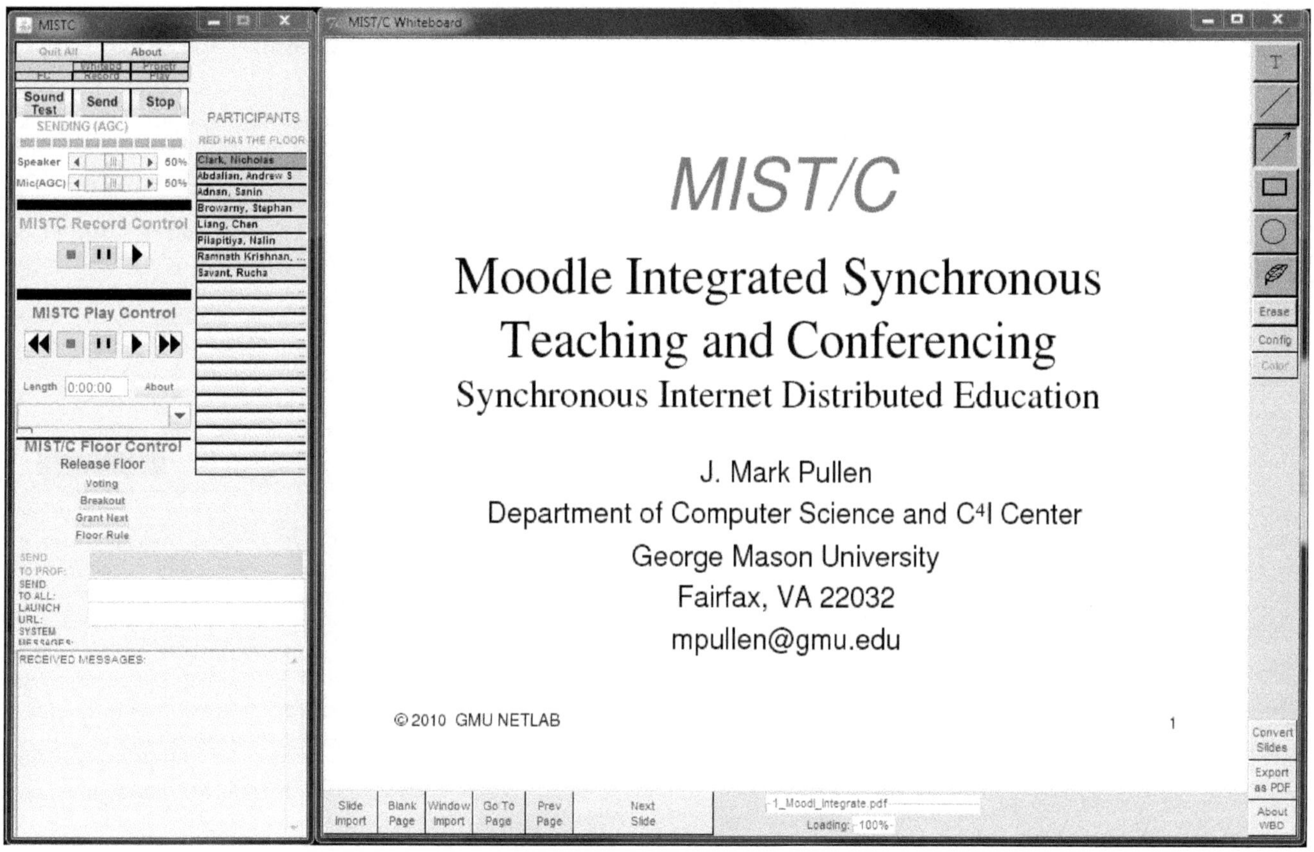

Figure 2. MIST/C User Interface.

SpecCheck: Automated Generation of Tests for Interface Conformance

Chris Johnson*
University of Wisconsin, Eau Claire
Eau Claire, WI, USA

ABSTRACT

Grading code in large introductory programming classes is fraught with difficulties. In particular, students deviate from the required specification—and these deviations in turn break instructors' test code, delay feedback, hurt grades, and drive instructors to create oppressive homework policies. We present a system called SpecCheck for automatically generating tests that inform students of these deviations *before* they submit their homework. Our system inspects a instructor's reference implementation of a homework and produces tests to validate student code for interface conformance. It aids in conditioning code for faster grading but avoids the hazards introduced by some autograders. We present the tool and an experience report of its effectiveness in a large first-semester programming course.

Categories and Subject Descriptors

K.3.2 [**Computer and Information Science Education**]: Computer science education

General Terms

Languages, Verification

Keywords

automated grading, large classes, interface conformance

1. INTRODUCTION

A typical programming assignment in a large introductory programming course passes through this unfortunate lifecycle:

1. The instructor devises a problem and details how students are expected to solve it in their code. Often the instructor describes the interface that students are to implement [12]. The interface may be specified in plain text or generated from documentation using tools like Javadoc.
2. Students develop their implementations, a non-trivial number of which deviate from the specification. Extra parameters are added to methods, classes and methods are renamed, or data is printed to the console instead of returned. These students submit their nonconforming solutions.
3. The instructor grades. Attempts at developing automated or semi-automated grading tools are thwarted by the solutions' numerous deviations from the specification. The grading process is slowed considerably, and students receive feedback too late to be useful.

In our experience, first-semester students are primarily focused on achieving correct final output. McCracken et al. [12] suggest that successful compilation alone may be the goal of many students. Details like correct method and class names, parameters, and return types are secondary requirements. Instructors, however, must inspect code in isolation—not just the final result—to adequately inventory a student's learning. It is convenient to develop unit tests or grading scripts that tease out students' achievement on individual requirements. Such code has a dependency on students' code, but if students' code does not conform to the specified interface, the instructor's code does not run.

Several unfortunate consequences may emerge from this situation. To save time and reduce frustration, the instructor reduces the number of graded coding assignments, likely to the disadvantage of students. Alternatively, students are penalized for not following directions, resulting in grades that may serve as poor proxy variables for their real ability to solve programming problems.

To avoid these consequences, we introduce the SpecCheck system for automatically generating test suites that verify conformance of student code to published specifications.

Generating a SpecCheck test suite is a simple operation. First the instructor develops a programming assignment and a reference implementation, as with any homework. Then, the instructor annotates each required class, method, and field with a custom annotation provided by the SpecCheck library and runs a test generator on the reference implementation. Using Java's reflection API, the generator inspects the code and automatically produces JUnit tests that check for the annotated structures. Students download and apply these tests to their own implementations, correct any problems that are reported, and ultimately submit a solution which the instructor can more successfully grade.

*johnch@uwec.edu

ITiCSE'12, July 3–5, 2012, Haifa, Israel.

Since SpecCheck relies heavily on the ability to programmatically inspect code, it's useful only for assignments in languages with an exposed reflection API. We have implemented our system for the Java programming language, but its concepts could be easily applied to C#, for example.

2. RELATED WORK

Automated grading has been a popular concept in computer science education since its development as a discipline. Though SpecCheck is itself not an autograder, it can be used to condition students' code for easier automatic grading. Therefore, many of the issues surrounding automatic grading are relevant to our work. The literature survey of Douce et al. [3] offers a more complete history of automatic grading in computer science classes.

One of the immediate benefits of autograding, as noted by Hollingsworth [7] in 1960, is the reduction in time spent compiling, inspecting, and evaluating students' code. Hollingsworth posits an untested hypothesis that with automated grading "students learn programming not only as well but probably better than they did" in laboratory groups of four or five students. SpecCheck's development was similarly motivated by the prospects of reducing time spent grading and helping students learn material more effectively by receiving feedback more quickly.

Jackson [8] identifies several problems that emerge from grading that is performed automatically. First, only those portions of student code which can be graded algorithmically are assessed. Most automated graded systems, for example, do not grade documentation and students therefore invest less time writing it. Second, the variability of program output leads to one of two problems: either a) the instructor falls back on code inspection and manual grading or b) instructors overspecify a problem to eliminate ambiguity. It seems that instructors are faced with a choice between spending a lot of time grading or eliminating creative, open-ended problems in assignments. Jackson proposes a middle-of-the-road workflow in which submitting, compiling, and some testing is performed automatically while documentation and code inspection requires human intervention. SpecCheck is a software tool that fits into such a workflow by checking student code for interface conformance, not just syntactic correctness.

SpecCheck shares its motivation with the AutoGrader framework described by Helmick [6]. With AutoGrader, instructors release Java `interface`s for each required class. Students implement the interfaces in the classes they write, and any deviations from the interface trigger compile-time errors. Thus, all submitted code is conditioned to have a uniform interface and is more easily graded by a machine. There are several limitations to this approach. While it is reported to work well in a data structures course, where students learn the strengths and weaknesses of competing implementations of a common interface, it is not clear that it would work well in a first-semester course. Students would be exposed very early to an advanced language concept which is typically not covered by textbooks until after inheritance [14]. Our SpecCheck system was designed for use in an introductory course and can be used even on the first programming assignment. A second limitation of AutoGrader is the `interface` mechanism itself. Examples of conformance checks outside the range of the Java compiler include verifying that a class is a subclass of another, determining the presence of `public` constants, and checking that a method has certain `throws` declarations.

3. SPECCHECK

SpecCheck is a system for automatically generating test suites that evaluate structural conformance to a defined software interface. The tests report whether the fields and methods in the classes under review conform in terms of modifiers (like `static`, `public`, and `abstract`), parameters, return values, and other language features. Testing functional correctness is not a feature of SpecCheck, but custom tests may be easily added to the generated suite.

This system has been designed for use in an introductory Java-based object-oriented programming course that regularly has an enrollment of 250 students. For each homework assignment, instructors publish a plain text specification of classes and methods that students are to implement. A SpecCheck test suite is also provided. Students run the tests against their code to ensure correct reading of the homework requirements.

The goal of the SpecCheck system is to turn grade-time errors into code-time errors. Students receive feedback before they even submit their homework, promoting learning and giving them a degree of confidence in their solution. Additionally, the homeworks that are submitted are more likely to conform to the specification, thereby reducing the time involved in grading and allowing feedback to be offered more quickly. It is our expectation that a tighter feedback loop will also improve students' learning.

The test suite does not provide any information that is not already available in the homework specification; it only aids students who are first learning to program in the task of parsing technical specifications and following directions.

The scope of this tool is narrow and independent of other grading mechanisms. It can be applied in conjunction with tools like manual inspection, rubrics, peer review, and functional tests. SpecCheck tests can be generated for any formally-specified assignment.

3.1 @Specified Annotation

Communicating the required interface to the testing framework is the necessary for first step to building a *SpecChecker*. This is done via a SpecCheck-provided annotation named `@Specified`. For most introductory assignments, this annotation serves as nothing more than a label that we can programmatically inspect. For advanced assignments, its properties can be tweaked to check for correct supertypes and exception handling.

The annotation's default values indicate that no particular superclass, exceptions, or `interface`s are required in students' implementations:

```
@Retention(RetentionPolicy.RUNTIME)
public @interface Specified {
  boolean checkSuper() default false;
  Class<?>[] mustThrow() default {};
  Class<?>[] mustNotThrow() default {};
  Class<?>[] mustImplement() default {};
}
```

This single annotation is applied to the specified classes, methods, and fields alike. Not all of its members apply to each structure—for example, a class doesn't throw exceptions and a method doesn't have a superclass. Irrelevant members are ignored during SpecCheck's execution.

The annotation is itself annotated with `@Retention` so that `@Specified` annotations are preserved in bytecode. This is necessary so that SpecCheck's test generator, which loads and queries the reference implementation in bytecode form, can determine the specification.

With the requirements of the code clearly labeled with `@Specified`, we then generate tests that ensure these requirements are met by students' implementations.

3.2 Workflow

To be effective, gains produced by automated grading systems must be offset by their development and maintenance costs. In order to maximize the benefits of SpecCheck, the production of tests for new homework assignments has been streamlined to the following process:

1. The instructor implements a reference implementation that satisfies the specified interface.

2. The instructor annotates any required classes, methods, and fields using the `@Specified` annotation described in Section 3.1.

   Suppose a homework requires a class named `Character` with a `public` constant, a constructor taking a single `String` argument, and methods `getHitPoints` and `load`. The annotated reference implementation at its simplest is:

```
@Specified
public class Character {
  @Specified
  public static final double DEFAULT_GOLD = 100;

  @Specified
  public Character(String name) {..}

  @Specified
  public int getHitPoints() {..}

  @Specified
  public void load()
    throws FileNotFoundException {..}

  protected void rename(String name) {..}
}
```

   Unspecified structures like `rename` may coexist beside their specified and annotated siblings. No tests will be generated for such members.

   Suppose the `load` method reads from a file, which may be missing. The specification states that the method should not handle this situation, and we enforce it by augmenting the annotation:

```
@Specified(mustThrow=
  new Class<?>{FileNotFoundException.class})
public void load()
  throws FileNotFoundException {..}
```

   A second class, an extension of the first, can also be specified:

```
@Specified(checkSuper=true)
public class Hero extends Character {
  @Specified
  public Hero(String name, int playerID) {..}
}
```

3. Next the instructor generates the JUnit tests that check for each `@Specified` field and method with:

```
SpecCheckGenerator.testClasses(
  Character.class,
  Hero.class
);
```

   Method `SpecCheckGenerator.testClasses` is a code generator that uses the Java reflection API to interrogate the classes passed to it. JUnit tests are produced for each `@Specified` structure in these classes. These tests are stored in a separate tester class. Following is an example of the generated test that verifies the existence of the specified `Hero` constructor:

```
try {
  Class<?>[] params = {
    String.class,
    int.class
  };
  Class<?> clazz = Class.forName("Hero");
  clazz.getDeclaredConstructor(params);
} catch (NoSuchMethodException e) {
  fail("You need a constructor in class " +
       "Hero taking 2 arguments, having " +
       "types String and int.");
}
```

   The test generated to verify the superclass of `Hero` is:

```
Class<?> clazz = Class.forName("Hero");
assertEquals("The superclass of class Hero " +
             "is not correct.",
             Character.class,
             clazz.getSuperclass());
```

4. The tester class is distributed to students, probably in a JAR file. The student adds JUnit and the JAR to the classpath. Included in the JAR is a `main` method so that students can simply run the JAR file without having to know anything about JUnit. When run, the tests use the Java reflection API to inspect the students' code and verify that it meets the specification modeled by the reference implementation.

The only activity outside the normal instructor workflow of an assignment is the annotation process and distribution of the generated tests, both of which are performed easily and quickly. The authors of this paper do not typically spend more than 5 minutes on this process in a CS1 course. For students, adding libraries to their class path is the only new activity. This can be done with just a few mouse-clicks in the Eclipse IDE. The SpecChecker, when run, gently reminds them to add JUnit if it is missing.

3.3 Design Considerations

Generated SpecCheck tests only verify structural conformance. Adding functional tests to check that fields have certain values or methods achieve certain effects is not a goal of our system. Such tests are orthogonal to the structural tests and are easily added to the tester class distributed to students.

A test for a field passes if the class under review has a field with the specified name, type, and modifiers. A test for a method passes if the class has a method with the specified name, arguments, return type, modifiers, and exception clauses. The annotation's `mustThrow` and `mustNotThrow` fields allow instructors to declare separately which exceptions must be declared thrown and which must not be. A test for a class passes if all its fields and methods are correct, if it has the correct modifiers, and (optionally) if it extends the proper superclass and implements the specified `interfaces`.

To avoid overwhelming students with screenfuls of failure messages, we deviate from the spirit of independently-evaluated unit tests and produce a single test for each class. Each test is run only until its first failed assertion. Students will likely have to run the tester multiple times to be certain all assertions are met.

In observing development patterns of students, we have identified several problematic behaviors for which we generate additional tests:

- Students have a tendency to create instance variables when local variables are more appropriate. This behavior leads to an exorbitant number of instance variables. Therefore, we test that each class has a number of instance variables less than some threshold set by the instructor. We added an integer field named `maxVariableCount` to the `Specified` annotation to allow this to be set on a class-by-class basis. This value is compared to the number of instance variables reported by Java reflection methods for a student's implementation of a class.

- The reasons for separating interface and implementation are not always immediately apparent to beginning programmers, and they may create `public` instance variables. SpecCheck optionally asserts that no unspecified public fields—either instance or `static`—exist in a class. This assertion can be enabled on a class-by-class basis using an additional boolean field in the annotation. Java's `Class.getDeclaredFields` method allows us to interrogate all of a class's fields and assert proper access modifiers.

- Students often add unspecified `public` methods to work around some limitation, real or imagined. These methods represent entry points into a class that students may rely on but which are unknown to the instructor's grading code. Therefore, we optionally integrate into each class's test an assertion that no unspecified `public` methods are present. Like the check for public fields, this assertion can be enabled on a class-by-class basis using a separate boolean field in the annotation. SpecCheck does allow for an unspecified `main` method since this is often included to test a class in isolation.

4. DISCUSSION

SpecCheck sits between the student and homework submission. Inserting tools into the student workflow can have its disadvantages, but SpecCheck is designed to avoid the common ones, keeping instructor accounts secure, helping instructors retain control over the grading process, and aiding in student learning.

4.1 Security

SpecCheck is not an automated grading system and is not vulnerable to problems that accompany these systems. For instance, Hollingsworth [7] warns that student code can potentially modify the grader code to produce a more favorable result. SpecCheck does not suffer this problem since tests only condition student code and do not actually assign a grade.

Modern operating systems hedge against the danger of modifying grader code, but other vulnerabilities remain, including faked grade reports [1] and file system access [13]. Restricted accounts and tools like Java's `SecurityManager` can minimize these problems, but their added complexity offsets the time benefits gained by automated grading. Since SpecCheck is run as a client process on a client machine, it in itself poses no threat to an instructor's account.

Additionally, no code from the reference implementation is included in the tester, eliminating the temptation of reverse engineering the test suite archive contents.

4.2 Control

SpecCheck is a middle-of-the-road approach to raising student awareness about the importance of following a specification. Though it does not automatically grade, it complements setups that do automatically grade. It guides students into developing code that can more easily be graded but keeps control in the hands of the instructor.

With SpecCheck, students must still functionally test their own code, an important skill which receives in an educational setting a fraction of the attention it's given in industry [2]. Automated grading systems which provide instructor-made tests further rob students of the opportunities to test their own code [5].

Additionally, the instructor does not need to develop tests for all possible scenarios before releasing an assignment. Rather, the instructor can defer producing functional tests until after having observed student solutions. The choice of grading content like documentation, efficiency, and style is also left open.

4.3 Learning

In contrast to online grading systems, feedback in SpecCheck is immediate. Online grading systems are appealing in their ability to centrally manage, add, or correct test cases, but they introduce an unnatural indirection to the development process, requiring students to submit their code to a grading server [4]. A SpecCheck test suite, on the other hand, is easily added to a development environment like Eclipse or NetBeans so that students can test their code by simply running the executable JAR.

Automatic grading is typically an impersonal process, producing confusing error messages when specifications are not met. Failed assertions in SpecCheck produce readable and specific messages that guide the student in correcting the noncomformance. Marceau et al. [11] suggest omitting these suggestions for educational compilers, despite students' clamor for them. It's unclear whether their removal is warranted for SpecCheck. The authors believe SpecCheck tests are more targeted and can recommend solutions that actually lead to a fix.

5. EVALUATION

Our SpecCheck system has been used in four semesters of an introductory Java programming course, three during the regular academic year and one during a compressed summer session. The first semester the software was under active development and no formal evaluation was done. At the end of the following three semesters and in exchange for a few points of extra credit, we asked the roughly 400 students still enrolled to complete a short online survey regarding their use of SpecCheck. We received 306 responses.

Figure 1 shows that a majority of respondents would like to receive homework grades back within 10 days time, with 45% stating that homework should be graded in 7 days. This confirms that students want grading done quickly. The feasibility of this deadline depends largely on the number of graders and students and the quality of submitted code. One of SpecCheck's major aims is to prevent overly-erratic code from being submitted and slowing down the grading process.

One related concern we had is that SpecCheck is only useful when an assignment is highly structured, with the necessary classes and methods already defined. Such structure can eliminate much of the creative design process from assignments. However, most students reported that they'd accept this structure if it meant quicker feedback, as shown in Figure 2. In an open-ended question on the survey, one student stated:

> As far as having highly structured assignments, although some may argue that having rigid specifications destroys creativity, I disagree. I believe that rigid specifications, which SpecCheck requires, ultimately increase creativity by forcing us to develop solutions that may be different from what we would naturally develop.

This structure also facilitates more objective grading. Requirements are communicated early [10], and students need not be surprised by poor grades.

Another aim of SpecCheck is to get students thinking about and more quickly understanding homework requirements. In particular, we want our system to enable students to better interpret the formalisms of a specification, including parameters, types, and names. Figure 3 shows that most respondents found SpecCheck helpful in this regard. Few respondents claimed it did more harm than good.

Students were asked what they did when they saw SpecCheck report an error. Several of their responses are:

> If I could tell where the error was I looked at my code to see where my code had gone wrong. If I couldn't see where the error was I then reread the assignment.

> It told me what I was doing wrong... I could go straight to the problem in my code. It made me think.

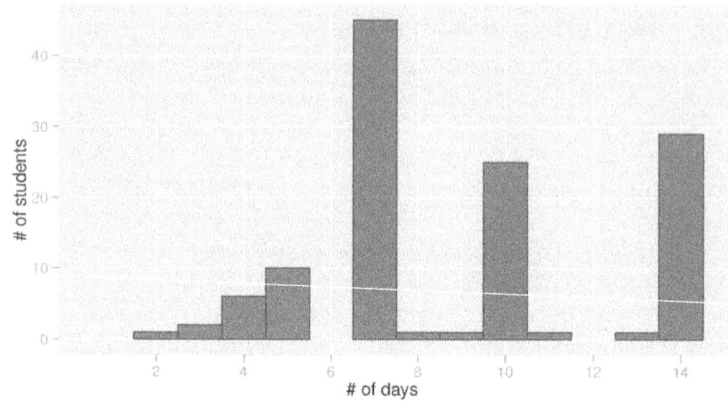

Figure 1: Students' maximum acceptable number of days between homework submission and receipt of grade and feedback.

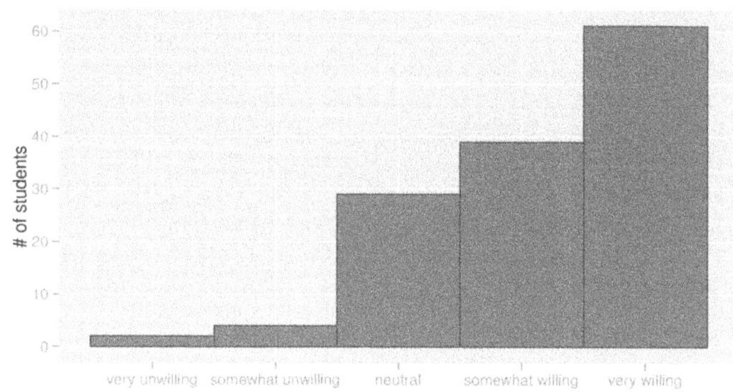

Figure 2: Students' willingness to accept highly-structured homework in return for faster grading times.

> Many times I would be working on something and leave a method or instance variable private or public for the purpose of testing and would forget I had made those changes when I would run the checker. Thankfully the spec checker caught them as they would have costed (sic) me points. The spec checkers are great for times when you go through really easy parts extremely fast. They're really a safety net which I am grateful for.

We expect SpecCheck to improve homework scores. Though Kinnunen and Malmi [9] cite fear of poor grades as only a minor motivation for drops, in the authors' experience, grades are extremely important for many students, and a botched exam or homework can cause a student to drop even if a passing final grade is still within a student's reach.

At present, our goal has been to develop the framework into a tool mature enough to use in a multiple-site experiment. As such, we did not establish a control group to assess the tool's relative impact on grades. We did ask the students how many errors they thought SpecCheck helped them catch. On average, students reported that SpecCheck helped them catch 14 errors in their code. Figure 4 shows their estimated number of errors. If students' perceptions are on par with the true number of errors caught, then the SpecCheckers saved graders a significant amount of time and frustration.

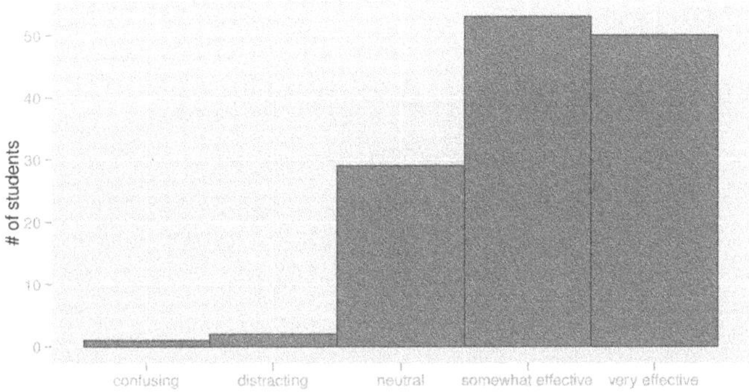

Figure 3: Students' perception of SpecCheck's effectiveness in helping them understand homework requirements.

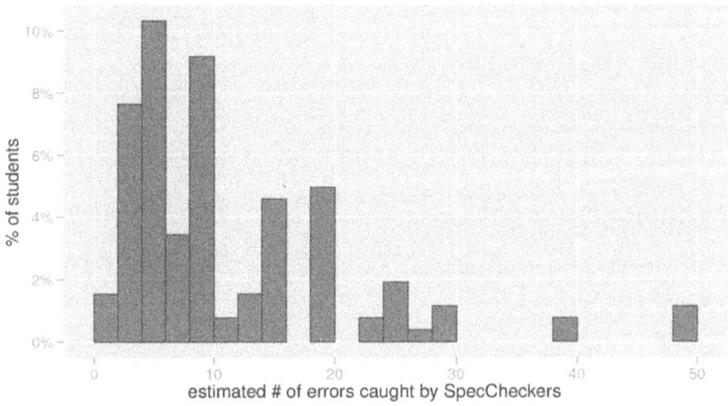

Figure 4: Students' estimated number of errors caught and fixed with the aid of SpecCheck.

6. CONCLUSIONS AND FUTURE WORK

We have described a software tool for automatically generating tests for verifying conformance to homework specifications. Its middle-of-the-road approach allows student code to be conditioned for easier grading. It can be used in either a manual or automated grading environment.

Through an informal evaluation, we have found that a majority of students in several offerings of an introductory programming course found SpecCheck useful. Almost all are willing to accept highly-specified, SpecCheckable homework in return for faster grades and feedback. Its impact on student grades is not as clear, but we can say that students certainly perceived it as helpful.

For future work, we intend to implement a rigorous evaluation of SpecCheck's contribution to student success. By making SpecCheck available only to an experimental group and using traditional means of grading for the control group, we can gain a better feel for its impact. Likely SpecCheck will not actually reduce instructors' overall grading time. It may be that students' increased passing of interface tests leads to the benign problem of more involved functional evaluation.

The SpecCheck software will be released under an open license on the developers' website for use at other institutions.

7. REFERENCES

[1] K.M. Dawson-Howe. Automatic submission and administration of programming assignments. *ACM SIGCSE Bulletin*, 27(4):51–53, June 1995.

[2] C. Desai, D.S. Janzen, and John Clements. Implications of integrating test-driven development into CS1/CS2 curricula. *SIGCSE Bulletin*, 41(1):148–152, 2009.

[3] Christopher Douce, David Livingstone, and James Orwell. Automatic test-based assessment of programming. *Journal on Educational Resources in Computing*, 5(3):4–es, September 2005.

[4] S.H. Edwards. Teaching software testing: automatic grading meets test-first coding. In *Conference on Object Oriented Programming Systems Languages and Applications*, pages 318–319. ACM New York, NY, USA, 2003.

[5] S.H. Edwards. Using Test-Driven Development in the Classroom: Providing Students with Automatic, Concrete Feedback on Performance. *International Conference on Education and Information Systems: Technologies and Applications (EISTA'03)*, 2003.

[6] Michael T. Helmick. Interface-based programming assignments and automatic grading of java programs. *ACM SIGCSE Bulletin*, 39(3):63, June 2007.

[7] Jack Hollingsworth. Automatic graders for programming classes. *Communications of the ACM*, 3(10):528–529, October 1960.

[8] David Jackson. A semi-automated approach to online assessment. *ACM SIGCSE Bulletin*, 32(3):164–167, September 2000.

[9] Päivi Kinnunen and Lauri Malmi. Why students drop out CS1 course? In *Proceedings of the second international workshop on Computing education research*, ICER '06, pages 97–108, New York, NY, USA, 2006. ACM.

[10] Raymond Lister and John Leaney. First year programming: let all the flowers bloom. In *Proceedings of the fifth Australasian conference on Computing education - Volume 20*, ACE '03, pages 221–230, Darlinghurst, Australia, Australia, 2003. Australian Computer Society, Inc.

[11] Guillaume Marceau, Kathi Fisler, and Shriram Krishnamurthi. Measuring the effectiveness of error messages designed for novice programmers. In *Proceedings of the 2010 Workshop on Scheme and Functional Programming (Scheme 2009)*, Montreal, Quebec, Canada, 2010.

[12] Michael McCracken, Vicki Almstrum, Danny Diaz, Mark Guzdial, Dianne Hagan, Yifat Ben-David Kolikant, Cary Laxer, Lynda Thomas, Ian Utting, and Tadeusz Wilusz. A multi-national, multi-institutional study of assessment of programming skills of first-year cs students. In *Working group reports from ITiCSE on Innovation and technology in computer science education*, ITiCSE-WGR '01, pages 125–180, New York, NY, USA, 2001. ACM.

[13] K.A. Reek. The TRY system-or-how to avoid testing student programs. *ACM SIGCSE Bulletin*, 21(1):112–116, 1989.

[14] Thomas VanDrunen. Java interfaces in CS 1 textbooks. *OOPSLA '06: Companion to the 21st ACM SIGPLAN conference*, pages 875–880, 2006.

PETCHA - A Programming Exercises Teaching Assistant

Ricardo Queirós
CRACS & INESC-Porto LA & DI-ESEIG/IPP,
Porto, Portugal
ricardo.queiros@eu.ipp.pt

José Paulo Leal
CRACS & INESC-Porto LA, Faculty of Sciences,
University of Porto, Portugal
zp@dcc.fc.up.pt

ABSTRACT

This paper presents a tool called Petcha that acts as an automated Teaching Assistant in computer programming courses. The ultimate objective of Petcha is to increase the number of programming exercises effectively solved by students. Petcha meets this objective by helping both teachers to author programming exercises and students to solve them. It also coordinates a network of heterogeneous systems, integrating automatic program evaluators, learning management systems, learning object repositories and integrated programming environments. This paper presents the concept and the design of Petcha and sets this tool in a service oriented architecture for managing learning processes based on the automatic evaluation of programming exercises. The paper presents also a case study that validates the use of Petcha and of the proposed architecture.

Categories and Subject Descriptors

D.3.3 [**Programming Languages**]: K.3.1 [Computer Uses in Education]: Computer-assisted instruction (CAI), Distance learning; K.3.2 [Computer and Information Science Education]: Computer science education, Self-assessment.

General Terms

Design, Experimentation, Standardization, Languages.

Keywords

Teaching Assistant, Automatic Evaluation, Programming Exercises, Interoperability, Learning Objects.

1. INTRODUCTION

A teaching assistant (TA) is a person who assists a teacher, typically in practical classes. The task of a TA in a programming course is usually to help students in solving exercises and assignments. They must help students to use programming tools (integrated programming environments, compilers, and debuggers), check if they have solved the exercises and provide feedback to help them to overcome their difficulties. Unfortunately, the number of TAs is frequently insufficient for the number of students enrolled in introductory programming courses, and they are only available in computer labs and on a certain timetable.

ITiCSE'12, July 3–5, 2012, Haifa, Israel.

This research aims to create an automatic TA specialized in programming exercises, a tool for bridging between the teacher and the students, while providing them with the best systems for each task. The automatic TA presented in this paper is called *Petcha*, an acronym of Programming Exercises TeaCHing Assistant.

Petcha can be described as a *scaffolding* tool since it complements existing tools and was designed to be easily removed once it is no longer needed. For instance, rather than providing its own environment for solving exercises Petcha promotes the use of existing Integrated Development Environments (IDEs) and different IDEs can be can be used with Petcha, such as Eclipse or Visual Studio.

More than just a scaffolding tool, Petcha is also pivot component on a network integrating other e-Learning systems. These e-Learning systems are used for: 1) automatic evaluation of programs and feedback generation; 2) authoring and storing of programming exercises as learning objects; 3) managing instruction and learning activities. A proper integration of these tools sets up the necessary foundations for the practice of solving programming exercises and has a great impact on the acquisition of programming skills.

The remainder of this paper is organized as follows. Section 2 reviews related work on the authoring of learning objects and evaluation of programming exercises. In the following section we present the design of Petcha and its role in the context of an e-Learning environment with a service-oriented architecture. The paper proceeds with a case study where Petcha was successfully used in the practical classes in an introductory programming course. Finally, we conclude with a summary of the main contributions of this work and a perspective of future research.

2. RELATED WORK

Petcha has two facets: it helps the teacher in exercise authoring and the students in the exercise solving. To the best of authors' knowledge, no other tool described in the literature integrates these two facets. Hence, we present in this section several systems addressing only one of these facets. Firstly we introduce systems that automate exercise authoring. Secondly we present systems for the automatic evaluation of programming exercises.

2.1 Exercises Authoring

In recent years, a large number of programming exercises have been developed and published mostly for use in programming contests. These exercises are generally stored in proprietary systems (e.g. online judges) for their own use (e.g. automatic submission, grading). Despite some efforts [8, 33] to define a common format to describe programming exercises, each of these systems has its own exercise format, hindering its sharing among instructors and students.

Trætteberg [31], presented a specification-based and test-driven exercise support plug-in for Eclipse, named JExercise. The plugin gives feedback to students about his/hers progress. An exercise in JExercise is based on three elements: 1) a textual specification of the Java elements that are required and their desired behavior; 2) a set of JUnit tests for checking whether the student's code meets the specification; 3) a model of the required solution. The exercises are wrapped in a Zip-file containing XML and HTML files describing the exercises and test files for testing the student's code, and may additionally contain Java source files and program skeletons.

Jena [11] presents a work regarding the authoring and sharing of programming exercises as learning objects. The work uses Labrat as the automatic grading system. The assignments are composed by an exercise statement, metadata, program solution and tests. All these resources are described with metadata based on the IEEE LOM specification and packaged in a single zip file structure conforming to the format required by Labrat. The exercises are stored in a repository called CollabX.

2.2 Automatic Evaluation of Exercises

The assessment of programming assignments poses significant demands on the teachers' time and other resources [5]. This demand stimulated the development of automated learning and assessment systems in many universities [1]. Most of these systems provide other features such as multi-programming language support, evaluation type (static or dynamic), feedback, interoperability, learning context, security and plagiarism.

Early efforts [10, 20, 24, 26] only support the assessment of exercises in a single programming language. With the advent of the Internet and the increase of platforms heterogeneity, web interfaces began to play an important role in the dissemination of several systems [3, 12, 13, 21]. These systems also share the common feature of supporting the submissions of exercises written in *multi-programming languages* such as Java, C++ and the C.

Regarding the *evaluation type,* the standard way of evaluating a program is to compile and execute it with a set of test cases with input and output files (black-box approach). The program is classified as accepted if compiles without errors and the output of each execution test is the same as the expected output. This strategy has been shown to bring undesirable pedagogical issues such as student frustration and confusion [28, 30]. Several systems [3, 10, 12, 18, 21, 26] test not only the behavior of single programs but also analyze the structure of source code (white-box approach). This approach allows the evaluator systems to guarantee that whether the program have been written in a particular way, following a particular algorithm or even using certain data structures. In the field of the output correctness determination, Edwards [6] and Auffarth [2] use also unit tests defined by teachers to validate students' submissions. Other main issue lies with the non-determinism of the program outputs where different correct (or acceptable) solutions to the same programming exercise may not always produce exactly the same output [29]. Leal [13], deals with this non-determinism using dynamic correctors as special evaluators that are invoked after each test case execution. For instance, if the solution is a set of values that can be presented in any order then a dynamic corrector can be used to reduce the output to a normal form.

Depending of the learning context (competitive or curricular) the systems must provide *feedback* to facilitate the students' comprehension about the correctness of their attempt to solve a particular exercise. The generation of feedback relies on static and dynamic program analyses [1]. The development of automatic program evaluation systems with high quality feedback (e.g. compilation errors, execution errors, execution tests) show good results [9, 17] and along with visual, incremental and personalized feedback should shape the future regarding this topic [27].

The *interoperability* of the evaluation systems is also a main issue. An evaluator should be able to participate in learning scenarios where teachers can create exercises, store them in a repository and reference them in a Learning Management System (LMS) and students solve the exercises and submit to evaluators who delivers an evaluation report back to students. Several systems [16] try to address this issue allowing the integration with course management systems. Nowadays with the advent of service oriented architectures the trend is service orientation rather than component-based systems. An evaluator system as a service will automate the existent business logic in distributed e-Learning scenarios allowing more flexibility in the comprised workflows and keeping the systems simple and easy maintainable. Leal [15] specified a service for programming exercises evaluation in a well-known e-Learning framework called the E-Framework. This work was used in Edujudge [32] with promising results.

Concerning the *security* issue, Luck and Joy [16] analyzed this issue covering robust environments, privacy, and data integrity. Security can be handled from ad-hoc solutions to solutions based on Virtual Machines (VM) to execute the programs on a safe and controlled environment.

Another issue is the increase in *plagiarism* [4, 7]. Various systems [3, 16] analyze the integration of plagiarism services in the assessment workflow.

Regarding the *learning context*, evaluation systems can be used in two contexts: curricular and competitive learning. In the former, teachers use practical classes, assignments and examinations to evaluate students' evolution. The latter relies on the competitiveness of students to increase their programming skills mostly in computer programming contests. In this last context, automated judge systems (or online judges) are used to run programming contests and to practice for such contests. These systems include automatic evaluators and many of these systems organize their own contests such as Mooshak [13], UVA-OJ (University of Valladolid Online Judge), SPOJ (Sphere Online Judge), DOMJudge and others.

3. PETCHA

As happens with a human TA, Petcha needs to interact both with teachers and students. Thus, these two use cases provide an overview of Petcha features. Unlike a human TA Petcha delegates most of its work to others, as it is fundamentally a coordinator of e-Learning systems.

The following subsections present the teacher and student use cases as well as the architecture of a network of e-Learning systems coordinated by Petcha.

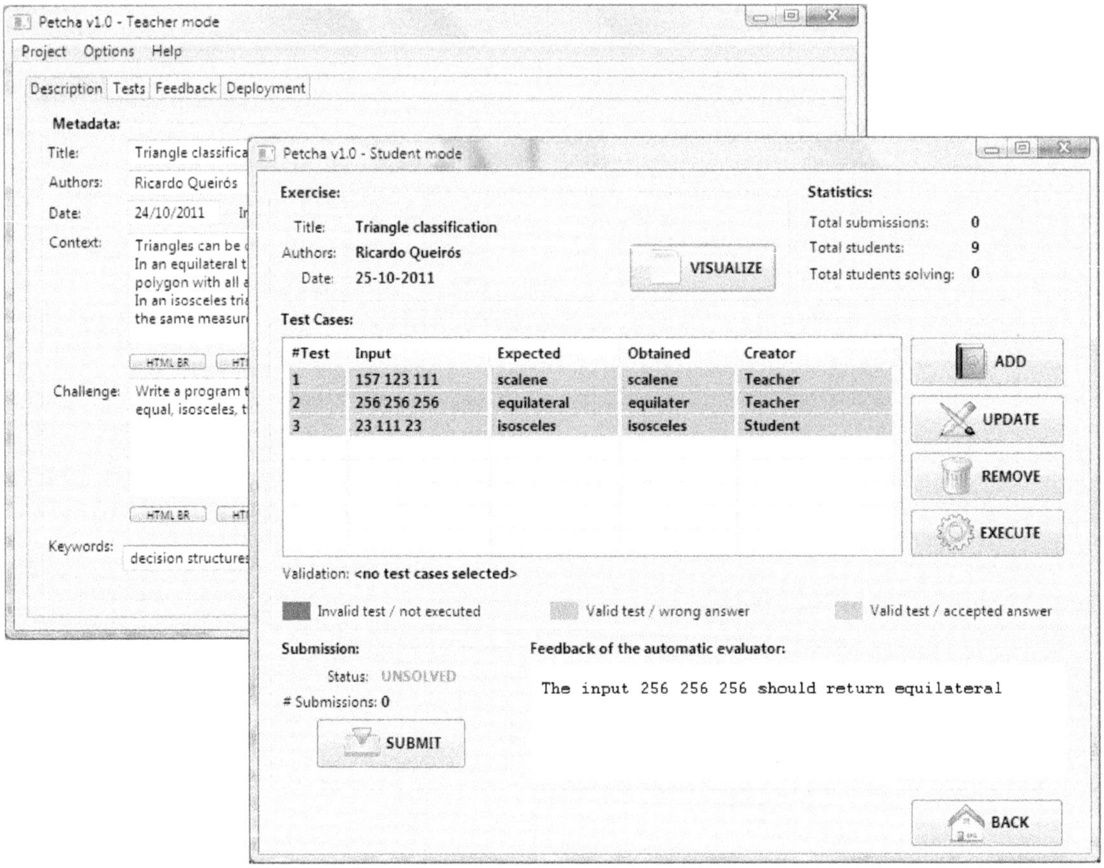

Figure 1. The GUI of Petcha with teacher and student modes.

3.1 Use Cases

Petcha is an automatic TA with two main tasks: to assist teachers in the authoring exercises and to help students in solving them. Although complementary, these two tasks share a number of requirements. Both teacher and student need to: code and test programs in an IDE; send and retrieve learning objects from a Learning Objects Repository (LOR); check program code against test cases. Thus, although the graphical user interface of both user profiles shown in Figure 1 is apparently very different, they actually share many Petcha internal functions. The following sub-subsections present both use cases in more detail.

3.1.1 Teacher

To author and deploy a programming exercise in Petcha teachers must perform the following three tasks:

Create programming exercises. In the authoring task, teachers automatically create most of the resources related with programming exercises such as expositive resources (e.g. exercise description) and evaluation resources (e.g. test cases, correctors, feedback files). The upper left window of Figure 1 shows an example where the teacher is defining a problem and setting related metadata. Other tabs in this window are used for defining tests, assigning feedback to error patterns and publishing the exercise. All the resources defined in these tabs are encoded using an XML dialect called PExIL (Programming Exercises Interoperability Language) [22]. The aim of PExIL is to consolidate all the data required in the programming exercise utilization, from creation to evaluation, covering also solving, the grading and feedback. The PExIL definition supports the concept of incremental feedback to control the appearance of both types of feedback upon a submission of a student's attempt.

Deploy programming exercises in a repository. In the deployment task, teachers can package and publish programming exercises in repositories. The packaging subtask consists on the selection of a package format and its generation. By default, Petcha supports the IMS Common Cartridge (IMS CC) specification as the package format. An IMS CC learning object assembles resources and metadata into a distribution medium, typically a file archive in ZIP format, with its content described by a manifest file. The generation of an IMS CC package is performed in two steps. First the manifest is generated from a valid PExIL instance and all the resources are assembled in a ZIP package. After that, teachers must publish the package on a repository. In order to be an eligible repository (Petcha uses the crimsonHex repository [14]) one must adhere to content (IMS CC) and communication specifications (IMS Digital Repositories Interoperability – IMS DRI).

Configure programming activity in LMS. For this task teachers search in repositories for suitable programming exercises and store a reference to them in a LMS as a Learning Tools Interoperability (LTI) activity. The LTI specification provides a uniform standards-based extension point in LMSs allowing the integration of remote web tools. Presently, most reference LMSs (Petcha is currently being used with Moodle) do not offer support for the full LTI specification. For this reason, Petcha uses a subset of the LTI specification known as IMS Basic LTI (bLTI). With bLTI a unidirectional link between the LMS and Petcha is created. On the invocation contextual information is provided to the launched process such as user identity, course information and role information. The full support of this specification will allow the access to run-time services on the LMS, enabling Petcha to send evaluation results back to the LMS grade book, for instance.

3.1.2 Student

To solve programming exercises using Petcha students performs the following two tasks:

Select an activity in the LMS. In this task, students should select the activity defined by the teacher in the LMS. This selection triggers an LTI launch of Petcha. The launch includes student's contextual information that can be used to presentation purposes (e.g. personalize the Petcha frontend) or for sequencing purposes (e.g. assign an exercises sequence model). After the selection of the activity Petcha is launched as a Java Web Start (JAWS) application on the computer of the student. This approach enables the interaction of Petcha with the IDE by using shell commands.

Execute the activity using the IDE and Petcha. When a student starts solving a problem Petcha automatically creates a project on the IDE of the student. Currently Petcha supports two IDEs: Eclipse and Visual Studio Express. Other IDEs could be used by extending Petcha's code. Then the student reads the exercise description in Petcha's GUI and solves it on the IDE. The student should test the code locally by executing the teachers' test cases and is encouraged to create new ones. If new test cases are created, a validation step is performed to verify that they meet the specification defined by the teacher in the authoring phase. The right window on Figure 1 shows an example where the student's code did not pass all the local tests (two provided by the teacher and one new test created by the student). Even so, the student decided to submit the code to the evaluator and received a feedback message indicating an input data that generated a wrong answer. After testing, the student should submit the solution to the Evaluation Engine (EE) where the submission is checked against the complete test set provided by the teacher. The report on the evaluation returned by the EE is presented to the student. The student may submit repeatedly, integrating the feedback received from the EE. In the end of this cycle, Petcha reports the exercise usage data back to the repository.

3.2 Architecture

In this subsection we present the overall architecture of a network of e-Learning systems participating in a network coordinated by Petcha. In this network Petcha acts as a pivot component mediating the communication among all components. The architecture depicted by UML component diagram in Figure 2 is composed by the following systems and tools:

Learning Objects Repository to store/retrieve exercises;
Evaluation Engine to evaluate students' exercises;
Learning Management System to present exercises to students;
Integrated Development Environment to code the exercises.

Petcha coordinates the communication among all the components of the network, from the LMS where students receives the activity to the IDE where students solve them. In order to fulfill this goal, the integration of the pivot component with the other systems must rely on content and communication standards. Using content and communication standards we can abstract the use of specific systems for each type of system. For instance, we can use on this network any repository as long it supports the IMS CC specification to formalize the description of programming exercises and it implements the IMS DRI specification for communication with other services.

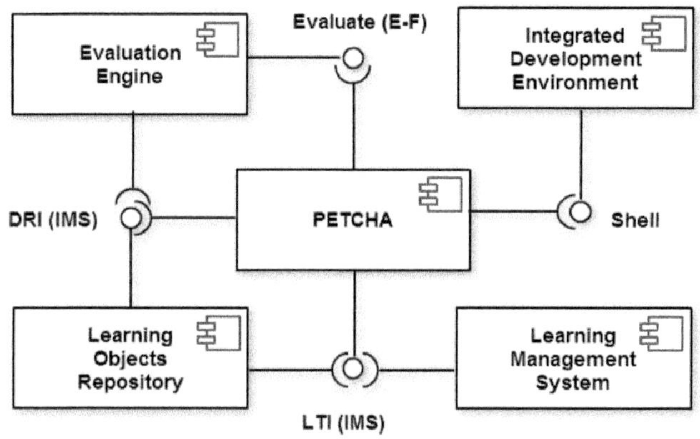

Figure 2. Network component diagram.

Another important point was the choice of the systems that comprise the current network. Since we made several efforts to address interoperability issues, the selection of the tools was straightforward. On the LMS side we choose Moodle since it is a popular and open source LMS, arguably the most popular LMS nowadays. We used the version 1.9 that supports the Basic LTI specification with the further installation of an IMS bLTI consumer[1]. Currently, the version 2.2 supports the IMS LTI 1.1 (a merge version of basic and full LTI) and import IMS CC packages. The exportation of CC packages will come in version 2.3. We successfully tested also the Sakai LMS on this network evidencing the interoperable characteristics of the proposed approach.

For the LOR selection, we had more difficulties to find a system that supports the defined content and communication specifications respectively the IMS CC and IMS DRI specifications. The final choice fell on a home-made system called CrimsonHex - a repository of programming exercises described as learning objects and complying with the IMS CC specification. The repository also adheres to the IMS DRI specification to communicate with other systems.

The EE system selected was Mooshak [13] Mooshak is an open source system for managing programming contests on the Web including automatic judging of submitted programs. The current version (1.6a2) supports the Evaluate service (E-F) [15].

On the IDE side we selected Eclipse. Eclipse is a free and open source multi-language software development environment comprising an IDE and an extensible plug-in system. We tested also the Visual Studio Express IDE on this network with success for C# assignments. In this case we need to install Mono to run .NET applications on the Mooshak server. Mono is a free and

[1] http://code.google.com/p/basiclti4moodle/

open source project to create a standard compliant .NET-compatible set of tools including a Common Language Runtime, C# compiler and others.

4. CASE STUDY

In order to validate Petcha as automatic TA and coordinator of a network of e-Learning systems, we conducted an experiment at ESEIG - a school of the Polytechnic Institute of Porto. First-year Mechanical Engineering students of the course Algorithmics and Programming participated in this experiment. The course aims to widen the students' programming skills using the C# programming language. The course has an average enrolment of 40 students per year divided in two classes. The experiment methodology was the following: only one class used the system – the experimental group - while the other class kept the traditional learning approach – the control group. The course is organized in two lectures of one hour each and one lab session of 4 hours per week. The experiment occurred in 6 lab sessions. In each lab session the classes (the experimental class with 21 students and the control class with 19 students) had 3 exercises to solve. After each lab session we surveyed both classes on the number of solved exercises and the feedback impact. Table 1 aggregates the answers given by students.

Table 1. Statistical data of Petcha usage

Questions	Experimental group	Control group
How many exercises were started in class?	89%	81%
How many exercises were finished in class?	83%	74%
How many exercises solved in class?	82%	66%
How many exercises got feedback?	59%	62%
What percent of students found feedback helpful?	55%	62%

The data collected in the surveys of the experimental class was checked against the logs of Petcha and other systems in the network. An average discrepancy of 4.6% between these two sets of values was found.

The first three lines of Table 1 show that Petcha increases the number of exercises solved by the students. They start and complete more exercises and they have a significantly higher number of exercises effectively solved. In the control class the exercises were manually assessed by the human TA. This clearly shows that students solve more exercises when helped by Petcha than when helped by a human TA.

The last two lines of Table 1 show that the automatic feedback provided by Petcha is inferior to the feedback provided by a human TA. Not only the students receive less feedback from Petcha but also this feedback is less helpful than the feedback provided by a human TA. Nevertheless on can argue that the automatic feedback provided by Petcha would be a remedy in a situation where the human TA is not available.

5. CONCLUSIONS AND FUTURE WORK

This paper presents Petcha, an automatic teaching assistant for programming exercises. This tool was conceived to mediate between the teacher and the students and act as an integrator of the best-of-bread systems involved in the process of automatic evaluation of programming exercises. Petcha is a scaffolding tool in the sense that it works with traditional IDEs, helping student to start using the tools they need to program effectively, and can be easily removed when it is no longer helpful. It helps also the teacher in authoring programming exercises for automatic evaluation, including the feedback to provide to students on common error patterns. To achieve these goals Petcha coordinates a network of heterogeneous e-Learning tools, namely program evaluators, learning management environments and learning object repositories.

The main contribution of the research described in this paper is the concept, design and implementation of a tool acting as a teaching assistant for computer programming classes. This tool was designed to coordinate an ensemble of e-Learning systems and the service oriented architecture of the resulting network is also a relevant contribution of this research.

Petcha is currently being used in the practical classes of an undergraduate programming course. The experience gained using Petcha in this context and the experiments designed to assess the impact of this tool were also presented in this paper. These experiments showed an increase in the number of exercises that the students attempted and successfully solve when Petcha replaced a human TA, which was the primary objective of this project. However, these results show also that the automatic feedback provided by Petcha is less effective than that of a human TA. There is clearly room for improving automatic feedback in Petcha, although it can be argued that automated feedback is still a remedy for situations where a human TA is not available.

The current and future work in this line of research contemplates both Petcha itself and the network it manages. Teachers and students reported a set of minor issues on the user interface that are being solved for the next version. There is also a long wish list with features such as: support for Sharable Content Object Reference Model (SCORM) object, support for MathJax for displaying math expressions, improved visualization of evaluation reports, and statistical data on student activity, among others.

Many of the requested improvements are not on Petcha itself but rather on the network of systems and tools it coordinates. To meet these requests we must either provide new features in those system and tools or to integrate new ones in the network. An intended addition is a sequencing and adaptation tool to guide the student through a collection of expository and evaluation resources. Petcha will report the exercise assessment to this new tool that will use it to propose the appropriate content or exercise to the student. Features that could be improved or added to existing systems include: a feedback mechanism using static analysis; a plagiarism detection component; the evaluation of languages that are not strictly programming languages, such as query languages (e.g. SQL), modeling languages (e.g. UML) and user interfaces (e.g. HTML).

6. REFERENCES

[1] Ala-Mutka, K. A survey of automated assessment approaches for programming assignments. *Computer Science Education*, 15(2), pp. 83±102, 2005.

[2] Auffarth, B. and Maite, L. System for Automated Assistance in Correction of Programming Exercises. *In V International*

Congress University Teaching and Innovation, pages pp. 104 (1-9)., Lleida (Spain), 2008.

[3] Blumenstein, M., Green, S., Nguyen, A. and Muthukkumarasamy, V. An experimental analysis of GAME: a generic automated marking environment. *In Proceedings of the 9th annual SIGCSE conference on Innovation and technology in computer science education*, pp 67-71, 2004.

[4] Cheang, B., Kurnia, A., Lim, A. and Oon, W. On automated grading of programming assignments in an academic institution. *In Comput. Educ.*, vol. 41, pp. 121–131, 2003.

[5] Douce, C., Livingstone, D. and Orwell J. Automatic test-based assessment of programming: a review. *Journal of Educational Resources in Computing (JERIC)*, 5(3), 2005.

[6] Edwards, S. H. and Pugh, W. Toward a common automated grading platform. *In SIGCSE '06: technical symposium on Computer science education*, ACM, 2006.

[7] Engels, S., Lakshmanan, V. and Craig, M. Plagiarism detection using feature based neural networks. *In SIGCSE*, pp. 34–38, 2007.

[8] Free Problem Set (FPS), Official Web site: http://code.google.com/p/freeproblemset/, 2010.

[9] Higgins, C. A., Gray, G., Symeonidis, P., Tsintsifas, A. Automated assessment and experiences of teaching programming. *Journal on Educational Resources in Computing (JERIC)*, 5(3), 2005.

[10] Jackson, D. and Usher, M. Grading student programming using ASSYST. *In Proceedings of 28th ACM SIGCSE Tech. Symposium on Computer Science Education*, San Jose, California, USA, pp 335-339, 1997.

[11] Jena, S. Authoring and Sharing of Programming Exercises. *MsC Thesis*http://scholarworks.sjsu.edu/etd_projects/19.

[12] Juedes, D. W. Experiences in Web-Based Grading. *33rd ASEE/IEEE Frontiers in Education Conference*, November 5–8, 2003, Boulder, CO, 2003.

[13] Leal, J.P. and Silva, F. Mooshak: a Web-based multi-site programming contest system. *In Software—Practice & Experience*, Volume 33, Issue 6, Pages: 567 - 581, 2003.

[14] Leal, J.P. and Queirós, R. CrimsonHex: a Service Oriented Repository of Specialized Learning Objects. *In ICEIS'09: International Conference on Enterprise Information Systems*, pages 102-113, Italy, May 2009, ISBN: 978-3-642-01346-1.

[15] Leal, José Paulo, Queirós, R. and Ferreira, D. Specifying a programming exercises evaluation service on the e-Framework. *In Advances in Web-Based Learning - ICWL 2010*, Shanghai, China, December, 2010, LNCS 6483, pp. 141-150, ISBN 978-3-642-17406-3

[16] Luck, M. and Joy, M. A secure on-line submission system. *In Software - Practice and Experience*, 29(8), pp721-740, 1999.

[17] Malmi, L., Karavirta, V., Korhonen, A., Nikander, J. Experiences on automatically assessed algorithm simulation exercises with different resubmission policies. In Journal on Educational Resources in Computing (JERIC), 5(3), 2005.

[18] Mandal, A.K., Mandal, C. and Reade, C.M.P. Architecture Of An Automatic Program Evaluation System. *In CSIE Proceedings*, 2006.

[19] Mandal, C., Sinha, V.L. and Reade, C. M. P. A Web-Based Course Management Tool and Web Services. In Electronic Journal of E-Learning, Vol 2(1) paper no. 19, 2004.

[20] Mansouri, F.Z., Gibbon, C.A., Higgins, C.A. PRAM: prolog automatic marker. *In Proceedings of ITiCSE'1998.* pp.166~170, 1998.

[21] Pisan, Y., Richards, D., Sloane, A., Koncek, H. and Mitchell, S. Submit! A Web-Based System for Automatic Program Critiquing. *In Proceedings of the Australasian Computing Education Conference (ACE)*, Australia, pp. 59-68, 2003.

[22] Queirós, R. and Leal, J.P. PExIL: Programming Exercises Interoperability Language. *XATA 2011 – XML, Aplicações e Tecnologias Aplicadas*, Junho 2011.

[23] Queirós, R. and Leal, J.P. A Survey on eLearning Content Standardization. *4th WSKS*, 2011, Mykonos, Greece.

[24] Reek, K. A. The TRY system or how to avoid testing student programs. *In Proceedings of SIGCSE*, pp 112-116, 1989.

[25] Rehak, D. R., Mason, R. Keeping the learning in learning objects. *In Littlejohn, A. (Ed.) Reusing online resources: a sustainable approach to e-Learning*, 2003. (pp.22-30).

[26] Saikkonen, R., Malmi, L. and Korhonen, A. Fully automatic assessment of Programming exercises. *In Proceedings of the Conference o Innovation and Technology in Computer Science Education (ITiCSE)*, UK, pp. 133-136, 2001.

[27] Striewe, M. and Goedicke, M. Visualizing Data Structures in an E-Learning System. *In Proceedings of the 2nd International Conference on Computer Supported Education (CSEDU)*, Valencia, Spain, volume 1, pages 172-179, 2010.

[28] Tang, C. M., Yu, Y. T., & Poon, C. K. Automated systems for testing student programs: Practical issues and requirements. *In Proceedings of the International Workshop on Strategies for Practical Integration of Emerging and Contemporary Technologies in Assessment and Learning (SPECIAL 2009)*, pp. 132±136, 2009a.

[29] Tang, C. M., Yu, Y. T., & Poon, C. K. An approach towards automatic testing of student programs using token patterns. *In Proceedings of the 17th International Conference on Computers in Education (ICCE 2009)*, pp. 188±190, 2009b.

[30] Tang, C.M., Yu, Y.T. and Poon, C.K. A Review of the Strategies for Output Correctness Determination in Automated Assessment of Student Programs. *Proceedings of Chinese Conference on Computers in Education,* 2010.

[31] Trætteberg, H, Aalberg, T. . JExercise: A specification-based and test-driven exercise support plug-in for Eclipse. *In Proceedings of the 2006 OOPSLA Workshop on Eclipse Technology eXchange, ETX 2006* (2006), 70-74.

[32] Verdú, E., Regueras, L.M., Verdú, M.J., Leal, J.P., Castro, J.P. and Queirós, R. A Distributed System for Learning Programming On-line. *In Computers & Education Journal*, 2011, ISSN 0360-1315

[33] Verhoeff, T. Programming Task Packages: Peach Exchange Format. In Olympiads in Informatics, 2008. Vol. 2 192-20.

Spaghetti for the Main Course? Observations on the Naturalness of Scenario-Based Programming

Michal Gordon
Dept. of Computer Science and Applied Mathematics
Weizmann Institute of Science
Rehovot 76100, Israel
michal.gordon@weizmann.ac.il

Assaf Marron
Dept. of Computer Science and Applied Mathematics
Weizmann Institute of Science
Rehovot 76100, Israel
assaf.marron@weizmann.ac.il

Orni Meerbaum-Salant
Dept. of Science Teaching
Weizmann Institute of Science
Rehovot 76100, Israel
orni.meerbaum-salant@weizmann.ac.il

ABSTRACT

Scenario-based programming is an approach to software development which calls for developing independent software modules to describe different behaviors that a system should or should not follow, and then coordinating the interwoven execution of these modules at run time. We show that patterns previously shown to exist in programs written in the Scratch environment, which is not specifically scenario oriented, by children who did not have other training, and were not guided to write in a scenario-based manner, are also characteristic to scenario-based programming. These patterns include extremely fine-grain decomposition and bottom-up development. This result suggests that scenario-based programming concepts are "natural" in some ways. Thus, with an appropriate environment and a matching set of tools, scenario-based programming concepts could have an important role in early-stage computer-programming curricula.

Categories and Subject Descriptors

K.3.2 [**Computers & Education**]: Computer and Information Science Education - Computer Science Education; D.1.m [**Software**]: Programming Techniques - Miscellaneous; D.3.3 [**Software**]: Programming Languages - Language Constructs and Features

General Terms

Human Factors, Design, Languages

Keywords

Scenario-based Programming, Scratch, behavioral programming, rule based systems, aspect-oriented programming, live sequence charts, LSC, BPJ, natural programming, habits

ITiCSE'12, July 3–5, 2012, Haifa, Israel.

1. INTRODUCTION

Scratch [18] is a visual programming environment intended "...to develop an approach for programming that would appeal to people who hadn't previously imagined themselves as programmers..." (Resnick et al [22]). While drawing ideas and inspiration from a number of other programming environments designed for young people or novice programmers, Scratch is designed to be "more tinkerable, more meaningful, and more social than other programming environments" [22].

Scenario-based programming is an approach to software development which calls for developing independent software modules to describe different behaviors that the system should or should not follow, and then coordinating the interwoven execution of these modules at run time. Implementations (or manifestations) of various facets of scenario-based programming are seen, e.g., in rule-based systems such as [14], aspect-oriented programming [15], the language of live sequence charts (LSC) [5, 10], and the package BPJ for behavioral programming in Java [11].

This paper reports on qualitative research carried out by re-interpreting pre-existing data reported by Meerbaum-Salant, Armoni and Ben-Ari in [21]. We find that patterns observed in Scratch programming are significant to the study of scenario-based programming — with a focus on traits related to naturalness of language constructs.

Meerbaum-Salant et al. [21] draw attention to emerging properties of Scratch projects written by children. They studied novices who used the Scratch environment and were not guided to write in a scenario-based programming approach. Their subjects were drawn from two middle school classes (46 students, ninth grade, ages 14-15 years old, boys and girls). Each class took place in one two-hour period a week for one semester. The teachers encountered the Scratch environment for the first time; one of them was experienced in CS, the other was not. The teachers received Scratch teaching materials as well as technical and pedagogical support. The researchers did not intervene in the actual teaching of the classes. Their investigation was based primarily on four sources of qualitative data: (a) documentations of class observations (b) analysis of students' projects and exams; (c) interviews with ten students and two teachers, (d) a discussion in a focus group of two students. During the data collection and its qualitative analysis, interesting findings arose serendipitously and appeared repeatedly in different types of data. For more details see [21].

The main patterns were defined as *extremely fine-grain programming (EFGP)* and *bottom-up development*. These patterns appear to be counter to some accepted programming design practices such as top-down design, and lead to a discussion of whether training in Scratch contributes or is detrimental to the teaching of principles of programming and computer science. We examine the patterns identified in [21] and the data supporting them, and observe that the patterns are shared with applications that are designed with *scenario-based programming* in mind. The fact that these patterns were found in Scratch programs of inexperienced students suggests that scenario-based programming concepts are "natural".

When discussing *natural* behavior or patterns throughout this paper we refer to the Merriam-Webster dictionary definitions of "produced by nature: not artificial " or "not cultivated". i.e., behaviors that are either inborn, or are acquired as part of normal and general child development, as opposed to specific training in computer programming. It appears that people describe behaviors using multiple scenarios, naturally, e.g., in sharing a cooking recipe: 'I do A and then B", "It is important to do C before doing D", and "If you see E don't do F". We will show in the following sections that scenario-based programming in Scratch was natural and intuitive to the students in the sense that Scratch constructs and operators were readily understood, and seem to connect to the tendency for scenario-based descriptions. The programming patterns we describe were found repetitively and in many student works, despite not being taught or discussed explicitly by teachers, hence we consider them natural.

Meerbaum-Salant et al. [21] expressed concern about the ability of students to deal with a multitude of simultaneous scenarios, and referred by analogy to the "go-to" debate and the emergence of *spaghetti* code from inappropriate or unwise use of available commands. However, we suggest to consider the extremely fine-grained programs not as spaghetti but rather as an application of scenario-based programming. In this case we can consider explicitly teaching these concepts in early-stage computer-science curricula, thus using tools from scenario-based programming platforms as utensils for enjoying the spaghetti meal. More research is required on how to associate this with current curricula.

This paper is structured as follows. Section 2 provides background on scenario-based programming. In Section 3 we examine the programming patterns identified in [21], as well as some additional characteristics in raw data of that experiment and re-interpret their significance in the context of scenario-based programming. In Sections 4 and 5 we discuss possible implications of these findings to programming education and to software engineering in general.

2. SCENARIO-BASED PROGRAMMING

The term *scenario* is commonly used in the context of requirements specification and use cases. In this paper we focus on executable scenarios - program parts or modules which can be run as part of the application, and are aligned with the system's behavior under a certain set of conditions. There is a variety of platforms and development environments which enable the developer to use scenarios not only in early design stages, but throughout the programming process.

In *rule-based systems* one codes a set of conditions, and associates each condition with one or more required actions. The infrastructure repeatedly evaluates all conditions and for any condition that is satisfied, it executes the actions associated with it. Figure 1 depicts some of the rules in a rule-based system for controlling a boiler in a steam generator [14].

#	IF			THEN		THEN	
	dt_Level	Status	WaterLevel	DoS	DrainValve	DoS	FeedValve
1		TankFill	AboveNormal	1.00	Closed	1.00	Closed
2		TankFill	BelowFull	1.00	Closed	1.00	OpMax
3		TankFill	StartUp	1.00	Closed	1.00	MinFlow
4		TankFill	Full	1.00	Closed	1.00	Closed
5		TankFill	CritFull	1.00	Open	1.00	Closed
6		StartPump	Full	1.00	Closed	1.00	Closed
7		StartPump	CritFull	0.70	Open	1.00	Closed
8		BoilerFill	CritEmpty	1.00	Closed	1.00	MaxFlow
9	StrongDecline	BoilerFill	Low	1.00	Closed	1.00	MinFlow
10	Decline	BoilerFill	Low	1.00	Medium	1.00	MinFlow
11	Steady	BoilerFill	Low	1.00	Open	1.00	MinFlow

Figure 1: Scenario-based programming in a rule-engine: rules in a steam-generation control system. The conditions involve a status variable, the water level and its rate of change, and the actions involve opening and closing feed and drain valves. E.g., rule number 5 requires that when filling up the tank, if the level becomes critically full, the drain valve must be opened.

In *aspect-oriented programming* (AOP) [15], the programmer uses the programming language to dictate when certain modules called *aspects* should be activated, by associating them with *join points* in the base code. Aspects and base code are interwoven such that at run time when a defined join point is reached, the relevant aspect code can be executed before, after, or instead of the original code. AOP was designed to enable implementation of cross-cutting concerns in a single module, rather than the previously standard practice of inserting appropriate method calls in every affected point in the base code. AOP is available as extensions of many programming languages, most notably ASPECTJ for Java.

Behavior-based architectures for constructing systems from desired behaviors were proposed in the context of robotics and hybrid-control. These include Brooks's subsumption architecture [4], Branicky's behavioral programming [3], and leJOS [16] (see the review in [1]).

The language of *Live Sequence Charts* (LSC) [5, 10] is a visual programming language in which behavior is described in multiple separate scenarios. Each scenario (see example in Figure 2) is a sequence chart enhanced with modalities that specify which events may, must or must not happen. The chart modalities play a role that corresponds to that of the modal verbs in natural language such as *shall, can, may or cannot.* Each chart describes a piece of behavior, or "story" that may involve multiple objects. A scenario is composed of a prechart and a main chart, where if the events in the prechart occur in the specified order, then the sequence of events specified in the main chart is executed by the system. During execution, all the charts are synchronized and coordinated: e.g., whenever conditions of precharts are satisfied, main charts are activated, and events that must be triggered are indeed triggered in the specified order if they are not forbidden by other charts. The LSC language enables interwoven execution (*play-out*) of scenarios each of which may involve sequences of conditions and events in multiple ob-

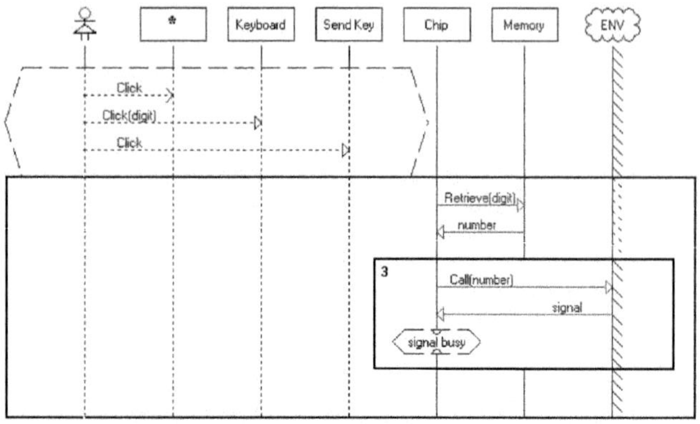

Figure 2: **Scenario-based programming example in LSC: Whenever a telephone user presses the sequence of a star, a digit and send (see hexagonal prechart), the chip must retrieve the corresponding number from memory and call it by sending a message to the environment. If a busy signal is returned, the call must be tried up to three times.**

Figure 3: **Scenario-based programming in Java with BPJ: Each behavior is coded as a separate Java thread. In the child's (and the application's) mind this part of strategy needs to wait for the events X(1,3) and X(2,2) (in green), and then attempt to trigger the event O(3,1) (in blue).**

jects. Inter-scenario dependencies are solved automatically, without requiring each scenario to be aware of the others. A feature called *play-in* enables the programmer to specify the required events by acting them out on a mock-up GUI of the application (e.g. *pressing a send button* on a simulated phone display).

Behavioral programming in Java (BPJ) [11] implements the principles of LSC in the realm of standard, procedural languages, and enables their integration with standard object-oriented programming. Each behavior is coded as a Java thread, independent of the others, and all threads are synchronized and coordinated at run time to produce integrated system behavior. For example, in an application that plays the game of Tic-Tac-Toe, each of the game rules and each playing strategy is coded in its own separate behavior thread. Figure 3 illustrates how, using BPJ, individual strategies conceived in one's mind can be coded directly as independent Java modules, to be interlaced by the infrastructure during execution.

A key feature of scenario-based programming is its alignment with the requirements, or the descriptions of the system behavior as perceived by humans. This feature can be observed from different angles. Structurally, the application (i.e. its modules) can be mapped to individual requirements, as opposed to having each module responsible for parts of different requirements, as is common in standard programming. From the time dimension, looking at the development process, a scenario-based design often enables incrementality. That is, adding, refining, or removing behaviors can be done by adding new modules (rules, aspects, scenarios, behavior threads, etc.) that influence the already-developed parts of the application. See [8] for a discussion of how such features can contribute to making the development process natural, intuitive, and fun.

3. ANOTHER LOOK AT SCRATCH PROGRAMMING PATTERNS

Meerbaum-Salant et al. [21] identified two programming habits, EFGP and Bottom-Up programming, that appeared repeatedly in the students' work and in the resulting projects. These habits emerged conspicuously during the data collection phase of an investigation of learning computer science concepts in Scratch [20]. The qualitative assessment in [21] focuses on how these behaviors of the students may affect the process of learning. Given that Scratch is not explicitly or inherently a scenario-based programming environment and that this concept was not one of the basic principles that were taught in the observed classes, we propose to use the emerging patterns to gain insight about scenario-based programming and people's tendencies in this context. For simplicity and clarity of the presentation, we use a few succinct code examples which represent what was observed in different forms in many students' projects.

3.1 Extremely Fine-Grained Programming

The pattern called EFGP in [21] revolves first around the fact that the programming modules are small, and second, around the fact that composite behaviors were decomposed into separate units, instead of being handled in a single module. For example, in a game application the player has to fight dragon guards. Every time the player touches a guard with his or her sword, the player obtains a magical item that was watched over by the guard. When the player collects six items, he or she can move to the next level. In standard programming, a script to handle the event of the player overcoming a guard would often be composed of the following steps: (a) move the magical item to the player's bag (e.g., by sending an appropriate message to the item); (b) update a counter of items in the player's bag; (c) if the counter is equal to six, move to the next level. The manifestation of EFGP shows that students broke the module into at least two parts:

in script 1, and

in script 2.

In the following subsections we discuss our observations relative to this decomposition

3.1.1 Naturalness

The extremely fine-grained structure reflects the ability of Scratch developers to align code modules with the requirements or with other natural human description of the system. As the students in the referenced experiment [21] were not required to document their projects, we rely on the common observation that game descriptions provide each of the basic rules of the game separately and independently, e.g., valid moves, how one can attack, defend and earn points, what are the winning conditions, etc. Sometimes, almost as an after-thought, these descriptions include exceptions, such as, what happens when the player gets a certain number of points (e.g., go up a level), or when a certain condition arises (e.g., a draw). The possibility in Scratch to create multiple independent modules was an opportunity for the students to separate the descriptions into different scripts. This is in contrast to standard programming practices where these behaviors are likely to be coded into a single or few modules, each with many conditions and branches. In some cases the program may even be structured very differently, e.g. replacing the conditions with a tree structure for usage by a minimax algorithm. The small scripts may have a confusing visual effect when floating in the scripts area in the Scratch development environment, however, the students seemed comfortable using these building blocks. We therefore observe in Scratch the ability to align the application structure with the requirements, which was discussed as key trait of scenario- based programming in Section 2.

3.1.2 Basic use of IF statements

A facet (or an enabler) of EFGP observed in [21] is the decomposition of *then* and *else* parts of an IF statement into separate scripts - one with `if <condition1> then <action1 >` and the other with `if <not-condition1> then <action2>`. This property is very much in line with the association of scenarios with "stories". In rule-based systems and in AOP, this style is the default. When coding in LSC one can write both standard conditions (with or without `else` blocks), and assertions - conditions with no `else` structure. In the latter - when the condition is not satisfied the scenario either terminates (i.e., becomes irrelevant), or is suspended until the condition is satisfied. Additionally, precharts and monitored events in LSC imply conditions that drive further actions, with no reference to `else` whatsoever. When the events listened for in the scenarios do not occur, the scenario simply (and naturally) remains inactive or suspended, allowing other scenarios to handle the situation. In natural language, it is common to find descriptions such as *"If a character is hit by dragon-fire it loses a life, but if it avoids the fire it earns bonus points"*. This style leads to separate scripts for each branch of the condition, with equivalent overall semantic to that of using *else*. In [21], this habit was described by a student during an interview:

Q: Can you define what is a 'condition"?

A: when I write: "If this is such and such then say move here"; "if this is such and such then go here". So if I lay down this kind of conditions, the moment I enter one situation, he goes here, and if the situation is different, it does something else.

In this context we note that when a particular action is desired following any of several conditions, many students did not program a disjunction, most likely because the topic was not covered in these classes. It is well known that disjunctions and conjunctions are indeed more complex constructs than simple conditions, and are often introduced at later stages, as reflected, e.g. in the textbook [2]. Instead, the students coded each term of the disjunction in a separate scenario: i.e., `if <condition1> then <action1>` and `if <condition2> then <action1>` — an approach which is readily accommodated in scenario-based programming and contributes to the EFGP phenomenon.

3.1.3 Preconditions and FOREVER loops

As already seen in the previous examples, many students' scripts began with conditional operations, implemented either by constant checking of variable values or by waiting for a message that is broadcast by other scripts when certain conditions are met. In contrast with more standard procedural programming where methods are called directly by other methods, and where conditions are tested mainly as part of a longer process, in scenario-based programming modules specify the conditions under which they are activated. In rule based systems the activation triggers are a complete set of conditions over the state of the system; in aspect-oriented programming they are the specifications of the join-points; and, in LSC they are the relevant scenarios' precharts - the sequences of events that trigger the main chart components of the scenarios; in BPJ this behavior is manifested by the fact that many b-threads begin by waiting for certain sequences of events.

In [21], students often performed the constant testing of conditions using the special construct of `forever_if`, which continually checks whether a condition is true and whenever it is, runs the blocks inside. Similar constructs are indeed an important part of the infrastructure in scenario-based programming platforms.

3.2 Bottom-up programming

Bottom-up programming is defined in [21] as starting from components which are later linked to form a larger subsystem. This pattern is observed based on examples of students dragging separate blocks and then combining them into a script. This is in line with the intention of Scratch designers as stated by Resnick et al [22] "to make bottom-up tinkerers as comfortable as planners". While these examples demonstrate bottom-up approach, in that the young programmers did not think about the structure of the entire system before beginning to program, we propose that scenarios coded early in the process can reflect also high level behaviors, or abstractions that are not necessarily aligned with classical bottom-up structures.

For example, in [21] there is a discussion of the decomposition of the `repeat until` loop

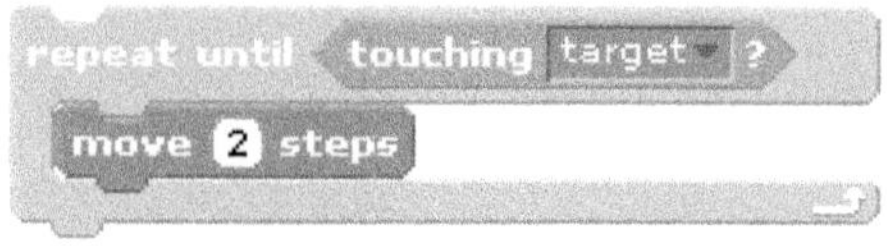

into the following three scripts:

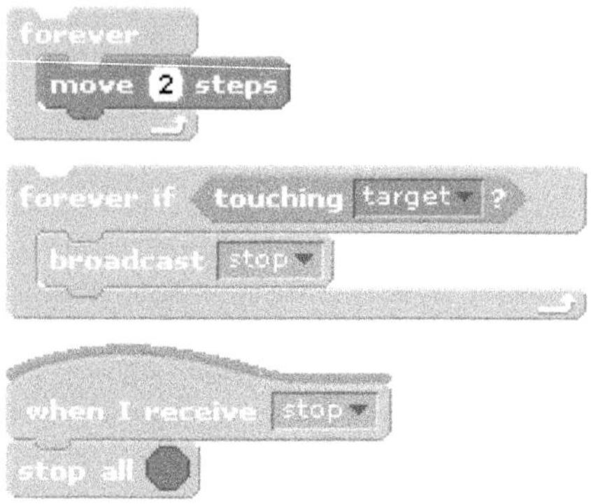

In scenario-based programming this decomposition would not be viewed as three tasks that were wrongly "separated at birth" and are now "desperately" trying to collaborate to accomplish a joint goal which would normally be better accomplished by a single module. Instead, these can be viewed as three behaviors that may be intrinsic to the sprite in their own right. One behavior is the constant moving, the other is the constant sensing whether the sprite touches other objects, and the third, reacting to such touching. Further, in a design review of such an application, one may even expect a discussion of whether the broadcasting of `stop` in reaction to the touch, is the right one, and perhaps instead, the broadcast should have been of the message `touched`, and then other behaviors could translate this to a request to stop, while others could use it for other purposes, such as touching again, or verifying the identity of the touched object, or escaping.

In other words, while the process of building the system may appear as bottom-up, the program structure suggests a decomposition which is orthogonal to the bottom-up dimension. The sprite has capabilities and/or routine behaviors, and what it does with them is programmed in the body of these behaviors. In general, these independent behavioral capabilities can be at abstraction levels that are high or low, and may not be restricted to a particular level. The programmer is not necessarily programming bottom-up, but rather, one behavior after another, as he or she thinks about them. Thus, not only can there be a mapping between the modules of the application to the sections and paragraphs of the requirements document - the process of developing some application components parts may indeed follow their sequential order in the requirements document (or in a sequential mental equivalent thereof). One may conceive the developer following a requirement document that is being read out aloud (with appropriate pauses), with little or no ability to go back in the text, beyond what is in his or her memory and with little or no modification to already completed scripts. Adjacent paragraphs may describe related or unrelated behaviors at different abstraction levels.

4. POSSIBLE IMPLICATIONS TO EDUCATION

In Scratch programming, a behavior may or may not be considered "scenario-based" based on its structure and the commands it uses. Perhaps with the right set of tools (as are available in many scenario-based platforms), scenario-based programming may be a central vehicle for teaching computer programming to young students in a way that will be natural, intuitive and fun. The required tools should cover, among others, organization of code, visualization and comprehension of code, visualization of interwoven execution and verification (see, e.g., [12, 6, 19, 9]). Such tools will help the students to not only get their scripts and sprites to run as desired, but also to "see the forest for the trees". They should be able to conceive of an application as a composite artifact whose design should have certain traits such as understandability or maintainability.

Additionally, when teaching top-down design and other accepted methodologies for creation of complex systems, the teacher's awareness of the natural tendencies for "bottom-up" construction and fine-grain design, may help clarify the points being taught.

The incrementality that comes with the scenario-based design, and the executability and feedback associated with it, are thus key ingredients in enabling tinkering, which is one of the goals of Scratch [22], and in line with the constructionism approach of Papert [13].

It should be noted that Scratch is not a full scenario-based platform, and that established scenario-based techniques and approaches have additional features such as automatic synchronization, and compact idioms for one behavior to suspend or otherwise influence the execution of all other behaviors without explicit interaction between modules. In the right setting, such concepts may prove easier to teach than the raw concepts of concurrency and interprocess communication where it is the programmer's responsibility to craft all aspects of the composite behavior.

Lastly, we conjecture that new design disciplines and practices will be developed where scenario-based programming concepts are first-class citizens among the methodologies and technologies that make up successful engineering practices. These disciplines will include, how to write independent behaviors, how to organize sets of behaviors, and what kind of inter-dependencies are acceptable. Subsequently, these practices will become a standard part of programming and computer science education at all levels.

5. DISCUSSION

While it is unlikely that humans are endowed with inherent/intrinsic skills specifically design for programming computers (as we know them today), "programming"-like skills are encountered in social human behaviors from the beginning of civilizations. From the wisdom of elders passed through generations, through social norms and laws, to everyday practices around nutrition, medicine, and art, humans were and are constantly engaged in telling others, or memorizing for themselves, how to do things. In computer science, the developers of various styles of scenario-based programming claim that the proposed techniques are "natural" in some ways - a claim that seems plausible in view of the prevailing styles of instruction manuals, cookbooks, books of law, spoken narratives with morales, etc. Qualitative studies such as [7] investigate what language features may or may not be natural or intuitive for programmers. The findings of Meerbaum-Salant et al. [21] and the findings of this paper suggest that the desire to compose full "operational descriptions" from small self-standing pieces, each of which is introduced shortly before it is needed, is manifested not only in verbal or documented descriptions, but, given a programming language that allows it, are a preferred way for constructing all or parts of the system.

We suggest that future research could shed light on what is it in scenario-based behavior description (and subsequently, programming) that is attractive to young programmers and whether the Scratch projects uncovered a pre-existing tendency, or led the students to a totally new behavior. From our experience as programming professionals and observers of novice and experienced programmers, it appears that part of the answer lies in reducing the amount of energy or resources required at any given point in time in the development process. Perhaps fine-grained, "bottom-up" development, allows one to reduce the number of pieces that one has to think about at each stage, at the cost of having more components in the final system. What we are observing may be the stages in the process described by Lochhead [17]: "before knowledge can be organized in comprehensive global structures it first must be collected piecemeal".

In summary, the seemingly unintentional new habits which are characteristics of students' Scratch programs, during early stages of learning programming skills, appear to be well aligned with key features of scenario-based programming. To the question posed in [21], namely, that *"why the control structures were not used in the ways they were designed to be used"* this paper proposes that the answer may be that the structures which were used instead are in some way natural.

6. ACKNOWLEDGMENTS

The authors thank Michal Armoni, Moti Ben-Ari, David Harel, and Gera Weiss for their valuable comments and suggestions. The reseasrch of Michal Gordon and of Assaf Marron was supported by an Advanced Research Grant from the European Research Council (ERC) under the European Community's 7th Framework Programme (FP7/2007-2013). The research of Orni Meerbaum-Salant was partially supported by the Israel Science Foundation grant 09/1277 and by a Sir Charles Clore Postdoctoral Fellowship.

7. REFERENCES

[1] R. C. Arkin. *Behavior-Based Robotics.* MIT Press, 1998.

[2] M. Armoni and M. Ben-Ari. *Computer Science Concepts in Scratch.* Weizmann Institute of Science, 2010. (In Hebrew).

[3] M. Branicky. Behavioral Programming. In *Working notes AAAI spring symp. on hybrid systems and AI*, 1999.

[4] R. Brooks. A Robust Layered Control System for a Mobile Robot. *IEEE J. of Robotics and Automation*, 2(1), 1986.

[5] W. Damm and D. Harel. LSCs: Breathing Life into Message Sequence Charts. *J. on Formal Methods in System Design*, 19(1), 2001.

[6] N. Eitan, M. Gordon, D. Harel, A. Marron, and G. Weiss. On Visualization and Comprehension of Scenario-Based Programs. *Int. Conf. on Program Comprehension (ICPC)*, 2011.

[7] I. Hadar and U. Leron. How Intuitive is Object-Oriented Design? *Commun. ACM*, 51:41–46, 2008.

[8] D. Harel. Can Programming Be Liberated, Period? *IEEE Computer*, 41(1), 2008.

[9] D. Harel, R. Lampert, A. Marron, and G. Weiss. Model-Checking Behavioral Programs. In *Int. Conf. on Embedded Software (EMSOFT)*, 2011.

[10] D. Harel and R. Marelly. *Come, Let's Play: Scenario-Based Programming Using LSCs and the Play-Engine.* Springer, 2003.

[11] D. Harel, A. Marron, and G. Weiss. Programming Coordinated Scenarios in Java. In *24th European Conference on Object-Oriented Programming (ECOOP)*, 2010.

[12] D. Harel and I. Segall. Visualizing Inter-Dependencies Between Scenarios. In *Proc. ACM Symp. on Software Visualization (SOFTVIS)*, pages 145–153. ACM, 2008.

[13] I. Harel and S. Papert. *Constructionism.* Ablex Publishing, 1991.

[14] INFORM Gmbh. *fuzzyTECH* Software Package `www.inform-ac.com/fuzzytech.htm`.

[15] G. Kiczales, J. Lamping, A. Mendhekar, C. Maeda, C. Lopes, J. Loingtier, and J. Irwin. Aspect-Oriented Programming. *European Conference on Object-Oriented Programming (ECOOP)*, 1997.

[16] LEJOS. Java for LEGO Mindstorms. http://lejos.sourceforge.net/.

[17] J. Lochhead. Some pieces of the puzzle. *Constructivism in the computer age. Lawrence Erlbaum Associates, Hillsdale, NJ*, pages 71–82, 1988.

[18] J. Maloney, L. Burd, Y. Kafai, N. Rusk, B. Silverman, and M. Resnick. Scratch: A Sneak Preview [Education]. In *Creating, Connecting and Collaborating through Computing, 2004. Proc. Second Int. Conf. on*, pages 104–109. IEEE, 2004.

[19] S. Maoz and D. Harel. On Tracing Reactive Systems. *Software and Systems Modeling*, pages 1–22, 2010.

[20] O. Meerbaum-Salant, M. Armoni, and M. Ben-Ari. Learning Computer Science Concepts with Scratch. In *Proc. of the Sixth Int. Workshop on Computing Education Research*, pages 69–76. ACM, 2010.

[21] O. Meerbaum-Salant, M. Armoni, and M. Ben-Ari. Habits of Programming in Scratch. In *Proc. of the 16th Annual Joint Conf. on Innovation and Technology in Computer Science Education (ITICSE)*, pages 168–172. ACM, 2011.

[22] M. Resnick, J. Maloney, A. Monroy-Hernández, N. Rusk, E. Eastmond, K. Brennan, A. Millner, E. Rosenbaum, J. Silver, B. Silverman, et al. Scratch: Programming for All. *Comm. of the ACM*, 52(11):60–67, 2009.

A New Curriculum for Junior-High in Computer Science

Iris Zur Bargury
The Ministry of Education
Tel-Aviv, Israel
Babeş-Bolyai University
Cluj-Napoca, Romania
iriszu@education.gov.il

ABSTRACT

Israel's Ministry of Education has launched a unique program to enhance science - technology education. It is a six year program for grades seven through twelve. The program introduces a new curriculum in computer science for junior-high school students. The computer science curriculum focuses on developing computational thinking. The purpose of this paper is to describe that curriculum and the preliminary evaluation of students' achievements.

Categories and Subject Descriptors

K.3.2 [**Computer and Information Science Education**]: Curriculum

General Terms

Algorithms, Experimentation, Human Factors.

Keywords

algorithmic thinking, computational thinking, computer science, curriculum, education, junior-high schools

1. INTRODUCTION

The current Israeli computer science (CS) curriculum for high school level is well known ([3], [4]) and successful. But up until now there was no official curriculum for the junior-high level.

Since Israel's Ministry of Education has decided to strengthen the sciences and technology studies, including computer science (based on the recommendation of the [6],) a new curriculum for CS for junior high was developed.

The CS curriculum was developed as a six year curriculum, meaning that the junior high curriculum should prepare the student for the high school curriculum. The curriculum emphasizes fundamental computational thinking and focuses on basic algorithmic structures such as conditions and loops.

2. BACKGROUND

Israel's Ministry of Education has launched a unique program to enhance science and technology education. The program seeks to increase the number of high school graduates that will have the skills and knowledge needed to become successful undergraduate students in sciences and engineering and be part of the Israeli High-tech industry.

In order to promote this issue, Israel's Ministry of Education defined, for the first time, a scientific – technology matriculation certificate. This scientific – technology matriculation certificate incorporates high level studies in three or more subjects: Mathematics, Science (Physics or Chemistry or Biology) and Science or Technology (One of the above or CS or one of five engineering technology subjects.) (To understand the Israeli' education system one can read the sidebar at [4])

The percentage of students currently achieving such a matriculation certificate is 6.5%. Israel's Ministry of Education wants to increase this percentage through the investment of resources in education. The long-term plan seeks to triple the above rate.

To reach that goal the program will be taught from the seventh grade to the twelfth grade. The principles of the plan and its implementation in high schools differ from those in junior high.

2.1 Principles for High Schools

Each school participating in the program will map its students and define the group of students participating in the program. Israel's Ministry of Education will assign those schools twelve additional weekly hours to reinforce that group of students in mathematics, sciences and technology. The school will appoint a program coordinator who will be responsible of monitoring students' learning and to help each of them as soon as they reveal any learning difficulties in one of the above subjects. Schools will be measured by the increase in the percentage of students that complete their studies with scientific – technology matriculation certificate.

Too few students learn science and technology of this magnitude in high school, for these studies are challenging and demanding. Undergraduate students who do not have the appropriate background in science and technology encounter great difficulties when enrolling into undergraduate courses. The program assumes that the students' exposure to science and technology studies at junior high, will help them in providing a background in mathematical and scientific thinking, and encourage them to choose these subjects in their high school and undergraduate studies.

2.2 Principles of the Junior High Schools

The principles and advantages of this program in junior high schools are:

- Routing students to this program in seventh grade
- Developing targeted curriculum and teaching materials in Mathematics, Physics, Chemistry, Biology and Computer Science. Physics and CS are new subjects at junior high.
- Instructional support to the school principal and leading staff.
- Additional teaching hours. Each student learns, in addition to the "regular" curricula, two hours of mathematical thinking, two hours of physics and two hours of CS.

3. THE CS PROGRAM

One of the subjects included in Israel's Ministry of Education's program is CS. This paper focuses on the CS curriculum. Since there was no official curriculum for CS studies at the Junior High level, a committee was established and a curriculum was specially developed for that purpose. (The author is a member of that committee)

3.1 Design Guidelines

Developing the new program was guided by some principles regarding the contents, chosen environments, alternative teaching and learning methods, and alternative assessments.

- *The program should provide the students with a set of basic concepts of CS.* The main goal of this program is to expose the students to algorithmic problems and their solutions and by that to enhance their algorithmic thinking. [2]

- *The program should provide basic concepts in logical thinking and algorithmic thinking.* The fundamentals of algorithmic thinking are conditions and loops and therefore the program will focus on these tools.

- *The program must be taught in fun and interactive ways.* Since the students in this program are young, it is easier to teach them through enjoyable experiential activities and the use of hands-on methods. The program aims to expose young students to computer science knowledge, to nurture their curiosity and encourage them to choose to continue studying this field in high school.

- *The programming environment for the first year should be translatable to different natural languages easily.* To avoid any language difficulties deterring the common junior-high student, it is better to choose an environment that can be translated to Israel's official languages: Hebrew and Arabic, but could still be used in English too, should any student choose so.

- *The programming environment should be free of charge (if possible), easy to use and graphically appealing.* Nevertheless, it is important to ensure that the focus of the students will be on the major goal – algorithms, and that he or she is not distracted by the graphics.

- *At least two different environments should be taught.* For the first year the environment should be one with no syntax debugging issues, so that the learning can be solely focused on algorithmic problems. The second environment should be designed to solve different kinds of problems than the first one. This environment may need syntax debugging. The use of at least two different environments enhances the understanding of using algorithms as a solution to algorithmic problems.

- *The program needs to motivate the students to be active learners.* The teaching techniques combine a number of methods that demand from the student to be an active learner, while encouraging taking responsibility on the learning process both in class and at home. The lessons will take place in a computer lab and will be based on building games or any other interactive system.

- *The program will empower teachers.* Teachers will be tutored and guided throughout the year, and will be equipped with a web forum and a blog for publishing teaching materials.

- *Alternative, unique and innovative students' assessment techniques will be applied.* Students' assessment is done both in traditional ways of exams, such as class work and homework, and in unique and innovative ways as well. Upon completion of the introduction to computer science module, the students will design and build a computer game using the algorithmic structures they acquired (conditions and loops). Writing a computer game will compel the students to plan and design the project before writing it, motivate them to study and make them proud of the product they produced. Writing a game gives the students the opportunity to express their creativity while using the knowledge and methods that they have acquired. The idea that games are good teaching tools is described in [7].

The program's goal is to impart knowledge and skills required for a person in the twenty-first century. It is not aimed to train students to be programmers or computer scientists.

3.2 Program's Structure

The curriculum contains five modules. Three of them are mandatory and two of them are elective and the teachers should choose one of them. All in all students are required to study four modules in total.

3.2.1 Mandatory Modules

There are three mandatory modules in this program:

1. "Introduction to CS" (60 hours, seventh grade.) This module is the core of the whole CS curriculum. The module includes serial execution, variables, conditions, loops (for and while,) counters, accumulators, messaging and event handling.

   The environment that was chosen is Scratch which was developed at MIT. The environment can be found in this link: http://scratch.mit.edu/. This environment was chosen since it's free, can be translated to many languages including Hebrew and Arabic with a click of a button, does not require syntax debugging, it is colorful (but still students remember their main goal: solving algorithmic problems) and it is easy to use. As [1] wrote: "Under these kinds of environments, students do not only have fun, but they also gain programming knowledge in many of the concepts that are taught in computer science foundation courses".

2. "Spreadsheet with an emphasis on its usage for scientific research" (20 hours, eighth grade.) This module is the contribution of CS for the whole program targets. Mathematics and Physics curricula are based on the basic knowledge of representation of functions using graphs, using mathematical functions and basic statistical functions and operations on the data base.

3. "Final programming project" (30 hours, ninth grade.) At the end of this program, and before graduating junior-high school, students will write a small project from scratch to the final product. This capstone project will include a project proposal, choosing an environment (Scratch or Robotics or Internet), modeling the problem, designing algorithms, writing the project and presenting it to the class. As we mentioned above, the student can choose one of the environments studied.

3.2.2 *Elective Modules*

At the second year, the teacher is obligated to choose between two modules. Both are based on the knowledge taught in the "Introduction to CS" module, and using it to solve new kinds of algorithmic problems.

1. "Introduction to Robotics" (70 hours, eighth and ninth grades.) This is the only module that its environment is not free of charge. The aim of this module is to use algorithmic thinking to solve robotic problems. The principles of this module are: to develop integrated logical and engineering thinking, teach basic concepts and principles of robotics, bestow access to mechatronic technologies (electronics, mechanics, software, control) and to provide an experimental and enjoyable learning environment. The student receives a complete robot ready to be programmed. The curriculum contains: controllers, actuators, sensors, electrical energy and mechanical energy, energy transformations, motors, an open-loop control and closed-loop control.

2. "Basic internet programming" (70 hours, eighth and ninth grades.) The module focuses on client side programming and does not contain server – client issues. The curriculum is based on HTML5, CSS, JavaScript and the 2Dim graphics using the tag canvas combined with JavaScript. The students will practice conditions and loops in JavaScript. The curriculum does not include handling of forms.

4. IMPLEMENTATION

4.1 Gradual Implementation

In 2011 a pilot program was conducted, comprising 30 schools. This year, 200 schools are participating in the program. This is only the beginning; the plan is to increase this number every year until we reach all of the 600 junior-high schools in Israel.

4.2 Teachers Training

Some of the teachers participating in the program are teachers that regularly prepare high school students for matriculation exams in computer science. Teachers with less experience need to join a course in order to be certified for teaching in this program. During this course they will deepen their understanding of the to-be-taught subjects and acquire new teaching methods and techniques.

The teachers were constantly guided during the year by two instructors from Israel's Ministry of Education (one of them is the author.) The instructors used email, a blog for learning materials, phone calls, face to face meetings and a dedicated web forum.

Teachers were offered training courses held all over the country. The courses included face to face meetings and a-synchronous virtual meetings. One of the courses was designed especially for exemplary teachers who were expected to develop and share teaching materials.

4.3 Materials Development

The program requires new learning materials. The material development is an ongoing process.

The instructors are constantly developing materials and so is the group of leading teachers. Any teacher in the program is invited to share his materials.

A dedicated blog has been opened and all the materials are published there. This blog is the most powerful tool to reach the participating teachers and share materials.

4.4 Implementing in High School

Data collected from tenth grade classes participating in the program, this year, shows that the average class is inhabited by about 30 students. It is an increase of 15.5 students compared to previous years at the same schools. Assuming a strict dropout rate of 50%, it is an increase of more than 50% within three years in the number of students achieving the scientific – technology matriculation certificate.

5. EVALUATION

Preliminary assessment of the CS program had been done by means of a nationwide exam aimed to evaluate the work of the teachers and the understanding of the students.

The national exam was comprised of 11 questions. A part of them were multiple choice questions and others were open-ended ones. The exam consisted of familiarity with the environment questions, language proficiency questions, variables questions and questions that require algorithmic thinking. We wanted to test the students' ability to cope with algorithmic thinking based on simple conditional and loops structures.

The exam was written specifically for the program by Israel's Ministry of Education (by the author of this paper) and took place simultaneously nationwide. The results are used to determine the extent of the implementation of the program content.

At the morning of the exam teachers were asked to download it from a web site. Since evaluation of the students' achievements is wanted, the teachers were prompted to download the solution and the guidelines for grading the students' answers, few days after the exam. That way, an objective and comparable grade for students across the country was ensured.

This was the first time junior high students took a nationwide exam in CS. 23 out of 30 teachers sent in their students' grades. The grades of 504 students were sent in total. The average score was 70.3%.

In the following passages, two questions: one about nested conditions statements and the other about loops statements, are described.

5.1 A Question about Conditions

5.1.1 The Question

Seventh graders at "The celebrating cat" school trace the following algorithm where each student punched his birthday month and current month:

1. write("What month were you born at?")
2. read(birthMonth)
3. write("What month is it?")
4. read(currentMonth)
5. if (birthMonth > currentMonth)
   5.1. write("You have not celebrated your birthday this year, yet")
6. else
   6.1. if (birthMonth < currentMonth)
      6.1.1. write("You have already celebrated your birthday, this year")
   6.2. else repeat birthMonth times
      6.2.1. write("Your birthday is in this month")

(For the script in Scratch see Figure 1,)

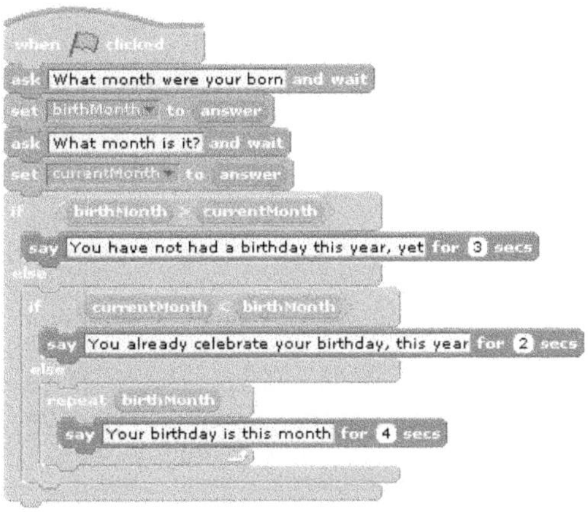

Figure 1. Scratch script of condition statement's question.

The birthdays of some of the seventh graders is listed below (see Table 1.)

Table 1. List of seventh grade students' birthday

Student name	Birthday's date
Abraham	16.3.1997
Naama	5.8.1996
Miriam	6.6.1997
Amir	24.12.1996
Joseph	6.1.1997

a. What will the program say to Abraham?

1☐ You have already celebrated your birthday, this year
2☐ You have not celebrated your birthday this year, yet
3☐ Your birthday is in this month
4☐ Say nothing

b. For how long will the program say the message to Abraham?

c. To whom will the program say "You have not celebrated your birthday this year, yet "?

d. What will the program say to Miriam, and for how long?

5.1.2 The Answer's Guidelines

As we mentioned above, the instructions given to the teachers included the solution and guidelines as to how to grade the students' answers (see Table 2).

Table 2. Answer and guidelines to the question about conditions

Item Type	The correct answer and guidelines for marking students' answers
Multiple choice	a. 2 = Answer 1 0 = Any other answer
Open-end question	b. 1 = 2 seconds 0 = Any other answer
	c. 2 = Naama and Amir 1 = Only one of them 0 = Any other answer
	d. 3 = Your birthday is in this month. 4 sec. 2 = If didn't mention the seconds 1 = If number of seconds is correct, but the statement isn't. 0 = Any other answer

5.1.3 Students' Achievements

The highest possible score for this question is 8 points, 504 students answered the question and only 54 of them (11%) got a score of less than 60%. The average score was 84.3%. Almost half of the students answered this question with a perfect score (see Figure 2.)

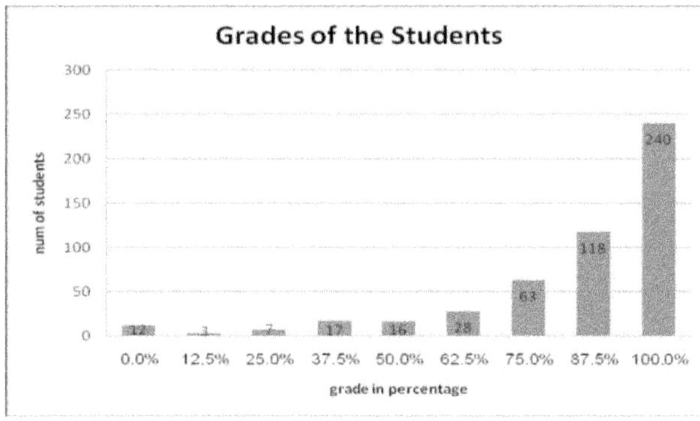

Figure 2. The question about conditions – students' grades

These results indicate students' ability to cope with algorithmic task based on conditional statements, including nested conditional sentences

5.2 A Question about Loops

5.2.1 The Question

Here are two algorithms written by students Omar and Jasmine:

Omar's Algorithm:

1. Write("Enter a positive digit")
2. Read(num)
3. repeat 3 times
   3.1. write(num)
   3.2. num = num*10
4. repeat 4 times
   4.1. write(num)
   4.2. num = num/10

Jasmine's Algorithm:

1. Write("Enter a positive digit")
2. Read(num)
3. repeat 7 times
   3.1. write(num)
   3.2. num = num*10
   3.3. write(num)
   3.4. num = num/10

(For the Scratch's scripts see Figure 3.)

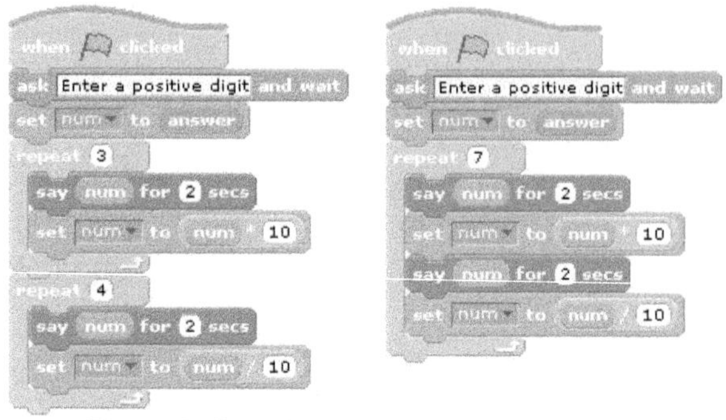

Figure 3. Omar's (on the left) and Jasmine's script.

a. Trace Omar's script. Choose the input 5 for the variable num and Fill in the table while tracing the script (see Table 3.)

Table 3. Tracing Table for the Condition Question

Iteration No.	num	The cat statement

Jasmine joined the two loops in Omar's script and instead of one loop iterating 3 times and the other loop iterating 4 times, she wrote a 7 iterations loop. (see Figure 3.)

b. Jasmine claims that both scripts are identical and Omar claims that they are different. Who is right?

1☐ Omar is right
2☐ Jasmine is right
3☐ Both are right
4☐ Both are wrong

c. Why?________________________________

The answer and the guidelines for grading the students' answer were given to the teachers.

5.2.2 Students' Achievements

The highest possible score for this question was 16 points, 504 students answered the question with 155 of them (31%) getting a score of under 60% of the highest mark. The average score was 65.4%. (see Figure 4)

This question is considered more difficult than the first one, not only because of the loop and mathematical calculations, but probably also because of the comparison skills that are needed.

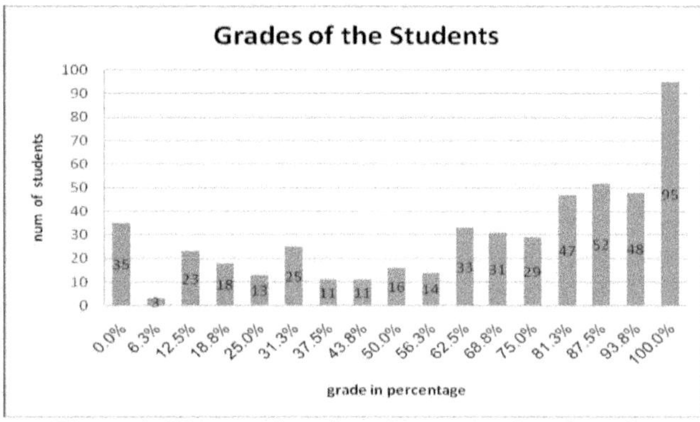

Figure 4. The question about loops – students' grades

5.3 Conclusions

As mentioned, the first national exam in computer science, for junior-high students took place in June 2011. 504 students attended the exam. One can see that the students, despite their young age, were able to deal with questions that require abstraction, algorithmic thinking and comparison.

6. SUMMARY

This is an ongoing research and there is still a lot to be done. Our plan is to expand the experiment each year, by adding new schools and by increasing the number of students enrolled in the program in schools that are already part of the program.

Study materials are regularly under development. The evaluation of materials is based on the comments of teachers and leading teachers, in particular, and on the student's achievements at the national test. The national test also provides an indication to the success in achieving the program's goal: to develop algorithmic thinking. Another assessment tool will be the number of students that are participating in this program, and will learn scientific and technological subjects in high school (in three years from now.) Within six years, the number of students that will complete their high school studies with a scientific – technology matriculation certificate, will be a decisive assessment to the success of the program.

7. ACKNOWLEDGMENTS

The author wishes to thank the many people who took part in developing and implementing the program: (a) members of the committee (beside the author): Reuven Hotoveli (chairman), Avi Cohen (inspector-in-chief, computer science and information technology, Ministry of Education, Israel), Dalit Levy, Orna Muller, Bruria Haberman, Shlomi Achnin, Avi Barak, Erez Sinai; and (b) Doron Zohar who is responsible for implementing the pilot program and for tutoring the teachers.

8. REFERENCES

[1] J.C.Y. Cheung, G. Ngai, S.C.F. Chan and W.W.Y. Lau 2006. *Filling the Gap in Programming Instruction: A Text-enhanced Graphical Programming Environment for Junior High Students*. SIGCSE '09 p. 276-280.

[2] G. Futschek, 2006. *Algorithmic Thinking: The key for Understanding Computer Science,* ISSEP 2006, LNCS 4226, pp. 159 – 168.

[3] Gal-Ezer J., C. Beeri, D. Harel and Yehudai, 1995. *A High-School Program in Computer Science*, Computer 28:10, 73–80.

[4] Gal-Ezer J. and D. Harel, 1999. *Curriculum and Course Syllabi for a High-School Program in Computer Science*, Computer Science Education Vol. 9, No. 2, pp. 114-147

[5] Harel, D. 1992. *Algorithmics: The Spirit of Computing*. Addison-Wesley

[6] Microsoft Research. *Towards Science 2020.* http://research.microsoft.com/towards2020science/downloads/T2020S_ReportA4.pdf [Accessed 9 January 2012]

[7] M. Papastergiou, 2009. *Digital Game-Based Learning in high school Computer Science education: Impact on educational effectiveness and student motivation*, Computers & Education, Volume 52 Issue 1, January, 2000

Outreach for Improved Student Performance: A Game Design and Development Curriculum

Katelyn Doran, Acey Boyce, Samantha Finkelstein, and Tiffany Barnes
Department of Computer Science
University of North Carolina at Charlotte
9201 University City Blvd., Charlotte, NC, USA
1-704-687-8577

ABSTRACT
We present a curriculum for computer science outreach using Game Maker. This curriculum has been adapted over six iterations of a 10-week, middle school apprenticeship on Game Design and Development. Through multiple iterations we have adjusted for many of the issues one could expect to encounter when running a similar outreach program. While many outreach curricula are independent from coursework, our video game design curriculum is targeted to address generalized student learning objectives (Math and English Language Arts) and designed for integration into middle school classrooms. We demonstrate that students' language arts and math classroom performance have improved with participation in this apprenticeship.

Categories and Subject Descriptors
K.3.2 [**Computers and Education**]: Computer and Information Science Education – *curriculum, computer science education.*

General Terms
Human factors, design

Keywords
Education, middle school, game design and development

1. INTRODUCTION
Among high school students taking the national Advanced Placement Computer Science exam, only 17% are women and the combined percentage for African-American and Hispanic students is about 6% (Durndell, 2000). This discrepancy in race and gender representation in Computer Science, as compared to the general population, is referred to as the *digital divide*. The STARS Alliance (starsalliance.org), an organization that spans 32 schools in the United States, is working to close the digital divide in computing disciplines through multi-faceted interventions, many of which are targeted at K-14 students. Through the STARS Alliance, we have been conducting game development outreach to middle and high school students every semester from Fall 2006 to the present. Our work has evolved into a computing after-school program for middle school students. We believe, as Margolis suggests, that one way to close the digital divide is to help students move from learning *how to use* technology to learning *how to create* technology (2003). This philosophy is central to our outreach, where we help students become creators.

ITiCSE'12, July 3–5, 2012, Haifa, Israel.

We partner with Citizen Schools, a non-profit organization that offers after-school services to middle school children with the long-term goal of teaching leadership and professional skills through apprenticeships, which are hands-on learning experiences with experts (citizenschools.org). For the past six semesters, we have led a Citizen Schools game design and development apprenticeship that teaches students how to develop a game prototype using Game Maker (yoyogames.com). Game Maker is an object-oriented programming environment that provides students with a drag-and-drop interface for creating the functionality of their object classes, which control in-game items. This software enables inexperienced students to learn high-level aspects of computing without being overwhelmed by issues of syntax. In this paper, we present our lessons learned over six semesters of outreach, our refined curriculum, and report on our program's effectiveness at improving student performance in standard curriculum as compared to other apprenticeships.

2. RELATED WORK
Games can be used to motivate students to engage in their coursework and to foster interest in programming (Repenning, 2007; Cliburn 2008, Kurvovsky 2007). It has been shown that using games to teach computer science concepts and providing students with game-based homework assignments results in higher class attendance (Burd, 2007), better grades, and increased student retention (Clua, 2006). Perhaps this is because games provide a context that many students can relate to, making the abstract ideas of computer science more socially relevant and grounded. The potential of games as a pedagogical tool has motivated a surge in game-based learning to clarify confusing concepts (Barnes et al., 2007, Leutenneger, 2007, Sweedyk, 2005) and tool development to increase student engagement (Bayliss, 2006, Clua et al., 2006). The results of research on the use of games in the computing curriculum suggest they are both popular with college students and effective: after departments began to implement game-based curriculums, professors noted an appreciable difference in attendance and retention, with students strongly preferring game-based assignments (Cliburn, 2008, Clua et al., 2006). Additionally, many students state that their reason for enrolling in a computer science program was due to their desire to create games (Parberry et al. 2005, Wallace et al., 2009).

3. EVOLUTION OF OUR PROGRAM
3.1 Single-Session Outreach
We began with *single session* outreach sessions at the middle, high school, and early college levels from 2007-2009. Our focus for these sessions was on the "My First Game" tutorial, provided by YoYoGames, which features a simple game called "Catch the Clown." During these sessions, students responded best when we encouraged them to make mistakes rather than avoid it. For instance, when students first ran the game, the clown began

moving in a random direction…right off the edge of the screen. Instantly hands were raised and students cried out "He went off the screen!" Calmly, we replied, "well, did you tell him not to?" What better way to teach the concepts of collision and AI than by showing the effects of not including necessary code? This resulted in our intentional inclusion of several *guided errors* in our curriculum. These errors encourage the students to utilize debugging logic, familiarize themselves with how game elements look when they go wrong, and avoid similar errors in the future.

3.2 Extended Outreach – First Iteration

In Spring 2009, we began teaching our first 10-week Game Maker Apprenticeship with Citizen Schools. Our aim in this initial foray into extended outreach was to give our apprentices a full understanding of the game design and development process. We made several mistakes, including

- Forming unreliable student pairs
- Allowing students to make any game they wished
- Not managing student expectations

We chose to have students work in pairs to model the success of pair programming in computing college courses. However, this did not work well for this iteration, as certain students were absent frequently or dropped out of the program. In these cases, some students were left without a partner and struggled to keep up with the pace of the apprenticeship. Had we worked with our Citizen Schools partners to identify students with behavioral and attendance issues, we could have likely reduced the impact of these issues. Additionally, had our lessons been more generalized, the absence of one partner from a group would not have resulted in that group falling behind.

Allowing students to make any game they could imagine meant we had to provide different instruction for each pair of students. All nine student pairs had their own game idea, varying from platform-based games to basketball games. To accommodate this, we had to have nine separate lessons every week to address the completely different games being made. While one group was learning how to add combat into their game, another was learning how to make a scrolling background. With only two instructors, we were quickly overwhelmed.

The largest problem we faced were student attitudes towards the apprenticeship. Students joined expecting to make *Halo* while we would have been impressed with *Space Invaders*. Young students, with no way of knowing how complex programming and game development can be, will have unrealistic expectations of what they can create in ten weeks. Our students had lofty goals for their games and, when they were unable to attain these goals in ten-weeks, they grew increasingly disappointed and frustrated throughout the apprenticeship.

3.3 Extended Outreach – Second Iteration

Based on the lessons learned in Spring 2010, we updated our approach to include more structure and more development time. Our primary focus during the Fall 2009 apprenticeship was to keep the students' ideas in check by making it clear to them the results they could expect by the end of the apprenticeship to avoid disappointment with their final products. We managed student expectations most effectively by showing them sample Game Maker games and avoiding referencing unfamiliar games.

To help create realistic expectations, we asked students to imagine they were working for a game design company. Students were asked to utilize the ten-week program to create prototype games that we could then play test to select our next big title. It was stressed that prototypes focus on the core game play mechanics rather than artwork and appearances. By informing students that they would be creating testable prototypes, rather than complete games, they had far more realistic expectations.

We limited the number of game types students could choose to make to three, which still let students feel they could choose what to make but helped reduce our preparation and support loads. Student groups could choose to make a platformer, a scrolling shooter, or a dungeon crawler. This allowed us to prepare just three lesson plans per session, rather than one for each student group. It also made it possible to maintain student pairs, because if a student's partner left the program they could easily join another pair working on the same type of game rather than be left with the task of completing an entirely unique game on their own.

Interestingly, groups making games within the same genre still felt their resulting game was unique and expressed their own creative ideas – even if many of the differences were only in the selected graphics. The end result was that students this session appeared to be far more satisfied with their final products than students in the previous session. We continued using this variation of our curriculum through Spring 2011.

3.4 Extended Outreach – Third Iteration

In Fall 2011 several changes were made to our existing curriculum. Most importantly, the games were limited to one game type – the dungeon crawler game. This change allowed for more focused lessons to the whole group followed by independent work by each student team. With this new approach, our curriculum resembles more of a traditional teaching style and better fits the Citizen Schools guidelines to focus on depth of subject.

In both of our previous iterations, we had many lessons where students simply followed along with the steps the instructors were completing. To amend this, we began placing more emphasis on instruction time and connecting with the students in order to help them better relate to the material and enable them to complete more tasks independently. Each lesson changed from having one primary goal to be completed to having a small lesson paired with a series of activities featuring a decreasing level of instructor guidance. This curriculum combines the lessons learned from six semesters of outreach and is our recommended curriculum.

4. RECOMMENDED CURRICULUM

Here we present an overview of our 10-week curriculum, which incorporates the lessons learned from our experiences. It was developed to engage 15-20 students in a once-per-week game development apprenticeship for 10 weeks. The goal of the curriculum is to foster student *creation* of technology, rather than student *use* of technology, as a way of attracting middle school students to computing and improving their overall classroom performance. Each 80-minute lesson follows the same basic structure including set objectives, a hook, a mini-lesson, activities, and a final check for understanding.

Table 1: Curriculum Scope and Sequence

Lesson 1: Catch the Clown	• ***Introductions*** • ***Hook:*** *Favorite game* • ***Mini-lesson:*** *Game Development Process* • ***Activity 0:*** *Play Catch the Clown* • ***Activity 1:*** *Create Game Objects* • ***Activity 2:*** *Debug Game* • ***Activity 3:*** *Expand Game* • ***Check for Understanding (CfU):*** *Exit Ticket*
Lesson 2: Main Characters and Basic Levels	• ***Hook:*** *Favorite main character* • ***Mini-lesson:*** *What a main character does* • ***Activity 1:*** *Create a placeholder character* • ***Activity 2:*** *Create user interactions* • ***Activity 3:*** *Create basic level* • ***CfU:*** *Review main character purpose and vocabulary*
Lesson 3: Treasures and Goals	• ***Hook:*** *Best in-game reward* • ***Mini-lesson:*** *The purpose of rewards in games* • ***Activity 1:*** *Create treasure that adds points* • ***Activity 2:*** *Create goal points* • ***Activity 3:*** *Create additional levels* • ***CfU:*** *Review if-then logic and pseudo-code*
Lesson 4: Sprites and Advanced Levels	• ***Hook:*** *Best art in a game* • ***Mini-lesson:*** *Importance of art in game design* • ***Activity 1:*** *Have pictures taken* • ***Activity 2:*** *Create advanced levels* • ***Activity 3:*** *Tie levels together* • ***CfU:*** *Review game art's value, explain game structure*
Lesson 5: Enemies and Title Screens	• ***Hook:*** *Best game enemies* • ***Mini-lesson:*** *How enemies affect game difficulty* • ***Activity 1:*** *Create Title Screen* • ***Activity 2:*** *Create Lives controller* • ***Activity 3:*** *Create basic enemy* • ***CfU:*** *Review pseudo-coding, discuss enemy importance*
Lesson 6: Attacks and Advanced Enemies	• ***Hook:*** *Best game ability* • ***Mini-lesson:*** *Balancing game attacks and enemies* • ***Activity 1:*** *Group pseudo-codes attacks and advanced enemies* • ***Activity 2:*** *Implement attacks* • ***Activity 3:*** *Implement advanced enemies* • ***CfU:*** *Review balancing and pseudo-coding principles*
Lesson 7: Variables and Loops	• ***Hook:*** *Best super power* • ***Mini-lesson:*** *How power-ups impact a game* • ***Activity 1:*** *Group pseudo-coding* • ***Activity 2:*** *Implement 360 attack* • ***Activity 3:*** *Add power up to game* • ***CfU:*** *Discuss pseudo-code, variable, and looping*
Lesson 8: Play Testing	• ***Hook:*** *What we've learned* • ***Mini-lesson:*** *Game design from beginning to end* • ***Activity 1:*** *Finish all art assets* • ***Activity 2:*** *Finish all level design* • ***Activity 3:*** *Play test game completely* • ***CfU:*** *Discuss game design process*
Lesson 9: The Elevator Pitch	• ***Hook:*** *A time we've spoken for an audience* • ***Mini-lesson:*** *Watch 6th grader T.Suarez's TEDx talk* • ***Activity 1:*** *Lecture on presentations, pitches, and constructive criticism* • ***Activity 2:*** *Prepare elevator pitches* • ***Activity 3:*** *Practice & critique pitches with partner* • ***CfU:*** *Present pitches for the class*
Lesson 10: Final Practice	• ***Hook:*** *Practice pitches* • ***Mini-lesson:*** *Review set up for final presentation* • ***Activity 1:*** *Final Play Test* • ***Activity 2:*** *Practice Group 1* • ***Activity 3:*** *Practice Group 2* • ***CfU:*** *Discuss final presentations, congratulate students*

4.1 In Depth Look at a Lesson

To provide a better explanation of how our Lessons cover materials and address certain classroom concerns, we present an in-depth look at one of the lesson plans from the curriculum – Lesson 2: Main Characters and Basic Levels.

4.1.1 Overview

Students will create player-controlled game objects that will serve as the main character of games. These objects will be controlled by keyboard interactions, which the students will program. Students will also create some basic, initial levels for their main characters to navigate.

4.1.2 Objectives

- Explain the uses of specific technological instruments and tools used in the apprenticeship
- Define technical terms and vocabulary associated with the apprenticeship

4.1.3 Connections

This lesson will focus on some key concepts in Computer Science including if-then statements and pseudo code

4.1.4 Materials

- A data projector capable of connecting to a laptop
- A projection screen
- Dry erase board and markers
- Enough computers for students to work in pairs

4.1.5 Lesson Preparation

- Space: Any classroom space is fine, but it is ideal to have space where students can easily sit side by side in pairs. Access to functional power outlets is helpful when working with laptops.
- Group: Students will be divided into pairs for this lesson; these pairs will remain consistent throughout the apprenticeship.
- Resources: Computers should have Game Maker already installed as well as pre-formatted sprite images. Ideally, the Game Maker short cut and the sprite images folder should be located on the desktop.

4.1.6 Hook: Who is your favorite main character?

- Do Now / Warm Up – Instructors introduce themselves and their favorite main character. We then go around the classroom, having each student introduce him- or her-self and state his or her favorite main character. Students can name any character, even if they are not from a video game, but cannot repeat a character that has already been named.
- Transition – After sharing their favorite main character, we ask students what it is that makes those characters their favorites. It is likely that all student answers will mention contributions main characters make to games, stories, and television shows. We will use these responses to talk about what contributions a main character makes to a video game during the Mini-Lesson.
- Student Perspective – Students might mock each other over their favorite characters. However, it should be emphasized that everyone has different preferences on characters, video games, and almost everything in life. One of the strengths of game design is the ability to make a game that includes all of the things one likes while leaving out the things they do not.

Mini-Lesson: What a Main Character does

The instructor gives an overview of what a main character does in general, and within the context of a video game. The focus should be on how main characters further plots, change stories, and create atmosphere in games. Possible examples are Mario (whose relationship with Princess Peach drives the game's plot), and The Hero of Oakvale from Fable (where the main character's choices change the story).

4.1.7 Activity 1: Create the Game Object

This will be a group-based activity with the Instructor leading by completing the task where it can be seen on the projector. Students should follow along, completing the steps with their partner on their computers, and participate in the discussion.

1. Create a placeholder sprite for the main character. This can be done as a group with students taking the lead, using the skills they learned in Lesson 1.
2. Associate the new sprite with a new game object . Again, students provide the steps based on the previous lesson.
3. Students should repeat the above steps, on their own, to create the Wall object.
4. Instructor should confirm that students have completed step three, and review the process one more time to ensure each student grasps how to create sprites and objects.

- Students might get caught up in what image is used for their Main Character. If this happens, remind them that a future lesson will focus on creating custom sprites using the students' own pictures and that these will then serve as the main characters, so art should not be a focus right now.

4.1.8 Activity 2: Program User Interaction

We will now add user interactions to the main character game object; these will control how the character moves when certain buttons are pressed.

1. Instructors talk through the code that controls the main character movement and write this out as pseudo code
2. Students implement the pseudo code in Game Maker, adding in movement for Up, Down, Left, and Right when the corresponding arrow keys are pressed
3. Have students create a basic room where they place walls and their character to test the new interactions. Students should rapidly realize that their character can walk off the screen and through walls.
4. Talk through the pseudo code for what actions should occur when the main character collides with the wall
5. Students will implement the pseudo code made in step four

Using pseudo code at this point helps make a connection beyond Game Maker to Computer Science in general. This also helps establish good problem solving practices, as students are encouraged to think about a solution before implementing it.

4.1.8.1 Activity 3: Create Basic Levels

Students should now have a moveable main character that cannot walk through walls. Students should use the objects they have created to design and implement new levels to navigate.

1. Do a quick refresher on how to create a new room and place elements inside
2. Have the students create their own, unique rooms that will serve as the game levels. Maze-like layouts are a great place to start.
3. Ask the students to share what new features and design decisions they made.

At this point in the apprenticeship, students will not yet be able to connect their levels to have one, linear game. Let the students know that this will be done in the future, but for now they will have to test each room separately.

4.1.9 Check for Understanding

- Ask students what the steps are to create a new game object.
- Ask students what role a main character serves in a game.
- Ask students to state what the pseudo code is for telling a character to speed up when the Space Bar is held.
- Ask students what other activities a game object could have, previewing Lesson 3 on Treasure and Goals.

4.2 Lesson Breakdown

As previously noted, lessons all follow the same basic format. Lesson 1 differs slightly with additional introductions and an extra activity that take up 10 minutes of the lesson time. Lessons 8 and 9 have a slightly different focus, but otherwise the format is the same. Here we will discuss the primary components of each lesson plan and what they contribute to our curriculum.

4.2.1 The Hook

Each lesson begins with an initial, 10 minute Hook activity. The purpose of the hook is three-fold. First, it provides an opportunity to learn (and remember) the names of students participating in the program. Secondly, it forms a connection between the students, their interests, and the subject matter of the day's lesson. Finally, it provides an important way for instructors to evaluate student improvement in speaking to an audience. Each Hook invites the students to introduce themselves to the class and share an opinion relating to a certain prompt.

For example during the Hook from Lesson 2 (detailed in 4.1.6), a student who selects Mario as their favorite main character probably likes cartoon-style, platform games while a student who selects Master Chief from the Halo series is likely partial to first-person shooter style games with high levels of combat. By identifying these preferences through the Hook activity, instructors can better connect to the students and help guide them in making a game that will suit their personal tastes.

Early in the apprenticeship, the Hook is handled informally. As the program continues, slight changes are made to provide students with experience presenting. These changes include standing up, removing hands from pockets, and projecting voices. A new change to how the Hook response must be provided is added each week until students are responding in a manner that closely reflects how they will deliver their final presentations. In this way, students are practicing for these presentations throughout the apprenticeship, not just in the final two lessons.

4.2.2 Mini-Lesson

From the Hook, each lesson moves into a 10 minute Mini-Lesson. The Mini-Lesson addresses one component related to the overall lesson plan. Mini-Lessons seek to provide context for the students to help them better understand how their apprenticeship activities are relevant to Game Design as a field.

By using the student responses from the Hook within the Mini-Lesson, the material has a direct connection to student interests, thus engaging them in what is otherwise more of a lecture than a hands-on component.

4.2.3 Activities

Lesson activities provide the hands-on component to our curriculum. Each Activity engages the students and requires their participation on computers. Activities total 55 minutes of each lesson. We provide a breakdown of time for each below, but these times sometimes differ due to the specific needs of a lesson.

4.2.3.1 *Activity 1: We do (10 minutes)*

This activity is referred to as the "we do" activity, which means the instructors complete the steps with the students following along. The instructor completes each step in Game Maker on their computer, which is projected for the students to see. Students follow along on their computers as the instructors complete each step of the activity. Activity 1 always provides the basic knowledge necessary for completing the Lesson.

4.2.3.2 *Activity 2: We do/ You do (20 minutes)*

Activity 2 is the "we do/you do" activity, building on Activity 1 to create a new, more complex game element. Instructors prompt the students here, but students are expected to determine the proper steps and their order. Instructors will ask the students what steps are necessary and guide them in the right direction as they seek to complete these steps. This work is done with a group discussion, where students are provided the opportunity to help each other and amend one another's incorrect responses. Only when the group reaches a consensus for the next step do we actually move forward into implementation.

Activity 2 is also where we incorporate pseudo code. For many Lessons, in the "we do" portion of the activity, instructors present and explain pseudo code to the students. The students then complete the "you do" portion by implementing that pseudo code within the Game Maker environment.

4.2.3.3 *Activity 3: You do (25 minutes)*

The third and final activity builds upon the topics covered in the previous two activities as well as those from all previous Lessons. During Activity 3, students are given a task to complete and then left on their own to complete it. In order to ensure that students are challenging themselves and truly mastering the material, rather than simply relying on their instructors, we use the first 5-10 minutes of Activity 3 for students to work with their partners with no instructor input. We have seen that, when given the option, students will tend to ask for help before they attempt to recall on their own how to complete a task. By leaving the students to their own devices for the first part of Activity 3, we encourage them to explore what they are capable of doing independently. Often, no instructor help is needed.

4.2.4 *Check for Understanding*

The Check for Understanding is a means of assessing how well the concepts taught in a lesson were understood by the students. This component of a lesson can take a variety of forms, including formal "Exit Tickets" that serve as written evaluation of the topics. Our Check for Understanding is a series of "teach-back" questions where the students are prompted to explain certain concepts in their own terms, walk through the steps of how to complete a task, or describe some insight they had during the lesson. If students struggle to respond to teach-back questions, it allows instructors to adjust their plans to cover the topics later in more depth. The Check for Understanding is also used to preview the next lesson with questions as shown in Lesson 2 (section 4.1.10).

5. RESULTS

Working with Citizen Schools, we have collected data from Fall 2009-Spring 2011, four of our six previous iterations of this apprenticeship. While our intent is to encourage a lifelong student interest and enthusiasm for computing, our short-term goal is to help middle school students improve performance in standard courses as we believe that doing so will provide us with a better basis for encouraging the integration of our curriculum into classrooms as part of the school-day. In seeking to address the digital divide, we have worked predominately with minority students. For the semesters presented, our students have been 89% African American.

In the four semesters for which we have data, we have consistently achieved improvement of below-B grades and maintenance of A-B grades among students in both English Language Arts (ELA) and Mathematics (the only courses with data collected through Citizen Schools). To better evaluate our performance, we compare our results to the average results from all Citizen Schools Apprenticeships. This allows us to compare our results to other, similar after school programs. These results do not include our most recent iteration for which our recommended curriculum was implemented. However, our version of the curriculum seeks to address shortcomings from our previous iterations including those that exist in the results presented here and we are confident that it is the strongest version of our work to date.

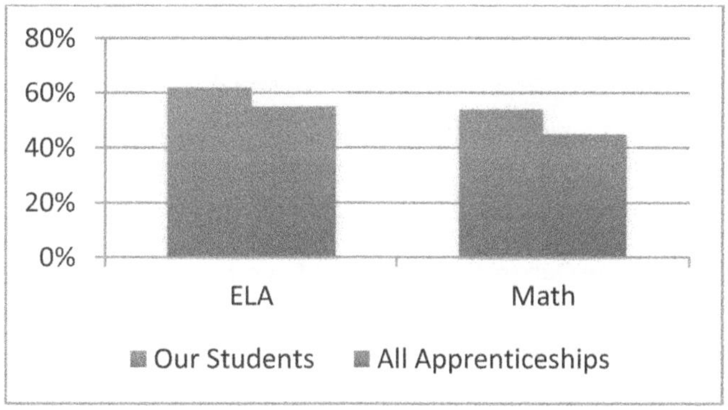

Figure 1: Fall '09 percentage who maintained/improved grade

From Fall 2009 (Figure 1) and Fiscal Year (FY) 2010 (Figure 2), we show high percentages of both grade maintenance and improvement, consistently exceeding the average performance of other apprenticeships. In addition, students in our apprenticeship demonstrated growth in both oral communication and leadership skills (Figure 4). In Spring 2011, 100% of our apprenticeship students maintained their A or B math grades. While no grade improvement is shown for this iteration, it is important to note that only 2 students were making below a B in ELA and only 3 in math, with such a small population as candidates for grade improvement we cannot draw strong conclusions, either positive or negative, regarding this particular measure (Figure 3).

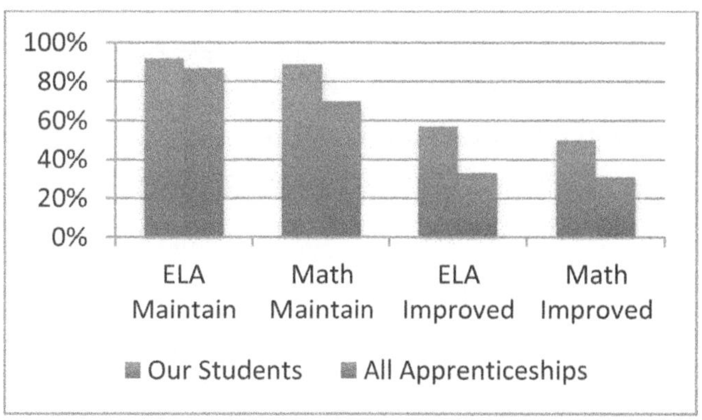

Figure 2: '10 percentage who maintained/improved grade

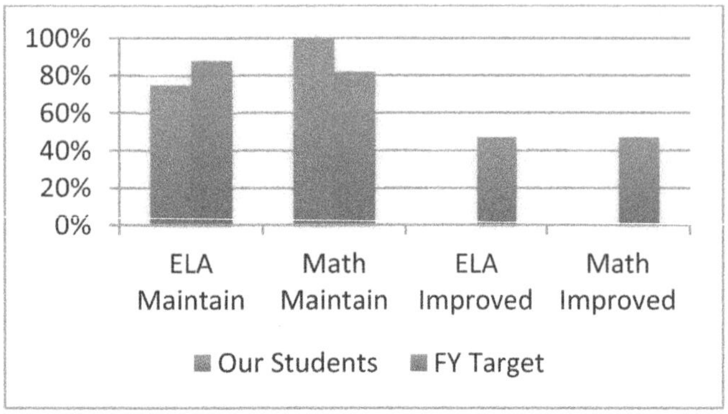

Figure 3: Spring '11 percentage who maintained/improved grade, compared to Citizen Schools FY Target goals

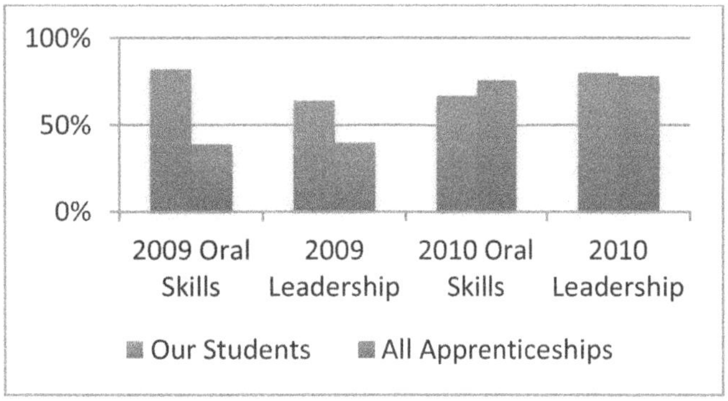

Figure 4: Percentage of students showing growth in Oral and Leadership skills

6. DISCUSSION and CONCLUSION

Having implemented this curriculum in multiple apprenticeships with Citizen Schools for over 80 middles school students, we feel that we have successfully addressed the issues we encountered during our early work and maximized student creativity and technical contribution while also contributing to improved student performance. This belief is strengthened by the increasingly positive feedback we have received each semester, from both our students and the Citizen Schools personnel.

7. FUTURE WORK

We are awaiting an annual report from our local school system that will provide us with a way to track how students who have participated in our apprenticeship perform in high school. Our hope is to see our apprenticeship alumni engaging in higher levels of math and science with strong grades.

8. ACKNOWLEDGMENTS

Our thanks to STARS Alliance for assisting us in our outreach efforts, UNC Charlotte's Chancellor's Diversity Fund for awarding us the funding necessary to provide our own mobile laptop lab to utilize during our outreach sessions, the Citizen Schools organization for their partnership and the work they do on behalf of underprivileged students across the country, Citizen Schools at MLK and Eastway middle schools for their guidance and support during our apprenticeships, and Cassie McIntyre and Michael Kubiak from Citizen Schools. This work was partially supported by NSF grants for the STARS Alliance (1042468, 0739216, 0540523), Culturally Situated Design Tools (0634342), and Game2Learn (0757521) and Graduate Training Grant awarded to Carnegie Mellon University by the Department of Education (R305B090023).

9. REFERENCES

[1] Barnes, T., Richter, H., Powell, E., Chaffin, A., and Godwin, A. 2007. Game2Learn: building CS1 learning games for retention. SIGCSE Bull. 2, 3 (Jun. 2007), 121-125.Ding, W. and Marchionini, G. 1997. *A Study on Video Browsing Strategies*. Technical Report. UMD at College Park.

[2] Bayliss, J. D., & Strout, S. 2006. Games as a "flavor" of CS1. SIGCSE Bull. 28, 1, 500-504.Tavel, P. 2007. *Modeling and Simulation Design*. AK Peters Ltd., Natick, MA.

[3] Burd, B., Goulden, J., Ladd, B., Rogers, M., and Stewart, K. 2007. Computer games in the classroom, or, how to get perfect attendance, even at 8 AM. SIGCSE Bull. 29, 1 (Mar. 2007), 496-496.

[4] Cliburn, D. C. & Miller, S. Games, stories, or something more traditional: the types of assignments college students prefer. SIGCSE Bull. 40, 1 (Feb. 2008), 128-142.

[5] Clua, E., Feijo, B., Rocca, J., Schwartz, J., das Gravas, M., Perlin, K., Tri, R., & Barnes, T. 2006. Game and interactivity in computer science education. ACM Siggraph 2006 Educators Program (Boston, MA, Jul. 30 – Aug 3, 2006). SIGGRAPH '06. ACM, New York, NY,

[6] Durndell, A., Haag, D., Asenova, D., & Laithwaite, H. 2000. Computer self efficacy and gender: East and West Europe." Women, Work, and Computerization: Charting a Course to the Future, E. Balka and R.K. Smith, Eds. Elsevier Science, 78-85.

[7] Kurvosky, S. 2009. Engaging students through mobile game development. In Proc. 40th ACM Technical Symposium on CSE (Chattanooga, TN, Mar. 4-7, 2009).

[8] Leutenegger, S. & Edginton, J. 2007. A games first approach to teaching introductory programming. SIGCSE Bull. 39, 1. Mar. 2007), 115-118.

[9] Margolis, J., Holme, J.J., Estrella, R., Goode, J., Nao, K., Stumme, S. 2003. The computer science pipeline in urban high schools: access to what? For whom? *IEEE Science and Technology,* 22(3), 12-19.

[10] Parberry, L., Roden, T., & Kazemzadeh, M. B. 2005. Experience with an industry-driven capstone course on game programming: extended abstract. SIGCSE Bull. 37, 1 (Feb, 2005), 91-95.

[11] Repenning, A. and Ioannidou, A. 2008. Broadening participation through scalable game design. SIGCSE Bull. 40, 1 (Feb, 2008), 305-309.

[12] Sweedyk, E., deLact, M., Slattery, M.C., & Kuffner, J. 2005. Computer games and CS education: why and how. SIGCSE Bull. 37, 1 (Feb. 2005), 256-257.

[13] Wallace, S. A., Russell, I., & Markov, Z. 2008.Integrating Games and Machine Learning in the Undergraduate Computer Science Classroom. In GDCSE 2008: Game Development in Computer Science (Celebrity Century, Feb. 28-Mar. 2, 2008.

CS1001.py* : A Topic-Based Introduction to Computer Science

Benny Chor and Rani Hod

School of Computer Science
Tel-Aviv University
Tel–Aviv, Israel

{bchor,ranihod}@tau.ac.il

ABSTRACT

We describe the curriculum, initial experience, and preliminary evaluation of an introductory CS course for students taking CS as their single or double major. The course is taught during the first or second semester of the first year of studies. It is centered around eleven to thirteen topics, offering a wide cover of major CS subjects. Many of these topics are not covered in "traditional" introductory CS courses, and some of them are not even covered through the standard undergraduate curricula. Examples: digital image representation and processing, error correction and detection codes, hashing (including Cuckoo hashing), and text compression.

The programming language used in the course is Python. The students are exposed to all standard programming language constructs (commands, assignments, functions, conditionals, iterations, recursion, etc.) and basic data types (*e.g.* integers, floating-point numbers, lists, dictionaries, and sets), as well as less basic constructs, like higher order functions, lambda expressions, classes and methods, and iterators.

We have set a dual learning outcome: the students are expected to acquire a good knowledge and proficiency of programming and understanding short programs. We also expect them to get a broad view of central subjects in Computer Science.

Categories and Subject Descriptors

K.3.2 [**Computer Science Education**]: computer science education, curriculum

*The standard introductory CS course is often named CS101. The nickname CS1001 reflects the extended nature of the new course, and the suffix, `.py`, indicates the choice of programming language used.

ITiCSE'12, July 3–5, 2012, Haifa, Israel.

Keywords

CS1: Introduction to Computer Science. Curriculum issues. Topic based course. Experience report (preliminary).

1. MOTIVATION

For almost 20 years, the school of Computer Science at Tel-Aviv University has taught its freshmen's introduction to Computer Science course based on MIT course 6.001 and the influential textbook "Structure and Interpretation of Computer Programs", by Abelson, Sussman, and Sussman [1]. In recent years, there was a wide spread sentiment among our faculty members and among students that time has come to revise the course our department teaches (this sentiment is wide spread, but by no means it is a consensus). As a response to this sentiment, we designed a new introductory CS course, taught using Python, which is now offered on a tentative ("pilot") basis to our first year students.

We planned this course as an introduction to Computer Science rather than as an introduction to programming. We teach and employ programming in every lecture and recitation of our course; but programming is used as a tool for implementing and explaining the ideas we wish to convey. Following the above mentioned goal, our course is a "topics course", designed around the choice of eleven to thirteen topics that represent central subjects in Computer Science. Our course is certainly not the only one using a "topics based" approach (see section 5). We feel that the novelty of our course is in the broad selection of topics, many of which are not covered in standard introductory courses, and some of them are not even covered in standard undergraduate CS curricula. These topics are integrally interleaved with the programming aspects of the course. Obviously, we do also cover many topics that are common to other introductory courses (Towers of Hanoi, or Euclid's algorithm, for example). There is yet no textbook for the course, but the course site, http://tau-cs1001-py.wikidot.com , contains detailed lecture presentations (along with additional material).

Students in our university choose a major (or double major) upon acceptance to the university. The course is offered to both single major and double major Computer Science students (even though a small number of Mathematics and Biology students took it as well).

In this manuscript, we explain the goals and design criteria of the course, and how both the teaching staff and the students have experienced it, during the two teaching cycles we had so far.

2. METHODOLOGY

The course is taught in a period of thirteen weeks. In every week, there are six weekly contact hours with the students – two lecture sessions, two hours each, and one recitation session of two hours. The first two weeks are mostly devoted to getting acquainted with basic programming principles and their realization in Python. From the third week onwards, we start discussing the course topics, and interleave this with more advanced programming aspects when they are relevant to the topic.

2.1 Choice of Programming Language

From the programming point of view, one choice we made is to use Python as the programming language. Like many instructors in other universities, we believe that Python's simplicity, on one hand, and expressiveness, on the other hand, make it an excellent first language. We believe that the reduced performance, inherent to agile languages such as Python, is not a problem in our context; the code we write and the code we ask our students to write are typically short and relatively simple. We feel that in the develop–debug–execute cycle, the ease of coding and the readability of the code more than compensate for the inefficiency of execution in computationally intensive tasks.

Moreover, we decided to use the new version (3.x) of Python. While the differences between versions are not grand, Python 2.x code is incompatible with Python 3.x, which is the main reason for Python 2.x to remain the dominant Python version in the industry. We, however, have the privilege of starting from a clean slate and thus we chose to promote the newer version, in which many of the legacy design problems have been resolved.

There are many fine Python development environments, even when limiting ourselves to version 3.x; to make it as easy for students to setup a programming environment on their own computers, we opted to encourage them to use the free, open-source one that comes bundled with the Python installation, called IDLE. It is a basic IDE with an integrated Python interpreter shell and a text editor; it supports auto-completion, auto-indentation and syntax highlighting; it provides a debugger (which we didn't use) and a GUI toolkit (exercised when dealing with image processing).

Python's extensive list comprehension capabilities often enable slick and elegant programming solutions, but the students are made aware of the fact that a short program is not necessarily an efficient one.

2.2 Object Oriented Aspects

An ongoing debate in the Computer Science Education community is "objects first" vs. "objects late" in introductory CS courses, both at the university level [5] and at the high-school level [3]. Most programs we write are written in a procedural manner. We introduce classes and methods relatively early in the course (week 5 out of 13), but both are used in a fairly simple manner.

We construct a `Student` class whose attributes are a name and an ID number. These are employed to demonstrate sequential search vs. binary search in an ordered list, so we can separate the key, `Student.name`, from the value, `Student.id`. We explain the motivation as encapsulation and ease of handling, compared to an alternative implementation using lists or tuples. We define a method for generating `Student.name` and `Student.id`, both at random, and other methods for comparing and testing equality in this class. The same class is later used for inserting items into large hash tables, and for measuring performance in terms of timing and maximum load.

We introduce a `Matrix` class and use it both for performing linear algebraic tasks (*e.g.* matrix multiplication, computing determinants), and later as the "infrastructure" for image representation. In the homework, students are asked to define an unbounded-precision `Rational` number class, implementing methods for arithmetic operators `+, -, *, /` in a way that provides interoperability with the built-in integer class.

However, we decided not to introduce inheritance, polymorphism or design patterns (note that [3] points out the difficulty of teaching these concepts in an introductory course, albeit their observations are mostly at the high-school level). The attitude towards procedural programming and the use of object oriented programming seems similar (but not identical) to the approach advocated by Stuart Reges [5].

3. COURSE TOPICS & ORGANIZATION

The major innovation in our course design is the decision to expose the students to a large variety of CS topics, and to challenge them in their homework assignments with problems that are similar to real world problems, often with no predefined preferred solutions. In this section, we list the topics studied in the course. We do this separately for the Computer Science topics and programming concepts. Each list is arranged more or less chronologically, in the order the topics were introduced. Most topics were covered both in the lectures and the recitations. Even with four weekly lecture hours and two weekly recitation hours, this program is fairly demanding. We consciously decided not to cover a number of important topics, either because we felt they were too advanced for a first course, or because they are covered in subsequent courses, or for lack of time. Among the subjects we chose *not* to cover are formal correctness proofs using invariants; data structures beyond lists, dictionaries, and sets; computability questions, including undecidability; and a number of software engineering topics, such as exception handling, inheritance, and polymorphism.

3.1 Computer Science Topics

- Integers: different representations, arithmetic operations. Integer base conversion.
- Measuring time complexity. O notation.
- Integer exponentiation and modular exponentiation. Fermat's little theorem. Randomized primality testing. Diffie–Hellman secret key exchange. Generating strong primes.
- Integer GCD: Naïve algorithm, Euclid's algorithm, and the binary gcd algorithm.
- Sequential search (in unsorted lists) and binary search (in sorted lists).
- Recursive definition and implementation of factorial and Fibonacci numbers.
- Recursion: quicksort and quicksort–inspired median selection.
- Addressing problems with naïve recursion in Fibonacci numbers. Memoization, replacing recursion by iteration, and solving using constant memory.

- Towers of Hanoi. Finding moves in towers of Hanoi: binary search in a huge space. Recursive and iterative solutions.
- Tail recursion.
- Numeric derivatives and integrals.
- Numeric computations: Finding roots of continuous real-valued functions via binary search.
- Numeric computations: Finding roots of differentiable real-valued functions via the Newton–Raphson iteration.
- Floating-point numbers.
- Numerical stability: floating-point numbers vs. unbounded precision rational numbers.
- Planar geometry computations.
- The dictionary problem (insert; delete; find). Hash functions and hash tables. Resolving collisions using chaining. Cuckoo hashing.
- Character representation: ASCII and unicode.
- Exact sequence comparison: three approaches to string matching. (*i*) naïve; (*ii*) randomized (Karp–Rabin); (*iii*) deterministic, based on deterministic finite automata (DFAs).
- Strassen's algorithm for matrix multiplication.
- Computation in the streaming model and infinite iterators. Sieve of Eratosthenes.
- Introduction to digital image representation and processing. Local noise reduction methods.
- Fractals: Sierpiński carpet; Julia and Mandelbrot sets.
- Introduction to error correction and error detection codes. Hamming distance and the induced geometry. Closest codeword decoding. The volume bound. Hamming $[7,4,3]$ code: encoding and decoding. Hadamard matrices and Hadamard code.
- Text compression. Fixed length and variable length coding. Huffman code. Ziv–Lempel compression.
- Paint-by-numbers.
- Dynamic programming. Inexact sequence comparison. Sequence alignment.

3.2 Programming Languages Topics

- Python basics.
- Program flow and conditional statements.
- Iteration constructs (`for` and `while` loops). Iterating over sequences (ranges, lists, strings).
- Built-in data structures: lists, tuples, sets, dictionaries.
- Equality vs. identity. Python's memory model.
- Mutable and immutable objects.
- Functions.
- Call by reference. Side effects of function calls.
- Higher order functions.
- Unnamed functions (λ-expressions).
- Standard input and output. File-based I/O.
- User-defined classes in Python: a gentle introduction to OOP.
- Recursion: definition and examples.
- Lazy evaluation. Iterables, iterators, generators.

3.3 Lectures

The lectures use prepared presentations, distributed to the students prior to the meetings. About 20% of classes are taught on the board, often as a response to questions raised during the lectures. Concepts taught during the lecture are always demonstrated via accompanying short Python code. We found that running code in `IDLE` during the lecture is a very effective mean to explain different notions that are not easily grasped otherwise. Specific examples include:

- The vast running time difference between naïve implementation of modular exponentiation and the efficient, repeated squaring method.
- Primality testing. Students were impressed by the ease of finding a witness for compositeness (in case the number in question is indeed a composite, of course).
- Measuring the maximal occupancy in chains formed when building hash tables with chaining. This gives a hands-on experience for the behavior of a random variable whose exact analysis is beyond the scope of this course.
- Performing simple operations on greyscale images. It helps to elucidate the representation and contents of a digital image, and suggests a concrete, visual realization (see [8] for a different use of image processing in an introductory CS course).
- Compressing books from Project Gutenberg. Measuring compression ratio and running time. Observing the compression vs. decompression running time asymmetry in Ziv–Lempel compression.

Running programs online in front of a few dozens of students is inherently an error prone process. Not only did we not try to avoid this, we explicitly told the students that errors are an inherent part of the programming and of the associated learning process. We often reached points where it was not clear to the instructor how Python will behave. We acknowledged that, and tackled the issue either by trying to run the interpreter, by using Python's built-in `help`, or by employing a search engine to look for solutions.

The course exposes the students to the standard notions of computational complexity, O notation, and the asymptotic difference between polynomial time and exponential time. In addition to the asymptotic analysis, we emphasize the importance of the actual time a task takes to complete (in miliseconds, seconds, or minutes). We make an extensive use of Python's timing package `timeit` to time executions of small pieces of code, and compare it to what we would expect from the asymptotic analysis.

3.4 Recitations

Despite the course stance as an introduction to Computer Science rather than an introduction to programming, the focus of recitations in the early weeks is on Python programming. Students vary in prior programming experience, and this aims to reduce the differences among their programming level, at least partially. Python's rich out-of-box library functionality makes it possible to skim quickly over programming prerequisites and plunge into computer science.

The instruction method employed in the recitations consists of writing *all* code from scratch during the recitation. This enables students to see how the program evolves, to notice the (intended or unintended) bugs in the code and to

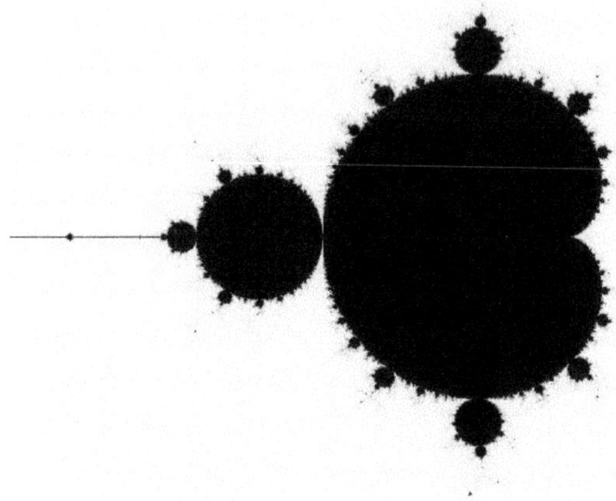

```
def mandelbrot(w,h):
  M = Matrix(h, w)
  for i in range(h):
    for j in range(w):
      z = 0
      c = complex(3*j/w-2, 3*i/h-1.5)
      for color in range(256):
        z = z**2 + c
        if abs(z) > 2:
          break
      M[i,j] = color
  return M

mandelbrot(800,800).display()
```

Figure 1: Mandelbrot fractal and the code used to generate the image

participate by suggesting how to solve them. The interactive interpreter allows to answer what-if questions by simply performing the suggested experiment. Besides teaching syntax, this format helps the students, especially those with little or no programming experience, to develop a sense of how to approach a CS problem, how to form in mind an algorithm solving it, and how to convert the abstract algorithm to a working implementation.

Further recitations complement the hands-on programming experience with a blackboard discussion of required mathematical or algorithmic background. To demonstrate OOP, we develop a `Matrix` class over a few recitations, which lends itself later in the course to applications such as image-processing (figure 1) and error correcting codes (figure 2).

3.5 Homework Assignments

Aside from the final exam, the home assignments are major triggers for the students to go over the material taught in class, and make sure they understand it. We had 6 assignments, approximately one every two weeks.

The assignments consist of diverse problems, varying in both the problem-solving and the programming difficulty levels. Some require students to explain the inner working of a given code; some present a computational task which has an immediate yet inefficient algorithm, and the students are expected to discover that their first attempt does not run quickly enough, and improve it; some ask to compare the performance of a few alternative heuristics that were presented in class; and some deal with extensions of the code written in lectures and recitations.

The advanced home assignments raise slimmed-down versions of real-world tasks, giving the students room for an open-ended solution. The aim here is to connect the theoretic techniques they learn about, with problems arising in actual circumstances.

Examples: measuring the performance of different hashing techniques on a large set of (randomly generated) items; writing an OCR program; finding long conserved subsequences in proteome sequences, as well as short sequences that are missing; generating several linear codes and determine their minimum distances; reconstruction of shredded documents (see also [9]), etc.

We use a semi-automated online exercise grading system. In each assignment, about half of the questions require code to be uploaded to a website, which then runs it on predefined inputs and compares this output with the anticipated output. Students are startled by the inflexibility of the online checking, which is a source to many complaints, but we believe that ambiguity should be kept within natural language and out of submitted code. Sadly, the current grading system performs with sub-par reliability, and this contributes to its unpopularity among students.

Figure 2: A graphical depiction of the Hadamard error correction code

3.6 Course Forum

In addition to reception hours and answering questions by email, we maintained a course forum. The forum is not password protected, and posts can be written in it anonymously. It is mostly used by the students to ask for clarifications regarding homework and exam questions, to discuss approaches for solutions (we announced that explicit solutions will not be allowed, and indeed did not have to deal with any), and to air complaints (mostly about the homework assignments). Prior to the submission of each homework assignments there are approximately 30 posts related to the assignment, and in the week before the exam the forum hosts discussions about questions from previous exams.

The communication in the forum is not limited to student questions and staff answers; we encourage students to answer their peers' questions. Aside from saving our time by not having to answer the same question multiple times individually, we feel that having to post these publicly forces the students to think again before posting trivial questions.

4. PRELIMINARY EVALUATION

We have run this new course twice, as an experimental "pilot". It was taught in two consecutive semesters, concurrently with the older, Scheme based course. During the first run of our course, a group of approximately 30 students were preselected to take it. These included Bioinformatics students (double major in Biology and Computer Science), double major students in Mathematics and Computer Science, and 3 Mathematics major students who were not preselected but have individually requested to join the course. During the second run of our course, it was offered to all first semester Computer Science students (most of whom are single major CS students). They could choose either this course or the older, Scheme based course. Registration to the course takes place using an on-line "bidding" system. Approximately the same number of students ($\sim$100) chose each course, so this does not indicate any preference on the students' side.

Early in the first lecture, we have pointed out to the students that the "old" course is stable, has a highly reputable textbook, and a large number of exams and homework assignments, including many with solutions, is available on the web. By way of contrast, the new course is not stable yet, has no textbook, and hardly any material directly relevant to it is available on the web. This did not seem to deter the students who did opt for the new course.

Students are strongly encouraged to raise questions during classes and recitations. The extent to which this is done typically reflects the level of understanding of the current topic. Complete silence is usually a reliable indication of a "lost class".

The students gave written feedback both via online forms, which are routinely employed university-wide to get feedback on all courses, and via written questionnaires that were distributed to them towards the end of the course. Some of these questionnaires were filled anonymously, while in others the students have chosen to fill their name. Overall, the students were positive about the course, and felt it gives them a worthwhile exposure to topics not covered by the "competing" introductory course.

There is a substantial variety among first year students in Israel with respect to their prior programming exposure and experience. About one third of the first year students have no programming experience at all, while about one third are highly experienced. Consequently, a major complaint by many students with no prior experience was that the pace of the course was too fast. Some students were critical about specific topics, saying they should either be covered in more depth, while for others they said they should not be covered at all. A common complaint was dissatisfaction from the way computational complexity and run-time analysis were covered. As a consequence, we gave more specific examples on this issue in the second run of the course. Another common complaint was that the load of homework assignments was too high. Another claim was related to more complex data structures, like a tree or a priority queue. While we avoided introducing them explicitly, we did use them implicitly, for example, in the construction of a Huffman code. Some students suggested that this should have been explicitly pointed out.

Finally, we approached the students who took the course last year, when they were in the first semester of their second year. We asked them what perspective on the course they had one semester later, and to what extent was it helpful in their second year courses. Overall the responses were, again, positive. One student had commented that the OCR homework assignment was helpful for him when he designed a program creating a collage from other pieces of photographs. Others said that their acquaintance with hashing helped them in the data structures course, where various hashing schemes are analyzed (but not implemented) and in the software project course, where hash tables are used. Some students have commented that they felt the course gave them a good "road map" to Computer Science. They also expressed a strong preference to the choice of Python over Scheme, and they said the mild exposure to OOP concepts was helpful for them. On the negative side, the students reiterated the high load of homework assignments. Some suggested that specific topics (e.g., image processing) could be dealt with in more depth.

5. PERSPECTIVES

Our own feeling is that overall, this was a successful pilot, and we expect it to be approved by our department and to replace the old introductory course. To evaluate it more thoroughly, it should be taught by a number of different instructors. We do see a process where a core of topics will be taught by all instructors, while a smaller fraction of topics will vary from one instructor to the next. We feel that the course is quite demanding intellectually, and hope it can be maintained at its current level.

The main difference between the new course and other contextual approaches (*e.g.* those based on biology [2], media [7], robots [6], or the web [4]) is that rather than focusing on one context, we cover a wide variety of topics. We made an attempt to distill "cores of ideas" from each topic we teach, and to expose the fundamental ideas in each. This often means we compromise either on generality or on efficiency. For example, when discussing error correction and detection codes, we only describe fairly basic codes with simple encoding and decoding procedures. We intentionally avoid any codes requiring knowledge about finite fields, for example. As a second example, when teaching the Ziv–Lempel compression algorithm, we describe a simple quadratic time algorithm for finding repeats in the text. We implement the algorithm and test it on large texts, and observe that this implementation is too slow for texts of lengths exceeding a few hundred thousand characters. We point out the ideas of improvements in "real life" scenarios. But we skip the details of such improvements, pointing the students to more advanced courses down the line, instead.

The introductory CS course described here is a substantial deviation from standard ones. In our opinion, putting the emphasize on Computer Science topics rather than on programming topics serves a number of goals. It exposes the students, very early in their studies, to major Computer Science topics. This helps them later make informed choices between alternative elective courses, and gives them a higher level view of the field. Of course, given such wide coverage, we cannot get very deep within any one topic, but we feel we do get deep enough to gain a nontrivial understanding of most topics. We expect that despite the obvious challenges and difficulties, our approach will be adopted as the standard introduction to CS in our own department, and hopefully in some universities elsewhere as well.

6. ACKNOWLEDGMENTS

We would like to thank Amir Rubinstein for helpful comments and suggestions.

7. REFERENCES

[1] H. Abelson, G.J. Sussman, and J. Sussman. Structure and Interpretation of Computer Programs. The MIT Press, Cambridge, Massachusetts, USA. Second edition, 1996.

[2] Z. Dodds, R. Ran Libeskind-Hadas, E. Bush. When CS 1 is Biology 1: Crossdisciplinary Collaboration as CS Context. In proceeding *ITiCSE* 2010, pages 219–223, ACM New York, NY, USA.

[3] N. Liberman, C. Beeri, and Y. Ben-David Kolikant. Difficulties in Learning Inheritance and Polymorphism. In *ACM Transactions on Computing Education*, Vol. 11, No. 1, Article 4, February 2011.

[4] J. Pearce and M. Nakazawa. The funnel that grew our cis major in the CS desert. In *SIGCSE*, pages 503–507. ACM New York, NY, USA, March 2008.

[5] S. Reges. Back to basics in CS1 and CS2. In *SIGCSE*, pages 293–297. ACM New York, NY, USA, March 2006.

[6] J. Summet, D. Kumar, K. O'Hara, D. Walker, L. Ni, D. Blank, T. Balch. Personalizing CS1 with Robots. In *SIGCSE*, pages 433–437. ACM New York, NY, USA, March 2009.

[7] A.E. Tew, W.M. McCracken, M. Guzdial. Impact of Alternative Introductory Courses on Programming Concept Understanding In *ICER*, pages 25–35. ACM New York, NY, USA, October 2005.

[8] R. Wicentowski and T. Newhall. Using image processing projects to teach CS1 topics. In *SIGCSE*, pages 15–26. ACM New York, NY, USA, March 2005.

[9] `http://www.shredderchallenge.com`

TVT: A Tableaux Verification Tool for the Interactive Learning of Formal Programming Techniques

Rafael del Vado Vírseda
Dpto de Sistemas Informáticos y Computación
Universidad Complutense de Madrid
rdelvado@sip.ucm.es

Fernando Pérez Morente
Dpto de Sistemas Informáticos y Computación
Universidad Complutense de Madrid
fperezmo@fdi.ucm.es

ABSTRACT

While Computational Logic plays an important role in several areas of Computer Science (CS), most educational software developed for teaching logic is not suitable to be used directly in more large portions of the CS education domain where the application of logical notions is usually required. In this paper we describe the logic teaching tool *TVT* based on semantic tableaux that has been developed to help students for using logic as a formal proof technique in other advanced topics of CS, such as the verification of algorithms, the algorithmic debugging of imperative programs, the formal design of invariants, and the design and derivation of algorithms from logical specifications, which are at the basis of the formal learning of programming techniques and a good development of software. We present the design, implementation, and results of the evaluation of this tool by means of several educational experiences during the academic courses 2009/2010 and 2010/2011. From these results we conclude that the use of the *TVT* tool in the current CS teaching can help our students to understand more advanced CS concepts and clarify the formal process involved in the design and analysis of correct and efficient imperative programs.

Categories and Subject Descriptors

F.3.1 [**Specifying and Verifying and Reasoning about Programs**]: Logic of programs; K.3.2 [**Computer and Information Science Education**]: Computer Science Education.

General Terms

Algorithms, Design, Theory, Verification.

Keywords

Semantic Tableaux, Verification, Debugging, Invariants.

1. MOTIVATION AND RELATED WORK

Computational Logic is a subject that is taught in the first courses of almost all the Computer Science (CS) universities around the world. The syllabus of the course usually includes the syntax and semantics of propositional and first-order logic, as well as some proof systems such as natural deduction, resolution, or semantic tableaux [2]. In some cases, there is also some lecture devoted to explain basic concepts on logic programming and practical work using a *Prolog* interpreter. However, while Computational Logic plays an important role in several areas of CS, most of the educational software developed for teaching logic ignores their application in a larger number of subjects of the CS education domain. Many educational tools in this area (e.g., logic inference assistants and proof visualizers) have been developed with different degrees of success, and its utility has been proved by means of several educational experiments and publications. An actual and extensive collection of them can be found at `http://www.ucalgary.ca/aslcle/logic-courseware` and [3]. Unfortunately, although advanced logical notions are applied in superior courses, this educational logic software is not suitable for being used in these subjects.

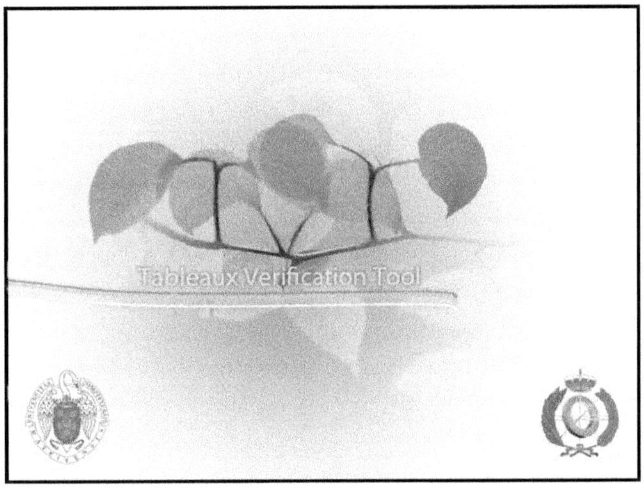

Figure 1: The Tableaux Verification Tool *TVT*.

The aim of this work is to describe an innovative methodology based on the logic teaching tool *TVT* (see **Figure 1**) that uses semantic tableaux to visualize formal proofs on advanced topics in CS, such as the design of correct and efficient algorithms from logical specifications. A *semantic tableau* [2] is a semantic but systematic method of finding a model for a given set of formulas Γ, usually classified as a refutation system because a theorem φ is proved from Γ by getting its negation $\Gamma \Vdash \neg\varphi$. Our major contribution is the implementation of new tableau methods that provide semantically reach feedback to the students in order to help them to understand the formal reasonings performed in the process of verifying the correctness of algorithms. Moreover, it allows to perform an algorithmic debugging of programs following a classical idea from Shapiro [6] that proposes to replace computation traces by computation trees with program fragments attached to its nodes

ITiCSE'12, July 3–5, 2012, Haifa, Israel.

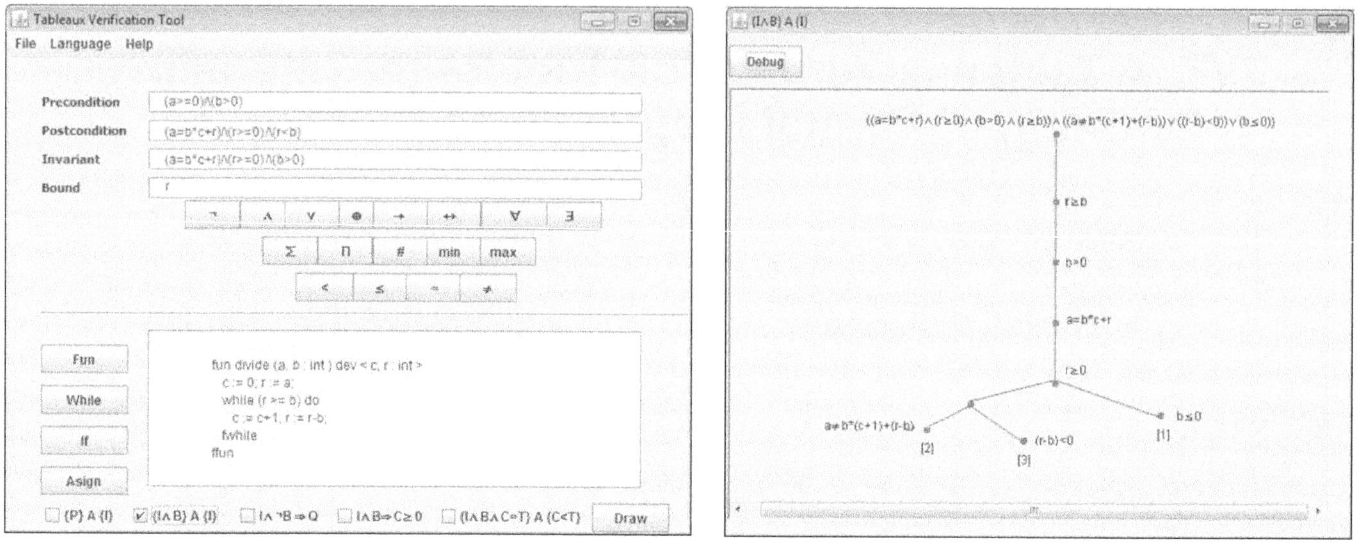

Figure 2: The *TVT* Tool for the Formal Learning of Programmming Techniques.

in the debugging process. As novelty in this work we propose to use semantic tableaux as computation trees to show the students that they can reason on the results of the execution of a program only considering the meaning of the program itself and ignoring complex operational details.

We have tested the *TVT* tool through the academic courses 2009/2010 and 2010/2011, performing some educational experiments to estimate the benefits for our students of using the tool as a complement to scheduled regular classes. This evaluation has been carried out by means of several tests, some of them managed in an online platform with open access to the students, and the other ones in a CS laboratory with a controlled group. We show the results of these educational experiments and the benefits of using the *TVT* tool in the teaching of advanced CS concepts involving the formal verification and the algorithmic debugging of imperative programs. We believe that these educational experiences prove that our implementation based on tableaux provides an excellent training to the students in the practical application of logic advanced concepts to perform different CS tasks.

2. THE TVT TOOL

Solving logical exercises is usually done with pen and paper, but educational tools can offer more useful pedagogical possibilities. The role of this educational software is to facilitate the student's grasp of the target procedures of education, and to provide teamwork and communication between teachers and students [7].

Our *Tableaux Verification Tool*, named *TVT* (the reviewer can find an an anonymized version at `gpd.sip.ucm.es/ITiCSE2012/TVT.zip`), is an educational application based on first-order semantic tableaux with equality and unification [2] used as a support for the teaching of deductive reasoning at an elementary university level for Computer Science students. The tool helps our students to learn how to build semantic tableaux and to understand the philosophy of this proof device using it not only to establish consistency/inconsistency or to draw conclusions from a given set of premises but also for verification and debugging purposes. Our first year students have learnt tableau calculus in the classroom and this software has helped them to understand advanced CS concepts visualizing and producing their own proof trees.

The tool consists of two main parts: one that produces first-order tableaux, and another one based on this tableaux methodology for verification and debugging of algorithms. In both cases, the application possesses a drawing window where the trees will be graphically displayed. The major functional interface of the *TVT* tool is shown in **Figure 2**. The user interacts with the prover through this graphical interface. In the following sections we describe the use of the tool and their main features by means of a running example.

3. VERIFICATION OF ALGORITHMS

The main novelty of the *TVT* tool is to train our students in the art and science of specifying correctness properties of algorithms and proving them correct. For this purpose, we use the classical approach developed by Edsger W. Dijkstra and others during the 1970s [1]. We use a guarded command language to denote our algorithms A, represented by functions **fun** A **ffun** that may contain variables (x, y, z, etc.), value expressions (e) and boolean expressions (B). The code of an algorithm is built out of the skip (`skip`) and assignment statements ($x := e$) using sequential composition ($S_1 ; S_2$), conditional branching (**if** B **then** S_1 **else** S_2 **fif**), and **while**-loops (**while** B **do** S **fwhile**). This language is quite modest but sufficiently rich to represent sequential algorithms in a succinct and elegant way. As an illustrative example, we consider a simple algorithm *divide* to compute the positive integer (*int*) division between a and b with quotient c and remainder r (represented in *TVT* on the left and bottom of **Figure 2**):

```
fun divide (a, b : int) dev < c, r : int >
   c := 0;  r := a;
   while r ≥ b do
            c := c + 1;  r := r − b
   fwhile
ffun
```

It becomes obvious that neither tracing nor testing can guarantee the absence of errors in algorithms. To be sure of the correctness of an algorithm one has to prove that it meets its *specification* [1]. A specification of an algorithm A consists of the definition of a *state space* (a set of program variables), a *precondition* P and a *post-*

condition Q (both predicates expressing properties of the values of variables), denoted as $\{P\}\ A\ \{Q\}$. Such a triple means that Q holds in any state reached by executing A from an initial state in which P holds. For example, a formal specification for the *divide* function (represented in *TVT* on the left and top of **Figure 2**) is:

$\{P : a \geq 0 \wedge b > 0\}$
`fun` $divide\ (a, b : int)$ `dev` $< c, r : int >$
$\{Q : a = b * c + r \wedge r \geq 0 \wedge r < b\}$

An algorithm together with its specification is viewed as a theorem. The theorem expresses that the program satisfies the specification. Hence, all algorithms require proofs (as theorems do). Following [4], the verification is based on a *loop invariant* I supplied by the designer or by some invariant-finding tool (in our example $a = b * c + r \wedge r \geq 0 \wedge b > 0$), a *bound function* C for termination (in our example r), and the following five proofs (see again **Figure 2**):

- $\{P\}\ c := 0; r := a\ \{I\}$.
- $\{I \wedge r \geq b\}\ c := c+1; r := r - b\ \{I\}$.
- $I \wedge r < b \Rightarrow Q$.
- $I \wedge r \geq b \Rightarrow C \geq 0$.
- $\{I \wedge r \geq b \wedge C = T\}\ c := c+1; r := r - b\ \{C < T\}$.

The *TVT* tool verifies algorithms A according to their specification $\{P\}\ A\ \{Q\}$ in a constructive way based on semantic tableaux $P \Vdash \neg wp(A, Q)$, where $\neg wp(A, Q)$ is the negation of the *weakest precondition* of A with respect to Q, which is the 'weakest' predicate that ensures that if a state satisfies it then after executing A the predicate Q holds (see [4] for more details). For example, we have the following tableau proof (graphically displayed by the *TVT* tool in the right side of **Figure 2**) to verify the proof corresponding to the preservation of the invariant I in the body of the loop: $\{I \wedge r \geq b\}\ c := c+1; r := r - b\ \{I\} \Leftrightarrow I \wedge r \geq b \Vdash \neg wp\,(c := c+1; r := r - b, I) \Leftrightarrow I \wedge r \geq b \Vdash \neg (I^{c+1, r-b}_{c,r})$, where $I^{c+1, r-b}_{c,r}$ represents the predicate I in which c and r are replaced by $c+1$ and $r-b$, respectively (see the root of the tree in **Fig. 2**).

To verify and check that this tableau is closed, the student must press the "*Debug*" button. The tool then begins to traverse the tree and tries to locate, for each of its three branches, a pair of atomic predicates that are contradictory with the interactive help of the student. Beginning with the first branch, the student finds that $b > 0$ and $b \leq 0$ are contradictory and marks the branch as "*Close*":

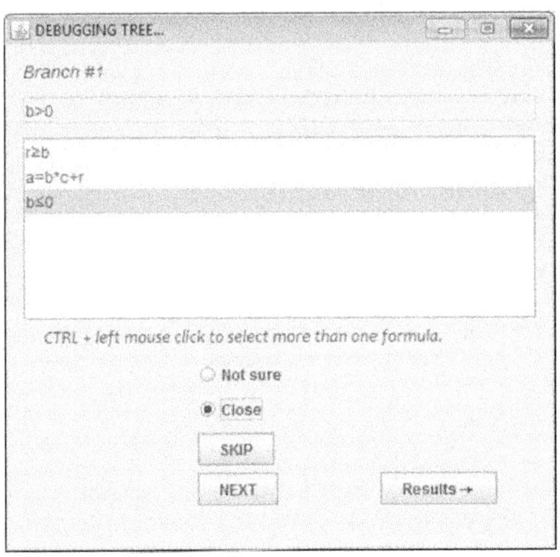

After pressing the button "*Next*", the tool finds in the second branch two possible atomic predicates that are contradictory: $a = b * c + r$ and $a \neq b * (c+1) + (r - b)$. The student marks the option "*Close*":

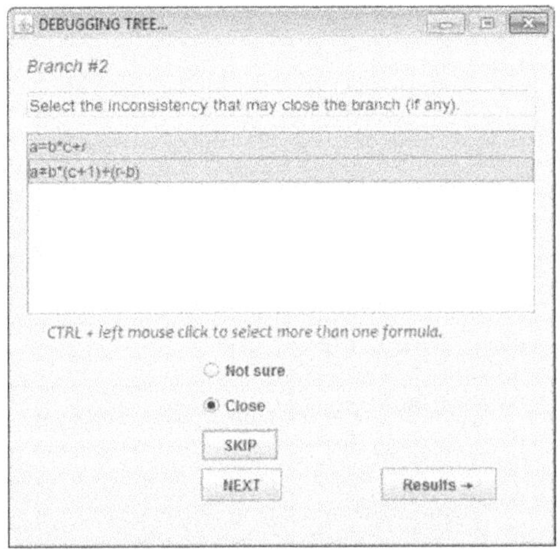

Finally, the tool analyzes the third branch and finds two atomic predicates that are contradictory: $r \geq b$ and $(r - b) < 0$. So, the student marks again the option "*Close*":

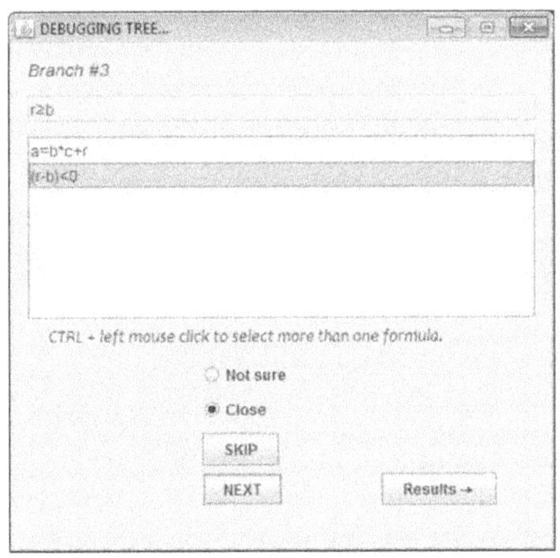

Finally, after pressing the button "Results", the tool summarizes the conflicting atomic predicates that have found for each of the tableau's branches. The formal verification session has finished.

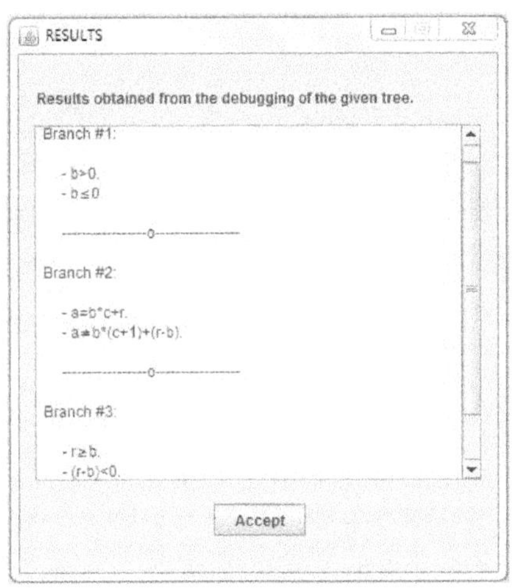

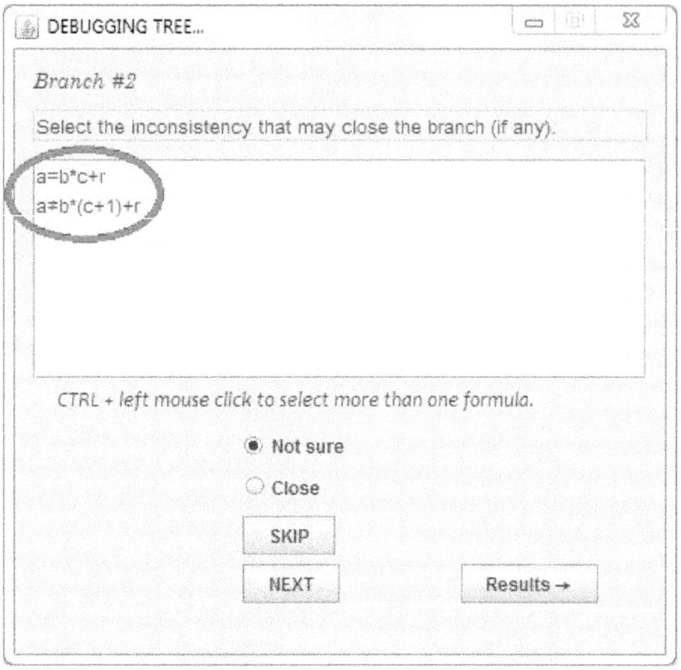

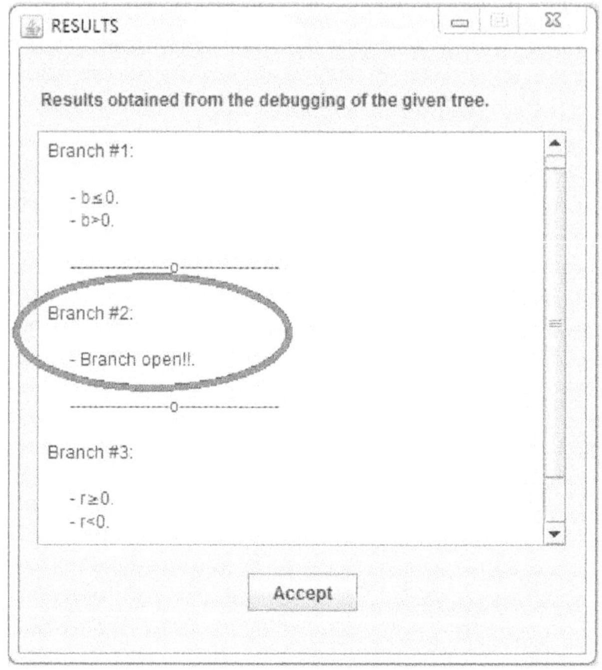

Figure 3: Algorithmic Debugging with the *TVT* Tool.

4. ALGORITHMIC DEBUGGING

Debugging is one of the essentials parts of the software development cycle and a practical need for helping our students to understand why their programs do not work as intended. In this section we apply the ideas of *algorithmic debugging* [5] as an alternative to conventional approaches to debugging for imperative programs. The major advantage of algorithmic debugging compared to conventional debugging is that allows our students to work on a higher level of abstraction. In particular, we have successfully applied our *TVT* tool based on semantic tableaux for the algorithmic debugging of simple programs to show how one can reason about such programs without operational arguments. Following a seminal idea from Shapiro [6], algorithmic debugging proposes to replace computation traces by *computation trees* with program fragments attached to the nodes. As novelty, in this work we propose to use semantic tableaux as computation trees.

As an example, we alter the code of the previous algorithm with a simple mistake: we omit the instruction $r := r - b$. If we try to verify this erroneous algorithm, we can execute again the *TVT* tool. If the student presses the "*Debug*" button to start now a debugging session on the proof tree of **Figure 2**, the *TVT* tool tries to close automatically all the possible branches from the stored information entered in the previous session. However, since it's not possible to close the second branch, the tool shows to the student the predicates $a = b*c+r$ and $a \neq b*(c+1)+r$ as possible opposite atoms that should be closed to close the branch and the proof tree (see the left side of **Figure 3**). The user checks that $a = b*c+r$ and $a \neq b*c+(r+b)$ are not necessarily contradictory for any value of the divisor b. Therefore, the student marks the option "*Not sure*", and the tool confirms that this branch cannot be finally closed and the proof tree remains open (see the right side of **Figure 3**). What failed to close this branch and how it could be solved? If the student compares again the atomic predicates previously showed by the tool, $a = b*c+r$ and $a \neq b*c+(r+b)$, easily concludes that the expression $r+b$ should be r for every b. But, how can this be done? Only if the code of the algorithm executes the instruction $r := r - b$. By examining the code, the student discovers that this assignment has been omitted, and introduces this piece of code into the body of the loop, because the tool is actually examining the proof tree $\{I \wedge B\}$ A $\{I\}$ corresponding to this part of the code. After running again the *TVT* tool, the student sees that all the proof trees remain closed. Then, the algorithmic debugging session finishes.

5. FORMAL DESIGN OF INVARIANTS

The design of suitable invariants I from formal specifications is crucial in the derivation of solutions to algorithm problems, and is an essential part of our educational process for the learning of formal programming techniques. The derivation of invariants is not a mechanical task and, in general, it is a challenging activity and it requires creativity. However, we can use the *TVT* tool to guide our students to obtain loop invariants from formal specifications.

For example, if we only provide to our students the postcondition Q for the *divide* algorithm, they usually infer only an incomplete predicate I' : $a = b*c+r$ as the loop invariant. When they apply the tool to verify the algorithm, they obtain an open branch in the semantic tableau for $I' \wedge r < b \Rightarrow Q$ (see the left side of **Figure 4**). Applying the algorithmic debugging method explained in the previous section, from the open branch our students learn to complete the invariant with $r \geq 0$ to obtain a more concise and complete predicate I'' : $a = b*c+r \wedge r \geq 0$. However, they still have an open branch in the tableau for $\{I'' \wedge r \geq b \wedge C = T\}$ $c := c+1; r := r-b$ $\{C < T\}$ (see the right side of **Figure 4**). Since $(r-b) \geq r$ (or equivalently, $b \leq 0$), they learn to insert $b > 0$ in the assertion I'' to complete the loop invariant $I : a = b*c+r \wedge r \geq 0 \wedge b > 0$. If they apply the tool again, all the tableaux remain closed and the formal design of the invariant finishes. This method does not only help our students in finding a solution, but it can also yield new solutions that are often quite surprising!

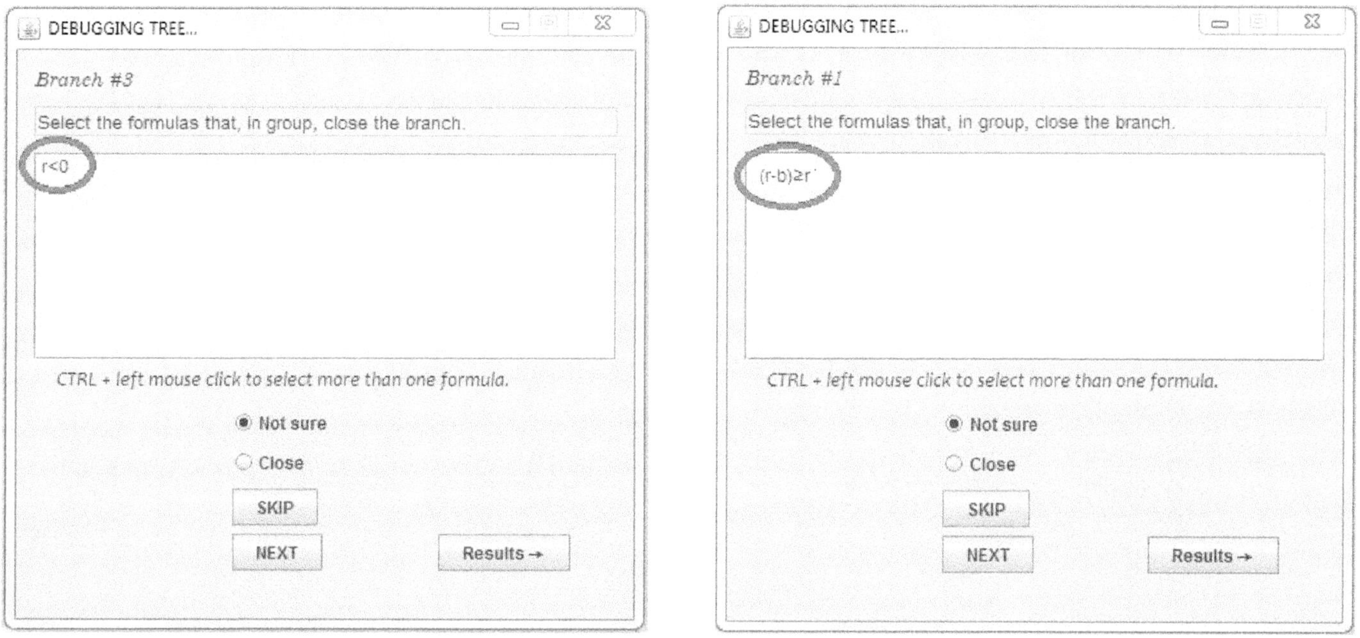

Figure 4: Formal Design of Invariants with the *TVT* Tool.

6. IMPLEMENTATION

An important design consideration in the implementation of the *TVT* tool is that the code must be easy to maintain and extend, guaranteeing its future development and support. We have made the choice of an open source *JavaFx* code in *Netbeans IDE*. The implementation is organized in 8 different packages: *GUI*, responsible of the graphical interface of the program's main window, *Indexicall* whose function along with the packages *WeakestPrecondition*, *LexLogAnalyzer* and *FormulaSimplifier* is to analyze the input strings which are formed by the five verification steps of iterative algorithms, *Drawing*, which is responsible for displaying on screen the semantic tableaux which leads to the decomposition of chains, *Debug* whose goal is to make the algorithmic debugging of each proof tree to ensure that all branches are closed correctly, and finally, *TVT* which is the main call of the application. The left side of **Figure 5** shows the corresponding class diagram, and the right side shows the execution path that traverses each formula from the selection of a proof tree to the end of the syntactic analysis.

7. EXPERIENCES AND RESULTS

The educational tool *TVT* is available for the students of the topics *Computational Logic* and *Design of Algorithms* in the Computer Science Faculty of our University through an online educational platform called *Virtual Campus*. The following results are based on the statistics from the 186 students who took the course in 2009/2010 and 2010/2011.

7.1 Design of the Experiences

We have carried out two educational experiences:

- One **non-controlled** experience: All the students may access the Virtual Campus and participate freely in the experience: download and use the *TVT* tool, and answer different tests.
- One **controlled** experience: Two groups of students must answer a test limited in time and access to material.

With respect to the **non-controlled** experience, the students may freely access the Virtual Campus without any restriction of time or material (slides, bibliography, and the tool) and answer the questions of several tests. For each of the explained topics in Computer Science we have provided a test that evaluates the knowledge of our students applying different kinds of semantic tableaux. The students may use these tests to verify their understanding of the different concepts. The questions are structured in three blocks: *propositional and predicate logic*, *specification and verification* of algorithms, and *debugging and derivation* of imperative programs. The resolution of the tests by the students is controlled by the Virtual Campus with the help of an interactive tutoring system. In the **controlled** experience we try to evaluate more objectively the usefulness of the tool. In particular we have chosen the application of *TVT* for the verification and debugging of simple searching and sorting algorithms [4]. We have chosen two groups of students answering the same questions: approximately half of the students works only with the slides of the course and the books at class; and the other half works only with the tool at a Computer Laboratory.

7.2 Results

7.2.1 Non-controlled experience

We outline here the main conclusions from the results of the **non-controlled** experience. With respect to the material the students used to study, as long as the exercises were more complicated the use of the tool (simulations, cases execution, and tool help) increased considerably. Better results were obtained in the verification and debugging of searching and sorting problems (linear and binary search, insertion and selection sort). The tool helped our students to visualize array manipulations in array assignments. In the rest of the algorithms (slope search and advanced sorting algorithms) they used only the class material or bibliography. When answering the tests questions, the students were also asked whether they needed additional help to answer them. In the case of linear and binary search they used the tool as much as the class material,

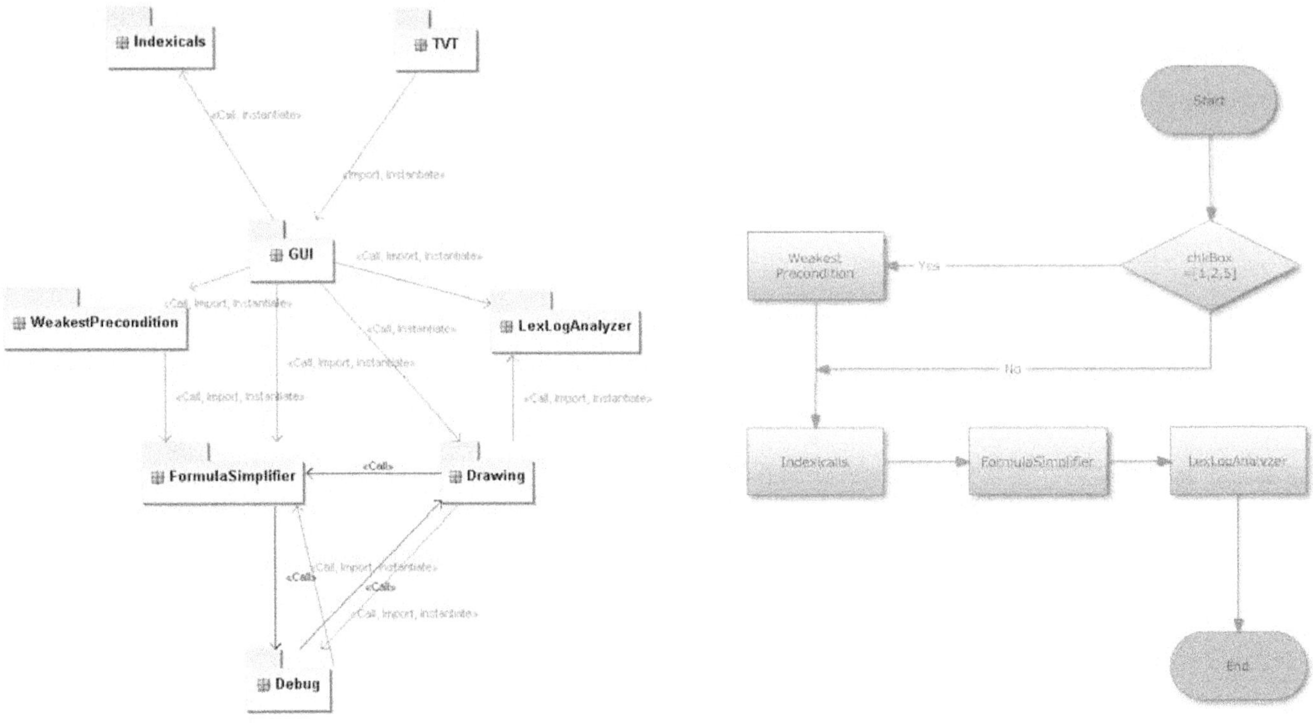

Figure 5: Design and Implementation of the *TVT* Tool.

which means that visualization of their own proof tableaux were a useful educational complement. We can conclude that the students consider the tool as an interesting resource and have used it to complement the rest of the available material.

	correct		errors		don't knows	
	mean	σ	mean	σ	mean	σ
slides/books	9.36	2.35	6.23	2.37	3.21	2.82
TVT tool	12.77	3.71	4.81	2.10	1.22	1.73

Figure 6: Means and standard deviations (σ).

7.2.2 Controlled experience

The **controlled** experience was carried out with 59 students. We gave 32 of them only the slides of the course and the books of the bibliography [2, 4]. The rest were taken to a Computer Laboratory, where they could execute the *TVT* tool. We gave the same test to both groups, consisting of 18 questions, 12 of them on specification aspects of the algorithms (inference of invariants and bound functions), and the rest on their verification and debugging from the code. In **Figure 6** we provide the means and the standard deviations of correct, errors, and *don't knows* answers. First, we observe that students using *TVT* answer more questions than the other ones. In addition, they make less errors than the others. This is due to the fact that most of the students of the *TVT tool* group performs the analysis of the algorithms directly from the corresponding semantic tableau displayed by the tool, while the *slides/book* group has to hardly deduce it directly from the code. All the students who used *TVT* indicated the benefits of using tableaux to understand the code of the algorithms from their specifications. Therefore, we can conclude that the methodology proposed in this work constitutes a good complement to facilitate the comprehension of the design and analysis of imperative programs. In addition, the methodology based on tableaux has helped us to detect in the students difficulties applying the formal techniques to derive correct and efficient imperative programs from specifications.

8. CONCLUSIONS AND FUTURE WORK

We have presented the educational and interactive tool *TVT* based on semantic tableaux for a specification language on predicate logic to perform verification and debugging of algorithms. This is a first step towards the development of a practical teaching technology for the formal learning of programming techniques. We have systematically evaluated the proposed methodology to confirm that *TVT* is a good complement to both the class explanations and material, making easier the visualization of proofs in the reasoning needed for the design of correct and efficient programs. We look forward to making good use of what we have learned from this evaluation to improve tool's usefulness in Computer Science Education.

9. REFERENCES

[1] E. Dijkstra. *A Discipline of Programming*. Prentice Hall, 1976.
[2] M. Fitting. *First-Order Logic and Automated Theorem Proving*. Springer, Graduate Texts in Computer Science, 1990.
[3] A. Huertas. Ten years of computer-based tutors for teaching logic 2000-2010: Lessons learned. In *TICTTL*, 2011.
[4] A. Kaldewaij. *Programming: The Derivation of Algorithms*. Prentice-Hall International Series in Computer Science, 1990.
[5] L. Naish. A declarative debugging scheme. *Journal of Functional and Logic Programming, vol. 3*, 1997.
[6] E. Shapiro. *Algorithmic Program Debugging*. MIT, 1983.
[7] H. van ditmarsch. *Logic software and logic education*. 2005.

Are Children Capable of Learning Image Processing Concepts? Cognitive and Affective Aspects

Khaled Asad
Alqasemi Academic College of Education,
Baqa-El-Gharbia 30100, Israel
Ben-Gurion University of the Negev,
Beer-Sheva 84105, Israel
kasad@qsm.ac.il

Moshe Barak
Ben-Gurion University of the Negev,
Beer-Sheva 84105, Israel
mbarak@bgu.ac.il

1. ABSTRACT

Many children are making extensive use of technological devices such as cellphones, digital cameras and music players. Are these children attracted to learning the computer principles on which these devices are based? Are they qualified to learn computer science concepts in an in-depth fashion? This study aimed at examining the case of teaching an advanced computer science course in image processing to middle school students. During the stage of learning the theory, the students exhibited rather low motivation; later, when they were involved in preparing individual projects on image processing, they demonstrated greater interest and success in learning the subject matter.

Categories and Subject Descriptors

K.3.2 [**Computer Science and Information System Education**]: Computer science education, Curriculum, Literacy.

General Terms

Measurement, Experimentation, Theory.

Keywords

Image processing, instructional approaches, contextual learning, project-based learning, computer science education.

2. BACKGROUND

The educational literature strongly supports the notion of 'contextual learning' [4], which is about engaging students in learning subjects that are close to their world and daily lives; and they learn best when they deal with subjects related to their own lives and interests [3]. Today's youth are making extensive use of advanced technological devices such as computers, digital cameras and cellphones. Kapp shows that we are living in a digital culture in which youngsters are not just influenced by culture but are actually shaping the culture of the 21st century [8].

ITiCSE'12, July 3–5, 2012, Haifa, Israel.

Roberson, from the other side, argues that schools holding on to the current curriculum and instructional methods are becoming more disconnected from the reality of the changing world [10].

For science and technology education to be successful, elements of the culture affecting third millennium students must be carefully considered and integrated into the curriculum. The new technologies should be seen not just as instructional tools but also as subjects for learning in order to contextualize the learning of computer science, technology and mathematics in the real world. In Addition to that, educators are increasingly recognizing the educational advantages of instructional strategies such as problem-based learning and project-based learning (PBL) in science and computer science education, in which students work in teams to investigate or solve real-life questions and problems [2,6,11]. In this sort of learning, the students often prepare a 'product,' such as a computer program or design an electronic simulator as a solution to a problem.

On the one hand, teaching basic concepts on which modern computers and systems are based could serve as a good platform for fostering student's interest in computers and developing higher-order intellectual skills such as problem-solving and creativity [1,7]. On the other hand, some educators still believe that young students are not capable of studying computer science subjects in an in-depth fashion and often recommend that schools should focus on core subjects such as science and math or they must support them with an appropriate guidance [9]. These issues guided the current study, which included the development, implementation and evaluation of an image processing course, which is considered a very challenging field [5], and it might interest today's youth since they making extensive use of images through advanced technological devices, such as smartphones and computers. The research was guided by the following questions: To what extent can middle school students having no background in computers learn an advanced computer science subject such as image processing? How could such a course affect their perceptions about the subject matter, their self-efficacy towards the subject and their desire to pursue a career in computers?

3. THE IMAGE PROCESSING COURSE

The course was designed primarily to teach junior high school students a range of image processing principles, as follows:

- Binary system and data representation: converting binary numbers into decimal or hexadecimal bases; Alpha numeric.
- Digital representation of an image: pixels, resolution, colors.

- Image enhancement for example, amending the brightness or sharpness of a picture, histogram equalization.
- Image compression methods: Run-Length Encoding (RLE) compression.
- Facial recognition; facial identification from a database.

Following are few examples of the subjects learned during the course. As illustrated in Figure 1, the students learned through this simplified example how a black & white picture is presented in pixels and how the pixels are converted into numbers.

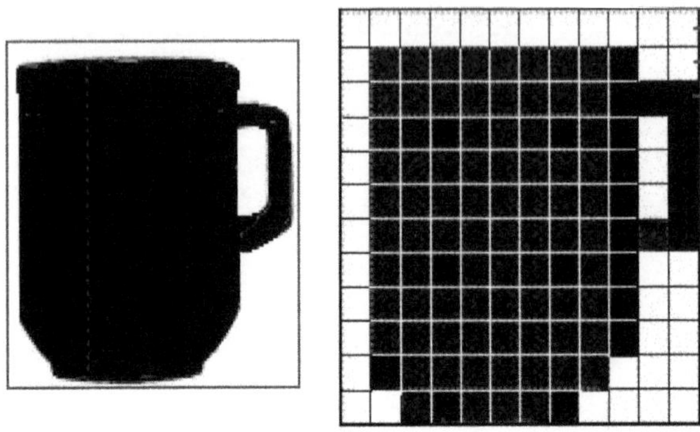

Binary	Hex	Decimal
111111111111	FFF	4095
100000000011	803	2051
100000000000	800	2048
100000000010	802	2050
100000000010	802	2050
100000000010	802	2050
100000000000	800	2048
100000000011	803	2051
100000000011	803	2051
100000000011	803	2051
100000000111	807	2055
110000001111	C0F	3087

Figure 1: Breaking down a black & white picture into pixels and converting them into binary, hexadecimal and decimal numbers.

During the course, the student learned how mathematical operations are used to change picture properties, for example, to change the contrast or the brightness of each pixel; or to get a negative image from a given one, as demonstrated in Figure 2.

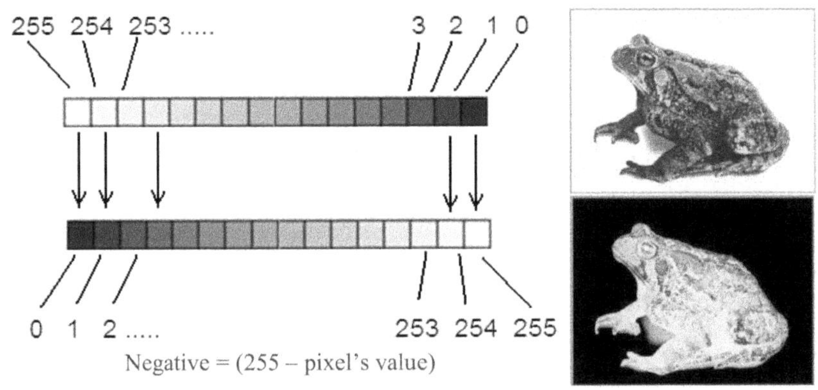

Figure 2: Gray scale (0-255) and negatives (255-0) values of a picture.

In the third example, as illustrated in Figure 3, the students learned how a colored pixel in a picture is represented by a combination of 3 basic colors: Red-Green-Blue (RGB), so its binary representation is a combination of these 3 binary numbers. Also, the students learned how a picture can be broken down into 3 one-colored pictures (three matrices).

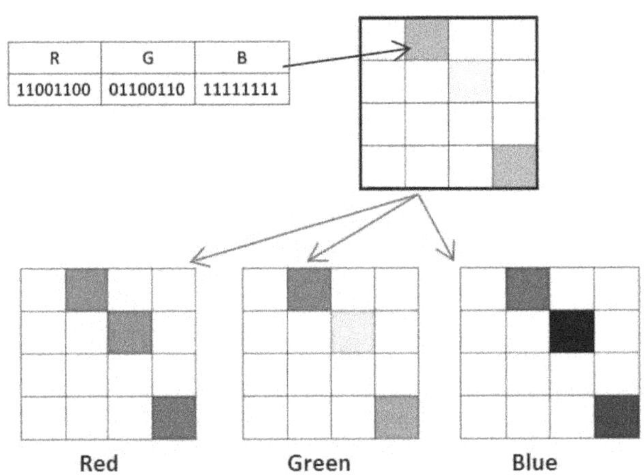

Figure 3: Breaking down a colored picture into three one-colored pictures (RGB).

At the end of the course, the students learned face recognition principles by identifying a set of parameters such as distance between the eyes or mouth width, as illustrated in Figure 4.

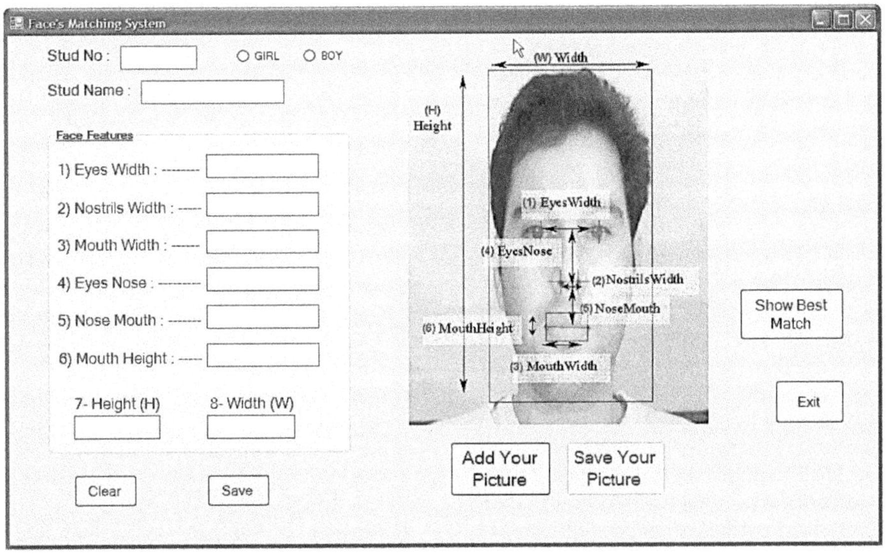

Figure 4: Face recognition according to basic face parameters.

4. THE STUDY

4.1. Participants

The participants in this study comprised three separate groups of 20 students each (9th grade): a total of 31 girls and 29 boys. Each group studied two classes a week over a period of 15 weeks (half of the school year).

The course was delivered to the students in two stages: in the first stage (seven weeks), the teacher presented theoretical image processing concepts and the students performed specific exercises on the computer; in the second stage, the students prepared individual projects, including editing and enhancing their own pictures or those of their family members. For example, some students brought old black & white photos of their parents or grandparents, scanned them and "colored" them artificially using computer software.

4.2. Data Collection

In this study, we intended to collect as much information as possible about students' activities in the class, their achievements, and their attitudes towards learning the subject of image processing. The data were gathered using diverse methods, which included:

1) Observing and documenting the teachers' and students' activities in each class, for example, taking pictures and videotaping the students during their work.
2) Delivering two attitude questionnaires: the first was a pre- and post-course questionnaire; the second was a questionnaire in the middle of the first stage and after the course.
3) Administrating a pencil-and-paper exam at the end of the first part of the course.
4) Documenting the reflections the students wrote about the course in their final projects.

In the current paper, we relate to only part of the findings, as detailed below.

5. FINDINGS

5.2. Students' Achievements

The research findings show that at the stage of learning image processing theory using traditional schooling, students had fair achievements. For example, in the written exam at the end of the first part of the course, the mean scores (on a 0-100 scale) were $\bar{x} = 76.3$ (n= 19, SD=17.97), $\bar{x} = 80.7$ (n=19, SD=20.18), and $\bar{x} = 89.1$ (n=20, SD=10.86) for groups 1, 2 and 3, respectively. In the second part of the course, in which the project-based learning approach was adopted, the students excelled in their performance. At this stage, the students prepared individual projects involving tasks that were meaningful to them such as enhancing their own pictures or those of family members.

The final projects were assessed according to a detailed scoring rubric that includes the following categories:

- Introduction, objectives and working method (10%).
- Picture enhancement (25%).
- Picture change (25%).
- Facial recognition (25%).
- Summary and reflection on the project (10%).
- General evaluation and portfolio editing (5%).

Table 1: Students' mean scores in the final projects (scale of 0-100)

Group	N	Mean	SD
9-a	20	90.4	8.78
9-b	19	89.6	11.54
9-c	17	95.2	7.08
Total	56	91.6	9.52

The mean scores in the final projects, as seen in Table 1, (on a scale of 0-100) ranged from 89.6 to 95.2.

Although it is difficult to compare students' scores on the final projects described here with their achievements in the mid-semester theoretical exam, it seems that the higher scores on the projects reflected the increase in students' motivation and efforts in accomplishing their projects at the end of the course (see next section).

5.2. Students' Attitudes

Although the students had fair achievements during the stage of learning the image processing theory, the participants did not demonstrate high motivation or interest in learning the course. Nevertheless, this situation changed significantly when the students prepared individual projects involving tasks that were meaningful to them, when their tasks involved enhancing their own pictures or those of their family members. They, for example, brought from home old black-and-white pictures of their parents or grandparents, scanned the pictures and "colored" them artificially using computer software. While working on their projects, students' attitudes to learning image processing changed considerably. They demonstrated greater interest and motivation in learning image processing compared to the earlier course stage. For example:

- The students often remained in class during the breaks to work on their projects.
- The participants had comments such as "*Now we understand the subject material*."
- One of the questions in the attitude questionnaire that a sample of students filled in was "*To what extent did the topic of image processing interest you?*(1 – very little, 2 – little, 3 – medium, 4 – much, 5 – very much). The mean score in the class (n=19) increased from $\bar{x} = 2.58$ (SD=1.54) in the in the first part of the course, where traditional schooling was adopted to $\bar{x} = 4.11$ (SD=1.1) in the second part, where Project-based Learning was the approach.

In the interviews during the first part of the course, the students had comments such as: "*The subject is difficult, why did you choose to teach it to us*" or "*This topic does not interest me at all.*" While working on their projects, however, the students had comments such as: "*We like what we are doing. We prefer that you teach us this way and not like during the previous semester.*"

A Likert-type questionnaire administrated to the classes pre- and post-course comprised 16 questions such as "I am interested in computer work." The students marked their answers on a scale of 1 (very little) to 4 (very much). Table 2 shows that the mean scores of students' attitudes increased significantly in three main aspects: interest to engage in computer work, ability to work with computers, and interest in learning computer science (rather than just using computers).

In their reflection on the projects, some students wrote:

"Working on the project contributed to my knowledge and motivated me to do things on my own at home"; "At first, we thought this subject was difficult, now after completing the project we saw how easy it is"; "I would like to work in this profession and learn more about computer technology and how it works."

Another interesting finding was that while learning the image processing course, the students naturally utilized mathematical concepts that were new for them without any special difficulties.

6. CONCLUSION

The research findings reveal that the instruction method is a critical element in achieving the goal of promoting computer science education among young students with no prior knowledge in the subject in order to have them learn basic concepts in the field and to increase their interest in learning advanced computer science courses.

Besides that, educators interested in developing a computer science curriculum or enrichment programs for young students, can use this study as an example to help them develop similar programs. In designing such a curriculum, it is important, though, to engage the students in challenging open-ended assignments that are meaningful to them personally throughout the program. It is important to prepare the conditions that contribute to meaningful learning, such as active learning, contextual learning, a positive emotional climate supporting learning and project-based learning.

In summary, teaching advanced computer science subjects to middle school students should be guided by constructive pedagogy while reducing the weight of formal instruction by the teacher or engaging the students in solving pre-designed exercises.

Table 2: Students' attitudes towards computers in the pre- and post-course questionnaire (scale of 1-4).

Item	Test	N	Mean	Std	df	t
I am interested in computer work	pre	57	3.167	.7278	102.73	2.078*
	post	51	3.422	.5420		
It is easy for me to do computer work	pre	57	2.904	.8683	106	2.301*
	post	51	3.245	.6432		
I want to learn computers in an in-depth fashion	pre	57	2.825	1.0286	104.09	2.161*
	post	51	3.206	.8011		

*$P<0.05$

7. REFERENCES

[1] Barak, M., & Zadok, Y. (2009). Robotics projects and learning concepts in science, technology and problem solving. *International Journal of Technology and Design Education, 19*(3), 289-307.

[2] Blumenfeld, P. C., Soloway, E., Marx, R. W., Krajcik, J. S., Guzdial, M., & Palinscar, A. (1991). Motivating project-based learning: Sustaining the doing, supporting the learning. *Educational Psychologist*, *26*(3/4), 369-398

[3] Brandt, R. S. & Brandt, R. (1998). *Powerful learning*. Association for Supervision & Curriculum Development (ASCD).

[4] Dewey, J. (1963). *Experience and Education. The Kappa Delta Pi Lecture Series*. New York: Macmillan Publishing Company.

[5] Gonzales, R.C. & Woods, R.E. (2002). *Digital Image Processing.* Upper Saddle River, N.J.: Prentice Hall.

[6] Hmelo-Silver, C. E. (2004). Problem-based learning: What and how do students learn? *Educational Psychology Review*, *16*(3), 235-266.

[7] Johnson, S. D. (1997). Learning technological concepts and developing intellectual skills. International Journal of Technology and Design Education, 7(1), 161-180.

[8] Kapp, K. (2011) A Cultural Perspective of Teaching and Learning ETE in a Digitally Connected World, in M. Barak & M. Hacker (Eds.) *Fostering human development through engineering and technology education (ETE).* Rotterdam: Sense Publishers, 207-232.

[9] Kirschner, P. A., Sweller, J., & Clark, R. E. (2006). Why Minimal Guidance During Instruction Does Not Work: An Analysis of the Failure of Constructivist, Discovery, Problem-Based, Experiential, and Inquiry-Based Teaching. *Educational Psychologist, 41,* 2, 75-86.

[10] Roberson, S. (2011). Defying the default culture and creating a culture of possibility, education, *131*(4), 885-904.

[11] Savery, J. R. (2006). Overview of problem based learning: Definitions and distinctions. *The Interdisciplinary Journal of Problem-Based Learning, 1*(1), 9-20.

OpenIRS-UCM: An Open-Source Multi-platform for Interactive Response Systems

Carlos Garcia
garsanca@dacya.ucm.es

Fernando Castro
fcastror@fis.ucm.es

Jose Ignacio Gomez
jigomez@dacya.ucm.es

Christian Tenllado
tenllado@dacya.ucm.es

Daniel Chaver
dani02@dacya.ucm.es

Jose A. Lopez-Orozco
jalo@dacya.ucm.es

Dpto. Arquitectura de Computadores
Univ. Complutense Madrid
Madrid, Spain

ABSTRACT

Interactive Response Systems (IRS) have been gaining acceptance within the educational community in recent years and a clear proof is the growing number of commercial systems available today in the market. However, most solutions are based on systems which are closed, rigid and dependent on proprietary keypad or platform. We have developed OpenIRS-UCM, a free teaching tool for interactive polling that solves these drawbacks. It is an open source software so it allows the development of new functions by anybody. It has a friendly interface that anyone without high computer skills can use. It enables the coexistence of several commercial clickers simultaneously with smart-phones, tablets or other modern electronic devices. It is developed in Java, thus its use is not restricted to systems based on *Microsoft®* *Windows* and it is independent of any proprietary software.

The excellent acceptance of this teaching tool at University Complutense of Madrid has encouraged the creation of a repository that holds all the source code and executables files [1], in order to facilitate its widespread use.

Categories and Subject Descriptors

K.3.2 [**Computer Uses in Education**]: Computer and Information Science Education—*Information systems education*; K.3.1 [**Computer Uses in Education**]: Information Systems Applications—*Collaborative learning, Distance learning*

General Terms

Design, Human Factors

Keywords

Free student response systems, multi-clickers, educational technology, virtual polling

1. INTRODUCTION

The Interactive Response System (IRS) is a learning technology for enhancing interaction between learners and teachers by transferring, collecting and displaying students' responses in a classroom. Unfortunately, there is not a standard terminology about this kind of systems in the literature. Thus, it is referred as Audience Response System (ARS), Student Response System (SRS), Classroom Performance System (CPS), Classroom Communication System (CCS), Hyper-active
Teaching Technology (H-ITT), Personal Response System (PRS) and so on. We will use IRS acronym in this paper.

It is clear that IRS software are interactive teaching tools that mitigate the lack of real time interactivity between the teacher and learners, as well as between students. Other research has evaluated the effectiveness of the interactive response systems [3, 11, 10] and described their features and advantages [8, 4]. There are previous studies that examine whether the use of clickers is truly a useful pedagogical tool [7, 5] and whether the effectiveness of clickers is solely related to the quality of the questions [2]. In order to allow the teacher to focus on the questions and to achieve all typical benefits from these systems, we have implemented an user-friendly IRS software called OpenIRS-UCM.

Any IRS tool is usually packaged as an integral hardware/software solution. The IRS hardware includes a personal hand-held signal transmitter called *clicker* –used by the students– and a response signal receiver that is connected to the teacher's computer. The remote communication transmitter and receiver can be the Internet (wired or wireless), radio or infrared. The IRS software is installed on the teacher's computer and it provides the following basic functionalities: collecting all responses within a time interval, storing and retrieving the individual responses, and generating reports.

There exist many commercial products based on proprietary IR/RF clickers and a survey can be found in [9]. However, many students have latest generation mobiles (like iPhone or Android based terminals) and WI-FI connection is available in almost all universities; therefore the use of phones as clickers has become a flexible and inexpensive alternative to proprietary clickers. [6]. Many companies (e.g. i>clickers, H-ITT or Turning technologies) have recently adapted their products in order to allow smartphones to be used as clickers. Furthermore, it is easy to extend its use to laptops, PDAs or tablets as clickers.

There are also open source initiatives like InfoCoral [14], which designs a hybrid low-cost open-source hardware to implement a clicker based on ZigBee technology. In the software side, Open Smart Classroom [12] or eRoster [13] are engaged in distance learning and improve the interactivity of active learning.

All products mentioned above exhibit lots of options regarding configuration, data analysis and question types. However, some of these functionalities turn the IRS software too complex to use, while most teachers would prefer a simpler tool that effectively performs the common day-to-day features.

In this paper, a new open software with the following properties is presented: (1) it is easy to use and it includes the tools and options required to get the responses of students; (2) it supports multiple response devices simultaneously: commercial clickers, smartphones and WI-FI devices; (3) it is multiplatform: Windows, Linux and Mac Os X; and (4) it is a free and open-source software that allows the inclusion of other clickers and the development of new functionalities.

The rest of the paper is organized as follows. Section 2 briefly explains the motivation to implement OpenIRS-UCM. Section 3 presents a general description of OpenIRS-UCM, its options and how it can be used. Section 4 details the major benefits and disadvantages that our software provides based on different experimental trials. Section 5 contains our conclusions regarding this work. Finally, Section 6 points out which projects have supported OpenIRS-UCM and how our previous works and software tools have helped to develop our system.

2. MOTIVATION

The increasing need for IRS has motivated a fast development of related software products. Most of them are closed proprietary solutionss that may have a very high cost for many educational institutions. Moreover, they have rigid system requirements, so the teacher is obliged to use other proprietary software, which further increases the deployment cost. OpenIRS-UCM tries to fill a gap in the IRS market providing a simple solution with the following characteristics:

- *User-friendly.* OpenIRS-UCM is not integrated in any presentation software. It performs the bare functionality of any IRS software: track students' answers for each predefined question.

- *Multi-platform.* The software is entirely developed in Java, with no low-level dependency other than communication libraries freely available for all platforms. OpenIRS-UCM has been successfully tested in Windows, Linux and Mac Os X.

- *Multi-clicker.* OpenIRS-UCM currently supports proprietary clickers from H-ITT[1] and SunVote[2] along with socket-based clients available for several platforms (including PC, iOS and Android based devices). All kind of clickers may be used simultaneously so most students will be able to work with their own mobile phone or laptop, largely decreasing the need for expensive commercial clickers.

- *It is free.* OpenIRS-UCM has been released under the GNU Lesser General Public License (LGPL)[3] which allows any user to freely use it and distribute it. If students have their own signal transmitter device, the software may be deployed at virtually zero cost.

- *Extendable.* The software is quite modular, so new extensions are easy to carry out. For example, adding a new clicker system is just a matter of implementing a Java interface. Moreover, thanks to its LGPL nature, any new functionality could be immediately available for the whole community.

3. SYSTEM DESCRIPTION

3.1 General Description

OpenIRS-UCM is a completely public and low-cost IRS that follows free software guidelines to facilitate its distribution, promote its use and accelerate functionality development. It allows to collect the student's opinions in a classroom, in a laboratory or even remote tests through the Internet.

This system organizes quizzes or a group of questions into different sessions that are saved in a database. Before starting the class, the teacher should assign a communication mechanism to each student, record it properly, and add a group of questions including the right answers. This can be done manually or importing them by means of a *Microsoft®* *Excel* or *comma-separated values* (CSV) file. The system is able to receive simultaneously answers from many devices such as H-ITT, SunVote frequency radio clickers, mobile phones (like iPhone, Android) and any other devices connected to the Internet (as PDAs or computers by means of sockets interface). We would like to emphasize that OpenIRS-UCM is completely independent of the teaching method and it can use any slide program (*Microsoft®* *PowerPoint*, *LibreOffice*, LaTeX, etc), or even just a blackboard to survey students.

Once this initial phase is completed, the teacher can gather students polls. The system provides a testing tool to check if everything has been properly configured and to verify its correctness. The *Student Test* mode, one of the available testers, incorporates the *Update Roster* option that automatically configures the system to collect questions only from the students who are present in the classroom. This aspect is useful to avoid distorting general view of the class group.

Once in the classroom, a questions bar manages the recollection of audience answers when the teacher starts a quiz. This bar is visible in the desktop or may remain resident in the System-Tray in order to not interfere with any teaching task. While students are clicking to send their options ,a list of those who have already answered is displayed. OpenIRS-UCM permits a real-time feedback by means of charts (answer bars, sectors, correct sectors, etc.) that reflect audience

[1]http://www.h-itt.com/

[2]http://www.sunvote.com.cn/fwzc.html

[3]http://www.gnu.org/copyleft/gpl.html

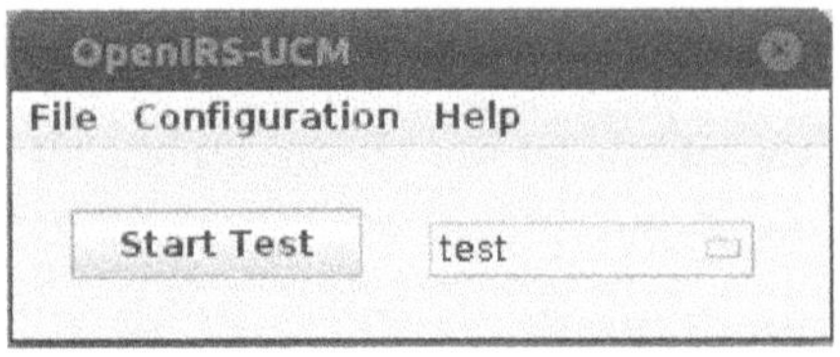

Figure 1: Main Window.

opinions. Also, the remaining time for each question is visible in a separate transparent -background window.

Once the test has been completed, the system allows to export the information associated with each session from the database to a *Microsoft® Excel* or *CSV* file so that the teacher can manage it at their convenience.

The utilization of a database has been motivated to prevent data loss in case of a temporary failure and to facilitate the arduous importing and exporting phase. The software also includes an auto-recording utility (associated with each session) for those teachers whose session involves more than one class, avoiding the configuration task in successive classes.

A setup file for each operating system has been uploaded in [1], including the required libraries for a correct use. Once it is installed, the OpenIRS-UCM Java file and the iTeletest client for the Internet (wired and wireless devices) are available.

3.2 Functional Details: A guided example

In this section we will describe in detail the different functionalities that our tool provides. In the user guide, available at [1], the user can find more extensive explanations about our software.

First of all, the teacher must create a new session or open an existing one. A session gathers all the information about students, questions, clickers-to-student association, answers (initially empty), etc. In the main window (Figure 1), the user chooses *File - Session - New Session* or *File - Session - Open/Load Session*. In the first case, a second window will open asking for a session's name and, optionally, for a student file, a question file, and a roster file (that defines the clickers-to-student association), with CSV or *Microsoft® Excel* format (the software provides some example files that the user can employ as a template). In the second case, the teacher displays the menu from the lower-right hand corner of Figure 1 for selecting the session to open among all existing ones.

Once the session is created or opened, the teacher can import the information about students, questions and roster, or, in case it was already inserted previously, the teacher can update it. Selecting the option *File - Session - Edit*, several options are available (next we only detail those concerning with questions, though for students and roster they would be completelly analogous):

- Option *File - Session - Edit - Questions - Add Questions File* opens a browser, from where the user can select a file containing the questions. The file should have an appropriate format (recall that the user can follow the example files provided with the software).
- Option *File - Session - Edit - Questions - Add Question* opens a new window where all the information associated with a new question can be added (time lapse to answer, question title, correct answer, etc.).
- Option *File - Session - Edit - Questions - Erase Question* opens a new window that allows the user to remove any question entered so far.
- Option *File - Session - Edit - Questions - Edit Question* opens a new window in which the user can edit the different fields of the questions.

Next, the user should properly configure all the devices. In the *Configuration* menu, the user selects the clickers and connection type to employ during the session.

Finally, the teacher can check the clickers operation using the option *Clickers Test Mode*, in the *Configuration* menu. A new window opens and the system moves into a listening mode. Besides, this option may be very useful for finding out the clickers' logic identifiers, required for creating the roster.

All this work should be done before the test. We next describe the tasks for carrying out the test during the class.

The teacher should first execute the *Students Test Mode*, in the *Configuration* menu. This mode opens a new window, in which the left part lists all the students associated with this session. When the *Start* button is clicked, the identifier will move to the right part of the window if the corresponding student pushes any key in his clicker. This allows to find out the group of students who are present in the classroom, as well as to update the roster.

After that, clicking the *Start Test* button from Figure 1, a new bar opens (bottom left corner of Figure 2). The teacher can navigate through the questions in the most advisable order. When the *Play* button is pushed, two windows opens: one that displays the remaining time for answering and another showing the students *id* as soon as they click. Figure 2 illustrates a complete example, where the first question among 19 is shown, students with clickers *HITT3*, *sunVote10* and *iPhone1* have already answered, and there are still 133 seconds left. In this example, a *Microsoft® PowerPoint* illustrates on the background the complete question and the 4 possible answers. Recall here that our tool is independent to the slide program used. When the predefined time assigned to respond a question ends, the application stores the answers in the database, and the system moves on to the next question. Optionally, the teacher can show a graph (for which several formats are possible) with the answers of the students.

The teacher can finish the test by just closing the application. The answers will remain stored in the database, allowing the teacher to easily export and analyze them.

3.3 Software architecture

The OpenIRS-UCM software [1] has been released under the GNU Lesser General Public License (LGPL), which gives the freedom to use, share and modify the software.

Figure 3 shows the software building blocks of OpenIRS-UCM. Even if some functionality is distributed across modules (which will be worked out in the future), this modular approach eases the task of maintaining and extending the tool functionality.

The central *Control* block works as the backbone of the system, interconnecting the other modules: it manages timing, queries the database for questions, activates the remote

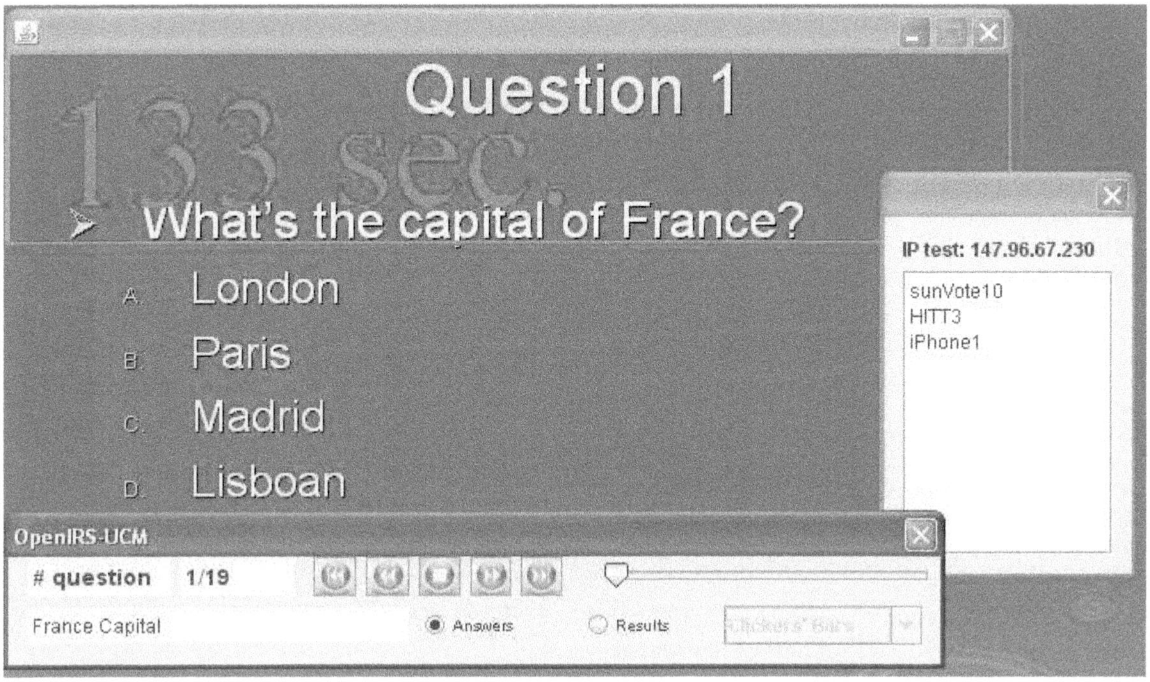

Figure 2: Example of a test execution.

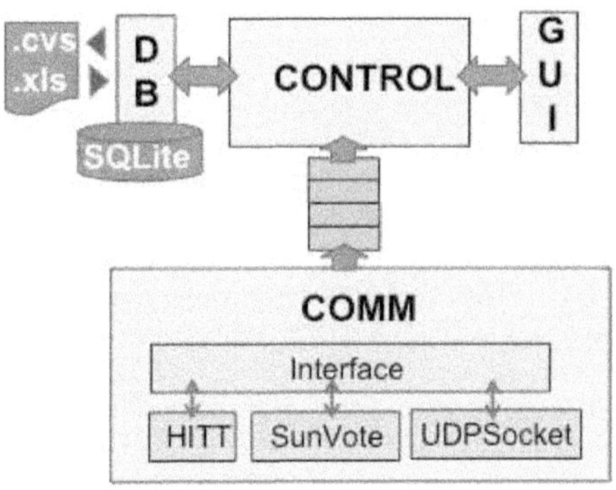

Figure 3: OpenIRS-UCM software modules.

devices to start accepting answers and dispatches user orders to the corresponding module.

The *GUI* module (corresponding to graphical support), is closely linked to the *Control* block: input from the teacher is collected through the *GUI* and usually implies actions on the communication or storage modules. Moreover, some output is also graphically represented so that functionality is also embedded in this module.

The *Communication* module encapsulates all the remote devices related functionality. Currently OpenIRS-UCM supports H-ITT and SunVote remote keypads and we have implemented UDP clients for PC and mobile phones (Android and iPhone) that work as soft-clickers. We developed a Java interface that must be implemented by any new device to be introduced in the system. All the featured devices may work concurrently, and all the answers are collected in a single answer queue. The *Communication* module also declares an interface to be used by the *Control* module to fetch answers from the queue and activate devices.

Finally, the *DB* module contains all the storage related functionality. OpenIRS-UCM uses *SQLite*[4] as database management system to keep data from current session, isolating the core from the input/output format desired by the user. The *DB* module provides an interface to query the session database. Currently, the session data can be imported/exported in two formats: proprietary *Microsoft® Excel* or *CSV* format. The tool could be easily extended to support other formats if needed.

As stated above, OpenIRS-UCM was developed under GNU LGPL licence. Some third party libraries were needed to support clickers from different manufacturers, that usually do not provide open source drivers. Most manufacturers provide a C dynamic library as driver. To use these C drivers from Java, we created appropriate wrappers using the Java Native Interface[5].

Support for the H-ITT clickers requires the copy righted and closed driver from the manufacturer[6]. The driver provides a virtual serial port that can be used to manage the clickers. To simplify the communication with the clickers, OpenIRS-UCM makes use of the RXTX[7] Java library, released under LGPL[8], which provides basic serial and parallel communication for the Java Development Toolkit (JDK).

---

[4]http://www.sqlite.org
[5]Java Native Interface in http://docs.oracle.com/javase/7/docs/technotes/guides/jni/index.html
[6]H-ITT Software Development Kit in http://www.h-itt.com/downloads.htm
[7]RXTX in http://rxtx.qbang.org/wiki/index.php/Main_Page
[8]GNU Lesser General Public License in http://www.gnu.org/licenses/lgpl.html

SunVote devices were also supported through the RXTX library. The manufacturer provides an USB reception device that shows up in the system as a virtual serial port. We developed the communication protocol on top of the RXTX services, using closed documentation from the manufacturer. Therefore this part of the software is released as a separate closed source library with copyright. Disclosing this library would need permission from the manufacturer.

The rest of the devices are supported as internet devices. We provide an UDP service to communicate with those devices, using the socket interface in the JDK.

Moreover, third party libraries were also needed in the other modules:

- Apache POI Java API[9] to manage Microsoft documents. It is composed of several modules for the different Microsoft file formats. We basically use the HSSF module for the traditional XLS *Microsoft® Excel* file formats. POI uses Apache license[10], which grants you the possibility to distribute your software as open or closed source.
- JFreeChart[11] to display charts with the statistics of the audience responses. It is a Java library distributed under LGPL.
- JDOM[12] to read and write XML files. JDOM is complete Java-based solution for accessing, manipulating, and outputting XML data from Java code. It is distributed under its own JDOM license, which is an Apache-style open source license, with the acknowledgment clause removed.
- OpenCSV[13] to read and parse *CSV* format files. It is available under Apache 2.0 license.

The multi-platform installers provided in the OpenIRS-UCM distribution [1] contain all the libraries required by the application to work except for the Java Virtual Machine (JVM). OpenIRS-UCM has been successfully tested in *Microsoft® Windows*, Linux and Mac Os X based systems with a 32-bit JVM. The developed code would work under a 64-bit JRE version, but some of the used libraries do not. Note that the only limitation is about the JVM version and does not affect the system itself that may perfectly be running a 64-bit operating system.

4. EVALUATION

In this section we detail the major benefits and disadvantages that our software reports based on different experimental trials.

At the same time the OpenIRS-UCM software was developed, some other interactive applications were analyzed in order to identify those additional elements that our tool could incorporate to provide the main required features keeping the operation mode simple enough. For this purpose, a team member assumed the supervision of two educational master works where the students evaluated some commercial software (for the available SunVote and Educlick[14] clickers) in the educational environment of two high schools of Madrid. The obtained information was employed as extra feedback in our software development.

Specifically, the ARS-SunVote and the H-ITTShow applications were analyzed in the mentioned works. Many different usages for these applications were tried, like attendance control, evaluation tests, student delegate election, *Trivial Pursuit competition*, students self assessments, collection of information about students preferences and habits, etc. Both applications –as well as our own software and other similar tools– share the same advantages according to students and teachers opinions: increase in students motivation, interest, participation –not only the less shy students answer the questions as in a conventional class–, attention, competitiveness, applicability to any subject, fast collected data processing and easinnes for creating new activities, constant evaluation, and so on. Among the main drawbacks detected in the commercial software evaluated, and already solved in our OpenIRS-UCM application, we should highlight the sporadic crash of some software versions, the incompatibility between different Windows Office versions and the restriction to just one slide program (*Microsoft® PowerPoint*).

An additional educational master work oriented to evaluate the students motivation in a high school using OpenIRS-UCM software was also supervised, confirming all aforementioned benefits and even revealing a significant increase in the students' qualifications.

In summary, and according to the mentioned trials and other tests performed with our tool in the classrooms of the university –corresponding to subjects like Robotics, Computer Structure, High Performance Techniques in Processor Design, and others– we can conclude that OpenIRS-UCM is straightforward, highly accepted by the educational community and as robust as similar commercial applications, since no important features are missing and even our tool managed to remove some significant drawbacks.

Finally, we outline that a potential future line related with OpenIRS-UCM could be to give virtual classes using this software, favoring students participation through the Internet.

5. CONCLUSIONS

In this paper we have presented the OpenIRS-UCM teaching tool which improves some properties from other commercial IRS systems. The most outstanding features of OpenIRS-UCM are:

1. **Cost**: it is free. Anyone can download it from a public repository in *http://sourceforge.net/projects/openirs-ucm*. Further versions will be uploaded in this url.
2. **Compatibility**: it is a multi-clicker system which allows to coexist commercial H-ITT and SunVote clickers with last generate smart-phones, and other devices connected to the Internet such as PDAs, tablets, laptops or PCs.
3. **System requirements**: it is portable to any computer with a Java Virtual Machine installed and it is

[9] Apache POI - the Java API for Microsoft Documents in http://poi.apache.org

[10] Apache License 2.0 in http://www.apache.org/licenses/LICENSE-2.0.txt

[11] JFreeChart in http://www.jfree.org/jfreechart/

[12] JDOM in http://www.jdom.org

[13] OpenCVS in http://opencsv.sourceforge.net

[14] http://www.educlick.es

not limited by any proprietary software or operating system.

4. **Development**: it is a free source code following open source software under the GPL license.

5. **Usability**: it is easy to use with a friendly interface that permits exporting and importing session information for further analysis.

OpenIRS-UCM has been tested with a variety of audiences and in different educational groups: higher education (undergraduate, masters, and post-graduate subjects), highschools and so on. Results have been satisfactory in all situations; its simplicity and robustness have been highlighted leading to a significant acceptance in the local teaching community.

OpenIRS-UCM versatility opens the possibility of exploring new teaching methodologies in a virtual classroom environment. Currently, web-based conferencing systems hardly include peer interaction between listener and lecturer tools, and those which do, are very basic. OpenIRS-UCM can be used as a complement in order to solve these weaknesses. Nowadays, it can even be used as an elementary score tool under these conditions.

6. ACKNOWLEDGEMENTS

OpenIRS-UCM has been supported by the University Complutense of Madrid Innovation Education Project PIMCD 211-2010/2011 and Spanish Project CICYT-TIN 2008/508.

It had two predecessor PIMCD projects: (1) the PIMCD 614-2007/2008 project where the ZigBee technology was analyzed in order to design keypads and a transmitter (student's keypad) as well as receiver prototypes were built; and, (2) the PIMCD 204-2008/2009 project where a set of clickers, making up ZigBee technology, were built. Besides, a first version of our IRS software was implemented. This software allowed the simultaneous use of WI-FI devices (PDAs or PCs) and the designed ZigBee clickers.

Although the ZigBee clickers were very useful, they were not competitive because of their high cost (related with the reduced amount of manufactured clickers and their assembly by hand). So, in the last project, the acquired experience has allowed to implement our open-free IRS software that also supports commercial and smart-phone clickers.

7. REFERENCES

[1] OpenIRS-UCM. http://sourceforge.net/projects/openirs-ucm.

[2] K. Anthis. Is it the clicker, or is it the question?. untangling the effects of student response system use. *Teaching of Psychology*, 38(3):189–193, July 2011.

[3] M. J. C. Dennis M. Shaffer. Evaluating the effectiveness of a personal response system in the classroom. *ACM Teaching of Psychology*, 36(4):273–277, 2009.

[4] C. Doe. Student response systems. *Multimedia and Internet@Schools [online]*, 17(4):32–35, July-Aug. 2010.

[5] J. Flynn and J. Russell. Personal response systems: is success in learning just a click away? *Educational Technology*, 48(6):20–3, November 2008.

[6] G. H.-N. John Stav, Kjetil Nielsen and T. Thorseth. Experiences obtained with integration of student response systems for ipod touch and iphone into e-learning environments. *Electronic Journal of e-Learning*, 8(2):179–190, January 2010.

[7] M. E. Lantz. The use of 'clickers' in the classroom: Teaching innovation or merely an amusing novelty? *Computers in Human Behavior*, 26(4):556–561, July 2010.

[8] T.-C. Liu. The features and potential of interactive response systems. In *Presented at the International Conference on Computers in Education. Hong Kong*, 2003.

[9] R. C. Lowery. Teaching and learning with interactive student response systems: A comparison of commercial products in the higher-education market. In *Prepared for presentation at the annual meeting of the Southwestern Social Science Association and its affiliates*, March 2005.

[10] B. S. M.A. Purvis and M. Purvis. Architecture for active and collaborative learning in a distributed classroom environment. *ACM Advanced Technology for Learning*, 3(4):225–232, January 2006.

[11] K. M. Moss and M. Crowley. Effective learning in science: The use of personal response systems with a wide range of audiences. *Computers and Education*, 56(1):36–43, January 2011.

[12] H. M. Yue Suo, N. Miyata, T. Ishida, and T. Y. Shi. Open smart classroom: Extensible and scalable learning system in smart space using web service technology. *IEEE Transactions on Knowledge and data engineering*, 21(6):814–828, June 2009.

[13] K. N. Yuji Tokiwa and M. Iwatsuki. Web-based tools to sustain the motivation of students in distance education. In *Proceedings of the 39th IEEE international conference on Frontiers in education conference. FIE'09*, pages 1438–1442. IEEE Press, October 2009.

[14] I. Zualkernan. Infocoral: Open-source hardware for low-cost, high-density concurrent simple response ubiquitous systems. In *11th IEEE International Conference on Advanced Learning Technologies (ICALT)*, pages 638–9. IEEE Comput. Soc., July 2011.

A Method to Construct Counterexamples for Greedy Algorithms

Jagadish M
Dept. of Computer Science and Engg.
Indian Institute of Technology Bombay
Mumbai 400076, India
jagadish@cse.iitb.ac.in

Sridhar Iyer
Dept. of Computer Science and Engg.
Indian Institute of Technology Bombay
Mumbai 400076, India
sri@iitb.ac.in

ABSTRACT

Problem solving is the focus of any algorithm design course. Being able to construct counterexamples is a critical part of the problem solving process. We address the following question: Is there a *teachable* approach to construct counterexamples? We present a technique, called the *Anchor Method*, that could prove useful in constructing counterexamples for greedy algorithms. The basic idea of the method is to get insight about the structure of a counterexample by weakening the greedy algorithm. We show the applicability of the method by constructing counterexamples for some classic problems in graph theory. We also investigate the teachability of the technique through experiments.

Categories and Subject Descriptors

K.3.2 [**Computers and Education**]: Computer and Information Science Education

General Terms

Algorithms

Keywords

Counterexamples, Greedy algorithms, Problem-solving

1. INTRODUCTION

In the design of algorithms, the discovery of a counterexample can help in discarding a wrong approach. Counterexamples developed for failed approaches usually serve as test cases for new approaches and may also yield insight into the problem structure.

Constructing counterexamples can be hard. Early research in cognition shows that people are more likely to look for examples to confirm a hypothesis than to disprove it[6]. For example, it is common for students to come up with an intuitive (but wrong) algorithm and use input cases only to assure themselves of its correctness, instead of finding a rigorous proof or searching for a counterexample[3].

ITiCSE'12, July 3–5, 2012, Haifa, Israel.

Greedy, divide-and-conquer, recursion, dynamic programming, reduction, etc. are some of the prominent algorithm design techniques that are taught at undergraduate level. Counterexamples often crop up in the context of greedy algorithms. For example, every third exercise problem in the chapter on greedy algorithms in the Klienberg-Tardos textbook[5] requests for a proof or a counterexample. "Exchange argument" is often helpful in proving the correctness of a greedy algorithm. To the best of our knowledge, there is no method aimed at constructing a counterexample to disprove a greedy approach. Students simply rely on their intuition or search for counterexamples by trying small cases.

We present a technique, called the *Anchor method*, that could prove useful in constructing counterexamples for greedy algorithms. We limit the scope of our work to simple greedy approaches since most of the problem solver's first plans of attack tend to be greedy in nature. We also limit the scope of our problems to graph theoretic problems on unweighted graphs, since many problems in computer science map to this class[8].

In the next section, we introduce the notion of *weak algorithm* and define three types of counterexamples: *weak*, *plausible* and *definitive*. We will use the Maximum Independent Set (MIS) problem as a running example to clarify these definitions and also illustrate the working of the anchor method (section 3). In section 4, we use the anchor method to construct counterexamples for a few well-known problems in graph theory–this shows the general applicability of our method. In section 5, we address questions related to the teachability of the method.

2. DEFINITIONS

Weak Algorithm. The greedy algorithm works by 'making the choice that looks best at the moment' [5]. We define a weak algorithm to be an algorithm that works by making an *arbitrary* choice at each moment.

Weak Counterexample. A weak counterexample is an instance on which the weak algorithm fails assuming the worst possible execution or, in other words, when choices are made in an adversarial manner (e.g. Fig. 4).

Plausible and Definitive Counterexample. If more than one choice looks best at a given step, the greedy algorithm makes a choice non-deterministically. Hence, the algorithm could have multiple execution paths for a given input instance. We call an input instance a *plausible counterexample* if one of the execution paths leads to a wrong answer. Similarly, an input instance is called a *definitive* *counterexample* if every possible path of execution leads to a wrong answer.

Maximum Independent Set Problem

A *graph* G consists of a set V of *vertices* and a set E of pairs of vertices called *edges*. For an edge $e = (u, v)$, we say e is *incident* on vertex u and v; vertices u and v are also the *endpoints* of e. The pair of vertices in an edge is unordered so $e = (u, v)$ is the same as $e = (v, u)$. The *degree* of a vertex is the number of edges incident upon it.

Problem. Let $G = (V, E)$ be an graph. The maximum independent set problem (MIS) is to find the largest vertex set $S \subseteq V$ such that no two vertices in S have an edge between them in E. See Fig. 1.

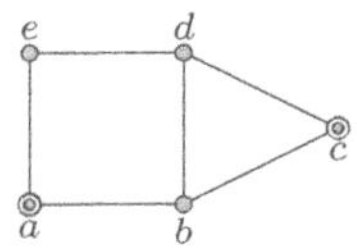

Figure 1: In the graph shown, $S = \{a, c\}$ is a maximum independent set.

Consider the following greedy approach to solve the MIS problem:

Algorithm. When a vertex is picked, we are prohibited from picking its neighbors. Since we want to pick as many vertices as possible, we start by picking vertices with low degree[7].

Algorithm 2.1: MIS(G)

Input: Graph G

Output: An independent set S from graph G

Initially the set S is empty.
1 : Sort the vertices according to their degree.
  Let V_s be the sorted sequence.
2 : **for each** vertex v in V_s
  if vertex v does not have a neighbor in S
    add vertex v to set S.
3 : Report S as the answer

Consider the input graph in Fig. 2: a cycle of length 6 (C_6). The size of the maximum independent set in this graph is 3 (set $\{a, c, e\}$ for example).

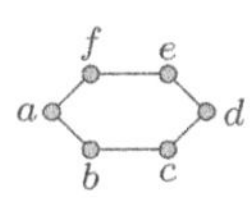

Figure 2: Cycle C_6 has 3 independent vertices.

As all the degrees of vertices are same, the algorithm could sort them in any order. If $V_s = [a, b, c, d, e, f]$, the algorithm returns $\{a, c, e\}$ as the maximum independent set. However, if $V_s = [a, d, f, e, b, c]$, the algorithm returns $\{a, d\}$ as the maximum independent set (incorrectly). Hence the input graph C_6 is a plausible counterexample for the given greedy algorithm.

In general, we can convert a plausible counterexample into a definitive counterexample with some modification. In the above example, we want the algorithm to pick vertices a and d before others. We can ensure that by adding the edges (b, e) and (c, f) as shown in Fig. 3.

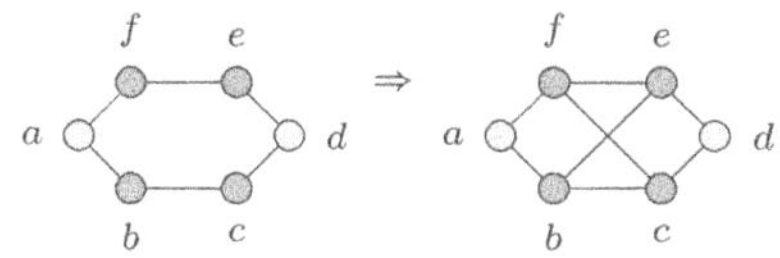

Figure 3: Converting a plausible counterexample to a definitive counterexample. The size of the MIS in the second graph is 3 ($\{a, c, e\}$), but the greedy algorithm 2.1 always returns a set of size 2 ($\{a, d\}$).

Although a definitive counterexample is more desirable, providing a plausible counterexample is a legitimate way of disproving a greedy algorithm.

3. WORKING OF THE ANCHOR METHOD

Our objective is to construct a counterexample to a given greedy algorithm. The anchor method follows a basic principle of problem-solving: solve an easier problem first. Instead of constructing a greedy counterexample directly, we first construct a counterexample for the weak algorithm. We call this a *weak counterexample*. Recall that a weak algorithm is obtained from the greedy algorithm by replacing the greedy choice with an arbitrary choice. The assumption is that the weak counterexample gives insight into the structure of the greedy counterexample. Our method consists of two steps:

Step 1 **Build an anchor** Use the weak counterexample to obtain an *anchor*. The anchor is a skeleton that captures the essence of a possible greedy counterexample. It serves as a starting point for constructing a counterexample to the greedy algorithm.

Step 2 **Add an auxiliary structure** Attach an *auxiliary structure* to the anchor to obtain a complete counterexample. The purpose of the auxiliary structure is to ensure that the greedy algorithm essentially mimics the weak algorithm (and hence fails in the same way). Auxiliary structures usually have 'extreme' or 'common' structures.

We apply the anchor method to construct a counterexample to Alg. 2.1 for the MIS problem. This algorithm picks the vertices in increasing order of degree, so the corresponding weak algorithm picks vertices in arbitrary order.

3.1 Maximum Independent Set: An illustrative example

Building an Anchor. Consider the weak algorithm that picks the vertices in arbitrary order to include in S. A counterexample to this algorithm is shown in Fig. 4.

The weak algorithm could pick the central vertex first and get an independent set of size 1, whereas the maximum independent set has size 3 ($\{a, b, c\}$). So this is our weak counterexample.

In the weak counterexample, the central vertex has the highest degree. We know that the greedy algorithm would pick the central vertex in the above graph first if the central

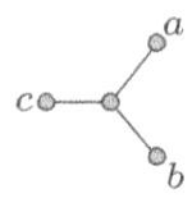

Figure 4: A counterexample to the weak algorithm for the MIS problem. A star graph with three outer vertices.

vertex had the *lowest* degree *somehow*. The anchor just captures this intuition (Fig. 5).

Notation. We use symbols ● and ○ to indicate a vertex we *wish* were of high degree and low degree, respectively.

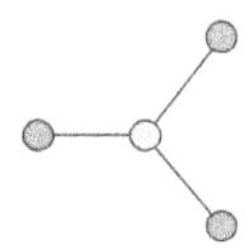

Figure 5: The anchor obtained from the weak counterexample.

Adding the auxiliary structure. Each high degree vertex needs to be connected to at least 3 vertices in order to exceed the low degree central vertex. Let K_n denote a complete graph with n vertices. Attaching the auxiliary graph K_3 gives a counterexample as shown in Fig. 6.

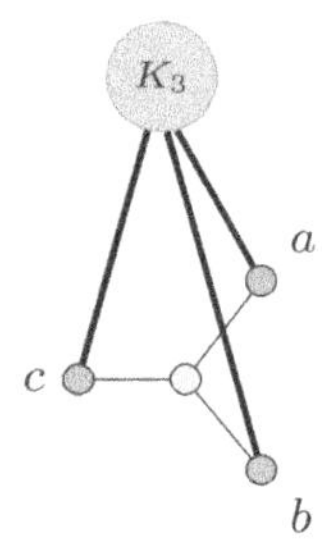

Figure 6: A counterexample to Alg. 2.1 for the MIS problem. A dark edge indicates that there are edges from the high degree vertex to all the three vertices in K_3. The central vertex has degree 3. Vertices a, b and c have degree 4 each. Each vertex in K_3 has degree 5. So the greedy algorithm picks the central vertex first and then picks one vertex from K_3. The maximum independent set is actually $\{a, b, c\}$. Hence, the greedy algorithm picks 2 vertices, while the optimal algorithm picks 3.

Approximation ratio. The approximation ratio is a measure of how good a counterexample is. It is defined as follows: Suppose $\mathcal{I}$ is an input to an algorithm $\mathcal{A}$. Let OPT be the value of the optimal solution to $\mathcal{I}$ and ALG be the value returned by the algorithm $\mathcal{A}$. The approximation ratio of the input $\mathcal{I}$ is defined the ratio of OPT to ALG, for maximization problems. For minimization problems, it is the ratio of ALG to OPT. For example, for the input shown in Fig. 6 OPT=3 and ALG=2, so the approximation ratio is 1.5.

Note that we can pick any star graph with $n(\geq 3)$ outer vertices as our weak counterexample. Attaching an auxiliary

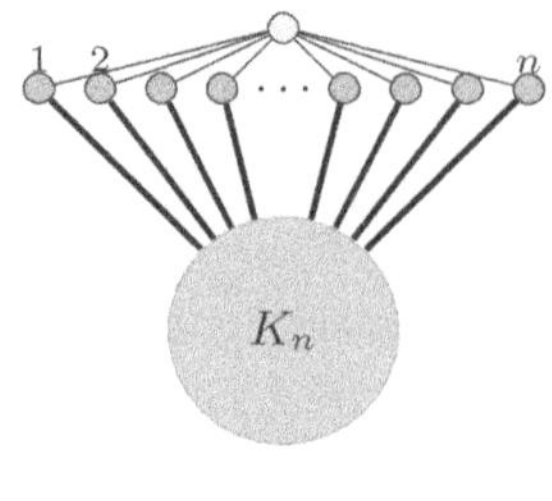

Figure 7: A general counterexample to Alg. 2.1 for the MIS problem with $O(n)$ approximation ratio. The greedy algorithm picks 2 independent vertices, while the optimal algorithm picks n vertices.

graph K_n to the corresponding anchor gives us a *general* counterexample (Fig. 7) with the best approximation ratio.

We may have to try a few weak counterexamples before hitting upon the one which extends to a greedy counterexample.

4. ADDITIONAL EXAMPLES

We show the applicability of the anchor method on many classic problems from graph theory. Most of the problem descriptions along with their applications can be found in standard texts like [2, 9].

4.1 Matching

A set of edges $M \subseteq E$ is called a *matching* if every vertex in G is an endpoint of at most one edge in M. A vertex is said to be *matched* if it is an endpoint of some edge in M; if not the vertex is said to be *unmatched*.

Problem Definition. Let $G = (V, E)$ be a graph. The maximum matching problem (MM) is to find a matching M of maximum size in G. An example is shown in Fig. 8.

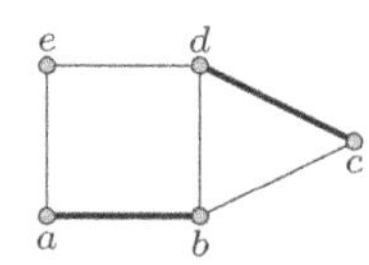

Figure 8: In the graph above, the dark edges form a matching of size 2 (which is also the maximum size).

Algorithm. A vertex with degree one has to necessarily be matched to its neighbor if it has to participate in the matching. In general, a vertex with fewer neighbors has fewer choices and is therefore more critical.

Notation. Let v_{min} denote the vertex with minimum non-zero degree in graph G and u_{min} denote the vertex with minimum degree adjacent to v_{min}.

The greedy algorithm is to pick the edge (v_{min}, u_{min}) and then remove the vertices v_{min} and u_{min} from G. Repeat the process on the resulting graph until an edge can be picked.

Counterexample

Building an Anchor. Consider the weaker algorithm that picks the edges in any order to include them in the matching. A path of four nodes is the simplest instance on which the weak algorithm fails (Fig. 9). The weak algorithm could pick just the middle edge, while the optimal algorithm picks the first and the last edge.

The anchor follows from the above weak counterexample:

Figure 9: A counterexample to the weak algorithm for the matching problem.

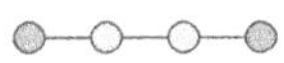

Adding the auxiliary structure. We attach K_2 to each of the end vertices. This gives a plausible counterexample–the greedy could pick a matching of size 3 instead of 4. Attaching K_4 gives a definitive counterexample.

Figure 10: Plausible and definitive counterexamples to the greedy algorithm for the matching problem.

4.2 Maximum leaf spanning tree

Problem Definition. Given a graph $G = (V, E)$, the maximum leaf spanning tree problem(MLS) is to find a spanning tree T in G that has maximum number of leaves; where leaves are vertices with degree 1. An example is shown in Fig. 11.

Algorithm. We would like to grow the tree along vertices that branch out well. One heuristic is to grow the tree along a vertex which has the maximum number of neighbors not in the tree[4].

Notation. For a vertex v in tree T, let $N'(v)$ denote the set of neighbors of v not in T.

The greedy algorithm initializes the tree T with the maximum degree vertex and then grows the tree along that vertex u for which the size of $N'(u)$ is maximized.

Counterexample

Building an Anchor. In the above algorithm, we grow the tree T along the vertex that has maximum number of neighbors outside the tree. Consider the weaker algorithm that does not exercise this choice and instead grows the tree along any arbitrary vertex.

An instance where the weak algorithm could perform poorly is shown in Fig.12. The optimal algorithm would pick the vertex with the highest degree r and obtain a spanning tree having $|V| - 1$ leaves. But if the weak algorithm picks vertex l first, it could end up with a spanning tree having only two leaves (as indicated with dark background).

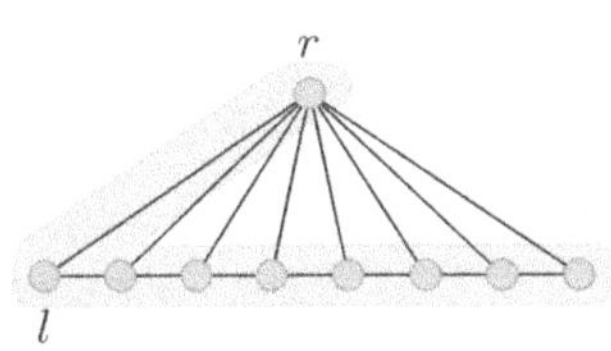

Figure 12: A counterexample to the weak algorithm for the MLS problem.

Notice that the key to designing the weak counterexample was to make the algorithm select a long path of vertices which should have been selected as leaves. Can we mimic that behavior for the greedy algorithm? We make the greedy algorithm start from the first node by increasing its degree.

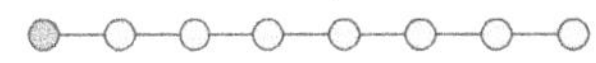

Adding the auxiliary structure. We need to make the vertices of this path as leaves of some tree. We need to attach an auxiliary structure such that the vertices on the path become leaves. The auxiliary structure cannot have a vertex with degree greater than 3 since we have forced the greedy algorithm to pick the the leftmost vertex in the anchor first. The complete binary tree serves this purpose. The counterexample is shown in Fig. 13.

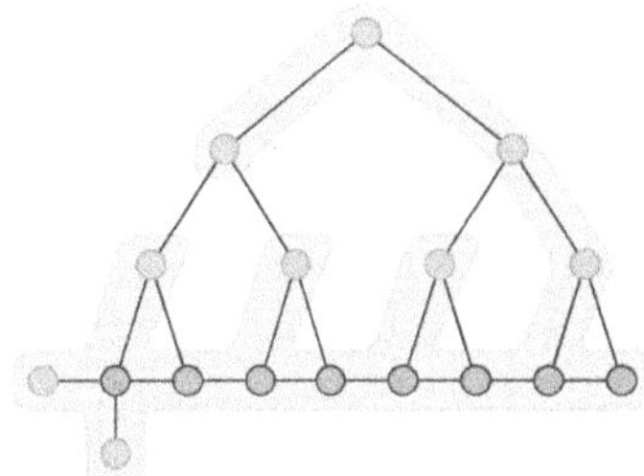

Figure 13: A plausible counterexample to the greedy algorithm for the Max-leaf Spanning Tree problem.

4.3 Minimum Steiner tree

Problem Definition. Given a graph $G = (V, E)$ and a set of *terminal* vertices $P \subseteq V$, the minimum Steiner tree problem (STP) is to find a tree T in G such that the following two conditions are satisfied:

1. Tree T contains all terminal vertices P.

2. The number of edges in T is minimized.

An example is shown in Fig. 14.

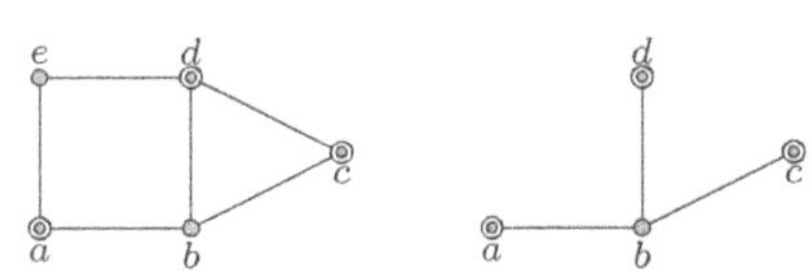

Figure 14: The input graph G with terminals $P = \{a, c, d\}$ has a minimum Steiner tree having three edges. Note that the Steiner tree can contain vertices not in set P.

Algorithm. Notice that the Steiner tree must connect all the terminals using the least number of edges. Since any two terminals must be connected, we try to grow the tree by connecting two vertices along their shortest path.

Definition. For a tree $T \in G$ and a vertex $v \in G$, a $v \rightsquigarrow T$ *connecting path* is the shortest path that connects vertex v to some vertex in T.

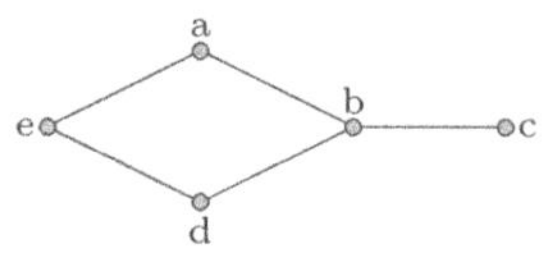

Figure 11: Two spanning trees for the graph given on the left: one with 3 leaves and the other with 2 leaves.

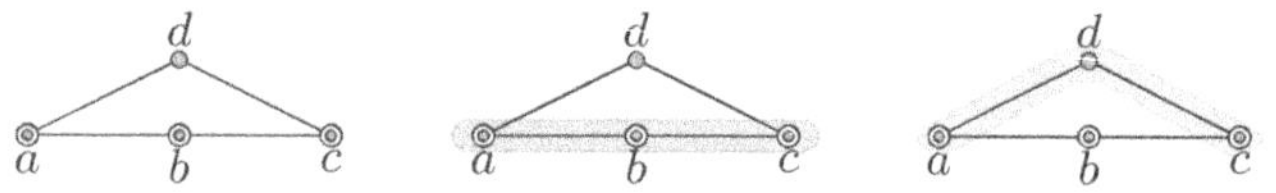

Figure 15: A weak counterexample for Steiner tree problem

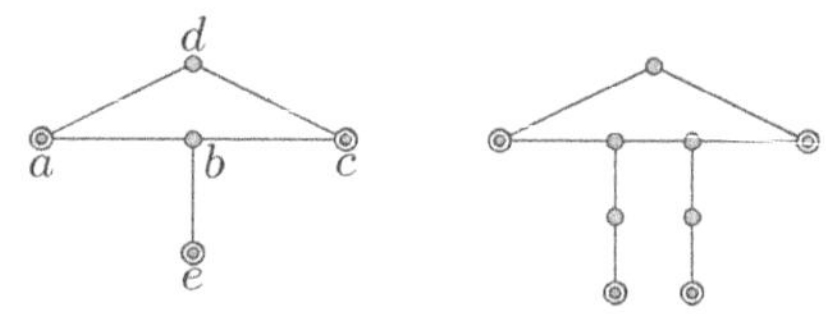

Figure 16: Plausible and definitive counterexamples to Alg. 4.1 for the Steiner tree problem.

Algorithm 4.1: STP(G)

Input: Graph G and a terminal set P

Output: A minimum Steiner tree of G

Initially, the tree T contains only the shortest path amongst all pairs of terminals in the set P.
repeat
 1 : Let u be the terminal not in T that has the shortest connecting path to T.
 2 : Add $u \rightsquigarrow T$ connecting path to T.
until the tree T contains all the terminals in the set P.
Report tree T as the Steiner tree for the graph G and terminals P.

Counterexample

Building an Anchor. Note that the greedy algorithm starts by picking the shortest path between all pairs of terminals. We weaken the algorithm slightly by saying the tree could be initialized with the shortest path between any two terminals.

Let us try to build a counterexample for the weak algorithm. It is possible to construct a counterexample having 3 terminals as shown in Fig 15. This is the simplest possible input since no counterexample is possible with only two terminals.

The optimal Steiner tree is the path containing 3 terminals. The weak algorithm could initialize tree T by picking the shortest path between a and c going via the non-terminal vertex d. This would result in a Steiner tree containing 3 edges. This serves as our anchor.
Adding the auxiliary structure. If the greedy algorithm has to take the path adc first, we cannot afford to have distance of 1 between any pair of terminals. We add an edge to move away vertex c so as to ensure all the shortest paths between terminals are 2. This is a plausible counterexample. We can extend the same idea to obtain a definitive counterexample as shown in Fig. 16.

5. EXPERIMENTS

We conducted two experiments to assess the educational value of the anchor method. Note that the anchor method assumes that the weak counterexample is easier to construct than the greedy counterexample. Though it seems like a reasonable assumption, we conducted an in-class experiment to test this assumption (Experiment 1).

The second experiment was of qualitative nature. The purpose was to find the strategies that students employ, common mistakes they make, while constructing counterexamples and to identify the difficulties they face in applying the anchor method. The small scale of this experiment does not allow us to establish that the anchor method is actually teachable, but going through the exercise has been helpful in identifying a few key aspects related to problem-solving. We describe the setup of two experiments below and then address questions related to the teachability of the method.

Experiment 1. Thirty eight students who were enrolled in a minor course on "Data structures and algorithms" took the test which had two questions on the MIS problem. The class consisted of top 5% second year undergraduate students (CGPA-wise) from different departments from a top ranked engineering institute. The first and the second question asked them to construct a counterexample for the weak and greedy algorithm for the MIS problem, respectively. The summary of results are given in Table 1.

Null Hypothesis. The number of students who are able to construct a weak counterexample (WCE) is same as the number of students who can construct a greedy counterexample (GCE) for the MIS problem.

	WCE	GCE
No of correct responses	37/38	19/38
Average time taken by those who solved the question	4 min	20 min

Table 1: Summary of students' responses

The result of the experiment rejects our null hypothesis with effect size (as defined in [1]) greater than 3.8. Hence, we conclude that students find it easier to construct the weak counterexample than the greedy counterexample for the MIS problem.

Experiment 2. A qualitative experiment with three graduate students: A (PhD student), B (Masters student) and C (PhD student). The purpose of the experiment was to observe how students approach problems in a detailed manner. A and B were part of the experimental group that was taught the anchor method after the pre-test, while C was the control subject.

Design. Pre-test and Post-test each followed by an interview. Pre-test contained MAX-INDEPENDENT SET and

STEINER TREE problems. Post-test contained MATCHING and MAX-LEAF problems. After the pre-test, Students A and B were taught the anchor method by using the pre-test problems as illustrative examples. Student C was not taught the anchor method but was simply given the solutions to pre-test problems.

Questions on teachability. We answer questions related to the teachability of the method based on the observations from the above experiments.

How difficult is it for a student to come up with greedy counterexamples?

In Exp. 1, only 19/38 gave the greedy counterexample for the MAXINDEPENDENT set problem, while 37/38 students were able to design a weak counterexample. In Exp. 2 pre-test, only student A was able to solve the the MAXINDEPENDENT set problem. The Steiner tree problem was solved by students A and C.

However, none of the students in both the experiments constructed a counterexample with $O(n)$ approximation ratio for the MIS problem. This shows that it is generally difficult for students to construct counterexamples for greedy algorithms, especially the ones with good approximation ratios.

What heuristics do students commonly apply while constructing counterexamples?

These observations are based on Exp. 2:

- *Force the algorithm to make the wrong choice first.* This by far seems to be the most popular heuristic. For the MIS problem, all three students wrote a star first and tried to tweak the example such that picking the central vertex leads to a bad choice. This heuristic was unsuccessful for the MIS problem.
- *Weaken the input.* For example, instead of building a Steiner tree with unweighted vertices student A first built a counterexample with weighted graph and then converted it into an unweighted graph.
- *Work backwards from the solution.* Student B and C reported having tried this heuristic on MIS and Matching problem, respectively.

In Exp. 2, were students in the experimental group able to apply the anchor method in the post-test?

Note that applying the anchor method consists of two steps: coming up with the weak counterexample and attaching a suitable auxiliary structure. Students A and B were able to construct weak counterexamples for MATCHING and MAX-LEAF problems. Both the students could construct the counterexample for the MATCHING problem by attaching a complete graph K_4. However, only student A was able to attach the auxiliary structure for MAX-LEAF problem. Student B was not able to think of using a complete binary tree as an auxiliary structure. This suggests that step 2 is harder than step 1 and requires some practice.

How did student C fare in the post-test? Student C was unable to solve both the MATCHING and the MAX-LEAF problems. During the post-test C looked at solutions to the pre-test problems to see if he could construct a counterexample along the same lines. He mostly tried the heuristics listed above and some ad-hoc methods before giving up. This shows that it is not easy to *intuit* the anchor method just by looking at the solutions.

6. CONCLUSION

A couple of points in favor of the anchor method are as follows. Techniques like greedy, divide-and-conquer, dynamic programming, etc. are quite general and hence the student does not usually know *when* a particular method is applicable. Unlike these techniques, the anchor method is tailor-made for constructing counterexamples for greedy algorithms, so there is a greater chance of recall. In the examples considered, our approach usually led to a general counterexample with good approximation ratio. No student gave a general counterexample for the greedy algorithm in our experiments.

We observed that students sometimes fail to acknowledge plausible counterexamples as legitimate counterexamples and seek to get a definitive counterexample directly. Hence, we recommend that the distinction between a plausible and a definitive counterexample be made clear to students.

The second step of attaching an appropriate auxiliary structure is still descriptive. What constitutes an auxiliary structure is problem-specific. For the examples discussed, the auxiliary structures turned out to be simple (complete graphs, complete binary tree, etc). But other problems may require more sophisticated auxiliary structures. We believe that a technique to identify auxiliary structures would strengthen the anchor method.

7. ACKNOWLEDGMENTS

We thank Soumitra Pal for suggesting improvements to the presentation of the paper.

8. REFERENCES

[1] L. Cohen, L. Manion, and K. Morrison. *Research Methods in Education.* Routledge, 6 edition, 2007.

[2] M. R. Garey and D. S. Johnson. *Computers and Intractability: A Guide to NP-Completeness.* Freeman, San Francisco, CA, USA, 1979.

[3] D. Ginat. The greedy trap and learning from mistakes. *SIGCSE Bull.*, 35:11–15, January 2003.

[4] S. Guha and S. Khuller. Approximation algorithms for connected dominating sets. *Algorithmica*, 20:374–387, 1996.

[5] J. Kleinberg and E. Tardos. *Algorithm Design.* Addison Wesley, second edition, 2006.

[6] J. V. Oakhill and P. N. Johnson-Laird. Rationality, memory and the search for counterexamples. *Cognition*, 20(1):79–94, 1985.

[7] S. Sakai, M. Togasaki, and K. Yamazaki. A note on greedy algorithms for the maximum weighted independent set problem. *Discrete Appl. Math.*, 126:313–322, March 2003.

[8] R. Sedgewick and K. Wayne. Undirected graphs applications. URL (accessed 2011-08-17). `http://www.cs.princeton.edu/~rs/AlgsDS07/11UndirectedGraphs.pdf`.

[9] D. B. West. *Introduction to Graph Theory.* Prentice Hall, 2 edition, September 2000.

Integrating AI and Machine Learning in Software Engineering Course for High School Students

Sperling, Ahuva
Leo Baeck Education Center
Haifa, Israel
97248300500
asperling@leobaeck.net

Lickerman, Dorit
Leo Baeck Education Center
Haifa, Israel
97248300500
dlickerman@gmail.com

ABSTRACT
This paper describes a unique software engineering curriculum for high-school students that includes subjects in artificial intelligence and machine learning. The students in the course deal with the implementation of solutions to riddles and games (complex algorithmic problems), use the DrRacket functional programming language as a tool that supports their comprehension and thorough understanding of blind search algorithms, informed search algorithms, search games trees and machine learning algorithms. During their studies, the students engage in self-learning, collaborative learning and peer teaching. At the end of the course, each student writes a final research project which integrates the main aspects that have been learned in the course.

Categories and Subject Descriptors
K.3.2 [**Computers and Education**]: Computer and Information Science Education – *Computer science education*, Curriculum.

General Terms
Algorithms, Human Factors, Languages.

Keywords
Computer science education, artificial intelligence, project based learning, machine learning, K-12.

1. INTRODUCTION
This paper describes a unique course in software engineering that was developed for high school students in the Leo Baeck Education Center (see Section 2). The course was developed as an advanced course for the functional programming unit of the Israeli high school CS curriculum (described in Sections 3 and 4). Section 5 describes the computer science curriculum in the Leo Baeck high school and Section 6 describes the software engineering course – the major contribution of this paper – which includes subjects in artificial intelligence (AI) and machine learning. In order to make the learning process more interesting and enjoyable, the students implement algorithms which enable them to write applications that solve riddles and play games. Apart from enjoying the learning process, this approach makes the learner active, encourages discussion between students, and stimulates the desire to continue studying and exploring the subjects being taught in class beyond the classroom hours [4]. Appendix A presents a letter that reinforces what has been said above.

ITiCSE'12, July 3–5, 2012, Haifa, Israel.

2. LEO BAECK EDUCATION CENTER
The Leo Baeck education center in Haifa was founded in 1938 for children who had survived the Holocaust. Its pluralistic approach is committed to democracy, egalitarianism and human rights, as well as to the teaching of the living values of progressive Judaism which inspires social change and imroving the world. The education center is one of Israel's finest institutions for academic excellence and it also promotes community outreach and social action.

Today, the Leo Baeck Education Center includes early childhood daycare, a middle school, a high school, an art school, a community center, a sport center, a Reform synagogue and the Lorry I. Lokey international center for Jewish studies.

In addition, the school runs many programs for the community, e.g., the World Youth Award[1], promotion of Jewish values, a district gifted class and a special education class for students with communication and other disabilities (PDD).

The Senior High School, in which we have been teaching during the last 20 years, is Leo Baeck's flagship, serving as one of Israel's premier high-school institutions. One hundred and fifty full and part-time teachers educate over 1,000 students from grades 10 through 12 (ages 16-18). The high school serves as an experimental school to develop leadership skills based on Jewish values. The school aims to educate its students to take personal responsibility for their actions and especially to fulfill their potential and to embark on an unrelenting climb to the summit of social, academic and ethical excellence. In addition, the school requires a personal contribution to the welfare of the community through extensive community service, develops an appreciation for the arts and culture, and instills a love of Israel.

The school encourages its students to innovation, initiative, independent thinking, originality and creativity, which are expressed in the class, in teaching and learning methods in various disciplines, in educational trips and in many additional community projects, where students improve and develop their leadership skills.

[1] This International Award is an exciting self-development program available to all 14 to 25 year olds. The program is intended to help young people and those concerned about their welfare. The program challenges youth, encouraging them toward personal achievement in sport, hobbies and contribution to the community. Young people, who achieve the Award, discover their potential, impact their community and develop a set of life skills.

3. COMPUTER SCIENCE IN ISRAELI HIGH SCHOOL

The high school computer science curriculum, as described in the article *A High-School Program in Computer Science* [5], aims to teach basic computer science concepts and principles of building computer systems. The program emphasizes the principles that stand the test of time [3] compared with technology-dependent concepts which quickly become outdated. The program provides learners with algorithmic reasoning ability, analysis and algorithmic problem solving skills, as well as basic concepts in the design of computerized systems.

The program's fundamental principles are [5, p. 5-7];

- Computer science should be taught on par with other scientific subjects.
- The program concentrates on the key concepts and foundations of the field. The main notion to be emphasized throughout the program is that of an algorithmic problem.
- The program contains required units as well as electives.
- Conceptual and experimental issues are interwoven throughout the program. This two-track approach, which is dubbed the "zipper principle" ([5] page 6), is one of the salient points of the program, and is elaborated on in a sidebar.
- Two different programming paradigms are taught. The students learn a "mother tongue" first, and then, on a more humble scale, they learn another language, of radically different nature, that suggests alternative ways of algorithmic thinking.

3.1 Teaching methods

According to the official website of the Computer Science Teaching Supervision in the Ministry of Education [3], the recommended teaching method is the one in which, in the course of their studies and led by the teacher, students experience independent development of computer programs to solve problems, some of which are set by the teacher and some of which are selected by the student. Emphasis is placed on the development process, product quality and process documentation.

The studies take place mostly in the computer lab. Work in the laboratory allows the demonstration of educational content by using the computer and projection equipment, in addition to the implementation of algorithms which are executed on the computer.

3.2 Target population

The program is designed for high school students (in both regular high school and vocational school[2]).

3.3 Curriculum structure

The curriculum, as written in the article *A High-School Program in Computer Science* [5] comes in two versions: a 3-unit and a 5-unit program. The former consists of 270 hours of study, and the latter, 450. The programs are constructed, as explained below, from the following list of modules:

1. Fundamentals 1 and 2 (2 units; 180 hours): This module provides the foundation for the entire program. It introduces most of the aforementioned central concepts, and at the same time teaches how to apply them in an object oriented programming language[3].

2. Advanced programming (1 unit; 90 hours): This module is based on Fundamentals. It concentrates on data structures, introducing abstract data-types, and also takes a step beyond stand-alone algorithms, to discuss the design of complete systems.

3. Second paradigm (1 unit; 90 hours): This module introduces the students to a second programming paradigm, which is conceptually quite different from the object oriented approach adopted in Fundamentals 1 and 2. Currently, the alternatives are: logic programming, system-level programming, functional programming, web programming, computer graphics and information systems[4].

4. Theoretical computer science choices (1 unit; 90 hours): This module exposes student to selected topics in theoretical computer science. The alternatives are: computational models (mainly automata), object-oriented programming, operations research and computer systems and assembly.

The 5-unit program is based on all the above, while the 3-unit program consists on fundamentals 1 and 2 and a second paradigm.

4. SOFTWARE ENGINEERING CURRICULUM IN ISRAELI HIGH SCHOOLS

The Israeli software engineering course (5 units; 450 hours) is an advance course, beyond the 5 units program described above and in [5]. It trains its graduates for systematic thinking and application capability of algorithms and complex systems in the world of high technology. The subjects taught in the course reflect the development of computer science, programming languages and technological innovations in software engineering, as well as addresses AI and selected topics related to technologies of the new millennium. Classes are held in a computerized environment and the students use the most advanced programming languages and systems. Curricula are based on knowledge and use of mathematics and scientific principles, as well as on planning and programming sophisticated systems.

The program's conceptual approach integrates three types of complexities [3]:

Computational complexity: Search for algorithmic solutions to algorithmic problems or proving non-existing solutions to these problems and complexity analysis of algorithmic problems and search for more effective solutions.

System complexity: Analysis and design of large software systems that combine modularization and reactivity.

Cognitive complexity: Design of intelligent systems, combining different disciplines of research in human and machine behavior.

---

[2] Vocational school is an educational institution in which students derive the benefits of a combination of study and practical work. The professional preparation of the students for the social and professional world is carried out in the ninth and tenth grade. In these years the students learn general and vocational subjects together with practical experience in the school workshops. The eleventh and twelfth grades combine three or four days of study at school with two or three working days, as paid apprentices in the workplace.

[3] The article [5] refers to procedural languages. Languages taught today are object oriented languages.

[4] We updated the curriculum in accordance with the article.

The curriculum has six alternatives:
1. Planning and programming operating systems
2. Planning and programming graphical systems
3. Planning and programming information systems
4. Planning and programming expert systems
5. Planning and programming Web network and service systems
6. Planning and programming mobile systems

5. COMPUTER SCIENCE CURRICULA IN LEO BAECK HIGH SCHOOL

The students in our school are offered with two options to learn computer science:

1. The 5 units program with functional programming (using DrRacket language) as the second paradigm unit and with computational models as the theoretical computer science choice. The students participate in the program for two years in the eleventh and twelfth grades (see Section 3.3).

2. A software engineering course, in which the students learn computer science for three years. They start learning the 5 units in the tenth grade for two years (as described above), and in the twelfth grade, they specialize in AI and machine learning in a unique program that is taught only at our school (described in Section 6).

During the seven years, in which the functional programming was taught as the second paradigm unit, the added value that the unit gives students, both in understanding of recursion and in top down design, became apparent. This understanding was reinforced when graduate students (5 units program) of our school expressed their opinion that their algorithmic problem-solving skills, regardless of the programming language, were considerably improved after they had studied this unit (see students' responses in Appendix B). When the school decided to start a software engineering course of study, it was found suitable to study it with this second paradigm in the same computational workspace. At this time, there was no suitable specialty in software engineering curriculum, and we could not find a similar course for high school students elsewhere; therefore, we had to develop our own curriculum. Prof. Shaul Markovitch[5] from the Technion's Department of Computer Science helped us in its development process, and once it was ready, it was submitted to the Ministry of Education and received the formal approval.

6. THE AI - MACHINE LEARNING CURRICULUM

This section describes the curriculum of the software engineering course that we developed. The course is based on cooperative and interactive learning as part of the pedagogical conception that students should be active in their learning.

Table 1 gives an overview of the curriculum. The 450 hours of the course can be divided into 4 major categories: theoretical basis (170 hours, 6.1-6.6), introduction to machine learning (100 hours, 6.7), advanced topics (60 hours, 6.8-6.9), and a final individual project (6.10).

[5] Prof. Shaul Markovitch's website: http://www.cs.technion.ac.il/people/shaulm/index.html

Table 1. Overview of the curriculum

	Topics	Hours
6.1	Introduction to Artificial Intelligence	10 hours
6.2	Extending the theoretical basis	40 hours
6.3	Problem solving by graph search	10 hours
6.4	Uninformed searches	40 hours
6.5	Heuristic searches (Informed searches)	30 hours
6.6	Non-cooperative games	40 hours
6.7	Introduction to Machine Learning	100 hours
6.8	Advanced topics in programming language I	15 hours
6.9	Advanced topics in programming language II	45 hours
6.10	Final personal project	120 hours

In what follows, we elaborate on each topic presented in Table 1.

6.1 Introduction to AI

The purpose of this introduction is to provide a theoretical background as the basis for the studying of the domain. The introduction is based on 6 parts as is shown in Table 2.

The teaching methods vary between classroom presentations and working in discussion groups on questions and answers for the Turing test.

Table 2. Introduction to AI: topics & subtopics

	Topic	Sub topics
1	What is artificial intelligence?	
2	Turing test	
3	Achievements in artificial intelligence	• Spacecraft managed by AI software • Computer program winning chess game Deep Blue • Automatic classification of documents • Medical diagnostics • Robotic assisted surgery • Computational Biology • Adaptive pets
4	Examples of unsolved tasks in artificial intelligence	• Understanding of natural language • Understanding a picture • Robot for housework
5	Intelligent agents	• Hardware agent • Software agent • Intelligent agents' structure (e.g. puzzle solving)
6	Research areas in artificial intelligence	• Multi-agents system with shared /conflicting goals • Computer vision • Understanding of natural language • Robotics • Learning

6.3 Extending the Theoretical Basis

The purpose of this section is to create a theoretical basis for further learning. This part of the course is based on 2 topics as shown in Table 3. The teaching methods are lectures and class discussions.

Table 3. Extending the theoretical basis: topics & subtopics

	Topic	Sub topics
1	Trees	• General trees • Knowledge representation using a tree • Directed trees • Minimum spanning tree
2	Algorithms and graph theory	• Graph characterization and description • Directed graph • Circular graph • Undirected graph • Shortest path algorithms • Knowledge representation using a graph

6.4 Problem Solving by Graph Search

The purpose of this section is to create a mathematical/theoretical basis for further learning, advancement from programming to theoretical/mathematical issues, and pupils' acquaintance with solving complex problems.

This part of the course is based on 3 topics as is shown in Table 4. The teacher formally defines a problem (for example, missionaries and cannibals), followed by students writing a formal definition of the other problems from the list; then, the class discusses the various definitions.

Table 4. Problem Solving by Graphs: topics & subtopics

	Topic	Sub topics
1	Formal definition of mathematical problems	• Missionaries and cannibals. • Puzzle problem 3×3. • Solution to the puzzle: "How to move a horse on all chessboards' slots without visiting a slot twice". • Solution to the puzzle: "How to fill 4 liters of water in a bucket with capacity of 5 liters using a bucket with capacity of 3 liters, without the option of measuring.
2	Formal definition of a complex problem	• Display problem • Set up a group of states in the graph illustrating the problem • Set a transition between two states in the graph depicting the problem
3	Solution of a complex problem by searching in the problem's states graph	• Develop a node • Introduction to search strategies with an emphasis on developing the next node, and "what is stored in the computer memory" as a distinction between the different algorithms • performance evaluation of search algorithms: o Memory Complexity o Runtime complexity o the nature of the solution: o Integrity o Optimal

6.5 Uninformed Searches

This part expands students' theoretical basis in algorithms as shown in Table 5, introduces the concepts of computational complexity of time and place, and emphasizes the finding of an optimal solution to complex tasks by utilizing integration programming in DrRacket computational workspace and theoretical content. The students implement:

- The breadth first algorithm to solve the problem of "missionaries and cannibals";
- The depth first search algorithm with depth limit to solve the problem of "leaping lizards";
- The backtracking search algorithm to solve the problem "How to place eight queens on a chess board".

The problems varied from one year to another.

Table 5. Uninformed Searches: topics & subtopics

	Topic	Sub topics
1	Breadth first search	Each algorithm is evaluated based on its completeness, optimality, time complexity and space complexity.
2	Depth first search	
3	Depth first search with depth limit	
4	Back tracking search	
5	Iterative depth first search	

6.6 Heuristic Searches (Informed Searches)

In this section, the students continue to acquire knowledge in computer science algorithms, as shown in Table 6, and deal with a complex task. They proceed from graph search to systematic search and finally heuristic search, finding the most significant factors leading to an optimal solution of a complex problem. The students implement and compare the solution paths (number of steps from a given state to the target state) of the following algorithms:

- The best first search algorithm to solve the 3×3 puzzle problem, using the evaluation function of Manhattan distance;
- The A* algorithm to solve the 3×3 puzzle problem, using the evaluation function of Manhattan distance.

Table 6. Heuristic Searches: topics and subtopics

	Topic	Sub topics
1	Differences between uninformed search and informed search	
2	Evaluation function	• Rule of thumb • Manhattan distance
3	Hill Climbing Search	Each algorithm is evaluated based on its completeness, optimality, time complexity and space complexity.
4	Best First Search	
5	Uniform cost search	
6	A* Search	

6.7 Non-Cooperative Games

In this part, a discussion on "How the computer can play and decide on its moves" takes place in the class.

The students are exposed to the idea that an opponent in a game chooses the best possible move s/he can make, and which is the worst move for the player in the algorithms presented in Table 7. The students implement the minmax algorithm in a given Tic Tack Toe game for two human players.

The game is prepared by the teacher in DrRacket computational workspace and the students replace one of the human players with a computer player. During implementation of the algorithm the students cope with changes in a complete program:

1. Understand the code written by someone else;

2. Write an alternative code fragment;

3. Make the adjustments necessary to incorporate the piece written instead of an existing code section.

Table 7. Non-cooperative games: topics & subtopics

	Topic	Sub topics
1	Game design as a system of two agents	
2	Tree game definition	
3	Game Tree Search	• Minmax algorithm • Minmax algorithm for games involving random (roll of the dice) • Alpha beta pruning.

6.8 Introduction to Machine Learning

According to Smith, [10], learning is quantitative increase in knowledge, storing information that can be reproduced, acquiring facts, skills, and methods that can be retained and used for the interpreting and understanding of reality in a different way. In addition, learning involves relating parts of the subject matter to each other and to the real world and comprehending the world by reinterpreting knowledge.

In this part, the students are exposed to the idea that percepts should be used not only for acting, but also for improving ability to act in the future [9, p. 649]. The students get knowledge of inductive learning from observations through the algorithms presented in Table 8. They are referred to U.C.I[6]- machine learning repository website to collect data in order to implement the ID3 (decision tree) learning algorithm [8].

Table 8. Introduction to Machine Learning: topics

	Topic	Sub topics
1	What is learning?	
2	Learning classifier	• Learning decision trees - id3 algorithm • Nearest neighbor algorithm • K closest neighbors algorithm
3	L.M.S algorithm	
4	Genetic algorithms	

6.9 Advanced Topics in Programming Language I

In this section, students expand their practical basis in DrRacket programming language as shown in Table 9. Knowledge is acquired with the aid of worksheets that help students become familiar with the learning material through guided inquiry, followed by discussion and summaries of the material. This method, according to Brunner's teaching model [2], places the responsibility for learning on the learner who learns concepts and ideas independently with only limited involvement on the part of the teacher, thus developing an independent learner.

Table 9. Advanced Topics in Programming Language I

	Topic
1	Flat Lists
2	Progressive list processing
3	Higher-order functions map, filter, reduce
4	Recursion depth
5	Deepening the assembly functions

6.10 Advanced Topics in Programming Language II

The content in this part is acquired through peer teaching. As an example of the deliverables expected from the students later, the teacher presents the first subject (structures) and distributes worksheets on this subject. Students are then divided into groups of 2-3 students. Each group studies one subject from the list shown in Table 10, searches for material on the subject and subject-related activities under guidance from the teacher, presents the subject to the other students in the class and prepares the overall work assignments page on the subject being studied.

Learning from examples (given by the teacher) was selected as a teaching method to illustrate abstract principles, thorough analysis of the example, generalization and abstraction of the example's components, and learning from others' experience. Peer teaching and collaborative learning were selected also since it is highly effective: It develops leadership skills, self-learning, team work, ability to present to an audience and develop learning outcomes (work pages). Group work encourages the transfer of knowledge, and develops discussion skills, an ability to listen to others, including preparing students for the real world [1, 7].

Table 10. Advanced Topics in Programming Language II

	Topic
1	Structures
2	Vectors
3	Files
4	Strings
5	Graphic viewport
6	GUI
7	Streams
8	Lambda expressions
9	Threads

6.11 Final Project

The final project is done individually. The work includes:

1. Implementation of at least a search algorithm and a learning algorithm

2. Small scale research that examines the system performance depending on various parameters of the learning algorithm

3. Graphical interface

4. User interface

5. Project portfolio

While working on the final project, the students fully utilize their personal potential, get experience in decision making, get a thorough understanding of issues arising during the writing of the final project and become active learners. The small-scale research requires coping with how to define of a research question, how to

---

6 http://archive.ics.uci.edu/ml/

propose a hypothesis to research question and check the validity of the hypothesis. Students write projects on a high level, characterized by originality and creativity. Developing the projects enables the students to develop themselves and learn topics outside of the academic program based on their interests. One reason that explains students' success in writing a final project at such a high level is the search algorithms and learning algorithms that have been written by the students throughout the course as mini projects, which prepared them for dealing with the final project. During the writing process, interesting phenomena occur in the class. For example:

- When a student has encountered a problem, s/he requests the teacher's guidance and, in addition, explains the difficulty to students in the class who try to locate the source of the problem and offer him or her ways to cope with it.
- After a student has overcome the difficulties arising during the writing of the project, there is a sense of "eureka – I found it".
- Students express great interest in each other's projects – even where no particularly difficulties are encountered. Private discussions take place on how to improve visual presentation, what can be added, how to improve performance, and so on.

7. CONCLUSION

To summarize, we are very satisfied with the material we teach in this advanced course. We have succeeded in adapting academic material to the needs of high-school students. Our students have dealt successfully with complicated algorithms that we think are even difficult for undergraduate students. We motivated our students to continue research in artificial intelligence and machine learning contents according to their ability.

Students' interest in the material and their will to develop projects at a higher level contributed to the improvement of the course. We plan to continue updating the contents learned and adjust it to our students.

Finally, we strongly believe that each student participating in this course improves his or her abilities.

8. ACKNOWLEDGMENTS

We would like to acknowledge the valuable contributions made by our advisor, Associate Professor Orit Hazzan. We wish also to thank Dr. Tami Lapidot, for her advice and support. Special thanks to Associate Professor Shaul Markovitch, for helping us recognize the domain and decide on the course content. We would like to thank also the Leo Baeck high school management: the CEO, Mr. Dan Fesler, former head of pedagogical department, Dr. Esti Schleyer, and former high school director, Mrs. Yona Katzir, for allowing us to carry out this unique advanced course, Finally, we would like to thank to Dr. Avi Cohen, Inspector-in-Chief, Computer Science and Information Technology, Ministry of Education, Israel, for giving us the formal permission to teach the course.

9. APPENDICES

9.1 Appendix A

This letter was written by a graduate student of the advanced course in Leo Baeck during his military service in one of the elite units of the intelligence corps. This unit recruits honors students in computer science from all over the country.

Dear Ahuva,
I would like to thank you, once again.

Only now, nearly two years after graduating from high school, I do understand how special the course you taught us was. While I was in high school, I didn't have contact with students from other schools so I didn't know how special the program you taught us was.

I couldn't wait to finish my military service and begin my studies at the Technion, where I had decided to learn computer science with specialization in artificial intelligence and Robotics.

Since graduating from high school, I have read many books on mathematics, statistics and game theory and I thank you again for revealing to me the fascinating area of artificial intelligence. In the near future I plan to rewrite the Checkers game I wrote in high school in Java language in order to improve efficiency.

These days, I am developing a minimax engine with some interesting add-ons, a generic engine that can be incorporated into zero-sum games, and hope to distribute it to a code-sharing site so that it can be developed by programmers from all over the world.

I hope to continue learning these subjects and do research by my own.

9.2 Appendix B

The following statements represent opinions of graduate students about the contribution of functional programming to their skills.

- I was exposed to a new way of thinking that was a little difficult at first. Over time I understood better this way of thinking. I enjoyed very much learning with the new programming language and I developed my ability to think.
- Project - I did it!!! I have learned to deal with things and not give up.
- I felt that I gained more from functional programming. ... I have developed my functional and logical thinking.
- I love this programming style because it makes me think, inquire, and improve my abstract logical thinking.

10. REFERENCES

[1] Brown, J. and Dobbie, G., (1999). Supporting and evaluating team dynamics in group projects. In the proceedings of the thirtieth *SIGCSE technical symposium on computer science education* ACM Press.

[2] Bruner, J. S., (1966). *Toward A Theory of Instruction*, W.W. Novton & company, NY.

[3] Computer Science and Information Technology Web site, Curricula (in Hebrew), http://www.csit.org.il/default.aspx?MenuShow=DOCS&Doc_ID=55

[4] David L. Parker (2003) Machine "learning" at all course levels, *Journal of Computing Sciences in Colleges* **18**(3).

[5] Gal-Ezer, J., Beeri, C., Harel, D. and Yehudai, A. (1995). A high-school program in Computer Science, *Computer* **28**(10), pp. 73-80.

[6] Leo Baeck Education Center Web site http://www.leobaeck.org.il/

[7] Koppelman, H., van Dijk, E.M.A.G., van der Mast, C.P.A.G., and van der Veer, G.C. (2000). Team projects in distance education: A case in HCI design. Proc. *ITiCSE 2000*. 97-100.

[8] Mitchel, Tom (1997). Machine Learning. McGraw Hill

[9] Russell, S. and Norvig, P. (1995). *Artificial Intelligence A Modern Approach.* Prentice Hall.

[10] Smith, M. K. (2003) 'Learning theory', the encyclopedia of informal education, www.infed.org/biblio/b-learn.htm

An Interactive Functional Programming Tutor

Alex Gerdes
School of Computer Science,
Open Universiteit Nederland
alex.gerdes@ou.nl

Johan Jeuring
Department of Information and
Computing Sciences,
Utrecht University
J.T.Jeuring@uu.nl

Bastiaan Heeren
School of Computer Science,
Open Universiteit Nederland
bastiaan.heeren@ou.nl

ABSTRACT

We introduce an interactive tutor that supports the stepwise development of simple functional programs. Using this tutor, students receive feedback about whether or not they are on the right track, can ask for a hint when they are stuck, and get suggestions about how to refactor their program. Our tutor generates this semantically rich feedback from model solutions, using advanced concepts from software technology. We show how a teacher can add an exercise to the tutor, and fine-tune feedback. We report on an experiment in which we used our tutor.

Categories and Subject Descriptors

K.3.1 [**Computer Uses in Education**]: Computer-assisted instruction (CAI); K.3.2 [**Computer and Information Science Education**]: Computer science education

General Terms

Languages, Human Factors, Measurement

Keywords

Functional programming, Haskell, tutoring

1. INTRODUCTION

Introductory functional programming courses often start with distinguishing the various steps a student has to take to write a program. A teacher usually explains by example how to develop a program: give the main function a name; if the function takes an argument, give the argument a name; if the value of the argument determines the action to be taken subsequently, analyse the argument, and depending on the form of the argument, develop the appropriate right-hand sides, etc. Once a student starts developing a program herself, in a lab session or at home, this kind of explanatory help is usually not present. Moreover, giving immediate help to large classes of students is almost always impossible. Especially beginning programmers are often at a loss about how to proceed when developing a program. We introduce an interactive tutor that supports the stepwise development of simple functional programs in the lazy, pure, higher-order functional programming language Haskell [19]. Using this tutor, students learning functional programming develop their programs incrementally, receive feedback about whether or not they are on the right track, can ask for a hint when they are stuck, and get suggestions about how to refactor their program. The interactive tutor gives hints at each step, generates worked-out solutions for exercises, and recognises common errors made by students. All of this functionality is calculated automatically from the teacher-specified annotated solutions and non-solutions for a problem.

To support learning programming, many intelligent tutoring programs have been developed. There exist intelligent tutors for Prolog [11], Lisp [1], Pascal [13], Java [23], Haskell [15], and many more programming languages. Evaluation studies have indicated that

- working with an intelligent tutor supporting the construction of programs is more effective when learning how to program than doing the same exercise "on your own" using only a compiler, or just pen-and-paper [5],
- using intelligent tutors requires less help from a teacher while showing the same performance on tests [18],
- using such tutors increases the self-confidence of female students [14],
- the immediate feedback given by many of the tutors is to be preferred over the delayed feedback common in classroom settings [17].

Despite the evidence for positive effects of using intelligent programming tutors, they are not widely used. An important reason is that building an intelligent tutor for a programming language is difficult and a substantial amount of work [20]. Some of these tutors are well-developed and extensively tested in classrooms, but most haven't outgrown the research prototype phase, and are not maintained anymore. Furthermore, deploying an intelligent tutor in a course is often hard for a teacher [2]. Most teachers want to adapt or extend an intelligent programming tutor to their needs. Adding an exercise to a tutor requires investigating which strategies can be used to solve the exercise, what the possible solutions are, and how the tutor should react to behaviour that doesn't follow the desired path. All this knowledge then has to be translated into the internals of the tutor, which

ITiCSE'12, July 3–5, 2012, Haifa, Israel.

implies a substantial amount of work. Other tutors have a fixed set of exercises, or enforce a strict order in which a program is constructed.

Our tutor is built on top of the Helium compiler for Haskell [10], which gives excellent syntax-error and type-error messages, and reports dependency analysis problems in a clear way. The most interesting feature of our tutor is that the hints and feedback given at intermediate steps are derived automatically from teacher-specified annotated solutions and non-solutions for a problem. This reduces the work required for using the tutor, and allows a teacher to use her favourite exercises. Furthermore, the order in which a student constructs a program using our tutor is quite flexible. The tutor is offered as a web application[1], which further reduces the burden to use it.

This paper describes a tutor that supports the step-wise, flexible development of simple functional programs, giving feedback and hints at intermediate steps, and showing worked-out examples. We make the following contributions:

- The feedback and hints are calculated automatically from teacher-specified annotated solutions for a problem.
- It discusses results of an experiment in which we used the tutor in a class-room setting.

This paper is organised as follows. Section 2 introduces our interactive functional programming tutor by means of an example session. Section 3 shows what a teacher has to do to add a programming exercises to the tutor. Section 4 discusses the result of using our tutor with a class of beginning functional programming students. Related and future work is discussed in Section 5, and Section 6 concludes.

2. AN INTERACTIVE SESSION

This section introduces our intelligent functional programming tutor by means of some interactions of a hypothetical student with the tutor. We assume that the student has visited lectures on how to write simple functional programs on lists.

The teacher has set a couple of exercises from the Ninety-nine Haskell Problems[2], in particular problem 22: Create a list containing all integers within a given range. We now show a couple of possible scenarios in which a student interacts with the tutor to solve this problem. At the start of a tutoring session the tutor gives a problem description:

```
Write a function that creates a list with all
integers between a given range:
```

$range :: Int \to Int \to [Int]$

```
For example:
```

$> range\ 4\ 9$
$[4,5,6,7,8,9]$

and displays the name of the function to be defined, along with its parameters:

$range\ x\ y = \bullet$

[1]http://ideas.cs.uu.nl/ProgTutor/

[2]http://www.haskell.org/haskellwiki/99_Haskell_exercises

The task of a student is to refine the holes, denoted by •, of the program. A student can use such holes to defer the refinement of parts of the program. After each refinement, a student can ask the tutor whether or not the refinement is bringing him or her closer to a correct solution, or, if the student doesn't know how to proceed, ask the tutor for a hint. Besides holes, a student can also introduce new declarations, function bindings, and alternatives.

Suppose the student has no idea where to start and asks the tutor for help. The tutor offers several ways to help. For example, it can list all possible ways to proceed solving an exercise. In this case, the tutor would respond with:

```
You can proceed in several ways:
- Implement range using the unfoldr function.
- Use the enumeration function from the
prelude[3].
- Use the prelude functions take and iterate.
```

We assume a student has some means to obtain information about functions and concepts that are mentioned in the feedback given by the tutor. This information might be obtained via lectures, an assistant, lecture notes, or even via the tutor at some later stage. The tutor can make a choice between the different possibilities, so if the student doesn't want to choose, and just wants a single hint, she gets:

```
Implement range using the unfoldr function.
```

Here we assume that the teacher has set up the tutor to prefer the solution that uses *unfoldr*, defined by:

$$\begin{aligned}
&unfoldr &&:: (b \to Maybe\ (a,b)) \to b \to [a]\\
&unfoldr\ f\ b &&= \mathbf{case}\ f\ b\ \mathbf{of}\\
& && \quad Just\ (a,b') \to a : unfoldr\ f\ b'\\
& && \quad Nothing \quad\ \to [\,]
\end{aligned}$$

The higher-order function *unfoldr* builds a list from a seed value, the second argument b. The first argument f is a producer function that takes the seed element and returns *Nothing* if it is done producing the list, or returns $Just\ (a, b')$, in which case, a is prepended to the output list and b' is used as the argument in the recursive call.

The student can ask for more detailed information at this point, and the tutor responds with increasing detail:

```
Define function range in terms of unfoldr,
which takes two arguments: a seed value, and
a function that produces a new value.
```

with the final bottom-out hint:

`Define:` $range\ x\ y = unfoldr\ \bullet\ \bullet$

At this point, the student can refine the function at two positions. In this exercise we do not impose an order on the sequence of refinements. However, the tutor offers a teacher the possibility to enforce a particular order of refinements. Suppose that the student chooses to first implement the producer function:

$$\begin{aligned}
&range\ x\ y = unfoldr\ f\ \bullet\\
&\quad \mathbf{where}\ f\ i \mid \bullet = \bullet
\end{aligned}$$

[3]The prelude is the standard library for Haskell containing many useful functions.

Note that the student has started to define the producer function in a **where** clause. She continues with the introduction of the stop criterion:

$$\begin{aligned}&\mathit{range}\ x\ y = \mathit{unfoldr}\ f\ \bullet\\&\quad \textbf{where}\ f\ i\ |\ i == y+1 = \bullet\end{aligned}$$

There are several ways in Haskell to implement a condition. Here the student has chosen to define the function f with a so-called guarded expression; the predicate after the vertical bar acts as a guard. The student continues with:

$$\begin{aligned}&\mathit{range}\ x\ y = \mathit{unfoldr}\ f\ \bullet\\&\quad \textbf{where}\ f\ i\ |\ i == y+1 = \mathit{Just}\ \bullet\end{aligned}$$

The tutor responds with:

```
Unexpected right hand side of f on line 3
```

Here the tutor indicates that the partial definition of f does not match any of the model solutions. Correcting the error, the student enters:

$$\begin{aligned}&\mathit{range}\ x\ y = \mathit{unfoldr}\ f\ \bullet\\&\quad \textbf{where}\ f\ i\ |\ i == y+1 = \mathit{Nothing}\end{aligned}$$

which is accepted by the tutor. If the student now asks for a hint, the tutor responds with:

```
Introduce a guarded expression that gives the
output value and the value for the next
iteration.
```

She continues with

$$\begin{aligned}&\mathit{range}\ x\ y = \mathit{unfoldr}\ f\ \bullet\\&\quad \textbf{where}\ f\ i\ |\ i == y+1 = \mathit{Nothing}\\&\qquad\qquad\quad |\ \mathit{otherwise} = \mathit{Just}\ \bullet\end{aligned}$$

which is accepted, and then

$$\begin{aligned}&\mathit{range}\ x\ y = \mathit{unfoldr}\ f\ \bullet\\&\quad \textbf{where}\ f\ i\ |\ i == y+1 = \mathit{Nothing}\\&\qquad\qquad\quad |\ \mathit{otherwise} = \mathit{Just}\ (n, i+1)\end{aligned}$$

which gives:

```
Error: undefined variable n
```

This is an error message generated by the compiler. Our tutor displays the syntax and type errors messages generated by Helium. The student continues with:

$$\begin{aligned}&\mathit{range}\ x\ y = \mathit{unfoldr}\ f\ x\\&\quad \textbf{where}\ f\ i\ |\ i == y+1 = \mathit{Nothing}\\&\qquad\qquad\quad |\ \mathit{otherwise} = \mathit{Just}\ (i, i+1)\end{aligned}$$

which completes the exercise:

```
You have correctly solved the exercise.
```

A student can develop a program in any order, as long as all variables are bound. For example, a student can write

$$\begin{aligned}&\mathit{range}\ x\ y = \bullet\\&\quad \textbf{where}\ f\ i\ |\ \bullet = \bullet\end{aligned}$$

and then proceed with defining f. This way, bottom-up developing a program is supported to some extent.

These interactions show that our tutor can:

- give hints about which step to take next, in various levels of detail,
- list all possible ways in which to proceed,
- point out errors, and where the error appears to be,
- show a complete worked-out example.

The next section shows what a teacher has to do to achieve the functionality of the tutor as described in this section.

3. SPECIFYING EXERCISES

The interactions of the tutor are based on *model solutions* to programming problems. A model solution is a program that an expert writes, using good programming practices. A teacher adds a programming exercise to the tutor by specifying such model solutions. For our running example of calculating a range, we have specified three model solutions. The first model solution uses the enumeration notation from Haskell's prelude:

$$\mathit{range}\ x\ y = [x\,..\,y]$$

The second model solution uses the prelude functions *take* and *iterate*:

$$\mathit{range}\ x\ y = \mathit{take}\ (y - x + 1)\ (\mathit{iterate}\ (+1)\ x)$$

The prelude function *iterate* returns an infinite list in which the next element is calculated by applying a given function, in this case a function that increases its argument by one, to the previous element, starting with a given value (x). The function *take* n returns the first n elements of a list. The last model solution uses the higher-order function *unfoldr* introduced in Section 2:

$$\begin{aligned}&\mathit{range}\ x\ y = \mathit{unfoldr}\ f\ x\\&\quad \textbf{where}\ f\ i\ |\ i == y+1 = \mathit{Nothing}\\&\qquad\qquad\quad |\ \mathit{otherwise} = \mathit{Just}\ (i, i+1)\end{aligned}$$

The tutor uses these model solutions to generate feedback. We not only recognise the exact specified model solution, but many variants. For example, although it appears entirely different, the following solution:

$$\begin{aligned}&\mathit{range}\ x\ y =\\&\quad \textbf{let}\ f = \lambda a \rightarrow \textbf{if}\ a == y+1\\&\qquad\qquad\qquad\qquad \textbf{then}\ \mathit{Nothing}\\&\qquad\qquad\qquad\qquad \textbf{else}\ \mathit{Just}\ (a, a+1)\\&\qquad\quad g = \lambda f\ x \rightarrow \textbf{case}\ f\ x\ \textbf{of}\\&\qquad\qquad\qquad\qquad \mathit{Just}\ (r, b) \rightarrow r : g\ f\ b\\&\qquad\qquad\qquad\qquad \mathit{Nothing} \quad\ \rightarrow [\,]\\&\quad \textbf{in}\ g\ f\ x\end{aligned}$$

is recognised from the third model solution. To achieve this, we not only recognise the usage of a prelude function, such as *unfoldr*, but also its definition.

We use techniques and concepts from software technology, such as parsing, rewriting, and program transformations, to calculate semantically rich feedback [9]. In a nutshell, our approach is as follows [12]: we derive a *programming strategy* from the set of model solutions. This programming strategy is used to generate many variants of the model solutions. Before we compare a student solution to the solutions from the strategy, we normalise all solutions using program transformations. In this normalisation procedure we, for example, rewrite a **where**-clause into a **let**-expression.

3.1 Adapting feedback

It is important that a teacher can easily adapt the feedback given to a student. Our tutor offers the possibility to fine-tune the generated feedback by means of *annotating* model solutions. The remainder of this section shows a number of such annotations, accompanied with an explanation.

A description of a particular model solution can be added to the source code using the following construction:

$\{-\#$ *DESC Implement range using the unfoldr...* $\#-\}$

The first hint in Section 2 gives the descriptions for the three model solutions for the range exercise. Next to a description for a single model solution, we can also give a description of the entire exercise. This description is given together with the model solutions in a configuration file for the exercise.

Another way to adapt the feedback is by specifying an *alternative* implementation for a prelude function. For example, the specification below shows how to give an alternative implementation for the *iterate* prelude function:

$\{-\#\ ALT$
$\quad iterate\ f = unfoldr\ (\lambda x \rightarrow Just\ (x, f\ x))\ \#-\}$

Using this annotation we not only recognise the prelude definition ($iterate\ f\ x = x : iterate\ f\ (f\ x)$), but also the alternative implementation given here. By adding an alternative a teacher expands the number of accepted solutions and therefore changes the way in which the tutor gives feedback. Alternatives give the teacher partial control over which program variants are allowed.

Besides adding alternatives to expand the number of accepted solutions, a teacher may want to emphasise one particular implementation method. For example, a teacher may want to enforce the use of higher-order functions and prohibit their explicit recursive definitions. The *MUSTUSE* construction allows a teacher to disable the recognition of the definition of a prelude function:

$range\ x\ y = \{-\#\ MUSTUSE\ \#-\}\ unfoldr\ f\ x$

Another way to modify the response of the tutor is to add specific feedback messages at particular locations in the source code. For example:

$range\ x\ y =$
$\quad \{-\#\ FEEDBACK\ Note...\ \#-\}\ take\ (y - x + 1)\ \$$
$\quad\quad iterate\ (+1)\ x$

Thus we give a detailed description of the *take* function. These feedback messages are organised in a hierarchy based on the abstract syntax tree of the model solution. This enables the teacher to configure the tutor to give feedback messages with an increasing level of detail.

Adding an exercise to our tutor is relatively easy. To support managing exercises, they can be arranged in *classes*. Using a class a teacher groups together exercises, for example for practicing list problems, collecting exercises of the same difficulty, or exercises from a particular textbook.

4. EXPERIMENTAL RESULTS

We have used our functional programming tutor in a course on functional programming for bachelor students at Utrecht University in September 2011. The course attracted more than 200 students. Around a hundred of these students have used our tutor in two sessions in the second week of the course after three lectures. 40 students filled out a questionnaire about the tutor, and we collected remarks at the lab session in which the students used the tutor. Table 1 shows the questions and the average of the answers on a Likert scale from 1 to 5. The first seven questions are related and indicate how satisfied a student is with the tutor. The last question addresses how students value the difficulty of the offered exercises.

The goal of the experiment is to analyse if students appreciate our approach, such as giving feedback on intermediate answers. The experiment does not check whether or not the tutor is more effective or efficient from a learning point of view. We hope to study this in the future.

Reflection on the scores.

The scoring shows that the students particularly like the worked-out solution feedback. A worked-out solution presents a complete, step-wise, construction of a program. Furthermore, the kind of exercises are as expected by the students. The results also show that the step-size used by the tutor does not correspond to the intuition of the student. We noticed this already during the experiment. The students often took larger steps than that the tutor was able to handle.

The average of the first seven question gives an overall score of the tutor of 3,4 out of 5. This is maybe sufficient, but there clearly is room for improvement.

4.1 Evaluation

In addition to questions about the usage of the tutor, the questionnaire contained a number of general questions, such as

1. We offer the feedback services: *strategy hint*, *step hint*, *step*, *all steps*, *solution*, and we check the program submitted by the student. Do you think we should offer more or different feedback services?
2. Do you have any other remarks, concerns, or ideas about our programming tutor?

The answers from the students to the first question indicate that the current services are adequate. We received some interesting suggestions on how to improve our tutor in response to the second open question. The remarks that appear most are:

- Some solutions are not recognised by the tutor
- The response of the tutor is sometimes too slow

The first remark may indicate that a student believes her own solution is correct, where in fact this might not be true. It could well be that the program is incorrect or contains imperfections, such as being inefficient, and hence is rejected by our tutor. This remark addresses the fact that we cannot give feedback on a student program that deviates from a path towards one of the model solutions. When a student program deviates from a path towards a model solution there are three possibilities. First, the student program is incorrect. We should be able to detect this and give a counterexample. At the moment our tutor cannot do this, but we are working onincorporating testing, based on the QuickCheck [3] library. Second, the student program is correct and uses desirable programming techniques, but

#	Question	Score
1	The tutor helped me to understand how to write simple functional programs	3,15
2	I found the high-level hints about how to solve a programming problem useful	3,43
3	I found the hints about the next step to take useful	3,05
4	The step-size of the tutor corresponded to my intuition	2,85
5	I found the possibility to see the complete solution useful	4,25
6	The worked-out solutions helped me to understand how to construct programs	3,55
7	The feedback texts are easy to understand	3,25
8	The kind of exercises offered are suitable for a first functional programming course	3,90

Table 1: Questionnaire: questions and scores.

our tutor rejects it. In this case the set of model solutions should be extended with this solution. Third, the student program is functionally correct but contains some imperfections, such as, for example, a clumsy way of calculating the length of a list xs: $length\ (x : xs) - 1$. The tutor cannot conclude that a student program contains imperfections when it passes the tests but deviates from the strategy, so it cannot give a definitive judgement. However, after using an exercise in the tutor for a while, and updating the tutor whenever we find an improvement, it is likely that the set of model solutions is complete, and therefore unlikely that a student comes up with a new model solution. Therefore, in this particular case we can give feedback that a student program probably has some undesired properties. We have used our approach for assessment of functional programming exercises [7], in which we could recognise almost 90% of the correct solutions based on only five model solutions. All of the other 10% of the correct solutions had some imperfections.

The second remark is related to the step-size supported by the tutor. When a student takes a large step, the tutor has to check many possibilities, due to the flexibility that our tutor offers. We have already addressed this problem and in the current version of the tutor it is not an issue anymore. We solved this problem by introducing a special search mode when recognising large steps.

In addition to the above experiment, we also asked a number of functional programming experts from the IFIP WG 2.1 group[4] and student participants of the Central European Functional Programming (CEFP 2011) summer school to fill out a questionnaire. We asked for input about some of the design choices we made in our tutor, such as giving hints in three levels of increasing specificity. Both the experts as well as the students support most of the choices we made. The main suggestion we got for adding extra services/functionality was to give concrete counterexamples using testing for semantically incorrect solutions. This suggestion corresponds to our own interpretation of the results from the experiment, and will be addressed in future work.

5. RELATED AND FUTURE WORK

There is a wealth of related work on intelligent programming tutors. We have not found other tutors that support the step-wise development of programs, automatically calculating feedback based on teacher-specified annotated solutions and non-solutions.

If ever the computer science education research field [6] finds an answer to the question of what makes programming hard, and how programming environments can support learning how to program, it is likely to depend on the age, interests, major subject, motivation, and background knowledge of a student. Programming environments for novices come in many variants, and for many programming languages or paradigms [8]. Programming environments like Scratch [21] and Alice [4] target younger students than we do, and emphasise the importance of constructing software with a strong visual component, with which students can develop software to which they can relate. We target beginning computer science students, who expect to work with real-life programming languages.

The Lisp tutor [1] is an intelligent tutoring system that supports the incremental construction of Lisp programs. At any point in the development a student can only take a single next step, which makes the interaction style of the tutor a bit restrictive. Furthermore, adding new material to the tutor is still quite some work. Using our approach, the interaction style becomes flexible, and adding exercises becomes relatively easy. Soloway [22] describes programming plans for constructing Lisp programs. These plans are instances of the higher-order function *foldr* and its companions. Our work structures the plans described by Soloway.

In tutoring systems for Prolog, a number of strategies for Prolog programming have been developed [11]. Strategies are matched against complete student solutions, and feedback is given after solving the exercise. We expect that these strategies can be translated to our situation, and can be reused for a programming language like Haskell.

Our work resembles the top-down Pascal editors developed in the Genie project [16]. These series of editors provide structure editing support, so that a student does not have to remember the particular syntax of a programming language. In our case students do have to write programs using the syntax of Haskell, but the intermediate steps are comparable. The Genie editors did not offer strategical support.

Our functional programming tutor grew out of a program assessment tool, which automatically assesses student programs based on model solutions [7] and program transformations to rewrite programs to normal form. Similar transformations have been developed for C++-like languages [24].

In the next couple of months we will add testing capabilities to our tutor. In addition to testing the student solution

[4]`http://www.cs.uu.nl/wiki/bin/view/IFIP21/WebHome`

against a model solution, we plan to offer the possibility to specify *properties*. A property is a statement that should always hold, and allows us to validate model solutions. For our running example, the following property states that the size of the generated list by *range x y* is equal to $y - x + 1$:

$$\{-\# \; PROP \\ prop\_range \; x \; y = \\ x \leqslant y \Longrightarrow length\ (range\ x\ y) == y - x + 1 \; \#-\}$$

Furthermore, we will extend the set of supported exercises. Once the tutor is sufficiently mature, we will add a service for teachers to upload their own annotated solutions and non-solutions.

6. CONCLUSIONS

We have introduced an intelligent tutor that supports the step-wise development of simple functional programs. A student can develop a program in many different ways. Our tutor automatically calculates hints and feedback at intermediate development steps from teacher-specified annotated solutions and non-solutions for a problem. This reduces the work required for using the tutor, and allows a teacher to use her favourite exercises.

We have conducted an experiment in which around a hundred students worked with our functional programming tutor. Furthermore, we asked functional programming experts about the design choices we made. The main conclusions of these two investigations are:

- Students appreciate worked-out solutions, and are moderately positive about the tutor.
- We need to judge student programs even when a student deviates from the model solutions. Therefore, we need to extend our tutor with testing capabilities.

Acknowledgements.

We thank Andres Löh and Doaitse Swierstra for allowing us to perform an experiment with our tutor in their classes. Furthermore, we thank Bram Vaessen for analysing the scores of our questionnaire.

References

[1] J. R. Anderson, F. G. Conrad, and A. T. Corbett. Skill acquisition and the LISP tutor. *Cognitive Science*, 13:467–505, 1986.

[2] J. R. Anderson, A. T. Corbett, K. R. Koedinger, and R. Pelletier. Cognitive tutors: lessons learned. *The Journal of the learning sciences*, 4(2):167–207, 1995.

[3] K. Claessen and J. Hughes. QuickCheck: A lightweight tool for random testing of Haskell programs. In *Proceedings of ICFP 2000: International Conference on Functional Programming*, 2000.

[4] M. J. Conway. *Alice: Easy-To-Learn 3D Scripting For Novices*. PhD thesis, University of Virginia, 1997.

[5] A. T. Corbett, J. R. Anderson, and E. J. Patterson. Problem compilation and tutoring flexibility in the Lisp tutor. In *Proceedings ITS'88: Intelligent Tutoring Systems*, pages 423–429, 1988.

[6] S. Fincher and M. Petre, editors. *Computer Science Education Research*. Routledge Falmer, 2004.

[7] A. Gerdes, J. Jeuring, and B. Heeren. Using strategies for assessment of programming exercises. In *SIGCSE*, pages 441–445, 2010.

[8] M. Guzdial. Programming environments for novices. In S. Fincher and M. Petre, editors, *Computer Science Education Research*. Routledge Falmer, 2004.

[9] B. Heeren, J. Jeuring, and A. Gerdes. Specifying rewrite strategies for interactive exercises. *Mathematics in Computer Science*, 3(3):349–370, 2010.

[10] B. Heeren, D. Leijen, and A. v. IJzendoorn. Helium, for learning Haskell. In *Haskell 2003: Proceedings of the 2003 ACM SIGPLAN workshop on Haskell*, pages 62 – 71. ACM, 2003.

[11] J. Hong. Guided programming and automated error analysis in an intelligent Prolog tutor. *International Journal on Human-Computer Studies*, 61(4):505–534, 2004.

[12] J. Jeuring, A. Gerdes, and B. Heeren. A programming tutor for Haskell. In *Proceedings of CEFP 2011: Lecture Notes of the Central European School on Functional Programming*, LNCS. Springer, 2011.

[13] W. L. Johnson and E. Soloway. Proust: Knowledge-based program understanding. *IEEE Transactions on Software Engineering*, 11(3):267–275, 1985.

[14] A. N. Kumar. The effect of using problem-solving software tutors on the self-confidence of female students. In *SIGCSE 2008: Proceedings of the 39th SIGCSE technical symposium on Computer science education*, pages 523–527. ACM, 2008.

[15] N. López, M. Núñez, I. Rodríguez, and F. Rubio. WHAT: Web-based Haskell adaptive tutor. In *AIMSA 2002: Proceedings of the 10th International Conference on Artificial Intelligence: Methodology, Systems, and Applications*, pages 71–80. Springer-Verlag, 2002.

[16] P. Miller, J. Pane, G. Meter, and S. Vorthmann. Evolution of Novice Programming Environments: The Structure Editors of Carnegie Mellon University. *Interactive Learning Environments*, 4(2):140–158, 1994.

[17] E. Mory. Feedback research revisited. In D. Jonassen, editor, *Handbook of research for educational communications and technology*, 2003.

[18] E. Odekirk-Hash and J. L. Zachary. Automated feedback on programs means students need less help from teachers. In *SIGCSE 2001: Proceedings of the 32nd SIGCSE technical symposium on Computer Science Education*, pages 55–59. ACM, 2001.

[19] S. Peyton Jones et al. *Haskell 98, Language and Libraries. The Revised Report*. Cambridge University Press, 2003. A special issue of the Journal of Functional Programming.

[20] N. Pillay. Developing intelligent programming tutors for novice programmers. *SIGCSE Bull.*, 35(2):78–82, 2003.

[21] M. Resnick et al. Scratch: programming for all. *Commun. ACM*, 52:60–67, Nov. 2009.

[22] E. Soloway. From problems to programs via plans: the content and structure of knowledge for introductory LISP programming. *Journal of Educational Computing Research*, 1(2):157–172, 1985.

[23] E. Sykes and F. Franek. A prototype for an intelligent tutoring system for students learning to program in Java. *Advanced Technology for Learning*, 1(1), 2004.

[24] S. Xu and Y. S. Chee. Transformation-based diagnosis of student programs for programming tutoring systems. *IEEE Transansactions on Software Engineering*, 29(4):360–384, 2003.

V-Lab: A Cloud-based Virtual Laboratory Platform for Hands-On Networking Courses

Le Xu, Dijiang Huang, Wei-Tek Tsai
School of Computing, Informatics, and Decision Systems Engineering
Ira A. Fulton School of Engineering
Arizona State University, Tempe AZ 85281
{le.xu, dijiang, wtsai}@asu.edu

ABSTRACT

For computer-network education, hands-on laboratories are essential in addition to lectures. Existing laboratory solutions are usually expensive to build, configure and maintain, while still lacking reusability, flexibility and scalability. This paper presents a cloud-based virtual laboratory education solution, called V-Lab, where instructors can use an interactive web GUI to configure computer network testbeds based on a set of dedicated virtual computers interconnected through VLAN-based virtual networks. The established virtual network system can be accessed by students via remote access using standard Secure Shell (SSH), Virtual Network Computing (VNC), or Remote Desktop Protocol (RDP). By using a flexible and re-configurable design, V-Lab greatly reduces the effort needed to establish and maintain a physical laboratory, while providing a secure and reliable environment that encourages students to use the resources based on their own schedule. V-Lab also helps re-design laboratory curriculum to focus on six educational factors, and the survey results show that V-Lab system is easy to use and setup and has satisfactory performance and reliability. It is also indicated that V-Lab helps students understand and solve real-world problems with sufficient laboratory resources and improved efficiency.

Categories and Subject Descriptors

J.1 [**COMPUTER APPLICATIONS**]: Administrative Data Processing—*Education*; K.3.1 [**COMPUTERS AND EDUCATION**]: Computer Uses in Education

General Terms

Experimentation

Keywords

Hands-on Laboratory, Computer Networks, Virtual Cloud Computing

1. INTRODUCTION

Hands-on laboratories are essential in computer network education. A good laboratory environment needs to be highly flexible and configurable to simulate a wide range of computer networks for experimentation. However, it is difficult for educational organizations to keep up with this complex and ever-changing area as computers and communication technologies keep on evolving.

Cloud-based virtual computing has received significant attention recently. It provides enormous and flexible computing power so that one system can satisfy different requirements with optimized computation and resources. This paper presents a cloud-based resource and service sharing platform for hands-on networking laboratory design, called V-Lab. It is built on top of Xen Virtualization [1] and Virtual LAN (VLAN) [2], which serves as a cost-effective, highly scalable and customizable Infrastructure-as-a-Service (IaaS) cloud platform where students and instructors can create, configure, perform and monitor laboratory resources via Web, SSH, VNC and RDP. Our main contributions are:

• We use Xen and VLAN to implement a cloud-based virtual resource sharing and configuring platform that provides laboratory computers using Xen Virtual computing and laboratory networks using VLANs. The virtual resources are dedicated to each student and isolated from other student's resources, providing a secure and private laboratory environment throughout the curriculum.

• We use ASP.NET, MSSQL and JavaScript to develop an interactive web 2.0 interface for V-Lab platform, where instructors and students can dynamically customize and configure laboratory virtual resources anytime throughout the semester. The web interface also helps students communicate with team mates, get support from Instructors, share and demonstrate laboratory works and results with other students.

• We design and refine several laboratory curriculums for computer and network security courses focusing on six educational factors: motivation, knowledge, creativity, collaboration, demonstration and feedback. For each factor, we define a few educational tasks to be performed by students and instructors using V-Lab platform. The re-designed curriculums show satisfactory educational results.

The next section provides a brief comparison between V-Lab and currently available computer network education solutions. Section 3 describes the design considerations and technical details of V-Lab. Section 4 presents the re-designed laboratory curriculums. Section 5 evaluates the survey results of V-Lab. The paper concludes at last.

Table 1: Virtual Laboratories Feature Comparison

Lab Type	Resource Sharing	Virtualization Type	Remote Access	Lab Scheduling	Reconfiguration Level	Private Data	Fidelity	Existing Labs
Physical Lab	Not sharable	None	No	Restricted time & space	Limited & expensive	No	High	[3] [4] [5]
Virtual Application Lab	In-campus sharable	Application-based	Yes	Restricted time	Application-level	No	Low	[6] [7] [8]
Shared-Host Lab	In-campus sharable	Session-based	Yes	Reservation-based & Restricted time	OS-level	No	Low	[9] [10]
Single-VM Lab	Cross-Campus sharable	Shared single-VM	Yes	Reservation-based & Restricted time	VM-level	No	Medium	[11] [12] [13] [14] [15] [16]
Multi-VM & Virtual Network Lab	Geographical multi-site sharable	Dedicated multi-VM & virtual networks	Yes	Unrestricted time or space	VM and Network-level	Yes	High	V-Lab

2. RELATED WORK

There are currently five types of hands-on laboratories among campuses. In this section, we compare V-Lab with existing laboratory solutions that are utilizing virtualization technologies at various extents. The comparison results are shown in Table 1.

• Physical Lab: is built with physical equipments such as routers, switches, hubs, PCs and etc. This type of laboratory can simulate real-world problems but it has drawbacks: (1) Physical equipments are difficult to be reconfigured when laboratory requirements change, therefore it is only useful for classes with similar needs; (2) Usually requires supporting staffs; (3) Students need to schedule laboratory times to share one physical laboratory.

• Virtual Application Laboratory: provides free use of expensive software to campus students via Internet connection. This type of virtualization is limited at application level and it does not allow students to perform system-level laboratory tasks. Moreover, it is stateless so that once the user session restarts, all the previous changes to the software are reset. This is not suitable in the cases where students perform progressive laboratories throughout the semester.

• Shared-Host Lab: provides virtualization with concurrent login sessions on a certain pool of hosts. This type of laboratory usually has limited and fixed computing resources, where students use RDP or VNC to remotely login and perform laboratory tasks. The host is usually shared among multiple concurrent users at same time therefore the types of laboratory task that can be performed are highly restricted. Also since students are sharing same computing hosts, there are potential performance and security issues.

• Single-VM Lab: provides single virtual machine for each student based on pre-defined VM templates. The laboratory is reservation-based and stateless. It also lacks the capacity of dynamically creating new VM templates or customizing existed VM configurations based on user's requirements, making it difficult to work with changing laboratory curriculums. The laboratory provides only single virtual machines to students, which restricts the capacity of simulating real-world problems where complex network topologies and devices are needed.

• Multi-VM & Virtual Network Lab (V-Lab): provides virtualization with multiple VMs and virtual networks based on students' requirements. The Xen and VLAN-based virtualizations provide a dedicated and private pool of resources to each student that can be configured and re-configured as virtually any type of network topologies and devices to simulate a wide range of real-world problems. With geographically multi-site support, the students are provided a global network resource pool, where they can simulate and solve problems at a global perspective. The laboratory also provides a 3-tier SDK on service tier, platform tier and infrastructure tier to laboratory developers and researchers so that they can design more comprehensive laboratory environments utilizing the full potential of cloud computing. With a private resource pool, students can store their own laboratory data without worrying about the data reset after signing off. Moreover, it provides dedicated computing and networking capacities to students so that the performance and security are guaranteed by the cloud.

3. V-LAB SYSTEM DESIGN

In this section, we present the implementation details of key components that build up V-Lab cloud system as shown in Fig. 1.

• Portal Gateway: serves as V-Lab firewall, which helps route web users to V-Lab website as well as logged-in users to their own virtual resources. V-Lab has a public IP so that users can access V-Lab anytime as long as they have Internet.

• Web Server: provides an interactive web interface to users. It works closely with user database to provide a role-based access control on the webpages. The web server also talks to Xen virtualization servers using Xen API calls to execute authorized user operations on the VMs and VLANs. A screenshot of V-Lab website in Fig. 2 illustrates the basic

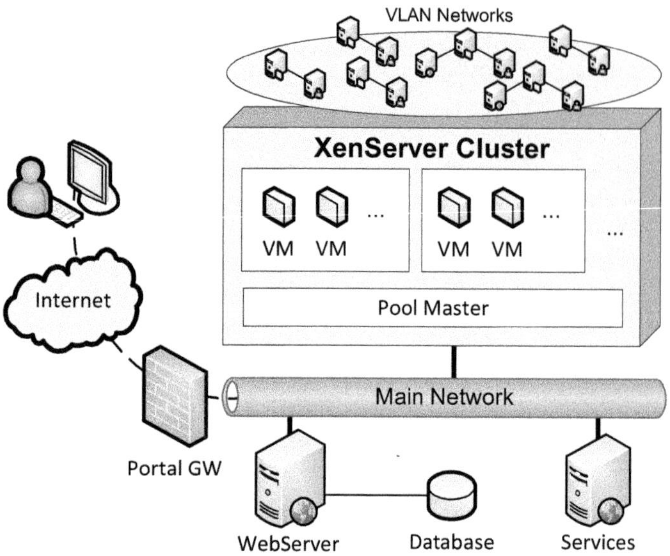

Figure 1: V-Lab System Architecture

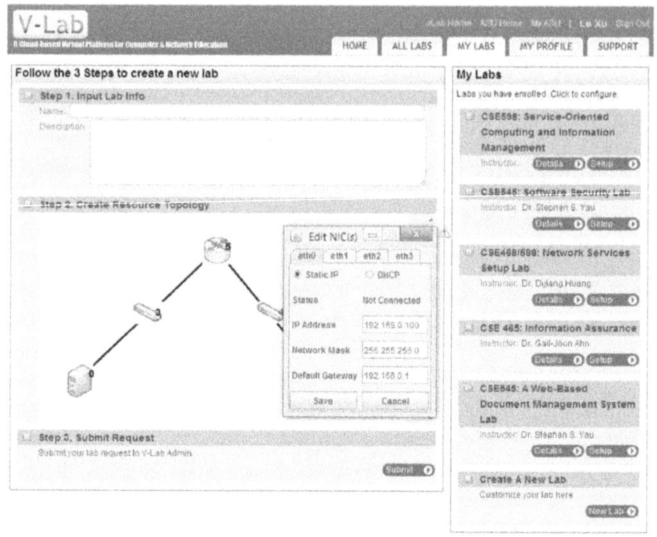

Figure 2: Virtual resource management panel of V-Lab website

features of customizable VMs and VLANs in V-Lab website. On the panel, users are free to create single or multiple VM nodes, configure them as any network devices, interconnect them with VLANs, and configure the IP address for each interface. Once the setup is submitted to V-Lab server, it will handle the request and create each resource for the user. The system will also configure the VLAN interfaces according to user's IP settings. Such mechanism provides a straightforward way for students to practice what they have learnt from computer network course and construct computer networks for laboratory tasks.

- Database: supports web server by providing user's profile and role information. The database also stores detailed specifications of each user's virtual resources for administrative purpose.
- Main Network: is V-Lab internal network, on which all the traffic between users and VMs or web server are handled. The network is protected using various security services and is transparent to end-users.
- V-Lab Server Cluster: contains a set of XenServers and other hardware to support the back-end of V-Lab system. All the VMs and VLANs are created and managed by pool master and hosted in XenServer for running. The cluster is easy to be duplicated and expanded with more laboratories and users. The server also contains a set of NFS storage servers which minimizes the storage footprint by only storing the changes made to VM comparing to its template VM.
- VLANs Network: is implemented with a physical switch with VLAN support. VLANs help isolate private networks from each other by specifying a VLAN tag on the network package. The VLAN functions are managed by Xen system and called from V-Lab website.
- Services: are a set of servers that provide various features for specific laboratories. For example, in computer network security laboratory, instructors usually do not want students to have access to Internet, while still be able to download required software packages. In this case, V-Lab can provide a software package site for the laboratory.

4. LABORATORY CURRICULUM DESIGN

The flexible configuration and web 2.0 capacities of V-Lab system have enabled instructors to extend traditional hands-on experiments with new elements such as more realistic demonstration and laboratory resource sharing. We define 6 factors: motivation, knowledge, creativity, collaboration, demonstration and feedback, which are critical to hands-on laboratories, and re-design several computer network related laboratory curriculums. Table 2 shows the factors and related curriculum design. In this section, we present the curriculum design of 2 laboratories using V-Lab system.

4.1 Computer Network Security Lab

Computer network security is an important area in computer education that helps students learn network foundation, applied cryptography foundation and network security techniques through various network analytic and diagnostic tools. The course at undergraduate level focuses on covering a wide range of network-related topics, providing students an overview of existing network protocols, tools and etc. In 2006, the course was offered to 40 students with lectures and a physical hands-on computer laboratory which had 2 Cisco switches, 40 computers and 2 Ethernet cards on each computer. There are some issues with the physical laboratory: (1) Lots of network security knowledges are confusing to the students who lack the knowledge base of networking. Lectures in classroom can only provide the first level of education: know-that [17]; (2) Setting up a physical computer network hands-on laboratory requires a great deal of investment and is costly to configure and maintain. Each laboratory computer has Ethernet interfaces connecting to 2 Cisco switches. In this way, all the Eth0 of laboratory computers are connected in one network and Eth1 in another one. Due to the restricted number of hardware, students have to schedule time slots to perform laboratories that require multiple computers. Also, since the laboratory only supports 2 networks, the capacity of simulating real-world networking problems is highly limited. Moreover, since no network iso-

Table 2: Lab Factors & Curriculum Design

Lab Factor	Curriculum Design
Motivation	• Instructors publish comprehensive grading criteria; • Importance & usefulness of course projects.
Knowledge	• Knowledge comprehensiveness; • Knowledge relevancy; • Knowledge correctness; • References and supporting materials.
Creativity	• Encouraging students to learn and research more; • Provides customizable virtual resources to students and encourage them to perform their own projects.
Collaboration	• Allow publishing and sharing design documents, components, services with team mates and users; • Allow designing and creating sharable VM and Virtual Network templates to be used by fellow students; • Use peer evaluations to encourage participation and collaboration.
Demonstration	• Construct more realistic demo environments with customized resources.
Feedback	• Allow web-based online survey and feedback; • Project review and discussion board.

lation is provided, a misuse of tools on the laboratory network may affect other computers in the same network. All these physical drawbacks result in compromised education outcomes.

With the above issues in mind, the curriculum was redesigned in 2011 using V-Lab system. A set of laboratories was created to simulate different network situations, one of which was the basic network configuring laboratory (BNCL). In BNCL, we create a dedicated private resource pool for each student that contains 3 VMs and 2 VLANs. Fig. 3 shows the virtual resources created for each student. Additionally, a background learning and a step-by-step laboratory instruction are presented by TA during the 75-minute laboratory time, followed-up with a 1-week laboratory assignment. The knowledges covered by BNCL include: (1) Learn how to perform laboratory tasks by using SSH and VNC clients to remotely access V-Lab VMs; (2) Configure IP address, netmask and gateway on the server, client and gateway VMs using Linux shell command. Specifically, VLAN1 is configured as *192.168.0.0/16* and VLAN2 as *172.16.0.0/16*; (3) Use ping, ifconfig and other commands to verify network settings; (4) Download, install and configure an Apache web server on server VM. Show that client VM cannot access to server VM's web server without a properly configured gateway; (5) Enable IP-Forwarding in gateway VM. Show that client VM can access server VM's website now. In this laboratory, students not only learn basic network knowledges through practicing, but are also encouraged to collaborate and communicate with team mates to construct and configure networks different than the given one. The instructors and TAs also provide online support via V-Lab website.

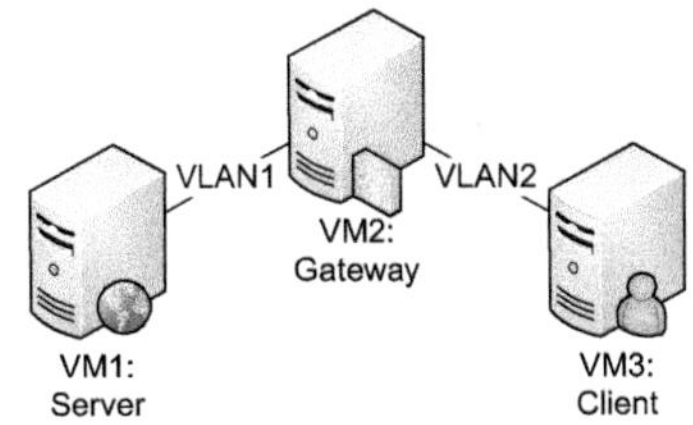

Figure 3: Basic Network configuring Lab

4.2 Service-Oriented Computing Laboratory (Online Course)

Today, more and more online courses are offered by universities. However, multiple issues can decrease educational outcome for online courses, especially the ones requiring hands-on laboratories: (1) Remote students have to configure the laboratory environment by themselves on their own computers; (2) Instructors and TAs are difficult to provide real-time laboratory support at a remote location; (3) Students have to pack all the files into a zip file and send to TA, who then unzips and imports it to a local computer and performs grading. In many cases, laboratory files developed on student's personal computer fail to run on TA's computer due to compatibility issues. In other cases when the laboratory is progressive (e.g., a web site with multiple web services added in at different development stages), or the laboratory file is in large size (e.g., a database with millions of records), it is impossible to pack it into a file. The TA will have to find other ways to grade the laboratory.

In Summer 2011, the online course Service-Oriented Computing and Information Management was offered to 20 students, focusing on application-layer networking laboratories such as web server configuration, XML parsing, SOAP and RESTful web services development and etc. For students to master these web-based technologies, a set of hands-on laboratories was designed using V-Lab system throughout the semester. According to the laboratory requirements, the VM has been pre-configured with a set of software packages and SDKs to help students get started with the laboratory. To fully emulate web server functions, we use port mapping on V-Lab gateway to open HTTP access from VMs to Internet. By publishing VM web access to Internet, students can quickly test their web services using any web browser as long as Internet is available. They can also peer-evaluate other groups' projects and improve their works. It also helps TAs and instructors to provide remote support and grading, by remotely access student's VM directly and check the laboratory projects as-is. This dramatically increases the communication efficiency and helps solve student's questions with minimized wait time. This also helps TAs and instructors keep track of user progress closely and adjust the curriculum according to the feedbacks in order to maximize the education outcome.

5. EVALUATION & RESULTS

Since the summer of 2011, V-Lab has served 5 different computer networking courses and provided more than 20 hands-on laboratories to over 250 students. Table 3 shows all the courses that have used V-Lab. In this section, we show the student survey results for V-Lab system and the 6-factor hands-on laboratory approach. We also show the

Table 3: Courses using V-Lab

Semester	Course Name	Students	Description	Virtual Resources
Summer & Fall, 2011	Service-Oriented Computing and Information Management	38	Use C#, ASP.NET and XML and learn to develop web services, web sites and databases.	38 VMs
Fall, 2011	Software Security Lab	74	Use Holodeck and IE6.0 to simulate various failures in a software system and test whether the software can securely handle failures.	74 VMs
Fall, 2011	Computer Network Security Lab	43	Use Apache, DNS Server, VNC, Iptables, SSH, SSL, Snort, Syslog, Openvas and etc. and learn to create, configure and protect computer networks.	129 VMs and 86 VLANs
Fall, 2011	Information Assurance	32	Use Apache to configure various access control models on a website with authentication, encryption and policies.	64 VMs and 32 VLANs
Fall, 2011	A Web-based Document Management System (WDMS)	68	Develop a WDMS to facilitate the management and access of all the documents of an organization.	68 VMs

evidences of V-Lab encouraging students to be creative in various projects.

5.1 V-Lab Survey Results

After each laboratory, a survey is collected asking students 14 single-choice questions with answers from Strongly Agree (5 points) to Strongly Disagree (1 point) targeting the 6 educational factors. The survey questions are:

- Knowledge:

Q1: *Comprehensiveness of knowledge provided by the course.*

Q2: *Relevancy of knowledge provided by the course.*

Q3: *Correctness of knowledge provided by the course.*

Q4: *Comprehensiveness of references and supporting materials.*

- Motivation:

Q5: *Comprehensiveness of grading criteria on projects and assignments.*

Q6: *Importance and usefulness of projects and assignments in the future, beyond the course.*

- Creativity:

Q7: *The course and V-Lab encourage you to learn and research more.*

Q8: *V-Lab provides customized virtual resources that help your projects and researches.*

- Collaboration:

Q9: *V-Lab provides a platform where it is easy to share and publish your work with the team and other users.*

Q10: *Course peer evaluation encourages participation and collaboration, which improves students' projects.*

- Demonstration:

Q11: *V-Lab is good for research and education because you can design, develop, test and demo your project in one platform.*

Q12: *V-Lab is capable of demonstrating in more realistic environment than personal computers.*

- Feedback:

Q13: *The instructors and TAs provide useful and quick response to your question.*

Q14: *V-Lab can recover your work from mis-configuration or system failure in less time than using personal computers.*

As shown in Fig. 4, most students give positive feedbacks to V-Lab system, provided that none of the students have used V-Lab before. The learning curve for V-Lab is so short that most students can setup and use V-Lab in minutes. Both students and instructors are able to finish the course laboratories throughout the semester, and produce a satisfactory education result. Because V-Lab is still a research project, it had lots of system-level upgrades during the summer and some of the users did suffer from reliability issues, which explains why Q14 has a relatively lower score. However, we manage to solve most of the technical issues by the end of the semester.

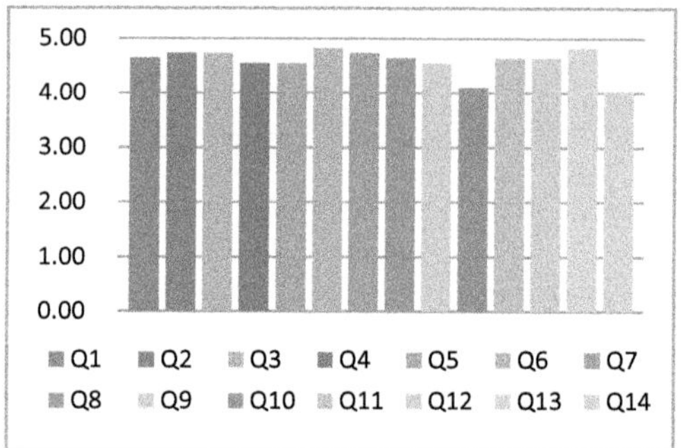

Figure 4: V-Lab Survey Results

5.2 User Creativities in V-Lab

In addition to supporting various networking hands-on laboratories, V-Lab system also works closely with Capstone student teams as well as independent developers to provide a variety of virtual resources and encourage them to explore innovative ideas in a wide range of research topics. Over the past 2 years, several research projects have made significant progress and some of them are integrated into seminar courses in the department, while others have been developed into research articles. In this section we present evidences that V-Lab promotes education strategies on students from *know-that,* to *know-how* and eventually to *know-in-action* where students develop and contribute to the system and open more educational opportunities for fellow students.

Among V-Lab projects, the Secure Search Engine (SSE) project which was initially proposed by a capstone student team is aiming to develop a cloud-based solution for phishing website searching, detection and blocking. The team used several virtual servers and networks in V-Lab to build up a comprehensive system that monitors web access requests of users and perform anti-phishing functions on the requests. The SSE project has been maintained over the past year and has now become part of a larger cloud research platform called MobiCloud [18], where mobile phone users will be able to benefit from SSE phishing website filtering.

6. CONCLUSION

This paper presents V-Lab, a cloud-based virtual laboratory design that is built on Xen virtualization and VLANs to customize, configure, monitor and manage virtual resources in computer and network laboratories. The system provides a web interface for end-users to sign in and manage their own virtual resources. A java-applet based virtual resource management panel is built in the website for users to configure the resources and view the remote access ports for each VM. By connecting to the VMs via SSH, VNC or RDP, students can perform laboratory tasks in a securely isolated resource pool where they do not need to worry about software misuse or misconfigurations. Survey results from classroom show a satisfactory feedback for V-Lab and the six-factor laboratory curriculums. The results also show that V-Lab provides sufficient laboratory resources that helps students understand and practice the knowledge in simulated real-world situations, promotes the education strategies from *know-that*, to *knwo-how* and eventually get to *know-in-action* where students develop themselves and contribute to education in return.

7. FUTURE WORK

Since V-Lab is currently a research project, it suffers reliability issues from time to time. The system needs to be divided into two isolated domains, while one is for public use the other one can be used for development. Currently we are purchasing more equipments to improve the system architecture design. Moreover, we are publishing V-Lab platform as an open-source project along with the laboratory curriculums so that they can benefit other universities. Eventually multiple V-Lab sites can inter-connect and become a powerful virtual resource platform.

8. ACKNOWLEDGEMENTS

The authors thank anonymous reviewers for their insightful comments. This research is sponsored by NSF-CCLI project: DUE-0942453.

9. REFERENCES

[1] "Xen Virtualization Open Source Project." [Online]. Available: http://xen.org

[2] "Virtual LAN Technology." [Online]. Available: http://en.wikipedia.org/wiki/Virtual_LAN

[3] "ASU IA Lab." [Online]. Available: http://snac.eas.asu.edu/IA-lab/

[4] T. A. Yang and T. A. Nguyen, "Network security development process: a framework for teaching network security courses," *J. Comput. Small Coll.*, vol. 21, pp. 203–209, April 2006. [Online]. Available: http://dl.acm.org/citation.cfm?id=1127389.1127428

[5] "Rochester Institute of Technology (RIT) NSSA Labs." [Online]. Available: http://www.nssa.rit.edu/?q=node/49

[6] "State University of New York Geneseo Virtual Computer Lab." [Online]. Available: http://www.geneseo.edu/cit/virtual_computer_labs

[7] "ASU My Apps." [Online]. Available: http://ets.fulton.asu.edu/software/software-home-page

[8] "Duke University Virtual Computing Lab." [Online]. Available: http://oit.duke.edu/comp-print/labs/vcl/index.php

[9] "Penn State University Virtual Lab." [Online]. Available: http://remotelab.psu-erie.bd.psu.edu/virtuallab.htm

[10] "Illinois Security Lab." [Online]. Available: http://seclab.illinois.edu/

[11] W. Du and R. Wang, "SEED: A Suite of Instructional Laboratories for Computer Security Education," *J. Educ. Resour. Comput.*, vol. 8, pp. 3:1–3:24, March 2008. [Online]. Available: http://doi.acm.org/10.1145/1348713.1348716

[12] H. E. Schaffer, S. F. Averitt, M. I. Hoit, A. Peeler, E. D. Sills, and M. A. Vouk, "NCSU's Virtual Computing Lab: A Cloud Computing Solution," *Computer*, vol. 42, pp. 94–97, 2009.

[13] W. Sun, V. Katta, K. Krishna, and R. Sekar, "V-NetLab: an approach for realizing logically isolated networks for security experiments," in *Proceedings of the conference on Cyber security experimentation and test.* Berkeley, CA, USA: USENIX Association, 2008, pp. 5:1–5:6. [Online]. Available: http://dl.acm.org/citation.cfm?id=1496662.1496667

[14] V. J. H. Powell, C. T. Davis, R. S. Johnson, P. Y. Wu, J. C. Turchek, and I. W. Parker, "VLabNet: the integrated design of hands-on learning in information security and networking," in *Proceedings of the 4th annual conference on Information security curriculum development*, ser. InfoSecCD '07. New York, NY, USA: ACM, 2007, pp. 9:1–9:7. [Online]. Available: http://doi.acm.org/10.1145/1409908.1409918

[15] "University of New Mexico (UNM) IA Lab." [Online]. Available: http://ia.mgt.unm.edu/labintro.asp

[16] "Idaho University VRAD Lab." [Online]. Available: http://seniordesign.engr.uidaho.edu/index.html

[17] P. Baumgartner and F. I. Hagen, "The Zen Art of Teaching Communication and Interactions in eEducation."

[18] D. Huang, Z. Zhou, L. Xu, T. Xing, and Y. Zhong, "Secure Data Processing Framework for Mobile Cloud Computing," in *Computer Communications Workshops (INFOCOM WKSHPS), 2011 IEEE Conference on*, april 2011, pp. 614 –618.

Serious Toys: Teaching the Binary Number System

Yvon Feaster[†], Farha Ali[‡], Jason O. Hallstrom[†]
[†]School of Computing, Clemson University, Clemson SC 29634-0974 USA
[‡]Department of Mathematics and Computing, Lander University, Greenwood, SC 29649-2099 USA
yfeaste@clemson.edu, fali@lander.edu, jasonoh@cs.clemson.edu

ABSTRACT

The binary number system is the lingua franca of computing, requisite to myriad areas, from hardware architecture and data storage to wireless communication and algorithm design. Given its significance to such a broad range of computing topics, it is not surprising that the binary number system plays a prominent role in K-12 outreach efforts. It is even less surprising that the topic is often viewed as a dreary introduction to the discipline. Motivated by these observations and the potential of binary arithmetic to connect future students to a wide spectrum of computing topics, we have developed a new approach to teaching binary arithmetic in the K-12 curriculum. The approach relies on the use of a *"serious toy"*, an embedded hardware platform designed to teach the binary number system while engaging visual and kinesthetic learners. We describe the design of the curriculum module and the supporting toy and detail our experiences using the approach in three independent outreach efforts. The results are largely positive, supporting our supposition that teaching the binary number system can achieve strong content understanding and improved attitudes toward the discipline.

Categories and Subject Descriptors

K.3.2 [**Computers and Education**]: Computer and Information Science Education—*CS education, Curriculum*

General Terms

Experimentation, Human Factors

Keywords

Binary numbers, computer science outreach, high school curriculum, experimental evaluation

1. INTRODUCTION

To borrow a quotation from the popular ThinkGeek t-shirt, *"There are 10 types of people in this world: Those who understand binary and those who don't."* At the risk of sounding flippant, our work is motivated by the belief that this quotation should be (at least mildly) funny to anyone with even a passing interest in computing.

Binary is one of the first topics introduced in the undergraduate curriculum because it is fundamental to so many subsequent topic areas. Proficiency in binary arithmetic is a requisite skill in the study of computer architecture, data storage, networking, and myriad other content areas. It is no surprise that the binary number system plays a prominent role in outreach efforts aimed at early learners [1,6].

Unfortunately, motivating K-12 students to learn binary is more difficult than motivating these students to learn, say, robotics or computer graphics. A number of experience reports note disproportionately low student engagement and satisfaction when compared to other topics [4,7]. Again, this is not surprising. Our supposition is that this is due to three factors. First, topics like robotics and computer graphics, which have strong visual components, naturally appeal to visual learners (e.g., creating a 3D graph). Similarly, these topics lend themselves to hands-on activities that provide immediate visual and/or tactile feedback, appealing to kinesthetic learners (e.g., playing a video game). Finally, these topics are more "real" for students; they involve physical technology components. Traditional modules for teaching binary arithmetic lack all three, which is unfortunate given the seeming universal agreement that the topic is fundamental, even for early learners.

To support the introduction of binary arithmetic in the K-12 curriculum in a manner that is both informative and engaging, we have developed a new approach to teaching the topic that, as with robotics, simultaneously addresses each of the three identified pedagogical challenges. Our approach relies on a *"serious toy"*— a small embedded hardware platform designed to teach binary arithmetic at the K-12 level. Students are guided through a series of arithmetic exercises that require the entry of operands, operators, and predicted results via short flashlight pulses that encode binary data. The display consists of an 8x8 LED matrix driven by an inexpensive microcontroller. We have piloted the approach in three independent outreach initiatives with largely positive results. In this paper, we describe the curriculum module, the design of the supporting hardware system, and the results of our evaluation. Our intent is to transform a traditionally dreary exercise format into an activity that engages students and positively impacts their perceptions of the discipline. The results suggest we are on the right track.

2. RELATED WORK

We are not the first outreach team to focus on binary. Sarkar et al. [11,12] describe a variety of kinesthetic activities designed to introduce students to computer organization based on the PIC microcontroller. In one activity, students are taught the basic concepts of bits, bytes, and binary numbers. They are then shown a PIC-based device that demonstrates binary numbers through the use of 8 LEDs. Subsequent lessons cover computer memory, LED matrix manipulation, displays, and speech generation. Each lesson emphasizes the importance of the binary number system in computing. Evaluation results indicate that 70% of the students were satisfied with the hands-on experience and would like more hands-on projects. In addition, 75% of students indicated the PIC project gave them a better understanding of hardware fundamentals, including binary. The activities described in this work differ from ours in that student interaction involved writing a desktop program to turn on the display. Further, their work does not cover arithmetic.

Sakala et al. [10] describe a software tool to teach the binary number system, with a focus on conversion from decimal to binary. The interface prompts the user to enter a number and demonstrates each step of the conversion process using division by 2, with the remainder representing the binary number. To evaluate the interface, a lesson on binary conversion was given to a control group using a traditional lecture method; the experimental group was taught using the interface. The results indicate that the tool-based approach was more effective. The primary difference in this work and ours is this group developed a software tool to teach binary conversion. We developed a hardware tool to teach students binary conversion, in addition to arithmetic.

Goldschmidt et al. [6] describe how several fundamental computer science concepts can be incorporated in the K-12 curriculum, including alternative number systems. They describe how to count in binary using rhythm in physical education. In addition, they explain how the Mayan base-20 system, the Enigma Code, and encryption/decryption can be used as discussion points in a social studies class. As with this group, we use lectures and activities to teach alternative number systems. Our activity consists of a hardware-based tool rather than group games.

Stanley [14] describes his experience using visualization to teach computer science concepts, including encryption/decryption and alternative number systems. As an example, he describes his use of MultiMedia Logic [13] in teaching binary and hexadecimal number systems. Stanley also presents an applet used to demonstrate the relationship between a binary number and its decimal representation using a circuit-based visualization. Again, this work involves learning through software-based visualization, whereas our work depends on hardware-based tools.

Waraich [16] describes a multimedia learning environment, used for lessons focused primarily on computer architecture, including binary arithmetic and logic gates. The target audience includes 1st year computer science undergraduates. Students using the instructional environment received higher test scores than those who did not. As with the previous work, this work uses software to teach binary and logic gates.

Chun et al. [1] describe a web-based system designed to help teach K-12 students and educators basic programming skills. An LED kit used to display binary numbers and images is used with the web application. The example discussed in their paper is based on lighting the LEDs to represent decimal numbers using a single row. This work incorporates both software and hardware to demonstrate binary conversion. However, with only a single row of LEDs, they cannot teach binary arithmetic.

CS Unplugged [3] uses games to teach computer science concepts, including binary numbers. The binary games focus on counting with binary and relating the importance of binary to computer science. Our module also discusses the importance of binary in computing, along with converting binary numbers and performing binary arithmetic.

3. WHY FOCUS ON BINARY?

According to the National Council of Teachers of Mathematics [9], number systems should be introduced to students as early as kindergarten. Similarly, new K-12 curriculum recommendations published by the Computer Science Teachers Association [15] include the binary number system. This includes the introduction of binary to K-3 students through a demonstration of data representation using 0s and 1s (page 13). Their report states that by completion of grade 9, students should be familiar with binary numbers and logic circuits (page 16). Their report also indicates that by the end of the 10th grade, students should know the relationship between binary and hexadecimal (page 18).

```
1. It is important for computing students to
   understand numeral systems other than base-10.
2. It is advantageous for incoming computing
   students to understand numeral systems other
   than base-10.
3. The binary number system is important throughout
   computing.
4. The binary number system is important in the
   course(s) I teach.
5. Learning the binary number system can be fun for
   students.
```

Listing 1: Survey Statements

Table 1: Computing Educator Survey Results

Choices	S1	S2	S3	S4	S5
Strongly Agree	9	5	7	3	3
Moderately Agree	1	3	2	2	1
Agree	0	2	1	2	5
Disagree	0	0	0	1	1
Moderately Disagree	0	0	0	1	0
Strongly Disagree	0	0	0	1	0

To gauge computing educators' perceived need for teaching binary to potential computing students, we developed a brief survey and sent it to 30 computing educators at a range of institutions (6) external to our own. The survey is shown in Listing 1. Participants were asked to rate their level of agreement with each of the 5 statements, choosing from *strongly disagree, moderately disagree, disagree, agree, moderately agree, and strongly agree.* We received 10 responses. While the sample size is too small to draw definitive conclusions, the results are informative, even anecdotally: Table 1 shows that the results were, overall, positive regarding the need for computing students to understand binary. One interesting observation is that while 30% of respondents indicated that binary is relatively unimportant in the courses they teach (statement 4), *all* respondents agreed that understanding number systems other than base-10 is important for computing students (statement 1).

4. APPROACH

Our approach to teaching the binary number system consists of a 75-minute lecture, followed by a review and active learning activities based on the embedded toy. The lecture occurs during one class period; the latter components occur during a subsequent period (on another day).

4.1 Lecture

We begin the lecture by reviewing base-10, motivating how and why we group by 10s. This is done by holding up two closed fists and asking students to count how many fingers are held up. When they respond with zero, we write the digit 0 on the board. Next, one finger is held up, and the exercise continues until we get to 10 fingers. We note that nine objects can be represented by a single digit, but another column is needed if we have ten or more objects. Similarly, if we have ten groups of ten objects each, a third column must be added. We conclude by noting one explanation for why we count by 10s: Humans typically have 10 fingers!

Next we introduce the binary number system. To continue the finger counting example, we ask students how many digits we might use, and how high we might be capable of counting if we were aliens with only two fingers, similar to [5]. While it may sound silly, the exercise motivates the concept well. As with base-10, we discuss the grouping principle and note when a new column must be added. Using an example similar to that shown in Figure 1, we illustrate how elements can be grouped by twos, as well as tens. As an exercise, we give the students several small numbers and ask them, using grouping, to write each number in decimal and binary.

This exercise was designed to help students understand

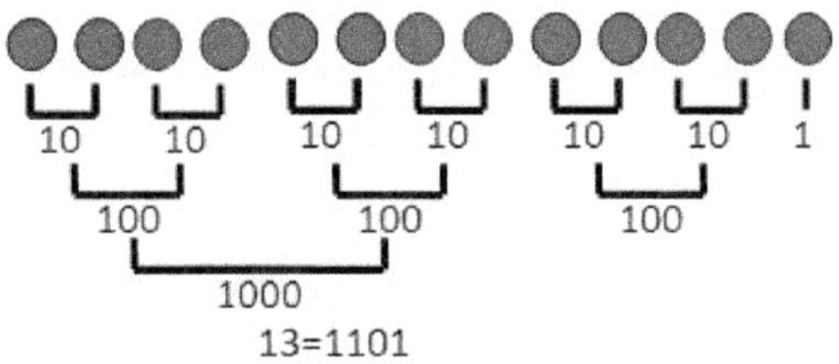

Figure 1: Grouping Example.

that 10 is effectively an arbitrary choice; any other base could be used. Next we discuss how tedious this translation approach would be for large numbers, and then introduce a decimal-to-binary conversion approach based on repeated division by 2. When demonstrating this method, we explain how the quotient represents the number of groups that could be formed, and the remainder represents the remaining elements. We next demonstrate the reverse approach, converting a binary number to a decimal number. We start the discussion by noting the value of each digit in a decimal number. We explain that the value is the product of the digit and a power of 10; the power value depends on the digit's position. We then adapt this idea to binary numbers. When students are comfortable with the conversion process, we introduce binary addition and subtraction.

We conclude with a discussion of why binary numbers are important in computer science, noting that the language used by computers is limited to 1s and 0s. We use the analogy of a light switch and explain that combinations of these switches allow the computer to operate using large numbers.

4.2 Binary Toy

We begin the second class period with a review, and then introduce the embedded toy, noting that the toy works on the same principle as a computer, i.e., it receives input, processes the input, and displays the results. The students are then divided into smaller groups, and the toy is demonstrated in each group. Students are assigned several binary conversion, addition, and subtraction problems, and are instructed to perform the operations on paper before validating their work using the toy.

Architecture. The embedded platform consists of an input device, two processors, and an output device. The input device is a photoresistor wired to a microcontroller (and triggered by a flashlight). When the beam of the flashlight is directed toward the photoresistor, a change in resistance is detected and read by an ATMega168 microcontroller. The duration of the resistance change is recorded and compared with a specified threshold. If the duration exceeds the threshold, a 1 is recorded; otherwise, a 0 is recorded. Using serial communication, the ATMega168 transmits the data to an ATMega8515 microcontroller. The ATMega8515 is responsible for receiving the data and driving the output device, an 8x8 LED display.

Six of the eight rows on the LED display are used, as shown in Figure 2. The first two rows are used to represent operands. The third is used to display the predicted addition or subtraction result. The fourth represents the correct answer to the problem. The sixth is used to display the operation being performed. Finally, the eighth row displays the last bit position entered.

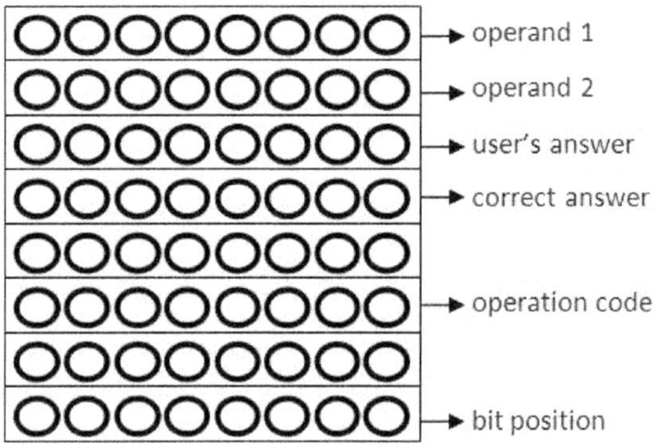

Figure 2: Display Setup

Toy Operation. To begin using the toy, students must direct the flashlight beam on the photoresistor for a count of ten. The display driver then turns on the first row of red LEDs to indicate that it is ready to receive the first operand. The operands must be entered from most significant bit to least significant bit. To enter a 1, the flashlight is focused on the photoresistor for three seconds. A 0 is captured by a shorter beam. The output display denotes a 1 by displaying a red LED; an unlit LED denotes a 0. To assist students in keeping track of the bits entered, the eighth row displays a red LED for each bit entered. After all eight bits are entered, the student must verify her entry. If satisfied, a 1 is entered; otherwise, the board will clear the row and allow the student to re-enter the number. This process is repeated for the second operand. After accepting the second operand, the red lights on the sixth row turn on, indicating the need to enter the operator. Two bits must be entered: '11' for addition,'10' for subtraction. The student must also confirm her choice of operation. At this point, the third row of LEDs is lit, indicating the toy is ready to receive the predicted answer. The students enters the predicted result beginning from the least significant bit. Upon confirmtion, the fourth row displays the correct answer, in green lights, for the student to compare with her's.

5. PILOT GROUPS

We piloted this approach with three groups of high school students. Two of the groups were participants in a university summer program. The third group consisted of students from a nearby high school.

5.1 Emerging Scholars

The Emerging Scholars program was established in 2002 with a mission to reach out to high schools located in areas which, according to the US Census Bureau, have a high poverty rating [2, 8]. Student participants are chosen because they exhibit the potential to succeed in higher education, but lack the economic and social support needed to make attending college a reality. Participants in this program are provided summer experiences for three consecutive summers. During the summers, the students are taught the importance of basic skills such as reading, writing, math, and science. During the students' third summer in the program, they follow a class schedule that mimics that of a freshman. This affords students the opportunity to experience, in a small way, what it is like to be a college student.

For our pilot project, we engaged two groups of Emerging Scholars, seniors and juniors. Each group was divided into two sections. Each senior section, referred to as ES Senior 1 and ES Senior 2 in our evaluation, had 12 students participate. The junior sections, referred to as ES Junior 1 and ES Junior 2, had participants totalling 15 and 17, respectively.

5.2 Local High School

The participating high school students were chosen from a mathematics course, Statistical Analysis, classified as College Preparatory (CP). The class was chosen because the students' expected abilities appeared similar to those of the Emerging Scholars groups. As with the Emerging Scholars groups, these students had no predetermined interest in computer science. There were 34 participants, 6 juniors and 28 seniors. This group will be referred to as HS.

6. PILOT STRUCTURE

To evaluate the role of the toy in improving students' knowledge of binary numbers, we taught the pilot groups using different approaches.

Lecture Only. We met with the ES Senior 1 and 2 groups for only one day. They were taught the binary number system using lectures only. This group was not introduced to the binary toy. Pre- and post-surveys were administered.

Lecture and Prototype Toy. We met with the ES Juniors 1 and 2 for two days. On the first day, we presented the lecture on the binary number system using the same material and style as the first groups. Pre-surveys were administered before this class. On the second day, we reviewed the lecture material and demonstrated a prototype of the binary toy. We also discussed the development process used to construct the toy. The prototype was developed using a breadboard setup, as shown in Figure 3a. Only two prototypes were available, so we divided the students into two smaller groups (7-8 per group) and let them take turns practicing addition and subtraction using the prototype. At the end of this meeting, students were given the post-survey.

Lecture and Assembled Toy. We met with the HS group for two days. The format of the first day was identical to the previous offerings. Since this group was twice the size of the ES Seniors and ES Juniors, we divided the students into two groups of 17. One group was introduced to the fully assembled version of the binary toy shown in Figure 3b. They were asked to practice converting, adding, and subtracting binary numbers using the toy. While the first set of students were playing with the binary toy, the second set of students were learning about the toy's development process. Students were given the opportunity to examine the breadboarded model of the toy and learn how the more complete prototype was constructed. To allow students ample time to use the toy, the groups swapped learning areas after approximately 25 minutes. At the end of the period, a post-survey was administered.

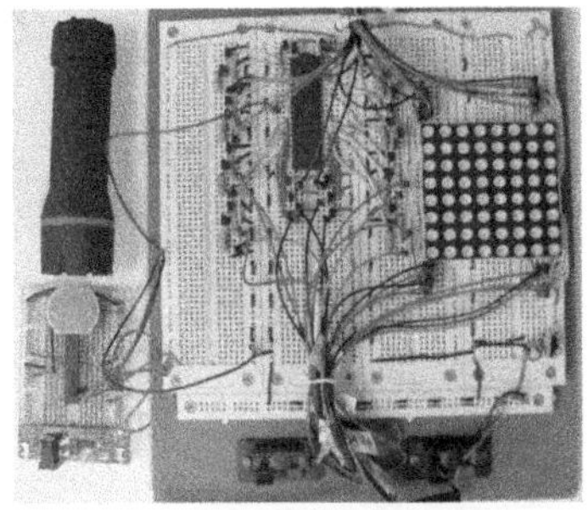

(a) Breadboarded Toy

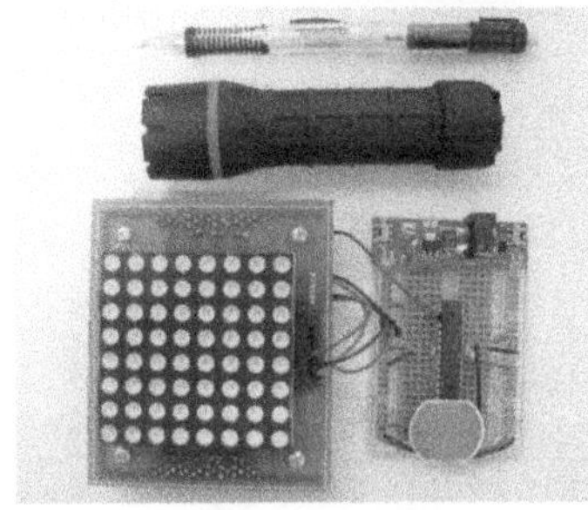

(b) Assembled Toy
Figure 3: Toys

7. EVALUATION

The pre-and post-surveys consisted of 15 Likert-style statements, shown in Listing 2. The students were instructed to rate their level of agreement with each statement, as in the educator survey: *strongly disagree, 1—strongly agree, 6.*

7.1 Emerging Scholars

Statements 12-15 were not included in the statistical significance analysis because these statements could not be answered until after the presentation of the material. For the remaining 11 statements, a two sample F-test for variance was performed. Once the variance was determined, the appropriate two sample t-test was performed to determine if the pre/post difference was statistically significant (5% p-level). Of the 44 statistical analyses performed, 31 (70%) indicated a significant change in the mean response. We categorized the statements into three groups: Of the 15 total statements, 2 were related to student interest (statements 1-2), 9 to student understanding (statements 3-11), and 4 to students' perception of the program (statements 12-15).

Interest in Computer Science. These statements were designed to measure the impact of the program on student interest in computer science. Although the change in mean for 7 of the 8 responses was not statistically significant (statement 1, ES Senior 2, significant decrease), we do

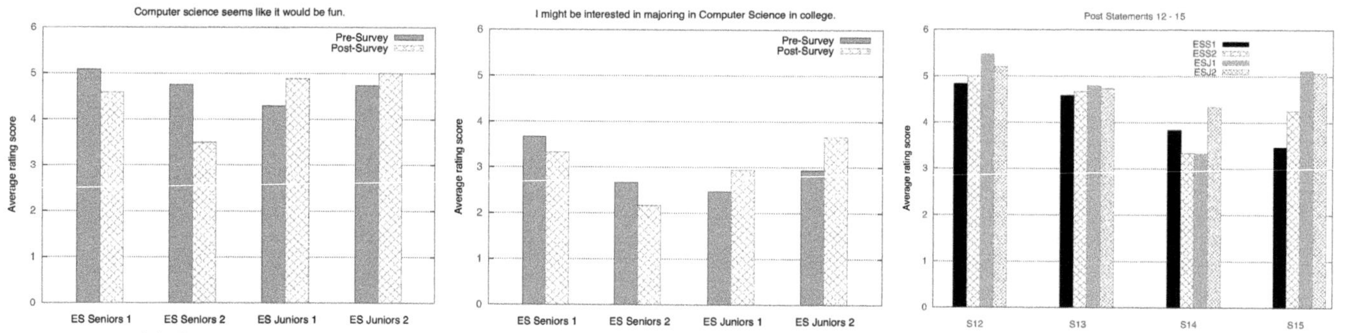

(a) Statement 1 (b) Statement 2 (c) Statements 12 - 15

Figure 4: Survey Results (S1, S2, S12-15)

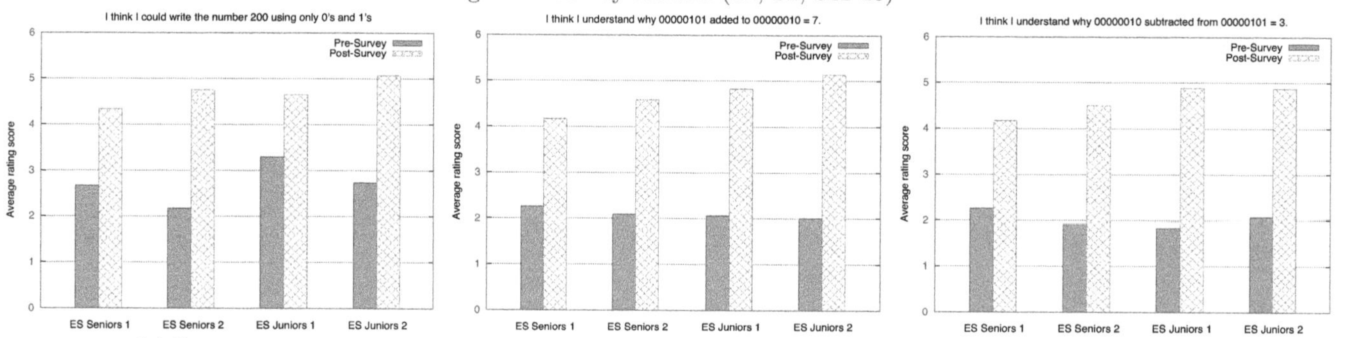

(a) Statement 9 (b) Statement 10 (c) Statement 11

Figure 5: Survey Results (S9-11)

observe interesting results. The ES Senior 1 and 2 groups both exhibited a decrease in interest, whereas the ES Junior 1 and 2 groups had an increase in interest, as shown in Figures 4a and 4b. As discussed in Section 6, the ES Senior 1 and 2 groups were not introduced to the binary toy; the ES Junior 1 and 2 groups were. We posit that the toy had a positive impact on students' interest in computer science.

Content Understanding. These statements were designed to measure student understanding of the material presented, in particular the impact of the toy. The statistical analysis showed that 30 of the 36 t-test analyses represent a significant change between the pre- and post-surveys. It is also notable that *all* of the results for this category indicate an increase in (perceived) content understanding. We focus on statements 9 - 11, which relate to student understanding of converting, adding, and subtracting binary numbers. Knowledge of each of these concepts is reinforced through the use of the binary toy. In each case, the analysis indicates a statistically significant increase between the pre- and post-surveys. In addition, the ES Junior 1 and 2 groups show a higher post-score on each of these three statements than the ES Senior 1 and 2 groups, as shown in 5a, 5b, and 5c. Since the ES Senior 1 and 2 groups were not introduced to the toy, we believe this suggests the binary toy had a positive impact on student understanding.

Structure of Outreach. These statements were designed to gauge whether students enjoyed the format of the program. Pre-survey data was not considered since students were unable to rate these statements until after the program was completed. As shown in Figure 4c, both ES groups, on average, agreed or moderately agreed that the instructors did an appropriate job. Also, on average, both ES groups enjoyed the format of the outreach module. However, the ES Junior 2 group was the only group that indicated they would like to participate in additional computer science outreach programs. This was not surprising since the ES Junior 2 group showed the highest interest in majoring in computer science. Lastly, three of the four ES groups indicated they enjoyed learning about binary. It is interesting to note that the ES Junior 1 and 2 groups averaged a score of 5.1 for this statement, whereas the ES Senior 1 and 2 groups scored 3.5 and 4.3, respectively. This suggests the binary toy had a positive impact.

```
 1. Computer science seems like it would be fun.
 2. I might be interested in majoring in
    computer science in college.
 3. I think I understand the need for
    alternate numbering systems.
 4. I think I understand why humans use the
    decimal number system.
 5. I think I understand the value of
    binary numbers in computer science.
 6. I think I understand the concept of
    a binary numbering system.
 7. I think I understand the relationship
    between decimal and binary numbers.
 8. I think I can understand a number
    system with any base.
 9. I think I could write the number 200
    using only 0s and 1s.
10. I think I understand why 00000101
    added to 00000010 = 7.
11. I think I understand why 00000010
    subtracted from 00000101 = 3.
12. I think the teacher did an appropriate
    job explaining the material.
13. I like the format of this outreach program.
14. I would like to attend more outreach
    programs related to computer science.
15. I liked learning about binary numbers.
```

Listing 2: Survey Statements

7.2 High School Classroom

Pre-treatment survey data was unavailable for this pilot group. Hence, our analysis is based only on the post-treatment survey.

As before, in the evaluation of the final pilot we group the survey statements into three categories, measuring interest, content understanding, and module organization. For each statement group, we compute the average and standard deviation across the response data for all of the constituent statements. The results are summarized in Table 2 below:

Table 2: High School Survey Results

Statement Category	Average	Std. Dev.
Interest in CS (S1-2)	2.40	1.28
Content Understanding (S3-11)	3.71	1.66
Module Organization (S12-15)	3.29	1.37

Recall that a score of 3 denotes moderate disagreement, and a score of 4 denotes moderate agreement. Accordingly, the average scores in the content understanding category indicate that students completed the program with a generally positive impression of their content understanding. Unfortunately, they had a less positive view of the module's organization and their likelihood of pursuing a computer science degree. It is interesting to note that the high standard deviation values indicate significant variation in the response data. Indeed, an analysis of the individual statements reveals that approximately half resulted in bimodal response distributions, with frequency peaks on either side of 3. This suggests that the class was partitioned in two — those who "got it", and those who didn't.

We posit several potential explanations for the underwhelming response data. First, with regard to interest, this was the only pilot group that was not self-selected to participate in an outreach module. They elected to participate in a statistical analysis course, and were then required to participate in the binary arithmetic module. Their pre-existing interest in the displaced statistical analysis content may have biased their attitudes toward the outreach content. With regard to module organization, these results are not surprising. The classroom setup made it difficult to power all of the toys in a manner that supported small group participation. The devices were arranged on a central table, and students took turns participating in a large group. Our impression is that only half of the students interacted with the toys, which aligns with the bimodal response data noted above. Finally, it is impossible to tell whether these figures represent improvements over students' baseline impressions given the absence of pre-treatment data.

8. CONCLUSION

We began with the observation that the binary number system is central to a host of areas across computing. It is widely regarded as a fundamental topic, featured in a number of popular outreach programs. Unfortunately, there is evidence that existing approaches to teaching this topic inadequately engage and excite students. In response, we described a new approach to introducing binary arithmetic in the K-12 curriculum using a supporting embedded platform that simultaneously engages visual and kinesthetic learners. The evaluation results are largely positive across the three pilot studies that have been conducted. Our hope is that this approach will serve as a model for introducing a fundamental topic that is often perceived as dull by young learners.

We are currently developing several software extensions to improve the toy's interface. As an example, upon completion of each task, the student will receive immediate feedback in the form of a scrolling message. Further, we are developing extensions to broaden the content coverage provided, including binary multiplication, division, and, logical operations. We are also scheduling pilots with middle and high school students to evaluate the effectiveness of the extensions.

We conclude by noting that the embedded platform presented in this paper is the first in a suite of *"serious toys"* that we are developing to support computer science education. These toys, when designed and used appropriately, have the potential to reenergize the pedagogical landscape around fundamental topics that are often difficult to teach in a manner that is both informative and fun.

Acknowledgments

This work was supported by the National Science Foundation through awards CNS-0745846 and DUE-1022941. Yvon Feaster is an NSF Graduate Research Fellow DGE-0751278

9. REFERENCES

[1] S. Chun and J. Ryoo. Development and Application of a Web-based Programming Learning System with LED Display Kits. In *Proceedings of the 41st ACM Technical Symposium on Computer Science Education*, SIGCSE '10, pages 310–314, New York, NY, USA, March 2010. ACM.

[2] Clemson University Emerging Scholars. http://www.clemson.edu/academics/programs/emerging-scholars/.

[3] CS Unplugged. http://www.csunplugged.org.

[4] Y. Feaster et al. Teaching CS Unplugged in the High School (with limited success). In *Proceedings of the 16th Annual Joint Conference on Innovation and Technology in Computer Science Education*, ITiCSE '11, pages 248–252, New York, NY, USA, June 2011. ACM.

[5] R. Garlikov. The Socratic Method Teaching by Asking Instead of by Telling. http://www.garlikov.com.

[6] D. Goldschmidt et al. An Interdisciplinary Approach to Injecting Computer Science into the K-12 Classroom. *Journal of Computing Sciences in Colleges*, 26(6):78–85, 2011.

[7] L. Lambert and H. Guiffre. Computer Science Outreach in an Elementary School. *Journal of Computing Sciences in Colleges*, 24(3):118–124, 2009.

[8] J. Martin. Enhancing Computer and IT Skills of Rural South Carolina High School Students. http://www.cs.clemson.edu/ jmarty/scholars/scholars.html.

[9] National Council of Teachers of Mathematics. Principles and Standards for School Mathematics. http://www.nctm.org.

[10] L. Sakala et al. The Use of Expert Systems Has Improved Students Learning in Zimbabwe. *Journal of Sustainable Development in Africa*, 12(3):1–13, 2010.

[11] N. Sarka and T. Craig. Teaching Computer Hardware and Organisation Using PIC-Based Projects. *International Journal of Electrical Engineering Education*, 43(2):150–312, 2006.

[12] N. Sarka and T. Craig. A Low-Cost PIC Unit for Teaching Computer Hardware Fundamentals to Undergraduates. *Inroads - The SIGCSE Bulletin*, 39(2):88–91, 2007.

[13] Softronix Inc. Multimedia logic. http://www.softronix.com/.

[14] T. Stanley. Using Digital Logic Circuit Simulation To Build Demonstrations of IT Concepts. *ACM SIGITE Newsletter*, 4(2):10–14, 2007.

[15] The CSTA Standards Task Force. CSTA K-12 Computer Science Standards. http://www.csta.org.

[16] A. Waraich. Using Narrative as a Motivating Device to Teach Binary Arithmetic and Logic Gates. In *Proceedings of the 9th Annual SIGCSE Conference on Innovation and Technology in Computer Science Technology*, ITiCSE '04, pages 97–101, New York, NY, USA, June 2004. ACM.

Bio1 as CS1: Evaluating a Crossdisciplinary CS Context

Zachary Dodds
Harvey Mudd College CS Dept.
301 Platt Blvd.
Claremont, CA 91711 USA
00+1+909-607-1813
dodds@cs.hmc.edu

Ran Libeskind-Hadas
Harvey Mudd College CS Dept.
301 Platt Blvd.
Claremont, CA 91711 USA
00+1+909-621-8976
hadas@cs.hmc.edu

Eliot Bush
Harvey Mudd College Biology Dept.
301 Platt Blvd.
Claremont, CA 91711 USA
00+1+909-607-0653
bush@hmc.edu

ABSTRACT
We present the curriculum, deployment, and initial evaluation of a course, BioCS1, designed to serve as an introductory course in *both* biology and CS. Co-taught by professors in both fields, BioCS1 interweaves fundamental biology and computational topics in a manner similar to contextual approaches to CS1. In contrast to other contextual approaches, however, BioCS1 emphasizes both CS and its context equally. The results suggest that such cross-disciplinary collaborations can thrive at the introductory level, just as they have later in the curriculum.

Categories and Subject Descriptors
K.3.2 [**Computers and Education**]: Computer Science Education

General Terms
Measurement, Design, Human Factors

Keywords
Contextualized CS, CS 1, Biology 1, contextual peers

1. MOTIVATION
Life computes – perhaps no aphorism better captures the spirit and challenge of modern biology. Life's computation spans orders of magnitude that dwarf that of our artificial machines. Its sophistication and intrinsic value offer a promise to which CS can, at its best, contribute both insight and intellectual resources.

Combined approaches to Biology and CS, even in shared spaces such as bioinformatics, treat each field as crucial but independent contributors. Specifically, introductory courses remain tethered to parent departments. Believing that Biology and CS will be even more interconnected in the future, we have run a three-year experiment with a novel, shared *BioCS1* curriculum. Distinct from media, robot, and web-based contexts for CS1 [16,20,23,24], in BioCS1 Biology was not only context but ***peer***: the course serves as both Bio1 and as CS1 for majors of either field as well as for non-majors.

ITiCSE'12, July 3–5, 2012, Haifa, Israel.

This paper reviews BioCS1's curriculum. We then present the student-generated evidence of its effectiveness. In brief, the results show that:

- Students in BioCS1 gained the same level of CS skills as a natural control group – and the entire cohort – of their peers in the standard CS 1 course.
- BioCS1 stimulated equal or greater student interest in both computing and biology as measured by (1) anonymous course evaluations, (2) the decision to take CS2, and (3) the choice of a biology or CS major course of study.

We also report on the student workload and affective response to BioCS1. We conclude with a vision of how BioCS1 might most usefully – and feasibly – evolve in the future.

2. BIO/CS BACKGROUND
This effort rests on the shoulders of at least a decade-long foundation of collaborative Biology and CS education. Each discipline's futurists foresee deeper links with the other [1,4]; for now, bioinformatics dominates the collaboration. Bioinformatics-specific courses [25,26] and programs [5,9,10,11] abound.

In the above-cited curricula, however, the disciplinary merge *follows* students' introductions to the fields. This late-curriculum convergence stems naturally from the specialized subsets of CS and Biology that make up bioinformatics. Other efforts tend to be asymmetric: they offer biologically-motivated projects for CS students [2,3,7,8] or computational thinking for biology students [17].

A second trend has seen introductory CS courses using biology and genomics as motivating context [12,13]. Such efforts continue to expand and mature [21]. In addition, there are wide-ranging examples of introductory Biology increasing students' computational savvy with domain-specific tools [14,27]. Recent examples also build with or from biology to span data-analysis skills important for all scientists [6,18]. Importantly, such efforts are not so new that all have succeeded [22]!

Perhaps Wellesley College's *BiSc303* course [25] is most similar to the course described here: like ours, it is co-taught – in Python – by a biologist and computer scientist and has a significant capstone project. Yet *BiSc303* is an advanced elective for majors of both disciplines; to our knowledge, there do not exist other *introductory* courses that interweave Biology and CS at a depth and breadth sufficient to fully support majors of either discipline. Indeed, since Bio1 and CS1 are solidly established curricula, a single-semester, full-fledged combination might seem impossible.

Yet contextualized CS has shown, compellingly, that adding more to CS1 is possible *with no reduction in students' CS skills and knowledge*. In fact, students' interest and performance can increase appreciably [24]. This work takes the next step: we hypothesize that a *peer*, Bio1, can succeed as a context for CS1. Symmetry dictates that we are making an equally strong statement about Bio1's use of a CS-based context. It is only the CS-themed venue that prompts the first formulation.

But why BioCS1? After all, a contextual peer is a far greater burden. Off-the-shelf contextualized curricula presume that an instructor will quickly pick up the context necessary to motivate the material [23,24]: this does *not* hold for Biology. Yet we believe that the following advantages of interdependence far outweigh our discomfort at losing independence:

1. students' equal or better mastery of CS1 & Bio1 skills
2. students' application of cross-disciplinary thinking
3. students' increased involvement in both fields
4. students' time-efficiency: two courses in one class

The next section reviews BioCS1's curriculum, emphasizing differences from the pilot three years ago [0]; the results then highlight points 1-4, above. We conclude with several lessons that this BioCS1 experiment has taught us.

3. CURRICULUM AND STUDENT WORK

The setting for this curricular experiment is a BioCS1 class that has now been taught three times -- in fall terms of 2009, 2010, and 2011 -- to a total of approximately 100 students. BioCS1 is a 14-week semester course comprising two 75-minute lectures and a two-hour computing lab per week, a structure similar to our CS1 and Bio1 courses.

All of our undergraduates, regardless of intended major, must take an introductory CS course in their first semester at the college. Students with prior experience can place into accelerated or advanced courses, but the majority take CS1. BioCS1 is a relatively recent addition to the curriculum and can be taken in lieu of CS1. Students indicate their course preferences and are placed accordingly. However, BioCS1 is intended exclusively for students with *no prior computing experience.*

By design, Biology and CS have equal footing in BioCS1. A biologist presents the first lecture each week and a computer scientist presents the second. The two lectures are tightly integrated in support of that week's topics. Students apply the week's computational idea in order to solve, model, and explore two to five biological questions for each week's homework assignment. As in CS1, BioCS1 students use Python throughout.

Module 1 Figure 1 presents an overview of BioCS1's topics and a small subset of student homework. The course is made up of seven two-week modules. By the end of the first module, students have written their own programs to simulate a bacterium's random walk in a Petri dish using the `turtle` package (a topic revisited with increasing sophistication through the term) and to implement the Central Dogma of Biology: the transcription and translation of DNA to proteins.

Module 2 increases comfort with computational problem-solving, asking students to write their own programs to simulate important biological ideas like genetic drift and natural selection. These fundamental processes become more concrete and meaningful when students write their own programs to model them and explore the effects of their parameters.

	Biology	CS	Subset of student HW
weeks 1-3	DNA, RNA, genes, and the central dogma	introduction to Python	gene-finding and modeling gene expression
weeks 4-5	population genetics + molecular evolution	randomness and Monte Carlo simulation	population genetics simulations
weeks 6-7	sequence alignment	recursion and larger-program design	sequence alignment algorithms
weeks 8-9	phylogenetics	recursion on trees	estimating phylogenetic trees from sequence data
weeks 10-11	structure and function: RNA folding	memoization	implementing polynomial-time RNA folding
weeks 11-12	systems biology: modeling chemotaxis	software modeling via objects and classes	modeling chemotaxis using Python's turtle graphics libraries
weeks 13-14	neuroscience	uncomputability	student capstone projects

Figure 1. Summary of BioCS1's syllabus, biological and computational topics, and a subset of student homework [0].

Module 3 provides a first exposure to recursion in the context of sequence alignment and other related problems. Questions like *Are humans more closely related to chimpanzees or to gorillas?* pique students' interest and motivate algorithms for determining the differences between genetic sequences. In this module, students design and implement a set of increasingly sophisticated recursive functions and apply them to small biological datasets.

Once students can compute the differences between different species' genes, these differences can be used to infer putative evolutionary or *phylogenetic* trees. **Module 4** explores both the biological basis of these phylogenies and the recursive algorithms to estimate them. Figure 2, left, shows one student-generated example. Here, the recursion is on trees – the data structures, not arboreal ones! – a topic that is also taught in CS1 course, but without the rich motivating application that biology offers.

Although recursion is an effective tool to explore data and answer biological questions, it is not an efficient one: the algorithms students develop have exponential running time. **Module 5** explores the efficiency of algorithms, including the difference between exponential and polynomial time, and a glimpse at NP-completeness.

Students then learn *memoization*, a form of dynamic programming that reinforces dictionary data structures and allows many of their exponential algorithms to run in polynomial time. As a result, students can handle data sets of a size relevant in current biological work. Memoization also allows investigation of biologically fundamental questions, e.g, *How does RNA fold?*, as depicted graphically and programmatically in Figures 2 and 3. This coupling of powerful CS techniques with compelling biological applications symbiotically motivates both disciplines in a way that would be difficult – perhaps impossible – to achieve in a CS1 or Bio1 course alone.

Module 6 introduces Systems Biology, whose mathematical models and computational implementations yield insights into complex biological systems. BioCS1 students build a classical chemotaxic model that explains how a bacterium can use chemical gradients to move toward a source of food. The interacting agents of systems biology are best modeled through object-oriented programming, and students build their own classes and objects to do so.

Module 7 concludes the semester with several fundamental CS questions. First, we examine basic ideas in neuroscience and what it means for biological systems to compute. Concurrently, we explore elementary ideas in the *limits* of computability, ultimately establishing the existence of uncomputable functions. During this module, students choose one of three medium-sized capstone projects for the course. Each option exercises the ideas of modularity, classes, and objects introduced in the previous module: one option returns to cell biology, modeling interactions and catalysis within an artificial chemistry; the second uses likelihood methods to deduce the structure of gene regulatory networks from micro-array data (Figure 2, at right); the third option uses genetic programming to optimize the behavior of a Karel-like automaton [15].

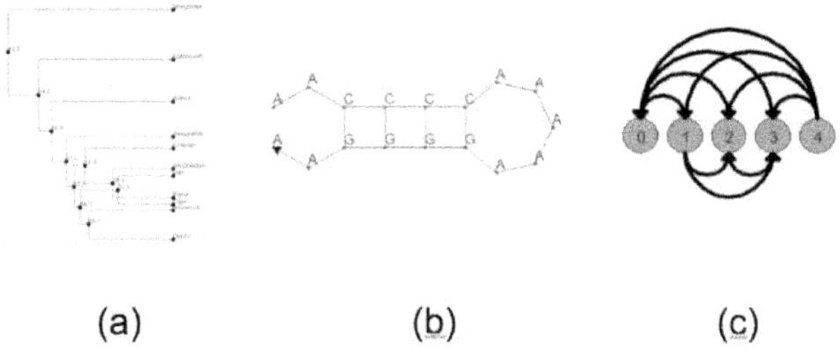

Figure 2. Example images from student work in BioCS1: (a) a deduced phylogenetic tree (week 9), (b) a computed fold within an RNA molecule (week 11), and (c) a maximum-likelihood gene regulatory network (week 14). Each image was created by a student submission that computed the structure in question and rendered via Python's turtle-graphics library.

Does BioCS1 cover all of CS 1 and Bio1? BioCS1 is a one semester course. In 2009-2010, we offered a follow-on "BioCS2" course. Of the 28 students who enrolled in BioCS1, 21 chose to take BioCS2. Students who took both of these courses saw the foundational topics in our one semester CS 1 course and our one semester Bio 1 course and satisfied both the college's CS and biology requirements.

In academic years 2010-11 and 2011-12, we offered BioCS1 without the BioCS2 follow-on course. In one semester it is clearly not possible to offer all of the material in CS 1 *and* Bio1. However, CS1 material not covered in BioCS1 is largely contextual, not fundamental. The CS1 course exposes students to a breadth of application areas, e.g., games, AI, and cryptography, in contrast to the single context that BioCS1 offers.

On the biology side, BioCS1 provides a first broad exposure to college-level biology by surveying some of the major ideas in the field and offering students weekly "dry lab" experiences that are not offered in the school's large Bio1 course. On the other hand, Bio1 does cover topics in both molecular and population biology absent from BioCS1. Even so, many students who complete BioCS1 can review those topics and successfully place out of Bio1. In 2010-11, every BioCS1 student placed out of Bio1, as did the vast majority of those who sought to pass out in 2011-12.

```
def compBase(base):
    """Returns the complementary RNA base."""
    if base == 'A': return 'U'
    if base == 'U': return 'A'
    if base == 'G': return 'C'
    if base == 'C': return 'G'

def adjust(pairs, k):
    """Takes a tuple of number pairs and
    increases the numbers by k."""
    output = ()
    for pair in pairs:
        adjPair = ((pair[0]+k, pair[1]+k),)
        output = output + adjPair
    return output

D = {}

def getFold(RNA):
    """ Returns an optimal folding of the given
    RNA string."""
    if len(RNA) <= 1: return (0, ())
    elif D.has_key(RNA): return D[RNA]
    else:
        maxUseIt = (0, ())
        for base in range(1,len(RNA)):
            if RNA[base] == compBase(RNA[0]):
                Int = getFold(RNA[1:base])
                IntPairs = adjust(Int[1], 1)
                Ext = getFold(RNA[base+1:])
                ExtPairs = adjust(Ext[1], base+1)
                useIt = (1 + Int[0] + Ext[0],
                        ((0, base),)+IntPairs+ExtPairs)
                if useIt[0] > maxUseIt[0]:
                    maxUseIt = useIt
        loseIt = getFold(RNA[1:])
        loseItPairs = adjust(loseIt[1], 1)
        if maxUseIt[0] >= loseIt[0]:
            RNAmax = maxUseIt
        else:
            RNAmax = (loseIt[0], loseItPairs)
        D[RNA] = RNAmax
        return RNAmax
```

Figure 3. A student's solution to the RNA folding problem of week 11, using recursion with memorization for efficiency.

4. EVALUATION AND RESULTS

Ultimately, it is student development that determines the success or failure of cross-disciplinary efforts such as this. In order to assess the choices and capabilities of the students taking BioCS1, we have tracked the first two cohorts (those taking BioCS1 in 2009 and 2010) through several measures of computational proficiency, through reported workload and affective feedback, and through subsequent choices of major. Because students at our institution do not choose a major program of study until the middle of the second year, we do not include the most recent cohort (2011) in these data. We are continuing the evaluation of BioCS1, however, and we do include that latest group where applicable, below.

Small-scale comparisons

In Fall 2009, we placed three identical fundamental computational questions on the CS1 and BioCS1 final exams. We also compared nearly identical questions between Bio1 homework problems and BioCS1 homework/exam questions. Although the details are reported elsewhere [0], the important outcome of these head-to-head problems was that student performance in BioCS1 did not differ significantly from that of students in Bio1 or students in CS1.

In the most recent cohort, Fall 2011, BioCS1 and CS1 shared one of the capstone projects (a genetic programming project). This capstone project requires a synthesis of a number of foundational CS topics including basic data structures and data types (e.g., two-dimensional arrays, dictionaries), object-oriented design, and, most importantly, the design, implementation, and testing of a mid-sized program (approximately 200 lines of code) from scratch. The BioCS1 and CS1 students performed equally well on this project, suggesting that both groups attained the desired level of computing proficiency.

	BioCS1 (2009-11)	CS1 Control (2009-11)	All students (2009-11)
cohort size	63	38	384
fraction taking CS2	49.2% (31/63)	44.7% (17/38)	44.0% (169/384)
average CS2 grade	3.69 (σ = 0.37)	3.53 (σ = 0.40)	3.56 (σ = 0.55)
choosing CS major	19.0% (12/63)	18.4% (7/38)	21.4% (82/384)
choosing Bio major	27.0% (17/63)	7.9% (3/38)	7.0% (27/384)

Figure 4. Data on how BioCS1 students fare in CS2 relative to the control cohort (those who wanted to join BioCS1 but could not because of space limitations) and all of the students in the 2009-2011 classes. In addition, we compare the rate at which BioCS1 students choose CS or biology majors with the control and institution-wide statistics. Note that BioCS1 students continue to take more CS and choose both CS and biology as a major more often than the control, though not significantly so. In addition, their performance in CS2 is *better* than both the control group's and the whole student body's.

Larger-scale comparisons

More important than individual exam problems or homework assignments is the question, ***How do BioCS1 students perform in subsequent CS courses?*** Figure 4 shows the rate at which BioCS1 students choose to take CS2 relative to the student body as a whole. Our CS2 course covers data-structures and programming-paradigms and has not changed significantly in the past 15 years. It is a required course for computer science majors, but a significant number of other majors choose to take it because of computation's growing role across many disciplines. Figure 4 also shows the average CS2 grades on a four-point scale for each cohort.

Although none of the differences in Figure 4's data are significant except the rise in biology majors within the BioCS1 students, this experiment is one in which the absence of difference is, in fact significant. After all, the students in BioCS1 received half the number of lectures on core CS that the control and the full student body received. Even so, they chose to continue with CS at the same rate – and performed as well in those subsequent courses as both the control and the college population as a whole.

Control cohort

Of course, students who sign up for an experience like BioCS1 may have academic interests and priorities distinct from the entire student body! Thus, we also break out a control cohort in Figure 4's results. The control group comprises those students who, like BioCS1's students, indicated a desire and interest in taking BioCS1 but could not enroll because of space limitations. Those placements were decided randomly and established before any of the students had even arrived for their first semester at college. We realize that *not* getting a placement in a desired course may have had some difficult-to-measure repercussions. Although few educational experiments – particularly those requiring open buy-in from students – can afford the scaffolding of a true scientific control, we do feel fortunate to have at least this approximation of a control cohort against which to measure BioCS1's effects.

Affective outcomes

Our institution's formal end-of-course evaluations are required of all students in all courses: they provide useful insights into student perceptions of BioCS1. On a Likert scale of 1 (low) to 7 (high), students were asked to indicate their agreement with the statements (a) *This course stimulated my interest in the material* and (b) *I learned a lot.* The means from the Fall 2011 offering are summarized here for BioCS1, CS1, and all courses at our college, along with one standard deviation σ reported for the final column:

	BioCS1	CS1	All courses
(a) Stimulated my interest	6.55	6.80	5.64 (σ = 1.43)
(b) I learned a lot	6.73	6.81	5.86 (σ = 1.28)

Certainly, both BioCS1 and CS1 are perceived positively by students. In light of the CS venue, we do not consider the biology scores here. We were particularly heartened to see such similar scores between these early offerings of BioCS1 and the college's older, better-established CS1 curriculum. A second indicator of interest emerges from the rates at which students choose to take CS 2: Figure 4 shows that the rate was no worse (in fact better, though not significantly) for BioCS1 students. This difference has widened in our most recent cohort (2011-12): 17 of the 33 BioCS1 students (52%) have chosen to take CS2 course as their sole spring elective. In contrast, only 51 of the 134 CS1 students (38%) have chosen to continue with CS2 next term.

Workload and student impressions

As part of those end-of-semester questionnaires, both BioCS1 and CS1 students reported identical averages of 5.6 hours per week outside of class. The average over all courses at the institution is 5.5 hours (with σ = 3.4). We have been deliberate and careful to keep the workloads of the two courses as equable as possible, in order not to favor one over the other.

We are excited, too, that open-ended student feedback has echoed the positive results borne out by the statistics above. In 2011, for example, one of the anonymous comments commended the pairing: "I was really impressed with the amount of both CS and bio I could learn in one course and the integration of the two fields was very interesting. Alternating CS and Bio lectures worked well." Another explained in more depth *why* alternating lectures worked: "I thought the split between biology one day and the programming the other worked well. This is because one day we grasped the concepts of what we were going to do and the next we learned the tools to carry out the programs." Still others pointed to how the course affected them: "I thought I was going to hate CS, but now I'm planning to study it further" and "I wasn't considering a CS major; now I am."

Negative comments focused on schedule (labs were held on Friday afternoons) or opportunities lost: "I wish we did

Mandelbrot sets"; the control and full cohorts had done so. Yet these knock the college experience, not BioCS1 *per se*.

5. PERSPECTIVE

The BioCS1 course described here offers one way to integrate an introductory computer science course with an introductory biology course. The merger provides a rich and compelling context in which to teach computer science along with powerful computational tools with which to explore biological phenomena. The BioCS1 combination thus benefits teaching of *both* disciplines, despite the fact that the course necessarily omits some peripheral material from parallel CS1 and Biology1 curricula.

This result is a promising one for CS educators: after all, it demonstrates that CS1's context can be expanded to full-fledged cross-disciplinary collaborations without compromising the students' resulting computational skills and enthusiasm. Put another way, BioCS1 shows that a course with only half the usual number of lecture-hours can succeed as well as a traditional CS1 offering – or even better, if *applications* of computer science are an important part of an institution's or department's goals.

With respect to biology education, BioCS1 presents a field-tested curriculum through which students begin to develop a skill set in demand by labs and universities alike. As with CS1, we believe the slightly reduced content is more than made up by the interdisciplinary problem-solving skills that a hybrid course fosters. What's more, BioCS1 enables hands-on experimentation, albeit *in silico*, of advanced topics such as sequence alignment and phylogeny estimation; more traditional approaches necessarily abstract away the field's computational foundations.

Thus, we hope that this effort might spark parallel peer-as-context approaches in chemistry, engineering, mathematics, physics, and beyond. More generally, we look forward to an era of integrative science education in which computation can act as both an effective collaborator and an inspiring catalyst.

6. COURSE MATERIALS

All course resources for BioCS1 including full lecture notes, assignments, labs, and capstone projects are available at [0].

7. ACKNOWLEDGMENTS

The authors thank HHMI award #52006301, NSF CPATH #0939149, and Harvey Mudd College for their generous support.

8. REFERENCES

[0] Dodds, Z., Libeskind-Hadas, R., and Bush, E. When CS 1 is biology 1: crossdisciplinary collaboration as CS context. ITiCSE '10, 219-223. Course URL: www.cs.hmc.edu/twiki/bin/view/CS6/

[1] 2020 Science Group. 2005. Towards 2020 Science Microsoft.

[2] Adams, J, Matheson, S, and Pruim, R. 2008. Blasted: integrating biology and computation. *JCSC* 24(1): 47-54.

[3] Beck, J, Buckner, B, and Nikolova, O. 2007. Using interdisciplinary bioinformatics undergraduate research to recruit and retain CS students. *Proc. SIGCSE 38* ACM Press: 358-361.

[4] Board on Life Sciences. 2003. Bio 2010 Nat. Acad. Press.

[5] Bruhn, R and Jennings, S. 2007. A multidisciplinary bioinformatics minor. *Proc. SIGCSE 38* ACM Press: 348-352.

[6] Burhans, D and Skuse, G. 2004. The role of CS in undergraduate bioinformatics education, *SIGCSE 35*: 417-421.

[7] Cutter, P. 2007. Having a BLAST: a bioinformatics project in CS2. *Proc. SIGCSE 38* ACM Press: 353-357.

[8] D'Antonio, L. 2003. Incorporating Bioinformatics in an algorithms course *SIGCSE Bulletin*, ACM Press 35(3): 211-214.

[9] Doom, T., Raymer, M., Krane, D., and Garcia, O. 2002. A proposed undergraduate bioinformatics curriculum for computer scientists. *Proc. SIGCSE 33* ACM Press: 78-81.

[10] Goode, E. and Trajkovski, G. 2007. Developing a truly interdisciplinary bioinformatics track: work in progress. *J. Comput. Small Coll.* 22(6): 73-79.

[11] Khuri, S. 2008. A bioinformatics track in computer science, *Proc. SIGCSE 39* ACM Press 508-512.

[12] LeBlanc, M. D. and Dyer, B D. 2004. Bioinformatics and CC2001: why computer science is well positioned in a post-genomic world, *SIGCSE Bull.*, ACM Press 36(4): PAGES.

[13] LeBlanc, M. D. and Dyer, B D. 2003. Teaching together: A three-year case study in genomics. *JCSC* 18(5): 85-95.

[14] McGuffee, J. 2007. Programming languages and the biological sciences, *J. of Comput. Small Coll.* 22(4): 178-183.

[15] Parlante, N. et al.. 2010. Nifty assignments. In Proceedings, SIGCSE '10. ACM, New York, NY, USA, 478-479.

[16] Pearce, J. and Nakazawa, M. 2008. The funnel that grew our CIS major in the CS desert. *Proc. SIGCSE 39* 503-507.

[17] Qin, H. 2009. Teaching computational thinking through bioinformatics to biology students. *Proc. SIGCSE 40* 188-191.

[18] Robbins, K. 2010. vip.cs.utsa.edu/classes/cs1173f2009

[19] Sadava, D., Heller, H, Orians, G, Purves, W, and Hillis, D. Life: The Science of Biology, W. H. Freeman and Co. NY, NY.

[20] Schaub, S. 2009. Teaching CS1 with web applications and test-driven development. *SIGCSE Bull.* 41(2): 113-117.

[21] Soh, L-K, et al. 2009. Renaissance computing: an initiative for promoting student participation in comp., *SIGCSE 40* 59-63.

[22] Stone, J. A., Medica, D. L., and Fetsko, L. A. 2009. Experiences with a CS1 for the health sciences. *SIGCSE Bull.* 41(2): 122-126.

[23] Summet, J., Kumar, D., O'Hara, K., Walker, D., Ni, L., Blank, D., and Balch, T. 2009. Personalizing CS1 with robots. *SIGCSE Bull.* ACM Press 41(1): 433-437.

[24] Tew, A E, McCracken, W M, and Guzdial, M. 2005. Impact of alternative introductory courses on programming concept understanding. *Proc. ICER 1* ACM Press: 25-35.

[25] Tjaden, B. 2007. A multidisciplinary course in comp. biology. *J. Comput. Small Coll.* CCSC Press 22(6): 80-87.

[26] Toth, C. and Connelly, R. 2006. A bioinformatics experience course. *J. Comput. Small Coll.* CCSC Press 21(6): 100-107.

[27] Wray, K.A. 2005. Perl algorithm to calculate and categorize φ and ψ angles in a protein. *J. Comp. Sci. in Coll.* 20(5): 98-99.

A Study of Stereotype Threat in Computer Science

Amruth N. Kumar
Ramapo College of New Jersey
505 Ramapo Valley Road
Mahwah, NJ 07430, USA
1 201 684 7712
amruth@ramapo.edu

ABSTRACT

A controlled study was conducted to detect stereotype threat on harder topics in introductory Computer Science. Students in the control group were asked to identify their demographic information before taking the test whereas students in the experimental group were asked to do so after completing the test. So, the control group was indirectly reminded of stereotypes before taking the test, when it could affect performance on the test, whereas the experimental group was reminded after the test when it could not affect test performance.

Tests on two different loops were used, along with a partial cross-over design: a random group of students served as the control group on one test, and the experimental group on the other and vice versa. Mixed factor ANOVA analysis of the data showed that all the students scored significantly higher when not reminded of stereotypes before the test regardless of sex or race. In addition, average/below-average students scored significantly higher when not reminded of stereotypes before the test, again, regardless of sex or race. So, on harder topics in Computer Science, stereotype threat affects all the students, and in particular, the less-prepared students. In light of this, some suggestions are offered for avoiding stereotype threat during tests.

Categories and Subject Descriptors

K.3.2 [**Computing Milieux**]: Computer and Information Science Education

General Terms

Experimentation, Measurement, Human Factors.

Keywords

Stereotype Threat, Online Testing, Computer Science I.

1. INTRODUCTION

When sex and race are associated with positive or negative stereotypes in a discipline, reminding students of the stereotype before a test can positively or negatively affect their performance. The effect has been termed stereotype threat (e.g., [14, 15]). Reminding students of stereotypes could happen explicitly or implicitly. Subtle gestures such as asking students for their race and sex, or holding the test in a classroom that contains "masculine" wall posters [6] are sufficient to elicit stereotype threat. Researchers have studied stereotype threat with women and minorities in mathematics (e.g., [13, 11]), and engineering (e.g., [3]). In Computer Science, stereotype threat is listed as one of the factors that could be contributing to problems with recruitment and retention of female and minority students (e.g., [4, 10]). Interventions have been tried to reduce students' susceptibility to stereotype threat [1], but have yielded mixed results in Computer Science [12].

A study was conducted earlier to see if stereotype threat could be detected in the context of testing in Computer Science [9]. In the study, stereotype threat was studied among introductory Computer Science students using online tests on logical and assignment expressions. Since stereotype threat was observed on assignment expression test, but not logical expression test, and students found assignment expressions to be harder, the study concluded that stereotype threat may be more readily apparent on harder topics in Computer Science. This result concurred with findings reported in literature for learning Math [13]. Another finding of the earlier study was that stereotype threat was significant on assignment expressions only when students who had scored 100% on the test had been eliminated from consideration. In other words, stereotype threat was more evident among students who had not already mastered the material.

The current study was conducted as a follow-up to see under what conditions stereotype threat could be detected on harder topics in Computer Science. The study was conducted with online tests on loops, which are harder than expression evaluation. In the study, stereotype threat was elicited by simply asking the students to identify their demographic information – sex, race, academic status and major. No other reference was made to positive or negative stereotypes during the test. Software tutors called problets (www.problets.org) were used to conduct the study entirely online.

The study was controlled – in the beginning, all the students entered their name and email address. At this time, the students in the control group were also asked for their demographic information, whereas the students in the experimental group were asked for it on a separate questionnaire presented after the test. So, the students in the control group were reminded of stereotypes before taking the test, which could affect their test performance, unlike the students in the experimental group. If stereotype threat was indeed detectable, a significant difference in test scores could be expected between control and experimental students. According to stereotype threat, the difference would apply in particular to female and minority students.

2. METHODS

Two tests were administered during the study in spring 2010 – one on `while` loops and another on `for` loops. The students answered the `while` loop test (usually 1-7 days) before the `for` loop test. During the tests, each limited to 30 minutes, the students solved 9-10 problems on program tracing. The tests and the demographic surveys were administered back to back, online. *Computer Science I* students participated in the study asynchronously, on their own time after class.

Participants were randomly assigned to one of two groups: A or B. Partial cross-over design was used: group A served as the experimental group on `while` loop and the control group on `for` loop test, and vice versa for group B. For analysis purposes, only the students who had answered both the tests were considered. As informed by the earlier study [9], students who had scored 100% on *both* the tests (N=13) were not considered.

A total of 193 students were included in the study – 129 male, 56 female, 117 Caucasians, and 54 non-Caucasians (including Black/African American, Hispanic/Latino, Asian and Other). Some students did not identify their sex/race and were not included in the corresponding analysis. The students had solved from 7 to 10 problems on the tests. In order to factor out the effect of the differences in the number of problems solved, the average score per problem with a range of 0 → 1.0 was considered for analysis rather than the raw score with a range of 0 → 10. Similarly, the average time spent per problem was considered rather than the total time spent on the test.

3. ANALYSIS AND RESULTS

Unless otherwise noted, 2 X 2 mixed factor ANOVA was used to analyze data in each of the following sections. In each case, the repeated measure and the between-subjects factor are listed. In the analysis, **treatment** refers to asking for demographic information before versus after the test.

3.1 Treatment versus group

Average score per problem was analyzed, with the treatment as the repeated measure for each student and the group (A versus B) as the between-subjects factor.

A significant main effect was observed for treatment [$F(1,191) = 13.910$, $p < 0.001$] - students scored:

- 0.8738 ± 0.02 (at 95% confidence level) when in the control group;
- 0.9105 ± 0.01 when in the experimental group.

The difference was statistically significant [$t(192) = -3.950$, $p < 0.001$]. The effect size (Cohen's d) is 0.31, indicating that the effect of treatment is small, but not negligible. *In other words, students scored higher when reminded of stereotypes after rather than before the test.* Note that this result applies to the general population, and not just women and minorities.

No significant main effect was observed for group - there was no statistical difference between groups A and B. The two groups of students were comparable, and it did not matter whether the students were in the control group first or in the experimental group first.

A significant interaction was observed between treatment and group [$F(1,191) = 4.608$, $p = 0.033$]: Group A scored more on the `while` test as the experimental group than on the `for` test as the control group, as shown in Table 1. But the difference between the two scores was not statistically significant. Group B scored less on the `while` test as the control group than on the `for` test as the experimental group. The difference between the scores was statistically significant [$t(1,106) = -4.642$, $p < 0.001$]. This eliminates the topic of the test (`while` versus `for` loops) as a confounding factor.

Table 1. Interaction between treatment and group: Score

Group (N)	`while` test	`for` test
A (86)	0.900 ± 0.022	0.885 ± 0.028
B (107)	0.865 ± 0.025	0.919 ± 0.020

Average time spent per problem was analyzed, with treatment as the repeated measure and group (A versus B) as the between-subjects factor. A significant main effect was found for treatment [$F(1,191) = 10.830$, $p = 0.001$] – students solved problems in:

- 91.739 ± 4.985 seconds per problem in experimental condition;
- 101.165 ± 5.978 seconds in control condition.

The difference was statistically significant [$t(192) = 2.940$, $p = 0.004$]. The effect size (Cohen's d) is 3.39, indicating that the effect of treatment is huge. *In other words, students answered the test faster when reminded of stereotypes after rather than before the test.*

Table 2. Interaction between treatment and group: Time

Group (N)	Control group	Experimental group
A (86)	104.992 ± 8.902	87.322 ± 7.424
B (107)	97.337 ± 7.981	96.156 ± 6.656

No significant main effect was found for group - there was no statistical difference between groups A and B. A significant interaction was found between treatment and group [$F(1,191) = 8.285$, $p = 0.004$]:

- Group B spent about the same amount of time per problem on the `while` loop test as the control group as it did on the `for` loop test as the experimental group, and any difference between the two was not statistically significant.
- Group A spent more time on the `for` loop test as the control group than it did on the `while` loop test as the experimental group as shown in Table 2, and the difference was statistically significant [$t(85) = 3.554$, $p = 0.001$].

This eliminates the topic of the test as a confounding factor, while attributing faster testing times to the treatment.

3.2 Treatment versus sex

In Computer Science, stereotype threat is expected to negatively affect female students in particular. So, the average score per problem was analyzed, with treatment as the repeated measure and sex as the between-subjects factor.

A marginally significant main effect was observed for sex [$F(1,183) = 3.242$, $p = 0.073$]: female students scored less than male students in both control and experimental groups as shown in Table 3. The difference between the sexes was marginally significant for the control group [$t(183) = 1.858$, $p = 0.065$] and not statistically significant for the experimental group.

Table 3. Interaction between treatment and sex – Score

Sex	Control group	Experimental group
Male	0.886 ± 0.023	0.915 ± 0.018
Female	0.847 ± 0.035	0.897 ± 0.028

The interaction between treatment and sex was not statistically significant since both male and female students scored higher when asked for demographics information after rather than before the test as shown in Table 3. The difference between control and experimental scores was statistically significant for both the sexes:

- Male students - [$t(128) = -2.610$, $p = 0.010$];
- Female students - [$t(55) = -2.747$, $p = 0.008$].

So, the data *did not support any greater influence of stereotype threat on female students than on male students.*

Analysis of the average time per problem yielded a significant main effect for sex [$F(1,183) = 14.450$, $p < 0.001$] – female students spent more time per problem than male students in control as well as experimental condition as shown in Table 4. The difference between the sexes was statistically significant in both the conditions:

- Control condition - [$t(183) = -2.184$, $p = 0.030$];
- Experimental condition - [$t(183) = -4.560$, $p < 0.001$].

The difference between control and experimental times was statistically significant for male [$t(128) = 3.164$, $p = 0.002$], but not female students. *So, the data supported a significant influence of treatment on the speed with which male students answered the test.*

Table 4. Interaction between treatment and sex – Time

Sex	Control group	Experimental group
Male	96.121 ± 7.200	85.232 ± 5.839
Female	110.606 ± 10.928	109.761 ± 8.862

3.3 Treatment versus race

Stereotype threat is also expected to negatively affect minority students in Computer Science. So, the average score per problem was analyzed, with treatment as the repeated measure and race as the between-subjects factor.

No significant main effect was found for race: non-Caucasians scored the same as Caucasians. The interaction between treatment and race was not statistically significant: both Caucasians and non-Caucasians scored higher when asked for demographic information after rather than before the test, as shown in Table 5. The improvement in score was statistically significant for both the groups:

- Caucasians - [$t(116) = -2.313$, $p = 0.022$];
- Non-Caucasians - [$t(53) = -2.979$, $p = 0.004$].

Asians are positively stereotyped in quantitative domains such as Computer Science (e.g., [7]). So, the analysis was repeated after combining Caucasians and Asians into one group and the rest into the other group. The results remained the same: no main effect for race since both the groups had similar scores; and no significant interaction between treatment and race since both the groups scored higher as experimental subjects than as control subjects. In other words, the data *did not support any greater influence of stereotype threat on minority students.*

Table 5. Interaction between treatment and race – Score

Race	Control group	Experimental group
Caucasians	0.878 ± 0.024	0.907 ± 0.020
Non-Caucasians	0.871 ± 0.035	0.913 ± 0.029

A similar analysis of the time spent per problem yielded a significant main effect for race [$F(1,169) = 9.336$, $p = 0.003$] – Caucasians spent less time per problem than non-Caucasians in both treatments, as shown in Table 6. The difference between the races was statistically significant in both the conditions:

- Control condition - [$t(169) = -2.543$, $p = 0.012$];
- Experimental condition - [$t(169) = -2.649$, $p = 0.009$].

The decrease in time from the control to the experimental condition was significant for Caucasians [$t(116) = 2.097$, $p = 0.038$], but not for non-Caucasians. *So, the data supported a significant influence of treatment on the speed with which Caucasian students answered the test.*

Table 6. Interaction between treatment and race – Time

Race	Control group	Experimental group
Caucasians	94.717 ± 7.482	87.779 ± 6.265
Non-Caucasians	111.870 ± 11.013	102.741 ± 9.222

The pattern that emerges from these analyses is that *students scored higher when reminded of stereotypes after rather than before the test. This was true and the increase in score was statistically significant regardless of the sex or race. The data did not support that stereotype threat affected the score of students in any one particular demographic group more than the other. On the other hand, being reminded of stereotypes after rather than before the test helped male and Caucasian students answer the test significantly faster.*

It might seem counter-intuitive that even male and Caucasian students who are positively stereotyped in Computer Science were affected by stereotype threat, i.e., they scored lower and solved problems slower when reminded of stereotypes before the test. However, this is explained as "choking effect" in literature [2, 5] – when male/Caucasian students have not mastered a topic, if they are reminded of stereotypes before a test, they may view the positive stereotype associated with their demographic group as being externally imposed. They choke, leading to poorer performance [2]. In other words, stereotype threat is a double-edged sword – *it could affect positively stereotyped students just as much as negatively stereotyped students in Computer Science.*

3.4 Preparation of the student

Could the level of preparation of students be a factor in eliciting stereotype threat? In order to test this hypothesis, the test performance of the students in the control condition was used as a measure of their preparation. The average test score of the control group was calculated and students were grouped into two – those who had scored above average and those who had not. The question was whether students who scored average/below-average were affected more from treatment than those who scored above average. The average score per problem was again analyzed with treatment as the repeated measure and preparation as the between-subjects factor.

As could be expected, a significant main effect was observed for preparation [$F(1,191) = 123.970$, $p < 0.001$] - the average was:

- 0.940 for students who scored above-average;
- 0.813 for those who scored average/below average.

Notably, the interaction between treatment and preparation was statistically significant [$F(1,191) = 96.663$, $p < 0.001$] as shown in Table 7:

- The score of above-average students *decreased* from control to experimental condition and the decrease was statistically significant [$t(119) = 2.891$, $p = 0.005$];
- The score of students at or below average *increased* from control to experimental condition and the increase was statistically significant [$t(72) = -8.312$, $p < 0.001$].

Table 7. Interaction between treatment and preparation

Preparation	Control group	Experimental group
Above-Average	0.951 ± 0.015	0.930 ± 0.019
Average or Below	0.747 ± 0.020	0.879 ± 0.024

It is not clear why the score of above-average students decreased from control to experimental condition. 20 of the 120 above-average students scored 1.0 on the control test, but scored less than 1.0 on the experimental test. Since the maximum score of 1.0 was observed in the control test and not the experimental test, ceiling effect cannot be blamed for the *decrease*. The 20 students who scored 1.0 on the control test were almost evenly distributed between groups A and B, which eliminates the topic of the test as contributing to the decrease. It is tempting to argue that in the absence of upfront reinforcement of positive stereotype associated with them, above-average students did not do as well in the experimental condition as they did in the control condition. But above-average student population was not homogeneous – it included female and minority students, whose traits are associated with negative rather than positive stereotypes in Computer Science. This unusual observation, however, concurs with the non-significant tendency reported in literature that "non-stereotyped groups seem to perform slightly worse in low stereotype threat conditions" [13].

A 2 X 2 X 2 mixed factor ANOVA with treatment as the repeated measure and preparation and sex as between-subjects factors did not yield any significant interaction between treatment, preparation and sex: the pattern of change in the score observed was the same for male and female students in the two groups of preparation as it was for the whole population. Similarly, a 2 X 2 X 2 mixed factor ANOVA with treatment as the repeated measure and preparation and race as between-subjects factors did not yield any significant interaction between treatment, preparation and race either. The pattern that emerges from these analyses is that *less-prepared students scored higher when reminded of stereotypes after rather than before the test. This is true regardless of sex or race.*

The students were asked to fill out a survey before each test. In the survey, the students were asked to respond to statements on how well they knew the topic of the test. They responded on a Likert scale of 1 (Strongly agree) to 5 (Strongly disagree). Their responses on the survey were used as an estimate of their self-confidence. Note that on the chosen Likert scale, the lower the numerical response, the more positive the student, and hence, the greater the student's self-confidence.

Analysis of the survey response with treatment as the repeated measure and preparation as the between-subjects factor yielded a significant main effect for preparation [$F(1,167) = 4.020$, $p = 0.047$]: not surprisingly, above-average students were more self-confident in control as well as experimental condition, as shown in Table 8. One hypothesis for the test score pattern observed earlier, which is the same regardless of sex or race, is that when average/below-average students are asked to identify their demographic information before the test, they are reminded that they are not confident in their knowledge of the topic.

Table 8. Students' estimation of their ability – treatment versus preparation

Preparation	Control	Experimental
Above-Ave	2.571 ± 0.161	2.548 ± 0.166
Ave/Below-Ave	2.836 ± 0.204	2.790 ± 0.210

4. DISCUSSION

This study was a follow-up to on an earlier study [9] that concluded that stereotype threat may be more readily apparent on harder topics in Computer Science. The results of the current study indicate that on harder topics such as loops, stereotype threat applies to *all* the students and not just those with whom negative stereotypes are associated. The reasons may be different – reminder of negative stereotypes for female/minority students, and choking effect [2] for male/Caucasian students, but the effect is the same – *all* the students scored higher on tests when they were not reminded of stereotypes before the test. Male/Caucasian students also solved problems significantly faster when not reminded of stereotypes before the test. The take-away message is that Computer Science educators must try to avoid eliciting stereotype threat during tests, and especially so when the tests are on harder topics.

The study found that on harder topics in Computer Science, the level of preparation of students is a strong predictor of stereotype threat – average/below-average students scored higher when they were not reminded of stereotypes before the test, regardless of sex or race. Additional analysis not included here showed that this was also true regardless of the major (Computer Science versus other disciplines), status (freshman versus others) or type of institution (4-year versus 2-year). The dearth of computing professionals is acute all around the world, whether in the United States (where enrollments have dropped significantly since the hey days of dot-com bubble), Europe (where talent is being imported on special visas) or in emerging markets (e.g., India cannot produce enough qualified computing professionals to meet its needs). So, the discipline cannot afford to ignore or lose average/below average students. Avoiding stereotype threat during testing would be an effort in the right direction.

In this study, stereotype threat was elicited implicitly by asking students to identify their demographic information, i.e., sex, race, academic status and major. In literature, other mechanisms have been listed for eliciting stereotype threat, e.g., researchers removed objects stereotypical of Computer Science such as Star Trek posters and video games from a classroom and replaced them with non-stereotypical objects such as nature posters to increase the interest of female undergraduate students to the level of their male peers, through a process called "ambient belonging" [6]. In another study, researchers used the gender of the experimenter as a subtle stereotype threat cue [16], and proposed a dual process for how blatant and subtle stereotype threat cues can impact performance. There are other ways in which stereotype threat can be elicited, and therefore, should be avoided – some are listed below:

- A class is separated by sex either during instruction or testing (as might be done in some cultures)
- Students are seated for a test not randomly but by some demographic criterion (such as major) to discourage unwanted collaboration during the test
- Two different tests are handed out, or students are asked to answer odd or even-numbered questions on a test based not on random order, but on some demographic criterion (such as academic status)
- An extra field is included on the test book for the student to enter "maiden name" or credits earned so far towards a degree.
- The wording of the test questions is not gender-neutral.
- The examples used in the test are known to appeal primarily to say male and not female students (i.e., are "boy-themed" [8]), e.g., a catch-as-they-drop game described as a warship catching falling bombs rather than a monkey catching falling fruits.

In each case, the instructor may inadvertently elicit stereotype threat, which can in turn lead to poorer performance on the test.

Given that stereotype threat can be elicited in any number of ways both overt and subtle, it negatively affects the test performance of both positively and negatively stereotyped students on harder topics in Computer Science, and it especially affects less-prepared students, Computer Science instructors should be cognizant of the potential for stereotype threat and take reasonable precautions to avoid it when administering tests. Such precautions are important to ensure that social factors do not affect student performance on the tests, and tests assess only technical knowledge. This is all the more important given the declined enrollment and continuing attrition problem in Computer Science and the projected increase in the demand for Computer Science graduates over the next decade all around the world.

5. ACKNOWLEDGMENTS

Partial support for this work was provided by the National Science Foundation under grant DUE-0817187.

6. REFERENCES

[1] Aronson, J., Fried, C. and Good, C. Reducing the effects of stereotype threat on African American college students by shaping theories of intelligence. *Journal of Experimental Social Psychology,* 38(2): 113-125, 2002.

[2] Baumeister, R.F., Hamilton, J.C., and Tice, D.M., "Public versus private expectancy of success: Confidence booster or performance pressure?", Journal of Personality and Social Psychology, 48, 1985, 1447-1457.

[3] Bell, A. and Spencer, S.J. "The Effect of Stereotype Threat on Women's Performance on the Fundamentals of Engineering Exam", Proc. 2002 American Society for Engineering Education Annual Conference and Exposition, Montreal, 2002.

[4] Beyer, S., Rynes, K., Perrault, J, Hay, K. and Haller, S., "Gender differences in computer science students", SIGCSE '03: Proceedings of the 34th SIGCSE technical symposium on Computer science education, Reno, NV, 2003, 49-53.

[5] Cheryan, S. and Bodenhausen, G.V. "When positive stereotypes threaten intellectual performance: The psychological hazards of 'model minority' status", Psychological Science, 11(5), September 2000, 399-402.

[6] Cheryan, S., Plaut, V.C., Davies, P.G. and Steele, C.M. Ambient Belonging: How Stereotypical Cues Impact Gender Participation in Computer Science. *Journal of Personality and Social Psychology.* 97(6): 1045-1060, 2009.

[7] Kao, G., "Asian Americans as model minorities? A look at their academic performance", American Journal of Education, 103, 1995, 121-159.

[8] Klawe, M. Girls, Boys, and Computers. *ACM SIGCSE Bulletin – Women and Computing.* 34(2). June 2002. 16-17.

[9] Kumar, A.N. "The Effect of Soliciting Demographic Data on the Performance of Students on Online Tests", FIE 2010, Washington, D.C., Oct 2010, Session T1A.

[10] Peckham, J., Stephenson, P.D., Harlow, L.L., Stuart, D.A., Silver, B., and Mederer, H., "Broadening Participation in

Computing: Issues and Challenges", Proc. of 12th SIGCSE conference on Innovation and Technology in Computer Science Education (ITiCSE 07), 2007, 9-13.

[11] Schmader, T., Johns, M., and Barquissau, M., "The costs of accepting gender differences: The role of stereotype endorsement in women's experience in the math domain", Sex Roles, 50(11-12), June 2004, 835-850.

[12] Simon, B., Hanks, B., Murphy, L., Fitzgerald, S., McCauley, R., Thomas, L., and Zander, C. Saying Isn't Necessarily Believing: Influencing Self-Theories in Computing. Proc. ICER 2008, Sydney, Australia, 2008, 173-184.

[13] Spencer, S.J., Steele, C.M., and Quinn, D.M., "Stereotype threat and women's math performance", Journal of Experimental Social Psychology, 35, 1999, 4-28.

[14] Steele, C.M., "A threat in the air: How stereotypes shape intellectual identity and performance", American Psychologist, 52, 1997, 613-629.

[15] Steele, C.M. and Aronson, J., "Stereotype threat and the intellectual test performance of African Americans", Journal of Personality and Social Psychology, 69, 1995, 797-811.

[16] Stone, J. and McWhinnie, C. Evidence that blatant versus subtle stereotype threat cues impact performance through dual processes. *Journal of Experimental Social Psychology.*44(2): 445-452, March 2008.

What Do Computer Scientists Do? A Survey of CS and Non-CS Liberal Arts Faculty

Hannah Fidoten
Knox College
2 East South St
Galesburg, IL 61401
hfidoten@knox.edu

Jaime Spacco
Knox College
2 East South St
Galesburg, IL 61401
jspacco@knox.edu

ABSTRACT

We asked all of the liberal arts faculty who advise undergraduates on course selection at the 14 colleges in the Associated Colleges of the Midwest a series of questions regarding their perceptions of the personality traits of Computer Science (CS) students, topics they think are covered in CS classes, and their overall impressions of CS. Our goal was to assess empirically the hypotheses that (1) many non-CS faculty do not really know what computer science is, and (2) many non-CS faculty are unaware of the differences between CS and Information Technology (IT). We received over 250 survey responses, which revealed that, among non-CS faculty, only 9% disagree or are neutral that CS should even be part of a liberal arts curriculum, but 32% think CS students learn to administer computers and computer networks, while 34% believe that CS students are taught to use Microsoft products in the classroom. However, over 95% of non-CS faculty also recognize the importance of both programming and algorithms to the study of computer science. The overall data suggests that a majority of non-CS faculty in the Associated Colleges of the Midwest have a a basic understanding of CS, while the remainder have an overly broad definition of CS (i.e. they think that CS includes IT).

Categories and Subject Descriptors

K.3.2 [**Computer and Information Science Education**]: Computer Science Education

General Terms

Human Factors

Keywords

cs education, survey, cs ed research

1. INTRODUCTION

When liberal arts Computer Science (CS) educators gather, it is not uncommon to hear anecdotes about colleagues in other academic fields who think that we teach our students to fix printers, or that we teach advanced typing and word processing, or some other gross misunderstanding of our discipline. These anecdotes are typically humorous stories that are told for amusement, and often revolve around our colleagues confusing CS with IT. If these anecdotes somehow represent a broader misunderstanding of CS, or a conflation of CS with IT in the minds of many faculty, then CS enrollments at liberal arts colleges could be negatively affected because of the dual-roles of professor and adviser that the majority of liberal arts faculty must take on.

A basic understanding of other academic disciplines is critical for liberal arts faculty because we must be both teacher and adviser to incoming students. The faculty at the majority of liberal arts colleges in the United States help students, typically first-and-second-year students who have not yet picked a major, select their classes each semester. If many of these faculty fundamentally do not understand what computer science is, they may be less likely to recommend the subject, or to recommend CS to student who are not as likely to enjoy or succeed in the discipline. Faculty cannot possibly be experts in every academic discipline, so they must do their best to match the student's interests with their understanding of other academic disciplines.

Outside of their own area of expertise, faculty are more likely to have experience with some academic disciplines over others. High school curricula in the US ensure that all high school graduates will have spent a year or more studying many academic disciplines, including literature, a foreign language, chemistry, physics, biology, history, and mathematics. Other academic disciplines, such as theater, fine arts, government, and music, are widely available as electives in high school. While taking a high school class is clearly not the same as studying a subject at the undergraduate or graduate level, a high school class is still more likely to convey a basic understanding of a discipline than no classes at all.

Computer Science, however, is not required of high school students in any state in the United States, and is only available as an elective (in other words, not as a core academic discipline) in many other states [4]. Many states also have a certification process for CS teachers that focuses on IT and basic computer literacy instead of CS, while other states lack any certification standards at all [4]. In 2010, about as many high school students took the first CS Advanced Placement (AP) exam took Art History, Music Theory, and Spanish Literature; about five times as many students took the Chemistry and Environmental Science AP exams, and

ITiCSE'12, July 3–5, 2012, Haifa, Israel.

about ten times as many students took the Psychology AP exam [1]. Finally, a survey of over 800 high school Calculus and Pre-Calculus students in the southwestern United States revealed that over 80% either had no idea what computer science is, or thought that computer science was something that it is not.

Given all of these factors, it seems pertinent to ask the question: Do faculty at liberal arts colleges have a basic understanding of CS? If the answer is "no", then our discipline must work harder to educate our colleagues about the exciting work that we do; on the other hand, if the answer is "yes", then we would be wise to recognize that those anecdotes about colleagues who think we fix printers and teach advanced typing skills are in fact anecdotes.

2. RELATED WORK

Our survey builds off of strong recent work in measuring the perceptions and understanding of CS by a number of different researchers. Some of our survey questions were borrowed from, or inspired by, these other surveys.

A survey by Carter [6] of eight hundred high school calculus and pre-calculus students revealed, among other things, that over 80% of these students, who ostensibly are the most likely to take CS in college, had no idea what computer science is. A survey by Ruslanov and Yolevich [10] of undergraduates revealed a number of key misunderstandings about CS, such as that 57% of undergraduates believing that using a computer regularly grants an advantage in CS courses, that over half of the undergraduates surveyed felt that only "computer savvy" people could succeed in CS, and that many of the survey respondents confused using a computer with being a computer scientist.

Lewis et. al. [8] found key differences of opinion between CS faculty and CS students regarding a number of important issues pertaining to the study of CS. Perrenet [9] follows up this work with a longitudinal study of a similar set of CS-related issues that compares the attitudes of undergraduates in their first, second, and third year with the attitudes of the faculty of the department. He finds that student attitudes towards most, but not all, of the survey items move towards the faculty attitudes as they progress through the undergraduate major (course).

Hewner and Guzdial study in careful detail essays about computing written by students who are preparing to graduate [7]. They find that, while CS majors "wrote expressively about the excitement and breadth of the discipline", the attitudes towards computing other majors who had taken introductory CS courses were not significantly changed by these courses. Hewner and Guzdial raise a number of important issues, such as whether one introductory computing course is enough to effect a change in the attitudes of non-majors towards computing, and whether an engaging introductory computing course is even the right vehicle to effect a change in attitudes. This work is significant because it addressees the difficulty of changing the attitudes held by a large, diverse group of people towards an academic discipline that they may not think about regularly.

3. FACULTY SURVEY

Given how poorly understood CS is at both the high school [6] and college [10] level, and given the rarity of CS programs at the high school level [4], we decided to ask all of the faculty at the 14 colleges of the Associated Colleges of the Midwest (the "other ACM" [5]) about their perceptions of CS. Our goal was to collect evidence that helps address two basic questions:

- Do non-CS faculty at liberal arts colleges have a basic understanding of CS?
- Do non-CS faculty recognize the differences between CS and IT?

The first question is important because liberal arts faculty also serve as advisors to undergraduates who need to select a course and a major; the second question matters because IT is usually considered too narrowly-focused of a field to be part of a typical broad-based liberal arts curriculum.

We emailed a link to our survey to about 2,150 faculty members at 13 of the 14 colleges in the Associated College of the Midwest (due to technical problems, the survey link was not sent to the faculty at St. Olaf College). At Knox College, we used the faculty email distribution list, but we had to cut-and-paste the email addresses from the department web pages of the other 13 schools.

We also sent the same survey to the SIGCSE mailing list (with the caveat that we wanted to hear from liberal arts faculty) in an attempt to establish a baseline perspective of CS faculty about the field of Computer Science.

Our survey questions are included in Table 1, and our survey data are available at `http://cs.knox.edu/jspacco/faculty-survey/`.

4. SURVEY RESULTS

Our survey of the Associated Colleges of the Midwest faculty received 213 responses out of about 2,150 faculty members surveyed, a 10% response rate. The survey of SIGCSE members yielded an additional 71 responses. The SIGCSE survey results was directed to liberal arts faculty, but was not restricted to liberal arts faculty, so comparisons between the the results of the two surveys are not perfect. Whenever possible, we indicate which populations are included in the results.

We found that over 95% of the non-CS liberal arts faculty surveyed reported knowing a computer scientist, which would be expected at a small college where faculty from a variety of departments intermingle on a regular basis. This is a cheerful result overall, although the very small number of respondents (5) who did not know a computer scientist make it difficult to conduct meaningful statistical analysis of that population.

4.1 Overall Results

Table 2 shows the overall breakdown of results comparing the non-CS faculty in the ACM with the CS faculty (combined SIGCSE and ACM). Categories that were statistically different at the $p<0.05$ level (as computed with the Mann-Whitney U Test) are starred. We report the modal value in addition to the mean values because we recognize that averages across Likert item responses, while commonly computed, can be misleading if the ordinal values are not equidistant (i.e. is the distance between *Slightly Agree* and *Agree* the same as the distance between *Slightly Disagree* and *Neutral*?).

Question Key	Full Question
Question: Please indicate how accurately these activities describe what computer science majors learn to do in their classes and labs Answers used a 5-point Likert Scale from 1=Disagree to 5=Agree	
Question Key	Full Question
fix printers	Fix computers and computer peripherals, such as printers
program	Write programs
administer	Administer and maintain computers and computer networks (install software, change passwords, configure wireless routers, etc)
group projects	Work on group projects or group assignments
analyze data	Analyze and interpret data
memorize formulas	Memorize and apply formulas
ms word	Learn to use different software products (i.e. Microsoft Word, Excel, etc)
algorithms	Design efficient algorithms to solve problems
web pages	Design web pages (choose color schemes and fonts, add images, manage links, etc)
organize info	Organize information effectively (can search and retrieve relevant items quickly)
Question: Please indicate how much you agree with the statements below Answers used a 5-point Likert Scale from 1=Disagree to 5=Agree	
Question Key	Full Question
good job	Knowledge of computing will not help students secure a good job.
sci. prog.	It is important for scientists to master a basic level of programming.
tech-savvy	Students do not need to be tech-savvy to be successful in a computer science course.
no life	A student who performs well in computer science will probably not have a "life" outside of computers.
gender	Women and men can both excel in careers that involve computing.
outsourcing	Due to outsourcing, employment opportunities for computer scientists in the US have decreased each of the last several years.
transferable skills	Skills acquired in a computer science course can be readily applied to other disciplines.
cs belongs	The computer science major belongs at a liberal arts college.
gender interest	Men are more interested in computing than are women.
prior experience	Students do not need prior experience to be successful in an introductory computer science course.

Table 1: Survey questions. The "Question Key" is a short textual key that can be used to identify each question in the tables of results throughout the paper.

	CS 66 resp.							non-CS 217 resp.						
question	D	SD	N	SA	A	mode	avg	D	SD	N	SA	A	mode	avg
*fix printers	55	8	2	1	0	1	1.23	123	49	20	16	5	1	1.74
program	0	1	2	8	55	5	4.77	0	1	4	38	171	5	4.77
*administer	26	21	8	7	4	1	2.12	65	38	41	43	25	1	2.65
group projects	0	1	1	21	43	5	4.61	0	2	9	41	162	5	4.70
*analyze data	2	6	9	26	23	4	3.94	1	8	24	58	122	5	4.37
*memorize formulas	13	26	17	10	0	2	2.36	26	42	57	64	24	4	3.08
*ms word	35	16	10	4	1	1	1.79	64	42	34	55	19	1	2.64
algorithms	0	0	0	7	59	5	4.89	0	1	2	23	184	5	4.86
make web pages	13	14	19	18	2	3	2.73	37	43	49	64	19	4	2.93
organize info	2	3	7	15	39	5	4.30	1	1	24	58	127	5	4.46
securejob	50	5	0	2	7	1	1.61	137	41	11	1	8	1	1.49
*basicprogsci	1	2	2	19	39	5	4.48	10	12	35	83	58	4	3.84
tech savvy	3	9	12	25	15	4	3.62	11	42	47	64	34	4	3.34
*no life	55	8	1	0	0	1	1.16	142	37	15	3	1	1	1.40
gender	0	0	0	1	62	5	4.98	2	1	1	7	186	5	4.90
*outsourcing	56	6	1	1	0	1	1.17	55	42	60	30	11	3	2.49
*transferable skills	0	0	0	15	49	5	4.77	1	6	16	67	108	5	4.39
*cs belongs	0	0	1	2	61	5	4.94	3	3	13	30	148	5	4.61
meninterested	6	5	13	31	9	4	3.50	23	22	48	78	26	4	3.31
*priorexperience	0	3	2	7	52	5	4.69	3	13	23	65	93	5	4.18

Table 2: Overall survey results to the Likert-scale questions comparing the non-CS ACM faculty with the CS faculty (SIGCSE and ACM combined). Statistically significant differences at the $p<0.05$ level, computed using the Mann-Whitney U test, are starred. Likert-scale responses were D=Disagree, SD=Somewhat Disagree, N=Neutral, SA=Somewhat Agree, A=Agree.

The survey results show statistically significant differences for a number of survey items, indicating that, overall, CS faculty and non-CS faculty hold different opinions on a number of these questions. For example, CS faculty are more likely than their non-CS counterparts to believe that CS classes do not focus on fixing printers or using Microsoft Office products, that CS students do not have to memorize many formulas, and that outsourcing has not decreased the number of jobs in the industry each of the last several years.

However, that there are statistically significant differences of opinion between experts and non-experts in a domain is hardly surprising. Our goal for the survey was to evaluate whether non-CS faculty have a basic understanding of CS, not whether they understand our discipline as well as we do. Closer inspection reveals that some statistically significant differences may not really indicate a poor understanding of CS. For example, none of the CS faculty felt that CS students would not have a "life" outside computers, while only 2% of non-CS faculty (4 out of 217) thought so. The modal response for the two populations was the same, and the mean response was very close (1.16 to 1.40). Non-CS faculty had a higher fraction of neutral responses to the question, but neutrality towards an issue may indicate something different than taking the stance opposite to the CS faculty. In other words, neutrality may simply represent a lack of buy-in to, or interest in, an issue.

Table 3 organizes the same data as Table 2 in a slightly different format, by combining the *Slightly Agree* and *Agree* reponse items, as well as the *Slightly Disagree* and *Disagree* items, and reporting percentages rather than counts. When the results are viewed in this fashion, a number of survey items that showed statistically significant differences do not appear to indicate that non-CS faculty have a poor understanding of CS or particularly negative impressions of CS. For example, while it may be disconcerting that 3% of our colleagues disagree that CS belongs in a liberal arts curriculum and another 6% are neutral on the issue, we can be encouraged that about 90% of our colleagues believe that our discipline should in fact be part of a liberal arts curriculum.

	CS			non-CS		
category	D	N	A	D	N	A
*fix printers	95%	3%	1%	80%	9%	9%
program	1%	3%	95%	0%	1%	97%
*administer	71%	12%	16%	48%	19%	32%
group projects	1%	1%	96%	0%	4%	94%
*analyze data	12%	13%	74%	4%	11%	84%
*memorize formulas	59%	25%	15%	31%	26%	41%
*ms word	77%	15%	7%	49%	15%	34%
algorithms	0%	0%	100%	0%	0%	98%
make web pages	40%	28%	30%	37%	23%	39%
organize info	7%	10%	81%	0%	11%	87%
securejob	85%	0%	14%	89%	5%	4%
*basicprogsci	4%	3%	92%	11%	17%	71%
tech savvy	18%	18%	62%	26%	23%	49%
*no life	98%	1%	0%	90%	7%	2%
gender	0%	0%	100%	1%	0%	97%
*outsourcing	96%	1%	1%	48%	30%	20%
*transferable skills	0%	0%	100%	3%	8%	88%
*cs belongs	0%	1%	98%	3%	6%	90%
meninterested	17%	20%	62%	22%	24%	52%
*priorexperience	4%	3%	92%	8%	11%	80%

Table 3: Percent of respondents who disagree (D), are neutral towards (N), or agree (A) with each statement, split up by CS and non-CS faculty. Statistically significant items are starred.

4.2 CS vs IT

One of the goals of this survey was to assess how well non-CS faculty recognize the differences between CS and IT, and the survey results may indicate some confusion, as 9% of non-CS faculty think we teach students to fix printers (only 1% of CS faculty think so); 32% of non-CS faculty believe CS students learn to administer networks and change passwords (surprising to us was that 16% of CS faculty also agree with this assessment); and 34% of our non-CS colleagues think we teach our students to use Microsoft products (only 7% of CS faculty think so). These results were all statistically significant, and provide some evidence that at least some non-CS faculty believe that CS and IT are more closely related than do CS faculty. On the other hand, we were surprised by the 16% of CS faculty who found that our students learned to administer computers and change passwords in the classroom.

On the other hand, non-CS faculty accurately recognized the importance of both programming and algorithms to our discipline, and were only slightly more likely to believe that students needed to be "tech savvy" to be successful in CS. Thus it may be the case that a significant minority of non-CS faculty have an overly broad definition of CS that includes some features traditionally part of IT. In other words, they accurately recognize that things like algorithms and programming are important to CS, but they are unsure of where to draw the boundary between CS and other disciplines, such as IT or Engineering.

4.3 Employment and Job Market Opportunities

Arguably the strongest point of disagreement between the CS and non-CS faculty had nothing to do with what students do in their CS courses, but rather with their employment opportunities after college. Twenty percent of non-CS faculty agreed that outsourcing caused a drop in CS employment opportunities for the last several years, while another 30% of respondents were neutral on the issue; on the other hand, 96% of CS faculty disagreed that this was the case. Bureau of Labor Statistics data in the United States expects a 24% increase in the number of jobs for computer scientists through 2018 [3]. Given that strong employment opportunities can be a powerful selling point for our discipline, it is important that we debunk myths about the effects of outsourcing, especially to our colleagues in other disciplines.

It is important to note that the categories used for employment data can be ambiguous regarding the training for each job, and the types of work done for each job category; furthermore, the cateogires may vary between reports. For example, the same Bureau of Labor Statistics report that expected a 24% increase through 2018 in the number of jobs for computer scientists also expects a 21% increase in employment for "computer software engineers" and a 3% decline for "comptuer programmers" [2] over the same period. The report also lists only about 30,000 jobs for "computer scientists", but 1.3 million jobs for "computer software engineers". It seems likely that some of the computer software engineers have computer science degrees, so it would be accurate to include those job opportunities as part of the "sales pitch" to undergraduates to encourage them to study CS. On the other hand, the report explicitly states that "[s]ome computer programmers hold a college degree in computer science, mathematics, or information systems", indicating that IT or Information Systems (IS) degrees can be a gateway to some of the same jobs also accessible with a CS degree. Similarly, the report says of "computer support specialist" jobs that "[a] bachelor's degree in computer science, computer engineering, or information systems is a prerequisite for some jobs", which suggests that a CS degree can also lead to IT jobs. It's possible that the many reports and newspaper articles touting the job opportunities for recent alumni with CS degrees may be a contributing factor in this confusion.

Given that non-CS faculty seem to be swayed by the media hype about the perils of outsourcing, they may also be swayed by the tendency of the media to lump all computer-related jobs together in the many reports and newspaper articles touting the excellent job opportunities for CS degree holders. When we point to these reports as a reason for studying CS, we may inadvertently make it more difficult for both our colleagues and our students to define the boundaries of CS as an academic discipline. Our survey certainly was not a powerful enough instrument to address this question directly, but it is something we'd like to study in the future.

4.4 Other Findings

One quirky finding of our survey was that non-CS faculty were significantly more likely than CS faculty (41% to 15%) to believe that CS involves a lot of memorizing of formulas, which could possibly be a result of confusing CS with Engineering-related disciplines, which, accurately or not, are known for the many formulas students must know. This particular confusion may also be additional evidence that non-CS faculty are unsure where CS ends and other disciplines begins, though we lack the data to do anything but guess at this sort of conclusion.

Finally, 62% of CS faculty agreed with the statement, "Men are more interested in computing than are women", while only 52% of non-CS faculty agreed. Our survey question did not ask to explain *why* men are more interested than are women; it is entirely possible that some respondents felt that men were *inherently* more interested in computing, while other respondents were merely observing that men are *effectively* more intersted in computing due to the staggering gender imbalance in our discipline. It's also possible that both populations were responding to the observed gender imbalance in CS, but that CS faculty are more aware of how skewed our gender ratio has become. It is also possible that faculty interpreted the word "computing" broadly enough to include computer activities such as video games, which, at least stereotypically, are considered to be male-dominated. Given the ambiguity of the wording, we have no way of knowing how respondents interpreted the question.

4.5 Qualitative Responses

We asked all faculty the free-response question, "What does a computer scientist do?". Table 4 shows the top 10 words for both the non-CS and CS faculty. *Computer* was the most common term for both populations, with *algorithm* was the next most popular term among CS faculty and *program* the second most popular term for non-CS faculty. While *algorithm* was the 7th most popular term for the non-CS faculty, it occured only 15% of the time, equivalent to the terms *problem, hardware*, and *data*. This data likely fits the hypothesis that many outside the field of CS recognize the importance of programming, but are less aware of the underlying algorithmic foundations of the discipline.

	CS (65 responses)			non-CS (213 responses)		
rank	word	#	pct.	word	#	pct.
1	computer	39	60%	computer	121	56%
2	algorithm	37	56%	program	116	54%
3	problem	29	44%	language	55	25%
4	solve	25	38%	software	46	21%
5	computational	19	29%	system	38	17%
6	software	18	27%	data	34	15%
7	system	18	27%	algorithm	33	15%
8	scientist	17	26%	problem	33	15%
9	design	17	26%	hardware	32	15%
10	hardware	15	23%	information	31	14%

Table 4: 10 most popular words written in response to the question "What does a computer scientist study?", for non-CS and CS (ACM and SIGCSE combined) faculty. Pct indicates the percentage of faculty who answered this question and mentioned the word at least once. Common words (and, or, the, for, and so on) have been removed, and the plural and singular form of nouns have been combined.

One of the background questions asked whether faculty have taken a CS course before; 84 of the non-CS faculty reported that they had, while 113 had not. Table 5 shows the 10 most popular words used by these two populations. Non-CS faculty who have taken a CS course are more than twice as likely (23% to 9%; algorithm was #17 for non-CS faculty) to use the word *algorithm* to describe what computer scientists do than are non-CS faculty who have not taken a CS course before. We did not ask how many CS courses faculty had taken, so we cannot draw any conclusions about how much experience is required for non-experts to begin to appreciate the critical importance of algorithms.

This sort of word-count analysis is an imprecise, imperfect tool for analysis of qualitative data. In the future we plan to perform a richer, more detailed reading of the answers to the free-response questions.

4.6 Threats to Validity

There are several threats to the validity of our survey and results:

- Faculty who are more interested in, or knowledgable about, CS may have been more likely to respond to our survey.
- Some faculty felt that the nature of the survey implied that we were looking for evidence of anti-CS bias or evidence that faculty advisees were not willing or able to give their advisees unbiased opinions about course selection; faculty members with this opinion may have

	Yes (84 responses)			No (113 responses)		
rank	word	#	pct.	word	#	pct.
1	computer	45	53%	program	70	61%
2	program	36	42%	computer	64	56%
3	language	24	28%	language	26	23%
4	algorithm	20	23%	software	24	21%
5	system	20	23%	design	17	15%
6	data	20	23%	problem	16	14%
7	software	17	20%	system	14	12%
8	structure	16	19%	theory	14	12%
9	problem	16	19%	study	14	12%
10	information	16	19%	application	13	11%

Table 5: 10 most popular words written in response to the question "What does a computer scientist study?", comparing non-CS faculty who have taken a CS course with non-CS faculty who have never taken a CS course. Pct indicates the percentage of faculty who answered this question and mentioned the word at least once. Common words (and, or, the, for, and so on) have been removed, and the plural and singular form of nouns have been combined.

been less likely to take the survey, or may have attempted to guess the "correct" answer to survey items rather than answering honestly.

- Because some of the questions may have been ambiguously worded, respondents may have thought they were answering a different question.
- The targeted population of non-CS liberal arts faculty all teach at residental midwestern colleges in the United States, and it is unclear that these results will generalize to other faculty populations.

5. CONCLUSIONS

Overall the survey results give a mixed response to our initial questions. A majority of non-CS faculty appear to have an accurate understanding of CS, which means that both CS and non-CS faculty seem well aware of the things that are integral to CS. However, a large minority of non-CS faculty seem unclear on where CS stops and other disciplines, such as IT or Engineering, begin. It's also possible that CS faculty are inadvertently helping to blur the CS/IT boundary by touting job opportunities in the technology sector through media reports that themselves tend to lump CS and IT together.

This is a better result than if non-CS faculty thought that CS students only did IT-related things, particularly at liberal arts colleges where faculty are responsible for helping students without a major to select their courses, and where disciplines that are perceived to be too narrowly-focused, such as IT, may not be viewed favorably by faculty.

6. FUTURE WORK

We asked faculty to rate how well certain traits and characteristics (athleic, adaptable, outgoing, perseverant, and so on) describe successful CS students; we have yet to analyze this data in detail. Similarly, we would like to perform a more detailed qualitative analysis of faculty responses to the free-reponse questions, "What does a computer scientist do?" and "Why have you advised (or why would you advise) a student to take a course in computer science?" An obvious question is what fraction of non-CS faculty give a more-or-less accurate definition of CS. Finally, we have not evaluated the correlations *between* questions in our survey.

7. ACKNOWLEDGMENTS

This work was funded by the Paul K Richter and Evalyn E. Cook Richter Memorial Trusts, and by the Ron Asplund Research Award. The authors would like to thank Janet Davis for her helpful feedback on early drafts of the survey, Matt Hewner for his insights into interpreting the survey results, and everyone who tooks the survey for taking the survey.

8. REFERENCES

[1] 7th Annual AP Report to the Nation. `http://apreport.collegeboard.org/sites/default/files/downloads/pdfs/ap_report_to_the_nation_Consolidated.pdf`, February 2011.

[2] Computer Scientists. `http://www.bls.gov/oco/ocos303.htm#outlook`, January 2012.

[3] Computer Software Engineers and Computer Programmers. `http://www.bls.gov/oco/ocos304.htm#outlook`, January 2012.

[4] Schools Fall Behind in Offering Computer Science. `http://www.edweek.org/ew/articles/2010/07/14/36compsci_ep.h29.html?qs=computer+science`, January 2012.

[5] The Associated Colleges of the Midwest. `http://www.acm.edu/index.html`, January 2012.

[6] L. Carter. Why students with an apparent aptitude for computer science don't choose to major in computer science. In *Proceedings of the 37th SIGCSE technical symposium on Computer science education*, SIGCSE '06, pages 27–31, New York, NY, USA, 2006. ACM.

[7] M. Hewner and M. Guzdial. Attitudes about computing in postsecondary graduates. In *Proceedings of the Fourth international Workshop on Computing Education Research*, ICER '08, pages 71–78, New York, NY, USA, 2008. ACM.

[8] C. Lewis, M. H. Jackson, and W. M. Waite. Student and faculty attitudes and beliefs about computer science. *Commun. ACM*, 53:78–85, May 2010.

[9] J. Perrenet. Differences in beliefs and attitudes about computer science among students and faculty of the bachelor program. In *Proceedings of the 14th annual ACM SIGCSE conference on Innovation and technology in computer science education*, ITiCSE '09, pages 129–133, New York, NY, USA, 2009. ACM.

[10] A. D. Ruslanov and A. P. Yolevich. College student views of computer science: opinion survey. *J. Comput. Sci. Coll.*, 25:142–148, April 2010.

Novices' Perceptions and Experiences of a Mobile Social Learning Environment for Learning of Programming

Mercy Maleko Margaret Hamilton Daryl D'Souza
School of CS & IT, RMIT University
PO Box 2476V Melbourne 3001, Australia.
{mercy.maleko, margaret.hamilton, daryl.dsouza}@rmit.edu.au

ABSTRACT

In this paper we report programming novices' perceptions and experiences of a Mobile Social Learning Environment (MSLE) designed to support the learning of programming through enabling increased novice-to-novice interactions. By capturing and analysing such interactions early it is hoped that instructors may identify misunderstandings and misconceptions of novice programmers, and provide timely feedback to alleviate novices' misunderstandings. The MSLE incorporates the use of mobile devices as well as the access to dedicated social networking sites. Novices from three different universities, each with different modes of delivery, participated in this research. Novices' perceived advantages of the MSLE include among other things instant access to discussions, increased interactions, instant feedback in a student-student context, and the ability to share ideas and views anytime, anywhere. Novices have experienced increased interactions among themselves and improved engagement with learning in the MSLE. Novices were able to form learning communities and able to share knowledge and ideas about programming language with each other. Some novices were able to provide assistance to others, hence indirectly, strengthening their own knowledge of programming. The cost of mobile devices and Internet charges on the other hand were perceived as disadvantages of a MSLE. Small screens, lack of programming applications for smart phones, laptops' battery life and distractions from other internet media were some of negative experiences observed by novices who used the MSLE.

Categories and Subject Descriptors

K.3.2 [**Computers and Education**]: Computer and Information Science Education-*Computer science education.*

Keywords

Novice programmer, Mobile Learning, Social Learning, Interactions, Social Networking, Facebook.

1. INTRODUCTION

Novice programmers (*novices),* by our definition, are students learning to program, and enrolled in a university-level, introductory programming course. Several studies have highlighted that learning is improved through increased interaction between teachers and learners and learners and learners. Social networking sites provide an opportunity for novice programmers to interact and to share knowledge and ideas related to programming. Our long-term goal is to establish a learning environment to enhance learning of programming, particularly in the early stages when students are most vulnerable to failures in understanding of programming and programming language concepts.

While there is no standard definition of mobile learning, the central principle applied to mobile learning is that it can be undertaken "Anytime" and "Anyplace" [20]. According to [18], mobile learning has been taken to mean the facilitation of learning and access to educational content using mobile devices. However, if technology is set aside and the learners' mobility is considered, mobile learning can then be defined to occur when the learner is not at any fixed, predetermined location [21]. In such a case, a learner may or may not have a mobile device. These learning interactions, when they occur between peers in a social network, may lead to social learning. The social learning may be both a process of peers learning from one another and an outcome, the learning that occurs as a result of these interactions [27].

The mobile social learning environment combines the mobile and social aspects of learning facilitated by mobile devices (mobile phones, smart phones, PDAs tablets and laptops). This includes learning while the learner is not confined in a physical space, and learning from others through social networks. This environment allows novices to use internet connected mobile devices to access a designated programming group within a social networking site, for discussions, brainstorming and for learning material related to their programming course. This environment is additional to what novices currently have in their respective universities.

Facilitation of learning through mobile devices has many advantages including supporting communication and increasing learner to learner interactions [10, 4]. Learner-learner interactions are known to play a fundamental role in the learning process [17] and are well facilitated by social networking sites [24, 9].

Learning to program has not been easy for many novices [14, 16]. Many interventions have been employed to help novices reduce difficulties they face while learning to program. This study will explore whether or not increased interactions and opportunities to share ideas and knowledge through the use of a mobile social learning environments can support novices further in their learning of programming.

Novices from three universities who were enrolled in introductory programming courses were invited to participate in the study. The selected programming courses in these universities are offered in three distinct ways: fully online, blended, and face-to-face. Each of the courses was allocated its own, separate environments for novices to discuss, brainstorm and share their knowledge and ideas relevant to their programming courses. This paper will report their perceptions and experiences of the MSLE, based on survey data collected at the beginning and end of the respective teaching periods.

While exploring and reporting novices' experiences with the use of this mobile social learning environment for supporting learning of programming, we sought to answer the following questions:

(1) What are novices' perceptions of a mobile social learning environment to support learning of programming?

(2) What are novices' experiences of a mobile social learning environment in terms of :-

(a) Engagement with learning.

(b) Student interactions.

The rest of this paper is organized as follows. Section 2 explores the relevant related work and briefly describes the MSLE. Section 3 presents our methodology employed to answer the foregoing research questions. Section 4 presents a discussion of our results obtained through student surveys, about their MSLE perceptions and experiences. Finally, we present our conclusion in Section 5.

2. RELATED WORK

Programming is not easy, especially for students with no background at all. Many students experience learning difficulties due to the abstract nature of the subject [14, 28]. Programming languages are artificial, they contain high-level concepts that beginning students (novices) do not readily grasp or indeed fail to grasp altogether, in a timely manner [22].

Different interventions have been developed to help novices reduce difficulties they face while learning to program [8, 30, 31]. Most of these interventions aim to increase interactions among learners.

Interactions have always been valued in all contexts of education, be they face to face or online [1]. Interactivity has been argued as a primary criterion for selecting media for educational delivery [3]. Despite these interventions to improve interactions they mostly serve their purpose for students who were on campus. Contemporary university students spend most of their time outside the campus [15]. However most of these students have mobile devices that make them more mobile, always on, and community oriented [25]. These students have been described as being focused on "connectedness" and maintaining social interactions [6], being in possession of an information technology mindset and highly developed skills in multitasking [25]. These traits can be exploited to increase interactions among students outside classrooms and to connect with others who are not spending much of their time on campus. These interactions could benefit some students in their learning process and, for novices, the learning of programming. Mobile technologies offer vast opportunities for students to support their learning [2, 6]. In studies where mobile devices have been used to support learning, many have yielded positive outcomes including collaborative learning and increased interactions [10], engaging reluctant learners, enabling learners to remain more focused and promoting learners' self-esteem and self-confidence [2].

The special kinds of interactions and communication that offer opportunities for students to share ideas, knowledge and activities, have enhanced the pedagogical potential of social networking sites [9]. Social networking sites offer students personal interaction and connectedness beyond traditional technologies, or Learning Management Systems (LMS) such as Blackboard [29]. These interactions can be used to address potential academic or social concerns of students. Through social networking sites, learning communities are formed that are important for students learning and achievement [23]. Studies have shown that some students are already using social networking sites specifically in connection with their studies [13, 5]. The attractiveness of social networking sites and their potential to increase interaction between users prompted us to establish course-related mobile social learning environments, which we briefly describe next.

2.1 The Mobile Social Learning Environment (MSLE)

The mobile social learning environment or MSLE introduced in our research exploits the traits of digital natives to increase interactions and to connect with one another anytime, anywhere and to create an online learning community. In the MSLE, novices are connected via a social networking site to a programming group dedicated to enrolled students for them to discuss, chat, brainstorm and access course material uploaded by researchers from time to time. Facebook was used for these activities because it is popular among university students [11, 19] and a large percentage of our students already had accounts on Facebook. Novices accessed the site using *mobile devices* including mobile phones, smart phones, PDAs, tablets and laptops that have access to the Internet at all times.

3. METHODOLOGY

As mentioned earlier, we are interested in finding out novices' perceptions and experiences on the use of MSLEs for the learning of programming. We designed online pre-surveys and post-surveys for data collection. The SPSS and Nvivo software were used to analyse quantitative and qualitative data, respectively. The open-ended questions were analysed using the inductive/conventional approach of qualitative content analysis. This approach derives categories or themes directly from the text data [12]. It has three steps. The first step is to read text data from the survey in order to make meaning of the data. The second step is to derive codes by reading the text again, word by word, to highlight words that appear to capture key thoughts that can be later grouped into themes or categories. The last step involves sorting related codes into categories/themes depending on the relationship and/or links that are observed from the codes.

Pre-surveys were administered during the second week of each teaching period. The mobile social learning environment was introduced in the third week. Students were free to use their previous Facebook accounts or create new ones for this study. Each student had to provide Facebook account-name to be used in the environment in the pre-survey. The MSLE was used as a complementary platform for discussions, chats, brainstorming, posting interesting links related to programming and forming friendships. Post surveys were completed during the last week of each teaching period.

3.1 Participants

We invited students studying introductory programming from three different universities to complete our pre-surveys and later invited them to the programming group before they completed the post-survey. Participation in the study was purely voluntarily and no assessment was carried out of user posts or interactions. The cohort details are as follows:

Cohort A: RMITU - RMIT University, Melbourne, 150 on-campus students studying Programming 1 (Java language), a traditional course offered in face-to-face mode with lectures, tutorials and laboratories. They also had Blackboard as LMS and mentoring sessions.

Cohort B: UDSM - University of Dar es Salaam, Tanzania, 120 on- campus students studying Programming in Java, a course offered in a blended learning mode with all resources online and facilitators delivering tutorials face-to-face. These students use Moodle as LMS.

Cohort C: OUA - Online Universities Australia, 230 fully online students studying CPT 121 (Java Language), with materials provided in Blackboard and a weekly chat session run using Elluminate.

3.2 Data Collection

We designed online surveys to collect data. We firstly wanted to know what proportion of these students has mobile devices for internet access. We asked students to list all the devices they owned. For students who had accounts on social networking sites, we asked them to mention the devices they use to access those accounts. Participation was voluntary, and those who were willing to participate were asked to list the devices they would prefer to use.

Three MSLEs were established for the three cohorts. Cohort A began their course first, in July 2011, while Cohort C commenced in August 2011 and Cohort B in September 2011. Each cohort was treated independently. Questions for discussions and links for self-study were uploaded to the MSLE. Each cohort had their course related documents loaded into Blackboard, but we uploaded some further questions relevant to the course content. Students were encouraged to also uploaded programming related links, so that other students could discuss their issues or pursue further information in their own time. During the last week of each teaching period, we gave novices post- surveys where we asked them to describe their experiences with the MSLE, whether or not the MSLE had increased their engagement with the course materials or interactions with each other.

4. RESULTS AND DISCUSSIONS

From Cohort A, 45 students representing 25% of those enrolled volunteered to participate in our research, while 89 students (74%) from Cohort B and 49 students (21%) from Cohort C volunteered and completed the pre-survey. From now on, we will refer to these students who completed the survey as simply Cohort A, B and C.

We noted that the majority of students had handheld devices and laptops. Cohort A had 91% of students with Internet-accessible handheld devices; Cohort B had 90% and Cohort C had 87%. Some students had laptops only, while others had laptops and home-based desktop computers. Cohorts A and C had higher percentages of students with smart phones than Cohort B, but Cohort B had a larger percentage of students with feature phones. All students from Cohort A had Internet-accessible mobile devices (handhelds and laptops). Only 9% of students from cohort B and 16% of students from Cohort C had no Internet-accessible mobile devices.

We noted that more than 90% of students from each Cohort had accounts on social networking sites, with more than 75% being accounts on Facebook. Students used different devices to access these accounts. More than 50% of students from each cohort have been using mobile devices (handheld or laptop) to access their accounts in social networking sites. Most of these students considered themselves as "always online", reflecting the true characteristics of digital natives [26]. Cohort A had more than 50% of students reporting themselves as being online 24/7, while Cohort B had 28% and Cohort C had 41% of students who are online anytime anywhere.

Cohort A had only 69% and Cohort C had 67% of students willing to participate further in the study. Cohort B students were more interested with this study with 99% of them volunteering to access the MSLE and continue further with this research. Compared with Cohort A, Cohort B had fewer opportunities for student-to-student interactions and had Internet access problems within their University.

4.1 Novices' Perceptions of MSLEs

Before we implemented our mobile social learning environment, we were keen to know what students thought about this environment in supporting their learning. We presented scenarios of mobile learning/MSLE in the survey and asked the following question: *Do you think the mobile learning scenarios expressed can support you in your learning? Can you give us reason(s) for any response on this question?*

Seventy-nine percent of students from Cohort A, 90% of students from Cohort B and 92% of students from Cohort C agreed that the MSLE would support their learning of programming. The mean scores results from a pre-survey, on a five point Likert scale showed that students from the three cohorts tend to agree that the MSLE would encourage them to engage more in learning of programming (m_A=3.89, m_B=4.43 *and* m_C=3.98). The environment would encourage them to interact with other students (m_A=3.68, m_B=4.45 *and* m_C=3.85); and that the MSLE would be useful for their learning of programming, (m_A=3.81, m_B=4.48 *and* m_C=4.06) for Cohort A, B and C respectively.

Students gave their reasons to support what they thought about the MSLE in supporting their learning. We analysed their responses using Nvivo and employing an inductive approach of qualitative content analysis. The following themes emerged: *instant access, instant feedback, interactions, mobility, knowledge sharing, costs, device capability, procrastination, collaboration, communication and motivation, cost of devices and distractions.* Instant access to discussions was considered to support learning by the majority of students. Access to social networking sites was considered faster than access to LMSs, regardless of the device. Students thought that with instant access many students would prefer to post their questions to the MSLE rather than in LMSs. Popular social networking sites have notification systems that alert users about activities that are happening in their pages. Facebook automatically notifies members when something has been changed, so members will know when and what changes have happened. Notifications of what and who posts a question or an answer were considered as the sort of feedback that would support learning in this environment.

Since the majority of students are already familiar with social networking sites, they thought there would be more students in this environment, friendships would be formed and questions would be answered instantly. With instant access to discussions and mobility of devices, procrastinations would be minimized. They would post questions whenever, wherever they have them and wherever they source them from, which is not the case with LMSs, as they cannot access them from their smart phones. Students expect to get more help from others in social networking sites, as the environment is expected to be more relaxed and familiar. Anytime, anywhere collaboration was seen as an advantage by many students. As there are many students with accounts in social networking sites, such environments will have many students, hence interactions would increase. Students thought that through sharing knowledge and ideas, they would have peace of mind as they would discuss their problems with each other and each would know what the other is doing, what problem are faced by others, etc.

On the other hand, less that 22% of students from each cohort thought the MSLE would not support their learning. Some, the minority, did not have mobile devices capable of connecting to the Internet and the cost of an internet connection was to some extent a hindrance. Other students did not like the idea of using social networking sites for academic activities. For them social networking sites are purely for entertainment. Distractions from other media available on social networking sites like games, advertisements were seen as a drawback to learning.

4.2 Novices Experiences of MSLEs

In this section we report novices' actual experiences with the mobile social learning environment, which they have used throughout their teaching periods. We wanted to know whether or not the MSLE had increased novices' engagement with their learning of programming and interactions with each other. Cohort A had 106 students using the MSLE, out of these, 33 (31%) completed our post-survey. Cohort B had 94 students and 36 (38%) completed the post-survey. Cohort C had 190 students, of which 25 (13%) completed the post-survey. Each cohort had their own MSLE. The mean scores results from a post-survey, on a five point Likert scale showed that students from the three cohorts tended to agree that the MSLE had encouraged them to engage more in learning of programming, (m_A=4.09, m_B=4.63 *and* m_C=3.96); it had encouraged them to interact with other students (m_A=4.00, m_B=4.68 *and* m_C=4.03); and it had been useful for their learning of programming (m_A=3.84, m_B=4.70 *and* m_C=4.42) for Cohort A, B and C respectively.

4.2.1 Student Engagement with Learning in MSLE

We asked students the following questions: *Do you think having this social site group has increased your engagement with learning of programming? Can you briefly explain your answer?*

78% of students from Cohort A, 97% from Cohort B and 71% from Cohort C agreed that having this social site group has increased their engagement with learning of programming; Figure 1 shows the results.[1]

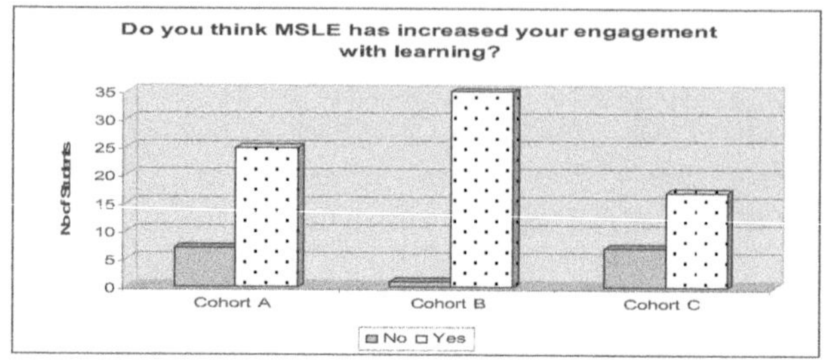

Figure 1. MSLE and Novices engagement.

According to students the environment has increased their engagement as they participated in answering questions that were posted on Facebook, which also has reinforced what they have learned. Some students appreciated corrections that others made to their posts as this was a useful way of learning. The tips and directions in approaching problems given by other students motivated some to engage more in learning. Instant feedback from students who were online has made some students appreciate the environment and have made them gain a lot of knowledge. Knowing who is struggling with what has made some students engage more as they find themselves not alone in the struggle especially during assignments. Ability to communicate with fellow students anytime anywhere has been useful to some students and had motivated them to ask questions and/or answer questions whenever possible.

On the other hand, engagement with learning for some students was not influenced by this environment. Most of these students did not find any difficulties in learning programming; some were there to help others, and indirectly engaging with learning.

"Programming all comes really easily to me - it all makes sense, so I don't think the group has influenced my own learning - but I have helped others via the group, so that should be accounted for I guess?"

4.2.2 Student to Student Interaction in MSLE

Students were asked the following questions: *Do you think having this social site group has increased your interactions with other students? Can you briefly explain your answer?*

75% of students from Cohort A, 95% from Cohort B and 88% from Cohort C noticed their interactions with each other increased through this environment; Figure 2 shows the results. Although Cohort A students had more opportunities for interactions than others as they had access to mentoring sessions, 66% found themselves interacting more in the MSLE than in any other places. Eight-four percent of Cohort B students reported more use the MSLE than Moodle. Online students, Cohort C, had Blackboard discussion forums and Elluminate chat rooms but 80% of students reported use of the MSLE for discussions in preference to Blackboard and Elluminate.

According to the students the MSLE provided instant access to discussions, enabled them to feel free to ask questions. They felt they had a more relaxed environment for discussions and chats,

[1] Other Figures and Tables can be found at http://yallara.cs.rmit.edu.au/~s3231569/VisualPresentations.html

and they asked other students for help which they might otherwise not have done in person or via Blackboard or Moodle.

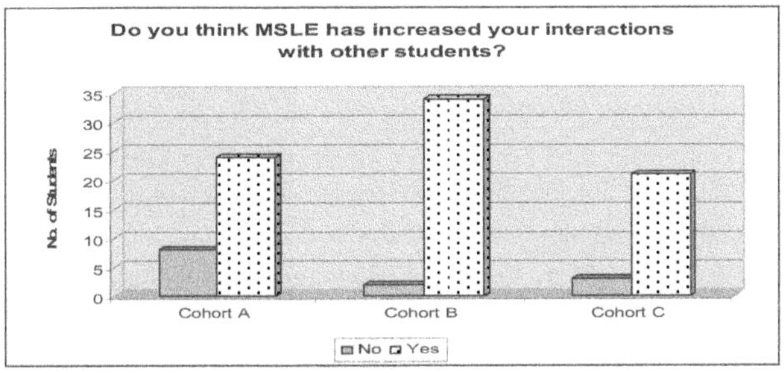

Figure 2. MSLE and Novices Interactions

"I have spoken to students via Facebook who I otherwise would not have talked to"

"Friendly common community to ourselves allows interaction to be easier within our course and therefore lessens the difficulty finding people to ask"

Some students managed to make more friends not only for this course but also beyond. Students, through giving and receiving help have found themselves interacting more in this environment.

"I have made new friends and have enjoyed learning more."

"Now I know more people who r studying the same course as me. And we can help each other"

"During first semester I had almost nothing to do with other students besides my immediate friends, but with this FB group i've actually just had some conversations with people I didn't know - helped out a few people I wouldn't have been able to otherwise".

Some students were encouraged to collaborate through interactions within the MSLE. As more students login to social sites, whatever that was posted was seen and perhaps answered instantly. The MSLE was therefore convenient to some.

"Discussing questions with students that I may not understand, also finding others that are in the same position as me and working together to get through it."

"It's more convenient. Nowadays, people login to social site like Facebook everyday. Any question post in the group will be notified by all members as soon as they log in."

Students who did not find their interactions increased through the MSLE reported themselves to have been not active or not having used social sites much.

5. CONCLUSION

This paper has reported novices' perceptions and experiences with the mobile social learning environment (MSLE) from three universities.

On perceptions, students thought the environment would encourage engagement with learning, encourage interactions with each other and be useful for their learning of programming. Although these students had just started their classes, had different backgrounds and different modes of course delivery, most of them were in favour of the MSLE for their learning.

The paper has reported the feasibility of the MSLE in terms of availability of participants who were ready to use their handheld devices for instant access and instant receipt of notifications. Students still needed laptops or desktop computers for compiling and running java code uploaded online. Handheld devices were however, useful for anytime, anywhere communication and interactions.

The MSLE was proposed with the expectation of increasing student-to-student interactions through discussions, chats, brainstorming and self learning; thereby supporting their learning of programming. From the students' experience, the MSLE increased their interactions with each other and motivated them to interact through asking and answering questions. Students from the three cohorts tended to agree that the MSLE encouraged them to engage more in their learning, to interact with other students and has been useful for their learning of programming. Independent sample t-tests were conducted to compare students' perceptions and experiences with the environment in terms of increased engagement, interactions and useful in learning of programming. The results showed the difference in mean scores between what students perceived about the MSLE and what they reported as their experiences was not statistically significant at $p=0.05$. This shows that students' experiences of the MSLE did not differ significantly with what they perceived. However, more than 70% of students from each cohort found themselves engaging more with their learning of programming and interacting more with each other in the MSLE, a key finding.

Some students learned vicariously [32], through observing and processing interactions that took place through others. Some logged on to the environment to post questions and wait for responses from other students. The rest logged in to see if there were links to follow or sample codes from others to run on their laptops.

Students were able to make more friends, hence forming an important component in their learning, the learning community [23]. The MSLE provided a tension-free platform where students at anytime, anywhere were able to communicate with each other with course-related materials and sometimes materials from other courses.

On the other hand, small screen and lack of durable programming applications for mobile phones (smartphones), mobile content being almost always in compressed format and, as such, omitting content such as photos or videos or having some details reduced to some extent hindered surfing of online materials uploaded by others on MSLE using smartphones. Battery life was another drawback for novices who used laptops to access the MSLE.

Apart from increased novice-to-novice interactions, the MSLE also intended to help instructors to grasp early misunderstandings and misconceptions of novice programmers through capturing novice posts on the MSLE. Although the reported novices' experiences with MSLEs were certain in supporting their learning of programming, increased engagement and interactions, the percentages of novices who completed the post-survey were relatively small, and yet, our results were based on student-reports. However, these self-reports have shown us that the environments had supported novices through anytime anywhere interactions. Handheld devices were used for instant chats and discussions and for receiving notification. Small learning communities were formed, where novices were able to share ideas and knowledge wherever they were.

In order to establish whether or not novices had meaningful interactions while using MSLE and to assess whether or not the reported attitude align with actual novices' behavior, our next step is to assess the messages posted on these MSLEs based on learning taxonomies and theories. Also, as part of next step, we will study how novices' background characteristics and modes of course delivery affect their attitudes towards MSLE.

6. REFERENCES

[1] T. Anderson, 2003. Getting the mix right again: An updated and theoretical rationale for interaction. *J. International Review of Research in Open and Distance Learning* 4, 1-14.

[2] J. Attewell 2005. From Research and Development to Mobile Learning: Tools for Education and Training Providers and their Learners. In *Proceedings of the mLearn Conference 2005.*

[3] A. Bates, 1990. Interactivity as a Criterion for Media Selection in Distance Education, in *Asian Association of Open Universities* Jakarta, Indonesia.

[4] T. Brown, 2005. Towards a model for m-Learning in Africa. *International Journal on E-Learning* 4, 299-315.

[5] J. B. Caruso and G. Salaway, 2010. The ECAR Study of Undergraduate Students and Information Technology, Educause Centre for Applied Research

[6] R. Cobcroft, 2006. Literature review into mobile learning in the university context. http://eprints.qut.edu.au/archive/00004805/

[7] R. Cobcroft, S. Towers, J. Smith, and A. Bruns, 2006. Mobile learning in review: Opportunities and challenges for learners, teachers and institutions. In *Proceedings of* Online *Learning and Teaching Confererence.* http://eprints.qut.edu.au/archive/00005399/

[8] D. D'Souza, M. Hamilton, J. Harland, P. Muir, C. Thevathayan, and C. Walker, 2008. Transforming learning of programming: a mentoring project. In *Proceedings of the 10th Australasian Computing Education Conference*, Wollongong, Australia.

[9] C. Dalsgaard, 2008. Social networking sites: Transparency in online education. *J. Learning* 2, 6.

[10] P. Dawabi, M. Wessner, and E. Neuhold, 2003. Using mobile devices for the classroom of the future. In *Proceedings of the MLEARN 2003*: Learning with Mobile Devices, London UK,55-60.

[11] D. M. Eberhardt, 2007. Facing up to Facebook. *J. About Campus* 12, 18-26.

[12] H. F. Hsieh and S. E. Shannon, 2005. Three approaches to qualitative content analysis. *J. Qualitative health research* 15, p. 1277.

[13] M. Ipsos, 2008. Great expectations of ICT: How higher education institutions are measuring up: Research study conducted for the Joint Information Systems Committee. *J. JISC* (June, 2008.)

[14] T. Jenkins, 2002. On the difficulty of learning to program. In *Proceedings of the LTSN-Center for Information and Computer Sciences*, Loughborough,UK,53-58.

[15] K. Krause, R. Hartley, R. James, and C. McInnes, 2005. The first year experience in Australian universities: Findings from a decade of national studies. Australian Department of Education, Science and Training, Australia.

[16] E. Lahtinen, K. Ala-Mutka, and H.-M. Jarvinen, 2005. A Study of the Difficulties of Novice Programmers. In *Proceedings of the 10th annual SIGCSE on Innovation and Technology in Computer Science Education*, Lisbon , Portugal.

[17] D. Laurillard, 2002. Rethinking University Teaching: A Conversational Framework for the Effective Use of Learning Technologies. Routledge-Falmer Taylor and Francis Group, New Fetter Lane, London.

[18] A. Litchfield, L. Dyson, E. Lawrence, and A. Zmijewska, 2007. Directions for m-learning research to enhance active learning. In *Proceedings of the ASCILITE - ICT: Providing choices for learners and learning,* Singapore, 587-596.

[19] C. Madge, J. Meek, J. Wellens, and T. Hooley, 2009. Facebook, social integration and informal learning at university:'It is more for socialising and talking to friends about work than for actually doing work'. *J. Learning, Media and Technology* 34, 141-155.

[20] S. W. McCombs, 2010. *Mobile Learning: An Analysis of Student Preferences and Perceptions Surrounding Podcasting.* Doctoral Thesis. ProQuest LLC. ERIC, EBSCO*host.*

[21] MOBILearn, 2004. *MOBILearn Project.*

[22] R. Moser, 1997. A fantasy adventure game as a learning environment: why learning to program is so difficult and what can be done about it. *SIGCSE Bulletin.* 29, 114-116.

[23] C. Munoz and T. Towner, 2009 Opening Facebook: How to use Facebook in the college classroom. In *Proceedings of the Society for Information and Technology and Teacher Education* Charleston, Carolina, 2623-2627.

[24] K. Murray and R. Waller, 2007. Social networking goes abroad. *J. International Educator* 16, 56–59.

[25] D. G. Oblinger and O. J.L (Eds), 2005. Educating the net generation. Retrieved from http://www.educause.edu/educatingthenetgen

[26] M. Prensky, 2001. Digital natives, digital immigrants Part 1. J. *On the horizon* 9, 1-6.

[27] M. S. Reed, A. C. Evely, G. Cundill, I. Fazey, J. Glass, A. Laing, J. Newig, B. Parrish, C. Prell, C. Raymond, and L. C. Stringer, 2010. What is social learning? *J. Ecology and Society* 15.

[28] A. Robins, J. Rountree, and N. Rountree, 2003. Learning and Teaching Programming: A Review and Discussion. *J. Computer Science Education 13*(2)137-172.

[29] N. Selwyn, 2007. 'Screw Blackboard... do it on Facebook!' an investigation of students' educational use of Facebook. [Available at: http://www.scribd.com/doc/513958/Facebookseminar-paper-Selwyn, accessed: 17.09.2011]

[30] I. Stamouli, E. Doyle, and M. Huggard, 2004. Establishing structured support for programming students. In *Proceedings of the 34th ASEE/IEEE frontiers in Education Conference,* Savannah, GA,F2G-5.

[31] L. Williams, E. Wiebe, K. Yang, M. Ferzli, and C. Miller, 2002. In support of pair programming in the introductory computer science course. *J. Computer Science Education* 12, 197-212.

Choosing a Study Mode in Blended Learning

Mikko Myllymäki
University of Jyväskylä, Kokkola University Consortium Chydenius
P.O.Box 567, FIN-67701
Kokkola, Finland
mikko.myllymaki@chydenius.fi

Ismo Hakala
University of Jyväskylä, Kokkola University Consortium Chydenius
P.O.Box 567, FIN-67701
Kokkola, Finland
ismo.hakala@chydenius.fi

ABSTRACT

Education providers aim to meet today's education requirements by employing, among other things, education technology solutions that increase flexibility. This has also happened with the master's level mathematical information technology degree directed to adults. In the degree program, lecture videos brought in together with face-to-face teaching provide good opportunities for flexible educational arrangements. Education with the help of videos can be arranged in such a way that students themselves will be able to choose their study mode in accordance with their needs. When students themselves can choose their study modes, many different ways to take advantage of the flexibility provided are created. It seems that students with different participation styles achieve the aims for their study progress in different ways. The purpose of this paper is to profile students with different study modes, the profiling being based on a structured questionnaire. In this way we try to find out what are the factors that affect the study mode. Our investigation focuses on both the effect of internal factors, such as motivation, and the effect of external factors, such as distance and time limitations, in the choice of a study method.

Categories and Subject Descriptors

K.3.1 [**Computers and Education**]: Computer Uses in Education—*Distance learning*; K.3.2 [**Computers and Education**]: Computer and Information Science Education—*Computer science education*

Keywords

study mode, student profile, blended learning, lecture video

1. INTRODUCTION

Education providers face a challenging task in attempting to meet the requirements that, for example, life-long learning and rapidly changing work life set for education. Work alongside study and education directed to adults force the education providers to adapt their own teaching to make it suitable for these purposes. Flexibility in study participation has, in fact, become the central element in education arrangements. Appropriate utilization of education technologies plays the key role in increasing flexibility. Diversification of traditional face-to-face teaching with the help of educational technologies enables arranging education in a form of so-called blended learning. Blended learning combines the traditional face-to-face study and online learning [4]. Realized in this way, education can be offered to students in a flexible manner regardless of time and place.

An educational technology solution that suits exceedingly well for the task of increasing flexibility is that of lecture videos made with streaming technology. These kinds of videos make it possible for the student to follow teaching in a face-to-face setting in real time and in a place better suited for students. With the help of on-demand videos the student is given the opportunity to participate in study when it is convenient to do so. Use of lecture videos is indeed a very popular solution that is becoming more and more widespread for diversifying education in higher education institutes [1, 9].

Blended learning realized with lecture videos brings about many kinds of changes to traditional study. The concept of study participation expands when it is possible to participate, in addition to a lecture room, in other places and even in other times. It has been proposed in earlier research that provision of lecture videos might have negative effects on face-to-face study participation [5, 9], or no effect at all [11]. On the other hand, it has been seen also that the flexibility brought about lecture videos on the whole could increase study participation, as long as study participation with videos is taken into account [7].

Participation with the help of lecture videos also differs in many ways from participation in face-to-face groups. Interaction changes its form, and the sense of cohesion and contacts to other students become more challenging. On the other hand, flexibility brings with it the ability for the student to study when his/her alertness is at its highest. It is possible to revise lecture topics, and, when so wished, pace the lecture with pauses made to suit to the student's own needs. It has been noted in various studies that the way students participate in education also has its effect on learning. According to some studies, study with lecture videos might have a positive effect on students' performance when examined in light of their grades and course completions [3, 8, 9]. There are also some study results according to which study with the help of videos has positive effect only on course

Figure 1: Students' study participation can be classified by video use.

completions but not on grades [10], or no effect on learning outcomes at all [2].

Earlier studies have mainly focused on the purpose and the way videos are used [5, 9, 11]. The main focus of these studies has been students' motivation and attitudes regarding the use of videos. Nevertheless, the research has not considered the suitability of different study modes for different kinds of students, learning opportunities for students participating in different ways and classification of students by their study mode. Nor has the profiling of students by these factors been considered.

When education is organized in such a way that students themselves can choose their study mode between face-to-face and distance learning, it becomes apparent that the students make use, in very different ways, of the flexibility provided. Some of the students continue studying almost without a fail in a face-to-face setting, whereas others keep studying almost always as distance students. Also, a great many of the students are so-called hybrid students, who evenhandedly take advantage of both face-to-face and distance study. The degree to which the students participate in study with the help of videos thus moves freely along the line in Figure 1.

This study includes, in addition to students whose study is clearly oriented towards video use or who study in a face-to-face setting, students who fairly evenly make good use of both study modes. It is important to include these students in the investigation because it seems probable that when their learning outcomes are examined no correlation with the outcomes of those who participate in other ways will be found. According to [8], these kinds of students did not achieve as good grades as students who generally participate in face-to-face mode or students who mainly participate with the help of videos.

The purpose of this paper is to find out how students themselves choose their study mode. The paper investigates the suitability of the study modes and the motivation and learning opportunities of students participating in different ways. In this way, we seek to find out what the students that typically participate in face-to-face mode and the students who take advantage of videos are like and to get an idea of those combining both study modes. The research data includes the results of an extensive interview of students in 2010.

2. STUDY DESIGN

This article investigates the differences between students who participate in organized study in different ways. The research data consists of the results of an extensive interview of students realized in the form of a structured interview during the latter part of 2010 as well as statistics collected in connection with the Master Studies in Mathematical Information Technology education at Kokkola University Consortium Chydenius of the University of Jyväskylä arranged between 2008 and 2010.

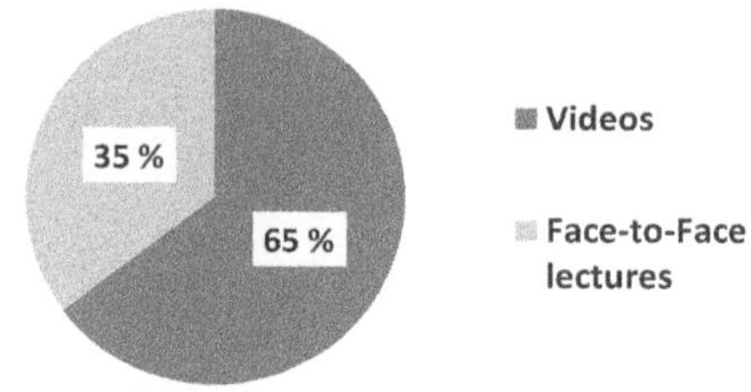

Figure 2: Relative shares of study modes of all lecture participations (n=2068).

All teaching in the degree program was arranged as face-to-face teaching. In addition, the face-to-face teaching was offered as real-time videos produced from a face-to-face setting. The videos transmitted in real time were also recorded and offered to students to be viewed later as so-called on-demand video. An unedited version of the recording was made available for the students in the evening of the lecture day, and a lightly edited video was also provided during the first weekday. The videos couldn't be stored on the student's own computer; they were kept in the media server. Thus, an active web connection was needed for their viewing. The web connection required for viewing of the videos was accessible for all the students of the degree.

The voice of the lecturer and a picture of the image source that the lecturer uses in the face-to-face teaching situation are recorded on the lecture video produced in the degree program. In other words, all electronic teaching material that the lecturer shows in the lecture room with a video projector is also shown on the video. Instead of using a traditional blackboard, a document camera, touch screen or smartboard were used during the lectures. In addition to the lecture videos, a web-based Learning Management System was used for the courses. The students could get via that system, in a written format, all the lecture material used in the course.

All the students that the data includes are adults, and almost all of them work. In addition, more than a half of the students live more than an hour's travel from the location where the face-to-face education takes place. The distance from the places of the farthest living students to the campus area is approximately 500 km. The students can participate in a lecture either by participating in face-to-face teaching, viewing a real-time video or watching the video later on at the time of their choosing. The students were not required to decide about their study mode beforehand; for each lecture session they could choose the mode that suited best for their own life situation. Thus, in each course the student could participate in education in many different ways by flexibly combining various alternatives.

The role of videos in study participation in the degree program under investigation was very important. Of all the single lecture participations between 2008 and 2010 approximately two-thirds took place with the help of videos and just one-third as face-to-face teaching, in other words without the help of videos. Figure 2 shows the shares of the students' study modes in all lecture participations for the students included in the data.

2.1 Student Classification

The results of student interviews are processed in accordance with the student classification made on the basis of the amount of video use. To help in student classification, attendance data collected in face-to-face teaching situations and log data accumulated of viewing lecture videos are used. The classification is based on the statistics gathered from 25 courses held between 2008 and 2010. The number of students classified who participated in at least one of the courses in question was 56. The number of course participations accumulated by the students during the investigation was 273 while the number of lecture participations during the same time period was 2068. For the classification purposes, a student was counted as a participant of a course if he/she participated at least in one of the course lectures, either through face-to-face education or with the help of a lecture video. The structure of the student classification is as follows:

Class 1: The student belongs to class [0, 1/3[, if the average share of his/her participations with the help of videos in all lecture participations is within 0-33.3%. The students that belong to this class are called face-to-face students.

Class 2: The student belongs to class [1/3, 2/3[, if the average share of his/her participations with the help of videos in all lecture participations is within 33.4-66.6%. The students that belong to this class are called hybrid students.

Class 3: The student belongs to class [2/3, 1], if the average share of his/her participations with the help of videos in all lecture participations is within 66.7-100%. The students that belong to this class are called online students.

Teaching for the master's degree in information technology is organized as intensive face-to-face teaching in such a way that the length of a single lecture is 3-4 times the length of a traditional lecture. Because of this even occasional absences from face to face teaching means that students participation percent with the help of videos will rise significantly. In order to reduce the importance occasional absences, the categories are selected as described above.

When the students in the research data are placed in the above categories, we get a distribution shown in Figure 3. As participations in the data are examined, it becomes fairly apparent that the use of videos to aid in participation is a well-established practice. When the students were completely free to choose their study mode between face-to-face teaching and videos, the focus of participation was on the participation with the help of videos. Only about 20% of the students participate mainly in face-to-face mode.

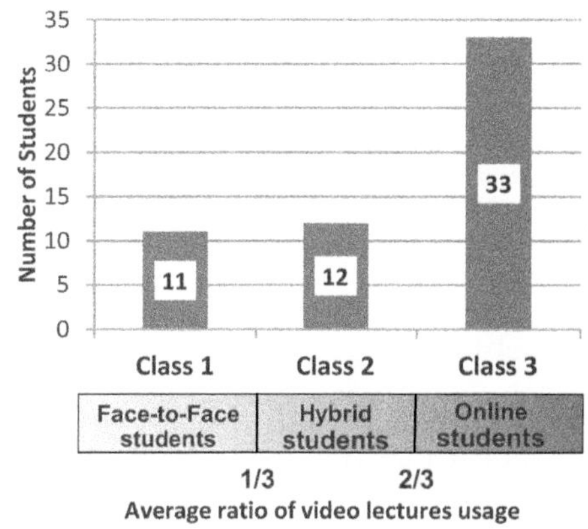

Figure 3: Classification based on the amount of video use, and the number of students in different classes (n=56).

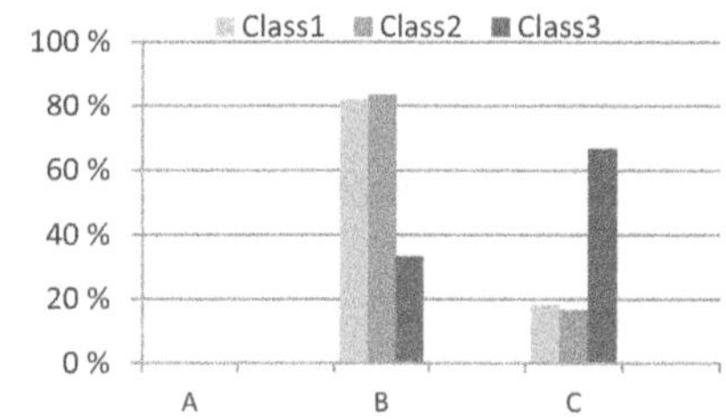

Figure 4: The ways of study that best suit for students (*A=written material only, B= face-to-face teaching and written material, C=utilizing videos one way or another*).

3. THE EFFECT OF INTERNAL FACTORS

3.1 Suitability of Different Study Modes

To map out the suitability of the different study modes, students were asked to evaluate them. In the master's degree program in mathematical information technology the study modes are participation in face-to-face teaching, participation with the help of real-time videos, participation with the help of recordings, and study by combining face-to-face teaching with videos. In all these modes, the student can make use also of all written course material available. Moreover, it is possible to study without resorting to videos or face-to-face teaching, just by getting to know the written material. To evaluate the study modes, the students were asked what their most preferred way of study would be.

In the opinion of the face-to-face students, learning face-to-face with written material would clearly be their most preferred study mode. This was the opinion of 82% of them. Also a clearly greatest share (83%) of the hybrid students were of the opinion that face-to-face teaching and written material would be the most preferred of the study modes. Hybrid students, therefore, show clear willingness to participate in face-to-face education. There were no hybrid students with the opinion that the most preferred way to study would completely exclude teaching and would merely consist of getting to know the written material. Of the online students, only 33% would prefer the use of face-to-face teaching and written material while 67% would prefer taking advantage of videos in one way or another (either videos on their own, or combination of videos and face-to-face education). There were no online students with the opinion that the most preferred way to study would consist merely of the use of written material. The responses concerning the most preferred way of study are shown in Figure 4.

When evaluating the different study modes, some students raised the issue that absences from face-to-face teaching make study, to a certain extent, more difficult. In this, there is not much difference between the responses of the hybrid students (25%) and online students (24%). The corresponding percentage for face-to-face students was 18%. Of the hybrid students who told of themselves being affected negatively by their absences from face-to-face teaching, all would expressly prefer face-to-face study. Of the online students who similarly told of themselves being negatively affected by their absences from face-to-face teaching, only half would prefer face-to-face study.

It may be thought that when compared with other study modes the benefit of face-to-face study typically is that of better communication opportunities. Perhaps, somewhat surprisingly, communication opportunity is not the explaining factor to that hybrid students would like to participate more in face-to-face study. There were no hybrid students who would regard the lack of communication opportunities as a factor that would make learning significantly more difficult. On the other hand, of the online students almost one-sixth (15%) felt that this was making their study more difficult.

When evaluating the suitability of different study modes, it behooves to raise the issue that, according to the questionnaire responses, those who study with the help of videos seem, in light of the study, achieve their study objectives better. Of the online students, 66% told of having progressed in their studies as they had expected. The corresponding figure for the hybrid students was 50% and for the face-to-face students 36%.

3.2 Motivation For The Choice of Study Mode

One of the aims of the questionnaire was also to find out about students' motivation for participation with the help of face-to-face teaching, on one hand, and with the help of recordings, on the other.

When asked about the motivation to participate in face-to-face teaching, 55% of the students told that they could learn best with it. Participation with the help of face-to-face teaching rather than with the help of videos was regarded more suitable by 73% of the face-to-face students. Compared with the responses of other student groups, their emphasis was more on the desire to ensure availability of teaching and on the opportunity to participate in the study within its schedule as well as on a better chance to concentrate on the education provided in the face-to-face study. When motivation for viewing recordings was examined, it turned out that only 27% of the face-to-face students were of the opinion that concentrating on study is best when it takes place with the help of recordings.

Also the hybrid students feel their learning is at its best in face-to-face study. This was the opinion of 67% of them. According to the responses, participation in face-to-face study suits also to hybrid students by far better than participation in lecture sessions with the help of videos. This was the opinion of 75% of them. As with the face-to-face students, the emphasis with the responses of the hybrid students was on the possibility to participate in study within course schedules and on a better chance to concentrate on the teaching provided in a face-to-face setting. These factors explain, for their part, why hybrid students want to participate in face-to-face study, and they might also explain why hybrids get worse grades than distance students. When motivation for viewing recordings was examined, it was noticed that only one quarter of the hybrid students were of the opinion that participation in lecture sessions with the help of videos would suit them better than participation in face-to-face study. Only 25% of them had the opinion that concentrating on study would be best when studying with the help of recordings. Similarly, only 17% of the hybrids told that they learn best by viewing the recordings.

Of the online students, who sometimes participate in face-to-face study, only 23% felt they learnt best in a face-to-face setting. Similarly, of the online students only 8% told that participation in face-to-face study suits them better than participation in lecture sessions with the help of videos. Compared with other student groups, the online students were motivated to participate in face-to-face study by a thought that face-to-face study transmits information that is not obtained via videos. When motivation for viewing lecture session recordings was examined, it was noticed that 73% of the online students were of the opinion that recorded lecture videos can substitute face-to-face study and participation in lecture sessions with the help of videos would suit them better than participation in face-to-face study. Here one should also pay attention to the fact 33% of the distance students had a different opinion in this question. Thus, even among them there is some willingness to participate in face-to-face study. Approximately a half of the distance students had the opinion that one can concentrate on teaching best when studying with the help of recordings.

When examining the motivation to participate with the help of recorded lecture videos, it became apparent that increase in flexibility is a very significant motivation factor for video use. In this, no differences between different student categories could be found. Of all the students who sometimes watch videos at all, 97% watches recorded lecture videos because they allow one to view a lecture at the time desired. In addition, 91% of all students view the recordings because they enable viewing a lecture in parts and 95% because they make it possible to view again the parts desired.

4. THE EFFECT OF EXTERNAL FACTORS

4.1 Timetables

The students were also asked about which study modes would best suit to their study schedules. Only about a quarter (27%) of the face-to-face students were of the opinion that participation in face-to-face study suits best also to their timetables. Combining face-to-face study with videos would be the best alternative, schedule-wise, for approximately half of them (46%). Only a quarter (27%) thought that studying with the help of recordings would be the most reasonable approach from the viewpoint of scheduling.

Of the hybrid students 92% were of the opinion that study in which videos are utilized (either just recordings or a combination of videos and face-to-face study) fits best to their schedules. Here one should pay attention to the fact that there were no hybrid students who would regard the use of real-time videos alone as the most suitable study mode in their study schedule. This tells us that the study mode of the hybrid students is defined, above all, by things related to time use rather than to distance. It also should turn our attention to that all hybrid students agreed, to a certain extent or completely, with that one reason why recorded lecture videos are used is because they facilitate watching the lectures at the time of one's choosing.

For online students' timetables videos naturally suit well. Of them 94% thought that study in which videos are utilized (either just recordings or a combination of videos and face-to-face study) fits best to their schedules.

Figure 5 depicts the responses related to the study modes that best suit for the students' study schedules.

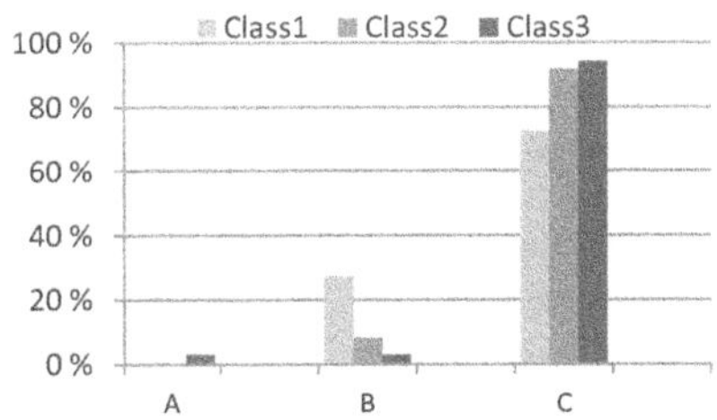

Figure 5: study modes that are suit best for the students' study schedules (*A=written material only, B= face-to-face teaching and written material, C=utilizing videos one way or another*).

4.2 Studying Alongside Work

The effects, on the study mode, of studying while working were mapped out for example by asking the students whether they could use work time for study when their work tasks allowed that. There was no difference to talk of in this issue between the hybrid and online students. Of the hybrid students 50% replied in the affirmative and also of the online students 44% did so. On the other hand, those participating in face-to-face study can use, on the basis of their responses, more work time for their study (73%). A great many of the hybrid students would regard participation in face-to-face study as suitable for them but do not, as a rule, participate in it. Therefore, it might be thought that, at least as far as they are concerned, the option to use work time for study means, first and foremost, that the students have better opportunities to view lecture videos during their work time but are not allowed to be off work for face-to-face study at the campus area.

4.3 Distance

Distance has a great impact on the use of videos. According to the responses of the students, the distance from which a student can participate at will in face-to-face study is about 70 km, which corresponds to about an hour's drive by car. It seems that the effect of distance is stronger for exclusively online students. Of the face-to-face students 36% told that the motivation for viewing recordings is their inability or unwillingness to travel. The corresponding figure for the hybrid students was 42%. Of the online students, 79% thought the same way. The importance of distance for the face-to-face and hybrid students seems, however, be mostly related to time spent on traveling rather than to impossibility to participate due to the distance involved. This can be concluded from the responses to a question mapping out the distance to the place of residence to which 90% of both groups replied that they are living near enough to participate also in face-to-face study if they so wish. Thus, in their case it appears that limitations in time use brought by work and family is one of the important factors that restrict participation in face-to-face education. Only 42% of the online students live close enough to the campus to participate at will in face-to-face study. A student's idea about whether he/she can participate in face-to-face study as far as distance is concerned is, naturally, subjective. A portion of the students who live quite far feel, however, that they can participate in face-to-face study if they so wish, whereas some of those living quite near cannot, in their own view, do so.

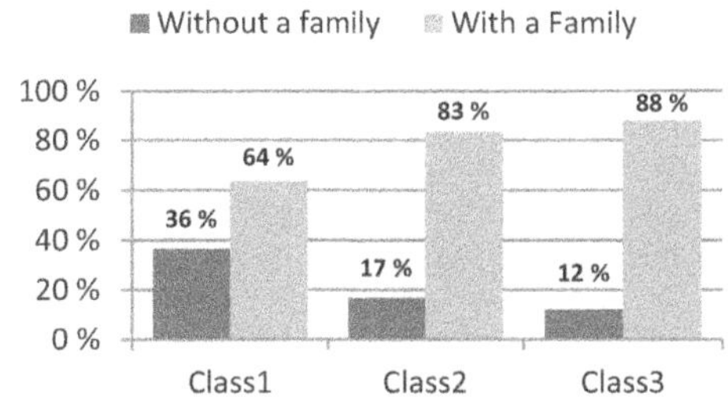

Figure 6: Distribution of students with a family and students without a family, in student categories.

4.4 Students' Life Situation

One important factor, especially when we consider adult students, is the effect of their life situation on study mode. Family creates limitations in time use for the student. The limitation in time use caused by family life is shown by the fact that the students who participate in studies more with the help of videos often are with a family. Figure 6 shows more accurate results of this.

5. CONCLUSIONS

The results of this study clearly argue for the important role that videos play in the search for teaching solutions that would be as flexible as possible. If the students are allowed to freely choose their mode of study, they will create strategies, which are quite distinct from each other, in order to complete their studies. Some of the students study with a fairly strong emphasis on face-to-face teaching, whereas others make good use of videos. In addition, some of the students utilize evenly both face-to-face mode and distance mode.

In the opinion of the face-to-face students, learning face-to-face is the best option for them. In fact, even for them it is not the best alternative as far as timetables are concerned. This clearly shows that the data consists of working adult students. Face-to-face students can choose their study mode freer than other student groups. Thus it is natural that 3/4 of the face-to-face students regarded face-to-face study as a study mode that is more suitable than participation with the help of videos. Their motivation to participate via face-to-face study was due to the desire to ensure availability of teaching and to the opportunity to participate in study within the course schedule as well as to a better chance to concentrate on the education provided in the face-to-face study. However, increase in flexibility sometimes motivated even face-to-face students to use videos. This outcome agrees quite closely with [5]. In their study, they noted that also students living close to the campus area need flexibility in their studies. Typically, the chances of a face-to-face student to use work time for study are good. Among the face-to-face students, the proportion of those with a family is smaller than in other student groups. It should be noted that only a third of the face-to-face students told of having achieved the objectives they had set for their study.

The desires and motivations of the hybrid students are very close to those of the face-to-face students. Based on the results of this study, it could be seen that the hybrid students would like to study in a face-to-face setting and that they did not feel that study with the help of videos would suit them as well as it would should to face-to-face students. They also feel that their learning is at its best in face-to-face study. As with the face-to-face students, the motivation of the hybrid students to participate in face-to-face study is the possibility to participate in study within course schedules and a better chance to concentrate on the teaching provided. Even though the hybrid students would be willing to participate in face-to-face study, it wouldn't suit to their schedules that well. The study mode of the hybrid students is defined, above all, by matters related to time use and not by the distance involved. In fact, the students utilize videos in their study participation due to reasons pertaining to scheduling. Approximately a half of the hybrid students can use their work time for studying. It doesn't seem, however, that this would lead to a situation where the hybrid students could participate more in face-to-face study. Typically, students with families are more common among the hybrid students than among the face-to-face students. A half of the hybrid students told of having progressed in their studies as they had expected.

Use of videos suits well to the online students and they think that videos can replace face-to-face teaching. This may be due partly to that in connection with student recruitment, flexibility brought about with the help of videos has been prominently displayed. Thus there are students who have found their way to the education and already at the beginning of their studies oriented towards the use of videos. It has been noted also in earlier research [10, 11] that a positive attitude towards and belief into videos as learning aids increases their use, and those who use videos a lot regard them as well suited for studying purposes. Also among the online students, however, the desire for participating in face-to-face teaching is smaller. Compared with other student groups, the online students were motivated to participate in face-to-face study by a thought that face-to-face study transmits information that is not obtained via videos. Among the student groups, the online students' chances to use work time for study are the worst. In addition, the portion of online students with a family is greater than average, and distance has a greater effect on their motivation to watch videos. The number of online students who feel that they cannot participate in face-to-face study even when they want to do so is, as a matter of fact, greater than the average. Increase in flexibility brought about lecture videos is, naturally, a very significant factor regarding their study mode. Absence from face-to-face teaching makes the study of some online students more difficult, but, nevertheless, it seems that those studying with the help of videos would achieve the objectives they have set for their studies. Two-thirds of the online students thought this way.

The face-to-face students and online students apparently study the way they prefer to study, and for that they have fairly good opportunities. The hybrid students, however, end up studying against their preferences for practical reasons. One should, moreover, notice that there is at least some willingness in all student categories to participate in face-to-face study. Similarly, in all categories the students use, to some extent, videos due to the increased flexibility they provide.

To ensure that the benefits that face-to-face participation and participation with the help of videos bring with them would be available as far as possible for the use of different students, one of the top priorities of the future is to reduce the differences between these study modes. This is aimed at, above all, by bringing participation aided by videos closer to participation in face-to-face study. For this, there is a novel application [6]. The application enables students' telepresence and communication and taking note of them better than before in a face-to-face teaching situation. In this way, participation with the help of videos is made to resemble more and more participation in face-to-face studies without, however, losing the added value that videos bring with them.

6. ACKNOWLEDGMENTS

The authors wish to thank the European Commission and The European Regional Development Fund for the grant to project "Ubiquitous Learning Environment for Adult Education", the Executive Agency for its help and all the partners of the project for their contribution.

7. REFERENCES

[1] S. Andberg and K. Tuononen. *Videoviestintä suomalaisissa korkeakouluissa 2008*. University of Helsinki. Educational Centre for ICT, Helsinki, 2009.

[2] C. Chiu, G. Lee, and J. Yang. A comparative study of post-class lecture video viewing. In *5th IASTED international conference on Web-based education Conference Proceedings*, 2006.

[3] P. Dean, M. Stahl, D. Sylwester, and J. Pear. Effectiveness of combined delivery modalities for distance learning and resident learning. *Quarterly Review Of Distance Education*, 2(3):247–254, 2001.

[4] C. Dziuban, J. Hartman, and P. Moskal. Blended learning. *EDUCAUSE Center for Applied Research, Research Bulletin*, 2004(7):1–12, 2004.

[5] M. Gosper, D. Green, M. McNeil, R. Phillips, G. Preston, and K. Woo. *The impact of web-based lecture technologies on current and future practices in learning and teaching*. Australian Learning and Teaching Council, Sydney, 2008.

[6] I. Hakala, T. Härmänmaa, and M. Myllymäki. Cinetvideo: video sharing application for educational use. In *22th EAEEIE Annual Conference Proceedings*, 2011.

[7] I. Hakala, S. Laine, and M. Myllymäki. The effect of lecture videos on participation in teaching. In *WBE Web-based Education Conference Proceedings*, 2010.

[8] I. Hakala and M. Myllymäki. The use of lecture videos: attendance and student performance. In *CATE 14th International Conference on Computers and Advanced Technology in Education Conference Proceedings*, 2011.

[9] T. Traphagan, J. Kucsera, and K. Kishi. Impact of class lecture webcasting on attendance and learning. *Educational Technology Research and Development*, 58(1):19–37, 2009.

[10] B. VonKonsky, J. Ivins, and S. Gribble. Lecture attendance and web based lecture technologies: A comparison of student perceptions and usage patterns. *Australasian Journal of Educational Technology*, 25(4):581–595, 2009.

[11] S. Walls, J. Kucsera, J. Walker, T. Acee, N. McVaugh, and D. Robinson. Podcasting in education: Are students as ready and eager as we think they are? *Computers Education*, 54(2):371–378, 2010.

cs4fn: A Flexible Model for Computer Science Outreach

Chrystie Myketiak
Queen Mary University of London
London UK
chrystie@eecs.qmul.ac.uk

Paul Curzon
Queen Mary University of London
London UK
pc@eecs.qmul.ac.uk

Jonathan Black
Queen Mary University of London
London UK
jonathanb@eecs.qmul.ac.uk

Peter W. McOwan
Queen Mary University of London
London UK
pmco@eecs.qmul.ac.uk

Laura R. Meagher
UK Technology Development Group
Fife, UK
Laura.Meagher@btinternet.com

ABSTRACT

There are a variety of initiatives to attract secondary school students to computer science. cs4fn is one such project. It combines a magazine, website and live shows, telling stories about computer science in spirited and creative ways. Here we focus on the use of the magazine and, using sociolinguistic discourse analysis, we analyze comments from students and teachers to understand why they have requested (free) subscriptions to the magazine and how they plan to use it. Our analysis shows that both students and teachers are attracted to the flexibility that cs4fn provides, and use it in a variety of learning contexts. We find that the flexibility of the magazine makes it a valuable tool to engage students and teachers and that they use it to further enthuse others (i.e., other students and teachers). We suggest that cs4fn magazine is a powerful form of outreach and that this approach can be widely disseminated within computer science and other academic disciplines, raising the profile of computing to both students and teachers, and spreading enthusiasm for computer science.

Categories and Subject Descriptors

K.3.2 [**Computers and Education**]: Computer and Information Science Education – Computer Science Education

General Terms

Human Factors.

Keywords

Public engagement, outreach, recruitment, K-12, teachers, diversity, cs4fn.

1. INTRODUCTION

There is a demand to attract students to science, technology, engineering and mathematics. As a result of this, there are a variety of initiatives to attract K-12 students to the field. The 'Computer Science for Fun' (cs4fn) project is a public engagement campaign that promotes computer science to school-aged children. Its underpinning philosophy is that public engagement in science works best when it emphasizes enthusiasm and interest through story-telling, rather than high-pressure recruitment of K-12 curriculum-directed activities. Our focus involves the development of a range of cs4fn branded materials that centralize innovative computing research, with our main aims of building intrinsic individual motivation and excitement for computer science among students.

cs4fn is based at a UK university (Queen Mary, University of London); however, its combination of a free magazine, website, and a series of talks and lectures are used by other universities in the UK and abroad to support their own outreach. The magazine, which is the focus of this paper, is sent to individual subscribers and classrooms in more than 80 countries. Our early evaluation data suggests that the cs4fn project is meeting its aims of sparking interest in computer science [4]. Data from the website shows that the average number of pages viewed per visit is increasing [4]. An evaluation of the talks and lectures, found that this style of kinesthetic teaching approaches provide learning and engagement activities that are successful for a range of age groups and levels of achievement [5, 6].

In this paper we explore how students and teachers use cs4fn magazine and discuss how the magazine is considered useful by a range of teachers and students, including those in subjects other than computing-related courses. A key finding is that, by basing the material and stories on exciting research topics with the aim of enthusing our audience, we encourage flexible use of the materials. This allows us to meet our aims, whilst allowing our users to address their own needs and interests. In addition, while the magazine is not directly tied to the K-12 curriculum of any jurisdiction, it lends itself to use by teachers in fulfilling curriculum objectives.

2. CONTEXT AND RELATED WORK

There are many approaches to computer science engagement that emphasize raising interest in the subject. One way to do this is to run workshops or events either in university computing departments or at schools. For example, Doerschuk et al. describe programming workshops in which students have 'cool' tasks such as building robots [8]. Other projects allow others to recreate their workshops, such as CS Unplugged who make their materials available in several languages such as Mandarin as well as English [1]. Wahla et al. adopt another approach to enthusing students in computing, using technology-assisted scavenger hunts to introduce school children to sensory networks [11].

An alternative to workshops can be the development of curriculum material that teachers can use to increase students' engagement whilst also fulfilling teaching requirements. For example, the Computing at Schools group (UK) and the US-based

ITiCSE'12, July 3–5, 2012, Haifa, Israel.

Computer Science Teachers Association aim to improve the curriculum while supporting teachers' professional development. There are also organizations that offer workshops that are directly tied to the curriculum. Two examples of programs that use workshops based on kinesthetic activities to provide curriculum support are Google's CS4HS program, which supports US computer science teachers through workshops [3], and the CS Inside project based in Scotland [7].

There are also a variety of approaches taken to enthusing students about computer science in order to improve recruitment at the university level. One commonality amongst large-scale campaigns is that many bolster motivation for taking the subject while also providing some support to teachers (e.g., CS Unplugged, Computing at Schools, and CS Inside). Workshops, away-days and teaching support provide excellent opportunities to participating students and schools. The cs4fn project proposes that it is also possible to increase motivation and support teachers through 'take away resources' such as magazines. The cs4fn approach makes the magazine a flexible resource that can support teachers and students to match their individual needs. The magazine format scales to audiences much larger than typical workshops (i.e., there are thousands of subscribers), which is an advantage. By sending out magazines to subscribers twice a year we have the opportunity to repeatedly re-ignite the interest of our readers.

3. MAGAZINE

cs4fn magazine is a professional quality magazine that is produced twice annually. Each issue is 20 pages in length and is printed on high quality, thick, glossy paper. All pages of the magazine contain graphics and vibrant colour alongside a distinctive font. Every issue has a main theme around which the articles are based, a short editorial note about the topic and an assortment of short, one-page, and two-page articles. We often choose themes to coincide with events. For example, the issue (14) in production at the time of writing is on Alan Turing and his work to coincide with the hundredth anniversary of his birth. Similarly, "Faces" (issue 13) matched the content we delivered at our stall at the Royal Society Summer Science Exhibition in summer 2011. This way we were able to give attendees copies of the magazine that matched the content that we displayed at the prestigious London science festival. We also attempt to maintain some variety in the themes: a very technical theme is likely to be followed by an interdisciplinary theme that relates more to the arts or social sciences.

In addition to the two regular issues published each year, we produce a third magazine, which we call an "annual"; a denser magazine that is usually three-times longer than the standard issues. Similar to standard issues, the annual usually has a theme around which we base our articles. The annual collates articles we published in earlier standard cs4fn issues on the topic as well as new articles written especially about the topic. Our most successful annual was 2010's "The Women are Here" which focused on women's historical and contemporary contributions to computer science [2]. We have also created other themed booklets, such as two magic books that support our magic of computer science shows [6].

Support for the production and distribution of the magazine currently comes from three main sources, each committed to improving recruitment into computer science. Base costs of printing and distribution are paid by a grant from EPSRC (Engineering and Physical Sciences Research Council) who also pay for staff time. Support from Google covers extra costs of printing and distribution, and our university provides support for additional overseas distribution as well as seed funding for new initiatives.

We do two types of mailing: the first is unsolicited mailings of new issues to teachers in the UK and the second is to those, including teachers, students and the general public, who have completed the webform to become subscribers to the free magazine. With regard to the unsolicited mailing, we send copies of the magazine to computing and ICT teachers in the UK based from a database of secondary schools in the UK that we developed. In addition to these teachers we also send copies of the magazine to teachers of other subjects that are relevant to a particular issue's interdisciplinary focus. For example, we sent "Animation" (issue 11) to arts teachers as well as computing/ICT teachers.

4. METHODOLOGY

Our aim in the study discussed here was to gain insight about teachers' and students' use of the magazine as represented in the (optional) comments that they left in the online request form when they subscribed. The cs4fn team is multidisciplinary and one member is also a sociolinguist. Drawing from her skill set, we embarked on a qualitative sociolinguistic discourse analysis of the comments, and that is the data we present and discuss here. Discourse analysis is a branch of sociolinguistics that emphasizes the importance of "language use above and beyond the sentence" [10]. Of importance to discourse analysts is not merely what is said, but the context in which it occurs, including its meaning and effect [9]. Many discourse analysts adopt a somewhat functional approach to language, as we do here, which means that our analysis emphasizes the *use* of language rather than its form [10]. For instance, we are concerned with social aspects such as examining the diversity of speakers – including teachers and students, as well as regional differences – rather than purely linguistic issues such as the syntax of comments.

Discourse analysts typically use 'naturally occurring' conversations rather than scripted or invented examples. Our study uses naturally occurring comments that individuals left when requesting copies/subscriptions of cs4fn magazine. Almost all requests for copies of the magazine come via an online form on the cs4fn website. The form has textboxes for individuals to leave their name, address, status (e.g., profession), position (e.g., job title), the number of copies they request, and an additional optional text box for them to provide a comment. We ask on the form that people who request multiple copies use the space to inform us of how they will use/distribute the additional copies.

When individuals submit these online webforms they go to a cs4fn email address, which has three recipients (all are members of the cs4fn team). We received an average of 18 new requests per week (01 January 2008 – 01 March 2010). The numbers of requests vary from month to month, with an overall increase over time. Spikes in the number of requests can be noted soon after we post copies of new issues to schools twice annually, and when school is in session.

We uploaded all of the data collected during this 26-month period into a qualitative data software package (Atlas.ti); the total number of requests over this time period was 2055 and included five issues of the magazine. The issues in chronological order are: "Images", "Space", "The Environment", "Mobile", and "Animation". Over this period the number of copies of the magazine we printed (and distributed) doubled from 11,000 copies of "Images" (issue 7) to 22,000 for "Mobile" (issue 10). Although the webform asks individuals to provide their name and address for mailing purposes, we did not upload that information when producing a data file. We included only: status, position, country, date and comment fields. We did not link the mailing list and the hermeneutic unit used to analyze the data.

Our qualitative discourse analysis approach meant that we coded the comments to note narratives in each comment. To this point, each comment could include multiple 'discourses', including a range of functions. Our coding process was iterative and we coded the data until we were satisfied that we had extracted meaning from each comment. While discourse analysis is a qualitative method, we also examined the demographic data pertaining to the numbers of requests from students and teachers.

4.1 Coding Scheme

We allowed the codes to emerge from the data, and did not assume that we knew what the speakers wished to convey in their statements. However, we also had specific research questions to guide our process. These included: how do users frame their requests and use of the magazine, and what if any patterns emerge in the responses in relation to the status or position magazine. In other words, we were interested in how users saw the magazine, their interest in the magazine or the interest of those who they wished to share it with, and if these points differed between the comments left by teachers and students.

4.1.1 Coding Status

In addition to the codes concerning the substantive matter of their comments, we also coded the status they provided in order to offer demographic data of the proportion of requests that came from students and teachers (as well as different types of teachers). Initially we coded only those statuses that were related to formal education contexts: students, teachers, librarians, and academics. During this process we realized that "teacher" was too generic a classification and that individuals were often more descriptive than that in describing what subjects they taught. Many identified themselves specifically as "Computing" or "Information and Communication Technology" teachers, a small number classified themselves as "Home School" teachers. Therefore we recoded these teachers as "computing/ICT teachers", "home teachers" and "other teachers". The "other teachers" category includes those who answered with "teacher" as well as those who listed that they taught the following subjects: arts, careers/work experience, English as an additional language, multimedia, maths, physics, and science. We also included primary school teachers who teach subjects across the curriculum in this category.

Some individuals left the status textbox empty when requesting their subscription to cs4fn magazine. However, there were instances when an individual left this empty but in their comment referred to themselves as a student or teacher. There were also cases of respondents writing "teacher" in the status space but who expanded upon their status in their comment; for example, one teacher states "for use with my year 9 computing students" and another "for use in my home school". Using a sociolinguistic discourse analysis perspective meant that we were able to classify those teachers as computing/ICT teachers and home teachers, respectively.

Of the 2055 requests for subscriptions to the magazine that we received during the time period, 1303 (63.41%) listed their status as a student or teacher). Our analysis focuses on these 1303 requests. Of those 846 (64.93%) were students and 457 (35.07%) were teachers (including computing/ICT teachers, home school teachers and other teachers).

While it may be intuitive that cs4fn magazine requests from teachers would be from computing/ICT teachers primarily, this is not the case in our data. Including requests from teachers who did not leave comments, we received 229 requests from computing/ICT teachers and 228 requests from other teachers (including the subset of seven home school teachers). It is possible that some 'other teachers' do teach computing/ICT but since they did not supply us with any information indicating this we include them in the category of 'other teachers'.

4.1.2 Coding Comments

The comments we received covered a wide range of topics and because we approached the comments as 'discourses', we found a large number of codes (n=20), which we organized thematically. While each request could contain only one comment, some comments were coded more than once because the speakers made multiple points relevant to our analysis. In total we coded 1585 points within the 805 comments that people requesting the magazine supplied. However, not all 805 comments were from teachers or students: 546 were from those who listed their status as teachers (n=167) or students (n=379). A discussion of the 546 comments from students and teachers follows.

5. DISCUSSION

Although the comments students and teachers left when requesting magazine subscriptions cover a range of topics such that 20 codes emerged from the data, in this paper we concentrate specifically on those comments that fall under the remit of the use and impact of the magazine (approximately 1127 of 1587 codes, or 71%) in education and learning. The importance of flexibility intersects comments related to both use and impact of the magazine. New subscribers to the magazine, who may have received hard copies sent unsolicited to their schools or downloaded soft copies of the magazine, find that cs4fn magazine can be used for a range of purposes – including curriculum activities, which aid in communicating enthusiasm for computer science. In addition, diverse student and teacher audiences find the magazine useful to their needs.

5.1 Teachers and Students

The anticipated readers of cs4fn magazine consist of secondary school students and teachers, the audience discussed here, and 67.83% (n=546) of all comments received can be attributed to either students or teachers. While it is likely that there are many more requests from students and teachers who did not inform us – either in the status/position textboxes or in the comment that they left in the comment textbox – we focus only on those comments that can be attributed to either students or teachers.

5.1.1 Teachers

One common reason that teachers, particularly computing/ICT teachers, requested copies of the magazine was for class sets and/or classroom/laboratory copies. For example, an ICT teacher in the UK wrote, "I have received a few copies of your magazine over the past months and find it incredibly informative, interesting and useful, and would like to provide access to your magazine for our students in our ICT suites." Providing copies of the magazine in computing labs means that any students interested in the subject may find the magazine and in turn become further sparked. It also allows students to be agents – the resource is there for them to pick up, should they wish. An alternative to this approach is to give copies to all students in a class. One computing/ICT teacher in the UK explained their request for a class set in the following terms: "I would love to hand out copies to my A-level computing classes as well as having a copy in our school library. We do struggle to get numbers studying the subject and struggle even more to get girls." One advantage to distributing class sets is that students who may not pick up a copy of the magazine left in a public, shared space such as a classroom or laboratory still have access to the magazine and its content.

5.1.1.1 Home school teachers

We had not considered the potential for cs4fn to reach home school students. However, a small number of home school teachers (n=7) visited our website and signed up for subscriptions to the magazine, showing the potential interest in computing resources among this community. In addition, it shows that the magazine is having a small but evident impact outside of traditional school environments. The home school teachers in our sample reported that they wanted copies for each of the children in their home schools as well as for themselves in order to teach the content of the magazine.

5.1.2 Students

While teachers often request multiple copies of the magazine as a classroom/laboratory resource or to distribute amongst their classes, students often request a single copy subscription to the magazine. In addition, many students report specific uses for the magazine, which is discussed in the next section "In Use". When students request multiple copies of the magazine it is often to distribute them to friends.

International (to the UK) students in particular reference their social network in their comments, including in how they came to hear of the cs4fn project. Take, for example, this student from the Philippines who wrote, "A friend of mine who received this magazine in her school referred me to your site and told me good things about this cs4fn magazine. Because of that I would like to have two copies of the magazine. One for me and the other one is for my brother." This student details how he found out about the magazine through his social network, and additionally requests an extra copy so that he can share cs4fn with a sibling. While students such as this one may not be requesting copies for formal distribution as teachers do, they detail how friendship circles among students further the reach of public engagement projects such as this one.

5.2 Uses

Students and teachers request copies of the magazine for diverse reasons, some of which we described above. While cs4fn does not create content specific to the computing/ICT curriculum, it appears to be a teaching resource among teachers in public/private schools and single/mixed sex schools, as well as amongst home school teachers. Purposes of the magazine given in the webform comments include: personal benefit, resource for teachers, enthusing others, interest and implied interest/benefit. Within these purposes we found variation in the comments indicating that those requesting copies of the magazine see the magazine as serving a function to them and their purposes. This diversity shows that cs4fn is versatile. Within the context of secondary school education, teachers left comments detailing use of the magazine in ways that both suit their teaching styles and can fit the needs of their pupils. For example, some teachers stated that they thought cs4fn would be particularly valuable in their gifted and talented student classes. Because cs4fn is based within a university and we use it in part to interest students in taking computer science at university, it reaffirms the project to have teachers of students who are advanced and likely thought to be on the university-track requesting copies. Yet, other teachers commented that they thought that the magazine would be useful for classes of students classified as 'at risk' as well as those who experience behavioural problems. The use of cs4fn in a variety of classrooms and a diverse set of students gives some evidence that public engagement with research can benefit all students, rather than only those students who are seen to be university-bound. Similarly, we have had requests from a small number of teachers working within the prison system who hoped that the magazine would help incarcerated persons to consider careers in computing following their release. While it may seem that in spreading enthusiasm for computer science that it is necessary to develop different tools for different target audiences, the responses that we have show that this is not the case. Rather, it is possible to create a single tool (such as cs4fn magazine) that teachers and students can use in ways that are useful and purposeful for them. It is especially encouraging that, as the comments we analyzed indicate, cs4fn is used to enthuse and inspire students with diverse educational needs. We intend to conduct further research to directly explore the impact of cs4fn on recruitment and with non-university-track groups.

5.2.1 Learning for Enjoyment

One of the uses of the magazine that emerged from the comments left by students is that of their own personal interest or pleasure. While the magazine contains some content that may be linked to their specific studies, many students explain their use of the magazine as personal. For example, a student in the UK wrote, "I am an enthusiastic ICT student and would like to find out lots about computer science. I really enjoy this subject and can't wait to read the magazine." Although their expressed aim was to learn, the student here framed their comment as learning for enjoyment rather than as a study aid. Another student from the UK made this point more explicitly: "I found cs4fn.org to be a motivating and inspiring site, and I would like to read more of the information as a hard copy. I am studying Computing for A-level, and am very interested in studying it further. I think that a copy of the magazine would add to my studies substantially, and add a bit of fun." This same theme of computing/ICT students wanting subscriptions of the magazine for enjoyment is also evident in comments from other students, many of them international; for example, a student from Kenya: "I am a student doing a computer science course and this will help me so much to love my course and explore more" and a student from Indonesia, "I'm a student from Indonesia and very interested in anything about computers, I like to read and learn computer stuff." While these are only a few examples of the hundreds of comments from students we analyzed, they indicate that students embrace this magazine that focuses on exposing the 'fun' of computer science.

Other students commented that they thought the magazine would be helpful for their courses in a general sense. For example, a student from the Philippines wrote, "I just want a large knowledge about my course." This student hopes that the magazine will serve as some kind of supplementary study aid to the resources in their course. This student hopes to gain general relevant knowledge for their course through the magazine. To this end, cs4fn can be seen as aiding proactive students in their attempts to seek out information geared towards further engaging them with their subject.

5.2.2 Basis for Classroom Activity

Both teachers and students reported using the magazine for specific activities. For exampled a UK computer science teacher wrote that the magazine would be useful for stimulating class discussion, "I teach programming and networking to high school students. My max class size is 20, so I will get them into groups of 3 and discuss a topic from the magazine in their group. Then summarise the article, even take a side if there is a side to take. Finally present it to the class." Another computer science teacher wrote that the magazine would be useful in a reading comprehension section of the course because "your magazine is the only one I have found with articles relevant to today's students." The quotes from these teachers represent discourses expressed by many teachers: they want to use the magazine to help them with specific objectives in their courses. In these two examples, they intend to use the magazine to help their computing students to develop essential 'soft skills' such as the articulation of points, debate, and reading comprehension.

For teachers of other subjects, the activities they developed also tended towards classroom assignments tied to their teaching needs. For example an art teacher in the UK wrote, "I am new to the school and Y8 [eighth grade] are doing a project on animation. I think your magazine could be very useful for the students to give them ideas and starting points." Here a teacher of a subject that can intersect computing plans to use the magazine to help them to master their projects. While this may not appear to be directly tied to increasing the profile of computer science, it does mean that students who might not otherwise engage with computing are given the opportunity, and that seed could lead to some students developing a passion for the subject. It is important that all students have a basic understanding of computing. Introducing it through the subjects students are already interested in is one way to accomplish this,

The thematic nature of each issue of cs4fn has meant that teachers can use the magazine for open-ended assignments. In addition, teachers report planning to share the magazine with their students in classroom exercises, giving students the opportunity to find articles in the magazine that interest them. This works as an alternative to a directed assignment through promoting flexibility for individual students. Teachers use cs4fn in the classroom and the analysis of their comments shows that they do so in ways that allows students to discover their own interests in the content and to explore computing perhaps more broadly than they would otherwise be able.

5.2.3 Deeper Knowledge for Computing Courses

While some students make general assertions about the usefulness of the magazine in providing knowledge for their courses, other student comments showed that they believed the magazine would help them gain specific types of knowledge and/or skills. Take for example a student from Sri Lanka who wrote, "I'm a computer networking student where I need to read lots of material for my student related assignments and projects and for this reason I believe cs4fn can help me." Similarly a student from India commented, "I have read the linked articles of this magazine [on the website]. They are very interesting including problem solving and communication. Since I am a computer science student, I find it can help me a lot to understand many things including programming." Students in the UK also requested subscriptions to help with specific elements of their studies. For example, one student wrote: "I would like a copy please. I am about to undertake my honours year doing computing and my project is going to focus on teaching children about programming. I am interested to see what is being done about the country to encourage children." All three of the students quoted here offer explanations of how they see the magazine as fitting into their study, and their requests for the magazine are focused on gaining knowledge in specific areas, such as their projects, programming, or networks.

5.2.4 Interdisciplinarity

Many teachers commented on the interdisciplinary approach of cs4fn. In the magazine we stress the connections between computer science and other fields. Because of cs4fn's attention to other disciplines and the ways in which computer scientists work with artists, biologists, psychologists and others, teachers write to us for copies to share with students of diverse subjects. A teacher in the UK wrote, I think this will be of great interest to our computing, multimedia and art students." This teacher is an example of one who wants to expose students in computing and other subjects to computer science topics. Other teachers explicitly state that they want to use the magazine to highlight the interdisciplinary nature of the real world. A teacher requesting copies of the magazine wrote, "additional issues would be an excellent resource for our students taking options in Year 9 who are interested in ICT and would benefit from seeing the links between ICT, science, art, and technology. This could enable them to make informed option choices based around areas of interest, links between subject areas, and would help them to understand their potential job opportunities." Other teachers remarked on the possibility of using the magazine to create links across teaching curriculums. For example, an art teacher in the UK wrote, "I was happy to receive the pack and want to use animation to create links across the curriculum." Some of the interdisciplinary elements of the magazine had been envisioned at the start. However, by making connections between computing and other fields in the magazine, especially through themed issues that intersect multiple areas, and by sending single unsolicited copies of themed issues of the magazine to teachers of other subjects we were able to engage more fully with teachers of other subjects. The fact that some of these teachers wrote to us requesting multiple copies would seem to underscore the value of interdisciplinary themes and the potential to enthuse or recruit students who may not be studying computing/ICT at secondary school.

6. Conclusion

In this paper we used a sociolinguistic discourse analysis to analyze comments people reporting to be students or teachers left when completing an online webform to become subscribers to the computer science educational magazine cs4fn. We examined comments made by 546 teachers (n=167) and students (n=379). Specific themes emerged from the data and these categories can be understood as reinforcing flexibility of the resource both in terms of attracting the attention of teachers and students outside of computer science and in how students and teachers use the magazine.

cs4fn magazine provides highly malleable computer science content that serves multiple educational audiences and most subscribers to the free magazine define themselves as students or teachers. This audience includes computing/ICT teachers; teachers of other subjects: arts, careers, English as an additional language, multimedia, maths, physics, and science; home school teachers; and students themselves. That a notable proportion of the number of teachers' requests for subscriptions were from teachers of subjects other than ICT/computing shows that the magazine can be seen as a tool for promoting computer science both in and outside of computing/ICT classrooms. The ultimate student audience, reached directly via their own requests and indirectly through teacher requests, is diverse in age and nationality and includes students across the spectrum, including gifted and talented students, standard classes, as well as students who are 'at risk' and those who are currently incarcerated.

Subscribers use the magazine in equally diverse ways to meet their own individual aims, ranging from personal interest to a variety of self-directed and formal educational uses. When teachers request multiple copies, they report that they will: 1) give the magazine to other teachers in their department; 2) leave copies in their laboratories/classrooms or libraries for students to pick up on their own initiative; or 3) distribute to students in their classes. Meanwhile, students do not report requesting additional copies to give out in formal educational contexts (i.e., to give to fellow students in their classes). Instead, we find that students are likely to request a single copy of the magazine, or if they request multiple copies these additional copies are to give to friends or family members who share their interest in computing.

These findings show that by emphasizing enjoyable, interesting content in an accessible, lively style, within an attractive format, cs4fn offers students and teachers flexibility in its uses. While not targeted as a form of curriculum support, the analysis of comments shows that the magazine does support teachers and students alike as a way to give greater depth of understanding of syllabus topics across a variety of learning scenarios, where it can be linked to computer science courses and materials. In addition, both students and teachers offer comments supporting that the magazine can be a tool for developing intrinsic motivation in and passion for computer science, and they write about enthusing others rather than strictly teaching them. Comments demonstrate that public engagement efforts that focus on celebrating the subject can have a meaningful effect on students and teachers both inside the classroom and in sparking their intellectual curiosity.

The popularity of the magazine by computing/ICT teachers as well as those teaching other subjects is in part due to cs4fn's interdisciplinary approach. However, it also goes some distance in demonstrating at least two major points: firstly, that teachers across subjects are interested in interdisciplinary computer science resources and secondly recruitment into computer science programs could be achieved via a variety of disciplines including the humanities, fine arts, and social sciences.

The success of cs4fn shows that there is room for flexible tools to ignite interest in computing. Content that can be used and adopted in different ways can provide students and teachers with material that appeals to a wide and diverse global audience. cs4fn shows that such flexible resources are a possibility. cs4fn's public engagement approach is a powerful form of outreach, encouraging tens of thousands of readers to think about computer science in new ways, both directly and through supporting teachers.

7. ACKNOWLEDGMENTS

This work is funded via EPSRC research agreement EP/F032641/1 with additional support from Google, ARM, and Microsoft.

8. REFERENCES

[1] Bell, T., Alexander, J., Freeman, I., and Grimley, M. Computer Science Without Computers: New Outreach Methods From Old Tricks. *Proceedings of the 21st Conference of the National Advisory Committee on Computing Qualifications*, 127-133. http://www.naccq.ac.nz/conferences/2008/127.pdf

[2] Black, J., Curzon, P., Myketiak, C., and McOwan P.W. 2011. A Study in Engaging Female Students in Computer Science Using Role Models. *Proceedings of the 16th Innovation and Technology Conference in Computer Science Education Conference*, 63-67 DOI= http://doi.acm.org/10.1145/1999678.

[3] Blum, L., Cortina, T.J., Lazowska, E., and Wise, J. 2008. The Expansion of CS4HS: An Outreach Program For High School Teachers. *ACM SIGCSE Bulletin,* 40(1), 377-378 DOI= http://doi.acm.org/10.1145/1352135.1352263.

[4] Curzon, P., Black, J., Meagher, L.R., and McOwan, P.W. 2009a. cs4fn.org: Enthusing Students About Computer Science. *Proceedings of Informatics Education Europe IV*, Hermann, C, Lauer, T., Ottmann, T. and Welte. M. Eds., (Freiburg, Germany, November 5 - 6, 2009), 73-80.

[5] Curzon, P., McOwan, P.W., Cutts, Q.I., and Bell, T. 2009b. Enthusing and Inspiring With Reusable Kinesthetic Activities. *Proceedings of the 14th Innovation and Technology Conference in Computer Science Education Conference*, 94-98. DOI= http://10.1145/1595496.1562911.

[6] Curzon, P. and McOwan, P.W. 2008. Engaging with Computer Science Through Magic Shows. *ACM SIGCSE* Bulletin, 40(3), 179-183 DOI= http://doi.acm.org/10.1145/1597849.1384320.

[7] Cutts, Q.I., Brown, M.I., Kemp, L., and Matheson, C. 2007. Enthusing and Informing Potential Computer Science Students and Their Teachers. *ACM SIGCSE* Bulletin, 39(3), 196-200. DOI= http://doi.acm.org/10.1145/1269900.1268842.

[8] Doerschuk, P., Liu. J., and Mann, J. 2007. Pilot Summer Camps in Computing for Middle School Girls: From Organization Through Assessment. *ACM SIGCSE* Bulletin, 39(3), 4-8. DOI= http://doi.acm.org/10.1145/1269900.1268789.

[9] Fairclough, N. 2003. *Analyzing Discourse: Textual Analysis for Social Research.* London: Routledge.

[10] Schiffrin, D. 2006. Discourse. *An Introduction to Language and Linguistics* (eds. R.W. Fasold and J. Connor-Linton). Cambridge: Cambridge University Press, 169-204.

[11] Taylor, D. 2007. Employment Preferences and Salary Expectations of Students in Science and Engineering. *Bioscience*, 57(February), 175-185.

[12] Wahla, S., Feaster, Y., and Hallstrom, J.O. 2011. A Technology-Assisted Scavenger Hunt for Introducing K-12 Students to Sensor Networks. *Proceedings of the 16th Innovation and Technology Conference in Computer Science Education Conference*, 73-77. DOI= http://10.1145/1999747.1999770.

Anatomy, Dissection, and Mechanics of an Introductory Cyber-Security Course's Curriculum at the United States Naval Academy

Christopher Brown, Frederick Crabbe, Rita Doerr, Raymond Greenlaw*,
Chris Hoffmeister, Justin Monroe, Donald Needham, Andrew Phillips, Anthony Pollman,
Stephen Schall, John Schultz, Steven Simon, David Stahl, Sarah Standard

United States Naval Academy
Annapolis, Maryland 21402
United States of America

ABSTRACT

Due to the high priority of cyber-security education, the United States Naval Academy rapidly developed and implemented a new cyber-security course that is required for all of its first-year students. During the fall semester in 2011, half of the incoming class (about 600 students) took the course through a total of 31 sections offered by 16 instructors from a variety of disciplines and backgrounds. In the following spring semester, the remaining half of the first-year students will take the course. This paper explains the motivation that instigated and drove course development, the curriculum, teaching mechanics implemented, personnel required, as well as challenges and lessons learned from the first offering of the course. The information contained in this paper will be useful to those thinking of implementing a technical course required of all students at the same level in an institution (in our case first-year students) and particularly those interested in implementing such a course in cyber security.

Categories and Subject Descriptors

K.3.2 [**Computers and Education**]: Computer and Information Science Education – *curriculum, information systems education, computer science education, literacy, self-assessment*

General Terms

Documentation, Security

Keywords

Active Learning, Computer Security Awareness, Cyber-Security Education, Cyberspace Policy Review, Freshmen Required, Information Assurance, Naval Academy, Networks

*Contact author phone and email: +1-410-293-6806, greenlaw@usna.edu.

ITiCSE'12, July 3–5, 2012, Haifa, Israel.

1. INTRODUCTION

In May 2009, President Obama's Cyberspace Policy Review included an action item to "expand and train the workforce, including cyber security expertise in the Federal government" [7]. In response to this charge, the United States Naval Academy's (USNA's) Academic Dean & Provost created a Cyber Warfare Ad Hoc Committee. This committee consisted of faculty and staff members with broad representation from across the campus. Their charge was to explore and define the scope of understanding of cyber security needed by Midshipmen (undergraduate students at USNA), as future naval officers. The committee consulted with the Office of the Chief of Naval Operations and Commandant of the Marine Corps staffs, and sought their input and perspectives on the education USNA's graduates should receive to help address the needs of the Navy and Marine Corps. The committee also analyzed the other service academies' inclusion of cyber-warfare concepts in their curricula, and examined graduate-level programs to determine the foundational education and skills necessary for entry into their cyber-warfare-related curricula.

In August 2009, USNA's Cyber Warfare Ad Hoc Committee delivered its Initial Report that included a recommendation to create a required core course providing a technical foundation for undergraduate cyber-warfare education for all students regardless of academic major [6]. The unanimous view of the committee was that the course be technically oriented, focused on naval applications and case studies, and delivered in a hands-on, lab-based format. This course was intended to form the technical basis for continued cyber-security education that could be expanded upon as appropriate within the various majors. In the spring semesters 2010 and 2011, a prototype course based on the Cyber Warfare Ad Hoc Committee's recommendations was developed, delivered, and refined by USNA's Computer Science Department.

In April 2010, USNA's Academic Dean & Provost formed an Ad Hoc Committee on Cyber-Security Curriculum Options. This committee, comprised of three senior professors from the Divisions of Engineering & Weapons, Humanities & Social Sciences, and Mathematics & Sciences, was charged with examining a variety of approaches for integrating cyber concepts in the core curriculum. Ultimately, the committee recommended a two-course, technically-oriented sequence: the first to be taken by all students during their initial year and the second, providing more technical depth, to be taken by all students during their third year. This paper focuses on the development of the first in that sequence of two cyber core courses. And while the term "cyber" is currently used in many ways, for the purposes of this paper, we use it to refer to the totality of the space in which new kinds of computer crime, terrorism, espionage, and warfare are taking place.

Although USNA settled on one course in the first year and a second course in the third year, numerous other options were considered. No other option was deemed as easy to implement; in fact, at the time the options were formally presented (February 2011), the general consensus of the Committee, and all others who had been involved, was that the earliest possible implementation date for any option selected would be August 2012. In February 2011, the Committee's recommendation was approved, but the implementation date was to be August 2011—a mere six months later. There were many roadblocks to overcome to meet this deadline, some that would be typical of any academic campus (such as faculty-led, curriculum-review processes and faculty-senate votes and recommendations). In this instance the ground rules usually applied at USNA were modified given the short deadline and the importance of the initiative. USNA leadership made two things clear from the outset: the implementation deadline of August 2011 was immovable, and the inclusion of the new cyber course as a first-year, lab-oriented, technical-core course was non-negotiable. Other than that, all other specific details from course content to faculty development to assessment measures were left up to the faculty to debate and decide. So, in that context and with only six months to act, all faculty approval processes were conducted in parallel with course development and implementation planning.

There were many other significant challenges as well, ranging from determining what technical content to teach, to who would teach the course and how USNA would identify and prepare those faculty members within a six-month time frame. Perhaps the greatest challenge of all was how to teach this technical course to a new class of 1,200 first-year students (600 each semester) in a way that did not simply add more work to an already very busy schedule for the first-year students. The phrase "very busy" is used because students at the service academies have many demanding military obligations that are not common at other institutions and classroom attendance is required. At USNA, all first-year students take the same "core" of courses in their first year, an academic workload that amounts to 11 courses consisting of 35 credits over two semesters. To make room for the new cyber-security course, one of the existing core courses was moved to the second year (which itself resulted in additional curriculum changes and shifts) thereby resulting in only a single hour increase in course time. While finding the "slot" in the first-year schedule was challenging, a greater challenge was how to teach another technical subject (in addition to the required science-and-engineering-focused calculus and chemistry core courses) in such a way that the students would be engaged in the material sufficiently so that the difficulty associated with the technical nature of the content would be compensated for by the motivation of learning about the practical aspects of both offensive and defensive cyber security. The mantra was "Make it Navy relevant and make it exciting!" That outcome was considered essential; in a technical course involving two lecture hours and two lab hours per week, the end result needed to be that the students really enjoyed and learned the content, and that their day-to-day behavior regarding the use of social media, the Internet, wired and wireless networks, and so on, would now be much-better informed and positively affected by their new understanding of the risks and threats associated with cyber security.

Teaching cyber security to computer science and related majors is not a particularly new idea; many higher-education institutions offer courses in computer/network security, and a few even offer full degree programs in cyber security. Finding undergraduate, graduate, and even certification courses in cyber security is not especially challenging. However, the Naval Academy was in search of a stand-alone, technical, hands-on course with a broad range of cyber-security content that could be taught to every first-year student, regardless of their intended major or computer knowledge/skills, and further which served to significantly enhance the student's awareness and understanding of the risks and threats associated with cyber security, especially those that are relevant to the U.S. Navy and Marine Corps.

Before launching our first-year, cyber-security course, we contacted the two other major military service academies to determine what cyber-security education was provided to their students. The United States Air Force Academy (USAFA) requires an introductory computer-systems and information-technology course that includes five lessons focused on the fundamentals of computer security. In the summer of 2011, USAFA rolled out an elective two-week, full-time program to about 90 cadets that provides them with a hands-on experience in cyber security [Gibson, personal communication, 2011]. The content of the elective course has perhaps a 40% overlap with the content of the USNA first-year course. Similarly, the United States Military Academy's curriculum includes an information-technology-related course, but the focus is not in computer or network security [1].

2. COURSE CONTENT

The Cyber Warfare Ad Hoc Committee's Initial Report describes Cyber Warfare as "...a technical academic core of tightly inter-related subject matter, as well as a wide range of important topics that, while dependent on the technical core for fullest appreciation, are not dependent on each other. Stated another way, cyber warfare is comprised of, first, a foundational component, dealing with a set of interconnected fundamental technical concepts, and second, a wide range of interdisciplinary topics, touching upon the areas of law, political science, strategy and tactics, policy, ethics, and the study of foreign languages and culture" [6]. The Initial Report recommended creating a required core course that covered the technical foundations of Cyber Warfare; a course that is technical in nature, relevant to naval officers, and delivered in a hands-on and engaging manner.

The required cyber-security course now offered at the Naval Academy meets the required recommended in the Initial Report. The fundamental goals for the course are that students acquire:

• an understanding of the basic physical and virtual architecture of cyberspace, including: the individual computer and program, the physical components and protocols of a network and the Internet, and the distributed client-server system that is the world wide web,
• hands-on experience with basic components of the physical and virtual architecture of cyberspace and the ability to relate that experience to the larger system,
• an understanding of the Department of Defense's pillars of Information Assurance (availability, integrity, authentication,

confidentiality, and non-repudiation), the inherent vulnerabilities of information systems that endanger these properties, defensive measures to ensure that information systems retain these properties, and offensive measures that can be used to violate these pillars, and

• hands-on experience with some basic defensive and offensive practices in cyberspace, and the ability to relate that experience to new or more sophisticated attacks and defenses.

2.1 Hands-On Aspects

The hands-on element of the course is crucial to delivering a meaningful academic, technical, and engaging experience. It provides students with concrete experiences that they can relate to new or more-complex situations and/or technologies they encounter in order to make sense of them. For example, the lessons devoted to programs look at only simple programs, but as a hands-on exercise, the students are asked to provide unexpected input that crashes these programs or that make them behave in unintended ways. The lessons ask students to modify these simple programs to deal gracefully with bad input so that they get concrete hands-on experience with "patching" these kinds of coding errors, and thus see firsthand how hard it is to anticipate all the ways that input might be problematic. For example, the students edit the programs to escape certain characters and they edit conditional statements. The bad-input concept recurs in the section on attacks against network services. A network service is simply a program that sits and waits for input from a network connection rather than a keyboard or mouse. If an attacker can send that program input that the programmer did not anticipate and deal with gracefully, the service can be made to crash or do unintended things. Through careful design, almost every class meeting involves hands-on activities. The activities provide students with concrete experiences from which to reason and generalize, and a strong foundation for critical thinking and problem solving.

2.2 Course Components and Premises

The cyber-security course is divided into three sections: the Cyber Battlefield, Models and Tools, and Cyber Operations. One cannot begin to instruct students in cyber attack and cyber defense until students actually understand the space in which these actions take place, so the first part of the course introduces students to the "Cyber Battlefield": digital data, computer hardware, operating systems, programs, the web, networks, wireless networks, and the Internet. By covering these elements of cyberspace, students get hands-on experience with them and also see a variety of "bad things" that can happen (for example, clicking on a hyperlink to some innocuous site but instead being sent somewhere else, crashing programs with bad input, injecting malicious code into a website to crash it, stealing user names and passwords with malicious e-mail attachments, and so on). The students not only see how systems are supposed to work, but also understand how malicious actions break them.

The second section of the course is "Models and Tools." In this section students learn formal models of "security" and "risk" for information systems. To make concrete and compelling what could be abstract and lacking motivation, these models are related back to the "bad stuff" that the students saw happening in the first part of the course. For example, we show how an injection attack that redirects one website to some other site is an attack on *availability*. The models are then used to understand and reason in a principled way about new situations. With this new-found understanding of what security really means for an information system (that is, what things we are really trying to protect) we look at some of the fundamental tools used to provide security: firewalls, symmetric encryption, cryptographic hashing, authentication, asymmetric encryption, and digital certificates.

Finally, once the students understand the battlefield, what they are trying to defend (or attack), and what defenses they can employ (or must defeat), we move to the third and final part of the course: "Cyber Operations." In this section of the course, we look at cyber reconnaissance, attack (including malware), defense, forensics, and case studies. The course culminates in a series of three hands-on labs in which each section of students is divided into two teams, with each team responsible for their own network. They reconnoiter their opponent's network, attack their opponent's network, and finally defend (that is, harden) their own network and re-attack their opponent's hardened network. These activities occur on virtual hosts and networks served from a system that is (students access the virtual sandbox environment via the VMware *Vsphere*™):

a) completely isolated from the Naval Academy's public network,

b) able to be reset in seconds to its initial configuration following each lab period, and

c) indistinguishable from a real physical network.

3. COURSE MECHANICS

In this section we discuss the "mechanics" involved in teaching the first-year, cyber-security course: the assumed background of the incoming students; the lecture and lab delivery; homework and exams; student perspective, student and instructor communication mechanisms during the semester; and the means by which additional tutoring and review were available.

3.1 Student Background

Realizing that the cyber-security course was required for each student entering their first year at USNA, it was anticipated that there would be a wide variety of backgrounds encountered with first-year students. USNA is a highly selective institution. In the class of 2015, there are 993 men and 236 women, or roughly 19% female [8]. The students come from all 50 states, U.S. territories, and several foreign countries. Over 50% of the class of 2015 ranked in the top 10% of their high school class, and 50% of the students scored from 590–720 (out of 800) on the SAT Verbal and 50% scored from 610–730 on the SAT Math [8]. We assumed that each first-year student had some (though not much) computer experience along with a basic understanding of the Windows™ operating system and its associated applications. But, given the first-year nature of this course, there could be no prerequisites.

3.2 Course Delivery

As noted earlier, instructors taught material through both lecture and lab format. Online student lecture or lab notes, as appropriate, were available for each of the 41 lessons. Both internal (available only on campus) and external (http://www.usna.edu/cs/si110/) websites were created. The course policies, support materials, and supplemental resources were also available on both websites. The internal website contained links to all software resources needed for the course;

however, not all these resources were available on the external site. The external site existed so that students could access course material when travelling for an athletic or extra-curricular event. Additionally, there was a website accessible only to instructors to provide lesson plans, laboratory guides, and homework solutions. All of the lectures included a link to a homework assignment that was due the next class period. Every instructor also utilized an in-class, individual message board for sharing links and demonstrating some web-based activities.

Following customary procedure at USNA, there were three exams administered for the course. In order to standardize exam grading across sections, a rubric was provided in order to determine the amount of partial credit to be awarded for wrong answers.

3.3 Student Perspective

We administered two in-class surveys at six and sixteen weeks as well as a course evaluation to all students in order to gauge whether the course objectives were met and the students improved computer security knowledge and awareness. Roughly 94% of the students felt that the hands-on activities were helpful. About two-thirds of the students indicated that they truly enjoyed the hands-on activities, while about 95% of the remaining third indicated that they enjoyed the hands-on activities somewhat. Roughly 27% of the students felt they lacked some of the requisite computer knowledge/skills at the start of the course, but of those just 13% felt that this deficiency was a problem. About 95% of the students said that they became more aware of the threats facing their computer than before they started the course, while about 4% indicated they were already highly aware of the existing threats. For each of the three main parts of the course (as described in section 2.1), between 88–95% of the students indicated that they either had a much-better or somewhat-better understanding of the key issues involved. In other words, as self reported, the course learning objectives were met by about 90% of the students.

3.4 Communication

Offering a new, required cyber-security course to first-year students with a newly-indoctrinated set of instructors, some who did not have a computer-science background and/or had never taught at USNA before, meant that communication (constant, consistent, and concise) was paramount. An email alias was created for each of the 31 course sections which were further grouped into an overall course email alias. Instructors regularly used their section's email alias for specific class updates, while the course coordinator was the primary user of the overall course alias for more-global course announcements. An instructor-email alias (consisting of the 16 course instructors) was also created and used for a wide variety of purposes.

While instructors maintained almost daily email contact, mandatory weekly instructor meetings were held to review the previous week's classes, as well as to prepare for the upcoming week's material. These meetings were also used to gauge the overall progress of the students, as well as to discuss any content issues for the course. Typical examples of content issues were discussions about the arrival of new hardware/software or how a lecture/lab could be better presented next semester. When a particularly involved lab was forthcoming, the weekly instructor meetings were devoted to stepping through the lab.

3.5 Additional Instruction

Since this cyber-security course had never been taught at USNA before, a support structure for student learning was critical. The offering of any required college-level course comes with it the responsibility of providing tutoring, additional review, and outside of class extra instruction. USNA's cyber-security course offered all three. Using the model of other USNA technical core courses, an evening, group-study program was instituted. This Midshipmen Group Study Program (MGSP) was available Sunday–Thursday evenings, led by junior- and senior-year computer science and information technology majors selected by USNA's Center for Academic Excellence and the Computer Science Department. MGSP was augmented with special review sessions for each of the 6-week, 12-week, and final exams. These well-attended sessions, held during the MGSP timeframe on a Sunday evening prior to the exam, reviewed key learning objectives and homework exercises while also answering student questions. For these reviews, numerous instructors and rooms were used. Some instructors supplemented exam reviews by offering evening online instruction using an online-meeting tool. Lastly, if more one-on-one tutoring was needed, students were encouraged to contact their instructor for additional help.

4. PERSONNEL REQUIRED

In order to successfully deliver this course, USNA needed to coordinate the efforts of personnel in diverse roles, from instructors, content developers, facility and technical support, to administrators.

4.1 Course Instructors

Having only six months lead time between the decision to deliver the cyber-security course and the start of the fall 2011 semester, there was considerable concern about where to find qualified instructors; hiring enough new faculty members (either part-time or full-time) with appropriate qualifications to teach cyber security is a very difficult proposition due to the high demand for this skill set. So, interested faculty members were sought from other departments, from the campus IT staff, and also from outside of the USNA academic community. As a result of these vigorous efforts, a diverse group of sixteen instructors taught the first semester. The faculty members assembled possessed various levels of technical expertise in cyber security. Some faculty members were active military officers who brought a great deal of relevant operational exposure gained during their previous career assignments. We should note that roughly 50% of the faculty members at USNA are military members who hold at least a Masters degree, and those percentages are the same for the Computer Science Department (CSD). Other instructors had a strong personal technical interest in the subject matter, while some had significant but non-technical experience.

4.2 Course Coordinator and Content Developers

Due to the technical nature of the course and the short timeline for implementation, several faculty members from the CSD were tasked with forming a course-coordination cadre to flesh out the course details fully. This group had four leaders. One developed much of the overall curriculum for the course, another led the hardware and software acquisition efforts and assisted with curriculum development, a third developed much of the lab-focused portions of the course, and a fourth formatted homework and solutions. The course content was developed mostly by the course coordinator, the instructors who taught the prototype of the course, and a small subset of the instructors. The development efforts began in earnest in April 2011 and continued full time throughout the summer and into the fall semester concurrent with the running of the cyber-security course. All courses at USNA have a course coordinator, so we did not need to create an entirely new model for developing and teaching this course. The benefits of a good course coordinator are that less-experienced instructors have a framework from which to deliver a strong class, and the efforts of one are leveraged so that faculty members do not need to duplicate work.

4.3 Facilities Manager

We designated an experienced faculty member as the course Facilitates Manager. This faculty member, who also taught the course, served as the main coordinator for hardware and software identification, acquisition and testing. We found that this approach worked well since it allowed the Course Coordinator to focus more fully on the task of developing course content. There were times when technical staff needed to drop everything they were doing to aid the facilities manager in addressing emergent problems with course hardware and software. Our facilities manager had the positional authority to expect immediate assistance from the technical support staff when required. Issues that prevented instructors from teaching the course effectively or prevented students from working on class material were given the highest possible priority, and the facilities manager and technical-support personnel did a good job in fixing any problems that developed unexpectedly.

4.4 Technical-Support Staff

This course required dedicated technical support. It was important to have technical-support staff available and ready to go to lab rooms to assist instructors with real-time issues. Although as we noted earlier, instructors practiced the labs during weekly instructor meetings, there were occasions when unexpected problems arose during labs. If instructors were not able to solve such problems themselves, they needed assistance from the technical-support staff, facilities manager, or course coordinator. Running such a course for the first time would be impossible with just faculty members supporting the course, as there are many network issues that need to be addressed. Our technical-support staff for the course included a contractor who had a high level of proficiency with computer security. Additionally, several staff members from the Academy's information technology staff were assigned to assist with the hardware and software support for the course.

4.5 Administrators

From the Superintendent to the Academic Dean & Provost to the Math & Science Division Director to the CSD Chair, administrators played a vital role in the successful rollout of the cyber-security course. (Note that at USNA the Academic Dean & Provost position is equivalent to the Vice President for Academic Affairs, and a Division Director is equivalent to a college level Dean.) They had to have vision; they had to instill the belief that this project could and would be implemented; they had to encourage faculty and set milestones; they had to provide resources and strong support for all personnel involved. And, most importantly, they had to remain flexible and keep expectations realistic. Our administration formed the appropriate committees, sought appropriate input for the course, listened to the feedback that they received, and helped guide the course through appropriate USNA approval channels. The administrators acted quickly in terms of hiring instructors and replacing lost technical staff. They helped as much as possible in expediting hardware and software requests which often can be notoriously slow in large organizations. And, they found creative ways to free up instructors to teach the course. The course received a great deal of media attention [2–5], and administrators worked on promoting the course both internally and externally. Without such a strong and dedicated administrative team, the course could never have been implemented. The challenge would simply have been too great for a department to take on alone.

5. LESSONS LEARNED AND RECOMMENDATIONS

Since many of the instructors were new to the course material, possessed varying levels of technical exposure to cyber security, and in some cases had never before taught at an undergraduate institution, USNA offered a two-week summer preparatory "boot camp" in August 2011. During this session, the entire course was presented and beta tested. The "boot camp" gave the instructors the opportunity to familiarize themselves with the content and provided the course coordinators the feedback necessary to refine material and test the support equipment. Fortunately, all instructors taught for the full semester without any emergency departures. Nevertheless, one recommendation is to train and maintain a list of possible replacement instructors in the event of an unexpected departure.

Section 3.4 discussed the weekly instructor forum, which was conducted in one of the student classrooms for faculty to review successes, challenges, and upcoming content. These meetings, together with the instructor-email alias, provided additional opportunities to test and improve upcoming labs and lectures. The instructor alias facilitated an ongoing exchange of ideas and a venue for capturing experiences and challenges encountered during the course. All email aliases that were established were keys to communicating successfully and efficiently.

As discussed in section 3.2, the primary reference for students was the course website, which was a very successful tool for students and instructors. The technical orientation and dynamic nature of the course necessitated the robustness and currency of the website, as it was the primary source of lesson material for the students. A secondary source of information was the required course textbook; however, most students never used their textbook for this course, and therefore the textbook requirement needs to be reassessed. The student notes posted by the course coordinator were extensive and students read those more than the textbook.

The previously discussed student-learning support structure with MGSP, exam reviews, and extra instruction were extremely popular among the students, and their student opinion forms highlighted that fact. As expected, the sessions dedicated to exam review were the best attended with about 50% of students attending. For MGSP sessions, typically 10–20% of the students attended. USNA will soon offer evening cyber-security tutors in its Center for Academic Excellence, and this service is seen as a necessity for the course. Additionally, an "extra-help" non-credit class is being offered starting with the spring 2012 course. This "extra help" period is available to students that anticipate needing additional assistance and study time for most of the first- and second-year technical core courses at USNA.

A key miscalculation when developing the content for this course was the expectation that students would have a much greater level of basic computer skills at the start of the course. The reality was that while students were adept end users of computer technology, they superficially understood the concepts and practical applications of computer technology and basic user security. As a result of this realization, future iterations of this cyber-security course must be adapted to take the lack of basic skills into account. All first-year students are issued laptops at USNA and are required to use those machines extensively in the fall. For this reason we expect the 600 students taking the course during the spring will not be burdened by a similar lack of basic computing skills; they will have been using the machines for four months.

While the cyber-security course was technically oriented and hands-on, it unintentionally lacked sufficient real-world contextual reinforcement of the technical concepts discussed in the classroom. USNA's Center for Cyber-Security Studies sponsors seminars and a lecture series with top-level, subject-matter experts discussing cutting-edge, cyber-security topics. And although these sessions were available to the student body at large and well attended, the incorporation of these events into the classroom would have provided one avenue for the needed contextual reinforcement. Additional contextual material should be integrated directly into course material. Since the required course textbook was insufficient at providing up-to-date content, online cyber-security articles may hold the key to deliver current and relevant supplemental and pre-read material.

The weekly utilization of hands-on laboratory exercises were instrumental in creating knowledge transfer and widely enjoyed by the majority of students, as indicated in course-wide evaluations. One downside to the exercises was the lack of laboratory assistants. Frequently, during the labs, the exercise was interrupted with competing individual technical issues or student questions. While the lab objectives were usually met, having (dedicated) assistance during the lab would have facilitated more-effective knowledge transfer for the class as a whole while providing the ability to address individual concerns.

Clearly, not all institutions can or would necessarily devote this amount of energy and resources to introducing an institution-wide course in cyber security. However we encourage other institutions to take some steps toward preparing students to handle emerging cyber-security threats. These steps might be any one of the following: the introduction of a non-technical, elective, cyber-security course that has no prerequisites, the introduction of a technical cyber-security course in a specific department such as information technology or computer science, the introduction of a short course on cyber security, or perhaps the incorporation of more cyber-security material into existing courses.

6. SUMMARY

By all measures the cyber-security course was successful. The course was implemented and provided to nearly 600 students in the fall semester with only six months notice. Overall, the learning objectives of the course as designed were met. The course was technically oriented with hands-on activities designed to reinforce the learning objectives. Although most of these students will not make their careers in cyber security, they will graduate with a better understanding of its fundamentals. Throughout this work we have highlighted many of the difficult challenges that were overcome to make the course a success. Finding qualified staff to teach/develop such courses and allocating the necessary resources are possibly the greatest challenges that an institution intending to design and implement a new curriculum will face. We did not observe meaningful differences in student outcomes attributable to a diverse set of instructors.

7. REFERENCES

[1] Academic Program. Curriculum and Course Descriptions. Office of the Dean. United States Military Academy. West Point, New York. DOI = http://www.dean.usma.edu/sebpublic/curriccat/static/index.htm.

[2] Brown, M. H. 2011. Naval Academy Preparing Officers for Cyberwarfare. Baltimore Sun. DOI = http://www.baltimoresun.com/news/maryland/education/bs-md-naval-academy-cyber-security-20111019,0,2371754.story.

[3] Carroll, C. 2011. Cyberwarfare Joins the Curriculum at Service Academies. Stars and Stripes. DOI = http://www.stripes.com/news/cyberwarfare-joins-the-curriculum-at-service-academies-1.158642.

[4] Witte, B. 2010. Military Academies Teach More Cyberwarfare. Navy Times. DOI = http://www.navytimes.com/news/2010/03/ap_cyberwarfare_030810/.

[5] Naval Academy Weaves Cybersecurity into Curriculum. DOI = http://defensesystems.com/articles/2011/03/08/naval-academy-adds-cybersecurity-courses.aspx.

[6] Needham, D., and Patrick, V. Initial Report of the Dean's Cyber Warfare Ad Hoc Committee, USNA-CS-TR-2011-02. U.S. Naval Academy Computer Science Department, Annapolis, MD, 2011.

[7] President's Cyberspace Policy Review: Assuring a Trusted and Resilient Information and Communications Infrastructure, May 2009. DOI = http://www.whitehouse.gov/assets/documents/Cyberspace_Policy_Review_final.pdf.

[8] United States Naval Academy. Class of 2015 Profile. DOI = http://www.usna.edu/admissions/USNA%202015%20Class%20Portrait.pdf

Fuzzy OOP: Expanded and Reduced Term Interpretations

Ronit Shmallo
Shamoon College of Engineering,
and Science Education Department
Tel-Aviv University
ronits1@sce.ac.il

Noa Ragonis
School of Education
Computer Science Department
Beit Berl College, Israel
& Department of Education
in Technology and Science
Technion – IIT, Israel
noarag@beitberl.ac.il

David Ginat
CS Group
Science Education Department
Tel-Aviv University
ginat@post.tau.ac.il

ABSTRACT

We display a novel perspective of novice OOP difficulties. In a thorough study of 120 undergraduates, in their first OOP course, we noticed a variety of misconceptions and difficulties with a wide range of basic terms and notions. Careful analysis revealed a recurring phenomenon, of fuzzy OOP conceptions, which derive from expansion and reduction of basic term features. Novices tended to expand and/or reduce properties not only of terms such as "class" and "object", but also of terms such as "static", "access", and "instance". Particular misconceptions were of the forms: "One vs. Many". We display a detailed categorization of our findings, in an ordered hierarchical structure, and discuss its cognitive characteristics.

Categories and Subject Descriptors

K.3.2 **[Computers and Education]:** Computer and Information Science Education – Computer science education.

General Terms

Performance, Design, Human Factors.

Keywords

Computer science education, Object-Oriented programming, expansion, reduction.

1. INTRODUCTION

Basic elements in object-oriented programming (OOP) involve terms such as: class, object, constructor, method, variable, attribute, and instance. Previous studies in the last decade revealed novice difficulties and misconceptions with these terms. In this paper, we shed further light on novice conceptions. We illuminate a common phenomenon among novices, which involves their inclination to expand and/or reduce the features characterising a wide variety of basic OOP elements.

In the next section, we describe previous studies of novices' OOP difficulties, and display the rationale for our study. In the two sections that follow, we display the framework and the findings of the study. The presentation of our findings involves hierarchical categorization, which yields two primary categories, four upper subcategories, and 25 detailed subcategories. We then discuss our findings (in the section that follows), with respect to related cognitive studies on problem solving in mathematics and computer science. We conclude with some suggestions for tutors.

ITiCSE'12, July 3-5, 2012, Haifa, Israel.

2. NOVICE OOP DIFFICULTIES

Various studies examined students' comprehension of basic OOP concepts, from different angles. Boustedt [2] examined senior students' understanding of particular, advanced object-oriented concepts, using a phenomegraphic approach. Sorva [15] studied novices' understanding of variables, and unfolded difficulties in discerning the differences and similarities between basic concepts (e.g., programming variables vs. math variables, objects vs. object-valued variables; primitives vs. object-valued variables).

Sanders et al. [14] used concept maps for examining novice beliefs of: which are the most important OOP concepts, and what are their inter-relationships. One primary finding in their study was the small amount of students who conceived modeling as one of the most important OOP concepts.

Eckerdal and Thuné [5] conjectured that the absence of students' beliefs of the essential role of modeling may be directly tied to their difficulties. A different study, by Eckerdal et al. [6] showed that teaching guided by conceptual hierarchy, may not be essential for teaching OOP concepts, and the order of teaching the concepts may vary.

Several studies particularly focused on novice conceptions of the fundamental notions of: Class, Object, and Constructor. We briefly describe them, and then offer the rationale to our study.

Difficulties in comprehending the term "Class"

Some studies indicate that students display difficulties in addressing a class as a pattern for object creation. Students find it difficult to understand how an abstract declarative description of a general entity can perform operations, and further, how is it possible to invoke an operation defined in the class on any of the class objects. Some students view the terms "class" and "object" as equivalent, perhaps due to the common theme of introductory examples, in which only one object of a class is used [5,7,8,9,14].

Ragonis and Ben-Ari [11] conducted a long-term study with high-school students, who learnt object-oriented concepts. They identified a total of 58 different difficulties and misconceptions, and categorized them into four primary categories. One of these categories focused on the *object vs. class* confusion, and the difficulties in comprehending the notions of *object creation* and the *link between objects and classes*. Subcategories in this category involved particular characteristics such as *difficulties in understanding the static aspect of a class definition.*

Difficulties in comprehending the term "Object"

Students find it difficult to understand that an object is an entity that consists of several characteristics, but is referred-to by only a single identifier. This misconception yields student selection of a simple feature instead, such as an object attribute called "name", which they believe is representative of the object. Students also tend to not distinguish between objects and the variables referring to them [7,8,9,11,13,16].

Difficulties in understanding constructors

The role of the constructor method is to create an object, that is, allocate an object in the memory, and set initial values to its attributes. Object creation is one of the fundamental operations in OOP. This concept is particularly difficult for novices, as it involves abstraction, and is related to memory allocation and pointer management [3]. Particular confusion arises from the characteristic that the constructor method may be defined explicitly in different forms, or not explicitly defined at all [1,7,8,10,11]. The advanced notion, of creating composite objects, where some of the attributes may be of an object type, poses additional difficulties [11].

3. RATIONALE FOR OUR STUDY

The above findings display various aspects of student difficulties with basic OOP concepts. They suggest different kinds of limited perceptions of terms, and confusion between terms. One characteristic that arises from many of these studies is the fuzzy perceptions that student demonstrate with respect to many basic terms and notions.

We noticed this phenomenon not only in previous studies, but also in our experience in class. As a result, we decided to conduct a study of student conceptions of basic OOP terms, and seek some unified characteristic of this "fuzziness". In what follows, we display our findings in this respect. The most dominant characteristic that we noticed was that of students' tendencies to expand or reduce term definitions; that is, students' inclination to associate, with many terms, features beyond their actual definition or feature that reduce their actual definition.

4. THE STUDY

The study involved 120 participants, in the latter part of their OOP course, with the Java language. The participants were second year undergraduates in a college department of Industrial Engineering and Management. Towards the end of the course, we posed three similar questionnaires to the students, focusing primarily on: class attributes and methods, the notions of static class variables and methods, instance class variables and methods, constructors, and composite objects. Each questionnaire consisted of three questions, to be answered in 90 minutes. Students were divided into three groups of 40 students. Each group answered one questionnaire of 3 questions. The division into 3 groups allowed 9 questions, about various aspects of the fundamental OOP notions indicated earlier. The questions required code design, code comprehension, and code completion. Some of the questions are exemplified in the findings below.

5. FINDINGS

A primary theme that evolved from our findings was students' tendencies to misinterpret and misuse basic OOP terms. The most common misinterpretations were characterized by expanding, or reducing the definitions of fundamental terms. We first present in section 5.1 a general characterization of the expansion/reduction phenomenon. Then, we exemplify this phenomenon in section 5.2 with particular examples. Finally, we display in section 5.3, a hierarchical structure of the accumulated expansions/reductions that we have observed. We discuss these findings in section 6.

5.1 Term Expansion and Term Reduction

We display the phenomenon of term expansion/reduction in a structure of categories and subcategories. The subcategories distinguish between different kinds of novice confusions.

1. **Expansion**
   - **1.1.** Many rather than one – the occurrence of multiple entities rather than one; for instance, a static variable may have many occurrences.
   - **1.2.** Expansion of properties – augmenting the properties associated with a specific term; for instance, object variables are reachable from other class methods.
2. **Reduction**
   - **2.1.** One rather than many – the occurrence of one entity, or event, rather than many; for instance, a constructor may only be invoked once, and create one object.
   - **2.2.** Reduction of properties – narrowing the properties associated with a specific term; for instance, there cannot be two objects of the same type that contain the same property values.

5.2 Examples of Expansion and Reduction

We exemplify below the phenomenon of term expansion and reduction with two questions that were posed to the students.

5.2.1 Example 1: Class Static Variables

The question presented in Figure 1 below examines student understanding of class variables. The class variable *x* is defined with public access, meaning that objects defined in the main method can access it directly.

- *The "Many rather than one" subcategory*

Static variables have one common occurrence for all the class objects. Nevertheless, students mistakenly thought that a static variable has many occurrences, since it can be accessed by either the class name or the class objects. They believed that there are "many" class variables, rather than only one. 17 out of 40 students (42%) demonstrated such misunderstanding.

In a post-questionnaire interview, the student T. said:

> *I don't understand how it is possible that we accessed a variable first through the class name and then later through the object name, and the same variable is updated in each case ... I understand that this variable is sort of a general variable... oh! It's actually global, but the output I got was 7,9,10 because each time we accessed variable x, a different variable was updated.*

Students demonstrated a difficulty understanding that it is possible to access a static class variables through either the class name or through objects of that class. They failed to understand that each time the variable is accessed, the access operation refers to the same memory cell. Similarly, the students "conceptually expanded" the creation of a single static variable in the memory into the creation of many variables in the memory. They did not realize that in fact, only one memory cell per static variable is created during program execution.

- *The "Reduction of properties" subcategory*

Some students demonstrated difficulties in understanding that a class variable can be accessed by the class name or by each of the class objects. Some students thought that the access is only through the class objects. This was evident in some students' claim that the line: "MyClass.x = 7;" is a mistake. 5 out of 40 students (12%) demonstrated this conceptual misunderstanding. Other students conjectured that the access is only by the class name. This was evident by their claim that the lines: "m1.x = 9; m2.x = 10;" are incorrect. 15 out of 40 students (37%) demonstrated this conceptual misunderstanding.

The following is quoted from an interview with one of the students:

> D.: *It is possible to access a class variable only by using the class name and not the object name.*
>
> Interviewer: *Why is that?*
>
> D.: *Because class variables do not refer to an object but to the class itself.*

Based on the term "class variable", the student interviewed above believed that the property referred only to a class, and therefore cannot be accessed through the class's objects. This misunderstanding narrows the properties of the term.

Figure 1. A question that focuses on static variables

Two classes are given: MyClass and Program. Please answer the questions displayed after the classes definitions.

```
public class MyClass {
    public static int x;
}

public class Program {
    public static void main(String[] args) {
        MyClass.x = 7;
        MyClass m1 = new MyClass();
        MyClass m2 = new MyClass();
        m1.x = 9;
        m2.x = 10;
        System.out.println(MyClass.x);
        System.out.println(m1.x);
        System.out.println(m2.x);
    }
}
```

A. Are there errors in the program? Explain

B. What will the output be? Explain.

Answer: Each of the 3 output sentences will yield the value 10.

5.2.2 *Example 2: Different Constructor Definitions*

The question presented in Figure 2 below examines the understanding of object creation by accessing different constructors.

- *The "Expansion of properties" subcategory*

Students believed that accessing the default constructor is done automatically. 5 out of 40 students (12%) created objects only while accessing constructors that have parameters, and did not use the default constructor, even though they were asked to use all the constructor versions defined in the class.

The following is a quote from an interview with J.:

> *There is no need to access the default constructor. It is invoked automatically.*

Students demonstrated difficulties in realizing the "language mechanism", which adds the definition of the default constructor, in cases in which the programmer does not define any constructor. The above student "conceptually expanded" the default constructor properties, and believed that it is invoked automatically. The student related to the compiler the capability of "calling this constructor automatically", even without explicitly "telling it" to do so.

- *The "Reduction of properties" subcategory*

Students demonstrated conceptual misunderstanding regarding the meaning of object creation, and thought that object creation is equivalent to variable definition. 16 out of 40 students (40%) demonstrated this misunderstanding.

The following quote is student B.'s response in an interview:

> *Object creation? I don't understand how this object is different from a regular variable, because a regular variable also gets memory allocated to it when it is defined.*

The student "conceptually narrowed" the constructor properties, and perceived the process of object creation as the process of simple variable allocation during program execution. (Language definitions emphasize the mechanism of object creation, using the saved word "new". Yet, some students regard it as an allocation of a single variable cell.)

Figure 2. A Question that focuses on different constructor definitions

The following is an Employee class code. Three constructors are defined for the class:

```
public class Employee
{
    private String  firstName;
    private String  lastName;
    private float   salary;


    public Employee() {
    }

    public Employee(String firstName, String lastName,
    float salary) {
        firstName = this.firstName;
        lastName = this.lastName;
        salary = this.salary;
```

```
    }

    public Employee(Employee e)
    {
        firstName = e.firstName;
        lastName = e.lastName;
        salary = e.salary;
    }
}
```

Create three objects in the next main method, each by a different constructor defined for the class:

```
public class Tester {
    public static void main() {
        ...
    }
}
```

<u>*An example of a correct solution*</u>:

```
public class Tester {
    public static void main() {
        Employee e1=new Employee();
        Employee e2=new Employee("John","More",2500);
        Employee e3=new Employee(e2);
    }
}
```

5.3 Categories of Fuzzy Perceptions

We analyzed the answers of all students through the lenses of term expansion and reduction. Our accumulated analysis yielded the following structure, which enclose subcategory indications of a variety of misconceptions. In each subcategory we display the percentage of those that held the erroneous conception. (As previously noted, the 120 participants were divided into three groups of 40 students, and each group answered a slightly different questionnaire. The percentages below refer to the number of wrong answers relative to each group's questionnaire.)

1. Expansion

1.1. Many rather than one

1.1.1. One identifier may refer to two objects or more (17%).

1.1.2. Any access to class properties, whether through an object name or a class name, is operated through different variables (42%).

1.2. Expansion of properties

1.2.1. The invocation of the default constructor is always possible (12%).

1.2.2. It is possible to access, from an outer class, a property that is defined with private access (12%).

1.2.3. It is possible to set an attribute value by assignment, instead of invoking an appropriate method (22%).

1.2.4. It is possible to access an instance method without invoking an object (15%).

1.2.5. There is no need to mention a class name or an object identifier upon accessing a method (25%).

1.2.6. It is possible to access instance properties via class methods (52%).

1.2.7. Operations of default constructors are conducted automatically (12%).

1.2.8. Objects may always be created using default constructors (17%).

1.2.9. If object properties' values are explicitly defined in the constructor, then the object exists (12%).

1.2.10. Upon accessing a method, the parameters may appear in any order (12%).

1.2.11. There is no need to create objects before using them (22%). (They are "just there".)

1.2.12. Assigning an object to another object creates a new object (22%).

1.2.13. Creating an object from a composite class automatically creates the simpler objects that are the values of its attributes (22%).

2. Reduction

2.1. One rather than many

2.1.1. It is allowed to define only one constructor in a class (5%).

2.1.2. A constructor may be used to create only one object (17%).

2.2. Reduction of properties

2.2.1. In order to invoke a class method that refers to a class property, it must be transferred as a parameter (30%).

2.2.2. It is possible to access an object that is a value of a composite object's attribute, as a primitive type (47%).

2.2.3. It is impossible to define public access for a property (45%).

2.2.4. It is impossible to access a static attribute through the relevant class name (12%).

2.2.5. It is impossible to access a static attribute through an object name (37%).

2.2.6. Assigning an object *obj2* to another object *obj1* updates the object *obj1*'s attribute values and does not override the object *obj1* itself (25%).

2.2.7. The creation of an object is equivalent to the allocation of a simple variable cell (40%).

2.2.8. The process of object creation does not yield memory allocation of the created object. It "only involves constructor execution" (15%).

6. DISCUSSION

Previous studies in computer science and mathematics education revealed various facets of misinterpretations and erroneous utilization of terms. Du Boulay [4] revealed novice's *improper use of analogies, metaphors, and projection* (from one entity to another), as well as *overgeneralization*. For example, he noticed that some novices perceive a variable as a box, which may keep several values at the same time. In addition, some students projected syntax and semantic properties from one entity to another. Rath and Brown [12] illuminated novice tendencies to relate capacities of "*independent thinking*" to the computer.

Vinner [17] observed student tendencies to turn to "concept images" rather than concept definitions, in mathematical problem solving. He noticed that some students "adopt" various associations from an example (possibly shown in class), of which some involve suitable features of an entity (such as a mathematical function) but others involve unsuitable features. Vinner conjectured that one's cognitive structure involves two different "cells": one of the entity's definition and one of the entity's association. In time, the "definition cell" may become inactive, and one repeatedly turns to her "association cell". Therefore, suitable "absorption" of a term should yield appropriate correlation between one's "association cell" and "definition cell".

The expansion and reduction tendencies illuminated in the previous section enhance and expand the above studies. The expansion component in our categorization involves overgeneralization and "independent thinking" aspects. Both of the expansion and reduction components involve improper analogies and projection, and inappropriate concept images.

More specifically, *overgeneralization* can be seen for example in the subcategories 1.2.6 and 1.2.8. In the case of 1.2.8: Since the default constructor may be invoked without explicitly specifying it for the class, students over-generalized this property and believed that objects may always be created with default constructors. This is wrong if another constructor is defined for the class.

"*Independent thinking*" is apparent in subcategories such as 1.2.7, 1.2.11, and 1.2.13. In the case of 1.2.13: An object of a composite class has attribute values that are objects. Students related independent thinking to the computer, and believed that it is sufficient to invoke the constructor of the composite object, and the "inner" object will be created automatically.

Improper analogies and projection are evident for example in subcategories 1.1.2, 1.2.3, 2.1.2, 2.2.4, and 2.2.5. In the case of 2.2.5: Since an object property may not be accessed directly from the class code, students projected the same limitation on the object, and did not realize that a class property may not be accessed using the class objects.

Many of the expansion and reduction elements are related to improper *concept images*. This may be particularly seen in subcategories 1.2.4, 1.2.9, 1.2.12, 2.1.1, 2.2.6, and 2.2.8. In the case of 2.2.6: Students misunderstood that the variable that identifies an object keeps a reference. They believed that an assignment of one object to another copies the object attributes.

The main contribution of this study is that it displays a framework, which combines the above, various facets in an ordered and detailed structure; and the structure construction is led by the observation that student tendencies to expand and reduce term interpretations is characteristic of many of the above phenomena. One may view the detailed statistics in section 5.3 and notice the variety of cases, all with non-negligible percentages of misconceptions (and some that are even close to 50%).

7. CONCLUSION

This study presents findings of undergraduate difficulties and misconceptions of fundamental OOP terms and notions. The novelty of the study is in the new perspective that it offers for characterizing and categorizing a wide and thorough collection of difficulties and misconceptions, with very basic terms and notions. The new perspective illuminates novice tendencies to expand and/or reduce the features of basic terms and notions, including those of "class", "object", "attributes", "access", "type", "static", "constructor", "default", "object creation", "composite objects", "instance", and more.

We offered an ordered categorization and sub-categorization, of the various misconceptions, which involved two primary categories, two upper subcategories, and 25 detailed subcategories – 15 in the primary category of *expansion*, and 10 in the primary category of *reduction*.

Two upper subcategories – *many rather than one* and *one rather than many* – are of particular interest, and nicely exemplify the contribution of this study. One of the key notions in OOP is that of many instances of an entity, particularly with respect to many objects in a class and several constructors of an object. As our findings show – this key notion is not easily conceived.

Novices demonstrate conceptual expansions and conceptual reductions of term features, with diverse characteristics, which relate to previous studies in mathematics and computer science education, among them: improper analogies, improper projection, overgeneralization, "independent thinking" of the computer, and erroneous concept images.

The latter aspect, of erroneous concept images, is of particular importance, as it pin-points a common process during learning, which involves the development of inaccurate associations of a term. Tutors should be aware of this phenomenon, which evolves primarily from the different examples that they pose to students.

Following the above observations, we offer several suggestions, for tutors and students:

- Be aware of inappropriate tendencies to expand and reduce term features.
- Some erroneous expansions and reductions should be particularly noticed, including: "Many rather than one", "One rather than many", as well as expansions and reductions related to object creation, composite objects, and the notion of "static".
- Novices tend to develop concept images according to the examples that they see and practice. Being aware of this tendency, embed diverse facets in your class and homework examples, with accordance to the subcategories of misconceptions displayed in this study.
- In addressing misconceptions pin-pointed in this study, pose and examine questions with erroneous answers, and elaborate, in a class discussion, on the delicate pitfalls of which one should be aware.

It is our hope that the findings displayed in this paper will help tutors and students to better recognize and address conceptual difficulties with basic OOP terms and notions. Future research may expand our findings further, in the domain of OOP, and in additional CS domains. In particular, it may be beneficial to examine tendencies to create and develop concept images, which expand and reduce definitions and roles of terms and entities in fundamental courses other than Object Oriented programming.

8. ACKNOWLEDGMENTS

We thank all the students who participated in the study.

REFERENCES

[1] Bishop, J. M. (1998). *Java Gently*. Harlow, Addison-Wesley.

[2] Boustedt, J. (2010). *On the Road to a Software Profession: Students' Experiences of Concepts and Thresholds*, Digital Comprehensive Summaries of Uppsala Dissertations from the Faculty of Science and Technology, ISSN 1651-6214; 734.

[3] Corradi, A. and Leonardi, L. (2000). Static vs. dynamic issues in Object-Oriented programming languages, *Journal of Object-Oriented Programming* [online], October, 2000.

[4] Du Boulay, B. (1986). Some difficulties of learning to program, *Journal of Educational Computing Research*, *2*(1), 57-73.

[5] Eckerdal, A. and Thuné, M. (2005). Novice Java programmers' conceptions of "object" and "class", and variation theory, *SIGCSE Bulletin*, 37(3), 89-93.

[6] Eckerdal, A. , Laakso, J. M., Lopez, M. and Sakar, A. (2011). Relationships between text and action conceptions of programming: A phenomenographic and quantitative perspective, *Proceedings of ITiCSE 2011*, 33-37.

[7] Fleury, A. E. (2000). Programming in Java: student-constructed rules, *SIGCSE Bulletin*, 32(1), 197-201.

[8] Garner, S., Haden, P. and Robins, A. (2005). My program is correct but it doesn't run: a preliminary investigation of novice programmers' problems, *Proceeding of ACE 2005 (Australasian Computing Education Conference)*, 173-180.

[9] Holland, S., Griffiths, R. and Woodman, M. (1997). Avoiding object misconceptions, *SIGCSE Bulletin*, 29(1), 131-134.

[10] Koffman, E. and Wolz, U. (1999). *Problem Solving with Java*, Addison-Wesley.

[11] Ragonis, N. and Ben-Ari, M. (2005). A long-term investigation of the comprehension of OOP concepts by novices. *Computer Science Education*, 15(3), 203-221.

[12] Rath, A. and Brown, D. E. (1995). Conceptions of human-computer interaction: A model for understanding student errors, *Journal of. Educational Computing Research*, 12(4), 395-409.

[13] Sanders, K., Thomas, L. (2007). Checklists for grading object-oriented CS1 programs: concepts and misconceptions, *SIGCSE Bulletin.*, 39(3), 166–170.

[14] Sanders, K., Boustendt, J., Eckerdal, A., McCartney, R., Moström, J. E., Thomas, L., and Zander, C. (2008). Student understanding of Object-Oriented programming as expressed in concept maps. *Proceeding of SIGCSE 2008*, 332-336.

[15] Sorva, J. (2008). The same but different – students' understandings of primitive and object variables, *Proceedings of the 8th International Conference on Computing Education Research (Koli Calling '08)*, New York, 5-15.

[16] Thomasson, B., Ratcliffe, M., and Thomas, L. (2006). Identifying novice difficulties in object oriented design, *SIGCSE Bullet*in., 38(3), 28–32.

[17] Vinner, S. (1983). Concept definition, concept image and the notion of function, *International Journal of Mathematics Education in Science and Technology*, 14(3), 293-305.

Formal Learning Groups in an Introductory CS Course: A Qualitative Exploration

Julie Krause
Colorado School of Mines
Golden, CO
+1 303-384-2465
jkrause@gmail.com

Irene Polycarpou
Colorado School of Mines
Golden, CO
+1 303-273-3462
ipolycar@mines.edu

Cyndi Rader
Colorado School of Mines
Golden, CO
+1 303-273-3195
crader@mines.edu

ABSTRACT
In this paper we present an exploratory study on students' learning experiences with formal learning groups in an introductory Computer Science course. To provide insights into ways to make learning groups productive in this setting, we report on the properties of learning groups that students indicated as more or less effective for various reasons. Additionally, we explore the impact of specific learning group characteristics such as the ratio of male to female students, length of time in the group, and inclusion of students with varying levels of knowledge and experience.

Categories and Subject Descriptors
K.3.2 [**Computers and Education**]: Computer and Information Science Education– *Computer science education.*

Keywords
Computer science education, introduction to computer science, collaborative learning, formal learning groups, gender

1. INTRODUCTION
Various active and collaborative learning constructs have been used in Computer Science (CS) education to improve learning, engage students, broaden participation, and promote retention in CS studies. For example, instructional techniques such as peer-led team learning [3], team-based learning [7], and active learning combined with peer instruction [2] have been shown to improve retention of students in CS courses or programs. Specific benefits with active learning include improved motivation, engagement in the learning process, and higher order thinking [1]. Collaborative learning offers several advantages over other types of learning such as individualistic and competitive learning [5]. With collaborative learning, students share learning goals, whereas with individualistic learning students have their own goals and do not share goals with others, and with competitive learning students work against one another to accomplish a goal that can only be reached by one (or only a few) student(s) [4, 5]. In collaborative learning, benefiting the self benefits others, whereas benefiting the self has no effect on others in individualistic learning and deprives others in competitive learning [5].

At Colorado School of Mines (CSM) we incorporate active and collaborative learning into our introductory CS course (CSCI 101) via formal learning groups [5]. In this paper we present a primarily-qualitative exploratory study that investigates the impact of specific learning group formations (e.g., different ratios of females/males, combinations of students with more/less experience with CS, etc.) on students' learning and enjoyment, as well as aspects of the formal learning groups that students perceived as either beneficial or unfavorable.

2. BACKGROUND

2.1 Formal Learning Groups
Formal learning groups are a specific type of collaborative learning that has been used in college courses since before the 1990s. While collaborative learning in various forms is used in CS education, the prevalence of the use of formal learning groups specifically is not currently known to be high in CS courses.

Formal learning groups, as defined and outlined by Johnson, Johnson & Smith [5] offer the opportunity for students to work collaboratively with other students, under the guidance of an instructor, in the following manner:

- Group work may be problem-solving oriented or may involve investigative sessions in which students break up tasks to learn content or solve problems on their own and later teach one another what they have learned. The latter type of learning group is typically used to introduce specific content.
- The same groups of students work together over a period of time (e.g., several days to several weeks).
- A key role of the instructor when using formal learning groups is to guide students; the instructor is "uncovering the material with the students" rather than giving material directly to them, as in a traditional lecture format.
- "Positive interdependence," or the notion that students rely on one another's successes in order to succeed themselves, is important in the success of formal learning groups. Positive interdependence can be achieved by giving all students the same reward for the whole group's performance or by giving all students the same goal to achieve.
- "Individual accountability," or a requirement that the performance of each individual in the group be assessed, helps to prevent single students from sitting out while other members of the group do the work, and helps to encourage all students to be engaged. Techniques for supporting individual accountability include calling on one student to respond for the group, and giving individual assessments where grades or other outcomes impact the group.

2.2 Group Learning in CSCI 101

Our study explored formal learning groups in the Introduction to Computer Science (CSCI 101) course at our university. Students who register for the course include CS majors as well as non-majors and students without a declared major. The course is offered every Fall and Spring semester. An estimated 200 to 400 students enroll in the course each academic year, with class sizes of up to 60 students. During Spring 2011 when our study was conducted, approximately 20% of the students enrolled in the course were female and 80% were male. Approximately 40% of the students enrolled were CS majors entering the course and 60% were either undecided or non-CS majors. Due to a change in the CS program bulletin, a larger than usual number of upperclass CS majors were enrolled in the course that semester (15% of the students were CS majors with Junior or Senior standing).

CSCI 101 is designed to provide an introduction to the field of Computer Science, especially for students who are new to the discipline. The course incorporates instruction on a broad variety of CS concepts, as well as computer programming in Python. Enrollment in the course does not require any prior experience in computer programming. CSCI 101 incorporates formal learning groups as a primary instructional approach.

Formal learning group work in the course involves both problem-solving activities and sessions in which students teach one another concepts they have learned through individual out-of-class work (learning group assignments, or "LGA's"). Groups are comprised of roughly five students each. During each class period, students are presented with a learning group assignment and are given time to decide which students will be responsible for each question assigned. Each student is then responsible for investigating specific topics and completing related problems on his or her own time. Groups are encouraged to duplicate coverage on topics between two or more students. At the beginning of the following class period group members teach one another and discuss their respective findings. As a motivation for students to be invested in teaching their peers, a portion of each student's course grade is dependent on their group members' performance on individually completed quizzes.

Groups change approximately three to four times during the course and all groups are assigned by the instructor. With the exception of the first group assignment which is completely random, groups are assigned using a randomized algorithm that minimizes the chance that pairings from previous rounds are repeated. The assignment process also utilizes students' scores from programming assignments and previous learning group quizzes to create teams with similar average performance. Gender composition in the groups is completely random.

As a result of the randomization, group formations typically include differing combinations of females and males, CS majors and non-majors, and class levels. Note that the presence of upperclass CS majors in the groups creates a different dynamic within the learning groups than might be expected in an introductory CS course.

3. METHODS

Our investigation included the collection of self-reported data related to students' perceptions of formal learning groups, including learning group formation and which aspects of learning groups students perceived as positive or negative. Data reported in this paper were collected via open-ended survey questions, interviews, and focus groups conducted at the end of the semester. Students' responses were categorized and common themes in their responses were identified.

3.1 Participants

Via announcements during class, all students registered in CSCI 101 during the semester of the study were given the opportunity to participate in the study. About 60 male students and 15 female students responded to each of the survey questions. A smaller number of students were selected at random to participate in an interview or focus group.

3.2 Surveys

Through open-ended survey questions at the end of the semester, students were asked to describe properties of the groups that worked well or did not work well based on different criteria. Specifically, they were asked what it was about their most and least effective groups that made them more or less effective. Similar questions were also asked regarding the groups that students considered to be most and least inclusive, where inclusive meant they "felt included in the group and felt comfortable teaching and asking questions of [their] group members." In order to explore specific group formation patterns, students were also asked to rank the different groups in which they participated based on the groups' effectiveness and inclusiveness.

3.3 Interviews and Focus Groups

In individual interviews and focus groups, students were asked to discuss their perceptions of learning groups in CSCI 101, including which aspects of learning groups they liked and disliked. Additionally, female students who were interviewed were asked whether they felt more comfortable in learning groups with no other females or groups with other females, or whether it made no difference. Finally, focus groups included discussions regarding which group formations (combinations of experience levels, gender, etc.) students felt were most and least effective and why.

The interviews and focus groups were approximately 20 to 30 minutes long and were semi-structured; a set of questions were asked to guide the discussion, but participants were given the opportunity to speak openly and provide additional details.

The interview and focus group participants were selected at random. All female students were invited to participate in an interview or a focus group, and whether they were selected for an interview or focus group was random; a total of 12 female students participated in one or the other. The number of male students selected was chosen to match the number of female participants. For each gender, four interviews and two focus groups were conducted. The focus groups were intended to have four students each. Due to the absence of two male students, however, both male focus groups had only three students each.

3.4 Categorizing Survey Responses

Open-ended survey responses were categorized for the purpose of identifying themes in students' responses to each question. Through an iterative process, categories, and typically subcategories, were created and then documented with specific codes. Similar responses were identified and categories were created for those types of responses. When appropriate, those categories were broken down further into subcategories based on dissimilarities. Once the specific categories were determined, each student's response was assigned one or more codes accordingly. To improve the trustworthiness of the coding a second person independently assigned codes to each student's response. Discrepancies were discussed and reconciled between the coders.

4. FINDINGS

4.1 Students' General Perceptions of Formal Learning Groups

As reported in [6], students generally enjoyed and learned from learning groups in CSCI 101. For example, when students were asked to rank five instructional methods used in the course (learning groups, lecture, textbook, programming in Python, and electronic educational games), 30% of students (40% of female students) ranked learning groups as the method they enjoyed the most and 20% (40% of female students) ranked learning groups as the method from which they learned the most. Moreover, more than 60% of students indicated at the end of the semester that they had fun working in formal learning groups.

In this paper, we explore the students' reactions to learning groups in more detail. Students' perceptions of working in groups were assessed through responses to the following questions:

- "Please provide any additional comments you have regarding your experience with learning groups in this course." *(Survey, Interview, and Focus Group question)*
- "What aspects of learning groups did you like/dislike most?" *(Interview question)*
- "How do you think learning groups compare to traditional learning methods (e.g. lecture and textbook)?" *(Survey question)*

In reviewing students' responses, details regarding perceived benefits of, problems associated with, and conditions for learning via learning groups became evident. Table 1 presents the emerging themes within each of these categories; the themes listed were cited by three or more students. Note that benefits include both educational aspects (e.g., ability to address misconceptions or ask questions) and social aspects (e.g., chance to meet others) and problems are primarily related to learning goals.

Table 1. Benefits and problems with learning groups that students identified.

Specific **Benefits** of Learning Groups	o Misconceptions (regarding content) can be avoided through discussions and explanations o They promote interactivity / active learning o The requirement of being responsible to the group promotes motivation to work harder o It is more comfortable asking questions in a small group setting (compared to asking in front of the whole class) o They present opportunities to meet people
Specific **Problems** with Learning Groups	o Wasted time can be problematic (e.g., a group may not utilize time to do work) o Working with groups can cause misconceptions or poor understanding of content o The fact that one's grade depends on others is problematic o Less material can be covered (learning groups are less productive than other methods) o There is often a need to teach oneself all the material anyway since the group's contributions are not always sufficient
Conditions for Learning from Formal Learning Groups	o Learning groups only work if sufficient lecture is incorporated as well o The success of a learning group depends on its members

4.2 What Makes Certain Groups Effective or Inclusive?

To obtain additional insights into properties of groups that were beneficial to students, they were asked *why* their most effective group was most effective and why their most inclusive group was most inclusive. Similarly, they were asked about their least effective and inclusive groups in order to identify properties of groups that may present less positive experiences for students.

The most frequent student response types are shown in Tables 2 and 3. Since similar categories emerged from responses to the questions regarding their most *effective* groups and *inclusive* groups, the categories for both questions are listed collectively.

Table 2. Top eight responses for specific groups being *most* effective or inclusive.

Response Types	Number of Students	Sample Responses
Group discussed LGA's/problems thoroughly	12	"Discussion was started promptly and all questions were discussed thoroughly."
Member(s) came prepared and did LGA	12	"Everyone came to class prepared to discuss the LGA."
Group *worked* well together	11	"[We] worked very well together."
Timing: Group took place in beginning of semester	9	"It was the beginning of semester and everyone was doing their work and contributing."
Member(s) were friendly/approachable	9	"All the members of the group were easygoing and approachable."
Group got along, meshed well, was conflict-free	9	"No conflicts, personalities meshed well."
Member(s) taught correctly/clearly	8	"Explained everything really well."
Group joked around, had sense of humor, was fun	8	"We joked around a lot after we got our work done."

Table 3. Top eight responses for specific groups being *least* effective or inclusive.

Response Types	Number of Students	Sample Responses
Member(s) were unmotivated/un-invested or did	13	"Negative view towards class, lower work ethic."
Group did not discuss LGA's/problems	12	"No one talked about the LGA."
Group did not talk/socialize much	12	"No one really socialized or got to know each other."
Timing: Group took place in end of semester	11	"At the end of the semester, focus dropped and the group didn't teach me as much as before."
Length of time in the group was insufficient	9	"We didn't spend much time together so it was harder to create the proper connections with each other."
Group did not get to know each other	9	"This one fell short because of the lack of group bonding."
Group did not discuss LGA's/problems *thoroughly enough*	9	"The group didn't focus too much on the small details of the problems."
Student felt his/her contributions were not needed or heard	6	"Group was more advanced in comp sci and so I felt like my contributions were not as worth while."

Regarding the groups that students considered least effective or inclusive, some students explicitly indicated that their least effective and least inclusive groups were not necessarily ineffective or non-inclusive, respectively, but rather those groups were simply less effective or less inclusive.

4.3 Issues to Consider in Promoting Learning

As reflected in Tables 2 and 3, students indicated a variety of explanations regarding their perceptions of learning groups and properties of specific groups that were more or less effective. Some of the specific issues are discussed in what follows.

4.3.1 Timing of Groups

Many students reported that their top ranked groups were most effective or inclusive because they took place in the beginning of the semester. Explanations included statements such as "Group members actually cared about the LGA's," "We were all more motivated to get the work done," and "The idea of LG's was fresh." Similarly, many students reported that their least effective or inclusive groups were the ones that took place toward the end of the semester; explanations included statements such as "[We were] all familiar with the subject so we were less motivated," "The team was burnt out," and "Focus dropped and the group didn't teach me as much as before."

Table 4 illustrates the effect of timing on students' perceptions of effective and inclusive groups.

Table 4. Percentage of students who considered a given group to be their most or least effective or inclusive group.

Group	% Who Ranked as Most Effective	% Who Ranked as Least Effective	% Who Ranked as Most Inclusive	% Who Ranked as Least Inclusive
1st	51%	6%	53%	10%
2nd	27%	24%	21%	22%
3rd	18%	19%	17%	19%
4th	4%	50%	10%	49%

In summary, approximately half of the students reported that their most effective (or most inclusive) group was the first group of the semester; similarly, about half of the students reported that their least effective (or least inclusive) group was the last group of the semester. The primary explanation that students gave was the presence or lack of motivation in the beginning or end of the semester, respectively.

4.3.2 Duration of Groups

As shown in Table 3, students indicated that insufficient time with a group was a negative factor. Several students also indicated that a group being together for a long time was a reason for the group being more effective or inclusive. During the semester in which data were collected for this study, there were four rounds of learning groups; the groups were together for approximately four weeks, six weeks, three weeks, and two weeks, respectively. The discrepancy in group lengths was not intentional; rather, transitions between groups occurred at section breaks in instruction and the group lengths depended on the timing of those transitions. As a result of the discrepancy, however, it became evident that some students perceived groups that were together longer as more effective and/or inclusive.

4.3.3 Student Preparedness and Participation

The characteristics of effective groups that appeared to be most important to students were preparedness and motivation along with willingness to contribute to the learning group discussions (especially providing thorough and clear explanations).

Concerns that students expressed regarding preparedness included group members sometimes coming into group discussions unprepared to teach their assigned content. In those cases, group members either did not do their assigned questions altogether or did not prepare sufficiently. For example, group members "didn't double-check the text for explanations."

Some students indicated that some of their group members did not participate fully in group work. For example, group members "kind of 'zoomed' over questions," presented content that "was wrong and mislead" the other students in the group, or did not engage in the group discussions (e.g., "there was a computer screen between me and some of the other group members").

Although learning group discussions in CSCI 101 were monitored and instructors provided clarifications regarding content misconceptions as needed, these findings indicate that a rigorous approach to observing and influencing learning group interactions is needed for learning groups to be most successful. For example, instructors could observe groups and assign grades for students' participation during the observation.

4.3.4 *Group Dynamics*

Certain group dynamics were reported by students as being integral to the effectiveness of a group. For example, groups must have good working relationships as well as have good social interactions.

To promote socialization and fun, instructors could include a small amount of time for socialization and/or encourage students to get to know one another, especially when each group is initially formed.

Students also indicated that a given group's success is dependent on its group members. Additionally, as shown in Tables 2 and 3, it is important to students that group members be friendly and approachable. It is also important for students, particularly female students, to feel that their group members listen to and value their input. For example, some comments from students regarding why their most inclusive groups made them feel included, were "everyone actually listened to what I had to say" and "I felt like I could make a difference by contributing within this group." To promote inclusive behaviors in group members and help students to feel that their input is valued, it may be beneficial for instructors to collect and act upon feedback regarding other group members' performance to encourage positive behaviors and discourage negative ones.

4.3.5 *Combinations of Students: Experience Levels*

In the focus group discussions surrounding the topic of specific group formations, students commented on the level of academic progress and CS experience of group members. Moreover, students provided explanations as to why certain combinations of students in learning groups were preferred or not.

Regarding the level of academic progress and experience with and knowledge of CS, the perceptions presented were varied, but many students preferred heterogeneity. In one of the female focus groups, three of the four female students commented that they preferred a mixture of CS knowledge or experience levels. Those students did not cite specific reasons as to why. The student who preferred more homogeneity stated:

> "My first group, ... we all had very like, similar knowledge level, and I liked that one, 'cause those were the ones where we were actually willing to teach each other and we were wanting to learn, 'cause we all knew about the same amount of stuff to start with."
> (Focus Group: Female, Sophomore, Non-Major)

In the other female focus group, the idea of the specific benefits of freshmen and upperclassmen arose. The "older" female students mentioned benefits of having freshmen in a learning group such as added motivation (e.g., enthusiasm from younger group members), as well as additional learning that came from teaching the material more. The student's explanation regarding enhanced learning was as follows:

> "Well, freshmen being in my group also helped me because when they were struggling with something, I could explain it to them, and then it made me learn that material better, more. So having freshmen in my group definitely helped."
> (Focus Group: Female, Junior, Non-Major)

The freshman student in that same focus group mentioned that as a freshman, having upperclassmen or students with more CS experience in a learning group was beneficial in receiving explanations of concepts.

> "As a freshman it was nice to have people who understood it 'cause when I was just completely lost they could explain it, and I didn't feel like I was going to fail the class."
> (Focus Group: Female, Freshman, Undeclared Major)

Concern was also expressed by some students, however, that having more advanced students in a group was problematic in cases where the students were over-critical or condescending. For example, regarding a group with a senior CS major, a student stated:

> "There were days [*pause*] well, maybe I shouldn't even do my homework because he's gonna tell me I'm wrong, or he's going to critique everything I've said, and it was really intimidating to have to go and [*pause*] it was like the first week of school, and so it was extra intimidating."
> (Focus Group: Female, Junior, Non-Major)

The male focus groups each had one student who mentioned the importance of variance in CS experience (as well as variety in majors and years). Reasons cited included the variety of opinions given, as well as advantages such as combining the in-depth explanations of experienced students with the fresh perspectives of less experienced students.

Students' responses suggest that there may be some benefits to constructing learning groups with students of varying experience levels, and that if students with CS experience are in learning groups with inexperienced students, those groups are only positive if the experienced students are willing to be teachers and not criticize or belittle inexperienced students for their lack of experience.

4.3.6 *Combinations of Students: Gender*

The topic of gender combinations was primarily discussed with female students to explore whether forming groups with multiple females would be beneficial in promoting female students' interest in CS. However, in one of the male focus groups, in the context of a discussion about preference for having variety in group composition, one male student mentioned the issue, indicating a preference for having at least one female in each group (when possible), since it was more fun and improved students' incentive to get along.

When female students were asked in an interview or focus group about their preferences regarding gender composition, varying perspectives were provided. Some of the students did not have a comparison since all of the learning groups in which they participated had similar female/male composition.

Two of the female interviewees, as well as three of the female students who participated in focus groups, reported that they did not have a preference. Examples of such responses included the following:

> "I don't think having another girl in the group really made any difference, it's just the personality type and not the gender."
> (Interview: Female, Junior, Non-Major)

> "I would say there is no difference simply because I go to [CSM] and I'm really used to being in groups of [*pause*] that don't have other females in them."
> (Interview: Female, Senior, Non-Major)

Three female students who reported that having more than one female in the group was preferable referenced feeling more comfortable working with other females and feeling ignored in a group where the rest of the members were male. In reference to one group that a student called "the perfect storm for the right group" in a focus group discussion, a female student stated:

> "It was nice to have another girl 'cause I think sometimes there's this thing where if you're a girl in a group of four guys, you can sometimes get kinda overlooked. They're like, 'oh, she's just doing something over there, let's not worry about her.'"
> (Focus group: Female, Sophomore, Non-Major)

Three female students during focus group discussions reported that they preferred being the only female student in a learning group. For example,

> "I worked better in groups with guys and I'm not quite sure why. ... I find that I function better with a bunch of guys, and I think it's because I have over-blatantly jealous issues, so if other girls are there I'm always comparing myself to them and that's not as good, whereas if it's a group of guys, I'm more relaxed, I guess, so I work better in groups where I am the only girl."
> (Focus Group: Female, Junior, Non-Major)

> *Directly following the above comment in a focus group, another student commented* "I also work better with guys. I don't know, I just get along better with guys. There's so much less drama."
> (Focus Group: Female, Sophomore, Non-Major)

Based on the interviews and focus group discussions, no strong conclusions can be reached regarding combinations of female and male students within learning groups. Findings suggest that having multiple female students in a formal learning group is preferred by some female students, while others prefer to be the single female in the group. Furthermore, the majority of female students in our study indicated that female/male combination is not a concern to them.

5. DISCUSSION

In this paper we presented an exploratory qualitative study on students' perceptions of formal learning groups in an introductory CS course. Based on open-ended survey responses, interviews, and focus groups, we've noted some characteristics of learning groups that students perceive as more or less beneficial, as well as strategies that might be used to optimize the success of implementing learning groups.

Our findings showed that there were no specific group compositions that contributed to students' positive or negative perceptions of learning groups, but that certain characteristics of groups such as motivation, preparedness, and approachability, were needed for fostering positive group environments.

Additional research on forming groups based on gender, personality, and CS experience within learning groups in CS courses may be productive. A study that incorporates controlled comparisons may be especially useful. Furthermore, there may be a need to structure groups differently for freshmen than for upperclassmen, so studying group formations separately for these populations may provide additional insights. Finally, based on results of this study, issues such as timing and duration of groups, maximizing accountability of group members, and instilling inclusive attitudes and behaviors among group members present opportunities for future research.

6. ACKNOWLEDGMENTS

The authors gratefully acknowledge the support of NCWIT in the form of external funding (NCWIT Academic Alliance Seed Fund Award supported by Microsoft Research) and The John U. and Sharon L. Trefny Curriculum and Development Program at CSM in the form of internal funding.

We would also like to thank all of the students who took the time to participate in our study as well as Keith Hellman, the faculty member who developed the curriculum for using formal learning groups in CSCI 101 at CSM.

7. REFERENCES

[1] Bonwell, C. & Eison, J. 1991. *Active learning: Creating excitement in the classroom.* ASHE ERIC Higher Education Report No. 1, Washington, D.C.

[2] Chase, J. D., & Okie, E. G. 2000. Combining cooperative learning and peer instruction in introductory computer science. *SIGCSE'00*. ACM, New York, NY, 372-376.

[3] Horwitz, S., & Rodger, S. H. 2009. Using peer-led team learning to increase participation and success of under-represented groups in introductory computer science. *SIGCSE'09,* ACM, New York, NY, 163-167.

[4] Hymel, S., Zinck, B., & Ditner, E. 1993. Cooperation versus competition in the classroom. In *Exceptionality Education Canada Vol. 3*. 103-128.

[5] Johnson, D., Johnson, R., & Smith, K. 1991. *Active learning: cooperation in the college classroom.* Interaction Book Company, Edina, MN.

[6] Krause, J., Polycarpou, I., & Hellman, K. 2011. Exploring formal learning groups and their impact on recruitment of women in undergraduate CS. *SIGCSE '12,* ACM, New York, NY, 179-184.

[7] Lasserre, P., & Szostak, C. 2011. Effects of team-based learning on a CS1 course. *ITiCSE'11*, ACM, New York, NY, 133-137.

Competitive Evaluation in a Video Game Development Course

Manuel Palomo-Duarte
Computer Languages and Systems Department
University of Cádiz
Cádiz, Spain
manuel.palomo@uca.es

Juan Manuel Dodero
Computer Languages and Systems Department
University of Cádiz
Cádiz, Spain
juanma.dodero@uca.es

José Tomás Tocino
Computer Languages and Systems Department
University of Cádiz
Cádiz, Spain
josetomas.tocino@uca.es

Antonio García-Domínguez
Computer Languages and Systems Department
University of Cádiz
Cádiz, Spain
antonio.garciadominguez@uca.es

Antonio Balderas
Computer Languages and Systems Department
University of Cádiz
Cádiz, Spain
antonio.balderas@uca.es

ABSTRACT

The importance of the video game and interactive entertainment industries has continuously increased in recent years. Academia has introduced computer game development in its curricula. In the case of the University of Cádiz, a non-compulsory course about "Video Game Design" is offered to Computer Science students. In the artificial intelligence lesson, students play a competition to earn part of their grade. Each student individually implements a strategy to play a predefined board-game. The different strategies compete in a software environment that implements it. Grading this part of the course depends on the results obtained in the competition. Additionally, before running the competition, students have to read the source code written by their classmates and bet a part of their grade on other teams' results. This way, they elaborate a critical analysis of the source code written by other programmers: a very valuable skill in the professional world. Students that are not so proficient in coding are still rewarded if they demonstrate they can do a good analysis of the source code written by others.

Categories and Subject Descriptors

I.2.1 [**Artificial Intelligence**]: Applications and Expert Systems; K.3.2 [**Computers and education**]: Computer and Information Science Education

General Terms

Experimentation

Keywords

Competition, video game development, artificial intelligence, expert system programming

1. INTRODUCTION

The importance of the video game and interactive entertainment industries has continuously increased in recent years [16]. Academia has introduced computer game development in its curricula. In the case of the University of Cádiz, a non-compulsory course about "Video Game Design" is offered to students of its degrees on Computer Science in their last year (third one). The recommended prerequisite is passing the Object Oriented Programming, Data Structures and Analysis and Design of Algorithms courses of the second year. There is also an elective Introduction to Artificial Intelligence course offered in the second year. But it is not a prerequisite as our experience gives all the necessary background on the topic and the course does not include lessons on expert systems.

The course mainly follows a project-based learning approach [13]. But in the artificial intelligence lesson, students play a competition (implementing a serious game [3]) to get part of their grade. Each student individually programs a strategy to play a predefined board-game. The different strategies compete in a software environment that implements it. Grading this part of the course depends on the results obtained in the competition, serving as a motivating factor [2].

To implement the competition, a specially designed free software tool provides a common environment where different strategies coded using rule-based expert systems compete against each other. The system models a square board in which players have a partial knowledge of the world (i.e., there is no "perfect strategy" to play the board-game). Using this application, the students can program and test their expert system rule sets against other rule sets or human players. After competing in a league, students can improve their systems before participating in a play-off tournament. This way, the students can develop the skill of critically analyzing the strategy they have implemented.

Table 1: Pieces in each army

Value	Number of pieces
1	1
2	8
3	2
4	2
5	2
6	1

Additionally, besides programming a strategy, students have to read source code written by their classmates and bet a part of their grades on other teams. This way, they review source code written by other programmers, which is a very valuable skill in the professional world. At the same time, students that are not so proficient in coding are still rewarded if they can do a good analysis of the source code written by others by identifying the future winner of the competition.

The rest of the paper is organized as follows: first, we describe the methodology followed in the classroom. Then, we discuss the results obtained last year. The fourth section comments similar experiences. Finally, we compile some conclusions and draw future works.

2. METHODOLOGY

The main aim of the experience is that students of the video game design course learn artificial intelligence programming using expert systems. All work for this lesson must be done within the allotted 8 hours in the classroom, so the game has to be very easy to play and code for.

2.1 The game

The game implemented for the competition is a simplified version of the Stratego board game [19]. It pits two armies made up by sixteen pieces against each other in a 8x8 grid. Both armies have the same pieces listed in table 1. Every piece has an associated value that is initially only visible to its owner. Players can initially place their pieces on the board in any order: one army is placed on the two lowest rows of the board and the other on the two highest rows. Figure 1 shows a possible initial set: brackets indicate that the value of the piece is hidden to the opponent.

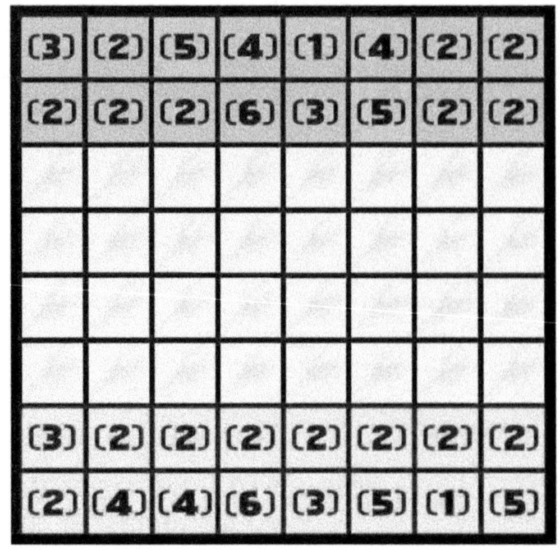

Figure 1: A possible initial set.

Players take turns moving one piece to an adjacent square (upwards, downwards, rightwards or leftwards). When a piece moves into a cell occupied by an enemy piece, their values are revealed and the lowest valued piece is removed from the board (*dies*). If they have the same value, both pieces die. The objective of the game is to capture the opponent's lowest valued piece. After a certain number of turns have passed, the match is tied.

A free software tool named Gades Siege [8] has been developed to support the competition. It improves upon a previous system called "Resistencia en Cádiz", and provides a common environment where the expert systems developed by the students and those saved from previous years can face off each other. Gades Siege allows for playing leagues, playoffs and single matches step by step, or collecting statistics from batches of 100 unattended matches against an opponent (using different random seeds). A human can also take control of a team to test the behavior of the strategy under certain situations. This helps students test and improve their strategies.

Figure 2 shows a screenshot of a match between two teams. Most of the window is dedicated to the game board. The right edge of the window shows the names of both teams and their dead pieces, along with the number of turns played and the remaining turns before the match is tied. Below the game board, four buttons with arrows allow for navigating the saved game states for the match. From left to right, they allow for replaying the match from the beginning, go back one step, go forwards one step, and fast forward to the last turn, respectively. Finally, three more icons on the bottom-right corner activate automatic simulation (advancing one turn per second), continue to the next match (or exiting if not inside a tournament), and exit the tournament, respectively.

On the one hand, the game implements a partial knowledge world for players. Thus, there is no "perfect strategy" to play the game, avoiding a loss of interest due to unbeatable teams. But, on the other hand, players have perfect knowledge of their armies. Since there is only one agent playing, the game is kept simple as there is no need to implement the fuzzy intelligence and communication protocols usually required by a multi-agent system. As a result, the problem is suitable to be solved using expert systems.

In particular, as the board is discrete, the artificial intelligence can be easily programmed using a rule-based expert system [5]. This way, the strategy is implemented as a set of prioritized if-then rules that are executed according to information from the current game state. Programming is as simple as adding, modifying, removing or re-prioritizing rules. This offers a wide variety of behaviors that can be implemented making slight changes in a rule set. It includes non-deterministic behaviors if several rules of the same priority can be activated at a certain moment. Even more, while general rules seem good for the beginning of a match, more specific ones play better in the last steps or in certain situations. So a good balance between both kinds of rules is required to create a winning team.

The system is programmed in Python using PyGame (a wrapper of the SDL multimedia library), and Glade for the GUI. As for the core, it is developed on CLIPS [15]. All sys-

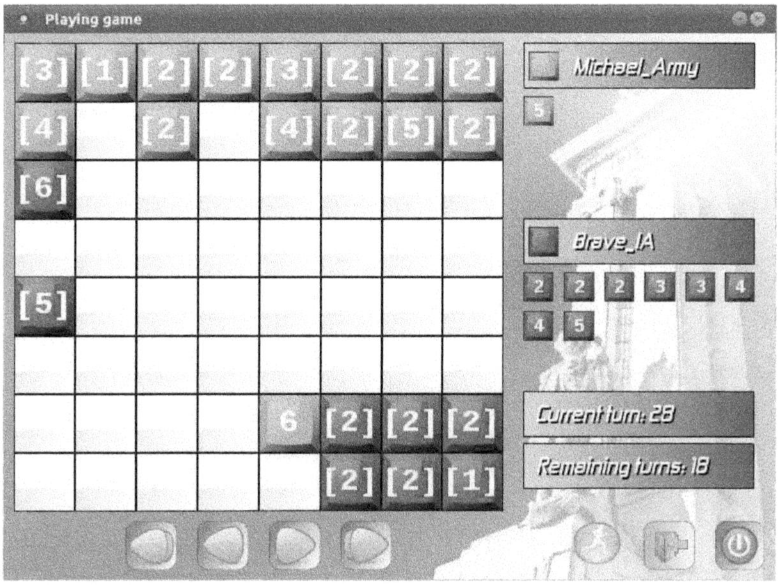

Figure 2: Screenshot of a match in Gades Siege. The value of the 6-point orange piece is revealed.

tems and our own code are multi-platform and free. Gades Siege is freely available for download at [8].

2.2 Schedule

The experience was performed throughout 2 weeks, using the weekly 4-hour blocks available for the course (2 hours of lectures followed by 2 hours of laboratory):

- A 2-hour lecture dedicates the first hour to provide the required conceptual foundations behind rule-based expert systems, emphasizing their practical applications in science and engineering. The second hour is used to show the game. Some sample rules are shown along, from simple cases to a reasonably complex system, so they can get familiar with the environment.

- After the lecture students move to the computer classroom. Due to the ease to program the system, they can code basic rule sets in 2 hours, learning expert system programming with the support of a teacher.

- Students have 5 days to code their strategies at home. Two of the features previously commented proved to be very useful for learning: playing a very large batch of matches automatically versus sample strategies to collect statistics on general performance, and playing against a human to test how the strategy behaves under certain circumstances and do fine tuning.

- One day before the competition starts, students have to upload their strategies into the Moodle virtual learning platform used in the course. When all the students have uploaded their strategies the teachers make them publicly available for the enrolled student, so they can read the code of colleagues. Note that only strategies and not initial formations are available for download. If they both could be downloaded, the students could actually play a competition and (except for light differences caused by random seeds) know the winner.

- Lecture time for the second week starts with students declaring which strategy or strategies will bet part of their marks. They can bet on one, two or three different strategies, and the sum of the grades bet must be between 10% and 50%. Then, a two-legged round robin league in which all students are confronted against each other is played. Some matches are watched by the entire class on a large wall screen so students can explain the behavior they implemented.

- Usually, after playing the league, students identify minor issues and weak points in their systems that could be easily fixed. Note that a change in the priority of a rule or the addition/deletion of one rule more is very easy to implement and can lead to a very different behavior. This improvement could include adding rules considered suitable from the strategies of a classmate. They have 1 hour in the laboratory to modify their rule set and then, the final strategies take part in a playoff tournament.

2.3 Grading

In order to pass the course, a strategy only needs to defeat a naive (*sparring*) team that is included in the system. This way, students can be confident they will pass this part of the course, even if the rule set ends up last in the competition. We do not consider fair that students able to program a good expert system in 2 weeks fail because their classmates are better programmers. Regardless of the quality of the strategies, one student must necessarily win the tournament, another must be second, and so on until the last place.

An additional point is given if the student explains clearly her strategy. This prevents cheating on one hand (or at least, it ensures that students know what their strategies do), and on the other hand, classmates can easily use some rules to improve their strategies for the play-off. In order to further improve their marks, students need to win matches against their classmates.

Table 2: Grades distribution

Mark (0-10)	Performance of the team	Range of teams
Fail (below 5)	No match won	0 or 1
5	Only defeats the sparring (DS)	0 or 1
6	DS and explains the strategy clearly	0 to All
7	DS and wins another match	0 to 2
8	DS and stays in upper half of the league or passes one play-off round	Half to all
9	DS, stays in upper half of the league and passes one play-off round Also DS and wins a tournament	Half to half+2
10	DS, stays in upper half of the league, passes one play-off and wins a tournament	0 to 2

Strategies get extra points (up to a total score of 10) for each of:

- Winning a match (not against the sparring opponent).
- Being in the top half of the league.
- Passing a play-off round.
- Winning a tournament.

The experience up to this point has been carried out since the first year of the course, in 2007–08. It has a clear problem: it implies certain restrictions on the number of teams that can get certain grades. For example, there can be only one winner in each competition, and only half of the teams will pass the first play-off round. This limits the distribution of grades according to teams' performance as shown in table 2.

This part of the course represents 15% of the course grade. As we have seen, getting 7 points in this part is quite affordable: students only need to program a strategy, explain it to their classmates and win a match against a real opponent. A student getting 7 points could get up to 9.55 points in the final general course grade (over a maximum of 10, allowing an A++ mark). Considering the relative value of the experience in overall course grade and the motivation of the competition, we think that the limitation of the range of teams obtaining certain grades is a good tradeoff. Nevertheless, a more flexible distribution of marks and grades according to students' skills was desired.

For this reason, in the 2010–11 academic year, besides programming an expert system, students had to read source code written by their classmates and bet a part of their final marks on other teams. This way, they elaborated a critical analysis of the source code written by other programmers, a very valuable professional skill. At the same time, students that were not so proficient in coding were still rewarded if they showed they could do a good analysis of the source code written by others, identifying the future winner of the competition.

It is important to note that the bet only concerned the performance of the strategies in the league. The play-offs were played using modified strategies that students improved in the lab, so they were different than those read by their colleagues before the competition. It would have been interesting to extend the betting system to the playoff, but it was not possible due to the strict time constrains (two blocks of 4 hours). The first block is dedicated to learning, and the second is for playing and making quick changes in strategies, leaving no time for analyzing and improving upon them.

This way, the relation between the performance of the strategy and the grade obtained by its author is further relaxed. If the final mark of a team in the league is X (of a maximum of 9), then the student who coded it could get a minimum grade of $X/2$ (by betting 50% for a team unable to beat the sparring opponent), and a maximum of $X/2 + 4.5$ (betting 50% for the best team, that obtains 9 points). But, if we suppose that every team gets at least 7 points, the minimum would be $X/2 + 3.5$ for betting half of the grade on a team that only got 7 points.

In any case, if a student preferred keeping the maximum of the mark of his team he could get a minimum of $X * 0.9$ (supposing that he bet for a team that won no matches) or $X*0.9+0.7$ if we suppose 7 to be the minimum actual mark. And the maximum would be $X*0.9+0.9$ (betting for a team that wins a competition).

As remarked before, the formulas concern only the league, covering up to 9 points. Two additional points could be obtained in the play-off of the improved strategies, up to 10 total points.

3. RESULTS OF THE EXPERIENCE

Due to the nature of the game (providing only partial knowledge of the world) and the limited knowledge of the undergraduate students on artificial intelligence techniques, there has been no "absolute best" team in any year. It is curious that quite often some of the teams in the top of the league had difficulties or even could not beat some in the lowest part. This demonstrates that even the best teams had some weak points.

Informally speaking with students, they reported that the competition between peers is a motivating factor to learn expert system programming, reinforcing conclusions of similar experiences [18]. They also commented that seeing the army evolve without their intervention against others was a nice way to understand the application of artificial intelligence to game development.

In this year 15 students joined the course, but only 14 attended the experience: a student uploaded a strategy but did not go to the sessions and got 0 points in the bet (as he did not provide a satisfactory reason to miss it). The 14 students bet an average of 24.29% of their marks: most bet below 30% except for one who bet 40% and another one who bet 50%. As for the lowest bets, three students bet the minimum 10% of their grade.

Only three students obtained lower grades due to their bets and seven improved it. The maximum gain was obtained by a student whose strategy had 7 points and bet half of his mark for the winning one (who obtained 8, the maximum available in the league). Highest losses were −0.85 and −0.65. The rest of students varied their strategy grades in a 0.2 points or less. Finally, four kept the same grade because they bet different rates for several teams whose weighted mean was the same grade their strategy got.

Interestingly, some students acknowledged that the main reason to bet for a certain team was not only their impressions when they reviewed the code, but the overall marks of the developers in previous courses. Although we do not have access to that information, in general seems that students who perform well in programming subjects, also do well in this experience.

Students were, on average, much more interested in this course than in others, judging from the anonymous surveys conducted near the end of the term. It included different aspects about the course, all of them rated from 1 (minimum) to 5 (maximum). Results showed a very high score:

- Evaluation method in the course: 4.69
- Competition of expert systems: 4.92
- Betting system included: 4.15
- General course value: 4.61

4. RELATED WORKS

There are similar experiences of competition between students in the literature. Concerning simulated robotic soccer, there are different experiences using RoboCup Soccerserver, an evolution of Javasoccer [10]. This systems uses a client-server architecture, so the artificial intelligence modules can be programmed not only using rule-based expert systems [12, 4], but also other techniques [11, 17]. In [7] groups of students had to implement the artificial intelligence for a RoboCup team during a course. At the end of it, a competition was run among the teams coded by students and some other from Robocup World Cup participants. The basis for the student's examination and grade was a written report on the team design and performance in the competition. The

Another example is Robocode [6]. Robocode is a game that implements a virtual battle field where two robots fight each other. Students use Java to implement different artificial intelligence techniques. Then, they observe how their agent performs compared to others by watching the agents compete.

There is an interesting experience using software based on the Ataxx game [14]. Groups of two or three students had to use Prolog to implement an agent which had to complete every game using a limited amount of CPU time. The assignment grade was determined by the ranking obtained in a free-for-all competition among these student programs.

Finally, even hardware competitions [9, 1] using robots are documented. They are developed in the laboratory sessions of the Artificial Intelligence course. This way, students can bring into practice the concepts learned and are highly motivated.

Nevertheless, all of the experiences commented use much more complex games than our proposal. So they would have needed more time than what was available. As we commented previously, time restrictions are very tight in this experience. As for the betting system, we have found no experiences using it, showing its originality.

5. DISCUSSION AND CONCLUSION

The importance of the video game and interactive entertainment industries has caused academia to introduce computer game development in their curricula. In an elective "Video Game Design" course offered in the Computer Science degrees of the University of Cádiz the grade in the artificial intelligence lesson is obtained competitively. Students code strategies to play a serious game. They compete in a software environment that implements a board-game, and the results obtained in the competition will be part of their grade.

Firstly, each student has to code a strategy as a rule-based expert system. Those strategies compete in a league. Then, students can improve them before participating in a play-off tournament. Another part of the grade depends on a bet on the strategies of their classmates. This way, they practice critical analysis on the source code written by other programmers, a very valuable skill in the professional world. At the same time, students that are not so proficient in coding are still rewarded if they demonstrate they can do a good analysis of the source code written by others identifying the future winner of the competition.

The experience has been rewarding both for the students and the teacher. Developing the environment was a time consuming task in the first year, but results showed it was a very interesting way to motivate students. As the system is open source, is has evolved year after year, mainly due to students who detected deficiencies or interesting features that could be added and coded them. Thanks to its automation, the experience is very easy to handle. Enrollment figures were 20 students in 2011, 16 in 2010, 27 in 2009 and 13 in 2008.

Skills developed include not only those specific for the lesson (programming rule-based expert systems, using it for video game artificial intelligence systems, etc.) but also general ones: improvement of a strategy by analyzing its performance and critical analysis of the source code written by other programmers.

In general, due to the generous grading system used for the strategies, all the students get good grades in this lesson. This way, students that are able to program a good expert system in 2 weeks cannot fail simply because their classmates are better. This is necessary, as regardless of the quality of the strategies, the range of teams in each place of the tournament is limited: one student must win the tournament, another must be second, and so till the last place.

The use of a betting system has an interesting impact in the experience, as it relaxes the relation between the performance of the strategy and the grade obtained by its author. In fact, most of the 15 students in the course increased their grades thanks to it (seven in particular), and only three decreased them. Students could bet from 10% to 50%, being the average almost 25%. Interestingly, some students acknowledged that the main reason to bet on a certain team was not only their impressions when they reviewed the code, but the overall marks of the developer in previous courses. Although we do not have access to that information, our general impression is that students who perform well in programming courses also do well in this experience.

Two lines of future work lie ahead. The first line of work is making it easier to change the rules of the board-game for each competition or match without having to code them, so the teams could play in different environments and avoid over-specialization. For example, there might be some unreachable square in the matrix that needed extra intelligence to play, or some pieces could be uncovered from the beginning of the match. Our second line of work would be applying log analysis techniques to detect weak rules in an strategy.

6. ACKNOWLEDGMENTS

This work has been funded by the Proyecto de Innovación Educativa Universitaria del Personal Docente e Investigador "La competitividad y el análisis crítico en la evaluación" (CIE44) of the Convocatoria 2010 de Proyectos de Innovación Educativa Universitaria para el PDI de la Universidad de Cádiz, funded by the Consejería de Innovación, Ciencia y Empresa of the Junta de Andalucía and the University of Cádiz (Spain), and by the Computer Languages and Systems Department of the same University.

7. REFERENCES

[1] M. Arevalillo-Herráez, S. Moreno-Picot, and V. Cavero-Millán. Arquitectura para utilizar robots AIBO en la enseñanza de la inteligencia artificial. *IEEE RITA (Revista Iberoamericana de Tecnologías del Aprendizaje)*, 6(1):57–64, 2011.

[2] J. C. Burguillo. Using game theory and competition-based learning to stimulate student motivation and performance. *Comput. Educ.*, 55:566–575, September 2010.

[3] M. J. Dondlinger. Educational video game design : A review of the literature. *Journal of Applied Educational Technology*, 4(1):21–31, 2007.

[4] R. Fathzadeh, V. Mokhtari, M. Mousakhani, and A. Shahri. Coaching with expert system towards robocup soccer coach simulation. In A. Bredenfeld, A. Jacoff, I. Noda, and Y. Takahashi, editors, *RoboCup 2005: Robot Soccer World Cup IX*, volume 4020 of *Lecture Notes in Computer Science*, pages 488–495. Springer Berlin / Heidelberg, 2006. 10.1007/11780519_45.

[5] J. C. Giarratano and G. Riley. *Expert Systems*. PWS Publishing Co., Boston, MA, USA, 3rd edition, 1998.

[6] K. Hartness. Robocode: Using games to teach artificial intelligence. In *Journal of Computing Sciences in Colleges*, page 2004, 2004.

[7] F. H. Johan, J. Kummeneje, and P. Scerri. Using simulated RoboCup to teach AI in undergraduate education. In *In Proceedings of the 7 th Scandinavian Conference on AI*, 2001.

[8] José Tomás Tocino et al. Gades Siege. `http://code.google.com/p/gsiege`, 2011.

[9] F. Klassner. A case study of LEGO Mindstorms' suitability for artificial intelligence and robotics courses at the college level. *SIGCSE Bull.*, 34:8–12, February 2002.

[10] B. López, M. Montaner, and J. L. de la Rosa. Utilización de un simulador de fútbol para enseñar inteligencia artificial a ingenieros. In *Actas de las Jornadas de Enseñanza Universitaria de la Informática*, 2001.

[11] I. Noda, H. Matsubara, K. Hiraki, and I. Frank. Soccer server: A tool for research on multiagent systems. *Applied Artificial Intelligence*, 12(2-3):233–250, 1998.

[12] M. Palomo, F.-J. Martín-Mateos, and J.-A. Alonso. Rete algorithm applied to robotic soccer. *Lecture Notes in Computer Science*, 3643:571–576, 2005.

[13] P. Recio-Quijano, N. Sales-Montes, A. García-Domínguez, and M. Palomo-Duarte. Collaboration and competitiveness in project-based learning. In *Proceedings of the Methods and Cases in Computing Education Workshop (MCCE)*, pages 8–14, 2010.

[14] P. M. P. Ribeiro, H. Simões, and M. Ferreira. Teaching artificial intelligence and logic programming in a competitive environment. *Informatics in Education*, 8(1):85–100, 2009.

[15] G. Riley. CLIPS home site. http://clipsrules.sourceforge.net, 2011.

[16] S. E. Siwek. Video Games in the 21st Century: the 2010 report, 2010.

[17] P. Stone and G. K. December. Publications related to the robocup soccer simulation league. *World*, 29(3):866–871, 2007.

[18] S. A. Wallace and J. Margolis. Exploring the use of competetive programming: observations from the classroom. *J. Comput. Sci. Coll.*, 23:33–39, December 2007.

[19] Wikipedia. Stratego. http://en.wikipedia.org/wiki/Stratego, 2012.

User Interface Evaluation by Novices

Dennis Bouvier
Southern Illinois Univ. Edwardsville
Edwardsville, IL 62025 USA
+1 (618) 650-2369
djb@acm.org

Tzu-Yi Chen
Pomona College
Claremont, CA 91711 USA
+1 (909) 607-8651
tzuyi@cs.pomona.edu

Gary Lewandowski
Xavier University
Cincinnati, OH 45207 USA
+1 (513) 745-2836
lewandow@cs.xu.edu

Robert McCartney
University of Connecticut
Storrs, CT 06269 USA
+1 (860) 486-5232
robert@cse.uconn.edu

Kate Sanders
Rhode Island College
Providence, RI 02908 USA
+1 (401) 456-8038
ksanders@ric.edu

Tammy VanDeGrift
University of Portland
Portland, OR 97203 USA
+1 (503) 943-7256
vandegri@up.edu

ABSTRACT
This study examines the extent to which novice computing students with minimal computer science coursework and no training in user interface (UI) evaluation consider UI concepts such as usability, user experience, and the context in which software will be used when evaluating an interface. In analyzing the responses of 149 novice computer science students who were asked to evaluate two interfaces for converting temperatures between Fahrenheit and Celsius, we observed that students generally considered usability and user experience factors, but were less likely to consider context. For educators, this exact task could be given to a class in order to initiate discussion of user-centered design; the study also provides a framework for structuring the discussion. More generally, the results of this study provide insight into some opportunities and challenges in teaching good interface design and evaluation skills.

Categories and Subject Descriptors
H.5.m. **[Information interfaces and presentation (e.g., HCI)]**: Miscellaneous. K.3.2 **[Computers and Education]:** Computer science education

General Terms
Design, Experimentation, Human Factors.

Keywords
user interface evaluation, novice, commonsense computing

1. INTRODUCTION
Strategies for evaluating interfaces include heuristic evaluation, cognitive walkthroughs, and usability testing. Previous work within the HCI community has considered how well these techniques work as a guideline for experts [5] as well as how effectively students in a UI class can apply a specified evaluation strategy [8]. In both cases the quality of a subject's response is judged by comparison to evaluations by experts.

ITiCSE'12, July 3- 5, 2012, Haifa, Israel.

In this paper we consider a slightly different question and use a different approach. Rather than analyzing individual evaluation techniques, we instead study how novices with minimal coursework in computer science, and none in user interface design, compare and contrast two interfaces when given relatively little guidance about what to look for or comment on. Rather than doing a point-by-point comparison of the novice responses against expert evaluation of the same two interfaces, we map their responses to metrics such as availability and affect that are commonly discussed within the user interface community. As a result, this study gives insight into the kinds of design issues that novices notice and consider important. It also gives insight into design issues that novices are likely to overlook or to dismiss and, as a result, suggests measures of interface quality that instructors may want to pay additional attention to in the classroom, as those metrics may be more likely to be ignored by students learning to evaluate or design user interfaces.

This project, like earlier commonsense computing projects, is grounded in constructivist learning theory, which holds that learning takes place by refining and extending what the student already knows [1, 9]. Bransford et al. [2] argue that learning must engage the students' preconceptions to be effective. Schwill [11], in applying Bruner's notion of fundamental ideas [3] to computing, argues that fundamental computing ideas provide a framework for learning constructively, have meaning in everyday life, and can be described in ordinary language. In other words, students have rich preconceptions about computer science when they enter college and, since their learning will build from these preconceptions, a deeper understanding of these preconceptions should allow for more effective teaching and learning. Earlier commonsense computing projects probed novice computing students' pre-existing knowledge of sorting, debugging, concurrency, and algorithm analysis [14, 4, 13, 7, 6]. These studies found that students did possess knowledge that translated well to computer science; for example, 69% of students could describe a coherent algorithm to sort a list of numbers [14], and 97% of students could identify a significant problem associated with concurrency [6]. On the other hand, there were also ways in which students' pre-existing knowledge did not translate well to computer science; for example, some common approaches to locating and resolving problems in the real world differ in fundamental ways from debugging strategies typically used in computer science [13].

In the rest of this paper we describe the study and our analysis in greater depth, and then explore implications for teaching UI design and evaluation.

2. METHODOLOGY

As a starting point, we asked students to compare and contrast two interfaces for converting temperatures between Fahrenheit and Celsius. These interfaces, shown in Figure 1, are both from Raskin [10]. Subjects were given links to URLs containing interactive versions of the two interfaces (written by one of the authors) and encouraged to experiment with them before responding. Some students were given additional information about a user named Hal and the context in which he would be using the interface (the *Hal version* of the task, also from Raskin [10]), other students were asked simply to evaluate the interfaces (the *No Hal version* of the task). The two tasks were given as follows:

[**Hal Version**] Hal works at a computer, typing reports; he is occasionally interrupted by one or another of the researchers in his room, asking him to convert a temperature reading from degrees Fahrenheit (F) or Celsius (C) to degrees C or F, respectively.

Below are two possible interfaces (ways to interact with a program) for an application which converts temperatures between Celsius and Fahrenheit for Hal to use. Using complete English sentences, describe, compare, and contrast the interfaces. Before giving your answer, click here to try the prototypes. (see Figure 1)

[**No Hal Version**] Below are two possible interfaces (ways to interact with a program) for an application which converts temperatures between Celsius and Fahrenheit. Using complete English sentences, describe, compare, and contrast the interfaces. Before giving your answer, click here to try the prototypes. (see Figure 1)

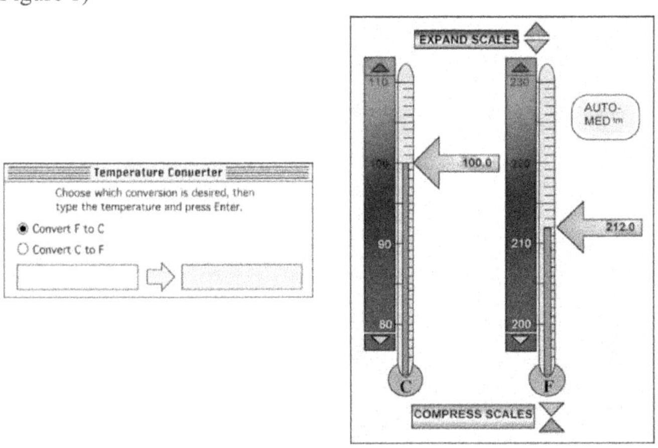

Figure 1: Interface A (left) and Interface B (right)

2.1 Participants and Institutions

The evaluation task was given to 149 students enrolled in introductory computer science courses (CS1) during the Fall of 2008 at one of four institutions in the United States. The Hal version was given to 68 students and the No Hal version was given to 81 students. Three of the institutions gave either only the Hal version or only the No Hal version of the task. The fourth institution used both the Hal and No Hal versions, but in different sections of the same course. The primary reason for giving students within a single course section the same task was to make it easier for the instructor to discuss student responses in class. Table 1 gives an overview of the institutions and of the data collected from each.

All students were enrolled in introductory computing courses that did not include human-computer interaction, user-centered design, or user interface design in their syllabi. The majors of the students included computer science, math, physics and engineering; some students had not yet declared a major.

Table 1. Study participants

Institution	# Subjects	Version
A. large public, East coast	40	20 Hal / 20 No Hal
B. small private, West coast	28	No Hal
C. small private, Midwest	33	No Hal
D. large public, Midwest	48	Hal

2.2 Data Collection

The evaluation task was given as a homework assignment during the first week of the term at each institution. We classified the participants as novices based on their extremely limited exposure to both programming and user interface evaluation, although students may have had computing courses before college. Students submitted responses electronically and the researchers prepared a common spreadsheet containing answers from all participants. The researchers received IRB approval and consent from participants to use the responses as data for this research study.

Below are two responses from students who were given the Hal version of the task. These responses illustrate how the subjects' responses varied in length, in detail, and in the metrics they use for analysis.

The first is a full response from a student who described how the interfaces work and compared the interfaces based on simplicity. The student also commented on the visual appearance of the interfaces.

> *Each of these interfaces gives the same end result, however due to different visual appearances they vary greatly. Interface A is fairly simple, the user inputs the temperature to be converted and the interface outputs the result. It is not intricate, with only two buttons for the type of conversion and one box for input. On the other hand, interface B is fairly more complex with many more options for usability. There is not a place for the user to input the initial temperature; instead there is a scale which the user is expected to manipulate. In addition, there are several different buttons which allow the user to change the scale as well as the values of the visual thermometer. Interface A is suitable for the task at hand, but it does not provide much more then the conversion. Interface B gives the user more options and flexibility in the way which they interpret the output. For beginner users, interface A will be far simpler than interface B, due to the simplicity of the interface. Visually, interface A is in black and white as oppose to interface B which is in color.*

The second is a complete response from a student who first evaluated each interface separately and then compared them specifically in regards to how well suited they were for the task facing Hal.

> *The first interface features a convenient radio button that allows the users to quickly choose their desired conversion method. The first user interface also features clear and easy to use instructions at the top of the program. The first interface allows for a great amount of precision. This is especially important for anyone in the scientific community where accuracy can mean all the difference. Overall the first interface is simple, easy to use, user friendly and allows for a great level of precision.*
>
> *The second interface is a little more confusing. This user interface contains two distracting brightly colored bars that show the temperature in Fahrenheit and Celsius. It is not immediately clear which thermometer represents Celsius as they are not labeled. The user interface is difficult to use and understand. The expansion and contraction of the scale causes there to be much more fiddling with the program before you are able to get it to run. While the graphic representation of the thermometers is a cute way of representing data, it makes the entire process infinitely more complicated. Overall the graphic representation of the data is a interesting and creative idea but in a practical sense it doesn't work as well as interface 1.*
>
> *Between the two interfaces I would choose interface 1 for a number of reasons. First of all, it's simple. Converting from Fahrenheit to Celsius does not need to be a complicated artistic task that requires the users to drag their mouse up and down hoping to find the temperature they are looking for. As it describes in the problem, Hal works on entering data into the computer. This is a task that I am sure does not welcome interruptions. Hal wants to convert the temperature for his colleague and then get back to work. With interface one, he can input the exact temperature with as much precision as is need and receive a result in a matter of seconds. With the second interface he would have to adjust the scale and move the sliders up and down until he found the temperature with a questionable level of accuracy. If for instance a researcher came to Hal with a temperature of 100.00235 degrees Fahrenheit, he could not computer degrees Celsius to the level of precision needed by the researcher. In the first user interface however, Hal could simply input the number 100.00235 degrees Fahrenheit and receive an equally precise 37.779083 degrees Celsius in a fraction of the time. My own criticism about interface 1 is that there is no blinking cursor or indicator as to which box you are typing in. Also there is no way to select the temperature for a quick copy and paste into a word document. However the same goes for interface 2. Again I believe that interface 1 is a smarter choice over interface 2 because of its ease of use and speed.*

2.3 Data Analysis

The two responses above illustrate the fact that students choose to focus on different aspects of the interfaces, that they use different techniques in discussing their observations (for example, the second response quoted above uses an example to clarify its point on accuracy and makes a recommendation on how to improve interface A by adding an indicator), and that they incorporate the user-context information about Hal in different ways.

To break down the analysis of these responses in a structured, repeatable way, each response was first divided into units. Ideally each unit, typically a phrase or a sentence, captured a single user interface evaluation idea. For each response, two researchers independently identified units and then argued to consensus for disagreements. For example, consider the following response:

> *Interface A is a lot simpler than interface B. B has options to expand or compress the scale depending on the temperature. Both display the temperatures but B also has graphics to accompany it. Interface A only has basic number, but the simplicity is desired since it only needs to convert temperatures. I would choose interface A because it is simpler.*

This response was divided into the following units:

- Interface A is a lot simpler than interface B.
- B has options to expand or compress the scale depending on the temperature.
- B also has graphics to accompany it
- but the simplicity is desired since it [Interface A] only needs to convert temperatures.

Once the units were extracted from the responses, two researchers independently categorized each unit, discussing disagreements with each other and, if necessary, with a third researcher who could break the tie. A given unit could fall into more than one category.

The initial list of categories consisted of the following features used by experts in designing and evaluating user interfaces (for a more detailed description of these categories, see [12]):

- *usability*, broken down into:
  - *utility*: whether the interface provides what is needed by, and useful for, the user to accomplish the necessary tasks.
  - *effectiveness*: a general goal capturing how good the interface is at allowing users to do what they need to do.
  - *efficiency*: whether a user can carry out common tasks with a minimal number of actions.
  - *safe to use*: how well the interface protects the user from errors and undesirable situations.
  - *learnability*: whether the user can determine how to use the interface correctly to accomplish the necessary tasks.
  - *memorability*: whether a user needs to repeatedly relearn how to accomplish specific tasks.
- *user experience*, abstracted as:
  - *affect*: the subjective quality of how interacting with and using the interface feels to a user.

Below are examples of units from subject responses that we assigned to each category.

- **Utility**: "The two interfaces for converting Fahrenheit and Celsius both give accurate answers."
- **Effectiveness**: "gives us a much more precise result" and "it gets much harder to get the exact temperature that you want. If I wanted a solid 43 C, I can only get 42.99 and 43.01 …

but with Interface A, you can just plug in 43, and convert it easily."
- **Efficiency**: "This is not a practical program simply because it is tedious to drag the bar to the required temperature to convert it" and "Interface A is more efficient if the user wants a specific number to be converted"
- **Safe to use**: "This interface makes it look like C is always larger than F, which is not the case at all."
- **Learnability**: "There are no instructions on how to use Interface B and there is no title to remind you what it is." and "The second converter doesn't have any instructions to follow and two sets of buttons that don't really explain what they do to the scale."
- **Memorability**: [no examples]
- **Affect**: "The multiple colors and images give the user a much more pleasant time using the application." and "Basically, the Temperature Converter is simple, boring, but effective."

In categorizing the units, we added five other categories that emerged from the analysis. *Visual appearance* and *Interactivity* relate to the user experience (without requiring an affective response), although we note Interactivity may be related (by the student) to usability factors such as efficiency and effectiveness. *Considers the user* and *Considers purpose* refer to the context in which the interfaces are to be used. *Implementation* relates the interfaces to how they might have been programmed. Examples of these are:

- **Visual appearance**: "Conversely, interface B was created in order to provide a visual aid, and focuses less on providing us with a concrete conversion." and "Whereas Interface A might be suited for technical calculations, Interface B provides a graphic representation of how the two units of temperature are related to one another."
- **Interactivity**: "I liked the drag function, it involves the user a little more and the visuals were good." and "Interface B is far more developed and interactive than Interface A."
- **Considers the users**: "There is a lot of temperature outside the range cannot be converted which is not very useful for researchers." and "This prototype would be better suited for the an experienced user looking to generate an answer quickly and does not require a visual illustration to better understand the relationship between the two measurements."
- **Considers purpose**: "the first one is better when one want to a exact number which they want to know" and "It seems to me that the Interface A may be more helpful if someone was wanting to know just an approximate temperature, or had a large range of numbers that needed to be converted."
- **Implementation**: "A is the more straightforward approach for both the programmer and the end-user." and "I actually prefer Interface A because it is a smaller file, which uses fewer system resources to accomplish the exact same task with far more precision."

3. RESULTS

In analyzing the data we focused on answering the following questions:

- Which evaluation criteria valued by experts are most likely to be used by novices? Which are most likely to be overlooked?
- Do novices consider the user and context when evaluating an interface?
- What effect does mentioning the user/context in the question have on the categories used in the evaluation?

3.1 Evaluation Criteria

Table 2 gives the number and percentage of subjects whose responses included at least one unit indicating use of that evaluation criterion.

Table 2: Novice use of expert criteria

evaluation criteria		# subjects	(%)
usability	Utility	103	(69.1%)
	effectiveness	65	(43.6%)
	Efficiency	80	(53.7%)
	safe to use	8	(5.4%)
	learnability	32	(21.5%)
	memorability	0	(0.0%)
user experience	Affect	38	(25.5%)
	visual appearance	110	(73.8%)
	interactivity	74	(49.7%)
context	considers user	29	(19.5%)
	considers purpose	35	(23.5%)
Implementation		19	(12.8%)

The five most common criteria were visual appearance, utility, efficiency, interactivity, and effectiveness – each used by over 40% of the students. Three of these are part of usability, two are part of user experience. Safe to use was quite uncommon, and we saw no mention of memorability.

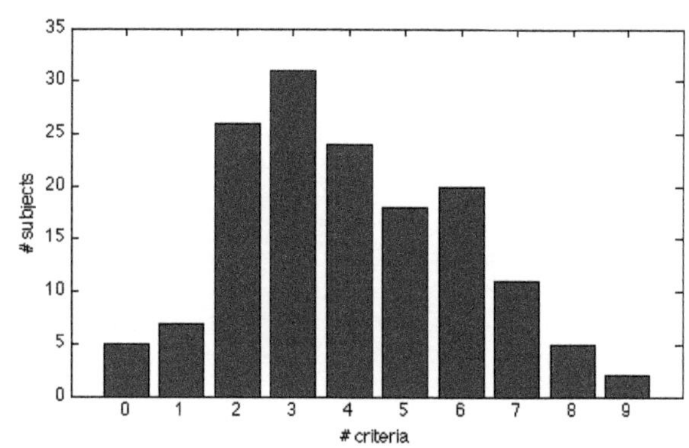

Figure 2: Number of subjects whose responses touched on a particular number of criteria

Figure 2 shows the distribution of number of criteria used by each student. Although this shows that individual students were unlikely to comment on more than 5 or 6 criteria (the average was 3.97), Table 2 shows that the students collectively used almost all of the criteria suggested by expert evaluators. This agrees with the findings in [8] that while individual evaluators do not do particularly well evaluating an interface – they miss things – aggregations of individual independent evaluations are quite good, even for relatively small numbers.

3.2 Contextual factors

Relatively few students considered the users or the software's purpose in their evaluations. We provided explicit contextual information in the Hal version of the task (given in Figure 1) with the goal of seeing how that affected student evaluation criteria. Table 3 again shows the number of subjects who used each evaluation criteria, but this time the count is separated into subjects who were asked the Hal version of the question and those who were asked the No Hal version of the question.

Table 3: Effect of mentioning Hal on novices' use of expert criteria

evaluation criteria		# subjects Hal version	# subjects no Hal version
usability	utility	41	62
	effectiveness	27	38
	efficiency	29	51
	safe to use	3	5
	learnability	14	18
	memorability	0	0
user experience	affect	18	20
	visual appearance	53	57
	interactivity	31	43
context	considers user	14	15
	considers purpose	14	21
implementation		11	8

Somewhat surprisingly, there were no significant differences in the likelihoods that they consider the user ($\chi^2(1,N=149)=.0087$, $p=.92$), or consider the purpose ($\chi^2(1,N=149)=.5860$, $p=.44$). Of the 68 students who were given the Hal version, only eight mentioned Hal by name. Six of the students with the Hal version mentioned other users, for a total of 14, as compared with 15 (out of 81) for the other students.

Those students who received the Hal version were less likely to mention either efficiency ($\chi^2(1,N=149)=6.14$, $p=.013$) or utility ($\chi^2(1,N=149)=4.57$, $p=.032$), and no differences were detected for any of the other criteria.

4. DISCUSSION

Based on the results of this study, we conclude that novices can collectively perform UI evaluations naturally, using the criteria used by expert evaluators. Individual students thought about usability and the user experience, but less so about the context of the temperature conversion tool. In fact, few students explicitly evaluated the interfaces with the context in mind, even when a user and a context were explicitly given. The responses collected are perhaps guided more by students' personal experiences with the applets than by their ability to imagine how someone else might use the tool. On the positive side, there is evidence that some students did think about potential users other than themselves, such as people learning about temperature scales and people with different learning styles.

Educators can apply these research results and materials in their own classrooms. For example, CS1 educators could ask beginning computing students to complete the Hal user evaluation exercise described in this paper. After students have completed their evaluations, the educator could present the list of expert user evaluation categories (utility, effectiveness, efficiency, etc) and ask students to determine which categories their evaluations include. It might be illuminating for the students and educator to see the percentage of students who consider the user. It might also be illuminating for students to see which categories they did not consider. This exercise could lead into a discussion about software usability and user-centered design. Even if an institution's CS1 class is not focused on these issues, having such a discussion in a first CS course might emphasize to students that "designing for users" is a recognized and valued goal. Such a discussion might also give CS1 students a sense of the breadth of areas of study within computer science.

This type of exercise could also be used in more advanced CS courses such as software engineering, human computer interaction, interface design, and capstone design courses. If the temperature conversion applications seem too simple, students could complete the evaluation task for two existing software applications. The professor could write a Hal-like scenario for the user task and ask students to complete the interface evaluation. The student responses could lead into a discussion about software usability and interface design.

In the future it could be interesting to compare the responses presented here to responses given by more advanced students as well as by professors and experts in the field. It has been conjectured that user-centered design is a "threshold concept" in computing [15]; a longitudinal study of how students respond to these questions over time might suggest additional ways to help students cross this threshold.

5. CONCLUSION

Overall, the students in this study used evaluation criteria similar to what could be expected from experts: most students consider both usability and user-experience factors. They seem much less likely, however, to consider the overall contextual factors of 1) who is going to use this interface? and 2) what is the purpose to which this interface will be put? It would seem that simply providing some contextual background is insufficient to change this.

Educators who teach HCI courses can apply these findings in their courses by putting additional emphasis on the importance of contextual factors in evaluating an interface. The exercise used here, or something similar, could be assigned to students as a starting point for discussion: it is simple enough to evaluate without formal training in HCI, but rich enough to illustrate the kinds of criteria that might be used.

6. ACKNOWLEDGMENTS

Thanks to Andy Carle for helpful discussions and to Beth Simon for helping with data collection. Thanks to our students for their insight and data. This work was supported in part by the National Science Foundation under grants DUE-0736343, DUE-0736700, DUE-0736572, DUE-0736738, DUE-0736859, and DUE-0736958. Any opinions, findings, and conclusions or recommendations expressed in this material are those of the authors and do not necessarily reflect those of the National Science Foundation.

7. REFERENCES

1. Ben-Ari, M. Constructivism in computer science education. *Journal of Computers in Mathematics and Science Teaching*, 20(1):45–73, 2001.
2. Bransford, J. D., Brown, A. L., and Cocking, R. R., editors. How People Learn: Brain, Mind, Experience, and School. National Academy Press, Washington, DC, expanded edition, 2000.
3. Bruner, J. The process of education. Harvard University Press, Cambridge, MA, 1960.
4. Chen, T.-Y., Lewandowski, G., McCartney, R., Sanders K., and Simon, B. Commonsense computing: using student sorting abilities to improve instruction. In *Proc. SIGCSE '07*, ACM Press (2007), 276–280.
5. Jeffries, R., Miller, J. R., Wharton, C., and Uyeda, K. User interface evaluation in the real world: a comparison of four techniques. In *Proc. CHI '91*, ACM Press (1991), 119-124.
6. Lewandowski, G., Bouvier, D., Chen, T.-Y., McCartney, R., Sanders, K., Simon, B., and VanDeGrift, T. Commonsense understanding of concurrency: computing students and concert tickets. *Communications of the ACM*, 53(7): 60-70, 2010.
7. McCartney, R., Bouvier, D., Chen, T.-Y., Lewandowski, G., Sanders, K., Simon, B., and VanDeGrift, T. Commonsense computing (episode 5): algorithm efficiency and balloon testing. In *Proc. ICER '09*, ACM Press (2009), 51-62.
8. Nielsen, J. and Molich, R. Heuristic evaluation of user interfaces. In *Proc. CHI '90*, ACM Press (1990), 249-256.
9. Perkins, D. The many faces of constructivism, Educational Leadership 57(3):6-11, 1999.
10. Raskin, J. The Humane Interface: New Directions for Designing Interactive Systems. Addison-Wesley Professional, 2000.
11. Schwill, A. Fundamental ideas of computer science. *Bull. European Association for Theoretical Computer Science*, 53:274–295, 1994.
12. Sharp, H., Rogers, Y., and Preece, J. Interaction Design: beyond human-computer interaction, 2nd edition. Wiley, 2007.
13. Simon, B., Bouvier, D., Chen, T.-Y., Lewandowski, G., McCartney, R., and Sanders, K. Commonsense computing (episode 4): Debugging. *Computer Science Education*, 18(2):117-133, 2008.
14. Simon, B., Chen, T.-Y., Lewandowski, G., McCartney, R., and Sanders, K. Commonsense computing: what students know before we teach (episode 1: sorting). In *Proc. ICER '06*, ACM Press (2006), 29–40.
15. Zander, C., Boustedt, J., McCartney, R., Mostrom, J.-E., Sanders, K., and Thomas, L. Student transformations: are they computer scientists yet? In *Proc. ICER '09*, ACM Press (2009), 129-140.

MyTuringTable: A Teaching Tool to Accompany Turing's Original Paper on Computability

Barry Fagin
Department of Computer Science
2354 Fairchild Drive, 6G-139
US Air Force Academy, CO 80840
719-333-7377
barry.fagin@usafa.edu

Dino Schweitzer
Director, Academy Center for
Cyberspace Research, 6G-101
US Air Force Academy, CO 80840
719-333-3945
dino.schweitzer@usafa.edu

ABSTRACT
MyTuringTable is a Turing Machine simulator designed to help students read and understand Turing's seminal 1937 paper on computability. We discuss our reasons for developing the tool, and report on its use in a "Great Ideas in Computer Science" course for the Air Force Academy Cadet Scholars program.

Categories and Subject Descriptors
F.1.1 [**Computation by Abstract Devices**]: Models of Computation – *Bounded-action devices, Turing Machines.* K.2 [**History of Computing**]: People, Theory. K.3.2 [**Computers and Education**]: Computer and Information Science Education – *Computer science education.*

General Terms
Algorithms, Theory

Keywords
Turing Machines, Educational Software, Computer Science Education, History of Computing

1. INTRODUCTION
Alan Turing's 1937 paper on the Entscheidungsproblem [9] marked the beginning of computer science as an academic discipline, and ushered in the computing era. As such, we believe it ranks as one of the most significant achievements in the history of ideas, a work that deserves a much larger audience.

Unfortunately, Turing's paper is dense and difficult to read, particularly for undergraduates. We faced this challenge in developing and teaching a course on "Great Ideas in Computer Science" in the Scholars Program at the US Air Force Academy.

The Scholars Program consists of the top one percent of cadets academically at USAFA, those likely to be competitive for national scholarships such as the Rhodes. These cadets take special versions of the Academy's core classes together, where they are expected to engage directly with original source materials, to think critically about them, and where possible to encounter and assimilate their important contributions through hands-on practice and implementation. Most Scholars courses are in the humanities and social sciences, but a few are in the sciences and engineering.

ITiCSE'12, July 3–5, 2012, Haifa, Israel.

Two years ago, the first author sought to create a computer science class for Scholars students, based on the theme of "Great Ideas in Computer Science". This course would be taught during the freshman year, with no prior knowledge of computing or programming assumed. Consistent with the intent of the Scholars Program, students would read original works by the most important contributors to the field, such as Babbage, Von Neumann, and of course Alan Turing. Similarly, they would implement the Method of Finite Differences as described in [6], write programs in assembly language for Von Neumann's IAS machine [1], and learn to write their own Turing Machines (TMs).

However, in the course of preparing the necessary instructional materials, it became quickly apparent that, even for students in an enriched program such as this, learning to write TMs solely from Turing's writing would be an extremely difficult task. To better acquaint students with the ideas in Turing's paper and to enable them to more easily write their own TMs, some sort of instructional support was required. We envisioned a TM simulator that was easy to use but at the same time closely tied to Turing's paper, to emphasize the specific nature of his ideas and originality of his thought.

2. PREVIOUS WORK
A number of interactive instructional tools have been developed to teach formal languages and theoretical models of computation. The idea of using a simulator for computational models is not new. For example, Curtis developed a program that simulated TMs over 40 years ago [3]. In more recent years, several software tools have been developed in an attempt to engage students by adding interactivity and experimentation into a traditional paper and pencil set of topics. The tools are written in different languages and environments with various types of interactivity, some graphical, some tabular. A common example is the TM simulator created at Princeton (http:// introcs.cs.princeton.edu/ java/74turing/).

Some of these tools focus on a single topic, such as finite automata or TMs, while others attempt to combine several related concepts into a package of tools with a common interface. Chesnevar, et.al., describe their experiences using multiple TM simulators, a state-based version created by Suzanne Skinner, and one with a graphical interface, called VisualTuring (http://sourceforge.net/projects/visualturing/) [2]. The Java Computability Toolkit (JCT) created by Robinson, et.al., provides a multiple-window environment for constructing finite automata and TMs graphically [7]. Hannay presents web-based tools with a tabular interface all written in JavaScript [5].

Educators at Duke have extended the idea of a single tool and created a collection of tools for experimenting with automata, grammars, and parsing called JFLAP [8]. Beyond TMs, JFLAP provides tools and demonstrations for several formal concepts in order to support an entire course on formal languages.

Work on other software developed for the Academy's "Great Ideas in Computer Science" course was first presented in [4]. It described the tools required for students to write programs for the original Princeton IAS machine.

3. MYTURINGTABLE

MyTuringTable contains a number of features unique to it among TM simulators, based on our desire to link it as closely as possible to the original presentation of the TM in [9]. In particular, while it shows the standard picture of a tape with symbols and a read-write head, the machine itself is *table-driven,* because Turing originally presented his "computing machines" in that form.

Programming a TM with MyTuringTable involves creating rows of a table with an arbitrarily named state, a symbol under the head, a symbol to write and a direction to move the head. Space is also provided for comments, and an editing column to add or delete rows. Machines can be saved and loaded from disk, and various buttons are provided for single-stepping forward and backward, running a specific number of steps, and resetting the machine. A slider is also available to speed up or slow down the computation.

Because Turing's paper makes use of a wide variety of symbols, MyTuringTable does as well, supporting any and all single-character symbols from the keyboard that can be drawn by Java. Smart pulldown menus are used whenever possible, for example in selecting the next state and in selecting the symbols that might appear under the head.

One particularly useful feature is the ability to aggregate sets of symbols together on a single row, similar to the shorthand notation occasionally used by Turing. Users can indicate that a transition is to be made for all symbols except a given one, or only for a specific set of symbols, and so on. An example will make this clearer.

4. USING MYTURINGTABLE TO IMPLEMENT THE FIRST TURING MACHINE

Turing's first machine, taken directly from [9], is shown below:

Configuration		*Behaviour*	
m-config.	*symbol*	*operations*	*final m-config.*
𝔟	None	$P0,\ R$	𝔠
𝔠	None	R	𝔢
𝔢	None	$P1,\ R$	𝔣
𝔣	None	R	𝔟

Figure 1, The First Turing Machine

Right away, we see the potential for confusion. *m-config* stands for machine configuration, what we would normally call a state. The phrase "final m-config" in the last column really means "next state". The operations column is clearer: "P0,R" means print a zero under the head and move the head right. This machine computes the infinite sequence "0 1 0 1…", alternating 0's and 1's between blank squares on the tape.

The initial screen of MyTuringTable is shown in Figure 2:

Note the special Start state at the top, highlighted in blue. For this machine, the symbol under the head is never checked, so we leave that entry at "any". To write a "0", we click in the "Write" column and select "new":

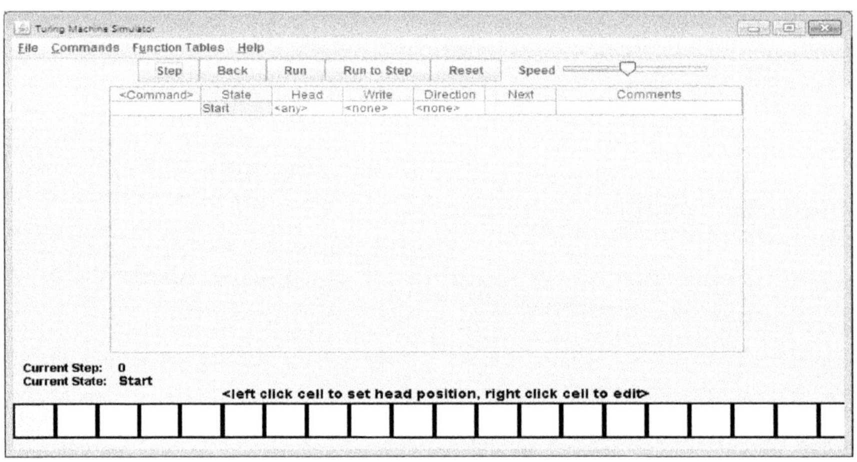

Figure 2, MyTuringTable Starting Screen

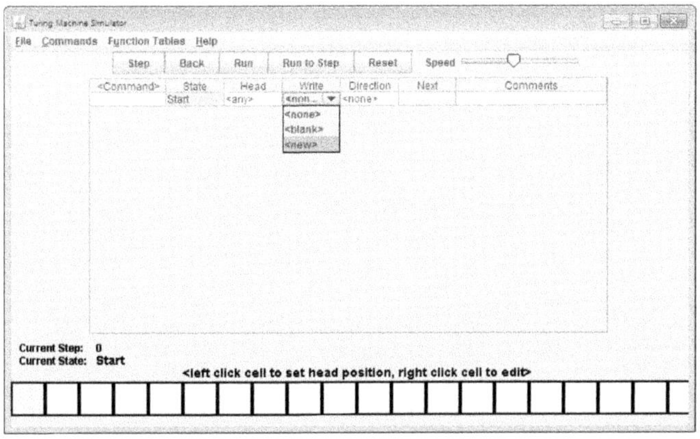

Figure 3, Choosing a Symbol

This brings up a text entry box, in which we type the symbol to be printed. Closing the box enters the new symbol in the table and creates a new row in the table in anticipation of further state entries:

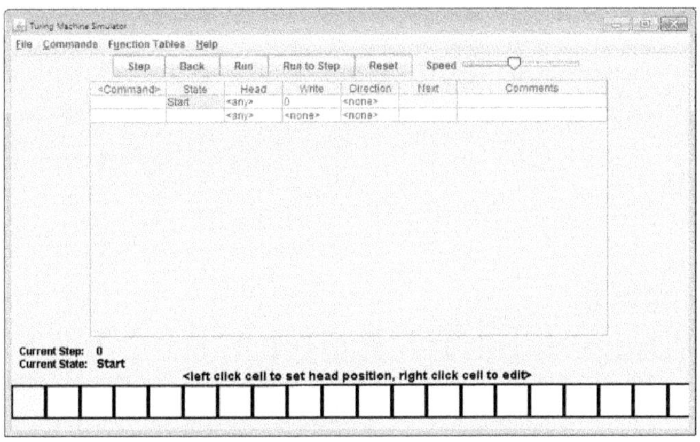

Figure 4, First Entry in the Table

Continuing to the "Direction" entry, we select either left or right from a pulldown as appropriate:

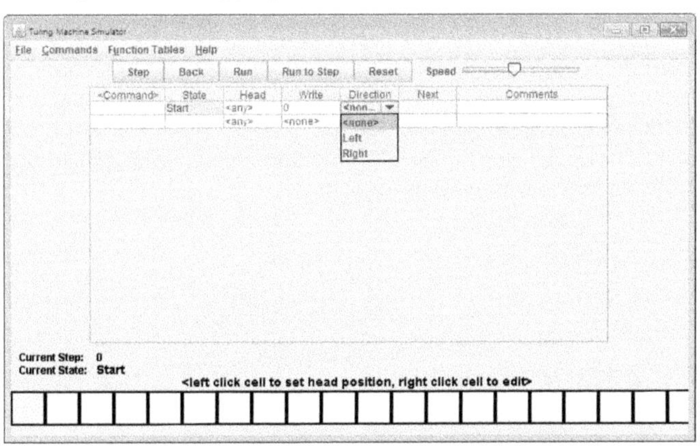

Figure 5, Selecting Direction of Head Movement

To create the "Next State" entry (highlighted in yellow), we click and choose from another pulldown. Initially, MyTuringTable knows about the special states Start and Halt, a default numbering scheme S1, S2, etc, and an option "new" if the user wishes to type in a custom state name.

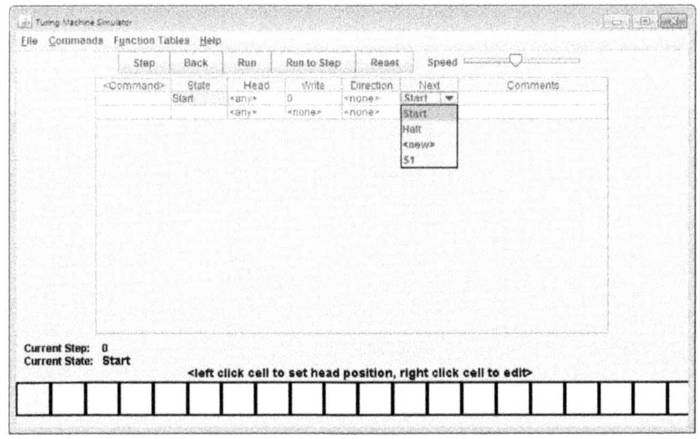

Figure 6, Selecting the Next State

Let's assume we select the default name of S1. Moving to the next row and selecting the next current state entry, the pulldown now shows possibilities of Start, S1, S2 (the next unused state in the default naming scheme), and "new". Note that "Halt" does not appear since it only belongs in the "Next State" column. Note as well that the entry for S1 in the "Next state" column is highlighted, to indicate that it does not (yet) appear anywhere in the current state column. This serves as a sanity check, as the existence of a "next state" entry without a corresponding "current state" entry may indicate an error. To allow for the possibility of testing incomplete machines, this condition is only flagged as a warning.

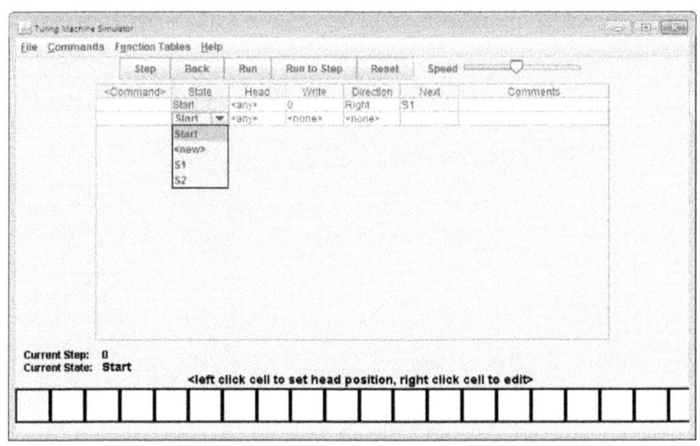

Figure 7, Pulldown for Current State

The correct state entry in this case would be S1, so we select that. This causes the highlighting of S1 to disappear, and moves to the next empty "Next State" entry:

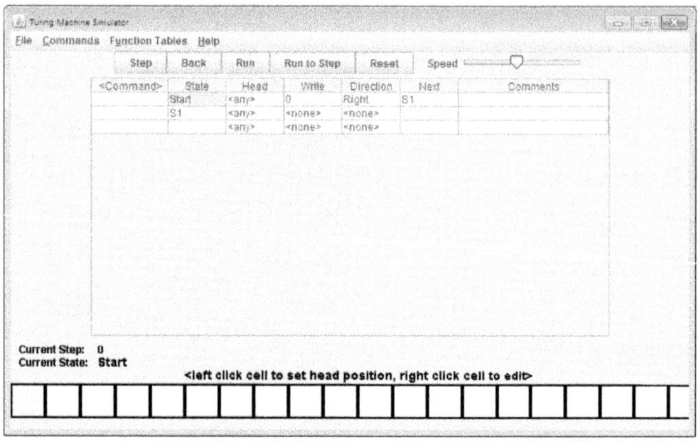

Figure 8, Current State Selected

Continuing the process a few more steps, we come to the entry where the machine must write a "1". Clicking in the "Head" column, we see the symbol "0" has been added to the pulldown.

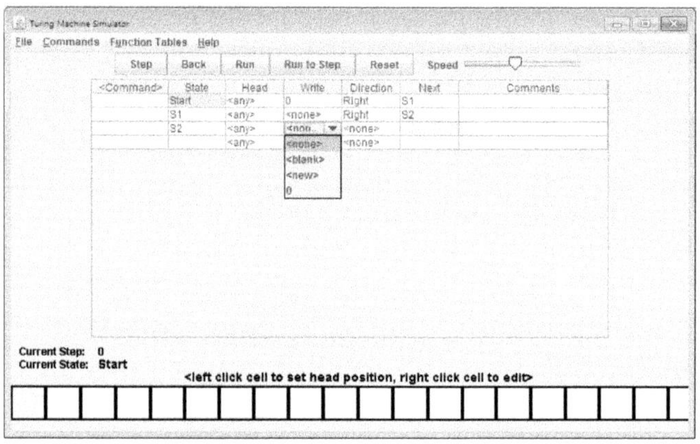

Figure 9, Writing a New Symbol

This is not the symbol we need, so once again we select "new" and type in a "1". Continuing the machine in this way gives the complete table below:

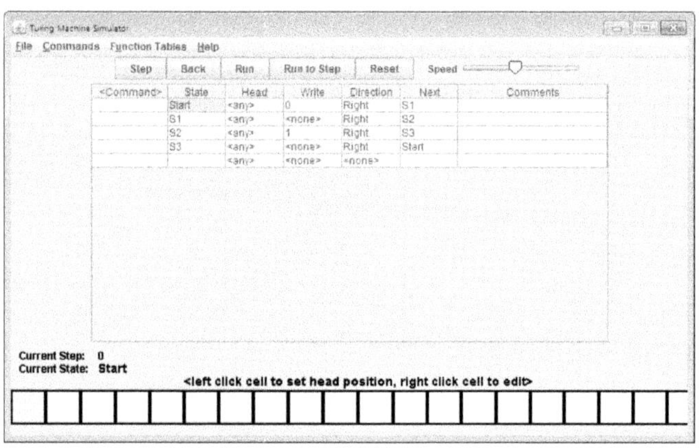

Figure 10, the First Turing Machine

Pressing "Step" causes the first row of the table to be executed. A 0 is printed under the head, it moves to the right, the next state becomes S1, and the new current state is highlighted:

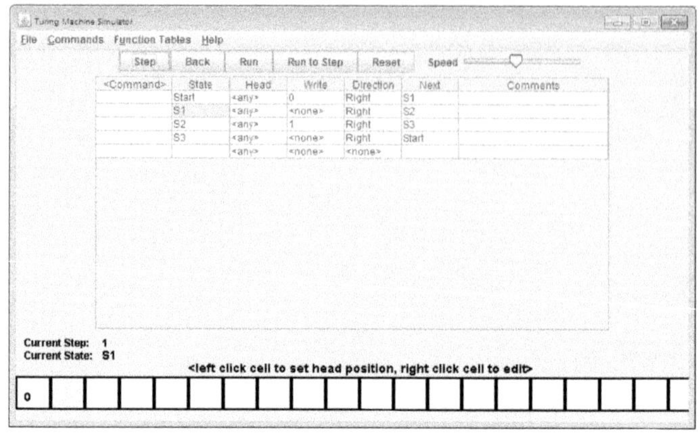

Figure 11, Single Step Computation

Pressing "Run" causes the expected sequence to appear on the tape:

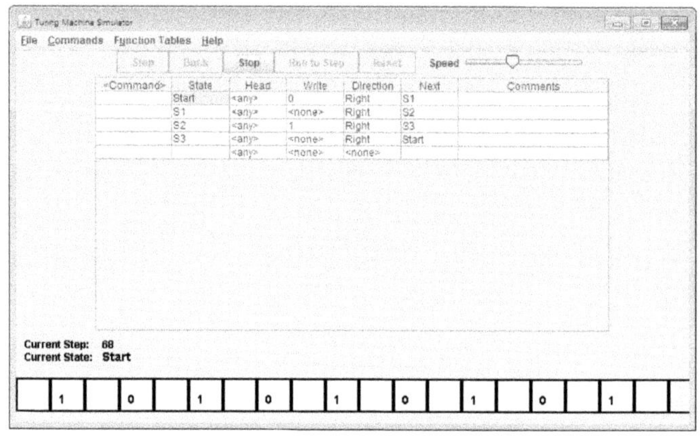

Figure 12, Running the Machine

The tape moves in the appropriate direction to keep the head on the screen. We chose to move the head as opposed to moving the tape to be as close as possible to the original description of TMs in [9].

5. A MORE COMPLEX EXAMPLE

Turing's second example illustrates considerably more features of the TM, and therefore of MyTuringTable. This example uses input, makes decisions based on the symbols under the head, and makes extensive use of shorthand notation to combine states. The table for this machine is shown below:

Configuration		*Behaviour*	
m-config.	*symbol*	*operations*	*final m-config.*
b		Pə, R, Pə, R, P0, R, R, P0, L, L	o
o	1	R, Px, L, L, L	o
	0		q
q	Any (0 or 1)	R, R	q
	None	P1, L	p
p	x	E, R	q
	ə	R	f
	None	L, L	p
f	Any	R, R	f
	None	P0, L, L	o

Figure 13, Turing's Second Machine

It produces the sequence “0010110111…” on alternate squares, with the squares in between used for bookkeeping purposes.

The first row in the table is shorthand for the states necessary to write the symbols “□□0 0” on the tape and move the head to the first “0”. While MyTuringTable does not as yet support this kind of notation, it does permit the user to edit tape cells directly (right click) and explicitly position the head (left click). Providing the designated input for the machine in Figure N produces the following:

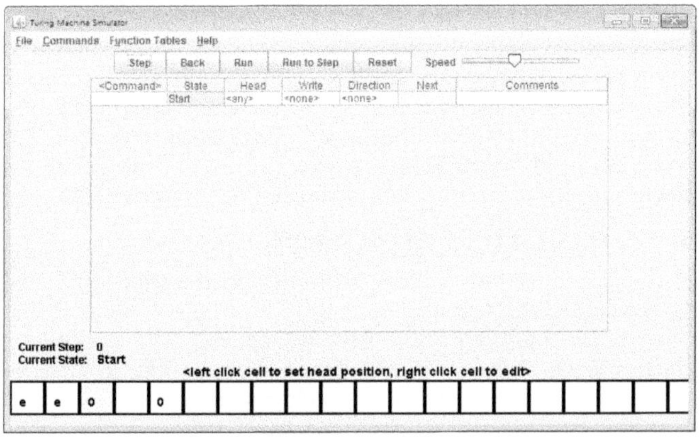

Figure 14, Setting Up the Input

Proceeding through the states from the top of the table down, we come to the entry where the transition should be triggered with either a 0 or a 1. Separate entries could of course be written for both, but in support of Turing’s notation and for similar reasons of convenience, MyTuringTable allows the user to specify a collection of symbols by selecting “Set” under the pulldown for symbols under the head:

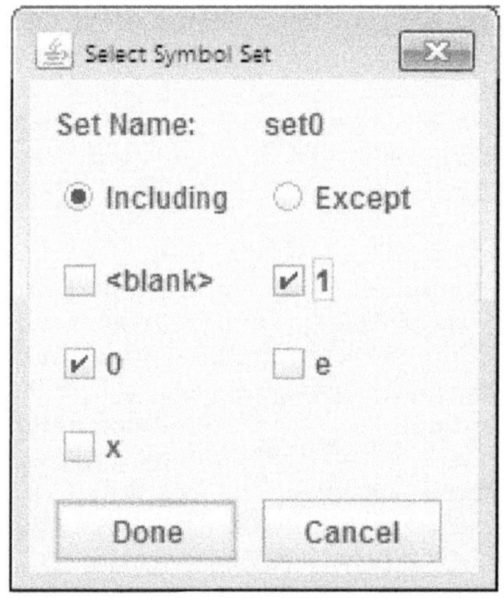

Figure 15, the Symbol Set Dialog

When this option is selected, all symbols currently in the machine are brought up in a dialog box. Individual symbols can be checked, and inclusion or exclusion selected. The use of a set for symbols under the head is indicated in the table with the word *setN,* which can be clicked on at any time to reveal its contents and to permit revisions as necessary. Sets can be reused as necessary.

The complete machine and its progress after several steps are shown below:

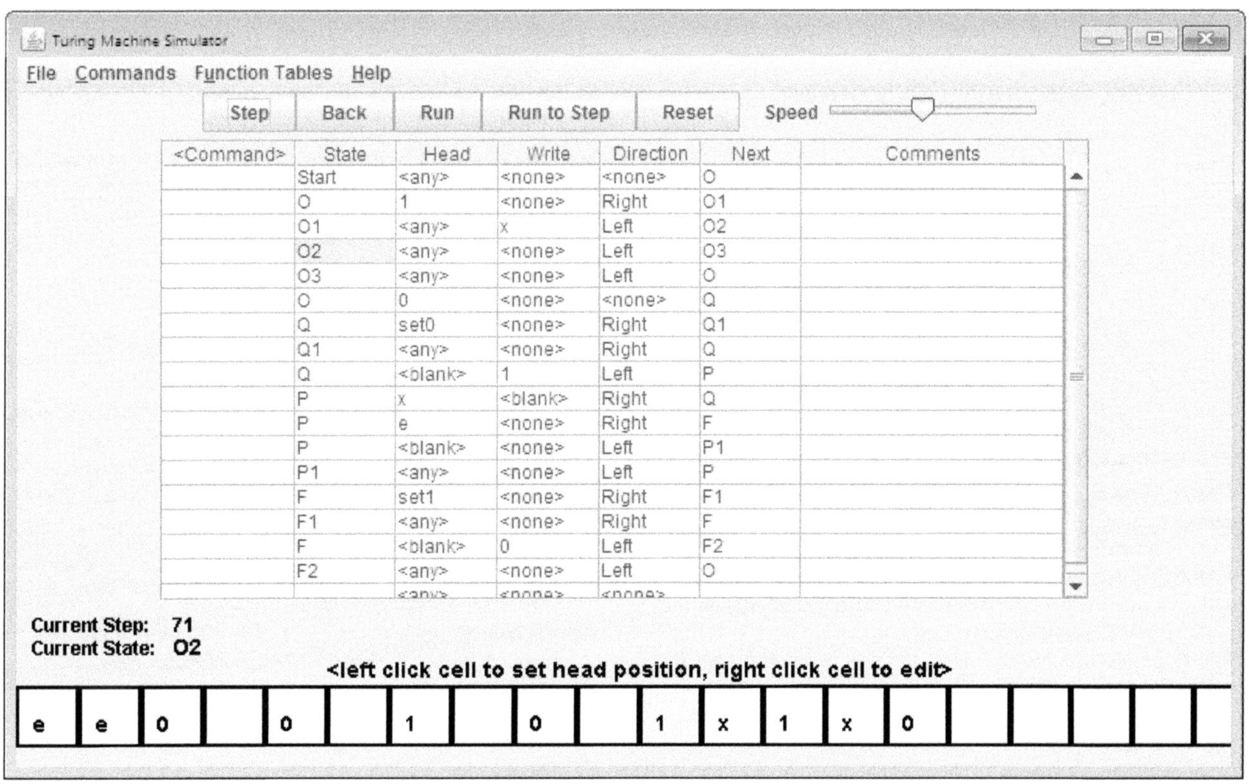

Figure 16, Turing’s Second Machine After Several Steps

Note the presence of the "x" symbols used by the machine for bookkeeping. State "F" makes use of a second set to mean "any symbols except a blank". Turing's paper uses "None" to indicate a blank, which is somewhat unclear. We permit the use of "None" in columns for consistency with Turing, but encourage the use of "blank" by students for clarity whenever possible.

6. OTHER FEATURES

To firmly establish the connection between TMs, computable numbers, and enumerability, Turing introduces the notion of a *standard form* for computing machines, in which all states are labeled as q_i along with some other simple conventions. Tables in standard form have a corresponding character string *standard description,* which in turn yields a unique *description number.* Since description numbers can be placed in one-to-one correspondence with the integers, this shows that the class of computable numbers is enumerable.

MyTuringTable includes commands to convert tables to standard form, to generate their standard description, and to calculate their description number.

7. ASSESSMENT

We now have two years' worth of data on the effectiveness of MyTuringTable, corresponding to two offerings of "Great Ideas in Computer Science". Students receive an extensive problem set requiring them to write simple TMs, ranging in complexity from the machine in Figure 1 up to a binary incrementer. We note that these students, while exceptionally motivated and talented academically, in the vast majority of cases will not be computer science majors and have never programmed before. They also have only four class sessions (about a week and a half) in which to read Turing's paper, become familiar with the concept of a TM, and complete the assignment.

Results for 44 students are shown below:

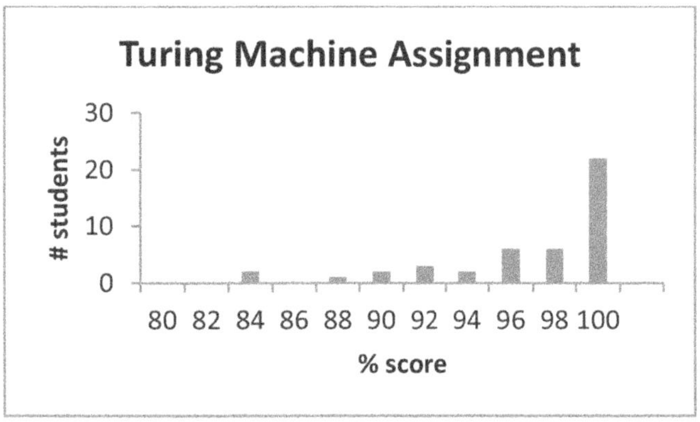

Figure 17, Student Performance in Writing Turing Machines

We see that despite having no computer science background, only one semester of college, four class sessions to spend on TMs, and no classroom resources other than Turing's paper, their teacher, and MyTuringTable, students were able to learn how to write non-trivial TMs very quickly; over half received perfect scores on the assignment. In fact, based on instructor notes from each offering, the difficulty of the assignment was increased each time, so far with little impact on student performance. All indications are students can learn to write still more complex machines within the context of the course, despite the time constraints.

8. FUTURE WORK

From the point of view of the history of computing, the most important aspect of the TM is its universality: The fact that TM can be constructed to read the description of any TM and perform its computations. To construct his universal machine, Turing makes extensive use of *function tables,* the rough equivalent of macro definitions. Function tables can be composed to produce successively more complex machines. In fact, it is effectively impossible to produce any TMs of reasonable utility without them, as their size and notation become too cumbersome.

In addition to minor tweaks and improvements in functionality, we hope to add function tables to MyTuringTable in a future release. This would significantly increase the complexity and utility of the TMs students can create. It is even conceivable that, eventually, MyTuringTable could be used to create a mathematically correct implementation of the Universal TM.

9. ACKNOWLEDGMENTS

The authors gratefully acknowledge support from the Air Force Academy Department of Computer Science in developing the Great Ideas course for the Scholars Program. The authors are grateful to the Academy Center for Cyberspace Research for its support for educational software development.

MyTuringTable is publicly available and can be downloaded from www.dinoonline.net.

10. REFERENCES

[1] Burks, A., Goldstine, H., and Von Neumann, J. 1946. "Preliminary Discussion of the Logical Design of an Electronic Computing Instrument", Report to US Army Ordnance Department.

[2] Chesñevar, C., Cobo, M., and Yurcik, W. 2003. Using theoretical computer simulators for formal languages and automata theory. *SIGCSE Bulletin* 35:2, 33-37.

[3] Curtis, M.W. 1965. A Turing Machine Simulator. *Journal of the ACM.* 12: 1, 1-13.

[4] Fagin, B. and Skrein, D. 2011. IASSim: a programmable emulator for the Princeton IAS/Von Neumann machine. *Proceedings of the 42nd ACM Technical Symposium on Computer Science Education,* 359-364.

[5] Hannay, D. 2002. Interactive tools for computation theory. *SIGCSE Bulletin* 34:4, 68-70.

[6] Lardner, D. 1834. Babbage's calculating engine. *Edinburgh Review.* Vol 59, 263-327.

[7] Robinson, M., Hamshar, J., Novillo, J. and Duchowski, A. 1999. A Java-based tool for reasoning about models of computation through simulating finite automata and Turing machines. *SIGCSE Bulletin* 31:1,105-109.

[8] Rodger, S., Wiebe, E., Lee, K.M., Morgan C., Omar K. and Su, J. 2009. Increasing engagement in automata theory with JFLAP. *SIGCSE Bulletin* 41:1,403-407.

[9] Turing, A. 1937. On computable numbers, with an application to the entscheidungsproblem. *Proceedings of the London Mathematical Society. 2:42,* 230-265.

Integrating the Teaching of Algorithmic Patterns into Computer Science Teacher Preparation Programs

Noa Ragonis
School of Education – Computer Science Department, Beit Berl College, Israel
and Department of Education in Technology and Science, Technion – IIT
noarag@beitberl.ac.il

ABSTRACT

The concept of patterns appears in the teaching of computer science in three main forms: algorithmic patterns, design patterns, and pedagogical patterns. A pattern is the identification of an abstract structure that can be further used in other, different contexts. This paper refers to algorithmic patterns as a tool that may be applied in computer science problem-solving processes, suggests an activity aimed at imparting algorithmic patterns to prospective computer science teachers, and presents part of an investigation of prospective teachers' understanding of algorithmic patterns. The main findings of the research support the inclusion of this topic in computer science teacher preparation programs, present the aspects of the concept for which the prospective teachers show meaningful understanding, and expose difficulties they experience when coping with patterns and composing recursion patterns. The focus is on abstract abilities demonstrated by computer science prospective teachers in the different stages of the activity.

Categories and Subject Descriptors

K.3.2 [**Computers and Education**]: Computer and Information Science Education – *Computer science education, Curriculum.*

General Terms

Algorithms, Management, Performance, Human Factors.

Keywords

Computer science education, computer science teacher preparation, Methods of Teaching Computer Science course, K-12 instruction, algorithmic patterns, abstraction, recursion.

1. INTRODUCTION

Computer science problem-solving processes involve different levels of abstraction that become more complicated the deeper you delve into the disciplinary knowledge. Assimilating problem-solving strategies is rooted in the teaching of computer science at any level, and pedagogical tools for teaching them are integrated into teacher preparation programs [13,19]. One common problem-solving strategy is based on the use of algorithmic patterns. The main approach of the current study is that patterns can reinforce learners' problem-solving skills that extend beyond programming, and hence must be explicitly included in teacher preparation programs. The importance of including the Methods of Teaching Computer Science course (MTCS) in computer science (CS) teacher preparation programs has come to be recognized as being very important [3,6,20,21,23]. The course aims to broaden the prospective CS teachers' pedagogical content knowledge [24] and so to set the basis for their in-school training. As presented in Section 2 – Background, it appears that, at present, there is only very minimal reference to the integration of algorithmic patterns into teacher preparation programs. One major reason for this may be the limited duration of the course as opposed to the broad spectrum of subjects it purports to impart. This paper presents an activity designed to expose this key population to algorithmic patterns and investigates its implementation in the MTCS course. The study is based on a three-stage query learning activity that was integrated into several MTCS courses and aimed to expose pre-service CS teachers to the concept. The objective of the research that accompanied the activity was to identify different levels of cognitive abstraction observed when CS prospective teachers implement the knowledge they acquire, and particularly when defining algorithmic patterns for recursion problems. The paper presents the activity and the research that investigated its implementation, and analyzes some of the research results. The activity itself can be interpreted as a pedagogical pattern but, due to space limitations, it will not be elaborated on in the current paper.

2. BACKGROUND

2.1 Patterns

Patterns are ways to describe best practices and good designs, and to capture experiences so as to enable their reuse. The concept of patterns appears within the discipline of computer science in three main different contexts: algorithmic patterns, design patterns and pedagogical patterns. *Algorithmic patterns* capture an algorithm idea that can be used when presenting solutions to other different algorithmic problems [9,18]; *design patterns* capture software structures that can be used in the implementation of software systems [1,18]; and *pedagogical patterns* capture teaching-learning activity forms that can be used in different educational situations [2,11,25]. Design patterns are used intensively in the industry and in courses offered towards CS degrees. Consequently, meaningful work has been done in the past two decades in developing pattern languages aimed at organizing principles that facilitate the use of patterns [7]. Four additional, necessary characteristics of patterns and pattern languages were offered: capture of practice, abstraction, organizing principle, and value system [7]. Nevertheless, when teaching CS, algorithmic patterns and, even more so, pedagogical patterns are not commonly used and are not usually pointed out directly. The use of algorithmic patterns is usually left to intuition and the concept is not presented explicitly so as to enable students to take full advantage of its potential.

2.2 Algorithmic Patterns

2.2.1 Algorithmic Patterns as a Problem-Solving Tool

Algorithmic patterns are generalized, elegant and efficient expert solutions for recurring algorithmic problems that appear in various algorithmic problems [4,5,8,14,15,18,22,24]. An algorithmic pattern is an abstract model of an algorithmic solution that can be adjusted or modified and integrated into the solutions of other, different problems. Patterns can appear overtly or covertly in problem texts in different contexts, and can manifest themselves directly in the problem or be entwined with other patterns. The use of algorithmic patterns, which is based on problem analysis, can assist learners in developing a solution to a given problem. The process of using algorithmic patterns starts with the recognition of the solution components and of similar problems for which solutions are already known. Then, the identified pattern (or patterns) is modified, adapted and integrated into the required solution of the given problem. In most cases, different patterns are combined to develop a new solution. The definition of a pattern traditionally contains: (a) the pattern name, which reflects its function; (b) the start point and goal; (c) the algorithm, usually written in pseudo code; and (d) clarifications and remarks, highlighting elements of the solution, giving examples of the use of pattern in concrete problems, or linking the pattern to other patterns, etc.

2.2.2 Algorithmic Patterns in Academic Studies

The literature reveals only few direct references to the use of algorithmic patterns in academic studies, either as a problem-solving strategy or as a teaching tool. Some researchers suggest pattern definitions, while others describe experiences or suggest methods for incorporating patterns into fundamental CS courses [1,5,17,18,28], into the teaching of OO programming [26] or functional programming [29]. Wallingford [26] and Ginat [10] describe the use of algorithmic patterns as a problem-solving tool for undergraduate CS students, aimed at developing the students' ability to combine different patterns into a new solution. Wallingford [26] relates to object patterns that are more similar to design patterns and dose not address algorithmic decomposition. Ginat [10] reports that the scaffolding learning approach using algorithmic patterns is suitable for students who experience difficulties in solving complex problems, since they gradually acquire the required skills which then increase their confidence and decrease their frustration.

2.2.3 Algorithmic Patterns in High School CS Studies

Resources dealing with the assimilation of systematic models of imparting problem-solving abilities based on algorithmic patterns to high school CS students are limited. Ginat, Muller and Haberman [9,12,15,16] applied this approach and investigated a model of teaching using pattern-oriented instruction (POI) as: a pedagogical approach, based on incorporating patterns into instruction design [16]; the way the POI teaching approach affects students' analogical reasoning [9]; and the uses of pattern-based problem-solving processes in teaching abstraction to novices [12]. The main reported findings were that POI is a significant tool that can serve as an organizing factor of CS courses, and that novices, who apply this learning approach, exhibit better problem-solving abilities when constructing solutions than those who do not.

2.2.4 Algorithmic Patterns in CS Teacher Training

Since the application of a pattern-based learning approach has been shown to enhance students' problem-solving skills, it seems reasonable to expect that it be used in CS teacher preparation programs. The group of researchers (Ginat et al.) that reported on using algorithmic patterns in high school CS studies went further as to assimilate the approach in in-service teacher training. Specifically, they presented a teacher guideline for pattern-based instruction [8] and described a workshop conducted for in-service teachers that addressed the topics of pattern-based instruction and pedagogical patterns [14]. Following the workshop, they reported, participating teachers shifted from programming-based instruction to problem-solving-oriented instruction. There was, however, no reference to the inclusion of the subject of algorithmic patterns in CS teacher preparation programs.

3. RESEARCH DESCRIPTION

The present research was based on a three-stage learning activity that was implemented in MTCS courses.

3.1 Research Objectives

The research objectives were:

(1) To characterize levels of abstraction that pre-service CS teachers express when implementing their new knowledge about algorithmic patterns.

(2) To explore attitudes pre-service CS teachers express, both as CS learners and as prospective CS teachers, about algorithmic patterns, the initiative to integrate the learning of the concept into CS teacher preparation programs, and the specific activity they experienced.

(3) To investigate attitudes of MTCS course lecturers about integrating the concept of algorithmic patterns into CS teacher preparation programs and about the specific activity used to implement it.

This paper presents results that relate to Research Objective No. 1.

3.2 Research Population

The research population consisted of students enrolled in MTCS courses at different academic institutions. Students enrolled in this course have already completed most of the requirements towards their CS degree. Data was collected from three groups of students from three different institutions: Group A – 10 students, Group B – 5 students, and Group C – 16 students (31 students in total). The findings, however, are not presented for each group separately for the following reasons: (a) The concept of algorithmic patterns was new to all students; (b) all interactions took place via direct e-mail exchanges between each of the students and the researcher; (c) the activity was conducted without any added, local guidelines, i.e., all instructions appeared in the activity itself; and (d) the data analyses did not reflect any meaningful difference between the three groups. Furthermore, not all students completed all three stages, and in one institution, students were allowed to submit their outcomes in pairs. Thus, data analysis refers to the students' outcomes rather than to the students themselves.

3.3 Research Data and Methodology

Research data included all learning outcomes handed in by students at the end of each of the three stages of the activity (see Table 1). Students and their instructors were also asked to reflect on the activity. The research methodology was based mainly on qualitative methods, including text analysis of students' outcomes.

Quantitative measures are also presented in some cases to support the qualitative analysis.

3.4 Research Course of Action

The activity comprised three main stages that build on each other (Table 1): Stage I – learn about algorithmic patterns and compose questions that are examples of the use of specific patterns; II – classify a collection of questions from two different aspects: (a) the correspondent pattern, and (b) the way the pattern is reflected in the question; III – write two patterns that capture the practice of recursion algorithms.

Table 1. Assignments and outcomes of the three-stage activity

Stage	Assignments and Outcomes
I	**Assignment**: Students were given a work sheet with a short explanation on the concept of algorithmic patterns and were directed to learn more about it from an internet resource [8]. The internet resource contained an explanation of the concept, different categories of algorithmic patterns, and the main algorithmic patterns in each category. Patterns were related to basic algorithmic patterns, like *find maximum value* and to patterns that involve array processing, like *shift segment of values in array*. Algorithmic patterns were presented in the structure described at the end of section 2.2.1. **Outcomes**: Students were asked to choose two patterns and for each pattern to compose a question whose solution is based on that particular pattern.
II	**Assignment**: The students' questions from Stage I (within each group of students) were collected and presented in a table. Students were then asked to elaborate on each question from two different aspects: (a) they had to match each question with a pattern or a combination of patterns that was supposed to be used in the solution of that question; (b) students were asked to classify the use of the pattern as it is manifested in the question. Categories are presented in Table 2. **Outcomes**: Each student assigned two different types of classifications to each question.
III	**Assignment**: Based on the knowledge gained in Stages I and II, students were asked to define two algorithmic patterns that relate to recursion algorithms, and to write an example of code that uses each defined pattern. **Outcomes**: Each student assigned two different types of recursion-related patterns according to the structure described at the end of section 2.2.1, including examples of their usage.

4. RESEARCH FINDINGS

Students' outcomes were analyzed from various perspectives and using different methods. The research findings are presented for each of the activity stages, focusing on the students' abstraction abilities as expressed in the activity outcomes.

4.1 Findings of Stage I – Composing Questions for Chosen Patterns

The outcomes of Stage I were analyzed according to two characteristics: (a) the ability to compose a question that matches the chosen pattern, and (b) the ability to classify the patterns used in the concrete questions.

Characteristic findings (a): All students composed questions that corresponded correctly to the pattern they chose (100% of 42 questions).

Characteristic findings (b): The students' questions were categorized into five types according to the way the pattern was reflected in the respective question. Table 2 presents the categories and frequencies with which they were used in the students' questions.

Table 2. Categories of ways patterns are reflected in the question and their frequencies of use, N*=42

Type	Category Interpretation	Frequency **	Percentage ***
1	**Direct use**: The pattern appears directly in the question. There is no "story" in the question, and the question contains straight-forward instructions as to which pattern should be used.	10	23.81%
2	**"Light story" with direct use**: The question relates to a cover situation (story) but still contains straightforward instructions as to which pattern should be used.	16	38.10%
3	**"Cover story"**: The question relates to a real situation (story), and the pattern is not presented directly in the question. To solve the question students must infer the pattern from the question text.	14	33.33%
4	**Comprehension question**: The question does not in fact present a problem to solve, but rather relates to the understanding of the underlying pattern concept.	2	4.76%
Total of Types 1-4		**N=42**	**100%**
5	**Pattern composition**: The question relates to more than one pattern.	23	54.76%

* N - total number of questions
** Frequency - the number of questions in the category type
*** Percentage - the percentage of the question category from all the questions

Type 5 category actually overlaps with Types 1-4 since they all can refer to a combination of two or more patterns.

Since the topic of study was patterns, it was reasonable to expect that the use of the pattern would not be as obvious as directly including the pattern wording in the question itself. Questions assigned to category Types 1 and 2 included direct references to the pattern and constitute 61.9% of the question collection. This finding may be interpreted as indicative of the students' lack of abstraction abilities.

Furthermore, only two questions were categorized by the researcher as *comprehension questions* that did not require any development of algorithm. For example, none of the questions gave an algorithm and asked which patterns are used in it as a basis for determining the purpose of the algorithm.

4.2 Findings of Stage II – Classify Questions According to Two Different Criteria

Stage II outcomes were also analyzed according to two measures: (a) the ability to match a suitable pattern (or patterns) to each question in the given list of questions, and (b) the ability to classify the way the pattern is used in the question according to the categorization described in Table 2. Note that the categorization of the question in Stage I, as presented in Table 2, was done by the researcher; students were asked to classify questions only in Stage II.

Characteristic findings (a): The lists of questions presented to each group of students comprised questions composed by their course mates and so were different for the three groups. Thus, the finding analyses and presentations are measured by percentage of success. Each student's outcome was scored so as to reflect the ratio between the number of questions assigned to a suitable pattern and the total number of questions. Figure 1 presents the percentage of students whose scores fall within the different 10-point grade ranges. For example, 23% of students' outcomes scored between 90 and 100. Note that since many students failed to classify questions as being composed of more than one pattern (see findings of paragraph b, below), a match was considered to be correct if at least one of the patterns involved in it was assigned to the question correctly.

Figure 1. Students' success in matching pattern types to questions

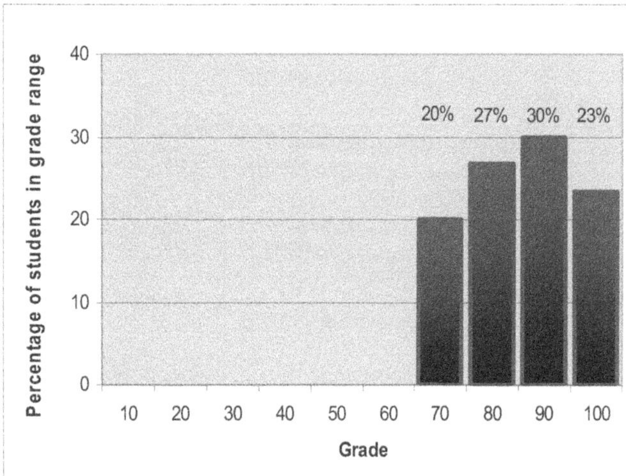

The findings reveal that students exhibited relatively high ability to match pattern types to questions. All of them scored above 60, more than half scored above 80 (53%), and the distribution between grades 60-100 was approximately normal.

Characteristic findings (b): The task of assigning a category of pattern usage to questions appears to be ambiguous. Students' answers were not consistent and were subject to explanations. Therefore, the data analyses are not presented in full and are rather discussed. Three main issues emerged from the data: (1) the distinction between *direct use* and *light story with direct use*, as well as the distinction that between *light story with direct use* and *cover story,* appear to be subject to interpretation. In some cases students clarified their decisions with explanations that illuminated their interpretation of the categorization. Such interpretations apparently led student to consider two different classifications as reasonable for a specific question and thus are not indicative of students' misunderstandings; (2) most students failed to address Type 5 – *Pattern composition*. Unexpectedly, none of the students succeeded in categorizing all of the questions in the list with respect to that category. In fact, 73% assigned this category in only less than half of the expected cases; (3) the attribute of category Type 4 - *Comprehension question*, was not originally given to the students as part of the category options. However, the worksheet's explicit guideline gave students the opportunity to define, explain and use additional categories. Only two questions composed by two different students from two different groups did not fit Types 1-4. Hence, students did not in fact have opportunity to deal with new categories. In Stage II of the activity, only 3 of the 21 students in those two groups referred to the question as belonging to a new category, 12 students ignored it and the remaining 6 did not understand the question. Thus it may be concluded that the topic of characterizing the pattern usage in questions should be further discussed and clarified in the course plenum, so that students can better integrate it into their future field work.

4.3 Findings of Stage III – Define Patterns That Relate to Recursion

Students were asked to compose patterns in order to capture the approach of recursive algorithms. The patterns were categorized according to five types with respect to the pattern's "abstract quality". Table 3 presents the interpretation of the categories and their frequency of appearance in students' patterns, and Table 4 presents examples of students' answers for each type.

Table 3. "Abstract quality" categories of patterns and frequency of their use by students, N* = 38

Type	Category Interpretation	Frequency **	Percentage ***
1	**A specific problem solution**: The defined pattern is not actually a pattern, but a specific answer to a specific question.	21	55.26%
2	**Half solution – Half pattern:** The defined pattern is in fact an answer to a specific question, and is accompanied by a general explanation of where and how it can be used.	3	7.89%
3	**Almost a pattern**: Most parts of the pattern definition are correct and generalized, but the pseudo-code contains reference to a specific assignment.	6	15.79%
4	**A pattern**: The defined pattern is correct, is generalized and does not contain reference to any specific assignment.	7	18.42%
5	**A meta-pattern**: The pattern aims to capture a global recursion structure.	1	2.63%

* N - total number of composed patterns
** Frequency - the number of questions in the category type
*** Percentage - the percentage of the question category within all the questions

The findings show that 55% of students failed to present a pattern, and in fact presented a specific algorithm. This misunderstanding could be better addressed by students if they could openly acknowledge their difficulties defining a pattern rather than presenting a specific solution to the problem. The other 45% of students exhibited an understanding of the concept even if they could not present a clear, abstract pattern.

Table 4. Examples of student-defined patterns by categories as defined in Table 3

Example of Type 1: A specific problem solution

Pattern name: factorial

Pattern start point: a positive number n

Pattern objective: return n!

factorial(n)
if (n<2) *return n*
else *return n * factorial(n-1)*

Categorization explanation: The "pattern" solves a very specific function and thus cannot serve as a pattern

Example of Type2: Half solution – Half pattern

Pattern name: prints digits of number starting from the digit on the far left

Pattern start point: a positive number n

Pattern objective: displays number's digits starting from the digit on the far left

display- digits(n)
if (n div 10 < 10) *print n*
else
display- digits(n div 10)
print (n mod 10)

Categorization explanation: The pattern solves a specific function, but can be generalized to different tasks that involve handling of elements starting with the one on the "far left".

Example of Type 3: Almost a pattern

Pattern name: computing the n-th element in a sequence

Pattern start point: a positive value n and a sequence rule

Pattern objective: return the n-th element of the sequence

sequence-n-th-element(n)
if (n = 1) *return* a_1
else *return sequence-n-th-element(n-1) + d*

Categorization explanation: The pattern computes elements of any systematic sequence. The student expressed the generalized idea for different sequences but failed to define it in the pseudo code, which relates specifically to arithmetic sequences.

Example of Type 4: A pattern

Pattern name: counting in a binary tree

Pattern start point: a binary tree

Pattern objective: return the number of nodes that match a condition

how-many-match-the-condition(tree)
if (tree is empty) *return 0*
else *if (root match the condition)*
return 1 + how-many-match-the-condition(tree left sun)
+ how-many-match-the-condition(tree right sun)
else
return *how-many-match-the-condition(tree left sun)*
+ how-many-match-the-condition(tree right sun)

Categorization explanation: The pattern fits a wide range of problems that require counting the number of nodes that fulfill a given condition.

Example of Type 5: A meta-pattern

Problem name: a problem that requires a recursion solution

Pattern start point: the problem and the required data structure

Pattern objective: a structure for recursion execution

function name(function parameters)
<optional> operations execution
condition: if halting state fulfill
then: return to previous assignation
else:
<optional> operations execution
function name(function iterated on reduced parameters)
<optional> operations execution

Categorization explanation: The student tried to capture a general recursion structure.

All students who did not present a pattern for the recursion algorithmic approach received additional guidance, via personal, written feedback, on how to improve their pattern definitions. This feedback included guiding questions that led students toward further abstraction. Students were asked to continue improving their patterns, and some of them did so. Future research will analyze the individual progression of students' level of abstraction regarding the identification of patterns for recursion.

5. DISCUSSION

The study suggests including the topic of patterns in CS teacher preparation programs due to its importance as a problem-solving tool. A three-stage activity, designed to be facilitated in the MTCS course, was presented along with analyses of students' outcomes. The analyses focused on different abstract abilities that prospective CS teachers demonstrate while self-learning about patterns through active learning. The different abstract abilities of students are manifested in the: (i) composition of questions that involve patterns of different clarity and complexity; (ii) recognition of pattern usage categories in questions; and (iii) definition of patterns. Results reveal that students have different difficulties acquiring knowledge about the abstract concept of patterns and that their varied performance indicates different levels of abstraction. This leads to the main conclusion and recommendation that the activity should be summarized in the course plenum. The course instructor should lead the discussion so that all students have the opportunity to complete and refine their understanding, in addition to direct and personal feedback on each student's outcomes. Wallingford [27] suggests a comprehensive analysis for a pattern language of recursive programming and describes seven recursion patterns that capture different recursive algorithmic ideas. Wallingford's model differs from the categories of recursion patterns offered here, which focus on five abstraction levels that appear in students' answers to the task of developing algorithmic patterns for recursion. Our research data analysis reveals that using patterns requires abstraction abilities. After students learn the concept, practice it by composing questions (Stage I), and have an opportunity to improve their understanding while classifying questions, including the way the pattern is used in a question (Stage II), it is foreseeable that they would be able to compose patterns on their own (Stage III) or at least exhibit an understanding of what is not a pattern. Our research showed clearly that this is not the case, and that the subject of patterns should be facilitated appropriately in the MTCS course. In any case, educators at all levels must be aware that *algorithmic patterns* are not merely a "concept", but rather a long-term tool to be assimilated and used throughout learning and teaching processes.

The research defined and used two pattern categorizations: (1) five categories of pattern usage in questions; and (2) five categories of pattern quality definition. Educators at all levels – high school teachers, instructors of the Methods of Teaching Computer Science courses, and CS lecturers – can benefit from those categorizations and use them in their teaching processes.

ACKNOWLEDGMENTS

I wish to thank all survey participants, instructors of the MTCS course, and students enrolled in the courses, who dedicated their time to learning and thinking. Thanks are also extended to Beit Berl College for its partial funding of this research.

5. REFERENCES

[1] Astrachan, O., Berry, G., Cox, L., and Mitchener, G. (1998). Design patterns: An essential component of CS curricula. *SIGCSE Bulletin*, 30(1), 153–160.

[2] Bergin, J. (2007). Fourteen Pedagogical Patterns, Pace University, New York, USA. http://csis.pace.edu/~bergin/PedPat1.3.html [2011, August]

[3] Blum, L. and Cortina, T.J. (2007). CS4HS: an outreach program for high school CS teachers. *ACM SIGCSE Bulletin*, 39(1), 19-23.

[4] Clancy, M.J., and Linn, M.C. (1999). Patterns and Pedagogy. *SIGCSE Bulletin 31(1)*, 37-42.

[5] East, J. P., Thomas, S.R., Wallingford, E., Beck, W., & Drake, J. (1996). Pattern-based programming instruction. *Proc. of the ASEE Annual Conference and Exposition.*

[6] EACEA P9 Eurydice (2011). *Key Data on Learning and Innovation through ICT at School in Europe.* http://eacea.ec.europa.eu/education/eurydice/documents/key_data_series/129EN.pdf [2011, August]

[7] Fincer, S. (1999). Analysis of Design: An Exploration of Patterns and Pattern Languages for Pedagogy. *Journal of Computers in Mathematics and Science Teaching: Special Issue CS-ED Research*, 18(3), 331-348.

[8] Ginat, D., Haberman, B., Cohen, D., Catz, D., Muller, O., and Menashe, E. (2001). *Patterns in computer science.* Tel-Aviv University (student and teacher guidelines, Hebrew).

[9] Ginat, D. (2004). Algorithmic patterns and the case of the sliding delta. *SIGCSE Bulletin,* 36(2), 29-33.

[10] Ginat, D. (2009). Interleaved pattern composition and scaffolded learning. *SIGCSE* Bulleting, 41(3), 109-113.

[11] Haberman, B. (2006). Pedagogical patterns – A means for communication within the CS teaching community of practice, *Computer Science Education*, 16(2), pp. 87-103.

[12] Haberman, B. and Muller, O. (2008). Teaching abstraction to novices in the course of pattern-based and ADTbased problem solving processes. *Proc. of the 2008 Frontiers in Education Conference*, T1A [1-6].

[13] Hazzan, O., Lapidot, T. and Ragonis, N. (2011). *Guide to Teaching Computer Science: An Activity-Based Approach*, Springer, UK.

[14] Muller, O., Haberman, B., and Averbuch, H. (2004). (An almost) pedagogical pattern for pattern-based problem solving instruction. *SIGCSE Bulleting*, 36(3), 102-106.

[15] Muller, O. (2005). Pattern oriented instruction and the enhancement of analogical reasoning. *Proc. of the First international Workshop on Computing Education Research.* ICER '05, 57-67.

[16] Muller, O., Ginat, D., and Haberman, B. (2007). Pattern-oriented instruction and its influence on problem decomposition and solution construction. *SIGCSE Bulleting*, 39(3), 151-155.

[17] Porter, R., and Calder, P. (2004). Patterns in learning to program – An Experiment? *Australian Computing Education Conference* (ACE2004), Dunedin, New Zealand.

[18] Proulx, V.K. (2000). Programming patterns and design patterns in the introductory computer science course. *SIGCSE Bulleting*, 32(1), 80-84.

[19] Ragonis, N. and Hazzan, O. (2009). Integrating a tutoring model into the training of prospective Computer Science teachers. *Journal of Computers in Mathematics and Science Teaching,* 28(3), 309-339.

[20] Ragonis, N., Hazzan, O. and Gal-Ezer, J. (2010). A survey of Computer Science teacher preparation programs in Israel tells us: Computer Science deserves a designated high school teacher preparation!, *Proc. f SIGCSE 2010,* 401-405.

[21] Ragonis, N., Hazzan, O. and Gal-Ezer, J. (2011). A Study on Attitudes and Emphases in Computer Science Teacher Preparation. *Proc. of SIGCSE 2011*, 559-564.

[22] Reed, D. (1999). Incorporating problem-solving patterns in CS1. *Journal of Computer Science Education*, 13(1), 6-13.

[23] Stephenson, C., Gal-Ezer, J., Haberman, B. and Verno, A. (2005). The new educational imperative: Improving high school computer science education. *Final report of the CSTA Curriculum Improvement Task Force* http://csta.acm.org/Communications/sub/DocsPresentationFiles/TCEAPres07.pdf [2011, August].

[24] Shulman, L. S. (1986). Those who understand: Knowledge growth in teaching. *Educational Teache*, 15(2), 4-14.

[25] The Pedagogical Patterns Project. Web site: http://www.pedagogicalpatterns.org/ [2011,August]

[26] Wallingford, E. (1996). Toward a first course based on object-oriented patterns. *SIGCSE Bulleting*, 28(1), 27-31.

[27] Wallingford, E. (1997). Roundabout: A pattern language for recursion programming. *Proc. of the Fourth Pattern Languages of Programs Conference.* http://hillside.net/plop/plop97/Proceedings/wallingford.pdf [2011, August]

[28] Wallingford, E. (2000). Using patterns in the CS curriculum. *Journal of Computing in Small Colleges, JCSC,* 15(5), 238-240.

[29] Wallingford, E., (2002). Functional programming patterns and their role in instruction. *Proc. of the Functional and Declarative Programming in Education Workshop, International Conference on Functional Programming*, Pittsburgh, Pennsylvania.

μPython: Non-Majors Programming from the Very First Lecture

John Aycock
Department of Computer Science
University of Calgary
2500 University Drive NW
Calgary, Alberta, Canada T2N 1N4
aycock@ucalgary.ca

ABSTRACT

We wanted to give first-year non-major students experience programming very early, right from the first lecture. To support this endeavor, we built a web-based subset of Python, called *μPython*. It allowed immediate use by students, overcame a number of practical constraints, and gave a gradual introduction and transition into the full version of Python.

Our data demonstrate that μPython has a miniscule impact on the server side, running easily on a desktop computer. A student survey shows an overwhelmingly positive response to programming in the first class; it also shows that a lot of students were using μPython to try examples from lecture, that they thought μPython was helpful for learning Python, and that they liked being able to write Python code within their browser.

Categories and Subject Descriptors

K.3.2 [**Computers and Education**]: Computer and Information Science Education—*Computer science education*; K.3.1 [**Computers and Education**]: Computer Uses in Education—*Computer-assisted instruction (CAI)*

General Terms

Experimentation, Languages, Measurement, Performance

Keywords

Non-majors, programming, Python

1. INTRODUCTION

At the University of Calgary, the Computer Science department offers a first-year course wordily called "Introduction to Computer Science for Multidisciplinary Studies I." The course is intended primarily as a service course for students in the natural sciences, but is also part of an alternate entry stream for CS majors. Students are taught how to program in Python, with an emphasis on application to scientific modeling and data processing.

The initial two times we taught the course, we noticed that some students would not touch the computer until an assignment due date neared, with the expected poor results. This makes perfect sense, assuming that students treat the course like other options, where they can simply "cram" close to a deadline or exam and achieve adequate results. No amount of professing that CS was much more like music performance, where frequent practice is essential, was able to turn the tide.

The key, we thought, was to have students program early and often. The limit of "early" is to have students programming in the very first lecture, of course – long before the first assignment, and a full week before students' first lab session. Could we have non-majors programming on Day One?

There were a number of constraints. Lectures are 50 minutes long, meaning that by the time the initial course administrivia is complete, at most 20–25 minutes remain in the first lecture. Installing software or explaining the use of an editor is thus extremely impractical. The lectures are scheduled in a traditional lecture theater without computers, although wireless Internet access is available. User accounts on the CS computers are not available until the second week of lectures; nothing could rely on the students' ability to run software in their CS account. Ideally, we also wanted something graphical for the students, not just textual, and something we could build on in later lectures.

The result, which we used for the last offering of the course, is "micro-Python" or *μPython*. We made it available for the first two weeks of class, starting from the first lecture, and presented it in class using some overheads (in Google Docs) that could be viewed using any web browser. μPython has five features that address the above constraints.

First, we assumed that almost all students now are comfortable using a web browser, and that they come equipped with (or readily have access to) devices with browsers already installed. μPython was therefore designed to work within a wide range of current browsers, with an extremely simple interface, where students enter only one Python command at a time. Being web-based, μPython could be accessed from anywhere – the lecture theater, the lab, the home, the coffee shop.

Second, μPython was designed so that it did not depend on the availability of CS user accounts, or indeed any support from technical staff. The creation of student accounts on μPython was directly under our control, and could thus

ITiCSE'12, July 3–5, 2012, Haifa, Israel.

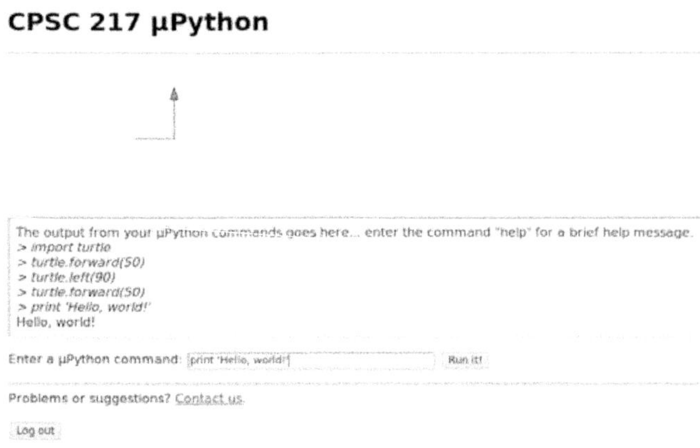

Figure 1: µPython screen shot

be updated easily and rapidly. Furthermore, µPython was lightweight enough to run on the author's desktop computer without impacting its normal use.

Third, a subset of Python was supported by µPython, allowing what students learned on µPython to transfer to the full version of Python, once labs had started and students had their CS accounts. In fact, the first lab assignment emphasized this connection by having students draw a picture in µPython then repeat the task in regular Python in their CS account. Programming topics in the first week of lectures were chosen so that they could all be run on µPython.

Fourth, drawing on past work, we supported turtle graphics [1, 14] in µPython. This is a very simple model that can be explained quickly and easily, yet students can use to develop very complex pictures. Turtle graphics are also supported in full Python, again enabling students' µPython knowledge to transfer over.

Fifth, µPython was not a reimplementation of Python, but a filter for a real Python interpreter. Students did not have to learn one version of Python, then a slightly different version; they simply saw a restricted view of the Python interpreter that they would eventually be using, again supporting a graduated transition.

Figure 1 is a screenshot of µPython in use. The top area is the canvas for turtle graphics output; the (red) triangle is the turtle. Below that is a text output window: the standard output from Python is in normal font, commands issued by the student are in italic, and error messages from the Python interpreter (not shown) are in boldface. Finally, a single-line input box is where the student enters a Python command.

Section 2 describes µPython's design and implementation. Data gathered from µPython's operation is presented and analyzed in Section 3, followed by the results of a student survey in Section 4. Related work is in Section 5, and Section 6 concludes.

2. µPython

Choosing what Python subset to support, we started with "straight-line" Python commands that would have a short, bounded execution time, i.e., loops and functions were excluded. The subset was further pared down to single-line commands, to maintain a simple interface. Potentially unsafe statements and functions were omitted too, such as `open`, `exec`, `eval`, and `__import__`. Others made no sense given the lack of standard input, e.g., `input` and `raw_input`. This left turtle graphics commands (to be rendered on the client side), `print` statements, variable assignments, and expressions. Appendix A has the final specification.

Initial experiments showed that loading and saving the variables a student may have defined to/from the Python interpreter took an imperceptibly short amount of time, assuming that this state information was small. As we did not expect students to be defining massive numbers of variables, this seemed like a reasonable design assumption.

µPython was designed to run over an unencrypted connection – HTTP rather than HTTPS – based on a risk analysis. If an adversary got access to a student's µPython account, either by guessing/stealing authentication information or hijacking a session, the worst case is that the adversary would see and be able to modify the student's variable names and values. This is not a terribly interesting or valuable ability. The other possibility is that commands being run by a student are sniffed off the network. In practice, an adversary skilled enough to perform any of these attacks is smart enough to do the first couple weeks of programming without cheating anyway.

A design decision was made to make µPython cookieless, to avoid any problems with unenabled cookies in students' browsers. Students were simply advised that refreshing the page in any way or closing the browser would log them out of µPython.

In terms of implementation, all the code was manually-written.[1] The client-side code was 360 lines of JavaScript, embedded in a smattering of HTML, and used the Raphaël JavaScript library [5] for rendering turtle graphics. The server side had 577 lines of Python code, which used the SPARK toolkit [4] for parsing; the HTTP server itself was Apache with mod_python [13] installed. µPython was tested and worked with recent versions of Internet Explorer, Firefox, Chrome, Safari, and even the browser on an iPod Touch.

Exchanges between the client and server were all JSON-encoded [6] and the client made all requests via HTTP POST. Of particular interest is the `runcmd` request that the client makes to run a µPython command, sending two strings: the session ID and the command.[2] The client gets a string in reply, prefixed by one of three characters:

- `>` Standard output from the command for client to display in output window.
- `!` Error message; client will render in boldface.
- `X` Meta-command to client, currently a turtle graphics directive to handle on the client side.

The server-side `runcmd` implementation is more involved, and is outlined in Figure 2 for session ID `sid` and command `cmd`. The session state consists of variables the student has defined, along with meta-information used internally to µPython (currently only a flag indicating whether or not the turtle module has been imported). We also attempt to identify commands that might work in full Python, but are not part of the µPython subset.

The grammar used for µPython commands (Appendix A) is actually an ambiguous grammar, but this does not matter because it is only used for filtering Python – all ambi-

[1] We had attempted use of a number of client-side and server-side frameworks, and invariably found them to be some combination of buggy and poorly documented.

[2] Arbitrary Python commands cannot be run accidentally or maliciously because filtering is done on the server side.

```
def runcmd(sid, cmd):
    validate sid
    load state for sid
    lexically analyze cmd
    parse cmd using grammar in Appendix A
    let rv be reply sent to client, initially nothing
    if lexical analysis and parsing succeeded:
        redirect standard output to a string buffer
        run cmd using Python "exec" command
        if error message or meta-command resulted:
            rv = error message or meta-command
        else:
            rv = standard output from string buffer
    else:
        try parsing cmd using Python's "parser" module
        if parsing succeeds:
            rv = error — cmd might work in full Python
        else:
            rv = error — no sense can be made of cmd
    save state for sid
    if rv is error message or standard output:
        escape any HTML characters in rv
    return rv
```

Figure 2: Pseudocode for running a μPython command

guities are resolved by the real Python interpreter underlying μPython. Also, some errors are deliberately caught. A grammar rule watching for the `cTurtle` module to be imported issues an error message to the student, to ward off the use of this nonstandard module that the students' textbook [11] employed. An error is also issued if the student enters an expression without a `print`, forcing awareness of the issue before students write full Python programs (where such expressions would quietly do nothing). Use of the `turtle` module before its import triggers a specific, instructive error message too.

3. μPython IN OPERATION

μPython was live and operational for two weeks, from January 8–22, 2011; for reference, the first lecture was January 10 and labs started the week of January 17. It ran on the author's desktop machine, an Intel Core 2 dual-processor computer at 2.66 GHz with 3 GiB of memory, running Ubuntu Linux 9.10. No software patches were applied during the two week interval so the system would be available continuously.[3]

3.1 User Accounts

We wrote a short Python script to take course registration data and convert it into the μPython password file format. The script was initially run a few hours before the first lecture, to make μPython available to all students initially registered; it was also run the day labs started in an effort to pick up any stragglers. All other (late) additions were done manually in response to individual student requests.

There was one instructor account, ten accounts for teaching assistants, and 249 student accounts. 25 of those student accounts – a full 10% – were added after the initial script run, illustrating why the ability to handle late registrants is needed when using a system early in a course.

[3]Collection and use of operational and survey data had ethics approval (University of Calgary file #6763).

Often, forgotten usernames and passwords are an operational concern. To mitigate this problem, and avoid having to distribute account information in the time-constrained first class, we used authentication information that would be known by the students and memorable: their first name, last name, and an easily-computed function of their student ID number. The function was used instead of the actual student number due to privacy concerns if it were sent in the clear. This scheme worked well, and we only had one case where a student had trouble logging in.

3.2 Usage

We gathered data on usage of μPython using system logs. There were 213 distinct users of the system (some students withdrew, which is normal for any course). 1265 successful logins happened, but only 239 logouts; fortunately, no aspect of μPython was critically dependent on a student logging out properly.

The logs contained eight instances where a command was issued from an IP address without any previous record of a login. These might indicate spoofing attempts, but are more likely cases where a student had logged in to μPython from a mobile device, moved the device to a new location, and got assigned a new IP address.

30,588 commands were run on μPython. Figure 3 shows the number of μPython commands run per minute, to illustrate the overall load pattern. The observed worst-case load was 31 commands run in a given second, and even that was rare – well below the theoretical worst case where all users would run commands simultaneously.

The class was split for administrative reasons into two back-to-back 50-minute lectures. Despite students having no warning that they may need their computers, something that could be done in the future, 245 commands were run during the first lecture time and 970 during the second. We speculate the number rose during the second lecture period as some students from the first lecture tried μPython after class. In any case, μPython was clearly used from day one.

3.3 State Size

The size of the Python state file was recorded on logout (after which the state file would be removed) or, alternately, on login if no logout had been performed – 991 were recorded in total. The largest state file recorded was 177 bytes long, but this was an anomaly. The arithmetic mean was 25 bytes ($\sigma = 13$), the median 24 bytes. This proves correct our intuition that the state size would be small.

3.4 System Impact

Qualitatively, the computer remained completely responsive during the entire time μPython was operational. Quantitatively, we gathered system statistics at one-minute intervals using `sar -urqS -n TCP 60` for the entire two-week time, yielding 20,126 data points.

Note that the computer μPython ran on was still in use by the author, although nothing more taxing than a web browser and window system were being used. One may argue that the author's use of the computer running μPython during the measurement period skews the statistics; on the contrary, this shows that μPython is lightweight and viable for use even in situations where no dedicated hardware is available.

Table 1 shows the overall system impact. The computer

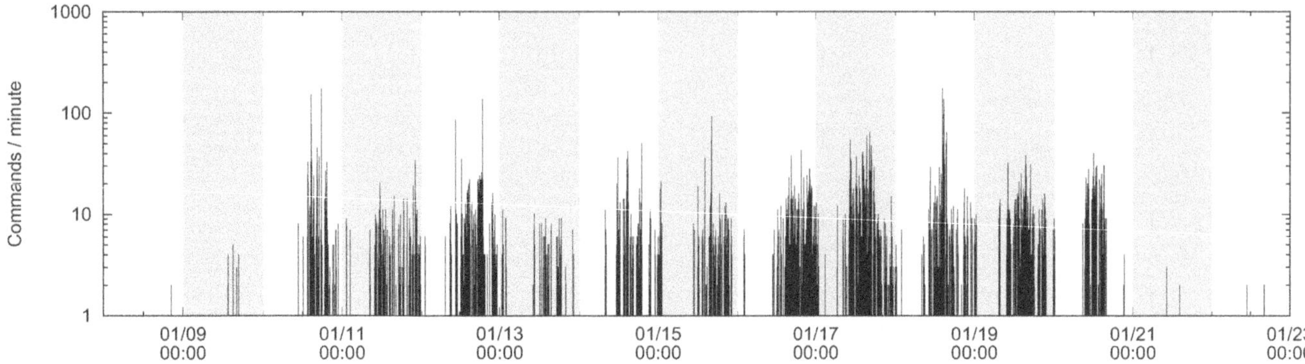

Figure 3: Commands per minute (log scale) issued on μPython

Table 1: Overall system impact, measured at 1-minute intervals

	Mean	Median	Max
Memory used	52.86%	54.87%	67.22%
Swap space used	0.01%	0.00%	10.19%
User-level CPU used	3.43%	3.28%	17.03%
System-level CPU used	0.24%	0.19%	17.72%
Load average (1 min)	0.64	0.63	1.94
TCP passive opens/s	0.02	0.0	0.63
Input segments/s	2.76	0.02	2436.59
Output segments/s	1.79	0.02	1190.20

Table 2: System impact at peak μPython load

Memory used	59.50%
Swap space used	0.00%
User-level CPU used	3.84%
System-level CPU used	0.25%
Load average (1 min)	0.74
TCP passive opens/s	0.05
Input segments/s	7.10
Output segments/s	6.63

is far from being overworked, even if the maximum values are considered. (The maximum values for TCP input and output segments were recorded just before the end of monitoring, and did not coincide with any μPython activity.)

Even looking at the one-minute interval containing the worst-case load mentioned above, where 31 commands were run in one second, the impact is negligible, as Table 2 shows.

3.5 Attack Probes

Although they are not germane to the educational value of μPython, there were some practical issues that arose during its use that must be considered when operating a system of this kind. Specifically, the computer running μPython was subject to a steady stream of probes from attackers once its firewall was changed to allow incoming TCP traffic for HTTP and `ssh` ports.[4] The first `ssh` probe came less than 12 hours after the `ssh` daemon was started on January 8; the first HTTP probe occurred *before* μPython was live, on January 7 (but after the HTTP server was running and the firewall was open).

All the probes we saw in the logs appeared to be crude script kiddie attacks, luckily, and were probing for known paths (HTTP) and username/password pairs (`ssh`). We finally moved the `ssh` server to a nonstandard port on January 12, and saw no further `ssh` probes, but we had no choice but to leave HTTP exposed.

[4]`ssh` was enabled to permit remote monitoring of μPython.

4. STUDENT SURVEY

We conducted an anonymous, in-class survey to get feedback on μPython, and got 126 responses from the 138 surveys handed out.[5] The survey was conducted in a lecture in early February, after μPython use had ended, and thus results are from lecture attendees that day. The surveys were collected by someone unaffiliated with the course to avoid influencing the results or finding out which students turned surveys in.

From the results, 90% tried μPython during the first week of classes, which was before they were required to use it in their labs. A substantial portion – almost 70% – were using μPython to try the examples shown on lecture overheads, either always (13%) or sometimes (55%).

The response to programming in the first class was overwhelmingly positive. 76%† strongly agreed or agreed with the statement 'I liked being able to write a program in the first class.' Only 6% disagreed in any way with the statement. We conjecture that this strong result occurs because μPython gives students a sense of immediate accomplishment, even though a number of students are (anecdotally) afraid of computers and computer science.

The graduated exposure to Python was also borne out. When asked if it was helpful to learn Python by first using μPython, 68% agreed or strongly agreed; only 12% disagreed in any way.

As far as the general web-based approach, our initial intuition was correct: less than 2% reported that they were uncomfortable with a web browser. 63%† liked the ability to write Python code within their browser, with 31% neutral on the matter. One obvious extension to this work would be to develop a Python-in-a-browser suitable for use throughout

[5]Sometimes the survey data were missing one response to a question. Where that occurred, the percentages for the question were based on 125 responses; we have marked those instances with a dagger (†).

the course (and we did, in fact, have a proof of concept functioning), but a notably smaller percentage – 38%† – reacted favorably to the idea, with 35% neutral.

The survey also included an open-ended set of questions, where students could write any μPython problems or suggestions. A number of comments were repeated independently on different surveys (including three separate requests to keep μPython available throughout the course!) and bear discussion.

Interface issues. The last command issued to μPython is always presented as the default, allowing editing, but some found it frustrating to delete it first, and others wanted more complete command history. This has been fixed. Others wanted the ability to enter multiple lines of code at once, perhaps an indicator of students cutting and pasting code.

Another request was the ability to save commands. Adding this would have potential security implications, as there would then be value in gaining access to another student's session, but one possible compromise might be the ability to email a record of μPython commands issued during a given session to the student.

Undo. The ability to undo a previous command is likely directed at turtle-based drawings in particular, although due to the limited μPython commands and the fact that state is reloaded for each new command, a more general undo would be possible too. For turtle commands, an undo command would be undoubtedly useful for novice programmers, and we note that Python's `turtle` module has an `undo` method [24]; this has now been added to μPython, implemented on the client side.

Differences from "full" Python. μPython is a subset of Python, but what version of Python is it a subset of? This problem is not specific to μPython. Students are routinely exposed to four different versions of Python: one in the textbook; one in the computer science labs; one in online Python documentation; one in any code excerpt they find. Apart from making students aware of the problem, which we do, there is probably little that can be done.

Limited commands. Some students mentioned the limited commands that μPython supported, and in particular asked for the ability to use constructs like loops. This would require a major architectural change, but we are looking at ways to efficiently support this as future work.

5. RELATED WORK

Papers discussing non-majors programming can be found in the literature thirty and forty years ago (e.g., [2, 12]) and continue up to the present day. Some even look at using Python as a language for non-majors, e.g., [17, 19]. To the best of our knowledge, none specifically address the challenge of programming as early as the first lecture. Two papers [7, 8] mention a Python graphics package suitable for use on 'the very first day of an introductory class' [7] but this is a nonstandard package and it is not clear how, or if, practical issues involving first-day programming (like software installation) were resolved; also, the students' reaction to the experience was not studied.

Generally, Kelleher and Pausch is a good survey of the whole "novice programming" area [9]. Our work fits best under their "simplify the language" category, but μPython is distinct from the systems they describe in that it acts as a filter for a full language underlying it.

Attempts have been made to support Python within a browser in some manner, by compiling it to or reimplementing it in JavaScript [15, 20]. These are currently fledgling projects, and do not correspond to a version of Python that students would eventually have to use. Others require specific software to be installed/used, like [10, 16, 23], and so are not usable solutions. One promising project has a full Python interpreter on the server side [3], hosted by Google, but it is not obvious how to change the version of the interpreter or how to integrate graphics. Yet another attempt has no turtle module and an interface unsuited to novices [21].

Finally, work similar to the filtering that μPython does also appears in the security area, such as JavaScript being rewritten for safe execution [18].

6. CONCLUSION AND FUTURE WORK

Our experience with μPython demonstrates that programming in the first lecture, even in a first-year non-major course, is possible, requires negligible resources, and is well-received by students. There is nothing precluding doing this in CS1 either. Now that this is established, while having students *like* something is no mean feat by itself, future work will look at the educational benefits of programming very early.

Based on student survey feedback, we will be enhancing μPython for future offerings of the course. We are also studying ways to extend the subset of Python we support without compromising the interface simplicity or the lightweight nature of μPython. The goal is to make μPython usable for a larger portion of the course. We have made modifications to make the transition to Python 3, and have moved to HTML5 for the turtle graphics implementation.

Finally, we note that the general approach, filtering a language interpreter to make an easy-to-learn subset that can later be expanded, is feasible for languages other than Python.

7. ACKNOWLEDGMENTS

The author's research is supported in part by the Natural Sciences and Engineering Research Council of Canada. Thanks to Ben Stephenson for helpful comments.

8. REFERENCES

[1] H. Abelson and A. A. diSessa. *Turtle Geometry: The Computer as a Medium for Exploring Mathematics.* MIT Press, 1980.

[2] J. M. Adams and D. H. Haden. Introductory service courses in the computer science curriculum. *ACM SIGCSE Bulletin*, 4(1):49–52, 1972.

[3] An interactive, stateful AJAX shell that runs Python code on the server. http://shell.appspot.com. Retrieved 20 December 2011.

[4] J. Aycock. Compiling little languages in Python. In *Proceedings of the 7th International Python Conference*, pages 69–77, 1998.

[5] D. Baranovskiy. Raphaël–JavaScript library. http://raphaeljs.com. Retrieved 20 December 2011.

[6] D. Crockford. The application/json media type for JavaScript object notation (JSON). RFC 4627, 2006.

[7] M. H. Goldwasser and D. Letscher. A Python graphics package for the first day and beyond. In *13th Annual SIGCSE Conference on Innovation and Technology in Computer Science Education*, page 326, 2008.

[8] M. H. Goldwasser and D. Letscher. A graphics package for the first day and beyond. In *40th SIGCSE Technical Symposium on Computer Science Education*, pages 206–210, 2009.

[9] C. Kelleher and R. Pausch. Lowering the barriers to programming: A taxonomy of programming environments and languages for novice programmers. *ACM Computing Surveys*, 37(2):83–137, 2005.

[10] B. McDonald. Python shell. Chrome Web Store. Retrieved 20 December 2011.

[11] B. N. Miller and D. L. Ranum. *Python Programming in Context*. Jones and Bartlett, 2009.

[12] W. Mitchell. Another approach to service courses. In *10th SIGCSE Technical Symposium on Computer Science Education*, pages 6–9, 1979.

[13] Mod_Python: Apache/Python integration. http://www.modpython.org. Retrieved 20 December 2011.

[14] S. Papert. *Mindstorms: Children, Computers, and Powerful Ideas*. Basic Books, 1980.

[15] Pyjamas. http://pyjs.org. Retrieved 20 December 2011.

[16] pythoninthebrowser. http://code.google.com/p/pythoninthebrowser. Retrieved 20 December 2011.

[17] A. Radenski. "Python first": A lab-based digital introduction to computer science. In *11th Annual SIGCSE Conference on Innovation and Technology in Computer Science Education*, pages 197–201, 2006.

[18] C. Reis, J. Dunagan, H. J. Wang, O. Dubrovsky, and S. Esmeir. BrowserShield: Vulnerability-driven filtering of dynamic HTML. In *7th USENIX Symposium on Operating Systems Design and Implementation*, pages 61–74, 2006.

[19] C. Shannon. Another breadth-first approach to CS I using Python. In *34th SIGCSE Technical Symposium on Computer Science Education*, pages 248–251, 2003.

[20] Skulpt. http://www.skulpt.org. Retrieved 20 December 2011.

[21] Sphere Research Labs. ideone. http://ideone.com. Retrieved 20 December 2011.

[22] tokenize – tokenizer for Python source. http://docs.python.org/library/tokenize.html. Retrieved 20 December 2011.

[23] Try Python. http://www.trypython.org. Retrieved 20 December 2011.

[24] turtle – turtle graphics for Tk. http://docs.python.org/library/turtle.html. Retrieved 20 December 2011.

APPENDIX

A. μPython SPECIFICATION

The context-free grammar used by μPython for filtering Python commands is below. The start symbol is "onestmt," and terminal symbols are shown in `typewriter` font. Lexical analysis is performed using Python's `tokenize` module [22].

```
     onestmt  ::=  stmt ENDMARKER
     onestmt  ::=  ENDMARKER
        stmt  ::=  NAME = expr
        stmt  ::=  expr
        stmt  ::=  import cTurtle
        stmt  ::=  import turtle
        stmt  ::=  turtlemodule NAME ( )
        stmt  ::=  turtlemodule NAME ( expr )
        stmt  ::=  print
        stmt  ::=  print arglist
        stmt  ::=  print arglist ,
turtlemodule  ::=  turtle .
        expr  ::=  expr op expr
        expr  ::=  ( expr )
        expr  ::=  unaryop expr
        expr  ::=  NUMBER
        expr  ::=  STRING
        expr  ::=  safename
        expr  ::=  safefunc ( )
        expr  ::=  safefunc ( arglist )
     arglist  ::=  arglist , expr
     arglist  ::=  expr
          op  ::=  **
          op  ::=  *
          op  ::=  /
          op  ::=  //
          op  ::=  %
          op  ::=  +
          op  ::=  -
          op  ::=  >>
          op  ::=  <<
          op  ::=  &
          op  ::=  |
          op  ::=  ^
          op  ::=  <
          op  ::=  >
          op  ::=  ==
          op  ::=  >=
          op  ::=  <=
          op  ::=  <>
          op  ::=  !=
          op  ::=  is
          op  ::=  is not
          op  ::=  in
          op  ::=  not in
          op  ::=  and
          op  ::=  or
     unaryop  ::=  +
     unaryop  ::=  -
     unaryop  ::=  ~
     unaryop  ::=  not
    safename  ::=  NAME
    safefunc  ::=  NAME
```

A "safe" name is a variable name the student has defined, or one of the Python values `None`, `True`, or `False`. "Safe" functions are any of the built-in Python functions: `abs`, `bin`, `bool`, `chr`, `dir`, `float`, `hex`, `int`, `len`, `long`, `oct`, `ord`, `str`, or `type`. Supported turtle commands are `reset`, `clear`, `home`, `ht` (or `hideturtle`), `st` (or `showturtle`), `pu` (or `up` or `penup`), `pd` (or `down` or `pendown`), `fd` (or `forward`), `bk` (or `back` or `backward`), `lt` (or `left`), `rt` (or `right`), and `seth` (or `setheading`).

Engaging Computer Science in Traditional Education: The ECSITE Project

Debra S. Goldberg[1] Dirk Grunwald[1] Clayton Lewis[1]

Jessica A. Feld[1] Sarah Hug[2]

[1]Department of Computer Science, University of Colorado Boulder, 430 UCB, Boulder, CO 80309, USA
[2]Alliance for Technology, Learning and Society Institute, U Colorado Boulder, Boulder, CO 80309, USA
{debra.goldberg, dirk.grunwald, clayton.lewis, jessica.feld, sarah.hug}@colorado.edu

ABSTRACT

Engaging Computer Science in Traditional Education (ECSITE, pronounced "excite") is a 5-year program that began in 2009 to bring computer science into traditional K-12 classrooms. Rather than seeking to draw students into computing courses, we bring computing into the courses that students are already taking. To date, these have included art, biology, health education, mathematics, and social studies courses as well as a Native American focus program. Middle school and high school students are introduced to computational thinking and computer science concepts including algorithms, graph theory, and simulations in interdisciplinary contexts, mirroring the ways in which computing technologies are utilized in research and industry. Teachers report that students increase their understanding and perception of computer science, and that participating K-12 teachers increase their knowledge about computing and will continue to include the computational curriculum after their involvement with ECSITE.

Categories and Subject Descriptors

K.3.2 [**Computers and Education**]: Computer and Information Science Education– *Computer science education.*

General Terms: Human Factors.

Keywords: K-12 instruction, computational thinking, interdisciplinary curriculum

1. INTRODUCTION

Computing, computational thinking and computer science are transforming society, but this has not been communicated clearly to the public. In particular, while K-12 students and teachers know the ways our lives change with the use of technology, they are largely unaware of the current ubiquity of computing and the revolutionary impact that computing has had on different areas of science. There are two ways this is apparent in the USA and other countries around the world – the underproduction of students with computing related majors [1, 2, 7, 14] and, equally important, the limited integration of computing into existing curricula (see [3, 5, 8, 16] for exceptions).

ITiCSE'12, July 3–5, 2012, Haifa, Israel.

The "computer science image problem" constrains the number and "types" of students who enroll in K-12 computing courses—in the US, K-12 computing classrooms are often full of white males of middle to high socioeconomic status [9, 10, 15]. Furthermore, as technological devices become ubiquitous in K-12 schools, computing education is often limited in K-12 to using rather than creating new technologies [4, 9]. This lack of interest in and access to high quality computational academic content is particularly troubling for fields important to our future.

Rather than seeking to draw students into computing courses in school, to address these issues we bring computing into the courses that students are already taking. Increasingly, "Computer Science" is an interdisciplinary field that encompasses researchers with backgrounds in biology, physics, psychology, applied math and other disciplines. Because this conceptual "cyberinfrastructure" has become essential in so many fields, importing a meaningful exposure to computing into students' studies in other fields can be done without compromising existing learning goals. For example, biology students can learn about the role of computing in understanding newly-sequenced genes in a way that enhances, not diminishes, their grasp of genetics.

The Engaging Computer Science in Traditional Education (ECSITE) Program is a 5-year program that began in 2009 to bring computer science into traditional K-12 classrooms. It is one of the first of the 400 programs funded by the U.S. National Science Foundation (NSF) GK-12 program to focus on computer science. An important goal of the NSF GK-12 program and ECSITE is to train future scientists to communicate effectively with the public about their contribution to science, but in this paper we focus on the K-12 programming. We are working with middle schools and high schools in three local school districts. We have partnered with other organizations to bring computer science to a diverse audience, and have provided mentors for high school students to engage in computer science research. Against this background, the goals of our project include:

- To inform K-12 students about the value of computing in fields they see as important to their further education, and expose them to areas of current research.
- To prepare K-12 teachers to communicate to their students the connections between computing and their fields of instruction.
- To develop and distribute materials that can be used to replicate our program in other settings.

2. THE ECSITE MODEL

Bringing computational content into traditional, existing courses is challenging because these courses typically must address a number of standards or requirements specified by the school district and/or school. Our model involves having our ECSITE fellows (computer science graduate students) work closely with classroom teachers to identify required elements of the curriculum that would benefit from a computational approach. The goal is to deliver required content in a way that improves student understanding *and* exposes students to methods and techniques of computer science. Often, the lesson simultaneously addresses National Educational Technology Standards for students (NETS•S) developed by the International Society for Technology Education (ISTE) for supporting technological fluency.

Each fellow is paired with one teacher, and meets with the teacher weekly to discuss curriculum development. Content teams typically include two or more teacher-fellow pairs and one university faculty member (see Figure 1). Each fellow attends some of the teacher's classes regularly, getting to know the students and describing how classroom topics pertain to computer science. The fellows in the team meet with each other weekly, and the supervising faculty member meets with the fellows monthly to discuss content-related issues and challenges in developing interdisciplinary curriculum. The teachers are kept informed about the activities in the other teachers' classrooms primarily through their fellow. The entire team meets to plan together three or four times during the school year. The ECSITE fellow delivers new content with teacher assistance. For example, the fellow may lead a discussion or activity while the teacher manages classroom behavior and circulates around the room.

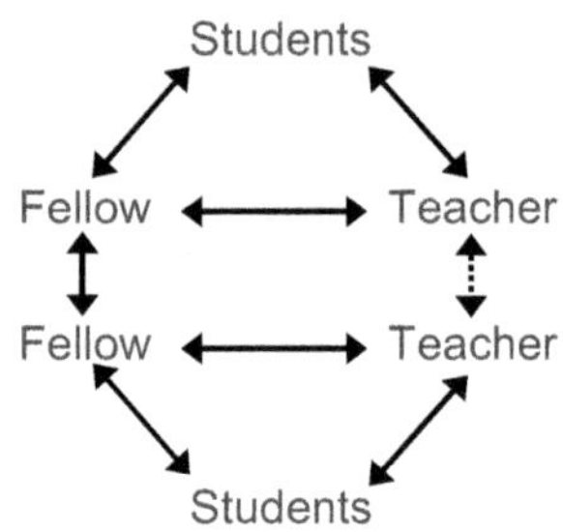

Figure 1. The ECSITE Model. Two teachers and their students are loosely coupled via their ECSITE fellows (Computer Science graduate students).

One important consideration in the development of ECSITE units is that we wish to include *computer science-based activities that allow students to reason about computational concepts* rather than lessons that simply showcase how computation is used in the chosen disciplines. The difference is subtle, but important for fellows' knowledge to be best utilized and shared with teachers and K-12 students. Providing opportunities for K-12 students to develop computational thinking and problem solving may be vital to their understanding of what computer scientists do.

3. CURRICULUM DEVELOPED

In each class, content is delivered either as one large unit (about five class periods spread over several weeks), typically in the second semester, or multiple small units (single class period) that may begin during the first semester. Here we give a sample of the units that have been developed by ECSITE.

3.1 Art

In a middle school multimedia course, an ECSITE fellow provided an in depth examination of Dreamweaver, Fireworks, Photoshop, and Illustrator to provide a deeper understanding of their purpose and the methods by which to use them. A month-long unit leveraged the software package Illustrator to teach students about vector graphics, to design their own vector images, and allow students to figure out how such images can be translated into laser cut objects. A third unit utilized the Arduino Lilypad, a small microcontroller designed for incorporation in soft, wearable computing projects. For a month students learned about microcontrollers, sensors, actuators, programming, and more while creating their own interactive plush puppets. This collaboration not only provided students with a non-traditional look at computer science applications, but also exposed a less obvious technical audience, students enrolled in an art class, to current university research projects, programming, and a creative, hands-on, engineering experience.

3.2 Biology

3.2.1 AP/IB Biology and Biotechnology

New curriculum includes an introduction to the concept of algorithms, an overview of the Basic Local Alignment Search Tool (BLAST) algorithm used to compare DNA sequences, and methods for building phylogenetic trees. These units were taught in an Advanced Placement (AP) Biology class, a combined AP and International Baccalaureate (IB) standard level (SL) Biology class, and an upper-level high school Biotechnology class.

Students were introduced to the vocabulary of algorithms by formulating algorithms for every-day tasks. Then they participated in a "living computer" algorithm: each student was given a numbered instruction that represented one step in the algorithm, performed their step, and handed the "output" to the next student in line until the final step was reached. Finally, students wrote algorithms to create Punnett squares, diagrams to predict the outcome of a cross-breed given the genotypes of the parents.

In the second lesson, DNA sequence comparison was explained in terms of word search puzzles containing progressively more error types. Students were asked to think about how they solve such puzzles (see Figure 2[1]). A "perfect" word search simulates the problem of finding an identical (unmutated) gene in another genome, and a "wrong key" word search simulates finding a gene with single nucleotide polymorphism (SNP) mutations. A "ditz" puzzle with wrong, missing, and inserted text (as if the person writing the word search forgot what he was doing and started typing in a shopping list) simulates the gene-finding problem in a genome that contains both SNP and insertion/deletion (indel) mutations. Students then obtained the DNA sequence for a gene associated with a disease and used BLAST to find similar genes in humans and other species. Students

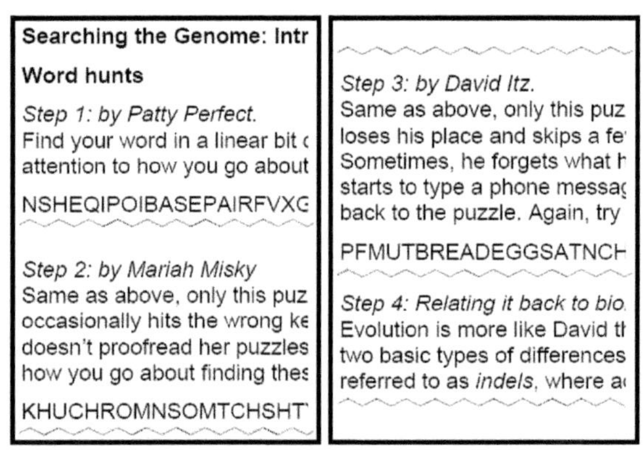

Figure 2. Advanced biology worksheet. Finding similar gene sequences to a query sequence is likened to finding words in a word search puzzle with errors. © DS Goldberg[1]

---

[1] Gallagher, et al. (2011). PLoS Computational Biology

then answered questions about the BLAST results to connect it to their understanding of genetics.

In the third lesson, students built phylogenetic trees from pairwise BLAST similarity scores for related genes from eight different species. Students were given different metrics for determining distance between clusters of genes: some students used the distance between the closest two points in the clusters (single linkage), some used the furthest two points in the clusters (complete linkage), and others used the average distance between all points in the clusters (average linkage). Students compared their results to find that seemingly minor differences in algorithm implementation can result in different biological conclusions, thus learning that biologists need to understand algorithmic details of the computational tools they use, even if they aren't themselves developing the tools.

3.2.2 Middle School Life Sciences

For an epidemiology simulation unit, students first act out how diseases spread and how they affect different age groups (kids, adults, elderly). In the second part, students used a computer simulation to implement vaccination strategies and see in what proportions age groups should be vaccinated to best reduce death and the spread of a generic disease.

In another school, data analysis activities were added to the curriculum and the number of long-term science projects were increased. These activities helped make quantitative data collection and analysis a regular part of the curriculum. Data analysis was added to activities where students build their own pond and grow "fast plants" (*Brassica rapa*) in the Science and Technology Concepts (STC) curriculum. In both cases, students made quantitative measurements for 6-8 weeks and had to graph their results. For the pond activity, about 10-20 percent of students did not understand the concept of graphing and that their measurements could be presented in this way. For the plant activity, this number was down to 1-2 percent. In the plant activity, students measured water use over time and graphed the relationship between plant growth and water use. This activity is based on the fellow's research optimizing residential landscape design for water conservation. Later activities repeated this process, and included sensors to show the value of computers in data collection. Following the long-term laboratory experiences, students in the long-term science course performed better on an assessment of research design and measurement error than did a control group classroom in the same middle school [Hoenigman, Donovan, Hug, under review].

3.3 Health Education

In our local school district, health education classes teach students the value of maintaining "overall" wellness in all areas of their lives, and is required for all 10th graders, making this an ideal course for reaching all students regardless of personal interests and aptitudes. We introduced three units into the health curriculum: how to search for authoritative health resources, aggregating data sources (e.g. Google maps mashup to identify the effects of food deserts on a population's health), and understanding the role of networks on health and wellness (e.g. flu transmission or gossip spreading).

To teach students how to effectively find health information and conduct research for projects online, students were provided information about "queries" and instruction on how search engines work. Students learned tips and tricks for doing good searches using Google or other search engines in order to find relevant, trustworthy information, and how to sift through complex scientific papers to find useful information.

For a unit about sexually transmitted infections (STIs), students learned the computational concept of graphs and networks. In one exercise, students in a group were each given a pile of candy of a different color, and then traded candies to simulate the exchange of sexual fluids during sexual contact, recording the names of their trade partners. After trading, students were informed that one of the colors represented Chlamydia, and had to find the sources of infection for another group using a graph representation of the recorded trades.

3.4 Social Studies

3.4.1 Geography

In our target schools, ECSITE fellows developed similar units on geography in both a middle school and a high school. Lessons were developed to show how computational cartography can explain social factors related to geography. Examples of these activities include exploring the Gapminder and WorldMapper.org website to understand how computation can be used to distort maps to better illustrate data (*e.g.* rates of disease or poverty). The students were introduced to computer visualizations of large amounts of data, as well as the topics of correlation and causation. They were then asked to come up with ideas for interesting graphs they would like to see, make predictions of what the graphs would look like based on their knowledge of history, geography, and other social science knowledge, and then discuss why the graph was or was not as they predicted. Students also developed an algorithm to identify "primate cities" (cities that are at least twice as large as the second largest city in its country).

3.4.2 Social and Civil Society

Social studies lessons were taught in high schools. Students participated in two modules, *The Pace of Cities* and *Variables of Hate*. In the first lesson, students monitored walking speed in their daily activities as a metaphor for the pace of life in their city, and compared that to experiences of students reported by the WNYC RadioLab report of the same name. Students used automated pace monitoring systems developed using Arduino computers and learned about the physics and computation of sensors, statistics, experimental design and data analysis. In *Variables of Hate*, students used data from the Southern Poverty Law Center Hate Map to understand hate groups, where they exist and why. Students used data from the US Census and the NY Times Mapping America tool to draw correlations of the factors that influence hate groups.

3.4.3 Civics and Government

ECSITE fellows frequently contribute to classroom discussions, adding topics related to computer science and citizenship, political information, and anonymous speech, to mention a few. The United States' "Founding Fathers" unit, which is a common lecture across our local K-12 educational setting, now asks students to use computational thinking to determine which decisions should utilize the wisdom of the crowds and which should be left to representatives. After learning Condorcet's Jury Theorem (which argues about the relative probability of a given group reaching a correct decision) the class is divided into two teams to play chess; one team votes on each move and the other team elects a representative to play. Another traditional US Government lesson about the Federalist Papers now involves a discussion of the importance of anonymous speech and an exercise explaining Tor and WikiLeaks. Finally, an encryption exercise helps to explain the Copyright Act's limitations on the First Amendment to the US constitution. These additions to the curriculum allow the fellow to discuss topics relevant to her work in Internet law while bringing a better understanding of computer science into the K-12 system. At the same time, the lessons gain relevance as they are revised to reflect 18th century ideas in a 21st century world.

4. OTHER ACTIVITIES

4.1 After-school and Summer Classes

ECSITE fellows led or helped with a variety of computer-related clubs. These included a FIRST Robotics team, a programming club, and an electronics club for high school students, as well as a craft technology club at an elementary school. These clubs incorporated curricula developed for classes as well as some unique content. On the robotics team, students learned fundamental computational thinking principles in order to accomplish a required task. In the electronics club, after deciphering a schematic diagram and locating the correct electronic components to build a simple circuit, students learned the simpler Arduino platform and were able to implement projects of their own design. The craft technology club combined computer science, craft, and engineering with the research of an ECSITE fellow.

An ECSITE fellow and teacher developed and implemented a two week summer program titled "Native Science Behind the Displays" in the Denver Museum of Nature and Science (DMNS; see Figure 3). In this program, ten Native American high school students were taught 21st Century computation skills to improve one of the museum's exhibits on Native American culture. Videos of past projects that involved Native American students were shown, so students could see other Native Americans in higher educational activities and their accomplishments.

Figure 3. Students in the *Native Science Behind the Displays* program. © DMNS

Another ECSITE fellow taught a class at the Colorado Association of Black Professional Engineers and Scientists (CABPES). CABPES is a non-profit organization dedicated to encouraging and helping African-American and underrepresented youth to pursue career choices in the engineering and applied science professions. Students created a simple Virus simulation like the curriculum lesson described above, a "Frogger" video game, and a "Space Invaders" game. Ultimately, students in CABPES created a science simulation in addition to creating a final game of their own. The students did everything from creating Frogger to the Sims to creating science simulations.

4.2 Mentoring

A number of high-ability high school students have been mentored one on one by ECSITE fellows. A mentor is able to expose these students to an area of research, often rekindling or increasing the student's passion for academic matters [6, 13].

Some students helped with a fellow's research without defining their own project. One fellow with expertise in graph theory and another with expertise in privacy considerations teamed up to help two students study the social network of their high school. Another high school student was able to produce original research in computational biology.

Some mentored high school students were previously very successful with computer science, but needed a mentor to go the next step. This was the case for one student who won the state science fair for a hydraulic modeling project, but asked for help to be able to include climate data in the following year. Another mentored student was a recipient of a computing award for women high school students. This student is now learning how to create tools for health improvement.

Many high-ability students get little challenge in their schools [6, 11], and some are quite discouraged about the prospect of continued academics [12]. Two such students that were referred to us by a high school counselor because they are very capable but unmotivated and despondent are now working on projects in game design and mobile applications.

5. RESULTS

Program evaluation is conducted by the Alliance for Technology, Learning and Society (ATLAS) Institute's Assessment & Research Center, which has extensive experience in examining student research experiences in CS, multi-institutional partnerships, and computing education. Evaluators use a mixed method design to triangulate information from multiple sources regarding fellow communication of computing concepts with teachers and students, and fellow and teacher perceptions of the impact of fellows in classrooms as well as teacher comfort and ability in incorporating the lessons into their regular curriculum after the fellow departs. Program outcomes and impacts were measured through analyses of surveys of ECSITE fellows and teachers. This evidence is supplemented with qualitative data analysis of survey items and interviews with fellows and teachers.

5.1 Impact on Students

ECSITE fellows reported a number of perceived impacts to students. They believe students now have more understanding of computer science and the important role that computers and computer science play in everyday life, often in unexpected ways. By discussing topics relevant to their research as well as introducing computing curriculum, fellows report they have improved students' impression of computing as well as educated students on computational thinking. Fellows have reported that their interaction with students has opened up discussions about careers in computer science as well as graduate school in general. In various settings, ECSITE fellows were able to form meaningful connections with students, and chat about options for college and the benefits of higher education, especially in the field of computer science.

In a geometry class, all but one of the women enrolled in an "Engineering Day for Women" put on by the University of Colorado Boulder. Many of the students interested in Robotics club were not initially interested in computer science, but after using computational thinking to program the robot to perform various tasks they were much more interested in pursuing a career in computer science.

Without the opportunity for direct student surveys, we view teacher perspectives as perhaps the most compelling for describing ECSITE student benefits[2], as the teacher has the most information about his or her students, and may best be able to ascertain differences among students with exposure to fellows and those without the same exposure. In the 2010-2011 school year, the surveyed teachers unanimously report that participation in ECSITE has not only increased students' understanding and perception of computer science, but has also improved students' problem-solving skills (see Figure 4). This indicates that ECSITE has met some of the key goals of the program, and also that there have been other positive outcomes as well.

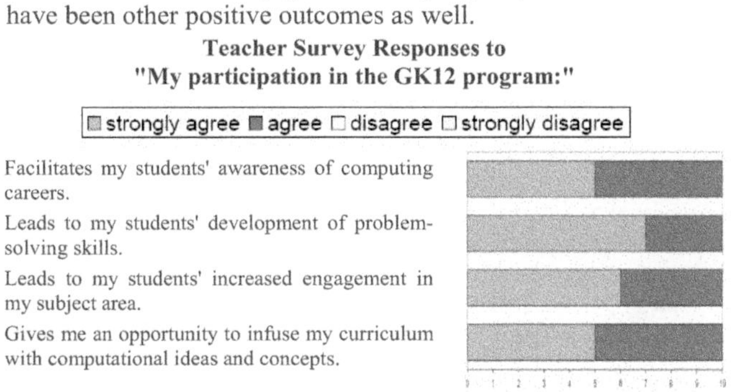

Figure 4. Teacher description of ECSITE fellows' impact on students.

Before the end of the second year, every fellow had an opportunity to discuss his or her research with K-12 students. These and other informal discussions between fellows and students seem to have had a significant impact on many students. A common theme emerging from evaluation data of teachers' responses is the impression that students are learning about computer science as a discipline. The fact that many K-12 students are learning about computing in their general education classes rather than in an elective computer science course ensures that the fellows are not "preaching to the choir", and instead reach a wide spectrum of students. The quote below is an example of this theme.

> *Students inquire about the fellow's studies and [research] projects. He has presented a few times on what computer science is and how he uses it, which has captured student interest.*

Another theme emerging from teacher responses regarding benefits for K-12 students is that their middle and high school students are becoming more interested in and knowledgeable about higher education options. The quote below is one example of this theme.

> *Students are discussing higher education with more of a sense that it is possible for them. They now freely use terms like master's degrees and PhD.*

5.2 Impact on Teachers

The longevity of activities and lessons depends on the teachers' attitudes and understanding, and there are promising indications of sustainability of this curriculum. All teachers interviewed said they planned to incorporate the computing lessons that they collaboratively created through ECSITE into their curricula in subsequent semesters, indicating teacher-fellow partnerships produced useful, sustainable content. Teachers' responses indicate that fellows expose teachers to new resources and tools, and inspire teachers to add computing into their curriculum. Teachers report development of new areas of interest and exploration of new activities with their fellow in the ECSITE program.

Because most ECSITE teachers are experts in other fields (e.g., social studies, civics, multimedia, and biology), they have increased opportunities to learn from their fellows about computer science. Every teacher indicated an increase in his or her knowledge regarding technology/computing education. All teachers interviewed agreed or strongly agreed with the following statements. "My participation in the GK12 program…"

- *Provides me with content knowledge about computing.*
- *Leads to the improvement of my technology skills and knowledge.*
- *Gives me an opportunity to expand my thinking about technology education.*
- *Exposes me to different resources and tools (e.g., websites, programs, or software).*
- *Gives me the opportunity to explore new teaching activities.*
- *Gives me the opportunity to explore new teaching content.*
- *Helps strengthen my curriculum development skills.*

An AP biology teacher described the content knowledge she gained in the program with regard to biology at the intersection of computing:

> *I learned a lot about how they program BLAST. In future years I can now explain BLAST. Also, the lesson gave me more ideas about career paths that I can talk about with students. [ECSITE lessons] got several students interested in the programming piece of biology.*

In order to persist in sharing ECSITE materials with students, it is important for teacher collaborators to value computer science as a discipline and career choice for their students. Survey results suggest that participating teachers recognize the importance of computer science not only in terms of the future career pursuits of their students but also the significant impact computer science can have in the classroom. All eight teachers surveyed believe that there are jobs in computing-related fields and all eight feel that their students can find jobs that combine their personal interests with computing. Overall, teachers shared a positive view on job prospects in the computing field. Teachers were less positive about their students' interest in computing careers, with only five out of eight teachers indicating that their students are interested in computing careers (63%). Exposing K-12 students as well as their teachers to a variety of computing careers can help inform teachers and students about new career fields that may incorporate their current interests with technology.

---

[2] Budget constraints and school district policies make direct surveys or interviews of students prohibitive in this case.

6. DISCUSSION

We have indications that the ECSITE curriculum can be easily sustained and disseminated. All ECSITE teachers plan to continue teaching the computational content, and some have brought it to other teachers in their school, who have also taught it in subsequent years. While we do not yet have any examples of teachers not involved in the project who incorporated ECSITE content, several fellows brought content developed with one teacher to a classroom in another school, spending only a day or two with this teacher, and these teachers indicated that they will incorporate the curriculum independently in the future. We plan to produce detailed guidelines to determine if teachers can make use of the curriculum without the intensive interactions that were part of the initial explorative stage.

We strive to be flexible so that our program is responsive to the differing needs of teachers and content areas. This led to diverse fellow experiences, with vastly different classroom roles when not delivering new content, and differing numbers and lengths of units developed. Not all went smoothly. Some units frustrated or failed to engage students. Each instance was evaluated by the teacher-fellow pair and often also by the entire content team, and the unit was either revised for future classes or dropped. For example, in one Advanced Placement Biology class (where end-of-year test success leads to college course credit), students felt that the computational content was a distraction from test preparation. As a consequence, this curriculum was revised to stay strictly closer to required course material, and this required coverage will be emphasized in future presentations.

Because our evaluations to date are based exclusively on the impressions of teachers and fellows, and not directly on what the students think, our evaluation is biased toward the curriculum designers rather than the overall experience of the students. While we hope to obtain funding to evaluate student experience directly, the external evaluator's formal classroom observations that focus on inquiry based learning principles, including student engagement, have supported the teachers' and fellows' reports.

7. CONCLUSION

As the need for computing expertise swells and the number of aspiring computer scientists stays relatively stagnant in countries around the world, the field must reach out to a larger audience of capable but currently uninterested young people. Promoting computer science at the intersections of other sciences and humanities highlights pathways into computing that resonate with students' current interests (e.g., health fields, social sciences) and prepares students for computing in interdisciplinary settings. An additional benefit is that ECSITE lessons can reach a much larger and more diverse K-12 population by meeting them in the courses they take out of interest or school mandate.

Initial results from ECSITE indicate teacher transformation and increased interest in computing topics, as well as increased K-12 student engagement in the hybrid subject matter. As we continue to investigate the benefits of GK12 ECSITE, we will track curriculum longevity in K-12 classrooms in which they develop as well as the spread of curricular units, lessons, and activities to novel settings. While interdisciplinary lessons will not replace a rigorous K-12 computer science curriculum, the lessons may plant seeds of interest and understanding of the possibilities that exist in the dynamic field of computer science.

8. ACKNOWLEDGMENTS

Our thanks to the fellows, teachers, administrators, and students involved with ECSITE. We thank A Goldberg for a critical reading of this manuscript and anonymous reviewers for helpful suggestions. This material is based upon work supported by the National Science Foundation under Grant No. DGE 0841423.

9. REFERENCES

[1] (2008). National Center for Education Statistics (NCES), Digest of Education Statistics, 2007 (NCES 2008-022), U.S. Department of Education, Institute of Educational Sciences, Washington, DC.

[2] Aspray, W., Mayadas, F. and Vardi, M.Y. (eds.) (2006). Globalization and offshoring of software: A report of the ACM job migration task force. Association for Computing Machinery. Available: http://www.acm.org/globalizationreport/.

[3] Eglash, R., Bennett, A., O'donnell, C., Jennings, S. and Cintorino, M. (2006). Culturally Situated Design Tools: Ethnocomputing from Field Site to Classroom. AMERICAN ANTHROPOLOGIST,, 108 (2). 347-362.

[4] Ericson, B., Guzdial, M. and Biggers, M., Improving secondary CS education: progress and problems. in Proceedings of the 38th SIGCSE technical symposium on Computer science education (SIGCSE), (2007).

[5] Freudenthal, E., Ogrey, A. and Gonzalez, R.Q., Work in progress — Eliciting integrated understandings of high school STEM curricula through programming in Frontiers in Education Conference (FIE), (Washington, DC, 2010).

[6] Gilman, B. (2008). Challenging Highly Gifted Learners. Prufrock Press, Waco, TX.

[7] Lacey, T. and Wright, B. (2009). Occupational employment projections to 2018. Monthly Labor Review, 132 (11).

[8] Lin, C.-C., Zhang, M., Beck, B. and Olsen, G., Embedding computer science concepts in K-12 science curricula. in Proceedings of the 40th ACM technical symposium on Computer science education (SIGCSE), (2009).

[9] Margolis, J. (2008). Stuck in the shallow end: Education, race, and computing. MIT Press, Cambridge, MA.

[10] Margolis, J. and Fisher, A. (2002). Unlocking the clubhouse: Women in computing. MIT Press, Cambridge, MA.

[11] Rimm, S.B. (2008). Why bright kids get poor grades and what you can do about it. Great Potential Press.

[12] Robertson, E. (1991). Neglected dropouts: The gifted and talented. Equity & Excellence in Education, 25 (1). 62-73.

[13] Ruf, D.L. (2005). Losing Our Minds: Gifted Children Left Behind. Great Potential Press.

[14] Schroeder, U., A Bouquet of Measures to Promote Computer Science in Middle & High Schools. in the 16th Annual SIGCSE Conference on Innovation and Technology in Computer Science Education (ITiCSE), (Darmstadt, Germany, 2011), ACM

[15] Weinberger, C.J. (2004). Just ask! Why surveyed women did not pursue IT courses or careers. IEEE Technology and Society Magazine, 23 (2). 28-35.

[16] Wolz, U., Stone, M., Pulimood, S.M. and Pearson, K., 2010. Computational thinking via interactive journalism in middle school. in Proceedings of the 41st ACM technical symposium on Computer science education (SIGCSE).

A Systematic Approach to Teaching Abstraction and Mathematical Modeling

Charles T. Cook[†], Svetlana Drachova[†], Jason O. Hallstrom[†], Joseph Hollingsworth[‡], David P. Jacobs[†], Joan Krone[♯], Murali Sitaraman[†]
[†]School of Computing, Clemson University
[‡]Computer Science, Indiana University Southeast
[♯]Mathematics and Computer Science, Denison Southeast
[†]{ctcook,sdracho,jasonoh,dpj,murali}@cs.clemson.edu,
[‡]jholly@ius.edu, [♯]krone@denison.edu

ABSTRACT

The need for undergraduate CS students to create and understand mathematical abstractions is clear, yet these skills are rarely taught in a systematic manner, if they are taught at all. This paper presents a systematic approach to teaching abstraction using rigorous mathematical models and a web-based reasoning environment. It contains a series of representative examples with varying levels of sophistication to make it possible to teach the ideas in a variety of courses, such as introductory programming, data structures, and software engineering. We also present results from our experimentation with these ideas over a 3-year period at our institution in a required course that introduces object-based software development, following CS2.

Categories and Subject Descriptors

K.3.2 [**Computers and Education**]: Computer and Information Science Education—*Computer science education, Curriculum*

General Terms

Design, Documentation, Reliability

Keywords

Abstraction, mathematical modeling, interface specifications, contract programming, formal methods

1. INTRODUCTION

The development community has seen a shift from systems spanning hundreds of thousands of lines of code, to systems spanning hundreds of millions of lines of code. The Software Engineering Institute's Ultra-Large-Scale Systems study projects a future of highly interconnected systems spanning *billions* of lines of code [10]. The days of the lone developer with end-to-end system knowledge are gone. Software size and complexity are quickly outstripping the capabilities of a single mind. The next generation of software practitioners must be trained in the principles and skills used to partition and isolate software complexity, and to communicate integration requirements across large teams.

The most fundamental tool for dealing with complexity in any domain is *abstraction*, the process of developing a simplified model of a more complex phenomenon. In the context of software development, the result is a conceptual model that explains how a software component is used and how it behaves. This model serves two purposes. First, it hides implementation details and other system components irrelevant to component clients. Developers needn't be concerned with the underlying representations or how they interact with other system components. Second, the model provides a logical partition that gives structure to the development process and enables parallel work to proceed. Put simply, abstraction is the cornerstone of any development paradigm that hopes to tackle large-scale software projects in a cost-effective manner.

Unfortunately, abstraction is rarely taught in a systematic fashion that provides deep coverage of the requisite principles and skills. Even when it is introduced, the rigor of presentation rarely matches the rigor of formal languages students learn in writing programs. In this paper, we focus on reconciling this coverage gap. We describe an approach to teaching software abstraction based on rigorous mathematical models of software behavior. Students are introduced to a small set of mathematical concepts that are sufficiently expressive to capture the behavior of an interesting set of software components. The state space of each component is represented in terms of these concepts, and the component operations are described by pre-conditions and post-conditions expressed in terms of this state. Within two or three lectures, students are capable of understanding mathematically rigorous specifications — and even developing specifications of their own. We present the approach through representative examples and present evidence of its effectiveness over a three year period in a sophomore-level object-oriented development course taught in Java.

2. RELATED WORK

The importance of abstraction in science and engineering has been well understood for many years [9]. The central role that it plays in managing complexity has not been lost on the computing community [7, 14]. The starting point for our work is the supposition that students who understand abstraction are more likely to succeed in computer science.

ITiCSE'12, July 3–5, 2012, Haifa, Israel.

Among the few systematic efforts to teach abstraction is the work of Bucci et al. [2] and Long et al. [8]. The authors emphasize the important role abstraction plays in distinguishing the "client" view of a software component from its implementation. The work of Sooriamurthi [13] aims to teach the basic principles of abstraction to beginning programmers. Unlike these prior efforts, the approach presented here is adaptable and incremental and may be used in introductory or later courses. The emphasis is on teaching abstraction through a series of mathematical models, as well as in assessing specifically how well students understand abstraction using these models.

3. APPROACH

Our instructional approach is guided by the supposition that abstraction and modeling are fundamental skills, which, if taught early, benefit students throughout the curriculum and beyond. Accordingly, we make few assumptions about the target audience. We assume only limited exposure to three areas: (*i*) basic discrete structures, including sets and tuples; (*ii*) boolean logic, including the primitive connectives; and (*iii*) basic imperative programming. The approach is applicable to most CS2- and CS3-level courses, and with some additional background coverage, may even be suitable for a CS1-level course.

We begin by highlighting the observation that if students have ever written a successful program, they must have already practiced abstraction and modeling at some level. Consider, for example, the following simple code fragment:

```
Integer i = ... ;
Integer j = sum(i, 5);
System.out.println(j);
```

When asked to explain what this code fragment does, most students immediately respond that it prints the value of `i` plus `5`. To arrive at this answer, students rely on their knowledge of integer arithmetic; they implicitly model the `Integer` data type as a mathematical integer. However, even for simple types like `Integer`, implicit modeling can lead to reasoning difficulties. Students' initial explanations for the short code fragment are often incorrect; few account for `max_int`, the largest possible `Integer`. At this point in the discussion we remind our students that a computer doesn't really store mathematical integers; it stores some representation of that concept. The example is trivial, but illustrates a powerful lesson: Informal, implicit models of software behavior are often insufficient; they tend to break down at the boundaries and introduce reasoning errors.

The implicit model can be used as a starting point to explicitly model the code fragment using annotations. The particular syntax used is not critical. Here we use a variation of the RESOLVE specification notation [12]:

```
// type Integer is modeled by: integer
// constraint:  min_int <= self <= max_int
// initial value: 0
```

The specification fragment documents the model for `Integer`. It specifies that all `Integer` variables may be thought of as mathematical integers. The associated `constraint` makes the integer bounds explicit. The `self` keyword refers to an arbitrary `Integer` value; all such values must be between `min_int` and `max_int`, platform-dependent constants. Finally, the `initial value` clause indicates that every `Integer` will be initialized to zero at the point of declaration.

Models of this type support a modest improvement in students' ability to reason about software by making implicit assumptions explicit. Students must also have a precise understanding of how the operations within their software influence these models. There are two aspects to consider. First, students must understand their client obligations, or "pre-conditions" — state requirements expressed in terms of the relevant mathematical models, which must be satisfied before an operation is called. Second, students must understand the guarantees provided by each function, or "post-conditions" — state assertions that an operation guarantees will hold upon termination, assuming its pre-conditions were met. We reiterate to our students that even if this is their first exposure to "contract programming" terminology, the ideas should be familiar. We are only making explicit a process that students must be using at some level if they are able to write correct software. Consider a potential specification for the `sum()` operation in our example:

```
public static Integer sum(Integer i, Integer j);
// requires: (min_int <= (i + j)) and
//           ((i + j) <= max_int)
// ensures:  (i = #i) and (j = #j) and
//           sum() = (i + j)
```

The `requires` and `ensures` clauses specify the function's pre-condition and post-condition, respectively. Each is represented by a mathematical assertion defined in terms of the `Integer` model. The pre-condition must evaluate to *true* before the function is called, and the post-condition must evaluate to *true* after the function returns. The pre-condition states that the sum of the integers `i` and `j` must be within the bounds of the model (otherwise, presumably, there could be an integer overflow within the operation implementation). The post-condition is a conjunctive assertion consisting of three clauses. The first two state that the arguments to `sum()` will be unchanged. The # notation is used in post-conditions to refer to the pre-conditional values of variables. The final clause states that the return value of `sum()` will be equal to the sum of `i` and `j`.

Equipped with the formal model of `Integer` and the specification of `sum()`, students are now able to reason precisely about the code fragment. They quickly identify a potential problem: If `i` is assigned the value of `max_int`, the pre-condition of `sum()` could be violated. If it is, there are no guarantees! An interesting exercise asks students how the code fragment might be modified to safeguard against an illegal call to `sum()` when `i` is sufficiently large. An interesting follow-up exercise asks how the specification of `sum()` might be modified to allow arbitrary argument values. These exercises reinforce the relationship between specifications and implementations and demonstrate that software correctness is about ensuring a match between them.

These exercises can be reinforced by making use of a web-based component development and reasoning environment we have developed for use in introductory and advanced undergraduate computing courses. The environment supports the RESOLVE specification notation, a subset of which can be rendered as simple Java code [3]. Consider, for example, the code and specifications for swapping two integers shown in Figure 1.

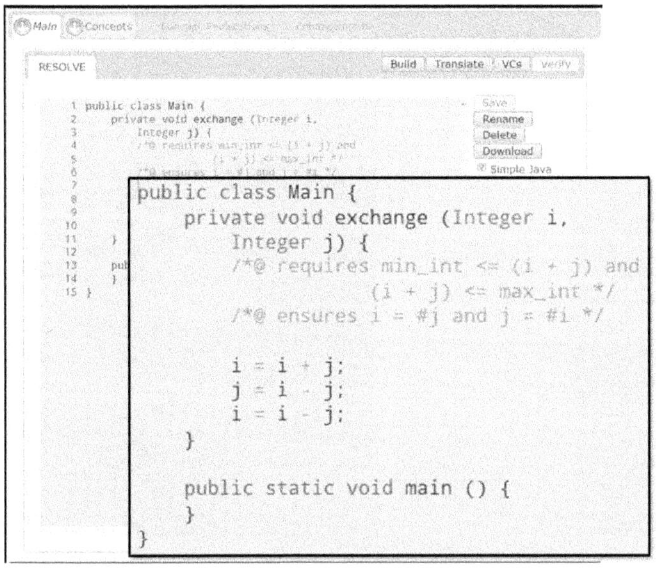

Figure 1: Web Environment (Integer Swap)

Students can also use the environment to generate *verification conditions* (VCs) for their programs. Each VC consists of a goal and a set of facts. The goal corresponds to a proof obligation raised by a program statement; it must be proven using the mathematical facts known to be true at that point [5]. Not surprisingly, VCs provide deep insight into code correctness. To reinforce this, the web environment highlights program statements that raise proof obligations, using a VC icon. Hovering the mouse over an icon expands the generated VC, reinforcing the connection between the code and the mathematical specifications. In Figure 2, for example, the VC raised by the addition of `i` and `j` (line 8) is shown. Note that the VC's goal matches the pre-condition of the addition operation (which is handled by `sum()`. This VC is easily proven using facts 6 and 7, given by the pre-condition of `exchange()`.

Figure 3 shows a portion of the VCs raised by the post-condition of `exchange()`. Both of the goals shown can be easily proven using the available facts. The goals are generated via substitution on the operation's post-condition.

3.1 Real World Modeling Examples

We have also found it useful to consider "real world" examples. In one exercise, students are asked to develop the formal model of a traffic light. A number of possible solutions typically arise, including a triple of booleans, a pair of booleans, and an integer. Each requires a constraint to limit the state space to three possibilities (i.e., red, green, yellow). Whereas the boolean triple requires a constraint that only one of the booleans be true, the integer version must restrict the value to be within 1 and 3. Once a model is identified, the specifications for needed operations, such as `turnRed()` or `isRed()`, can be developed. This exercise serves as a catalyst for a discussion of what it means for one model to be "better" than another. It also raises the point that the desired operations can influence model selection.

Another useful discussion considers the modeling space. For example, a suitable model for the state of a paper weight might simply be a real number; but depending on the problem, the dimensions may also need to be captured.

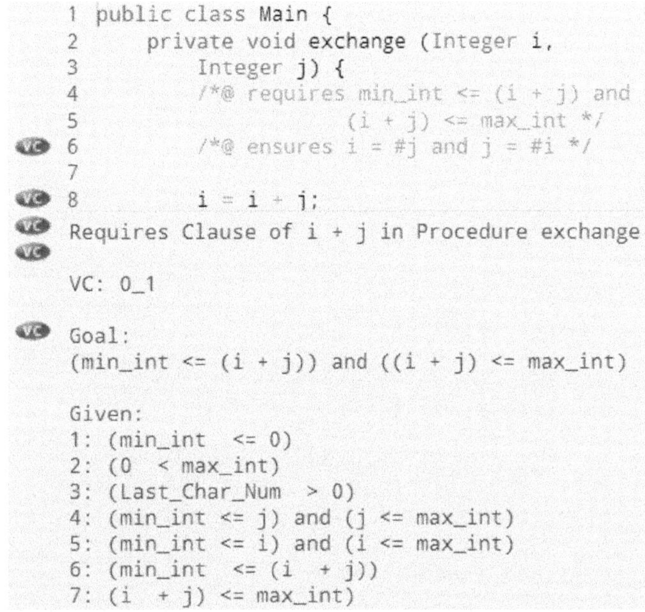

Figure 2: Generated VCs (pre-condition of `sum()`)

3.2 Component Examples

We now focus on data structures found in standard class libraries (e.g., stacks, queues, lists)[1] often introduced in sophomore-level courses. The development environment provides a drop-down system to navigate (and modify) many of these (and other) models, as well as to create new models, as shown in Figure 4; see [4].

Consider, for example, attempting to document the interface of a simple stack component (i.e., with `push()`, `pop()`, `length()`, and `clear()`). It is useful to ask students to work in pairs and pretend that one member of the pair has never heard of a stack. The other member is tasked with explaining how the data structure works without assuming a particular implementation and without using any self-references (e.g., "A `stack` is like a stack of ...", "`push()` pushes an element..."). This is surprisingly difficult. Students' descriptions are likely to be both verbose and ambiguous. The exercise demonstrates that natural languages are a poor choice for documenting software operations, which exhibit precise requirements and behaviors.

To specify the `Stack` interface, a mathematical model must be selected that captures the state space in a way that is descriptive to developers and supports the documentation of pre-conditions and post-conditions. A mathematical *string* is a good choice. (A useful discussion asks why a *set* would be a bad choice.) A string over some set of elements —the same notion as Σ^* over an alphabet Σ used in formal languages courses— is an ordered sequence of elements expressed as a comma-separated list enclosed within angle brackets. The string $< 4, 6 >$, for example, contains two integers; $<>$ denotes the empty string. This model is a convenient first example because, in addition to the notion of an empty string, there are only two string operations, *length* and *concatenation*. The length operator is unary, represented as vertical bars placed on either side of

[1]These models are not meant to be novel; variants are routinely found in the specification literature.

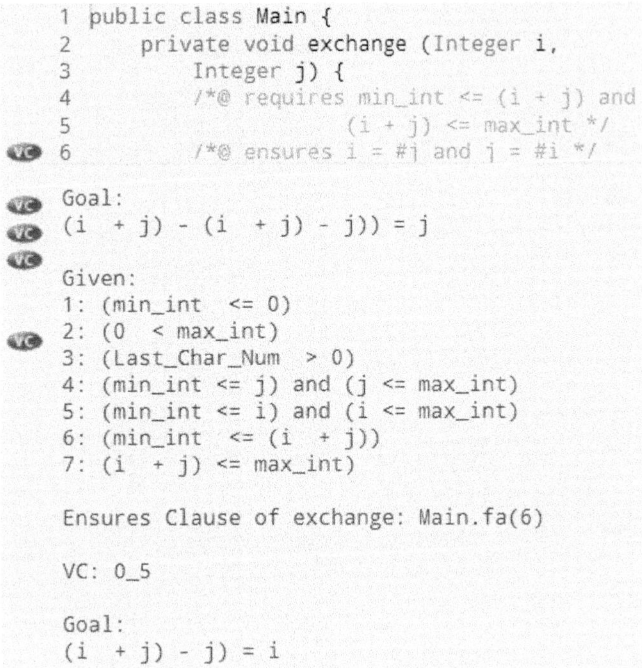

Figure 3: Generated VCs (post-con. of `exchange()`**)**

the argument. The expression $| < 4,6 > |$, for example, evaluates to 2. Concatenation, the second operator, is *binary*, represented by a lower case o between its arguments. The expression $< 4,6 > o < 1 >$, for example, yields the string, $< 4,6,1 >$[2].

Students are now prepared to consider the `Stack` model:

```
public interface Stack<E> {
// Stack<E> is modeled by: string of E
// initial value: <>
```

The `modeled by` clause states that each `stack` should be thought of as a mathematical string of `E`, where `E` is a generic type parameter; it could be anything[3]. The `initial value` clause states that all `stacks` are initially empty.

Now consider the interface operations, beginning with the specification of `push()`:

```
void push(E e);
// requires: true
// preserves: e
// ensures: self = <e> o #self
```

The pre-condition is trivial; it indicates that `push()` does not impose any calling requirements. (In later examples, we will omit such pre-conditions by eliding the `requires` clause.) The `preserves` clause states that the argument `e` will not be modified by the operation. Finally, the post-condition states that upon return, the final value of the `stack` (i.e., its *post-conditional value*) will be equal to the string containing the argument `e` concatenated with the value of the `stack` prior to the call (i.e., its *pre-conditional value*). Note that the `self` keyword is analogous to `this` in popular languages like Java and C^{++}. It refers to the "current" instance. The key difference is that `self` refers to the instance's model. Note that a new type of specification has been introduced — the preserves statement. The listed elements will not be changed; this is a short-hand for omitting post-conditions of the form, **ensures:** `e = #e`.

[2]It is important to make clear that these mathematical strings are quite different from the `String` type in Java.

[3]The generic parameter `E` will eventually be replaced with an actual programming type, say `Integer`. This type will also be specified mathematically. When its mathematical type is substituted for `E` in the `modeled by` clause, a *fully instantiated* model will result, namely, a string of integers.

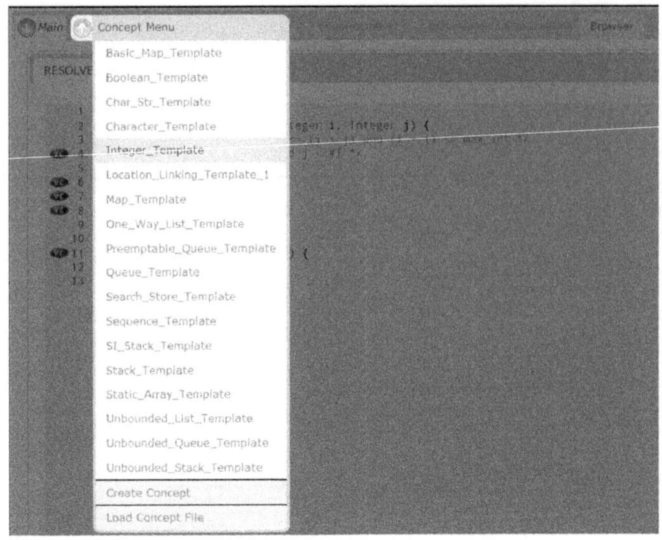

Figure 4: Additional IDE Interface Specifications

Next consider the specification of `pop()`:

```
E pop();
// requires: |self| > 0
// ensures: #self = <pop()> o self
```

The pre-condition states that `pop()` may not be called on an empty `stack`. (A useful exercise asks students to develop an alternative expression of this requirement — e.g., `self != <>`.) The post-condition states that the string containing the element returned by the function, concatenated with the post-conditional value of the `stack` will be equal to the `stack`'s pre-conditional value. (The specifications of `length()` and `clear()` are easily expressed using the same format; we omit them here.)

One surprising outcome of introducing this material in introductory courses is that most students are able to read and understand specifications of similar complexity almost immediately. Even more surprising, many are able to write specifications after only one or two lectures. A good first exercise asks students to work in pairs to develop the formal specification of a queue component that provides a minimal set of operations (i.e., `enqueue()`, `dequeue()`, `length()`, `clear()`). The most obvious solution mirrors the `Stack` example, but requires `dequeue()` to operate on the opposite side of the string as `enqueue()`. An equally appropriate solution concatenates the new entry to the end of the string. Beyond reinforcing basic modeling skills, the exercise underscores that the specification is merely a "cover story". What matters is that the specifications be meaningful when the operations are considered in their totality.

To introduce students to the modeling techniques used to describe composite types, we next consider the `SplitList` interface, adapted from [2]. `SplitList` represents a partitioned list of elements. The interface provides operations for moving the list partition and accessing the element to its right. Formally, `SplitList` is modeled as a pair of strings:

```
public interface SplitList<E> {
// SplitList<E> is modeled by:
//    (l: string of E, r: string of E)
// initial value: (<>,<>)
```

The model designates the first element of the pair as `l`, for "left", and the second element of the pair as `r`, for "right". Initially, both strings are empty. A subset of the operations used to move the list partition are shown below:

```
void moveToFront();
// ensures: self.l = <> and
//          self.r = #self.l o #self.r

void advance();
// requires: |self.r| > 0
// ensures: (self.l o self.r =
//           #self.l o #self.r) and
//          |self.l| = |#self.l| + 1
```

Consider a list with the value $(<1,3>, <9,1>)$. The first operation, `moveToFront()`, moves the partition to the left side of the list. According to the post-condition, this empties the left string and prepends its elements to the right string — $(<>, <1,3,9,1>)$. The final operation, `advance()`, is more complex. The pre-condition requires that the operation be called only when the right string is non-empty. The post-condition states that the contents of the left and right strings taken together remain unchanged by the operation, but the length of the left string is increased by one. Essentially, it states that an entry is moved from the right to the left string. An alternative expression of this condition may be used to introduce existential quantifiers.

The remaining methods —`addRightElement()`, `removeRightElement()`, `leftLength()`, `rightLength()`, and `clear()`— are omitted; they are immediately understandable to students after their exposure to the `Stack` interface.

With the limited experience these examples and exercise provide, students are able to understand a surprisingly broad set of specifications. One of the more complex involves the `Sequence` interface, used to model an unbounded, indexed sequence of elements, similar to Java's `List` interface and many other index-based data structures. Consider the partial `Sequence` specification:

```
public interface Sequence<E> {
// Sequence<E> is modeled by: string of E
// initial value: <>

void addElement(Integer pos, E e);
// requires: 0 <= pos <= |self|
// preserves: pos, e
// ensures:
//   there exists l,r : string of E
//   s.t. #self = l o r and
//        |l| = pos and
//        self = l o <e> o r
  ... remaining operations elided ...
```

The interface is modeled as a string, and instances are initially empty. The pre-condition on `addElement()` indicates that an element may only be added adjacent to an existing element, or at position zero when the string is empty. The first two clauses of the post-condition state that the pre-conditional string can be partitioned into two substrings, `l` and `r`, where the length of the first substring is equal to the desired insertion point. The final clause states that the post-conditional string will consist of the same two substrings, with the argument `e` inserted between them. The specification of `removeElement()`, omitted, is similar.

While the presentation has focused on string-based abstractions, the same approach can be used across a wide range of models and software components. Consider, for example, the partial specification of a basic `Set` interface:

```
public interface Set<E> {
// Set<E> is modeled by: finite set of E
// initial value: {}

void add(E e);
// requires: e ∉ self
// preserves: e
// ensures: self = #self ∪ {e}

void remove(E e);
// requires: e ∈ self
// preserves: e
// ensures: self = #self - {e}
  ... remaining operations elided ...
```

The interface is modeled as a finite set. The `add()` operation is used to add an element, assuming it was not a member of the set prior to the call; `remove()` is similarly specified (using set difference). An interesting exercise asks students to consider the omission of the pre-condition on `add()` and the associated impact on the performance of possible implementations of `add()` and `remove()`.

By selecting mathematical models that are well matched to the interface abstractions, the resulting specifications are generally straightforward, even when the components are themselves rich. In our own classes, we introduce students to models involving strings, sets, tuples, functions, and other structures, with nearly uniform positive results.

3.3 Example Exercises

We conclude the overview of our approach with a brief summary of three types of exercises used to reinforce these abstraction and modeling skills. The simplest asks students to develop test cases for a `mystery()` operation based only on an associated model and mathematical pre- and post-conditions. A more challenging question asks students to write a formal specification given a formal model, an *informal* natural language description of a `mystery()` operation, and a series of valid test cases (i.e., input and output values). An even more challenging question asks students to devise a mathematical model for a new software component.

4. EVIDENCE FOR LOWER-PERFORMERS

Over three years, in a sophomore-level Java course, we have collected evidence that undergraduate students are able to understand mathematical abstraction, as exhibited by their ability to read, write, and use specifications based on these abstractions. To avoid the bias introduced by top performers, who tend to do well regardless of the instructional approach, we focus our analysis on the bottom half of the performance curve, based on graded assignments and exams. At the end of each semester, these students were given assessments that test specific skills required to think abstractly, model data structures with a variety of models, and understand and develop rigorous specifications.

The most basic questions ask students to create test points (i.e., pre-conditional and post-conditional values) based on their understanding of a component's mathematical model. The most complex ask them to apply their knowledge by developing formal proofs of code correctness that involve application of theorems from relevant mathematical theories. Other interesting questions ask them to develop formal specifications based on these models:

```
public void mystery(Sequence s1,
        Sequence sub, Sequence s2, int p);
```

requires:

- `sub` must be a substring of `s1`
- `p` must be less than or equal to the length of `s2`

ensures:

- `sub` will be removed from `s1`;
  no other changes will be made to `s1`
- `sub` will not be modified;
  it will be inserted at position `p` within `s2`
- no other changes will be made to `s2`
- `p` will not be modified

example:

#s1=<1,2,3,4,5>; #sub=<3,4>; #s2=<1,2,3>; #p=1
s1=<1,2,5>; sub=<3,4>; s2=<1,3,4,2,3>; p = 1

Q2. Provide the formal pre-condition for this method.
Q3. Provide the formal post-condition for this method.

The assessment questions are based on a *Reasoning Concept Inventory* (RCI) that has evolved over several years to capture the analytical reasoning skills CS graduates must possess to develop and maintain high quality software [6, 11]. Assessment results are summarized in the table below. Columns represent the average performance on the concept, the number of students scoring above 70%, and the corresponding percentage, respectively. The results span 4 sections of an introductory programming class offered over the course of 3 years. A total of 94 students completed the class; the top-scoring 44 were exempted from assessment.

Concept Item	Avg.	$\# \geq 70\%$	$\% \geq 70\%$
Specification basics	80%	30	81.1%
Reading specifications	97.7%	48	96%
Writing pre-conditions	70.8%	28	56%
Writing post-conditions	56.6%	23	46%
Reasoning basics	80%	29	78.4%
Proof assumptions	90%	33	89%
Proof obligations	73.6%	24	64.9%
Correctness proofs	22.5%	8	21.6%

Rows 1–4 correspond to reading and writing mathematical specifications. Rows 5–8 correspond to applying specifications to support reasoning. Naturally, students found writing specifications (as in the exercise above) to be more difficult. Students had the most trouble with proofs. This data informs us that while we have been successful in teaching mathematical abstraction and its use in reasoning to lower-performing students, we still have work to do in teaching them how to write specifications and proofs, either in this course or elsewhere (e.g., discrete structures).

5. CONCLUSION

We conclude with a well-known quote from Aho and Ullman [1]: *"Computer Science is a science of abstraction — creating the right model for a problem and devising the appropriate mechanizable techniques to solve it."* The quote reflects our belief that abstraction and modeling are central to computing; every CS graduate should be able to demonstrate proficiency in these skills. Yet surprisingly, little emphasis has been placed on teaching them sytematically.

We have described a systematic approach to teaching abstraction based on formal interface models. We have presented representative interface examples, classroom exercises, a web-based reasoning environment, and summarized our experiences teaching these skills in our courses. The ideas can be integrated in a variety of CS courses. We have shown that lower-performing students can be taught abstraction, and we are in the process of replicating our efforts at other institutions.

This work is supported by the National Science Foundation through awards DUE-1022941 and CNS-0745846.

6. REFERENCES

[1] A. Aho and J. Ullman. *Foundations of Computer Science*. W. H. Freeman & Co., New York, NY, 1994.

[2] P. Bucci, T. Long, and B. Weide. Do we really teach abstraction? In *The 32nd SIGCSE*, pages 26–30, New York, NY USA, February 2001. ACM.

[3] C. Cook. A web-integrated environment for component-based software reasoning. Master's thesis, Clemson University, School of Computing, August 2011.

[4] C. Cook et al. Specification engineering and modular verification using a web-integrated verifying compiler. In *The 34th ICSE*, page (*to appear*), New York, NY USA, June 2012. ACM.

[5] H. Harton. *Mechanical and Modular Verification Condition Generation for Object-Based Software*. PhD thesis, Clemson University, School of Computing, December 2011.

[6] J. Krone et al. Mathematics throughout the CS curriculum. *J. of Computing Sciences in Colleges*, 27(1):65–73, October 2011.

[7] B. Liskov and J. Guttag. *Program Development in Java: Abstraction, Specification, and Object-Oriented Design*. Addison-Wesley, Boston, MA USA, 1st edition, 2000.

[8] T. Long et al. Client view first: An exodus from implementation-biased teaching. In *The 30th SIGCSE*, pages 136–140, New York, NY USA, March 1999. ACM.

[9] D. Norman. *Things That Make Us Smart: Defending Human Attributes in the Age of the Machine*. Addison-Wesley, Boston, MA USA, 1993.

[10] L. Northrop et al. Ultra-large-scale systems: The software challenge of the future. Technical report, Software Engineering Institute, Carnegie Mellon, June 2006. www.sei.cmu.edu/uls/downloads.html.

[11] RSRG, Clemson University. Reasoning concept inventory, 2011. resolve.cs.clemson.edu/wiki/.

[12] M. Sitaraman and B. Weide. Component-based software using Resolve. *SIGSOFT SEN*, October 1994.

[13] R. Sooriamurthi. Introducing abstraction and decomposition to novice programmers. In *The 14th Annual ITiCSE*, pages 196–200, New York, NY USA, July 2009. ACM.

[14] J. Wing. Computational thinking. *Communications of the ACM*, 49:33–35, March 2006.

The New CSTA K–12 Computer Science Standards

Steven Cooper
Stanford University
coopers@cs.stanford.edu

Barbara Boucher Owens
Southwestern University
owensb@southwestern.edu

Chris Stephenson
Executive Director, CSTA
cstephenson@csta.acm.org

Judith Gal-Ezer
Open University of Israel
galezer@openu.ac.il

Abstract

In this panel, we describe the new CSTA K-12 Computer Science Standards, their organization, and their hoped-for impact.

Categories and Subject Descriptors

K.3.2 [**Computers and Education**]: Computer and Information Science Education – *computer science education, curriculum*

General Terms

Management, Design, Standardization

Keywords

Computer Science Education, K-12 Curriculum

1. SUMMARY

In 2003, ACM's K-12 Education Task Force released a document entitled "A Model Curriculum for K-12 Computer Science" [1]. This document represented an attempt by the Task Force to develop a comprehensive set of learning standards for pre-college educators and their students. In the ensuing years, this document became the de facto national (United States) standards for K–12 computer science and had significant impact on the development of standards at the state and district level and on courses at the high school level. With the formation of the Computer Science Teachers Association) (CSTA), they also became the first K-12 computer science standards with the support of a national association for computer science teachers.

Over the years, however, it became apparent that there were flaws with this document. It was constructed in a format computer scientists were comfortable with but school administrators were not. Unlike other curriculum documents, which were organized by thematic strands and focused on student learning outcomes, the Model Curriculum was organized by topics and lab work. The document had also failed to provide a compelling argument for the teaching of computer science in high schools. A second edition released in 2006 addressed this latter deficit with a new preface provided by thought leaders in computer science education. But the basic contextual and structural problems remained.

In 2011, CSTA created new standards that would address these deficiencies and provide cohesive and coherent learning outcomes that would more directly resemble standards documents

This special session brings together project leaders to report on the current status of the standards and next steps to disseminate these standards with educators and policy makers internationally.

ITiCSE'12, July 3–5, 2012, Haifa, Israel.
ACM 978-1-4503-1246-2/12/07.

2. Objectives and Organization

We will report on the CSTA K–12computer science standards project from four perspectives represented by each of the participants. The goal of the session is to help the computing education community understand the organization, scope, and contents of the CSTA standards and to engage in a dialogue that will strengthen such efforts internationally.

3. Motivation (Steve Cooper)

There are several projects aimed at making changes in high school computer science. Many of these are referenced and accessible from the CSTA web site [2]. For example, the *Exploring Computer Science* project based on work by Margolis *et al* [3,4,5] is transforming Computer Science education in the Los Angeles Unified School District. Elsewhere the *Georgia Computes!* [6] Project is having a broad impact in Georgia. A more wide spread (national) and systemic change to K–12 computer science education, however, requires foundational learning standards upon which all such projects can build. The new CSTA K-12 learning standards are intended to fill this role and to continue the work begun with the ACM Model Curriculum. At this session we will talk about the role of standards in educational change, the process used for creating these standards and the challenges encountered, the organization and content of these standards, and how they compare to the current Israeli standards.

Dr. Steve Cooper is a professor of computer science at Stanford University and Chair of the CSTA Board of Directors.

4. Process and Pitfalls (Chris Stephenson)

Few practices in the United States education system are more fraught with controversy and dissention than the creation of national learning standards. Perceived by some as a contravention of the rights of individual states to set their own education policy and by others as the end of individual creativity among teachers, learning standards have none-the-less become the litmus test of academic rigor and acceptance within the cannon of learning in public schools. In the absence of standards, individual courses have little perceived value.

CSTA's efforts to revise the ACM Model Curriculum for K-12 Computer Science and develop new standards must therefore be seen in the context of a highly politicized system that, in addition to its polarized view of standards in general, suffers from significant differences of opinion about what computer science is and what it should be in schools. By assembling a diverse and dedicated committee of experts and paying close attention to the comments and critiques of its intended community, however, CSTA was able to develop a new set of standards that incorporates new learning about what and how to teach.

Dr. Chris Stephenson is the executive director of CSTA and is responsible for managing the standards project

5. Organization (Barbara Boucher Owens)

The CSTA computer science standards were developed with the perspective that computer science is a core academic discipline and that all students would benefit from a foundational knowledge of its principles and concepts. They are intended to serve as a catalyst for widespread adoption of computer science education for all K–12 students in the United States.

The standards provide a three-level framework for computer science where each level represents a specific set of grades and courses. The first two levels are aimed at grades K–6 and 6–9 respectively. The learning outcomes in Level 1 are addressed in the context of other academic subjects. The Level 2 learning outcomes may be addressed through other subjects or in discrete computer science courses. Level 3 is divided into three separate courses: *Computer Science in the Modern World*, *Computer Science Concepts and Practices*, and *Topics in Computer Science*. The standards in *Computer Science in the Modern World* reflect learning content that should be mastered by all students; *Computer Science Concepts and Practices* and *Topics in Computer Science* are intended for students with interest in computer science and other computing careers, whether they are college-bound or not.

Within each level and course, the standards are further organized by five strands (or general themes): computational thinking; collaboration; computing practice; computers and communication devices; and community, global, and ethical impacts. These strands not only demonstrate the richness of computer science but also help organize the subject matter for students so that they can begin to perceive computer science as more engaging and relevant, and as more than a solitary pursuit.

The standards themselves are presented in a learning objective-based format that identifies the specific computer science concepts and skills students should achieve at each of the three levels (grades K–6, 6–9, and 9–12).

Barbara Boucher Owens served as the SIGCSE representative on the standards development committee and is the former Chair of the SIGCSE Board.

6. Comparisons with Israel's Standards (Judith Gal-Ezer)

The Israeli standards were developed when the CS high school curriculum, was designed [7]. These standards guided the work of the committee that put together the curriculum and took care of its implementation. The curriculum was updated continuously. It was examined thoroughly about three years ago and no radical changes in the standards were introduced. The main and most important ones are:

1. Computer science is a full-fledged scientific subject. It should be taught in high school on a par with other scientific subjects, like Physics, Chemistry and Biology.
2. The program should concentrate on the key concepts and foundations of the field. The main notion to be emphasized throughout the program is that of an algorithmic problem, and an algorithm as a solution thereof.
3. The "zipper principle": Conceptual and experimental issues should be interwoven throughout the program. The word `conceptual' refers to subjects that are taught in the classroom, rather than in the laboratory.
4. A well-equipped and well-maintained computer laboratory is mandatory.
5. Teachers certified to teach the subject must have adequate formal CS education. An undergraduate degree in computer science and formal teacher training are mandatory.
6. The program should focus on the most basic and lasting concepts of CS, and should be challenging, in the sense that it will not only teach the foundations, but will also relate them to the practical side of computing.

After years of implementing the program, the main consequence was that more emphasis should be placed on the laboratory issue, and integrating the experimental issues more intensively into the program. We should mention, however, that we still struggle to convince policy makers, especially university committees responsible for the admission policy, that computer science has a main role in the 21st century and should be on the same par as the other sciences in high school programs.

Dr. Judith Gal-Ezer is the Vice President of the Open University of Israel. She served many years as member and chair of the Ministry of Education professional committee for computer science.

7. Intended Audience

This session is intended to report on the current status and future directions of the CSTA/ACM's K-12 computer science standards. These standards and their relationship to the current Israeli standards will be of interest to all computer science educators at all levels. After brief remarks by the session leaders, thirty minutes will be available for discussion with audience members.

8. REFERENCES

[1] Tucker, A., McCowan, D., Deek, F., Stephenson, C., Jones, J., & Verno, A. (2006). *A model curriculum for K–12 computer science: Report of the ACM K–12 Task Force Computer Science Curriculum Committee*, 2nd Ed. NewYork, NY: Association for Computing Machinery.

[2] csta.acm.org

[3] Exploring Computer Science, Margolis, Goode, Chapman http://intotheloop.gseis.ucla.edu/exploring.html

[4] Jane Margolis, Rachel Estrella, Joanna Goode, Jennifer Jellison Holme, Kimberly Nao. Stuck in the Shallow End. MIT Press, 2008.

[5] Jane Margolis and Allan Fisher. Unlocking the Clubhouse: Women in Computing. MIT Press, 2003.

[6] Georgia Computes! http://gacomputes.cc.gatech.ed.

Computer Science as a Community Involvement Activity

Assaf Zaritsky
Blavatnik School of Computer Science
Tel Aviv University
Israel
assafzar@cs.tau.ac.il

Ohad Barzilay
Blavatnik School of Computer Science
Tel Aviv University
Israel
Ohad.Barzilay@cs.tau.ac.il

ABSTRACT
In the proposed panel we discuss the efforts made by the academy and industry to bring computer science (CS) to audience that is not exposed to CS education, not represented in the CS workforce or not accessible due to lack in technological solutions.

Categories and Subject Descriptors
K.3.2 [**COMPUTERS AND EDUCATION**]: Computer and Information Science Education.

General Terms
Human Factors.

Keywords
Community involvement, engaging computer science. volunteering, students, computer science unplugged.

1. INTRODUCTION
The fundamental ideas of computer science (CS) go beyond numbers and formulas. However, CS education takes place at high schools and universities addressing mainly homogeneous target audiences. In this panel we explore four initiatives aiming to make it accessible and appealing to larger audiences, which currently are intimidated by CS or not aware of its beauty due to prejudices or the manner in which it is usually introduced.

The 4 initiatives to be discussed include Tel Aviv University students who teach CS ideas to underprivileged high school kids; Google's program encouraging female pupils to learn math and CS in high school; Microsoft's technologies exploited by students to assist non-governmental organizations; HP encouragement of minorities to consider careers in technology, to learn about some practical technologies and to participate in hands-on activities.

2. CS UNPLUGGED FOR STUDENTS FROM ECOMICALLY LESS PRIVILEDGED BACKGROUND
The Blavatnik school of CS in Tel Aviv University initiated an undergraduate elective academic course entitled "Teaching Computer Science in the Community", and has run it for the last four years, providing a community service. Undergraduate CS students in their final year teach CS topics to diverse audience from economically under-privileged communities. The major emphasis this year was teaching an international program entitled "Computer Science Unplugged" (CSU) [1,2], a collection of learning activities that teach CS through engaging games and puzzles. Around thirty undergraduate students participate in the course for academic credit. After several meetings at the university, during which students are exposed to CSU and teaching methodologies, they are sent to various sites where they taught two hours weekly, for twelve weeks. The major target audience was middle-schools pupils (ages 12-15), but there were groups of younger (down to 7 years old) and older (even adults) pupils. As the major academic requirement, the students were prepared a new teaching module in the style of CSU. All these modules are freely available online (in Hebrew, https://sites.google.com/site/computersiencesincomputers/home). The program is considered a success for both the students and the pupils, and the reactions from school principals and site leaders have been enthusiastic.

2.1 Panelist - Benny Chor
Benny Chor did his B.Sc. and M.Sc. in Mathematics at the Hebrew University of Jerusalem, did his Ph.D. at the MIT working on public key cryptography under the supervision of Ron Rivest, and spent post-doctoral periods at MIT and Harvard. He was a faculty member at the CS department, Technion, between 1987-2001, and is with the CS school of Tel-Aviv University since 2001. He was a visiting fellow at Massey University, Palmerston North, New Zealand, and at the European Bioinformatics Institute (EBI), Cambridge, UK, and a Visiting Fellow in Clare Hall, Cambridge Univ., UK. His research interests are computational biology and educational issues and teaching of CS and computational thinking at the high school and university levels – both to CS and non CS majors.

3. ENCOURAGING HIGH SCHOOL GIRLS
As part of Google Israel's pre-university diversity efforts, this project is aimed at encouraging high school girls to select CS and math as their high-school major. The program has had so far 2500 girls coming from over 100 schools, with outstanding results of 40% of the participating girls indeed choosing CS as a major [3]. The diversity program is in the process of evolving as a key factor in helping more women progress to significant positions in the high tech industry.

3.1 Panelist – Michal Segalov
Michal Segalov is a Software Engineer working on improving Google's backbone-network infrastructure. Previously, she has worked on YouTube's monetization platform and launched several of Google's international search products. Prior to joining Google's R&D center, Michal worked at IBM research labs, focusing on hardware verification techniques. She holds B.A. in CS from the Technion and M.Sc. in CS from Tel Aviv University.

ITiCSE'12, July 3–5, 2012, Haifa, Israel.
ACM 978-1-4503-1246-2/12/07.

4. TAILOR-MADE SOLUTIONS FOR NON-GOVERNMENTAL ORGANIZATIONS

The Third Sector in Israel includes tens of thousands of non-governmental organizations (NGOs) that assist millions of people each year. The sector is highly skilled in providing services to populations in need, but is still lacking in its IT infrastructure and capabilities. Computer engineering students from universities across the country implement their development skills to create tailor-made solutions for NGOs participating in the project. Working closely with the NGOs, the students identify their needs, investigate the subject, and develop appropriate applications. Microsoft R&D volunteers guide and tutor the students throughout the entire process – from research and planning to implementation and integration. The programs runs for the second year, ending (last year) with a competition demonstrating 20 student projects including cognitive games for the elderly suited for smart phones, call for help button on the phone for emergency matters, text to voice SMS system for the blind, etc.

4.1 Panelist –Dana Shoushan-Whol

Dana Shoushan-Whol is the community affairs and social responsibility manager in Microsoft Israel who brings vast experience in both bridging between the business world to the social arena with former positions as head of the development resources of ELEM – for Youth at Risk org.; VP of flowers of medicine org. turning it into a national social org.; consultant for the Beyond Business co. brining business companies to realize their roles as responsible players in the community; and initiating the office of community affairs and social responsibility at the Israel's Microsoft's R&D Center. Dana holds a Master's degree from the Hebrew University in conflict solutions and a BA in political science and communication from Bar-Ilan University. She is a graduate of the MA'ALA course for corporate affairs managers and ethics in the business world from Tel Aviv University, and served as volunteer using her fundraising abilities for the benefit of small NGOs around Israel.

5. ENCOURAGING MINORITIES

HP Israel recently launched a social innovation project entitled "It's all about people" with the objective of promoting technological education and employment among young people from minorities' populations by guidance and mentoring from HP volunteering employees. The program focuses on Arab pupils, young immigrates from Ethiopia, and young women from Jaffa. HP employees participate by providing pupils business and technological mentorship towards participation in national innovation competitions and towards achieving their career goals. In addition, HP also invests in organizing lectures given by HP professionals on technology, marketing and business. Visiting HP headquarters for the first time, the students, many of which come from low-income families, are exposed to a lifestyle very different than their own. Our team's motivation to mentor and embrace the students inspires them to pursue a career in technology, as some of them claim - a mere dream not long before.

5.1 Panelist – Anna Levinson

After completing her BA in Economics at Tel Aviv University, Anna Levinson joined HP's Graduate Program and worked as sales representative in the HP Enterprise Business group. She later moved to Product Management in the Business Critical Solutions team, a position she's been holding for almost two years now.

6. TEACHING KIDS TO PROGRAM USING SCRATCH

Scratch is an early computer language learning environment enabling young beginners to get results without having to learn syntactically correct writing first. Created by the MIT Media Lab, it is intended to motivate for further learning through playfully experimenting and creating projects, such as interactive animations etc. Panelist Oren Zuckerman, one of the leaders of the Israeli Scratch team, will share his experience teaching Scratch to kids.

6.1 Panelist – Oren Zuckerman

Oren Zuckerman (PhD MIT Media Lab 2007) is the founder of the Media Innovation Lab at IDC Herzliya's school of communications. Zuckerman's research areas include mobile technologies & wellbeing, tangible interfaces for learning, contextual media, and analysis of participation patterns in online & mobile communities. At MIT Media Lab, Zuckerman completed his Masters and PhD, looking deeply into the convergence of physical and digital interactive experiences. Prior to MIT (1999-2001), Zuckerman was the co-founder of an Internet startup that created a "decentralized blogging community" on top of the Web. On 2001, the World Economic Forum recognized Zuckerman as a "Technology Pioneer" at the annual forum in Davos, Switzerland.

7. REFERENCES

[1] Bell, T., Whitten, I., and Powell, M. Computer science unplugged; www.unplugged.canterbury.ac.nz

[2] Bell, T., Fellows, M. and Witten, I. Computer Science Unplugged: Off-line Activities and Games for All Ages. 1998. Available at: www.lulu.com

[3] Eidelman, L., Hazzan, O., Lapidot, T., Matias, Y., Raijman, D., and Segalov, M. Mind the (gender) gap: can a two-hour visit to a hi-tech company change perceptions about computer science? *ACM Inroads*. 2011

Assessing the Benefits of Integrating Social Issues Components in the Computing Curriculum

Paul M. Leidig
Grand Valley State University
School of Computing & Info. Systems
Allendale, MI 49401 USA
+1-616-331-2060
leidig@gvsu.edu

Michael Goldweber
Xavier University
Dept. of Math & Computer Science
Cincinnati, OH 45207 USA
+1-513-745-3936
mikeyg@cs.xu.edu

Barbara Boucher Owens
Southwestern University
Dept. of Math & Computer Science
Georgetown, TX 78626 USA
+1-512-863-1513
owensb@southwestern.edu

ABSTRACT
The inclusion of social issues, including ethical and professional topics, in computing curricula has become commonplace two decades after being incorporated into the ACM Computing Curricula. However, authors of academic papers and conference presentations often concentrate on integrating the broader issues of societal impact and best practices into computing curricula, while neglecting the assessment of their benefits. This panel explores how the institutions of the panelists include social issues in projects and the curriculum as a whole, and additionally how they assess the benefits of doing so. Special attention is given to an appreciation of the social good emanating from the use of community-based and non-profit organizations in student projects. Additionally, ways to assess the effectiveness of these approaches are presented in an effort to help meet model curriculum guidelines and accreditation requirements.

Categories and Subject Descriptors
K.3.2 [**Computers and Education**]: Computer and Information Science Education – *curriculum, accreditation.*

K4.2 [**Computers and Society**]: Social Issues

K.7.4 [**The Computing Profession**]: Professional Ethics.

General Terms
Measurement, Human Factors.

Keywords
Social issues, community-based projects, assessment, curriculum.

1. INTRODUCTION
Many computing programs expect that graduates will be prepared for practice as professionals in their discipline [7]. In addition to possessing technical knowledge and skills, graduates need the ability to assess the societal impact of their work and have a commitment to the standards of computing professional ethics. Coverage of these attributes is not new to the computing curricula. The ACM/IEEE Computing Curricula 91 articulated these goals two decades ago, stipulating that students need to: (1) *understand the basic cultural, social, legal, and ethical issues inherent in the discipline of computing, and* (2) *develop the ability to ask serious questions about the social impact of computing* [10].

ITiCSE'12, July 3–5, 2012, Haifa, Israel.
ACM 978-1-4503-1246-2/12/07.

Unfortunately, there is no clear consensus on where and how social issues should be integrated in the computing curriculum. Homkes and Strikwerda [5] conducted an analysis of ABET accredited undergraduate programs in information technology, computer science, and information systems to characterize how different programs implement these curricula recommendations and address accreditation requirements for professional, ethical, societal, privacy, and discipline impact issues.

Several ACM sponsored ITiCSE conferences offered various methods and practices of collaborative efforts, and in 1997 an ITiCSE working group produced an array of exercises that could be used to incorporate social issues as modules within computing courses [4]. Other ITiCSE working groups followed: historical perspectives on the computing curricula [2]; a report offering ways to incorporate professional issues [6]; and, incorporating cultural issues [7].

The use of service learning based projects is an increasingly popular method used to provide practical experience for students while contributing to the local community. This panel presents approaches taken to apply service learning in student projects, and then explores ways to assess the effectiveness of these projects.

One critical piece missing from the evolving use of service-learning based projects in computing curricula, is attention to the assessment of the effectiveness of the inclusion of various social computing aspects in the curriculum. The Seoul Accord [8] is an agreement among computing accreditation organizations. Signatories of the accord assess the equivalency of the programs, including the attributes graduates must develop related to professional responsibilities to society, ethics, and lifelong learning. As documented in the accord, graduates must be able to (1) *understand and assess societal, health, safety, legal, and cultural issues within local and global contexts*, and (2) *understand and commit to professional ethics, responsibilities, and norms of professional computing practice* [9].

Accrediting bodies generally do not define curricula. Instead, their role may be better characterized as providing a quality assurance assessment process. ABET, one of the signatures of the Seoul Accord, provides a framework to define, measure, and evaluate the effectiveness of the delivery of curriculum components. This framework may be used to evaluate the coverage of social issues, including but not limited to, social issues embedded in community-based projects. This panel will explore ways to use the assessment tools of accreditation bodies to assess the effectiveness of the use of community-based service-learning projects to introduce the social issues aspects of computing curricula.

2. DISCUSSION

This panel has a two-fold purpose. First, it presents the approaches taken by the panelists' institutions to including these social issues in existing computing curricula; including coverage of an appreciation of the social good emanating from the use of community-based and non-profit organizations in student projects. Secondly, suggestions will be presented on ways to assess the effectiveness of these approaches in meeting the model curriculum guides and accreditation requirements.

3. PRESENTERS BIOGRAPHIES

The following panelists represent a diverse set of institutions and computing programs with a variety of experiences. All believe in the value of social-learning projects for computing students. The panelists will present their approach to using social-learning projects and how they assess the effectiveness of their efforts.

Paul Leidig, Professor of Computing and Information Systems, Grand Valley State University, Allendale, MI, USA. Dr. Leidig has over 35 years of experience in the information technology industry and computing education. In addition to early efforts helping develop tools for implementing community-based projects, he was instrumental in developing a curriculum that requires all students to experience community-based service with senior capstone experiences with non-profit organizations. A member of the Computing Accreditation Commission of ABET, he presents the need to assess the effectiveness of efforts to integrate social issues in computing programs.

Michael Goldweber, Professor of Computer Science, Xavier University, Cincinnati, OH, USA. Dr. Goldweber has over 30 years of experience in both computer science education and the information technology industry. With a diversified portfolio of computer systems expertise, he has been at the forefront of several computing education initiatives, including efforts to increase the use of social issues in the computing curriculum. Currently he is working with a couple of community partners: (1) a local school in a disadvantaged neighborhood running a Scratch after school club; (2) an NGO in Honduras called Shoulder-to-Shoulder, working on a database project dealing with their medical records, and (3) a study abroad program in Bogota, Colombia for American computer science students. While there, students take a software engineering course where the projects are all service learning based. The students also volunteer at local centers in the shantytowns teaching interested kids Scratch. This summer's project will either be working with a local shantytown medical clinic to develop a database to track the health of pregnant girls, or working with a trade school in the same slum to track the progress of their graduates.

Barbara Boucher Owens, Associate Professor of Computer Science, Southwestern University, Georgetown, TX, USA Dr. Owens has over 40 years of experience in computer science education, holding numerous leadership positions including the chair of the ACM special interest group on computer science education. She has most recently been involved in the documentation of the computing educators oral history project and in recruiting and retaining women in computing. She has demonstrated a passion for the active use of non-profit clients in service learning projects for computer science students.

4. REFERENCES

[1] ACM Interim Review Task Force. (2008). *Computer Science Curriculum 2008: An Interim Revision of CS 2001. http://www.acm.org/education/curricula/ComputerScience2008.pdf.*

[2] Goldweber, M., et al., Historical perspectives on the computing curriculum (report of the ITiCSE '97 working group on historical perspectives in computing education), in The supplemental proceedings of the conference on Integrating technology into computer science education: working group reports and supplemental proceedings. 1997, ACM: Uppsala, Sweden. p. 94-111.

[3] Goldweber, M., et al., Enhancing the social issues components in our computing curriculum: computing for the social good. *INRODES, volume 2 Issue 1,February 2011, ACM*

[4] Granger, M.J., et al., Using information technology to integrate social and ethical issues into the computer science and information systems curriculum. Report of the ITiCSE '97 working group on social and ethical issue in computing curricula in ITiCSE'97. 1997, ACM SIGCSE: Uppsala, Sweden. p. 38-50.

[5] Homkes, R. and R.A. Strikwerda, Meeting the ABET program outcome for issues and responsibilities: an 47. evaluation of CS, IS, and IT programs, in Proceedings of the 10th ACM conference on SIG-information technology education. 2009, ACM: Fairfax, Virginia, USA. p. 133-137.

[6] Little, J.C., et al., Integrating cultural issues into the computer and information technology curriculum (ITiCSE 2000 working group reports). SIGCSE Bull., 2001. 33(2): p. 136-154.

[7] Little, J.C., et al., Integrating professionalism and workplace issues into the computing and information technology curriculum: report of the ITiCSE'99 working group on professional- ism, in Working group reports from ITiCSE on Innovation and technology in computer science education. 1999, ACM: Cracow, Poland. p. 106-120.

[8] Seoul Accord. *Seoul Accord.* 2010 June 4 2010]; Available from:http://www.abeek.or.kr/accord/contents.jsp?menu_l=85

[9] Seoul Accord. *Seoul Accord Foundation Documents: Section D (Graduate Attributes).* 2010 June 4 2010]; Available from: http://www.abeek.or.kr/accord/contents.jsp?menu_l=144&menu_m=199.

[10] Tucker, A.B., et al., Computing curricula 1991: Report of the ACM/IEEE-CS Joint Curriculum Task Force. 1991.

Programming Studio: Advances and Lessons Learned

Charlie Meyer and Michael Woodley
University of Illinois at Urbana-Champaign
Department of Computer Science
201 N. Goodwin Ave, Urbana, IL, 61820
{cemeyer2, mwoodley}@illinois.edu

ABSTRACT

In [1] we previously described an innovative approach to teaching programming fundamentals to undergraduate students in a course called Programming Studio. This required program is designed to be given shortly after CS2. We teach topics such as high quality code design, proper problem decomposition and methods of code documentation, as well as practical subjects such as correct usage of various types of version control and a variety of programming languages that are not usually introduced in other CS courses. Here we build on what was previously written with the new methods of assessment, types of assignments, and the lessons learned from expanding the course from less than 75 students to nearly 150 students.

Categories and Subject Descriptors

K.3.2 [**Computers and Education**]: Computer and Information Science Education

General Terms

Measurement, Design, Human Factors

Keywords

Programming, undergraduate education

1. ADVANCEMENTS

Over the past 5 years, we have learned many lessons from teaching our programming studio course to over 1000 undergraduate students. One of the most interesting advancements that we have incorporated into the course is a new method of structuring assignments to students. Previously, we gave roughly independent assignments each week. Recently, we have reworked our syllabus to have a progression of assignments where each week builds on the previous one, lasting as long as 5 or 6 weeks. This forces our students into real-world scenarios where they are forced to rework the code they wrote in previous weeks. This reinforces valuable skills such as proper design from the onset of the assignment sequence, proper documentation and the need for refactoring.

We have also introduced a new component to these multi-week assignments that adds another aspect of real-world programming that we call customer/client weeks. In the first week of the assignment sequence, our students will design the interface for the given problem along with a test suite that is intended to excercise all branches of their design. After the first week is submitted, the staff will randomly assign another student's design to every student in the discussion section. During the second week, the students have to implement to the specification they were given until the test suite they were given passes. The code is then returned to the original author for the remainder of the sequence.

Another new aspect to our course is our innovative method of assessment. As we described previously in [1], our discussion sections involve 1 moderator and 5-6 undergraduate students. With nearly 150 students enrolled in the course, it is essential to have a large course staff. With so many people grading student work, it was a necessity to come up with a system of assessment that removed as much subjectivity as possible while still maintaining fairness. To accomplish this, we have created a standard rubric that lists out various criteria to be graded, along with detailed descriptions of what merits earning various levels of points for each. With each assignment given, various criteria from the standard rubric are selected and are each given a weight. Our moderators grade each student on each criteria selected out of 3 points based on how the student's performance aligns with the descriptions for each in the standard rubric.

Lastly, we describe how the course has evolved as enrollment in it has doubled over the past five years. As noted in [1], the cost for this course is quite high and has grown almost linearly with enrollment. We have had to add extra graduate TAs as well hire many more undergraduates to act as section moderators. We have found that the course scaled well as we proposed earlier, and is easily adoptable at other universities that are willing to allocate the required resources to it.

2. REFERENCES

[1] M. Woodley and S. Kamin. Programming studio: A course for improving programming skills in undergraduates. In *Proceedings of the ACM SIGCSE conference on computer science education*. SIGCSE, March 2007.

ITiCSE'12, July 3–5, 2012, Haifa, Israel.
ACM 978-1-4503-1246-2/12/07.

Sample Courseware for Introductory OO Programming

Rikki Fletcher
California State University, San Marcos
333 S. Twin Oaks Valley Rd,
San Marcos, CA 92096, USA
1.760.750.4000
fletcher@csusm.edu

Rocio Guillen
California State University, San Marcos
333 S. Twin Oaks Valley Rd.
San Marcos, CA 92096, USA
1.760.750.8046
rguillen@csusm.edu

ABSTRACT
In this paper, we describe a programming assignment for first semester computer science students that requires them to apply object-oriented (OO) programming and design skills in order to successfully complete their work. The students work in an interactive 3D environment that gives them immediate visual feedback.

Categories and Subject Descriptors
K.3.2 [**Computers and Education**]: Computer and Information Science Education –*Computer science education, Curriculum*

General Terms
Algorithms, Design, Human Factors, Languages

Keywords
Object-oriented-programming, OO design, CS0, computational thinking

1. INTRODUCTION
As Computer Science educators we want students to focus, pay close attention to detail and develop the problem-solving skills necessary to design and implement software solutions. They have to be able to reason systematically, think creatively, logically and abstractly. To facilitate student success we have developed a first programming course using Alice [1], a 3D programming environment where the outcome of each assignment is an animated movie. A study by Moskal [2] found that at-risk students taught with Alice showed significant improvements in their attitude toward programming over two separate control groups who did not use Alice.

2. COURSE SUMMARY
The introductory CS0 course developed presents all the basic programming concepts to CS majors and non-CS majors without concern for syntax rules. The students become comfortable as they apply OO concepts while creating animations. We expect the students to follow good programming style and create documentation with flowcharts. Using Alice, students are able to start writing programs on the second day of class. As the course progresses, they learn how to decompose problems, write custom methods and apply control structures to solve problems. Students report that "the course was fun", and "they learned a lot." Some go on to pursue CS as their major or minor.

3. COURSE ACTIVITY
The following is one of the final assessment activities for the course. Students are asked to design and implement a program as an animation based on the following narrative:

> *A performer can juggle three balls. These are special balls that will slowly disappear. When one of the balls touches the performer's left hand, it starts to fade. The performer keeps juggling until two of the balls are completely invisible. He then drops his hands and his head in dismay. The balls all reappear and drop to the ground.*

In order to successfully complete the assignment, students must design a solution. The program solution must be decomposed into small modules. Design considerations include the following: a) The balls must move correctly; b) they must fade (Figure 1) slowly and correctly, c) the performer's hands must move correctly and d) the juggling must end at the correct moment.

Figure 1. The balls fade as the performer juggles

Students must implement their solution using loops and conditional logic. In addition, the students are asked to create movie credits, and a flowchart to document the movie action.

4. ACKNOWLEDGMENTS
Our thanks to ACM SIGCHI for templates they developed; to NSF for partial funding grant #0940575 and to Carnegie Mellon who developed the Alice programming environment.

5. REFERENCES
[1] DOI= http://Alice.org.

[2] Moskal, D. Lurie, and S. Cooper. Evaluating the effectiveness of a new instructional Approach. In ACM SIGCSE Bulletin, volume 36, pages 75-79. ACM

A Web-Based Problem Solving Tool for Introductory Computer Science

Petr Jarušek
Faculty of Informatics
Botanická 68a
Brno, Czech republic
xjarusek@fi.muni.cz

Radek Pelánek
Faculty of Informatics
Botanická 68a
Brno, Czech republic
pelanek@fi.muni.cz

ABSTRACT

We present a "Problem Solving Tutor" (`tutor.fi.muni.cz`) – a web-based educational tool for learning through problem solving. The tool contains more than 1 400 problems, mainly introductory programming problems, math and logic puzzles. All problems are interactive and the system gives students immediate feedback on their performance. The tool makes individual predictions of problem solving times and therefore is able to recommend each student a problem of suitable difficulty.

Categories and Subject Descriptors

K.3.2 [**Computing Milieux**]: Computers and Education—*Computer and Information Science Education, Computer science education*

General Terms

Human Factors

Keywords

Problem solving, intelligent tutoring systems, computer science education

1. MAIN APPROACH

For efficient learning it is important to respect individual learning pace. Difficult problems may be frustrating, easy problems boring. Our Tutor makes learning individualized. It uses machine learning algorithms to predict solving times for every student (see [1]). Based on these predictions, the Tutor recommends problems for further solving.

When students finish a solving task the Tutor displays an immediate feedback – their solving time and comparison with others. Moreover for each problem set students gather "learning points", which reflects number and difficulty of successfully finished problems.

Compared to usual intelligent tutoring systems, our system is easy to extend with new problems. Problem ordering and recommendations are done automatically by machine learning techniques and thus it is not necessary to use human experts.

ITiCSE'12, July 3–5, 2012, Haifa, Israel.
ACM 978-1-4503-1246-2/12/07.

2. PROBLEMS

The Tutor is an online application, therefore all problems run in a web browser and do not require any installation. To make learning topics more attractive, all problems are interactive. This means, that students do not only fill in a multiple choice test, but they usually have to widely interact with a learning environment to solve a presented task. We believe that a good problem solving formulation can make even less interesting topics (like learning binary numbers) quite entertaining.

Currently, the Tutor contains 20 different problem sets (more than 1 400 individual problems). Eight problem sets are directly oriented on computer science education. Particularly popular are robot programming problems, where students have to program a robot to perform a particular task. These problems have very simple syntax and semantics, yet can provide challenging problems which illustrate important concepts (particularly recursion). Other computer science problems include "programming by selection" in C and Python, data filtering by regular expressions, and binary numbers crosswords.

3. APPLICATION

The Tutor provides two modes. In an individual mode, students may pass through all problem sets and compete with other students for the best results. In a class mode, teachers can create a virtual class for their students. Students then solve problem sets chosen by their teacher and teachers can see detailed statistics of their students. Based on these statistics, teachers can suitably target their behavior in a real class – focusing on problems with which students struggled the most or helping specific students.

The Tutor was launched in March 2011 and is already used by more than 5 500 users who have spent more than 8 200 hours by problem solving and solved more than 260 000 problem instances. The Tutor is used both at introductory university courses and at more than 20 high schools in information technology lessons.

4. REFERENCES

[1] P. Jarušek and R. Pelánek. Analysis of a Simple Model of Problem Solving Times. In *11th International Conference on Intelligent Tutoring Systems*, 2012. To appear.

Techniques at the Intersection of Computing and Music

Jesse M. Heines
Dept. of Computer Science
Univ. of Massachusetts Lowell
Lowell, MA 01854
1-978-934-3634
heines@cs.uml.edu

Gena R. Greher
Dept. of Music
Univ. of Massachusetts Lowell
Lowell, MA 01854
1-978-934-3893
Gena_Greher@uml.edu

S. Alex Ruthmann
Dept. of Music
Univ. of Massachusetts Lowell
Lowell, MA 01854
1-978-934-3879
Alex_Ruthmann@uml.edu

Abstract

Our work on *Performamatics* aims to enhance students' computational thinking (CT) by engaging them in fundamental concepts that unite computing and music. Our approach leverages students' near universal interest in music as a context for rich CT experiences. The techniques we share are used in a General Education course open to students in any major called *Sound Thinking*, which is now being offered for the fourth time.

Categories and Subject Descriptors

K.3.2 [**Computers and Education**]: Computer and Information Science Education – *computer science education, curriculum.*

Keywords

Performamatics, computer science education, interdisciplinary programs, music+computing, Audacity, Scratch.

Course Structure

Our course teaches both music and computing. We begin by having students analyze music through listening exercises and sequencing and manipulating sounds using Audacity (audacity.sourceforge.net). We then have them begin to work with pre-recorded sounds in Scratch (scratch.mit.edu) before getting into composing in Scratch with MIDI.

Audacity-Based Techniques

Students begin the course by making instruments from "found objects," that is, common things that they find in their living area. We specify that they should look for objects that can produce multiple pitches with multiple timbres. This gets them thinking about what, exactly, constitutes "music."

The next step is to record the sounds their instruments make and load them into Audacity. They learn to use the editing capabilities of that program to break their sounds into component elements and the various effects to manipulate them. They then arrange the component sounds and apply effects to create a composition that further explores their own interpretation of "music."

In the third assignment, students choose a song of their own liking and listen to it critically to identify the components from which it is built. With these in hand, they create a flowchart of the song to illustrate how those components go together.

Scratch-Based Techniques

We then get into programing with Scratch, which is very easy for students of all majors to pick up and has some terrific capabilities for working with music.

ITiCSE'12, July 3–5, 2012, Haifa, Israel.
ACM 978-1-4503-1246-2/12/07.

Students begin by sequencing sounds in Scratch in a manner similar to what they did in Audacity. There is much more they can do, however, using loops and control structures. They also learn about the limitations of computer software as they try to do things that the system just can't handle.

Next we introduce intervals, focusing on the major 2nd and the perfect 5th. We show students how to program these and we have them create a composition using only these intervals. More advanced students program the intervals algorithmically and add randomization to have the music change each time it is played.

To introduce lists, we have students work on a piece that they must transpose from one key to another. This forces them to use offsets controlled by variables.

Finally, we introduce physical interaction between Scratch and the IchiBoard, a small device packed with sensors, a slider, a button, and accelerometers from which Scratch can read values that control the notes it plays (see www.cs.uml.edu/ecg/index.php/IchiBoard/IchiBoard). This technique gets students doing the most sophisticated programming in the course, as they must scale the sensor values to ranges that are appropriate for playing music.

Culminating Performances

Our course builds to a "recital" in which students showcase final projects based on the course assignments. Performances are in a venue other than our normal classroom, and students are welcome to invite their friends and family. Middle and secondary school students also attend, not only for their own benefit, but for the benefit of our students, as well. By explaining their work to younger students, our students expand and deepen their own understanding of the intersection between computing and music.

Our presentation will feature videos, recordings, and live examples of student work to demonstrate the types of results that students produce for the assignments described above.

Project URLs and Locations of Materials

Further information on our work and the materials that we use in our classes may be found at:

- *Performamatics:* http://www.performamatics.org
- *Sound Thinking:* http://soundthinking.uml.edu

Acknowledgments

This work is currently supported by National Science Foundation Award No. 1118435, "Computational Thinking through Computing and Music." *Principal Investigator:* Jesse M. Heines. *Co-Principal Investigators:* Gena Greher and S. Alex Ruthmann. *Senior Personnel:* Fred G. Martin and Sarah Kuhn. Any opinions, findings, and conclusions or recommendations expressed in these materials are those of the author(s) and do not necessarily reflect the views of the National Science Foundation.

Nintendo® DS Projects to Learn Computer Input-Output

Edurne Larraza-Mendiluze, Nestor Garay-Vitoria, Jose Ignacio Martín, Javier Muguerza, Txelo Ruiz-Vazquez, Iratxe Soraluze, Jose Francisco Lukas & Karlos Santiago
University of the Basque Country, (UPV/EHU)
Manuel Lardizabal Pasealekua, 1, 20018 Donostia (Gipuzkoa) - Spain
{edurne.larraza, nestor.garay, j.martin, j.muguerza, txelo.ruiz, iratxe.soraluze, jf.lukas, karlos.santiago}@ehu.es

ABSTRACT
Being the Input/Output subsystem an important topic in the area of Computer Architecture [1], in this work we propose a Project-Based Learning (PBL) methodology enhanced by the use of a Nintendo®1 DS machine. The use of both, methodology and platform, is endorsed by students' comments, the projects themselves and the scores obtained in the subject.

Categories and Subject Descriptors
B.4.0 [**Hardware**]: Input/Output and data communications – *General.* K.3.2 [**Computers and Education**]: Computer and Information Science Education – *Computer Science Education*

Keywords
I/O, Education, Game Console, Project Based Learning.

OUR PROPOSAL
A Project-Based Learning (PBL) methodology fits perfectly to learn computer I/O, as expressed in [2]. As a project, we proposed developing vending machines simulators that run on a Nintendo® DS machine (following other experiences as [3]).

To begin, students had to design the behavior of their vending machine using a state machine, and the lecturers had to verify whether the restrictions were taken into account. Afterwards, students had to program the main program and the interrupt service routines, using as a reference the notes handed out by the lecturers, in which I/O notions and the NDS devices' specifications were given.

The code was written in C under the devkitPro toolchain, an open toolchain that can be used to program several game consoles.

OBTAINED RESULTS
Most of the students went deep into their project's development and they obtained very positive results, emulating with the Nintendo DS different options, for instance, a train ticket vending machine, a sandwich vending machine, a soft drinks vending machine, a photo booth, an automatic gas station, and a candy machine, where they had to control the touch screen, the keyboard (either by poll or by interruption) and a timer.

The scores obtained, compared to previous the control group that followed a classical lectures methodology, were very good. As Figure 1 shows, the drop-out and Not Pass (<5) rates were lower, and out of 10, most of the students got a score between 7 and 9.

The methodology was mostly satisfactory and motivating for the students: "*We feel comfortable.*", "*We learn more*". "*Motivation is maintained for the whole semester. These things could be done on a PC, but it is not so appealing. It is better with a Nintendo®.*". "*You can see that you are learning*".

ITiCSE'12, July 3–5, 2012, Haifa, Israel.
ACM 978-1-4503-1246-2/12/07.

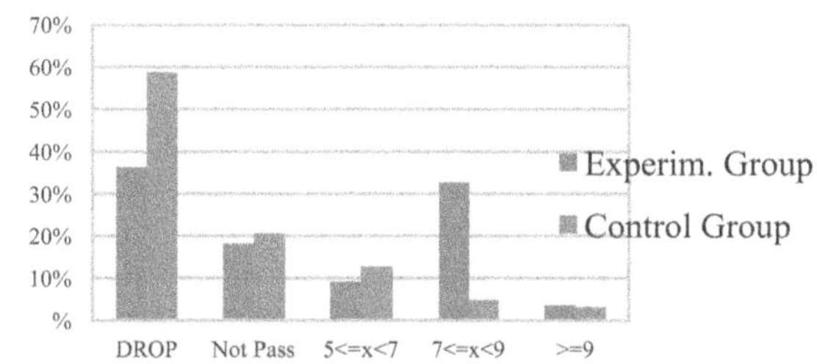

Figure 1. Scores in different situations

The weak point was the theoretical part. Although students admit that the theoretical content is contained in the class notes, they constantly said that there should be more theoretical explanations. "*With this methodology theoretical concepts are not explained as necessary*", "*We didn't have lectures. We had the notes and had to manage ourselves. But did we understand?*", "*I would give more theoretical explanation, since I had many doubts during the development of the project.*". However, the projects were completed successfully.

CONCLUSIONS
Although a single experience is not enough to draw conclusions, the proposed methodology and platform appear to be suitable for our purposes. Most of the evidence indicates that the results obtained were better than in previous years. The students felt lost without theoretical explanations, but they found themselves and emerged from the labyrinth stronger, even if they didn't realize it.

In the future, we would like to continue making both quantitative and qualitative research to observe the benefits and damages of the methodology and the platform, and also the problems experienced by students when faced with the topic. We also would like to address the sense of lack of theoretical explanations.

ACKNOWLEDGMENTS
This work has been funded by SAE/HELAZ, UPV/EHU.

We also would like to acknowledge all the students that took part in the experience.

REFERENCES
[1] ACM/IEEE Curricula recommendations http://www.acm.org/education/education/curricula-recommendations

[2] Martinez-Monés, A., Gómez-Sánchez, E., Dimitriadis Y.A., Jorrín-Abellán, I.M., Rubia-Avi, B., Vega-Gorgojo, G. Multiple Case Studies to Enhance Project-Based Learning in a Computer Architecture Course. IEEE Transactions on Education, Vol. 48, No. 3, August 2005, 482-489.

[3] Tew,A.E., Dorn, B., Leahy Jr.,W.D., and Guzdial, M. Context as Support for Learning Computer Organization. *Journal on Educational Resources in Computing (JERIC).* 8, 3, (Oct. 2008). DOI=http://dx.doi.org/10.1145/1404935.1404937

Using Professional and Ethical Themes

John Impagliazzo
Emeritus, Hofstra University
Department of Computer Science
Hempstead, New York 11549 USA
+1 631 463 6774
John.Impagliazzo@Hofstra.edu

ABSTRACT

This presentation describes ways in which teachers could use computing professionalism and ethics to enrich topics in their courses. These enrichment techniques could become a very effective extension to teaching computing courses. Using professionalism as a pedagogical technique could contribute to the better understanding of course material and to the foundations of lifelong learning experiences of students. Professional extensions and ethics also encourage students to appreciate the subject at hand and foster a sense of natural inquiry surrounding their area of study that includes the human dimension.

Categories and Subject Descriptors

K.4.1 [Public Policy Issues] *Ethics, Privacy*; K.4.2 [Social Issues]; K.7.4 [Professional Ethics]; K.3.2 [Computer and Information Science Education]: *Curriculum*

General Terms

Human Factors

Keywords

Computing professionalism, computing ethics, computing education, course enhancement

SUMMARY

The inclusion of professional elements in a computing course has advantages by allowing students to think beyond immediate technical topics. Computing professionalism and ethics has a way of encouraging students to look beyond the machine and broadens their outlook on the social implications of computing. Professional interludes could include a recitation of anecdotes to perk student interest or they could include undertakings to engage students in critical thinking about a computing topic. Professionals and students tend to overlook ethical areas of computing. Therefore, teachers should strive to include elements of the subject in their courses.

This presentation suggests ways in which teachers could include professionalism and ethics in their courses by incorporating relevant topics as a thread or theme associated with technical topics. The approach encourages students to explore these areas using various methods and websites that inspire professional and ethical awareness within computing courses.

In support of this professional theme, the author provides examples whereby teachers and students might engage in brief interludes to encourage professional responsibility and lifelong learning in their classes. Some topics highlighted at the presentation include:

- Computers harming other people
- Interfering with other people's computer work
- Snooping for computer files of others
- Stealing with computers
- Using computers to bear false witnesses
- Copying or using proprietary software
- Using computer resources of others without authorization
- Appropriating intellectual products of others
- Considering the social consequences of programs written or systems designed
- Using computers to ensure respect for other people

The above list (adopted from the "Ten Commandments of the Computer Ethics Institute" [i]) is a good starting point for instructors who wish to explore the use of professionalism and ethics in their courses.

Students should also realize that they will eventually work in global environments. What should be their ethical responsibilities as computing professionals when they practice in global settings? They should understand that their own local customs and practices may not necessarily conform to external thinking in a world where practice in global situations and endeavors represent the normal and modern way of doing business. Students should understand mutual respect for the ethical, moral, and legal customs of others in a way that affects positively the social connections they make and likely endure.

Bridging professional and ethical storytelling with technical content could form a unique opportunity to connect technical material to real life. All teachers of computing should at least try this approach. The rewards derived from the experience should well offset any preparation needed to present the material. So, try a bit of ethics in your courses. You just might enjoy it while making your courses more uplifting, more informative, and more relevant to today's world.

[i] http://computerethicsinstitute.org/publications/tencommandments.html

ITiCSE'12, July 3–5, 2012, Haifa, Israel.
ACM 978-1-4503-1246-2/12/07.

Breadth First Search (Animation and Obstacle Avoidance)*

Arnold Rosenbloom
University of Toronto at Mississauga
Mississauga, Ontario, Canada
arnold@cs.toronto.edu

ABSTRACT

A simple, motivating first year assignment which animates a Breadth First Search solution to a graphical obstacle avoidance problem is presented.

Categories and Subject Descriptors

K.3.2.4 [**Computers and Education**]: Computer & Information Science Education—*computer science education*

General Terms

Algorithms

Keywords

Data structures, algorithms, visualization, queues

1. INTRODUCTION AND ASSIGNMENT

Breadth First Search (BFS) is particularly challenging for first year students. In [1] they use graphics to motivate and illustrate BFS. Their students generate static colorized images to compare the Depth First Search and BFS approaches to background detection. In contrast, our assignment uses animation and focuses specifically on BFS and the intuition behind the queue, the reachable vertices and generating a shortest path back to a source vertex. We have students modify a graph based BFS algorithm to solve a graphical version of the obstacle avoidance problem. Each student's program animates the breadth first search for a destination from a source which avoids obstacles in an image.

In preparation for this assignment, students have been introduced to stacks, queues, Object Oriented programming in Python, the BFS algorithm, image and colour representation. Students also attend a tutorial introducing the Python Image Library (see the author's website).

The assignment website includes samples of the animations their code will produce and a zip file with an images directory, and starter code, stripped down from a solution. It also includes instructions on generating animations(gif89) from a collection of images using ImageMagic's `convert`.

The starter code includes a `Queue` class, a `PathDetails` class, used to generate a destination to source path. When completed by the student, the `ObstacleAvoider` class can create a random obstacle image with a source and destination, display and save snapshots of the breadth first search algorithm in progress.

Students complete the assignment by supplying code at specified locations inside the `ObstacleAvoider` class. They adapted a graph based BFS algorithm to the present context, including the notion of neighbouring pixels in place of adjacent vertices. Snapshots of the algorithms datastructures are taken when the BFS queue advances by two pixels. These were assembled into an animation. Challenges include knowing when to take a snapshot, identifying and visualizing the data structures that appear as the blue reachable pixels, the yellow frontier between reachable and unexplored pixels, and the path from the destination back to the source.

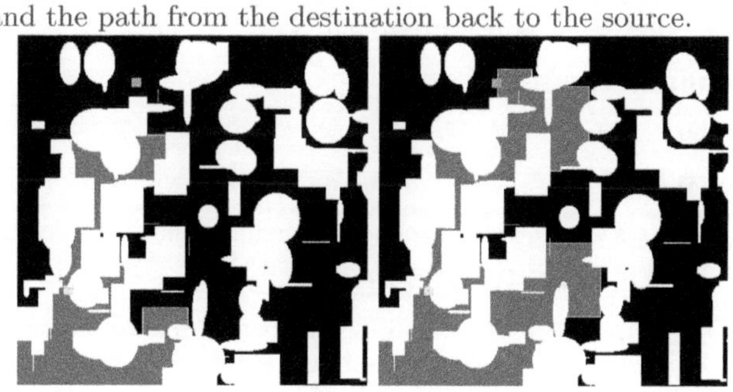

Marking this assignment was easy. Style and simplicity were marked by examining submitted code. A script executes their code on sample problem instances generating algorithm animations. Correctness is marked by comparing these with the solutions animations to 'see' whether students understood the BFS algorithm, the queue, the reachable pixels and the obstacle avoiding path. By looking at the advancing yellow frontier, we see whether a student understands and properly populates the queue. By comparing the sizes of the generated animations, we easily see whether a student generates snapshots at the proper frequency and so understands the notion of distance.

*Related resources can be found at `http://www.cs.toronto.edu/~arnold/teaching/bfs.zip`

2. REFERENCES

[1] A. Erkan and D. Gochev. An image background detection project for a visual exploration of dfs and bfs. In *Proceedings of the 39th SIGCSE technical symposium on Computer science education*, SIGCSE '08, pages 483–487, New York, NY, USA, 2008. ACM.

ITiCSE'12, July 3–5, 2012, Haifa, Israel.
ACM 978-1-4503-1246-2/12/07.

Teaching Labs on Pseudorandom Number Generation

Elizabeth Patitsas
University of Toronto
40 St George St.
Toronto ON M5S 2E4
patitsas@cs.toronto.edu

ABSTRACT

This presentation describes our approach to teaching pseudorandom number generation (PRNG) in CS labs. We use PRNG at two universities as an example of an application of sequential circuitry in our digital logic courses. Our goal is for our students to have meaningful assignments, and to relate digital logic not only to the larger CS curriculum, but to the students' lives. This also us a motivation to discuss "what is randomness?", security issues relating to seeding and encryption, and why and how we use randomness in computing.

Categories and Subject Descriptors

K.3.2 [**Computers and Information Science Education**]: Pedagogy, education research

General Terms

Design

Keywords

Digital logic, labs, computer science education

1. THE PRESENTATION

This "Tips, Techniques, and Courseware" session presents two lab activities aimed at teaching pseudorandom number generation (PRNG). Our goal in this presentation is to give CS educators a compelling example for students to practice with when learning sequential circuitry in a digital logic or hardware course. We believe this will be interesting to the ITiCSE community as it provides a new example for teaching sequential circuitry which can be related to "big picture" CS topics such as stochastic algorithms, cryptography, and computer security.

1.1 The Lab Activities

We will be presenting two lab activities on PRNG, a first-year lab from the University of British Columbia, and a second-year lab from the University of Toronto. The former is freely available under a Creative Commons License [1]. Both activities have students build PRNG circuits in courses which cover digital logic. In both cases, the activities provide a new example for teaching sequential circuitry. Learning how to design sequential circuits is analogous to learning to write recursive programs; the design approach is different from the combinational circuitry that we begin by teaching them.

In both labs, students implement linear shift feedback registers (LFSRs). These circuits have the advantage of being simple, yet the results are interesting to the students. For the students, the activity of building an LFSR is rated as being fun, interesting, and rewarding. They see it as a real-world problem that engages them. Previously, when teaching sequential circuitry, we opted to use "toy problems". This new activity has grounded this portion of the course by presenting a real world problem.

1.2 Benefits of teaching PRNG

We have found a number of benefits of teaching PRNG beyond how its grounds digital logic for the students:

1. Learning PRNG gives the students experience with the concept of seeding. Not only does this give them more familiarity with sequential circuitry, but it also teaches them the need to seed a PRNG properly. TAs in courses downstream of ours have reported that students who complete this lab activity now properly seed their C++ code when dealing with random algorithms.
2. The discussion of seeding bridges into a discussion of security. We also take this activity as an opportunity to teach students about cryptography, particularly one-time pads and stream ciphers.
3. It allows us to engage students in the discussion of "what is randomness?"
4. When students ask what random numbers are used for in CS, it allows a discussion of how randomness is used in the field. This also gives us an opportunity to bridge hardware-level topics with the CS theory students are learning concurrently.

2. ACKNOWLEDGMENTS

For feedback in lab development: Meghan Allen, Patrice Belleville, Steve Engels, Simon Hastings, Vanessa Kroeker, Kimberly Voll, Steve Wolfman, Bob Woodham, and the TAs of the two courses. For the author's supervision and funding: Steve Easterbrook.

[1]Available at `http://www.ugrad.cs.ubc.ca/~cs121/2011W2/Homepage/labs.html`

Best Practices for Time-Management of Student Groups with Heterogeneous Effort

André Schäfer, Matthias Mielke, Rainer Brück
Institute of Microsystem Technology
University of Siegen
andre.schaefer@uni-siegen.de, matthias.mielke@uni-siegen.de
rainer.brueck@uni-siegen.de

ABSTRACT
The daily work of an engineer in industry is affected by project work; often more than one project at a time. Consequently, time and self-management is an important part of the education of future engineers and scientists. Students of electrical engineering and computer science at the University of Siegen have a student project work in their curricula to deepen hard skills and to learn soft skills, like teamwork, organization and time-management. Often these groups consist of students with heterogeneous requirements in terms of working hours. In this contribution, the authors present a good practice for time-management of groups with heterogeneous working-time.

Categories and Subject Descriptors
K.3.2 [**Computer and Education**]: Computer and Information Science Education - *Self-assessment*

General Terms
Management, Human Factors

Keywords
Time Management, Project Work, Heterogeneous Working-Time

1. INTRODUCTION
The curricula of students, studying electrical engineering or computer science at the University of Siegen, contain a project work to deepen hard skills and to learn soft skills. Here, the students have to deal with an engineering task. Additionally, they have to manage and coordinate the complete work by themselves. A detailed description of the concept and realization of project groups at the Microsystems Engineering Group can be found in [1].

To keep track of the time spent and gain a better intuition for the time necessary to complete a task, the students' group has to do time and resource management. Complicating, the participants in the project groups are studying different subjects, e.g. computer science and electrical engineering, with different intended degrees, e.g. Bachelor and Master. Each subject imposes other requirements in terms of working hours for a project group, with an intended effort between 300 and 900 hours.

Best practices were setup to cope with the diversity of the intended effort.

2. BEST-PRACTICES
The students have to score their hours working on a project in spreadsheets, which are necessary for later time management and allocation of duties. Comparing the work times for homogeneous

ITiCSE'12, July 3–5, 2012, Haifa, Israel.
ACM 978-1-4503-1246-2/12/07.

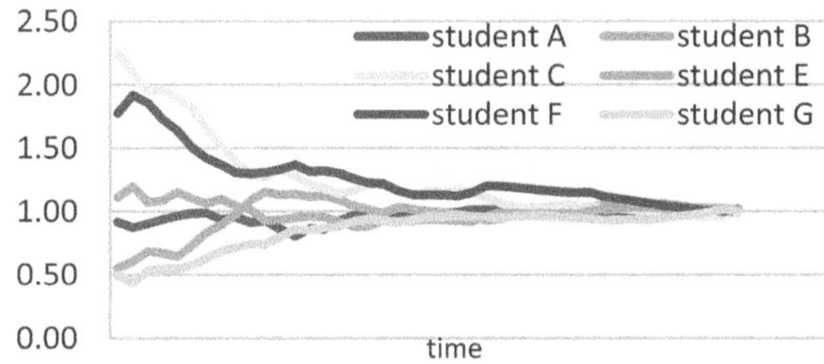

groups, i.e. a group in which all members have the same requirements in terms of working hours, is relatively simple. For a group with members, that have all the same requirements in terms of working hours, the absolute working hours can be directly used to compare the individual students' investment in time. For a group of students with heterogeneous time requirements, this approach alone is not meaningful, since the individual students' time requirement has to be taken into account.

A practical technique to judge the invested working time of a student i in relation to the other n students of the group is given by the formula

$$normed\ actual\ value_i = \frac{\frac{worked\ hours_i}{\sum_{j=0}^{n} worked\ hours_j}}{\frac{total\ working\ hours_i}{\sum_{j=0}^{n} total\ working\ hours_j}}.$$

The equation is evaluated for all students every week. If all students have a value of 1, they have invested an equal amount of their time on the project. The value for all students is plotted in a chart to visualize the development. The Figure above shows the working hours of seven students in proportions to each other and in proportion to their own needed working hours.

A group of inexperienced students has always problems with planning and allocation of tasks. Hence, it is important that they update their schedule regularly. However, the students learn directly from their mistakes. With the help of the chart and the spreadsheets containing the absolute working time, the tasks for the next week can be planed easily.

3. EXPERIENCES
We tested this technique with five student groups with heterogeneous working-time in the last four years. We experienced, that the groups which adopted the approach early and used it thoroughly, had less difficulties in time management. It is possible to combine this technique with other methods for time management.

4. REFERENCES
[1] Schäfer, A., Mielke, M., and Brück, R. 2011. Design of innovative integrated circuits in education. ITiCSE '11. ACM Press, 53–56, 2011.

Developing Contexts for Teaching Java Using AGUIA/J

André L. Santos[*†]
andre.santos@iscte.pt

[*]Faculty of Sciences, University of Lisbon
LASIGE, Bloco C6, Piso 3, Campo Grande
1749-016 Lisboa, Portugal

[†]Instituto Universitário de Lisboa (ISCTE-IUL)
Av. das Forças Armadas, Edifício II
1649-026 Lisboa, Portugal

ABSTRACT

Teaching programming in *context* [1], i.e. having exercises dealing with artifacts of a familiar domain (e.g. images, card games), has demonstrated convincing results in terms of raising student retention and interest in CS. This session addresses the development of contexts for Java by means of AGUIA/J plugins [3].

Categories and Subject Descriptors

K.3.2 [**Computers and Education**]: Computer and Information Science Education; D.1.5 [**Programming Techniques**]: Object-oriented Programming

General Terms

Design, Human Factors

Keywords

Object-oriented programming, contextualized programming, Java

1. AGUIA/J ENVIRONMENT

AGUIA/J [2] is an open-ended environment for teaching Java for which contexts can be provided through the development of plugins. This tool has been used at our institution during the last delivery of the Introduction to Programming course, customized with the contexts of *images*, *card games*, and *board games*. Its adoption yielded good results in terms of approval rates and student satisfaction, especially in the case of non-CS majors [3].

In order to develop a context to use with the tool one has to provide a *domain model* and *view widgets* for the objects of that model (see Figure 1). The domain model represents an abstract description of the objects of the context, being conceptually pure and independent from any form of visualization. The view widgets are graphical components that are capable of rendering objects of a certain domain model. In turn, the AGUIA/J environment acts as the *controller* that coordinates models and views. The domain model and the view widgets are wired by means of an Eclipse plugin. Several context plugins may coexist in the environment.

2. DEMONSTRATION

This session demonstrates how to develop a context plugin for AGUIA/J, explaining the essential steps together with a small example context. A context may be basically anything that can be

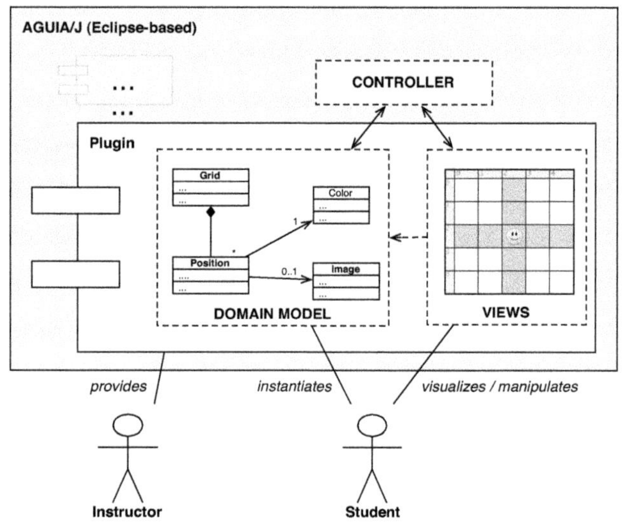

Figure 1: Context plugins in AGUIA/J: Instructors develop plugins that consist of a domain model and view widgets for that model, whereas students instantiate objects of the domain model in their programs and visualize them in the environment.

modeled and graphically rendered. Having a domain model as a set of simple Java classes totally independent from the environment, the main task is to develop view widgets against the domain model, while conforming to an environment-specific Java interface.

We show that by writing a few tens of lines of code, an instructor is able to extend the environment with a custom context for programming exercises. The proposed approach stands as a low-cost solution for customizing a programming course for a specific audience, which may vary with respect to age, social context, or discipline.

3. REFERENCES

[1] S. Cooper and S. Cunningham. Teaching computer science in context. *ACM Inroads*, 1:5–8, March 2010.

[2] A. L. Santos. AGUIA/J: a tool for interactive experimentation of objects. In *Proceedings of the 16th annual conference on Innovation and technology in computer science education*, ITiCSE '11. Darmstadt, Germany, June 2011.

[3] A. L. Santos. An open-ended environment for teaching Java in context. In *Proceedings of the 17th annual joint conference on Innovation and technology in computer science education*, ITiCSE '12. Haifa, Israel, July 2012.

The Presenter First Design Approach

Zachary Kurmas
School of Computing
Grand Valley State University
kurmasz@gvsu.edu

ABSTRACT

Presenter First is a design technique that combines the Model-View-Presenter design pattern with the concept of "user stories." We have found that Presenter First helps students decompose their programming projects into manageable tasks.

Categories and Subject Descriptors

D.2.2 [**Software Engineering**]: Design Tools and Techniques

General Terms

Design

Keywords

Presenter First, Model-View-Presenter

1. INTRODUCTION

CS 2 at our university covers a fairly standard list of topics, including two-dimensional arrays, recursion, algorithm analysis, and linked lists. In the process of teaching these topics, we also strive to develop students' software design skills. One goal for CS 2 is for students to be able to define and implement a small set of classes that work together and exhibit good design (avoid duplicate code, separation of concerns, etc.).

Our CS 2 is not an analysis and design course; and many students are still novice programmers who need a lot of guidance to complete a project. We have struggled to find the right balance between giving the students enough direction to keep them reasonably on track while also keeping the requirements flexible enough to allow them to make non-trivial design decisions (i.e., choose their own classes and methods).

A design process called "Presenter First" has helped us find this balance.

2. PRESENTER FIRST

Presenter First is a design technique developed by Atomic Object, a software development company in Grand Rapids, Michigan [1, 2]. It is a process of iteratively defining and implementing user stories using a variant of the Model-View-Presenter (MVP) design pattern. MVP organizes application code into three main pieces:

- The **view** is responsible for rendering the user interface (UI) and displaying the state of the application.
- The **model** contains the application state and logic.
- The **presenter** is responsible for interacting with both the view and the model.

The presenter (not the view) responds to UI events (such as button pushes) and calls the appropriate methods on the model. The presenter is also responsible for detecting changes to the model's state and passing updated data to the view. With MVP, the model and the view do not directly interact: All interactions go through the presenter.

Students often feel overwhelmed by projects and don't know where to begin. Presenter First provides a clear starting point: user stories. Students develop, then implement, a story of the form "When the user `xxxx`, then `yyyy`." An example story would be "When a user clicks on a game square, then a new token should appear in that square."

The MVP design pattern is useful because the presenter provides a single, well-defined place for the code that implements a user story. Students implement a user story by implementing a private method in the presenter that

- detects when the user does `xxxx`,
- calls methods on the model to cause `yyyy`, then
- calls an update method on the view.

Notice that it is the presenter, not the view, that responds to UI events. This design helps students by separating their "story" code from the basic UI implementation. With a traditional model-view design, user stories can get spread over several view classes. With MVP, all the user story code remains in the presenter. This design also allows students to use an instructor-provided GUI without having to modify the code to add listeners. Instead, the students simply place the listeners they write in the presenter.

3. REFERENCES

[1] M. Alles, D. Crosby, B. Harleton, G. Pattison, C. Erickson, M. Marsiglia, and C. Stienstra. Presenter first: organizing complex gui applications for test-driven development. In *Agile Conference, 2006*, july 2006.

[2] D. Crosby and C. Erickson. Big, complex, and tested? just say 'when'. *Better Software*, 2007.

ITiCSE'12, July 3–5, 2012, Haifa, Israel.
ACM 978-1-4503-1246-2/12/07.

A Hardware Simulator for Teaching CPU Design

Michael Black
Department of Computer Science, American University
4400 Massachusetts Ave, NW
Washington, DC, USA
mblack@american.edu

ABSTRACT

This presentation describes a GUI-based tool for teaching CPU design to computer architecture students. A datapath builder allows microarchitecture building blocks, such as registers, ALUs, and multiplexors, to be laid out and wired together. A control builder allows a control state machine to be developed for the datapath. Because the processor design is simulated within a full PC emulator, student-designed processors can use emulated devices, such as drives, video, and I/O ports. A tutorial teaches students to use the simulator to build and simulate a pipelined RISC processor.

Categories and Subject Descriptors

C.0 [**Computer Systems Organization**]: General

General Terms

Design,Experimentation

Keywords

Processor, Simulator, x86

1. INTRODUCTION

Hardware simulators are frequently employed in computer architecture courses, allowing students to experiment with the course materials and produce designs without having to physically construct the device. This presentation describes a new hardware simulator that allows students to develop their own CPUs. The simulator is entirely graphics-based and does not require the user to have programming experience. It nevertheless is powerful enough that more advanced architectural techniques, such as pipelining, speculation, and caching, and real instruction sets can be modeled. The simulator is closely integrated with a PC emulator, allowing student processor designs to access memory and devices.

2. SIMULATOR

Our simulator has two basic user interfaces: a Datapath GUI, and a Control GUI, both of which are integrated with the PC emulator. The Datapath contains the components, their layout and connections, and the Control models the control state machine and signals sent to manage data flow and clock registers. To run a hardware simulation takes four steps: 1) opening the PC emulator, 2) creating or loading a datapath with the Datapath Builder, 3) creating or loading a control with the Control Builder, 4) instantiating the a "custom processor", which simulates the design and allows the user to see it run.

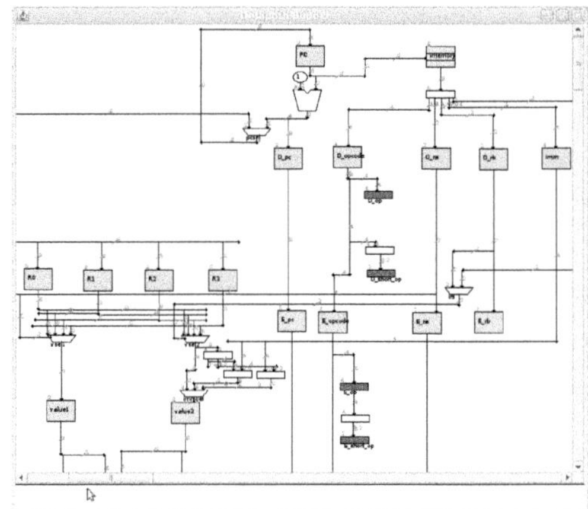

Figure 1: Pipelined RISC Processor, Execute Stage

Accompanying the simulator is a tutorial intended for undergraduate students taking a computer architecture course. In a series of labs, students 1) make the control for a 10-instruction RISC processor, 2) make a 4-stage pipeline for that processor, and 3) detect and remove pipeline hazards to improve performance. The tutorial was tested as part of a computer architecture course for computer engineering majors at the University of Maryland, College Park. Of these, all 30 teams successfully completed the RISC processor lab, 22 teams completed the pipelined processor, and 2 teams implemented the optional hazard detection unit. The tutorial and simulator are freely available under the GNU Public License and are posted at `rodent.cs.american.edu/mblack/simulator`.

3. ACKNOWLEDGEMENTS

This work was made possible by NSF CCLI grant 0941057.

4. REFERENCES

[1] Black, M., Komala, P. A full system x86 simulator for teaching computer organization. SIGCSE Technical Symposium on Computer Science Education, 2011.

Introvert Educators: Techniques to be Effective in the Traditional Face-to-face CS Classroom

Karina Vashta Assiter
Wentworth Institute of Technology
550 Huntington Avenue
Boston, MA 01255
1.781.866.6050
assiterk@wit.edu

ABSTRACT

This purpose of this session is two-fold: first, to consider an initial set of strategies that introvert educators could adopt (and then adapt) in order to be effective in the traditional face-to-face computer science classroom; and, then, to initiate research (and dialogue) about educator personality types, in general, and their associated best teaching practice, since, just as preferred learning style depends on the personality of the learner, best teaching practices should be determined based (among other things) upon the personality type of the instructor.

Categories and Subject Descriptors

K.3.2. [**Computer Milieux**]: Computer and information Science education – *Computer science, education, curriculum.*

General Terms

Performance.

Keywords

Computer Science Education, Pedagogy, Personality Types.

1. INTRODUCTION

Today's multi-tasking students have a limited ability to pay attention in class, so the responsibility of keeping attention has shifted from the student, who in the past was expected to put in the effort to *pay attention*, to the instructor, who must now attempt to *hold student attention*. Thus, the educator becomes more of an entertainer, as the just a conveyer of knowledge; to be effective in the classroom they need to be (or act) outgoing, gregarious, to dance from the board to the front of the classroom, and to relate jokes and personal stories to a class full of students. The image of the outgoing instructor is in contrast to what we envision to be the natural characteristics of the introvert personality type. [1, 2]

This does not imply that introverts can't be excellent educators; the key is identifying strategies that can adopted (and then adapted) in order for them to be effective even in the traditional face-to-face (versus online) setting.

This session will start off with a presentation of an initial set of strategies that have worked for the author and several colleagues, but that have not been *proven* to be effective, nor implemented in all teaching/learning contexts (with all learner types and within all instructional environments). Thus, the second part of the session will be a dialogue (between the audience/presenters), and an opportunity to explore areas of further research within the realm of educator personality type and associated best teaching practices

2. REFERENCES

[1] Eysenck, H.J. 1971. Readings n Extraversion-Introversion, Wiley, New York.

[2] Hall, C. and Nordby, V. 1999. *A Primer of Jungian Psychology.* Meridian, New York.

ITiCSE'12, July 3–5, 2012, Haifa, Israel.
ACM 978-1-4503-1246-2/12/07.

The Effect of Mathematical vs. Verbal Formulation for Finite Automata

Tali Dror
Kiryat Sharet high school, Holon, Israel
Tel: ++972-54-2344717
dror.tali@gmail.com

Dafna Levi Rashti
Kiryat Sharet high school, Holon, Israel
Tel: ++972-52-2653173
dafna81@bezeqint.net

ABSTRACT

This study examines the capability of high-school students to solve problems related to the Computational model of finite deterministic automata. Specifically, we compared student's achievements when solving verbal "story like" questions to solving the similar problem but formulated mathematically. A questionnaire composed of two questions, each formulated in two ways (verbal and mathematical), was given to the students as part of an exam. Generally, average or weak students got lower grades when they had to solve verbal questions. It was also found that the gap between the student achievements in verbal vs. mathematical questions widened for weaker students and when the teaching and practicing time was reduced. The student mistakes originated from their difficulties to extract a formal language from the story and to translate constrains given in the verbal formulation of the questions correctly. It was also found that when the students were unfamiliar to the content and the context of the story they had difficulties comprehending the text. This in turn caused the student to inaccurately describe the formal language (alphabet and constrains) and thus to design an incorrect automata.

Categories and Subject Descriptors

F.4.3 Formal Languages - Classes defined by grammars or automata; K.3.2 Computer and Information Science Education – Computer science education; Curriculum.

Keywords: Computational models, finite deterministic automata, word problem, story-like problems, mathematical formulation, verbal formulation.

1. INTRODUCTION

The Israeli CS high school curriculum includes 5 units [2], the fifth of which is considered a "Theoretical" unit; one of the options for this unit is a 'Computational Models' course.

There are various explanations for the difficulty in solving problems in computer science in general and in the 'Computational Models' course in particular. One possible explanation is that the basic difficulty lies in understanding the tasks and in the student's problem solving skills [3]. Difficulties in problem solving in general and in verbal questions in particular, are not unique to the field of computer science education [1].

2. THE RESEARCH QUESTION

The research question of this study was: *Does the formulation of a problem (verbal vs. mathematical) influence the student achievements?*

Therefore the goals of this study were (1) to compare the success ratio of students receiving a verbal question to students that receive similar questions in a mathematical formulation; and (2) to identify the students' difficulties in solving verbal questions.

3. RESULTS

Among the 63 high school students that participated in the research the average grade of the verbal question was 83 points; this score was 10 points lower than the average grade of the mathematical question (93 points). Among the best students (whose scores in the entire exams was 85 and over) the gap was of only 3 points between the grades in the mathematical formulation question and verbal question and average achievements were excellent, 95 and 98 respectively. In contrast, the gap among average and weak students (whose average grade in the entire exams was 84 and under) was much wider, 20 points, the average grade for the verbal question was 62 points compared to 82 points in the mathematical question. Students' showed difficulties in 'translating' verbal formulations to mathematical terms. From interviews with the students it was found that students, particularly the weak students, preferred the verbal questions because these appeared to the students clearer and more direct. The reason for this was that the students preferred questions that did not include mathematical descriptions and / or mathematical signs. These verbal questions also did not use terms that often the students are not confident about their meaning.

4. DISCUSSION AND CONCLUSION

Based on the above results students that show good and very good achievements in the Computational models course are able to solve problem that are formulated either in mathematical or in verbal format. The average and weak students however were found to have more difficulties when the questions are given in verbal "story like" format. As the amount of elements given in the verbal formulation of the questions increase more difficulties in defining the terms or structure of the word in the language is observed. It was further found that exposing students to verbal questions improve their achievements. Additional training and in turn extended experience in problem solving improves the rate of success in general but also the exposure to a specific questions-style directly contributes to the student ability to solve a larger variety of questions. The questionnaire, as well as interviews with the students, will both be elaborated in our Poster.

5. ACKNOWLEDGMENTS

We thank Prof. Ben Ari and Dr. Lapidot for fruitful discussions and mentoring. We thank Dganit Muchtar-Ebel for assistance with the distribution of the questionnaires.

6. REFERENCES

[1] Croteau E.A., Heffernan N. T. and Koedinger K.R. (2004). Why are Algebra Word Problem Difficult? Using Tutoring Log Files and the Power Law of Learning to Select the Best Fitting Cognitive Model, In J.C. Lester et al. (Eds.): *Proceedings of Intelligent Tutoring Systems 2004*, 240-250.

[2] Gal-Ezer, J., Beeri, C., Harel, D. and Yehudai, A. (1995). A high school program in computer science, *Computer*, 28, 73-80.

[3] Ginat, D. (2000). Colorful examples for elaborating exploration of regularities in high-school CS1, *Proceedings of the 5th annual SIGCSE/SIGCUE ITiCSE conference on Innovation and technology in computer science education*, 81-84.

A Model of CS Teachers' Knowledge Growth

Neomi Liberman
The Hebrew University of Jerusalem, Israel
+972-588-2056
neomilib@gmail.com

Yifat Ben-David Kolikant
The Hebrew University of Jerusalem, Israel
+972-588-2056
yifat.kolikant@mail.huji.ac.il

Catriel Beeri
Dan Academic Center
Petach-Tikva, Israel
+972- 073-706-7020
catriel.beeri@dan.ac.il

ABSTRACT

Our poster suggests a spiral model of CS teachers' knowledge growth in laboratory sessions, based on Shulman's model of pedagogical reasoning. Our proposed spiral model deals with much smaller units of time, e.g. a session or a part of a session in class, and with small units of knowledge. It is based on observations in laboratory sessions of regressed experts in the first, second and third time they taught inheritance and polymorphism, as well as on interviews with them.

Categories and Subject Descriptors

K.3.2 [**Computer and Information Science Education**]: Computer Science Education.

General Terms: Human Factors

Keywords: *Inheritance; polymorphism; laboratory session; pedagogical reasoning*

INTRODUCTION

Due to a reform in the Israeli CS high school curricula, and the development of a new program based on object-oriented programming (OOP), in-service teachers who studied and taught procedural programming were required in the last decade to cope with the new paradigm of OOP. Since most teachers were trained in procedural programming, they were offered courses in OOP, to enable them to teach the new paradigm. Consequently, these in-service teachers found themselves in a rather unique situation: on the one hand they were experienced CS teachers who knew the craft of teaching in general, and teaching programming to high-school students in particular; on the other hand they were novices with respect to the content they had to teach.

In the years 2006-2008 we investigated how such teachers coped with this challenge. We studied both how they learn the new paradigm, and how they teach it, concentrating on the topic of inheritance and polymorphism, an advanced topic in OOP.

FINDINGS AND CONCLUSIONS

In a previous report on this research, we argued for a new teacher state, a hybrid of the novice and the expert states, which we suggested to name a *regressed expert*. This is the state of an expert teacher, who needs to learn and then teach a new body of knowledge, quite different from that which he or she has been teaching. In this poster we focus on the process by which these teachers' knowledge grows as they teach, based on three case studies from this investigation. We propose a model of knowledge growth, based on Shulman's model of pedagogical reasoning [1].

Recall that Shulman's model has 6 stages that a teacher passes through when she teaches a subject (issue): Comprehension, Transformation, Instruction, Evaluation, Reflection, and New comprehension. This model assumes a complete circle of knowledge growth is measured on large time quanta (such as a season of teaching), as well as large quanta of knowledge.

In contrast, our proposed spiral model deals with much smaller units of time, e.g. a session or a part of a session in class, and with small, units ("bits") of knowledge. It is based on observations in laboratory sessions of regressed experts in the first, second and third time they taught inheritance and polymorphism, as well as on interviews with them, in which we observed a series of several completed circles of knowledge growth within 90-computer lab session. The teachers who taught second and third time inheritance and polymorphism behaved as experts. The teacher who taught that subject for the first time improved her knowledge, as demonstrated in figure 1 and figure 2. In fact, we observed a series of several completed circles of knowledge growth within 90-computer lab session. The speed of knowledge growth can be explained as a result, at least in some part, of the characteristic of laboratory sessions combined together with the teachers' experience.

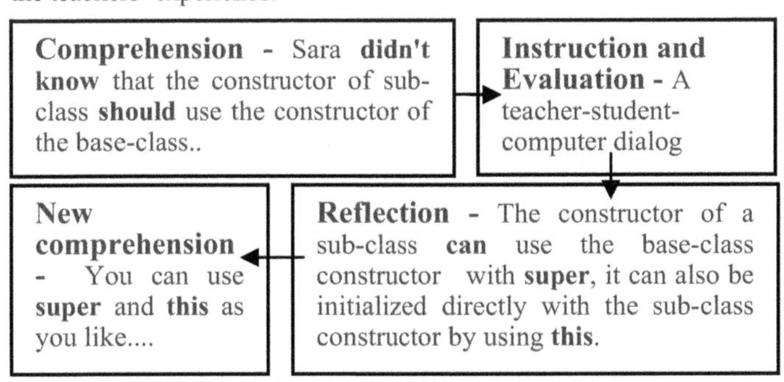

Figure 2: Another **pass** in the same laboratory session

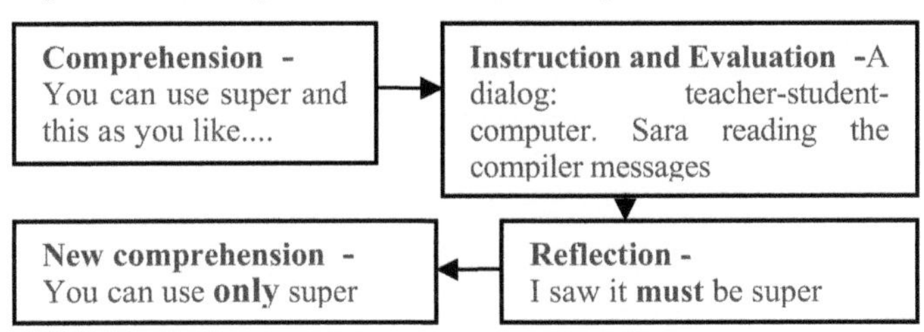

Figure 1: One pass on the new model by Sara

REFERENCES

[1] Shulman, L.S., (1987). Knowledge and Teaching: Foundations of the New Reform. Harvard Educational Review, 57(1), 1-22.

ITiCSE'12, July 3–5, 2012, Haifa, Israel.
ACM 978-1-4503-1246-2/12/07.

Cryptography for the Million

Yonatan Chen
Department of Computer Science
Charedic College
Jerusalem, Israel
yonatanhen@gmail.com

Eran London
Department of Computer Science
Hadassah Academic College
Jerusalem, Israel
eran@hadassah.ac.il

Moshe Munk
Department of Computer Science
Charedic College
Jerusalem, Israel
moshemunk@gmail.com

ABSTRACT
As part of the Centenary events of the Alan Turing Year, the Bloomfield Science Museum in Jerusalem is planning an exhibition that will present different aspects of Computer Science, whose center will be Alan Turing. Cryptography is one of the major fields associated with him. Our goal is to present an intriguing family of hands-on exhibits that will be both recreational and educational for the general audience, suitable for a wide spectrum of visitors, starting at the age of (about) 8 and going up to 120.

Categories and Subject Descriptors
K.3.2 [**COMPUTERS AND EDUCATION**]: Computer and Information Science Education.

General Terms
Theory, Security, Human Factors.

Keywords
Exhibition, Cryptography, General Audience, Science Museum.

1. MOTIVATION
We wish to develop a series of hands-on exhibits attracting visitors of all ages (starting at around the age of 8), that will teach and demonstrate basic notions of cryptography in a game-like atmosphere. The challenge lies in the fact that this is a "wandering audience", walking around in the museum. There are other exhibits in the neighborhood, and we get a single chance to get attention.

2. BASIC CRYPTOGRAPHY
Nowadays, the importance of cryptography is clear. The need for secure and private channels is essential. Examples begin with passwords for private computers and phones, continue with secure communication over the internet and reach the high end of military needs. Although techniques and ideas did change over the years, especially with the invention of public key cryptography (allowing two parties that had never met before to communicate securely), basic notions are still the same: two parties should be able to communicate without worrying about eavesdropping. In order to do so, they (classically) share a secret key – known only to them, that allows one of them to encrypt messages, while the other can decrypt them. An eavesdropper that does not know the secret key should not be able to learn anything about the message. The goal of the eavesdropper is to *break the code*, i.e., decipher the encrypted message, or even better – calculate the secret key, thus allowing him to decipher any future message transmitted between the two.

Perhaps the most simple, and probably the earliest example of a cryptographic algorithm is the substitution cipher. Working with an alphabet of 26 letters, the two parties may agree beforehand on one of the 26! possible permutations to serve as the secret key. A variant of this idea, is to partition the 26 letters to pairs and use only transpositions. For example, the following key may be used:

a	*b*	*c*	*d*	*e*	*f*	*g*	*h*	*i*	*j*	*k*	*l*	*m*
↕	↕	↕	↕	↕	↕	↕	↕	↕	↕	↕	↕	↕
z	*y*	*x*	*w*	*v*	*u*	*t*	*s*	*r*	*q*	*p*	*o*	*n*.

This means that when one wishes to encrypt the letter "a", "z" is used, and vice versa. This results in "all" being encrypted as "zoo". Knowing the permutation, it is a simple task to decrypt the message. Actually the given example is very old – it appears in the bible and is being used by the prophet Jeremiah (in Hebrew, not English …). This encryption scheme is called "ATBASH" due to the Hebrew first letter "aleph" changing places with the last letter "tav", and the second letter "beth" changing places with the second-to-last "shin".

Breaking such a code is easy, assuming the encrypted message is long enough. This is due to the fact that in any given language, each letter has its relative frequency. For example, in English, "e" appears about 12.7%, while "z" only 0.1%. Therefore, given a long-enough encrypted message, an encrypted letter appearing ~12.7% is most likely really an "e". Recognizing several letters (the more frequent ones) and using a dictionary – the full permutation is easily calculated.

An excellent reference for all background material (and much more) may be found in [1].

3. EXHIBITS
Our exhibits include the following:

1. ATBASH – the visitor sees a picture on the screen and is asked to type what he sees (for example: "zoo"). The encrypted result ("all") appears on the screen. Various such examples challenge him to understand what is going on.
2. Various other simple substitution ciphers are presented.
3. Manipulating letters to numbers and using mathematical functions to transform them to other numbers and then back to letters.
4. Code breaking of substitution ciphers via frequency tables: two players – each chooses a famous text and a key and sends to the other one. The first to decrypt wins.

All these ideas may be implemented via games between two players, as explained in the last example.

We may also try to present the basic ideas of modern cryptography and public key, but are not sure yet how.

4. REFERENCES
[1] Singh, S. 2000. *The Code Book*. Anchor Books, NY.

The Scientific Method and Software Testing Integrated into the Same Lesson

Hanania T. Salzer
HP OMS
9 Daphna St.
Ra'anana 43662, Israel
hanania.salzer@013net.net

Bruria Haberman
Davidson Inst. of Science Education,
Weizmann Inst. of Science,
Rehovot 76100, Israel
bruria.haberman@weizmann.ac.il

Cecile Yehezkel
Davidson Inst. of Science Education,
Weizmann Inst. of Science,
Rehovot 76100, Israel
cecile.yehezkel@weizmann.ac.il

ABSTRACT
In our poster, we propose a hands-on activity intended to educate students to the notion that neither the claim that a software application is free of a certain bug, nor a scientific hypothesis can be proven. Yet, we can increase our confidence in either's validity by genuine attempts of falsification.

Categories and Subject Descriptors
K.3.2 [**Computers and Education**]: Computer and Information Science Education – *computer science education.*

General Terms
Human Factors.

Keywords
Software testing; the scientific method; falsification.

1. SOFTWARE TESTING AND SCIENCE
While the reputation of testing in the software industry is from mediocre to belittled, the ACM and the IEEE-CS [1] situate testing as an essential part of the core of undergraduate software engineering education. According to common belief, the purpose of software testing is to ensure its correctness. This misconception needs to be substituted with the real goal of testing, namely, finding discrepancies.

An integral component of the scientific method is the disposition for critical thinking, overcoming cognitive biases [2]. An example bias is the tendency to prove a hypothesis rather than the genuine attempt to disprove it.

Several publications, such as [3], expressed strong intuitions that the process of software testing is, somehow, analogous to the scientific method, or at least to the scientific experiment. They pointed to similarities between a hypothesis and a test goal, between running an experiment and a test, and between the a-priori expected results in both disciplines. Salzer [4] formalized the homology between the two. He proposed capitalizing on the correspondence between the scientific method and software testing by combining the teaching of both in the same lessons.

1.1 The Teaching Aid
We developed a set of four versions for an interactive application. All have the same user interface. We implemented a few random behaviors, each of which is likely to be perceived as a bug. All bugs are present in all versions. The versions differ in their behavior only as a result of different frequencies in which the bugs are revealed in the output of each one, ranging from very frequently through none. The application has a graphical user interface with no text or graphics to hint the user about the application's functionality. A log file tracks the user's input and the application's output for later analysis by a researcher.

ITiCSE'12, July 3–5, 2012, Haifa, Israel.
ACM 978-1-4503-1246-2/12/07.

1.2 Teaching Highlights
Students will be instructed to try out each of the four versions of the application. For each one, they will be asked to list its properties, and indicate for each property whether, in their opinion, it represents a correct behavior or a bug. The teacher will pick a bug from the student's list, and instruct her to plan tests that target the selected bug.

The student will test each of the versions. After completing the tests, the teacher will ask the student to consider the version in which she easily demonstrated the existence of the bug, the version where this task was harder, the one where the task was really challenging, and, finally, the version where the student failed to do so. At this point they will discuss the question: How confident is the student about the existence of the selected bug or about its lack in each of the applications?

Students should internalize with the help of this exercise that it is not possible to prove the hypothesis that a software application is free of a certain bug, just as it is impossible to prove the correctness of a scientific hypothesis. Yet, the more we try to genuinely falsify a hypothesis, the larger will be our confidence in its validity.

2. REFERENCES
[1] ACM/IEEE Computer Society. 2004. *Software Engineering 2004, Curriculum Guidelines for Undergraduate Degree Programs in Software Engineering.*

[2] Halpern, D. F. 1998. Teaching critical thinking for transfer across domains: Disposition, skills, structure training, and metacognitive monitoring. *American Psychologist*, 53(4):449–455.

[3] Pettichord, B. 2000. Testers and Developers Think Differently. *Software Testing and Quality Engineering Magazine*, January/February 2000.

[4] Salzer, H. 2008. *Atomic Requirement Specifications and their Abstraction Level Hierarchy in Software Engineering Education.* Doctoral Thesis. Tel-Aviv University. The School of Education. (http://primage.tau.ac.il/libraries/theses/humart/free/002219606.pdf)

An Animation as an Illustrate Tool for Learning Concepts in Oop

Yael Mussai
Jerusalem College
Jerusalem
Israel 91160
+972-6750-949
ymussai@gmail.com

Neomi Liberman
Jerusalem College
Jerusalem
Israel 91160
+972-6750-948
neomilib@gmail.com

ABSTRACT

An animation as an illustrate tool for learning concepts in oop was created. It based on previous research that recognized misconceptions in inheritance and Our research checked how viewing the animation impacted on the CS students' understanding the main concepts of oop. The main finding was that viewing the animation improved the CS students' performance, especially the concept: casting. It especially helped them to build proper programming modules.

Categories and Subject Descriptors

[Computer and Information Science Education]

General Terms

Human Factors

Keywords

animation, misconception, object oriented programming, inheritance, polymorphism, casting.

INTRODUCTION

Inheritance and polymorphism are abstract, complex concepts. They are central concepts in object oriented programming. Therefore, a proper understanding of them is important and basic to the learning process. We created an animation that demonstrates concepts like: inheritance; polymorphism and casting. The animation is based on previous research that recognized misconceptions in inheritance and polymorphism [1]. The base class in the animation is a button-class and it has 4 scenes, figure 1 shows one image of a scene in the animation.

Our research checked how viewing the animation impacted on the CS students' understanding the main concepts of oop.

FINDINGS

We checked it on 30 students using open questionnaires. The students were asked to follow 10 program segments , to write the output of each segment and give an explanation. After viewing the animation, they were asked to describe their feeling about the animation contribution. We also asked their teachers about their positions toward the animation as a learning tool.

The main finding was that viewing the animation improved the CS students' performance, especially the concept: casting. It especially helped them to build proper programming modules.

In the poster, we will describe the conceptual environment of the animation coupled with the rationale of it. A few parts of the animation will be displayed. We will also show the study's results and implications for better ways to teach the inheritance and polymorphism concepts.

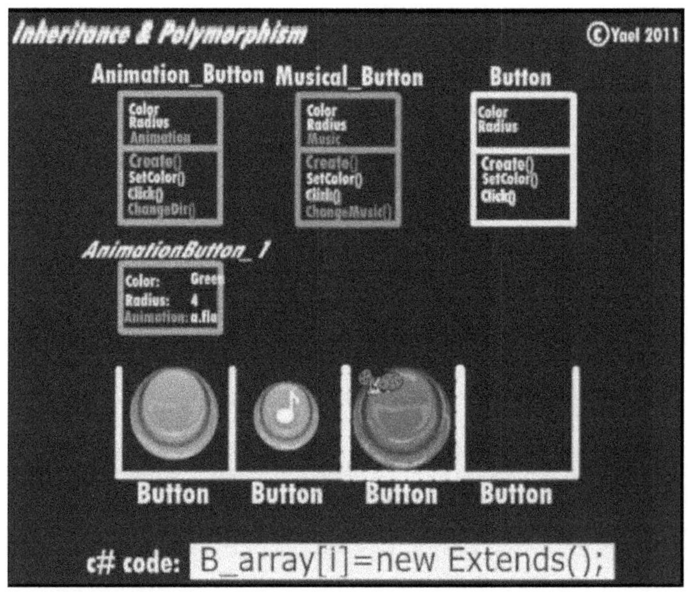

Figure 1: One image of a scene in the animation

REFERENCES

[1] Liberman, N., Beeri, C. ,Ben-David- Kolikant, Y., (2011). Difficulties in Learning Inheritance and Polymorphism.Jeric, ACM Transactions on Computing Education.

ITiCSE'12, July 3–5, 2012, Haifa, Israel.
ACM 978-1-4503-1246-2/12/07.

How Innovative Technology Tools Can Be Used to Create New Methodology for Teaching Knowledge

Eti Hershkovich
Maccabim-Reut Mor High School
Modi'in Maccabim Reut 71908, Israel
etihershko@bezeqint.net

Bruria Haberman
Computer Science Department,
Holon Inst. of Technology, Holon, Israel, and Davidson Inst. of Science Education, Weizmann Inst. of Science,
Rehovot 76100, Israel
bruria.haberman@weizmann.ac.il

ABSTRACT
Knowledge Management (KM) is a new, evolving computing paradigm based on a collection of processes that govern the creation, dissemination, and utilization of knowledge. We present and discuss a novel method, Systematic Knowledge Pattern (SKP), based on utilizing innovative technology tools for teaching KM to high school students. The SKP builds on powerful computing tools employing generic logic-based problem-solving methods that provide an insight into and an understanding of common problems and knowledge processes in any area of KM.

Categories and Subject Descriptors
K.3.2 [Computers and Education]: Computer and Information Science Education – *computer science education.*

General Terms
Human Factors.

Keywords
Knowledge Management, knowledge pattern, pedagogical pattern.

1. CHALLENGES IN TEACHING KM
The Knowledge Management new, evolving computing paradigm has emerged from a number of areas in computer science, notably artificial intelligence, databases, software engineering, and information systems. Teaching Knowledge Management, especially since it is a young discipline, is challenging to computing educators. Teaching various aspects of KM and related learning strategies involve solving typical problems, designing systems, and understanding human behavior. Teaching should be planned to develop students' abstraction abilities and their computational thinking [2]. Since KM deals with the creation, dissemination, and utilization of knowledge, which is a complex ongoing task usually performed by a group of people, it is important to emphasize to students the collaborative aspect of distributed and shared knowledge.

Regarding computing studies in Israeli high schools, high achievers would usually prefer to major in computer science or in software engineering, whereas average achievers may benefit more from learning KM and practice how to use fluently and reflectively innovative computing tools to create and process knowledge. However, problem-solving processes in the KM area require abstract thinking and integrating the following levels: (a) understanding the problem, (b) acquiring relevant information; and (c) using tools effectively and wisely; combining the levels might be very difficult for average students.

ITiCSE'12, July 3–5, 2012, Haifa, Israel.
ACM 978-1-4503-1246-2/12/07.

Specifically, learning fundamentals of KM require students to develop and use skills related to various aspects of knowledge: (a) *Explicit knowledge*: Emerging assumptions; codifying known knowledge; (b) *Systematic and reflective processing:* Finding implicit knowledge by repetition; (c) *Differentiating vital knowledge*: Abstracting and focusing on the main issues; (d) *Sharing knowledge*: Sharing distributed knowledge and integrating it into a deduced (implicit) knowledge base to obtain insights about the organization; and (e) *Smart use:* Using innovative tools in an intelligent way. These skills are required for understanding the essence of KM and for internalizing knowledge patterns discussed in class.

Average students might have difficulties in comprehending the complexity of knowledge and the compound structure of an abstract problem. These considerations motivated the first author to develop a suitable pedagogical approach.

2. THE PEDAGOGICAL APPROACH
In our poster we present a novel approach to teach KM, which builds on the power of innovative computerized tools, and combines disciplinary principles, pedagogical tools (i.e. pedagogical patterns), and intelligent use of technology. The tool, called Systematic Knowledge Pattern (SKP), features a new style of teaching and learning; it enables average students to systematically organize and process explicit and implicit knowledge, and eventually to create collections of knowledge patterns (i.e. general, proven, and beneficial solutions to common, recurring problems in knowledge design) for a variety of organization-related problems [1]. We discuss pedagogical aspects of employing the method for teaching and demonstrate how it can be specifically adapted to teach the Information and Knowledge Systems course to high school students with average problem-solving skills. Results of a preliminary study aimed at classifying students' KM processes, as well as their perception of knowledge will be presented.

3. REFERENCES
[1] Rech, J., Feldmann, R.L., Ras, E. (2011). Knowledge Patterns, *Encyclopedia of Knowledge Management 2011*, 833-841.

[2] Wing, J.M. (2006). Computational thinking, *Communication of the ACM*, 49(3), 33-35.

Mobile Game Development Projects in CS 1

Stan Kurkovsky
Department of Computer Science
Central Connecticut State University
kurkovskysta@ccsu.edu

ABSTRACT

Using computer games in the computing curriculum has been generally accepted as a viable tool to increase student engagement with the material and motivation to study. However, the process of design and implementation of a complete game offers a number of substantial challenges. Consequently, game development may be best suited for advanced courses, in which students already have sufficient hands-on experience with software development and exposure to a variety of advanced topics, such as computer networking, databases, and artificial intelligence. At the same time, games typically found on mobile devices may offer the advantage of being simpler by nature and, thus, easier to program. This could make it more feasible for students in introductory courses to develop playable games as a part of their classroom experience. Furthermore, a large majority of students find it much easier to relate to mobile applications and devices (as opposed to their desktop counterparts) due to the increasingly important role that mobile technology plays in their lives.

A number of current studies suggest that today's students may quickly become disillusioned with Computer Science because many of them perceive their classroom experience as irrelevant or having very little to do with the real-world applications of computing. At the same time, a certain percentage of students may be interested in other areas of computing that emphasize design or theory over coding. By exposing students to a wide range of advanced topics early in their academic career, we are working on an approach that aims to show students that computing can be much more than coding and that there are many areas in which programming plays a supplementary role. This work is supported by a number of research works that suggest that more participatory learning methods such as those used in mobile game development can level the playing field for different types of students.

Supported by NSF TUES/CCLI award DUE-0941348, we are currently working to produce a comprehensive set of learning modules consisting of laboratory projects and accompanying instructional materials for introductory Computer Science courses taught using Java. We use mobile game development early in the curriculum as a motivational learning context. Each learning module serves as a platform to introduce students to an advanced topic, such as artificial intelligence, computer security, or networking, as well as to practice a fundamental topic, such as arrays or inheritance. By demonstrating these and other non-programming and diverse aspects of the discipline to the students early, this approach may help dissolve a widely popular misconception that "CS is all about coding." Research literature and our own experience demonstrate that most Computer Science students seem to be very interested in computer game development and mobile computing, and introducing students to these topics early in the curriculum could serve as a good tool to increase student retention. More broadly, current research literature indicates that students perform better when they find their course material relevant and motivating.

Each learning module contains a number of components:

- *Learning objectives and outcomes* clearly states what students will do in the project and what they will accomplish upon completing it;
- *Problem statement* describes a game, typically a well-known puzzle or board game, that is in the core of this project;
- *Programming project* provides the scaffolding for the students to use as they add their own code to implement the missing features of the gameplay or add new ones;
- *Demonstration game and a sample solution* is a resource that can aid instructors explain the learning objectives;
- *Lecture notes* introduce the students to the theoretical topics covered by the project;
- *Taking a step further* suggests how students could take a step above and beyond this project by extending the existing game or reusing the code to create a new game.

Learning modules developed so far have been tested in several courses at two different institutions. We are currently in the process of making changes and finalizing the modules to address the concerns raised in the interim assessment report. A few of the learning modules have been presented to the CS community also and they were well received.

Categories and Subject Descriptors

K.3.2 [**Computers and Education**]: Computers and Information Science Education – *Curriculum*; K.8.0 [**Personal Computing**]: General – *Games*

General Terms

Design, Experimentation, Human Factors

Keywords

Mobile games, curriculum, engagement, motivation, project.

ITiCSE'12, July 3–5, 2012, Haifa, Israel.
ACM 978-1-4503-1246-2/12/07.

Applying Advanced Technology Tools in Distance Learning - Case Study: Traffic Data and Road Safety

Muna Baghdadi, Khaled Asad, Jamal Raiyn
Computer Science Department, Alqasemi-Academic College of Education
Baka El-Gharbiah, Israel
raiyn@qsm.ac.il

Abstract

This paper introduces new technology tools for e-learning system. We aim to increase the performance analysis of the e-learning platform by adding new technology tools based on mobile cloud computing and simulation. Simulations have been used as a tool for teaching in many area and disciplines. Using the simulation in distance learning can provide tools for teachers to demonstrate and explain the behavior of complex and dynamic systems.

Categories and Subject Descriptors

D.0 **[Software]**

General Terms

Design, Management

Keywords

E-learning, cloud computing, simulation

1. INTRODUCTION

Conventional simulations start from a set of equations to derive statements about cause-effect relationships. However, finding all relevant relationship in complex dynamic environments is a nontrivial task, therefore, these models often state very strong assumptions which limit their plausibility. To avoid these deficiencies, we base our simulations on the behaviour of the mobile cloud computing (MCC) to improve the e-learning tools. The use of mobile computing in the distance learning will leading to significant changes in the meaning of the e-learning field. MCC offers impressive environments in which the user has great possibilities of interaction. Interactivity is one of the major challenges that facing providers of e-learning. The meaningful interactive courseware that is responsive to learners, allowing them actively participates in the learning process.

2. CONCEPT

In our research project we will use the agent goal oriented simulations to search and update the e-learning systems that extend the e-learning tools toward mobility. The major task of the agent is to present the material of academic unit based on different teaching tools. e.g. by using multimedia, games, third dimension environment in comprehensive and simply form. We are high motivated to develop new e-learning methods based on mobility, due several pedagogical, political and social reasons. The study that we have carried out showed, that making the e-learning mobile will improve the quality of education level in our society[1].

ITiCSE'12, July 3–5, 2012, Haifa, Israel.
ACM 978-1-4503-1246-2/12/07.

Applying the mobile cloud computing in the e-learning will improve the performance of the e-learning methods. Furthermore using cloud computing in courses, which was focused exclusively on developing and deploying SaaS application, makes the distance learning attractive. Colleges and schools seem to have bought the idea of cloud computing. It is important to mention that the use of cloud computing in the virtual machine eliminate the need for a hard drive on the local computer. The best example for using cloud computing in the education is google services.

3. IMPLEMENTATION

Figure 1 illustrates the accomplishment of Computerized Project-Based Learning (CPBL). CPBL is new learning toolkit that aims to bring the theoretical knowledge into practice. To bring the designed algorithm from the theory to practice, we can use Micro Control Unit (MCU). The MCU kit is controlled by visual programming language. Three students participated in this CPBL. Each participant got a brief overview of the toolkit and requirements of the CPBL. CPBL highlights implementation of the proposed case study. The case study focused on traffic education and road safety. The second part of the CPBL will deal with designing Platform as a Service (PaaS). PaaS is a set of cloud delivered services that provide an environment for application development and integration in the cloud.

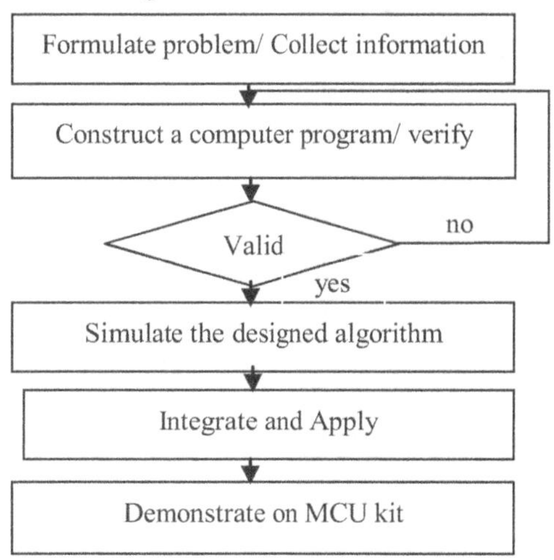

Figure 1: CPBL steps

4. REFERENCES

[1] Raiyn, J. 2011. Developing E-society Cognitive Platform Based on the Social Agent E-learning Goal Oriented, *Advances in Internet of Things*, April, pp.1-4.

Junior High School Students Performing Image Smoothening and Noise Filtering by Applying Mathematical Operations

Khaled Asad
Alqasemi Academic College of Education, Baqa-El-Gharbia 30100, Israel
Ben-Gurion University of the Negev, Beer-Sheva 84105, Israel
kasad@qsm.ac.il

ABSTRACT

This poster describes the successful development and implementation of an approach to getting junior high school students to study and deal with advanced topics in image processing. The students had no prior knowledge in image processing nor in computer science. Our instructional approach can be briefly outlined by four steps. Early results of the study show that the students succeeded to perform challenging tasks and to deal with a variety of advanced topics in image processing.

Categories and Subject Descriptors

K.3.2 [**Computer Science and Information System Education**]: Computer science education, Curriculum, Literacy.

Keywords: Computer Science education k-12, Image Processing, Math in Context, Instructional Approaches.

1. INTRODUCTION

Getting junior high school students, with no prior knowledge in computer science, to study advanced topics in image processing is not an easy task. They need appropriate support to deal with open-ended projects in topics like facial recognition and image smoothening. Thus, the most challenging questions are: what kind of support can we provide those learners in order to deal with such topics? What is the best instructional approach should we adhere? These questions are part of what the study tries to answer.

Image processing is considered an inter-disciplinary field that combines knowledge of computer science, mathematics and physics. It needs deep understanding of mathematics of several levels. For example, image smoothening and noise removing is actually done by means of mathematical operations. As illustrated in figure 2, the best way for removing a Salt and Pepper noise from an image is applying a Median Filter over blocks of surrounding pixels of sizes [3×3] or [5×5]. For other distortions one should study the distortion type in order to decide what are the best math operations or Spatial Filters to be applied.

Having young students learn and do such advanced things is nontrivial, and it is a challenging task. Teachers should carefully adopt pedagogical and instructional strategies such as problem-based learning and project-based learning (PBL) while students work in teams to investigate and solve real-life problems [1].

2. THE INSTRUCTIONAL APPROACH

In the current study in order to overcome the mentioned obstacles and to bring young students to perform advanced tasks and manipulate images mathematically, we provided them with a preliminary stage. In this stage, they got basic image processing concepts, such as pixel representation in memory for gray and color images, basic math operations to change images and etc.

After this necessary stage, the students learned authentic topics, such as face recognition, methods of image enhancements and noise removal. In the study, as illustrated in figure 1, learning these advanced topics essentially is done through four main steps:

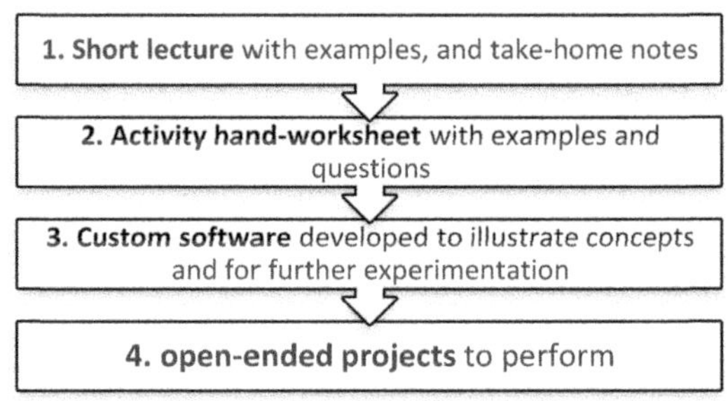

Figure 1: Four steps for teaching advanced CS topics

3. THE CASE OF NOISE REMOVAL

The topic of noise removal is presented here as an example to apply the above four steps. Step 1, students get explanations about the Noise concept, like the Salt & Pepper Noise, and about Spatial Filtering. Step 2, they learn the Median Filtering Algorithm and work the algorithm out by pencil and paper, in order to get the concept. Step 3, they make experiments with a software, compare images before and after and try other filtering effects. Step 4, they perform an authentic open-ended project in spatial filtering.

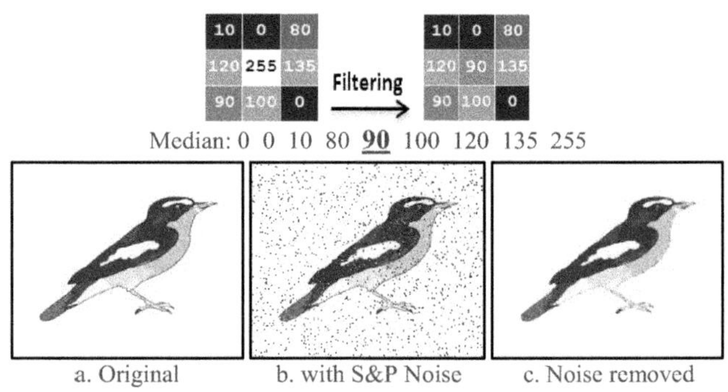

Figure 2: The effect of applying the Median Filter to remove Salt & Pepper Noise using a [3×3] surrounding block.

4. CONCLUSION

In order to teach advanced technology subjects to young students in a successful way, it should be designed carefully and guided by constructive pedagogy rather than by traditional schooling.

5. REFERENCES

[1] Asad, K. Barak, M. (2010). Teaching image processing concepts in junior high school: The role of student-centered vs. traditional instruction, *Technological Learning & Thinking conference* (TL&T), University of British Columbia, June 17-21.

Intuitive Thinking While Dealing with Abstract Data Types

Waleed Khalifa
Computer Science Department
Sakhnin College of Education, Sakhnin, Israel
Tamra, East Galilee, 19328, Israel
972-4-6620139
khwalid@hotmail.com

ABSTRACT

This paper describes a research conducted in computer science high-school classrooms while the students were learning Abstract Data Types ("Software Design"). The students were studying abstract data type's module after completing three modules based on the paradigm of procedural programming. The study researches the strategies used by the students and the conceptions they developed during their exposure to the paradigm. The main goal is to characterize high school students' practice with abstract data types.

Categories and Subject Descriptors

Algorithms, data structures, abstract data types.

General Terms

Algorithms, Design.

Keywords

Abstract data types, dual system, operations on objects.

1. INTRODUCTION

The field work of this study included collection of data, interpretation and presentation of data. It is directed by the guiding principles of ethnographic research. The data was collected from computer science high school students over a four-year period. Throughout the initial stages, participant observations in the classes served as the main tool for data collection; later on, special kind of interviews were conducted with the students as they were working on programming or algorithmic assignments. The findings of the research reveal pupils' difficulties in connection to representation of data types and their related operations.

2. THEORETICAL FRAMEWORK

Data analysis revealed several factors that affect the ability of understanding new concepts. The overall theoretical framework of this study is based on a combination of a cognitive psychology theory called "the dual system" (which is composed of two systems: system 1 and system 2) [1] that differentiates between intuitive and analytical thinking, and a theory which declares that most human thinking is mainly metaphoric.

3. ANALYSIS

It seems that the intensive indulgence of human beings with objects and their constant endeavor to map between two allegedly separate fields, influence the way people deal with new knowledge. In the case of abstract data types, the students tried to bridge the gap between their current knowledge and the new knowledge by giving daily meanings to software operations (that are mostly related to objects and the operations on them - such operations already exist in system 1, The students master them almost completely and they can be brought to mind immediately). This on the one hand, and on the other hand, they are related to metaphors and to their attempt to bridge between the fields of the explanatory (the metaphor) and the explained. That is to say, the students take something known and adopt it (its meaning) for a meaning of an operation or a statement in a programming language. For example, the operation of taking a physical object in everyday life will leave a void in its place. The effect of this daily operation intuition in programming language will be excluding the element from the data type and leaving a void in its place. This can be explained as moving it, although in programming language we take a copy of this element. In other words, the students mistakenly use operations because they give them a programming meaning depending on previous knowledge of daily physical objects and depend on language.

4. FINDINGS

As a consequence of this analysis, the findings have been organized in a main category: **the influence of intuition of daily operations on students' writing in formal language in the course of their study of abstract data types.** This category includes two main sub-categories: 1) giving a daily meaning to operations on abstract data types in the transition from an idea to formal language, and 2) the influence of intuition of daily operations on successful working strategies.

5. REFERENCES

[1] Leron, U. and Hazzan, O. 2009. Intuitive vs. Analytical Thinking: Four Perspectives. Educational Studies in Mathematics, 71, 263-278.

ITiCSE'12, July 3–5, 2012, Haifa, Israel.
ACM 978-1-4503-1246-2/12/07.

Similarities in CSE and Gemara Education

Bracha Daum-Reiter
Yeshivat HaShomron
Karney-Shomron
972-544939780
baki@netvision.net.il

Shriki Galit
Leyada High School
Pisgat-Ze'ev Jerusalem
972-0543376274
Galits7@gmail.com

ABSTRACT

In this poster, we suggest several similarities between computer science education (CSE) and Gemara that could help CS educators.

Categories and Subject Descriptors: K.3.2 Computer and Information Science Education – Computer science education

General Terms: Human factor.

Keywords: Computer science education, Gemara.

1. INTRODUCTION

After many years of teaching in *yeshivas* (religious colleges), it is impossible not to be aware of the many parallels in teaching both Gemara and computer science and of the significance they can contribute to each other. This poster will attempt to illustrate some tools that are common to both subjects.

2.1 Study Groups (*Hevruta*) vs. Pair Programming

Traditionally, over the past 700 years, the Gemara was studied in pairs (called *'Hevruta'* in Hebrew). Recently the CS academic world has discovered the benefits of this learning method. For example, an experiment [1] conducted on pair programming produced the following results: Exam results improved; A higher percentage of students successfully completed the course; The majority of students reported an improvement in code quality; Improvement in team work, communications skills, comprehension and learning ability; Students greatly enjoyed this study format and expressed a desire to continue this style of study.

2.2 In-Depth Gemara Study vs. Agile Software Development

The essence of studying the Gemara in depth is the exchange of opinions that is created during pair study. In the realm of CSE, parallels can be seen in agile software development. For example, we offer the following quotation from a manifest that was designed to alter preconceptions of software engineering [2]: "We expose better ways of developing software during work and mutual help; these are our values and principles: *People and interpersonal relations* in preference to processes and tools; *Working software* in preference to detailed records; *Client cooperation* in preference to contractual negotiations; *Response to change* in preference to program follow-up"; What this means in effect is that as long as the values of each of the first phrases above are observed, *we are better able to appreciate the second phrases*.

Hazzan has written at length on this subject and identifies the following inherent advantages, including: Software educates towards team work; Software encourages diversity; Software stimulates thinking practice; Software underlines ethical norms and more.

2.3 Division for Assignments

In computer science, we teach students to design algorithms, define the problem and divide the solution up into assignments. The following quotation from the introduction to *Gemara Berura* software [3], a program used as an auxiliary tool for Gemara students, might help understand the study of Gemara: "... With the help of designated auxiliary tools, the student breaks_down the question into units (sections), defines the goal of each unit and finds a connection between inter-related units. Each stage of Gemara study is a step towards unraveling the complexities of the question and urging the student on towards a greater understanding of it."

2.4 Think Aloud

The Jewish world in general and the world of Gemara in particular tend to believe that a "think aloud" strategy is more productive than silent learning. The Gemara says: *Samuel said to Rabbi Judah, open your mouth and read the Scriptures, open your mouth and learn the Gemara, that your studies may be retained and that you may live long, since it is said: 'For they are life unto those that find them, and a healing to all their flesh'; read not 'To those that find them' but 'To him who utters them with his mouth [4]'*

The commentators explain that when a student "thinks aloud" he is able to understand everything accurately and learn one thing from another while also concentrating on his studies. The "think aloud" method requires students to use intelligible language down to the finest detail.

A recently introduced methodology in CSE, known as the "Think Aloud Protocol"[5], is used to stimulate thought processes and problem solving skills.

3. CONCLUSION

There are many more similarities on this subject, and examples from the Gemara learning that could be beneficial to CSE as well. If our poster will be accepted, we will present these in the conference.

4. REFERENCES

[1] Mendes, E. Al-Fakhri, L., Luxton-Reilly, A. (2006). A Replicated experiment of pair-programming in a 2nd year Software development and design CS course *ITiCSE06*.

[2] Hazzan, O., Dubinsky, Y. (2007). Why software engineering Program should teach agile software development. *ACM SIGSOFT Software Engineering Notes*. 32 (2).

[3] http://www.gemaraberura.com/whatisgb.htm

[4] Gemara Eiruvin 54a.

[5] Arshad, Naveed. (2009). Teaching Programming and Problem Solving to CS2 Students Using Think-Alouds. *SIGCSE '09*, pp 372 – 376.

Teachers' Perception of Teaching Problem-Solving Strategies to Novices

Lavy Bunimovich
Ort Michlala, Givat-Ram, Jerusalem
P.O.B. 11516, Jerusalem, 91114, Israel
972 2 6768518
lavy.bnm@gmail.com

ABSTRACT
This poster presents a pilot study whose aim is to determine whether and how CS1 high school teachers provide algorithmic problem-solving skills: which aspects are expressed in teaching problem-solving, which strategies are used, and what are the difficulties in teaching problem-solving.

Categories and Subject Descriptors
K.3.2 [**Computer and Information Science Education**]: Computer Science Education.

General Terms
Algorithms, Human Factors.

Keywords
K-12, Problem-Solving Strategies

1. INTRODUCTION
Problem solving (PS) is a basic skill needed by today's learners. According to Schoenfeld [2], the term "Problem Solving" refers to dealing with an unfamiliar task, that the student does not have a prepared procedure for solving it. Polya [1] proposed a dictionary-style set of heuristics (strategies) such as analogy, induction, auxiliary elements, etc., which are intended to help students solve math problems.

PS is a central aspect of computer science and also a significant part of the CS1 course. The pilot study presented in the poster tests whether CS1 teachers include PS strategies in their curriculum, and if so, which strategies are used.

2. METHODOLOGY
Six CS1 high school teachers participated in the qualitative study and were interviewed. All informants teach in schools in the Jerusalem area in Israel, and have a rich teaching experience. Each teacher was introduced with an algorithmic problem from a matriculation exam. Teachers were asked to solve the problem and then to answer the questions of a semi-structured interview, which contained open questions about teaching this problem in particular, and teaching PS in general. Teachers' answers were recorded and transferred into text.

3. RESULTS
Informants' answers reflect significant differences in teachers' approach to teaching PS. To describe the diversity, teachers' responses were classified into four categories according to PS approaches or strategies they introduce in class:

Category 1: Understanding a problem

This category is associated with the teachers' comments to the issue of understanding a problem.

Category 2: To solve a problem in stages.

This category includes sayings of teachers who report that they teach the students to solve a problem in stages

Category 3: Strategies to obtain an algorithm.

This category brings together statements concerning different approaches to obtain an algorithm.

Category 4: Teaching strategies to obtain an algorithm.

To this category belong reports of the interviewees who explicitly teach PS approaches.

The first three categories of teachers' reports refer to teaching PS only in the context of a specific problem. Category 4 is associated with cases in which teachers describe the explicit teaching of a PS approach.

4. CONCLUSIONS
The study's results can be concluded as follows:

1. Surveyed teachers do not teach PS strategies explicitly, but assume that the PS skills of their students improve as students solve more problems.
2. Most of the teachers think that the principal difficulty of students is understanding the text of a problem.

Following the study several questions arise:

- Does explicit teaching of problem-solving strategies promote problem-solving abilities of students?
- What strategies can be taught to students? In what ways can a teacher incorporate PS strategies in the curriculum?
- If teachers are aware of the existence of PS strategies, how will this affect their teaching?

5. ACKNOWLEDGMENTS
I wish to thank Dr. Orna Muller for her help with the research and the poster, David Howard for his help with editing, and Dr. Tami Lapidot for her help with the poster.

6. REFERENCES
[1] Pólya, G. (1945). How to Solve It. *Princeton University Press.*

[2] Schoenfeld, A. H. (1985). Mathematical problem solving. *Orlando, FL: Academic Press.*

ITiCSE'12, July 3–5, 2012, Haifa, Israel.
ACM 978-1-4503-1246-2/12/07.

An Integrated Educational Tool for Testing Data Type Implementations from Formal Specifications

Rafael del Vado Vírseda
Dpto. de Sistemas Informáticos y Computación
Universidad Complutense de Madrid
rdelvado@sip.ucm.es

Fernando Pérez Morente
Dpto. de Sistemas Informáticos y Computación
Universidad Complutense de Madrid
fperezmo@fdi.ucm.es

ABSTRACT

This poster presents an educational and integrated software tool for testing abstract data types and data structures implemented in C++ from algebraic specifications written in the formal specification language *Maude*. Our software testing tool is fully integrated in the *Eclipse* programming environment and is platform-independent. We have developed an *Eclipse* plug-in that calls the *Maude* system to generate the test cases and translates them into a sequence of C++ instructions. The C++ instructions are compiled and executed, and the results are compared with the results obtained from the *Maude* execution of the corresponding formal specification. The educational tool has been used during the academic year 2010-11 by the Computer Science students in a data types course. The experience is being very useful as it allows students to test their implementations and correct their errors, encouraging the use of formal specification methods in their programming developments and resulting in an improved software quality.

Categories and Subject Descriptors

D.2.5 [**Testing and Debugging**]: Testing tools; D.3.3 [**Language Constructs and Features**]: Abstract data types; K.3.2 [**Computer Science Education**]: Computer Science Education.

General Terms

Algorithms, Design, Theory, Verification.

Keywords

Integrated educational tools, formal specifications, abstract data types, data structures, testing software tools.

1. INTRODUCTION

There is little incentive and motivation for writing formal specifications in Computer Science students unless they can be used to prove the correctness of their implementations in a simple and friendly way. For this reason, the development of an educational software tool[1] in an integrated programming environment, familiar to the students, in which they can define formal specifications, write implementations and prove them to correct their errors, can be useful to show students the usefulness of formal methods, not demotivating them with long formal proofs, but encouraging their use in future software developments. This poster presents an educational software tool[1] for testing abstract data type implementations from algebraic specifications [2] written in *Maude* [1], which is a formal specification language based on rewriting logic that allows the specification of abstract data types and data structures in a clear and concise manner.

[1] `http://gpd.sip.ucm.es/Testing/ITiCSE2012/`

ITiCSE'12, July 3–5, 2012, Haifa, Israel.
ACM 978-1-4503-1246-2/12/07.

2. TESTING IMPLEMENTATIONS

Maude specifications can be executed under the *Eclipse* programming environment by means of special *plugins*[1]. This environment facilitates the usage of *Maude* by integrating the text editor with the execution commands of the system. The student writes the specification in a *Maude* file and reduces terms by using the command line or by writing them on the file and sending them to the *Maude* system. The results are shown in the *Maude console*. When the student is convinced of the algebraic specification correctness by means of the execution of several term reductions in *Maude*, he/she selects an appropriate representation for the abstract data type and implements it in C++. The testing tool checks that the data computed by the C++ implementation is equivalent to the one obtained from the *Maude* specification. The tool shows a dot in the console for each test that passes. When a test fails, the tool finishes and writes in the console the specification term that fails, the result obtained from the execution of the specification, and the result obtained from the execution of the implementation.

3. STUDENT EXPERIENCE

The software testing tool has been used during the academic year 2010-11, by the Computer Science students in the "Data Structures and Algorithms" academic subject at the second year[1]. The experience has proved very useful as it allows students to test their own implementations and correct their errors:

	complex numbers	stacks	lists	binary search trees	tables
2010/2011 Tool	83 (93.26%)	82 (92.13%)	74 (83.15%)	72 (80.90%)	75 (84.27%)
2009/2010 No Tool	71.48%	67.84%	60.39%	51.07%	41.47%

4. REFERENCES

[1] M. Clavel, F. Durán, S. Eker, P. Lincoln, N. Martí-Oliet, J. Meseguer, and C. Talcott. *All About Maude: A High-Performance Logical Framework, LNCS 4350*. Springer, 2007.

[2] M.C. Gaudel and P. Le Gall. Testing data types implementations from algebraic specifications. In *Formal methods and testing*, pages 209-239. Springer, Berlin, Heidelberg, 2008.

Are Students Learning Object Oriented Programming in an Object Oriented Programming Course? Student Voices

Desmond Wesley Govender & Irene Govender
University of KwaZulu-Natal, South Africa
Govenderd50@ukzn.ac.za

Categories and Subject Descriptors
K.3 [Computers and Education]
K.3.2 [Computer & Information Science Education]

General Terms
Performance, Human factors, Languages

Keywords
Object Oriented Programming, Teaching strategy; Objects first approach.

1. INTRODUCTION

The integration of the Object Oriented Programming (OOP) into Computer Science introductory programming courses has become a necessity dictated to by global software companies. When designing software projects, programmers have an array of languages to choose from, and lecturers of computer science programming courses are faced with decisions about programming paradigms that have to keep abreast with the ever changing computer programming environments.

The key features of OOP are the use of classes and objects, and design principles of encapsulation, inheritance and polymorphism [1]. Object oriented program developers design class hierarchies, focus on encapsulation, think in terms of class constructs and use language features of inheritance and polymorphism.

In contrast, the procedural programming paradigm (PPP) is characterized by three properties: "execution of instructions sequentially, separate data and methods and the use of assignment operators to change the values of variables directly" [2].

Programming is seen as a complex and difficult intellectual activity that requires a great number of problem-solving skills [3]. Lecturers of computer science programming require a great deal of dedication and perseverance to adapt their teaching to an ever changing programming environment, that satisfy firstly the curriculum norms and secondly the information technology industry.

2. THE STUDY

Presently, at a University of Technology's Information Technology (IT) department the curriculum includes a course in programming using the programming languages visual basic and .Net. Earlier programming courses followed command-driven and procedural programming languages. The inclusion of object-oriented programming languages introduced greater flexibility and a shift from the rigidity associated with earlier procedural programming writing styles; however, the teaching pedagogy remains focused on the procedural programming approach and consequently students lack the ability to comprehend OOP concepts at a first year level, and the IT department succumbs to the "norms of the national student dropout rate" [4].

In this paper we explore students' perceptions and experiences in an introductory object oriented programming course at this university of technology. Questionnaires and interviews were used in the study. Students were asked using a Likert scale to respond to statements which indicated their perceptions and experiences. Thereafter, interviews were conducted with an extracted random sample of students. Student perceptions and experiences reflected that they were being taught using the procedural programming approach which interestingly brings to light that lecturers may have some resistance to embrace OOP as a programming paradigm for an introductory programming course. The results point to evidence that students are not fully knowledgeable on the different concepts in OOP. Where students were doubtful they simply responded by indicating a neutral response to statements pertaining to OOP. The interviews further supported the evidence in that students were quite honest in revealing that classes and objects were only introduced much later in the module. It seems that lecturers are quite steeped into the procedural approach as an introduction to programming and only much later introduce the concepts of true OOP.

3. CONCLUSION

The authors suggest that lecturers and students embrace OOP from the very first lecture/lesson and adopt innovative strategies into their teaching. This could be used as a spring board to increase the understanding of OO programming principles and ultimately the pass rate of these courses.

Although the use of an OOP language at tertiary institutions is slowly gaining acceptance, there exists a tendency for computer science lecturers at this university of technology to continue adopting the characteristics of procedural programming as listed above, even though the institution may teach an object-oriented programming language.

4. ACKNOWLEDGEMENTS

Part of the data was collected by a masters student, Mr. P. Govender, and is acknowledged.

5. REFERENCES

[1] Barker, J. (2005). *Beginning Java Objects. From Concepts to Code (*2nd ed.): New York. Springer-Verlag.

[2] Louden, K.C. (1993). *Programming Languages, Principles and Practice*: PWS Publishing Company, Boston

[3] Govender, I. & Grayson, D. (2007). Pre-service and in-service teachers' experiences of learning to program in an object-oriented language. *Computers & Education,* (51)2, pp 874-885.

[4] Kinnunen, P, & Malmi, L. (2006). Why Students Drop Out CS1 Courses? *ICER,*Sept 2006, pp 97-98.

ITiCSE'12, July 3–5, 2012, Haifa, Israel.
ACM 978-1-4503-1246-2/12/07.

Problem Presentation in CS1 Courses

Carmen Morgado
CITI/Dept. de Informática, FCT,
Universidade Nova de Lisboa
Quinta da Torre, Caparica, Portugal
cpm@fct.unl.pt

Fernanda Barbosa
CITI/Dept. de Informática, FCT,
Universidade Nova de Lisboa
Quinta da Torre, Caparica, Portugal
fb@fct.unl.pt

ABSTRACT

Several research activities have been made related to the domain of computer science education, in order to increase learning effectiveness in CS1 courses. These works address the programming language used [1], the use of tools and environments [4], the human factor [2], the problem domain [3], and so on. Teaching programming presents several difficulties and one of the biggest obstacles to achieve a solution to the problem is its interpretation.

In our opinion, the presentation of the problem is a very important issue in teaching programming. The problem must be attractive to the students [2], and should engage the students in structured reasoning. Although the diversity of forms in problem presentation could be an advantage, it may be an obstacle in CS1. It may pose difficulties to the easy understanding of the problem by the students, which, in our opinion, is one of the greatest obstacles in solving problems. In order to minimize the "blank page trauma" on students and to maximize a good structuring of the proposed solutions, we defined a structured way to problem presentation. This presentation should focus mainly on: problem goals; problem concepts; and user interactions. The document describing a problem presentation must be composed by: (1) a title, (2) a short description of the problem goal, (3) a functionalities description, and (4) an application interaction description using scenarios as a way to illustrate application behaviors. We also give to the students a prototype so they can test user interactions and general behavior. Next we present an example of a simple problem, that was proposed to our CS1 students.

Problem title: Coverage of the classroom floor.

Problem description: Find out how many square tiles are needed to cover the largest possible square in the center of the classroom floor.

Functionalities description: The floor of the classroom is a rectangular surface with a width and a length measured in centimeters. The tile is a square with side measured in centimeters, and is unicolor.

Interaction description: At the beginning the user must provide the width and the length of the classroom floor, and the tile side, then the number of tiles needed to cover the largest possible square will be presented.

Interaction scenarios:

Scenario 1

Classroom floor	Tile
Length (in cm): 40 Width (in cm): 30	Side (in cm): 20

Result: Number of tiles = 2

Our experience led us to conclude that a structured problem presentation helps students to increase high-level skills in programming activity, in order to propose structured problem solution. In a study conducted in our CS1 courses, we observed that the resulting problem solution was more structured when the presentation problem follows the rules defined above.

Categories and Subject Descriptors

K.3.2 [**Computer and Education**]: Computer and Information Science Education—*computer science education*

General Terms

Human Factors

Keywords

Problem presentation, teaching programming

Acknowledgments

The authors would like to thank the FCT/MCTES, PEst-OE/EEI/UI0527/2011 Centro de Informática e Tecnologias da Informação (CITI/FCT/UNL) 2011-2012, for the support given to this work.

1. REFERENCES

[1] P. J. Burton and R. E. Bruhn. Teaching programming in the oop era. *SIGCSE Bull.*, 35:111–114, June 2003.

[2] M. K. Hamza, B. A. Alhalabi, and D. M. Marcovitz. Creative pedagogy for computer learning: eight effective tactics. *SIGCSE Bulletin*, 32(4):70–73, 2000.

[3] O. L. Oliveira, A. M. Monteiro, and N. T. Roman. From concrete to abstract?: problem domain in the learning of introductory programming. In *Proc. 16th annual joint conf. ITiCSE*, pages 173–177. ACM, 2011.

[4] J. A. Villalobos, N. A. Calderon, and C. H. Jiménez. Developing programming skills by using interactive learning objects. *SIGCSE Bull.*, 41:151–155, July 2009.

A Learning Tool for MP3 Audio Compression

Mohamed Hamada
Graduate School of Computer Science
University of Aizu
Aizuwakamatsu, Fukushima, Japan
+81-242-372617
Hamada@u-aizu.ac.jp

Hyato Namae
Graduate School of Computer Science
University of Aizu
Aizuwakamatsu, Fukushima, Japan
+81-242-372617
hyato@u-aizu.ac.jp

ABSTRACT
In this paper, we describe a learning tool for helping learners to study MP3 audio compression technique. Our system is designed for engineering learners with active preferences.

Categories and Subject Descriptors
K.3 [**Computers & Education**]: Computer & Information Science Education – *Computer Science Education*

Keywords: Learning systems, MP3, media compression.

1. INTRODUCTION
The concepts of audio compression are important in many applications and in information theory related courses. These concepts are abstract in nature and hence used to be taught by a traditional lecture-driven style, which is suitable for learners with reflective preferences. Since computer engineering learners tend to have strong active preferences [1], a lecture-driven teaching style is less motivating for them.

To tackle this issue we introduce a learning tool for MP3 audio compression technique. MP3 is one of the most popular audio compression techniques and it is widely used in practice. That is what motivated us to implement a learning tool for it. The learning tool is suitable for engineering students with active learning preferences.

2. TOOL DESIGN
The tool was designed in Java language which makes it portable and platform independent. Figure 1 describes the tool's diagram.

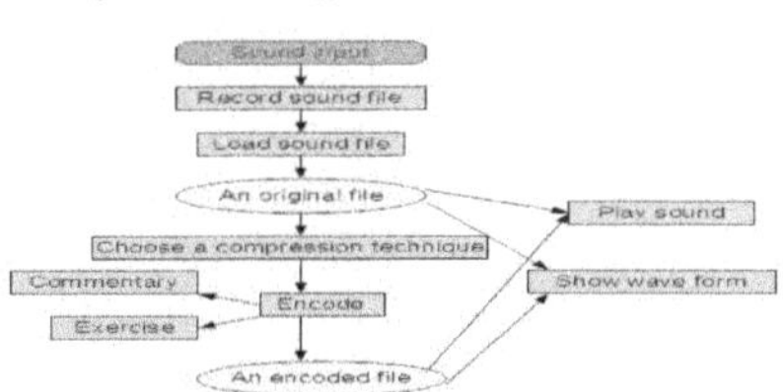

Figure 1. The process chart of the learning tool.

The system start with the input sound file (it can also be a live recording by the student), which is a wave file. After the file is loaded (recorded) it can be played and its wave form is shown. Then the student can chose a compression technique. For the current version of the system we have only MP3 compression technique, other compression techniques will be implemented in future versions of the tool. During the compression process comments on the ongoing process is displayed in the commentary interface, so the student can follow the compression process in a step by step manner. An additional component in the system is the exercise interface which allows the students to check their progress during the learning process. Figure 2 shows the tool's interface.

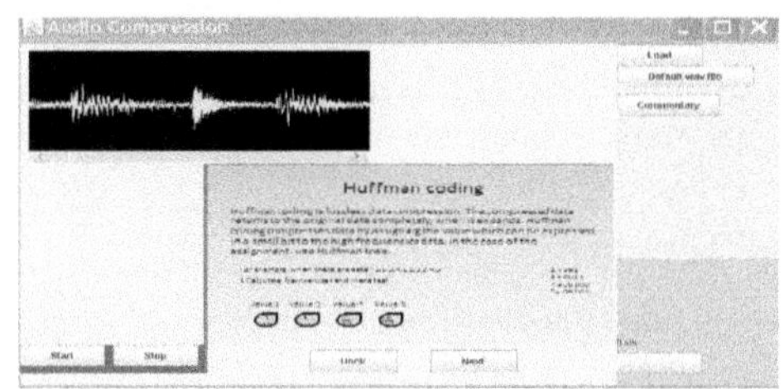

Figure 4. The User Interface of our learning tool.

The user can chose to load an existing audio file, use system default wave file, or record his file through the "Load", "Default Wave file", and "Record" buttons respectively. The window in the upper left corner shows the wave of the used audio file. During the compression process the student can learn more details about the underline algorithms through the "Commentary" button. When the commentary button is pressed an additional window is displayed showing details of the current step of the compression process. By this way the learner can listen, see, and read all the compression process in step by step manner. This way of learning help in motivating students and get them deeper knowledge by using many of their sensors.

ACM 978-1-4503-1246-2/12/07. In a preliminary study on several students the tool was appreciated and told to be a promising one. However several improvements are needed, for example to show an animated compression process and to have more evaluation study on the system in classroom. These issues will be address in the future versions of the tool.

3. REFERENCES
[1]. P. Rosati, The learning preferences of engineering students from two perspectives. Proc. Frontiers in Education, Tempe, AZ, pp. 29-32, 1998.

ITiCSE'12, July 3–5, 2012, Haifa, Israel.
ACM 978-1-4503-1246-2/12/07.

A Qualitative Framework for Comparison and Evaluation of Computer Science Doctoral Programs

Maria del Carmen Calatrava Moreno
Vienna University of Technology
Vienna, Austria
mc.calatrava.moreno@ec.tuwien.ac.at

ABSTRACT

This work aims to provide a better understanding of the process, content and outcome of different programs' models of doctoral education in Computer Science. Our approach compares them on the basis of the analysis of empirical data gathered about the experiences and career paths of doctoral students, as well as the impacts of the initiatives themselves.

Categories and Subject Descriptors

K.3.2 [**Computer and Information Science Education**]: Computer Science Education

General Terms

Management, Human Factors

Keywords

Doctoral Education, Evaluation

1. INTRODUCTION

With the implementation of the third cycle of the Bologna Process, European universities are currently involved in an intensive reform of doctoral structures, across a range of scales, from the macro-contextual through to the micro-practices of everyday. A core part of these initiatives is the offer of PhD studies in doctoral colleges, which resemble the Anglo-American doctorate and differ from the traditional European Master-apprentice model [2]. The latter is typically conceived as a single-supervised approach based on a close relationship between supervisor and PhD candidate. The matching process is personal, left to the professor and the prospective student, who is not necessarily integrated into a formal study program but is involved in individual research work. Instead, doctoral colleges set clear rules for the application and selection of new candidates, have a structured curricula with general and subject-related courses and milestones, all under continuous supervision [4].

Our work aims to analyze the actual effects of the organization and structure of new-style doctoral programs and fill an evident lacuna in the literature on CS doctoral education.

ITiCSE'12, July 3–5, 2012, Haifa, Israel.
ACM 978-1-4503-1246-2/12/07.

2. OUR APPROACH

We believe that the circumstances in which postgraduate programs are offered have a major impact on their quality. Students play an important role, as we enlist them as agents and products of change and improvement. Our qualitative research is based on grounded theory method [1] to build an explanatory framework, differentiating three stages of students' doctoral experience: pre-admission, ongoing studies and post-graduation. For each, we select indicators to scrutinize in-depth and longitudinally academic performance and professional development. Case studies are conducted in three different doctoral programs offered in CS at our faculty – one follows the traditional model and two are doctoral college initiatives. We utilize data of open-ended interviews and organizational information. The sample consists of 24 male and female PhD candidates in their first and second year. To analyze the interview statements we use Qualitative Comparative Analysis [3], a comparative case-oriented research technique based on set theory and Boolean algebra, with which we develop explanatory models on the basis of a systematic comparison of a limited number of cases.

3. RESULTS AND FUTURE WORK

Preliminary results identify empirical patterns and relations among students' experiences in different PhD stages and program models, which could be transformed into hypotheses about correlations between variables. We intend to extend this framework with quantitative criteria. We plan to select a sample of European doctoral colleges based on similarity to ours, and apply our framework to benchmark them and analyze their effect on the doctoral experience.

4. REFERENCES

[1] B. G. Glaser and A. L. Strauss. *The Discovery of Grounded Theory. Strategies for Qualitative Research.* Aldine Pub, 1967.

[2] B. Kehm. Doctoral education in Germany within the European framework. *CIRGE*, 2005.

[3] C. C. Ragin. *The Comparative Method: Moving Beyond Qualitative and Quantitative Strategies.* Berkeley: University of California Press, 1987.

[4] J. Sadlak. Doctoral studies and qualifications in Europe and the United States. *UNESCO, CEPES*, 12(2), 2004.

A Structured Approach to Problem Solving in CS1

Carmen Morgado
CITI/Dept. de Informática, FCT,
Universidade Nova de Lisboa
Quinta da Torre, Caparica, Portugal
cpm@fct.unl.pt

Fernanda Barbosa
CITI/Dept. de Informática, FCT,
Universidade Nova de Lisboa
Quinta da Torre, Caparica, Portugal
fb@fct.unl.pt

ABSTRACT

Teaching programming in CS1 presents several difficulties [1]. Problem solving is a complex process that requires various skills, one of which is the ability to correctly identify and understand the problem [2]. One of the biggest obstacles is the analysis and interpretation of the problem. Before teaching a programming language it is important that students are able to understand the problem and the steps that must be followed to solve it. Preliminary steps needed to enable the student to reach a solution are often ignored in many text books that focus on programming languages. In our opinion the use of an approach in CS1, that helps students to understand the problem and to develop a structured solution, is essential.

So, we defined a sequence of steps, each one with a set of rules, that must be followed during the development of a program. The main steps that we considered are: (1) problem analysis: there are two distinct components that must be identified and processed separately: the problem solution (a set of application concepts) and the application interactions with the user; (2) solution formalization: the aim of this step is the final description of all the concepts of the problem solution. For each concept, we need to describe its attributes and its behavior.

The use of this method in the problem "MyFarm an experimentation of cultivations in a farm", which is a simulation of a set of cultivation experiments by a farmer in a farm, had the following results:

- solution model: includes all domain concepts and a detailed description of all concepts (figure 1 illustrates the concepts and the specification of one them, the Farm);
- interaction model: includes a structured description of data and behavior interaction.

This approach in CS1 courses allows students to increase their ability to solve problems, independently of the programming language, and reduces the problem of "blank page", which is a discouraging aspect both for students and teachers. In our computer sciences courses with around 150 students, this approach increased the approval rate by 25% (on average, there are about 30 students per lab class).

Concept Name	Concept Description
Farm	The farm where the cultivation experiments are done by the farmer, in order to obtain a plantation that gives a greater skill level to the farmer.
Farmer	The worker of the farm, which makes plantations and has associated a skill level and a profit given by plantation.
Cultivation	Seeds sequence, which gives skills and profits to the farmer.
Seed	The seed to plant in the farm, which as a cost, plantation time, profit and experience.

Concept Name: Farm

Attributes:

Name	Type	Description
worker	Farmer	The farmer that works in this farm.
seeds	Set<Seed>	The seeds that may be planted in the farm.

Functionalities:

Name: experiment
Goal: simulation of a cultivation on a given period of time.
Data:

Input	Description	Output	Description
time	The period of time	Cultivation	The seeds sequence planted in the experiment

Behavior:

```
return worker.experiment(time,seeds);
```

Name: greaterSkillExperiment
Goal: return the experiment done in the farm, which gives a greater skill level to the farm worker.
Data:

Output	Description
Cultivation	The seeds sequence planted.

Behavior:

```
return worker.skillExperiment();
```

Name: greaterProfitExperiment
Goal: return the experiment done in the farm, which gives a greater profit to the farm worker.
Data:

Output	Description
Cultivation	The seeds sequence planted.

Behavior:

```
return worker.profitExperiment();
```

Figure 1: Solution Concepts and Farm Concept

Categories and Subject Descriptors

K.3.2 [**Computer and Education**]: Computer and Information Science Education—*computer science education*

General Terms

Human Factors

Keywords

Problem solving, teaching programming

1. ACKNOWLEDGMENTS

The authors would like to thank the FCT/MCTES, PEst-OE/EEI/UI0527/2011 Centro de Informática e Tecnologias da Informação (CITI/FCT/UNL) 2011-2012, for the support given to this work.

2. REFERENCES

[1] M. Guzdial. From science to engineering. *Commun. ACM*, 54:37–39, Feb. 2011.

[2] T. Jenkins. On the difficulty of learning to program. In *Proc. of 3rd Annual Conf. of the LTSN-ICS*, 2002.

DSS for the Group Estimating of the Graduation Papers

Vsevolod Kuzmitskiy
Russia, Khabarovsk, Seryshev St.47
Far Eastern State Transport University
+7 4212 407152
vsevolod.kuzmitskiy@mail.ru

Boris Davydov
Russia, Khabarovsk, Seryshev St.47
Far Eastern State Transport University
+7 4212 407152
dbi@rambler.ru

ABSTRACT

We describe the approach and the decision support tool for the effective estimating of the graduation papers by the group of experts. We apply the Analytic Hierarchy Process (AHP) as the method of the expert's judgments coordination and the computer system for the evaluation indexes calculating.

Categories and Subject Descriptor

J.m **[Computer Applications]**; Miscellaneous;

General Terms

Human Factors, Measurement

Keywords

AHP, group decision making, decisions support system, graduated papers, examination

AHP make decision model that combines both qualitative and quantitative factors. The decision is made through the hierarchy of criteria and the flexible scale of evaluating. Hierarchical model of the group decision making pursue the aim helps to compare the approximation degree of the graduation paper with the specified level.

The grade of the student paper's level is the focus of hierarchy. It may offer the degree of approximation to the specified graduated work level.

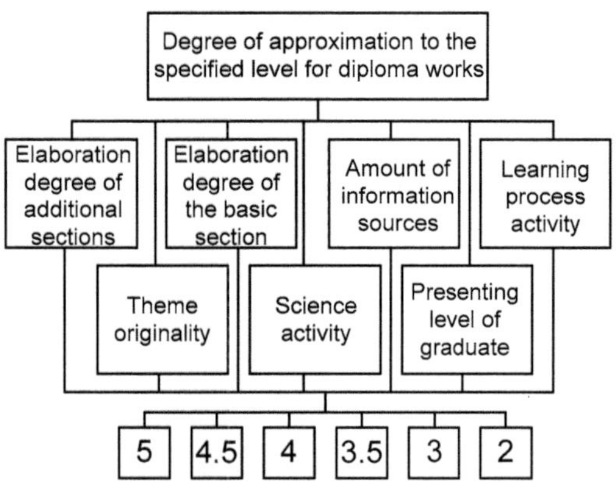

The comparison criteria of the works being examined have been defined during the interviewing process of the senior teaching staff. The set of the main criteria includes the following ones: elaboration degree of the basic section and additional sections, amount of information sources, learning process activity, theme originality, science activity, presenting level. The expert's weights (ratings) are applied in the process of the raw grades combining.

The criteria priorities must be calculated in advance by the inquiry of the senior teaching staff. The coordinational process of the professor's judgments is resulting of the compromise grade. Priority vector of the every paper is building-up by the T. Saaty's algorithm.

The raw grade definition consists of the three stages. Each expert grades received by the matrix calculation are based on the expert's judgments. In the second stage these weights are compiling with taking the own expert status into account and weighted values are summarized. And the thirds stage is definition of the raw grade.

At the conclusion graduate group examination is carried out the alignment private experts' scale procedure. It's applied for the adaptation private experts' scale to the real graduation papers' level. This procedure implements by the filling the table, in which each expert makes a correction ratio for each graduate paper. It's conveniently to make corrections using three point scale: overestimate, retain the assessment and understate the estimate. Each expert fills the correction matrix column and the correction ratio defined by reading matrix line. Further, this ratio is used to conversion of the raw grades. As a result the aligned grade is determined for each graduation paper.

To simplify and expedite the evaluation process the quality grades of flexible AHP scale are correlated with quantity grades through a five point scale which is easy to understand for any expert who makes the decision.

The flexibility of the DSS applying is increased due to use of the simulation and calculating of expert group grades. It results for the reduced group working time and increased the evaluation quality.

The developed approach and decision support system can be used for the new soft tools quality evaluation and in all spheres which require group decision making.

REFERENCES

[1] Edgar Osuna, & Ernesto Coello "AHP as a tool for conflict resolution", ISAHP, Berne, Switzerland, August 2, 2001

[2] Kadarsah Suryadi "Empirical experience on combining AHP with non-AHP decision models in managing cross functional conflicts", ISAHP, Vica Del Mar, Chile, August 2, 2007

[3] Saaty L.Thomas, Kirti Peniwati, "Group Decision Making: Drawing Out And Reconciling Differences", RWS Publications, 2007

ITiCSE'12, July 3–5, 2012, Haifa, Israel.
ACM 978-1-4503-1246-2/12/07.

Using Quick Response Codes for Student Interaction During Lectures

Robert Law
Glasgow Caledonian University
70 Cowcaddens Road
Glasgow
+441413313921
Robert.law@gcu.ac.uk

ABSTRACT

This poster will describe an ongoing attempt to encourage student interaction during lectures through the use of quick response (QR) codes and Google forms to generate rapid response polls and quizzes.

Categories and Subject Descriptors

K.3.2 [**Computer and Information Science Education**]: Computer Science Education:

General Terms

Human Factors.

Keywords

QR Codes, Student Interaction.

1. INTRODUCTION

The rise in popularity of smartphones in the UK, and elsewhere, over the last few years has been evidenced by recent figures showing "Over half of the British population (50.3%) now owns a smartphone" [1]. A recent survey by Edinburgh University of their student population showed that 67% had ownership of a smartphone "an increase of seventeen percent from those students surveyed seven months earlier." [2] The uptake in smartphone ownership within the student population opens a new dimension for interaction.

With this increase in smartphone popularity there has been a tangible increase and use of Quick Response (QR) codes by many companies as a form of marketing. This ability to allow smartphone users to interact with products in situ has allowed companies to reinforce brand presence in a new and engaging manner. Education has already harnessed this potential to extend learning materials through the use of QR codes. They have been used to enhance learning materials by providing "just in time support materials" [3] such as videos, explanatory text, URI's and staff details.

From this the next logical step is to combine the technologies to allow students to interact during lectures through quick multiple choice based questions. The students' responses can be compiled to show the result in a timely manner.

2. LECTURE INTERACTION

Interaction within the lecture is based on three key components: smartphones, QR codes and a Google spreadsheet. The process used to create this interactive lecture was based on designing a set of suitable questions that could be used to strategically punctuate the lecture to gain maximum benefit for the students. It was decided that the questions would be slotted into the lecture at the end of the first topic and at the end of the lecture itself. Although Google forms can handle a number of different inputs the decision was taken to keep the question to a simple Boolean style question thus presenting the student with two QR codes per question.

To create the QR codes requires the compilation of an http request based on the URI for the Google spreadsheet and the data to be sent to the spreadsheet. Once the http request was constructed and tested an online QR code generator was used to generate the required QR codes. These QR codes were subsequently saved as image files for insertion into the lecture slides. At the appropriate point in the lecture the slide would be shown, paper copies of the slide were also distributed. This allowed for the difference within the quality of phone cameras to focus on the projected QR codes. It was fully explained to the students the nature of the experiment and the procedure which should be followed to correctly participate with experiment.

The students then used their smartphones to scan the QR code of their choice, submitting the data request. This in turn populated the spreadsheet with the students' choices, activating a simple script, allowing the results to be observed in near real time.

3. CONCLUSION

A "buzz" was created within the participant group generating a positive reaction from the students. It also created a focus point for the students to reflect on their understanding of the material taught and to apply that understanding. In conclusion the positive feedback suggests that this technique is worthy of further exploration.

4. REFERENCES

[1] Kantar Worldpanel. (2012). The smartest way to communicate: over half of the GB population owns a smartphone. Available: http://goo.gl/Z1n7u. Last accessed 9th March 2012.

[2] EUSA. (2011). Campus app now available for download. Available: http://www.eusa.ed.ac.uk/news/article/6001/290/. Last accessed 9th March 2012.

[3] Ramsden, A., 2008. The use of QR codes in Education: A getting started guide for academics. Working Paper. University of Bath

Zawilinski: Helping Beginning Programmers Conduct MediaWiki-based Research

Zachary Kurmas
School of Computing
Grand Valley State University
kurmasz@gvsu.edu

ABSTRACT

Zawilinski is our Java library that helps undergraduates conduct research on Wikipedia and Wiktionary. It simplifies the loading and filtering MediaWiki XML dumps so that the resulting object tree will fit into the memory of a typical PC, thereby eliminating the need for advanced programming techniques to access Wikipedia and Wiktionary data.

Categories and Subject Descriptors

H.5.3 [**Information Interfaces and Presentation**]: Group and Organization Interfaces

General Terms

Design

Keywords

Wiktionary, Wikipedia, MediaWiki, XML, undergraduate research, SAX, DOM, JAXB

1. MOTIVATION

One of the main challenges in mentoring undergraduate research (especially at a university without a Ph.D. program) is developing projects that are both interesting to undergraduates and within their abilities. Wikipedia and Wiktionary are excellent sources for such projects: (1) Students are familiar with them; (2) they represent a large, free data set; and, (3) students with relatively little programming experience can design and conduct interesting analyses. However, Wikipedia and Wiktionary data sets are so large that loading them into an easily accessible data structure requires advanced programming techniques.

To address this challenge, we developed *Zawilinski*: a Java library that provides access to MediaWiki history and content in a manner that is simple enough to make Wikipedia and Wiktionary-based research accessible to sufficiently motivated undergraduates who have as few as two semesters of programming experience.

2. PROBLEM DETAILS

Wikipedia and Wiktionary make their content available for analysis by publishing a large (tens of gigabytes) XML file. Naïvely processing XML files this large can overwhelm the typical desktop PC (especially the memory).

ITiCSE'12, July 3–5, 2012, Haifa, Israel.
ACM 978-1-4503-1246-2/12/07.

There are two basic approaches for loading XML files: stream parsers and tree-based parsers. Stream (e.g., Simple API for XML – SAX) parsers are efficient, but require the programmer to handle each XML event. The typical undergraduate needs considerable help writing a stream parser.

Tree-based parsers (e.g., Document Object Model – DOM) load the entire document into an object tree. Writing code to access data in the tree is much easier than processing stream parser events. Most strong CS 2 students could effectively use a DOM parser. However, a document's object tree is typically 2 to 10 times the size of the document itself. Thus, it is impractical, if not impossible, to load the entire Wikipedia or Wiktionary XML file into an object tree.

3. ZAWILINSKI

Our Zawilinski Java library allows researchers to provide two sets of filters that together allow programmers to easily leverage both the efficiency of a stream-based filter and the simplicity of a tree-based filter. The first set of filters (called "pre-filters") are placed on the stream parser and remove article text that can be identified as irrelevant without examining meta-data, buffering text, or buffering XML elements. The second set of filters (called "post-filters") examine each article's object subtree as it is created and decide whether to keep or discard it.

Pre-filters reduce the processing load and memory requirements of the tree parser, but they cannot easily remove entire articles. The post-filters provide an easy way for programmers to remove an irrelevant article's object tree.

Zawilinski users will likely need to write a custom post-filter for their particular study. Post-filters consider only a single article's object-tree, and should, therefore, be within the ability of an intermediate programmer. We anticipate that the pre-filters provided by Zawilinski will be sufficient for most studies.

For more information and to download, see `http://www.cis.gvsu.edu/~kurmasz/Software/Zawilinski`

4. REFERENCES

[1] Z. Kurmas. Zawilinski: A library for studying grammar in wiktionary. In *WikiSym '10: Proceedings of the 6th International Symposium on Wikis and Open Collaboration*, 2010.

Kielce: Configurable HTML Course Documents

Zachary Kurmas
School of Computing
Grand Valley State University
kurmasz@gvsu.edu

ABSTRACT

Kielce is a JavaScript library that provides a simple, light-weight, *client-side* technique for moving configurable static content from an HTML document into a separate file where it can more easily and accurately be managed. For example, Kielce simplifies the process of updating a syllabus each semester by collecting the content that changes (semester name, office hours, exam dates, etc.) into a separate file.

Categories and Subject Descriptors

H.3.2 [**Information Storage and Retrieval**]: Information Storage

General Terms

Documentation, Management

Keywords

JavaScript, HTML, Course Management

1. MOTIVATION

Many course documents change in only a few very predictable ways from semester to semester. Consider a syllabus: Most semesters, only the name of the semester, office hours, and important dates change. The standard search-and-replace technique is not terrible; but, it can be tedious and error-prone. For example, it is easy to forget to update one of the dates.

Kielce helps simplify the process of maintaining and updating course documents by allowing authors to move content out of the HTML document and into a JavaScript file. Thus, instead of searching through the entire HTML file for data that must be updated (and having to remember what they all are) instructors need only modify the external JavaScript file. Unlike the HTML document, the JavaScript file contains only those data that require updates, making it easier to find the needed updates and harder to overlook any needed changes.

2. BASIC OPERATION

To use Kielce, take the content to be made configurable and replace it with a tag like this:

ITiCSE'12, July 3–5, 2012, Haifa, Israel.
ACM 978-1-4503-1246-2/12/07.

```
Final exam:  <span kkey="finalExam"></span>
```

Then create a file named `kielceData.js` and add a key-value pair like this:

```
({
  Override: {
    finalExam: "15 December 2012.  8:00 a.m."
  }
});
```

Finally, include the following in the HTML document:

```
<script type="text/javascript" src="kielce3.js">
</script>
<script type="text/javascript">
  Kielce.run();
</script>
```

The `run` method searches the HTML document for tags with `kkey` attributes and replaces the tag's content with the value for the specified key.

3. ADVANTAGES

Kielce's primary advantage is that it runs completely on the client side and does not require any special configuration or software. As a result:

- Authors need not "compile" or "pre-process" documents (as is necessary when using a search-and-replace script).
- Authors don't need to specially configure a server or their web space to publish documents (unlike PHP).
- Authors need not run a full-featured web server to edit documents off-line (as is necessary when using PHP).
- Kielce is a single JavaScript file. Authors can disseminate documents by simply delivering all required files.

The values in the data file can be any valid JavaScript expression; they need not be string literals. Thus, users can automate their configuration files as much as their comfort with JavaScript allows. For example, instead of individually editing each exam date, users can add code to kielceData.js that calculates all exam dates based on the date on which the semester begins.

Kielce also loads one data file from each level in the URL's directory hierarchy, which allows configurations to be shared among many documents, sections, courses, and semesters.

4. AVAILABILITY

For more information or to download, see
`http://www.cis.gvsu.edu/~kurmasz/Software/Kielce/`.

Teaching Programming on a Mobile Device

Nikolai Tillmann, Judith Bishop
Microsoft Research
One Microsoft Way
Redmond, WA, 98052, USA
{nikolait, jbishop}@microsoft.com

ABSTRACT

From paper to computers, the way we have been writing down thoughts and performing symbolic computations has been constantly evolving. Teaching methods closely follow this trend, leveraging existing technology to make teaching more effective and preparing students for their later careers with available technologies. At present, we are in the middle of another technology shift: instead of using PCs and laptops, mobile devices are becoming more prevalent for most everyday computing tasks. We propose that computer programming, and thus the teaching of programming, can and should be done directly on the mobile devices themselves, without the need for a separate PC to write code. Programming on mobile devices engages students in new ways, allowing them to access and manipulate programmatically their most personal digital data such as pictures, videos, and music in an easy and intuitive way.

The poster highlights opportunities and challenges of teaching and learning in the context of TouchDevelop, and writing programs on mobile devices in general. The poster will depict data from surveys conducted before and after class with students learning to program for the very first time. The poster will also introduce teaching and learning resources available to teachers.

TouchDevelop is freely available as an app in the Windows Phone Marketplace and is supported by a book, slides, tutorials and many sample programs. See www.touchdevelop.com.

Categories and Subject Descriptors

D.2.3 [**Software Engineering**]: Program editors; D.2.3 [**Software Engineering**]: Structured programming; D.2.6 [**Programming Environments/Construction Tools**]: Integrated environments; D.2.11 [**Software Architectures**]: Languages

General Terms

Human Factors, Design, Languages.

Keywords

Evolution, Mobile Devices, Touchscreen, Cloud, Type inference.

1. PROGRAMMING ON A PHONE

Teaching to program by writing code for mobile devices has been tried before [1, 2]. However, developing mobile applications (by using a PC) has been found to be more difficult than developing desktop applications (on a PC), since the mobile programming models are typically a restricted subset of the PC model. TouchDevelop [3] (screenshots shown in Figure 1) is a new programming environment and language for mobile devices where, in contrast, no PC is required at all. All the action happens on the phone, and the focus is on the phone, its data and its capabilities.

At the core of TouchDevelop is a typed, structured programming language (Fig. 1(a)) that is built around the idea of using only a touchscreen as the input device to author code. A complex predictive engine ensures that the programmer is presented with tiles that anticipate the next part of a construct and can quickly be chosen and tapped (Fig. 1(b)). Very little actual typing of letters has to be done.

After five months, more than 2000 games and applications have been written and published by users of TouchDevelop. Many games written by users leverage the accelerometer of the phone as a controller, measuring how the phone is tilted. Examples include a fully-featured Tetris-like game and warehouse games where boxes need to be moved to particular locations. Other applications are useful tools and utilities, including a program that queries the calendar on the phone and connects to currently scheduled meeting, and a program that queries current state of parking meters via a web service and projects the information on a map.

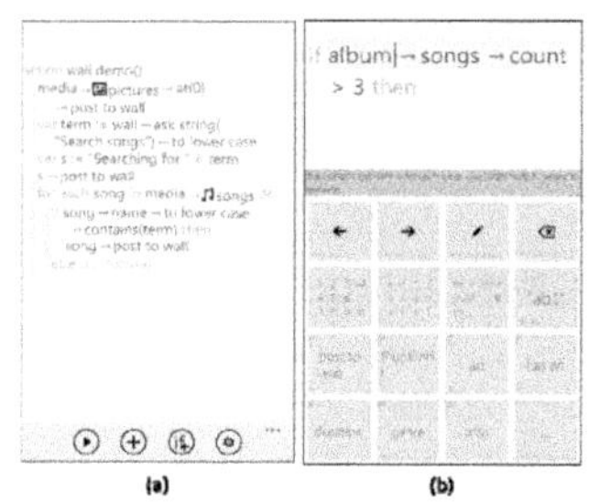

Figure 1. Screenshots of (a) TouchDevelop program and (b) the programming environment on Windows Phone 7.

2. REFERENCES

[1] Q. H. Mahmoud. Best practices in teaching mobile application development. In G. Robling, T. L. Naps, and C. Spannagel, editors, ITiCSE, page 333. ACM, 2011.

[2] Q. H. Mahmoud and A. Dyer. Mobile devices in an introductory programming course. Computer, 41:108-107, June 2008.

[3] Nikolai Tillmann, Michal Moskal, Jonathan de Halleux, and Manuel Fahndrich. 2011. TouchDevelop: programming cloud-connected mobile devices via touchscreen. In Proceedings of the 10th SIGPLAN symposium on New ideas, new paradigms, and reflections on programming and software (ONWARD '11). ACM, New York, NY, USA, 49-60.

ITiCSE'12, July 3–5, 2012, Haifa, Israel.
ACM 978-1-4503-1246-2/12/07.

Visual Search with Deep Zoom to Explore Curriculum Resources Interactively

Arkady Retik
Technical Education Group
Microsoft Corporation
Redmond, WA, 98052 USA
+1-425-705-8973
a.retik@microsoft.com

ABSTRACT

In this poster session, we introduce and describe the Faculty Connection repository including Visual Search with Deep Zoom to help higher education academic faculty and instructors explore thousands of curriculum resources interactively – from presentation slides to software tools.

Categories and Subject Descriptors

H.5.2 [**Information Interfaces and Presentation**]: User Interfaces – *graphical user interfaces (GUI), interaction styles, user-centered system.*

K.3.2 [**Computers and Education**]: Computer and Information Science Education - *Computer science education, Curriculum*

General Terms

Documentation, Design, Human Factors.

Keywords

Curriculum Resources, Faculty Connection, Visual Search, Open Educational Resources

1. SUMMARY

Microsoft Faculty Connection [1] is a web portal providing curriculum resources, training materials, and software tools direct to faculty to help integrate software technology into teaching computing and technical classes. Faculty Connection facilitates development and sharing curriculum resources. The materials, both developed by Microsoft and faculty, are for non-commercial, academic use and available to download free of charge.

The portal contains around 3,000 learning objects including labs, presentations, videos, source code, etc. The users can use a dedicated search or browse information by topics such as CS Area, technology, author, etc. However, many of the objects are zipped packages consisting of courseware for a semester-long class - lessons, labs, source code, tools and other material. The courseware itself may have materials in different formats (from source code to videos), several dozen files and often reaches hundreds of megabytes. Having to download and examine this kind of materials is a very time consuming task.

To speed up exploration and make it easier for users, we implemented Visual Search with Deep Zoom feature [2] allowing users to preview the resources before downloading them (see Fig 1). One can zoom through zip files, folders and view pages of Word and PDF documents, Power Point slides, text files, etc. This feature has been implemented using Silverlight technology [3].

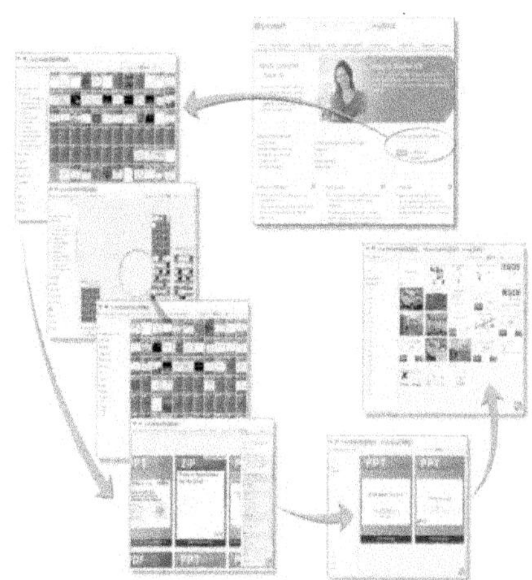

Figure 1. Visual exploration of curriculum resources

2. REFERENCES

[1] Faculty Connection repository: www.microsoft.com/faculty

[2] Visual Search http://www.facultyresourcecenter.com/curriculum/visual

[3] Silverlight Development Platform http://www.silverlight.net/

ITiCSE'12, July 3–5, 2012, Haifa, Israel.
ACM 978-1-4503-1246-2/12/07.

Author Index

www.ingramcontent.com/pod-product-compliance
Ingram Content Group UK Ltd.
Pitfield, Milton Keynes, MK11 3LW, UK
UKHW051510290926
15471UKWH00008B/1546

9 781450 317368